FOURTH EDITION

PSYCHOLOGY
BEING HUMAN

Zick Rubin · Elton B. McNeil

Brandeis University   *Late, University of Michigan*

HARPER & ROW, PUBLISHERS, New York

1817

Cambridge, Philadelphia, San Francisco, London, Mexico City, São Paulo, Singapore, Sydney

Sponsoring Editor: Susan Mackey
Development Editor: Jackie Estrada
Project Editor: Ellen Meek Tweedy
Text and Cover Design: Gayle Jaeger
Cover Photo: Bill Longcore
Text Art: Eric Hieber
Photo Research: Mira Schachne
Production: Jeanie Berke
Compositor: York Graphic Services, Inc.
Printer and Binder: Kingsport Press

PSYCHOLOGY: BEING HUMAN,
Fourth Edition
Copyright © 1985 by Zick Rubin

The previous edition of this book was
published as *The Psychology of Being
Human,* Third Edition.

Library of Congress Cataloging in
Publication Data
Rubin, Zick.
  Psychology: being human.

  Rev. ed. of: The psychology of being
human. 3rd ed., c1981.
  Bibliography: p.
  1. Psychology. I. McNeil, Elton
Burbank, 1924–1974.
II. Rubin, Zick. The psychology of being
human.
III. Title.
BF121.R75 1985   150   84-25230
ISBN 0-06-044378-2

84 85 86 87 9 8 7 6 5 4 3 2

TEXT AND ILLUSTRATION ACKNOWLEDGMENTS

TEXT
CHAPTER 6 Page 178, reprinted from *Psychology Today* Magazine, Copyright © 1982, American Psychological Association.
CHAPTER 8 Page 250, from *Adolescent development*, by R. M. Lerner and G. B. Spanier. New York: McGraw-Hill, 1980, p. 56.
CHAPTER 9 Page 267, from *The seasons of a man's life*, by Daniel J. Levinson, et al. Copyright © 1978 by Daniel J. Levinson. Reprint by permission of Alfred A. Knopf, Inc./ p. 277, from *The view from 80*, by Malcolm Cowley. Copyright © 1976, 1978, 1980 by Malcolm Cowley. Reprinted by permission of Viking Penguin Inc.
CHAPTER 13 Page 412, from *A child called Noah*, by Josh Greenfeld. Copyright © 1970, 1971, 1972 by Josh Greenfeld. Reprinted by permission of Holt, Rinehart and Winston, Publishers; from *A place for Noah*, by Josh Greenfeld. Copyright © 1978 by Josh Greenfeld. Reprinted by permission of Holt, Rinehart and Winston, Publishers/ p. 418, from *Vivienne: the life and suicide of an adolescent girl*, by John E. Mack and Holly Hickler. Boston: Little, Brown, 1981. Copyright © 1981 by David Loomis and Paulette Loomis.

ILLUSTRATIONS
PART 1 Page 2, © Albertson, Stock, Boston.
CHAPTER 1 Page 6 (left), Granger; (middle, top and bottom), National Library of Medicine; (right), John Hopkins University/ p. 8, Jan Lucas, Photo Researchers/ p. 11, AP/Wide World Photos/ p. 12, Granger/ p. 16, Van Bucher, Photo Researchers/ p. 18, Wolinsky, Stock, Boston/ p. 19, Wolinsky, Stock, Boston/ p. 22, Van Bucher, Photo Researchers/ p. 23, NASA/ p. 24, © Ken Heyman/ p. 25, © Hrynewych, Southern Light/ p. 26, Forsyth, Monkmeyer/ p. 30 (left and right), The Bettmann Archive/ p. 31, *New York Post*, July 26, 1980, p. 25.
CHAPTER 2 Page 36, © Gray, Jeroboam/ p. 38 (top), © Carey, Image Works; (bottom), Hays, Monkmeyer/ p. 42, Science Photo Library, © 1982, Rotker/ p. 43, © Rotker, Taurus/ p. 44, © Joe Munroe, Photo Researchers/ p. 45, © David Powers/ p. 46, Monte S. Buchsbaum, M.D./ p. 47, Ray Ellis, Photo Researchers/ p. 53 (top), Thompson, Jeroboam; (bottom), © Liftin, Archive Pictures/ p. 61, © Alexander, 1984,

Woodfin Camp/ p. 62, Charlotte Brooks, Magnum/ p. 63, Freed, NIH/ p. 64, Freed, NIH.
CHAPTER 3 Page 67 (top), Weisbrot, Stock, Boston; (bottom), © Kroll, 1979, Taurus/ p. 68, Constantine Manos, Magnum/ p. 69 (left), Carey, Image Works; (right), © Cavanaugh, Archive Pictures/ p. 70, Mitchell Payne, Jeroboam/ p. 72, © Ken Heyman/ p. 74, Lejeune, Stock, Boston/ p. 75, Arthur Tress, Photo Researchers/ p. 79, Owens, Jeroboam/ p. 80, Gatewood, Image Works/ p. 81, Michael C. Hayman, Photo Researchers/ p. 82, Dr. Peter M. Witt, North Carolina Department of Mental Health/ p. 83, Culver/ p. 85, Forsyth, Monkmeyer/ p. 86, © Hrynewych, Southern Light/ p. 90, Bernard Wolff, Magnum/ p. 91, Morrow, Stock, Boston/ p. 93 (top), © Preuss, 1972, Jeroboam; (bottom), Malave, Stock, Boston.
PART 2 Page 94, © Bellerose/Picture Group.
CHAPTER 4 Page 99, © Lennart Nilsson, *Behold man*, Delacorte Press, N.Y./ p. 102, © Dodge, DPI/ p. 104, Rotmil, DPI/ p. 105, William Vandivert and *Scientific American*, April, 1970/ p. 107, © Bodin/ Picture Group/ p. 110, Franken, Stock, Boston/ p. 111, Jill Freedman, Archive Pictures/ p. 113, © Spragen, Jr./ Picture Group/ p. 114, Mercado, Jeroboam/ p. 118, Bintliff, DPI/ p. 122, Audrey Ross, Berkeley/ p. 127 (top), © Hrynewych, Stock, Boston; (bottom), Bill Stanton, Magnum/ p. 128, Saidel, Stock, Boston.
CHAPTER 5 Page 132, Library of Congress/ p. 134, Courtesy of Dr. Ben Harris, Vassar College/ p. 137 (top), Hugh Rogers, Monkmeyer; (bottom), © Ken Heyman/ p. 138, Forsyth, Monkmeyer/ p. 140, Photo Researchers/ p. 142, Cheney, EKM-Nepenthe/ p. 145, © Menzel, Stock, Boston/ p. 146, David Shapiro/ p. 147, © Fortin, 1980, Stock, Boston/ p. 149, Robert Smith, Black Star/ p. 150, © Crews, Stock, Boston/ p. 152, © Hayman, 1981, Click/ Chicago/ p. 153, © Druskis, Jeroboam/ p. 157, © Joel Gordon, 1978/ p. 158, E. Scott Geller/ p. 160, AP/ Wide World Photos.
CHAPTER 6 Page 164, Cornell Capa, Magnum/ p. 165, B.F. Grunzweig, Photo Researchers/ p. 167, The Bettmann Archive/ p. 169, © Elizabeth Crews/ p. 171, © Diakopoulis/ Picture Group/ p. 173, Adena Rubin/ p. 176, UPI/ Bettmann Archive/ p. 177, Van Bucher, Photo Researchers/ p. 178, Wayne Miller, Magnum/ p. 183, © O'Brien, Archive Pictures/ p. 184, *New York Times*

Pictures/ p. 185, AP/ Wide World Photos.
CHAPTER 7 Page 189, United Nations/ p. 191, Beatrice T. Gardner/ p. 192, © Campione, 1982, Taurus/ p. 193, McKenna, Taurus/ p. 194, © Abigail Heyman, Archive Pictures/ p. 196 (top left and right), A.W. Ambler, National Audubon Society, Photo Researchers; (bottom), Allan D. Cruickshank, National Audubon Society, Photo Researchers/ p. 199, © Hall, 1976, Stock, Boston/ p. 200, Kohler, *The mentality of apes*, Routledge & Kegan Paul PLC, London, 1956/ p. 203, Ruth Silverman, BBM Associates/ p. 209 (top left), © Lejeune, Stock, Boston; (top right), © Moore, 1977, Taurus; (bottom), Carey, Image Works/ p. 211, Vandermark, Stock, Boston/ p. 212, Will McIntyre, Photo Researchers/ p. 213, © Pfleger, 1982/ p. 215, Rotker, Taurus/ p. 218, AP/ Wide World Photos/ p. 219, John Alexandrowicz/ p. 220, Courtesy, Control Data.
PART 3 Page 222, © Lejeune, Stock, Boston.
CHAPTER 8 Page 226 (left), © Ken Heyman; (right), © Kalman, Image Works/ p. 227, Nina Leen, Life Magazine, © 1964 Time Inc./ p. 228, Howard Gardner, *Artful scribbles: the significance of children's drawings*, Basic Books, N.Y./ p. 229, UPI/ Bettmann Archive/ p. 230, Dr. C. Reather, Omikron, Photo Researchers/ p. 231, Suzanne Arms, Jeroboam/ p. 233, Carol Rubin/ p. 234, World Health Organization/ p. 235, Erika, Photo Researchers/ p. 237, Wisconsin Primate Laboratory/ p. 238, Maher, EKM-Nepenthe/ p. 240, Forsyth, Monkmeyer/ p. 241, © Welsch, Stock, Boston/ p. 244, Suzanne Szasz, Photo Researchers/ p. 245 (top), © Hrynewych, Stock, Boston; (bottom), Eckert, EKM-Nepenthe/ p. 246, Kalman, Image Works/ p. 248, Lejeune, Stock, Boston/ p. 249 (left), Zeiberg, Taurus; (right), © Siteman, EKM-Nepenthe/ p. 250, © Zeiberg, Taurus/ p. 253, UPI/ Bettmann Archive/ p. 254, © Lejeune, Stock, Boston/ p. 255, Gross, Stock, Boston/ p. 256, Franken, Stock, Boston.
CHAPTER 9 Page 259 (top left and right), AP/ Wide World; (bottom left), NASA; (bottom right), AP/ Wide World/ p. 260, Brody, Stock, Boston/ p. 262 (left), Bruce Roberts, Photo Researchers; (right), © Abigail Heyman, Archive Pictures/ p. 263, © Grace, Stock, Boston/ p. 265, © Abigail Heyman, Archive Pictures/ p. 266, Southwick, Stock, Boston/ p. 268, UPI/ Bettmann Archive/ p. 271,

© Burk Uzzle 1984, Woodfin Camp/ p. 272, Gene Daniels, Black Star/ p. 273, © Hella Hammid, Rapho/ Photo Researchers/ p. 275, Siteman, EKM-Nepenthe/ p. 277, Nancy Crampton/ p. 278, © Zucker, Stock, Boston/ p. 279, © Hazel Hankin, 1982/ p. 280, © Abigail Heyman, Archive Pictures/ p. 281 (top), © Siteman, Taurus; (bottom), Carey, Image Works/ p. 284, David Seymour, Magnum/ p. 286, Chester Higgins, Photo Researchers/ p. 287, © Jewett, EKM-Nepenthe.

PART 4   Page 288, Bellerose, Stock, Boston.

CHAPTER 10   Page 291, Rogers, Monkmeyer/ p. 293 (top left), Simon, Stock, Boston; (top right), © Morrow, 1977, Stock, Boston; (bottom), Shackman, Monkmeyer/ p. 296 (left), © Kroll, Taurus; (right), Running, Stock, Boston/ p. 297, Meyers/ Picture Group/ p. 298, Courtesy of Philip Teitelbaum, University of Pennsylvania/ p. 299, Kalman, Image Works/ p. 301 (top), Wolinsky, Stock, Boston; (bottom), © Anderson, 1980, Stock, Boston/ p. 304, © Kruse, Jeroboam/ p. 308, Courtesy of Dr. Paul Ekman/ p. 309, Courtesy of Dr. C. Izard, University of Delaware/ p. 313, Paul Ekman and Wallace V. Friesen, *Unmasking the face,* reprint edition, Consulting Psychologists Press/ p. 314, © Charles Harbutt, Archive Pictures/ p. 318, Culver/ p. 319, Constantine Manos, Magnum/ p. 320, Courtesy of Albert Bandura, Stanford University/ p. 321, Gatewood, Image Works/ p. 322, AP/ Wide World Photos.

CHAPTER 11   Page 325 (left and right), AP/ Wide World Photos/ p. 326, AP/ Wide World Photos/ p. 327, © Enrico Ferrorelli/DOT/ p. 328 (left), © Matusaw, Archive Pictures; (right), © Cannefax, EKM-Nepenthe/ p. 329 (left), AP/ Wide World Photos; (right), Atlan/ Sygma/ p. 330, The Bettmann Archive/ p. 331 (top and bottom), Sigmund Freud Copyrights, Ltd./ p. 334 (top left), © 1976, Fritz Henle, Photo Researchers; (top right), Magnum; (bottom), Homer Sykes, Woodfin Camp/ p. 335 (left), Eve Arnold, © 1961, Magnum; (right), John Veltri, Photo Researchers/ p. 338 (top), National Library of Medicine; (middle), The Bettmann Archive; (bottom), Association for the Advancement of Psychoanalysis of the Karen Horney Psychoanalytic Institute and Center/ p. 339 (left), Westenberger, Gamma/Liaison; (right), AP/ Wide World Photos/ p. 341, © Reno, 1979, Jeroboam/ p. 342, The Bettmann Archive/ p. 343, Herwig, Stock, Boston/ p. 344, Courtesy of Bertha G. Maslow/ p. 345, Siteman, The Picture Cube/ p. 347, National Computer Systems, Courtesy of University of Minnesota Press/ p. 352,

© Hamlin, 1976, Stock, Boston/ p. 353, © Crews, Stock, Boston/ p. 354, UPI/ Bettmann Archive.

CHAPTER 12   Page 358, © Grace, Stock, Boston/ p. 361 (left), Costa Manos, Magnum; (right), © 1981, Stratford, Photo Researchers/ p. 363, Sidney, Monkmeyer/ p. 365 (top), American Heart Association; (bottom), Rothstein, Jeroboam/ p. 366 (top), © Grace, Stock, Boston; (bottom), Southwick, Stock, Boston/ p. 368 (top left), © 1980, Kinne, Photo Researchers; (right), Courtesy of Dr. John C. Roder, Department of Microbiology, Queens University, Kingston, Canada/ p. 370, © Bucher, Photo Researchers/ p. 372, © Preuss, Jeroboam, 1978/ p. 374, © O'Brien, Archive Pictures/ p. 375, Jane E. Brody/ NYT Pictures/ p. 376, © 1981, Falco, Photo Researchers/ p. 378, © Ellis, Photo Researchers/ p. 379, © Menzel, Stock, Boston/ p. 380 (left and right), Courtesy, Kelly Brownell/ p. 383, Bemis Company, Inc./ p. 384, Forsyth, Monkmeyer/ p. 385 (top), Holmgren, Jeroboam; (bottom), Alper, Stock, Boston/ p. 386, © 1983, Hedman, Jeroboam.

PART 5   Page 388, Weisbrot, Stock, Boston.

CHAPTER 13   Page 394 (top), Museo del Prado; (bottom left), L.J. Bruce-Chwatt, The Wellcome Museum of Medical Science, London; (bottom right), Brown Brothers/ p. 396, © Ries/ Picture Group/ p. 397 (left), Burk Uzzle, Woodfin Camp; (right), © Abigail Heyman, Archive Pictures/ p. 399, Lejeune, Stock, Boston/ p. 401, George Rodger, Magnum/ p. 402, Culver/ p. 403, © Ken Heyman/ p. 405, © Buryn, Jeroboam/ p. 406, © Buck, The Picture Cube/ p. 407, UPI/ Bettmann Archive/ p. 409, AP/ Wide World Photos/ p. 411, *Newsweek,* June 23, 1980. Copyright 1980 by Newsweek, Inc. All Rights Reserved. Reprinted by Permission/ p. 412, Cal Bernstein/ p. 413, Costa Manos, © Magnum/ p. 416, Malave, Stock, Boston/ p. 419, © Fortin/ Picture Group.

CHAPTER 14   Page 423, Jan Lukas, Photo Researchers/ p. 425, Deke Simon/ p. 426, © Roth, 1979, The Picture Cube/ p. 428, Don Hogan Charles, *The New York Times*/ p. 429, Costa Manos, © Magnum/ p. 430, Alex Webb, © Magnum/ p. 431, AP/ Wide World Photos/ p. 433, © Hrynewych, Southern Light/ p. 435, © Paul Fusco, Magnum/ p. 436, Ken Stein/ p. 438, Delevingne, Stock, Boston/ p. 439, © Morrow/ Picture Group/ p. 440, © Hankin, Stock, Boston/ p. 444, © Hella Hammid, Photo Researchers/ p. 445, © Hedman, Jeroboam/ p. 446, © Kalvar, Magnum/ p. 447, © Kalvar, Magnum/ p. 449, © Lei, Omni-Photo.

PART 6   Page 450, © 1981, Bachman, Photo Researchers.

CHAPTER 15   Page 454, Herwig, Stock, Boston/ p. 456, Forsyth, Monkmeyer/ p. 458, © Burt Glinn, Magnum/ p. 459 (top), © Lubin, Jeroboam; (bottom), © Siluk, EKM-Nepenthe/ p. 461, Franken, Stock, Boston/ p. 462, Courtesy of Bennington College/ p. 463, Grace, Stock, Boston/ p. 464, from "Opinions and social pressure," by Solomon E. Asch. In *Scientific American,* November 1955/ p. 467, AP/ Wide World Photos/ p. 468, Courtesy of American Cancer Society/ p. 469, © Burk Uzzle 1984, Woodfin Camp/ p. 470, Carey, Image Works/ p. 471, Eckert, EKM-Nepenthe/ p. 472, Copyright © 1965 by Stanley Milgram. From the film "Obedience" distributed by the New York University Film Library/ p. 475, UPI/ Bettmann Archive/ p. 479, AP/ Wide World Photos/ p. 481, © Burk Uzzle 1983, Woodfin Camp/ p. 482, © Marc & Evelyne Bernheim 1980, Woodfin Camp.

CHAPTER 16   Page 487 (top), © Gupton, Southern Light; (bottom), © Crews, Stock, Boston/ p. 489 (top), Strickler, Monkmeyer; (bottom), © 1982, Morrow/ Picture Group/ p. 491, Courtesy, Carol Gilligan/ p. 492, © Smith, 1982, Jeroboam/ p. 493, Robert Goy, Wisconsin Primate Center/ p. 495, AP/ Wide World Photos/ p. 496 (left), Leonard Freed, Magnum; (right), © Joanne Leonard 1983, Woodfin Camp/ p. 497 (top and bottom), UPI/ Bettman Archive/ p. 498, Shelton, Monkmeyer/ p. 501, © Mahler, 1980, EKM-Nepenthe/ p. 502, Siteman, Stock, Boston/ p. 503, © Siteman, Stock, Boston/ p. 505, © Eckert, Jr., EKM-Nepenthe/ p. 506, Beckwith Studios/ p. 508, Bodin, Stock, Boston/ p. 509 (left), AP/ Wide World Photos; (middle), NASA; (right), AP/ Wide World Photos/ p. 510, © Abigail Heyman, Archive Pictures/ p. 511, Antman, Image Works.

CHAPTER 17   Page 514, © Mercado, Jeroboam/ p. 515 (left), Charles Harbutt, Archive Pictures; (right), Weldon, Leo de Wys Inc./ p. 516, Brody, Stock, Boston/ p. 518, Eric Hartmann, © 1970 Magnum/ p. 519 (top and bottom), UPI/ Bettmann Archive/ p. 520, AP/ Wide World Photos/ p. 521, Carey, Image Works/ p. 522, Richard Kalvar, © Magnum/ p. 523 (top and bottom), Courtesy of Dane Archer/ p. 524, Eckert, EKM-Nepenthe/ p. 526, AP/ Wide World Photos/ p. 527, UPI/ Bettmann Archive/ p. 529, Carey, Image Works/ p. 530, Siteman, Stock, Boston/ p. 536, © Burk Uzzle 1984, Woodfin Camp/ p. 537, Herwig, Stock, Boston/ p. 538, Sidney, Leo de Wys Inc./ p. 539, © Dietz, 1982, Stock, Boston.

CONTENTS IN BRIEF

CONTENTS

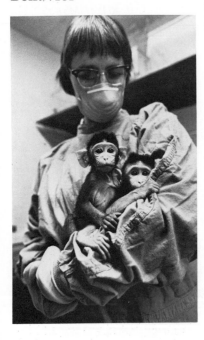

PREFACE

When Elton McNeil wrote the first edition of *Psychology: Being Human*, he wanted to share with his readers his own fascination with the field of psychology. He wrote as a person with a full range of feelings about psychology—respect for its historical foundations, excitement about its research frontiers, bemused skepticism about its fads and foibles, apprehension about its possible misuses, and faith in its ability to better people's lives—and he let these feelings be known. Elton McNeil wrote about psychology in a personal way rather than standing behind a cloak of anonymity. And although Dr. McNeil took his psychology seriously, he also found it to be great fun—and he let you know it. His death in 1974, a week before the publication of the first edition, was a great loss to the field of psychology.

I am, of course, a different person from Elton McNeil and my own special loves and pet peeves about psychology are not identical to his. But I share Dr. McNeil's basic approach to psychology—his fascination with the field, his desire to communicate his enthusiasm to others, and his feeling that a solid and comprehensive introductory psychology textbook can be written in a way that is personal, related to students' own concerns, and fun to read. In revising *Psychology: Being Human*, I've tried to follow Dr. McNeil's example and, by doing so, to help make the study of psychology a lively and involving enterprise.

This fourth edition of *Psychology: Being Human* retains two distinctive features that Elton McNeil introduced in the first edition—Psychological Issues and "teasers." The Psychological Issues, self-contained sections that follow each chapter of the text, focus on applications of psychology to current social issues or to topics of personal concern to students. For example, there are Psy-

chological Issues on "Noise Pollution," "Brothers and Sisters," "Happiness," "Prejudice and Racism," and "Marriage and Divorce." The Psychological Issues emphasize the many ways in which psychology relates to our lives and to the society in which we live.

Scattered through the margins of this text are paragraphs that Elton McNeil called "teasers." These are humorous, dramatic, or offbeat pieces of information that both students and instructors seem to like. They can be used as pick-me-ups from more tedious stretches of prose, or as conversation openers at parties. Although many of the teasers you will encounter are new to the fourth edition, I hope they are as irreverent and enjoyable as ever. Read and enjoy them when you're in the mood. Ignore them when you're not.

CHANGES IN THE FOURTH EDITION

Although it retains the spirit that Elton McNeil instilled into the first edition, this fourth edition embodies many significant changes. In particular, advances in the neurosciences and in cognitive science continue to transform the face of modern psychology. New work in the neurosciences—the biological underpinnings of mind and behavior—is reflected in major revisions throughout the book, especially in the chapters on biological foundations, consciousness, and memory. The new work in cognitive science is reflected especially in the chapters of Part Two, "Perceiving, Learning, and Thinking," which include new discussions of such topics as learning cognitive skills, autobiographical memory, and problem solving. Both the biological and the cognitive revolutions are also reflected in the revisions of the chapters on psychological disorder and therapy.

Not only does the science of psychology change, but so do the problems and challenges facing society. These changes, too, have led to changes in this book. New discussions of such topics as the role of computers in education, the insanity defense, the mental patient's right to refuse treatment, and psychology's own sex bias all relate to current issues and concerns. New or extensively revised Psychological Issues on such topics as biological engineering, artificial intelligence, and changing sex roles all reflect the status of these social phenomena in the mid-1980s.

This edition also includes a completely new chapter on "Psychology and Health," reflecting the emergence in the past decade of health psychology and behavioral medicine as a major subfield of psychology. Until recently it was commonly believed that the biological and the psychological were separate domains and that, as a result, psychology had only tangential relevance to medical practice and the promotion of physical health. It is now recognized, however, that people's emotions and behavior are closely related to their health, and psychological approaches to health maintenance are becoming increasingly influential.

This fourth edition of *Psychology: Being Human* also *looks* different from previous editions. The textbook has been redesigned in what I think is a highly attractive and readable format. A completely new set of scientific illustrations has been prepared to highlight biological and psychological function rather than simply depict anatomical structure. Full-color drawings and photographs are included in the first four chapters, not merely as decoration, but as a striking way of illustrating principles of brain function and of perception.

PEDAGOGY

The fourth edition includes three new pedagogical features to help the student master the book's content. First, an *outline page* at the start of each chapter provides both a list of the sections and subsections of the chapter and a one- or two-sentence overview of each major section. This combination of section headings and overviews is intended to provide the student with a coherent organizing framework for dealing with the material in the chapter. Second, a list of *key terms* at the end of each chapter will help in reviewing the material. Third, the *glossary* at the end of the book now includes the number of the page on which each term was introduced in the text, so that the student can easily retrieve the context in which the term was introduced. Students may also be interested in applying the method known as *PQ4R* (a close relative of another method called *SQ3R*) to studying this textbook, as a way of increasing their comprehension and retention of the material. This method is briefly described in the chapter on memory (page 179), as part of a more general discussion of study strategies. The PQ4R method is also explained in greater detail in the Student Guide and PSI Manual that accompanies the text.

A NOTE ON PRONOUNS

In the first edition of *Psychology: Being Human*, Elton McNeil did not hesitate to use the first-person singular in presenting his own views and experiences. In the second and third editions I shied away from the first-person singular. After all, I reasoned, how could a jointly authored book address its readers in this way? Occasionally, when I wanted to relate a personal experience, I referred to myself as "Zick Rubin." This approach made me feel like those political candidates who always refer to themselves by their full names, just in case their audience doesn't know who they are. It avoids confusion, but it's also a bit awkward. In this fourth edition, therefore, I have taken the liberty of using the first person. So, when you read about my earliest memory (in Chapter 6) or my son's language development (in Chapter 7) or my college alumni magazine (in Chapter 16), you'll know what "I" means.

The following additional materials have been prepared to help both students and instructors make the most effective use of this text.

FOR THE STUDENT

STUDY GUIDE AND PSI MANUAL

Prepared by Richard P. McGlynn of Texas Tech University and Ann P. McGlynn, the Guide will aid the student in mastering the concepts presented in the text. It can be used with a traditional course format or a PSI (Personalized System of Instruction) format. There are three sections in each chapter: open-ended study questions, a programmed review unit, and a self-quiz.

The study questions can be used as learning objectives for the student who is reading the chapter for the first time since they highlight the material that is most important. The questions ask for definitions, identifications, summaries of theories or research, and finding relationships between concepts. Once the chapter has been read, the questions can be used as a study aid. Space is provided beneath each question so the student can make notes and learning becomes an active process. In PSI courses, chapter or unit quizzes can be coordinated with these study questions/objectives, and feedback on missed items can direct the student back to specific areas for further review.

Each chapter also contains a programmed review unit which promotes active review by asking the student to fill in the blanks with important concepts and terms from the chapter. The chapter summary format for these questions provides a context for the concepts to cue the student's response. Missed items signal areas for further review. Both the study questions and the items in the programmed review contain references to page numbers in the text to facilitate review.

Depending on the level of mastery the student wishes to attain, he might work through the study questions or the programmed review or both. To test the student's mastery, each chapter contains a twenty-item multiple choice self-quiz (with answers provided). The items vary in difficulty depending on the difficulty of the material. By returning to the sections of the text that correspond to missed items, a student can determine whether the problem lies in failure to commit important terms to memory, failure to comprehend, or failure to conceptualize. To facilitate this process, each self-quiz question is referenced with the number of the corresponding study question which indicates the kind of understanding of each section that is required.

The Guide contains an introduction with a more detailed description of its use in both traditional and PSI courses.

STUDY-AID

Study-Aid is a new computer program for the Apple II, IIe, and IIc and the IBM-PC computers. It is keyed directly to the text and Study Guide, for easy reference and learning. After reading each chapter, Study-Aid allows the students to test themselves with fill-in-the-blank, multiple choice, and review exercises. Automatic scoring allows students to check themselves as they learn.

FOR THE INSTRUCTOR

TEST ITEM FILE

Prepared by Mary Lou Zanich of Indiana University of Pennsylvania, Test Item File consists of 105 multiple choice questions for each chapter. These test items reflect a careful balance among factual, conceptual, and applied questions, and are keyed to pages in the text.

MICROTEST

A recent innovation in the Harper & Row college text package, MicroTest is a microcomputerized test generation system that includes: a program diskette for creating test files and for selecting, adding, deleting, and editing questions from the test file diskette; test file diskettes containing the complete test item file for the book; a User's/Author's Manual with step-by-step instructions and examples for setting up and using the system. MicroTest is compatible with two microcomputer series—the Apple II and the IBM-PC.

INSTRUCTOR'S MANUAL

Prepared by Joe W. Rode of Tarrant County Junior College, the Manual includes chapter reviews, classroom discussion questions, lecture ideas, lists of key terms, suggestions for films, and supplemental readings.

SLIDES

A set of 194 slides, suitable for use with any introductory psychology text, is available to adopters of *Psychology: Being Human.*

ACKNOWLEDGMENTS

In preparing the fourth edition of *Psychology: Being Human,* I have profited from the reactions and suggestions of many people. I owe a special debt of gratitude to a panel of three reviewers who read the entire draft of the fourth edition and provided extensive suggestions, often under great time pressure. These reviewers are Richard McGlynn, Texas Tech University; Katherine Noll, Elmhurst College; and Mary Lou Zanich, Indiana University of Pennsylvania. In addition, both Richard McGlynn and Christina Munson of Monroe Community College provided helpful reviews of the entire third edition.

Several of my colleagues at Brandeis University helped me out by reviewing chapters of the third edition in their areas of specialization: Teresa Amabile (social psychology; creativity); Margie Lachman (adulthood and aging); James Todd (perception); Arthur Wingfield (cognitive psychology); and Edgar Zurif (brain and language). Ricardo Morant advised me on figures illustrating perceptual processes, and Becky Thompson reviewed the Psychological Issue on changing sex roles. The following psychologists at other colleges and universities also provided expert reviews of third edition chapters: Bruce Baker, University of California, Los Angeles (disorder and therapy); Sheila Brachfeld-Child, Wellesley College (development); David Buss, Harvard University (motivation, emotion, and personality); Gerald Davison, University of Southern California (disorder and therapy); Ronald Finke, University of California, Davis (perception); Bernard Gorman, Nassau Community College (development); Carroll Izard, University of Delaware (motivation and emotion); John Kihlstrom, University of Wisconsin (consciousness; memory); Richard Leavy, Ohio Wesleyan University (development); Nora Newcombe, Pennsylvania State University (development); Stuart Oskamp, Claremont Graduate Center (attitudes and influence); Letitia Anne Peplau, University of California, Los Angeles (male and female; social relationships); Joseph Pleck, Wellesley College Center for Research on Women (male and female); William Ray, Pennsylvania State University (disorder and therapy); Robert Sternberg, Yale University (cognitive psychology); Jeffrey Wine, Stanford University (biological foundations); Steven Zarit, University of Southern California (adulthood and aging).

In addition, the following professors provided valuable reactions to the third edition and/or the preliminary plans for the fourth edition:

William Beaver, Robert Morris College

Ellen Beck, Sinclair Community College

Florence Berger, Cornell University

Susan Bond, Manchester Community College

Sam Bottosto, Palm Beach Junior College

Robert Bowden, Quinsigamond Community College

John Brackmann, California State University, Sacramento

Larry Brandstein, Berkshire Community College

Robert C. Brown, Jr., Georgia State University

R.L. Calhoun, Humboldt State University

Dudley Campbell, L.A. Pierce College

Larry Christensen, Utah Technical College

Jan Cleveland, Colorado State University

Ruth Cline, Los Angeles Valley College

John Cross, St. Louis University

Michael Cunningham, Elmhurst College

Fred Culler, Florence-Darlington TEC

Lisa Davis, Pasadena City College

Douglas Degelman, Eastern Nazarene College

Nancy Dixon, Tennessee Tech University

Warren Fass, University of Pittsburgh at Bradford

Samuel Feldman, New York University

Linda Flickinger, St. Clair County Community College

Charles Fry, University of Virginia

William Gannon, Quinebaug Valley Community College

Victor Garlock, Cayuga County Community College

Michael Garza, El Centro College

Thomas Gerry, Columbia-Greene Community College

Richard Glessner, Mount Ida College

Randall Gold, Cuesta College

Stephen Grammatico, Greater New Haven State Technical College

Jacob Halberstam, Baruch College

Jerry Harris, Tarrant County Junior College

James Hart, Central State University

Donald Helms, Mitchell College

Warren Hills, Jordan College

Lyllian Hix, Houston Community College

John Hoffman, Quinsigamond Community College

Cort Holdgrafer, Santa Ana College

Henry Houde, Dean Junior College

Marilyn Howe, Quinsigamond Community College

Ted Hsieh, Judson College

Sallie Hume, Schenectady County Community College

Idell Jacobson, Embry-Riddle Aeronautical University

Louis Kahn, Bellevue Community College

Carol Laman, Houston Community College

Edwin Kurlander, Sullivan County Community College

Irving Lane, Louisiana State University

Denis Laplante, Lambton College

Bert Levine, Pan American University

Judith Levine, Fashion Institute of Technology

Ruby Lewis, DeKalb Community College

Nancy Lobb, Alvin Community College

Barbara Long, Goucher College

Paul Lu, Walters State Community College

Joseph Lucas, St. Clair College

Robert Mathews, Louisiana State University

Matthew Merrens, State University of New York College at Plattsburgh

Jerry Meyer, University of Massachusetts

Richard Miller, Navarro College

Robert Moffie, Oglethorpe University

E.E.D. Mullin, Royal Military College of Canada

Richard Nickeson, St. Louis University

Gary Noll, Elmhurst College

Anne Noury, Allan Hancock College

Robert Nye, State University of New York College at New Paltz

Joan Oliver, St. Louis University

R.W. Olson, Saddleback College

Ginger Osborne, Santa Ana College

John Pennachio, Adirondack County College

Gregory Pezzetti, Santa Ana College

Walter Reichman, Baruch College

Daniel W. Richards, III, Houston Community College

Tom Ritzdorf, Northeastern Junior College

Douglas Robbins, Pratt Institute

Barbara Robinson, Portland Community College

Ronald Rogers, University of Alabama

Lawrence Rosenkoetter, Bethany College

Tirzah Schutzengel, Bergen Community College

Dale Septeowski, Concordia College

Mark Sherman, State University of New York College at New Paltz

Darlene Smith, Cuesta College

Nancy Smith, College of the Canyons

George Smrtic, Cayuga Community
College

Doug Soderstrom, Wharton County
Junior College

Richard Stellar, Lasell Junior College

Kenneth Steere, Manchester Community College

Adolph Streng, Eastfield College

Deborah Taylor, Colby-Sawyer College

Sister Trinitas, College of Notre
Dame

David Trueman, William Paterson
College

Mary Vander Goot, Calvin College

Marc Wayner, Hocking Technical
College

Sarah White, J. Sargeant Reynolds
Community College

In the course of preparing the revision, I was assisted by several talented psychologists. Jone Sloman of the Children's Hospital of Boston worked closely with me throughout the revision process and drafted material for many portions of the text. Martha Farah of the Massachusetts Institute of Technology, Anne Sandoval of the University of New Hampshire, and Marilyn Geller also provided assistance in their special areas of expertise. Alan Stein, a Brandeis undergraduate, provided library assistance. I could not have asked for a more talented and conscientious group of collaborators. I am also grateful to Howard Friedman of the University of California at Riverside, who worked with me on the draft of the new chapter on "Psychology and Health," and to Lois Biener of the Wellesley College Center for Research on Women and Joan Borysenko of the Harvard University Medical School who provided valuable advice on this chapter.

As development editor for this textbook, Jackie Estrada once again did an outstanding job of polishing the prose, preparing the chapter summaries and glossary, and compiling the bibliography. I also want to thank the many people at Harper & Row who contributed in vital ways to the book's preparation and production. These include, among many others, Susan Mackey (psychology editor), Gayle Jaeger (designer), Ellen Meek Tweedy (project editor), and Mira Schachne (picture editor).

Finally, I would like to thank my wife Carol and my sons Elihu and Noam for their stimulation and support. You will find each of them featured at one point or another in the course of this book .

Zick Rubin

ABOUT THE AUTHORS

Zick Rubin

ZICK RUBIN, who prepared the second, third, and fourth editions of *Psychology: Being Human,* received his B.A. in 1965 from Yale University, where he was a psychology major and managing editor of the *Yale Daily News.* He received his Ph.D. in social psychology from the University of Michigan in 1969. He served on the faculty of Harvard University before assuming his current position as Louis and Frances Salvage Professor of Social Psychology at Brandeis University. Dr. Rubin is widely known as a researcher and popular writer in psychology. His research has centered on social interaction and relationships among both adults and children. He has received the Socio-Psychological Prize of the American Association for the Advancement of Science for his research on romantic love and the National Media Award of the American Psychological Foundation for his book *Children's Friendships.* He is also the author of *Liking and Loving: An Invitation to Social Psychology* and a contributing editor of *Psychology Today* magazine.

ELTON B. McNEIL, who wrote the first edition of *Psychology: Being Human,* received his B.A. from Harvard University and his Ph.D. in clinical psychology from the University of Michigan. He was on the faculty of the University of Michigan for 22 years, teaching undergraduate and graduate courses in introductory psychology, clinical psychology, and psychotherapy. Before his death in 1974, Dr. McNeil wrote and edited many books, including *The Quiet Furies, The Nature of Human Conflict,* and *Human Socialization.* He was also director of the clinical training center for emotionally disturbed and delinquent boys at the University of Michigan Fresh Air Camp, and he served in the Peace Corps as a field selection officer.

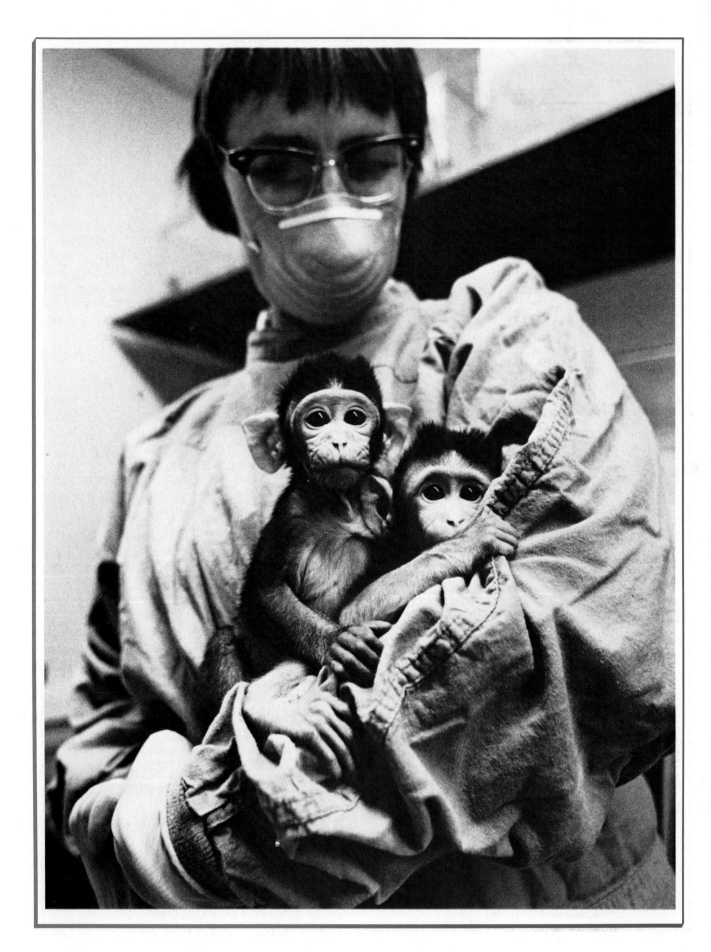

BRAIN, MIND, AND BEHAVIOR

A toddler utters his first sentence.

A young adult has a mental breakdown.

A man and a woman fall in love.

Psychologists try to understand these and other aspects of human behavior and mental processes. In Chapter 1, What Is Psychology?, we will introduce psychology and examine the methods that psychologists employ to study mind and behavior systematically. In the Psychological Issue on Parascience that follows the chapter, we will look at some of the alternative approaches to understanding human behavior that have been taken through the ages, from counting the bumps on people's heads to charting the movement of the planets.

One approach to understanding our thoughts, feelings, and actions involves probing the workings of a three-pound glob of matter called the brain. In Chapter 2, Biological Foundations of Behavior, we will survey what is known about the brain and, more generally, the links between our bodies and our behavior. As scientists learn more about the biological foundations of behavior, they also become increasingly capable of changing these biological processes, a controversial enterprise discussed in the Psychological Issue on Biological Engineering.

The links between brain, mind, and behavior are highlighted in Chapter 3, which explores the nature of Consciousness. We will examine the connections between brain functioning and such mental states as being awake or asleep, having dreams, and being under the influence of drugs. As discussed in the Psychological Issue, Biological Rhythms, our states of mind and behavior are influenced by daily, monthly, and annual rhythms that reflect the interplay of our biological nature and the rhythmic environment in which we live.

WHAT IS PSYCHOLOGY?

Psychology is the science of behavior and mental processes.

THE RESEARCH ADVENTURE

The case of the Good Samaritan
The case of the flashbulb memory
Where do psychologists get their ideas?

As researchers, psychologists begin with a mystery they want to solve and then gradually trace a series of clues that they hope will lead to a solution.

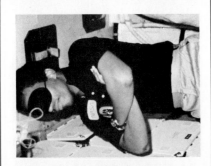

THE METHODS OF PSYCHOLOGY

Whom do psychologists observe?
What do psychologists observe?
Where do psychologists observe?
Description, correlation, and experimentation
Research and application

Psychologists strive to study behavior in ways that are systematic and objective.

WHAT DO PSYCHOLOGISTS DO?

The professional activities of psychologists range widely, from conducting brain research to counseling students about careers.

PSYCHOLOGICAL ISSUE
PARASCIENCE

BOXES
1 Psychology's roots
2 The day Lincoln was shot
3 The personal side of psychological research
4 Finding what you're looking for

The parasciences, such as astrology, offer alternative ways of looking at reality.

Even though this is probably your first course in psychology, you are a psychologist already. That's because the kinds of questions that psychologists ask and try to answer are very similar to the kinds of questions that all of us ask and try to answer in our everyday lives. The essential difference between you, as an "everyday psychologist," and the professional psychologist lies in the specific ways in which the questions are posed and in the specific techniques used to answer them.

For example, here are a few questions that you might have asked yourself at one time or another:

• Why is it that people who witness an emergency sometimes rush over to help but at other times walk right on by? (See pages 8–10.)

• Where do dreams come from, and why do we dream the particular things we do? (See Chapter 3.)

• Why do people remember so little about their early childhood? And why do some long-lost memories sometimes come rushing back? (See Chapter 6.)

• How are children able to learn language so quickly, within the first three years of life? Is it just a matter of imitating others, or is it somehow built into their brains? (See Chapter 7.)

• How do some people manage to keep slim without much apparent effort, while others find weight control a terrible ordeal? Is it simply a matter of self-control, or are fundamental biological or psychological differences involved? (See Chapter 10, Box 1.)

• How can the crimes of violence that fill our daily papers be explained? Does this violence reflect something basic about the human species, or is it a product of the times in which we live? (See the Psychological Issue for Chapter 10.)

• Why do people have such different personalities—why, for example, is Linda so outgoing and Dorothy so shy? Are they going to keep the same personalities as they grow older, or are they likely to change? (See Chapter 11.)

• What leads some people to become afraid of everyday situations or to become extremely depressed? And what can be done to help people with such psychological difficulties? (See Chapters 13 and 14.)

• What leads two people to fall in love and two other people to feel nothing special for each other? And, vows of love notwithstanding, why do so many of today's marriages end in divorce? (See Chapter 17.)

These are the sorts of questions that people are likely to ask themselves even if they have never heard of the academic discipline called psychology. But they are also the sorts of questions that are the professional psychologist's bread and butter.

There is a simple explanation for the fact that most people ponder the same sorts of questions that psychologists do. *Psychology* is the study of behavior and mental processes, primarily among humans. And human behavior and mental processes are nothing less than the substance of our lives: our actions, our thoughts, our attitudes, our moods, even our hopes and dreams. It is no wonder, then, that psychology is a subject that all of us ask questions about. The purpose of psychology as a science and profession is twofold: first, to provide better answers to questions about behavior and mental processes than the "everyday psychologist" is likely to

SOUL, MIND, AND BEHAVIOR

The term psychology *(actually* psychologia *in Latin) was apparently first used around 1530 by a German scholar, Phillip Melanchton, as a title for some lectures. Its original meaning—from the Greek* psyche *(or soul) and* logos *(or study)—was the "study of the soul." Later* psyche *became translated as "mind" rather than "soul." In this century, psychology was redefined as "the science of behavior and mental processes."*

BOX 1

PSYCHOLOGY'S ROOTS

The first people to speculate formally about the nature of human beings and their behavior were the early Greek and Roman philosophers. They were concerned with the question "What is the mind?" and came up with some interesting answers. Aristotle (384–322 B.C.) thought that mental functions were located in the heart. Centuries passed before this view was corrected and mental functions were linked to the brain. Meanwhile, questions that today would be considered psychological were left to the realm of philosophy. It is only within the last century that psychology has become recognized as a distinct discipline.

Aristotle

Two streams of thought, one in philosophy and the other in the physical and biological sciences, eventually led to the development of psychology as a separate field of study. The seventeenth-century British philosopher John Locke attempted to answer the question of how we can obtain valid information about the physical world. He concluded that at birth a person's mind is a "blank slate" on which sensory experience makes its marks. All knowledge, Locke believed, derives from sensory encounters with the physical world. Later British philosophers continued Locke's inquiry into the nature and origin of thoughts and ideas.

John Locke

Whereas these philosophers *thought* about the nature of mental processes, it was a group of German biologists and physicists in the late nineteenth century who first investigated these processes systematically. In 1879 Wilhelm Wundt, a German physiologist, opened the first psychological laboratory. For this reason, he is often considered to be the "father of scientific psychology." Wundt's studies were aimed at discovering the nature of consciousness. Subjects were asked to describe their sensations, images, and feelings as they were exposed to vari-

Wilhelm Wundt

ous experiences, such as flashes of light, colors, or tones.

Wundt's psychology was referred to as *structuralism* because it focused on the anatomy or structure of conscious processes. Structuralism was considered by the German psychologists to be a "pure science" because there was no practical application of the findings. But Wundt's followers in America—William James, John Dewey, and others—became interested in the practical applications of psychological research. Early American psychology—referred to as *functionalism*—became an applied discipline that developed into the fields of child psychology, educational psychology, and mental testing, among others.

John B. Watson

In the early twentieth century, John B. Watson, a former functionalist, founded *behaviorism* as a reaction to the structuralists, who were then occupied with such unanswerable questions—it seemed to Watson—as "Do all thoughts involve images?" Watson asserted that the only proper subject matter for psychology was observable behavior. This viewpoint, coupled with the development of objective experimental methods, brought the study of conscious processes to a virtual end. The behaviorist approach, carried on by B. F. Skinner and others, has been the predominant one in American psychology for most of the past 50 years.

While structuralism, functionalism, and behaviorism were developing, mainly in the universities, another crucial development in psychology sprang from medicine and the treatment of mental illness: psychoanalytic theory. This theory, developed by Sigmund Freud around the turn of the century, emphasized unconscious motives and the importance of early life experiences in shaping personality.

During the past 20 years certain themes from the history of psychology have reemerged and other new emphases have developed. Among the most important of these recent developments:

First, although behaviorism has not been forgotten, many psychologists have returned to questions about consciousness, mental imagery, and thought processes. But now they use more sophisticated tools than those employed by the early structuralists. This influential new approach is known as cognitive psychology.

Second, psychologists have strengthened their links with biologists and other scientists to study the biological foundations of behavior and mental processes, including the biological aspects of mental illness. Because this research focuses on the operation of the nervous system (which includes the brain), this interdisciplinary approach is often referred to as neuroscience.

Third, psychologists have been concerned with new applications of their research to the problems of society. In particular, there has been a burst of interest in applications of psychology to health, to the legal system, and to problems of the environment.

Psychology has come a long way since the time of Aristotle. Nevertheless, many of the same questions about the mind and behavior that were first asked over 2000 years ago are still being asked today.

come up with; and, second, to help people make use of these answers in shaping their own lives.

Although questions about human behavior and mental life have been asked throughout recorded history, psychology remains a young science (see Box 1). There were virtually no psychologists before the twentieth century, and psychologists are still a long way from having all the answers. Nevertheless, the approach that psychologists take toward understanding human behavior and thought represents significant progress from the approaches that have been taken by "everyday psychologists" throughout history. (For a glimpse at some other approaches to explaining and predicting human behavior, see the Psychological Issue on parascience following this chapter.) Because the psychologist's methods of research are so central to understanding what psychology is about, most of this chapter is devoted to examining these methods.

Despite psychology's advocacy of a scientific approach to human behavior and mental life, there are some perceptive observers who have doubts about the "scientific" study of the human condition. The Nobel Prize-winning storyteller and novelist Isaac Bashevis Singer is one who admits to such doubts. In his view, the attempt of psychologists to make predictions about human behavior runs up against the ability of human beings to make their own personal choices and, thus, to defy all predictions. "I think that psychology can never become a real science," Singer (1982) has written, "because when you deal with free choice you can never know what free choice will do." Singer's point has a certain validity: human beings are indeed endowed with free will, and their behavior often seems mystifying. As a result, the predictions of psychologists—especially those who deal with human motivation, personality, and social behavior—tend to be less precise than the predictions of scientists in such fields as biology, chemistry, or physics. Moreover, novelists such as Singer are often able to provide great insights into human behavior through their perceptive (albeit "unscientific") observations of people. It should be stressed, how-

ever, that despite people's ability to make free choices, behavior and mental life still rely on certain basic processes and are influenced by specifiable sets of causes and conditions. The systematic study of these processes, causes, and conditions is the task of the psychologist. In fact, scientific and literary approaches to human life need not be set in opposition to each other. The two approaches can complement each other and, together, enhance our understanding of the human condition.

THE RESEARCH ADVENTURE

What does the word research mean to you? Perhaps it brings to mind a white-coated scientist scurrying around a laboratory with test tubes in hand. Or perhaps it evokes memories of being holed up in the library, surrounded by a pile of reference books, trying to gather the information you need for a term paper. Psychologists do a great deal of work in the laboratory (where some of them even wear white coats) and in the library. But neither the laboratory nor the library is essential to psychological research. In fact, research can be done in a wide variety of locales—in board rooms and bars, airports and laundromats, nursery schools and retirement communities. Important psychological research has even been done underwater (see page 171) and in outer space (see page 23). No matter where it is done, there is a sense in which psychological research is like a detective story. As researchers, psychologists begin with a mystery that they want to solve. Then they gradually trace a series of clues that, they hope, will ultimately lead to a solution.

To help give you the flavor of this research adventure, we will trace two psychological detective stories in some detail. Each comes from a different area of psychology: the first deals with a troublesome aspect of people's behavior toward their fellow human beings; the second, with a remarkable aspect of human memory.

The case of the Good Samaritan

While walking down the street, have you ever seen a person collapse on the sidewalk? Or seen a fight break out between two children, with one of them really seeming to hurt the other? In some such cases, a bystander will immediately come to the aid of the victim. If the helper can't handle the situation, she might recruit other people* or call the police for assistance. In other cases, however, incidents like these—or worse—occur in the presence of many bystanders, yet nobody does anything at all. Some years ago, for example, a young woman named Kitty Genovese was attacked by a male assailant one night as she returned to her home in New York City. Thirty-eight of her neighbors watched from their apartment windows without doing anything to intervene—even though it took her attacker over half an hour to murder her (Rosenthal, 1964). Since that time, many similar cases have been reported in the news, usually in urban locations.

What determines whether or not a person will come to the aid of a victim in an accident or emergency? It was the desire to answer this question that motivated two psychologists, John Darley and C. Daniel Batson (1973), to investigate the case of the Good Samaritan. In setting up their study of factors that affect helping, Darley and Batson got *their* help from an expected—well, perhaps not so unexpected—source: the Bible. "Fortunately," Batson later recounted, "Jesus showed us the way—with his parable of the Good Samaritan" (1976, page 207).

In the parable of the Good Samaritan, told in the Gospel of Luke, Jesus described the situation of a man who had been robbed, beaten, and left half dead along the road from Jerusalem to Jericho. A priest came down the road but walked right on by without stop-

ping. Later a Levite (a member of the group who assisted the priests in the temple) came down the road, but he did not stop to help either. Finally, a Samaritan—a member of a group of religious outcasts—stopped, took care of the man's wounds, and took him to an inn where he could recover. The message of the parable is that we should not be like the priest or the Levite, so-called "religious" people who did not stop to help; instead, we should emulate the Good Samaritan, an "irreligious" person who had compassion for a fellow human being.

The parable of the Good Samaritan suggested to Darley and Batson two factors that might have an effect on whether a person would offer to help in an emergency: first, what the person happens to be thinking about when he or she notices the victim, and second, the person's time schedule. Darley and Batson speculated that the priest and Levite, as religious functionaries, had their heads full of prayers, rituals, and Biblical passages; they may have been so preoccupied with "religious" thoughts that they could not pay attention to the plight of the victim. Darley and Batson also reasoned that the priest and Levite, as busy public figures, might have been in more of a rush than the Samaritan and that this, too, might have decreased their willingness to help.

Psychologists are interested in finding out why bystanders sometimes come to the aid of victims in an emergency, but at other times fail to help.

*When referring to people in general, the usual convention is to use the male pronoun ("he" or "him") but this convention can make it sound as if all human beings are male. To avoid this implication, in this textbook we will switch back and forth between male and female pronouns.

Finally, the parable of the Good Samaritan suggested to Darley and Batson a way to set up their experiment. They selected as their experimental site a narrow alley that ran between two campus buildings at Princeton University. The students who took part in the study (the *subjects*) were sent from one building to the other. As a student walked along the deserted alley, he encountered the victim—a young man slumped in a doorway, with head down and eyes closed. As the student went by, the victim coughed twice and groaned, keeping his head down. Darley and Batson's main interest was in whether or not the student offered to help the victim. The victim was an accomplice of the researchers; he went into his act on a signal from the experimenter. If the subject stopped and offered help, the victim assured him that he was all right and thanked him for his concern.

Because Darley and Batson's study had a religious theme, they decided to recruit divinity school students as their subjects. The students were told that they would be sent to the other building to tape-record a short talk. Half of the subjects were asked to give a talk on a nonreligious topic. The other half of the subjects were to give a talk that was not only religious but specifically relevant to the ideal of helping victims: they were to talk on the parable of the Good Samaritan. All of the students were given a chance to think about their talk briefly before being sent over to the other building. We can assume, therefore, that subjects in the two different experimental conditions had rather different thoughts on their minds as they walked along the narrow alley.

The experiment had another variation, crosscutting the first one (see Figure 1.1). One-third of the subjects were told that the experiment was running late and that they would have to get over to the other building in a hurry. Another one-third of the students were simply told to go right over to the building. The remaining one-third were told that they could take their time because it would be a few minutes before the assistant in the other building would be ready for them. Thus, some subjects were in a big hurry as they walked down the road, some were in a moderate hurry, and some were in no hurry at all.

What was the evidence in the case of the Good Samaritan? All told, 40 percent of the subjects helped the victim, either by stopping to offer help or at least by telling someone else about the emergency; 60 percent did not help. But these rates were markedly

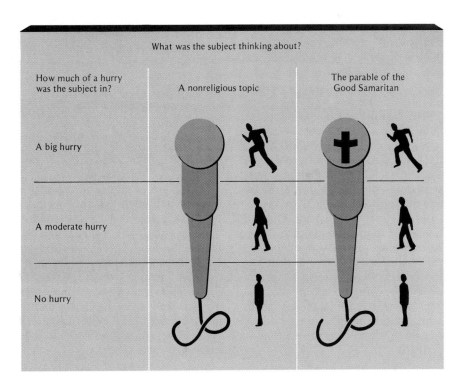

FIGURE 1.1

The experimental conditions in the Good Samaritan study. There were about seven subjects in each of the six conditions.

affected by the experimental variations. How much of a rush the subjects were in clearly affected their behavior: 63 percent of the no-hurry subjects offered help, compared to 45 percent of the moderate-hurry subjects and only 10 percent of the big-hurry subjects.

The subjects' thoughts as they walked along the road also had an effect on their helping behavior: 53 percent of those preparing to give a talk about the parable of the Good Samaritan offered aid to the victim, compared to 29 percent of those who were preparing to talk about a nonreligious topic. These results indicate that thinking about the religious ideal of compassion for victims can itself promote compassion. It should be stressed, however, that thinking helpful thoughts does not always lead to helpful action—after all, almost half the subjects in this condition did *not* offer any assistance to the victim. "On several occasions," Darley and Batson report, "a seminary student going to give his talk on the parable of the Good Samaritan literally stepped over the victim as he hurried on his way" (page 107).

In planning and conducting their research, psychologists must give careful attention to ethical issues: Does the research invade subjects' privacy? How will the subjects feel about their participation after the study is over? Studies like Darley's and Batson's, in which subjects are misled about the researchers' purposes and methods, raise special ethical questions that will be discussed in Chapter 15, Box 4.

The case of the Good Samaritan is not closed. Much more research needs to be done before we will have a full understanding of why people are sometimes Good Samaritans and sometimes not. A great deal of research is now being conducted on the sorts of situations that are more or less likely to promote helping. Other research focuses on the values and personality traits of people who are especially likely to help others in emergency situations. In the last analysis, we need to learn more about which sorts of people are most likely to help in which sorts of situations—and why.

The case of the flashbulb memory

Like the case of the Good Samaritan, our second research adventure also has its roots in personal experience. Practically everyone in the United States who was at least 10 years old in 1963 can tell you, often in great detail, the exact circumstances under which he first heard of President John F. Kennedy's assassination—where he was and what he was doing, who told him the news, and the first thing he did after hearing it.

Psychologist James Kulik recalls, for example:

I was seated in a sixth-grade music class, and over the intercom I was told that the president had been shot. At first everyone just looked at each other. Then the class started yelling, and the music teacher tried to calm everyone down. About ten minutes later I heard over the intercom that Kennedy had died and that everyone should return to their homeroom. I remember that when I got to my homeroom my teacher was crying and everyone was standing in a state of shock. They told us to go home.

Psychologist Roger Brown, an older colleague of Kulik's, recalls:

I was on the telephone with Miss Johnson, the Dean's secretary, about some departmental business. Suddenly she broke in with: "Excuse me a moment; everyone is excited about something. What? Mr. Kennedy has been shot!" We hung up, I opened my door to hear further news as it came in, and then resumed my work on some forgotten business that "had to be finished" that day.

These are examples of memories so sharp and vivid that they seem to have been recorded in the sudden glare of a flashbulb. For that reason, Brown and Kulik (1977), who decided to investigate such memories systematically, named them *flashbulb memories.* They are not memories for an historical event itself, but rather enduring memories of the setting and manner in which one heard of the event. (For another example, see Box

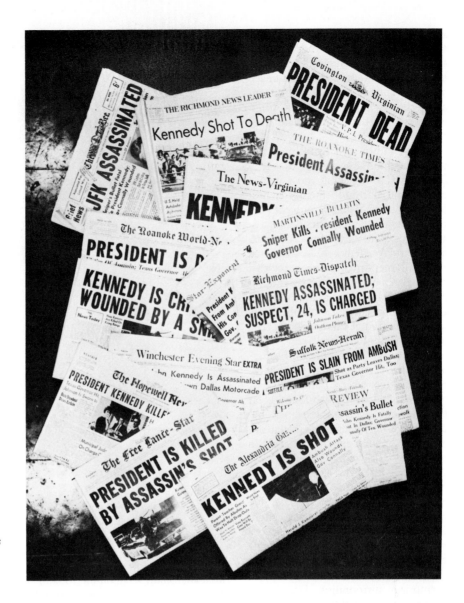

Many people remember exactly what they were doing when they first heard the news of President Kennedy's assassination. Brown and Kulik call this phenomenon a flashbulb memory.

2.) Brown and Kulik suspected that people experience flashbulb memories at certain special times in their lives. They proceeded to design a study that would shed light on the circumstances that give rise to such memories.

The two psychologists had certain educated guesses—or *hypotheses*—about the cause of flashbulb memories. First, they suspected that the event around which such a memory occurs must be sudden. Second, they believed that the event had to be personally important—it had to be perceived as having a real impact on the person's life. The more consequential the event, Brown and Kulik believed, the more likely it would be to create a flashbulb memory that would remain vivid for years to come—perhaps for one's entire life. Brown and Kulik set out to test their hypotheses by administering a questionnaire to a sample of people about their flashbulb memories.

In their questionnaire, the researchers described what they meant by flashbulb memories and then asked their subjects—eighty Americans ranging in age from 20 to 60—to indicate whether they had such memories for each of nine events that had occurred during the previous 15 years. The events included the assassinations of President Kennedy in 1963 and of Martin Luther King and Robert F. Kennedy in 1968. In addition, the subjects were asked whether they had a flashbulb memory for any personal events in their lives, such as the death of a friend or relative. Those subjects who did have flashbulb memories were asked to recount those memories in detail. The subjects were also asked to indicate how important each of the events was for them personally—that is, how much of a difference they felt the event had made in their lives.

When Brown and Kulik analyzed the questionnaire responses, they found, first of all, that most people indeed had flashbulb memories. All but one of the eighty subjects reported flashbulb memories connected with President Kennedy's assassination, and seventy-three reported flashbulb memories connected with a personal shock—most often the unexpected death of a parent. Many of the accounts were extraordinarily vivid, including such details as "The weather was cloudy and gray," "We all had on our little blue uniforms," and "I was carrying a carton of Viceroy cigarettes, which I dropped."

Brown and Kulik also found clear evidence for the link they had hypothesized between the personal importance of an event and flashbulb memories. For example, the blacks in the sample rated the assassination of Martin Luther King, the great civil rights leader, as being of considerably greater personal importance to them than the whites did. And, in accord with the researchers' prediction, the blacks were considerably more likely than the whites to have flashbulb memories surrounding Dr. King's murder: thirty of the forty blacks in the study, but only ten of the forty whites, had such memories.

While the Good Samaritan study is an *experiment*, in which the researchers set up different conditions and then observed their effects on subjects' behavior, the flashbulb memory study is a *correlational study*. The researchers did not set up conditions but instead gathered information from their subjects and then looked at the relationships (or correlations) among different pieces of information. As will be explained later, correlational studies cannot identify cause-and-effect relationships as clearly as experiments can. From Brown and Kulik's data, we cannot be sure that the personal importance of events is what *caused* the flashbulb

BOX 2

THE DAY LINCOLN WAS SHOT

THE ASSASSINATION OF PRESIDENT LINCOLN AT FORD'S THEATRE ON THE NIGHT OF APRIL 14, 1865.

Long before Roger Brown and James Kulik coined the term "flashbulb memory," another psychologist observed the same phenomenon. Consider this report, provided in the 1890s by a middle-aged man:

My father and I were on the road to A_____ in the State of Maine to purchase the "fixings" needed for my graduation. When we were driving down a steep hill into the city we felt that something was wrong. Everybody looked so sad, and there was such terrible excitement that my father stopped his horse, and leaning from the carriage called: "What is it, my friends? What has happened?" "Haven't you heard?" was the reply—"Lincoln has been assassinated." The lines fell from my father's limp hands, and with tears streaming from his eyes he sat as one bereft of emotion. We were far from home, and much must be done, so he rallied after a time, and we finished our work as well as our heavy hearts would allow.

This account was one of the many vivid recollections obtained by the psychologist F. W. Colegrove in 1899 when he asked people where they were when they heard that President Lincoln had been shot. Of 179 middle-aged and old persons interviewed, 127 gave full details of where they were. "Inasmuch as 33 years have elapsed since Lincoln's death," Colegrove concluded, "the number who made an affirmative reply must be considered large, and bears testimony to the abiding character of vivid experiences."

CHAPTER ONE: WHAT IS PSYCHOLOGY?

memories. But the fact that it does not pin down cause and effect does not reduce the importance of the study. Before psychologists can move to a full understanding of cause and effect, they must devote their attention to *describing* people's behavior, thoughts, and feelings (for example, the experience of flashbulb memories) and to determining the relationships between different events and experiences.

It is also important to realize that a single study almost never provides the final answer to a psychologist's question. Psychology, like other sciences, is *cumulative*, with one study building on another in a continuing quest for fuller understanding. In recent years, for example, other researchers have followed up on Brown and Kulik's study. In 1981, soon after an attempt had been made on the life of President Ronald Reagan, David Pillemer (1984) probed people's memories of the circumstances under which they had heard about the event. A large proportion of Pillemer's subjects, interviewed either one or seven months after the attack, had vivid memories of the event. Pillemer's results suggested that the impact of an event on a person's life may not, in fact, be the primary cause of a flashbulb memory. After all, President Reagan survived the attack, and the event turned out to be rather inconsequential for most of the subjects. What did seem to relate strongly to the fullness and vividness of the subjects' flashbulb memories was how strong an emotional reaction they initially had to the news of the attack: the stronger the reaction, the more vivid the memory. Thus, Pillemer's study helped to refine our understanding of the flashbulb memory mechanism, and additional studies will surely refine this understanding further.

Just why we are likely to form flashbulb memories for sudden and highly emotional events remains an unanswered question. As Brown and Kulik point out, however, there is reason to think that the ability to remember the circumstances surrounding sudden and important events probably had great value to our ancestors in prehistoric times. After all, the hunter who could remember the precise circumstances under which he first encountered a dangerous animal would be more likely to avoid those circumstances in the future—and, therefore, be more likely to survive. Because of this survival value, Brown and Kulik speculate, our brain structures may have evolved in such a way as to make flashbulb memories likely. Researchers are just beginning to get a handle on the physiological mechanism that may underlie flashbulb memories. Recent work (described in Chapter 6) suggests that the hormones epinephrine and norepinephrine, which are released into the bloodstream when people are emotionally aroused, play an important role in fixing material in memory. More generally, the whole field of neuroscience—the study of brain mechanisms underlying human behavior and mental life—is an exciting research frontier. We shall encounter some of the research on this frontier in Chapter 2 and at other points throughout the book.

Where do psychologists get their ideas?

Psychologists get their ideas for research questions and ways of answering them from many sources. Personal experience is one of the most important sources of research questions and hypotheses, whether it concerns people's readiness to help others, their memories, or their emotions. As the examples in Box 3 illustrate, the events of psychologists' own lives can have an important impact on the research they choose to conduct.

Psychologists get their ideas from more than just personal experiences, however. Events in the news may suggest important research questions. The widely publicized case of Kitty Genovese and her thirty-eight neighbors inspired many valuable studies of helping behavior. Similarly, the horrors of the Nazi era in Germany led psychologist Stanley Milgram to conduct important experiments on people's obedience to authority (see Chapter 15). As the case of the Good Samaritan indicates, psychologists can also get insights from religious,

SERENDIPITY

Sometimes a psychologist's insights arise by accident, as an outgrowth of other work that the psychologist happens to be doing. For example, the Russian physiologist Ivan Pavlov was studying the process of salivation in dogs when they were fed. He noticed that after a while the dogs began to salivate even before they were fed, as soon as they saw the experimenter who was about to feed them. This unexpected observation led Pavlov to discover the type of learning known as classical conditioning (see Chapter 5). An incident such as this—finding something you're not looking for—is called serendipity.

BOX 3

THE PERSONAL SIDE OF PSYCHOLOGICAL RESEARCH

Why do psychologists decide to do particular sorts of research? The reasons they usually give are scientific ones—the desire to test a theory or to continue the work of other researchers in a given area. But the decision to investigate particular topics often has its personal roots, too. Frequently, something about a psychologist's own life and personal concerns motivates her to explore particular questions. The following first-hand accounts by four researchers provide good examples.

Daniel Levinson is a clinical and social psychologist at Yale University. Beginning in the late 1960s, Levinson embarked on a major study of men's development in the middle years of life—especially the years between 35 and 50. (We will be looking at this research in Chapter 9.) Levinson explains that he had an intellectual interest in the process of adult development. But he adds:

The choice of topic also reflected a personal concern. At 46, I wanted to study the transition into middle age in order to understand what I had been going through myself. Over the previous ten years my life had changed in crucial ways; I had "developed" in a sense that I could not articulate. The study would cast light on my own experience and, I hoped, contribute to an understanding of adult development in general. (Levinson, 1978, page x.)

Teresa Amabile, a social psychologist at Brandeis University, has done extensive research on some of the factors that influence—and in many cases inhibit—people's creativity (her results are described in Chapter 7, Box 3). She traces her interest in this inquiry to some important early experiences:

When I was in kindergarten, I remember overhearing the teacher tell my mother that I showed a lot of potential for "artistic creativity." Unfortunately, the potential is yet to be realized. The problems started the next year when I entered a strict parochial school. Each art period began with the teacher handing out a miniature of one of the Great Masters' paintings for us to copy with our crayons. This was an impossible task, and it was doubly frustrating by the fact that we were graded on our accuracy. Once, in a later grade, we were allowed to do whatever we wished with our crayons. I started drawing something abstract and garish when I heard the teacher, who had been pacing the aisles, stop by my desk. She was silent for a moment and then pronounced her verdict: "I think we're being a little too creative." My interest in how external constraints can dampen creativity stems from the feeling that my own "creative potential" in art was extinguished by a restrictive school environment.

Toni Falbo, a psychologist at the University of Texas, decided to undertake research on the personalities of only children—for reasons that came close to home. She frequently heard the view expressed by educators, psychologists, and physicians that a child without siblings is likely to become selfish, lonely, and maladjusted. As an only child herself, Falbo was not convinced. "I was getting a bit peeved by the stereotype," she later admitted, "[so] I decided to see whether the only child was really as unfortunate as reputed" (Falbo, 1976). We'll learn about what she discovered in the Psychological Issue for Chapter 8.

C. Daniel Batson, one of the psychologists who conducted the Good Samaritan study, also had personal reasons for deciding to study helping behavior, stemming from his religious concerns and his prior training as a minister. When I asked him about this, Batson wrote back:

It's true that I had some designs on "tending the flocks" before being called by the Lord of Wundt, James, and Watson [see Box 1]. Actually, I carried through to the point of being ordained (still am—Presbyterian), getting a Ph.D. at Princeton Seminary, and teaching part-time while I completed my Ph.D. in psychology. My difficulty with the Seminary was that I kept wanting to know what religion actually did in people's lives (quite apart from whether it was true or not). Did it, as advertised, encourage them to be more caring? Or the opposite? Both, neither, etc.? Pursuit of these questions led me across campus to psychology—and research on helping behavior.

So, as you see, psychologists' decisions to study particular aspects of other people's lives have a great deal to do with their own lives as human beings.

philosophical, or literary writings. In addition, research is often prompted by the desire to find ways of solving pressing psychological and social problems, whether it is to develop ways to help people study more effectively (see Chapter 6), to help people stop smoking (see Chapter 12), or to reduce racial prejudice (see the Psychological Issue for Chapter 15).

In addition to these sources of research ideas, most of psychologists' ideas and methods are closely related to previous research questions and answers. As noted earlier, scientific research is a cumulative process, in which each researcher builds on the work that has already been done in a particular area. In this process, psychologists are often guided by *theories*. You have probably heard of some theories in other sciences, such as Darwin's theory of natural selection or Einstein's theory of relativity. Each theory, whether in biology, physics, or psychology, is a set of ideas that fits together to provide a perspective on some aspect of the world. In Chapter 11, for example, we will survey several different theories of personality, including psychoanalytic theory and social learning theory.

A psychologist's theoretical perspective affects the way he is likely to interpret events or findings. Thus, for example, a psychoanalytic theorist might explain a 5-year-old boy's attempt to do things the way his father does in terms of the notion of *identification*, while a social learning theorist might explain the same behavior in terms of the notions of *reinforcement* and *modeling* (see Chapter 11). At the same time, theories point the way to new research. Beginning with the concepts and hypotheses of a particular theory, the researcher derives specific predictions about behavior that she can then design a study to test.

While psychoanalytic theory and social learning theory are both wide-ranging perspectives on behavior, other theories are more narrowly focused sets of concepts and hypotheses that concern a specific problem, such as the theories of emotional activation that will be considered in Chapter 10. A great deal of research is done in an effort to test and refine theories and, in the long run, to replace inadequate theories with better ones. For a theory to survive, it must generate a body of findings that are consistent with it.

THE METHODS OF PSYCHOLOGY

Although psychological researchers often derive important insights from their personal experience, such experiences usually constitute a rather small and unreliable body of evidence. Human experiences are likely to be colored by motives and moods, so that two people in the same situation may observe quite different things. Depending on how you feel about yourself and what sort of mood you are in, for example, you may interpret the expression on another person's face as either a friendly glance, a puzzled look, or a hostile stare. In contrast, psychologists strive to study behavior in ways that are *systematic* (based on a thorough and well-organized search for facts) and *objective* (based on careful measurements that different observers can agree on, rather than on one person's intuitions).

In their efforts to gather systematic and objective information, psychologists use a wide variety of methods. No single method, such as the laboratory experiment or the nationwide survey, is the best method for psychological research, any more than a hammer is the best tool for the carpenter or a putter is the best club for the golfer. The particular method a researcher chooses will depend on the nature of the problem, the methods that previous researchers have used, and the researcher's own experience, skills, and preferences. Here we will consider some of the most commonly used methods of psychological researchers.

Whom do psychologists observe?

The psychologist's business is to make systematic observations of behavior. But no psychologist can study

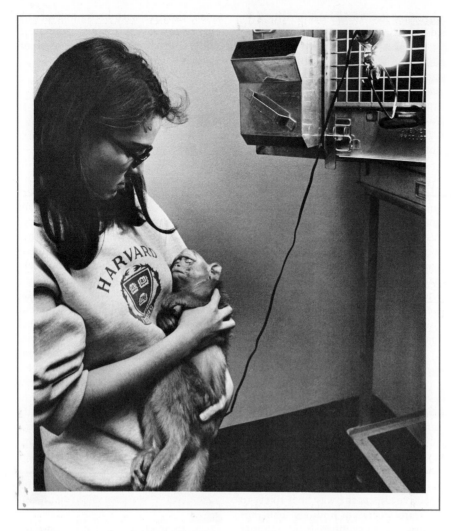

Primates such as this monkey are used in many kinds of psychological research. Although results of experiments with animals cannot be directly applied to humans, they can provide clues to some fundamental aspects of human behavior.

everyone's behavior. Instead, the researcher chooses a *sample* of people to study. Just as a geologist may attempt to determine the composition of the moon by analyzing a small sample of rocks, so the psychologist attempts to discover principles of human behavior by studying a small but representative sample of humans. In some cases, the nature of the psychologist's sample is dictated by the problem being studied. If the researcher is interested in alcoholism, he will study a sample of alcoholics—and, preferably, a sample that reflects as closely as possible the characteristics of alcoholics more generally. Similarly, a psychologist interested in child development will study children; one interested in mental illness will study people suffering from psychological disorders.

The psychologist's choice of a sample of subjects is also likely to be dictated by convenience. Roughly 75 percent of psychological research with humans has made use of college students as subjects (Rubenstein, 1982). This is not too surprising: because most psychological researchers work in colleges and universities, students—especially those taking psychology courses—provide their most readily available supply of subjects. The heavy reliance on college students as subjects presents certain problems, however. College students are not representative in all respects of the population at large. Students tend to be young, white, and middle class, and to score higher on measures of self-esteem and intellectual ability than their noncollege peers. Can one generalize from the behavior of this particular set of people to that of other segments of society?

In fact, the degree to which the results of research can be generalized from one group of people to another depends in large measure on the particular problem being studied. Whereas basic processes of learning and memory may work in much the same way for almost all human beings, patterns of social behavior are more likely to depend on people's social and cultural background. There is no easy answer to the problem of selecting subjects for psychological research. Being aware of this difficulty, you should ask yourself when reading about a psychological study: "Who were the subjects?" "How would other sorts of people be likely to behave in the same situation?" "Do these findings apply to me?"

In most cases, the psychologist includes a fairly large number of subjects in any given study. By observing the behavior of 30 or 50 or 100 people, the researcher can look for common patterns, as well as individual differences, in the subjects' behavior. Sometimes, when researchers are trying to describe the behavior or attitudes of a large group of people, they conduct *surveys* of hundreds or even thousands of subjects. At the other extreme, the psychologist can sometimes learn a great deal about human behavior by closely observing a single subject. For example, clinical psychologists often learn and communicate a great deal about personality from intensive *case studies* of individuals.

Since most psychologists are ultimately concerned with human behavior, it may seem surprising that much of their research is conducted with nonhumans. The best-known animal subjects are pigeons, monkeys, and most popular of all, laboratory rats. But psychologists have also conducted research with many other species, including houseflies, worms, elephants, kangaroos, and cockroaches. Psychologists use nonhuman subjects for a variety of reasons. For one thing, animals can be kept captive in laboratories for long periods of time, so it is easier to observe their behavior. Animals are also less likely than humans to try to second-guess the experimenter or to be suspicious of the researcher's stated intentions. There are also certain techniques, such as brain surgery or severe electric shocks, that cannot ethically be used with humans but sometimes— although ethical concerns remain— can be used with animals.

Some critics argue that research with nonhumans is not likely to be applicable to human behavior. It certainly is true that some human problems have no known parallels among other animals. As Robert Zajonc (1972) notes, "No amount of experimentation with animals would tell us whether the possession of handguns by private citizens enhances crime and violence, or what to do about industrial conflict or how to deal with poverty" (page 2). On the other hand, there are often striking similarities between animal and human behavior. Much of what we know about human

learning, for example, is based on studies of learning in pigeons, rats, and other animals (see Chapter 5). In addition, as Zajonc points out, studying other animals helps to keep us honest about our own behavior. Human beings are a unique species in many ways, but we must remember that we, too, are members of the animal kingdom.

What do psychologists observe?

Psychologists cannot observe everything about a person's (or animal's) behavior at once. They must instead devise ways of observing and measuring those specific aspects of behavior that they are most interested in. In many instances, the researcher will record particular aspects of a subject's overt behavior—for example, the number of times a baby smiles or cries, the amount of food a person eats in a given situation, or the length of time it takes for a cat to figure out how to open the door to its cage. In the case of the Good Samaritan, there was a direct measure of helping behavior: whether or not the subject stopped to help the victim. In addition, researchers sometimes use special equipment to record a subject's physiological responses, such as heart rate, blood pressure, or sweat gland activity. Researchers also frequently ask people to provide *self-reports*— their own assessment of their thoughts or behavior. The flashbulb memory study relied on such self-reports of subjects' memories and emotions. Finally, researchers often make use of specially constructed tests of people's cognitive skills or personality. (Intelligence testing is given special attention in Chapter 7, and personality assessment is described in Chapter 11.)

As with methods of research more generally, there is no single best measure for the psychologist. In

Psychologists often make direct observations of people's behavior. In this case, the researchers are observing and tabulating the subject's playful and aggressive behaviors in a laboratory situation.

Psychologists often gain information by interviewing people about their thoughts, feelings, and behaviors.

UNOBTRUSIVE MEASURES

When people know that their behavior is being observed, they are likely to behave differently than they might otherwise. To get around this problem, psychologists sometimes use unobtrusive measures: measures that are unlikely to have any effect on the attitude or behavior being studied. For example, one investigator wanted to find out—without asking—how much liquor was being consumed in a town that was officially "dry." His solution: count empty bottles in trashcans. In a study of another delicate topic, researchers investigated cultural differences in sexual attitudes by comparing the inscriptions on toilet walls in the Philippines and the United States (Webb et al., 1966).

many cases, the researcher will do best to use several different measures simultaneously, to find out how they compare with one another. For example, I once attempted to define and measure one of the more mysterious facets of human behavior, romantic love (Rubin, 1973). My primary approach was to obtain college students' self-reports of their attitudes and feelings toward their boyfriends or girlfriends. To do this, I asked the students to indicate how much they agreed or disagreed with a series of statements like, "If I were lonely, my first thought would be to seek _____ out," and "I would do almost anything for _____." In each case, the blank space denoted the student's boyfriend or girlfriend. In addition to this self-report "love scale," I obtained a behavioral measure of love by recording the amount of time couples spent looking into each others' eyes while they were waiting for an experiment to begin. I found, as I had hoped to find, that the two measures related to each other: The more the students indicated that they loved each other on the attitude scale, the more eye contact they tended to make (see Chapter 17).

Where do psychologists observe?

A large proportion of psychological research is conducted in laboratories. There are many different sorts of psychological laboratories. For example, an animal learning laboratory may have rooms full of cages in which the animals are kept and special boxes and mazes in which the animals are tested. A human group laboratory may have rooms in which groups of people can meet around a table and equipment for observing and videotaping group discussions. Laboratories help psychologists to study behavior under precise, well-regulated conditions. Because the laboratory is a rather artificial environment, however, it is sometimes difficult to generalize from the ways subjects behave in the laboratory to the ways they would behave in other situations. For example, studies of aggression in the laboratory can never give us a complete understanding of the determinants of violence in the streets. An additional limitation is that when people are studied in the laboratory, they *know* they are being studied. This awareness may lead people to be on their best behavior or to respond in ways that are not typical of their usual behavior.

To get around these problems, many psychologists conduct research in nonlaboratory settings. It is often worthwhile to study an animal's behavior in its natural habitat, whether jungle, marsh, or stream. Similarly, psychologists often study human behavior in natural settings, including dormitory rooms, parks, churches, subways, and factories. The Good Samaritan study was unique in making use of both laboratory and natural settings. The subjects began the study in the laboratory but then were sent across campus, encountering the emergency in the natural setting of an alley between two buildings.

Description, correlation, and experimentation

In addition to deciding where, what, and whom to observe, the psychologist must decide on a research plan or strategy for addressing the questions she is particularly interested in. We will consider three major research strategies: description, correlation, and experimentation.

Description. When a researcher is engaged in *description*, she is primarily concerned with setting forth a clear account of the subject's behavior or self-reports. One approach to description is the *observational study*, in which the researcher observes behavior as it occurs in a particular setting. For example, a psychologist might observe the social behaviors of several children in a nursery-school classroom, either taking notes in narrative form or counting the occurrences of specific behaviors (such as "plays alone," "plays cooperatively," "fights," and "calls for the teacher"). Other descriptive studies make use of *interviews*, in which the researcher summarizes the subjects' own appraisals of themselves. In Chapter 17, for example, we will discuss research on loneliness that makes use of extensive interviews with people who have experienced separation or loss. Descriptive studies are a central part of the psychologist's effort to come to terms

with human behavior. However, they do not in themselves permit the researcher to test specific hypotheses about cause-and-effect relationships. A good description of behavior can tell us *what* is happening, but it can't tell us with any certainty *why* it is happening.

Correlation. In a correlational study, the researcher tries to discover the relationship (or *correlation*) between two or more aspects of people's behavior, attitudes, or background. Brown and Kulik's flashbulb memory study is an example of a correlational study—subjects' ratings of the personal importance of events were related to their flashbulb memories of those events. To take another example of a correlational study, suppose that you were interested in determining the relationship between people's training in psychology and their sensitivity to other people's feelings. You might go about such a study by choosing a sample of students, asking each one how many psychology courses he has taken, and finally giving them a test of social sensitivity. You would then be able to chart the relationship between your two measures. Figure 1.2 presents one possible set of results from such a study, suggesting that the two measures (sometimes called *variables*) are in fact related to one another. (For more on correlations and how they are computed, see the Appendix.)

Such a correlational study has its limitations, however. Although our hypothetical study demonstrates that training in psychology and social sensitivity are related to each other, it does not provide a clear test of hypotheses about cause and effect. One hypothesis is that training in psychology increases people's sensitivity to others. But the casual link might go in the other direction: People who are sensitive to others may be especially interested in taking psychology classes. It is even possible that neither of the variables has any effect on the other and that both of them are caused by a third factor that we neglected to measure. For example, students who come from particular family backgrounds may be especially likely to be socially sensitive and to take psychology, while people from other family backgrounds may tend

DOES SEX CAUSE HAPPINESS . . . OR DOES HAPPINESS CAUSE SEX?

According to one study, a married couple's frequency of sex minus their frequency of arguments is highly correlated with their marital happiness (Howard and Dawes, 1976). This correlation could mean that sex enhances marital happiness and that arguments detract from it. However, it could also mean that happy couples are predisposed to have sex more and argue less. The causal sequence may even go in both directions, in a continuing cycle. Unfortunately, manipulating any of the variables experimentally is probably out of the question.

FIGURE 1.2

The results of a hypothetical study relating training in psychology to scores on a test of interpersonal sensitivity. Each dot represents one subject. The results show a high correlation between the two variables.

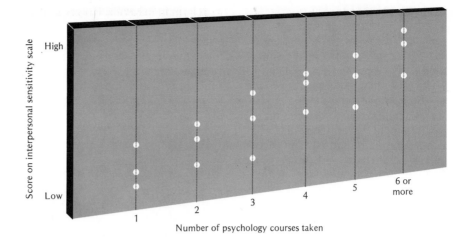

to lack sensitivity and to avoid taking psychology. Similarly, in the flash-bulb memory study, we can't be completely sure that the personal importance of events is what caused the flashbulb memories. Perhaps it worked the other way around, and the experiencing of flashbulb memories led the subjects to believe that the associated events must have been important. The moral of the story is that *correlation does not imply causation.* In other words, simply knowing that two variables are related does not in itself tell us what is causing what.

Experimentation. In order to test cause-and-effect hypotheses more definitely, psychologists also conduct experiments. An *experiment* is a study in which the researcher exerts direct control over some aspects of the subject's environment and then assesses the effects. The Good Samaritan study is an example of an experiment. Subjects were assigned to different conditions—what they were thinking about, how much of a hurry they were in—by the researchers, who then observed the effects of these conditions on the subjects' behavior.

Let's say you wanted to conduct an experiment to check out the hypothesis that training in psychology will increase people's sensitivity to others' feelings. You might do it in the following way: First, select a sample of incoming freshmen who have not yet taken psychology. Next, randomly divide your sample into two groups (you might do this by putting the subjects' names on slips of paper, mixing them up, and then dividing

them into two piles). Give the students in both groups a test of social sensitivity. Now give the students in one group a weekly assignment from a psychology textbook. Give the students in the other group a weekly reading assignment of the same length but in some other field, such as history or economics. Finally, at the end of the term, give all the students another test of social sensitivity. If the psychology training increased sensitivity to others' feelings, you should find that the average sensitivity scores of the first group increased significantly more than the average sensitivity scores of the second group. (A statistically significant difference is one that is highly unlikely to have come about by chance, and therefore can be attributed to the impact of your experimental treatments. For a discussion of statistical significance and how it is determined, see the Appendix.)

Because in this experiment you had direct control over your subjects' psychology training, it was possible for you to find out whether it actually *caused* increases in social sensitivity. In experiments, the variable that the researcher has control over (in this case, training in psychology) is called the *independent variable,* and the variable that may be affected by the independent variable is the *dependent variable* (in this case, social sensitivity). The group of subjects who receive the special treatment (in this case, the training in psychology) is called the *experimental group,* and the group of subjects they are compared with (in this case, those who were assigned reading in some other field) is called the *control group*.

The control group plays a vital function in an experiment by ruling out the effects of extraneous factors on the dependent variable. It is possible, for example, that college freshmen generally tend to become more socially sensitive over the course of a year, as they gain maturity and accumulate experiences with other people. If our experiment did not include a control group, we would not know whether changes in social sensitivity were caused by the independent variable (training in psychology) or by the personal growth that would have taken place anyway. By including the control group, whose subjects also got older during the year but who did not get training in psychology, we can determine whether the psychology training in fact made the difference.

Some experiments do not compare an experimental and a control group but rather include comparisons between a variety of conditions. In the Good Samaritan study, for example, there were six groups involved (as shown in Figure 1.1). In that study, there were two independent variables: the topic of the talk to be given and the hurry in which the subjects had to cross the campus. The dependent variable—whether the subject stopped to help the victim—was compared across all six conditions of the experiment.

One of the pitfalls of experiments, as well as of descriptive and correlational studies, is that the researcher's own expectations may influence the results that are obtained. This difficulty is examined in Box 4.

Research and application

Psychological research has been applied to a wide variety of practical issues, from energy conservation to crime prevention. The translation from research to application is not easy or automatic, however. While some psychological research has immediate applications, other research has no apparent application at all. To understand the links between research and application, it is useful to distinguish two sorts of psycholog-

BOX 4

FINDING WHAT YOU'RE LOOKING FOR

The researcher's facial expression or tone of voice can sometimes provide subtle signals to the subject about what sort of response is expected.

One of the pitfalls of psychological research is the possibility that the researcher will sometimes inadvertently produce precisely the results he or she expects to find.

Robert Rosenthal (1976) has conducted many studies demonstrating the existence of such *experimenter expectancy effects*. In one study, for example, a group of ten college students were recruited to serve as "experimenters" in a supposed research study. The experimenters were all given the same set of instructions about how to conduct the study and were told not to deviate from them. They were to show subjects a series of photos of people's faces and to ask them to guess the degree of "success" or "failure" expressed in each face. However, half of the "experimenters" were told that most people tended to rate the faces as quite successful, while the other half were told that people tended to rate the faces as quite unsuccessful. The result? The experimenters who were led to expect "success" ratings in fact obtained more such ratings from their subjects than did the experimenters who were led to expect failure ratings.

How do experimenter expectancy effects work? The best guess is that experimenters do not intentionally set out to shape their subjects' responses. Nevertheless, subtle nonverbal cues such as facial expressions and tone of voice can provide signals to the subject as to what sort of response is expected. Once they have picked up on these cues, subjects may unconsciously shift their responses in the direction that the experimenter seems to expect.

You can probably demonstrate similar effects yourself. Go up to a friend with a smile on your face and ask, in a bright tone of voice, "How often do you get depressed?" Go up to another friend and ask the same question, but this time wear a sorrowful expression and use a somber tone. There's a good chance that the way you ask the question will affect the response you get.

As a result of the work of Rosenthal and others, psychologists have become aware of this problem of unintentional influence and they have taken measures to combat it. One device is to present instructions to subjects in writing or on tape, so that the experimenter will not be able to behave differently toward different subjects. Another precaution is for the researchers to keep themselves in the dark about the experimental condition being run. In the Good Samaritan study, for example, the "victim," who had to record the subjects' helping responses, remained unaware of (or "blind" to) the experimental condition of the subjects who came down the road. The less the experimenters know about what to expect from subjects, the reasoning goes, the less likely they will be to unwittingly influence the results.

ical research: basic research and applied research.

The purpose of *basic research* is to advance our understanding of behavior, without any immediate concern for the practical uses of this understanding. The flashbulb memory study is an example of basic research. It adds to our understanding of human memory, but it does not have any direct application to the solution of personal or social problems. Although basic research seldom has any direct application, in the long run it may prove to be of great practical importance. For example, basic research on helping behavior, such as the Good Samaritan study, may eventually lead to ways of encouraging people to be more responsive to the plight of others.

Applied research is work that attempts, from the outset, to help solve a practical problem. For example, research into biofeedback techniques (use of equipment that monitors and reports such physiological processes as heart rate and blood pressure) may help people to improve their health (see Chapter 5, Box 3). Applied research is conducted in such areas as designing equipment (such as airplane instrument panels) to suit human perceptual and motor abilities and preparing educational materials that motivate students. In other instances, psychologists have done research that has direct bearing on court cases or on decisions about

government programs. For example, Sandra Bem and Daryl Bem (1973) conducted experiments that demonstrated that certain newspaper want ads were worded in such a way as to steer women into particular sorts of jobs and men into others. Their findings played an important role in the court decision that one of the largest American corporations had engaged in discriminatory hiring practices.

In addition to conducting basic and applied research, many psychologists are also involved in the *practice* of psychology—that is, in making direct applications of psychological knowledge. These activities include providing psychological counseling to individual clients, working with groups and organizations, and helping to develop social policies and programs. In the next section we will take a closer look at the variety of activities, including both research and practice, that psychologists are involved in.

WHAT DO PSYCHOLOGISTS DO?

Many people have a specific image of what psychologists do. One popular conception is that psychologists spend most of their time talking to people about their emotional problems. Another is that psychologists can usually be found showing people

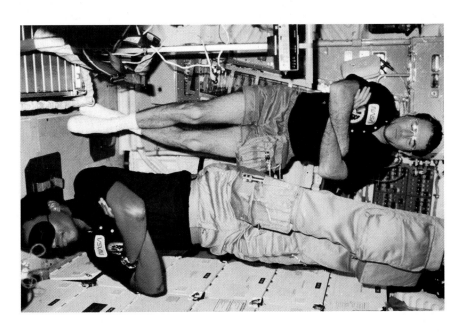

One example of applied research by psychologists has been studies of people's adaptation to the weightless conditions of spaceflight.

inkblots and asking them what they see in them. Still another image is that of people with stopwatches and clipboards who tirelessly watch rats run mazes until, after a while, they begin to look a little like rats themselves. All these images have a grain of truth to them in that psychotherapy, psychological testing, and research with laboratory animals are all among the activities of psychologists.

As you probably realize by now, however, no one of these images provides an accurate picture of the psychologist. There are well over 100,000

psychologists in the United States and Canada, and they are not all alike. Psychologists work in different settings: in colleges and universities, hospitals and clinics, government agencies, schools, businesses, and their own independent practices. In addition, psychologists specialize in different subfields of the discipline. In this section we will take a brief tour through the subfields of psychology to give you a fuller idea of what psychologists do.

Experimental psychology. Although psychologists in several dif-

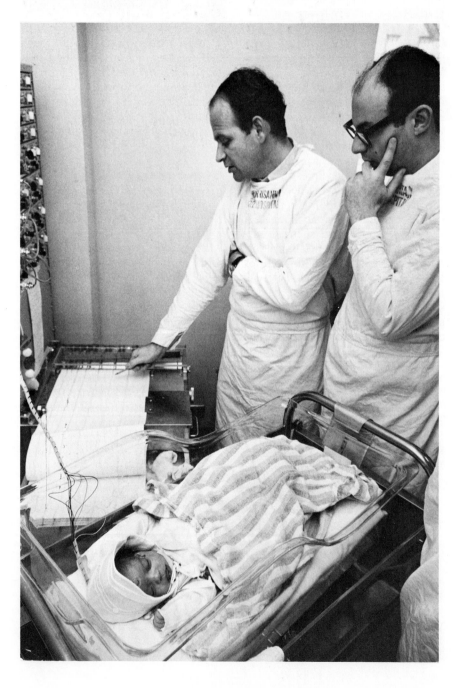

Experimental psychologists have studied sleep patterns in infants.

CHAPTER ONE: WHAT IS PSYCHOLOGY?

Clinical psychologists sometimes conduct group therapy sessions, in which participants share their feelings and concerns.

ferent subfields conduct experiments, the term *experimental psychology* is generally reserved for research on the most fundamental psychological processes, such as perception, learning, memory, motivation, and emotion. Experimental psychologists do much of their work in laboratories, using both animal and human subjects. Included in the general category of experimental psychologists are *comparative psychologists,* who compare the behavior patterns of different animal species, and *physiological psychologists,* who study the biological foundations of behavior and mental processes. One experimental psychologist might be engaged in studying the impact of people's emotions on their memory; another might be conducting research on how loud noises affect people's ability to solve problems; and a third might be concerned with explaining why lesions in particular areas of the brain cause rats to overeat.

Developmental, personality, and social psychology. *Developmental psychologists* are concerned with the development of human capacities and behavior, from conception and birth through old age and death. A developmental psychologist might study the

effects of day care on children's adjustment or the effects of retirement on older people's mental health. Psychologists in the related fields of *personality* and *social psychology* are concerned with the nature of human personality and the ways in which people's attitudes and behavior are affected by their social environment. A personality psychologist might study the function that religious or racial prejudice serves for some people, while a social psychologist might examine the processes that take place when groups—such as a jury in a court case—have to arrive at decisions.

Clinical, counseling, and community psychology. These subfields of psychology are all concerned with helping people deal with problems and decisions in their lives. *Clinical psychologists* work in schools, hospitals, and mental health centers and in private practice; they diagnose psychological difficulties and provide therapy for those who need it. The work of clinical psychologists overlaps with that of *psychiatrists,* who are also concerned with the diagnosis and treatment of psychological problems and mental illness. But clinical psychologists are trained in graduate schools, where they receive M.A., M.S., Ph.D., or Psy.D. (doctor of psychology) degrees, whereas psychiatrists attend medical schools, earn M.D. degrees, and obtain additional training in psychiatry. Clinical psychologists more often use psychological tests in their work, and they are more likely to draw on theory and research from other areas of psychology. Psychiatrists, because they are medical doctors, are able to prescribe drugs and make use of other medical treatments.

Counseling psychologists also work with people experiencing psychological problems; they also advise people who are, for example, trying to choose a career (vocational counseling), pondering decisions about marriage (marriage counseling), or trying to cope with a severe illness or injury (rehabilitation counseling). *Community psychologists* specialize in preventing and treating psychological problems at a community level—for example, by working with organizations of elderly people or with youth groups. Psychologists in any of these fields may also do research, such as

investigation of the causes of psychological disorders or the effectiveness of particular modes of therapy.

Educational and school psychology. Psychologists in these subfields focus on educational issues and problems. *Educational psychologists* are involved in the design of educational settings and techniques, and they help train teachers. *School psychologists* work within the school setting. They work with children who are having difficulty in school, consult with teachers and parents, and help to design special school programs, such as those for retarded or gifted children.

Personnel, organizational, engineering, and consumer psychology. Psychologists in these areas generally work in commercial or industrial settings. *Personnel psychologists* are concerned with selecting workers for particular jobs and with handling questions of morale and job satisfaction. *Organizational psychologists* are called upon to develop ways for businesses and other organizations to function more effectively. *Engineering psychologists* work to ensure that

Teaching is a primary activity of about one-fourth of psychologists.

CHAPTER ONE: WHAT IS PSYCHOLOGY?

the design of equipment, from telephone systems to nuclear power plants, takes into account the abilities and limitations of the people using it. *Consumer psychologists* are concerned with questions involving the purchase and consumption of goods and services, from packaging a new brand of shampoo to developing a campaign to encourage people to conserve electricity.

Even though psychology consists of a diverse set of specialties, these specialties are often closely related. An educational psychologist, for example, may call upon research generated in experimental psychology (on principles of learning), developmental psychology (on the development of intellectual abilities), social psychology (on students' interracial attitudes), clinical psychology (on psychological disorders that may affect the educational process), and organizational psychology (as it relates to the workings of a school system).

Because of these many interconnections, there are in fact no sharp dividing lines between the various specialties. And the careers of individual psychologists often span several of the subfields. For example, Elton McNeil began as an experimental psychologist, was then trained to be a clinical psychologist, worked as an educational consultant to school systems and as a school psychologist, directed a training center for persons planning to work with emotionally disturbed and delinquent boys, worked on psychological aspects of disarmament proposals, and was a field selection officer for the Peace Corps.

There is one more activity of psychologists that should not be omitted from our list: *teaching* psychology. Teachers of psychology often engage in other psychological work as well, such as research, counseling, or therapy. But teaching remains a primary activity of about one-fourth of all psychologists (Stapp and Fulcher, 1983). For most teachers of psychology, teaching is another way of putting research into practice. By presenting psychological theory and research to our students, we hope to inspire them to think about how this work applies to their own lives.

SUMMARY

- **1** *Psychology* is the science of behavior and mental processes. Psychologists attempt to systematically ask and answer questions about why people act, think, and feel the way they do.
- **2** The science of psychology is relatively new; in the late nineteenth century the German Wilhelm Wundt founded the first psychological laboratory. His theory of *structuralism*, which focused on conscious processes, became an applied science for *functionalists* in America. As a reaction against structuralism, Watson developed *behaviorism*, in which mental processes were discounted. Now things seem to have gone full circle with renewed interest in the conscious mind.

The research adventure
- **3** Darley and Batson designed an experiment to see what factors affect helping behavior. In their Good Samaritan study, they learned that people's mental preoccupations and hurriedness can influence whether or not they will stop to help someone who is in trouble.
- **4** Brown and Kulik hypothesized that *flashbulb memories*—vivid memories of what one was doing when one heard of a certain event—are more likely to occur with events that are personally important. They used a questionnaire to examine people's experiences with flashbulb memories and found support for their hypothesis.
- **5** Psychologists get their research ideas from a variety of sources: personal experience, events in the news, philosophical and literary writings, a need to solve an urgent psychological or social problem, and previous research.
- **6** Psychological *theories*—sets of ideas that fit together to provide a perspective on some aspect of behavior—serve to organize knowledge and point the way to new research.

The methods of psychology
- **7** Psychologists use a wide variety of methods for systematically gathering objective and reliable in-

formation about human behavior. These methods range from laboratory experiments to nationwide surveys.

• **8** The subjects in a psychological study may be chosen on the basis of appropriateness, convenience (most subjects are college students), and the nature of the problem being studied. The *sample,* or group of subjects representing a larger population, may range from a single person to thousands. Animal subjects are widely used in psychological research, but the applicability of results to humans depends greatly on the aspect of behavior being studied.

• **9** Psychologists must narrow down the focus of their study; they may choose to measure overt behavior, to record physiological responses, or to gather *self-reports* in the form of interviews, questionnaires, or tests. Often more than one type of measure is used in examining a single phenomenon.

• **10** Research may take place in a variety of settings, from different types of laboratories to factories, parks, and subways. Because the laboratory is an artificial environment, it is often difficult to be sure that subjects are behaving "normally" there.

• **11** *Descriptive studies* are primarily concerned with observing and recording subjects' behavior or self-reports.

• **12** *Correlational studies* are those in which a researcher tries to discover a relationship between two factors by measuring each separately and comparing the results. A limitation of such studies is that a high correlation does not necessarily imply that one factor has caused the other.

• **13** In an *experiment,* the researcher exerts direct control over one factor (the *independent variable*) to see what effect, if any, it will have on another factor (the *dependent variable*). The group for whom the independent variable is being manipulated is called the *experimental group;* the results for the experimental group are then compared with those for a second group, called the *control group.*

• **14** One problem in psychological research is the influence of *experimenter expectancy effects:* If a researcher expects an experiment to turn out a certain way, that expectation can subtly influence the outcome of the experiment.

• **15** *Basic research* is work that aims to advance our understanding of behavior without any immediate concern for its practical implications. *Applied research* attempts, from the outset, to help solve a practical problem. The *practice* of psychology involves making direct applications of psychological knowledge.

What do psychologists do?

• **16** Psychology contains numerous subfields, each devoted to research and practice of psychology in a specific area. However, a working psychologist is likely to draw from many of the subdisciplines in doing her own work.

---

*KEY TERMS**

applied research
basic research
case studies
control group
correlation
correlational studies
dependent variable
descriptive studies
experiment
experimental group
experimenter expectancy effects
flashbulb memories
hypotheses
independent variable
interviews
observational studies
psychology
sample
self-reports
subjects
survey
theory
variable

*Definitions for the key terms in each chapter are included in the Glossary that begins on page 547. The Glossary also lists the page on which each term was introduced.

PARASCIENCE

Psychology is based on the traditional methods of science, including systematic gathering of data, putting hypotheses to careful tests, and cumulative building of knowledge. But there are alternative ways of looking at human behavior that are not based on such a scientific approach to reality. The worlds of mysticism and the occult, for example, begin with a set of premises that differ sharply from those of the scientific world. Such alternative views are often referred to as "pseudoscientific" or "parascientific." The authors of this book prefer the term *parascience* (*para* meaning "beside or apart from") to the traditional derogatory label *pseudoscience* (meaning "false science").

One reason we prefer the term *parascience* is that it is not always as easy as one might suppose to distinguish "real science" from "false science." Scientists laughed at the germ theory of disease when it was first proposed in the nineteenth century, but now it is taken for granted. Astronomers are now making serious attempts to listen for signals from intelligent beings in other galaxies, an idea that would have been ridiculed a generation ago. As James Trefil (1978) has pointed out, what is "accepted science" shifts over time. Ideas that are on the outer fringe of science sometimes become the next decade's research frontiers, and some of this research, such as Einstein's work on relativity, moves on to a

Ideas that are on the outer fringe of science today can become tomorrow's research frontiers.

position of universal scientific acceptance.

Scientists often find it difficult to treat parascience in an objective, impartial manner. The authors of this book, like other psychologists, have accumulated certain convictions over the years about the approaches that can legitimately be taken toward human behavior. We label these convictions "scholarly conclusions." But those who disagree with us might call them "personal biases." So as you read the rest of this Psychological Issue, subtract what you take to be the authors' personal biases and keep your own mind open. And keep your skepticism about what you read, with the possibility in mind that those of us who have gone before you have figured it out all wrong. What we would urge most, however, is that you retain a healthy respect for the search for the facts, as opposed to unsubstantiated claims.

In discussing some of the parasciences concerned with human behavior, we will begin with one that has seen its day and is no longer in vogue: phrenology. Then we will turn to three parasciences that currently enjoy a great deal of popularity: graphology, biorhythms, and astrology. (In Chapter 4, Box 2,

we will examine the debate about the existence of extrasensory perception, which also remains beyond the bounds of accepted science.)

PHRENOLOGY

Phrenology is the study of personality characteristics through examination of the bumps and hollows of the skull. It is based on the idea that the shape and size of the various parts of the growing brain represent the overdevelopment or underdevelopment of specific personality traits.

The discipline of phrenology began in the early nineteenth century with Franz Joseph Gall (1758–1828). He was curious about a possible relationship between the physical characteristics and psychological traits of people. After examining the skulls of his friends and of imprisoned criminals, he came up with a list of 37 powers or propensities (from "combativeness" to "marvelousness") that could be equated to specific areas of the brain, as reflected in bumps on the skull (see the poster on the next page).

By 1840 phrenology had become a popular craze, offering a quick, "scientific," inexpensive way to get vocational guidance and assure happiness. There were phrenology parlors scattered across the country, and traveling phrenologists crisscrossed the nation on lecture tours. Phrenology had a reasonable ring to it in that day and age, but today's scientists reject the notion that bumps on the skull have anything to do with brain function.

People grasp at ways—including supernatural ones—to increase their certainty about life.

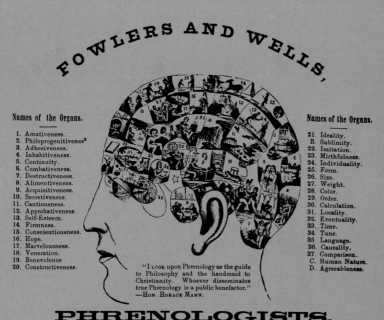

FOWLERS AND WELLS,

Names of the Organs.

1. Amativeness.
2. Philoprogenitiveness
3. Adhesiveness.
4. Inhabitiveness.
5. Continuity.
6. Combativeness.
7. Destructiveness.
8. Alimentiveness.
9. Acquisitiveness.
10. Secretiveness.
11. Cautiousness.
12. Approbativeness.
13. Self-Esteem.
14. Firmness.
15. Conscientiousness.
16. Hope.
17. Marvelousness.
18. Veneration.
19. Benevolence
20. Constructiveness.

Names of the Organs.

21. Ideality.
B. Sublimity.
22. Imitation.
23. Mirthfulness.
24. Individuality.
25. Form.
26. Size.
27. Weight.
28. Color.
29. Order.
30. Calculation.
31. Locality.
32. Eventuality.
33. Time.
34. Tune.
35 Language.
36. Causality.
37. Comparison.
C. Human Nature.
D. Agreeableness.

"I LOOK upon Phrenology as the guide to Philosophy and the handmaid to Christianity. Whoever disseminates true Phrenology is a public benefactor."
—Hon. HORACE MANN.

PHRENOLOGISTS,

142 WASHINGTON ST., BOSTON,

308 BROADWAY, NEW YORK,

231 ARCH ST., PHILADELPHIA.

OUR CABINETS OR MUSEUMS

Contain Busts and Casts from the heads of the most distinguished men that ever lived; also Skulls, human and animal, from all quarters of the globe—including Egyptian Mummies, Pirates, Robbers, Murderers and Thieves; also numerous Paintings and Drawings of celebrated Individuals, living and dead. Strangers and citizens will find our Phrenological Rooms an agreeable place to visit.

PHRENOLOGICAL EXAMINATIONS

AND ADVICE, with Charts and full Written Descriptions of Character, given, when desired. These MENTAL portraits, as guides to self-culture, are invaluable.

THE UTILITY OF PHRENOLOGY.

PHRENOLOGY teaches us our natural capacities, our right and wrong tendencies, the most appropriate avocations, and directs us how to attain self-improvement, happiness, and success in life.

VALUABLE PUBLICATIONS,

FOWLERS AND WELLS have all works on Phrenology, Physiology, Phonography, Hydropathy, and the Natural Sciences generally.

GRAPHOLOGY

Graphology is another method that purports to provide insight into personality—this time by handwritting analysis. The possibility that people's personalities are revealed in their handwriting is plausible enough to many people to encourage them to obtain—for a fee—a personal analysis from a graphologist. Some business organizations have also made use of such analyses. Indeed, the practitioners of graphology have made astonishing claims about its uses. One modern advocate, Daniel Anthony (1967), has suggested that graphology would be useful in hiring personnel, evaluating therapy patients, helping young people choose careers, and making medical diagnoses. In our view, however, these claims are vastly overstated. Graphology is more of an art than a science, and it is not an art that is likely to yield particularly accurate results.

This is not to say that people's handwriting is totally unrelated to their personalities and emotional styles. Recent studies have suggested, for example, that the size of people's signatures is positively related to their status and self-esteem. The more confident people feel about themselves, the larger their signatures tend to be (Zweigenhaft, 1977). John Hancock, whose signature on the Declaration of Independence was twice as big as anyone else's, certainly seemed to be a man with a mighty ego.

When research on handwriting is done systematically and objectively, it becomes a legitimate part of the science of psychology. But most of the practice of graphology is not based on systematic research. The reliance of graphologists and their clients on handwriting analysis is based on faith, rather than on objective evidence.

BIORHYTHMS

Don't get *biorhythms* and *biological rhythms* confused with each other. *Biological rhythm* is a general term referring to a wide variety of cyclic variations in biological systems, such as the wake-sleep cycle and the menstrual cycle. Biological rhythms are real, and we'll discuss them in the Psychological Issue for Chapter 3. *Biorhythms*, on the other hand, is a popular fad that sometimes purports to be "scientific" but really is—here go our personal biases again—a lot of malarkey.

Biorhythms theory was first developed in the late nineteenth century by Wilhelm Fliess, a nose-and-throat specialist and acquaintance of Sigmund Freud. This theory is based on the assumption that there are three important biological rhythms: a 23-day "male" or physical rhythm, a 28-day "female" or emotional rhythm, and a 33-day intellectual rhythm. Everyone is supposed to be influenced by all three of these rhythms, which are said to begin at birth and to continue uninterrupted until death. You can calculate whether you are at a high or low point on one or more of the rhythms simply by counting the number of days since your birth. As a result of the growth of the biorhythm fad in recent years, you can even buy a calculator that will compute your biorhythms for you.

Unfortunately, there is no scientific evidence for the whole idea. Yes, we *do* have mood cycles. For women, mood swings may sometimes correspond to the menstrual cycle, and there is some evidence for comparable sorts of emotional rhythms among men. But there is no good reason to believe that such cycles are as regular as the proponents of biorhythms would have it or that such cycles begin at the moment of birth.

"So," you ask, "what about all the research *proving* the importance of biorhythms?" You may have seen headlines reading something like "Japanese Bus Drivers Have Fewer Accidents When Warned of Critical Days." Unfortunately, this kind of study doesn't prove anything, except maybe that workers will be more careful when they are warned to be. Sure, accidents were reduced when workers were warned on critical days, but accidents would probably be reduced just as much if they were warned on *noncritical* days. There have been some systematic attempts to compare people's biorhythms with events in their lives, including professional golfers' scores (Holmes et al., 1980), performances in baseball and boxing (Louis, 1978), aircraft accidents (Wolcott et al., 1977), and even introductory psychology students' performance on exams (Floody, 1981). The evidence from such studies is uniformly negative.

Still, biorhythms are touted as the key to health and riches. Bestsellers have been written about them, and gamblers are supposed to bet by them. "My uncle went to Las Vegas on one of his 'up' days and won a bundle," writes psychologist Joseph Dewhirst (1979). "But he went back on the next 'up' day and lost it all. It looks like the only way to make money using biorhythms theory is to write a book about it."

ASTROLOGY

The belief that the planets and stars exert an influence on human behavior and events has been entertained for at least as long as recorded history. And today many thousands of people look past their morning newspaper's headlines to first check their horoscopes for the day. Depending upon their

birth sign—Aquarians were born between January 20 and February 18, Pisces between February 19 and March 20, and so on—they will receive advice to guide them in their day's activities:

- Take time for a long talk with associates.
- Don't act in too forceful a manner with superiors.
- Use tact in handling a personal matter.
- Get in touch with a neglected friend in the evening.

Sound a little like Chinese fortune cookies? The basic principle is the same. Each of the twelve messages, one for each birth sign, contains advice that would be suitable for almost anyone in almost any circumstances. The horoscopes are sufficiently vague to be highly applicable to most people. Most of us, for example, have a neglected

---

Horoscope

By JEANE DIXON

FOR SUNDAY, JULY 27

YOUR BIRTHDAY: This summer sees your pet project get a big boost. Financial progress is slow but steady. Hope to achieve greater happiness in love, marriage? — guard against unconventional behavior.

ARIES (March 21-April 19): Financial schemes demand careful scrutiny. Settle an old argument. New love interest on way.

TAURUS (April 20-May 20): Take a long-range view of what you hope to accomplish. Influential people will not accept ideas now.

GEMINI (May 21-June 20): Seek legan advice before signing contracts. Be alert, you may be watched.

CANCER (June 21-July 22): Work schedule may be changed. Financial affairs require careful handling. Rearrange priorities.

LEO (July 23-Aug. 22): There is profit in real es-tate deals Timing is vital. Travel, romance featured.

VIRGO (Aug. 23-Sept. 22): Troubled associates may be feeling down in the dumps. Take the initiative.

LIBRA (Sept. 23-Oct. 22): Don't let reason be ruled by emotions. Be moderate in speech. Declaration of intent nets positive response.

SCORPIO (Oct. 23-Nov. 21): Top is where you'll get straight answers. There is more to public disagreement than meets the eye.

SAGITTARIUS (Nov. 22-Dec. 21): All in authority are quite impressed with your performance. Maintain positive outlook.

CAPRICORN (Dec. 22-Jan. 19): Long delayed news arrives. You feel great because of stroke of luck. Celebrate at home.

AQUARIUS (Jan. 20 Feb. 18): Where money is concerned you need to act with considerable restraint. Begin a "rainy day" fund.

PISCES (Feb. 19-March 20): A "lone wolf" role is to your advantage today. This is a day others cannot be relied upon. Business before pleasure.

friend somewhere in our lives, a personal matter that requires tact, and a superior who doesn't take well to being pushed around.

Most people who consult their horoscope every day don't take it too seriously and certainly don't think there is anything "scientific" about it. Many astrologers believe their work has a scientific basis, however, and they demand to be taken seriously. They point out that some rhythms on earth are clearly influenced by forces emanating from the sun (our day-night rhythms) and from the moon (the rhythm of the tides). And they take that link to its "logical" conclusion: Heavenly bodies influence more than a few limited aspects of life on earth; in fact, they influence *all* of them.

There is, to be sure, little evidence for these claims. Systematic attempts by psychologists to check out astrological predictions have repeatedly yielded negative results. Nevertheless, there are at least a handful of scientists who are unwilling to write off the claims of astrologers altogether. Two French psychologists, Françoise and Michel Gauquelin, for example, have collected information on people's date and time of birth and claim to have found links between planetary positions at the time of birth and people's later traits and skills. In particular, they found that the position of Mars at the time of birth seemed to influence success in athletics and in military careers—both endeavors that demand a high degree of competitiveness and aggression. This discovery received worldwide recognition and was heralded by some as a major breakthrough in the scientific study of astrology. Yet careful attempts by other researchers to confirm this "Mars effect" have not been successful (Abell, 1982), and most psychologists would regard this finding as a fluke.

THE APPEAL OF PARASCIENCE

The appeal of parasciences such as biorhythms and astrology does not really seem to depend on their scientific credibility. Rather, their popularity seems to reflect needs that run deep in many of us. There have always been people who like to believe that control of their lives is out of their own hands, that the ultimate responsibility lies elsewhere—whether in their "rhythms" or in the stars. These people have consulted ouija boards, tarot cards, the I Ching, and horoscopes for clues about what these outside forces have planned.

But to some degree the parasciences appeal to all of us, and belief in such phenomena has been rising in recent decades (Bainbridge and Stark, 1981). Belief in the occult seems to rise and fall according to the social and political climate (Singer and Benassi, 1981). In today's uncertain world, with its changing values, economic shifts, and the threat of nuclear war, people grasp at ways—including supernatural ones—of increasing their certainty about life.

Whatever the climate of the times, human beings are quite susceptible to illogical beliefs. We tend to give the most credence to information that confirms our expectations and to discount information that disconfirms our expectations (Nisbett and Ross, 1980). So, we are likely to remember the few times our horoscope precisely matched our experience and to forget the many other times it had no relevance. Or we may focus on the two or three correct statements in our graphological analysis and ignore the seven or eight incorrect ones.

The mass media feed into these cultural and cognitive biases. If an astrologer correctly predicts the date a world leader will be assassinated, for example, it will be picked up as "news," while the thousands of times such predictions are false do not make the headlines. And movies, books, and magazines capitalize on our need to have explanations for events science cannot currently explain. Some of the most popular movies and books of recent years—including *Star Wars* and its sequels—have emphasized mysterious forces influencing our lives.

Finally, part of the appeal of the parasciences may be the very fact that they are *not* scientific—that their "predictions" cannot be accounted for in terms of accepted scientific principles. As Trefil (1978) writes, "Perhaps it serves some deep need of human beings to believe that there is still some mystery—something unknown—left in life."

SUMMARY

- *1* The *parasciences* are alternative ways of looking at reality that are not based in science. It is difficult to examine the parasciences objectively.
- *2* *Phrenology*, the study of personality via examination of the bumps and hollows of a person's skull, was a popular fad in the 1800s.
- *3* *Graphology*, or handwriting analysis, is not typically based on systematic research and is more a matter of faith between graphologist and client.
- *4* According to *biorhythms* theory, our lives are influenced by three biological cycles. However, there is no scientific evidence to support this theory.
- *5* *Astrology*, the belief that our lives are influenced by the stars and planets under which we were born, has not been proved to have a scientific basis.
- *6* The appeal of parasciences seems to reflect some people's need to believe in outside forces controlling their lives or in mysteries of life that science cannot explain.

Attempts to confirm the "Mars effect" have not been successful.

BIOLOGICAL FOUNDATIONS OF BEHAVIOR

All our behaviors and thoughts are based in our biological makeup—the workings of our bodies and our brains.

CHAPTER **2**

EVOLUTION AND GENETICS

Human evolution
Principles of genetics
Behavior genetics
Genetic disorders

Our biological heritage begins with our evolution from earlier primates. The heritage continues through the genetic transmission of characteristics from one generation to the next.

THE NERVOUS SYSTEM

The organization of the nervous
 system
Neurons and their messages

The human nervous system, made up of billions of neurons, allows us to receive, process, and act on information.

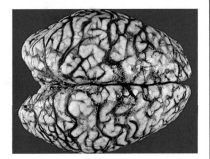

THE BRAIN

Unlocking the brain
The structure of the brain
Specialization of brain function
Our two brains

The central headquarters of the nervous system is a mushy three-pound glob called the brain.

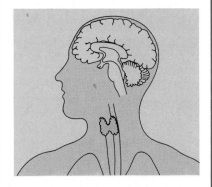

THE CHEMISTRY OF BEHAVIOR

Neurotransmitters
Hormones
Neuropeptides

The brain's and body's own chemicals play a vital role in regulating behavior and mental life.

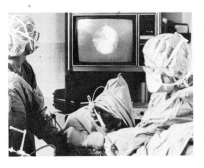

PSYCHOLOGICAL ISSUE
BIOLOGICAL ENGINEERING

BOXES
1 The brain and the computer
2 Biofeedback
3 Happy brain, sad brain
4 "That time of the month":
 Menstruation and moods

New technologies—from "test-tube babies" to "brain transplants"—are enabling us to alter our biological functioning. The prospects are exciting—and troublesome.

All our thoughts and actions, our moods and memories, are based in our biological makeup: the workings of our bodies and our brains. Because we share a biological heritage with other animals, our needs and patterns of behavior resemble those of other animals in many respects. But the human brain has evolved to a point that allows us to do things that are unique in the animal kingdom: create works of art, build machines, communicate by means of language, contemplate the meaning of life, and explore the workings of the brain itself.

In this chapter we will explore the biological foundations of human thought and behavior. We will begin by discussing the biological evolution of the human species and the principles of genetics that underlie the transmission of characteristics from generation to generation. We will then turn our attention to the *nervous system*, the complex network that provides the links between the mind, the body, and behavior. At the center of our inquiry will be the central switchboard of the system, the brain itself. Finally, we will discuss one of the new frontiers of brain research: the chemicals, some only recently discovered, that transmit messages through our brains and bodies and thereby regulate our experiences.

EVOLUTION AND GENETICS

"There are one hundred and ninety-three living species of monkeys and apes," wrote the zoologist Desmond Morris (1967). "One hundred and ninety-two of them are covered with hair. The exception is a naked ape self-named *Homo sapiens*" (page 9). *Homo sapiens* is, of course, us. The scientific name for the human species

comes from the Latin *homo*, meaning "man," and *sapiens*, meaning "knowing" or "wise." How did *Homo sapiens* get here? And how do human beings pass on their characteristics from one generation to the next?

Human evolution

Over the billions of years of the earth's existence, simple one-celled organisms have given rise to life forms as diverse as hyacinths, herrings, hippopotami, and humans. How did this process come about? The key elements of the answer were provided by Charles Darwin in his world-famous book, *On the Origin of Species By Means of Natural Selection* (1859). The basis of Darwin's account was the principle he called *natural selection*. Darwin noted that although the members of any given plant or animal species share basic characteristics, they also vary markedly among themselves. Take dogs, for example. Although they all share the same general features, they vary widely in size, shape, coloring, and temperament. And the same holds true for every other sort of plant or animal, from cockroaches to human beings.

Of all the members of a particular species, only some bear offspring and only some of these offspring ever reach adulthood. The ones "selected" to survive are those best able to adapt to their environment. This is what Darwin meant by the phrase "survival of the fittest." In a particular species of fish for example, those with a darker coloring may be most likely to survive because the coloring provides camouflage against predators. Darker fish, in this environment, will be more likely to grow to adulthood and produce offspring, which will inherit the darker coloring. Over the course of many generations, the species as a whole will gradually take on that darker color. Thus, natural selection does not in itself produce variations, but it channels the variations that naturally occur by perpetuating some and eliminating others.

Can this principle of natural selection explain the evolution of the human species as well? Darwin believed that it could. He suggested that just as frogs evolved from primitive lizards, and dogs evolved from wolves, so humans evolved from apes. In Darwin's time, this was a heretical suggestion. After all, the Bible tells us that God placed man and woman on earth on the sixth day of creation, and it doesn't say anything about evolution. Even today, some people contend that the biblical account of creation is a valid explanation of the origins of the human species. This viewpoint is called *creationism*. The advocates of creationism argue that the biblical account of human origins should be taught in school science classes, along with the theory of evolution.

Despite the claims of creationists, however, the scientific evidence indicates that humans evolved from other species. The great apes, including the gorilla and the chimpanzee, are our closest living relatives (see Figure 2.1). We did not evolve directly from any of the apes that inhabit the earth today, however. Instead, we are distant cousins, with our closest common ancestors being creatures that lived millions of years ago, long before the emergence of today's humans or chimps. The earliest of our direct ancestors to be discovered through fossil evidence is the apeman *Australopithecus*, who walked upright and used tools from about 4 million to 1.3 million years ago. *Homo sapiens* is only a toddler in the perspective of evolution—we've only been around for about 250,000 years.

THE PRICE WE PAY

One of the most important differences between humans and the apes is that we can walk continuously on two legs. But our bipedalism, accomplished through the course of evolution, was not bought without a price. As a result of our two-legged posture, members of the human species suffer from backaches, rupture easily, and have far more trouble bearing children than any other animal (Curtis, 1975).

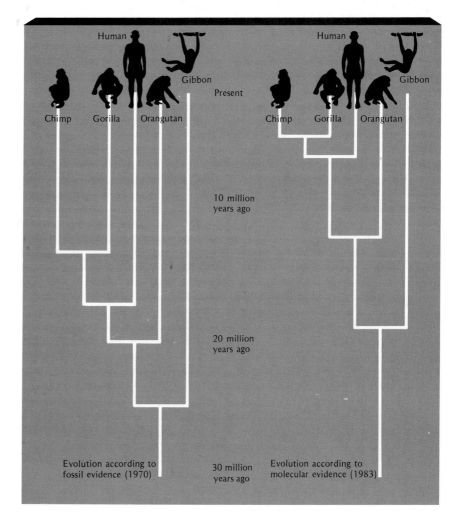

FIGURE 2.1

Two accounts of human evolution. Until recently it was estimated, on the basis of fossil evidence, that humans and apes began evolving in separate directions some 14 million years ago (left). But new techniques, which examine the molecular structure of the genetic material (DNA) of different animals to determine how closely they are related, suggest that humans and apes split off only about 5 million years ago (right) (McKean and Brownlee, 1983).

As indicated in Figure 2.1, humans do not descend directly from any of the apes that inhabit the world today. We are distant cousins.

Like species of fish, our species evolved through the natural selection of those of our prehistoric ancestors who were best adapted to survive in their environment. Those early primates whose bone structure enabled them to walk on two feet were better able to use their hands to gather food and to use tools. Thus, they were more likely to survive and produce more offspring having the sort of bone structure that made walking possible. Over millions of years, other human traits—most notably a large and highly developed brain—were similarly selected.

Principles of genetics

To understand evolution more fully, one needs to understand some basic principles of genetics. The word *genetics* comes from the word *gene*. Genes are the tiny structures within the nuclei of the body's cells that carry the messages of heredity. The genes are segments of a chemical called deoxyribonucleic acid—DNA, for short—that serves as the carrier of genetic information. When a child is conceived, the genes received from the sperm cell of the father and the egg cell of the mother jointly serve as chemical instructors to the developing organism. These genetic instructions affect the physical characteristics of the child; it is because of such messages that a child can have "her

father's nose" or "his mother's eyes." In addition, genes influence the child's developing brain and nervous system in ways that can affect intellectual capacities, personality, and behavior.

If parents' characteristics are passed on to their children through their genes, why aren't children exact carbon copies of their parents? One reason is that genes usually act in pairs, one from each parent. A combination of two sets of characteristics often leads to a result that resembles neither very closely. More fundamentally, genetic information is only indirectly reflected in visible characteristics. We must distinguish between a person's *genotype*, or genetic makeup, and the person's *phenotype*, or outward expression of the genetic makeup. For example, Jerry's genes for eye color may be one brown (say, from his father) and one blue (from his mother). So Jerry's genotype for the characteristic of eye color is brown-blue. But this doesn't mean that Jerry will have one brown eye and one blue eye. In fact, he will have brown eyes, because the gene for brown eyes outranks the gene for blue eyes in the determination of eye color (the phenotype). In this case, the gene for brown eyes is said to be *dominant* and the gene for blue eyes is said to be *recessive* (see Figure 2.2).

In addition to eye color, several other human traits are controlled by a

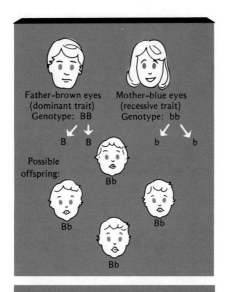

All children have brown eyes (phenotype) and are Bb (genotype).

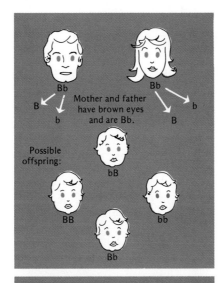

Three-fourths of children have brown eyes; one-fourth have blue eyes.

FIGURE 2.2

Inheritance of eye color. The gene for brown eyes (B) is dominant over the gene for blue eyes (b). Thus, when a parent who has two genes for brown eyes (BB) mates with a parent who has two genes for blue eyes (bb), all their children will have brown eyes. However, when both parents have a genotype that includes a gene for brown eyes and a gene for blue eyes (Bb), it is possible for them to have a child with blue eyes (bb). Thus, brown-eyed parents can have blue-eyed children. The actual eye color is the person's phenotype for the trait; the particular genes involved (such as BB and Bb for brown eyes) make up the person's genotype for the trait.

single gene pair, including color vision, hair curliness, hair color, and certain genetic diseases. However, most human traits involve an interaction between many genes, so tracing the genetic origins of most traits is much more complex than tracing the origins of a person's eye color.

Behavior genetics

Genes can affect not only our physical characteristics but our psychological characteristics as well. Heredity has a substantial influence on people's intellectual capacities (see Chapter 7), their personalities (see Chapter 11), and their likelihood of developing depression and schizophrenia (see Chapter 13).

The study of hereditary factors affecting personality and behavior is called *behavior genetics.* Much of the data in this area comes from other animals, because selective breeding experiments (which would be unconscionable with humans) can be done with laboratory animals. For example, studies have shown that heredity has a great deal to do with the degree of savageness in laboratory rats. The white rat is tamed easily; the gray rat is not. When white rats are mated with gray rats, some of the offspring show the tame disposition of the white parent, while others exhibit the savageness of the gray parent (Sprott and Statts, 1975).

Researchers can explore the impact of genetics on human traits by comparing the characteristics of people with different degrees of relatedness, such as parents and children, cousins, and siblings (brothers and sisters). Studies comparing pairs of identical and fraternal twins are often particularly valuable. Identical twins develop from a single fertilized egg and have identical sets of genes. Fraternal twins develop from two different fertilized eggs and share only half their genes—they are no more similar genetically than any other pair of siblings. One such twin study examined genetic influences on people's fears. Fears are often assumed to be a product of early learning experiences. Yet when researchers compared the fears of identical and fraternal twins, both adolescents and adults, they found that identical twins were more similar in what they feared than fraternal twins were (Rose and Ditto, 1983). For example, if one identical twin was afraid of deep water or small animals, the co-twin was likely to share this fear.

In acknowledging that our genes influence psychological characteristics, it is important to emphasize that these effects are indirect. Genes don't produce behavior—people do. There is no gene for intelligence, for emotionality, or for any other psychologi-

Identical twins, such as the pair shown above, develop from a single fertilized egg and have identical sets of genes. Fraternal twins, such as the pair below, develop from two different fertilized eggs and are no more similar genetically than any other pair of siblings.

cal trait. Rather, genes exert their effects on the development of bodily structures, including the brain and nervous system, and on the body's complex chemical processes. These physical and chemical legacies can then play a part in determining our intellectual capacities, personalities, and behavior—but only in complex interaction with the environment in which we grow up. (This issue is explored in further detail in Chapter 11.)

Genetic disorders

Genetic disorders—about 2000 different types have been identified so far—are believed to account for about 40 percent of infant deaths and 80 percent of all cases of mental retardation (Halcomb, 1977). Most genetically caused disorders are recessive genetic traits. Take *phenylketonuria* (PKU), for example. This disease occurs only in individuals who have received the defective gene from both parents—those with only one defective gene show no signs of the disease. Children born with this disease lack an important enzyme that normally functions to help break down phenylalanine, an amino acid found in milk and other high-protein foods. Without this enzyme, the phenylalanine builds up in the body and eventually disturbs brain and nervous system functioning by causing the destruction of brain cells. Children with PKU show severe mental retardation, hyperactivity, skin disorders and discoloration, and seizures. Fortunately, this disease can be controlled when it is discovered early enough, and today most states require a routine blood test for PKU in newborns. If PKU is discovered, the infant is put on a diet that regulates the amount of phenylalanine consumed, so that it will never reach dangerous levels.

Some genetic diseases are found primarily among particular ethnic and racial groups. For example, a nervous system disorder called *Tay-Sachs disease* is found almost exclusively in the descendants of European Jews, the serious blood disease *sickle-cell anemia* is found primarily among blacks, and the respiratory and digestive disorder *cystic fibrosis* is found mainly among Northern European whites.

THE NERVOUS SYSTEM

The nervous system is a marvelously complicated network of pathways that allow us to receive information from the outside world; to learn, think, feel, and plan; to speak, write, and act. First we will look at the overall organization of the nervous system. Then we will examine the ways in which individual nerve cells (*neurons*) send and receive messages.

The organization of the nervous system

The nervous system is organized to perform several crucial functions. Let's say that you see a friend across the street and you wave to her. To accomplish this feat, your brain—which is the nervous system's central operating headquarters—first needs a means of *receiving* information, in this case the image of your friend from your eyes. Second, the brain needs a means of analyzing or *processing* information, as in recognizing that the image is in fact your friend. And third, the brain needs a means of *sending* instructions to different parts of the body, as in the order it issues to the muscles in your arm that are needed for the act of waving. A different kind of neuron performs each of these three functions. *Afferent neurons* (also called sensory neurons) carry incoming information to the brain from the sense organs. *Association neurons* process the information. And *efferent neurons* (also called motor neurons) carry outgoing information and instructions from the brain to other parts of the body.

The afferent and efferent neurons make up the *peripheral nervous system;* they provide the channels of communication between association neurons and the rest of the body. The *central nervous system* consists of the brain and spinal cord; it is made up of the association neurons, which actually carry out the information processing. The *brain* is responsible for language, thought, and intelligent action. For example, the brain carries out the process of recognizing and deciding to wave to a friend. The neurons of the *spinal cord* are not able to perform such complex processing. Their specialty is the fast, automatic processing known as *reflex action*. When your hand touches a hot stove, for example, only a simple reaction is needed, but it is needed fast. The association neurons in the spinal cord receive the "hot" message from afferent neurons in your hand and imme-

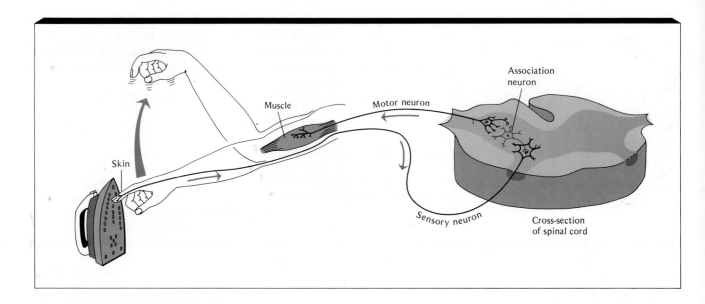

diately send a "pull back" message to the muscles in your hand and arm (see Figure 2.3). In this type of reflex response, the brain need not be involved at all.

The peripheral nervous system, with its afferent and efferent neurons, is organized into two main divisions: the somatic and autonomic systems (see Figure 2.4). The *somatic nervous system* carries information to and from the muscles that we can move voluntarily, whether it is to smile, to talk, or to wave. It also carries information from the sense organs to the brain. The *autonomic nervous system* controls the muscles of the inter-

nal organs, such as the blood vessels and the stomach, which we cannot control voluntarily. (If you have ever blushed when you wanted to appear "cool" or heard your stomach rumble all through a lecture, you will appreciate that the autonomic system is not under voluntary control.)

The autonomic nervous system can be further divided into the *sympathetic* and *parasympathetic* branches. These two branches have opposite functions in many parts of the body. The sympathetic branch is active whenever the body is under stress: It causes the heart to pound, the pupils to enlarge, digestion to

FIGURE 2.3

An example of a reflex. When the finger touches the hot iron, a "hot" message is sent along a sensory neuron to the spinal cord. Association neurons in the spinal cord receive the signal and relay it to a motor neuron, which in turn sends a "pull back" message to muscles in the hand and arm.

FIGURE 2.4

The divisions of the nervous system.

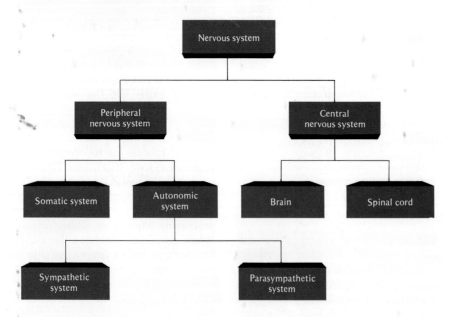

stop, breathing to increase, and blood to rush to muscles. The parasympathetic division, on the other hand, sends messages that reduce the emergency reaction. It signals the heart to beat a little slower, the pupils to contract, the stomach muscles to relax and resume digestion, and breathing to slow down (Figure 2.5). Thus, the sympathetic system arouses the body, while the parasympathetic calms it down. Just before the start of a race, for example, a runner's sympathetic system will be especially active. After the race is over, the parasympathetic will come to the fore.

One way in which the autonomic nervous system affects the body is by stimulating the glands of the *endocrine system* to produce chemicals called *hormones*. Once hormones are in the blood, these chemicals travel to different parts of the body, where they can affect body functions and reactions. The endocrine system and hormones will be discussed later in the chapter, when we consider the chemistry of behavior.

FIGURE 2.5

The parasympathetic (left) and sympathetic (right) divisions of the autonomic nervous system have opposing effects in many parts of the body. Parasympathetic neurons originate from the brain and the base of the spinal cord, while sympathetic neurons originate from the remainder of the spinal cord.

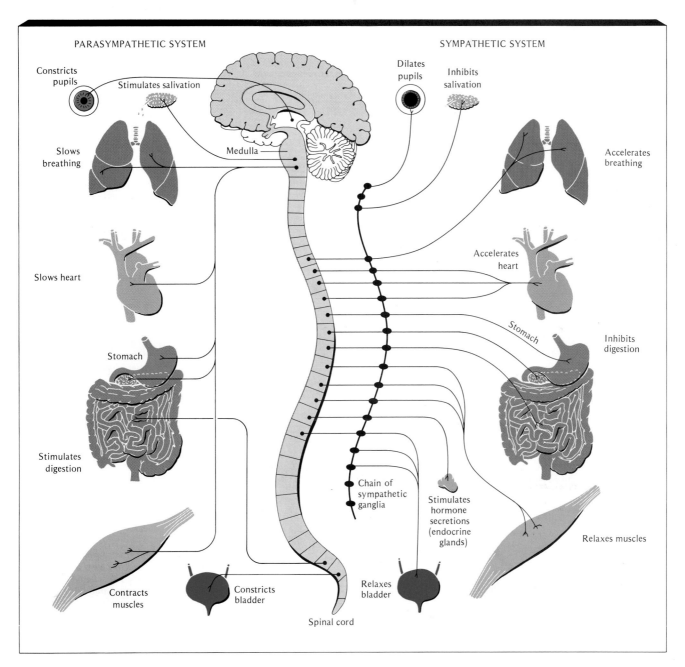

PARASYMPATHETIC SYSTEM

Constricts pupils
Stimulates salivation
Slows breathing
Medulla
Slows heart
Stomach
Stimulates digestion
Contracts muscles
Constricts bladder

SYMPATHETIC SYSTEM

Dilates pupils
Inhibits salivation
Accelerates breathing
Accelerates heart
Stomach
Inhibits digestion
Chain of sympathetic ganglia
Stimulates hormone secretions (endocrine glands)
Relaxes muscles
Relaxes bladder
Spinal cord

Neurons and their messages

When we talk about the various divisions of the nervous system we are actually talking about an immense network of billions of interacting neurons continuously exchanging information and carrying messages throughout the body. The processing done by each individual neuron is complex: some researchers have compared a single neuron to a small computer. To understand the way in which these microscopic "computers" interact to create a functioning nervous system, we must first look at the process of *neural transmission:* how separate nerve cells communicate with one another.

Neurons are specially designed for communication. A typical neuron has three main parts: the cell body, dendrites, and an axon. The *cell body* contains the cell nucleus, and projecting from it are numerous *dendrites,* short fibers that receive messages from nearby cells. The *axon* is a longer fiber that extends from one side of the cell body and transmits messages to other neurons or to muscles or glands (see Figure 2.6). Although most neurons have these general features, they may differ greatly in their dimensions. A neuron in the

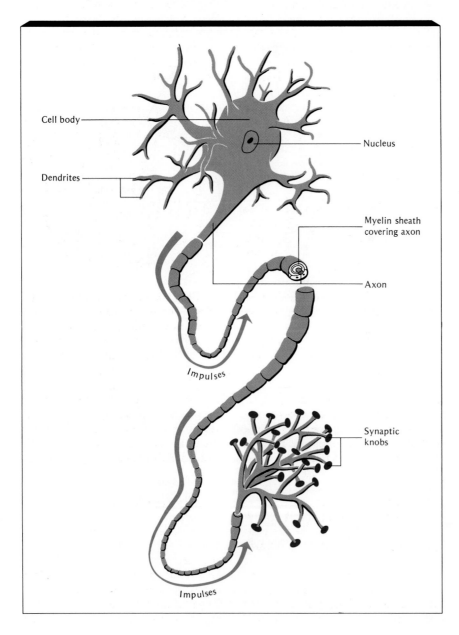

Cell body

Nucleus

Dendrites

Myelin sheath covering axon

Axon

Impulses

Synaptic knobs

Impulses

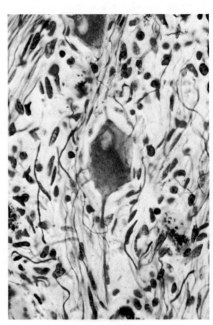

FIGURE 2.6

(Above) A neuron from a portion of the human nervous system called a sympathetic ganglion. (Left) A schematic drawing of a neuron. The nerve impulse travels from the dendrites through the cell body and along the axon, terminating in the synaptic knobs at the end of the axon. The myelin sheath is a fatty tissue that covers the axon and enhances its ability to carry electrical messages.

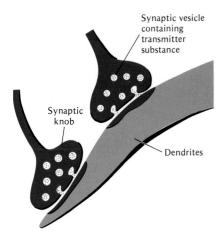

Synaptic vesicle containing transmitter substance

Synaptic knob

Dendrites

FIGURE 2.7

Schematic drawing of a synapse. Synaptic knobs at the end of the terminal branches of axons contain chemical transmitter substances. When a message travels along the axon, these knobs are stimulated to release their chemicals into the tiny gap between the knob and the cell membrane of another neuron. These chemicals make the receiving neuron either more or less likely to fire.

spinal cord, for example, may have an axon 2 or 3 feet long, whereas axons in the brain may be as short as a few thousandths of an inch.

Nerve messages normally move in one direction. Within a cell, messages pass from the dendrites through the cell body and along the axon. Messages also pass between cells, from the end of the axon, across the microscopic gap between the cells called the *synapse*, to the dendrites of the next cell (Figure 2.7). Transmission along a neuron's surface is called *axonal transmission*; transmission between neurons is called *synaptic transmission.*

In axonal transmission, an electrical impulse is sent from one end of the neuron to the other, and the neuron is said to have *fired.* The stimulation to an axon must exceed a certain threshold—or minimum level—before the axon will fire. If the stimulus, whether from a sense organ or from other neurons, does not reach this threshold, the neuron will not fire. But once a stimulus is strong enough to cause the neuron to fire, it will fire completely. This is called the *all-or-none principle.* In some ways it is like the firing of a gun: You must pull the trigger hard enough to fire, but pulling harder on the trigger will not cause the bullet to travel any faster or any farther. If the stimulation to an axon is continued, however, it will fire repeatedly, up to a maximum of 500 impulses per second in some neurons.

Once a neuron has fired, synaptic transmission from one neuron to another can occur. When an impulse reaches the tip of an axon, it causes a chemical *neurotransmitter* to be released. This substance crosses the synapse and gives a message to the next neuron. This message may be *excitatory,* increasing the likelihood that the next neuron will fire, or *inhibitory,* decreasing the likelihood of such firing. In either case, the effect is that a message is communicated from one neuron to the next. Nerve cells are not usually hooked up in a single chain, however. Especially in the brain, it is common for one neuron to receive messages from hundreds of other neurons simultaneously (see Box 1). Whether or not any one neu-

ron will fire depends on the sum total of all the excitatory and inhibitory signals reaching it at any given time.

THE BRAIN

The mind has always been dumbfounded by the brain. That three-pound glob of matter hardly seems up to the task of writing Paradise Lost, *composing* Eroica *or discovering relativity. Yet for 2400 years, ever since Hippocrates located the seat of the intellect inside the skull, the mind has been forced to admit that its greatest achievements, its loftiest thoughts, its deepest emotions all arise from something with the consistency of Jell-O and the color of day-old slush. (Begley, 1983, page 40.)*

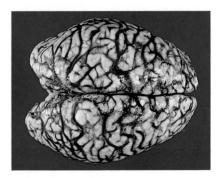

At first glance, this mushy, three-pound glob seems an unlikely candidate for its role as commander-in-chief of the entire nervous system. But in cellular terms, the brain is impressive. The human brain is believed to contain about 100 billion neurons—about as many as the number of stars in our galaxy (Stevens, 1979). It also contains perhaps ten times as many *glia*—cells that provide nourishment and support for the neurons.

Unlocking the brain

The brain is a difficult organ to study. It is locked up inside a bony skull and is protected by several layers of membrane and cushioning fluid. In the early days of brain study, the brains of lower animals or of humans were removed after death and sliced into

BOX 1

THE BRAIN AND THE COMPUTER

Can the human brain really be likened to a computer?

It is fashionable to liken the human brain to a computer—in the words of an advertisement for a book about the brain, "the most complex, sophisticated and powerful computer on earth." This analogy has a good deal of intuitive appeal. Both the brain and the computer receive information (or *input*), process this information rapidly, and produce responses (*output*).

For many of us in today's computer era, thinking of the brain as a computer may make this mysterious organ seem just a bit more comprehensible.

But whereas the analogy between the brain and the computer has its appeal, it can also be misleading. Recent brain research has made it clear that there are some fundamental differences between the operations of the

brain and those of the computer. Francis Crick (1979), the Nobel Prize-winning biologist, has summarized some of these differences:

- In a computer, information is processed at a staggeringly rapid rate, and the process is serial—that is, messages are sent one at a time from one point to another. In the brain, the rate of transmission is slower, but the information can be handled on millions of channels in parallel. That is, as part of any one mental act, millions of neurons may be sending messages in millions of directions, all at the same time.
- The components of a modern computer are extremely reliable—they almost always work precisely as they are supposed to—but removing even one or two of them can ruin an entire calculation. The neurons of the brain are less reliable, but the deletion of quite a few of them is unlikely to make much of a difference.
- Whereas the computer makes use of a very strict and inflexible electronic code, the brain is much less precise and more flexible in its operations. The brain is apparently able to adjust the number and complexity of its own synapses in order to adapt its operations to its needs.

Because of fundamental differences such as these, the brain and the computer are best suited for rather different sorts of functions. A computer can far surpass the brain in performing intricate mathematical computations. Computers can even be programmed to play chess at a higher level than any but the most skilled human chess-players. But the brain can recognize faces and patterns in ways no existing computer can begin to approach. And the brain can make judgments, exercise imagination, and even reflect on itself in ways that will forever be beyond the computer's reach.

We will pursue the comparison between human mental processes and the computer's information-processing capacities in the Psychological Issue following Chapter 7, entitled "Can Computers Think?"

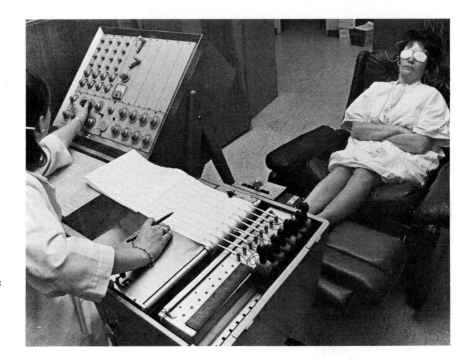

Brain waves are detected by electrodes attached to a person's skull. The brain waves are amplified by an electroencephalograph (EEG) machine, which creates a written printout that can be examined. Having an EEG made is a simple and painless procedure.

BRAIN WAVES ON MADISON AVENUE

As scientists learn more about how to assess the brain's activity, folks in the advertising business have been interested in putting this research to use. The evoked potential is a computer-derived average of the brain waves produced in response to a particular stimulus. Advertising researchers have begun to make use of the evoked potential as an index of a person's interest in commercials that are being tested. For example, one airline used the test to measure people's reactions to film clips of twenty-five British actors and actresses. The one who stimulated the most brain arousal presumably had an inside track for a job in the airline's commercials (Goleman, 1979).

sections for examination. Such studies helped reveal the brain's basic anatomy. However, since then a variety of techniques have been developed to help us learn more about the functioning of the brain.

One important technique involves *electrical stimulation* of parts of the brain to discover their specific functions. Most such studies have been done with animals. In the 1940s and 1950s, however, important work on mapping the human brain was conducted by Wilder Penfield (1959) and his colleagues at the Montreal Neurological Institute. During brain surgery, they stimulated specific parts of the cerebral cortex with tiny electrodes while the patients—who remained conscious—reported what they felt. Depending on where the electrode was placed, Penfield's patients reported feeling tingling in their hands, seeing lights, or experiencing vivid memories of the past. More recently, another neurosurgeon, George Ojemann (1983), has used a similar technique to "map out" the parts of the cortex involved in speaking, naming objects, and even doing arithmetic.

The study of people with *brain damage*—from injury, tumors, or strokes—has also provided important clues to brain function. Because people often suffer damage to only a lim-

ited area of the brain, the nature of the resulting impairment can help scientists to discover the function of the damaged area. Studies with animals have also made use of *brain surgery*, in which specific areas of the brain are destroyed or removed. Brain surgery has occasionally been resorted to in humans as well, for treating people with severe neurological disorders, such as uncontrollable seizures. By observing people who have undergone such surgery, researchers have been able to determine some of the functions of particular parts of the brain.

Another method for studying the brain relies on the electrical activity of its neurons. In the 1920s scientists learned how to amplify the brain's overall pattern of electrical activity and record it on graph paper. When such brain recordings, or *electroencephalograms* (EEGs), are examined, they reveal regular fluctuations in patterns that change in a consistent manner, depending on what the person is doing or thinking. We now call these rhythmic fluctuations of brain impulses *brain waves*. There are four basic brain waves—called alpha, beta, theta, and delta waves—each with a characteristic pattern that shows up on the EEG. Although none of these waves is ever emitted exclusively by the brain at any one time, one wave

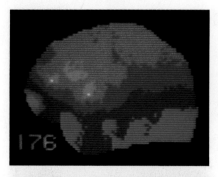
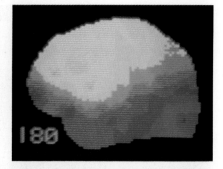
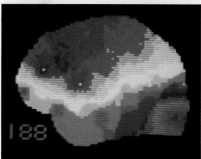
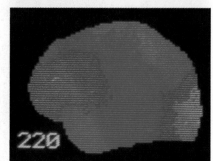

Evoked-potential imaging shows the rise and fall of a subject's brain response, over the course of a small fraction of a second, to a single electric shock administered to the arm. The computer-generated images are color-coded with red indicating a high level of brain-wave activity in a particular region of the cerebral cortex, and decreasing amounts of activity indicated by orange, yellow, green, blue, and purple. The response to the shock begins to appear 176 milliseconds (176 thousandths of a second) after the shock is administered (upper left), reaches a peak in the central sensory regions of the cortex 12 milliseconds later (lower left), and dies when it is barely a twentieth of a second old (lower right).

may be more pronounced than the others (see Box 2). Brain waves can be detected by attaching electrodes to a person's forehead or skull. Physicians can use EEG patterns to help diagnose such diseases as brain tumors or epilepsy, and psychologists can use EEG readings to learn about dreams, sleep, and other states of consciousness (see Chapter 4). Researchers have recently been making use of *evoked potentials*, computer-generated averages of brain-wave activity in different regions of the brain in response to a specific stimulus such as a word or, as in the photos above, an electric shock.

In recent years researchers have been developing other techniques for monitoring the activity of specific brain areas. For example, microelectrodes can be implanted in an animal's brain to record the firing patterns of individual neurons as the animal engages in different behaviors. Using this technique, researchers have found evidence of single neurons in the monkey's brain that respond to stimuli as specific as the sight of a monkey's hand (Gross, 1973). Other neurons in the brain have been found to fire as animals make decisions to perform different actions, such as to push a button to obtain a drink (Kojima and Goldman-Rakic, 1984). Although we cannot safely implant microelectrodes into human

brains to record the activity of single cells, new techniques are making it possible to monitor the activity of specific portions of the brain from outside the skull. In one such procedure a radioactive substance is injected into the brain's blood supply, and the amount of blood flowing in different parts of the brain is measured as the subjects perform different activities. Such *blood-flow measurement* is a good indicator of the functioning of certain parts of the brain, since the more activity in any part of the brain—that is, the more frequently nerve cells are firing—the more blood is needed to provide oxygen to support the activity (Lassen, Ingvar, and Skinhøj, 1978). Another new technique, called *positron-emission tomography* (PET), monitors the concentration of the sugar glucose in different parts of the working brain; the more active a part of the brain, the more glucose is used in that area.

Our current understanding of the structure and function of the brain relies on a combination of all these techniques for unlocking the brain. Our understanding still remains preliminary, however. Because of the current explosion in research on the brain, we can expect to learn much more about the brain's functions in the rest of the 1980s.

BOX 2

BIOFEEDBACK

Can you learn to control your own brain waves? With the use of *biofeedback,* it's possible that you can. Biofeedback is the use of electronic devices to amplify, record, and display various physiological responses so that the person can see exactly what his body is doing. With the help of such continuous readings, people can sometimes consciously alter their internal responses. For example, biofeedback has been used successfully to train people to alter their heart rate and blood pressure (see Chapter 5, Box 3).

When biofeedback is used to monitor a person's brain waves, electrodes are attached to the subject's skull and the brain wave patterns are indicated by sounds or lights. With the help of this feedback, the person may be able to shift his pattern of brain activity, such as from a state of alertness to a state of relaxation.

To investigate the emotional states associated with different patterns of brain waves, Barbara Brown (1970) asked subjects to write down their feelings, moment-by-moment, as their brain waves were being recorded. She found that most subjects described their experience as pleasant and tranquil when they were producing a large number of alpha waves. However, when they were producing a large

number of beta waves, many of the subjects reported feelings of anger, fear, and excitement. Brown and other researchers went on to show that people could be trained through biofeedback to produce more alpha waves.

It is often claimed that high alpha wave production is associated with a pleasant, relaxed state of consciousness, much like states of meditation (see Chapter 3, Box 4). But the claim is controversial. Some people experience high alpha states as unpleasant and it is possible to feel anxious even when in such a state (Orne and Wilson, 1978).

Regardless of whether or not people get high on alpha waves, brain wave biofeedback may have important medical uses. For example, it has been used to treat epilepsy, a condition in which people are likely to have uncontrollable seizures. M. B. Sterman (1978) has found that epileptics have a deficiency in a pattern of brain waves called the sensorimotor rhythm. Although the results of studies are not entirely consistent, it appears that training epileptics to produce this pattern of brain waves can help them to control their seizures.

The structure
of the brain

The human brain is composed of four basic sets of structures: the brain stem, cerebellum, limbic system, and cerebral cortex (see Figure 2.8). At the base of the brain lies the *brain stem*. From an evolutionary point of view, the brain stem is the "oldest" part of the brain. In lower animals, whose behaviors are largely automatic and instinctive, the brain stem structures make up virtually the entire brain. In humans, the brain stem also concerns itself with automatic functions, as well as with the "gut reaction" aspect of emotion. The brain stem comprises several connected structures. One of these, the *medulla,* lies at the bottom of the brain stem. It controls such basic physical rhythms as heartbeat and breathing, and it contains the reflex centers for vomiting, sneezing, coughing, and swallowing. The *hypothalamus,* located higher in the brain stem, monitors the automatic aspects of such behaviors as eating, drinking, sexual activity, and sleeping, and it plays a role in such emotions as rage, terror, and pleasure.

The *cerebellum* is positioned behind the brain stem and is largely concerned with automatic control of body position and motion. For example, it monitors the tension of arm muscles and keeps track of where the arm is in relation to the rest of the body and its surroundings. A patient with damage to the cerebellum will have a hard time getting a cup of coffee to his mouth without spilling it.

The *limbic system* is an interrelated set of structures located in parts of the brain stem and the lower part of the cerebral cortex. The limbic structures are evolutionarily "newer" than other parts of the brain stem or the cerebellum, having made their appearance with the first warm-blooded animals on earth; in fact, only mammals have a limbic system. Although its functions are not well understood, the limbic system appears to be involved with emotion. For example, electrical stimulation of one limbic structure, the *amygdala,* can cause "sham rage" in animals—frenzied displays of aggression without apparent cause. Removal of the amygdala can have the opposite effect; a naturally wild animal such as the lynx can become as gentle as a kitten after having the amygdala surgically de-

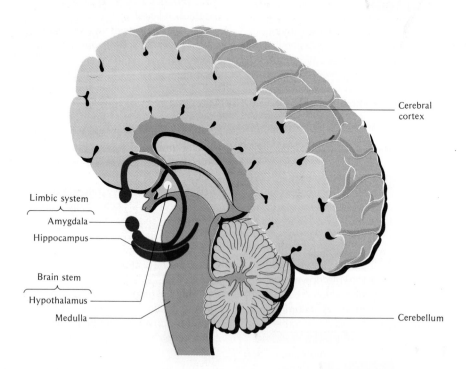

Limbic system
Amygdala
Hippocampus

Brain stem
Hypothalamus
Medulla

Cerebral cortex

Cerebellum

FIGURE 2.8

A cross-section of the brain showing some of its major structures: the brain stem, cerebellum, limbic system, and cerebral cortex.

CHAPTER TWO: BIOLOGICAL FOUNDATIONS OF BEHAVIOR

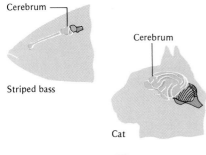

Cerebrum

Striped bass

Cerebrum

Cat

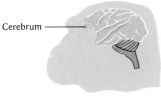

Cerebrum

Macaque monkey

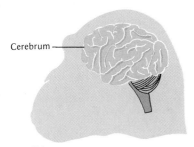

Cerebrum

Chimpanzee

Cerebrum

Human

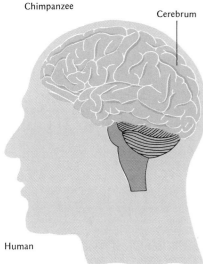

FIGURE 2.9

As we move up the evolutionary ladder, the cerebral cortex (or cerebrum) constitutes a larger and larger proportion of the brain.

FIGURE 2.10

The cerebral cortex is divided into four lobes on each side, each playing a distinctive role in sensation, thought, and behavior. A narrow band of the cerebral cortex at the top of the head controls the body's sensory and motor responses (see Figure 2.11).

stroyed. The amygdala seems to have similar functions in humans. In a few cases, brain disorders causing both seizures and violent behavior have been linked to abnormalities of the amygdala (Mark and Ervin, 1970). Another structure in the limbic system, the *hippocampus*, appears to play a critical role in memory. As we will see in Chapter 6, surgical removal of both right and left hippocampi of the patient known as H. M. produced an inability to form new memories.

Perhaps the most distinctively human part of the brain is the *cerebral cortex*. As one comes up the evolutionary scale, from the simple to the complex animals, the cerebral cortex grows markedly in size (see Figure 2.9). In a shark, for example, the cerebral cortex is a very small portion of the brain. In contrast, a human brain is 80 percent cerebral cortex. As the cortex has grown larger, it has assumed many tasks originally performed by the brain stem. Thus, if you cut away the section of the cerebral cortex associated with vision in a rat, the rat can still see, although it will be unable to distinguish patterns. Do the same to a man, and he will become blind. The lower portions of the rat's brain perform basic visual functions, but in humans these functions have been passed on to the more developed cerebral cortex. As two

prominent brain scientists have noted, "A man without a cortex is almost a vegetable, speechless, sightless, senseless" (Hubel and Wiesel, 1979, page 150).

In humans, the cerebral cortex is the place where sensory impulses concerning sight, sound, taste, smell, and touch are interpreted. It is the site of thought and intelligence. Portions of the cerebral cortex integrate the sensory and motor systems, acting as a sort of final switchboard between what comes in and what goes out.

Using as reference points two prominent grooves, or *fissures*, that run through the cerebral cortex, it can be divided into four regions, or *lobes*, on each side of the brain: the left and right frontal, temporal, parietal, and occipital lobes (see Figure 2.10). We still have only a preliminary understanding of the functions of the various parts of the cortex, but it seems clear that the lobes—and specific areas within each lobe—play distinctive roles in sensation, thought, and behavior. The *occipital lobes* receive most of their input from the eyes and are largely concerned with vision. The *parietal lobes* help to keep us physically oriented in our environment—literally, to know which end is up. The *temporal lobes* seem to be involved with hearing, language, and memory. The *frontal lobes* contribute to our sense of time and the ability to

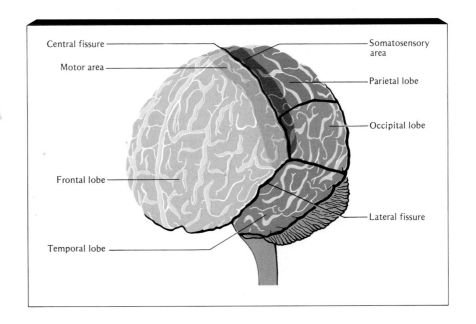

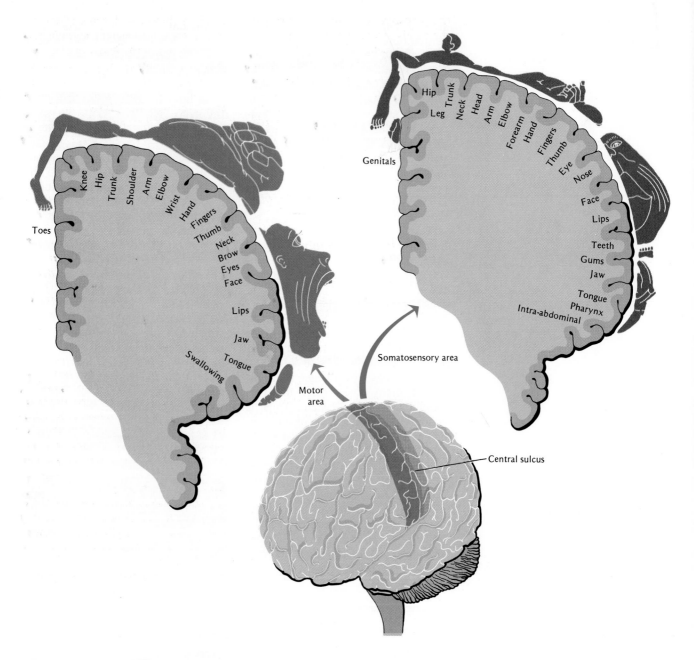

Toes

Knee
Hip
Trunk
Shoulder
Arm
Elbow
Wrist
Hand
Fingers
Thumb
Neck
Brow
Eyes
Face
Lips
Jaw
Tongue
Swallowing

Motor
area

Hip
Leg
Trunk
Neck
Head
Arm
Elbow
Forearm
Hand
Fingers
Thumb
Eye
Nose
Face
Lips
Teeth
Gums
Jaw
Tongue
Pharynx

Genitals

Intra-abdominal

Somatosensory area

Central sulcus

plan and anticipate events; they are also involved in speech and in the experience and expression of emotion. It is not surprising that patients who underwent the now extremely rare surgical procedure of frontal lobotomy, in which a portion of the frontal lobe is separated from the rest of the brain, showed striking personality changes. Because the frontal lobes are important both to experiencing emotions and to planning future actions, these lobotomized patients generally became easy-going and obedient, with little independence or "willfulness."

A narrow band of cortex at the top of the head, on the border of the frontal and parietal lobes, controls the body's motor and sensory processes (Figure 2.11). The *motor strip*, on the frontal lobe side of the border, controls body movement. Just behind it, on the parietal lobe side, is the *sensory strip*, which receives sensory input such as heat, touch, and pressure from different parts of the body. The amounts of sensory and motor tissue devoted to particular body parts are not related to the size of the body parts themselves but rather to the complexity of the functions that

FIGURE 2.11

Specific portions of the motor area of the cerebral cortex (left-hand drawing) are responsible for movement of different parts of the body. Similarly, specific portions of the somatosensory area (right-hand drawing) are responsible for sensation in different parts of the body.

the part must perform. For example, the hands and mouth make up only a small percentage of body volume, yet they merit almost half of the motor cortex, as shown in Figure 2.11.

The entire cerebral cortex is divided into two halves, the right and left *cerebral hemispheres.* The two hemispheres are, for the most part, mirror images of each other. As we will see later in this chapter, however, there is reason to believe that in most people the two hemispheres perform rather different functions.

Specialization of brain function

Different regions of the brain perform different jobs. We have already seen that specific areas of the cerebral cortex control the sensations and the movements of specific parts of the body. Specialized brain areas seem to handle higher mental functions, as well. Much of our knowledge of such specialization comes from studies of brain-damaged patients. For example, damage to different sites in the cortex has been found to give rise to different forms of *aphasia,* or language breakdown (see Figure 2.12). If there is damage to an area in the left frontal lobe known as *Broca's area,* patients have difficulty articulating words and their grammar is faulty. When asked about a dental appointment, for ex-

ample, a patient with Broca's aphasia might say, in a hesitant and blurred voice, "Yes . . . Monday . . . Dad and Dick . . . Wednesday 9:00 . . . doctors . . . and . . . teeth." If there is damage to another area, known as *Wernicke's area,* located in the left temporal lobe, the patient's pronunciation and grammar are normal but the words chosen are often inappropriate or nonsensical. For example, a patient with Wernicke's aphasia was asked to describe a picture that showed two boys stealing cookies behind their mother's back. He reported: "Mother is away here working her work to get her better, but when she's looking the two boys looking in the other part." These defects have enabled researchers to develop a general understanding of the ways in which brain centers must work together to produce normal language (Geschwind, 1979).

Another example of brain localization of a complex mental function comes from a condition called *prosopagnosia*—the inability to identify people from their faces. A patient with this disorder is unable to name a person she sees face to face or in a photograph. Such a patient may even fail to recognize her own spouse and children. In fact, when given a mirror and photographs, she may even fail to recognize herself (Shuttleworth et al., 1982). The identity of familiar people is not lost to the patient, for when the

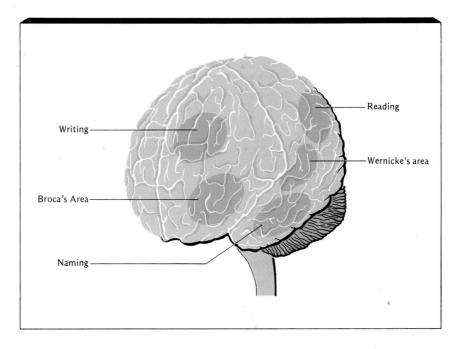

FIGURE 2.12

Areas of the left hemisphere of the cerebral cortex that are typically responsible for specific aspects of language. Damage to different sites will give rise to different forms of language breakdown.

other person speaks the patient recognizes the voice and can say the name immediately. Moreover, the patient can perceive and describe facial features quite accurately. The deficiency seems to be confined to the specific mental function of forming associations between faces and identities. In prosopagnosia the damage is found in the underside of both occipital lobes. In normal people, these areas of the brain apparently are entrusted with the task of linking faces and identities (Geschwind, 1979).

These examples of specialization of function show that different lobes within the brain serve different functions. As will be seen in the next section, moreover, the left and right halves of the brain also specialize in different functions.

Our two brains

Imagine what it would be like to have two brains, one controlling the left side of your body, the other controlling the right side. Each brain would control one hand and one leg, and each brain would have a separate consciousness. You could think with one brain, daydream with the other. Or you might write a paper with one brain while playing the harmonica with the other. Quite literally, your left hand might not know what your right hand is doing.

Actually, this description contains a small grain of truth, since the cerebral cortex is composed of two separate halves, or hemispheres. Each cerebral hemisphere is capable of functioning independently of the other, and each controls one side of the body. In fact, the right side of the brain controls the left side of the body, and the left side of the brain controls the right side of the body. This is because most peripheral nerve fibers cross over when they reach the brain. As a result, everything touched with the right hand is initially registered in the left hemisphere, and vice versa.

But the two hemispheres do not function identically. During the course of evolution of the human species, the two halves began to specialize in their functions. In right-handed people, the left hemisphere has primary control over linguistic abilities such as speaking, reading, and writing, while the right hemisphere has primary control over certain nonverbal skills, including the recognition of complex visual patterns, the recognition of emotion, and, in most cases, musical ability. In left-handed people the different functions of the two hemispheres are shared more evenly.

One sort of evidence for this specialization of hemispheric function comes from studies of patients with brain lesions caused by strokes, tumors, or head injuries. For example, 95 percent of brain-related language disorders result from damage to the left hemisphere, which is in charge of linguistic abilities. Similarly, a large proportion of cases of "visual neglect," in which the patient can see but does not pay attention to visual stimuli, occur with right-hemisphere damage. There is also evidence from recent studies of brain damage that the two hemispheres are specialized for different kinds of emotions (see Box 3).

Researchers have also found evidence for specialization of function in normal brains. For example, when the brain waves of people engaged in verbal tasks are recorded, the left hemisphere shows more activity than the right. But when spatial activities, such as recognizing patterns, are involved, the right hemisphere becomes more active (Ornstein, 1972). Recent studies also suggest that such hemispheric specialization is greater in men, while the functions are more equally shared by the hemispheres in women.

For most of us, the division of labor between the two halves of the brain is difficult to detect. This is because the two hemispheres are connected by a body of nerve fibers called the *corpus callosum*. Messages are constantly being transferred through this cable from one hemisphere to the other, enabling them to work together on most tasks. In this way the two hemispheres let each other know what they are up to.

But there are a few human beings walking around today whose two hemispheres cannot communicate with each other, because their corpus callosum has been surgically cut.

IT'S A RIGHT-HANDED WORLD

For the almost 94 percent of us who are right-handed, the left hemisphere is "dominant." Unfortunately for the left-handers among us, we seem to live in a right-handed world. Try playing the violin, cutting with scissors, or opening a refrigerator door with your left hand; you will learn just how right-handed our culture is. Pilots find that most of the aircraft controls are on the right. The same thing is true of TV sets. There are only a few settings, such as professional baseball, in which left-handers seem to get an even break.

BOX 3

HAPPY BRAIN, SAD BRAIN

The two sides of the brain may not only *think* differently but may *feel* differently as well. Recent evidence suggests that the left brain is more responsible for feeling and expressing positive emotions, while the right brain is more responsible for negative emotions. In other words, we might call the left hemisphere our "happy brain" and the right hemisphere our "sad brain."

The following true account of two patients, reported to me by a neurologist, illustrates one kind of evidence for this speculation. Mrs. Bright and

Mrs. Grimm (not the women pictured above) were both women in their seventies who had recently suffered strokes. (In a stroke, the blood supply to part of the brain is temporarily cut off, as a result of blockage or leaks in the blood vessels that feed that part of the brain, which may then become damaged or destroyed.) The two elderly women were admitted to a stroke rehabilitation center at about the same time and shared a semiprivate room there.

When the neurologist at the center first looked at special brain x-rays (called CAT scans) of her new patients, she noted that the areas damaged by the strokes were of almost identical size and location in the two women. The only difference was that Mrs. Bright's stroke damaged the *right* frontal lobe and Mrs. Grimm's stroke damaged the *left* frontal lobe.

Both patients' families expressed

concern over changes in the women's temperaments since the strokes. The nature of these emotional changes couldn't have been more different, however. Mrs. Grimm was terribly depressed and irritable and, to the dismay of her family and friends, felt that she was to blame for her own stroke. Mrs. Bright, in contrast, was forever joking, smiling, and laughing, and she never complained. "The problem was," her neurologist said, "no one could make Mrs. Bright see the seriousness of her condition."

Although these two cases are unusually dramatic, they are in accord with studies suggesting that the left hemisphere is more important for feeling and expressing happy emotions and the right is more important for feeling and expressing sad emotions. Thus, damage to the left hemisphere is likely to tip the balance of a patient's emotions toward depression (as in

Mrs. Grimm's case), whereas damage to the right hemisphere is likely to tip the balance toward the brighter side of things (as in the case of Mrs. Bright).

In one recent study (Sackeim et al., 1982), researchers surveyed the most extreme cases of these emotional changes—cases in which the patients would either cry or laugh uncontrollably as a result of their brain damage—and found that the criers tended to be left brain damaged, and the laughers tended to be right brain damaged. The same researchers also examined cases of laughing and crying during epileptic seizures, in which a portion of the brain is overactive, and found the opposite trend: a left hemisphere seizure is more likely to cause uncontrollable laughing, while a right hemisphere seizure is more likely to cause uncontrollable crying. This, too, makes sense given the notion that the right hemisphere specializes in the positive emotions and the left hemisphere, the negative emotions.

When it comes to perceiving other people's emotions, a different picture emerges. There is evidence to suggest that the right hemisphere is better at *perceiving* all emotions, both positive and negative, from such nonverbal cues as facial expressions and tone of voice. For example, patients with right hemisphere damage often fail to understand that another person is speaking with an angry or humorous tone of voice (Geschwind, 1979).

Brain surgeons have performed this operation on people afflicted with uncontrollable epilepsy in the hope of confining seizures to one side of the brain. The operation proved to be remarkably successful, producing an almost total elimination of attacks. Roger Sperry and Michael Gazzaniga devised several experiments to determine how cutting the corpus callosum has affected these patients (Gazzaniga, 1967). They set up situations in which information would be sent to only one side of the brain. For example, pictures would be flashed in only the right visual field (the area seen by the right half of each eye), or placed in the right hand, so that they would be "seen" or "felt" only by the left hemisphere.

Whenever items were shown to the left hemisphere, the person could verbally describe the items because speech is located in the left hemisphere. But when objects were presented to the right hemisphere (such as by being placed in the left hand), the person was unable to identify them verbally. Instead, the person would guess at what had been shown or would deny that he had seen anything. However, if the person was asked to use his left hand to point to or pick up the object that had been shown, the right hemisphere had no problem picking the right one. In one experiment, for example, some patients were shown the word "heart" with the "he" positioned in the left of the visual field and the "art" in the right (see Figure 2.13). When asked to pronounce the word they had seen, the patients would say "art," for that is what the speaking left hemisphere saw. But when patients were asked to point with their left hand to the word they had seen, they pointed to the word "he," for that is what the right hemisphere, which controls the left hand, saw. Remarkably, it was only in these types of experiments that the patients demonstrated their "split brain" condition. Otherwise, the patients seemed perfectly normal.

Even though different portions of the brain perform highly specific functions, any complex human activity is likely to involve many areas of the brain working together. Recent studies of blood flow in the brain have indicated, for example, that when we read silently, at least four areas of the brain are activated, including the visual association area in the occipital lobes and Broca's area in the left frontal lobe. When we read aloud, additional brain areas related to the mouth and hearing are also activated (Lassen, Ingvar, and Skinhøj, 1978). A current challenge for brain scientists is to map more precisely the neural messages that are being sent from one area to another during such activities.

In addition to the transmission of neural messages from one part of the brain to another, the brain's functioning seems to depend on the overall level of activation—or rate of neural firing—of the cerebral cortex. When people are given difficult mental tasks or are placed in stressful situations, neural activity increases in certain pathways throughout the cerebral cortex. These pathways fan out from a portion of the brain stem called the *reticular formation.* Such overall activation of the brain seems necessary to allow more specific neural messages to travel between widely separated parts of the brain.

THE CHEMISTRY OF BEHAVIOR

"It's that special chemistry," we sometimes say, as a way of explaining why two people fall in love. When we say that, we are speaking metaphorically: we mean that they are attracted to each other, just as the molecules of certain chemicals are always ready to unite with the molecules of certain other chemicals. But as research on the chemical bases of behavior and mental life continues, such phrases may begin to take on a more literal meaning. The messages sent by our brain and nervous system depend on the operation of specific chemical substances—neurotransmitters, hormones, and neuropeptides. The exploration of these substances, which can alter our state of mind and shape our behavior, is an important frontier of brain research.

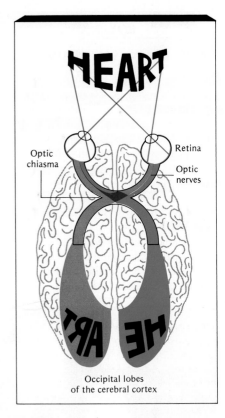

FIGURE 2.13

The left hemisphere of the brain "sees" material presented to the right visual field (ART), and the right hemisphere "sees" material presented to the left visual field (HE).

Neurotransmitters

As we have seen, neurons must communicate with each other across synapses, the microscopic gaps that occur between the axons of the "sender" neuron and the dendrites of the "receiver" neuron. Neurons accomplish this by means of neurotransmitters released by the axon on one side of the synapse that then drift across to the dendrites on the other side. So far, about thirty types of proteinlike molecules are known or are suspected to be chemical transmitters in the brain (Iverson, 1979). Among the best known are *dopamine, norepinephrine,* and *serotonin.* Many more transmitter substances—perhaps as many as 200—remain to be discovered (Snyder, 1980).

It is now known that neurons in specific areas of the brain and spinal cord will send and receive only specific transmitter substances. When molecules of the "right" substance cross a synapse, they fit precisely into regions of the receptor neuron's surface, much like a key fits into a lock. Once the "key" is inserted, a chain of chemical events takes place that makes the receptor neuron more likely or less likely to fire, depending on whether the substance is excitatory or inhibitory.

Scientists are especially interested in the role that brain chemicals play in neurological and psychological disorders. For example, dopamine has the effect of inhibiting neurons in the *substantia nigra,* a portion near the center of the brain that regulates complex motor activity. A deficiency of dopamine in this area has been linked to the muscular rigidity and tremors found with Parkinson's disease (Côté, 1981). As a result of this discovery, forms of dopamine that can be manufactured in the laboratory are being used to treat the disease. Dopamine also transmits messages to portions of the limbic system that regulate emotional responses. An excess of dopamine in these areas is now believed to be a cause of the hallucinations and other disruptions of thought and emotion that characterize schizophrenia (see Chapter 13). As we will see in Chapter 14, drugs (such as Thorazine) that are used to treat schizophrenia work by attaching themselves to dopamine receptors, thus preventing the dopamine from reaching them. Other psychoactive drugs, such as amphetamines and LSD, work by influencing or mimicking the effects of the brain's own chemical neurotransmitters (see Chapter 3).

Hormones

The passage of neurotransmitters across synapses from one neuron to another is one way in which chemical messages travel through our brains and bodies. In addition, the brain can send messages throughout the body by stimulating our endocrine glands to release *hormones* (Figure 2.14). Hormones are secreted directly into the bloodstream and then are carried by the blood through the entire body. When the hormones reach specific targets in other parts of the body, including the brain itself, they exert specific effects. Even though only minute quantities of hormones are secreted into the bloodstream, they have massive effects on our physical and mental functioning.

The *pituitary gland,* located at the base of the brain, secretes *growth hormone* that plays a crucial role in children's physical growth. If too little growth hormone is released, the child may become a midget; if too much, the child can grow to be a giant. The pituitary gland is often called the "master gland" because it also secretes hormones that move through the bloodstream to other endocrine glands and signals them, in turn, to release their own hormones.

The *thyroid gland,* located in the neck, secretes a hormone called *thyroxin* that regulates aspects of the body's metabolism—the rate at which the body converts food to energy. If too little thyroxin is released, the heart rate and other physical processes are slowed down, and the person is likely to become overweight and lethargic. If too much thyroxin is released, the person is likely to have an elevated heart rate, to lose weight, and to become hyperactive. As in the case of other hormones, it is essential

SOYBEANS, LIVER, AND THE BRAIN
Yes, eating the right food can make you smarter. At least that's the suggestion of recent research examining the links between nutrition and brain chemistry. For example, foods rich in lecithin, such as soybeans, eggs, and liver, can increase the supply of the neurotransmitter acetylcholine, which is believed to be involved in memory, sleep, and motor coordination. Neuroscientist Richard Wurtman (1978) has speculated that we will eventually know enough about how diet affects brain chemistry to be able to reduce pain, control our moods, and improve our concentration.

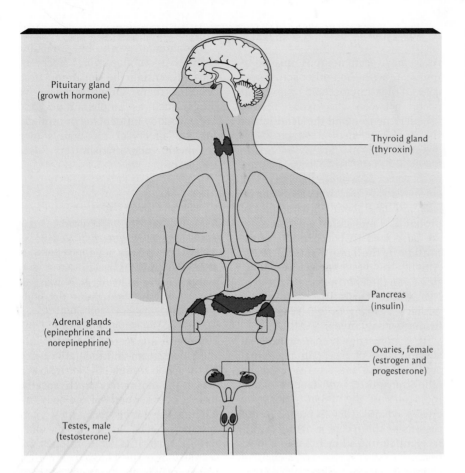

FIGURE 2.14

The endocrine glands secrete hormones into the bloodstream. These chemical messengers proceed to exert effects on different parts of the body.

Pituitary gland (growth hormone)

Thyroid gland (thyroxin)

Pancreas (insulin)

Adrenal glands (epinephrine and norepinephrine)

Ovaries, female (estrogen and progesterone)

Testes, male (testosterone)

for the brain to closely monitor the level of thyroxin in the blood and to send messages back to the thyroid gland that fine tune its rate of secretion.

The *adrenal glands*, located just above the kidneys, produce many different hormones. Two of them, *epinephrine* and *norepinephrine* (also known as adrenalin and noradrenalin) play a key role in the body's response to emergencies. When a person faces a sudden challenge or danger, the brain signals the adrenal glands to secrete these hormones, which increase heart rate, speed up breathing, and help supply extra blood sugar to the muscles and brain. This burst of epinephrine helps the body to take action to deal with the challenge, whether it involves the extra energy needed to prepare a last-minute legal brief or the ability to run on overdrive to catch the last train home before it leaves the station. These hormonal effects closely resemble the direct messages the sympathetic nervous system sends to the heart, lungs, and other organs in times of emergency. When

we are faced by danger, the direct action of the sympathetic nervous system and the chemical messages sent by the adrenal glands provide two complementary ways of getting the body revved up for action. We will return to these effects in Chapter 12 when we discuss the effects of stress on people's health.

The *gonads*, or sex glands, secrete hormones that affect many aspects of sexual development and behavior. In males, the *testes*, located in the scrotum, secrete the hormone *testosterone*, which triggers the development of secondary sex characteristics, such as a deepening voice and facial hair, at the time of puberty. In females, the *ovaries*, located on each side of the uterus, secrete *estrogen*, which leads to such secondary sex characteristics as breast development. Both estrogen and *progesterone*, another hormone released by the ovaries, are secreted at regular intervals during a woman's reproductive years, creating the menstrual cycle (see Box 4). As we will see in Chapter 10, the gonads also affect sexual motivation and behavior.

RUNNING YOUR STRESS AWAY
Many people claim that regular exercise gives them a sense of increased well-being in the face of all the stresses and strains of life. One reason for this effect, according to recent research, is that aerobic exercise—which pushes the heart and lungs to their maximum capacity—helps to train the adrenal glands to respond to stress more efficiently. In a preliminary study, a semester of aerobic running led college students (previously nonrunners) to show increased levels of epinephrine and norepinephrine when the students were placed in a stressful situation (Dienstbier, 1982). And other research has demonstrated that efficient production of epinephrine and norepinephrine does help people to deal with stress (Frankenhaeuser, 1979).

BOX 4

"THAT TIME OF THE MONTH": MENSTRUATION AND MOODS

Menstrual syndrome is a label for the physical and emotional experiences that many women undergo each month at the time of menstruation. The symptoms include weight gain, abdominal cramps, backache, headaches, intestinal problems, depression, irritability, and a generally negative mood. These symptoms are described as being most severe for a day or two preceding the menstrual period and during the first few days of the period: "I bloat up, feel fat and klutzy"; "My temper is short; I am near tears; I am depressed"; "My most tense time is just prior to my period when physical and emotional states are at their worst" (Weideger, 1977).

Such periodic changes in mood and physical symptoms seem to result in part from hormonal changes that occur in all healthy females throughout their reproductive lives. The pituitary gland and the hypothalamus control the process by signaling the ovaries to release the hormones estrogen and progesterone according to a monthly timetable. During menstruation, levels of estrogen and progesterone are extremely low. After the first day of the period, the levels of these hormones gradually increase until they peak, roughly in the middle of the monthly cycle. For a few days, the hormone levels remain high—this is the time in the cycle when an egg is released. The hormonal levels then begin to drop until the next menstrual period, when the whole process starts all over again (unless the woman becomes pregnant).

These physiological changes may have a direct effect on a woman's moods. But researchers have begun to suspect that such changes cannot fully explain women's emotional and physical responses to menstruation. Although hormonal shifts occur in all women—from the first menstrual period until menopause—reports on how many women experience negative menstrual symptoms vary widely, ranging from 15 percent to 95 percent of women in different populations (Paige, 1973). If hormones are the basis of such symptoms, why aren't all women similarly affected?

In some cases cultural expectations may increase the likelihood of experiencing menstrual symptoms. No known culture has viewed menstruation positively (Weideger, 1976). In primitive societies, menstruating women are sometimes seen as dangerous and are isolated from their social group. In our own society, menstruation is often expected to be a negative experience. Many girls receive inadequate explanations of menstruation from their parents, and menarche (the first period) is often shrouded in secrecy. It is therefore not surprising that Anne Clarke and Diane Ruble (1978) found that 12-year-old girls who had not yet started menstruating anticipated physical pain, disruption of social activities, and negative moods. These negative expectations may contribute to negative experiences when girls start to menstruate. If a women *expects* to be upset and distressed at "that time of the month," the chances become greater that she will be.

It remains likely that hormonal shifts have a direct effect on the psychological, as well as the physical, states of many women. In some cases, moreover, menstrual syndrome can be relieved by the administration of hormones or other drugs, or by certain dietary changes. It also seems clear, however, that social learning shapes women's perceptions of the cyclical changes in their bodies. As long as little girls continue to learn that menstruation is a "curse," women will be likely to attribute a variety of negative experiences to "that time of the month."

Neuropeptides

Some of the most exciting research in the field of brain chemistry concerns a recently discovered family of chemicals called *neuropeptides*. These chemicals are found throughout the body, as well as in the brain, sometimes traveling across synapses between neurons (as neurotransmitters) and sometimes traveling through the bloodstream (as hormones). Although these chemicals are found in only minute quantities, they have major effects on experience and behavior. In particular, the *enkephalins* and *endorphins* are similar chemically to the pain-killer morphine and have the same ability to reduce pain. These chemicals are concentrated not only in the brain's pain centers but also in emotional centers, such as the amygdala, where they may serve to keep our moods under control.

Other neuropeptides have been found to have direct effects on drinking behavior, sexual behavior, and memory—at least in laboratory animals. The "neuropeptide revolution," as some scientists are calling it, has raised hopes that synthetic versions of neuropeptides can be developed as pain-killers, as relaxants, and even as ways of enhancing intellectual skills and memory (see Chapter 6, Box 3). "In the future," one psychologist predicts, "we may all go to a pharmacy to pick up brain pills that give us whatever mental or emotional traits we may want at a given time" (Edson, 1978). Of course, not everyone views such future possibilities with eager anticipation.

The past two decades have seen tremendous advances in our knowledge of the biological foundations of behavior. Scientists now have a reasonably good understanding of basic brain structure and of how nerves send messages. But for all this increase in knowledge, most of what is important about the brain's functioning still remains to be learned. As David Hubel (1979) has written, "Brain research is only at its beginning. The incredible complexity of the brain is a cliché, but it is a fact." For the time being, it is clear that we cannot address many of the most important questions about human behavior and experience in terms of the brain mechanisms that underlie them. Instead, we must continue to explore behavior with the tools we have available and to develop new tools that give us even greater insights into the biological foundations of behavior. With the knowledge currently available, scientists and physicians are already finding ways to *change* biological functioning in potentially beneficial, if controversial, ways. Some of these methods of *biological engineering* are discussed in the Psychological Issue that follows.

SUMMARY

Evolution and genetics

- **1** According to Darwin's principle of *natural selection*, those organisms best able to adapt to their environment are the ones that are most likely to survive to produce offspring. Natural selection provides the basis for the evolution and diversity of species, including *Homo sapiens*, the human species.

- **2** *Genes* are the carriers of genetic information. A child receives two sets of genes (one from each parent) that interact to provide the child with a unique set of characteristics. The genetic inheritance constitutes the person's *genotype;* the outward expression of the genetic makeup is the person's *phenotype*. A *dominant gene* for a trait is one that is always expressed, while a *recessive gene* is expressed only when the dominant gene is absent.

- **3** *Behavior genetics* is the study of hereditary factors that affect personality and behavior. Genetic effects on behavior are primarily indirect, through their effects on bodily structures and chemical processes.

- **4** Genetic disorders account for about 40 percent of infant deaths and 80 percent of cases of retardation. One of the major genetic disorders is *phenylketonuria* (PKU).

The nervous system

- **5** The nervous system is composed of three main types of neurons: *afferent neurons*, which collect messages and carry them *to the* brain and spinal cord; *efferent neurons*, which carry messages *away* from the brain and spinal cord; and *association neurons*, which make connections between incoming and outgoing messages. Afferent and efferent neurons make up the *peripheral nervous system*; association neurons make up the *central nervous system* (brain and spinal cord).

• **6** The peripheral nervous system is subdivided into the *somatic nervous system*, controlling voluntary movements, and the *autonomic nervous system*, governing glands and involuntary muscles. The autonomic nervous system is further subdivided into two branches, the *sympathetic* and the *parasympathetic*.

• **7** A typical neuron consists of a *cell body*, short *dendrites*, which receive messages, and a long *axon*, which transmits messages. In the process of *axonal transmission*, messages travel along the surface of the neuron from the dendrites, through the cell body, and along the axon.

• **8** Messages move from one neuron to the next through the chemical process of *synaptic transmission*. For such transmission to occur, the neuron must fire. The *all-or-none principle* refers to the fact that neurons will fire only if the impulse they receive is above a certain threshold intensity. The firing of a neuron causes a chemical *neurotransmitter* to cross the *synapse* between neurons, thereby exciting or inhibiting the firing of the next neuron.

The brain

• **9** Although comparing the brain to a computer is an interesting analogy, there are significant differences between the two.

• **10** The brain contains about 100 billion nerve cells and about 1000 billion *glia*—cells that provide nourishment and support for the neurons.

• **11** Our knowledge of the brain has come from the use of a variety of techniques, including *electrical stimulation of the brain*, study of brain-damaged people, use of brain surgery, analysis of *brain waves* as recorded on *electroencephalograms* (EEGs), *blood-flow measurement*, and *positron-emission tomography*.

• **12** *Biofeedback* techniques have been used to monitor and control brain waves, particularly the alpha rhythm.

• **13** The human brain comprises four basic sets of structures: the brain stem, cerebellum, limbic system, and cerebral cortex.

• **14** The *brain stem* is the most primitive part of the brain and is concerned with automatic functions. Among structures found in the brain stem are the *medulla*, which controls basic physical rhythms and reflexes, and the *hypothalamus*, which monitors such behaviors as eating, drinking, and sleeping. The overall level of activity in the brain appears to be governed by a portion of the brain stem called the *reticular formation*.

• **15** The *cerebellum*, located behind the brain stem, is involved in balance and coordination.

• **16** The *limbic system*, including such structures as the *amygdala* and the *hippocampus*, is found only in mammals. It appears to be involved in emotional expression and short-term memory.

• **17** The *cerebral cortex* contains centers for sight, hearing, taste, smell, and touch. It is the site of thought, intelligence, and memory. Two major *fissures* serve to divide each side of the brain into four functionally separate lobes: the *frontal*, *parietal*, *occipital*, and *temporal*. Two narrow strips of cortex at the top of the head control the sensory and motor responses of the body.

• **18** Evidence of specialization of brain function often comes from studies of brain-damaged patients. Patients with damage to *Broca's area* in the frontal lobe have difficulty articulating words and have faulty grammar. Patients with damage to *Wernicke's area* in the left temporal lobe often choose inappropriate words. Patients with damage to the underside of the occipital lobes may suffer from *prosopagnosia*—the inability to recognize faces.

• **19** The cerebral cortex is divided into two halves, the left and right *cerebral hemispheres*. The left hemisphere has primary control over verbal abilities, while the right hemisphere has primary control over such nonverbal skills as musical ability, recognition of complex visual patterns, and expression and recognition of emotion. The right side of the brain controls the left side of the body, and vice versa.

• **20** The hemispheres are connected by a band of fibers called the *corpus callosum*. When this band is severed, the individual in effect has two separate brains.

The chemistry of behavior

• **21** Several types of chemicals are involved in the functioning of the nervous system. At least thirty different substances act as neurotransmitters, and neurons in the brain and spinal cord will send and receive only specific neurotransmitters.

• **22** Behavior is also influenced by the chemical *hormones* produced in *endocrine glands* and sent, like messages, to target tissues in the body. More recently discovered nervous system chemicals are the *neuropeptides*, including *enkephalins* and *endorphins*.

• **23** *Menstrual syndrome* is a set of psychological and physical symptoms that, although based in hormonal changes, may also be influenced by culture and expectations.

BIOLOGICAL ENGINEERING

- In January 1982, Elizabeth Carr was born in Norfolk, Virginia. She weighed 5 pounds, 12 ounces, and was perfectly normal in all respects except one: Elizabeth was the first baby in America to have been conceived outside of her mother's body, in a glass dish.
- Babies with the dangerous condition of hydrocephalus—in which excess fluid puts pressure on the brain—can now be treated before they are born. Techniques have been perfected that allow physicians to install drainage shunts in a fetus that is still inside the womb.
- In Sweden a 45-year-old woman has received an unusual treatment for her severe case of Parkinson's disease: Doctors transplanted one of her own adrenal glands into her brain.

Our rapidly developing knowledge of human biology and brain functioning is spawning new technological advances that are enabling us to alter our biological functions in ways that, until very recently, were the stuff of science fiction. From "test-tube babies" to "brain transplants," one of the most remarkable stories of the 1980s has been the development of techniques of *biological engineering*. These new methods have tremendous potential for reducing human disease and misery, but they also raise troublesome ethical questions.

TEST-TUBE BABIES

Although most couples want to have children, about one in six have difficulty conceiving, and a significant proportion never succeed. In some cases, the husband has too low a concentration of

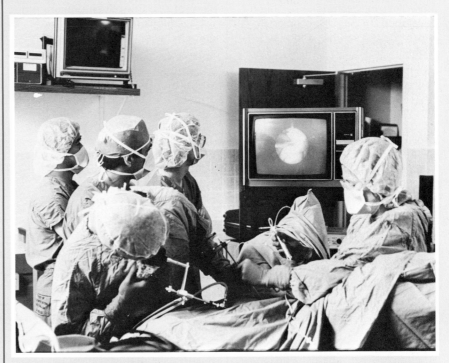

As part of the process of in vitro fertilization, doctors remove egg cells from a woman's ovary, using an instrument called a laparoscope. Afterward, an attempt will be made to fertilize one of the eggs outside the woman's body.

sperm for conception to occur; in other cases, the wife has problems with her reproductive organs that make conception difficult or impossible. In about 40 percent of the cases of female infertility, the Fallopian tubes, which carry the egg cell from the ovaries to the uterus, are blocked, preventing the woman from conceiving. However, the new technique of *in vitro fertilization*—fertilizing an egg outside of the woman's body—has changed this state of affairs.

On July 25, 1978, a healthy baby, named Louise Joy, was born to Mr. and Mrs. Gilbert Brown of Bristol, England, and a new era in human reproduction had begun. Louise Brown's birth marked the first time in history that a human egg had

been surgically removed from a woman's ovary, fertilized by her husband's sperm in a glass dish, returned to the uterus once it had reached the eight-cell stage, and allowed to develop to a full-term baby. (Although the infant does not actually develop in a test tube, the image of conception taking place in a glass dish has led people to refer to infants conceived by the technique of in vitro fertilization as "test-tube babies.")

Since the birth of Louise, she has been joined by a sister, also conceived outside her mother's body, and by hundreds of other "brothers" and "sisters" around the world (including Elizabeth Carr). The technique is not foolproof, however. The chances that it will work on any given attempt are only about 20 percent—and at about $4000 a try, it is not an option for every couple. But the success rate will almost certainly improve as the technique is perfected.

More recently, another, even more amazing technique has been developed for helping couples in which the woman has a fertility problem. In January of 1984, a baby boy was born in California to a woman who was genetically unrelated to him (Bustillo et al., 1984). The mother, who could not produce her own egg cells, had been implanted with the fertilized eggs of another woman. In this procedure of *embryo transfer,* the husband of the infertile woman provides sperm that are implanted in the womb of a fertile woman. Four or five days later, if fertilization has occurred, the embryo is washed out of the uterus and transferred to the wife's uterus. In this way, a woman who is infertile or who has a genetic disease can have the experience of carrying and giving birth to a baby. Instead of adopting a baby after it is born, the couple, in effect, adopts an embryo—with the extra advantage that it carries the husband's, if not the wife's, genes.

Another potential use of embryo transfer procedures is for women who are fertile but who are, for health reasons, unable to carry a child for nine months. In such cases the fertilized ovum might be transferred to another woman—a "surrogate mother"—who would take on the responsibility of carrying and giving birth to the child.

These new techniques for achieving conception have already begun to relieve the anguish of many couples who until now would not have been able to have their own children. At the same time, these techniques bring to many people's minds the future envisioned by Aldous Huxley in *Brave New World,* where all reproduction takes place in laboratories and embryos developed in test tubes are subject to state regulation and control. Critics

of "embryo technology" argue that these techniques involve "playing God" and that they entail tampering with potential human lives. They add that when fertilized eggs are discarded as part of these attempts at conception, it is the moral equivalent of abortion. Such difficult ethical questions must be asked and grappled with. They have no easy answers.

GENETIC COUNSELING

Until recently, a couple had no way of knowing whether their child would have genetic disorders or other diseases until it was already born. But recent advances have made it possible to know in advance whether a child is likely to be born with genetic disorders, such as forms of severe mental retardation or serious diseases that are likely to be fatal within the first few years of life. Analyzing the blood of prospective parents is one method used to test for certain types of genetic risks. Another useful technique is *amniocentesis,* in which fluid containing fetal cells is removed from the mother's womb and the cells analyzed for biochemical and chromosomal abnormalities.

These techniques of parental screening and prenatal diagnosis can help couples who are in high-risk groups (often because of a history of genetic disorders in their family) decide whether it is safe for them to have children. Prenatal diagnosis can also make it possible for a couple to decide to terminate a pregnancy rather than give birth to a severely retarded or fatally ill child. For example, as a result of screening programs in cities with large Jewish populations, only 13 children with Tay-Sachs disease, a fatal neurological disorder, were born in the United States in 1980, compared with 100 in 1970 (Clark, 1981).

But in spite of the potential benefits of genetic screening and prenatal diagnosis, these methods may also have great costs. Sometimes the knowledge that they are carriers of genetic disorders makes prospective parents feel so fearful, ashamed, or guilty that they would prefer never to have had the knowledge at all.

Dealing with the fears and doubts of prospective parents is part of the task of a new group of professionals called *genetic counselors.* Genetic counselors may be psychologists, physicians, nurses, or social workers, and often members of different disciplines work to-

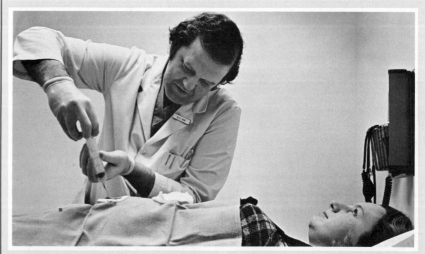

A physician inserts a needle through a pregnant woman's abdominal wall in order to withdraw amniotic fluid for analysis. Through this procedure of amniocentesis, various genetic abnormalities in the fetus can be detected.

Any attempt to identify "defects" can be troubling. Who is to decide what is defective?

gether in teams. They have the extremely sensitive job of informing prospective parents about genetic facts, risks, and potential courses of action.

People's individual values about what to do in such situations differ widely. Many people believe that it is proper and humane to prevent the birth of a child whose life would be one of great suffering. But many others believe that abortion under any circumstances is morally wrong. And still others are troubled by any attempt to identify particular conditions as "defects." Who is to decide what is defective?

Indeed, the possibility of deciding to destroy a "defective" fetus before birth raises awesome questions about our general attitudes toward the sick and disabled. Leon Kass asks how we will regard a child who is born with a genetic disorder in an era when most others with the same disorder have been destroyed before birth: "[The child] is likely to be looked upon by the community as unfit to be alive, as a second-class (or even lower) human type. He may seem as a person who need not have been, and who would not have been if only someone had gotten to him in time" (Restak, 1975, page 22).

But in spite of these dilemmas, most scientists and students of ethics believe the potential value of genetic screening and prenatal diagnosis in reducing human suffering is too great to disavow. It is clear, moreover, that these techniques can sometimes lead to the birth of healthy babies who otherwise would never have been born at all. One New Jersey couple vowed not to have another child after their first daughter died of sickle-cell anemia, a genetic blood disorder that occurs mainly among blacks. But after the woman got pregnant again she underwent tests that showed the un-

born child to be free of the disease. "We were overjoyed," the mother said, "because we knew it was going to be OK. If they didn't have genetic counseling I probably wouldn't be having it" (Clark, 1981, page 122).

The highly emotional issue of abortion has occupied a central role in discussions of the ethics of genetic screening and prenatal diagnosis. But this issue may become less central as new methods of treating unborn babies and of curing genetic diseases are developed. It is already possible for physicians to perform surgery on fetuses, while still in the mother's womb, to correct certain problems that would otherwise have killed or severely handicapped the child. For example, doctors have successfully treated *hydrocephalus* (a condition in which excess fluid accumulates in the skull and puts pressure in the brain) by installing drainage shunts on a fetus. Further off lies the possibility of using new techniques of genetic engineering to splice normal genes into the place of abnormal ones, thus correcting many of the genetic disorders that today are incurable.

BRAIN TRANSPLANTS

The term *brain transplant* is not loved by the neuroscientists who are working on this technique. It conjures up Frankenstein-like images of putting one person's brain—or a sizable chunk thereof—into another person's skull. Even though the past decade has seen the widespread use of heart, kidney, and liver transplants, no serious scientist has the remotest plan to attempt such procedures with the brain.

But what *is* being attempted—more properly referred to as *brain-tissue transplants*—is almost as startling as the idea of transplanting en-

tire brains. Until recently it was believed that once a portion of the brain or spinal cord was destroyed, there was no way to repair the damage, because neurons—unlike other body cells, such as blood or skin—are unable to regenerate. But brain-tissue transplants may provide a solution to the problem. By grafting neurons from another person or from another part of the body into the portions of the brain that have been destroyed, it appears to be possible to restore the functioning of that part of the brain.

So far, research on brain-tissue transplants has been done with rats and other animals, not with humans. Most of the initial research has been aimed at Parkinson's disease, which involves the gradual loss of control over one's body movements. The disease, which afflicts half a million Americans, occurs when the *substantia nigra*, a

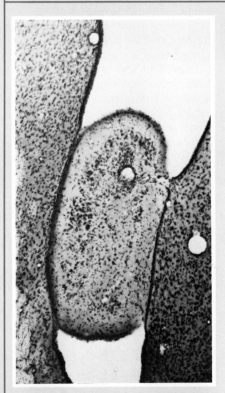

A transplant of tissue from the brain of a fetal rat is shown inside a fluid-filled ventricle in the brain of a rat with a type of Parkinson's disease. The graft makes normal new connections with the damaged areas of the brain.

group of about 3500 neurons on both sides of the brain, gradually dies. These neurons produce the neurotransmitter dopamine, which is involved in the control of movement. The symptoms of Parkinson's disease apparently result from a deficiency of dopamine.

In a series of recent studies, researchers destroyed the substantia nigra in rats. This produced a rat version of Parkinson's disease, and the rats showed such symptoms as an abnormal circling movement. Then the researchers transplanted cells taken from the substantia nigra of unborn rat fetuses into the rats' brains. They found that the transplants "took" and that the rats' abnormal symptoms were greatly reduced (Freed et al., 1983). So far, the transplants have been successful only when the transplanted cells come from fetuses, whose neurons are still relatively undeveloped. More highly developed neurons appear to already be set in their ways and thus are unable to make new connections after they are transplanted.

In another approach to repairing destroyed brain tissue in Parkinson's disease, tissue from one of the organism's own adrenal glands is transplanted into its brain. In experiments with young rats, it has been found that after the adrenal cells have been transplanted into the spot that had been occupied by the substantia nigra, they become less like gland cells and more like brain cells. And these cells, which in the adrenal gland produce the hormones epinephrine and norepinephrine, now begin producing dopamine (which, in fact, is one of the chemical components of epinephrine and norepinephrine) (Freed et al., 1983). The result is a clear reduction in the rat's Parkinson-like symptoms.

Could this technique help to cure Parkinson's disease in humans? In two dramatic attempts made in the early 1980s, doctors in Sweden transplanted a portion of the adrenal gland into the cells of two human patients with severe cases. One patient was a 58-year-old man, the other the 45-year-old woman mentioned at the beginning of this Issue (Knox, 1983). In neither case, however, was there any evidence that the transplant improved the patient's condition. Most scientists believe that these attempts to perform brain-tissue transplants in humans were premature and that scientists must learn more about techniques for transplanting brain tissue in primates before performing any more human surgery.

But even if the use of brain-tissue transplants is premature, it also seems inevitable. Within the next 10 to 20 years, brain-tissue transplants will almost certainly be used to treat people with Parkinson's disease and with other degenerative human diseases, such as Alzheimer's disease and Huntington's disease. With the development of other new surgical techniques for grafting neurons, it is also possible that doctors will be able to perform spinal cord transplants to restore movement in cases of spinal cord injury.

What is most sure of all is that along the way, as researchers pursue such possibilities as using tissue from human fetuses for transplants or implanting brain tissue from other animals into human brains, we will have new ethical issues to grapple with. For with the tremendous advances in our ability to alter our biological functioning, there also come tremendous new responsibilities for us to handle these new possibilities in thoughtful and enlightened ways.

SUMMARY

- **1** One technique of biological engineering being used to help women who are infertile is *in vitro fertilization,* in which sperm and ovum are united in a glass dish and the fertilized egg is implanted in the mother's uterus. Another new technique is *embryo transfer,* where a fertilized egg from a fertile women is transferred to the infertile woman.

- **2** *Genetic counselors* inform couples about the potential risks of having children with birth defects and describe possible courses of action. Techniques such as parental screening and prenatal diagnosis can help high-risk couples decide whether to have a child.

- **3** People with serious brain disorders, such as Parkinson's disease, may benefit in the future from techniques of *brain-tissue transplant.*

Rats with a form of Parkinson's disease walk in endless circles. Brain-tissue transplants reduced or eliminated the circling.

CONSCIOUSNESS

Consciousness refers to our subjective awareness of ourselves and the world.

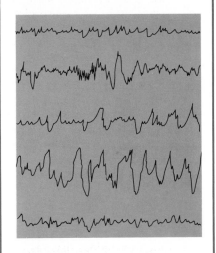

Our state of consciousness can range from subdued to intense, from ordinary to remarkable.

Each night we pass through several stages of sleep, from light to deep, each with its own pattern of brain waves.

Dreams may reflect our unconscious wishes and may help us to work through our daytime problems.

Drugs affect people's moods and perceptions by mimicking or interacting with neurotransmitters in the brain.

Hypnosis, once written off as a gimmick, is now taken seriously. It can make severe pain feel like a tingle.

Daily, monthly, and annual rhythms all exert an influence on our lives.

Cindy wakes up in the morning and lies in bed for a while, no longer asleep but not quite awake. Groggily she pulls herself from the bed, and before long she feels alert enough to get ready to face the day. She puts on her clothes, not really paying attention to what she's doing since she's done this so many times before. As she thinks about the test coming up, she absentmindedly squeezes a tube of handcream onto her toothbrush. At school she is "up" for the test and puts her total attention into answering the questions. But her after-lunch class is dull and she finds herself drowsing in the middle of the lecture, especially since she stayed up so late studying the night before. After class she heads to the track to run a few miles. She alternates between being absorbed in the running itself and letting her mind wander to wherever it wishes to go. That night she drops into bed and enjoys a deep sleep, punctuated by vivid dreams.

Sound familiar? In the activities of Cindy's typical day, she experiences many different states of consciousness, from full alertness to deep sleep. Similarly, we all go through our lives alternating between different modes of consciousness. *Consciousness* refers to our subjective awareness of our own actions and of the world around us. In this chapter we will explore what is still a largely uncharted area of psychology—human consciousness. After a preliminary survey of the nature of consciousness, we will focus on several specific states of consciousness, including the ordinary states of waking, sleeping, and dreaming and the altered states induced by drugs and hypnosis. In some of the boxes we will look at still other states of consciousness: daydreaming and meditation. In the Psychological Issue that follows the chapter, we will

explore biological rhythms, such as the daily wake-sleep cycle, that are closely linked to our states of consciousness.

THE NATURE OF CONSCIOUSNESS

Consciousness is a difficult concept to describe, because it is fundamental to everything we do. In fact, it is somewhat artificial to use "consciousness" as the title for a single chapter of this book, because it is involved in all forms of behavior, perception, thought, and emotion. Here we will discuss some central characteristics of consciousness and how it has been studied by psychologists.

Characteristics of consciousness

Consciousness can vary in its quality. Our subjective experiences can range from subdued and ordinary to exciting and intense. At some times we become totally absorbed in our environment, while at other times we focus most of our attention on ourselves, displaying a high degree of self-consciousness. Consciousness can also vary in the accuracy with which we perceive the environment. In our normal waking state we perceive our surroundings accurately, but when we dream or daydream, we perceive things that are not really in our environment at all. And people in drug states experience a variety of distortions in their perceptions of the world.

Our consciousness of our own activities also varies greatly from one time to another. Most of us are quite conscious or aware of our own movements or mental activities when we are learning a new skill, whether it is a physical skill, such as skiing, or a cognitive skill, such as solving algebra problems. As we will see in Chapter 5, however, as we master a skill, the movements and thoughts that go into it become more and more automatic. As a result, most of our routine activities—tying shoes, descending stairs, speaking English—are performed quite automatically and unconsciously. For instance, we are seldom aware of the movements our legs and bodies make when we are walking. We may be talking with someone or looking at things around us. However, we can focus our attention on walking if we want to, thus making it a conscious behavior. In some cases, focusing attention on an automatic behavior can actually hinder it. Try running down a flight of stairs while thinking about what your feet are doing—but be sure to bring plenty of bandages.

Consciousness also plays a role in the choices we make. Many of our choices are deliberate—we speak of making a "conscious decision" about something, such as which course to register for or what movie to see. But other choices are less intentional and thus involve less conscious thought. For example, we go to the supermarket and select specific items from the shelves. Although there are many alternatives available, we often automatically and unconsciously choose particular items and brands out of habit.

Behaviors that are performed automatically or without awareness are often referred to as being "unconscious." We can usually make such activities conscious when we want to. Sigmund Freud had a different meaning for the term *unconscious*. He saw the unconscious part of the mind as a repository for sexual and aggressive thoughts and impulses that are too threatening to think about consciously. It is very difficult for a person to bring this material to a conscious level. As we will see, Freud believed that one way to probe the unconscious mind is through dreams.

As many of our examples suggest, a central aspect of consciousness is *attention*: focusing on certain things while ignoring others. As will be seen

When we first learn a new skill (top), we are very conscious of our own movements and mental activity. But as we master a skill (bottom), the movements and thoughts become more and more automatic.

later in this chapter, certain states of consciousness such as hypnosis and meditation are achieved by learning to focus attention in special ways.

The study of consciousness

The study of consciousness has had its ups and downs in psychology. In the early days of the field, in the late nineteenth century, the structuralists (see Chapter 1, Box 1) felt that psychology's central concern should be the study of consciousness. E. B. Titchener and other structuralists sought to learn about consciousness through *introspection*—the careful examination of their own conscious experience. For instance, Titchener was concerned with determining the number of "mental elements" and in 1896 had determined that there were more than 44,000 sensory elements, such as colors, images, and tones, that come together to form perceptions and ideas.

It soon became apparent, however, that the introspective method was unreliable: introspective reports could not be checked, because no one can get inside anyone else's skull to share the experience. As a result, structuralism gave way to a new school, behaviorism, which focused on the study of overt behavior, employing observations that everyone could agree on. Declared John Watson (1913), the founder of behaviorism: "The time seems to have come when psychology must discard all references to consciousness; when it need no longer delude itself into thinking that it is making mental states the object of observation" (page 164).

In the past quarter century, the tide has turned again, with psychologists returning to the study of such subjective states as sleeping, dreaming, hypnosis, mental imagery, and drug-altered states of consciousness. One example of the new approach is current research on daydreaming, as presented in Box 1. This shift can be seen as part of the more general resurgence of interest in cognitive approaches, including the systematic study of perception, memory, and other mental processes.

This burst of new research on con-

BOX 1

DAYDREAMING

Frank is driving to a job interview. He wants the job very badly, and as he weaves in and out of the busy early morning traffic, he considers the upcoming conversation. In the midst of organizing his presentation, he has an image of the interviewer making fun of him and virtually laughing him out of the office. The image is gone as quickly as it came, and if you were to ask Frank about it later he would probably say he has no memory of it.

Janet has received a C+ on her sociology paper. She had worked hard on the paper and really thought she'd get an A. As she rereads the paper and goes over her professor's comments, Janet imagines herself storming into the teacher's office, hurling the paper on the teacher's desk, and telling the woman just what she thinks of her. This fantasy passes in a moment.

Lou is in Janet's sociology class and got an A− on his paper. He's quite excited. As he walks to his car, he starts to think about graduate school for the first time and wonders what it's like to be a professor. He imagines himself sitting in a cluttered office, surrounded by adoring students who are taking notes as he outlines his latest research project.

Frank, Janet, and Lou are daydreamers. Like most of the rest of us, their days are made up of more than looking, touching, responding. As they move through their varied activities, their behavior is accompanied by a private stream of consciousness. The total stream of consciousness includes the information they process, the events they remember, the plans they make. But a part of that stream is daydreaming, and it is as much a part of most people's lives as eating.

After questioning hundreds of people about their daydreams, Jerome L. Singer (1975) has concluded that virtually everyone daydreams, and he has identified three different types of daydreamers. The first type, like Frank, typically has anxious daydreams, often centered on fears of failure. These daydreams are unorganized, fleeting, and vague. The second type of daydreamer, like Janet, is given to self-

criticism and self-doubt and is most likely to have hostile fantasies. The third type, whom Singer calls the "happy daydreamer," has positive fantasies, with clear visual images, like Lou's. Not surprisingly, people in the third group enjoy daydreaming the most.

Our daydreams and night dreams are probably related to each other. Anxious or hostile daydreamers tend to have anxious or hostile night dreams; happier daydreamers have correspondingly positive night dreams (Starker, 1974). Daydreaming appears to peak every 90 minutes or so (similar to night dreaming), and this peak is associated with reduced eye movement and a particular type of brain wave (Kripke and Sonneschein, 1973). Thus it is possible that some of the same brain mechanisms are involved in both daydreaming and night dreaming.

But there are important differences between daydreaming and night dreaming. As we will see later in this chapter, night dreaming is associated with rapid eye movements—our eyes dart about during dreams as if we were watching a movie behind our closed lids. While we daydream, however, we tend to move our eyes less than usual, as if we were staring at

some far-off point in space (Singer and Antrobus, 1965).

Why do we daydream? Singer believes that daydreaming promotes intellectual functioning, self-control, and a peaceful inner life. Our fantasies can keep us from going bananas when we perform boring tasks and can provide periodic relaxation when we do demanding intellectual work (Singer, 1976).

Singer suggests that daydreams can help insulate people from some of the lures of the external world. In the absence of an inner world, rich in images and interest, nondaydreamers may respond to the demands of the external world in nonadaptive ways, such as by engaging in crime, overeating, or drug abuse. Singer found, for example, that delinquent adolescent boys daydreamed very little.

Of course, the absence of daydreaming does not necessarily produce delinquents or drug addicts. But daydreaming does appear to be important to psychological well-being. The thread of daydreaming woven through our fabric of thought may serve an important function in tying the rest of consciousness together.

sciousness is also closely connected with the current revolution in brain research, as scientists try to discover how states of consciousness are related to measurable brain activity. Although the work has barely begun, researchers may ultimately be able to identify the physical and chemical processes within the brain that account for consciousness.

SLEEP

There are two major states of consciousness that each of us experiences every day: being awake and being asleep. Even within the waking state there are, as noted earlier, variations in our conscious experience. Within the state of sleep, too, there are different states of consciousness, including that special state of consciousness we call *dreaming*. But the distinction between being awake and being asleep remains a fundamental one. When we are awake, we are more physically active and responsive to the outside world. When we are asleep, our physical activity is greatly diminished and our responsiveness to the environment is greatly decreased.

One-third of our lives

We spend about one-third of our lives in the state of consciousness called *sleep*. Sleep appears to be an automatic behavior necessary for survival. Rats that are kept awake for more than a week or two, for example, suffer severe physical breakdown and ultimately die (Rechtschaffen et al., 1983). Yet one of the biggest mysteries about sleep is just why it is necessary. Some of the theories that have been put forth are summarized in Box 2.

As far as we know, people in cultures all over the world generally sleep 5 to 9 hours in every 24 hours and usually do so at night. A study of American college students found that the average student slept 7.4 hours on weeknights (White, 1975). But the "average" amount is not necessarily the right or best amount for you. In fact, there are wide variations in what makes a "normal" night's sleep.

The amount people sleep varies with age. A 3-day-old infant may sleep anywhere from 12 to 22 hours per day (with an average of 16), spread over five or six periods during the day and night. As the infant matures, the amount of sleep during the day slowly decreases, while the length of night sleep stays at about 10 hours. Adults sleep 7 to 8 hours a day on the average. Those in middle and old age tend to sleep less than younger adults and to wake up more frequently during the night.

Sleep patterns can also vary from day to day. Physical exercise in the

As we get older, the amount of sleep we need decreases.

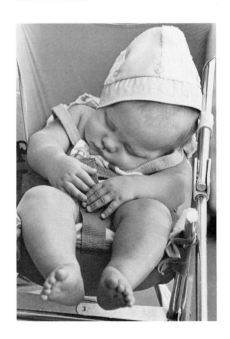

BOX 2

WHY DO WE SLEEP?

Although people cannot survive without sleep, just why we sleep remains a mystery. Many different explanations have been put forth. Here are a few of them.

Sleep evolved to protect us from predators. During the course of human evolution, it was probably dangerous for our apelike ancestors (whose vision wasn't too good) to roam around at night. They were all too likely to encounter night-hunting animals, to get lost, or to fall into unseen pits. Members of the same species who were fortunate enough to be immobilized by sleep during the dark hours had the best chance to live to see the dawn. After millions of years of evolution, this theory suggests, sleep has become an instinct in humans that is tied to the light-dark cycle of day and night (Webb, 1982).

Sleep is a means of restoring brain chemicals. REM sleep may help to restore the effectiveness of certain brain pathways that make use of the neurotransmitter norepinephrine. Ernest Hartmann (1973) believes that this restorative function of sleep helps explain why some people need more sleep than others. Whereas some people flourish on four to six hours of sleep a night, others need at least eight hours. The differences seem to be at least partly hereditary (Webb and Campbell, 1983), and they may stem from genetically based differences in people's levels of norepinephrine in the brain.

We sleep in order to dream. The need to dream appears to be as basic as the need to sleep. People who are deprived of the opportunity to dream become anxious and irritable, and they make up for the deprivation by dreaming more on subsequent nights. Some psychologists, such as Carl Jung, have pointed to the valuable roles that our dreams play in helping us to work through our daytime problems and to achieve psychological balance. From this point of view, the ultimate purpose of sleep may be to allow us to dream.

We sleep in order to clear our minds. In the course of a typical day,

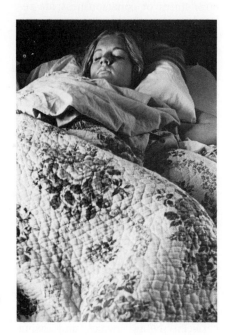

we accumulate many thoughts, memories, and mental associations. Many of these thoughts are utterly useless. Worse than that, some of the bizarre connections that reverberate through our brains will interfere with new learning. As a result, we need a method of clearing our mind of these worse-than-useless thoughts. Francis Crick and Graeme Mitchison (1983) have proposed that the intense electrical activity of REM sleep has the effect of wiping our brains clear of extraneous information, leaving our brains ready for new learning. Without such nightly cleanings, they suggest, our minds would be too cluttered to work properly.

To all of these ideas about why we sleep, still others can be added. There are times, it seems, when we sleep to rest our weary bodies, times when we sleep to ease our emotional burdens, and times when we sleep simply because we have nothing better to do. All of the theories may be correct, at least in part, or none of them may be. The question of why we sleep remains a scientific mystery that has attracted a lot of attention but has yet to be solved. Better sleep on it.

afternoon is likely to lead to longer sleep that night. People also tend to sleep less soundly during their first night in a new place, such as when they are on vacation or during their first night in a sleep laboratory, where volunteers take part in systematic studies of sleep (Webb and Bonnet, 1979).

When we want to go to sleep, we ordinarily seek a quiet room, turn the lights off, lie down, and close our eyes. These actions have important effects on our nervous system. The quiet environment and closed eyes reduce external sensory input. By lying down, we cut off a significant portion of the feedback from muscles that keep the brain aroused when we are sitting or standing. All these changes decrease the general level of activation in the brain, thereby helping us move from waking to sleeping.

We usually think of "falling asleep" as being a slow, gradual process. In fact, however, it happens in an instant. As William Dement (1972), a leading sleep researcher, put it, "One second the organism is aware—the next second it is not. Awareness stops abruptly, as if 10 billion furiously communicating brain cells were suddenly placed on 'standby' status."

Stages of sleep

A major discovery made by sleep researchers is that sleep is not a single state. Rather, during a single night's sleep we move through a sleep cycle that consists of several stages, each with its own distinctive pattern of brain waves (see Figure 3.1).

Stage 1 is falling asleep, the stage that usually occurs a few minutes after climbing into bed. Brain waves are irregular, and they lack the pattern of alpha waves that characterize the relaxed waking state. The heart rate begins to slow, and muscles relax. The person in stage 1 is easy to waken and may not realize that he has fallen asleep.

FIGURE 3.1

Each stage of sleep is indicated by a specific pattern of brain waves.

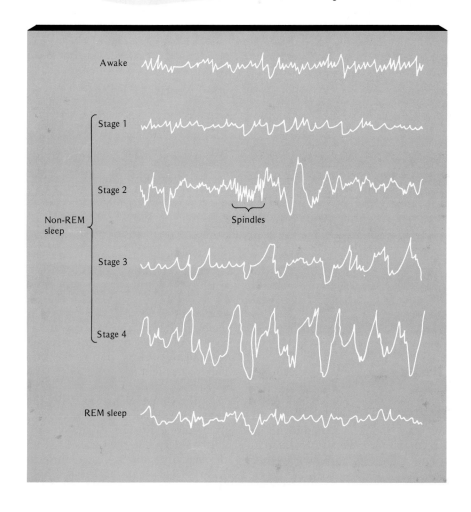

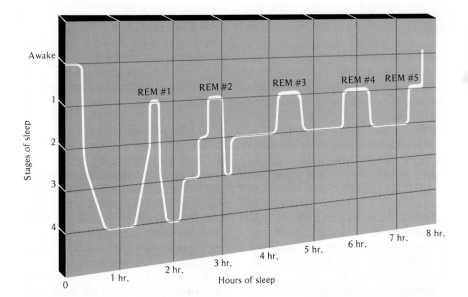

FIGURE 3.2

A typical night's sleep. Through the course of the night, we cycle through the stages of sleep. The deepest sleep occurs primarily in the first few hours. The REM periods, during which we dream, become longer as morning approaches.

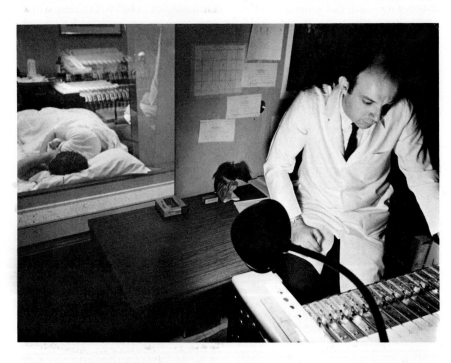

In a sleep laboratory, subjects are made comfortable for the night and are hooked up to EEG monitoring equipment. In addition to the brain-wave tracings, researchers can observe the subjects through one-way windows to record any movements or behaviors.

In *stage 2*, brain waves show bursts of activity called *spindles*, so named because their tracings on an EEG chart resemble thread wrapped around an old-fashioned spindle. Stage 2 is a deeper stage of sleep than stage 1.

In *stage 3*, even deeper sleep, the spindles disappear and long, slow (about one wave per second) brain waves called delta waves appear. At this stage the sleeper is difficult to waken and unresponsive to external stimuli. Heart rate, blood pressure, and temperature continue to drop.

Stage 4 is the deepest stage. It is called *delta sleep* because it is characterized by the slow delta waves. In young adults, delta sleep occurs in 15- to 30-minute segments, interspersed with lighter stages, during the first half of the night. As one grows older, the amount of delta sleep is reduced.

In the course of a sleep cycle, the sleeper goes from stage 1 to stage 2, from stage 2 to stage 3, and on into deepest sleep. He then goes back up through the stages—back through stage 3 to stage 2. But when the brain waves again reach stage 1, the sleeper does not awaken. Instead, his eyes start darting and rolling around under his closed eyelids. This is the start of a stage of sleep called *REM (rapid eye movement) sleep.* It is during REM sleep that we dream. The REM periods are easily visible to anyone who looks closely at the sleeper's eyelids. Ninety minutes or so after the person has gone to sleep, the first REM period of the night usually starts and lasts about 5 to 10 minutes. Later in the night, REM periods last as long as 25 minutes. Because such eye movements do not occur in stages 1 through 4, they are referred to as *non-REM (NREM) sleep.*

During a typical night's sleep, a person goes up and down through the stages, but with each cycle the REM period becomes longer and the slow-wave stages become shorter. In later cycles, it is common for the sleeper to go only to stage 2 and then back to REM. These cycles are about 90 minutes long (see Figure 3.2).

REM and NREM sleep differ greatly in their mental activity. Almost every time people are awakened during a REM period they report that they have been dreaming. But people who are awakened during NREM sleep rarely report that they have been dreaming, and the mental content they do report usually seems more like random thoughts than real dreams with vivid images. It seems, therefore, that REM sleep and dreaming are almost synonymous. When the sleeper's eyes dart about during REM sleep, she may well be looking at the various people and events of the dream.

During REM sleep, the brain seems to be highly activated, even though the person is clearly asleep. The pattern of brain waves is similar to that of the waking state. During REM sleep, pulse rate and respiration are a bit faster than during NREM sleep, blood pressure is higher, and all three processes are less regular. At the same time, there is a major decrease in muscle tone during REM sleep. This reduced muscle tone helps prevent the dreamer from moving about and acting out her dreams.

DALI'S NAP

What is the shortest nap a person can take? The story goes that Salvador Dali, the surrealist painter, used to put a tin plate on the floor and then sit on a chair beside it, holding a spoon over the plate. He would then go into a doze. The moment that he fell asleep the spoon would slip from his fingers and clang onto the plate, immediately awakening him. Dali claimed that he was completely refreshed by the sleep that took place between the time the spoon left his hand and the time it hit the plate (Dement, 1972).

Sleep disorders

A surprisingly large number of people have trouble falling or staying asleep, a problem called *insomnia.* Some people toss and turn restlessly until they get to sleep but then sleep well the rest of the night. Others wake up repeatedly throughout the night. In a survey in Los Angeles, over 40 percent of adults reported having a current or past problem with insomnia, and it was most prevalent among older people (Bixler et al., 1979). Insomniac clubs have been formed in some cities and, as you might expect, meetings are held late at night when no one can fall asleep.

There are several causes of insomnia. Some people take all their daytime worries to bed with them, which prevents them from relaxing enough to sleep. Others are actually afraid of falling asleep, for fear of nightmares or of emergencies that might arise. Insomnia is also a common symptom of depression (see Chapter 13). In addition, people with irregular schedules often have difficulty dropping off. Sleep is one of the body's natural rhythms, as we will see in the Psychological Issue following this chapter, and changing schedules can throw the rhythm off balance. Paradoxically, both sleeping pills and alcohol can produce insomnia. Although these drugs are sometimes helpful in small doses, they require ever-increasing amounts to be effective, and they disrupt the natural sequence of sleep stages. On the other hand, several methods of relaxing the mind and muscles have proven to be effective in beating sleeplessness. Some of these methods involve progressive relaxation of body muscles, starting with the toes and moving up toward the shoulders and neck. Others emphasize concentrating on pleasant, relaxing mental images.

Insomnia is the most common sleep disorder, but it is not the only one. Most of us have had the embarrassing experience of falling asleep in an inappropriate situation, such as in class or at a movie with friends. Fatigue and boredom are usually the culprits. But a small number of people have a far more serious problem with

Insomnia is the most common sleep disorder. Worries and tensions from the day are among the factors that can keep people up at night.

"sleep attacks," a disorder called *narcolepsy*. At any time of the day, they may suddenly drop into a deep sleep for up to 30 minutes. The attacks may even come at inopportune moments, such as while driving a car. In attacks of narcolepsy, the person is plunged directly into REM sleep, unlike the normal sleep pattern in which REMs appear after 90 minutes or so. Although the precise causes of narcolepsy are not known, it apparently involves a disorder in the brain mechanisms that control REM sleep (Browman et al., 1982).

Sleepwalking, another sleep disorder, is most common among children. Sleepwalkers are not acting out dreams; in fact, this activity occurs during stage 4 sleep, when there is little, if any, dreaming. In some cases, sleepwalking may involve other unconscious acts, such as going to the refrigerator for a snack (Restak, 1979). Sleepwalking is usually outgrown, but some adults continue to walk in their sleep.

Some people experience attacks called *night terrors* that waken them directly from a deep stage of sleep. Night terrors are different from nightmares, which are scary dreams that occur during REM sleep. Nightmares raise the heartbeat only slightly and may be forgotten with the morning light. But night terrors involve sudden awakening from deep sleep (stage 4). The person awakens in a panic, may scream or cower in fear, has an elevated heart rate, and may break out in a cold sweat. Night terrors are most common in children. They peak between the ages of 3 and 5 but are occasionally seen in adults.

DREAMING

I have a key that opens a closed drugstore. I go in as if I'm looking for something. I am a sweet, young, responsible girl, like Teresa Wright in Shadow of a Doubt. *I also have a key to the beauty parlor next door. I go in in order to leave something (a comb and mirror?) in the window. I come back to the drugstore when it is open and decide to have a dessert. I inquire about a letter I sent to myself at this address but it hasn't arrived. I finally find it on a counter—this is what I have been looking for in the drugstore—and I leave. Next I am playing hopscotch with some little girls as it grows dark. Police come and arrest me. They ask me why I killed the little girl (some days earlier, I assume). I say it was because she was very unhappy. They take me away.*

This account, taken from one woman's "dream diary," emphasizes the fact that in dreams we do things that we cannot do in real life. We fly, we change identities, we even kill people. Through most of the world's history, humans have regarded dreams as magical states, as ways of exchanging one's worldly identity and limitations for new selves and new capacities, and as messengers of divine instructions and prophecies. In many cultures people who interpreted the dreams of others were likely to be highly respected leaders. Today we are still fascinated by dreams and their meanings. The interpretation of dreams and their symbols was given new impetus by Sigmund Freud, who saw dreams as the "royal road to the unconscious." More recently, systematic studies are exploring the physiological bases of dreaming and its contributions to our emotional well-being.

The interpretation of dreams

Freud came into prominence with the publication in 1900 of *The Interpretation of Dreams.* Freud stated that dreams represent the fulfillment of unconscious impulses, both sexual and aggressive, that are unacceptable on a conscious level. (Freud's ideas about these unconscious impulses are discussed in greater detail in Chapter 11.) While we sleep, Freud believed, our repressed wishes—especially our sexual desires—thrust to the surface and are fulfilled. If we were to experience these wishes directly, we would be filled with anxiety and guilt. But the impulses are disguised in our dreams, so we can continue to sleep peacefully. Freud suggested that our wishes and impulses are disguised through three processes: symbolism, condensation, and displacement.

By *symbolism* Freud meant that unacceptable ideas are translated into a more acceptable—symbolic—form in dreams. Freud focused primarily on sexual symbols, suggesting that sharp, elongated objects (umbrellas, swords, sticks) were symbols of the penis and that containers (cups, boxes, houses) were symbols of the vagina. By *condensation* Freud meant that one image in a dream could represent several elements in a person's life. For example, a dream about scoring a touchdown may bring together a man's feelings about competition, fame, and sexual accomplishment. By *displacement*, Freud meant that in a dream unacceptable wishes can be focused on an object different from the real object of the wishes. For in-

The surrealistic world of our dreams lends itself to many interpretations that can provide insights into our waking lives.

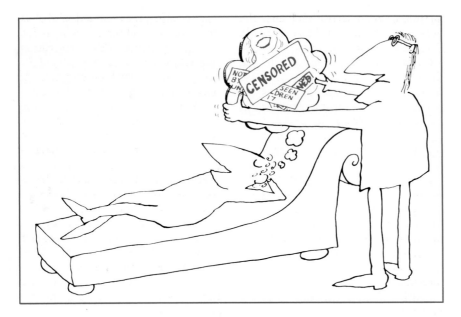

stance, dreaming of hitting a tiger with a baseball bat might represent a wish to harm an authority figure in one's life.

Freud distinguished two types of content in dreams: the latent content and the manifest content. The *latent content* is the underlying meaning of the dream. The *manifest content* is the disguised form of the dream that we remember when we wake up. For example, a woman may dream that she is playing a carnival game in which she tosses a ring onto a bottle and wins a giant teddy bear. That is the manifest content of the dream. The latent content may be that she wishes she could conceive and have a baby.

Because sexual impulses play a central role in Freud's theory of personality, Freud almost always found sexual desires in the latent content of dreams. Other dream theorists do not give sex such important status in their interpretations. Today, most dream analysts feel that dreams can have a much wider range of meanings and functions than Freud believed. Calvin Hall (1966), a leading dream researcher, has suggested that each dream be viewed as "a personal document, a letter to oneself." Hall has also pointed out that gathering and interpreting a series of dreams—looking at the common themes that run through them—can be more helpful than focusing on a single dream.

Where do dreams come from?

People in some cultures believe that dreams come from the travel of the soul outside the body. Freud believed that dreams originated in unconscious wishes. Recent research provides another perspective: the idea that dreams originate in the activity of different portions of the brain during REM sleep. According to the *activation-synthesis model* of dreams put forth by Allan Hobson and Robert McCarley (1977), the dream process begins with the periodic firing of nerve cells known as *giant cells* in the brain stem. This firing leads to the rapid eye movements and brain waves characteristic of REM sleep, and it also leads to high levels of activation (the firing of nerve cells) in other areas of the brain, including those areas concerned with sensation (especially vision), motor activity, and emotion. At the same time, this neural firing greatly reduces the tone of the major muscles of the body, such as in the arms and legs, producing a kind of paralysis.

During a dream, of course, the activation of sensory areas of the brain does not correspond to actual events, as it does when we are awake. And the inhibition of muscles during REM sleep prevents the actual acting out of motor impulses. Instead, we *synthesize* a dream mentally, coming up with content that corresponds to the

A WELL-EXECUTED DREAM

We often incorporate external stimuli into our dreams, sometimes in highly creative ways. If water is squirted on a dreamer, he may dream of being caught in a thunderstorm. Or a pinprick may become an injection in a doctor's office. In a book written in 1861, André Maury reported a dream set during the French Revolution. The dream included his trial, conviction, and travel to the place of execution. Maury climbed onto the scaffold, was bound, and felt the guillotine fall. He awoke to find that the top of his bed had fallen and had struck him in the back of the neck (Webb and Bonnet, 1979).

pattern of brain activation (hence the term *activation-synthesis model*). For example, stimulation of brain centers for vision, as well as feedback from rapid eye movements, may lead to the rapidly shifting scenes that are characteristic of dreams; stimulation of the brain centers for the sense of balance may lead to sensations of spinning or floating. According to the activation-synthesis model, it is the unusual intensity and rapidity of the brain stimulation, often activating simultaneously areas of the brain that are unlikely to be activated simultaneously when we are awake, that accounts for the highly changeable and sometimes bizarre content of our dreams.

Although the Hobson-McCarley model helps to link physiological events with the events of dreams, it raises more questions than it answers about the content of dreams. What leads a person to synthesize a dream that includes specific persons and incidents? Our memories, emotions, and personality styles, as well as the previous day's events are all likely to play a prominent role. In the dream quoted at the beginning of this section, for instance, the woman might have seen Alfred Hitchcock's movie *Shadow of a Doubt* on the day before she had the dream or she may have taken a trip to the drugstore. Dreams may still serve as wish-fulfillments, as Freud believed, even as they correspond to patterns of physiological activation.

The functions of dreaming

The need to dream appears to be as basic as the need to sleep. Young adults dream about two hours a night on the average—whether or not the dreams are remembered. In one experiment, people were awakened for five consecutive nights just as the periods of REM sleep began (Dement, 1960), so they were prevented from dreaming. These dream-deprived individuals became anxious, irritable, and angry; they had difficulty concentrating, and some began to hallucinate. Moreover, as subjects were deprived of REM sleep their need for it seemed to build. When they went

back to sleep, they entered REM sleep more often. And for as many as five nights following REM deprivation, the subjects spent more time in REM sleep than usual—sometimes as much as double the normal amount.

Why do we have such a strong need to dream? Freud's view, as described earlier, was that dreams provide for the expression of repressed impulses, albeit in disguised form. Carl Jung (1964) took another view of the function of dreams. He argued that dreams compensate for things that we lack when we are awake and thus serve to restore our overall psychological balance. In some cases, Jung believed, dreams can bring us messages from our unconscious minds, including warnings of personal weakness.

Recent research has begun to document the ways dreams can help people deal with problems in their waking lives. Rosalind Cartwright (1978) has found that people sometimes handle emotional situations more realistically after dreaming. In one study, she presented students with incomplete "problem stories" before bedtime in a sleep laboratory. The stories dealt with common concerns of young adults, such as separation from home. The subjects then went to sleep. Some were allowed to dream (they were awakened only during NREM sleep), while others were not (they were awakened only during REM sleep or were not allowed to sleep at all). In the morning, when asked about possible solutions to the problem posed in a story, the subjects who had been allowed to dream were better able to acknowledge the realistic dimensions of the problem. On the basis of this and other studies, Cartwright has proposed that dreams provide "a kind of workshop for the repair of self-esteem and competence."

DRUGS AND CONSCIOUSNESS

Throughout history people have taken various chemical substances, often derived from plants, to change their moods, perceptions, and thought processes. Today is no excep-

SEX DIFFERENCES IN DREAMS

Men and women tend to dream different sorts of dreams. For example, men are more likely to report dreams that have outdoor settings and that include acts of aggression. Whereas women are more likely to dream about people they know or recognize, men are more likely to dream about strangers. In men's dreams, about two-thirds of the other characters are males; in women's dreams about half are females. All of these sex differences were found in extensive sets of dream reports collected from college students in 1950 and again in 1980 (Hall, 1984).

tion, with a wide variety of drugs available to lift one up, bring one down, expand one's consciousness, or shake up one's senses. Such substances that have a noticeable impact on mood, perception, or thought are called *psychoactive drugs*. Although different psychoactive drugs have different effects, they all work by altering chemical events in the brain. Many psychoactive drugs are chemically similar to certain of the brain's neurotransmitters (Chapter 2). Some of these drugs exert their effects by attaching themselves to receptor neurons and mimicking the brain's own neurotransmitters. Other psychoactive drugs produce chemical reactions that either stimulate or inhibit the production of neurotransmitters.

Types of psychoactive drugs

There are hundreds of psychoactive drugs, but they can be grouped into four major categories: depressants, psychedelic drugs, stimulants, and marijuana (see Figure 3.3).

Depressants include alcohol, narcotics such as heroin and morphine, and the barbiturates and other sedative drugs often taken as sleeping pills. Although these drugs can be taken to achieve a psychological "high," they actually depress the activity of the central nervous system and decrease its ability to respond to stimuli.

Psychedelic drugs, including LSD, mescaline, and psilocybin, have the effect of "opening the floodgates" of brain activity, so that the user may be deluged with internally produced perceptions—colors, odors, and sounds. Because these perceptions sometimes resemble hallucinations, these drugs are also called *hallucinogens*.

Stimulants, including the amphetamines and cocaine, are drugs that stimulate the activity of the central nervous system and thus may intensify the user's perceptions and produce heightened activity and restlessness. Caffeine, found in coffee, soft drinks, and chocolate, is also a stimulant.

Marijuana, the most widely used of the psychoactive drugs (other than the "common drugs," such as nicotine and caffeine, discussed in Box 3), combines some of the effects of the psychedelic drugs and the stimulants and is generally placed in its own category.

In this section, we will look more closely at the effects of several of the best known psychoactive drugs: LSD and other psychedelics, marijuana, amphetamines, and cocaine. In later chapters of this book, you will encounter discussions of other psychoactive drugs: alcohol use and abuse are examined in the Psychological Issue following Chapter 12, and drugs used to treat psychological disorders are described in Chapter 14.

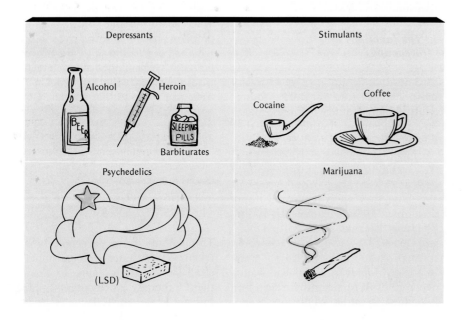

FIGURE 3.3

The four major categories of psychoactive drugs.

CHAPTER THREE: CONSCIOUSNESS

BOX 3

THE COMMON DRUGS

Caffeine (in coffee) and nicotine (in cigarettes) are drugs that millions of people take every day.

A nation of drug addicts? Well, not quite, but most of us do use drugs a great deal more than we are aware.

Cigarettes, for example, are a common source of nicotine, a drug that seems to have both stimulating and depressant effects on the central nervous system. Smoking can bring people up when they are groggy and down when they are tense (Stepney, 1983). Nicotine also constricts the peripheral blood vessels, elevates heart rate and blood pressure, and increases stomach activity. Perhaps for this reason smokers often find cigarettes after meals quite pleasurable.

Caffeine, in coffee, tea, and soft drinks, acts as a central nervous system stimulant. People who consume too much caffeine may experience tremors, rapid heartbeat, overactivity, restlessness, and nausea. Caffeine is the "extra ingredient" in many common pain relievers, although its effects on pain are not clear.

People can become psychologically dependent on caffeine, just as they can on nicotine—a fact that has been discovered by millions of people who feel they can't function unless they begin the day with a cup of coffee (or, for some people, a can of cola). Indeed, it has been suggested that if caffeine were a newly introduced drug, it would not be made available without a prescription (Timson, 1978).

Ethyl alcohol is consumed in huge quantities in beer, wine, and liquor. Alcohol abuse is the biggest drug problem in America today, in all age groups. Small doses cause dilation of the pupils, slight increases in blood pressure, and temporary elevation of blood-sugar level. Larger doses interfere with fine discrimination, motor control, and self-restraint. Excessive doses can cause coma and death (see the Psychological Issue for Chapter 12).

There are many other drugs that are not quite as popular as caffeine or alcohol but are still quite common. Codeine, a narcotic, is used for pain relief and for remedy of coughs. Sedatives and tranquilizers are used by thousands of people to promote relaxation, reduce anxiety, and induce sleep. Large numbers of people trap themselves in a vicious cycle, taking one pill for pep in the morning, various other stimulants or anxiety-reducers during the day, and a sleeping pill at night.

Because drugs can have pleasant effects on people's states of consciousness, drug-taking has become a recreational activity for millions of people. It should be borne in mind, however, that taking any of these drugs involves risks. For one thing, most of these drugs are illegal. And in all cases, drug use involves risks to health. The risks are greater with some drugs than with others, of course. Some psychoactive drugs, particularly depressants, can be *physiologically addictive*; when an addicted person stops taking the drug, he goes through a painful illness called *withdrawal syndrome*, during which the body adjusts to removal of the drug. Common withdrawal symptoms include increased blood pressure and severe cramps, as well as anxiety, irritability, and restlessness. Moreover, even those drugs that are not physically addictive can lead to *psychological dependence*, in which the person feels a strong need to continue taking the drug at practically any cost.

LSD and the psychedelic drugs

LSD–25 (lysergic acid diethylamide) is a psychedelic drug—that is, a drug that causes profound alteration of sensory, perceptual, cognitive, and emotional experiences. It takes only a tiny speck of this substance to produce intense hallucinations and distortions of vision, sound, time, and feelings. Sensations merge into each other, and the person may say he can taste color or see sounds. Although LSD experiences are often described as pleasant or even as mystical, users may also have painful or frightening experiences, sometimes called "bad trips." The effects of the drug depend to a great extent on the personal characteristics of the user, on the setting in which the drug is taken, and on the purity of the substance being used.

There are several other psychedelic drugs that produce effects similar to those of LSD. *Peyote*, a Mexican cactus, is made up of alkaloids (one of which is mescaline) that produce intense color awareness and hallucinations. Reflexes seem heightened, hearing and vision seem intensified, and ideas flow rapidly (Nabokov,

1969). Some Indian tribes have used mescal buttons, made from the peyote cactus, for centuries in religious ceremonies. Another psychedelic drug, *psilocybin*, is derived from mushrooms that have been used in Indian religious rites since ancient times. Psilocybin is not nearly as potent as LSD, but it produces similar hallucinations and distorted sensations.

The manner in which LSD and the other psychedelics operate is still far from clear. However, one prominent theory holds that LSD may work by blocking the effects of the neurotransmitter serotonin. Serotonin usually acts to inhibit thought processes and emotions. LSD, which is chemically similar to serotonin, may attach itself to serotonin receptors in the brain. This may prevent the normal functioning of the neurotransmitter, causing the consciousness to become flooded with remote associations and feelings (Siegel and Jarvik, 1975).

Marijuana

Marijuana is made from the flowering tops of the hemp plant, *Cannabis sativa*. Aside from alcohol, it is probably humanity's oldest drug. It was used in ancient China and eventually found its way to India, North Africa, and Europe. Marijuana has been used for centuries in Central and South America but became important in the United States only after 1920.

During the 1960s, marijuana became identified with the counterculture of the day and had an explosion in popularity. In the 1980s marijuana remains by far the most widely used of the illegal psychoactive drugs. In 1982, over 25 percent of young adults in the United States between the ages of 18 and 25 reported using marijuana at least monthly (National Institute of Drug Abuse, 1982). In the early 1980s, however, there has been some decrease in the proportion of high-school students using marijuana (Collins, 1983).

For many users, marijuana provides a "high"—a sense of elation or well-being. Some people say it enhances enjoyment of food and sex and that it heightens all sensory perceptions. In addition, users often report

LSD can produce major distortions of vision, sound, time, and feelings.

In the 1960s the use of marijuana became identified with the counterculture of the day. In the 1980s marijuana is still widely used.

MARIJUANA AS MEDICINE

Marijuana may have medically beneficial effects for certain groups of people. It has been found to be helpful for some patients suffering from glaucoma, a painful eye disease that can cause blindness (Schmeck, 1979). Marijuana has also been administered to cancer patients receiving chemotherapy or radiation therapy. The marijuana sometimes seems to alleviate the severe nausea and loss of appetite that are side effects of these treatments. Researchers have also investigated the use of marijuana to treat asthma, epilepsy, and pain (Cohen, 1978).

that marijuana makes time seem to pass more slowly. However, the perceptual changes produced by marijuana are of a much milder sort than those produced by LSD. Marijuana has two easily observable physiological effects: it increases heart rate and it enhances appetite. It also affects brain function, producing detectable changes in brain waves. But researchers are not yet sure just how it works. While many researchers believe that marijuana operates on neurotransmitters in the brain (Maugh, 1974), it has also been suggested that the drug has a direct effect on nerve fibers (Byck and Ritchie, 1973).

Because of the extensive use of marijuana and the ongoing debate about its legalization, researchers have been concentrating on the long-term effects of marijuana use. The results are conflicting, however. Emotions tend to run high on this issue, and even "objective" scientists are prone to show some personal bias for or against marijuana use. Nevertheless, it is possible to draw some general conclusions regarding the effects of marijuana on health and behavior. Some of the most serious

charges leveled against the drug—such as that it causes permanent brain damage or intellectual impairment—do not seem to be justified (Schaffer et al., 1981). Nor does it appear that marijuana is physiologically addictive (Zinberg, 1976).

But the effects of marijuana are not totally benign. Because marijuana reduces perceptual acuity and motor coordination, driving or operating machinery while high can be dangerous. And because of its unpredictable effects on judgment and emotions, use of marijuana—like all other intoxicants—can be risky for the young or the emotionally troubled. There is also reason to believe that heavy marijuana smoking can lead to lung cancer, just as cigarette smoking can. A recent report on the effects of marijuana smoking on physical and mental health, sponsored by the National Academy of Sciences (1982), concluded that the available evidence justifies "serious national concern."

Amphetamines

Amphetamines are a group of drugs that act as central nervous system stimulants. In 1932, the first amphetamine—Benzedrine—was made available to the public in drugstores across the country. It was taken as a medicine for hay fever, asthma, and other disorders involving nasal congestion. At the time, physicians were not aware of the great dangers of this drug. By the end of World War II, at least seven different inhalers containing large amounts of amphetamine could be purchased without a prescription.

In recent years, amphetamines as prescription drugs have been produced in the billions of tablets per year. They have been prescribed as "pep pills" and have been used by countless students staying up all night cramming for exams and by long-distance truck drivers trying to stay alert on all-night hauls. Amphetamines can also suppress the appetite, and they were widely prescribed as diet pills until the Food and Drug Administration banned them for this purpose, judging them to be ineffective and dangerous.

Amphetamine is a dangerous drug on which people can become dependent. People who abuse amphetamines ("speed freaks") take the pills in large doses or even inject amphetamine in liquid form. They sometimes spend several days on a "run," keeping a continuous high by injecting the drug every few hours. When the amphetamine high is over, the physical and psychological effects can be devastating. The user may suffer extreme lethargy, anxiety, headaches, muscle cramps, nightmares, severe depression, and disorientation; he may also become extremely irritable and demanding.

Amphetamine use can also lead to *amphetamine psychosis,* a group of symptoms remarkably similar to those of the psychological disorder called paranoid schizophrenia (see Chapter 13). In fact, without prior knowledge of a patient's history of drug abuse, a psychiatrist or psychologist may misdiagnose amphetamine psychosis as schizophrenia. Solomon Snyder has described the state of amphetamine psychosis: "The harbinger is vague fear and suspicion— *What was that? I heard something. Is somebody trying to get me?* Soon the

paranoia centers around a specific delusion. . . . Acting on his delusions the speed freak may become violent— *to get them before they get me"* (1972, page 44). The person caught in amphetamine psychosis may also spend hours in a compulsive stereotyped behavior, such as counting grains of sand, without seeming to be fatigued or bored.

Because of the similarity of amphetamine effects to schizophrenia, researchers believe that if we could understand how amphetamines affect the brain we might get important clues about the biological bases of schizophrenia. As with the psychedelic drugs, amphetamines produce their psychological effects by influencing neural transmission. Specifically, amphetamines seem to trigger the release of dopamine, a neurotransmitter associated with the arousal and emotional functions of the brain (Iversen, 1979).

Cocaine

Cocaine, like amphetamine, is a stimulant. It is a chemical compound extracted from the leaves of the coca plant. This plant has been grown for thousands of years in South America, where peasant workers regularly chew its leaves. In the eighteenth century European explorers noted that the leaves seemed to help the workers tolerate hunger, cold, and fatigue. Considered a boon to good health, the drug was gradually introduced to Western Europe and, from there, to North America. By the late nineteenth century, cocaine was a featured ingredient in dozens of patent medicines. Its benefits were extolled in the treatment of disorders ranging from colds to loss of sexual desire. Even Sigmund Freud, the founder of psychoanalysis, used cocaine and recommended it to others. By the 1920s, however, public attitudes had turned against cocaine use. The Coca-Cola company eliminated cocaine from its product. In 1922 Congress prohibited import of the plant and drug (Grinspoon and Bakalar, 1977).

In the 1980s, use of cocaine has risen faster than that of any other drug, with an estimated 4 to 5 million

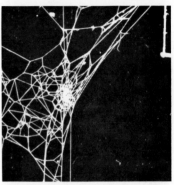

The effect of amphetamine on the web-spinning of a spider. The top photo is a normal web. After being given amphetamine, the spider became severely disturbed and spun the middle web. After 24 hours, the spider spun the bottom web, which shows signs of recovery.

Cocaine was once considered to be a boon to good health. Until the 1920s it was one of the ingredients of Coca-Cola (which explains how the drink got its name).

DRINK
Coca-Cola
DELICIOUS   REFRESHING

Coca-Cola

5¢

THE STRENUOUS
LIFE
On the street or curb or any phase
of endeavor loses much of its
nerve racking and physically ex-
hausting terrors, if you drink
Coca-Cola
Refreshes! Invigorates!
Sustains!
5¢ Sold Everywhere 5¢

Americans using cocaine at least once a month. The fastest-growing group of users seems to be young adults in their twenties and thirties. And whereas cocaine used to be associated with high-flying occupations and social scenes, such as rock music and sports figures, its use has now become more common across all strata of society (Anderson, 1983).

Cocaine can be taken in many different forms: it can be chewed, drunk as tea, inhaled in powder form, smoked, injected, or breathed as a vapor. Regardless of how it is taken, cocaine typically produces feelings of alertness, mastery, and self-confidence, often accompanied by talkativeness. It may also produce nervousness, irritability, restlessness, and exhaustion from lack of sleep.

Cocaine acts by stimulating the central nervous system. Like other stimulants, cocaine increases heart and breathing rates, raises body temperature and blood-sugar levels, increases muscle tension, and dilates pupils. Cocaine clears from the blood very quickly, so its effects usually last for no more than 20 or 30 minutes. Scientists do not know for sure how cocaine produces its effects. It is believed, however, that cocaine prevents the breakdown of norepinephrine in the brain, thereby affecting the transmission of nerve signals at synapses that involve this neurotransmitter.

With cocaine's burst of popularity, there has been increased concern about its harmful effects on physical and mental health. Many extremely harmful effects have been linked to cocaine abuse, including paranoid reactions similar to those observed in cases of amphetamine psychosis, as well as serious damage to the heart and lungs. In one recent year, overdoses of cocaine were held to be responsible for at least 300 deaths in the United States (Anderson, 1983).

Part of the danger of cocaine seems to result from the fact that it produces strongly pleasurable, even if short-lived, reactions. People sometimes find cocaine so pleasurable that they develop a compulsion to take it at all costs—and the cost of cocaine on the underground market can be great indeed.

In the past, it was often claimed that cocaine is not addictive. But although cocaine does not lead to the sort of extreme physiological dependence and withdrawal symptoms that may be produced by narcotics such as heroin, it now seems clear that many people become so psychologically dependent on cocaine that their problem can be called an addiction. Although many people take cocaine in small doses without any apparent ill effects, others have had their health and lives ruined by cocaine addiction. As a result, cocaine abuse has become a central concern of mental health professionals in the 1980s.

HYPNOSIS

Don't look up while you're reading this. There may be someone nearby whose piercing eyes are waiting to catch your attention, hypnotize you, destroy your willpower, and make you a slave. At least, that's what you might believe if you watch too many old movies. Mystery has surrounded hypnosis since Anton Mesmer introduced it to Europe in the 1780s. Eighteenth-century scientists rejected hypnosis as a hoax and a fraud. Now, two centuries later, researchers are taking a new look at hypnosis. Hypnosis isn't magic, and for the first time we are getting some insight into how it works.

The hypnotic state

Hypnosis is a state of increased suggestibility (or willingness to comply with another person's directions) that is brought about through the use of certain procedures by another person, the hypnotist. These procedures vary from one hypnotist to another. The subject may be asked to stare at a thumbtack on the wall, or just to close her eyes and relax. The exact method of inducing hypnosis doesn't seem to matter. As long as the subject has confidence in the hypnotist, any procedure that focuses the subject's attention and puts him in a relaxed, responsive mood will do.

Ernest Hilgard (1977) has described the characteristic changes observed in a hypnotized subject. A hypnotized person becomes very passive, never initiating activity but waiting for instructions from the hypnotist. Attention becomes very selective; if told to listen only to a particular voice, the subject may become completely unresponsive to music or to other voices in the room. Hypnotized subjects are apt to believe practically anything the hypnotist tells them, even things that would ordinarily seem preposterous. If, for example, a subject is told that there is a puppy on the empty table in front of her, she may begin to play with the imaginary dog. Similarly, subjects may take on new and uncharacteristic roles at the hypnotist's suggestion. The timid young man, ordinarily too shy to even speak in public, may become quite willing to sing and dance like Michael Jackson. There *are* limits to the effects of hypnosis, however. Despite their increased suggestibility, hypnotized subjects will not do things they are fundamentally opposed to.

Increased suggestibility is the basis for another phenomenon associated with hypnosis: the *posthypnotic suggestion*. This occurs when a hypnotized subject is instructed to act on a suggestion when she is back in the waking state. For example, the suggestion might be for the subject to stand up whenever the hypnotist says the word "day." After the subject comes out of the hypnotic state, she is not aware of this posthypnotic suggestion and is baffled by the fact that she stands up when the hypnotist says, "This sure is a beautiful day."

Memory processes, too, may be altered by hypnosis. Subjects may

"YOU WILL BE ABLE TO PITCH!"
Hypnosis is often used to help people get over mental blocks and to reduce tensions that affect their job performance. One group of professionals who has been helped by hypnosis are baseball players. For examples, Los Angeles Dodgers pitcher Jerry Reuss says a hypnotist helped him to conquer his fear of Wrigley Field, the Chicago Cubs' stadium, after he had pitched a couple of bad games there. Such ball park hypnosis doesn't always work, however. In 1977 a hypnotist treated the entire California Angels team when their manager decided they needed some pepping up. Despite the hypnotic efforts, the team finished fifth in its division (Leo, 1983).

People who are highly susceptible to hypnosis will focus their attention on the hypnotist and follow his suggestions quite completely.

cannot be hypnotized at all, about 15 percent are highly susceptible, and the rest of us fall somewhere in between.

On the average, men and women are equally susceptible to hypnosis. People with high susceptibility scores are not particularly suggestible in normal circumstances, as when others are trying to persuade them to change their beliefs or attitudes, nor are susceptible persons especially passive, compliant types (Hilgard, 1979). But susceptible persons do have some things in common. They are able to become deeply absorbed in activities that interest them, whether it is reading, listening to music, or bird-watching. When the susceptible individual picks up a novel, he can become oblivious to the activity around him, conscious only of the characters and events in the book. The susceptible person apparently brings the same capacity for absorption to the hypnotic session, when he becomes absorbed in the world of fantasy created by the hypnotist.

Hypnosis and pain control

Some people can free themselves from even severe pain through hypnosis. In fact, hypnosis was the anesthetic most commonly used for patients undergoing surgery until the discovery of ether and chloroform in the nineteenth century. Today, dental patients, burn victims, women in childbirth, and cancer patients have all been relieved of pain through hypnosis (Hilgard and Hilgard, 1975). In the laboratory, psychologists have studied the effects of hypnosis on the pain that occurs with the *cold-pressor response.* Subjects are asked to place their hand and forearm in ice water. Normally, people can tolerate this discomfort for only 30 to 45 seconds. But hypnotized subjects placed in this situation and told that the experience will not be painful report very little pain. Instead, they may describe what they feel as "a slight tingle" or "like a cold wind blowing on my arm." In one study of cold-pressor pain, hypnosis was found to be a more effective pain reliever than acupuncture, mor-

demonstrate *posthypnotic amnesia.* If so instructed while hypnotized, when wakened some subjects may fail to recall any or all of the events that occurred in the hypnotic state. The effects of hypnosis on memory aren't limited to forgetting; memory for past events may also be affected by the hypnotic state. This phenomenon will be examined further in the Psychological Issue for Chapter 6 on memory and the law.

Who can be hypnotized?

Not everyone responds to the hypnotic procedure in the same way; some people are more susceptible than others. The Stanford Hypnotic Susceptibility Scale (Hilgard, 1965) provides a measure of an individual's responsiveness to hypnosis. After a short attempt by the hypnotist to induce hypnosis, the subject is given a series of suggestions—for example, to close her eyes, to imagine that her left arm is rigid, to imagine that a bottle of ammonia is a bottle of perfume. The more suggestions that the subject "passes"—for example, by closing her eyes, or sniffing pungent ammonia without a grimace—the higher her score. Individuals vary widely in their susceptibility scores. It appears that about 5 to 10 percent of all people

BOX 4

MEDITATION

The search for the meaning of life and for ways to cope with life's pressures is as ancient as mankind itself. Monks and mystics have long offered *meditation* as a possible answer. In recent decades the practice of meditation has extended from the Himalayan monastery to the college campus and the business office, as individuals from all walks of life have sought relief from the stresses of daily existence.

Meditation makes use of different techniques of focusing one's attention in order to achieve a state of deep passivity combined with awareness. In our usual rat race of mental and physical activity, our mind bounces from one idea to another, reacting to every sensation, thought, or stimulus. When we meditate, we suspend our familiar ways of thinking and perceiving and seek to experience things in a fuller way.

In one type of meditation, called *concentrative*, the goal is to focus attention exclusively on a single object, a repeated word, or a part of the body. In *opening-up* techniques, on the other hand, the meditator opens herself to all sensations: air moving in and out of her lungs, sounds within

and without, familiar and unfamiliar odors. As different as these two states are, they are achieved by very similar methods. In both cases, meditation requires a quiet environment, a comfortable and relaxed posture, and a positive mental attitude (Benson, 1975).

In the last 20 years, over a million Americans have learned some form of meditation. At least half of these people have learned *transcendental meditation* (TM), a concentrative system developed by an Indian guru (or spiritual guide) named Maharishi Mahesh Yogi. Each person initiated into TM receives his own personal *mantra*—a word or phrase on which he is to meditate for the rest of his life. But the mystic and religious overtones of TM are not a necessary part of meditation— they are just the philosophical icing on the cake.

Research has demonstrated that meditation has both psychological and physical benefits. Meditators tend to score high on tests of self-esteem and mental health (Murray, 1982). Furthermore, such benefits are not limited to those who might be in good psychological condition to begin with. One

study found that individuals who suffered from chronic anxiety were substantially less fearful after 18 months of regular meditation (Raskin, Bali, and Peeke, 1980).

Meditation appears to have dramatic physical effects as well. For example, Wallace and Benson (1972) found that during meditation, less oxygen was consumed, the heartbeat and respiration were slower, and brain waves were altered. Meditators were found to be extremely relaxed, yet wide awake—a state that Benson (1975) calls the *relaxation response*. In some clinics patients are being taught to meditate in order to manage high blood pressure, coronary artery disease, migraine headaches, and chronic pain.

Some researchers suggest that meditation is no more effective reducing physiological arousal than any other form of relaxation, such as just sitting down quietly and taking it easy for a while (Holmes, 1984). Nevertheless, a special sense of serenity—that blend of relaxation and alertness—still seems to be unique to meditation.

phine, Valium, or aspirin (Stern et al., 1977).

The "hidden observer"

Psychologists are uncertain as to how hypnosis works; indeed, there is considerable debate over just what hypnosis is. Some psychologists argue that hypnosis isn't a separate state of consciousness at all. They believe that the hypnotic "state" is nothing more than the willingness of subjects to get involved and play a role. In this view, hypnosis is more like asking an actor to play a part—the role of someone in a hypnotic trance—than a truly different state of consciousness (Spanos and Barber, 1974).

But the prevailing opinion among psychologists today is that hypnosis represents a real shift from normal consciousness. This view has been taken by Ernest Hilgard (1977), who has developed a fascinating theory to explain hypnosis. Hilgard's theory began with the unexpected discovery that a part of the hypnotized person's mind—a part of which the person is not aware—is watching and remembering everything that is going on. Hilgard called this the *hidden observer.*

The discovery of the hidden observer was a dramatic one. Hilgard was giving a classroom demonstration of hypnosis with a subject who happened to be blind. Hilgard suggested to the hypnotized man that he would be unable to hear anything until a hand was placed on his shoulder. The subject then became quite unresponsive to any type of sound. One of the student observers asked if the man was really unable to hear. Hilgard turned to the man and quietly asked whether "some part of him" might be able to hear; if so, the man was to raise a finger. Slowly, the finger rose.

No one was more surprised than the subject, who wanted to know what was going on and why he had moved his finger. Hilgard placed a hand on the man's shoulder to remove his hypnotically induced deafness, then asked the subject what he had experienced. The man recalled that everything had become very quiet—in fact, downright dull. He

had just started to think about a problem in statistics when he felt his finger move. Then Hilgard addressed the same question about what the subject had experienced to "that part of you that listened to me before and made your finger rise," telling the man that he would not be able to hear his own words. That second part of the man's mind proceeded to report quite accurately everything that had gone on. Hilgard called this unconscious witness the "hidden observer."

Hilgard and his colleagues do not believe that the hidden observer is any more "mystical" than consciousness itself. We've all had experiences of attending to different things with different parts of our mind. For example, you may have found yourself planning next weekend's activities while typing a term paper. In such instances, consciousness seems to be divided or *dissociated;* one portion manages the typing while the other is concerned with planning the weekend. Hilgard (1977) believes that hypnosis represents just such a dissociated state. What Hilgard calls the hidden observer is a part of the mind separate from the remainder of consciousness. It seems to take note of everything that is going on, but without any awareness on the part of the subject. For example, in one of the cold-pressor response experiments, hypnotized subjects who verbally reported no discomfort were asked if "some part" of them was conscious of any pain. Many responded that indeed there was some pain. But the part of them that felt the pain—the hidden observer—was not communicating with their conscious self (Hilgard and Hilgard, 1975).

This research strongly suggests that we can have two or more states of consciousness simultaneously. And it is supported by other research (to be discussed in Chapter 4) on processes of attention. As a result, hypnosis—once a highly suspect outsider among psychological phenomena—is now a topic of active research that is helping to shed light on the remarkable mental processes of our everyday lives: how we routinely bring off the feat of simultaneously thinking and doing different things with different parts of our mind.

SUMMARY

The nature of consciousness

• **1** *Consciousness* refers to our subjective awareness of our own actions and of the world around us. Conscious mental processes can vary in quality, from subdued to intense. Consciousness can also vary from accurate perception of one's surroundings to major distortions (as in dreaming or drug-induced states).

• **2** In the late nineteenth century the structuralists used *introspection* to study consciousness. But the behaviorists declared that consciousness was not a proper subject for psychology. In recent times psychology has returned to the study of consciousness.

• **3** *Daydreaming* is a state of consciousness that differs from night dreaming in that daydreaming has minimal eye movement and more sensory interference from the environment. Singer suggests that daydreaming is necessary for our mental well-being.

Sleep

• **4** We spend about one-third of our lives in sleep. The human propensity to sleep at night appears to be universal. The amount of time people spend sleeping varies with age: infants sleep more than 12 hours a day, whereas old people sleep less than 8 hours.

• **5** Among the explanations for why we sleep are (1) it evolved to protect us from predators; (2) it restores brain chemicals; (3) it allows us to dream; (4) it clears our minds.

• **6** The process of falling asleep seems to be triggered by the reduction of sensory input afforded by a quiet, dark environment and a reclining position.

• **7** While sleeping we pass through *sleep cycles*, each running about 90 minutes and consisting of four distinct stages. As we pass from stage 1 to stage 4 and back to stage 1 again, we go into progressively deeper, then lighter levels of sleep. Brain-wave patterns are different for each stage.

• **8** Returning to stage 1, we enter a new stage—*REM (rapid eye move-ment) sleep*—during which we dream. Dreamless stages 1 through 4 are called the *non-REM*, or *NREM*, stages.

• **9** Among the sleep disorders that plague certain individuals are *insomnia* (inability to sleep), *narcolepsy* (attacks of REM sleep), *sleepwalking*, and *night terrors* (anxiety attacks suffered primarily by children).

Dreaming

• **10** Sigmund Freud thought that dreams provide wish fulfillment and in so doing reduce the tension created by unacceptable desires. He also thought that dreams preserve sleep by disguising unacceptable impulses in the form of *symbolism, condensation,* and *displacement.* He referred to the surface events of dreams as their *latent content* and to the outer description of dreams as their *manifest content.*

• **11** Freud's approach has been criticized for its emphasis on sexual interpretations and for its basis in the dreams of selected disturbed patients. Other dream theorists give a wider range of meanings and functions to dreams.

• **12** According to the *activation-synthesis model* of dreaming, dreams begin with the firing of giant cells in the brain stem. This firing leads to the activation of certain areas of the brain. The dreams we then synthesize depend on which areas of the brain were stimulated. Stimulation of the brain center for our sense of balance, for example, might lead to a dream that involves spinning around.

• **13** Dreaming appears to be a basic need. People deprived of REM sleep become anxious, irritable, and confused. Sometimes they hallucinate. Such REM-deprived individuals seem to need to "catch up" on their REM sleep once they are allowed to return to it.

• **14** Some researchers believe that dreams can help us to deal with problems in our waking lives. Dreams may help us handle emotional situations better, and analyzing dreams may give us insights into our problems.

Drugs and consciousness

• **15** *Psychoactive drugs* are those

that have a noticeable impact on mood, thought, or behavior. Many drugs work by affecting the action of neurotransmitters in the brain.

• **16** Psychoactive drugs can be grouped into four main categories: *depressants* (alcohol, narcotics, sedatives), *psychedelics, stimulants* (amphetamines, cocaine), and *marijuana.*

• **17** *LSD* is a *psychedelic drug* that produces profound alterations of sensory, perceptual, cognitive, and emotional experiences. Other psychedelics include *peyote* (mescaline) and *psilocybin.* LSD appears to work by blocking the action of the transmitter substance serotonin.

• **18** *Marijuana* is a drug, made from the hemp plant, that generally creates a feeling of well-being when smoked. Use of the drug carries some risks, although the most serious charges against it are probably not justified.

• **19** *Amphetamines* are drugs that stimulate the central nervous system. People who use amphetamines for dieting or staying awake usually take pills, whereas true "speed freaks" inject the drug while on a several-day "run." Excessive use of amphetamines can lead to *amphetamine psychosis,* in which the user has delusions and paranoia similar to those of paranoid schizophrenia. Amphetamines appear to exert their effects by stimulating production of the neurotransmitter dopamine.

• **20** *Cocaine* is a stimulant extracted from coca leaves. Cocaine use has increased greatly in the United States in the last decade, causing increasing concern about its potential psychological and physical dangers.

• **21** Among other drugs commonly used in America are nicotine (in cigarettes), caffeine, alcohol, sedatives, and tranquilizers.

Hypnosis

• **22** *Hypnosis* is a state of increased suggestibility that is brought about through certain induction procedures. The hypnotist may suggest that the subject perform certain behaviors, forget specific material *(posthypnotic amnesia),* or perform some act on a signal after coming out of the trance *(posthypnotic suggestion).*

• **23** People vary in their susceptibility to hypnosis. Those with a capacity for deep absorption in an activity tend to be most susceptible.

• **24** Hypnosis has been used to reduce pain in dental patients, burn victims, and terminal cancer patients, among others.

• **25** Hilgard has explained hypnosis in terms of the "hidden observer" theory—the idea that there is a part of the unconscious mind of the hypnotized person that is watching and remembering everything that is going on. Hilgard sees hypnosis as a *dissociated* state in which a person experiences two or more states of consciousness simultaneously.

• **26** *Meditation* is a state of deep passivity combined with awareness. In concentrative meditation, one focuses on a single object or word; in opening-up meditation, one accepts all sensations. Meditation has become popular because of its psychological and physical benefits.

KEY TERMS

activation-synthesis model
amphetamines
condensation
consciousness
depressants
displacement
dissociated consciousness
"hidden observer"
hypnosis
insomnia
introspection
latent dream content
manifest dream content
marijuana
meditation
non-REM sleep
physiological addiction
posthypnotic amnesia
posthypnotic suggestion
psychedelic drugs
psychoactive drugs
psychological dependence
REM sleep
stimulants
symbolism
unconscious
withdrawal syndrome

BIOLOGICAL RHYTHMS

The sun rises and sets. The moon passes regularly through its phases. Spring turns to summer, which gives way to autumn. This may sound more like the stuff of poetry than the domain of psychology. But there are daily, monthly, and annual rhythms—as well as other, quicker rhythms—in our lives that reflect the interplay of our biological nature with the rhythmic environment in which we live.

"In adapting over evolutionary time to a periodic environment," writes psychiatrist Peter Whybrow (1979), "animals including man have developed within themselves many sophisticated clocklike mechanisms. . . . Partly innate and partly shaped by the individual's prevailing surroundings, the rhythms serve to keep us functioning at an optimal level in a predictable but ever-changing environment." We are not ordinarily aware of our own biological rhythms, or of the social and cultural rhythms that accompany them. But psychologists and other scientists have begun to explore these cycles of human behavior and experience.

CIRCADIAN RHYTHMS

Some of the best-known biological rhythms take place over a 24-hour period. Most of us regularly sleep about one-third of the 24-hour day and are active for the other two-thirds. This type of pattern—one that goes through a full cycle in about 24 hours—is called a *circadian rhythm*. The term *circadian* comes from the Latin meaning "about a day."

There are many circadian rhythms in our bodily functioning. Body temperature, blood pressure, heart rate, blood-sugar level, and secretion of certain hormones all reach a peak and drop to a low once in each 24-hour period (Luce, 1971). Blood sugar begins to drop slowly in the late afternoon. It reaches its low point by about 3 A.M. to 6 A.M. and then begins to rise again. Blood pressure is generally highest at about 6 P.M. Pulse rate and respiration also have daily rhythms, although they rise and fall at different times for different people.

Although we are not usually aware of many of our circadian rhythms, we may notice some of their effects. If you have ever stayed up all night, you probably felt cold by about 4 A.M. despite a constant room temperature. That's because body temperature drops to its lowest point a few hours before dawn.

Sensory acuity also shows rhythmic variations. Even though our bodies use food most efficiently in the morning, many people eat their biggest meal in the evening. Our reason for such a preference may be that our senses of smell and taste tend to be most sensitive in the evening hours. Such heightened sensitivity may be related to daily fluctuations in the production of adrenal hormones, which influence taste and smell (Luce, 1971).

Not everyone runs on the same biological clock. Although most people share basic patterns, there are also wide variations between individuals. "Morning people" awake refreshed and alert and are most productive in the early part of the day. "Night people" drag themselves out of bed, stay half asleep for an hour or two after rising, and prefer to work in the evening hours. Being a night or morning person may be related to rhythmic changes in the levels of certain hormones (Fitzgerald and Bundy, 1975) Several investigators have found

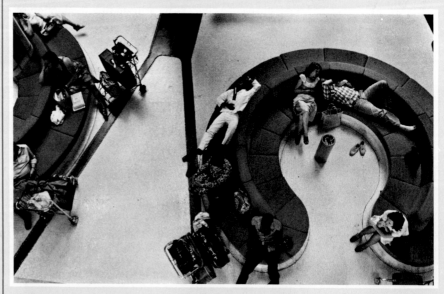

Jet lag can temporarily throw our biological rhythms out of sync.

that most people can readily identify themselves as morning or night people. Barbara Watts (1982) found that college roommates who are "mismatched"—that is, a morning person with a night person—have more trouble getting along than "matched" roommates. Such mismatching can also affect marriages. Mismatched spouses may have to rely on creative compromise to overcome the lack of synchrony in their personal rhythms (Adams and Cromwell, 1978).

Our biological clocks are normally synchronized with the day and night cycles of our environment—when it is daytime we are awake and alert; as night approaches our bodies prepare for sleep. But if you've ever traveled across a time zone, you know what it is like to have your biological rhythms "out of sync" with your surroundings. The discomfort travelers experience, commonly known as jet lag, results from the desynchronization of biological rhythms. For example, a traveler arriving in London at 9 A.M. from New York may be prepared intellectually to begin the day. But for her body it is only 4 A.M. and not yet time to get up.

One problem is that some rhythms adjust to changes more quickly than do others. Sleep rhythms may become reestablished after a few days, while body temperature and hormonal fluctuations appear to take longer to adjust (Goldberg, 1977).

You can imagine what happens to the performance of an executive engaged in delicate negotiations when her body is on New York time and the negotiations are in London. When her counterparts are refreshed, relaxed, and ready for the day's business, her body is crying, "Help! I should be sleeping!" Many governments and corporations have attempted to reduce such problems by insisting that their representatives leave early for trips overseas so their bodies have time to adjust. Travelers may also try to remain on "home time" whenever possible, a trick long used by pilots. For example, a sales representative from Boston who lands in San Francisco might eat dinner at 3 P.M., retire to bed at 7 P.M., and rise for breakfast at 3 A.M.

One scientist recently suggested that jet lag can be reduced through diet control prior to changing time zones. His plan includes limiting intake of caffeine and alcohol and concentrating on high-protein and high-carbohydrate foods to prepare the body for resetting its internal clock (Ehret and Scanlon, 1983).

Problems similar to those experienced with jet lag arise when workers switch from the day shift to the night shift. Eighty percent of rotating workers report having problems of adjustment, such as insomnia and fatigue. Although a direct causal relationship cannot be proved, it is worth noting that the nuclear power plant accident at Three Mile Island in 1979 occurred at 4 A.M., with a crew that had just been rotated onto the night schedule. This is a low point on the daily cycle of alertness, when a slow response to warning signals is most likely (Moore-Ede, 1982).

Workers who switch from the day to the night shift commonly report problems of adjustment.

ULTRADIAN RHYTHMS

The daily rhythms of sleeping and wakefulness are themselves composed of shorter cycles of biological activity. These shorter cycles are called *ultradian rhythms* (from the Latin for "more often than daily"). Our regular, rhythmic patterns of heartbeats and breathing are examples of ultradian rhythms. Another sort of ultradian rhythm is the 90-minute sleep cycle we pass through several times each night.

Scientists have suspected that a similar 90-minute cycle may occur through the waking hours, as well as during sleep. Sleep researcher Nathaniel Kleitman (1970) suggests that there is a "basic rest-and-activity cycle" built into our nervous system that programs continuous alternations between activity and rest. For example, Michael Chase (1979) has found a pattern in human brain waves marked by a peak in mental activity about every 90 minutes; there is a low point in activity 45 minutes after each peak. Chase refers to the peaks as "brainstorms." Students have also shown 90-minute cycles in people's susceptibility to visual illusions, in stomach contractions (Hiatt and Kripke, 1975), and in daydreaming (Kripke and Sonneschein, 1973).

Why do all of these changes occur at approximately 90-minute intervals? What sort of internal clock leads to patterns of neural firing in the brain at these intervals? So far, researchers simply don't know.

INFRADIAN RHYTHMS

Our bodies also show cycles of activity that take longer than a day to complete. These cycles are called *infradian rhythms* (from the Latin for "less often than daily"). One infradian rhythm is the female menstrual cycle, which lasts about 28 days. The menstrual cycle is defined by shifts in the levels of female sex hormones. The cycle begins when these hormones are at the lowest levels, at the time of menstrual bleeding. The hormone levels peak about two weeks later, at the time of ovulation, and then begin to drop again. As we saw in Chapter 2, Box 4, variations in these hormone levels have sometimes been associated with fluctuations in women's moods.

Is there a comparable cycle in men's hormones? When Charles Doering and his colleagues (1975) studies the levels of testosterone in a group of men, they found cycles in hormone level that varied from 3 to 30 days from one peak to the next. They did not find that fluctuation in testosterone levels corresponded to mood reports, however. Nevertheless there do seem to be male mood cycles, ranging from 6 to 90 days. In fact, Mary Brown Parlee (1978) found more cyclical mood changes in men than in a control group of women. Parlee did not measure hormone levels, so it wasn't possible to tell whether the men's mood changes were related to hormonal fluctuations. Parlee suggests that social conventions—for example, working Monday through Friday and relaxing on Saturday and Sunday—may also be important influences on infradian rhythms.

INTERNAL CLOCKS AND EXTERNAL FORCES

Many scientists believe that our biological rhythms are set by an internal *biological clock,* a mechanism in the central nervous system that programs the timing of changes in biological functions. From this point of view, biological rhythms may become synchronized with external rhythms (such as the day-night cycle), but the rhythmicity itself is internally regulated. The specific biological source of these rhythms—the nature of the internal pendulum, as it were—is not yet understood. Nor is

the relationship between these internal cycles and the external rhythms in nature clear to scientists. It is well known, for example, that the rhythms of the ocean's tides are set by the shifting gravitational pull of the moon. Are our own biological rhythms influenced by external cycles such as the phases of the moon?

Throughout recorded history people have speculated about the relationship between the moon's phases and human behavior. Murder and madness have been associated—at least in folklore—with the full moon. (In fact, the word *lunatic* comes from the Latin word for "moon.") Recently there have been suggestions that the association is not entirely mythical. One extended study of homicides in Ohio and Florida found that homicides were most common after the new and full moon phases (Lieber and Sherin, 1972). The researchers who conducted this study suggested that the moon might influence "biological tides"—including levels of hormones and brain chemicals—just as it influences ocean tides.

However, other researchers have failed to obtain similar findings in different geographical areas. And examinations of the links between psychotic episodes, suicides, and the lunar phase have not shown any relationship (Campbell and Beets, 1978). If the moon does exert an influence on human affairs, it has not yet been conclusively documented.

SEASONAL RHYTHMS

In addition to all other rhythms we have considered, our physical and psychological functioning is also affected by the annual cycle of the seasons. Greek and Roman scholars believed that each season was associated with a dominant humor, or bodily substance, that was accompanied by a corresponding temperament. For example, the

"sanguine," or cheerful, humor (associated with blood) was thought to dominate in the spring, while the "melancholic," or depressed, humor (associated with black bile) was thought to dominate in the fall.

Today's scientists have little use for the theory of the humors, but they are still faced with explaining the variations in health, mood, and behavior that occur over the course of the year. Birth rates, for example, are highest between March and June in Canada and between July and October in the United States. Deaths are most likely to occur in the winter, especially those caused by heart disease, stroke, and respiratory disease (Kevan, 1979).

Do these variations mean that there is some sort of "biological calendar" inside us, causing annual cycles in our behavior? Probably not. But they do suggest that the changes that occur with the seasons—day length, weather, and social and cultural events—have important effects on our experience.

Perhaps not surprisingly, national surveys suggest that Americans tend to be the happiest in the spring and summer and gradually decline in mood throughout the fall and winter (Smith, 1979). One factor that may be associated with the upsurge of happiness in the spring and summer is increased day length and the increased likelihood of sunshine. In one study, Michael Cunningham (1979) found that the sunnier it was, the more positively people rated their moods and the more willing pedestrians were to stop and answer questions for an interviewer. These heart-warming effects of sunshine may be in part biological. For example, solar radiation can increase the concentration of negative ions (electrically charged particles) in the atmosphere, which may in turn be related to levels of serotonin in the brain and to relaxation (Krueger and Reed, 1976). But sunshine may also brighten our mood for aesthetic and symbolic reasons.

The seasons of the year can exert a profound influence on our moods and behavior.

The sunlight brightens everything around us, recalls memories of happy times, and makes the world look shiny and pleasant.

Among the best-documented seasonal effects in behavior is the rise in suicide rates and in mental hospital admissions during spring and early summer. It is possible that emotional disorder increases in spring as a result of increased secretion of hormones, triggered by increasing day length. For many people, such stirrings of the glands may contribute to the feelings of optimism and "thoughts of love" that are associated with springtime.

But some vulnerable individuals may experience excessive glandular activity, precipitating emotional disorder and breakdown. Such biological effects of increasing day length clearly play a central role in the reproductive lives and migrations of many animals and birds. But their operation among human beings remains a topic of controversy.

A different sort of explanation of the springtime upturn in emotional distress involves the interplay of weather and people's self-perceptions. In the spring, as the weather warms, people spend more time out-of-doors and a general mood of optimism prevails; people who feel alone, unloved, and unsuccessful are likely to feel most acutely distressed by comparison. What's more, people in northern climates can blame their troubles during the winter on the cold, the ice, the frostbite, the stalled cars, the frozen pipes, the perpetually to-be-shoveled snow. When the spring comes, there is nothing left to blame troubles on but oneself, one's fears, one's ruined relationships, one's unfulfilled dreams. In the spring, we must account to ourselves more honestly for our failings, which may push some troubled people over the edge of despair.

SUMMARY

- *1 Circadian rhythms* occur on a 24-hour cycle. They include rhythmic peaks and drops in body temperature, blood pressure, heart rate, blood-sugar level, and secretions of certain hormones, as well as changes in sensory acuity. Biological rhythms can go "out of sync" with the environment when one travels across time zones.
- *2 Ultradian rhythms* occur in cycles that are shorter than 24 hours. The most obvious example is the cycle of stages that occurs every 90 minutes during sleep.
- *3 Infradian rhythms* occur in cycles that last longer than a day. The menstrual cycle, for example, occurs about every 28 days. There may be similar cycles of hormone changes in men.
- *4* Many scientists believe that biological rhythms are controlled by an internal *biological clock*.
- *5* There is little evidence that the changing phases of the moon influence human biology or psychology.
- *6* Seasonal changes appear to have effects on people's moods and behavior. Both biological factors (such as glandular activity) and psychological factors (such as self-perceptions) may account for these variations.

Human beings are information processors. We receive and interpret information about the world, we learn to make new mental connections, we store and retrieve information, and we use information to make decisions and solve problems. In this part, we will explore these information-processing capacities of human beings. Chapter 4 is devoted to the processes of Perception, *Chapter 5 to* Learning, *Chapter 6 to* Memory, *and Chapter 7 to* Language, Thought, and Intelligence. *We often take these cognitive capacities for granted, but their importance is pointed up when we reflect upon instances in which they are impaired. For example, we will consider color blindness in Chapter 4, memory disorders in Chapter 6, and mental retardation in Chapter 7.*

The processes of perceiving, learning, and thinking are linked not only to our lives as individuals but also to the workings of society. After Chapter 4, we will discuss Noise Pollution, *a social problem that can affect not only our hearing but even our social relationships. In the Psychological Issue for Chapter 5, we will consider the ways in which our knowledge of principles of learning can lead to* Behavior Control, *the regulation of some people's behavior by other people. Following Chapter 6, we will discuss* Memory and the Law, *focusing on the questionable reliability of eyewitness testimony. Finally, after Chapter 7, we will ask the challenging question* Can Computers Think? *Computers, too, are information processors. And now that computers can be programmed to act "intelligently"—to do everything from playing chess to making medical diagnoses—the question of computer "intelligence" has become an issue of profound social importance.*

PERCEPTION

Perception is the process by which the external world becomes part of our inner experience.

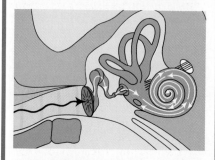

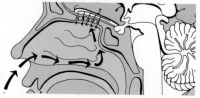

You are sitting in a darkened theater, watching a movie. You see the images on the screen and listen to the music and dialogue. You feel the seat beneath you and you sense the position of your limbs as you lean back. You smell the buttery aroma of your friend's popcorn and reach over for a handful; it tastes too salty. Through all of these sensory avenues—sight, hearing, smell, touch, taste, and so on—the world out there becomes part of your inner experience. In addition, your brain is hard at work, not just passively receiving signals from the different senses but also actively interpreting those signals, in order to form a meaningful impression of reality.

Perception refers to the processes by which people come to experience the stimuli in their environment. Our study of these processes will begin with a discussion of the human *senses*, the organs and neural pathways through which information about our environment is received. Our senses include vision, hearing, the skin senses, kinesthesis (awareness of our own body movements), equilibrium (balance), smell, and taste. When we "sense" something we are actually experiencing activity in our brain and nervous system. Physical energy (such as light, sound waves, heat) emanating from objects must be transformed by the sense organs into a code that can be relayed to and interpreted by the brain. The first step in the process is the work of the *receptor cells*, which respond to particular forms of energy. These receptors include cells in the retina of the eye that are sensitive to light and structures in the ear that are sensitive to sound waves. The energy is next converted into electrical impulses, which travel from the sense organs

along nerve fibers to the central nervous system and eventually to the appropriate area of the cerebral cortex (see Chapter 2).

In the brain, information from the senses is organized so that it has some meaning for us. We don't experience isolated lights, colors, shapes, or sounds; rather, our perceptual world is filled with recognizable people, objects, and events. When you answer the phone, for example, you immediately recognize a friend's voice. Your sensory receptors are responding to physical sound waves, but you experience the familiar voice of someone you know well. Perception thus relies not only on our sense organs but also on our learning, memory, and knowledge of the world. How we translate light waves, sound waves, and other types of physical energy into a coherent meaningful experience is a central problem in the study of perception.

VISION

We learn more about the outside world through our sense of vision than through any of our other senses. Indeed, vision dominates our life. Vision has played a dominant role for researchers as well: Scientists have studied sight more than any of the other senses.

The eye

The human eye is the "camera" that we always carry with us. Like a camera, it admits light through a small hole and passes it through a lens that focuses an image on a photosensitive surface. In the eye, light first passes through the *cornea*, a transparent protective coating over the front part of

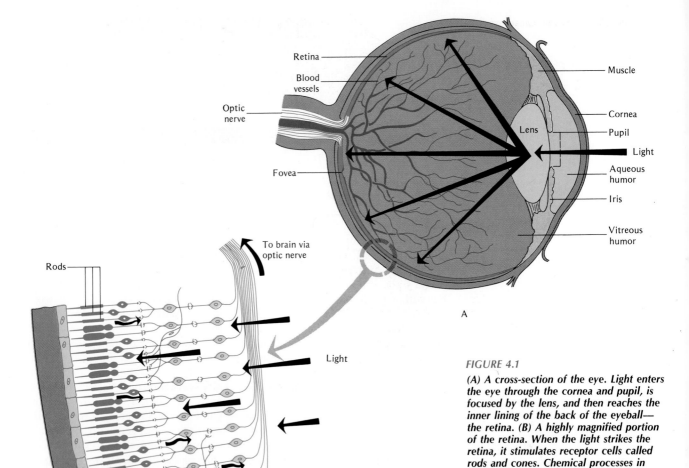

Retina
Blood vessels
Optic nerve
Fovea
Muscle
Lens
Cornea
Pupil
Light
Aqueous humor
Iris
Vitreous humor

A

Rods
To brain via optic nerve
Light
Sensory neurons
Cone
Pigment layer
Choroid layer

B

the eye (see Figure 4.1A). Light next passes through the *pupil*, an opening that can be enlarged or reduced to let more or less light in by contractions in the muscles of the *iris*, the colored part of the eye. Light passes through the pupil to the *lens*, which can be adjusted to bring near or far objects into focus. The light is focused through the lens onto the inner lining of the back of the eyeball, the *retina*, analogous to the film in a camera. The light stimulates chemical processes in receptor cells on the surface of the retina, similar to the effects of light on the photosensitive coating of film. The retina's receptor cells, which respond to light energy and transmit the message back toward the brain, are called *rods* and *cones.*

More than 6 million cones and 100 million rods are distributed on the retina. Rods are slim nerve cells that contain a light-sensitive chemical called *rhodopsin*. Cones are thicker than rods, with a cone-shaped tip at one end, and contain other light-sensitive chemicals. When light waves strike the retina, they break down the chemicals in the rods and cones, which in turn leads to the firing of sensory neurons (Figure 4.1B). These

A scene as reflected in the human eye.

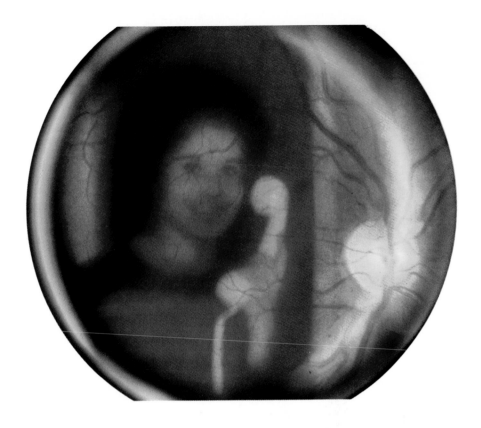

sensory neurons are connected to other neurons that converge to form the *optic nerve*, which then carries the nerve impulses to the brain.

The cones are color receptors and are packed together in the center of the retina. The *fovea*, a depressed spot on the retina directly behind the lens, has a high concentration of cones, but no rods. The rods are not sensitive to color and are more densely concentrated away from the fovea. A few cones are mixed with rods all the way to the outer edges of the retina, but the center of the eye is the most color-sensitive portion.

When you first go into a dark movie theater, you stumble around, barely able to make out the shapes of people or the seats. After you have been in the theater for a while, however, you are able to see quite well. That is because, as you go from bright light to dim light, the rods and cones must go through a period of *adaptation* to the changes in illumination. In order to see in dim light, you need a greater amount of light-sensitive chemicals in your rods and cones.

The greater the concentration of these chemicals, the lower the *visual threshold*—the smallest amount of stimulation needed for the rods and cones to respond. Thus, adaptation to darkness is in part a matter of building up a surplus of rhodopsin in the rods and of the color-sensitive chemicals in the cones.

The cones adapt quickly in the dark (10 minutes or so), but the rods adapt slowly and continue to adapt even after 30 minutes or more of darkness. When completely adapted, however, the rods are much more sensitive to light than the cones. Thus, if you want to see a dim light in pitch darkness, don't look directly at it, since the center of the eye contains only the less sensitive cones. If you look away from the object, the image will fall on the edge of the retina, where the rods are concentrated, and you are more likely to see it. Stargazers usually learn this trick: A star that can barely be seen when viewed directly will seem to become brighter and more distinct if viewed from an angle.

Visual acuity

Visual acuity is the ability to discriminate the details in the field of vision. One way this ability can be measured is by using the familiar eye chart. Standard perfect vision is often called 20/20 vision, because a person with normal vision can clearly see material on a standard eye chart from a distance of 20 feet. A person with 20/50 vision is someone who sees clearly at 20 feet what people with normal vision can read at 50 feet; such a person is said to be *nearsighted*. A person who sees distant images well but has trouble focusing on near objects is said to be *farsighted*. The conditions of nearsightedness and farsightedness are caused by variations in the shape of the person's eyeball or by irregularities in curvature of the cornea, so that images are focused in front of or behind the retina rather than directly on it (see Figure 4.2).

Part of the retina, the *blind spot*, has no visual acuity. This spot is the point at which the nerves of the eye converge to form the optic nerve. The optic nerve exits through the back wall of the eyeball and connects the eye to the brain. People are usually unaware of the blind spot; the brain compensates for this blank portion of vision by mentally filling in uniform patterns. You can discover your own blind spot by following the instructions in Figure 4.3.

Color vision

How does the visual system work to give us the experience of color? Different colors are associated with light of different wavelengths (see Figure 4.4). Researchers have discovered that our retinas contain three types of cones: one sensitive primarily to red wavelengths, one sensitive to green, and one sensitive to blue (Wald, 1964). When, for example, light of the wavelength we perceive as red hits the retina, only those cones sensitive to that wavelength will react. This information is passed to neurons called *opponent cells* (Hurvich and Jameson, 1957). Opponent cells code pairs of colors and are of three types: red-green, blue-yellow, and dark-light. These cells receive their name from the fact that the two colors they code "oppose" each other. For example, some opponent cells are "turned on" by red light and "turned off" by green light; others are activated by green light but inhibited by red light. Similarly, when yellow light hits the

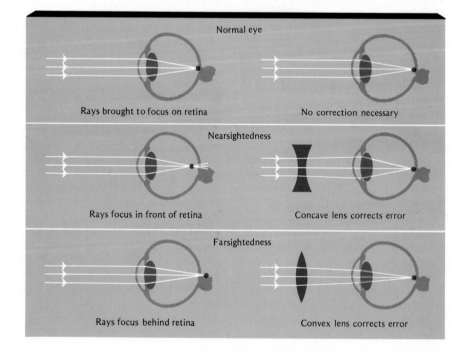

FIGURE 4.2

In the normal eye, the lens focuses light rays directly on the retina. In nearsightedness and farsightedness, variations in the shape of the lens cause the light rays to focus either in front of or behind the retina. Eyeglasses can correct these errors by refocusing the image before it reaches the lens of the eye.

FIGURE 4.3

Exercises to help you find your blind spot: (A) Close your right eye and look at the magician. Move the page closer or further away until the rabbit disappears. (B) Close your right eye and look at the fairy. Move the page closer or further away until the wand appears unbroken. It's not really magic. The images of the rabbit and of the break in the wand are falling on your blind spot, where the optic nerve connects to the retina.

A

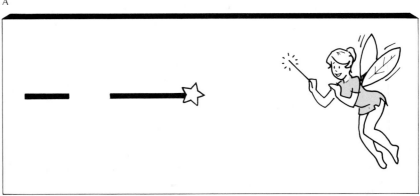

B

FIGURE 4.4

The full spectrum of electromagnetic radiation. Only the narrow band between 400 and 700 nanometers (nm.) is visible to the human eye. (1 nanometer = 1/1,000,000,000 meter)

visual system, some blue-yellow opponent cells become active, while other blue-yellow cells are inhibited. The sensation of yellowish-red (orange) occurs when red light and yellow light excite red-green and blue-yellow cells at the same time. It is the overall pattern of activation that gives us our rich experience of color. The opponent-process theory also helps to explain the phenomenon of color *afterimages*—the sensory impressions that persist after the removal of a stimulus (see Figure 4.5).

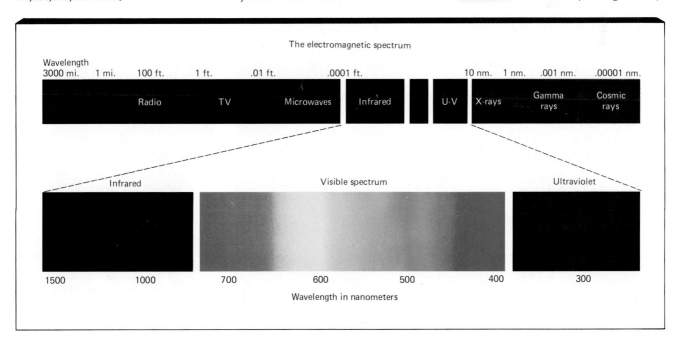

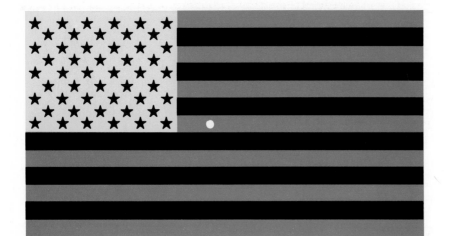

FIGURE 4.5

A color afterimage. Stare at the oddly colored American flag for 45 seconds, keeping your eyes fixed on the white dot in the center. Then look at a blank piece of white paper. You should see a quick afterimage of a more familiar flag.

A

B

CHAPTER FOUR: PERCEPTION

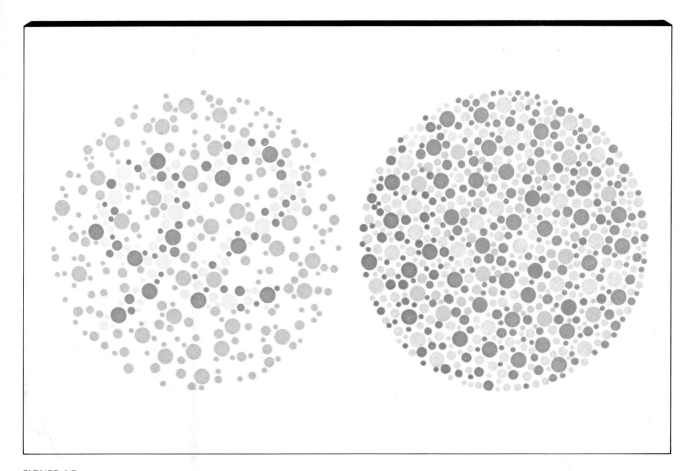

FIGURE 4.7

These plates are commonly used to diagnose color blindness. Because the dots in
the numerals are of the same brightness as
the dots in the background, one can distinguish the numerals only by distinguishing
the colors. The plate on the left is used to
detect yellow-blue color blindness, and the
plate on the right is used to detect red-
green color blindness.

FIGURE 4.6

The scene on the left contains a wide
range of colors. Figure 4.6A provides an
approximation of what the scene would
look like to a person with red-green color
blindness, and Figure 4.6B approximates
what it would look like to a person with
yellow-blue color blindness.

About 7 percent of the people in
the world cannot see one or more colors. Most of these partially color-
blind people are men, since color
blindness is an inherited, sex-linked
characteristic. The most common
type of color blindness is *dichromatic:* Color vision is normal in two
of the three primary colors but deficient in the third, perhaps because
one of the three types of cones is deficient (Figure 4.6). In one type of dichromatic color blindness—red-green
deficiency—the person sees the world
almost entirely in blues and yellows.
A red fire engine appears dull yellow,
and grass is blue. The person with
yellow-blue color blindness, in contrast, sees a world of reds and greens.
Red-green color blindness is by far the
most common, and blue-yellow is the
least common. People with *monochromatic* color blindness see nothing but black, white, and shades of
gray, because they have no cone cells.

Although color-blind people may
miss out on one sort of experience

that other people have, they can still
function quite well without color
cues—so much so that some people
don't even know they're color-blind.
For example, it's not hard for a red-
green color-blind person to know
whether a traffic light is green or red,
since the red light is always at the top
and the green light is at the bottom.
Color-blind people can also discriminate between different colors because
there is usually a perceivable difference in brightness and such persons
learn to be highly sensitive to these
brightness differences. Special tests
have been devised to eliminate such
cues when determining whether a
person is color-blind. Most commonly these tests consist of buried
figures composed of dots of different
colors but of equal brightness to surrounding dots, as in Figure 4.7. A person who is red-green color-blind, for
example, won't be able to distinguish
the red dots from the green ones and
won't be able to see the number
formed by the red dots.

A Overlap

B Relative size

C Perspective

D Texture gradient

Depth perception

How do we know how close or how far away objects are? How can we tell that objects are three-dimensional just by looking at them, when all that is recorded on the retina is a two-dimensional image? We automatically make use of a variety of perceptual cues to help us perceive depth (see Figure 4.8). For one thing, objects *overlap*, which gives us a clue that one is in front of another. Another cue is the *relative size* of objects: if one tree appears larger than another, we assume that it is closer. And all art students know about *perspective*—the fact that lines converge when stretched into the distance, such as the lines that form railroad tracks. Another important set of perceptual cues to depth are called *texture gradients.* A texture gradient is an apparent change in the surface of an object as it extends away in space. Imagine, for example, standing in a field of grass. You can see the blades of grass near your feet quite distinctly, but as you

look at the grass farther away, the blades become less defined until the field becomes a mass of green. Still another powerful cue to depth perception is *motion parallax*—the fact that images of objects close to the eye move across the retina faster than images of objects farther away. When you are riding in a car, for example, you see the telephone poles whiz by, yet the farmhouse in the distance moves by much more slowly. All of these cues—overlap, relative size, perspective, texture gradients, and motion parallax—are called *monocular cues* because they work even when we use only one eye.

For more precise depth perception, we rely on *binocular vision,* in which the two eyes cooperate to give solidity and distance to objects. If you close one eye and survey a scene, you will perceive depth less clearly. And if you squint that one open eye, the scene may begin to look like a two-dimensional canvas rather than a three-dimensional world. Binocular vision adds three-dimensionality be-

FIGURE 4.8

A variety of cues help us to perceive depth: (A) **Overlap.** *Objects overlap, indicating that one is closer than the other. (B)* **Relative size.** *If one object appears larger than another, we may assume it is closer. (C)* **Perspective.** *Parallel lines converge as they extend into the distance. (D)* **Texture gradients.** *Surfaces of objects become less clearly defined the further away they are. These are all called* **monocular cues,** *because they work whether we use one eye or two.*

cause each eye gets a slightly different image of what is being looked at. If you cover your right eye and then your left, you will see the object you are focusing on jump from left to right. But when you look at the object with both eyes, you get a unified, central three-dimensional image.

Some of the cues for depth perception, such as the evaluation of the relative sizes of objects, seem to result from experience. Many psychologists used to believe, in fact, that learning is necessary for depth perception to occur at all. But studies with the *visual cliff* have provided convincing evidence that much of depth perception is innate. Eleanor Gibson and Richard Walk (1960) devised the original visual cliff apparatus (see Figure 4.9). It is a large tabletop with a wide wooden board down the center. On one side of the board is a glass-cov-

ered checkerboard pattern. On the other side is a clear sheet of glass, with the same checkerboard pattern painted on the floor three-and-a-half feet below the table. When viewed from above, the entire tabletop appears to contain the checkerboard pattern. When infants from 6 to 14 months old are placed on the tabletop and allowed to crawl about, very few venture onto the "deep" side, even when urged to do so.

The fact that 6-month-old babies have depth perception does not in itself prove that this ability is innate—a good deal of learning might take place during the first 6 months of life. But other experiments, using animals such as lambs and chickens that can walk within a day after birth, have demonstrated that newborn animals also avoid the deep side of the cliff, suggesting that the reaction is in fact

FIGURE 4.9

The visual cliff. Infants as young as 6 months old will not crawl past the apparent "edge" of the cliff, indicating that they already have depth perception.

innate. As a result of millions of years of evolution, we seem to be born "prewired" with whatever connections in the nervous system are needed to perceive depth when we receive the appropriate stimulation (Hochberg, 1978). Nevertheless, depth perception continues to improve as we gain greater experience in dealing with our three-dimensional world.

THE OTHER SENSES

Although researchers have devoted more time to vision than to the other senses, we know, of course, that a great deal of our information about the world comes to us through our other senses. In this section we will briefly examine these other senses: hearing, the skin senses, kinesthesis, equilibrium, smell, and taste. The importance of all these senses is pointed up when researchers investigate situations in which sensory stimulation is severely limited (see Box 1).

Hearing

To understand hearing, imagine what happens when a swimmer practices kicking in a pool. Wave after wave of ripples circles out from the swimmer, striking the edge of the pool and bouncing back. Similarly, whenever any object is struck, causing it to vibrate, the molecules of air around it are pushed away—just as the swimmer's feet push water molecules away. Such movements of air molecules are called *sound waves*. Most surfaces of the human body are not sensitive enough to detect these vibrations in the air, but when these waves reach your ear, they set in motion a series of mechanical processes in the outer, middle, and inner ears (see Figure 4.10). The *outer ear* is composed of an inch-long canal and the *tympanic membrane* (eardrum). Changes in air pressure cause vibrations in this flexible membrane. The *middle ear* is composed of three bones, the *malleus*, the *incus*, and the *stapes*. (These terms are Latin for "hammer," "anvil," and "stirrup,"

and are derived from the shapes of the three bones.) These bones make up a system that conducts sound waves to the *inner ear*. In the inner ear, the vibrations are transmitted to the fluid inside the snail-shaped *cochlea*. Like the retina with its rod and cone receptor cells, the cochlea contains tiny *hair cells* that are the receptor cells for hearing. When sound vibrations reach the hair cells, they are translated into nerve impulses, which are then sent on to the brain via the *auditory nerve*.

The sounds we actually perceive are related to different qualities of sound waves. *Loudness* is related primarily to the *amplitude* of the sound wave—the amount of expansion and contraction of the pressure changes that form a sound wave. When you turn up the volume of a radio, you increase the amplitude of the vibrations and therefore the sound is louder. (*Very* loud sounds can be bad for health, as we will see in the Psychological Issue following this chapter.) *Pitch* refers to the high or low quality of a sound. It is determined primarily by the frequency of wave vibrations—the faster the vibration, the higher the pitch. Another property of sound is *timbre*, the richness or quality of a sound that comes from a particular sound source. Each sound source actually produces a distinctive combination of sound waves, and it is this combination that determines the sound's timbre. Thus, a note played on a violin will not sound exactly like the same note played on a trumpet or a piano.

The ears are far enough apart to allow people to locate the position of a sound source. If a noise is two or three feet away from your left ear, it will reach that ear a tiny fraction of a second before it reaches your right ear. The sound will also be louder in your left ear than in your right ear. The time lag and difference in loudness allow you to localize the sound as being on your left. Thus, to properly locate a sound, both ears are necessary. That is why, if you listen to music through headphones, it sometimes sounds as though the sound source is in the middle of your head: Both ears are getting the same input at exactly the same time.

THE SOUND OF BORSCHT

Most of us see with our eyes, hear with our ears, and taste with our tongue. But there are people who report occasional mixups in links—when, for example, sounds may be experienced as colors or tastes. This experience of sensory blending is called synesthesia. *The Russian psychologist Alexander Luria gave an account of a person for whom a pure tone of 1000 cycles per second produced "a brown stripe against a dark background that had red, tonguelike edges [and] the taste . . . of sweet-and-sour borscht." Some researchers believe that synesthesia may result from a mechanism in the nervous system that connects the senses with each other (Marks, 1975).*

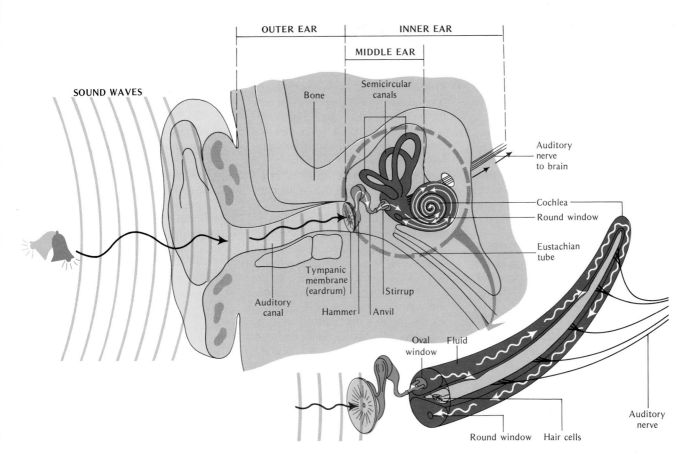

OUTER EAR   INNER EAR

MIDDLE EAR

SOUND WAVES

Bone

Semicircular
canals

Auditory
nerve
to brain

Cochlea

Round window

Eustachian
tube

Tympanic
membrane
(eardrum)

Stirrup

Auditory
canal

Hammer   Anvil

Oval
window

Fluid

Round window   Hair cells

Auditory
nerve

FIGURE 4.10

*Sound waves pass through the outer ear
and cause vibrations in the tympanic membrane (eardrum). These vibrations are
transmitted by the bones of the middle ear
to the fluid inside the cochlea (in the inner
ear). These vibrations are received by hair
cells inside the cochlea. They are translated into nerve impulses which are sent
along the auditory nerve to the brain.*

*Each musical instrument has its own
unique timbre, or quality of sound, resulting from a distinctive combination of
sound waves.*

BOX 1

SENSORY DEPRIVATION

During practically all of our waking lives, we are constantly bombarded with stimulation to our senses. What would happen if we were deprived of this sensory stimulation?

Psychologists became interested in studying the effects of sensory deprivation in the early 1950s. Researchers enlisted volunteers to spend days at a time in environments that permitted virtually no sensory stimulation. In one well-known study, Woodburn Heron (1957) paid male college students $20 a day to lie on a bed in a lighted cubicle, around the clock, for as many days as they could. The subjects wore translucent plastic visors, permitting them to see only constant, diffuse light, but no objects or patterns. They wore gloves and cardboard cuffs to restrict skin sensation. Hearing was limited by a U-shaped foam rubber pillow and by the unchanging hum of air-conditioning equipment. There were only brief time-outs for meals and for going to the toilet.

After one or more days in this setting, subjects' performance on a variety of intellectual tasks was markedly impaired. In addition, they were found to be highly persuasible: When a tape recording arguing for the reality of ghosts was played, the subjects found it to be much more believable after the period of sensory deprivation than before it. Some students reported that they were afraid of seeing ghosts for several days after the experiment.

The most dramatic results of Heron's experiment were the hallucinations subjects experienced while in the chamber. At first, they "saw" dots of light, lines, or geometrical patterns. Later, they began to see more complex images, such as marching squirrels with sacks over their shoulders or processions of eyeglasses walking down the street. After emerging from several days of sensory deprivation, subjects experienced perceptual distortions—straight lines seemed curved, and stationary rooms seemed to be in motion.

Heron concluded: "A changing sensory environment seems essential for human beings. Without it the brain ceases to function in an adequate way."

These effects of sensory deprivation point to real dangers. Many crucial jobs are typically done in highly monotonous, unchanging settings. If radar operators scanning screens for enemy missiles were to begin to see nonexistent blips—or if they were to miss real ones—the consequences could be disastrous.

On the other hand, Peter Suedfeld (1975) suggests that sensory deprivation may also have some unexpected benefits. In some cases, sensory deprivation may sharpen subjects' visual and auditory acuity. It can also lead to greater openness to new experiences, and thus may help to foster artistic creativity.

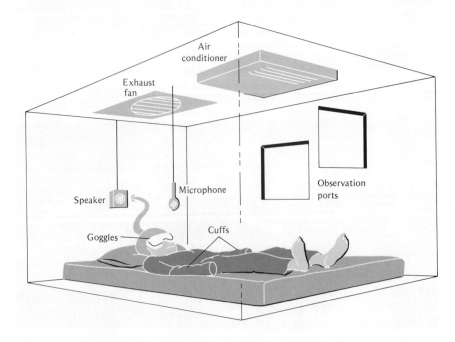

A sensory deprivation chamber, such as the one used in Heron's experiment.

CHAPTER FOUR: PERCEPTION

FIGURE 4.11

A cross-section of the skin. The skin contains a number of different kinds of receptor cells—for cold, heat, pressure, and pain.

The skin senses

The sense of touch is actually a combination of at least three sensations: pressure, temperature, and pain. If you unbend a paper clip and probe an area of your skin lightly, you will feel pressure at certain points where the wire contacts your skin, but not at every point. If you do the same thing with a cold wire, you will feel cold at other specific points. If you probe your skin with a warm wire, you will feel warmth at still other points. A pin point will produce spots of pain. Thus, different points on the skin are serviced by receptors that are sensitive to different kinds of stimuli (see Figure 4.11).

The experience you have when you are touched lightly with a single hair is called *pressure* or *touch*. The amount of pressure required to produce this experience varies for different parts of the body. The tip of the tongue, the lips, the fingers, and the hands are the most sensitive areas. The arms, legs, and body trunk are less sensitive. People experience pressure not only when an object touches the skin but also when the hairs on the body are slightly moved.

In addition to pressure receptors, the skin contains receptors for both *heat* and *cold*. There are about six times as many cold receptors as heat receptors in the skin. These temperature receptors are more concentrated along the trunk of the body, which is why the hands and feet can withstand greater temperature extremes than can the bare back. Hot and cold are relative terms: Anything that you touch that is colder than your skin will be perceived as cool; anything you touch that is hotter than your skin will seem warm. Interestingly, a really hot stimulus excites both cold and heat receptors.

A third type of receptor in the skin is the *pain* receptor. Psychologists are still debating whether pain is a separate sense with its own nerve structures or whether it results from a pattern of intense stimulation to any of a number of receptors. Pain seems to be received by a variety of nerve endings—not only in the skin but in other organs as well; very bright lights, loud noises, high or low temperatures, or great pressures all yield pain sensations. Pain serves to warn us of tissue destruction. However, most internal organs of the body do not have sense receptors for pain and are unable to inform us when they are in trouble.

How do we experience pain? Ac-

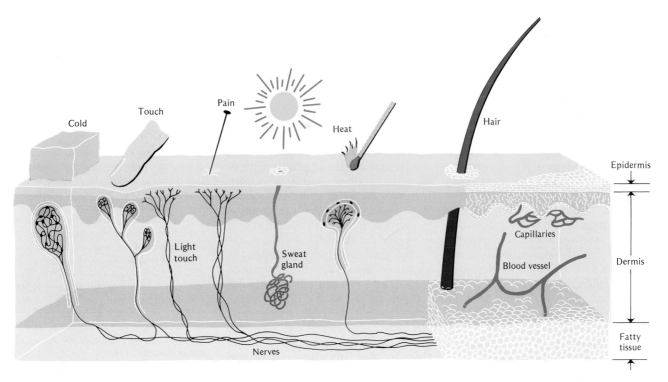

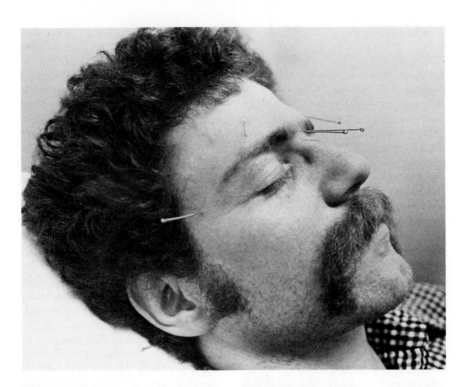

In acupuncture, the insertion of needles into various sites on the body surface sometimes relieves pain in other parts of the body.

cording to the *specificity theory*, there are specific pain receptors that relay signals of pain to the spinal cord, and from there directly to the pain centers of the brain. A person should therefore feel pain exactly where the stimulation occurs, and the amount of pain felt should depend on the amount of stimulation at the pain site. But this theory does not account for the phenomenon of *acupuncture*, in which the insertion of needles into various sites on the body surface sometimes relieves pain in body regions quite distant from the needle site. Chinese physicians regularly use acupuncture as the only form of anesthesia in major operations. Ronald Melzack and Patrick Wall came up with a new theory of pain that would account for the effects of acupuncture (Melzack, 1973). They proposed that the transmission of pain signals depends on *gate-control mechanisms*, which permit or block the transmission of pain signals to the central nervous system. Stimulation of certain areas will open the gate to allow pain signals to pass; stimulation of other areas will close the gate, so that pain signals from any part of the body cannot reach the pain reception areas of the brain. In the case of acupuncture, Melzack and Wall believe, the needles themselves are inserted at the sites that activate the reticular formation of the brain stem—one of the gate-control areas of the nervous system. As a result, pain signals are blocked before they reach the brain, and no pain is perceived.

Kinesthesis and equilibrium

Close your eyes and raise your hand. You still know where your hand is. Now touch your nose with your finger. You know where both parts are. The sense that tells you the positions and movements of your muscles and joints is called *kinesthesis*. Some kinesthetic receptors are embedded in the muscles and send information to the brain about the load on the muscle and its state of contraction. Other receptors are in tendons and joints. With these sensors you can detect a movement as slight as one-third of a degree in the shoulder and wrist.

The kinesthetic senses provide information about active body movement. Thus, you can tell the relative weights of objects by lifting them. You can walk along the street without watching what your legs are doing. And you can talk without thinking about moving your tongue and jaw.

Kinesthesis is extremely important to daily life. When kinesthetic sensitivity is destroyed somewhere along the spinal cord, impulses coming into the spinal cord below the point of damage cannot find a path to the brain. If this were to happen to you, you would sway and have trouble keeping your balance with your eyes closed. You might not be able to lift your foot onto a curb without first looking at the foot, and you would walk with a peculiar gait.

The sense of balance, or *equilibrium*, works in conjunction with kinesthesis. Together, these senses keep track of body motion and body position in relation to gravity. The major sense organs for equilibrium are the *semicircular canals*, located in the inner ear. These structures, which are oriented in different directions, are filled with a fluid that moves when the head rotates. The fluid movement allows perception of the body's movement. If movement is extreme, the individual gets dizzy. Vision also plays a role in our sense of balance. By watching objects in our environment "move" as we move around, we are better able to figure out what is "up" and what is "down." And just watching film footage shot with a spinning camera can make people feel dizzy.

We all have a basic sense of balance, but some people are able to refine this sense into a specialized ability.

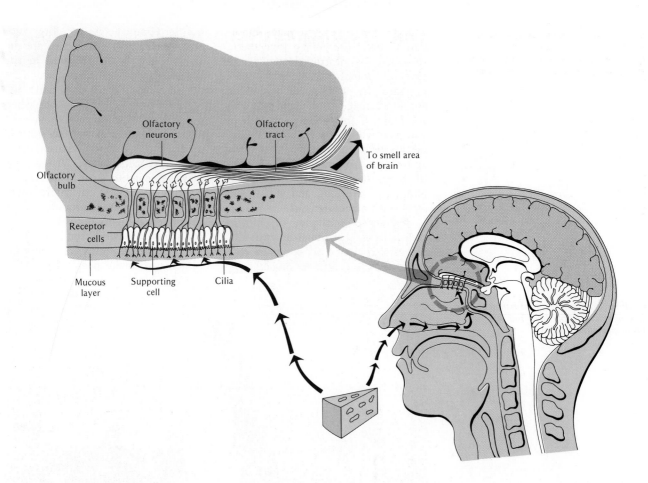

Smell

Our experience of *smell* (or *olfaction*) results from the stimulation of receptor cells in the nose by chemical molecules in the air. When the molecules reach the *olfactory neurons*, located high in the nasal cavities, they trigger a message that is sent to the *olfactory bulbs* in the brain (Figure 4.12). Sniffing helps us to smell better by forcing air currents into the upper portions of our nose, where the olfactory neurons are. When we eat, molecules from the food go up the back of our nose to the olfactory neurons and thus contribute to our experience of taste. Although the human sense of smell is not as acute as that of many other animals, such as dogs, it remains quite keen. For example, the average person can detect even one small drop of perfume that is diffused through a house (Engen, 1982).

There are about 5 million olfactory neurons in each of our nasal cavities. These receptor cells are unique in being the only neurons in the body that regenerate, replacing themselves every month or two. Thus, people whose olfactory neurons are damaged, such as by a blow to the head, may regain their sense of smell when new neurons grow and establish links to the proper area of the brain.

Over the years, scientists have proposed various classifications of the basic odors that we smell. Carolus Linnaeus, an eighteenth-century Swedish botanist, proposed seven basic odors: aromatic, fragrant, musky, garlicky, goaty, repulsive, and nauseous. (If just reading this list makes you nauseous, you are probably not alone.) But today's researchers have largely abandoned the attempt to classify odors, focusing instead on the ways in which people detect and interpret odors. People can detect the differences between hundreds, and perhaps even thousands, of odors. But we can *name* only a much smaller number of odors. Our ability to discriminate odors clearly outstrips our ability to label them (Cain, 1979).

FIGURE 4.12

When we smell something, molecules from the object we smell trigger a chemical reaction in receptor cells located high in the nasal cavities. The message is transmitted along olfactory neurons to the olfactory bulbs, and from there to the smell area of the brain.

This man's job is made tolerable by the fact that we adapt to smells that we are exposed to for an extended period of time. After a while we scarcely notice them.

THY BROTHER'S SMELL

You know that you can identify people by recognizing their faces and voices. But you may not know that you can recognize their smell, too. Studies have shown, for instance, that people can distinguish the two sexes by smell alone and that people can correctly identify their spouse's odor (Schleidt, 1980). In one study, pairs of young brothers and sisters wore new T-shirts for three consecutive nights. Afterward, the T-shirts were placed in plastic-lined cardboard buckets with small openings for sniffing. The children were asked to guess which of two buckets contained the shirt worn by their sibling. Nineteen of the 24 children guessed correctly. (Porter and Moore, 1981).

Some smells are highly pleasurable experiences—think of the scent of an alluring perfume, or the aroma of fresh-baked bread. Other smells, such as rotten meat or bad breath, are perceived as unpleasant or even disgusting. These preferences are not inborn but are learned as a result of our growing up in a particular culture. Children have few preferences among odors, but as they get older more preferences develop (Engen, 1982). And scents that are perceived as pleasant in one culture may be perceived as unpleasant in another. For example, members of certain African tribes "perfume" their hair with rancid fat, an odor most Westerners find unpleasant.

Fortunately, we *adapt* to smells that we are exposed to for an extended period of time, so that after a while we are hardly aware of them. In one study, people who were repeatedly exposed to sweaty socks soon began to downgrade their unpleasantness. And my dentist, who spends much of his time in close contact with people's mouths, reports that he is virtually unaware of the powerful odors emanating from them. The adaptation process seems to take place both in the olfactory neurons (which, after a while, will not respond as strongly to particular scent molecules) and in the brain (Cain, 1981).

Taste

Our *taste buds*, which are the receptor cells for the sense of taste, are scattered across the upper surface and sides of the tongue. They respond to four basic taste qualities—sweet, sour, bitter, and salty—and our taste experiences are mixtures of these four basic qualities. The sense of taste by itself provides a quite restricted sensory experience. The rich sensations that we get from food result from the fact that what we call "taste" is really the product of several sensations. Foods from anchovies to zucchini all take on their distinctive flavors because of their combinations of taste, odor, color, and texture. The other most important contributor to flavor is smell. If you could not smell your food, you would not know what you were eating. (If you find this hard to believe, try holding your nose the next time you eat a steak or a baked potato.) Color, too, influences your taste experience. In one study, a soft drink tasted very different to subjects, depending on the color it was dyed. Subjects sipping the red-dyed liquid tended to identify it as cherry soda, while many other subjects tasting the same drink dyed yellow thought it was mouthwash (Hyman, 1983). Because of the impact of color on taste, food manufacturers devote a great deal of attention to the colorings they add to foods.

The flavors we prefer seem to change as we mature. Infants prefer sweet liquids to bland ones. This preference for sweet foods becomes more marked through childhood, peaks in early adolescence, and then declines in adulthood. Children also seem to like saltier foods than do adults. It is not clear whether these changes are the result of learning or of physiological changes in our sensory functioning (Cowart, 1981). It is clear, however, that learning does play a role in taste preferences. For example, most children reject the bitter taste of beer, but many adults have learned to appreciate its flavor. Indeed, our preferences for flavors are often referred to as "acquired tastes." People of different cultures also learn to like some tastes and reject others. Diets in India include many more sour and bitter tastes than Western diets do. As a consequence, Indian adults show a greater preference for these flavors than for the blander foods chosen by most Westerners (Moskowitz et al., 1975).

We have briefly examined the major human senses here. In addition to these known senses, some people believe there are still other channels through which we perceive the world. This idea of *extrasensory perception* is explored in Box 2.

Some people have learned to make very subtle distinctions among different tastes.

CHAPTER FOUR: PERCEPTION

BOX 2

EXTRASENSORY PERCEPTION

At 11:30 on a Thursday night in 1976, Mrs. G. was startled out of her sleep by a tapping sound that seemed to come from her radio. The radio was off but the tapping noise continued. The tapping was clearly an SOS signal—a call for help in an emergency. After a few minutes it stopped. Mrs. G. was disturbed by the episode and slept badly that night. The next morning she told her brother about the strange occurrence and tried to put it out of her mind. The following day Mrs. G. was informed of her granddaughter's hospitalization: the young woman had been mugged on Thursday night at 11:30 (Nisbet, 1977).

This episode, and others like it, might be considered a dream, a coincidence, or a fantasy. Or it might be regarded as an example of *extrasensory perception,* commonly known as ESP. Many people believe that they can receive impressions of distant realities that do not reach them through sight, hearing, or any of the other "ordinary" senses—hence, they are called extrasensory. In practically every culture, the belief in extrasensory phenomena is common (Sheils, 1978).

J. B. Rhine (1934) was one of the first researchers to examine ESP, and his methods became widely used by others. Rhine used a special deck of 25 cards that included five different symbols: a cross, a circle, a star, a square, and a set of wavy lines. Subjects had to guess the order of the cards in the shuffled deck, either when the order was known to no one (to measure *clairvoyance*) or when the experimenter or another subject looked at the cards first (to measure mind-reading, or *telepathy*).

Following Rhine's lead, many recent studies have reported results that seem to show ESP. In such "successful" studies, subjects are never 100 percent correct in their guesses (called "hits"), but they do hit at rates that are slightly better than might be expected by chance.

Most ESP experiments are conducted by researchers who themselves believe that ESP exists, and they use subjects who are also "believers."

When nonbelieving researchers have tried to verify the findings, they have generally been unsuccessful. In addition, the more rigorous the experimental procedures in ESP studies, the harder it is to obtain statistically significant results.

This state of affairs has led most psychologists and other "conventional" scientists to doubt that ESP abilities exist at all. In one survey, only one-third of the psychologists polled thought ESP is at least a likely possibility, and more than half said that ESP is impossible.

Despite the general skepticism, there are some highly reputable psychologists (for example, Child, 1982) who are convinced that ESP abilities do exist and who are attempting to explore the links between ESP and more conventional topics in psychology.

And the Pentagon seems to be hedging its bets on ESP. Recent reports, although they have been officially denied, indicate that the U.S. Defense Department has investigated the possible use of ESP for such purposes as locating enemy submarines and pinpointing the location of groundbased missiles. The Russians have apparently been exploring similar applications, and the Americans, for all their skepticism, do not want to be left out in the psychic cold (Broad, 1984).

ESP may in fact exist, but it has yet to be demonstrated conclusively according to the rules of established science. If ESP does exist, it will eventually enter the halls of science, despite strong resistance by the scientific establishment. And then we will be faced with the mind-boggling task of explaining how it works.

PERCEPTION AS AN ACTIVE PROCESS

Perception was once thought to be a passive process. All you had to do was keep your eyes and ears open, and the world would automatically represent itself in your head. We now know that this view was mistaken. In fact, the achievement of meaningful perceptions is an active process, with the individual perceiver playing a major role in determining his or her own experiences. This role goes far beyond simply deciding where to look or what to touch. We rarely experience just one sensation at a time. Instead, we are constantly bombarded with a multitude of messages that must be sorted out, identified, and interpreted. We must select certain messages from the incoming array, identify them, and figure out how they relate to one another, in order to construct a meaningful picture of reality. This process depends not only on the sensations themselves but on our past experiences, expectations, and needs.

Principles of perceptual organization

Objects can often be perceived in more than one way. It is the perceiver who actively gives structure to these objects by employing various principles of *perceptual organization:* the way individual sensations are organized into meaningful perceptions of reality. These structural principles were first identified by the *Gestalt psychologists,* a group of German psychologists who did much of their work in the 1920s. (Many of them later came to America.) The German word *Gestalt* means "whole" or "con-

figuration," reflecting the emphasis these psychologists gave to our perception of figures and forms as whole units.

The Gestalt psychologists concentrated on the ways in which we interpret images in two-dimensional space, such as the images that appear on the pages of a book. One basic feature of perceptual organization that they identified is our tendency to differentiate between *figure*—the part of an image that seems to be an object—and *ground*—the background against which the object stands. In many drawings it is possible to see one portion as being either figure *or* ground, depending on how we look at it. In Figure 4.13, for example, we can see either a vase or two faces, depending on which part of the drawing we perceive as the figure and which part we perceive as ground.

Another central aspect of perceptual organization is the principle of *closure:* when we see a figure that is disconnected or incomplete, as in Figure 4.14, we are mentally primed to fill in the gaps and to see it as a complete figure. The Gestalt psychologists also noted that we tend to organize our perceptions in terms of the *proximity* of their elements. In Figure 4.15A, we can see the sixteen dots as either horizontal rows or vertical columns. As the dots get closer together horizontally, as in Figure 4.15B, we are more likely to view them as rows; as they get closer together vertically (Figure 4.15C), we are more likely to view them as columns. This tendency to view objects in terms of the proximity of their elements is relied on in printed photographs, comic book panels, and television pictures, which are all actually arrays of dots or lines that we perceive as shapes and objects.

FIGURE 4.13

As you keep looking at this drawing, what is figure and what is ground is likely to shift back and forth.

FIGURE 4.14

The principle of closure. Although parts of the letters are missing in the word, we tend to fill in these gaps and to perceive the whole letters and, therefore, the whole word. Similarly, we tend to fill in the gaps between the dots and see the figure as a circle.

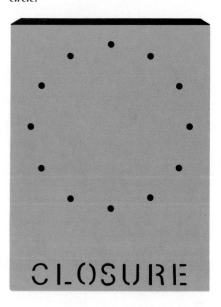

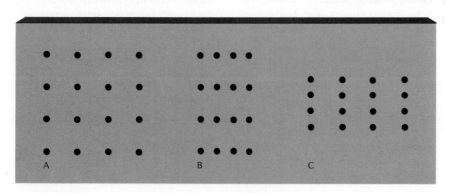

FIGURE 4.15

The principle of proximity. We tend to see things that are near each other as going together. The same set of dots can be arranged so that they can be perceived as either columns or rows (A), as rows (B), or as columns (C), depending on the proximity of the dots to each other.

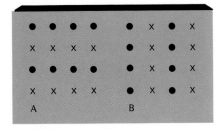

FIGURE 4.16
The principle of similarity. We tend to perceptually group things that are alike. Thus, in (A) we see rows and in (B) we see columns.

Still another Gestalt principle of organization is *similarity*. In Figure 4.16A, we are likely to see horizontal rows, while in Figure 4.16B, we see vertical columns. In each case, we are predisposed to organize the elements in terms of their similarity to one another. All of these Gestalt principles emphasize the strong tendency we all have to give our perceptions a total structure.

Where do these principles of perceptual organization come from? Although experience with the world may help us to refine our use of these principles, the basic tendencies to organize our perceptions in terms of figure-ground, figure completion, proximity, and similarity seem to be innate. Our minds themselves seem to be organized in a way that readies us to perceive the world in meaningful ways.

Paying attention

As you sit reading this page, stop and look around the room for a minute. The room you are in is full of objects, surfaces, colors, shapes. The room is probably full of sounds as well: distant voices, footsteps, perhaps music from a radio or traffic sounds from outside. If the room has a window, there is even more for your eyes to see and your ears to hear. Feel the soft pressure of your clothes against your body and your feet against the floor. Sense the rhythm of your breathing and your heartbeat. Notice any little itches, twinges, or aches in your body. All these stimuli have been present as long as you have been reading, but you have selected only the printed page (perhaps with greater or lesser success) for concentration. The process of focusing on a few stimuli while ignoring others is called *attention*. We never attend to all the stimuli around us at once. Our nervous systems would be hopelessly overloaded if we did. Instead, we select the item we want to attend to—a book, a conversation, a TV show, even our own thoughts—and the surrounding events seem to fade into the background of consciousness.

How do we manage to focus attention in this way? Some stimuli capture attention almost automatically, without any effort on our part. Among the characteristics that consistently grab our attention are *contrast* and *novelty* (Berlyne, 1970). A brightly lit neon sign captures our attention because it stands out in sharp contrast to its surroundings. And although the red and blue mailbox that you pass each day may go unnoticed, a purple mailbox would probably catch your eye because it would be novel and unexpected.

But even when we are not confronted with striking stimuli we manage to keep our attention focused. Consider, for example, a crowded, noisy party. You are surrounded by voices, as dozens of people engage in loud conversation. Yet you are able to keep track of your own conversation and to ignore others. One way you accomplish this is by relying on physical cues, such as the sound pattern of particular voices and the direction they are coming from (Broadbent, 1958). Perhaps even more important, you can follow a single conversation despite surrounding noise by "tuning in" to the meaning of what is being said. If one person standing near you is talking about existential philosophy and another is talking about football, you will probably be able to keep track of what one speaker is saying without being derailed by the other.

Some psychologists have described attention as mental effort, or a pool of mental resources (Norman and Bobrow, 1975). All of our mental activities—perceiving, understanding, remembering—require such a mental effort or attention. The more energy we give to one task, the less is left over for coping with other stimuli. Some tasks require a great deal of attention or mental effort because the stimuli are difficult to process: you have to concentrate very hard to understand a garbled voice on a bad telephone connection or to read a distant road sign at dusk. Other tasks, such as writing a term paper or listening to a chemistry lecture, involve a great deal of attention because they require you to make many mental links between different pieces of information. If the stimulus or the task you have selected for concentration is a difficult one, you'll have that much less

WAIT A MINUTE— ARE YOUR SHOES ON?

Our senses are better suited to informing us about changes in stimulation than about stimulation that remains constant. Our visual system is designed to give special attention to contrast and movement, and our skin receptors generally respond better at the beginning or end of a stimulus (such as pressure on the skin) than they do to constant stimulation. This makes sense in terms of what we need to know about the outside world. As David Hubel (1979) writes, "We need to know about changes; no one wants or needs to be reminded 16 hours a day that his shoes are on" (page 51).

Objects that stand in sharp contrast to their surroundings are most likely to capture our attention.

attention to pay to surrounding events; you have to devote more "attention energy" to difficult stimuli. So, as you read a textbook, you may be less aware of the surrounding sights and sounds than you would be if you were doing something that requires less attention, such as washing dishes.

What becomes of the surrounding sights and sounds that fade into the background while we focus on a particular task? We probably do take note of most of what is going on around us at some level of awareness (Lewis, 1970). One rainy day, for example, I was sitting by myself at McDonald's, totally absorbed in making corrections on one of the boxes for this book. There was music coming through the piped-in system and conversations at nearby tables. I was not consciously aware of any of this—it was all a blur in the background. But all of a sudden I was aware of three words that had just been said by a man at one table to a man at another table. The words were "Buick . . . lights on." I looked up with a start, thought for a moment, and then said to the man, "Did you say that there's an old Buick with its lights on?" The man confirmed that he had indeed said so. I immediately ran out into the rain to turn out the lights on my car, just in time to save the draining battery.

Although I was absorbed in my work, at some level I was monitoring the conversations around me. It is as though we can set our levels of attention for different kinds of stimuli. We might set the attention level at high for a particular stimulus—a person talking, a television screen, a book— while keeping a low setting for the remaining environmental activity. While the background events may not reach full awareness, neither are they completely blocked out. When something happens that is unusual or important enough, it will arouse sufficient attention to spring to our conscious awareness.

CHAPTER FOUR: PERCEPTION

THE BETTER, THE BIGGER

People sometimes perceive objects they value highly as being larger than objects they value less highly. In one study, poor children—for whom the value of money must be particularly great—perceived coins as being larger than rich children did (Bruner and Goodman, 1947). Similarly, voters have been found to view their preferred candidates as taller than they really are (Kassarjian, 1963). There is a common assumption in our culture that bigger is better. As a result, we may be predisposed to view objects—or people—that are "better" as "bigger," too, even when they really aren't.

Seeing what you're looking for: selective perception

In interpreting the messages that bombard our senses, we tend to see (or hear, feel, smell, or taste) what we're looking for—that is, what we expect to see. This phenomenon is called *selective perception.* E. M. Siipola (1935) demonstrated this phenomenon in his studies of individuals' responses to words. He told one group of people they would be shown words that referred to animals. He then showed them, for brief time intervals, combinations of letters that did not really spell anything (*sael, dack,* or *wharl*). Most of the group perceived the letters as the words *seal, duck,* and *whale.* He told a second group he was going to show them words pertaining to boats. He showed this group the same combinations that the first group saw. People in this group reported seeing the words *sail, deck,* and *wharf.* Each group saw what they expected to see.

You can demonstrate the phenomenon of selective perception using Figure 4.17. Show a friend Picture A and ask what he sees. Then present Picture C and ask what he sees. Most likely the friend will say that A shows an old woman and that C is another picture of the same woman. Now show another friend Picture B and Picture C. Most likely, she will report that B is the picture of a young girl and that so is C. Thus, each friend will see something different in Pic-

ture C—and, of course, each will be right, since C includes both an old woman and a young girl, depending on how you look at the picture (Leeper, 1935). But the particular image that each friend sees depends on what he expects, based on previous experience. Researchers have shown that once a person is primed to see a picture in a particular way, it is very hard to change that set and see things differently. (You can try this with your friends: Ask them whether they see anything *else* in the picture, and find out how long it takes for them to come up with another possibility.)

Motivation can also affect selective perception. If you need to mail a letter, you will suddenly be aware of that red and blue mailbox that you normally ignore each day. If you are hungry, you are especially likely to notice signs saying "restaurant" or "food" and you may even misread signs so that "claims" becomes "clams." Selective perception seems to reflect people's need to predict their environment and to get what they want (Bruner, 1957). As a result, people pay attention to stimuli that conform to their expectations, needs, and values. We find things we are looking for, and we avoid things that don't fit our interest.

Selective perception is closely connected to the phenomenon of attention. When we expect a particular event, we focus our attention in advance so that we are especially alert to cues for the event. Suppose, for example, that you know that you are

FIGURE 4.17

An illustration of selective perception. (See the text for explanation.)

A

B

C

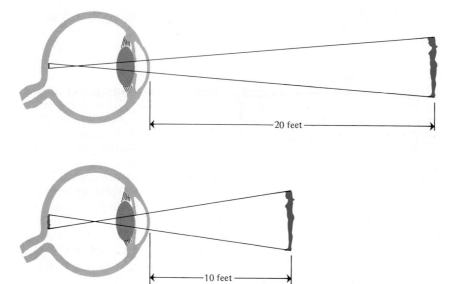

FIGURE 4.18

As you move closer to or farther away from an object, the size of the image on your retina gets larger or smaller. Yet you still perceive the object as being the same size. This phenomenon is known as size constancy.

going to hear a one-syllable English word. Experiments show that if you know the word will be one of two alternatives—say, "book" or "pen"—you can accurately determine which word is being used, even if it is played at a very low volume in a very noisy setting. But if instead you are waiting for *any* English monosyllable, your chance of recognizing it at that low volume is very small (Ferrell, 1983).

Another factor that influences perception of stimuli and events is our tendency to compare the present stimulus with the stimuli that directly preceded it. This idea is discussed in Box 3.

Experiencing a stable world: perceptual constancy

You are sitting in the cafeteria at some distance from the food lines. You look up as a woman carries a tray from the food line, walks past your table, and sits down. What are the successive patterns of visual stimulation that register on your retina as you watch this scene?

Every time the woman moves closer to you, the image on your retina gets larger (see Figure 4.18). As she moves from 20 feet away to 10 feet away, the height of the image on your retina doubles. The opposite occurs if the person moves away from you. In addition, as the woman moves nearer

the window, more light is available, and her image on your retina gets brighter. When the woman moves away from the window, the image gets darker. That is what your retina senses. But what do you actually perceive? A changeable chameleon of a person who constantly gets larger and smaller, lighter and darker? Not at all. Instead, you see the same woman, who remains more or less the same size and brightness, regardless of the games her retinal image may be playing. We make automatic adjustments in our perception of objects that take into account changes in the distance and lighting. By so doing, we manage to convert what would otherwise be a bewildering pattern of stimulation into a stable and meaningful world. These processes by which we take into account changing patterns of stimulation and perceive the world as stable are aspects of *perceptual constancy* (for example, Figure 4.19).

Our tendency to perceive objects as staying the same size despite changes in the size of the image on the retina is called *size constancy*. Some aspects of this process are apparently innate, but it also seems to depend on experience. Size constancy may be especially difficult to achieve when distance cues are not available or when we are dealing with unfamiliar objects. Colin Turnbull (1961) tells of the Bambuti Pygmies who live in the forests of the Congo and are not

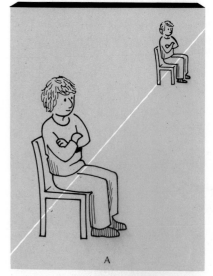

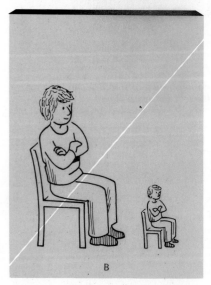

FIGURE 4.19

In evaluating the size of objects, we take their spatial location into account. In (A), we assume that the two men are of about equal size, because one is closer to us than the other. In (B), we do not make the same assumption.

BOX 3

PERCEPTUAL ADAPTATION

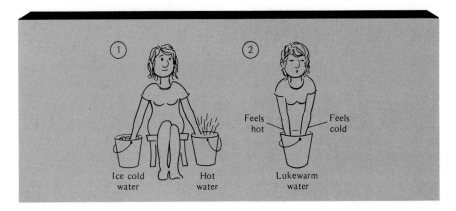

Try the following demonstration: Fill one bucket with ice-cold water and another bucket with water as hot as you can stand. Plunge your left hand into the cold water and your right hand into the hot water. After a minute, put both hands into a bucket of lukewarm water. You will immediately feel an odd sensation: The water will feel hot to your left hand (which had gotten used to the cold water) and cold to your right hand (which had gotten used to the hot water).

This demonstration illustrates the process of *sensory adaptation:* Our sensations depend not only on the current stimulus but also on the stimuli that immediately preceded it. Such adaptation is based on the tendency of our sense organs—such as the heat and cold receptors in the skin—to adjust themselves to a particular level of stimulation, as when our rods and cones adapt to low illumination and our olfactory receptors adapt to on-going smells.

Other cases of *perceptual adaptation* involve our judgments rather than our sense organs. In such cases, an initial perception provides a frame of reference against which subsequent perceptions are judged. For example, a standard weight will feel heavier if you lift it after lifting a light weight than after lifting a heavier one (Helson, 1964).

Analogous effects occur in the social domain, such as in our perceptions of physical attractiveness. In one study, male subjects were given a set of photographs of college women and were asked to evaluate each woman's attractiveness on a rating scale. Half of the subjects rated the photos while watching an episode of "Charlie's Angels," a TV show that featured a group of beautiful women. These subjects rated the women in the photos as being less attractive than did the subjects who were not watching the show (Kenrick et al., 1980).

It seems that a sort of perceptual adaptation takes place when we are evaluating other people's qualities. Just as lukewarm water feels cooler after we have gotten used to hot water, so people seem less attractive after we've gotten used to a higher standard of attractiveness. To my knowledge, the "Charlie's Angels" experiment has not been done with female subjects watching TV shows featuring Tom Selleck or other male sex symbols. If it were, the same effect would almost certainly be found.

familiar with wide-open spaces. Turnbull took a Pygmy to a vast plain, and when the Pygmy looked at a herd of buffalo several hundred yards away, he asked what type of insects they were. He refused to believe they were buffalo. Because he rarely looked at objects more than a few yards away, the Pygmy had not learned to take distance as well as retinal image into account. In most cases, however, people make such adjustments automatically and unconsciously.

Our tendency to perceive objects as maintaining the same brightness, even as lighting conditions change, is called *brightness constancy*. For example, white paper looks white and black paper looks black whether viewed in sunlight or indoors. The black paper outside may actually reflect more light than the white paper does inside, yet it will still look darker. How do we manage to perceive the actual brightness of an object despite changing lighting conditions? It is certainly not a conscious process. But we seem to have the ability to evaluate the brightness of the object by comparing it to other objects viewed under the same lighting conditions. The black paper in bright sunlight still reflects less light than other objects in bright sunlight, so we see it as being dark. Finally, our tendency to perceive objects as maintaining the same color, no matter what the lighting, is called *color constancy*.

Perceptual illusions

Magicians are sometimes called masters of illusion because they can make us "see" things that aren't really there, such as rabbits coming out of hats or cut ropes joining back together. Psychologists have a special interest in *perceptual illusions*—instances in which perception and reality do not agree—not only because of their intrinsic fascination but because such illusions can help us to understand the process of perception.

One of the best known illusions is called the *Müller-Lyer illusion*, after the person who devised it in 1889 (see Figure 4.20). The illusion is an extremely powerful one. Even after you measure the two lines and prove to yourself that they are equal, you will still perceive the line with the reversed arrowheads (B) as being longer than the line with the standard arrowheads (A). What causes this misperception? Many hypotheses have been offered, but the most likely explanation has to do with the phenomenon of size constancy (Gregory, 1968). The arrangement of lines in A looks like the lines in the outside corner of a building (C in the figure), whereas the lines in B resemble those of an inside corner of a building (D in the figure). This resemblance leads us to operate as if the line in A is closer to us than the line in B. To maintain

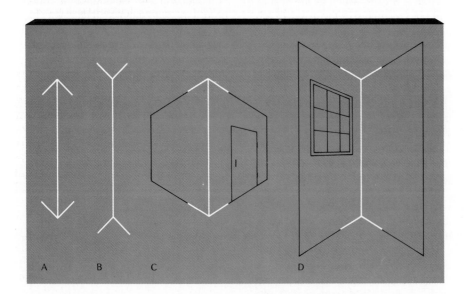

FIGURE 4.20

The Müller-Lyer illusion. Line B appears to be longer than line A, yet they are both the same length. This illusion may be explained by the fact that our knowledge of perspective may lead us to see line A as if it were the outside corner of a building (C) and line B as if it were the inside corner of a room (D). (See the text for explanation.)

FIGURE 4.21

The Ponzo illusion. The two horizontal lines in the drawing above are of the same length, yet the top line appears to be longer than the bottom one. The illusion may be explained by the fact that our knowledge of perspective leads us to see the vertical lines as if they were railroad tracks receding into the distance (see text).

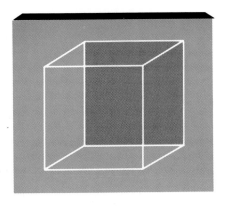

FIGURE 4.22

The Necker cube, an ambiguous figure.

size constancy, we perceive the line in B to be longer than the line in A because it seems to be more distant from us. Because distant objects will produce smaller retinal images, we compensate and see the "distant" object as *larger*. Normally, this type of correction enables us to see a world that corresponds to reality, but when three-dimensional objects are presented on a two-dimensional surface, these corrections can lead us astray. These correction processes are so deeply ingrained that we keep using them even when we know them to be inappropriate.

Other perceptual illusions can similarly be understood as special cases in which the corrections that usually insure accurate perception are inappropriately applied. One of these is the Ponzo illusion (also known as the railway ties illusion), shown in Figure 4.21. Although both horizontal lines in A are the same length, we perceive the top line as being longer. Why? If this were a picture of a three-dimensional scene, such as railroad tracks receding in the distance, the

top line would be seen as more distant. As with the Müller-Lyer illusion, our unconscious knowledge of perspective tells us that the top line must be larger than the bottom line, so we automatically compensate and perceive it that way, even though, in a two-dimensional drawing, there is no difference in the lines.

Another famous illusion is the *Necker cube*, devised in 1832 by a Swiss scientist named L. S. Necker. He noticed that a cube drawn in two dimensions will spontaneously reverse its direction (Figure 4.22). The tinted area in the figure can appear as either an outer surface or inner surface of a transparent box. When such three-dimensional figures are drawn in two dimensions, they become ambiguous. Our perception reflects this ambiguity, alternating back and forth between one interpretation and another.

In everyday living we rarely encounter illusions such as these that trick our perceptions. Our perceptual abilities function well in normal circumstances and give us a quite accurate picture of the world. It is only under special conditions, such as when magicians and psychologists deliberately try to trick us, that the very processes that usually improve the accuracy of our perception lead us to perceive things inaccurately.

SUMMARY

• **1** *Perception* is the active process of integrating and organizing information collected by the sense organs. The first step in the process of perception is for *receptor cells* in the sense organs to respond to energy in the environment. The energy is then converted to electrical impulses that can be transmitted to and interpreted by the brain.

Vision
• **2** *Vision* is the dominant human sense. The eye admits light (through the *pupil*) and focuses it (via the *lens*) onto the light-sensitive cells of the *retina*. These cells, the *rods* and *cones*, contain chemicals that break down when struck by light. The breakdown of chemicals triggers the sending of messages to the brain along the *optic nerve.*

• **3** The cones, which are packed together in the center of the retina, are the color receptors. The rods, which spread to the outer edges of the retina, are not sensitive to color but are more sensitive to light than cones. Adaptation to dim light occurs because chemicals in the rods and cones build up faster than they are broken down when there is little light stimulation.

• **4** *Visual acuity* is the ability to discriminate the details in the field of vision. Poor visual acuity may be in the form of *nearsightedness*, in which only near objects are seen clearly, or *farsightedness*, in which only distant objects are seen clearly. The *blind spot* is an empty spot in one's vision corresponding to the place on the back of the eye where the optic nerve exits to the brain.

• **5** Color vision results from the "mixing" of stimulation of three types of cones, each sensitive to a different primary color. The cones pass information on to *opponent cells* that are activated or inhibited.

Defects in cones result in *color blindness*, which may be *dichromatic* (in which only two of the three types of cones are functioning) or *monochromatic* (in which none of the cones are functioning.)

• **6** *Monocular cues* to *depth perception* include overlapping of objects, size differences, perspective, and texture gradients. Depth perception is also produced by *binocular vision*, in which the images received by the two eyes combine to give objects three-dimensionality. Experiments with the *visual cliff* indicate that depth perception is innate, although it improves with learning.

The other senses
• **7** Studies of *sensory deprivation* in the 1950s showed that students who were placed in a room without sensory stimulation experienced hallucinations, were impaired in performance of intellectual tasks, and were more susceptible to persuasion.

• **8** *Hearing* occurs when a *sound wave* causes the eardrum to vibrate, which in turn sets the three bones of the middle ear into motion. These bones transmit the vibrations to fluids in the *cochlea* in the inner ear, where receptor cells are stimulated, causing messages to be sent along the *auditory nerve* to the brain.

• **9** Among the qualities of a sound are *loudness* (determined primarily by the amplitude of the sound wave), *pitch* (determined primarily by the frequency of wave vibrations), and *timbre* (determined by the distinctive pattern of sound waves produced by the sound source).

• **10** Locating the source of a sound generally requires two ears: Sounds reach one ear a fraction of a second before the other, and they are also louder for the first (and closer) ear they reach.

• **11** The *skin senses* include receptors for pressure, heat, cold, and pain. The experiencing of warmth and cold is relative, depending on the temperature of the skin. Psychologists are uncertain whether pain is a sense in itself or a result of the intense stimulation of any of a number of receptors. According to the *specificity theory*, pain receptors send signals directly to the brain. According to the *gate-control theory*, there are areas in the nervous system that control whether or not a pain sensation will reach the brain.

• *12* *Kinesthesis* is the sense of body movement and position. Receptors for this sense are located in the muscles, tendons, and joints. The sense of balance, or *equilibrium* (based in the *semicircular canals* in the inner ear), works in conjunction with kinesthesis to make one aware of body position in relation to gravity.

• *13* The sense of *smell* involves the reception of chemical molecules by olfactory neurons in the nasal cavity. Preferences for particular odors appear to be culturally ingrained.

• *14* The receptors for *taste* are the *taste buds*. There appear to be four basic *taste* qualities: sweet, sour, salty, and bitter. Preferences for flavors are also culturally acquired.

• *15* Many people believe that they can learn about objects and events through means other than the ordinary senses. Such *extrasensory perception* is treated with skepticism by most scientists.

Perception as an active process

• *16* Among the principles of *perceptual organization* identified by *Gestalt psychologists* are *figure-ground* distinctions, *closure, proximity* of elements, and *similarity* of elements.

• *17* Perception is *selective*—people pay *attention* to only a small percentage of the stimuli in their environment. According to one theory, we have a limited pool of energy to use for attending to things; the more difficult the task, the more energy we use for it and the less we use to notice other stimuli.

• *18* People tend to perceive what they expect to perceive; this phenomenon is called *selective perception*. Selective perception is influenced by a person's needs and values.

• *19* The phenomenon of perceptual *adaptation* is the tendency to use previous perceptions as a basis

against which to judge subsequent perceptions.

• *20* People view objects as stable and unchanging despite changes in the pattern of stimulation received. This ability is called *perceptual constancy*. The process of perceiving objects as staying the same size no matter what the distance is called *size constancy*, and perceiving them as maintaining the same brightness despite changing lighting conditions is called *brightness constancy*.

• *21* Perceptual *illusions* are instances in which perception and reality do not agree. Famous illusions include the Müller-Lyer illusion, the Ponzo illusion, and the Necker cube.

KEY TERMS

afterimages
attention
auditory nerve
binocular vision
cones
depth perception
equilibrium
extrasensory perception (ESP)
figure-ground
gate-control theory of pain
Gestalt psychologists
kinesthesis
monocular depth cues
olfactory neurons
opponent cells
optic nerve
perception
perceptual adaptation
perceptual constancy
perceptual illusions
perceptual organization
receptor cells
retina
rods
selective perception
semicircular canals
senses
sensory deprivation
size constancy
skin senses
specificity theory of pain
taste buds
visual acuity
visual cliff

NOISE POLLUTION

American cities, with their screeching cars, thundering trucks, roaring motorcycles, wailing sirens, blaring horns, and bellowing factories, are tremendously noisy places, and they are getting noisier. City dwellers are constantly exposed to the cacophony of street noises, and many people work in settings where equipment raises the noise level to frightening extremes.

It is not only cities and workplaces that are noisy. Even in suburban areas, traffic and airplane noise is becoming an increasing problem. And modern technology has brought a constant din inside our homes, with appliances such as hair dryers, food processors, vacuum cleaners, air conditioners, stereo systems, television sets, and lawnmowers taking turns to prevent peace and quiet. Even if we try to get away from it all, chainsaws, speedboats, snowmobiles, and minibikes assault our ears in the countryside. Although we enjoy a high standard of living, we pay for it in part through the noise our technology creates. All these noises can have harmful effects on our hearing, our state of mind, and even our social relationships.

EFFECTS ON HEARING

High levels of noise can literally be deafening. The Environmental Protection Agency estimates that more than 16 million people in the United States suffer from hearing loss caused by noise. When the cells of the inner ear are bombarded with loud sounds, they can be damaged, leading to hearing loss. Even a relatively mild noise level of 70 decibels (see table), about the level of a crowded business office, can damage hearing if

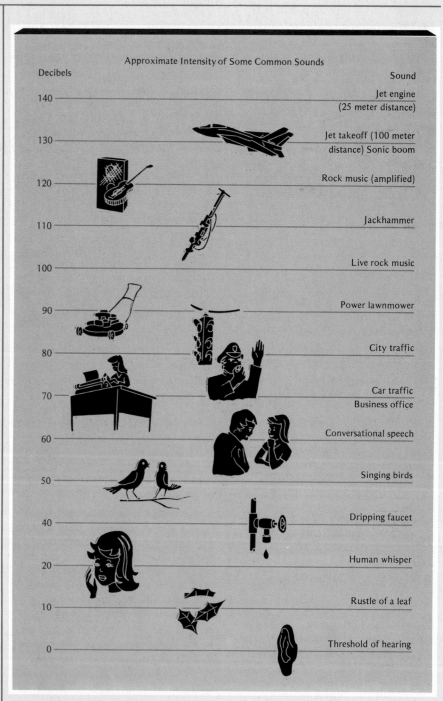

Decibels	Sound
140	Jet engine (25 meter distance)
130	Jet takeoff (100 meter distance) Sonic boom
120	Rock music (amplified)
110	Jackhammer
100	Live rock music
90	Power lawnmower
80	City traffic
70	Car traffic / Business office
60	Conversational speech
50	Singing birds
40	Dripping faucet
20	Human whisper
10	Rustle of a leaf
0	Threshold of hearing

Approximate Intensity of Some Common Sounds

The column on the left shows the decibel intensity of some common sounds. A decibel is the smallest difference in intensity of sound that the human ear can detect. The scale is a mathematical power function. At around the middle of the scale, every increase of 10 decibels represents approximately a doubling of the sound intensity.

Amplified rock music can be as loud as 120 decibels. Continued exposure to it can be harmful to hearing.

one is subjected to it year in and year out. And higher levels of noise can have much worse effects. Noise levels between 90 and 100 decibels put people at risk of hearing loss, and noise levels of 120 decibels or more are clearly harmful to hearing. When we are exposed to sounds of 130 decibels or more, we actually feel pain.

Noise in industrial settings is a major health hazard. For example, coal miners work each day with noise levels between 95 and 120 decibels from mining equipment. (If you've ever stood next to a jackhammer, you know how loud that is.) It is estimated that half of America's coal miners have impaired hearing by the time they are 50. Construction workers and some airline employees are at similar risk for hearing problems (Raloff, 1982).

Damage can also be done by sounds we enjoy and bring upon ourselves. A recent examination of Japanese students found a previously unknown cause of hearing problems: "headphone addiction." Some students who suffered from unexplained hearing loss had listened to stereo headphones more than 24 hours a week at a volume

that averaged 88 decibels (Brody, 1982). American college students, too, have been showing increased levels of hearing impairment that seem to result from exposure to amplified sound (Lipscomb, 1982).

Even if we avoid noisy workplaces or leisure pursuits, we may still be exposed to damaging noise levels. The street noise in many urban neighborhoods approaches or exceeds 90 decibels—the legal level to which workers can be exposed without ear protectors (Raloff, 1982).

WHAT IS NOISE?

Noise batters not only our ears, but our minds as well. When it comes to predicting psychological effects, there is an important distinction to be made between *sound* and *noise*. When psychologists talk about "noise," they are referring to sounds that are unpleasant or unwanted (Cohen and Weinstein, 1981). As a result, what is "noise" remains to a certain extent in the ear of the beholder. Some people find loud rock music enjoyable (and hardly noisy) and loud opera music annoying (and therefore "noisy"); other people have exactly the opposite reaction.

More generally, what we perceive as tolerable sound or intolerable noise depends on our attitudes toward the source of the sound. In one study, people rated automobile sounds as "noisier" if they thought the sounds came from a teenager's car than if they thought the sounds came from a taxi (Cederlöf et al., 1961). Another study found that people living next to an Air Force base were less annoyed by the aircraft sounds when they were persuaded that the base was a vital part of their community and country (Sorenson, 1970).

NOISE AND PSYCHOLOGICAL STRESS

There is a common response that we have to unwanted noise, especially if it persists over time: It produces stress. The body responds to such noise as it does to any threat, by showing signs of physiological arousal (see Chapter 12). Recent research suggest that continued exposure to noise can contribute to high blood pressure, heart disease, and ulcers (Cohen and Weinstein, 1981).

Some researchers have suggested that prolonged exposure to noise makes people more vulnerable to anxiety, irritability, and even emotional breakdown. People exposed

to high noise levels at work report experiencing greater tension, more conflict with other people at home and on the job, and more psychosomatic complaints, such as nausea and headaches (Miller, 1974). And a study of people living near London's Heathrow Airport found that those living in the corridor of greatest noise from the airplanes were more likely to check into mental hospitals than were those living in quieter neighborhoods (Herridge and Chir, 1972). These studies do not prove that noise is a primary cause of psychological problems. People living in the noisiest neighborhoods and working in the noisiest jobs may also be the most likely to experience other, non-noise-related stresses that are linked to a lower standard of living. Yet given the stressful effects of noise, it would not be surprising to find that high noise levels aggravate existing emotional problems.

When we are continually exposed to noise, we are likely to adapt to it, so that we are no longer startled by it or even aware of it much of the time. Indeed, some people in very noisy places seem almost oblivious to the noise. But even in such cases, the noise is likely to have harmful effects. In one series of studies, David Glass and Jerome Singer (1973) played students tape-recorded bursts of either loud (110 decibels) or soft (56 decibels) noise over a period of 20 minutes. After a short while, the subjects adapted to the noise, and they were able to perform clerical tasks successfully. But the loud noise had unwelcome aftereffects: Immediately after the noisy period, subjects who had heard the loud noise were impaired in their ability to work efficiently on problem-solving and proofreading tasks.

In this and other studies, Glass and Singer found that the predictability and controllability of the noise made a big difference in subjects' reactions to it. When subjects knew when the loud noise was coming, its harmful aftereffects were greatly reduced. And when the subjects knew they could stop the noise if they wanted to, the effects were also reduced—even though the subjects didn't actually make use of their "stop" button. Unfortunately, most of the noise that pervades our cities is of the worst kind—it comes in unpredictable bursts, and it comes from sources over which we have no control.

NOISE AND INTELLECTUAL ABILITIES

When noise continues over a period of years, it can have adverse effects on intellectual abilities. In four New York City apartment buildings spanning a noisy highway, elementary school children who lived on the lower floors (where noise was loudest) were found to have less ability to discriminate between sounds than children who lived on higher floors (Cohen, Glass, and Singer, 1973). Children on the lower floors also had poorer reading skills than those on the higher floors.

Glass and Singer suggest that in tuning out a noisy environment, children may fail to distinguish between speech-relevant sounds and speech-irrelevant sounds. The unhappy result is that the longer children must endure noise, the more likely they are to ignore all sounds, and this, in turn, may make reading more difficult.

Another study compared children who attended school near an airport, where they were subjected to the noise of aircraft landings and takeoffs at unpredictable times, with children who attended an otherwise similar school in a quieter neighborhood (Cohen et al., 1980). At both schools, the children were tested in a soundproof trailer. Children from the noisy school found it harder to solve puzzles and math problems and were more likely to give up in frustration. These children were also found to have higher blood pressure than those in the quieter school. Some of these effects of noise do not seem to disappear quickly. A few classrooms in the noisy school were soundproofed. When the children were tested a year later, those who had soundproofed classrooms did better on the puzzles and problems than those who remained in the noisier rooms, but they still did not persist at difficult tasks for as long as the children from the quiet classrooms

Children who attended school near an airport, where they were subjected to the noise of airplane landings and takeoffs, found it difficult to solve problems and were more likely than other children to give up in frustration.

CHAPTER FOUR: PERCEPTION

When a power lawnmower was running, people were less likely to help a stranger.

from the other neighborhood (Cohen et al., 1981).

The noise levels of our homes can also have subtle effects on cognitive abilities. In one study, infants raised in homes rated as having a high noise level—for example, with kitchen appliances near the children's rooms and the TV left on all day—scored lower on tests of intellectual development than did infants raised in otherwise comparable homes that were not so noisy. Although it is unclear whether these effects are lasting ones, the researchers speculated that the noise caused the infants to tune out other stimuli, especially verbal communication from adults (Wachs, 1982).

NOISE AND HELPING

The noise level in our environment also affects the way we relate to other people. Various studies have shown that people are less likely to be helpful and friendly to others in noisy places. Kenneth Mathews and Lance Canon (1975) set up a field experiment to investigate this phenomenon. As people walked down a residential street, they encountered a confederate of the experimenters who "accidentally" dropped several books. In half of the encounters, a power lawnmower was running at full throttle; in the other half it was turned off. When the lawnmower was off, half of the passersby helped pick up the books; when it was going, only one-eighth of the passersby came to the stranger's aid.

Why should the noise of a lawnmower influence people's desire to help? The most plausible explanation seems to be that the noise distracts the attention of the passersby. As noted in this chapter, we have the capacity to attend to only a limited amount of stimulation at one time. Noise in the environment makes it harder to take in any other

information. Because of the noisy lawnmower, the passersby were less able to pick up on the cues indicating that the person needed help. In some cases the confederate wore an armcast—a clear sign that he needed help. The cast increased helping when the lawnmower was off, but it did not affect the frequency of helping when the mower was on. Apparently, the noise led people to overlook this indication of another person's need.

Noise influences our friendships as well. In a study in San Francisco, residents of lightly trafficked, quiet streets were found to have three times as many friends and twice as many acquaintances on the street than residents of comparable but more heavily trafficked streets. On a busy street, casual conversation with neighbors is unpleasant, if not impossible. As a result, people on the noisy street made fewer friends. In fact, they described it as "a lonely place to live" (Appleyard and Lintell, 1973).

WHAT CAN WE DO ABOUT IT?

As we have seen, noise deafens us, stresses us, impedes intellectual performance, and reduces our sense of fellowship and community. What can we do about it? Unfortunately, little is being done to curtail the general noise level in our cities, neighborhoods, and homes. Indeed, many of us seem to welcome noise. One manufacturer found that people would not buy his newly designed, quieter vacuum cleaner. Because it didn't make a lot of noise, consumers assumed that it couldn't be doing a good job. And reducing noise represents a financial threat for many enterprises, from automobile manufacturers to bar owners. When informed of a study in which the eardrums of guinea pigs shriveled up after exposure to loud rock music, a club

owner replied, "Should a major increase in guinea-pig attendance occur at my place, we'll certainly bear their comfort in mind" (Dempsey, 1975).

On several important fronts, however, progress is being made toward reducing the harmful effects of noise. In industry, federal regulation has been imposed on the level of noise to which workers can be exposed. Precautions, from required ear protectors to screening programs for susceptibility to hearing impairment, have been instituted. There has also been recognition of the hazards for those living near airports. The California Supreme Court has awarded compensation to a group of people living in the pathway of jets landing at the Los Angeles airport, for mental and emotional distress as well as for lowering of property values. In the eyes of the law, noise is beginning to be acknowledged as a threat to people's well-being. As a result, employers, transit authorities, and other noise producers may become a bit more careful about all the noise they are making.

SUMMARY

- *1 Noise* (loud, annoying sounds) can damage hearing if it is sufficiently loud or if the exposure is over a long period.
- *2* Noise can be damaging to emotional health by being stressful, especially if the noise is unpredictable and comes from sources over which we have no control.
- *3* Long-term exposure to noise can also have adverse effects on intellectual abilities, even if one is adapted to the noise.
- *4* Studies indicate that environmental noise can reduce our sense of fellowship and community by distracting us from helping others and by preventing us from forming friendships.
- *5* Although in many ways environmental noise continues unabated, efforts are being made in the workplace and in other areas to reduce harmful noise.

LEARNING

From teaching animals new tricks to teaching people new skills, most of what we know and what we can do results from learning.

CHAPTER *5*

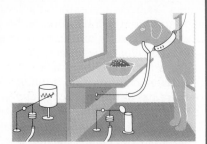

CLASSICAL CONDITIONING

Pavlov's discovery
Classical conditioning in humans
Principles of classical conditioning

In classical conditioning, involuntary responses—reflexes, fears, and even attitudes—become linked to particular objects and events.

OPERANT CONDITIONING

Shaping behavior
Reinforcement
Schedules of reinforcement
Punishment

In operant conditioning, our behavior is shaped by the reinforcements and punishments that we receive.

COGNITIVE LEARNING

Learning cognitive maps
Learning by observation
Learning cognitive skills

We learn not only responses but also knowledge and skills, such as mental "maps" of our environment and skills for solving problems.

PSYCHOLOGICAL ISSUE
BEHAVIOR CONTROL

The principles of learning can be used to change people's behavior.

BOXES

1 Learning to be superstitious
2 My teacher, the computer
3 Training your heart
4 Laughing while you learn

Is this something like your typical day? You walk or ride or drive to school. You go to the correct rooms for your classes, and you make your way to the library almost without thinking. There, you read a book effortlessly. On your way to the student union you see someone you know and say, "Hi, Sue!" When you get home, you make yourself a snack and do some studying. Later, you play cards with some friends.

How is it that you can do all these things? When you were much younger, you couldn't do any of them. Gradually, you've come to be able to do more and more. The basic process underlying all of these changes (from not being able to do something to being able to) is called *learning*. Learning is defined in psychology as a relatively permanent change in behavior or knowledge as a result of experience or practice (Wingfield, 1979). Because so much of our behavior is learned—and because this simple fact has so many implications—learning has long been the cornerstone of American psychology.

In this chapter and the next, we will deal with learning and with the related process of memory. To be able to say "Hi, Sue!" you must have learned Sue's name in the first place and you must have been able to remember it over some period of time. To be able to play cards, you must have learned the rules of the card game and how to keep track of the cards play by play. And to do well in classes you need to learn and remember course material. The processes of learning and memory are thus closely interrelated. Each has its own distinctive issues and problems, however, so we will take them up in separate chapters.

Before beginning our discussion of learning, we should point out that not *all* of our behavior is learned—some animal and human behaviors are inborn. Reflexes and instincts are examples of inborn behaviors. As noted in Chapter 2, *reflexes* are automatic responses (such as blinking at a flashing light) that do not have to be learned at all. *Instincts* are more complex fixed patterns of behavior that are exhibited by all members of a species. Instinctive behaviors are found in many animals, particularly birds, insects, and fish. For example, mother birds build nests, lay eggs, find food, and return to their nest without ever having "learned" to do so. Behaviors such as these are instinctive because they meet three conditions: (1) all members of the species (of the appropriate age and sex) exhibit them; (2) they are not learned; and (3) they are not mere reflexes (simple automatic responses to specific stimuli). The term *instinct* is sometimes used incorrectly in referring to human behaviors. We may talk about the "maternal instinct" of a new mother or of the "killer instinct" of a mass murderer. But when we do so we are confusing behaviors that may be emotionally involving or impulsive with those that are in fact instinctive. In reality, the concept of instinctive behavior appears to have little relevance for higher animals, especially humans. There is such a wide variation in human maternal behavior, for example, that it cannot be called instinctive.

Our biological heritage also determines to a large extent what we can and cannot learn. For one thing, our physical and mental capacities limit the behaviors we can learn and perform. No matter how much they practice, birds will not learn to speak (although some birds can imitate speech sounds), and people will never learn to fly. In addition, organisms of particular species seem to be biologically *prepared* to learn certain behaviors—particularly actions that help them to survive. Rats, for example, seem to learn certain kinds of responses to danger (such as running away rather than fighting) and it is difficult to teach them other kinds of responses for avoiding danger (Bolles, 1970). Human beings, too, may be biologically prepared to learn some things more easily than others. Take our fears, for example. We are not born with our fears; we learn to be fearful of specific things as a result of both cultural precepts and our own experience. But researchers have speculated that people are biologically prepared to learn to fear certain naturally occurring phenomena (such as fire and insects) more readily than manmade objects (such as cars or guns) (Seligman, 1972). Human beings also seem biologically prepared to learn language (a topic we will return to in Chapter 7). We will discuss the interplay of biology (or heredity) and learning more generally in Chapter 8, when we consider the nature of human development.

In this chapter we will concentrate on two basic forms of learning: *classical conditioning* and *operant conditioning*. Both of these learning processes involve learning to make new responses to particular *stimuli:* objects or events in the world. Some psychologists believe that these two processes can account for all the phenomena of learning. Other psychologists, however, feel that there is more to learning than making connections between stimuli and responses. Thus, in the last part of the chapter we will consider *cognitive learning*, an approach that emphasizes the fact that people learn not just behavioral responses but information about their environment.

CLASSICAL CONDITIONING

We have defined learning as a relatively permanent change in behavior or knowledge as the result of experience or practice. We typically assume that someone has "learned" something when his behavior changes in a

certain way. The term *conditioning* is used for the basic learning processes of classical and operant conditioning, because in each case we focus on the conditions under which particular responses are made. In both types of conditioning, particular stimuli set up the conditions for the occurrence of our *responses* (the behaviors we perform). *Classical conditioning* focuses on the way in which involuntary responses (such as heart rate, blood pressure, or aspects of emotion that we cannot control directly) may be linked to particular objects or events. *Operant conditioning* focuses on the way in which voluntary responses (such as walking, writing, or talking) may be linked to the rewards and punishments we receive for making them. We will consider classical conditioning in this section and operant conditioning in the next section.

Pavlov's discovery

The story of conditioning begins with the work of the Russian physiologist Ivan Pavlov (1849–1936). A Nobel Prize winner in physiology, Pavlov was experimenting on the salivary and digestive glands of animals—primarily dogs—to learn how digestion works. He found that animals would begin to salivate when food was placed in their mouth. This is a reflexive response that does not have to be learned. But Pavlov also discovered, to his surprise, that animals would begin to salivate as soon as the experimenter who had previously fed them entered the room. The same thing happens when you pick up your dog's feeding dish; it starts to respond as if it were time to eat. That is, stimuli that are merely *associated* with food produce the same response that the food does. Pavlov's curiosity was aroused by this phenomenon, and he began a long series of experiments on it. These experiments demonstrated the basic principles of what is now called classical conditioning.

Let us look at a typical experiment in Pavlov's laboratory to analyze classical conditioning. The animals were prepared so that their saliva flowed into a small glass funnel outside the cheek, allowing their salivation to be measured (see Figure 5.1). During the experiment the dog was placed in a

IVAN PETROWITCH PAWLOW.

Ivan Pavlov, who discovered the process of classical conditioning.

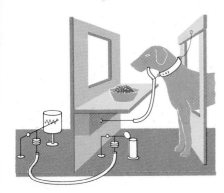

FIGURE 5.1

The laboratory apparatus used by Pavlov. The tube, connected to the salivary gland, collects any saliva secreted, and the number of drops is recorded on a revolving drum outside the chamber. An attendant can watch through a one-way mirror and deliver food by remote control.

harness while the experimenter sat on the other side of a partition, presenting stimuli to the dog and recording its responses. At this point in the experiment, before the conditioning begun, two things could be observed:

1 Food placed near the dog's mouth elicited salivation. This is a reflex; it occurs automatically. Since no conditioning had yet taken place, Pavlov called food the *unconditioned stimulus* and salivation the *unconditioned response*.

2 Other stimuli that were irrelevant to salivation would evoke other responses from the dog. A bell, for example, would cause the dog to prick up its ears and turn toward the sound but would not cause saliva to flow. At this point, the bell would be called a *neutral stimulus*.

The next part of the experiment was the conditioning phase, which took place over a period of several days. During conditioning, a bell was rung and a few seconds later a small amount of food was placed near the dog's mouth, causing it to salivate. A dog would never, under normal circumstances, salivate at the sound of a bell. Yet, after about thirty such presentations of the bell and food together, the bell alone was sufficient to elicit a strong flow of saliva. The bell was now called the *conditioned stimulus*, and the salivation was called the *conditioned response*. This is the essence of classical conditioning: The subject learns to attach an existing response (such as salivation) to a new stimulus (such as the bell). For a summary of the classical conditioning process, see Figure 5.2.

FIGURE 5.2

The process of classical conditioning.

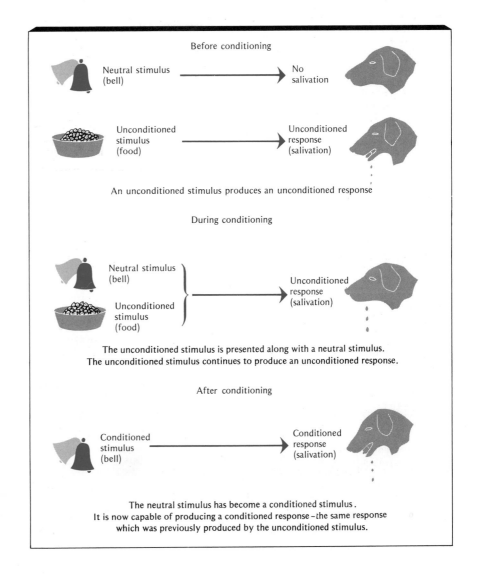

One way of looking at classical conditioning is to observe that the animal has learned an *association* between two events in the environment—that they "go together"—in this case, the bell and the food. Once this association has been made, the animal reacts to the bell in the same way it would react to the food. It is as if the animal hearing the bell anticipates that the food will soon arrive and therefore responds accordingly. Yet this is all accomplished at a physiological level, with apparently no thought involved.

Classical conditioning in humans

In humans, classical conditioning plays an important role in learning emotional responses, such as fears, attitudes, and feelings toward particular objects. Such classical conditioning is likely to occur when we are young, and as adults we may have many feelings and reactions that are leftovers of long-forgotten childhood experiences. Take the case of Jackie, who feels revulsion every time she hears the classical piece "Sabre Dance" by Khatchaturian. It's not that she has listened to the piece and judged it to be poor music; rather, she traces the bad feelings back to a childhood cross-country road trip during which she had a major case of car sickness. At that time, a popular radio commercial featured "Sabre Dance," and the 8-year-old Jackie came to associate the piece with nausea—an association that has persisted over the years.

Children can also learn certain fears through classical conditioning, as was demonstrated in one of the nastier experiments in the psychological literature. In this famous experiment, John B. Watson and Rosalie Rayner (1920) classically conditioned an 11-month-old boy named Albert to fear a variety of furry things. They began by putting a white rat in Albert's room. At first Albert was not afraid of the rat at all. But as he reached to touch it, the researchers struck a steel bar near Albert's head, creating a terrifyingly loud noise. They continued to do this six more times, until Albert showed a strong fear of the rat, crying and shrinking away whenever the rat was placed near him. What's more, Albert showed fearful reactions to a variety of other furry objects, including a rabbit, a Santa Claus mask, and even Dr. Watson's hair. Watson and Rayner speculated that such conditioned fears are likely to persist indefinitely, but they didn't study Albert long enough to know for sure (Harris, 1979). Still, if you should happen to see a man in his sixties who turns pale and quickly crosses the street whenever he sees someone wearing a fur coat, shout "Albert!" and see whether he answers.

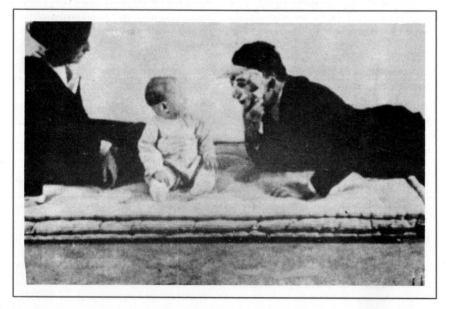

Little Albert was conditioned to fear a variety of furry things, including a Santa Claus mask. This photograph of Little Albert and John Watson is taken from a film made in 1919 of this famous demonstration of classical conditioning.

Although Albert's case is unique, the conditioning of fear to objects that are not themselves harmful is a common phenomenon. If you are the sort of person who feels shivers whenever you pass the street where your dentist's office is located, you know about such fears. Most such conditioned fears, although "irrational," are harmless enough. But when a person has strong irrational fears that interfere with his functioning, such as an intense fear of venturing out-of-doors, he is said to have a *phobia* (Chapter 13). Therapists have developed a technique for eliminating classically conditioned fears by reversing the conditioning process. In this technique, called *densensitization*, the person learns to link the feared object with a new response (such as relaxation) that replaces the fear (see Chapter 14).

Advertisers often make use of classical conditioning techniques in their attempts to produce positive attitudes toward their products. By repeatedly pairing images of people having a good time (the unconditioned stimulus) with a product (such as Coke), the advertiser attempts to make people associate the product with the good feelings (unconditioned response) produced by the unconditioned stimulus. If the technique works, simply drinking a Coke can make you feel good, even when the commercial is not playing in the background.

Classical conditioning helps explain the formation of attitudes that may seem quite irrational. When we take a look at our attitudes about certain people or groups, we are sometimes forced to say something like, "I don't know why I feel that way; I just do." This uncertainty may be due to the fact that the attitude does not have any logical or rational base at all. Instead, it may be based on repeated pairings of emotional stimuli with the attitude object. That fact that Dave dislikes people with red hair and freckles, for example, may stem from the childhood experience of having been beaten up several times by a freckled redhead. We will be returning to the topic of classical conditioning of attitudes when we get to Chapter 15.

Principles of classical conditioning

For a classically conditioned response to be learned, the unconditioned stimulus and the conditioned stimulus must be presented together repeatedly. This is referred to as the *acquisition* of the conditioned response. If the conditioned stimulus is repeatedly presented *without* the unconditioned stimulus, however, the response becomes weaker—less vigorous and less likely to occur. Thus, when Pavlov would ring his bell (the CS) over and over without giving his dogs food (the UCS), the dogs salivated less and less. Such weakening of a learned response is called *extinction*. In our example of Dave and freckled redheads, suppose that he goes to work in an office where several of the other employees have red hair and freckles and they all turn out to be nice people. Eventually, Dave's dislike for people with this characteristic is likely to disappear—it will be *extinguished*.

Although extinction involves a gradual decrease in the strength of a response, it is important to note that the response does not just fade away. Rather, there is an active "unlearning" of the conditioned response as the animal or person discovers that a given consequence (such as food) no longer follows the conditioned stimulus. Many responses are never completely extinguished, as Pavlov observed with his dogs. Sometimes after a conditioned response has been extinguished it will suddenly reappear. Pavlov called this phenomenon *spontaneous recovery* (see Figure 5.3). If Dave runs into a redhead who closely resembles the one who beat him up years earlier, he may experience a sudden return of his dislike for freckles and red hair.

The phenomenon of spontaneous recovery indicates that even though a learned response may have been suppressed, it is not totally gone. Traces remain in some form in the nervous system. The more strongly a response is learned, the more resistant it will be to total extinction.

Two other principles that are involved in classically conditioned responses are generalization and dis-

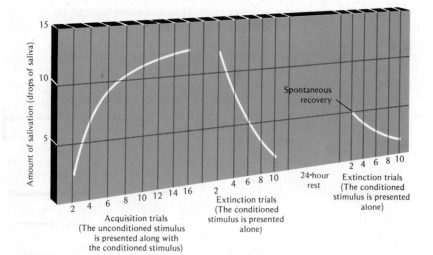

Amount of salivation (drops of saliva)

15

10

5

2 4 6 8 10 12 14 16
Acquisition trials
(The unconditioned stimulus
is presented along with
the conditioned stimulus)

2 4 6 8 10
Extinction trials
(The conditioned
stimulus is presented
alone)

24-hour
rest

Spontaneous
recovery

2 4 6 8 10
Extinction trials
(The conditioned
stimulus is presented
alone)

FIGURE 5.3

Over a series of trials, learned responses may gain strength when they are reinforced (acquisition), lose strength when they are not reinforced (extinction), or regain strength after a rest period (spontaneous recovery).

crimination. Pavlov found that a dog that was conditioned to salivate at the sound of a bell would also salivate—although to a lesser extent—at the sound of a tuning fork or a buzzer. And recall that Little Albert came to fear many other furry things besides rats. The fact that stimuli similar to the conditioned stimulus can produce a similar conditioned response is called *generalization*. Pavlov also found that he could teach his dogs to make distinctions between stimuli. For example, he taught a dog not to salivate at the sight of a piece of dyed bread, which it was never allowed to eat. However, the dog continued to salivate to the stimulus of undyed bread, which it *was* allowed to eat. Thus, the dog had learned to *discriminate* between the two stimuli. One way to think of discrimination is that it involves the conditioning of a response to one stimulus while extinguishing the response to a different stimulus.

OPERANT CONDITIONING

A classically conditioned response is an involuntary one—Pavlov's dogs had no control over their salivation, and we typically have no control over sweaty palms or blushing cheeks. But most human behavior is voluntary. We do some things because we feel they will benefit us, and we do other things in order to avoid having a bad experience. And we can change our behavior if we stop receiving the benefits or if we get punished. It is this capacity to change or shape behavior on the basis of its consequences that is explained by the principles of operant conditioning.

The central principle of operant conditioning is that animals will produce particular behaviors if they learn that those behaviors will be followed by *reinforcement* (some event that is rewarding to them) and that they will stop producing behaviors that they learn will be followed by *punishment* (some unpleasant event or consequence). If a baby discovers that by bringing a bottle to his mouth he will be rewarded by the pleasant taste of milk, he will proceed to bring the bottle to his mouth repeatedly. Or if a woman discovers that by turning the radio dial to a particular station she will hear the kind of music she likes, she will learn to tune in that station in the future. Thus, the baby or the woman "operates" on the environment in order to get a reward or to avoid a punishment—hence the term *operant conditioning*. As described in Box 1, even "superstitious" behaviors can be acquired through operant conditioning.

Most of the research on operant conditioning has been conducted with animals such as rats and pigeons. In his pioneering studies of operant conditioning in the 1930s, B. F. Skinner designed a chamber—popularly known as a *Skinner box*—with enough room to allow the ani-

GUIDED MISSILES—FOR THE BIRDS?

During World War II, B. F. Skinner came up with the idea of using pigeons to control guided missiles. Using operant conditioning techniques, the pigeons were taught to peck continuously for four or five minutes at the image of a target on a screen. The birds were then placed in the nose of a missile, harnessed in front of a similar screen. The idea was that when the missile was in flight, the pigeons would peck the moving image on the screen, which would produce corrective signals that would keep the missile on course. The missile was never used in actual warfare, however. A basic problem, Skinner later said, was that no one would take the idea seriously.

A psychologist records the responses of a pigeon in a Skinner box.

B.F. Skinner and friends.

BOX 1

LEARNING TO BE SUPERSTITIOUS

Old-time Brooklyn Dodger pitcher Alan Foster forgot his baseball shoes on a road trip and borrowed a pair from a teammate. That night he pitched a no-hitter, and later he bought the shoes from his friend. They became his most prized possession.

Rube Waddell, a Philadelphia Athletics pitching great of long ago, always had a hairpin in his pocket when he pitched. However, the hairpin was only powerful as long as he won. If he lost a game, he would look for another hairpin (which had to be found on the street), and he would not pitch until he found one (Gmelch, 1971).

Most people who act superstitiously defend their actions by saying that they don't really believe that an object causes good or bad luck, but they're just not taking any chances. So there are a great many "unsuperstitious" people who carry rabbit's feet, knock on wood, and wear a lucky shirt to a tough interview. Why do so many seemingly trivial acts continue to hold so much importance for so many individuals? It's simply a matter of operant conditioning, say the learning theorists.

In 1957, Morse and Skinner demonstrated that "superstitious" behavior can be produced in animals. They put hungry pigeons in small cages and fed them every so often. The animals were fed regardless of what they did in the cage. Yet most of the birds developed patterns of "superstitious" behavior. Whatever the pigeons happened to be doing when the food was delivered became a reinforced response and thus was likely to occur more often subsequently. Thus, one bird learned to make two or three counterclockwise turns about the cage trying to cause the food hopper to drop more food. Another bird learned to jerk its head repeatedly, and still another learned to make pecking or brushing movements toward the floor. In reality, of course, being fed was not contingent on any of these behaviors.

B. F. Skinner (1953) argues that humans resemble pigeons in forming superstitions. If you wear or do something just before a good experience (reinforcement), there is a chance that you will mistakenly associate the reward with your actions. This is what happened to Alan Foster with his lucky shoes and Rube Waddell with his hairpin.

All of this is based on the principles of operant conditioning. When the reward is *really* a consequence of your actions, your subsequent repetition of the reinforced response makes a good deal of sense. But even when a reward is only coincidental, you may still respond to it as if someone is shaping your behavior.

mal to move about and with devices to deliver food and water. The animal must perform specific responses in order to trip the mechanism that delivers reinforcement. For example, the box may contain a small bar or lever for a rat to press or a circular key for a pigeon to peck, in order to receive a food pellet. The animal's rate of responding (such as number of bar presses per minute) can then be recorded automatically. The Skinner box makes it possible to experiment with different types of reinforcement under highly controlled conditions, and animals can be taught specific responses using operant conditioning principles.

Shaping behavior

The basic idea of operant conditioning is well known to animal trainers, who teach animals from parrots to whales to obey by selectively rewarding their behaviors. They can teach an animal a complex behavior through the process of *behavior shaping*. At first the trainers reward any response that is roughly similar to the desired behavior. Then, one step at a time, they reward responses that are progressively more like the desired response. For example, if you want to teach your dog to roll over, you reward her at first when she lies down. Then you reward her only for making rolling movements while lying down. When she finally rolls over, you reward her only for that behavior from then on. Through this method of *successive approximation*, partial behaviors are shaped in a sequence that eventually produces the desired behavior.

Although most of the research on operant conditioning has involved nonhuman animals, the same principles have been used to alter human behavior. The alteration of behavior through the systematic application of principles of learning is called *behavior modification*. In one experiment nursery-school teachers used a powerful reinforcement—their attention and praise—to increase the amount of time that 4-year-old children played with children of the opposite sex (Serbin, Tonick, and Sternglanz, 1977). When the teachers saw a boy and a girl playing together cooperatively, they commented approvingly, indicating the children's names and what they were doing. They would say, for example, "I like the tower John and Kathy are building." Such reinforcement was administered approximately every five minutes during a two-week experimental period. During this period, the rate of cross-sex cooperative play increased dramatically in each of the two classes in which the experiment was performed—from about 5 percent to 25 percent of the children's time.

After the experimental period, the teachers discontinued their reinforcement to see whether the new behaviors would be maintained without reward. They were not. The amount of cross-sex play declined to the same low level it had been at initially. In the absence of reinforcement, the new behavior was *extinguished*. In other cases, however, new responses may continue even after reinforcement is discontinued. In such instances, the person has discovered that the new behavior is rewarding in its own right.

Recent work on behavior modification has gone beyond the simple application of rewards and punishments and makes use of models, verbal instruction, and other aspects of cognitive learning that we will discuss later in this chapter. We will return to the topic of behavior modification, including the ethical issues that it poses about the control of human behavior, in the Psychological Issue that follows this chapter.

The ideas of generalization and discrimination between stimuli that we encountered in the case of classical conditioning are involved in operant conditioning as well. If you've learned to perform a response in one situation in which it has led to reward, you may generalize the response to similar situations. If you have learned, for example, that kicking a soft drink machine in a certain way often gets you a free drink, you may generalize the response and start kicking other food-dispensing machines.

Discrimination plays an especially important role in operant conditioning. Imagine the operant response of asking your father for money. In such a situation you want to be able to tell whether or not your father is in a good mood: A good mood signals reinforcement (money), while a bad mood signals nonreinforcement. In this example, your father's mood would be called a discriminative stimulus. A *discriminative stimulus* is one that becomes associated with the delivery of reinforcement because reinforcement is forthcoming in its presence if the appropriate response is made. In a Skinner box an animal can learn that bar pressing is reinforced with a food pellet only when a light is turned on. Under these conditions, the animal does very little bar pressing when the light is off but is quite active when the light is on. When a behavior such as bar pressing occurs consistently in the presence of a discriminative stimulus such as a light (but not in its absence), the behavior is said to be under *stimulus control*. Thus, if you were to ask your father for money only when he shows signs of being in a good mood, your behavior would be under stimulus control.

Reinforcement

A *reinforcement* is any event that strengthens the response it follows—that is, that increases the likelihood of that response occurring again. One of the most important challenges for anyone trying to teach something to an animal or a person is to figure out just what things are reinforcing to that individual. Some rewards seem to be naturally reinforcing, such as food, water, and affection; these are called *primary reinforcers*. Other events become reinforcing as a result of their association with primary reinforcers; these are called *secondary reinforcers*. Secondary reinforcers play a big part in shaping our behavior: Think of all the behaviors we engage in to earn awards, pats on the back, and grades. We have learned that the awards, pats, and grades are rewarding, because they tend to go along with other more basic rewards, such as affection and esteem.

One of the most important secondary reinforcers for human beings is money. Consider a dollar bill. To a

BARNABUS PERFORMS

Animal trainers can make use of operant conditioning to get animals to do remarkable things. Pierrel and Sherman (1963) taught their rat Barnabus to climb a spiral staircase, cross a narrow drawbridge, go up a ladder, pull a toy car over by a chain, get into the car and pedal it to a second ladder, climb this ladder, crawl through a tube, board an elevator, pull a chain to raise a flag, and lower himself back to the starting platform, where he would press a lever to get a food pellet. After he ate the pellet, he began the remarkable sequence of behavior all over again. In such a sequence, each behavior that is performed serves as the stimulus for the next one, with the delivery of food serving as the ultimate reward for the entire sequence.

Operant conditioning techniques are used to train animals to do things they might never do in their natural environment.

small child a dollar may not seem to be much of a reinforcement. It doesn't taste particularly good, it's not much fun to rub against, and the expression on George Washington's or (in Canada) Queen Elizabeth's face looks, if anything, rather forbidding. But dollar bills become reinforcers once we have learned that they can be exchanged for food, clothing, and other items that are primary reinforcers. Similarly, poker chips, which in themselves have little value, are highly reinforcing to gamblers, who know that they can cash in the chips for money—and that they can later exchange the money for whatever it is that they really find rewarding. Even monkeys can be taught new behaviors using poker chips as a reward if the monkeys have previously learned that the chips can later be exchanged for food (Wolfe, 1936).

Words—such as *yes* or *right*—can also serve as reinforcers because of their association with other rewards, such as a parent's affection or a teacher's approval. As we saw in the experiment with preschoolers, a teacher's comment was enough to reinforce cross-sex play.

Reinforcement can be either positive or negative. In *positive reinforcement,* a rewarding stimulus is presented after a response in order to strengthen the response. In *negative reinforcement,* a response is strengthened by the *removal* or avoidance of an unpleasant stimulus. If a father praises his child for dressing nicely, that is positive reinforcement. If he keeps nagging the child until she changes into nicer clothes, that is negative reinforcement.

Psychologists use both positive and negative reinforcement in studying learning in animals. A dog can learn to jump over a barrier in order to get food (positive reinforcement) or to avoid or escape an electric shock (negative reinforcement). In either case, the response of jumping over the barrier is strengthened.

Positive and negative reinforcers play a central part in our daily lives. We buy food that tastes good and that fills us. We read books by authors who have pleased us in the past. We avoid parking in places where we have received tickets. In each instance, we behave in a way that will produce rewards and avoid unpleasantness. Of course, people differ in what reinforces them. Some people enjoy horror movies, while others are repelled by them. Some people love spinach but would never touch an artichoke, while others have the opposite reaction. In Chapter 10, when we consider the psychology of motivation, we will examine further what is reinforcing for different people.

For reinforcement to be effective, it must be well timed. *Delayed reinforcement,* administered some time after the response, is less likely to be effective than more immediate reinforcement. If an animal receives food a long time after it has pressed a bar, it may never make a clear connection between the behavior and the consequence, so the behavior is not likely to be repeated. Humans are better able to tolerate delays because of our ability to think about the long-term consequences of a behavior. Thus, a student may study hard now in order to get a good grade in a few months. Even so, it is often frustrating, rather than rewarding, to have to wait for a reward that we think we have earned. If you tell me a joke and I laugh a minute later, your joke-telling behavior will probably not be reinforced at all. Some of these principles of reinforcement and its timing are now being incorporated into educational computer programs, as described in Box 2.

Schedules of reinforcement

If a learned response is no longer reinforced, the person or animal will eventually stop producing the response; at this point the response is said to be *extinguished.* Thus, if a rat in a Skinner box is no longer reinforced with food for pressing a bar, the bar pressing will eventually cease. And as noted earlier, when nursery-school teachers stopped reinforcing children for cross-sex play, the children went back to their previous behavior. Similarly, you will stop shopping at a store that gives you bad service and you will stop putting your money in a slot machine that never pays off.

The ease with which a response can be extinguished often depends on

BOX 2

MY TEACHER, THE COMPUTER

In a classroom with 30 students, a teacher cannot carefully monitor each child's abilities and give consistent and immediate rewards for progress. To remedy this situation. B. F. Skinner (1958) suggested the use of "teaching machines" that would relate information, pose a question about it, and give immediate feedback and reinforcement for correct answers. With the explosion of computer technology, Skinner's notion of widespread use of teaching machines is becoming a reality. In the mid-1980s, millions of schoolchildren are learning from computers in the classroom.

As Skinner foresaw, there are many ways in which computers can enhance learning. Richard Atkinson (1974) has used *computer-aided instruction* (CAI) with great success to help children in the early school years learn to read. His system makes use of a typewriter keyboard, audio earphones, and a video display. The following is an example of an exercise in word recall:

Thus, the child gets immediate feedback from the computer and is rewarded for correct answers. In addition to typing a "+" for a correct answer, every so often the program will give an audio or visual feedback message, from a simple "great" or "you're doing brilliantly" to cheering, clapping, or bells ringing. The computer is ideally suited to *individualize* instruction. It has a complete response history for each student, and it uses this information to make trial-by-trial decisions as to which instruction to present next.

Today, learning programs are available for virtually every age level and topic, from arithmetic to zoology. And they seem to work. A careful review of over 50 evaluations of computer-based teaching in grades 6 through 12 showed that computer-based teaching raised students' final examination scores dramatically and that it also gave the students more positive attitudes toward their courses (Kulik, Ban-

gort, and Williams, 1983).

In many educational programs, children can learn skills while seemingly playing a game. In Alphabeam, for example, a preschooler shoots down letters or words to match those in his rocketship. In Math Grand Prix, a 7- to 10-year-old earns the right to move a car along the race track by solving math problems (Segal and Segal, 1983). Critics worry that with programs like these we may be turning our schools into videogame arcades. But many educators feel that learning should be fun and that if a child is reinforced by shooting down the right letters or words, he will learn from the experience.

	Teletypewriter display	Audio message (taped voice)
PROGRAM OUTPUT:		**Type crept.**
Student responds:	CREPT	
PROGRAM OUTPUT:	+	**That's fabulous!**

Learning programs are available for virtually every age level and subject.

its original *schedule of reinforcement,* the frequency or rate at which reinforcement occurs. Some of our behaviors are reinforced every time we produce them. When you press the elevator button, the elevator stops at your floor. When you go to a cafeteria for lunch, you get food. This is called *continuous reinforcement.* But it is at least as common for responses to be rewarded on some occasions and not on others. If you are familiar with a soft drink machine that works only intermittently, you will understand the concept of *partial reinforcement.*

When responses are first acquired, continuous reinforcement is most effective in producing a strong response. However, such responses are easily extinguished. But if a response is reinforced on a partial or intermittent schedule, it takes longer for the response to extinguish when reinforcement is withdrawn. Why is this the case? With partial reinforcement, the person or animal comes to learn that not every response will be reinforced. As a result, the individual may keep trying even when reinforcement is withheld, in the hope that sooner or later reinforcement will be provided.

For example, suppose you have a very reliable car. It has always started without trouble, and you've never had a problem with it. Then one morning it simply won't start. You try to start it several times, but nothing happens. In this case, you will probably give up and call for a mechanic. But suppose you have an old clunker that starts right up some days and is sluggish on others. Again, one morning you try to start it and nothing happens. Because you know that this car is erratic, you will probably spend a much longer time trying to start this car. With the reliable car your starting response is likely to extinguish rather quickly, but with the clunker extinction may take hours. In fact, you may keep returning to the car at various points during the day to see if "just this time" it might start.

Schedules of partial reinforcement can be set up in various ways. If you use partial reinforcement to train an animal, you could decide to schedule reinforcement so that it is delivered after a certain number of responses, such as after every third or every fifth

response. This is called a *ratio* schedule of reinforcement. On the other hand, you could schedule the reinforcement according to the clock, so that a certain amount of time must pass before a response is reinforced. When time is the main factor, the schedule is called an *interval* schedule.

For both ratio and interval schedules another distinction can be made. If either the ratio or the interval is constant, the schedule is referred to as *fixed;* if the ratio or interval is not constant and varies somewhat each time, the schedule is called *variable.* Thus, there are four basic schedules of reinforcement based on these two distinctions (see Figure 5.4).

Fixed-ratio schedules involve reinforcement after a fixed number of responses—after every tenth response, for example. In this case there would be nine nonreinforced responses followed by one reinforced response. If you had a job in which you were paid for every twenty pieces of work that you turned out, you would be working on a fixed-ratio schedule.

Variable-ratio schedules also involve reinforcement after a certain number of responses, but the number varies around some average. Slot machines reward gamblers on a variable-ratio schedule. The machine pays off after a certain number of responses—say, once every ten handle pulls, on the average—but the gambler does not know in advance which particular attempt will pay off. This schedule of reinforcement has proven to be highly effective in keeping gamblers at the machines.

With *fixed-interval schedules,* it is the first response after a set period of time that gets reinforced. The number of responses made during the interval does not matter. Animals such as rats do not learn to measure time in quite the same way as humans do; nevertheless, a rat in a Skinner box will increase the number of bar presses as the time for reinforcement draws near. Similarly, students are likely to respond to the fixed intervals at which examinations take place by cramming just before the exam, laying off right afterward, and starting to study again as the next exam approaches.

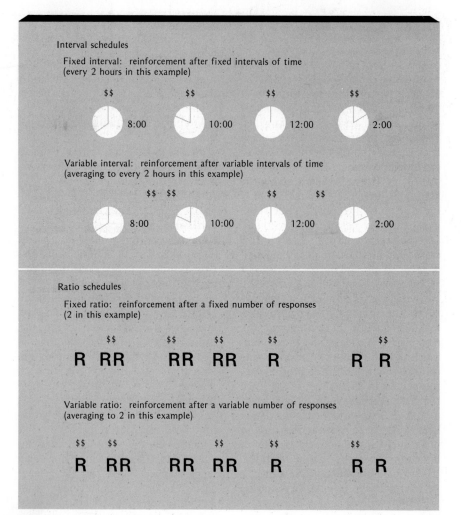

Interval schedules

Fixed interval: reinforcement after fixed intervals of time (every 2 hours in this example)

Variable interval: reinforcement after variable intervals of time (averaging to every 2 hours in this example)

Ratio schedules

Fixed ratio: reinforcement after a fixed number of responses (2 in this example)

Variable ratio: reinforcement after a variable number of responses (averaging to 2 in this example)

FIGURE 5.4

Schedules of reinforcement. Interval schedules are based on the time intervals between reinforcements; ratio schedules are based on the number of responses produced.

With *variable-interval schedules,* the only response reinforced is the first one after a time interval has passed, but the length of the interval varies around some average. An animal in a Skinner box might be rewarded after intervals averaging out to five minutes, with some intervals as short as a minute and some as long as fifteen minutes. Similarly, an instructor might have you on a variable-interval schedule for studying by giving surprise quizzes. The quizzes may come once a week, on the average, but some come a day after the last one, while others come as long as a week later. A variable-interval schedule typically produces a steadier rate of responding than a fixed-interval schedule, as when a student has to study regularly to be prepared for pop quizzes.

On the whole, both kinds of interval schedules result in lower response rates than those produced with ratio schedules. Both kinds of ratio schedules tend to produce high rates of responding. Pigeons in a Skinner box will peck the response key up to several hundred times a minute on ratio schedules. And why not? The more pecking, the more food; if the pigeon slows down, so does the reinforcement.

In real life it is difficult to find pure examples of these four basic schedules. The schedules of partial reinforcement that most often occur are *mixed* schedules that are combinations of ratio and interval, fixed and variable. You may be paid on the first and fifteenth days of every month (fixed interval), but pay raises are more likely to be determined by the number of responses—such as the number of encyclopedias you sell—which is more like a variable-ratio schedule.

LEARNING TO PERSEVERE

In his novel Walden Two, *B. F. Skinner (1948) envisioned the widespread use of operant conditioning techniques, which he called "cultural engineering." Partial reinforcement was used in Skinner's fictional community to develop frustration tolerance in children. Beginning at about age 6 months, babies were given certain toys designed to build perseverance. In order for the toy to be rewarding—for a music box to play a song or for a pattern of flashing lights to go off—the child had to give a certain response, such as pulling a ring. At first every pull of the ring was rewarded, but then the reward came after about every second response, every third, or even every tenth response, on a variable-ratio schedule. As Skinner pointed out, this method could be used to build up great perseverance "without encountering frustration or rage."*

Slot machines reward gamblers on a varia-ble-ratio schedule of reinforcement. This schedule proves to be very effective in keeping gamblers at the machines.

As we have seen, operant conditioning can be applied to responses that are under our voluntary control. Recent research has suggested, however, that even involuntary responses—such as our heart rate—may be altered by operant conditioning. This research is discussed in Box 3.

Punishment

So far a lot has been said about rewarding behavior that we wish to encourage and little has been said about the other side of things: punishing behavior that we wish to eliminate. With *punishment*, the undesired response is followed by an unpleasant event or consequence; as a result, the strength of the undesired response decreases. Punishment can be physical, such as a spanking, or psychological, such as a harsh word or a frown. Sometimes the most painful punishments involve depriving someone of expected rewards, such as sending a child to bed without his dinner or depriving him of a favorite television show.

Punishment is *not* the same as negative reinforcement. Whereas punishment is the application of an unpleasant stimulus after a response, with the goal of *decreasing* the response, negative reinforcement involves the removal of an unpleasant stimulus when the response occurs, with the goal of *increasing* the response. If a rat is shocked each time it presses a bar (a punishment), it will quickly learn to press the bar *less* often. If an electric shock is turned off each time the rat presses a bar (a negative reinforcement), it will learn to press the bar *more* often.

Punishments are often extremely effective in suppressing responses. Dogs and cats will starve to death rather than eat if they have been subjected to severe electric shock when eating. On a cheerier note, people who have been criticized by their friends for smoking in class are likely to avoid this behavior in the future—at least while their friends are watching.

But although punished responses are temporarily suppressed, they are not actually "unlearned." Once the punishment is discontinued, these behaviors—assuming they were rewarding to the person in the first place—are likely to reappear. Thus, once the friends stop mentioning smoking, the smokers may resume their annoying habit.

A basic problem with the use of punishment in teaching and learning is that a punishment tells people or animals only what they should *not* do, and not what they *should* do. Thus, someone who is trying to connect an electrical appliance and gets

BOX 3

TRAINING YOUR HEART

Research on operant conditioning makes it clear that, given an adequate reward, animals and humans can be trained to perform new behaviors. These behaviors can range from pressing levers to changing eating habits, but they all have one thing in common: they are voluntary actions. At first glance, operant conditioning seems inapplicable to "involuntary" behaviors, such as your heartbeat.

How could someone ever learn to change his own blood pressure or heart rate, regardless of how much he was rewarded for doing so? But think again.

In recent years, psychologists have found that people can in fact learn to control such involuntary responses as heart rate and blood pressure. Such control has been achieved through operant conditioning coupled with bio-

feedback techniques (see Chapter 2, Box 2), in which people are wired to monitoring devices that give them information about their heart rate or blood pressure. In a typical experiment, a subject watches a needle registering her blood pressure on a meter as she tries to raise or lower the pressure. Movement of the needle indicates that she is succeeding in her efforts. This is as clear an example of operant conditioning as rewarding a rat with food for learning to press a lever, even though it involves responses that are thought to be involuntary.

How do biofeedback subjects learn to regulate internal responses that most of us aren't even aware of? No one knows for sure, not even the subjects themselves. Some subjects report that they rely on visual images or thoughts to produce the physiological changes. A subject trying to lower his blood pressure, for example, might visualize a peaceful scene, such as lying on a beach. Other subjects say they "just did it"; they thought about the response being studied and concentrated on producing the requested change. It will take more research to determine just what these subjects really did to produce their results.

Most of these experiments have been done with healthy subjects. But researchers have begun to apply operant conditioning and biofeedback techniques to treat people with high blood pressure. Patients who have improved the most have used biofeedback in combination with other techniques, such as relaxation training (Katkin, Fitzgerald, and Shapiro, 1978). In such programs, patients may in fact be taught to control their hearts successfully, with great benefit to their health. This and other techniques of behavioral medicine will be discussed further in Chapter 12. An attractive feature of such programs, as Neal Miller (1983) has pointed out, is that instead of having doctors do something to patients, patients are taught to do something for themselves.

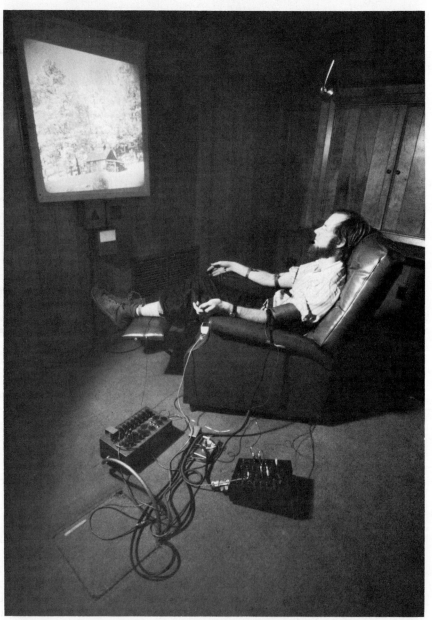

A subject tries to lower his blood pressure. If he succeeds, he is "rewarded" by the display of relaxing slides.

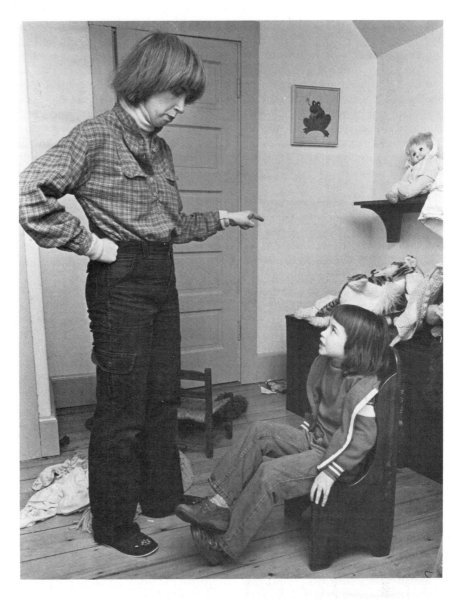

Punishment can sometimes be effective in child rearing, but its use involves certain problems. Some instances of "punishment" are actually rewarding to the child, because they provide her with the attention that she craves.

shocked in the process may learn that he's doing it wrong, but it won't teach him how to connect the appliance correctly. Similarly, a child who tries to get attention by telling wild stories may be punished by people who don't believe her, but that does not help her find other, more acceptable ways of getting attention. The person must still figure out what the correct or appropriate response is—or better yet, have someone else demonstrate it. Punishments can be effective, however, in compelling someone to switch from one response to a clearly available alternative response, which is then rewarded. For example, shocking a rat for taking a particular route in a maze may be a quick way of teaching it to take a different route

instead. Animal trainers may also use punishment as a way of signaling an animal to discontinue one response and to replace it with another one, which is then rewarded.

The use of punishment involves some other common problems. One problem is that in some instances a "punishment" actually turns out to be rewarding and, as a result, strengthens the response that it was intended to eliminate. If little Morris is ignored whenever he is being a good boy but is yelled at (supposedly a punishment) whenever he does something wrong, he may find that doing "bad" things is an effective way of getting the attention he craves. Another problem is that the person may come to associate the punishment not so much with the behavior that was punished as with the person administering the punishment. A worker may do her best to avoid a supervisor who frequently criticizes her, which in turn reduces the supervisor's opportunities to employ positive reinforcement. Still another problem is that punishment often gives rise to stress and anxiety, states that do not usually make for efficient learning (Kahneman, 1973).

Because of all these problems with punishment, psychologists much prefer to use reinforcement in altering behavior. They often recommend, for example, that parents make a point of rewarding a child's good behavior and simply ignoring the child's misbehavior.

COGNITIVE LEARNING

Classical and operant conditioning involve simple stimulus-response processes of learning—people or animals come to associate a particular behavioral response with a particular set of stimuli. When a hungry rat in a Skinner box sees a bar, it presses. When a student is asked to spell a word, he responds with the right spelling. These stimulus-response associations are believed to be made as a direct result of rewards and punishments. For a long time, most psychologists viewed learning in such stimulus-response terms. They gave relatively little attention to the ways in which people learn more complex stores of information about the world. One reason for the emphasis on stimulus-response learning is that most of the research on learning was conducted with animals such as rats and pigeons, whose capacity to think is far less developed than people's. Another reason for this emphasis was the insistence of psychologists of the behaviorist school (Chapter 1, Box 1), such as John B. Watson and B. F. Skinner, that only observable responses can be studied scientifically. Because we can't observe the knowledge that may be inside people's heads, these psychologists felt, it could not be seriously considered.

More recently, however, many psychologists have taken a more *cognitive* approach to learning, emphasizing the ways in which people acquire and organize information. The word *cognitive* comes from the Latin word meaning "to know," and that is what cognitive learning is all about—how people come to know about their world. In fact, people acquire, store, and organize information even when they are not rewarded for doing so. Psychologists studying cognitive learning are interested in exploring our mental representations of our environment—how we acquire and store facts, ideas, images, rules, and expectations.

Both classical and operant conditioning may in fact be looked at from a cognitive viewpoint. In classical conditioning, an animal may be seen as learning not so much as automatic response as an *expectation:* "That bell is a signal; it means that some food will be coming soon." Of course, a dog wouldn't put it quite that way, but some unspoken expectation may still be part of the process. In operant conditioning, the animal may be acquiring information about what actions lead to what effects in its environment. A rat may learn (once again putting words into an animal's mouth): "If I turn right, then left, and then left again, I'll get to the end of the maze, where the food usually is." Or a student may learn: "When I approach Professor Plum at the end of class, rather than before, when he's nervous, I'm more likely to get his full attention." From this point of view, what behaviorists view as the learning of stimulus-response associations is reformulated as the acquisition and application of information about the world.

In the remainder of this chapter we will consider three types of cognitive learning: the learning of cognitive maps, learning by observation, and learning cognitive skills. In each case, we will be looking at particular types of mental representations and how they are acquired. Recent research on cognitive learning has also become closely linked with the field of educational psychology, as psychologists try to determine the most effective ways of presenting material to chil-

LEARNING WITH WORDS

An additional way in which human beings learn—sometimes overlooked because it is so obvious—is with words. As one college professor put it, "If I want to teach a student how to focus the slide projector, I might reward any move he makes toward the focusing dial, but that would take quite a while. A better way would be to demonstrate how to do it. But still another way is to ask him to fiddle with the dial on the left side of the machine." Words can provide powerful and efficient ways of teaching and learning new behaviors.

dren and adults in school settings. One example of such a link is discussed in Box 4.

Learning cognitive maps

Although cognitive learning is largely concerned with the acquisition of information by humans, it was first studied in the animal laboratory. In many experiments on learning, rats have been taught to run mazes. Rats are able maze-learners, quite capable of learning to run along a path that will take them toward some reward or away from some punishment. It had been assumed that this learning is the result of a series of stimulus-response associations—that the rat learns to associate a left or right turn with each choice point in the maze. For example, a rat might learn to associate a right turn with the first corner, a left turn with the first door, another left turn with the second door, and so on until it reaches the food, which serves as a reward for this chain of responses.

But a psychologist named Edward Tolman challenged this associationistic view. Tolman suspected that a series of stimulus-response associations was not the primary basis for the rats' learning. First, Tolman (1938) noticed that even rats who were not rein-

forced with food seemed to learn their way around the mazes quite well. One group of rats was allowed to wander freely in mazes without reward each day for a week and a half. When a reward was offered to these animals, they were able to travel quite directly through the maze to the food—just as quickly as rats who had been trained for the same period of time *with* reinforcement. This suggested that reinforcement is not really necessary for learning. Learning of this sort, that occurs without any direct reinforcement or intent to learn, is called *latent learning.*

Second, Tolman and his associates (1946) noted that in maze-learning rats learned the location of places rather than a sequence of turns. After they had learned a route to food or to safety, the rats could find their way to this location even when they were placed in different starting points and so had to alter the left-right sequence they had originally learned. Other researchers have shown that rats whose learned routes to a goal were blocked were able to switch to a different route to the goal (Gleitman, 1963). Thus the rats didn't seem to be simply memorizing a series of turns to reach the goal; instead, they appeared to be making use of a kind of "mental map."

A rat running a maze develops a cognitive map or mental representation of the maze.

BOX 4

LAUGHING WHILE YOU LEARN

Cookie Monster and Grover are illustrating the concepts of "near" and "far," with Grover repeatedly running away from Cookie Monster ("That's far") and then returning ("Now he's near"). Grover eventually falls over a cliff because he has gone so far.

All of a sudden the scene switches to Oscar the Grouch in his garbage can, slinging humorous insults at a confused Big Bird who misinterprets everything Oscar says.

In a flash the scene changes again. This time to Bert and Ernie, who are finding all the things they have in their household that begin with the letter P. Bert can't understand why Ernie has brought out the scissors but Ernie explains it is a pair of scissors.

This segment of *Sesame Street*, with its abundant humor and rapid shifting of scenes, is characteristic of much of children's educational television programming. The result is highly entertaining, and it helps to motivate children to keep tuning in. But some critics wonder whether the rapid-fire shifts from one scene to another, while they may keep children laughing, might also interfere with their learning by reducing their attention span and discouraging reflective thought.

Does rapidly paced humor help or hinder the learning process? Dolf Zillmann and his coworkers (1980) conducted a series of experiments to investigate this question. In one study, they showed kindergartners and first-graders brief educational films on such topics as stamp collecting and exotic plants. For some of the children, funny one-liners from *The Muppet Show* were spliced into each film; for the other children they were not. The researchers recorded how attentive the children were to the films and later asked the children questions about what they saw. It turned out that children viewing the humorous inserts not only paid more attention to the films but also learned more from the educational segments.

This research supports the intuitions of producers of educational television programs. Humorous inserts grab children's attention, and this attention carries over to whatever comes next. Moreover, fast-paced humor reinforces children for staying attentive to the screen. Thus, children may sometimes learn more from fast-paced humorous programs—when they are always on the lookout for what comes next—than programs where things move more slowly and seriously.

Among young children, for whom grabbing and maintaining attention can be a real challenge, even humor that is irrelevant to the topic (as in the Zillmann study) seems to facilitate learning. But among older children

and adults, who have longer attention spans, humor seems to aid learning only when it is relevant. Studies of college students have found that humor used to make a point increases learning, but forced, unrelated humor makes the teacher seem less competent and actually decreases learning (Bryant, Comisky, and Zillmann, 1979). Thus, if your geology professor were to intersperse his lecture with comments like "That's gneiss, but don't take it for granite," you might laugh some and learn more at the same time. If, instead, he were to tell nongeological knock-knock jokes every few minutes, he might garner a few laughs, but at the expense of your learning.

Tolman believed that rat maze-learning was based on latent learning rather than on a series of rewarded associations. He thought this learning was possible because in walking through the mazes the rats formed *cognitive maps* of their environments. A cognitive map is a mental representation of the relationships between locations, just as a real map provides a visual representation of these relationships. Human beings also form cognitive maps of their physical environments. If you are driving to school in the morning and encounter a road block you can probably find a new route to campus even if you have never traveled the alternative route before. This is because you have formed a cognitive map of the area your school is situated in.

Some researchers view cognitive maps as *mental images*—almost like pictures inside our head that we can mentally examine (Kosslyn, 1983). We can scan these mental images and even rotate them in our heads (Shepard and Metzler, 1971). Of course, we do not have actual pictures of places inside our brains. But we do seem to have a form of mental representation of the spatial relationships between locations—the mental images—that are analogous to pictures that we can call to mind and examine. In one study, University of Michigan students were asked to estimate the distance between specific pairs of landmarks on campus. The researchers found the greater the actual distance between the landmarks, the longer it took students to make their estimates—suggesting that they were scanning their mental representations of the campus (Baum and Jonides, 1979).

Despite the fact that we are able to form such cognitive maps of our surroundings, it is not always easy to do so. Our environments, such as the cities we live in, are often very large and complex, and the amount of spatial information we can process at one time is limited (Anderson, 1980). As children grow older, their cognitive maps seem to progress from being *route maps* to being *survey maps*. Younger children typically rely on route maps—that is, their understanding of the sequence in which particular landmarks occur on their

accustomed routes: "First we pass the gas station, then the toy store, then the church, and then we get to Linda's house." But such route maps are more like lists than two-dimensional maps, and the child has little notion of which direction Linda's house is from his own. By the time children are about 11 or 12 they are able to develop the more "adult" sort of survey maps—mental pictures that represent the relationships between locations, much as real maps represent these relationships on paper (Siegel, Kirasic, and Kail, 1978).

Even adults seem to go through the same sequence from route maps to survey maps, as they learn to get about in a new environment. In one study, researchers investigated secretaries' knowledge of the Rand Building, a large mazelike building in Santa Monica, California (Thorndyke and Hayes-Roth, 1982). The secretaries who came to work at the Rand Building quickly learned to find their way from one specific place to another, such as from their offices to the photocopy room or from their offices to the lunchroom. But secretaries had to have ten years' experience, on the average, before they were capable of making such survey-map determinations as the direction from the lunchroom to the photocopy room.

Learning by observation

Especially among human beings, a great deal of learning takes place without any direct reward or punishment, simply as a result of our observing the behavior of other people. For example, a boy who is beginning nursery school may learn how to build block castles simply by watching the activity of the older children in the class. A college student who is beginning a part-time job at an ice cream parlor will learn how to make milkshakes by following the example of her more experienced coworkers. This important process of learning is called *learning by observation*, or *modeling*.

Studies of modeling point up the distinction between *learning* and *performance* (the actual production of a learned response). A person who listens to a popular music station regularly may never sing along while she listens, yet she may be acquiring a great deal of information. This fact is finally revealed when she is asked by a friend for the lyrics to "Yesterday" and she discovers that she knows them all. The learning had clearly taken place, in the form of the person's mental representation of the lyrics, even though it had not previously been performed. Studies have shown that children can quietly watch adults or other children engage in a novel sequence of actions and then some time later—especially if they expect to be rewarded for doing so—will repeat the sequence themselves (Bandura, 1977).

In observational learning, two different sorts of things may be learned. One is a specific set of behaviors, such as a new dance step or the procedure for answering a phone in an office. Although such behaviors can also be taught by verbal instruction or with a training manual, a good model is often worth a thousand words. When Elton McNeil was learning to fly, the instructor (often in despair) would execute the maneuver and have McNeil follow him by doing what he did, rather than trying to explain. The second sort of thing that is

learned by observation is whether or not a particular behavior is likely to be rewarded. If a student observes that when his classmates ask questions they are regarded approvingly by the instructor, he will be more likely to follow suit himself. If, on the other hand, he observes that the questioners are treated brusquely, he will learn to avoid making the same mistake. Similarly, Albert Bandura (1973) found that if a child observes an adult being rewarded for performing aggressive responses—such as hitting an inflatable doll with a rubber mallet—the child is likely to engage in similar behavior herself when given the opportunity (see the Psychological Issue on violence that follows Chapter 10). Thus, we learn by observation not only how to behave in a novel way but also about what behaviors can be expected to lead to particular consequences.

What we learn by observation clearly goes beyond simple stimulus-response associations to a more complex set of information about our environment. Many of our habits, values, skills, and beliefs are the products of observing others. For example, adolescents are more likely to drink

SLEEP LEARNING: DA OR NYET?

Can people learn new information by having recorded material played to them while they are asleep? American psychologists have generally answered the question with a "no," and Russian psychologists have generally answered with a "yes." Are Russians better sleep learners than Americans? Almost certainly not. But researchers in the two countries have studied sleep learning under different conditions. The Americans typically make use of one-session studies and meaningless materials, and they concentrate on the deepest stages of sleep. The Russian researchers typically make use of extended sessions and meaningful materials, and they include the lighter stages of sleep in their research (Aarons, 1976).

We learn many behaviors by observing other people, or modeling.

We learn various skills through a series of stages, during which the skill becomes more and more practiced and automatic.

alcohol if they observe their parents and friends drinking (Newcomb, Huba, and Bentler, 1983), and are more likely to start smoking if they have older brothers or sisters who smoke (McCaul et al., 1982). We will return to learning by observation at several points in this book: in connection with the learning of aggressive behavior (in the Psychological Issue following Chapter 10), the shaping of personality (Chapter 11), and the development of sex roles (Chapter 16).

Learning cognitive skills

Let's say that you want to learn to program a computer. Or to prove some geometry theorems. Or to do well at word-analogy problems. In each of these cases skilled performance is not so much a matter of knowing specific pieces of information as knowing how to approach the task. Such approaches or procedures useful in solving a particular set of problems are called *cognitive skills.* As Lee Shulman (1982) has pointed out, "We all can recall the frustration

of staring at a geometry theorem we have been assigned to prove, believing we know all that is needed, and yet being stymied about where to begin and how to proceed." In recent years, researchers have begun to look into the ways in which cognitive skills—such as knowing how to approach a geometry problem—are learned.

Just as when we learn a motor skill, such as riding a bicycle or playing the piano, we learn cognitive skills through a series of stages, during which the skill becomes more and more practiced and automatic. As outlined by John Anderson (1980), there are three basic stages of skill learning:

1 Cognitive stage. In this stage, we learn a set of step-by-step rules to be followed in performing the skill. In the case of a motor skill such as shifting gears in a car, we memorize the gear locations and the rules for shifting gears. Similarly, a novice computer programmer may learn a set of rules to be followed in writing a program. But this knowledge remains quite inadequate for performing the skill quickly or easily. We can perform the skill only laboriously, by consciously going through the rules in our mind and then trying to follow them. If someone is at this stage of learning how to drive a car, you ride with him at your own peril.

2 Associative stage. In this stage our initial errors in understanding the relevant facts and rules are gradually eliminated. As we continue to practice the skill, the mental connections required for successful performance are strengthened. John Anderson reports on the associative stage of his own learning to drive a stick-shift: "I slowly learned to coordinate the release of the clutch in first gear with the application of gas in order not to kill the engine . . . [and] I no longer had to sit for a few seconds trying to remember how to get from second gear to first" (page 226).

3 Autonomous stage. In this stage the procedure becomes more and more automatic and rapid, until it becomes almost second nature to us. In fact, once a person gets to the third stage of a skill, he may no longer be able to explain the facts and rules learned in the cognitive stage. A pianist may not be able to tell you how she goes about the fingering of an arpeggio; she just does it. The same holds true for cognitive skills, such as proving theorems or programming computers.

Once we have learned to perform a skill at the autonomous stage, it requires less of our attention. Now we can perform the skill without interfering with other tasks that we may be performing at the same time. In one study, subjects practiced performing two tasks at the same time: reading a text for comprehension, and copying words dictated by the experimenter. At first these tasks were difficult to do simultaneously, and subjects read much more slowly than their normal rate. But after six weeks of practice, subjects were able to copy words while reading at their normal speed, without any loss in comprehension. At this point, when the copying task had become autonomous, reading while copying was no more difficult than, say, reading while walking (Spelke, Hirst, and Neisser, 1976).

To become expert in most domains, it is important to achieve this autonomous stage of skill. If a tennis player becomes autonomous in the basic strokes, she can then devote more attention to the fine points of strategy. Similarly, if a computer programmer becomes autonomous in performing certain basic routines, she can then devote more attention to unexpected problems that may arise. In many domains, however, it may take a long time to master the basic skills at a fully autonomous level. In such fields as music, chess playing, and physics, mastery may require concentrated practice for many years.

One important element in learning cognitive skills, as in learning motor skills, is receiving *feedback* as to whether one has performed the skill correctly and, if not, how one is in error. A computer programmer, for example, may be able to run her program and find out immediately whether the program works—and, if not, where it fails. For the feedback to be useful it should come rapidly—while the person clearly remembers the thoughts and actions he has performed. It is also important for the person to try out the skill again soon after the feedback, while the details are still fresh in mind (Anderson, 1980).

We will discuss cognitive skills in greater detail in the next two chapters, as we explore several areas in which particular cognitive skills are necessary: memory, language, problem solving, and intelligence.

The more we learn about the process of learning, both the basic processes of conditioning and the more complex processes of cognitive learning, the better able we may be to apply this knowledge in teaching people more effective ways of behaving. At the same time, such applications raise difficult questions about the control of human behavior. We turn to both the potentials and dangers of behavior control in the Psychological Issue that follows this chapter.

SUMMARY

- **1** *Learning* is a relatively permanent change in behavior or knowledge as a result of experience or practice. Some behaviors, such as reflexes and instincts, are inborn rather than learned, and what we can learn depends on our inherited capacities or what we are biologically *prepared* for.

Classical conditioning

- **2** In *classical conditioning,* a neutral stimulus is paired with an *unconditioned stimulus* that elicits an *unconditioned response.* After repeated pairings, the neutral stimulus itself comes to elicit the response, and it is then called a *conditioned stimulus* and the response is called a *conditioned response.*
- **3** Classical conditioning involves making an association between two events in the environment and tying them to an involuntary response. In humans, classical conditioning is often involved in learning emotional responses and attitudes.
- **4** *Extinction* is the weakening of a learned response. In classical conditioning, extinction is accomplished by repeatedly presenting the

conditioned stimulus without the unconditioned stimulus. Sometimes an extinguished response suddenly reappears; this is called *spontaneous recovery.*

• **5** *Generalization* is responding in the same way to more than one stimulus with similar characteristics. *Discrimination* involves responding to one stimulus while not responding to a very similar stimulus.

Operant conditioning

• **6** In *operant conditioning,* an operant response (one that operates on the environment to produce some effect) that is rewarded is more likely to be repeated; a response that is not rewarded or that is punished is not likely to be repeated.

• **7** The *Skinner box* is a chamber in which animals can be taught new behaviors using operant conditioning techniques, under carefully controlled conditions.

• **8** Skinner has suggested that superstitious behavior occurs when a reinforcement is accidently paired with a particular response. The subject will view the desired event as being contingent on his performing the "reinforced" behavior even when it isn't.

• **9** *Shaping behavior* involves rewarding responses that are closer and closer to the desired behavior until the desired behavior is produced. The systematic use of rewards and punishments to achieve alteration in behavior is called *behavior modification.*

• **10** The principles of extinction, generalization, and discrimination all apply to operant conditioning, as well as to classical conditioning.

• **11** A *discriminative stimulus* is one that becomes associated with the delivery of reinforcement because reinforcement occurs in its presence. When a behavior consistently occurs only in the presence of a discriminative stimulus, the behavior is said to be under *stimulus control.*

• **12** A *reinforcement* is any event following a response that increases the likelihood of that response occurring again. Naturally reinforcing rewards are called *primary reinforc-*

ers; events that become reinforcing through their association with primary reinforcers are called *secondary reinforcers.*

• **13** In *positive reinforcement,* a reward is used to increase the frequency of a response. In *negative reinforcement,* an unpleasant stimulus is removed in order to increase the frequency of a response. For reinforcement to be effective, it must be well timed.

• **14** The principles of operant conditioning have been used to develop *computer-aided instruction* (CAI) methods for use in the classroom.

• **15** The *schedule of reinforcement* influences the rate of response and resistance to extinction. In *continuous reinforcement* every response is rewarded. In *partial reinforcement,* responses are rewarded after a certain number have been emitted (*ratio* schedule) or after a certain amount of time has elapsed (*interval* schedule). Responses are more resistant to extinction when reinforced on a partial schedule. Ratio schedules produce higher and steadier rates of responding than interval schedules.

• **16** Using operant conditioning techniques and biofeedback, people can learn to alter such involuntary responses as heart rate and blood pressure.

• **17** *Punishment* is following an undesired behavior with an unpleasant event or consequence. Punishment can be effective in suppressing responses but it does not really eliminate them. Problems with using punishment include the possibility that the punishment may actually be rewarding, the association of the punishment with the person doing the punishing, and the creation of stress and anxiety.

Cognitive learning

• **18** Not all learning is of a stimulus-response, conditioned nature. *Cognitive* aspects of learning involve acquiring and organizing information about one's environment—making sense out of things rather than learning associations.

• **19** Cognitive learning can be seen in the formation of *cognitive maps* of our surroundings. Cognitive maps usually begin as route maps and progress to survey maps, with age or experience.

• **20** A great deal of learning comes from observing the behavior of others; this process is called *modeling*. In this type of learning, people can acquire new behaviors or they can learn what behaviors are likely to produce positive or negative consequences.

• **21** Cognitive learning requires certain *cognitive skills*, which must themselves be learned, much like motor skills. There are three basic stages to skill learning: the cognitive stage, the associative stage, and the autonomous stage.

KEY TERMS

behavior modification
classical conditioning
cognitive learning
cognitive maps
conditioned response
conditioned stimulus
continuous reinforcement
discrimination
discriminative stimulus
extinction
generalization
instincts
latent learning
learning
modeling
negative reinforcement
operant conditioning
partial reinforcement
primary reinforcer
punishment
reinforcement
schedules of reinforcement
secondary reinforcer
shaping of behavior
spontaneous recovery
stimulus control
unconditioned response
unconditioned stimulus

BEHAVIOR CONTROL

It's 1984, or sometime thereafter, and you're getting ready for work. You smile into the bathroom mirror and soothing strains of Brahms' "Eternal Love" fill the air. When the smiling stops, so does the music.

You greet your fellow workers with a cheerful "good morning," and they respond with warm handshakes and grins. Any other greeting, and they would ignore you.

Those are the rules.

The rest of the day, and month, and year, are governed by similar "rewards" and "non-rewards." Your behavior becomes nearly automatic. You are "happy." (Greenberg, 1976)

Even now that 1984 has come and gone, the issue of behavior control remains a pressing one. As we learn more and more about the conditions that shape people's behavior, we also become more capable—at least potentially—of *controlling* their behavior. In particular, the principles of operant conditioning have been espoused by B. F. Skinner (1971) and others as ways of changing people's behavior in positive ways, thereby making our society more productive, just, and humane. Many other social observers are frightened by this vision of utopia, as caricatured in the above description of 1984.

Scientific behavior control—often called *behavior modification*—can in fact have great practical benefits. By changing people's behavior—and helping them to change their *own* behavior—in desired ways, psychologists can do a great deal to alleviate human misery. But such behavior modification also raises serious issues about possible threats to individual freedom and autonomy.

A patient cashes in his tokens for purchases that he wishes to make at a hospital store.

BEHAVIOR MODIFICATION: FROM THE LABORATORY TO SOCIETY

Behavioral psychologists—especially those who focus on the principles of operant conditioning—began to move out of campus laboratories and into the larger world some 30 years ago. The first attempts to make practical use of learning principles were in the context of psychotherapy. As we will see in Chapter 14, many therapists make use of procedures based on principles of learning when they deal with problems ranging from shyness to alcoholism.

One innovation derived from behavioral theories is the *token economy*, which was first established as a way to encourage socially constructive activities among chronic psychotic patients in mental hospitals (Ayllon and Azrin, 1968). The token economy relies on the fact that people will often behave in ways that they know will lead to future rewards. Mental patients can be given tokens (such as poker chips) whenever they engage in desired activities, such as keeping clean. The patients can later exchange the tokens for things they want, such as cigarettes, a walk out-

Learning principles have been used to encourage wearing seat belts, seeing the dentist, and conserving energy.

side, or a chance to watch television. This technique has led to striking improvement in many patients, including some who were previously totally withdrawn. Similar token economies have been successful in improving the performance of "problem" children in school and in keeping juvenile delinquents out of trouble (Kazdin, 1982).

One problem with token economies is how to get people off them. For example, a juvenile delinquent cannot expect to continue receiving tokens for good behavior the rest of his life. Psychologists have tried various strategies to deal with this problem. In some instances they gradually phase out the tokens, moving from a continuous to an intermittent schedule of reinforcement, while at the same time encouraging clients to start reinforcing *themselves* for the desired behaviors (Kazdin, 1982).

Today behavior modification techniques are used not only in hospitals and schools but also in such diverse settings as business offices, restaurants, movie theaters, and parking lots. The techniques have been used to encourage such behaviors as wearing seat belts, taking children to the dentist, and conserving energy. For example:

- When people who were wearing seat belts as they entered a campus parking lot were given flyers that gave them a chance to win a prize (the reinforcement), the number of people using seat belts rose from 26 percent to 46 percent, and the percentage stayed high even when the flyers were no longer distributed (Geller, Paterson, and Talbott, 1982).
- After a medical screening of children at a health center, some parents were offered a choice of prizes if they sought out dental care for their children. Not surprisingly, these parents were more likely to contact a dentist than those not given this extra incentive (Reiss and Bailey, 1982). In a similar vein, when parents of

If people were wearing their seat belts when they entered this campus parking lot, they were given flyers that gave them a chance to win a prize.

handicapped children were offered prizes and lottery tickets for gains in their children's development, the children's scores on standardized tests improved markedly (Muir and Milan, 1982).

- When, during a hot summer, some of the residents of a community in New Jersey were given daily feedback on how much electricity they had consumed, the feedback proved to be effective in getting the residents to raise the settings on their thermostats to reduce air-conditioner use (Seligman and Darley, 1977). Feedback seemed to work by providing information about the consequences of particular behaviors and, when positive, by serving as a reinforcement that motivated people to keep up the good work.

Other behavior modifiers have made effective use of learning principles to encourage such activities as interracial interaction in schools (Hauserman, Waylen, and Behling, 1973), riding the bus rather than driving to work (Everett, Hayward,

and Meyers, 1974), and refraining from smoking in public places (Jason, 1979).

"What's new about all this?" you might ask. Certainly, public officials, business executives, merchandisers, teachers, and parents have always known that they could influence people's behavior by selectively rewarding them. That's what tax incentives, merit raises, give-away offers, and gold stars are all about. What *is* new about the approach of behavior modifiers, however, is that their efforts are more careful and systematic and are patterned specifically after techniques developed in laboratory research. In particular, psychologists who specialize in behavior modification place a heavy emphasis on careful measurement and evaluation of their programs. The result, they believe, is a technology of behavior change that will be more effective than those techniques used in the past. And this possibility that behavior control techniques will in fact become more and more effective is exactly what scares many other psychologists.

THE HUMANISTS VERSUS THE BEHAVIORISTS

Few people would deny that techniques of behavior modification can be used for laudable purposes, whether to help a severely retarded person learn language or to help a phobic person conquer incapacitating fears. But as behavior modification programs spread to "healthy" populations—schools, businesses, towns—some doubts began to be raised. Among the most vocal doubters have been the *humanistic psychologists*, who emphasize people's potential for self-determined growth and development.

The debate between the behaviorists and the humanists revolves around a central philosophical issue. The behaviorists emphasize control of our behavior by external forces—we act in ways that are dictated by the reinforcements and punishments of our environment. The humanists, in contrast, emphasize our internal control of our lives, our ability to make choices and judgments on our own. The behaviorists stress determinism—we are a product of the conditions that shape us; the humanists stress free will—we set our own terms, our own conditions in life.

In B. F. Skinner's view, the idea of "freedom" is actually a myth. In his book *Beyond Freedom and Dignity* (1971) Skinner argues that even without scientific behavior control, our behavior is entirely controlled by external forces. Whether we are stopping at a red light, buying a certain brand of toothpaste, studying for an exam, kissing our spouse, or feeding the cat, we are behaving in ways designed to gain rewards and avoid punishments. Behavioral techniques simply enable us to make use of such control more efficiently, and for socially desirable ends. Thus, Skinner talks of "designing a social environment in

which people treat each other well, keep the population size within reasonable bounds, learn to work productively, preserve and enhance the beauty of the world, and limit the use of energy and other resources." Now, who can argue with that?

Some of the humanistic psychologists can—and do. The fatal flaw of Skinner's approach, argues Carmi Harari, is that ultimately one person or group must decide what is desirable for other people. And that smacks of totalitarianism. "You either view people as innately good," Harari says, "or as wild, antisocial beings that need control. The aim of control is to suppress the human spirit" (Greenberg, 1976).

WHO DOES THE CONTROLLING?

The control of people's behavior seems to be a basic aspect of life in society. The basic moral issue, then, is not *whether* people's behavior will be controlled but rather by whom, by what specific means, and for what purposes. As Skinner himself writes, the techniques of behavior modification "can be used by a villain or a saint. There is nothing in methodology which determines the values governing its use" (1971, page 150).

Critics of behavior control sometimes maintain that it constitutes a set of tools used by powerful people to keep the powerless down. In token economies and other uses of behavior modification in mental hospitals and prisons, the controllers are the powerful authorities and the controlled are the powerless patients and inmates. Even though the authorities may have the best intentions, one may wonder whether their exercise of behavior control is justified. Recent court decisions have addressed this issue. In the case of *Wyatt v. Stickney*, for example, the court ruled that certain items that had been used as reinforcers in token economies

were in fact basic rights of the patients and therefore could not be withheld from them for not having enough tokens to "buy" them. In this and many other instances, including those involving the control of children by adults, we must ask the question: Who controls the controllers?

Another concern is that the techniques of behavior control will be in the hands of a scientific elite who will in effect become the decision makers for all of society. Behavioral psychologists stress, however, that they have not been keeping the techniques secret. To the contrary, they have been active in teaching behavior modification techniques to others who might be able to use them productively, including teachers and parents.

In one study, a group of seven "incorrigible" junior high school students were taught to use rewards such as smiles, praise, eye contact, and shows of interest to shape their *teachers'* behavior. During a five-week conditioning period, positive teacher-student contacts increased 400 percent while negative contacts dropped to zero. In the end, the teachers were happy because the students were learning, and the students were happy because they could control their relationship with the teachers (Gray, Graubard, and Rosenberg, 1974). As this example makes clear, techniques of behavior control can be used effectively by relatively powerless, as well as powerful, people.

Critics of behavior modification also protest that it turns people into machines whose behavior can be manipulated without their even realizing it. But, as Albert Bandura (1974) points out, this fear is largely unfounded. In general, people will not behave in a certain way just because they have been reinforced for this behavior in the past. Rather, a key element in behavior modification is that people *recognize* that a particular behavior will produce a desired reward and then change the way they act accordingly. In behav-

I*n Skinner's view, the idea of "freedom" is a myth.*

ioral approaches to psychotherapy, patients are themselves making the decision to be "controlled." The patient says to the therapist, in effect, "You teach me to stop smoking, or to stop eating so much, or to not be afraid of flying, and I'll not only go along with you, I'll pay you for it." In cases like these, one can argue that behavior modification is *increasing* people's freedom by helping to liberate them from confining habits or behaviors.

CONTROLLING YOUR OWN BEHAVIOR

The debate between free will and determinism may finally be resolved when we realize that people can also make use of behavioral techniques to control *themselves.* Indeed, helping people to change themselves in ways that they desire is now a major emphasis of work in the area of behavior modification.

Behavioral psychologists have had considerable success in teaching people techniques of self-modification. Such procedures are especially valuable in cases in which a particular behavior, such as buying and eating candy, may lead to immediate reinforcements (it tastes good) but brings long-term punishments (being overweight). In such cases, people can be taught to use *stimulus control* techniques. For example, an overweight person who knows that passing a candy store is likely to result in buying candy can control his behavior by avoiding candy stores or by passing them only after eating a big meal (Kazdin, 1975).

When people want to motivate themselves to perform tasks that are not immediately reinforcing, they can be taught to make use of *self-reinforcement.* For example, someone who is trying to learn to play a musical instrument but who finds it difficult to keep practicing might specify a reinforcement of 5 minutes of free time following each 15 minutes of continuous practice.

Rewards can be used to shape people's behavior in desired ways. Here, a company president pays off employees who were successful in losing weight.

After a while, she might increase the practice time required for reinforcement. In other cases, a person might promise himself a reward after completing a specified activity. If you keep your promise not to bite your nails, for example, you might reward yourself with a small present—or, better yet, a manicure (Morris and Charney, 1983).

The trick with such self-reinforcement procedures is that the reward must really be contingent on the desired behavior. If you decide to give yourself the reward *before* you've done the activity, the technique won't work. Psychologists have developed procedures to help train people to use self-reinforcement. In some cases, an external agent, such as a therapist or teacher, may at first reward a client or student for using self-reinforcement effectively. Once the basic technique is learned, the external reinforcements may no longer be necessary (Kazdin, 1975).

Carl Rogers, one of the most eminent of the humanistic psychologists, once put his doubts about external behavior control in the following terms: "The human being is a trustworthy organism, and has vast abilities to improve himself if exposed to the right attitudinal climate. The individual modifies his own behavior, rather than having someone else in control" (quoted

by Greenberg, 1976). And this principle would be endorsed by many behavioral psychologists, especially those who have been working on procedures for self-modification. By enabling people to select their own goals and helping them to achieve them, self-control techniques can actually increase people's individual freedom.

SUMMARY

- *1* Behavior modification refers to the use of learning techniques to alter people's behavior. One popular method of behavior modification is the *token economy.*
- *2* Behaviorists, who emphasize control of behavior by external forces, are in favor of careful and systematic behavior control. Humanistic psychologists, who emphasize internal control of one's life, find behavioral techniques to be dehumanizing and possibly totalitarian.
- *3* Behavior modification implies that someone will be controlling someone's else's behavior. *Who* does the controlling is a major issue.
- *4* Behavioral techniques can be used by individuals who want to change themselves in some way, and thus may in fact increase individual freedom.

MEMORY

Without memory we would live only in the present, without the ability to recall the past or to relate new experiences to our store of knowledge.

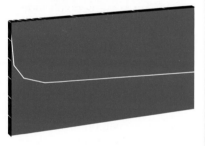

The man known to his doctors as N.A. lives in the perpetual present. Injured in 1960 when a fencing foil pierced his brain, he is virtually incapable of forming new memories. He has no memory of events since the time of the accident. What the rest of us remember for weeks, N.A. retains for only a few minutes.

"Don't dwell on the past," we are sometimes told. "Live in the present!" But the case of N.A. reminds us that without memory, we would live *only* in the present. Everything would, in effect, go in one ear and out the other. Although certain sorts of skill learning might still be possible—N.A. has steadily improved his performance on certain puzzles while consistently denying that he has ever seen them before—we would not be able to relate new experiences to our existing store of knowledge. Without memory, there would be no sense of identity, no history, no civilization.

In this chapter we will explore the workings of this remarkable aspect of our mental lives. First, we will consider two basic types of memory, short-term and long-term, and how they work together to register, store, and retrieve information. Then we will examine forgetting—why we can't always "find" the information that we want when we want it. After that, we will explore what is known about the brain mechanisms underlying memory; in the process, we will examine cases of serious memory disorders, in which these brain mechanisms go awry.

Finally, we will see how psychological research on memory provides some suggestions for more effective study habits and methods for improving memory. In the Psychological Issue that follows the chapter, we will delve into another application of research on memory: the accuracy—or inaccuracy—of eyewitness testimony in the courtroom.

SHORT-TERM AND LONG-TERM MEMORY

Almost a century ago, the pioneering American psychologist William James noted that there seem to be two distinct types of memory, one that is fleeting and another that appears to be permanent and indestructible. James wrote:

The stream of thought flows on, but most of its elements fall into the bottomless pit of oblivion. Of some, no element survives the instant of their passage. Of others, it is confined to a few moments, hours, or days. Others, again, leave vestiges which are indestructible, and by means of which they may be recalled as long as life endures. Can we explain these differences? (James, 1890)

James's remarks agree with everyday experience. Some thoughts—such as a telephone number we've just looked up—seem to be immediately present in our consciousness but do not stay there for very long. Other thoughts—such as the capital of Iowa—may be somewhere in our memory stores but we can't bring them to consciousness without an active search; such memories seem to be quite enduring, however.

Research conducted over the past several decades has suggested that James was right about the existence of two distinct sorts of memory—short-term and long-term. Short-term memory appears to hold a small amount of material at a time and to lose it quickly. Long-term memory holds a huge amount of material and loses it much more slowly—if at all. A model of memory that includes these two types has been proposed by Richard Atkinson and Richard Shiffrin (1968). If the model of memory that we are about to describe reminds

FIGURE 6.1
A model of memory.

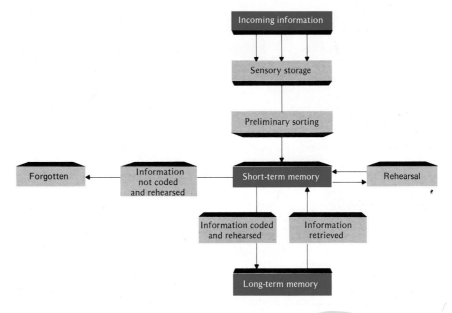

you of a computer program, it is no
accident (see Figure 6.1). In fact, this
model was developed as a direct analogy to the ways in which computers
register, store, and retrieve information.

Short-term memory

At any moment, thousands of pieces
of information impinge on our eyes,
ears, and other sense organs. Very little of this information actually
reaches our consciousness, however.
From all of the incoming sensory
stimulation, most is held in a stage of
sensory storage, lasts but a fraction of
a second, and then is lost (Sperling,
1960). Sensory storage holds information in "raw" form—the colors,
shapes, flashes of light, tones, and
other stimuli that impinge on our
sense organs but that have not yet
been sufficiently analyzed in our
brains to have any meaning. Only a
small fraction of the material in sensory storage goes into our short-term
memory, and it does so in a form that
has some meaning, such as words,
numbers, or images.

Short-term memory lasts much
longer than sensory storage. But it,
too, can hold only a limited amount
of information. For example, if you
recite a list of unrelated letters or
numbers to people and ask them to
repeat the list, they can usually handle lists of up to seven (or sometimes
eight or nine) items, but not much

more. Thus, short-term memory appears to have a capacity of about
seven items (Miller, 1956). That's one
reason why it makes sense for telephone numbers to have seven digits.
We can usually look up a number and
then keep it in mind long enough to
dial it.

Although short-term memory is
limited, its span can be increased by
organizing inputs into larger
"chunks." Short-term memory is not
limited to seven letters or numbers
but rather to about seven pieces of
information, which could be seven
numbers, seven words, or even seven
sentences. If we can manage to code a
set of letters or numbers into a single
piece of information (such as a word
or phrase), the amount of information
we can hold in short-term memory
will be increased. For example, try
reading the following list of letters to
a friend and ask him to repeat them
back to you:

U S A L S D F B I N F L

This string of letters is well over the
seven-item limit. But if your friend
memorizes them as well-known
chunks (USA, LSD, FBI, and NFL), the
list consists of only four items and
can easily be remembered.

Even though short-term memory
can be expanded in this way, its capacity remains limited, and the information is kept in mind for only a
short time. Sometimes the information doesn't stay in mind for as long

as we need it. You've surely had the experience of looking up a phone number, then being distracted before dialing and forgetting the number by the time you turn to dial. Or, when you are introduced to a lot of people, you may forget their names almost as fast as new names are introduced. In this instance, new information is arriving in short-term memory at a time when the storehouse is already full. In such a case the new information may bump the older information out of short-term memory before it can be readied for long-term storage.

In general, short-term memory can hold items fairly well for the first few seconds. After about 12 seconds, however, recall is poor, and after 20 seconds the information has disappeared entirely, unless we have kept repeating the material to ourselves (Peterson and Peterson, 1959). A phone number that we look up and dial is often forgotten by the time the call is answered. But a certain relatively small proportion of the material that enters short-term memory is not lost along the way. Instead, we manage to transfer this material to long-term memory for later reference. Thus, there are some telephone numbers that we once had to look up but that we now know without looking. These are the numbers that are important enough for us to have filed in our long-term memory store.

Long-term memory

Sherlock Holmes, the fictional detective who was, among other things, a master of memory, likened the brain to a "little empty attic" in which we store all the things we know. He emphasized that if we want to be able to find the information that we need, we must stock our brain attic with great care. What Holmes referred to as the "brain attic" is what today's psychologists call *long-term memory*, the process by which we can retain information for days, years, or even a lifetime. Recent research suggests that Holmes was right in recommending that we stock the attic carefully. Unless information is carefully coded and filed, it will become impossible for us to retrieve it when we need it—the task would be like trying to find a book in a large library where the books are arranged randomly and the card catalog is disorganized.

How, then, do we get information from short-term memory into long-term storage? There are two basic processes: *rehearsal* of the information (repeating it to yourself or keeping a picture of it in your mind) and *encoding* it (linking it to concepts and categories that you have already learned). Of these two processes, psychologists now believe that encoding the material in a meaningful way is the more important. In fact, rehearsal

SILVER
LETTUCE
TYPEWRITER
TOMATO
DESK
COPPER
CELERY
FILE CABINET
BRONZE
ZINC
BOOKCASE
CARROT

Long-term memory has been likened to a library card catalog. Access to our memories depends on how well we have set up our filing system.

may be important only insofar as it provides a better opportunity for meaningful encoding. Encoding is like filing things in a complicated, cross-referenced file system. The encoding process may either simplify or elaborate on the information to be stored (Bower, 1972). The process is analogous to labeling books, cross-listing them on cards, and storing the material in specified places in a library.

As part of our attempt to stock our brain attics carefully, we have all learned to package the material in meaningful clusters. To demonstrate this process, you can do the following simple experiment, using a friend as

your subject. Read the adjacent list of words to your friend, telling him to remember as many of the words as possible. After you've read the list of words, ask your friend to start with the number 42 and count backward by threes to zero. The purpose of this counting task is to provide some mental interference so that the memory task won't be too easy. Now ask your friend to tell you as many of the words as possible, in whatever order he likes. If your friend is like most subjects in this sort of experiment, he will remember a large proportion of the words—but he will report them in a different order from the order that you read them. Your friend will prob-

ably report them in clusters or categories—for example, first vegetables, then office furniture, then metals. It is, in fact, much easier to learn and remember a list of words that includes meaningful clusters than it is to learn a list of unrelated words because we can use the natural categories to file the material.

In order to establish material in long-term memory, we need to pay attention to the meaning of the material and to link it to concepts and knowledge we already have. The importance of meaning has been demonstrated in many research studies. In one series of experiments, college students were presented with long lists of words, such as "bear," "vest," "apple," "string," and so on (Craik and Tulving, 1975). After each word was presented, the subject was asked a question about it. Some of the questions directed the subject's attention to the *meaning* of the word (for example, "Is it a wild animal?"), while other questions directed his attention to the *sound* of the word (for example, "Does it rhyme with 'chair'?"). In later memory tests, the students were much more successful at remembering the "meaning" words than the "sound" words.

Whatever method is used to get material into long-term memory, the next problem is being able to *retrieve* the information at the moment that we need it—to get it out of the crowded attic and back into consciousness. What *is* the capital of Iowa? It's likely that you know the answer—that it's somewhere in your long-term memory—but that you can't get it out at the moment. Or can you remember the name of your third-grade teacher or what she looked like? That information, too, is in your long-term memory. The question is, can you retrieve it? One type of retrieval problem—the tip-of-the-tongue phenomenon—is described in Box 1.

As already noted, one way to improve information retrieval is to store and encode things carefully in the first place. The more completely we inspect the incoming material and mentally connect it with things we already know, the more likely we are to remember it later (Craik and Lock-

hart, 1972). You probably know from your own experience that it is difficult to remember the contents of a textbook chapter that you didn't really understand when you first read it. As your understanding of the material improves, the better you remember it.

In addition to meaningful storage of information, retrieval is best when you have reminders, or *cues*, available that you can associate with the material to be retrieved. In the exercise with the word list, for example, if you ask your friend to recall the words the next day, he may be unable to list more than a few of them. But if you remind him that the words were metals, vegetables, and office furniture, he may then be able to retrieve many more of them. As will be discussed shortly, forgetting is often due to the fact that we lack sufficient cues to retrieve a piece of information.

Memory as a reconstructive process

Sherlock Holmes's image of the "brain attic" seems to imply that the pieces of information filed away in our long-term memories—like the old clothes, books, and furniture that might be stored in an attic—are fixed entities, unchanged by the passage of time. But most psychologists have come to doubt this notion. Instead, they view memory as a *reconstructive* process, in which our wider knowledge of the world affects the way we remember a specific event. Remembering may actually be a process of mentally "rebuilding" an event rather than simply finding a permanent record of it in our long-term memory. For example, your memory of the first time you rode on a bicycle may be influenced not only by that event but also by your more general knowledge of how a bicycle works, your general picture of what you were like at that age, and stories your parents have told you about yourself as a child. In recalling such events, you may tie them into the context of your life at the time, rather than remembering every detail as it actually was.

To illustrate the ways in which more general knowledge may influ-

BOX 1

"IT'S ON THE TIP OF MY TONGUE"

I was watching a news reporter on television. I had seen him before, and I knew that I knew his name, but I couldn't quite remember it. I struggled to get the name off the tip of my tongue and into my consciousness. Was it John Calhoun? That was close, but it didn't seem right. Was it John Coltrane? That seemed even closer, but it wasn't the name I was groping for. When I finally managed to get the right name in my mind—it was John Cochran—I felt tremendous relief.

This *tip-of-the-tongue (TOT) phenomenon*—the feeling of being almost but not quite able to recall a word—is something that most people are familiar with but have a difficult time explaining. The phenomenon involves an essential puzzle: How can you know that you know something without actually knowing what that something is? This puzzle also intrigued two psychologists, Roger Brown and David McNeill. They conducted an important study of the tip-of-the-tongue phenomenon that helps to explain aspects of the way we store names and other words in long-term memory.

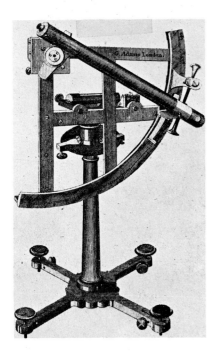

What is this object called?

To study the TOT phenomenon, Brown and McNeill (1966) read the definitions of obscure words to their subjects and recorded the words that came to mind for subjects who said they knew the correct word but could not quite recall it. For example, they gave their subjects the definition: "A navigational instrument . . . stars at sea." The correct answer, or target word, was *sextant*. This definition put some subjects in the TOT state—they said they knew what the word was but couldn't bring it to mind. When asked which words *did* come to mind, the subjects generally listed words that were similar to the target word either in meaning or in sound. The words of similar meaning included *astrolabe, compass, dividers,* and *protractor*. The words of similar sound included *secant, sextet,* and *sexton*.

The similar-sounding words were of particular interest to Brown and McNeill. The fact that these words came to mind made it clear that the subjects knew a great deal about the target word even though they could not quite remember it. As further evidence of this knowledge, subjects in the TOT state were remarkably accurate in identifying the first letter and the number of syllables in a target word.

On the basis of their results, Brown and McNeill proposed that our verbal storage is like a complex filing system, cross-referenced by both meaning and sound. One part of the filing system is arranged something like a thesaurus, indexed in terms of word meanings. The definition of a navigational instrument calls forth the mental file drawer for that category, including words like astrolabe and compass, as well as sextant. The other part of the filing system is organized something like a conventional dictionary, but with a difference: it is organized not only according to the way words are spelled but also according to the way they sound. The meaning-filing system helps us to recall the right word when speaking or writing: we retrieve the appropriate file from the appropriate file drawer and then search through it for the word we want. The sound-filing system is especially helpful in enabling us to recognize and understand words—if someone says something remotely like *sextant*, we can usually figure out what he or she means.

ence specific memories, college students in one experiment were asked to read a brief biographical passage, such as the following (Sulin and Dooling, 1974):

_____ _____'S SEIZURE OF
POWER

_____ _____ *strove to undermine the existing government to satisfy his political ambitions. Many of the people of his country supported his efforts. Current political problems made it relatively easy for _____ to take over. Certain groups remained loyal to the old government and caused _____ trouble. He confronted these groups directly and silenced them. He became a ruthless, uncontrollable dictator. The ultimate effect of his rule was the downfall of his country.*

For half of the subjects the blanks were filled in with the name of Adolf Hitler; for the other half they were filled in with the name of a fictitious person, Gerald Martin. After reading the passage, the subjects were given a list of sentences and were asked which ones had appeared in the story. All of the sentences but one had actually appeared: "He hated the Jews particularly and so he persecuted them." Significantly more subjects who read the description of "Adolf Hitler" thought they had seen this sentence than did subjects who read the description of "Gerald Martin." The subjects' prior knowledge of Hitler's life affected the way they remembered the passage, allowing them to

"recognize" a sentence they had never seen before. The reconstructive nature of memory is discussed further in the Psychological Issue on memory and the law following this chapter.

WHY DO WE FORGET?

Given the impressive capacities of human memory, why do we forget things at all? The issue of forgetting was first explored systematically by a turn-of-the-century German psychologist named Hermann Ebbinghaus. Using himself as his subject, Ebbinghaus spent thousands of hours memorizing nonsense syllables (such as KEJ, GOK, and PUM) and then measuring his memory performance. Ebbinghaus made use of nonsense syllables because he wanted to focus on those aspects of learning and memory that did *not* involve meaning—what is sometimes called *rote learning*. His basic finding was that the greatest memory loss occurs soon after learning and that the rate of loss declines as time passes (Ebbinghaus, 1913). This decelerating rate of forgetting is summarized in what is referred to as the *forgetting curve* (see Figure 6.2). More recent research has gone beyond Ebbinghaus's basic principle of forgetting to an investigation of the reasons that forgetting occurs and the circumstances that make it more or less likely. In most of the recent research, central attention is given to the meaning of the material to be remembered—or forgotten.

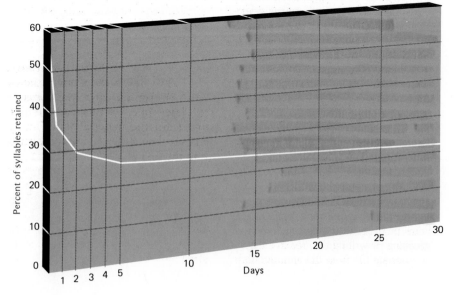

FIGURE 6.2

Ebbinghaus's forgetting curve, showing the decreasing percentage of nonsense syllables remembered as time goes by.

People find it hard to recall the names of their high-school classmates. But they are still able to recognize most of their classmates' names if they are presented with them.

Recall, recognition, and relearning

How can we tell whether a person remembers or has forgotten something he has learned? Much of the research in this area has involved laboratory studies of *verbal learning*—the circumstances under which we remember or forget words or other verbal material.

Researchers studying verbal learning have used three basic measures of memory (or retention): recall, recognition, and relearning. In *recall*, the individual must recount or reproduce something previously learned, with the help of only the barest cues. In *recognition*, the individual must simply identify something that he has encountered before. As you might expect, people's recognition of words, faces, or events tends to be considerably better than their recall. In one study, subjects ranging in age from 17 to 74 were asked to remember names of their high-school classmates. On a *free recall* test, in which they were simply asked to list as many of their classmates as they could, the more recent graduates could recall an average of 47 names; those out of school for 40 years could recall an average of 19. But when the subjects were given a *name recognition* test, in which they had to pick out classmates' names from sets of five, even subjects who had graduated from high school 40 years before could identify almost 75 percent of their classmates (Bah-

rick et al., 1975). Results such as these suggest that in many cases the person has the information stored somewhere in memory but is simply unable to find it. But if the person encounters this information as part of a list, as in the name recognition test, the retrieval problem is solved and the information can then be recognized.

A third measure of retention is *relearning*. With this measure, a researcher sees how quickly the subject can learn material she has learned previously. The length of time required to master the relearned material can be compared with the length of time it took to master it originally. The difference between the first and second learnings is the savings in time. (For this reason, the relearning method of measuring memory is sometimes called the *savings method*.) Of the three measures, relearning generally shows the greatest amount of retention over the longest period of time. Individuals who have once learned something often cannot recall or even recognize the material at a later time, yet they are still able to relearn the material much more quickly than if they had never learned it in the first place. This ability to relearn material quickly can be of great practical value later in life—when, for example, one wants to brush up on French before taking that long-awaited trip to Paris, or one needs to relearn shorthand to move into a desired job.

Interference

In presenting his advice about memory, Sherlock Holmes added that it is a mistake to try to cram one's "brain attic" with too much material. "Depend upon it," he told his friend Dr. Watson, "that there comes a time when for every addition of knowledge you forget something you knew before" (Doyle, 1937, p. 21).

Since Sherlock Holmes's time, researchers have confirmed that this observation holds true, at least in certain circumstances. One of the reasons that we sometimes forget things is that one bit of learning is interfered with by another. Studies of verbal learning have identified two types of interference—the influence of activities *prior* to the learning and the influence of activities *following* the learning. The first type is called *proactive interference*—material learned earlier interferes with the retention of something learned more recently (Figure 6.3A). For example, students who have learned the French words for certain objects often have trouble learning the Spanish words for the same objects because the previous learning interferes with the retention of the new information. Benton J. Underwood (1957) demonstrated the effects of proactive interference in the laboratory. Subjects learned nine different lists of words on successive days and were asked each day to recall the list learned the previous day. Subjects remembered 71 percent of the first list but only 27 percent of the last list. Apparently, the previously learned lists interfered with the ability to recall the later lists.

The second kind of interference is called *retroactive*—when newly learned information hinders the recall or recognition of information that was learned previously (Figure 6.3B). In a language class, a student may do well on the first few vocabulary tests, but as the number of vocabulary items increases through the semester, more recently learned items may begin to interfere with the retrieval of items learned earlier in the semester. Almost anything can be an interfering activity. This may help to explain the finding that subjects who sleep after learning new material tend to retain more of the material than subjects who remain awake (Ekstrand, 1967). When you are asleep, there are fewer new inputs that can interfere with what you have learned. For years, students have used such results to justify abandoning their books and going to sleep the night before a big exam. Keep in mind, though, that sleep works to reduce interference only when the material has been learned well in the first place.

UNFINISHED BUSINESS

In a classic study of memory, Bluma Zeigarnik (1927) gave her subjects a number of simple tasks to do. She allowed some of the tasks to be completed, but she interrupted others. Several hours later, when the subjects were asked to recall the tasks, they recalled more of the incomplete tasks than the complete ones. This tendency to recall incomplete tasks is now called the "Zeigarnik effect." It apparently stems from our greater need to remember things that are still unfinished so that we can go back and finish them. Usually, there is less need to remember completed tasks.

A Proactive Interference	Step 1	Step 2	Step 3
Experimental Group	Learn List A	Learn List B	Recall List B
Control Group	Rest or engage in unrelated activity	Learn List B	Recall List B

B Retroactive Interference	Step 1	Step 2	Step 3
Experimental Group	Learn List A	Learn List B	Recall List A
Control Group	Learn List A	Rest or engage in unrelated activity	Recall List A

FIGURE 6.3

Design of experiments on interference in verbal learning. In proactive interference, earlier learning (memorizing list A) interferes with later learning (recalling list B). In retroactive interference, later learning (memorizing list B), interferes with earlier learning (recalling list A).

Retrieval failure

As noted earlier, some information is forgotten almost as soon as it is learned. This is information, such as a telephone number, that is held for a brief period in short-term memory but is never transferred to long-term memory. Once such information drops out of short-term memory, it seems to be lost to us forever. When we talk about forgetting things, however, we are usually talking about information that we once knew—that was once part of our long-term memory store—but that we can no longer bring to mind. This type of forgetting is referred to as *retrieval failure*.

Psychologists once believed that information in long-term memory would "decay" over time if it were never used or that it would fade as the result of interference from new material. But recent research suggests that this is not the case. In fact, long-term memories seem to remain in indefinitely long—and perhaps permanent—storage, embedded in chemical codes in the brain that scientists are just beginning to understand.

Endel Tulving (1974) has concluded that much of what we call forgetting is actually a failure to locate information in one's memory. In his experiments, subjects memorized lists of words. When they were asked to recall these words later, they seemed to have forgotten many items. But when the subjects were given cues to jog their memories—such as the category to which the word belonged ("four-footed animal") or words that rhymed with the word to be recalled ("it rhymes with *chair*")—they remembered much of the "forgotten" material.

You have probably had your own memory prompted by retrieval cues on many occasions. Suppose a friend mentions a day several months ago when you joined a group of people in the cafeteria for a cup of coffee. You have no recollection of the event. But then she reminds you that it was raining, it was the day that Joel showed up with his arm in a cast, and the group was discussing a particular movie. Suddenly the incident comes back to you—an event you had "forgotten."

The importance of retrieval cues is illustrated in the phenomenon of *state-dependent memory*—the tendency for people's memories to be best when they recall material in the same locale or the same physical or mental state they were in when they first learned it. For example, when scuba divers were asked to learn lists of words either on the shore or 10 feet beneath the ocean's surface, they were later found to recall more words when they were in their original learning environment (Godden and

When divers learned words beneath the surface, they remembered them best when they were beneath the surface again. When they learned words on the shore, they remembered them best when they were on the shore again. This phenomenon is called state-dependent memory.

Baddeley, 1975). Similarly, many studies have shown that memories acquired under the influence of drugs, such as marijuana or alcohol, are most accessible when the same drug is taken again (Swanson and Kinsbourne, 1979). Memory of word lists also seems to be better when subjects are in the same mood as they were when they learned the lists (Bower, 1981). In all of these cases, the person's physical or emotional state appears to be closely associated with the memory and can therefore be used as a retrieval cue. Returning to the same state makes this cue highly available, increasing the chances of recalling the rest of the original memory.

With the right sort of prompting, even long-lost information can eventually be dredged up from our memories (see Box 2). One way to help may be to return to the situation or condition in which we initially stored the material. Criminal investigators make use of this principle when they bring witnesses back to the scene of the crime, in the hope of jogging their memories. Another implication, which may or may not work in practice: Study for exams in the exam room.

Motivated forgetting

We sometimes forget material that is in our long-term memory not because we *can't* retrieve it but because we don't really want to—because remembering it would be embarrassing or painful. This process is called *motivated forgetting*. This type of forgetting sometimes comes out when families exchange reminiscences about days gone by. Someone will bring up an incident in which another family member appears in a bad light, and the second person will say, "I never did that!" and profess no memory of the event.

Sigmund Freud's concept of *repression* deals with motivated forgetting on a deeper level. According to Freud, we are unable to retrieve some memories because they are related to emotional conflicts. If we remembered certain feelings and events, such as our early sexual and aggressive feelings, we would experience severe anxiety (see Chapter 11). To avoid this anxiety, we manage to repress this material and keep it from coming to the surface. In this way, "forgetting" serves to protect our self-concept. In other cases, though, such as the flashbulb memories discussed in Chapter 1, strong emotions may help to fix certain memories firmly in our minds.

Could we recall *everything* we ever knew, if only we had adequate retrieval cues and were highly enough motivated to do so? Some researchers believe we could; others remain doubtful. The question of the ultimate limits of our memories is one that psychologists cannot yet answer.

MEMORY AND THE BRAIN

Although psychologists have learned a great deal about the way memory works, the biological processes that underlie memory remain shrouded in mystery. How can a first kiss, a plot of a novel, or a scientific formula be imprinted permanently in the folds of gray matter that make up our brains? And how are our brains organized so that such memories—even "long-lost" ones—can be called back by the proper cues? Scientists are still far from able to answer these questions, but in recent years they have made dramatic progress in approaching them. Some of this research has focused on the chemical processes that underlie memory storage, and some of it has focused on persons with serious memory disorders.

The chemistry of memory

For a long time it was thought that long-term memory depended on electrical circuits in various parts of the brain that laid down lasting patterns, called *engrams*. Karl Lashley, a noted neurophysiologist, spent a good part of his life searching for such engrams in the brains of laboratory animals. Lashley would teach a rat a new skill—to run a particular maze, for example—and then remove a portion of

BOX 2

CHILDHOOD MEMORIES

I was 4. I was standing at the water fountain in the park with my bloody chin hanging down. I had crashed into the picket fence with my tricycle. Then I was at the hospital waiting for someone to find my mother. She had to sign permission forms before they would stitch up my chin. I remember lying on the couch in the study a week or so later while my father, a doctor, took out the stitches.

Most of us have a few such memories of our early childhood—a birthday party, a trip away from home, perhaps just a fleeting image of a room or a toy. As with my own memories of a bloody chin, these recollections are often tinged with feelings of joy or fear or sadness. But while we have a few vivid images of our earliest years, these are what one author calls "islands in a sea of oblivion"; there are a few moments that we can recapture, but the rest is lost to us (Salaman, 1970).

Few of us can recall being delighted with a rattle, taking our first steps, or blowing out the candles on our third birthday cake. When John Kihlstrom and Judith Harackiewicz (1982) asked college students to describe their first memory, only a few of them could reach back before the age of 3 or 4. These first memories were usually fleeting visual images. As individuals move on through the years of childhood, they generate more abundant and sharper memories. Memories that originate in the early school years (from the age of 6 or so) are more likely to be clear, coherent stories (White and Pillemer, 1979).

Why do we remember so little of our first few years of life? Sigmund Freud (1901) was the first to discuss the phenomenon of *childhood amnesia*—the tendency to forget the events and emotions of these early years. Freud proposed that the first few years of life are fraught with so much inner conflict that all our memories of these years are *repressed*, or banished from consciousness.

More recent explanations for the lack of early memories have emphasized the different cognitive capacities of young children and adults. Before the age of 3 or 4, children lack the cognitive skills that adults use to encode material in long-term memory. Young children do not have access to precise verbal labels, clear time sequences, and well-understood causal schemes. Moreover, young children seem to focus on only one aspect of experience at a time, making richly cross-referenced encoding impossible. By the age of 5 or 6, however, children's language and thought become more sophisticated and their attention capacities broaden, enabling them to encode information in more adultlike ways. As a result, memories dating from about age 5 or 6 tend to be more complete and more easily brought to mind (White and Pillemer, 1979).

Even very early memories may come flooding back to us, however, if they are triggered by the right cue, such as a sight, smell, sound, or emotion. In Marcel Proust's famous novel *Swann's Way* (1928), the narrator tells how the taste of a piece of cake, dipped in tea, brought back a torrent of memories from his childhood. Similarly, a young father told me that doing things with his 2-year-old son unexpectedly brought back memories of his own early childhood: "One day I was putting my son's shirt on, and his hands sort of popped out of his shirt. I found myself counting my son's fingers out to him. And then I remembered that my father used to play that game with me—count my fingers when they came out of the shirt."

Why do certain early memories stay with us, while others fade? Alfred Adler (1937) believed that our earliest memories reveal the central concerns of our lives. In one study, for example, a hard-working premedical student described her first memory as sitting in her pink, frilly room reading *The Little Engine that Could,* a well-known children's book about overcoming obstacles to success (Kihlstrom and Harackiewicz, 1982). Followers of Adler have been able to document links between people's early memories and their later personality traits (Barrett, 1980) and vocational choice (Attarian, 1978). Particular events may stay with us, it appears, both because they reflect stable aspects of our personality and because they have the most meaning for our current situation.

In addition, some early memories stay with us because we are frequently reminded of them, through old photographs, family stories, or returns to the locales of our early childhood. In some cases, what was originally no more than a series of fleeting images may later be elaborated into a more complete, coherent memory. Thus, my memory of my early tricycle accident may have survived not only because the event was traumatic but also because I have told the story many times—whenever anyone asks me how I got that scar on my chin.

the rat's cortex. He would then put the rat back into the maze to see whether it still retained the skill. Lashley found, to his dismay, that no matter which part of the rat's cortex he removed, the memory remained. Looking back over his research, Lashley came to the tongue-in-cheek conclusion, "I sometimes feel, in reviewing the evidence on the localization of the memory trace, that the necessary conclusion is that learning is just not possible" (1950, pages 477–478).

In the mid-1960s, researchers began to turn from the search for localized electrical circuits to an emphasis on the chemistry of memory. It is now believed that memories are created by chemical changes that affect neurotransmitters (the chemicals that carry messages across synapses) or that affect neurons' sensitivity to neurotransmitters (see Chapter 2). As learning progresses these chemical changes seem to make particular synapses in the brain more efficient at passing messages. In recent studies of these chemical processes, Gary Lynch and his coworkers (Lynch and Baudry, 1984) have administered high-frequency bursts of electrical stimulation to neurons in an area of rats' brains called the hippocampus (see Chapter 2). When these neurons are subsequently given low-frequency stimulation, they respond more actively than they did previously. The high-frequency stimulation apparently leads to the release of an enzyme that makes dendrites (the receiving ends of neurons) more sensitive to certain neurotransmitters. The elevated response may last for weeks or months. Lynch calls this phenomenon *long-term potentiation.* He points out that this electrical-chemical process matches the needs of long-term memory: it is turned on by a specific event, it appears very quickly, and it lasts for a long time.

In many cases, however, it seems to take time for chemical changes to have a permanent impact on the brain. This period of time is called the *consolidation phase.* If brain processes are disrupted during this period, the memory is lost. If no disruption occurs, the message consolidates into long-term memory (McGaugh, 1966). For example, people who suffer

brain injury often have no memory of the events that occurred just before the accident. This loss of memory, called *retrograde amnesia,* may cover a period from several minutes to more than an hour before the accident. The injury apparently interferes with chemical changes in the brain before the changes have a chance to consolidate. Memory loss of this sort can also be produced in the laboratory. If an electroconvulsive shock—an electric current that produces temporary unconsciousness—is passed through the brain of a laboratory animal shortly after it has learned a new task, the learning may be forgotten. But although such memory consolidation seems to be important, in some cases the animals subjected to electroconvulsive shock may actually retain the memory that was "lost"—but it is harder for them to retrieve it (Miller and Marlin, 1979). Electroconvulsive therapy, which is sometimes used to treat people suffering from depression (see Chapter 14), can have similar sorts of disruptive effects on memory.

Other recent research by James McGaugh (1983) and his coworkers has shown that the hormones epinephrine and norepinephrine play an important role in memory. As noted in Chapter 2, these hormones are released by the adrenal glands in times of stress. When rats are taught to avoid a shock and then are given epinephrine or norepinephrine, they remember the lesson better. If, on the other hand, the secretion of these hormones is blocked, the lesson is lost. McGaugh points out that organisms that can remember stressful situations are better equipped to survive; thus, the impact of epinephrine and norepinephrine on memory may have developed as a way of enhancing survival. These hormonal influences may help to explain the phenomenon of flashbulb memories that we examined in Chapter 1: When people experience a highly stressful or significant event, such as the assassination of President Kennedy, they are likely to form an unusually clear and enduring memory of where they were and what they were doing at the time. It is as if the brain is given a signal at such times to "Print it!"—to lock short-term changes into memory.

FROM ONE FLATWORM TO ANOTHER

Some researchers have had the notion that memories are stored in specific molecules in the nervous system. To test this idea, James McConnell (1962) classically conditioned flatworms to respond to a flash of light. He then chopped up the conditioned flatworms and fed them to untrained flatworms, which were then put through the same learning process. McConnell reported that these flatworms learned to react to the light faster than did ordinary flatworms. Perhaps they had incorporated the "memory molecules" from their food and acquired the memories they contained. Other experimenters have had difficulty replicating McConnell's results, however, and it now seems doubtful that memories are stored in specific molecules.

McGaugh's research suggests that epinephrine and norepinephrine may play this vital signaling role.

The recent research on the chemistry of memory has also given rise to the hope that new drugs will be developed to help improve memory, especially in the treatment of severe memory disorders. This area of memory research is discussed in Box 3.

Disorders of memory

One way in which we can learn more about the workings of memory is by studying cases in which it does not work normally. For example, brain-damaged patients sometimes experience a condition of *transient global amnesia*, in which they are unable to hold on to any information for more than a few seconds. The patient retains all memories that were formed up to a few hours before the attack, but he or she cannot remember what is happening from one moment to the next. Such patients can drive a car, but they don't know where they started from and have a hard time remembering where they are going. They can't boil an egg unless they are watching a clock and have written down the time the egg was placed on the stove. The attack usually lasts about a day, and then it gradually clears up. The patients eventually return to normal, except that they can't remember anything that happened during the period of the attack (Gardner, 1975). This condition is similar to the sort of retrograde amnesia that can be caused by a head injury. Retrograde amnesia is apparently caused by a disruption of the chemical processes by which new learning becomes consolidated into long-term memory. In the case of transient global amnesia, however, the disruption is caused by attacks within the brain that can recur periodically.

In another, even more serious condition, called *Korsakoff's syndrome*, the patient's inability to place new information in long-term storage is a lasting one. Named for S. S. Korsakoff, a Russian psychiatrist, this syndrome is associated with excessive intake of alcohol over a period of many years. Korsakoff patients can remember their lives up to the time

the syndrome took hold, but they remember little else since that point. Howard Gardner (1975) recounted the following conversation he had with a man suffering from Korsakoff's syndrome:

"How old are you?"
"I was born in 1927."
"Which makes you . . ."
"Let's see, Doctor, how I always forget, the year is . . ."
"The year is what?"
"Oh, I must be thirty-four, thirty-five, what's the difference?" He grinned sheepishly.
"You'll soon be forty-six, Mr. O'Donnell, the year is 1973."
Mr. O'Donnell looked momentarily surprised, started to protest, and said, "Sure, you must be right, Doctor. How silly of me. I'm forty-five, that's right, I guess."
(pages 178–179)

A famous case of memory disorder is that of a man who has been referred to as H.M. in the scientific literature. H.M.'s disorder is similar to that of N.A., with whom we began this chapter. Whereas N.A. was injured in an accident, H.M. had both hippocampi of his brain removed to treat a severe epileptic condition. The surgery succeeded in curing the epilepsy, but this operation has never been done again because it caused H.M. to suffer a profound memory deficit. Like patients with Korsakoff's syndrome—but to a more complete degree—H.M. lives only in the present. He lacks the capacity to store any new information in memory. As a result, H.M. reads the same magazine over and over again, never realizing that he has seen the material before. The case of H.M. helps to illustrate the distinction between short-term and long-term memory: Whereas H.M. has a short-term memory—for example, he can repeat things that are said to him—he lacks the ability to store information in long-term memory.

Although researchers initially thought that H.M. could not learn anything at all, later tests showed that he was in fact capable of motor learning (Milner, 1966). With practice, he steadily improved in his ability at mirror drawing, such as drawing a line around the border of a star

THE MAN WHO COULDN'T FORGET

The eminent Russian psychologist A. R. Luria (1968) described a man with a very unusual memory disorder: he couldn't forget anything. The man, known as "S.," could remember lists of numbers or words of any length, reciting them either frontward or backward. Years later, he could produce copies of entire previous lists without ever confusing any two of them. S.'s astounding memory was apparently due to his extraordinary sensory imagery: every letter, number, or scene evoked an array of colors, sounds, and feelings that fixed the experience in his mind. But while S. remembered every concrete experience, he had difficulty with any job that required the ability to organize, classify, or evaluate. The only way he could make a living was as a professional mnemonist—a stage performer of memory tricks, regarded by most people as something of a freak.

BOX 3

MEMORY DRUGS

"Having a hard time remembering what you've been reading in your textbooks lately? No problem. Just take a memory pill."

Right now this idea seems far-fetched, but some day in the not-too-distant future students may be able to follow such advice. After years of experimenting with animals, researchers have begun to try out drugs that may enhance memory—and prevent its loss—in humans.

One such drug, called DDAVP, is a synthetic form of the pituitary gland hormone vasopressin. In one study, college students took DDAVP in the form of a nasal spray daily for several weeks. These students showed a 20 percent improvement in their scores on memory tests. A control group of subjects who used a nasal spray with no active ingredients showed no such improvement. DDAVP improved memory even more strikingly in a small group of middle-aged women who were suffering from depression. In addition, DDAVP seemed to minimize the amnesia that occurs after patients receive electroconvulsive therapy (Weingartner et al., 1981). Researchers suspect that DDAVP acts on portions of the brain involved in motivation and reward, which play an important role in learning and memory.

Other researchers have focused on drugs and foods that may increase the level of the neurotransmitter acetylcholine in the brain. A sharp reduction in levels of acetylcholine occurs in Alzheimer's disease, which is the most common cause of mental deterioration in old age (Coyle et al., 1983). There is at least some evidence that foods high in choline (including milk, eggs, and fish), a chemical precursor of acetylcholine, can improve memory. Other studies have achieved some success with a drug called physostigmine that seems to slow down the breakdown of acetylcholine in the brain. Such research offers hope of reducing the memory impairments of Alzheimer's disease.

And how about a drug for the night-before syndrome—the tendency

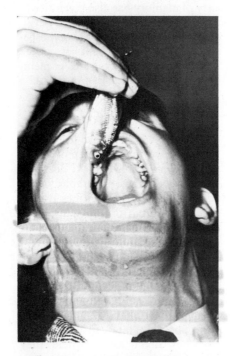

Folk wisdom has it that fish is a good memory food. And it now appears that foods high in choline (including fish) may in fact be able to improve memory.

for heavy drinkers to forget what went on when they were in their soggy state? In one study, subjects were given either a placebo (a "drug" that actually has no active ingredients) or a drug called zimelidine and then asked to drink a series of precisely measured cocktails. While they were intoxicated, the subjects listened to lists of words. Later, while they were sobering up, they were asked to recall the lists. Among the subjects who had received the placebo, the alcohol produced a 40 percent memory loss, but there was no such loss among subjects who had received zimelidine (Weingartner et al., 1983).

Researchers believe that alcohol dampens memory by reducing the levels of the neurotransmitter serotonin in the brain and that zimelidine works by restoring these levels. This effect appears to be quite specific: while zimelidine improves the impaired memory that is caused by drinking, it does nothing for normal memory.

The research on human memory drugs is too new to be conclusive. And, unfortunately, the memory drugs often have harmful side effects. For example, DDAVP tends to constrict blood vessels, and physostigmine can lead to heart and digestive problems. But as research on the chemistry of memory continues, it is a good bet that safe and effective memory drugs will eventually become available.

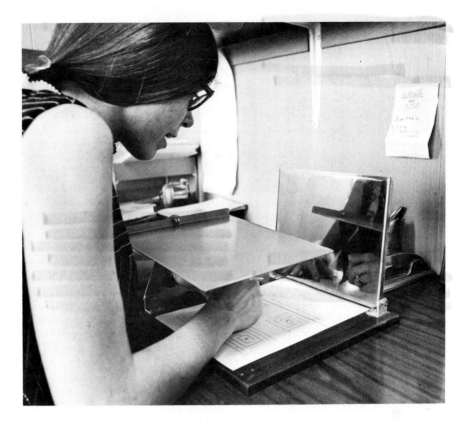

A subject performing a mirror drawing task similar to the one used to assess H.M.'s memory for motor skills.

when he could only observe what he was doing in a mirror. (If you've ever tried mirror drawing, you know that it takes a great deal of practice to get it right.) Each time H.M. was asked to do the task, he reported that he had never seen it before, and it had to be explained to him anew. At the verbal level, therefore, he didn't remember it at all. But his performance got steadily better, indicating that at the motor level he came to remember the task quite well. This discrepancy suggests that our verbal memory (or memory for facts) and our motor memory (our memory for skills) are in fact distinct systems. Recent studies of patients with a variety of memory disorders have supported this conclusion, leading to the current belief that verbal memories and motor memories are processed by different portions of the brain (Cohen and Squire, 1982).

IMPROVING MEMORY

When you want to remember something important, what do you do? Tie a string around your finger? Write it down? Say it over and over to yourself? Ask a friend to remind you? We all have our own ways of making sure that we remember certain things, but some ways are better than others. Thus, when some people say they have a "bad memory," they are probably just using an inefficient method of remembering. By applying some of the principles psychologists have discovered in their study of memory, you can improve your recall.

Study strategies

As we have seen, the ways in which we learn or encode information in the first place are of prime importance in memory. Research on memory and learning suggests a number of practical strategies to use in studying for your classes: spacing study periods, active recitation, reviewing the material, and giving the material meaning.
1 Spacing study periods is usually more effective than trying to learn material all at once. For most students, four one-hour sessions of study would result in better recall of the material than one four-hour session. When study sessions are extended for too long, attention

tends to wander and fatigue begins to set in. In addition, when you are trying to learn too much in a single session, old and new material may start interfering with each other. The best length for study periods depends, however, on the material to be learned. As long as you can place the material in a meaningful context, relating one fact or principle to another, it may be useful to lengthen the study session. But when the connections become elusive and you find yourself trying to learn by rote, it's time to take a break.

2 *Active recitation* involves stopping every so often as you read and repeating to yourself what you have just learned. This procedure focuses your attention on the material at hand and gives you repeated practice in retrieving information that has been stored. Perhaps even more important, such recitation can provide more opportunity for you to think about what the material really means—and, thus, to encode it in an efficient way. As a result, active recitation helps to ensure that you will be able to recall—not merely recognize—the material when it is needed.

3 *Reviewing* material follows the principle of savings (see page 169):

it is easier to relearn material that has been learned previously. Therefore, if you know you will be tested on information learned early in the term, it pays to review the material every so often to refresh your memory about the parts you know and to learn those parts you had trouble with the first time. The more you review during the term, the less time you will need to spend going over old material for the final examination.

4 *Giving meaning* to the material is probably the most important of all study strategies. Rote learning is not nearly so efficient as learning accompanied by an understanding of how the material fits together with other materials and ideas that you already know. For example, instead of just memorizing these four study strategies, you could think about whether each one has been useful to you in the past, and you could think about how each of them relates to principles of memory introduced earlier in this chapter.

One way to help give meaning to what you read is to take notes, putting the central ideas in your own words, or to make an outline of the important points. Such note taking serves two purposes. First, it may be useful to refer back to the notes

WHEN VERSE IS WORSE

The results of a series of studies of children's memory (Hayes et al., 1982) were aptly summarized by Christopher T. Cory (1982):

What kids read in rhyme
They'll forget in no time;
Psychology knows
They do better with prose.

Thirty-two preschoolers
Tested by researchers
Liked rhymed stories best
But booted a test

Of what they recalled.
Adults were not stalled:
They remembered just fine
Short stories in rhyme.

Taking notes helps make the material you are studying more meaningful to you— and, therefore, easier to remember.

later to refresh your memory of the material. Second, in the process of taking the notes you will be mentally organizing the material in a way that is meaningful to you and, hence, easier to remember.

The *PQ4R method* is an approach to studying textbook material that incorporates several of these study strategies (Thomas and Robinson, 1982). "PQ4R" gets its name from the six stages that it advocates for studying a textbook chapter: *Preview, Question, Read, Reflect, Recite,* and *Review.* The central feature of the PQ4R technique is the enterprise of making up questions about each section of the chapter and then reading the section with the specific aim of answering the questions. Often you can make up satisfactory questions simply by transforming section headings (Anderson, 1980). If a section is titled "Study Strategies," for example, some appropriate questions would be "What are the key study strategies suggested?" and "What makes each strategy effective?" Generating such questions for yourself—and then trying to answer them—helps guarantee that you will read and organize the material in a way that is meaningful to you.

Memory systems

Many memory techniques and systems are based on the idea that careful and systematic coding can greatly increase our ability to store and retrieve information. Suppose, for example, you were asked to learn the following list of unrelated words: tree, magazine, swimming pool, shoelace, hospital, faucet, potato chips, stocking, convertible, cigarette. Instead of saying the words over and over to yourself, try to make up a story in which all of the words are used in the right order. For example: *Susan was sitting under a tree, reading a magazine, with a swimming pool on the cover. As she leaned over to tie her shoelace, she developed a sprained back and had to be taken to the hospital. In the hospital, she was kept awake by the sounds of a dripping faucet and of her roommate's crunching on potato chips all night long. To make things even worse, a man wearing a stocking over his head broke into her room the next day and carried her off in a convertible. Most unpleasant of all, he kept blowing cigarette smoke into her face.*

The story doesn't have to be a terribly plausible one. All it has to do is place the list of words into a meaningful framework. Now when you are asked to recall the list of words, you simply run the story through your mind and report the key words as you get to them.

An experiment by Gordon Bower and Michal Clark (1969) demonstrated the tremendous effectiveness of this method. Subjects were asked to learn twelve lists of ten unrelated nouns. Half the subjects (the experimental group) were instructed to learn the words by making up a story that included the ten words in the proper order. The other subjects (the control group) merely studied the words for an equivalent amount of time. In a test at the end of the session, subjects who made up stories recalled an average of 94 percent of all the words, while subjects in the control group recalled only 14 percent.

An additional reason for the effectiveness of this memory system is that it adds vivid visual images to the verbal material to be recalled—for example, the man with the stocking over his head, driving a convertible, and smoking a cigarette. Allan Paivio (1971) has suggested that recall tends to be best when we can make simultaneous use of verbal and visual systems of coding. The presence of both a name and a picture of an object or a person—what Paivio calls *dual coding*—helps us to get a better handle on the information than we could have with only the name or picture.

Another effective memory system that also involves simultaneous verbal and visual coding is the *method of loci.* This time-honored system—it is said to have been used by the ancient Greeks—makes use of a set of familiar locations (*loci* means "places" or locations) that follow in a known order. You might imagine a familiar walk between two points on campus and identify a dozen or more distinctive locations along the way—first

ABSENTMINDEDNESS

Harry Lorayne and Jerry Lucas, authors of The Memory Book *(1974), suggest that many cases of absentmindedness (forgetting where you put your glasses, etc.) are simply matters of not having fully registered the information in the first place. For example, have you ever gone to the refrigerator and then forgotten what you wanted? Lorayne and Lucas have a simple solution: "Just make an association the moment you think of what it is you want from the refrigerator. If you want a glass of milk, see yourself opening the refrigerator door and gallons of milk flying out and hitting you in the face! Try this idea, and you'll never stare into a refrigerator again" (page 79).*

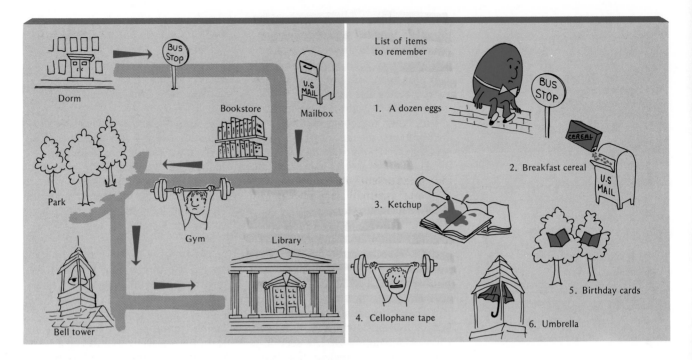

the bus stop, then the mailbox, and so on (see Figure 6.4). Then you would form images of the items you want to remember and mentally place each object in a distinctive location. As with the story method, the important thing is that the images of the items vividly interact with the images of the locations. If, for example, the first location on your walk is a mailbox and the first item on your list is a dozen eggs, you might form a mental image of Humpty Dumpty perched upon the mailbox. When it is time to recall the list of items, you need only take a mental walk through your familiar mental map and pick up the images of the items one by one.

In one experiment (Groninger, 1971) half of the subjects learned a twenty-five-item list by the method of loci while the other half were given no instructions. The method of loci resulted in better recall after one week (92 percent to 64 percent) and after five weeks (80 percent to 36 percent). Gordon Bower (1975) has identified three reasons for the method's success. First, the mental image provides a ready-made route to guide you effortlessly from one item to the next. Second, when you find an empty location or one with a vague image, you know that you have forgotten something. And third, arriving at the end of your mental walk is a signal that re-

call is complete. Bower views the method of loci as taking advantage of our vital ability, discussed in Chapter 5, to learn cognitive maps of our environment.

Similar kinds of memory systems have been developed for specific purposes. For example, Richard Atkinson (1975) describes a procedure that has proved effective in the learning of a foreign language vocabulary. Called the *key word method*, it consists of two steps: (1) the foreign word (such as the Spanish word *pato*) is linked to an English key word on the basis of similar sound (*pato* = "pot"); and (2) the key word is then linked to the correct English translation (duck) by an interacting mental image (a duck in a pot). In one test, subjects using the key word method had 88 percent correct recall, while subjects who learned by rote had only 28 percent correct recall.

We should note, finally, that when we talk about improving memory we are not really talking about the *ability* to remember. That ability is a given, and it seems to be pretty much the same for all normal humans. What we are talking about, rather, is improving our methods of putting information into long-term memory in the first place—stocking that brain attic carefully—so that we can retrieve it when we need it. And the key

FIGURE 6.4

The method of loci. To remember a series of items, such as your shopping list, imagine a set of landmarks on a familiar walk from one point to another. Then form a mental image that links each item on your list with one of the landmarks. When it is time to recall the list, take a mental walk through your familiar map and pick up the images of the items one by one.

DON'T FORGET THESE TRICKS

Tricks for improving memory—"mnemonics"—have been used for thousands of years. One popular device is to develop an acronym for the material to be learned. For example, the acronym STAB helps one to remember the four members of a quartet: soprano, tenor, alto, and bass. Similarly, letters that must be remembered in sequence can be used to make up a sentence, such as "Every Good Boy Does Fine" for remembering the musical notes on the staff lines of the treble clef (EGBDF). Another common method is to develop a rhyme—"I before E except after C," or "Thirty days hath September . . ." All these methods work by adding meaning to hard-to-remember information so it can be stored and retrieved more easily.

CHAPTER SIX: MEMORY

to doing this is meaning—making things fit together in coherent ways. In many cases, as in studying from a textbook, the meaning is inherent in the material itself, and the trick is to make sure that you capture this meaning. In other cases, as in lists of objects, memory systems are useful because they give artificial organization or meaning to otherwise meaningless materials. In either case, the more meaningful the material to you, the better you will remember it.

SUMMARY

Short-term and long-term memory

● **1** There appear to be two distinct sorts of memory—short-term and long-term. Information from the environment is first held in *sensory storage* for a fraction of a second and is then either discarded or passed on to short-term memory.

● **2** *Short-term memory* has a limited capacity of about seven items. The amount of information held in short-term memory can be increased by organizing inputs into "chunks." Short-term memory lasts about 20 seconds at most without rehearsal. Information is either then forgotten or is passed on to *long-term memory*.

● **3** Information can be transferred from short-term memory to long-term memory by rehearsal or by encoding. The way material is encoded is a major factor in its later accessibility for retrieval. One useful coding method is to package information in meaningful clusters.

● **4** Retrieval of information from long-term storage is facilitated by using a meaningful process for storing the material in the first place and by using reminders, or cues.

● **5** One interesting retrieval problem—the tip-of-the-tongue phenomenon—seems to indicate that our verbal storage system is coded according to both meaning and sound.

● **6** Remembering may be a process of mentally reconstructing the event rather than simply finding a permanent record of it in long-term storage.

Why do we forget?

● **7** Studies of *verbal learning*, such as those done by Ebbinghaus, have demonstrated a *forgetting curve*: the greatest memory loss occurs soon after learning and the rate of loss declines with time.

● **8** The three basic measures of *verbal learning* are recall, recognition, and relearning. In *recall*, one recounts or reproduces something previously learned. In *recognition*, one identifies something that one has encountered before. In *relearning*, one is able to quickly relearn material that was learned at some earlier time.

● **9** Verbal learning can be hindered by interference. In *proactive interference*, previously learned material interferes with something learned more recently. In *retroactive interference*, new learning interferes with old. Interference may cause its disruptions by preventing rehearsal of material.

● **10** *Retrieval failure* is an inability to locate information in memory. It may be, however, that appropriate cues can trigger the memory. The importance of retrieval cues is illustrated in the phenomenon of *state-dependent memory*—the tendency to remember better when in the same locale or emotional state as when one first learned the material.

● **11** *Motivated forgetting* is the inability to recall information because it would be embarrassing or painful to do so. Freud called such purposeful forgetting *repression*.

Memory and the brain

● **12** Although the physiological bases of memory are poorly understood, memory appears to be a chemical process, involving chemical changes in neurotransmitters in the brain. It is believed that as learning progresses, these chemical changes cause certain synapses to become more efficient at passing messages.

● **13** In most cases, the chemical changes associated with learning require about an hour to consolidate. If the *consolidation phase* is disrupted, the memory is lost, producing *retrograde amnesia*. The hormones epinephrine and norepinephrine also play an important role in locking in memories associated with stressful situations.

- **14** Scientists are following several paths in their search for a "memory drug." Among the drugs that have shown promise are DDAVP, physostigmine, and zimelidine.
- **15** Among unusual disorders of memory are *transient global amnesia*, in which the victim is temporarily unable to hold on to new information for more than a few minutes, and *Korsakoff's syndrome*, in which the victim has a lasting inability to put new information into long-term storage.

Improving memory

- **16** Among methods of improving memory that are particularly helpful in studying are spacing study periods, active recitation, reviewing, giving meaning to the material, and the *PQ4R method*.
- **17** Careful and systematic coding of information can be accomplished with various memory systems. One approach is to make up a story containing the information to be remembered. Another, called the *method of loci*, involves imagining the items to be remembered as being placed in a set of familiar locations. One memory system developed for a specific purpose is the *key word method*, used for learning foreign words.

KEY TERMS

childhood amnesia
consolidation phase
encoding
forgetting curve
key word method
Korsakoff's syndrome
long-term memory
method of loci
motivated forgetting
PQ4R method
proactive interference
recall
recognition
reconstructive memory
rehearsal
relearning
repression
retrieval
retroactive interference
retrograde amnesia
sensory storage
short-term memory
state-dependent memory
tip-of-the-tongue (TOT)
   phenomenon
transient global amnesia
verbal learning

MEMORY AND THE LAW

"Where were you on the night of August 22nd?"

"Is this the man you saw running from your house?"

"What happened immediately after the man took your wallet?"

As these questions illustrate, memory plays an essential role in criminal investigations and trials. Courtroom proceedings place heavy emphasis on eyewitness testimony. This emphasis is based on the assumption that witnesses can see and hear accurately—and, what's more, that they have a clear memory of what they saw and heard, even when the event occurred a year or more before the trial. Unfortunately, these assumptions are not fully justified.

THE UNRELIABLE WITNESS

Despite the heavy reliance on eyewitness testimony, such reports are often much less complete and much less accurate than is commonly believed. In the Warren Commission Report on the assassination of President John F. Kennedy, for example, there was conflict between eyewitnesses as to the number of shots fired, the direction from which the shots were fired, the size of the rifle bag Lee Harvey Oswald carried, and other details (Marshall, 1969).

In classroom exercises, eyewitness testimony has been demonstrated to be unreliable. In one study, 141 students witnessed a staged attack on a professor. After seven weeks had gone by, the students were asked to pick out the assailant from a set of six photographs. Even though the incident had been highly dramatic, 60 percent of the witnesses, including the professor himself, picked the wrong man. Further, 25 percent of the students identified as the assailant a person who had been an innocent bystander at the scene of the crime (Buckhout, Figueroa, and Hoff, 1972).

What accounts for the discrepancy between the law's heavy reliance on eyewitness testimony and the actual unreliability of such recollections? In criminal proceedings, it is often assumed that memory is complete, easily accessible, and totally accurate. The fact of the matter, however, is that memory has

none of these qualities. It is not complete, since many aspects of events are not noticed or transferred into long-term storage. Furthermore, memory is not always easily accessible—it is often quite difficult to retrieve material from long-term memory. And above all, as we will see, memory is not always fully accurate.

IMAGINATIVE RECONSTRUCTION

We sometimes talk about memories for past events as if they were located on videotapes in our brain: To recall the event, all we need to do is replay the tape. But that metaphor is not a very appropriate one. It would be better to think of memories for past events as a kind of blurry slide show—a loose assortment of images and phrases that often requires a good deal of interpretation before it makes sense. Sir Frederic Bartlett (1932) had this sort of interpretation in mind when he described remembering as "an imaginative reconstruction" of experience.

Here is an illustration of imaginative reconstruction, from another classroom demonstration (Erlich, 1974):

Some twenty students sit in a classroom, their heads bent over examination papers. Suddenly the door pops open, and a young woman, about five feet tall and dressed in levis, a plaid hunting shirt, and green tyrolean hat, bursts into the room. She quickly levels a carrot at a student seated in the first row and shouts, "Federal herring! You stole my marks!" Outside in the corridor, a popping sound is heard.

A student in the front row clutches his breast, screams and falls to the floor. As the assailant runs out, two men dressed as ambulance attendants enter the room, drag the victim to his feet, and quickly carry him away.

The whole scene has taken almost one minute from the time the assailant enters until the victim is removed.

The students in this class were immediately asked to write a complete description of the events they witnessed. Considering that these witnesses were all graduate students in psychology, the results are enlightening:

Who was the assailant? One student wrote, "a big Germanic type . . . like a Hollywood storm trooper."

What did the assailant wear? Another student described her dress as "a European-style railroad conductor's uniform."

What was the weapon? And the motive? According to one account, the murderer "used a switch-blade knife on the victim . . . and said . . . 'You are a Marxist and are working to destroy our republic.'"

Who was the victim? "A white male dressed in khaki trousers and a blue sweater," testified one witness. Actually, the victim was a black male in an ROTC uniform.

In all of these reports, we see how the students gave structure and meaning to their recollections of the event they saw—and, came up with quite distorted reports. Such reconstructions of observed events are likely to take place in the courtroom as well.

THE WORDING OF QUESTIONS

One factor that may have a large impact on eyewitnesses' recollections is the wording of the questions that investigators and lawyers put to them both before and during the trial. To demonstrate such effects, Elizabeth Loftus (1979) showed students a short film depicting a traffic accident. Some of the student witnesses were subsequently asked, "About how fast were the cars going when they hit each other?" For other witnesses, the verb "hit" was replaced with "smashed," "collided," "bumped," or "contacted." It

turned out that the witnesses' estimates were influenced by the particular verb used. Those questioned with "contacted" gave the lowest speed estimates (30.8 mph on the average), while those questioned using the verb "smashed" gave the highest (40.8 mph).

In another study, Loftus brought subjects back to the laboratory a week after viewing a filmed accident and asked them some more questions about it. A critical question was whether the witness had seen any broken glass—although in fact there had been none in the film. Loftus reasoned that if the verb "smashed" really influenced witnesses to remember the accident as more severe than it had been, they might also "remember" details that would be congruent with a high-speed accident—like broken glass. This is just what she found. Over 30 percent of the subjects who had been questioned a week earlier with "smashed" reported seeing the nonexistent glass, compared to 16 percent of those who had been questioned with "hit." And subjects who were asked, "Did you see *the* broken headlight?" were more likely to say they had than were subjects who were asked, "Did you see *a* broken headlight?"

On the basis of this and other studies, Loftus concludes that human memory is much more changeable than is often assumed to be the case. The witnesses in her study were not lying to the questioner. Rather, the form of the questions influenced their recollections—or, in Bartlett's terms, reconstructions—of the events.

MISTAKEN IDENTITY

The changeability or *malleability* of memory is also demonstrated in cases of mistaken identifications of "criminals." In 1972 in Queens, New York, for example, Lawrence Berson was charged with raping five women. The 17-year-old college freshman was identified by all five women as their attacker. Berson was released only after another man, Richard

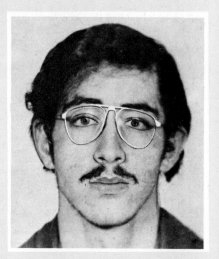

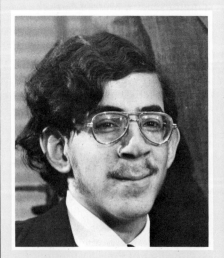

George Morales (top) and Lawrence Berson (bottom) were each arrested for crimes later admitted to by Richard Carbone (center).

Police lineups are most likely to lead to accurate identifications when no one person in the lineup "sticks out like a sore thumb."

Carbone, was arrested for the same crimes. Carbone was later convicted. Two years later, a man named George Morales was arrested for robbery, only to be cleared when the same Richard Carbone admitted the crime. Both Berson's and Morales's only "crime" was that they looked like Carbone (Loftus, 1975).

Even less striking resemblances can lead to mistaken identifications. This is especially likely when the witness is asked to select an assailant from a lineup that is biased or "stacked" in particular ways. In one case, the suspect was at least ten years older than the other men in the lineup. In another case, the suspect was at least four inches shorter than any of the others. And in still another case, the suspect was the only man in the lineup not wearing a tie and glasses.

In such cases, the witness is likely to pick out the distinctive looking person in the lineup, even if that person resembles the actual criminal only slightly. The witness feels pressure to identify *somebody.* So he may think to himself: "The person who attacked me was not wearing glasses or a tie. And neither is that man over there—so it must be him." Clearly, lineups in which one person sticks out like a sore

thumb are not fair (Ellison and Buckhout, 1981). Such lineups increase the likelihood that witnesses will make "imaginative reconstructions" that are far from the truth.

In spite of the unreliability of eyewitness testimony, jurors often appear to be heavily influenced by it. In another of Loftus's studies, 68 percent of student-jurors in a mock trial voted to convict a defendant in a murder case on the basis of a single eyewitness report, even when it was proved that the eyewitness had 20–400 vision, was not wearing his glasses, and therefore could not possibly have seen the face of the murderer from where he stood.

(When there was no eyewitness, only 18 percent of the jurors voted for conviction.) Given the malleability of human memory, jurors might well take eyewitness testimony with a larger grain of salt. Indeed, in many recent cases psychologists have testified as expert witnesses to warn juries of the limitations of eyewitness testimony (Brigham, 1981).

HYPNOSIS AND EYEWITNESSES

Some law enforcement officials believe that one way to improve the memories of eyewitnesses is to make use of hypnosis. In some cases, people who were unable to remember the details of crimes they had witnessed were able to come up with such details when they were hypnotized. This technique has led to the solution of several dramatic cases. In 1976, for example, a busload of California schoolchildren was forced off the road and the children held captive. The bus driver managed to escape but couldn't remember anything about the kidnapper. When put under hypnosis, he was able to remember all but the last number of the license plate of the kidnapper's van. This information enabled police to track down the kidnapper and release the children.

Because of successes such as this one, most major police departments use hypnosis to elicit information from witnesses in certain cases. But it is not at all clear that hypnosis does enhance accurate memory. For every case in which hypnosis has been able to elicit truthful and useful information there have been others in which the information has proven to be inaccurate. In one case, a woman had disappeared. Hoping to find what had become of her, police investigators hypnotized her young son. The boy was able to recount an event that until then he had apparently repressed: he had

seen his father murder his mother. The father was charged with first degree murder, tried, and convicted. Long after the trial, the woman turned up alive in another state. The "memory" elicited from the boy turned out to have been based in fantasy, not reality.

Cases such as this one raise serious questions about the validity of memories extracted during hypnosis. Recent research by psychologists raises similar questions. Psychologists have found that, in general, hypnosis does not increase the accuracy of people's recollections. If anything, hypnosis may make people's reports less reliable (Smith, 1983). As noted in Chapter 3, hypnosis heightens people's motivation to behave in ways suggested to them by the hypnotist. Under hypnosis, people may be very highly motivated to retrieve memories of the crime they witnessed. But this motivation, as often as not, leads people to reconstruct details that did not actually occur.

In one study, subjects were shown a series of pictures and were asked to describe them immediately afterward. A week later the subjects were called back to the laboratory and questioned again. This time, half were hypnotized before being questioned and half were not. The hypnotized subjects came up with more new information about the pictures than did those who weren't hypnotized, but most of what they "remembered" was inaccurate—their own reconstruction of what they had seen (Dywan and Bowers, 1983). Similar results have been reported in studies where subjects viewed film clips of crimes (Buckhout et al., 1982). Thus, in a police investigation or a court of law, hypnosis may reveal either a true clue (and thus help in solving the crimes) or it may reveal a false clue (and thus possibly lead to a miscarriage of justice).

The use of testimony from eyewitnesses who have been hypnotized is thus highly controversial. Martin Orne (1979) has suggested that hypnosis should be used in some instances to gain leads in a case but that such recollections should not be admitted as evidence in a trial. In recent years, some states (such as California) have banned testimony from eyewitnesses who have been hypnotized, while other states (such as New Jersey) will admit such evidence only if certain precautions have been taken, such as requiring the hypnotist to be someone with no knowledge of the case, to minimize the chance of biasing the subject's memories. Few would deny that hypnosis represents a valuable investigative tool, but it is a tool that should be used only with great caution.

SUMMARY

- **1** Eyewitness testimony in trials and criminal investigations is not as reliable as is commonly believed. This discrepancy arises from the fact that memory is incomplete, not always easily accessible, and not always accurate.
- **2** People often give structure and meaning to their recollections—a phenomenon Bartlett called *imaginative reconstruction*
- **3** A person's memory of an event is often influenced simply by the way he or she is questioned about the event.
- **4** The malleability of memory is further demonstrated by the fact that mistaken identification is a common occurrence in criminal cases.
- **5** Although it has become popular to use hypnosis to "improve" the memories of eyewitnesses, hypnotized eyewitnesses may actually reconstruct details that did not occur.

LANGUAGE, THOUGHT, AND INTELLIGENCE

Language, thought, and intelligence are among our "higher mental processes," involving complex sorts of information processing.

Producing even a simple sentence is a complicated act. Yet we all learn to speak fluently by the age of 4 or 5.

Concepts—our mental groupings of objects or events—affect the way we interpret the world and organize our experience.

When we have a goal that we don't know how to achieve, we have a problem to solve. Research provides some hints on how we can improve our problem solving.

People vary in their abilities to acquire and use knowledge—their intelligence. IQ tests are widely used, if controversial, measures of these abilities.

People at both extremes of intelligence—the mentally retarded and the intellectually gifted—present special challenges to society.

Researchers in the field of artificial intelligence program computers to "think." But can computers really think the way humans do?

• It is fourth down and a foot to go. The quarterback must decide whether to try for a first down or go for the field goal. As the team goes into its huddle, he quickly asks one of his linemen a question and nods at the answer. Then he calls the play.

• As managing editor of the school newspaper, Sarah must go over all the front-page headlines before the paper goes to press. She realizes that one of the headlines could easily be misinterpreted. She picks up her pencil, thinks for a moment, then crosses out the old headline and writes in a new one that is more precise.

• Steve, Alicia, and Brian are sitting around the lunch table arguing about politics. Each of them is supporting a different candidate in the upcoming primary election. "Your candidate is so wishy-washy that he ought to open a laundromat," Steve explodes at Brian. "Better to be wishy-washy than plain dumb," Brain retorts.

In the last three chapters we have reviewed research on the basic mental processes of perception, learning, and memory. In addition to these processes, however, there are other sorts of mental processes that are almost constantly involved in our daily activities. Language, thought, and intelligence, to be discussed in this chapter, are sometimes called *higher mental processes* because they involve some of the most complex sorts of mental activities that we perform.

As suggested by the above examples, language, thought, and intelligence are often closely connected with one another. Language is central to the ways in which we interpret situations and solve problems. The quarterback uses language to confer with his teammates, in the process of making his strategic decision. The editor must think *about* language and deal with the problem of using language effectively. The three students at lunch use language to formulate their thoughts about the various candidates. In all of these cases, people are making use of their intellectual skills—their "intelligence"—in evaluating information. And as Brian's comment reminds us, we often make appraisals of other people's intelligence as indications of their ability in particular jobs or spheres.

In this chapter we will first consider language, a capacity that most—although not all—researchers believe is a unique property of human beings. We will focus on the question of how language is acquired in the first years of life. We will then turn to two important aspects of thought: the use of concepts to categorize objects and events, and the methods people use to solve problems. Finally, we will consider the nature and measurement of intelligence, including a discussion of people who are at one or another extreme of intelligence—either mentally retarded or intellectually gifted.

LANGUAGE

Language is the primary means by which we communicate with other people. In addition, we use language as a means of formulating our thoughts. Clearly, language is much more than a set of sounds. Whether English, Hungarian, or Vietnamese, a language is a system of symbols that can be used to represent our activities, our thoughts, and our worlds. How this system works, and especially how each of us comes to acquire it, is one of the most important

Each of the world's languages is a system of symbols that can be used to represent objects, activities, and ideas.

questions that can be asked about the human mind.

How is language acquired?

We engage in dozens of conversations each day. Yet producing even a simple sentence such as "I'll have a cup of tea" is in fact a very complex act. We must make the organs of our larynx and mouth produce the right sounds; we must link the sounds together into words; we must know and choose among thousands of words to use; and we must know the intricate rules of joining words together to produce a meaningful sentence. And this is only half of it. We must also be able to interpret the sounds, words, and phrases of the other person's responses to us.

Speaking our native tongue is probably at least as complicated as applying calculus or astrophysics. Yet quite miraculously, we all learn to speak fluently, without any specific training, by the time we are 4 or 5 years old. Before children can add 2 and 2, they have mastered the basic rules of grammar. They can modify tenses, pluralize nouns, choose pronouns, and correctly apply many other rules. That a 3-year-old can say,

with perfect adherence to the rules of grammar, "But I don't want to take a bath!" is no mean accomplishment.

What accounts for this remarkable and rapid process? How is language acquired? During the first half of this century, the generally accepted explanation came from learning theorists—notably B. F. Skinner (1957)—who believed that language was learned in the same way as any other behavior: according to principles of reinforcement and imitation, discussed in Chapter 5. According to this view, when a small child correctly copies an adult word or group of words, she is given a reward, such as attention, a smile, or an immediate response. On the other hand, if the child makes an inappropriate sound or statement, she is ignored or corrected. Through a gradual shaping process, the child acquires correct, adultlike language.

Learning undoubtedly does play an important role in language learning. Children do utter words or phrases that gain them rewards, and they do imitate the words and phrases of others. Research of the last few decades has found, however, that learning principles offer an inadequate explanation of how children learn language. For one thing, adults do not generally reward only grammatically correct statements (Brown, 1973). A child who says "Me want Teddy" is just as likely to get what she wants as a child who uses the proper pronoun. And while a small child will imitate phrases she hears from adults, many of her statements are quite unique constructions. For example, a child may say "Allgone milk" or "Truck bye-bye," statements she is unlikely to have heard from adults and that seem to reflect her own system of language.

The linguist Noam Chomsky (1968) proposed that in learning language children do not learn a list of words and phrases but rather a complex set of rules for producing and understanding sentences. Chomsky has described language in terms of *transformational grammar*—a set of rules about how words are usually joined in a sentence and how sentences can be transformed, or changed around, without changing their meaning. With such rules, we can understand and produce an infinite number of sentences. For example, if we hear the simple statement "John kissed Mary," we immediately know from the word order that "John" is the actor, "kissing" is the action, and "Mary" is the object. If we hear the statement "Mary was kissed by John," we still get the same meaning by using the transformational rule of English that inserting the verb auxiliary "was" reverses the actor-object relationship. And if we hear "The man who kissed Mary is called John," we can apply other transformational rules to get the meaning. Each language has its own specific rules, but they all serve the purpose of regularizing the way words are joined so that we can effortlessly understand and produce even the most complicated sentences.

Whether a child learns English or Swahili, the rules are far too complex to learn simply by listening to others. Chomsky proposed that some knowledge of language must be innate—that certain rules, categories, and strategies of processing language are built into our brains. This innate capacity for language enables the child to "soak up" the rules of whatever language he is exposed to and guaran-tees language to all members of our species.

Many psychologists and linguists agree that there must be a biological predisposition for language. In fact, as discussed in Box 1, this capacity may be unique to the human species. But just how language is built into our brains is only dimly understood. As was noted in Chapter 2, certain areas of the cerebral cortex seem to play specialized roles in language produc-tion and comprehension. For exam-ple, patients with damage to an area of the left hemisphere called Broca's area retain an understanding of indi-vidual words but have difficulty join-ing the words into sentences (Zurif, 1980). The fact that particular parts of the brain seem to be specialized for the grammatical aspects of language lends support to Chomsky's argu-ment that some aspects of language are biologically determined.

It is possible that there are biologi-cally based *critical periods* for lan-guage learning—periods of time dur-ing which language must be learned if the learning is to be complete and ef-fective. If one puts a young child into a new language environment, he or she soon speaks it like a native. But for older children and adults, learning a new language is much harder and never as successful. The fact that young children learn language much more easily than older children or adults has been linked to the develop-ment of the brain. As explained in Chapter 2, in adults the two hemi-spheres of the brain each have pri-mary control over separate sets of abilities. Language is usually con-trolled by the left hemisphere. The process of *lateralization*, or the spe-cialization of the hemispheres, occurs gradually throughout childhood and seems to be linked to language acqui-sition. Once lateralization is com-plete, at about age 10, language is never as easily acquired (Lenneberg, 1967).

The biological predisposition for language does not necessarily depend on speech. Deaf children learn sign language in a way that parallels the acquisition of speech in hearing chil-dren. They produce their first "words" and "sentences" at about the

THE LANGUAGE OF MUSIC

In most right-handed people the left hemi-sphere of the brain has primary control over linguistic abilities, such as reading, writing, and speaking, while the right hemisphere has primary control over cer-tain nonlinguistic skills, including musical ability. Among accomplished musicians, however, the left hemisphere has been found to be more involved in understand-ing music than the right hemisphere is. For these musicians, it seems, music has be-come a kind of language, with its own set of "linguistic" rules for combining and representing musical notes and phrases, much like the rules for combining and rep-resenting words and phrases in spoken lan-guage. Among musicians, therefore, musi-cal skills become more closely linked to the "linguistic" side of the brain (Bever and Chiarello, 1972).

BOX 1

IF I COULD TALK LIKE THE HUMANS

"When we study human language," wrote the linguist Noam Chomsky (1972), "we are approaching what some might call the 'human essence,' the distinctive qualities of mind that are, as far as we know, unique to man."

Is Chomsky right? Is language in fact a unique human ability, something that separates us from all other members of the animal kingdom? As one approach to answering this question, a number of investigators have attempted to do what others said couldn't be done: to teach language to chimpanzees, our closest animal relatives. It is unfair, though, to expect a chimpanzee to speak, since its vocal apparatus is not as well developed as ours. So researchers have tried to teach chimpanzees sign language.

The best known of these attempts was conducted by Allen and Beatrice Gardner (1969), who began their study of a female chimpanzee named Washoe in 1966, when she was about 1 year old. Washoe would spend much of each day interacting with humans speaking to her in American

Sign Language (Ameslan), the language commonly used by deaf people in America. After six months of training, Washoe used only a few signs. By age 4, however, she had a vocabulary of 85 signs, and by age 5 it had nearly doubled to 165.

Washoe's use of Ameslan remained crude, but the Gardners believe that she used it as a real language. She produced sequences of signs in ways that resembled sentences, and she sometimes seemed to create expressions of her own that she had never seen her trainers use. On one occasion, for example, Washoe signaled "Open food drink" while pointing at the refrigerator. On another occasion, when she saw a swan for the first time, she created her own name for it, making the two signs "water bird." During the past 15 years, psychologists have taught many other apes extensive sign language vocabularies as well.

It is clear that apes can, indeed, learn to understand and use individual signs that represent specific objects and events. But there is considerable

debate over whether the apes' accomplishments qualify them for the distinction of being "language users." The skeptics claim that the animals have merely memorized specific sequences of signs and are not applying general rules of language. Even pigeons can be trained to peck at four keys in a specific sequence in order to obtain food, but no one would argue that they are using "language" when they do so.

One psychologist who arrived at a negative conclusion about ape language is Herbert Terrace (1979). Terrace and his colleagues raised a chimpanzee named "Nim Chimpsky" in New York City apartments. Nim was treated much like a young child and was toilet trained at 2½. Like the sign-learning chimps before him, he developed an extensive vocabulary in Ameslan, used signs in their proper order, and sometimes created new sentences. After an extensive analysis of the videotape record, however, Terrace noted that Nim's course of "language" learning was very different from that of human children.

Whereas children come to imitate parents' exact utterances less and less, Nim imitated more and more. In fact, over half of his sentences were exact imitations of what his trainers had just signed to him. Terrace concluded that all of Nim's language could be accounted for in terms of prompting by and imitation of his trainers, rather than of any capacity of Nim's to produce language on his own. After looking back at films that had been made of Washoe's interactions with her trainers, Terrace suggested that a similar explanation probably accounts for Washoe's signaling as well.

Although the question is still hotly debated, the current evidence suggests that whereas chimpanzees can certainly learn to use signs (usually to get things they want), they cannot use *language*, a rule-governed system of symbols in which new sentences can be generated.

Nim Chimpsky with one of his trainers. Although Nim developed an extensive vocabulary of signs, it is not clear that he could really use language.

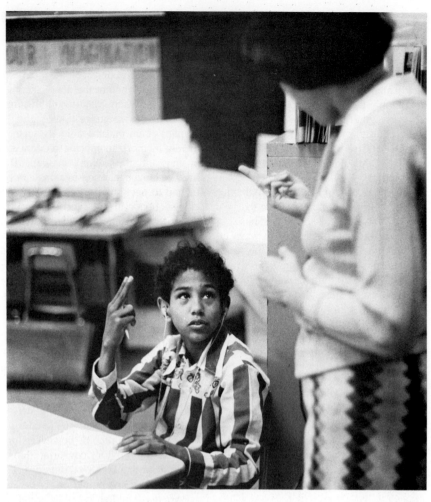

Deaf children learn sign language in a sequence that parallels the acquisition of speech in hearing children.

same time as hearing children (Newport and Ashbrook, 1977) and even make the same sorts of mistakes in grammar. For example, deaf children first produce negative sentences by just adding the "no" sign to other signs, and only later do they learn other, more correct, ways of signing negatives. A hearing child does the same thing. He might first say, "Me no go" and only later learn to say, "I won't go" (Klima and Bellugi, 1979).

Although we seem to be biologically "prewired" to learn language, input from the environment is still necessary. In order to learn the rules of their language, toddlers must be spoken to and have opportunities to respond in turn. Adults also seem to facilitate children's language learning by speaking to them in ways that fit their needs as language learners. When speaking to toddlers, adults tend to use short sentences, limited vocabulary, and straightforward grammar, with lots of questions and

plenty of repetition (Snow, 1972). Thus, a father is much more likely to say, "See the birdie, Franny?" than "Do you remember the bird we saw yesterday in the park?" This simplification of speech makes the meaning of words and rules of grammar stand out for the beginning speaker.

The course of language development

The general timing and sequence of language acquisition seems to be the same the world over (Slobin, 1973). Although there is a good deal of individual variation, most children begin to babble at about 6 months of age. They say their first word at about 1 year and begin to combine words when they are about 1½ or 2. By the age of 4½, the basic grammar of adult speech is in use.

Infants make relatively few different sounds during the first months of life, but by about 6 months they are producing a great variety of sounds and putting them together in various combinations. The babbling of infants the world over sounds pretty much the same. All seem to prefer a few repetitive vowel-consonant combinations, such as "ba-ba" and "da-da." At around 9 months, however, babies begin to sound different, as they begin to use the basic sounds that make a difference in the particular language that they are exposed to. The recognizable sound units of a language—or *phonemes*—differ from one language to another. In Japanese, for example, no distinction is made between "l" and "r" sounds, and whereas there is only one "n" sound in English there are five different "n" sounds in Spanish. These sound distinctions prepare the infant to combine the sounds into her first syllables and words, beginning at about 1 year.

The baby's first words are typi-cally the names of the people and objects that matter most in his world—words such as "Mommy," "Daddy," "cookie," and "teddy." The first words also include those that achieve effects important to the child, such as "more" and "no." At first, children are likely to pronounce their words in simplified ways, and they may *over-extend* words, using them in ways broader than the ways they are used by adults. When my son Elihu was a little over a year old, "da" meant both "Daddy" and "Mommy," and "duh" meant not only "duck" but most other small animals and birds. Babies usually understand the differences between words before they themselves can produce them (deVilliers and deVilliers, 1979). For example, Elihu could point to pictures of ducks, dogs, pigs, and cats when he was asked to, even when he was still calling all of them "duhs."

By the age of 6 months, infants produce a great variety of sounds and put them together in different combinations. The babbling of infants all over the world sounds pretty much the same.

At about age 2 (although there is a great deal of variation from child to child), children form their first sentences, combining two words in a meaningful way. Among the earliest sentences are those that indicate possession ("Adam ball," "Jill cup") or that link a subject with an action ("Adam fall," "Jill run") (Brown, 1973). Early language is marked by errors that often seem "cute" or amusing to adults. But these errors reflect the fact that children are not simply imitating what they have heard but are producing language by discerning and applying *rules*. For example, the usual rule for forming the past tense in English is to add "d" or "ed" to the end of a verb. Once this rule is learned by about age 2½ or 3, the child will *overregularize* it and apply it even in cases in which it happens to be incorrect. Thus, the child is likely to say, "I goed to the zoo" or "I maked my bed." Similarly, children commonly form plurals such as "mans" and "foots" by overregularizing the rule that plurals are formed by adding an "s."

Between the ages of 2 and 5, children continuously refine their understanding of the rules of language. At the same time, they are adding more and more words to their vocabulary. By one estimate, it works out to an average of about five new words a day. And children's sentences become increasingly complex as new elements are plugged into the sentence. While a 2-year-old might say, "See ball," the 3-year-old comments, "See the red ball" and the 4-year-old exclaims, "Look, Mommy, the ball is rolling down the hill!" All of these linguistic developments go hand in hand with the child's cognitive development—his ability to understand the world in fuller and more sophisticated terms (see Chapter 8). Before the child can use the past tense, for example, he must understand what it means for something to have already occurred. Before the child can use adjectives such as "big," "tall," and "fat," he must acquire some initial concepts about size and space. By age 5 or 6, the process of learning language is largely complete. A first grader continues to learn new words, and parents may remind children not to say "ain't," but this is icing on the cake.

All human children learn a language, and learn it in a similar sequence, no matter what their environment. This commonality provides further evidence of the existence of a biological predisposition for language. But the style of language they are exposed to and the amount of language they hear has an impact on how quickly and how well they learn to speak (Hoff-Ginsberg and Shatz, 1982). For example, one recent study found that children in day-care centers where adults spoke frequently to them produced longer and more complicated sentences than children of the same age and background in day-care centers where interactions with adults were less frequent (McCartney, 1984).

As children become more fluent speakers, language takes on even greater proportions. It is used not only in conversation with others but goes "underground" to become a part of private thoughts, to refine their concepts of the world, and to help in solving problems. As adults we often do our thinking with the help of words and sentences. In deciding what to order for lunch, we may go through a mental monologue: "The lasagna looks good—but all those calories! I'd better stick to the tuna salad." Our thoughts do not *always* involve words; some of our thoughts rely on nonverbal mental images. But a large proportion of our thoughts, including the formation and application of concepts (to be discussed in the next section), involves the private use of language.

CONCEPTS

You are strolling through the park with a friend. Suddenly, an object flashes through the air, startling you both. Then your friend says, with relief, "Oh, it's only a bird." In those few seconds between the initial perception and the ultimate labeling of the "bird," some complex mental events have occurred. In order to use the label, your friend has had to recognize important attributes of the flying object and then to categorize it among similar objects while distinguishing it from all others. You are categorizing objects when you call apples, peaches, and plums "fruits"

and when you call Barbra Streisand, Luciano Pavarotti, and Michael Jackson "singers." Categories such as these are called *concepts*. A concept is a mental grouping of a set of objects or events on the basis of important common features. Concepts are basic to our use of language, our thought processes, and our experience of life.

How concepts are learned

People are not born with ready-made concepts. Concepts have to be learned. Some concepts are communicated through explicit definitions, as when your chemistry instructor defines "molecule" or your sociology instructor defines "social movement." But most concepts are learned from examples. When a boy is told, "Go feed the birdie," he learns that the particular object hopping around on the ground is an instance of the concept "bird." And when the boy is later scolded for throwing crumbs to a cat, he learns that not all objects hopping around on the ground are birdies. Psychologists call examples that fit within a concept *positive instances*; robins, sparrows, eagles, and chickens are all positive instances of the concept "bird." Cats, dogs, rocks, and trees would be *negative instances*. Given enough encounters with both positive and negative instances, the person develops a refined picture of the attributes that characterize a bird. In other words, the person learns the concept. Concept learning is vitally linked to language since it involves developing a vocabulary—we depend on words as labels for categories of objects, actions, and attributes.

As we learn concepts, whether as children or as adults, our attention is not drawn equally to all attributes of the objects in question. Rather, we focus on those attributes that seem to be most common and that distinguish this object most clearly from other kinds of objects. As the child learns the concept "bird," for example, he is likely to focus on the bird's small size, its feathers, and its ability to fly. As a result, robins and sparrows, which have these characteristics, are considered to be better, or more *prototypical*, examples of the bird con-

THE "BEST" DISEASE YOU CAN FIND

What is the first thing that comes to mind when you think of a disease? of a crime? of a sport? If you are like the subjects studied by Eleanor Rosch (1973), certain instances of these concepts are more likely to come to your mind than others. For Rosch's subjects, cancer and measles are better examples of a disease than is rheumatism; murder is a better example of a crime than blackmail; and hockey is a better example of a sport than archery. In each case, the "better" examples, or prototypes, contain the attributes of the concept that are central and important to most people.

Which looks most like a "bird" to you? Some birds are more "birdlike" than others. Thus, a robin is a better prototype of the concept of a "bird" than an ostrich or a penguin.

cept than are ducks and ostriches (Rosch, 1973). Similarly, most people consider apples and oranges to be more "prototypical" fruits than avocados or figs, because their size, shape, and texture correspond more closely to our general concept of fruit.

How concepts affect our lives

Concepts have a large impact on our everyday lives because they affect the way we interpret the world. In particular, concepts help us to predict and control events. For example, until we learn to incorporate "sharp teeth" into our concept of "dog," we risk being bitten. But concepts help us only if they *appropriately* organize our experience. The child who thinks that a rat is a "kitty" or that orange-

flavored aspirins are "candy" is clearly in danger.

We are most likely to apply our expectations about categories of objects to the more prototypical (or "best") instances of the category (Rosch, Simpson, and Miller, 1976). Thus, if someone asks us to buy some "fruit," we're more likely to bring home apples and oranges than figs or prunes. Or when we enter a living room, we're more likely to sit down on a piece of furniture with a back and four legs (a prototypical "chair") than on a modernistic chair that looks like a piece of sculpture.

We also come to categorize objects at different *levels of generality*—as instances of either broader, more inclusive categories or narrower, more specific categories. For example, is a particular object a "piece of furniture," a "chair," or a "Chippendale"? Is another object a "book," a "text-book," or "the fourth edition of Ledger's *Introduction to Accounting*"? The level of generality that we employ depends on our experiences and on our needs. Thus, a particular object may be a "book" to someone who needs a convenient flat object to prop up a slide projector, a "textbook" to someone who is thinking of selling some possessions, and "Ledger's *Introduction to Accounting*" to someone studying for final examinations.

Roger Brown (1958) has noted that children learn to use different levels of generality as they grow older. For example, most children first learn to call all coins "money." Money is what Mommy and Daddy buy things with, and it is something you do not swallow or throw away. When the child is old enough to go to the store herself, it becomes important for her to distinguish the different coins; she must be able to tell nickels from dimes and pennies. At this point parents will begin using the new words "nickel" and "dime" and "penny." Hearing the new words and having the opportunity to use the coins, the child begins to differentiate her simple concept of "money" into a more refined one. Concepts, then, are mental categories that we use to help organize our experience. Other sorts of mental categories that affect our lives—the "mental accounts" that underlie many of our decisions—are discussed in Box 2.

Concepts and culture

As the above examples suggest, there is no single, objectively correct way to classify most of the objects in our experience. Classifications are determined to a great extent by social and cultural factors. Thus, we who speak English have only one word for snow, while the Eskimos have separate words for falling snow, fallen show, packed snow, slushy snow, wind-driven snow, and still other varieties. Such distinctions make good sense for a people whose survival may depend on knowing snow conditions. In contrast, the Aztecs reportedly used variations of a single word to communicate the concepts "snow," "cold," and "ice." In their hot climate, more extensive categorization was unnecessary (Whorf, 1956).

Culture has a particularly important effect on our concepts of other people. Concepts about entire groups of people are called *stereotypes*. When you have a stereotype of blacks as being musical or of women as being emotional, it means that being musical or emotional is part of your concept of a black person or of a woman, in much the same way that having feathers may be part of your concept

of a bird. And, because stereotypes are so often based on small numbers of observed instances (and sometimes on no observed instances at all), they are particularly prone to error. We will come back to stereotypes and their effects in Chapter 16 when we discuss sex roles, and in the Psychological Issue following Chapter 15, when we look at racial prejudice.

PROBLEM SOLVING

As we go through life we are constantly faced with problems, from solving crossword puzzles to planning a family budget or patching up an argument with a friend. By studying the ways in which people go about solving problems, we may be able to get some ideas about how we can improve our problem-solving performance.

What is a problem?

A person is confronted with a problem when he wants something (a goal) and does not immediately know what set of actions he can take to achieve the goal (Newell and Simon, 1972). Not all of our mental processes involve solving problems. Sometimes we already know exactly how to perform a task. Thus, for most of us writing our names or riding a bicycle is not really a "problem." When we don't have all the information we need at the outset, then we face a problem. Morton Hunt (1982) has dramatized the difference between a situation that does not present a problem and one that does: "You are flying in the right front seat of a two-place plane with a friend who is a pilot. He falls unconscious and you grab the controls. If you happen to be a pilot, you have a task to perform; if you have never flown a plane, you have a problem to solve" (page 238).

In all cases, a problem begins with an initial set of information (sometimes called the *givens*) and the *goal*. Some problems are quite *well-defined*: both the givens and the goal are clearly specified. For example, the problem of preparing all of the dishes in a meal so that they are ready at the

COLORFUL CONCEPTS

Different cultures have different color concepts, as revealed in the ways in which people categorize and describe different portions of the color spectrum. In English, for example, we identify six basic color ranges: purple, blue, green, yellow, orange, and red. Shona, an Afrian language, uses one word for the range of colors between purple and red, a second for blue and green, and a third for orange and yellow. As Roger Brown (1965) notes, many color names derive from specific objects. The English color word orange *is one example. Many coastal cultures that combine green and blue derive that color name from their word for sea.*

BOX 2

MENTAL ACCOUNTS

Imagine that you have decided to see a play and have paid the admission price of $10 for your ticket. When you arrive at the theater you discover that you have lost your ticket. The seat was not marked and the ticket cannot be recovered. Would you pay $10 for another ticket?

When 200 students were asked this question, slightly more than half said they would not buy another ticket. The annoyance of paying twice to see the same play was apparently too much for them.

But now consider the following, slightly different situation. You decide to see a play for which the admission price is $10. When you arrive at the theater, you discover that you have lost a $10 bill. Would you still pay $10 for a ticket for the play?

When this situation was presented to another 183 students, an overwhelming majority—88 percent—said they would go ahead and buy the ticket.

The difference between responses to the two situations is intriguing. Why do so many people balk at spending $10 after losing a ticket if they would readily spend the same sum after losing an equivalent amount of cash?

Daniel Kahneman and Amos Tversky (1984), who conducted this study, attribute the difference to the way people keep their "mental accounts"—the categories under which they evaluate gains and losses. Most people view theater-going as a transaction in which the cost of a ticket is exchanged for the experience of seeing the play. Buying a second ticket increases the cost of seeing the play to a level that most people find unacceptable. But the loss of the cash is not posted to the mental account of the play and, therefore, has little influence on the decision to buy a ticket.

An interesting effect was observed when the two situations were presented to the same subjects. When students were first presented with the lost-cash version, many of them became more willing to replace a lost ticket. The lost-cash version apparently suggested to many students that they could set up their mental accounts in a different way—they could simply think of the lost ticket as lost cash.

Tversky and Kahneman have used many different sorts of problems to study the psychological factors that underlie people's choices and decisions. Their results make clear that we do not typically make decisions on strictly logical grounds. As in the lost-ticket study, our decisions can be affected by the different ways in which choice situations are described—or "framed"—even when the information turns out to be logically equivalent.

The way our choices are framed can have implications that reach far beyond the decision of whether or not to see a play. In one study, physicians were found to make very different decisions about alternative treatments for lung cancer patients, depending on whether the choices were framed in terms of the probability of the patient's *living* or the probability of the patient's *dying*—even though the two sets of choices were logically identical (McNeil et al., 1982).

Similarly, presidential advisers might influence the decisions made by a president, including crucial decisions of war and peace, by the way they choose to formulate a set of alternatives—such as in terms of the risk of *losing* lives or the chance of *saving* lives.

There are ways in which we can defend against such inconsistent reasoning. One way is to practice framing choices in two or more different ways and seeing whether one's preferences remain the same in both cases.

In problem solving, it often helps to make a written list or diagram that summarizes the givens of the problem.

same time has a clear starting point (all of the items are present but unprepared) and a clear goal (to have them all ready at about the same time) (Wessells, 1982). Many of the problems of daily life are *ill-defined*, however, with neither the givens nor the goal being clear at the start. In deciding what subject to major in, for example, a student is facing a problem, but it may not be at all clear just what the givens or the goals are. In such cases, the givens and the goal may become clear only gradually, as the person undertakes the task. Most research on problem solving makes use of well-defined problems, such as various games and puzzles, as the best way to learn more about the processes people use to solve problems of all sorts.

The first step in solving a problem is to define the problem as clearly as possible. The problem solver must begin by forming a clear *mental representation* of the givens of the problem. Sometimes this mental representation is in the form of sentences and ideas (a list of the dishes needed for the meal we want to prepare), and sometimes it is in the form of mental images or pictures. It often helps to make a written list or diagram that summarizes a given problem. Jill Larkin (1981) found, for example, that the best predictor of people's success on a physics problem was the ability to represent the givens in an appropriate diagram. Once the problem has been defined, a strategy or plan of attack must be devised, the strategy must be executed, and one's progress

FIGURE 7.1

In a flash of insight, Sultan figured out how to get the banana that had been placed beyond his reach.

toward the goal must be evaluated (Wessells, 1982). In the ideal case, these steps form a straightforward sequence. In practice, however, people often switch back and forth between steps. Thus, a person may explore one possible strategy, decide that it is leading nowhere, and then try a new strategy. Such an approach is sometimes called *trial and error*. In other cases, the problem solver must go back to the drawing board and redefine the problem.

Insight

During World War I, one of the leading Gestalt psychologists, Wolfgang Köhler, found himself on one of the Canary Islands, where there was a colony of chimpanzees. With time on his hands, Köhler decided to study the way chimps solved problems. In what has become one of the most famous demonstrations in psychology, Köhler (1925) placed a banana outside the cage and beyond the reach of a chimpanzee named Sultan. Two sticks were inside the cage, neither of them

long enough to reach the banana. After vainly reaching for the banana with one stick at a time, Sultan sulked in his cage, holding one stick in each hand. While manipulating the two sticks, he happened to hold them in a way that made a straight line (Figure 7.1). Suddenly, he inserted the thinner stick inside the thicker one, ran to the edge of the cage, and raked in the banana. Köhler used the term *insight* to refer to the chimp's discovery. Sultan seemed to have mentally organized the sticks into a new pattern, which he instantly recognized as the solution to the problem. Many of us have had similar experiences in which, after struggling with a problem for a long time, we suddenly see it in a new light and thereby discover the solution. These are the times when we say to ourselves, "Aha, now I've got it!"

The basic feature of insight is the mental representation of a problem in a new way. Consider the following problem:

Two police officers stood behind a large billboard to wait for speeding

*violators. One of them looked up
the highway, the other looked
down it, so as to cover all six lanes.
"Mike," said one without turning
his head, "what the heck are you
smiling at?" How could he tell that
Mike was smiling? (Raudsepp, 1980)*

EUREKA!

*Archimedes, the Greek physicist, provided
one of the most famous examples of insight. He had been wrestling with a difficult problem: The king, suspecting that a
golden crown contained more silver than it
was supposed to, had asked Archimedes to
devise a method for determining the
crown's purity. While sitting in the bath-
tub, Archimedes noted that the bath water
was overflowing. All of a sudden he came
up with an ingenious method for solving
the problem, involving the amount of
water that would be displaced by a pure
gold crown. According to legend, Archimedes was so excited by his discovery that he
rushed naked out into the streets of Syra-
cuse shouting, "Eureka!" ("I've found it!").*

One could spend a long time pursuing different ways of solving the problem. But the solution will come in an instant, as soon as the problem solver mentally represents the givens of the problem in a new way. Whereas you might have assumed that the two police officers were standing back to back as they scanned the highway, they were actually facing each other.

One of the factors that often prevents us from gaining insight into problems is that we become used to solving particular sorts of problems in a particular way. In many cases, our familiarity with particular methods of solving problems is helpful to us: we can apply our past experience to new situations. Such learning from experience is called *positive transfer*. However, when we confront a new problem for which the tried-and-true method doesn't work, it is often difficult to shift gears and find an appropriate solution. One such difficulty involves our perception of the tools or equipment needed to solve a problem. We tend to think of an object in terms of its usual function and then have trouble conceiving of using it in a dif-

ferent way. This tendency to perceive only the familiar functions of objects is called *functional fixedness*. Consider the problem depicted in Figure 7.2. Given the materials present in the picture—a candle, a box of tacks, and a book of matches—your task is to mount the candle vertically on the wall, so that the wax does not drip on the floor. Before reading on, see if you can solve the problem.

The correct solution to this problem, which was made famous by the Gestalt psychologist Karl Duncker (1945), is presented in Figure 7.3. The solution is to empty the tack box, then tack the box to the wall and mount the candle on the box with wax. Duncker had subjects sit at a table on which the materials had been placed and try to solve the problem. He found that when the box was full of tacks, as in Figure 7.2, fewer than half of the subjects solved the problem. These subjects remained "fixed" on the box's use as a container and failed to recognize its other possible uses. This functional fixedness could be reduced or eliminated, however: When other subjects were presented with tacks loose on the table, alongside an empty box, all of them solved the problem. Separating the container from its usual function helped the subjects arrive at a new use for it.

More generally, the insightful solution of problems often involves representing the problem in a new way

FIGURE 7.2

*How can you mount the candle vertically
on the wall, using the materials provided?
The solution appears on page 202.*

FIGURE 7.3

Solution to the candle-tack problem. In attempting to solve this problem, many people are hindered by functional fixedness. They think of the box only as a container for tacks and not as a possible candleholder.

that gets beyond the constraints that we might tend to place on it. Figure 7.4 presents three more problems that help illustrate this principle. In each case the solution to the problem requires you to free yourself of certain assumptions in order to conceptualize the problem in a new way.

Some people try to solve problems like these by working and working at them, but to no avail. Without the essential flash of insight—the new way of viewing the problem—it's a little like beating one's head against a wall. In such cases it sometimes helps to stop working on the problem and then to come back to it with a fresh mind a few hours or days later. After such a break, a person may be less likely to persist in the same old ways of approaching the problem and instead come up with a new approach. Sometimes the person may actually be working on the problem "unconsciously." When she returns to the problem, she may find that she already has some new glimmerings of how to solve it. This process of moving toward the solution of a problem while ostensibly thinking about something else is called *incubation* (Silveira, 1971). Incubation is one of the techniques that may facilitate creative problem solving. Some other conditions that may suppress or enhance creativity are discussed in Box 3.

Information processing and problem solving

When solving problems, people often engage in extended sequences of evaluating information, planning a strategy, trying the strategy out, and evaluating their progress toward a solution. The *information-processing approach* to problem solving has focused on the mental processes that go into these sequences, often making use of computer programs as models of human problem solving.

Allen Newell and Herbert Simon (1972), who pioneered the information-processing approach, began their research by asking subjects to think aloud as they worked on various problems. They recorded each of the steps—including the false steps and blind alleys—that the subjects reported taking toward the problem goal. This method of obtaining and analyzing subjects' thoughts while working on problems is called *protocol analysis*. Newell and Simon reasoned that if they could accurately describe the steps by which subjects got from givens to goals, then a computer programmed with a repertoire of these steps should be able to solve the problem. Newell, Simon, and their coworkers proceeded to develop one of the first *computer simulations* of human thought processes, called the General Problem Solver (GPS).

1. Two men play five games of checkers. Each of them win an equal number of games, and there are no ties. How could that come about?

2. Begin with six matchsticks or toothpicks of equal length. Your task is to make them into four equilateral triangles, the sides of which are one stick long.

3.

Connect the nine dots with four straight lines, without taking your pencil off the paper.

FIGURE 7.4

The solutions to these problems appear on page 205.

BOX 3

CREATIVITY

POEM A
Laughter
Edgy, breathless
Fracturing, puncturing breaks
Bullet-like gasps, uncontrolled
Laughter

POEM B
Laughter
Cheerful, excited
Sharing, Opening, Expressing
A clear moment of peace
Laughter

These poems are what two different writers produced when they were asked to write a Japanese Haiku-style poem with the first and last lines consisting of the word "laughter." Which poem is more creative?

In answering this question, chances are you had to stop and think about the word "creative." What does it mean: the best? the strangest? the most pleasing? *Creativity* is an elusive concept, but an important one. We speak of creativity in many domains—in the arts, in sciences, and in business. And we recognize creativity in solving day-to-day problems, such as figuring out how to do something without the usual tools. But what is it that makes one solution seem creative and inspired and another seem ordinary?

Teresa Amabile (1983) has defined creative products as having three components. First, a creative piece of work must be *novel*—different from what has been done before. Second, the product must be *appropriate*—correct, useful, or valuable, and not just different. Third, the task must be one that has *no fixed solution*—the person must find his own way, rather than following a preset formula.

Amabile has found that people generally agree on what is considered creative, especially if they are experts in the particular field of endeavor. Painters tend to agree as to what is a "creative" painting, mathematicians to agree on what is a "creative" proof.

Evaluating the Haiku poems, a group of poets rated Poem A as more creative than Poem B—presumably because it includes a more novel set of words and ideas while still remaining cogent and appropriate (Amabile, 1985).

What accounts for a person's ability to come up with a creative idea or product? Some aspects of people's personalities, such as the ability to become absorbed in a task and the willingness to take risks, seem to be conducive to creativity. And a certain level of intelligence and specific knowledge helps. But creativity remains distinct from intelligence or technical skill.

All of us have the capacity to be creative in certain areas. But how creative we will be depends on our motivation. Amabile (1983) has proposed that we are most creative when we are *intrinsically motivated*—pursuing an activity for its own sake simply because we are interested in it. We are least creative when we are *extrinsically motivated,* or doing it to gain approval or reward. (Intrinsic and extrinsic motivation are discussed further in Chapter 10.) When we engage in an activity primarily for its own sake, Amabile suggests, we are likely to be playful with ideas and materials, to take risks,

and to explore new pathways —all of which promote creativity. When we are working to gain financial rewards, high grades, or the approval of others, on the other hand, we are more likely to stick to safe and uninspired approaches.

When both intrinsic and extrinsic goals are present, we may concentrate on one more than the other, and this emphasis may affect our creativity. Amabile (1985) explored this possibility in the Haiku study. Before writing the poems, half of the writers were reminded of extrinsic concerns by being asked to rate their agreement with such statements as "You enjoy public recognition of your work" and "The market for freelance writing is constantly expanding." The others were reminded of intrinsic goals by rating such statements as "You derive satisfaction from expressing yourself clearly and eloquently" and "You enjoy becoming involved with ideas, characters, and events in your writing."

All of the subjects in the study were committed writers. But those who had been induced to focus for the moment on extrinsic concerns, such as public recognition, wrote poetry that was rated as less creative than those who were induced to focus on intrinsic concerns. Poem A, for example, was written by a subject in the intrinsic motivation condition, and Poem B was by a subject in the extrinsic motivation condition.

Because of the importance of intrinsic motivation for creativity, Amabile suggests that school systems which place a heavy emphasis on grades and strict requirements may be limiting children's creative potential. Albert Einstein (1949), for one, recalled that his experience of studying for exams in a highly competitive school almost wiped out his emerging interest in science. Amabile advises educators and parents to try to minimize extrinsic rewards and constraints in order to let children's creative potential blossom.

When combined with the basic rules of specific games or problems, GPS can be applied to a wide range of problems, including even playing chess. In many cases, GPS has not only solved the problem it was working on but has also seemed to go about solving problems in the same way that people do, thus shedding light on the ways in which human problem solvers process information (see Figure 7.5). In the Psychological Issue that follows this chapter we will survey some of the more recent developments in the field of *artificial intelligence*—programming computers that "think."

One of the most powerful problem-solving methods identified by Newell and Simon is *means-end analysis*. This strategy is seen in the following everyday problem:
I want to take my son to nursery school. What's the difference between what I have and what I want? One of distance. What changes distance? My automobile. My automobile won't work. What is needed to make it work? A new battery. What has new batteries? An auto repair shop . . . and so on.

In this sort of reasoning, the problem solver goes back and forth between goals to be achieved (ends) and the methods (or means) to achieve these goals. Each of the intermediate goals, such as finding a new battery for one's car, is a *subgoal*. Similarly, a computer can be programmed to use the means-end strategy. First, the program analyzes the difference between the current state of affairs and the goal; then, it focuses on ways to reduce that difference. In the process, the computer—just like the human problem solver—sets up a series of subgoals that it attempts to achieve on the way to the final solution.

Improving problem solving

How can we use our knowledge of problem-solving processes to improve our own problem-solving performance? Several of the techniques just discussed can be translated into principles for use in everyday life.

First, you should recognize the central importance of representing and classifying a problem appropri-

ately. For example, if a friend does not want to fly and your statistics about air safety are not helping, perhaps you have misclassified an emotional problem as an intellectual one. If the problem is emotional, then a different kind of solution—such as helping your friend to relax, to get used to airports, and to meet friendly pilots—may be called for. More generally, keep in mind that situations can be classified in more than one way and that our particular classification is bound to affect the decisions that we make.

Second, if you are having trouble with a problem, examine your mental set—the assumptions you are making about the problem. Are you adding constraints to the problem that are not really necessary, as in the candle and tack box problem? This might be the case for a large family in which everyone likes to take a bath but there is not enough hot water for everyone in the mornings. Although cooler baths or alternate days are possible solutions, they fall short of the goal of a daily hot bath for everyone. Having some family members take their baths at night, on the other hand, enables everyone to have a daily hot bath. (Who said everyone has to take a bath in the morning?)

Third, become explicitly aware of various techniques that are useful for a wide range of problems, such as means-end analysis. One frequently useful technique is to begin by making a small-scale plan or model of the problem. Some simplified plans, much like an architect's rough plans for a house, may leave out many details that remain to be resolved, but the plans help by providing an overall structure for solving the problem. Practice using these techniques whenever you can. Many books on problem solving, such as *The Complete Problem Solver* by John R. Hayes (1981), provide opportunities for such practice. But note that there are limits on the effectiveness of general techniques in solving problems in specific domains, such as medical diagnosis, chess playing, or human relations. To become an expert at solving problems in a specific area, there is no substitute for years of experience.

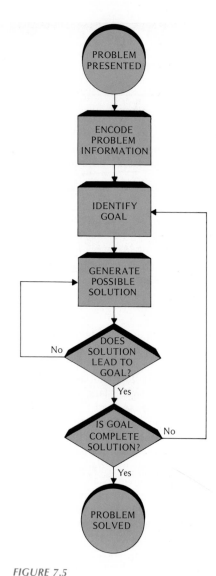

FIGURE 7.5

An information-processing model of problem solving.

Each of the solutions involves liberating yourself from certain assumptions that you might have made.

1. The two men were playing against two different opponents. (Who said they were playing each other?)

2.

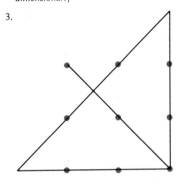

(Who said the answer had to be two-dimensional?)

3.

(Who said the lines had to stay within the nine dots?)

Solutions to the problems presented on page 202.

INTELLIGENCE

Although we all make use of concepts and solve problems every day of our lives, some people seem to be capable of thinking and reasoning at a higher level than others. We refer to such differences in mental abilities as being differences in intelligence. But what exactly is intelligence? Although psychologists differ in their definitions of the term, most would agree with the general notion that *intelligence* is the capacity to acquire and use knowledge.

A key feature of this definition is that intelligence is a *capacity* rather than the possession of particular information or skills. It is possible for someone to have a great deal of information drummed into him without knowing what to do with it—and, therefore, without being particularly intelligent. On the other hand, it is possible for someone to have little knowledge of many subjects, perhaps because of limited experience, and still be highly intelligent.

Measuring intelligence

Much of what psychologists have learned about intelligence is based on research making use of *intelligence tests*. These tests yield scores called *intelligence quotients*, or *IQs*. IQ tests are used extensively to evaluate people's intellectual capacity.

The first IQ tests were devised in the early 1900s by a group of French educators led by Alfred Binet and his colleague Theodore Simon. Their goal was to produce a method of determining which schoolchildren required special instruction and which should go to a regular school. Binet assumed that intelligence develops with age and therefore decided that test items should be graded by both age and difficulty. As a result, he developed the concept of *mental age.* If a child could successfully answer the test items that the average 9-year-old got right, she was said to have a mental age of 9 years, regardless of her chronological age. The child's intelligence quotient was computed by dividing mental age by chronological age and multiplying by 100. Thus, a 9-year-old with a mental age of 9 had an IQ of 100 (% × 100), which is average intelligence. Similarly, a 6-year-old with a mental age of 9 had an IQ of 150 (% × 100), which is an extremely high intelligence. For adults, an IQ of 100 is equal to the average score of a large sample of adults of all ages, and a higher or lower score means that the person did better or worse than this average.

In 1916 Lewis Terman of Stanford University revised Binet's tests, producing what is now called the *Stanford-Binet test.* This revised test (further changed in 1937, 1960, and 1972) emphasized the scholastic aspects of intelligence: reading, writing, and arithmetic (Terman and Merrill, 1937). For example, 8-year-olds were asked to give the similarities and differences between words, such as "orange" and "baseball." In adult tests, more difficult items were included. For example, people were asked to distinguish more subtle verbal differences, such as between "laziness" and "idleness."

In the 1930s David Wechsler observed that the Stanford-Binet test relied heavily on verbal skills, so he decided to develop a test that would include not only verbal abilities but nonverbal performance skills—for example, the abilities to complete an incomplete picture or to arrange a series of pictures in a logical sequence (see Figure 7.6). The tests he developed are the Wechsler Adult Intelligence Scale (WAIS) and the Wechsler Intelligence Scale for Children (WISC). Wechsler thought that including performance tests would provide a fairer assessment of an individual's intellect, especially for those whose social backgrounds did not promote verbal skills. A person's overall IQ score on the WAIS is derived by combining scores from several subtests (vocabulary, picture completion, and so on), but it is also possible to look at individual subtest scores to identify areas in which the person does particularly well or poorly.

A person's IQ score is a relative matter—it is an expression of his standing in comparison to those who were used to standardize the test. An intelligence test is *standardized* by administering it to a large sample of people and calculating their scores. The tests are constructed in such a way that the majority of test-takers achieve scores in the middle range, while increasingly fewer achieve scores toward the higher and lower ends of the range. This sort of distribution of scores is called a *normal distribution* (see Figure 7.7 and Table 7.1).

If the distribution of IQs follows a normal curve (as in Figure 7.7), the odds of having a given IQ score may be determined. The average score on most IQ tests is around 100. About half of the people taking a test will fall within 10 points of the average (between 90 and 109), and about 80 percent will fall within 20 points of the average (between 80 and 119).

FIGURE 7.6

Items similar to those used on the Wechsler Adult Intelligence Scale.

FIGURE 7.7

When the distribution of IQ scores listed in Table 7.1 are plotted, the result is a normal curve. About 80 percent of the population falls within the "average" range.

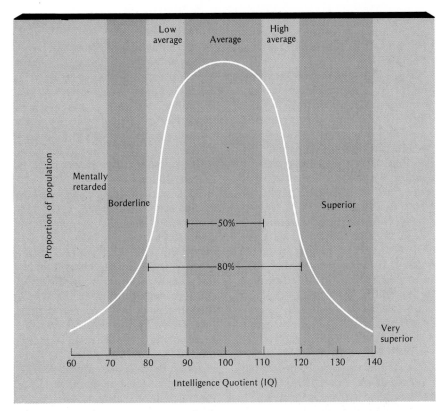

TABLE 7.1

NORMAL DISTRIBUTION OF IQ SCORES

IQ	Classification	Approximate percentage in standardization sample
140 and above	Very superior	1
120–139	Superior	10
110–119	High average	18
90–109	Average	47
80–89	Low average	15
70–79	Borderline	6
69 and below	Mentally retarded	3

Source: From L. M. Terman and M. A. Merrill, *Measuring Intelligence: A Guide to the Administration of the New Revised Stanford-Binet Tests of Intelligence* (Boston: Houghton-Mifflin). Copyright © 1960, 1937.

The use and misuse of IQ tests

About 95 percent of the schools in the United States administer group IQ tests to assess students' needs and abilities (Haney, 1981), and many employers use the tests to select and evaluate personnel. IQ tests have proved to be of great value, especially as predictors of success in school (McCall, 1975). But the extensive use of IQ tests has been highly controversial. One major criticism is that the tests may discriminate against blacks, Hispanics, other minorities, and poor people. On the average, peo-ple from these groups score lower than whites, Anglos, and more afflu-ent people. Even though the tests in-clude nonverbal subtests, they still reflect to a large extent the traditional academic skills that have been most highly emphasized in white, middle-class culture. Critics contend that to use such "culture-specific" measures as a basis for making educational de-cisions about members of other cul-tural groups, such as blacks and the poor, is inappropriate and discrimina-tory (Garcia, 1981). The critics also note that the use of IQ tests has led educators to place many children from minority groups in "slow" classes or in vocational programs rather than academic courses, further restricting their opportunities (Olmedo, 1981).

Critics also argue that IQ tests are often used inappropriately by employers. In 1981, for example, a group of firefighters sued the city of St. Louis because job promotions were based in part on scores on an IQ test. The firefighters claimed that the academic skills the test measured had nothing to do with their ability to fight fires (Bersoff, 1981). Many psychologists would agree. Although IQ tests have been shown to be fairly good predictors of success in school (McCall, 1975), they do not necessarily predict success in other areas of life. As will be discussed in the next section, what is considered "intelligence" may vary from one situation to another and may not depend on the few skills measured by IQ tests.

Because of these problems, critics advocate doing away with standardized intelligence tests. Instead of testing "intelligence," they suggest, we should test for the specific skills relevant to each academic job or decision (McClelland, 1973). Others defend the usefulness of IQ tests, noting that the intellectual skills that the tests measure remain central to many jobs and activities. But if intelligence tests continue to be used—and it seems certain that they will be—they need to be used and interpreted with great care. An IQ score should not be placed on a pedestal as the total evaluation of the person's potential, but used only in conjunction with other measures of ability.

The nature of intelligence

Just what is the capacity called intelligence? Is it a single, unitary entity, or is it a mixed bag of abilities that are only slightly related to one another? Charles Spearman (1904), a British psychologist, took the view that intelligence is a single entity. He proposed that a single general-intelligence factor—which he labeled *g*—accounted for the correlations that are regularly found between different measures of mental ability. He described *g* as a wellspring of mental

energy that flows into everything an individual does.

In contrast, L. L. Thurstone (1938) proposed that intelligence consists of eight primary abilities that are relatively independent of one another, including verbal comprehension, numerical ability, spatial visualization, and deductive reasoning. Excelling in any one of these, Thurstone believed, has little to do with excelling in any other.

Most of the evidence suggests that a compromise between these two positions is probably closer to the truth. Intelligence—at least as it is measured on intelligence tests—seems to include a general ability that underlies scores on a wide variety of subtests (such as those of the WAIS). The higher a person scores on any one subtest, the higher she will probably score on any of the other subtests. But there also seem to be clusters of intellectual abilities that are somewhat independent of one another; thus, some people are better at visual tasks, others at verbal ones.

In recent years researchers have been reconsidering the basic question of just what skills are to be included in the domain of "intelligence." In day-to-day situations, "intelligent behavior" seems to involve far more than the verbal, spatial, and logical skills identified by Thurstone. One leading researcher, Robert Sternberg (1984), favors a view of intelligence that recognizes the ability to adapt to one's environment. By this definition, what is considered "intelligence" may vary from one situation to another according to what skills are required and how well the person matches his particular skills to the demands of the situation.

Howard Gardner (1983) proposes a particularly broad view of intelligence. Drawing from a wide range of biological, psychological, and cross-cultural studies, Gardner has concluded that there are eight different and independent "intelligences": linguistic intelligence, musical intelligence, logical-mathematical intelligence, spatial intelligence, bodily-kinesthetic intelligence (control of the body), interpersonal intelligence (knowledge of others), and intrapersonal intelligence (knowledge of self).

THE GREAT ESCAPE

Psychologist Seymour Sarason recalls that he began to question the validity of IQ tests early in his career. One of his first jobs was to administer tests to students at a school for the mentally retarded. He arrived just after some students had escaped from the school's restricted grounds. After the escapees were caught, Sarason gave them intelligence tests, including a measure of spatial relationships called the Porteus Maze Test. To figure out how to leave the grounds, the students must have had a pretty good sense of spatial relationships. Yet they were unable to solve even the first problem on the test. This anomaly left Sarason wondering which was a better measure of spatial intelligence, the Porteus Maze Test or the successful escape from the institution (reported by Sternberg, 1984).

Howard Gardner suggests that there are eight different "intelligences," including logical-mathematical intelligence (top left), musical intelligence (top right), and bodily-kinesthetic intelligence (above).

Gardner's suggestion that each of these abilities should be called an "intelligence" is a controversial one; others might call them "talents." But his suggestion helps to challenge the prevalent assumption that the verbal, spatial, and logical reasoning skills are somehow more basic than other human capacities.

Still another approach to defining intelligence is to shift attention from "abilities," whether general or specific, and to look more closely at the step-by-step processes people use when they tackle intellectual problems. In such an information-processing approach to intelligence, researchers attempt to analyze what happens to the information in an intelligence test problem, from the time the test-taker perceives it until he provides a response. Consider, for example, the following analogy problem, similar to those found on intelligence tests:

LAWYER is to CLIENT as DOCTOR is to
(a) Patient   (b) Medicine

It took subjects an average of 2.4 seconds to solve a form of this problem used by Robert Sternberg (1979). These subjects were timed from the moment the choices were displayed on a screen until the moment they pressed a button to signal their response.

Some people can solve such problem more quickly and more easily than others can. Sternberg notes that solving such an analogy problem in-

volves several different steps, or *components*. First, the subject must *encode* the terms of the analogy—he must identify what each of the words means, together with their various connotations. For example, a subject might retrieve from his memory the facts that lawyers provide legal services to their clients in offices and courtrooms and that doctors provide services to their patients in offices and hospitals. Next, the subject must *infer* the relationship between the first two terms of the analogy (lawyers serve clients) and then *apply* this relationship to the second half of the analogy (doctors serve patients). At this point, the subject is ready to respond with the right answer.

Sternberg has devised ways to estimate the time taken by subjects to perform each of the problem-solving components. He has found that on certain sorts of problems people who have high IQs actually take *longer* than people with lower IQs to perform the first step in the process, encoding. They are then able to perform the remaining steps more quickly and efficiently. As was noted in the previous section, categorizing or mentally representing a problem is a crucial part of problem solving. From Sternberg's point of view, g—the general factor in intelligence that Spearman described—may refer most fundamentally to people's ability to decide ahead of time what sort of problem they are faced with and what sorts of strategies are needed to solve it.

Heredity and environment

One extreme view of intelligence is that it is a part of one's inheritance, transmitted from one's parents through the genes, much like eye color or blood type. Another extreme view is that heredity has nothing to do with one's intelligence—that it is totally a function of one's environment and experience. Neither of these extreme views is correct. In fact, intelligence is a product of both heredity and environment. But although virtually all psychologists would agree with this statement, there is still a great deal of controversy—and some confusion—about the relative importance of each of these factors in determining intelligence.

The *heritability* of a trait is an estimate of how much of the variation between individuals in that trait is due to genetic factors. To make estimates of heritability, researchers study the similarities between the traits of individuals who stand in different degrees of kinship to one another. Most scientists conclude that IQ has a substantial heritability. One revealing comparison is between similarities of IQ scores for pairs of identical twins and for pairs of fraternal twins. If IQ is highly heritable, then we would expect the IQs of identical twins (who are genetically identical) to be more highly correlated than the IQs of fraternal twins (who are no more similar genetically than ordinary siblings). This turns out to be the case. On the basis of such data, it is estimated that heredity accounts for 40 to 60 percent of the variation in people's IQ scores within the populations that have been studied (Loehlin, Lindzey, and Spuhler, 1975).

The fact that IQ has a substantial heritability does not imply that environment has little impact on intelligence or that one's IQ score cannot be changed. Many studies have indicated that people's experiences—especially early in life—can influence their intelligence. In one successful program at Yale University (Trickett et al., 1983), a group of infants from disadvantaged homes were provided with special help from the time they were

3 months old until they were 2½. Some of the infants, whose parents provided little intellectual stimulation, were put into a special day-care center where they had toys, the freedom to explore, and time with adults that was not available at home. For other families, in which the parents were willing and able to give their children attention but faced too many outside pressures to do so, financial, employment, and marital counseling were provided. It turned out that the children in this program scored higher on measures of intelligence than did a comparable group of children not given the extra stimulation and support. And the program had long-lasting effects. The children's scores were higher than the comparison group not only at the end of the program but even when they were 8 years old.

Even when there is no dramatic intervention in children's lives, particular experiences can have a major impact on IQ scores (McCall, 1983). For example, having many opportunities to explore one's environment may boost IQ scores; a long illness or living under stressful conditions may lower scores. Our genetic endowment may set a certain potential range of intelligence, but within that range, IQ may vary considerably depending on the individual's experience.

Many studies have shown that there are social-class differences in IQ. James Coleman and his colleagues (1966), for example, reported that children from lower socioeconomic backgrounds scored below the national averages on both verbal and nonverbal tests at all grades tested. There are also racial differences in IQ scores. On the average, the tested IQ of blacks is about 15 points lower than that of whites. Both whites and blacks score at all points along the IQ continuum, but there are proportionately more blacks at the lower end of the scale and more whites at the higher end (Loehlin, Lindzey, and Spuhler, 1975).

How can we account for these relationships between IQ and social class, and between IQ and race? Hereditary influences can't be entirely discounted. It is important to note, however, that estimates of heritability of

IS SMART FAST?

Is intelligence "fast" or "slow"? We often assume that intelligent people are those who absorb and process information quickly. Some researchers have even tried to assess IQ by precisely measuring the speed with which people make simple choices (Jensen, 1982). But we also commonly assume that intelligent people think carefully and deliberately. Jumping into problems without adequate reflection is likely to produce false starts and mistaken conclusions—hardly an intelligent way to operate. Robert Sternberg (1984) concludes that intelligence, as a whole, is neither "fast" nor "slow." At bottom, what is important is not how much time one takes to solve problems, but how one allocates one's time among various components of the problems.

A child's environment—including the intellectual stimulation provided by parents—can have an impact on intelligence.

a trait refer only to the genetic influence on variations within the group that has been studied. These estimates do not shed any direct light on differences between groups—for example, different races—in the general population. To account for the relationships between social class, race, and IQ, most researchers have emphasized the role of the environment, including the nutritional, educational, and cultural factors that may determine the extent to which intellectual skills flourish. One study that helps to document the enormous role that environment can play in black-white IQ differences was conducted by Sandra Scarr and Richard Weinberg (1976). They measured the IQs of black children who were adopted and raised by white families in Minneapolis. In all cases, the children were reared in a more affluent environment than the one they were born in. The researchers found that the children's IQs were considerably higher than would have been ex-

pected if they had remained in an impoverished environment. Moreover, the earlier in life the children were adopted, the higher their IQs tended to be, pointing to the influence of experiences in early life.

Another study that attests to the impact of environmental factors on intelligence was conducted by Arthur Jensen (1977). He analyzed the IQ scores of black and white schoolchildren in a rural area of Georgia, a section in which blacks are greatly disadvantaged, both economically and educationally. Jensen found that as the black children grew older, from age 5 to 16, their IQ scores tended to decrease, whereas no such decline was found for whites. As Jensen points out, it is difficult to account for this pattern (which he calls a *cumulative deficit*) in terms of any genetic differences between the races. Rather, it seems to reflect the impact of an environment that limits the opportunities for disadvantaged people to develop their intellectual skills.

EXTREMES OF INTELLIGENCE

Most people have intelligence that is in the "normal" range, with IQs between 70 and 135. But there is also a significant minority of people whose intelligence is higher or lower than this range. Although the specific IQ cutoff points are rather arbitrary, those people with IQs lower than 70 are regarded as *mentally retarded* and those with IQs higher than 135 are regarded as *intellectually gifted*. Each of these groups of people presents special challenges for society.

The mentally retarded

About 3 out of every 100 children born in the United States are diagnosed as mentally retarded at some time in their lives. The range of intellectual abilities included under this label is extremely broad. Some mentally retarded individuals are so profoundly handicapped that they have no speech and must be cared for as if they were infants. Others have no noticeable intellectual impairment until they are confronted with mathematical problems or reading. Some mentally retarded individuals have physical handicaps as well, but many others are physically normal. As noted in Box 4, some retarded persons also have exceptional talents in spe-

cific areas. Thus, no one description can encompass all persons with the label of mental retardation (Edgerton, 1979).

Most diagnoses of mental retardation are based on IQ scores. The classification of retarded persons commonly employed includes four categories: *mild retardation* (IQ of 55–69), *moderate retardation* (IQ of 40–54), *severe retardation* (IQ of 25–39), and *profound retardation* (IQ below 25). Whereas the profoundly retarded require constant medical supervision (only about 1.5 percent of the retarded are in this category), mildly retarded persons can be educated, can hold jobs, and in many respects can lead normal lives.

An important distinction among retarded persons is between the *clinically retarded* and the *socioculturally retarded*. Clinical retardation, accounting for 20 to 25 percent of all retarded individuals, is a condition that is usually diagnosed at birth or in the first few years, and the retardation ranges from moderate to profound. Clinical retardation usually has an identifiable biological or genetic cause. The most common cause of clinical retardation, is a genetic disorder called Down's syndrome (formerly known as "mongolism"). Most people with Down's syndrome have IQs between 35 and 54 (moderately retarded), but some have IQs near 70 and a few have normal intelligence.

Retarded adults can lead fairly normal lives if they are given the training and opportunities needed to work and to live independently. These two individuals are enrolled in a program designed especially for people who might not otherwise be able to maintain jobs.

BOX 4

ISLANDS OF GENIUS

- Nineteen-year-old Michael Hickey has never spoken an intelligible word and spends much of his time rocking back and forth, making grunting sounds or quick, nervous gestures. But on his first try Michael realigned a scrambled Rubik's cube in less than 40 seconds (Restak, 1982).
- Leslie Lemke, born mentally retarded, blind, and suffering from cerebral palsy, sat down at the piano for the first time and played an almost perfect rendition of Tchaikovsky's First Piano Concerto (Schmidt, 1983).
- Bob, now in his sixties, is a "calendar calculator"—he can name the day of the week for any given date since 1937. He gives most answers in less than 8 seconds. Yet Bob is mentally retarded; he lives in a foster home because he cannot manage even simple daily living skills on his own (Hill, 1975).

Though Michael, Leslie, and Bob would perform below normal on any conventional measure of intelligence, they have prodigious abilities in specific areas. In the past, psychologists have referred to such people as *idiot savants*, a term that literally means "learned idiots." This term is inappropriate, however, since they are not idiots (those at the lowest possible IQ level), nor are they savants (those with great knowledge). Their amazing talents—most often in the areas of music, art, mechanical dexterity, mathematics, calendar calculation, or memory for obscure facts—contrast sharply with their low levels of general functioning. An estimated 0.6 percent of mentally retarded people and 10 percent of autistic people have some sort of "savant" talents (Restak, 1982). (Autism, to be discussed in Chapter 13, is a disorder that affects communication, learning, and emotions and sometimes includes mental retardation. Michael Hickey has been diagnosed as autistic.)

Researchers still cannot explain the rare abilities of these retarded and autistic persons. Some claim that savant abilities are based on photographic memories, or analogous "phonographic memories" for music. After

Michael Hickey was able to unscramble a Rubik's cube on his first try.

Leslie Lemke hears any piece of music just once, for example, he can reproduce that piece on the piano. Others have speculated that savants' talents are based on a remarkable ability to concentrate without getting distracted, tired, or bored. One psychologist concluded, "I think retarded savants tune out everything else in the world but the one thing that is of interest to them" (Restak, 1982).

Researchers have also noted that the special abilities of savants are of the type that most people process in the right hemisphere of the brain. Language, logic, and abstract thought are processed in the left hemisphere, and IQ tests emphasize left-hemisphere functions. But music, art, and spatial skills are processed primarily in the right hemisphere. The method used by calendar calculators such as Bob may involve some sort of visual or spatial images of calendarlike configurations, which would also involve the right hemisphere.

Although most types of mental retardation affect both hemispheres, it is possible that some types of retardation affect the left hemisphere while permitting development of the right hemisphere. Such development of the potential for right-hemisphere skills, far out of proportion to the person's linguistic and conceptual abilities, may lead to the development of a single, very special skill—what might be referred to as an "island of genius" (Restak, 1982).

The remaining 75 to 80 percent of retarded persons are said to be socioculturally retarded. They have IQs in the 55 to 69 ("mildly retarded") range. This type of retardation is usually not diagnosed until the child reaches school age and encounters problems with schoolwork. Whereas clinically retarded children can be found in families from all walks of life, socioculturally retarded children tend to be from families that are economically, socially, and educationally disadvantaged. Sociocultural retardation has no specific genetic or biological cause. Some of the factors that may contribute to it are disease, malnutrition, environmental hazards suh as lead-paint poisoning, and lack of intellectual stimulation at home or of encouragement to succeed in school (Edgerton, 1979).

Clinical retardation is usually easy to identify, but diagnosing sociocultural retardation is controversial. Critics say that sociocultural retardation is no more than a discriminatory label, applied to those who are deficient in certain intellectual skills that are valued by middle-class society. The critics also note that a disproportionate number of minority children are labeled as retarded, at least in part because of bias in IQ testing.

Until recently, children diagnosed as retarded were generally placed in special classes of their own. Recently, however, there has been a trend toward *mainstreaming*—allowing retarded students to attend regular classes for at least part of the school day. The extent to which the retarded child can be integrated into regular school programs depends on the individual child's needs. Some moderately retarded children may attend separate classes but with some opportunities during the day to mix with nonretarded children—for example, in recess or gym classes. Many mildly retarded children can spend part of the day in regular classrooms and several hours a day in a "resource room" where special instruction is available (Goldstein et al., 1980).

Once retarded individuals have completed their schooling and have reached adulthood, their options in society are limited. They can live in institutions for the mentally retarded,

or they can remain at home and be cared for by their families. However, there is now a concerted effort in America toward *normalization* of the lives of retarded individuals. That is, they are given opportunities for independent living arrangements, regular employment, and conditions of everyday life that are as nearly normal as possible. They are taught how to manage money, how to use public transportation, and how to cope with other common problems of everyday life. Many mildly retarded adults have benefited from such programs and now live normal lives in their communities, without noticeably being "retarded." In order for retarded individuals to live relatively normal lives, it seems, they must be treated as human beings capable of controlling their own lives. But they must also be given access to assistance when it is needed; for example, a hotline to call in emergencies (Edgerton, 1979).

The intellectually gifted

At the other end of the range of intellectual capacity are those people who have extremely high intellectual potential—the *intellectually gifted*. As we noted earlier in this chapter, people's measured intelligence may have relatively little to do with their success in nonacademic aspects of life. It remains true, however, that people who achieve eminence in science, law, politics, literature, the arts, and other fields are likely to have unusually high intelligence.

The most famous study of gifted children was begun by Lewis M. Terman in 1921. He located 1528 children with IQs of 135 or higher to use in his study. The purpose of the research, in his words, was "first of all, to find what traits characterize children of high IQ, and secondly, to follow them for as many years as possible to see what kind of adults they might become" (Terman, 1954).

In fulfilling the first purpose of his study, Terman found that the gifted children were, in general, healthier, better adjusted, superior in moral attitudes (as measured by certain tests of character), and far more advanced in mastery of school subjects than a control group of normal-IQ children.

AND NOW WE MEASURE FAMOUS MEN
Cox (1926) made use of extensive biographical information to estimate the IQs in early life of 300 famous people. The average of the estimated IQs was 155. The following are some of her estimates:

Sir Francis Galton	200
John Stuart Mill	190
Johann Wolfgang von Goethe	185
Samuel Taylor Coleridge	175
Voltaire	170
Alfred, Lord Tennyson	155
Sir Walter Scott	150
Wolfgang Amadeus Mozart	150
Henry Wadsworth Longfellow	150
Thomas Jefferson	145
John Milton	145
Benjamin Franklin	145
Napoleon Bonaparte	135
Charles Darwin	135

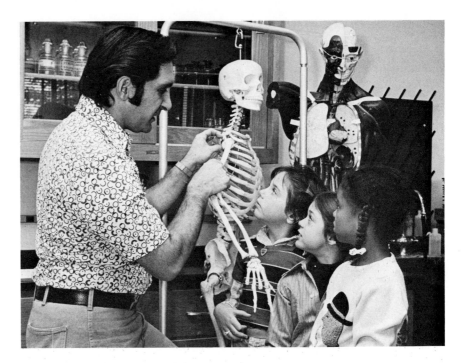

Many programs to identify and nurture gifted children have been established. These 7-year-olds, enrolled in such a program, are learning how body joints work.

The second part of Terman's study is still continuing (even though Terman died in 1956). The gifted individuals in the study have taken part in follow-up interviews and questionnaires many times since the 1920s. By 1984, the average age of the subjects was 74, and the focus of the study had turned to processes of aging. The follow-up research has been conducted by Pauline Sears and Robert Sears, who, it turns out, was himself one of Terman's "little geniuses." The follow-ups have found that the gifted individuals encountered a wide range of outcomes in life. The most successful members of the sample not only had great intelligence but also had a special drive to succeed that had been with them from grade school on. The least successful people often said they felt guilty about not living up to their potential (Goleman, 1980).

Terman's "geniuses" attended ordinary classes and took part in no special programs. But today many educators and psychologists believe that gifted children need to have their talents nurtured—otherwise they are likely to get bored (some gifted children get labeled "learning disabled" for this reason) and to fail to realize their potential. This viewpoint has led to an upsurge in special programs to identify and nurture gifted children, such as programs to train grade-school children in the creative use of computers and to teach college math to junior-high students (Rice, 1980). The "elitist" idea of special programs for the gifted rubs some people the wrong way. But most educators believe that the educational system should be responsive to the special needs and potentials of the intellectually gifted as well as to the special needs of the mentally retarded.

SUMMARY

Language

• **1** *Language* is the system of symbols that we use to communicate with each other. Learning theorists believe that children learn language by being reinforced for imitating adult speech. Other theorists, such as Chomsky, contend that humans have an innate capacity to acquire language. But input from the environment is still necessary.

• **2** Many attempts have been made to teach chimpanzees to use language. The Gardners taught Washoe, a chimpanzee, American Sign Language, and she has been able to create a few novel sentences. Terrace has suggested that such apes have not really learned to use language but rather have simply learned to make signs through imitation and reinforcement.

- **3** Children all over the world develop speech in a predictable sequence. They start with babbling, which at around 9 months starts to narrow to the basic sounds (or *phonemes*) of their culture, and then they begin making single-word utterances. By the age of 2 they are combining words into two- and three-word sentences. By the age of 4½, they have learned the basic grammar of adult speech.

Concepts

- **4** *Concepts* are categories that we use to group a variety of objects or events according to their similar characteristics. A concept is learned by discovering both positive instances and negative instances in which the concept applies.
- **5** The more *prototypical* an object is as a member of a category, the more quickly we will recognize it as belonging to that category. We also come to categorize objects more broadly or more narrowly—that is, at different *levels of generality*—depending on our experiences and needs.
- **6** Concepts are to a great extent socially and culturally determined. Once learned, concepts can influence our perceptions and our behavior. For example, concepts about groups of people—*stereotypes*—can influence the way we behave toward people in these groups.

Problem solving

- **7** To solve a problem, one must move from an initial set of information (the *givens*) to a *goal*. In *well-defined* problems, the givens and goals are quite clear; in *ill-defined* problems, neither the givens nor the goals are clear at the start.
- **8** Some problems are solved through *insight*—the sudden discovery of a solution after having struggled with the problem for a while. Insight requires the mental representation of a problem in a new way.
- **9** We are aided in problem solving by *positive transfer* of learning from past experiences with similar problems, but we are hindered if the tried-and-true methods are not appropriate to the problem. We are

also hindered by *functional fixedness*—the tendency to see objects only in terms of their familiar functions.

- **10** Creative products are novel and appropriate responses to tasks that have no fixed solution. We tend to be most creative when we are *intrinsically motivated*—pursuing an activity for its own sake, rather than to gain a reward.
- **11** The *information-processing approach* to problem solving utilizes computer simulations of human thought processes to arrive at solutions to problems. One such process is *means-end analysis*, in which the solver sets up a series of subgoals that must be reached on the way to achieving the ultimate solution.

Intelligence

- **12** *Intelligence* may be defined as the capacity to acquire and use knowledge.
- **13** Among the tests developed for assessing intelligence are the Stanford-Binet and the Wechsler. A child's *intelligence quotient (IQ)* is computed by dividing *mental age* (as measured by an intelligence test) by chronological age and multiplying by 100. An adult's IQ score is determined by comparing his results with those of a *standardized* sample. Scores on a standardized IQ test are distributed on a *normal*, or bell-shaped, curve.
- **14** IQ tests are under criticism for unfairly placing people into categories. It has been suggested that use of IQ tests for such things as job placement discriminates against minorities and the poor because IQ tests are aimed at skills emphasized in white, middle-class culture.
- **15** Spearman considered intelligence to be a single factor (which he called *g*), while Thurstone thought intelligence comprised eight primary abilities. Gardner has proposed an even broader view of intelligence, including artistic and interpersonal skills.
- **16** Researchers using the information-processing approach to intelligence have studied the step-by-step processes people use to solve problems. The first step is *encoding* the problem. People with higher IQs appear to take a longer time encod-

ing but are then able to perform the rest of the steps more quickly.

• **17** The *heritability* of a trait is a measure of how much of the variation between individuals in that trait is due to genetic factors. Most scientists conclude that IQ has a substantial heritability, although environment also has a major influence.

• **18** Children of lower socioeconomic backgrounds tend to score below average on IQ tests, and blacks tend to score lower than whites. Most researchers emphasize nutritional, educational, and cultural factors in accounting for this disparity.

Extremes of intelligence

• **19** Mental retardation is usually divided into four categories: mild, moderate, severe, and profound. An important distinction is between the *clinically retarded*, whose retardation has an identifiable biological cause, and the *socioculturally retarded*, whose retardation has no identifiable biological cause and is usually not diagnosed until a child enters school.

• **20** *Mainstreaming* of retarded students in regular classes seems to improve their academic performance. Socioculturally retarded adults can be taught to live relatively normal and independent lives in their communities.

• **21** Terman found that *intellectually gifted* children—those who score above 135 on IQ tests—grew up to be healthier, better adjusted, and more successful than people from similar backgrounds with lower IQ scores.

KEY TERMS

clinical retardation
computer simulation
concepts
creativity
functional fixedness
g
heritability
information-processing approach
insight
intellectually gifted
intelligence
intelligence quotient (IQ)
intelligence tests
language
mainstreaming
means-end analysis
mental age
normal distribution
overregularization
phonemes
problems
sociocultural retardation
stereotypes
transformational grammar
trial and error

CAN COMPUTERS THINK?

There are no computers today that approach the abilities of C3PO and R2D2. But perhaps some day there will be.

Of the many futuristic marvels in the *Star Wars* movies, perhaps the most technically marvelous are the droids R2D2 and C3PO. These characters think, feel, and communicate much like their human comrades, even though they have no brain—only a computer—guiding their behavior.

There are no computers today that approach the abilities of R2D2 and C3PO, such as the abilities to carry on conversations, to recognize people, and even to crack jokes.

Even today's most "intelligent" machines cannot understand English as well as a 4-year-old child can. But will there some day be such intelligent computers? Many researchers working in the field of *artificial intelligence* believe there will be.

These researchers take the controversial view that computers can already "think" and that it is only a matter of time before computers will be able to handle just about any intellectual problem that people can. What's more, many researchers believe that as we program computers to perform more and more intelligently, we will learn more about human intelligence as well.

ARTIFICIAL INTELLIGENCE

Artificial intelligence (AI) is the science of programming computers to behave intelligently. AI was born in the 1950s, as researchers tried to program computers to simulate the ways in which human subjects solved problems. The General Problem Solver, described in Chapter 7, was one of the first AI programs. In the past decade, AI research—often conducted by teams including both psychologists and computer scientists—has advanced dramatically.

AI researchers have focused on programming computers to perform operations that seem basic to human thought: storing and retrieving information, and using logical principles to solve problems. In the view of many AI experts, the programming steps that a computer follows in processing information are fundamentally the same as the mental steps taken by humans in carrying out these same activities (Simon, 1981). If this view is correct, an intelligent computer can serve as a model of the human mind, and programs for solving specific problems amount to models of how humans solve these problems.

Such "intelligent" computer programs have forced researchers to be more precise in their models of how human thought might work. Until recently, as one AI researcher put it, "We [were] to thinking as the Victorians were to sex"—everyone was doing it, but no one knew how to talk about it (Huyghe, 1983). In order to teach a computer to perform a logical operation, researchers first needed to describe the process in terms of the specific steps of a computer program. As a result, work in artificial intelligence has been widely hailed for helping researchers think more clearly about thought itself.

In addition to helping us think about basic mental processes, work in artificial intelligence has had, as we will see, some exciting practical applications.

COMPUTERS AS "EXPERTS"

The patient's diagnosis was complicated, so Dr. Jack Myers brought in his best consultant. They quickly examined the elderly man's medical background: a history of chest and abdominal pains, heavy smoking, and high blood sugar. The consultant asked the doctor a few terse questions: "Numerous attacks of chest pain per day?" "No," responded Myers.

"Skin lesions present?" "No."

"Is the pain radiating to the upper extremities?" "Yes."

The specialist pondered briefly and asked for the results of two more tests. Then came a crisp diagnosis: obesity, diabetes mellitus, angina pectoris. (Carey, 1983)

This may sound like an ordinary conversation between two doctors, but Dr. Myers's associate was, in fact, a computer program called INTERNIST-1, which can deal with roughly three-fourths of all major diseases. In a study published in the *New England Journal of Medicine* (Miller, Pople, and Myers, 1982), INTERNIST-1 did about as well in diagnosing puzzling cases from the medical literature as human doctors had done with the actual patients. INTERNIST-1 can review a patient's medical history, suggest questions, follow up the answers with more questions, and eventually arrive at a diagnosis. Although INTERNIST-1 is not yet widely used, other more specialized diagnostic programs—such as PUFF, which specializes in lung disease—are already in general use.

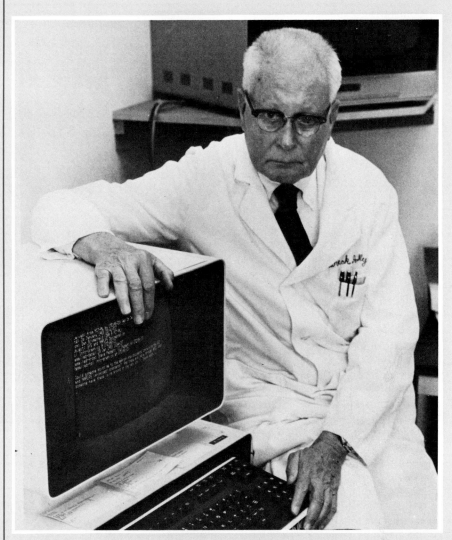

Dr. Jack Myers and his best consultant. The INTERNIST-1 program did about as well as human doctors in diagnosing puzzling cases.

INTERNIST-1 is a product of a branch of artificial intelligence research called *expert systems*. In recent years, expert systems have been developed in many different areas. For example, PROSPECTOR is a geological "expert" that was recently used to pinpoint a deposit of molybdenum worth $100 million. MYCIN is a program that helps doctors diagnose bacterial infections. Other expert systems are being used to help chemists determine the molecular structure of compounds, to help biologists plan cloning experiments, and to help the Air Force plan attacks on air bases (Rheingold, 1983).

To develop these expert systems, computer scientists work closely with human experts in the respective fields and try to capture as much as they can of the expert's problem-solving methods in the form of a computer program. The human experts often rely on intuitive strategies that are hard to reduce to a set of logical rules that a computer can follow. But by building and refining models of these problem-solving processes, AI researchers have made great progress in their ability to codify the experts' rules.

When a model of how human experts solve problems in a particular domain is combined with the computer's ability to store vast amounts of information and to process this information almost instantaneously, the power of the new computer experts becomes immense. In the future, these computer systems are likely to serve as indispensable "assistants" to doctors, lawyers, business executives, scientists, and engineers.

BUT CAN THEY REALLY *THINK*?

Despite these dramatic accomplishments, there is still debate over whether what these computer programs do can actually be called *thinking*. Is artificial intelligence really "intelligent" at all?

From one point of view, it seems clear that computers programmed in this way *are* thinking. After all, the computers accept information, manipulate symbols, store items in memory, and retrieve them again when they are needed. If this isn't thinking, AI researchers argue, what is?

But critics argue that all the computers are doing is slavishly following the rules that are programmed into them—hardly what we would want to characterize as "thought" or "intelligent" behavior. The critics also emphasize that, in practice, many AI programs call for computers to process information in distinctly nonhuman ways.

Take the case of chess-playing programs. Such programs can now beat all but the top several hundred human players in the world (Hilts, 1982). But the methods used by the best computer chess-playing programs are entirely different from those used by the human chessmasters. The computers use "brute force" methods. With their ability to consider as many as 50

A computer chess tournament. Computer chess-playing programs can now beat all but the top several hundred human players in the world.

million moves on a single turn, the computers are programmed to explore so many moves and to look so many moves ahead that sooner or later they find a "good" move. The human chessmasters, in contrast, focus on a small number of moves on every turn. The humans, relying on their extensive experience and on a well-developed sense of position, have an intuitive sense of the game that no computer program has yet been able to capture.

More generally, in their efforts to develop more and more powerful programs, many AI researchers have been programming computers to "think" in ways that seem less and less similar to human thought. The computers are strong on computational skills and strict logic and

weak on imagination and inspiration. Indeed, it has proven to be extremely difficult to teach computers to do certain sorts of information processing that humans seem to do automatically—to understand language, to learn from experience, and to exercise what may best be called "common sense."

As a result of these differences, some observers have come to doubt that AI research will shed much light on human intelligence after all. "How computers work seems to have no real relevance to how the mind works," declares psychologist George Miller, "any more than a wheel shows how people walk" (in Ferrell, 1982). The philosopher Hubert Dreyfus pinpoints the reason

We may deprecate computer thought simply because it is unlike human thought.

Can computers ever get smarter than the humans who programmed them?

for what he sees as the inevitable differences between human and computer problem solving: "Without the bodies we have and without being raised like humans, computers can't acquire the background knowledge needed to behave intelligently" (in Carey, 1983).

But despite these differences between people and computers, a strong case can still be made for the argument that computers *are* thinking and that artificial intelligence *is* intelligence. The answer to the question "Can computers think?" may boil down to a matter of definition. We may deprecate computer thought simply because it is unlike human thought. But perhaps we humans should be wary of our tendency to make ourselves the measure of all things. Instead, we might want to broaden our notion of what constitutes thinking. As Seymour Papert has put it, "When we ask if a machine thinks, we are asking whether we would like to extend the notion of thinking to include what machines might do" (in Carey, 1983).

HOW SMART CAN THEY GET?

Even as it is acknowledged that humans and computers often "think" in different ways, some AI researchers are redoubling their efforts to program computers to think the way people do.

In recent years, for example, AI researchers have made progress toward one of their most challenging goals: programming computers to understand human language. A program called FRUMP can now read news stories and then provide one-sentence summaries of them in English, Spanish, and Chinese. As modest as this feat may seem, FRUMP's accomplishment is substantial because the program must not only understand words but must be able to link words to con-

cepts in a way that enables it to extract the gist of the story. (Of course, FRUMP sometimes makes mistakes. When FRUMP was asked to summarize a wire-service story that reported the shooting of the mayor of San Francisco in 1978, an event that "shook" the city, FRUMP concluded that there had been another earthquake there [Stockton, 1980]).

Progress has also been made in programming computers to learn from experience—to take into account feedback on their performance in order to improve their problem-solving strategies.

Some AI researchers are trying to go even further—to program computers to capture some of the intuitive, creative, and even subconscious aspects of human thought. In one approach, taken by computer scientist Douglas Hofstadter, the computer is programmed to work on different small aspects of a problem simultaneously and then is given the opportunity to make connections between the products of the different subroutines—something like a human thinker making intuitive connections between diverse thoughts (Gleick, 1983).

If such efforts succeed, computer intelligence may some day include such aspects of human intelligence as creativity, insight, and even self-consciousness—that is, the thinker's awareness of its own thoughts. At such a point some AI researchers believe that even emotions will be programmable. If such a time comes, the idea of computer intelligences such as those of R2D2 and C3PO will have moved from the realm of science fiction to the realm of reality.

Can computers ever get so intelligent that they will be smarter than the humans who programmed them? Although many people would consider this notion absurd, not all

AI researchers would rule it out. Marvin Minsky, one of the fathers of AI, remains open to the possibility that computers will some day outthink their creators. "There are people who think that evolution has stopped and there can't be anything smarter than human beings," Minsky says, "but why should that be the case?" (Stockton, 1980).

No one seems seriously worried about computers taking over the world. What does worry researchers, however, is the possibility that we may become too dependent on computers to provide the solutions to all sorts of problems, from medicine to foreign affairs. For in the last analysis, no matter how smart, creative, witty, and charming computers may become, human beings must take ultimate responsibility for the computer's recommendations—the humans, after all, put the "intelligence" into the computer in the first place—and for deciding whether or not to follow them.

SUMMARY

- *1* Artificial intelligence is the science of programming computers to behave intelligently. Most AI research to date has focused on programming computers to store and retrieve information and to use logical principles to solve problems.
- *2* The branch of AI research called *expert systems* is involved in developing computer programs that solve problems in a particular field of expertise.
- *3* There is a great deal of debate over whether artificial intelligence can really be called "intelligence" and whether computers running AI programs can be characterized as "thinking." One reason for the disagreement is that computers process information in ways much different from those used by humans.
- *4* Current research efforts are geared toward programming computers to perform such humanlike processes as intuitive thinking and creativity.

DEVELOPMENT THROUGH LIFE

A large part of being human is becoming human. We grow and develop throughout life, not only physically, but also in our intellectual abilities, motives, values, and social relationships. Our development is directed both from within, in the unfolding of our biologically given capacities, and from without, as we are shaped by the experiences of life. These processes of psychological development are the subject of the two chapters in this part.

Chapter 8 deals with the portion of life that extends From Birth to Adolescence. It explores cognitive, personality, and social development in the years of infancy, childhood, and adolescence. The Psychological Issue that follows deals with the relationships between Brothers and Sisters, psychologically important relationships that begin with the birth of a younger sibling and continue throughout the span of life.

Psychological development is not limited to the first two decades of life. As emphasized in Chapter 9, on Adulthood and Aging, we continue to develop and change throughout our adult lives, through the years of early, middle, and late adulthood. This part concludes with a Psychological Issue on Facing Death. Death is the final stage of life for each of us, and it is a reality that we all must face.

FROM BIRTH TO ADOLESCENCE

The first two decades of life are years of dramatic change in skills, modes of thought, and relationships to others.

CHAPTER *8*

THE NATURE OF DEVELOPMENT

Learning and maturation
The importance of early experience
Sequences, ages, and stages

Development is directed from within, in the maturation of our inborn capacities, and from without, as we learn from the experiences of life.

PRENATAL DEVELOPMENT AND THE NEWBORN

Prenatal development
The newborn child

Development begins before birth, inside the mother's womb. The newborn child is ready to start learning about the world.

INFANCY

Motor skills
Cognitive development
Social development: attachment
Individual differences in infancy

Physical, cognitive, and social changes take place more rapidly during the first two years of life than during any later period.

CHILDHOOD

Cognitive development
Broadening perspectives
Moral development
Child rearing and the growth of competence

In the years between 2 and 12, children develop new modes of reasoning, broader perspectives, and the ability to act independently.

ADOLESCENCE

Physical development
Cognitive development
The formation of identity
Parents and peers

A central challenge of adolescence is to establish a sense of identity—an answer to the question "Who am I?"

PSYCHOLOGICAL ISSUE
BROTHERS AND SISTERS

From earliest childhood through adulthood, brothers and sisters experience feelings of both love and rivalry.

BOXES
1 Erikson's eight stages of psychosocial development
2 Born too soon
3 Children of divorce
4 "Steve asked me out and I'm going"

The years from birth through childhood are years of dramatic change—physical, intellectual, emotional, and social. When the last edition of this book went to press, my younger son Noam had just been born. He could cry, turn his head, suck, and sleep, and not do much more than that. Now, just three years later, Noam brandishes the tinfoil sword that his older brother has made for him and loudly sings, "I am a pirate king!" which he has learned from the movie version of *The Pirates of Penzance*. Noam's big brother Elihu, himself a preschooler at the time of the last edition, now pops back into the house after playing basketball in the driveway and, after a bit of parental prodding, reviews the words for tomorrow's first-grade spelling test.

In this chapter we will explore psychological development during the first two decades of life, from birth through adolescence. These early years of life are of interest to psychologists not only because they are periods of dramatic development and change but because the patterns of thought, feeling, and behavior that develop in childhood provide insights into how people think, feel, and act as adults.

We begin the chapter by discussing the nature of development, including the joint roles of maturation (biological programming) and learning (experience). We then consider development at each early stage of life, starting before birth and going through infancy, childhood, and adolescence. At each stage, our tour includes both cognitive development (the changes that take place in modes of thought) and social development (the ways in which people come to relate to others). In Chapter 9 we will continue our examination of development through the years of adulthood.

THE NATURE OF DEVELOPMENT

Development refers to the relatively enduring changes in people's capacities and behavior that occur as they grow older. We develop both physically—in size, biological functions, and physical skills—and psychologically—in intellectual abilities, personality, and social behavior. In this section we shall examine some of the basic issues in development: the interplay of learning and maturation, the significance of early experiences for later development, and the idea that aspects of development occur in a fixed sequence of stages.

Learning and maturation

How does development take place? How, for example, do babies come to tell familiar adults from strangers? Why do 1- and 2-year-olds display an increased desire to explore their environment? Why do school-age children often become preoccupied with playing games "according to the rules," and why do adolescents often show a new sort of self-consciousness that they did not have at an earlier age?

Each of these questions is complex, because in each case the answer involves a combination of several factors. Throughout this chapter, it will be helpful for you to keep in mind two sets of processes that jointly account for psychological development: learning and maturation. *Learning*, as discussed in Chapter 5, refers to relatively enduring changes in behavior that take place as the result of experience. *Maturation*, in contrast, refers to changes that take place without any specific experience or practice, as

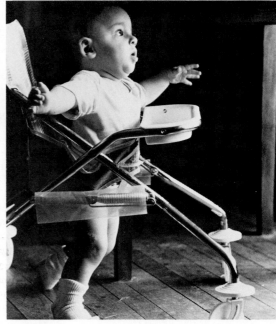

long as environmental conditions stay within a normal range. For example, children will begin to crawl when they are 10 months old and to walk when they are about 15 months, even if they are not given any special training or reinforcement. Even when infants are prevented from walking by being wrapped in swaddling clothes during the first year, as is the custom in some cultures, the infants begin walking at the usual age (Orlansky, 1949). Whereas learning reflects the impact of the environment on behavior, maturation reflects the unfolding of inherited biological patterns that are "preprogrammed" into the individual.

There has long been a debate over which of these two processes is more important in development. At the end of the seventeenth century, the philosopher John Locke claimed that the mind of a newborn is a "blank slate," to be filled in by what could be learned; in Locke's view, development is a product of experience (see Chapter 1, Box 1). In the eighteenth century, Jean Jacques Rousseau espoused the opposing view, that development is the unfolding of innate tendencies. This debate has continued into our own century, with some scientists emphasizing the role of learning and others stressing maturational factors. But most psychologists now emphasize the *interaction* of

learning and maturation in human development.

Our consideration of language development in Chapter 7 provided one example of this interplay. Babies all over the world start talking at roughly the same age and go through the same grammatical stages (from single word to the two-word phrase and so on). This development probably reflects a biological program that is "prewired" into all human beings. But whether the child comes to speak in French or Chinese, in short simple sentences or long complex ones, is *not* part of the biological program—these specific features of language must be learned. The biological program provides the readiness to acquire language at a particular age and in particular ways, but the specific words and grammatical rules that are used depend on experience. The same interplay between maturation and learning is characteristic of psychological development more generally.

The importance of early experience

Another controversy among psychologists concerns the impact that experiences early in life have on later development. Most of us would agree that development is *cumulative*; that is, later advances depend and build on earlier achievements. A baby must be

Maturation, rather than learning, plays the primary role in the development of walking. Indian babies bound to cradleboards in their first year start walking at about the same age as infants in other cultures. And practice with walkers does not lead babies to walk on their own any sooner.

able to babble before he can talk, to stand before he can walk. The question remains, however, as to how necessary it is to have certain experiences in order to develop normally. According to one viewpoint, if a child does not have certain essential early experiences he will not develop optimally, and any damage cannot be undone. A contrasting view considers early experience less critical and holds that later learning can make up for earlier deficits.

Those who believe that early experience is crucial point to the role of *critical periods* in the development of some animals. These are specific periods of time during which the presence or absence of something in the environment irreversibly determines later development. Perhaps the best-known example of critical periods is the phenomenon of *imprinting* in certain waterfowl. Konrad Lorenz (1937) noticed that soon after ducklings are born they start following the mother duck around, and he wondered why this particular response occurred. By arranging things so that he would be the first moving object seen by a group of newly hatched ducklings, Lorenz found that they would follow him around instead of their mother. These ducklings had "imprinted" on Lorenz during a critical period, in which any object that fit certain characteristics became the mother figure to be followed. Subsequent experimenters have confirmed that ducks are imprintable during a short period immediately after hatching.

Such critical periods do not seem to exist for humans, however. And the importance of early experience for later development has been the topic of considerable debate. One well-known study found that infants who were confined to institutions and who were deprived of a loving, responsive caretaker during the first six months of life were more likely to become emotionally maladjusted than infants institutionalized at a later age (Goldfarb, 1947). This finding suggested that the first six months are a critical period for establishing the social attachments that are necessary for normal emotional development. But other studies of children who were adopted after the stage of infancy indicate that a good home can overcome severe early disadvantages (Kagan, Kearsley, and Zelazo, 1978).

Psychologists have also energetically debated the importance of early experience for children's intellectual development. Burton White (1975) has argued that stimulation provided during the first three years of life—especially between 8 and 14 months—can determine whether children reach their full intellectual potential. Reasoning of this sort has led many parents to push their children to learn earlier than ever, using techniques ranging from music lessons for toddlers to letter and number flashcards for infants still too young to talk. There is little evidence that such early training has any lasting positive effects, however. And many psychol-

Soon after hatching, ducklings will follow the first moving object they see. In this case, they saw the famous biologist Konrad Lorenz. This is an example of the process of imprinting.

ogists and pediatricians worry that early parental pressures for achievement can set children up for later failures (Langway, 1983).

On the other hand, intellectual stimulation in the early years of life can be helpful for children from disadvantaged backgrounds who otherwise might get little such stimulation in the preschool years. At least one major study found that children from disadvantaged backgrounds who attended federally funded Head Start programs were much more likely than their peers to get through school without failing (Lazar and Darlington, 1979). The positive effects of Head Start may be to a large extent motivational: when the disadvantaged child has successful "academic" experiences in early life, he may be more likely to approach school with a positive attitude, and his parents may be more likely to support and encourage his academic progress. When we sort out all the diverse findings, we are led to conclude that the first years of life do have special importance for later development but do not necessarily set the child on an irrevocable course (Rutter, 1979).

Sequences, ages, and stages

Although there is still controversy about the critical importance of early experiences, researchers have generally found that psychological development occurs in fixed *sequences* and that later developments build upon earlier ones in a predictable order. A great deal of research in developmental psychology has focused on charting these sequences as precisely as possible in specific areas of development, including physical, cognitive, and social development. For example, there are consistent sequences in children's drawings—from first scribbles to lifelike representations (Gardner, 1980), and in their evolving musical abilities, from first bangings and clappings to the humming of entire melodies (McKernon, 1979).

In what follows, it will sometimes be noted that particular behaviors or capacities typically emerge at a particular age. You should bear in mind,

however, that these are *average* ages and that there is a wide range of variation among individuals. Babies may start walking as early as 9 months or as late as 18 months; girls may begin to menstruate as early as age 10 and as late as 17. Whereas the *sequences* of developmental milestones are relatively constant across individuals, the specific ages are not. Moreover, a rapid rate of early cognitive development does not necessarily imply that the person will be an unusually intelligent adult, nor does a slow rate of early development mean that the person will always be at the bottom of the class.

Some of the most important theories of psychological development depend heavily on the notion of stages. A *stage* is a description of the way children's thought or behavior is organized during a particular period of time. As children move from one stage to the next, their responses are organized in more complex ways that build upon the preceding stage. In this chapter we will give special attention to three stage theories: Erik Erikson's theory of psychosocial development (see Box 1), Jean Piaget's theory of cognitive development, and Lawrence Kohlberg's theory of moral development. Although stage theories imply relatively abrupt jumps from one stage to the next (like ascending a staircase), a great deal of recent research suggests that psychological development is more likely to be gradual and continuous (more like walking up a ramp) (Flavell, 1982). Nevertheless, stage theories provide useful descriptions of the changes in thought and behavior that take place between birth and adolescence.

PRENATAL DEVELOPMENT AND THE NEWBORN

A child's development begins long before birth. In this section we will examine *prenatal development* (development before birth) and some of the capacities that newborns bring into the world.

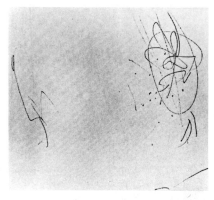

Children's drawings develop in consistent sequences. At 18 months, this child produced his first "picture" (top). By 25 months, he was making much more carefully controlled lines and shapes (middle). By the age of 4½, he could produce lifelike representations, such as this "Batman" (bottom) (from Gardner, 1980).

BOX 1

ERIKSON'S EIGHT STAGES OF PSYCHOSOCIAL DEVELOPMENT

Erik Erikson

Erik Erikson was born in Germany in 1902. As a young man he moved to Vienna, where he became a disciple of Sigmund Freud. He later went on to become the foremost theorist of the development of personality through the life cycle. The initial impetus for Erikson's theory was Freud's theory of psychosexual development, which we will discuss in Chapter 11. But whereas Freud's stages covered only the years between birth and puberty, Erikson's stages extended through adulthood and old age. And whereas Freud focused on the relationships between children and their parents, Erikson took into account the impact of the larger society on development.

In *Childhood and Society* (1950), Erikson presented each of eight *psychosocial stages* as a polarity, with a positive pole representing successful development at that stage and a negative pole representing unsuccessful development. Erikson did not see these stages as fixed or rigid, however. To some degree, we all continue to work on these eight challenges or crises throughout our lives. Erikson's eight stages are as follows:

1 *Trust versus mistrust.* In the first year of life infants depend on others to feed them, dress them, and carry them about. The parents cuddle them, talk to them, and play with them, and these interactions determine the children's attitude later in life. If a child's physical and emotional needs are met, he learns to trust his environment. If not, he will become fearful and mistrust the people and objects around him.

2 *Autonomy versus doubt.* In the second and third years, when children learn to walk, talk, and do things for themselves, parental encouragement and consistency in discipline can help the child to develop autonomy and independence. But if parents are overprotective, are inconsistent in their disciplinary techniques, or show disapproval when the child does things on her own, she will become doubtful and ashamed of herself.

3 *Initiative versus guilt.* By ages 4 and 5, children are ready to roam about, to explore unfamiliar places, and to get to know new people. If the child's inquisitiveness and exploration of his environment are encouraged by his parents, he will find it easier to use his initiative to go out on his own. But if parents inhibit such actions, the child will develop guilt feelings whenever he tries to take initiative.

4 *Industry versus inferiority.* From about ages 6 to 11, children learn to manipulate objects and events by themselves. If encouraged, the child will develop a sense of industry, will enjoy solving problems and completing tasks, and will seek intellectual stimulation. If not, she will develop a sense of inferiority and will have to be bribed or cajoled to complete a task.

5 *Identity versus role confusion.* Between the ages of 12 and 18 sexuality emerges and the adolescent faces the task of finding himself. He must integrate all that he has previously experienced in order to develop a sense of ego identity. If he is unable to reconcile his various roles in life into one identity, he is said to be suffering from role confusion.

6 *Intimacy versus isolation.* If the adult has achieved a sense of identity, then she can form close relationships and share with others. Failure at this stage consists of being unable to relate intimately to others. The person may develop a sense of isolation, feeling there is no one but herself she can depend on in the world.

7 *Generativity versus self-absorption.* By middle age the individual must have taken a stance toward the world, the future, and his readiness to contribute to it. Generativity is the ability to look outside oneself and be concerned with other people. The generative individual is productive and happy. The person who fails at this stage becomes self-centered.

8 *Integrity versus despair.* If life has been satisfying and the individual has achieved a sense of unity within herself and with others, old age will be a happy time. But if the old person feels that her life has been full of disappointments and failures and she cannot face life at this age, she will develop a sense of despair.

We will make reference to the last three of Erikson's stages in Chapter 9, when we discuss development through the course of adulthood.

Prenatal development

The development of a new human being begins at the moment of conception, when a sperm cell contributed by the father fertilizes the ovum, or egg, of the mother. Within the egg and sperm are the genes, the tiny structures that carry the messages of heredity. As we learned in Chapter 2, these genetic instructions affect not only physical characteristics but psychological characteristics as well.

For purposes of discussion, pregnancy can be divided into three 3-month periods, or *trimesters*. At the start of the first trimester, for about the first two weeks after conception, the fertilized egg is called the *zygote*. When the ball of dividing cells implants itself in the uterine wall (on about the fourteenth day), it becomes an *embryo*. During the embryonic period—between the third and eighth weeks of pregnancy—all the essential elements of anatomy begin to form. The heart begins to beat, the liver begins to manufacture red blood cells, and the limbs appear in budlike form. By the eighth week, the eyes, ears, nose, and mouth are clearly recognizable. By the end of the second month the organism is unmistakably human, and from this point on it is called a *fetus*. Now the external sex organs can be identified as male or female. The fetus weighs about 2 grams—only about the weight of two paper clips—and is about 1½ inches long. It continues to grow rapidly, however, so that by the end of the sixth month it weighs about 2 pounds and is about 14 inches long.

During the second trimester of pregnancy (the fourth through sixth months), the internal organs become more fully formed and start to function. The fetus in the second trimester can open its eyes, move its arms and legs, and go through wake-sleep cycles. A baby delivered at six months of pregnancy has a good chance of surviving, especially as a result of recent medical advances (see Box 2).

In the final trimester (the seventh through ninth months), the fetus is growing larger and undergoing the finishing touches. Many fetuses are quite active at this stage, kicking, tossing, turning—even hiccuping and sneezing. In the last month fat forms over the body and hair and fingernails grow.

During prenatal development, the child can be affected in various ways by the external environment. Nutrients and oxygen from the mother's blood system pass through the *placenta*—a network of blood vessels and membranes attached to the wall of the uterus—to the blood system of the fetus. Some infections may be transmitted across the placenta and affect the child's development. In addition, poor nutrition in the mother and her use of certain drugs (including nicotine, alcohol, caffeine, and some medicines) can harm the fetus.

There is also evidence that the mother's emotions can affect the unborn child. Women who are anxious during pregnancy are more likely than less anxious mothers to have infants who go into distress during delivery, who cry more before feedings, and who are more active in the hospital nursery (Simmons, Ottinger, and Haugh, 1967). The anxiety the expectant mother feels could lead her to get insufficient rest, to be careless about her diet, and to act in other ways that might contribute to a more troublesome newborn. In addition, studies of animals point to the possibility of more direct transmission of emotions from the mother to the fetus. The hormones in the mother's bloodstream circulate through the child's system. Thus, when the mother is stressed, increased epinephrine goes into the bloodstream of the fetus, and it may "feel" stress, too.

The effect that the mother has on the child continues right up to the moment of birth. Any medication she takes during delivery crosses over to the infant, making him groggy in the first days of life (Brackbill, 1978). Thus, many obstetricians (physicians who perform deliveries) advocate *natural childbirth,* in which the mother uses breathing and relaxation techniques instead of anesthesia to ease the pain of labor and delivery.

The newborn child

The newborn human is helpless in many ways. It will take many months

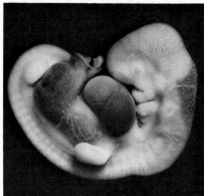

A

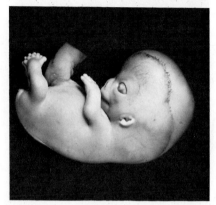

B

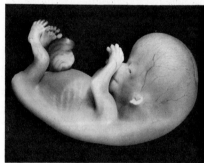

C

Early prenatal development. (A) The embryo at 31 days. At this point it resembles the embryo of any mammal, since it has not yet taken on a human appearance. (B) At 44 days the embryo has already developed hands, feet, and ears, and facial features are beginning to form. (C) At 56 days all the basic humanoid features are visible and the embryo is now referred to as a fetus.

A newborn infant, minutes after birth.

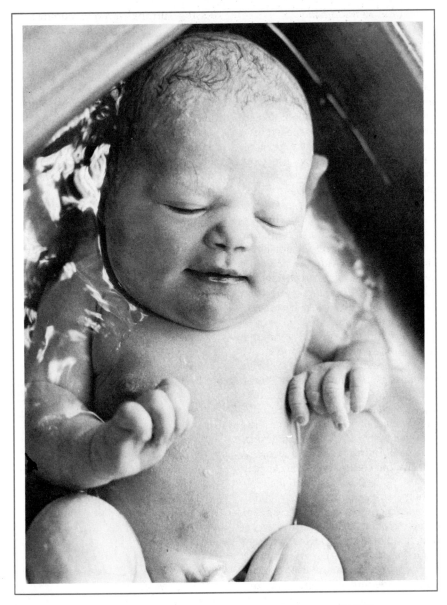

"THE CAT IN THE HAT"?
I'LL HAVE MORE OF THAT!

Can babies recall sounds that they heard when they were still in the womb? The case has not been proven, but it's possible that they can. Anthony DeCasper and his coworkers asked sixteen women to read Dr. Seuss's The Cat in the Hat *to their fetuses for a total of five hours during the last month and a half of their pregnancies. After the babies were born, the researchers used a test in which the newborns sucked on a nipple connected to a tape recorder. By sucking in one pattern of shorter and longer sucks, the babies could hear a recording of their mothers reading* The Cat in the Hat; *another pattern would produce a recording of their mothers reading a different book. The babies, some only hours old, chose* The Cat in the Hat *most often. The researchers concluded that the child's preferences are greatly affected by what they hear before they are born (Lewis, 1984).*

before the infant can begin to crawl about, and it will be over a year before she can walk alone. In addition, the infant is totally dependent on others for food, clothing, and shelter. Nevertheless, recent research has shown that the newborn is considerably more competent than had previously been thought. The newborn comes into the world equipped with reflexes to protect her, to help her find food, and to obtain stimulation. For example, she will put out her arms to protect herself if her head drops down, will suck on whatever is put near her mouth, and will grasp whatever is put into her hands. And although a generation ago it was thought that newborns could not see or hear, we now

know that all the senses are well-developed and functional at birth.

The infant not only senses what is around her but has distinct preferences. Newborns prefer to hear high-pitched rather than low-pitched sounds, to see moving rather than still objects, and to taste sweet rather than nonsweet substances. In order to get what she wants and avoid what she doesn't want, a newborn will follow a pleasant sight or sound with her eyes or turn away from something unpleasant.

The newborn infant shows a special interest in human beings and a special sensitivity to human communication. By 12 hours after birth, the infant moves his body in synchrony

| BOX 2 |

BORN TOO SOON

The remarkable development of a new life from a tiny cell occurs on a rigid timetable during the nine months of pregnancy. Each day adds a portion of the strength and maturity needed to sustain life outside the womb. Unfortunately, approximately one out of ten babies in the United States is born prematurely. Premature infants are doubly handicapped. Their fragile systems cannot yet function optimally on their own, and their special medical problems can make it more difficult for them to establish the sort of positive relationship with their parents that is so important in early development. Recent research, however, has made great progress in identifying these problems and suggesting ways of coping with them.

Any degree of prematurity places the child at some medical risk. As a result of recent medical advances, however, the survival rates—even of very young and very small infants— have increased dramatically in the past 15 years. An infant born at seven or eight months' gestation and weighing more than 5 pounds has excellent chances for survival, and even "younger" and smaller infants can often be saved.

With more and "younger" infants surviving, the effects of early birth on later development are of central interest. It is clear that premature infants lag behind their full-term peers for the first year of life (Hunt and Rhodes, 1977). For example, an infant two months premature will probably smile, sit up, crawl, and utter his first words about two months later than a full-term infant with the same birthday. Thus, the child's abilities seem to unfold on a schedule independent of his birth. By 2 years of age, the premature infant seems to have caught up to full-terms on most physical abilities (Sigman and Parmelee, 1979). But premature infants remain more susceptible to various perceptual, motor, and learning difficulties in later childhood. In addition, children born prematurely score slightly lower on IQ tests in middle childhood (Caputo, Goldstein, and Taub, 1981).

Whether or not a premature infant has any lasting difficulties may depend to a large extent on the way the child is raised *after* she leaves the hospital. Two infants with the same birth weight and complications may develop quite differently, depending on the resources available to them as they mature.

The circumstances of premature birth may sometimes get the relationship between parents and infant off to a bad start. After the shock and worry of the early birth itself, parents must turn over their newborn to medical personnel and machines for possibly months at a time. The parents can only view and touch their child

through the window of an incubator. Even though many hospitals now encourage parents to visit and take care of their infant, mothers often report feeling as if the child belongs to the nurses and is not their own at all.

Once the premature infant comes home from the hospital, he is likely to be more difficult to care for. Not only will parents have to wait longer for a good night's sleep, but they are faced with a more irritable and less responsive infant well through the first year (Crawford, 1982).

Susan Goldberg (1978) has documented some of the early difficulties in interactions between premature infants

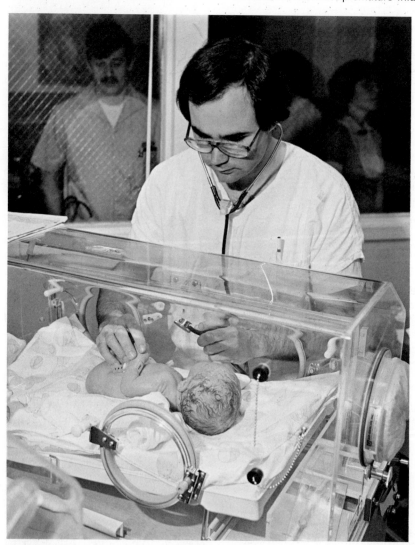

Premature infants are cared for in incubators until they can survive without artificial assistance.

and their parents. After ten days home from the hospital, parents of preterm infants did not hold them as close or smile and talk to them as much during feedings as did parents of a comparison group of full-term infants. When the babies were 8 months old, parents of premature infants worked harder during play sessions, showing them toys and touching them more, but had less success at engaging them than parents of full-term infants. Their infants cried more and smiled less than full-term infants.

By the child's first birthday, however, no differences in the parent-child interactions were found between the preterm and full-term groups. The improvement may be due in part to the fact that premature infants at this age could do more and had in effect almost caught up with the full-term infants. In addition, the infants studied by Goldberg were from two-parent, middle-class homes and were born in a hospital in a community that provided valuable advice and support to the parents. In fact, being in the study itself probably helped parents adjust to their infants' special needs.

We cannot be assured of such a happy ending in homes with more stress and fewer advantages. Indeed, premature infants have been shown to be overrepresented in cases of child abuse (Klein and Stern, 1971). Intensive medical care in the hospital has increased the survival rate of infants born early. But these children's subsequent development must also be optimized. For that, their parents, too, will need some "intensive care."

Elihu Rubin at 5 months and 20 months. Changes take place more rapidly during infancy than during any other period of life.

to human speech (Condon and Sander, 1974). While a newborn's sounds seem quite random, at 3 days of age the infant is more likely to make noise if someone is speaking to him (Rosenthal, 1982). By the time he is 3 or 4 months old, the baby prefers to look at faces more than any other sight and prefers the human voice to other sounds (Macfarlane, 1977).

Of special importance, the newborn is primed to start learning about the world. For example, he will look at the objects around him in systematic ways. When Marshall Haith (1980) used an apparatus that records exactly where the infant looks, he found certain "rules" that newborns seem to follow when looking at something. If the newborn is in the dark, he will look toward light. After he has found the light, he will look for some pattern, such as the frame of a window. Once he has located a pattern, he will look at the point of maximum contrast, such as the corner of the window frame. Thus, the infant does not merely open his eyes and stare straight ahead but actively seeks out particular features. Haith suggests that this pattern of looking provides the most information about what is in the environment and also provides maximal stimulation to the growing brain.

INFANCY

Excerpts from a mother's baby diary:
• *2 months:* Elihu is holding his head up for a long time and smiling more. He stares at his musical mobile and coos. He recognizes me now.

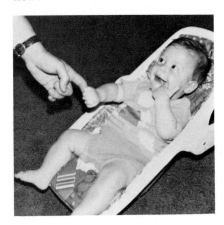

• *5 months:* Elihu turned over for the first time from his tummy to his back, stretching to see his mobile. He is much more aware of my presence.
• *7 months:* Elihu sits up perfectly straight and tall. He loves to sit at the piano and play. He is crawling everywhere. . . . He loves playing hide and seek, peeking below and above the table to see Mommy.
• *11 months:* Elihu is standing by himself for 15–30 seconds. . . . He is waving his hand all the time, to say bye-bye and hello.
• *14 months:* Elihu is learning to say "duck" (he uses this word to refer to all animals he does not know), "na na" (no), "yeah" (yes), "da da" (for Daddy), "eh eh" (for dog).
• *15 months:* Elihu has given up crawling. He walks everywhere. I guess you could say he's a toddler now. . . . He does a number of very cute things. The other day I found his blanket in the toilet.
• *20 months:* Elihu loves Ernie and Bert and Cookie Monster and Captain Kangaroo. . . . He neatly places blocks side by side or in a tower. . . . He's using three-word sentences—"Sit here, Mama" and "Come here, Dada."
• *23 months:* When Zick says good-bye in the morning, Elihu says "Don't say bye-bye, Daddy!" When the doorbell rings, he yells, "Who dat is?" When he builds something, he exclaims, "I did it!"

Changes take place more rapidly during infancy—the first two years of life—than during any other period in the life span. In this section we will describe some important features of the infant's physical, cognitive, and social development.

Motor skills

Compared with those of other species, human *motor skills*—the ability to control the movement of body parts—develop at a very slow pace. Many animals walk within a few moments of birth, but it takes humans about 15 months to master this skill. The average ages at which children acquire various motor abilities are summarized in Figure 8.1. There are wide individual differences in the ages at which children acquire particular skills, and yet all children follow this same sequence.

In general, the development of motor control goes in two directions: from head to toe and from the center of the body to the periphery. For example, the infant first learns to control the trunk and arms, and only later controls the feet and fingers. Physical development is in large part controlled by maturation—children learn to reach or crawl or walk without any special training. But the environment also plays a role in the emergence of particular skills. Burton White (1967) found, for example, that infants who had been given mobiles in their cribs started reaching earlier than infants who had nothing to try to grab.

Cognitive development

Much of our knowledge of cognitive development comes from the research of the Swiss psychologist Jean Piaget. Piaget was originally trained as a biologist and then worked briefly at Alfred Binet's laboratory where intelligence tests were being developed (see Chapter 7). While doing some routine intelligence testing, Piaget became intrigued with the reasoning behind children's answers to questions. He devoted the next 50 years of his life to exploring the development of children's ways of thinking and of perceiving the world.

According to Piaget (1952; Piaget and Inhelder, 1958), an individual's cognitive abilities progress through four stages in infancy and childhood:

Jean Piaget

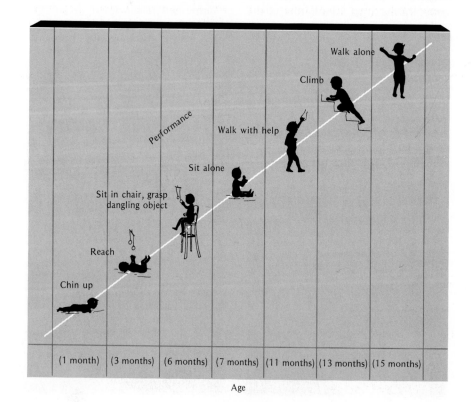

FIGURE 8.1

Although there are individual differences, children usually develop their motor skills in this sequence. The average age at which each event occurs is indicated.

CHAPTER EIGHT: FROM BIRTH TO ADOLESCENCE

FEEDING THE BABY: BREAST OR BOTTLE?

One of the first decisions a new mother must make is whether to feed her infant by breast or by bottle. Recent studies have shown that breast milk is particularly suited to infants' nutritional needs and provides protection against disease and allergies (Consumer Reports, 1977). Nature also provides variety and pacing in the meals of the young gourmets. At the beginning of a feeding, breast milk is relatively dilute; it becomes more concentrated toward the end. So the baby gets his fluids at the beginning of the meal and his food at the end. Shifting from one breast to another has been likened to having a drink in the middle of a meal (Macfarlane, 1977).

1 The *sensorimotor stage* (from birth to age 2). Through his senses and motor activities, the infant comes to understand the workings of the world. But knowledge is limited to what the child can directly see or do.

2 The *preoperational stage* (from 2 to 6). The child forms mental representations of objects and thus can think about things even when he cannot see or touch them.

3 The *concrete-operational stage* (from 6 to 12). Mental representations of the world become more flexible. The child can now solve problems through logic and reasoning, rather than relying on direct action.

4 The *formal-operational stage* (from 12 on). With mature thinking, the child or adolescent can now consider theories and imagine possibilities that are not within her own experience.

As the child progresses through these stages, cognitive processes gradually shift from a focus solely on the immediate, observable present to a conception of the world in symbolic and abstract terms. Thought becomes more highly organized, and the individual becomes able to consider the world from perspectives other than his own.

In infancy, the individual is in Pia-get's first stage, the "sensorimotor period," so called because the newborn's knowledge of the world is limited to what she perceives through her senses and acts on with motor activities. At first the infant has only a few reflexive behaviors, which she applies indiscriminately to any object she encounters—she will suck anything placed near her mouth and grasp anything near her hand. Very quickly, however, the infant learns that she must suck differently on a breast than on a bottle and that she receives different sensations from grasping a toy than from grasping a blanket. She then gradually begins to make distinctions between objects and accommodates her behavior to each. For example, a 6- or 7-month-old infant given a toy will inspect it, bang it, and feel it to see how the object fits into her scheme of things, but a 12-month-old will have had enough experience with objects to know how to respond to them. Given a ball, a 12-month-old will respond as if thinking, "Aha, this feels smooth and is round—it needs to be rolled."

As infants learn about the properties of objects, they also learn about cause and effect. At first all events seem quite random; if a light is turned on or a mobile begins to chime, the infant does not wonder why or look for a cause of the event.

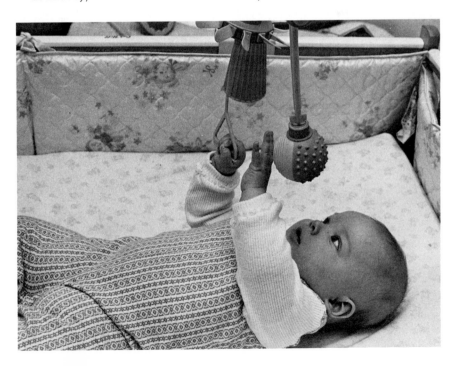

During the sensorimotor period, the infant learns to associate sensory information (such as sights and sounds) with motor experiences (such as reaching and grasping).

INFANCY

235

But by 2 or 3 months of age, the infant begins to realize that certain actions tend to go with certain results. He may note that every time he moves, the musical mobile over his crib begins to chime. At first he may engage in generalized motion and pause to hear the sound or may try to make the sound happen by crying or babbling. But by age 1 the infant engages in careful experimentation, trying different kinds of movements to see what indeed will cause the mobile to chime and will begin to invent new ways to cause the sound. At this point, according to Piaget, the infant has a notion of cause and effect—of the fact that varying our behavior will vary the results.

With the increasing understanding of the properties of objects and some notion of what causes events, the infant is also acquiring the concept of *object permanence*. As adults we take for granted that when we look away from our desk, the book opened in front of us still exists. But the infant makes no assumptions about the world beyond what he can directly perceive. To the young infant, what is not seen or felt does not exist. However, by the end of the first year, the child begins to learn that objects exist even when not being directly perceived. As Piaget has shown, if you take a small toy that a 6- or 7-month-old is interested in and place it behind a pillow, she will not reach behind the pillow for the toy. As far as she is concerned, out of sight is out of mind. But if you repeat this exercise a few months later, the baby will reach behind the pillow for the toy. By this time the baby knows that the toy continues to exist, and she knows just where to find it.

By the time the baby nears the end of the sensorimotor period (about age 2), these concepts are developed to such a point that an adult can move an object around several times without fooling the baby as to its whereabouts. With her new understanding of object permanence, the infant begins to have a mental representation of the object not tied to her own vision or actions. And with this understanding, the child has advanced from purely sensorimotor experience to *thought*.

Social development: attachment

Infancy is an important period not only in the development of a basic understanding of the physical world but also in the development of social behavior. During the first two years of life, infants typically develop a strong *attachment* to a small number of people. The baby's attachment is reflected in his selective responding to his mother, father, or other caretaker. The baby is much more likely to approach these persons than any others, is more willing to be cared for by them, and is least afraid in their presence.

In the first few months of life, the baby will respond to all adults. She does not care much who feeds her, rocks her, or picks her up. But by 6 months the infant is much more discriminating. She is likely to withdraw from people she doesn't know and to gurgle and coo only with familiar persons. And starting at about the age of 6 months, the baby is likely to protest or withdraw when approached by an unfamiliar person, a phenomenon known as *stranger anxiety*. You can tell the baby, "But she's your grandmother!" or "It's only Harry, my old roommate," but unless the baby has had a great deal of contact with these people, it won't do much good. The baby shows less distress if his mother or father is present, and whether he will cry hysterically or merely stop smiling depends on his individual temperament and on the circumstances. The reaction of stranger anxiety typically reaches its peak at about 8 months and generally disappears by 15 months, when the baby has gotten used to the idea that these other people are humans, too, and are not to be feared (Sroufe, 1977).

What causes the baby to become attached to a particular person or persons and not to others? Psychologists used to believe that it was a matter of learning—specifically, of secondary reinforcement (see Chapter 5). They thought that since the mother provides the infant with food, either by nursing or bottle-feeding, the baby learns to approach the mother whenever he is hungry. As a result, the

LINUS'S BLANKET

During the second year of life there is a period of necessary "separation" between the mother and toddler as they break away from the intimacy and dependency that characterized the first year of their relationship. About two-thirds of the children in this stage have what psychologists call a transitional object—a blanket, a teddy bear, or some other toy to which they are intensely attached. With these objects, children are sure they always have something familiar nearby to reassure them if need be. The transitional object is also something that can be controlled, which is not always true of mothers (Busch et al., 1973).

mother herself was thought to take on more general reward value for the infant. But this view of attachment has changed, partly as a result of pioneering research by Harry Harlow (1959) with infant rhesus monkeys. Harlow separated the infant monkeys from their mothers and raised them instead with wire and terrycloth constructions that he called *surrogate mothers.* In one study, the infants had access to both a "wire mother" fitted with a nipple that the monkey could obtain milk from and a "cloth mother" that did not provide milk but that the baby could cling to much more comfortably (see Figure 8.2). If the infant's attachment were the result of associating a particular object with the receipt of nourishment, we would expect the monkeys to become attached to the wire mother rather than the cloth mother. But Harlow found the opposite to be true. The infants became attached to the cloth mother. Not only would they cling to her, but they also were less fearful and more venturesome in her presence, just as human infants are in the presence of an attachment figure. When the infant monkeys were hungry, they would go to the wire mother to feed but then return immediately to the cloth mother.

As a result of his research, Harlow concluded that attachment is *not* a learned response to a food-giving object but rather an innate tendency to love a mother (or a mother surrogate) for the sheer pleasure of contact with her body. *Contact comfort,* as Harlow called it, may play a role in the development of human attachments as well. More generally, human infants appear to develop attachments toward people they repeatedly interact with in a variety of situations, whether or not they happen to be the ones who supply their food.

John Bowlby (1969) came to similar conclusions regarding human infants. Bowlby began with the assumption that over the course of evolution each animal species takes on the capacities that are most likely to ensure their survival. For human infants, who cannot move about on their own, the protection of an adult is essential. Thus, human infants are born with the capacity to seek out others, to pick out a particular adult who has provided the most comfort, and to use a variety of behaviors, such as crying and clinging, to ensure that contact with that adult is maintained.

Mary Ainsworth (1978) and her colleagues have studied differences in the quality of infants' attachments to their mothers and the effects of these differences on later development. In their experimental setup, they observed infants in a strange room. In-

FIGURE 8.2

In Harlow's experiments, infant monkeys preferred terrycloth-covered "mothers" to wire "mothers." The monkey would venture to the wire mother to obtain milk but would quickly return to the cloth mother as a base of security. Harlow stressed the importance of "contact comfort" in the development of the infant's attachment to its mother.

fants whom the researchers identified as *securely attached* played freely while their mother was present, protested vigorously when she left, and greeted her happily when she returned. Infants whom the researchers termed *anxiously attached* showed a very different pattern. They did not leave their mother's side to play, perhaps because they were unsure of her availability when they did not stay close. Nor did they protest when their mother left the room, presumably because they were unsure that their efforts would have any effect. They did not greet the mother upon her return, and some even avoided their mother, as if angry at her unpredictable behavior. This relatively brief experimental situation is thought to reflect more enduring qualities of the mother-infant relationship: Some infants have learned that mother can be counted on, while others have not built up this knowledge.

The trust that securely attached infants develop has positive long-term effects. Infants who are securely attached at age 1 have been found to do better at problem solving at ages 2 and 3 (Matas et al., 1978). As the infant grows up, his trust in the mother or another adult seems to be general-

ized to others. Thus, securely attached infants have been found to be more sociable to other adults at age 2 (Thompson and Lamb, 1983) and to be rated as more socially competent in kindergarten (Arend, Gove, and Sroufe, 1979).

Although most research focuses on relationships with the mother, infants become attached to fathers as well (Main and Weston, 1981). Most infants do seem to be more secure with their mothers than with their fathers when in an unfamiliar situation; however, these findings may simply reflect the fact that in most families fathers spend less time with the baby. Although the mother may be more comforting in times of stress, the father is more likely to be sought out for playing. Mothers generally do more of the caretaking and talk more to infants than fathers do, but fathers engage in more physical play. Thus, fathers can serve as a source of security much as mothers do, and they can also enrich the child's experience by providing a somewhat different kind of interaction (Lamb, 1981).

Because attachment to parents is so crucial for later development, many people have worried about the growing number of infants who spend

Attachments to parents develop in infancy and persist through the course of childhood.

CHAPTER EIGHT: FROM BIRTH TO ADOLESCENCE

their days in day-care settings, away from parents. But most of the studies comparing infants placed in day care to infants reared at home have concluded that day care has no ill effects on the child. Children in well-run day-care programs develop as strong an attachment to their parents as those whose days are spent at home (Belsky and Steinberg, 1978). It appears that the quality of time spent with parents is more important than the quantity.

Individual differences in infancy

All infants follow the sequence of physical, cognitive, and social development just described. Yet infants are still quite different from one another. From the moment of birth each has his or her own *temperament,* or consistent style of responding to the world. Alexander Thomas and Stella Chess (1977) have identified nine dimensions on which infants differ, including their activity level, distractibility, and tendency to approach or avoid new people and situations. These dimensions have been found to be relatively stable through the period of infancy and, to a lesser degree, through the childhood years. Thus, the active infant who thrashes about in her crib in the early months is likely to be toddling busily about the house at age 2, while the infant who lies quietly in the early months is likely to be sitting calmly in a playpen when she is 2.

Will an active infant be an active child or an energetic adult? We are unable to predict with certainty. Nevertheless, studies that have followed infants for long periods of time have shown that there is at least some degree of continuity in people's activity level and sociability (whether they are shy or outgoing) from infancy to adulthood (Kagan and Moss, 1962). Some differences in infant temperament are inborn (Goldsmith, 1983). But the environment often plays a strong role in perpetuating such characteristics. For example, the sociable infant who smiles at all adults and receives smiles in return learns that it is rewarding to greet others. Thus, the infant's tendency to be sociable is

strengthened. In contrast, a more fearful and withdrawn infant will not elicit many glowing smiles from adults and may therefore continue to be wary of others.

In other cases, experiences can cause dramatic changes in temperament. For example, if a child who finds it difficult to adapt to new people or situations is introduced to new experiences slowly and patiently, she may eventually become quite venturesome. For this reason, Thomas and Chess suggest that it is important for parents to recognize their child's individual style and to adapt their own behavior accordingly, rather than coming to parenthood with preconceived ideas about what is best for *all* children.

CHILDHOOD

During the years between ages 2 and 12, children gradually develop modes of reasoning that are essentially identical to those of adults. It is also during this period that individuals first venture from home and develop a sense of mastery and competence. The psychological developments of childhood are too numerous for us to cover in only one chapter. We have already covered language development (in Chapter 7), and we will examine personality development in Chapter 11 and sex-role development in Chapter 16. In this section we will continue Piaget's account of cognitive development in children, describe how the child's broadening view of the world extends to his relationships with others, outline the process of moral development, and examine ways in which child-rearing patterns can affect children's sense of competence.

Cognitive development

Children between the ages of about 2 and 7, according to Piaget, are in the preoperational period of cognitive development. While the infant in the sensorimotor stage knows only what he can immediately perceive, the preoperational child has mental representations of the world that go be-

---

"WE'LL LOOK AT MY DREAM TOGETHER"

During the earliest years of childhood—between the ages of 2 and 4—children cannot easily distinguish between fantasy and reality. Fictional events on TV shows may be taken to be real, and incidents that take place in dreams may be confused with the happenings of waking life. The Russian writer Kornei Chukovsky (1963) tells of a 3-year-old who complained to her mother one morning, "Mother, why don't you ever appear in my dreams?" And on the evening of the same day, she said, "Lie down on my pillow, Mommy, we'll look at my dream together."

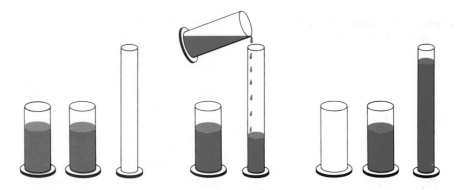

yond the here and now. The child no longer has to see or feel an object in order to bring that object to mind; for example, simply hearing or saying a word—such as "ball"—will bring the image of a ball into the child's mind.

But the thought of children in the preoperational stage remains quite limited. Children in this stage do not yet have what Piaget referred to as *operations*, or the ability to mentally manipulate objects or ideas. Operations are basic thought processes that adults take for granted. Preoperational thought is closely tied to immediate perceptions—what the child can see or do, rather than what she can figure out in her mind. Thus, if you were to show a young child a row of sticks and ask her to select the same number of sticks from another pile, she would do so by matching the sticks one by one. An older child, in contrast, would count the sticks mentally.

At around age 7, the child overcomes this limitation in thought and enters Piaget's period of concrete operations. In this stage the child still focuses on the concrete—on what is immediately present in the situation rather than what can be inferred or abstracted—but now, for the first time, he can mentally manipulate the objects that he perceives. He can think, "If I do this, then . . ." without having to actually perform the action. A prime sign that the child has reached the level of concrete operations is the attainment of *conservation:* understanding that a substance's weight, mass, or volume will remain the same even if its form or shape changes. Conservation of volume is illustrated in Figure 8.3. If you pour water from a short, wide beaker into a tall, thin one, a preoperational child will usually say that you now have more water than you did before. After all, the water now comes to a higher level. But a child who has attained concrete operations will realize that as long as no water has been added or subtracted the volume will remain the same, regardless of the shape of the beaker. In solving this problem, the older child makes use of the operation of *reversibility*—he can imagine pouring the water back into the wide beaker and realizes that the

amount is the same as before. With the attainment of concrete operations, the child becomes capable of many new skills, including the use of arithmetic.

Because concrete operations are such necessary skills, parents and teachers often wonder whether it is possible to hasten the development of this mode of thought. Americans seem to be particularly concerned with "getting there faster"—so much so that Piaget called the issue of accelerating cognitive development "the American question." Recent studies suggest that, within limits, such acceleration is in fact possible. By using techniques in which children are confronted with contradictions in their own judgments, researchers have been able to teach 4-year-olds to master the principle of conservation (Brainerd, 1977). Yet attempts to train 3-year-olds have not been successful, indicating that a child must be close to getting it on his own for training to be effective (Field, 1981). There is no evidence that such acceleration has long-lived effects on intellectual ability.

Broadening perspectives

Another major change in children's thinking between ages 2 and 12 is an increasing ability to take another person's point of view. Infants and very young children, according to Piaget, are *egocentric*. Piaget did not use this term to connote selfishness but rather to signify the fact that young children are able to view their world from only a single perspective—their own. A colleague of mine, knowledgeable in child development, took advantage of

FIGURE 8.3

A problem used to study the development of conservation of volume, one of the concepts acquired in the concrete-operations stage. Children of different ages agree that the amount of water in the two identical beakers (top left) is the same. But when the water in one of the beakers is poured into a tall, thin beaker, children under about age 7 are likely to say that the taller beaker now has more water, whereas older children recognize the amounts are still equal.

his child's lack of perspective-taking ability. When his 3-year-old called out from another room, "Dad, is this the finger a ring goes on?" he answered, "Yes, that's right," without getting up to look. The child went on playing contentedly. The boy could not put himself in his father's place and realize that his father had no way of knowing which finger he was talking about.

Piaget studied egocentrism using what he called the three-mountain task. A child placed on one side of a model landscape is asked to describe what someone standing on the other side would see. Younger children typically described their own personal view, not realizing that the view would be different for someone else. Older children are able to mentally put themselves on the other side and to accurately describe the view.

Whereas Piaget focused on the child's broadening perspective in reasoning about physical space, more recently researchers have turned their attention to children's broadening perspectives in their reasoning about other people and social relationships. Just as a child comes to understand what other people see, so she comes to understand what other people think and feel.

Between the ages of about 4 and 6, the child typically equates his own attitudes with objective reality. When a preschool child says that "tuna fish tastes good," he does not stop to think that tuna tastes good to *him* but might not taste good to someone else. By the early school years, however, he comes to recognize that different people have their own distinctive attitudes and that one person's preferences may not be the same as another's (Selman, 1980). In addition, children gradually develop a broader view of their own friendships. At first, they view friendship in a one-sided way, solely in terms of what a friend can do for them. A friend is a friend because "I like him" or "He plays with me." Only at later stages do children become able to step back and take the other person's viewpoint ("She doesn't like it when I act too wild") or to appreciate their interlocking needs ("We share a lot of the same values") (Selman, 1980).

Thus, both physical and social perspectives become broader over the course of childhood. In both the physical and the social domains, there is a progression from what the child directly sees or feels to more complicated inferences about the perceptions and feelings of others.

Over the course of childhood, children develop a broader view of their own friendships. As children become able to take other people's feelings into account, their friendships come to include more helping and sharing.

Moral development

Paralleling shifts in the child's understanding of the physical and social world are shifts in the child's view of right and wrong—her *moral development*. Piaget (1948) proposed that moral reasoning evolves through stages that are dependent, in part, on cognitive abilities. Before the age of 6 or 7, the child is in what Piaget called the stage of *moral realism*. She sees rules as sacred and permanent. A 4-year-old would be surprised to learn that her friend plays a card game by different rules than she does, or that different countries have different laws. In this stage, the rules have an objective reality of their own. Between the ages of 7 and 10, the child gains experience with rules, as she plays games with friends and adjusts to the different rules of her home, school, and other settings. In the process, the child's unbending view of rules breaks down. By about age 10, the child enters the stage of *moral independence*, in which she can recognize the need to devise and modify rules to fit particular situations. For instance, a child may decide that it is okay to play a baseball game using four outs per inning if everyone consents and if it will make the game more enjoyable.

As children progress from the stage of moral realism to the stage of moral independence, their feelings about the seriousness of wrongdoing change dramatically. During the stage of moral realism, it seems to the child that the amount of damage counts more than the intentions. The worse the mess, the more guilty the child, and whether or not the culprit "meant" to do it is not taken into account. By the time the child reaches the stage of moral independence, he regards intentions as more important than the amount of damage. He now considers it worse to smash a small vase on purpose than a large one by accident.

Of course, moral issues are more complex than simply balancing consequences and intentions. Lawrence Kohlberg (1969) extended and revised Piaget's analysis by studying the moral reasoning of adolescents and adults as well as children. To measure moral development, Kohlberg explored the ways that subjects resolved the conflicts in a series of moral dilemmas. In one such dilemma, a man named Heinz must decide whether to steal a drug that he cannot afford in order to save the life of his dying wife. Subjects were asked what they would do in such a situation and—more important—to explain their reasons for their decision.

On the basis of responses to dilemmas such as these, Kohlberg identified three basic levels of moral reasoning (Figure 8.4). At the first, or *preconventional*, level, "morality"

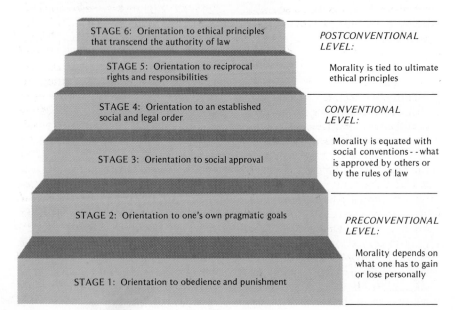

STAGE 6: Orientation to ethical principles that transcend the authority of law

STAGE 5: Orientation to reciprocal rights and responsibilities

POSTCONVENTIONAL LEVEL:

Morality is tied to ultimate ethical principles

STAGE 4: Orientation to an established social and legal order

STAGE 3: Orientation to social approval

CONVENTIONAL LEVEL:

Morality is equated with social conventions - - what is approved by others or by the rules of law

STAGE 2: Orientation to one's own pragmatic goals

PRECONVENTIONAL LEVEL:

Morality depends on what one has to gain or lose personally

STAGE 1: Orientation to obedience and punishment

FIGURE 8.4

The stages of the development of moral reasoning postulated by Lawrence Kohlberg.

depends simply on what Heinz has to gain or lose personally. Some children at this level say that Heinz shouldn't steal the drug because he might be punished and go to jail; others say that he should steal the drug because he needs his wife to take care of him. At the second, or *conventional*, level, "morality" is equated with the conventions of society—what is approved by others or by the rules of law. At this level, some children say that Heinz shouldn't steal the drug because stealing is illegal; others say that Heinz should steal the drug because his marriage vows require him to protect his wife. At the third, or *postconventional*, level of reasoning, right and wrong are tied not to any existing laws but rather to more abstract ethical principles. People at this stage might say that Heinz shouldn't steal the drug because the druggist has a right to his own property or that he should steal the drug because life is a higher value.

Kohlberg proposes that these three stages make up an invariant and universal sequence in development: everyone goes through the first stage before the second and the second before the third. In general, research has indeed shown that children proceed through the earliest stages as Kohlberg would predict (Walker, 1982). Not all people ever reach Kohlberg's third level of morality, however, even as adults.

Recent studies have also focused on the impact of children's social relationships on their moral development. Advances in moral reasoning seem most likely to take place as a result of encounters with other people—especially peers—in which the person must consider and debate his own and others' views about moral issues (Damon and Killen, 1982).

Although Kohlberg's approach to moral development has been highly influential, his proposed stages of moral development have been criticized by Carol Gilligan (1982) as reflecting a prototypically male view of morality, which emphasizes impersonal systems of rights, and as neglecting a female view, which emphasizes interpersonal caring and communication. Boys tend to score "higher" than girls on Kohlberg's

measure, but Gilligan believes that this is because the measure itself is biased. Future researchers may be expected to take this criticism into account and to develop a more comprehensive view of what constitutes "morality."

It is also important to note that the level at which a child or adult reasons about hypothetical moral dilemmas does not necessarily predict the way in which that person will make his real decisions about right and wrong—whether he will be honest or dishonest in particular situations, whether he will speak out or remain silent in the face of injustice. The fact that a person can reason at a sophisticated level does not guarantee that he will *act* at that level.

Child rearing and the growth of competence

Most parents hope that their children will become competent people, capable of making decisions for themselves, taking initiative, and relating effectively to others. For Robert White (1959), competence is the most central of human motives (see Chapter 10). Erik Erikson, as mentioned in Box 1, sees elements of competence involved at several stages of development. The 2- or 3-year-old must learn to act confidently on his own *(autonomy)*, the 4- or 5-year-old must set forth boldly to explore his environment *(initiative)*, and the older child must develop a sense of accomplishment in solving problems and completing tasks *(industry)*. The extent to which children develop such competence depends greatly on their parents' approach to child rearing. (In Box 3 we consider the special problems of child rearing that must be faced by parents who have divorced.)

Several different approaches to child rearing have been distinguished. One approach, often associated with the "old school," is the *authoritarian* style. Authoritarian parents try to shape the behavior of the child according to their own standards of conduct. These parents put a premium on obedience, and they may use punishment to keep the child in line. In an authoritarian family, there is little room for discussion and debate; "do it

BOX 3

CHILDREN OF DIVORCE

Divorce—increasingly prevalent in the United States—has a psychological impact not only on the divorcing couple (see the Psychological Issue following Chapter 17) but on their children, as well. By 1990 approximately one-third of all 18-year-olds will have experienced the divorce of their parents (Glick, 1979). With so many children and adolescents affected, researchers have focused on the short- and long-term effects of divorce on children.

Children involved in the divorce situation often live disrupted lives. First, they must deal with the trauma of their parents' separating and of one parent leaving home. "I remember it was near my birthday when I was going to be 6 that Dad said at lunch he was leaving," one 8-year-old recalled. "I tried to say, 'No, Dad, don't do it,' but I couldn't get my voice out. I was too much shocked" (Francke et al., 1980).

In addition, the child of divorce now has only one parent to turn to on a day-to-day basis, and that parent—usually the mother—may often be too busy with work, housekeeping, or establishing a social life to offer sufficient support and guidance to the child. Divorce also usually leads to a decrease in available income, which in turn leads to greater stress for both parents and children (Colletta, 1983).

Children of divorce must often deal with the continuing conflict between warring parents. This conflict is especially traumatic in cases of child custody battles, where the parents vie with each other for custody of the child, while the child awaits the outcome.

Judith Wallerstein and Joan Kelly (1980) interviewed the parents and children in sixty families who had gone through a recent divorce, then interviewed them again 18 months and five years after the divorce. They found a prevailing sense of sadness, loneliness, and anger in children of all ages. Young children, unable to understand the reason for the separation, often blamed themselves for the breakup, thinking that perhaps they were

being punished for being bad. Older children were less likely to blame themselves but were often torn by the loyalty dilemma—the feeling that whenever they sided with one parent they were betraying the other. By the end of the first year, most of the children had learned to cope at least moderately well; yet many of them remained intensely unhappy and dissatisfied with their home life even five years after the divorce.

In another study, E. Mavis Hetherington and her coworkers compared forty-eight 3- and 4-year-olds whose parents had recently divorced with other children attending the same nursery school. Preschoolers from divorced homes showed less creativity and imagination in their play than their counterparts, and they also played less often with other children. These effects were more pronounced and long-lasting for boys than for girls (Hetherington, Cox, and Cox, 1978, 1979).

The effects of divorce on children are not necessarily all bad. Studies of long-term psychological effects suggest that children from broken homes may well experience less unhappiness in the long run than children in unbroken

homes that are full of conflict and hostility (Emery, 1982). Children of divorced parents sometimes become more self-reliant and responsible, as a result of their increased participation in household tasks and decisions; in some ways, children of divorce "grow up a little faster" (Weiss, 1979b).

Moreover, surveys of adult personal adjustment do not point to clear differences between those who did and did not grow up in broken homes (Kulka and Weingarten, 1979). Children of divorce *are* more likely to get divorced themselves, however, perhaps in part because of the model their parents provided—the idea that divorce is a legitimate solution to family conflict (Pope and Mueller, 1979).

In recent years, the idea of *joint custody* for the children of divorced parents has gained popularity. In such arrangements, child-rearing decisions are shared by both parents, and the children may divide their time between the two parents' homes. Joint custody can be hard to bring off successfully. The former spouses are likely to remain hostile toward each other long after the divorce, which can make it difficult for them to cooperate in raising the children. One psychia-

trist who opposes joint custody contends that the child needs to know that there is one adult who will have responsibility for his daily care: "He needs an anchor. In joint custody there are only two half anchors" (Dullea, 1980). In many cases, however, joint custody seems to provide the best way for the child to remain closely connected to both parents after the divorce. Psychologists are beginning to study joint custody systematically to find out more about the conditions under which it is most likely to succeed (Clingempeel and Reppucci, 1982).

Most children of divorce eventually emerge from the experience in good shape. Nevertheless, divorce remains a traumatic experience for the child, one that can lead to many months or years of pain and deprivation, and one that probably no one gets over completely.

because I told you to" is sufficient reason for obedience.

At the other extreme is a *permissive* style of child rearing. Instead of trying to shape the child's behavior, permissive parents adopt the policy of keeping hands off and letting children "be themselves." These parents hope that by maximizing the children's freedom, they will encourage the development of initiative and self-reliance. As Robert White (1976) wisely points out, however, when parents really care about their children's well-being (as most parents do), it is very hard to live up to this permissive ideal. Devoted parents can't help worrying about how far they should go in letting children make their own deci-

sions. "Parents who care about their children," White writes, "inevitably harbor wishes and hopes for their future. They do not want to see this future compromised by shortsighted impulsiveness and youthful impatience" (page 46).

Neither an authoritarian pattern nor a pattern of total permissiveness seems to be as effective in the development of competence as is a child-rearing pattern that combines acceptance of the child's behavior within certain limits with relatively firm control. On the basis of extensive observations of parents and their preschool children, Diana Baumrind (1971) concluded that the most independent, creative, and cooperative

Parents who take an authoritarian approach to child rearing place a premium on obedience (top). Parents who take a permissive approach, in contrast, place few limits on their children's behavior (bottom). Neither extreme seems to be the best way to build a child's competence.

children tend to have parents who have definite standards but also encourage their children's independence and solicit their opinions. Similarly, Stanley Coopersmith (1967) found that 10- to 12-year-old boys were most likely to develop high self-esteem when their parents provided them with clearly defined limits and respected the boys' right to make decisions for themselves within those limits.

ADOLESCENCE

Whereas the changes that take place in childhood are relatively slow and gradual, adolescence begins (at about age 12) with changes that are abrupt and dramatic. Along with the rapid physical and sexual development that occurs early in adolescence, cognitive development enters a new stage. The growth of adolescents' bodies and the continuing development of their modes of thinking provide the backdrop for several other critical developments of adolescence (roughly ages 12 through 17), including formation of a stable sense of identity and changing relationships with parents and peers.

Physical development

The beginnings of adolescence are marked by physical changes, including the maturing of the reproductive system and rapid changes in body size and shape. For girls, the budding of the breasts and the onset of menstruation are especially dramatic changes. For boys, the changes include the sprouting of facial hair and deepening of the voice.

There is wide variation in the ages at which these developments take place. Although the average age of menarche (first menstrual period) for American girls is about 12½, it can take place anywhere between ages 9 and 17 (Bullough, 1981). The height spurt can begin for girls anywhere between 7½ and 11 and for boys between 10½ and 16. As a result, it is quite possible for three girls or three boys of the same age in early adolescence to look as if their ages are widely different.

Because of these differences, girls and boys are likely to be acutely self-conscious about their size and shape during early adolescence. Late-maturing boys, in particular, are likely to feel less adequate, less self-assured,

The rate of physical development in adolescence varies greatly from one person to another. Despite their different sizes and shapes, these girls are all 12 years old.

When adults comment, "Those kids are growing up faster than ever!" they're right, in more ways than one. Over the past century the age of puberty in the Western world has declined sharply, at least in part because of better nutrition. In 1900, the average age of menarche (first menstruation) for American girls was about 14; it is now about 12½. Boys are also undergoing the physical changes of puberty earlier than before. Will the decline continue? Probably not to any large extent. The evidence suggests that by now young people in America are growing up at something close to the fastest possible speed (Tanner, 1972).

and more anxious than boys who mature earlier (Mussen and Jones, 1957; Simmons et al., 1979), and some of these differences may persist into adulthood (Jones, 1957). Among girls, there are fewer personality differences between early and late maturers (Tobin-Richards, Boxer, and Petersen, 1983). In at least some cases, however, early maturing reduces a girl's popularity with her peers—until the peers catch up (Faust, 1960). To minimize such negative effects, it is important for young people to be informed that wide variations in the age of the height spurt and sexual maturation are perfectly normal.

Cognitive development

At about age 12, children enter Piaget's stage of formal operations. Whereas children at the concrete-operational stage require the presence of objects in order to mentally manipulate them, at the stage of formal operations children can manipulate thoughts and ideas without physically perceiving the objects they are thinking about. For example, a child of 8 may play checkers very well and be able to plan several moves ahead—she is mentally manipulating objects in physical space. But she may be less proficient at playing 20 Questions. She will ask a series of unrelated concrete questions ("Is it a dog?" "Is it a banana?" "Is it Daddy?") instead of asking questions that logically close in on the target ("Is it alive?" "Is it animal rather than vegetable?" "Is it a person?"). The latter sort of strategy requires the child to manipulate concepts and categories systematically; these are formal operations (Flavell, 1977).

It is not until early adolescence that most people can play complex word games, learn algebra, and do other tasks that involve the mental manipulation of complex thoughts and concepts. Formal operations are necessary for a fuller grasp of historical time (what does it mean for something to have occurred "five centuries ago"?) and geographical distance (how far is "a thousand miles"?).

Does the adolescent acquire formal operations all of a sudden, or are

they acquired singly and gradually? Piaget implied that there is an abrupt reorganization of the child's mode of thinking in early adolescence (Inhelder and Piaget, 1958). However, recent research has cast doubt on this notion. In fact, even relatively young children often show the beginnings of formal-operational thought, and the general picture appears to be one of continuous development rather than abrupt change (Keating, 1980). Thus, whereas the physical changes from childhood to adolescence are sudden and dramatic, the changes in modes of thought are more gradual.

The formation of identity

In Erik Erikson's view, identity formation is the central developmental task of the adolescent years. From all the separate roles that the adolescent plays—as son or daughter, sibling, boyfriend or girlfriend, athlete, student, and so on—he or she must struggle to emerge with a clearly defined sense of self. The adolescent must answer the question, "Who am I—and where am I headed?" In Erikson's words:

The identity the adolescent seeks to clarify is who he is, what his role in society is to be. Is he a child or is he an adult? Does he have it in him to someday be a husband and father? What is he to be as a worker and an earner of money? Can he feel confident in spite of the fact that his race or religious or national backgrounds make him a person some people look down upon? Overall, will he be a success or a failure? (1951, page 9)

Identity takes shape gradually, and it develops along several fronts. As the adolescent forms his sense of identity, he considers who he is in several different domains—his occupational goals, his political and social values, his self-definition as male or female. In the process, the individual considers different possible paths or definitions before committing himself to a particular one. The adolescent's acquisition of formal operations seems to be a necessary ingredient in this process of forming an identity (Rowe and Marcia, 1980). With formal operations, the adolescent can try out new ideas, think about possibilities, and think about *himself* in a contemplative way.

Elizabeth Douvan and Joseph Adelson (1966) have suggested that because of the lower status of women in American society, girls find it harder than boys to develop a strong sense of identity and that girls often postpone this task until after marriage. At this time their identity may depend in large part on the accomplishments and plans of their husband. One of the concerns of the women's movement is to remove this sort of socially imposed obstacle to women's identity formation.

But the formation of a stable sense of identity is not an easy task for anyone, regardless of sex. The rapid physical changes and sexual awakening of adolescence often lead young people to be confused about the continuity between their past and present. The many changes taking place in today's society only serve to compound the difficulty. It is no wonder, then, that many adolescents fail to establish a clear identity and instead experience what Erikson calls *role confusion*. Indeed, recent research suggests that the most extensive advances toward forming a clear sense of identity do not take place until the college years (Waterman, 1982).

Even at the end of adolescence, people's identities are not fully formed and unchangeable. In fact, as we will see in Chapter 9, people continue to form and re-form their identities throughout much of the course of life. Nevertheless, the adolescent years remain the period when people are first likely to achieve a real appreciation of who they are and what makes them special.

Parents and peers

As children become adolescents, they typically become less closely attached to their parents and become more involved with their friends and their "crowds." As with the shift from concrete to formal operations, the shift in the relative importance of parents and peers is not sudden. From birth onward, infants and children gradually gain independence from their parents: they learn to feed themselves, to venture away from home on their own, and to pursue their own interests and activities. Starting as early as the preschool years, moreover, relationships with age-mates become increasingly important (Rubin, 1980). In adolescence, however, the shift from parents to peers is heightened.

Adolescents often feel impelled to distinguish themselves from being "the Jones's boy" or "the O'Malleys' girl," to develop a clear sense of their individual identity. As the teenager comes closer to being an adult herself, she may also begin to question her parents' authority over her. After all, she reasons, "I'm not a kid any more." But as the adolescent becomes more independent of her parents, she remains in need of support from others. Especially as the adolescent struggles with the biological changes of puberty and the psychological changes that go along with it, she is likely to gain security by associating with others who are in the same boat.

As a result, the friendships of adolescence are often very close. Adolescents have been found to spend more hours talking to friends than any other waking activity and to rate themselves as happiest when they are with their friends (Csikszentmihalyi et al., 1977). Compared to younger children, adolescents typically cooperate more with their friends and share more intimate information with them (Berndt, 1982). At the same time, teenagers are strongly motivated to conform to the standards of their peer group. Groups of adolescent friends often have astonishingly similar attitudes about a variety of topics, ranging from tastes in clothing to standards of sexual behavior. "Teen culture" serves some useful functions. It helps adolescents feel that they are accepted members of a world of their own, rather than junior members of a world of their parents. On the other hand, for those teenagers who do not have friends or a peer group, adolescence can be a tremendously lonely period of life (Brennan, 1982).

Despite the great influence of friends, parents still have a strong in-

Adolescence is a time to forge a sense of identity—to come up with an answer to the questions, "Who am I and where am I headed?"

fluence on teenagers' attitudes and values. Parents and peers often have their greatest influence in different areas. For example, teenagers report themselves to be more influenced by peers when it comes to styles of dress, hair length, and hours of sleep but more influenced by parents when it comes to religion, moral values, and such personality traits as thrift and responsibility (Lerner and Spanier, 1980). In many areas, such as cigarette smoking, both parents and peers are likely to have an influence: teenagers who smoke are more likely than nonsmokers to have both parents and friends who smoke (Krosnick and Judd, 1982).

When people think about teenagers and parents, the first word that comes to mind is likely to be "conflict." And, indeed, there is usually some conflict between adolescents and parents. As illustrated in Box 4, at least some of this conflict stems from the fact that parents' and peers' standards for appropriate behaviors are sometimes at odds. But the extent of conflict in adolescents' relationships with their parents can easily be overestimated. In fact, teenagers and their parents seldom differ greatly on important values, and more often than not teenagers select the sorts of

friends who share their parents' standards about such matters as the importance of school achievement (Offer and Offer, 1975).

Interestingly, when adolescents are asked to predict their parents' attitudes about various issues, they tend to overestimate the differences between their parents' views and their own (Lerner and Knapp, 1975). Because of their desire to distinguish themselves as unique individuals, teenagers seem to perceive the small differences that do exist as larger than they really are. The fact remains, however, that adolescents and their parents usually have a great deal in common; the influences of parents and peers are likely to be congruent, rather than contradictory.

Despite all the talk about adolescent rebellion, studies have shown that rebellion against parents—and against society's standards more generally—is not a "normal" aspect of adolescence. Rather, such rebellion is a response by a relatively small number of adolescents, often in cases where parents do not provide the sort of support and guidance that the adolescent needs (Block, 1982). In most cases, parents continue to be important sources of support, guidance, and affection throughout the teenage

As children become adolescents, they typically become less closely attached to their parents and more involved with their friends. In most cases, however, parents continue to be important sources of support, guidance, and affection.

BOX 4

"STEVE ASKED ME OUT, AND I'M GOING"

As adolescents assert their own individuality and are increasingly influenced by their peers, certain conflicts with parents seem almost inevitable. Richard Lerner and Graham Spanier (1980) have provided some apt illustrations of these conflicts:

• **Steve asked me out, and I'm going**
Shari just turned 15, and has recently begun high school. She has never been on a date before, and has now been asked out by Steve, a junior, who has his own car. Shari asked her parents for "permission," and they said that Steve is too old for her, that she is too young to be dating, and that they don't want her driving around in this boy's car. After a bitter argument about the problem, Shari announces that she is going anyway.

• **I'll smoke if I want to**
Ted, a 16-year-old, began smoking about 18 months ago. He started out smoking one cigarette each day on the way home from school with a friend. After about six months of that, he began smoking more often—at parties, at school athletic events, during breaks around the school grounds, and at the shopping center where all the kids "hang out." Ted's parents suspected this because they smelled smoke on his clothes, but Ted denied it every time it came up. Then his parents

were told by friends of theirs that they saw Ted smoking at the shopping center. The parents were furious and announced that they forbade Ted to smoke. Ted reported that he planned to continue smoking; but he never smokes at home. Ted and his parents argue daily about the smell of smoke on his clothes.

• **Get off the phone, or I'll rip it out**
Wendy, age 17, talks on the phone about two hours every night. On some nights, she talks even longer. Wendy's parents constantly insist she should restrict her calls to ten minutes. Wendy says that she has as much right to use the phone as anyone, and often talks on the upstairs extension so that her parents don't know she is on the line. Wendy has suggested getting a second phone number, but her parents absolutely refuse. (page 56)

In some families, arguments like these occur only occasionally, and the family is able to cope effectively with the conflict. After the argument, such families are able to return to a state of good feelings. In other families, however, fighting is continual and the hostility extends from one quarrel to another (Haan, Smith, and Block, 1968).

years—and beyond (Klos and Paddock, 1978). Many parents share actively in the activities and accomplishments of their adolescent children, and many teenagers wish to please their parents more than anyone else.

My two children, with whom I opened this chapter, are in the backyard right now. Noam, the 3-year-old, is happily chasing and catching bubbles that his 7-year-old brother Elihu is blowing in his direction. Minutes later, the mood shifts. Noam is crying, explaining through his tears that "Elihu screamed at me." Elihu, in his own defense, claims that he was only trying to teach Noam that he is not allowed to throw rocks. Like Elihu and Noam, most children grow up with brothers and sisters, and the relationships between them are an important aspect of development. In the Psychological Issue that follows, we will discuss the relationship between brothers and sisters in both childhood and adulthood.

SUMMARY

- *1* *Development* refers to the relatively enduring changes in people's capacities and behaviors as they grow older. People develop both physically and psychologically.

The nature of development
- *2* *Maturation* refers to the unfolding of inherited biological patterns. Maturation and learning interact to produce psychological development.
- *3* Many psychologists believe that experiences very early in life can have a significant influence on all subsequent development. They point to the crucial role of *critical periods* in the early development of animals such as waterfowl to prove their point. Although some studies have indicated that the first few months of life can have special importance for social development, experiences at this time do not necessarily set the child on an irrevocable course. Furthermore, there is little evidence that very early intellectual training will have lasting positive effects.
- *4* Psychological development

occurs in fixed sequences, with later developments building upon earlier ones in a predictable order. But while the sequences of developmental milestones are relatively constant, the ages at which they occur can vary widely. There is some debate among psychologists as to whether most development occurs gradually and continuously or through relatively abrupt jumps from one stage to the next.
- *5* Erik Erikson has identified eight stages of psychosocial development, each characterized by a specific task that must be mastered.

Prenatal development and the newborn
- *6* Development begins long before birth, starting at the moment of conception. The development of the *embryo* and *fetus* within the mother can be affected by the mother's nutrition, use of drugs, and even emotions.
- *7* Newborn babies are more competent than they were once assumed to be. They are equipped with a number of reflexes and all their senses are well-developed and functioning. They also show a special interest in human faces and voices and seem to seek out particular features in their environment.
- *8* The newborn period is important for establishing strong bonds between infant and parents. This period is made more difficult if the infant is born prematurely.

Infancy
- *9* Although the development of *motor skills* in infancy is largely controlled by maturation, experience can influence emergence of particular skills.
- *10* According to Piaget, cognitive development progresses through four qualitatively different stages: the *sensorimotor period* (birth to age 2), the *preoperational period* (2 to 6), the *concrete-operational period* (6 to 12), and the *formal-operational period* (from 12 on).
- *11* In the sensorimotor period, the infant comes to understand the world through explorations with his senses and motor activities. Infants also begin to learn about cause and effect and acquire the concept of *object permanence*.

• **12** During the first year of life, the infant develops a strong *attachment* to a small number of people. The presence of the attachment figure helps to reduce the reaction of *stranger anxiety* that typically occurs at this stage.

• **13** Harlow's studies with infant monkeys imply that attachment is not a learned response to someone else who provides food but rather an innate tendency to bond with someone who provides pleasurable physical contact.

• **14** Infants who are "securely attached" to their parents appear to be more socially competent than their peers. Mothers are often the primary attachment figures because they usually spend more time with the infant, but babies commonly become attached to their father as well.

Childhood

• **15** Children between the ages of 2 and 7 are in Piaget's preoperational stage of cognitive development. They tend to be *egocentric* and have not yet attained an understanding of concepts such as *conservation*. At about age 7 children enter Piaget's concrete-operational stage and are able to mentally manipulate objects. During this period they also begin to develop an understanding of other people's perspectives and feelings.

• **16** Accompanying changes in cognitive abilities are changes in the child's view of right and wrong. Piaget saw a shift from *moral realism* to *moral independence* as children grow older. Kohlberg identified three basic levels of moral reasoning: preconventional, conventional, and postconventional.

• **17** *Authoritarian* parents deliberately try to shape their children's behavior according to their own standards of conduct. *Permissive* parents let their children "do their own thing." Parents who set definite standards but also encourage their children's independence and opinions are more likely to have children who are independent, creative, and cooperative.

• **18** Children of divorced parents must cope with the disruption caused by the divorce and with the fact that they have only one parent available to them on a day-to-day basis. Although children of divorce encounter many psychological difficulties, most emerge from the experience successfully.

Adolescence

• **19** Adolescence begins with maturation of the reproductive system and rapid bodily changes. There is wide variation in the age at which major developments occur, and early or late maturation can significantly affect the person's self-concept and personality.

• **20** Most adolescents are in Piaget's stage of formal operations. At this stage the individual is able to manipulate concepts and categories systematically. The acquisition of formal operations seems to be a necessary ingredient in the process of forming a sense of identity.

• **21** During adolescence the individual tends to become less attached to parents and more involved with friends. However, parents continue to be a major influence on the teenager's attitudes and values.

KEY TERMS

attachment
authoritarian child rearing
concrete-operational stage
conservation
critical period
development
egocentrism
embryo
Erikson's psychosocial stages
fetus
formal-operational stage
imprinting
learning
maturation
moral development
object permanence
operations
permissive child rearing
prenatal development
preoperational stage
reversibility
sensorimotor stage
stage
stranger anxiety
temperament

BROTHERS AND SISTERS

The Marx Brothers

"If I answered quickly, I'd say she's always been a real pain in the ass," the young woman answered when asked how she felt about her older sister. Then she thought for a moment and gave a fuller reply: *I'm sorry that we always gave each other so much trouble. But at the same time, there's some kind of indescribable closeness between us. No matter how many fights we had as kids, I think we'll always keep getting back to each other. . . . I wonder about her, and I worry about her. I guess I'm really glad that she's my sister, even though, at times, I could wring her neck. (Bank and Kahn, 1982, page 49)*

This woman's sentiments, though expressed in her own distinctive way, are not unusual. In fact, it is common for people of all ages to have strong ambivalent (mixed) feelings about their siblings (brothers and sisters), including elements of both love and hate.

In this Psychological Issue, we will discuss sibling relationships in both childhood and adulthood. We

will begin with a fascinating area of research that is closely linked to sibling relationships: how people's *birth order* in their families—particularly whether they are first-borns or later-borns—may influence their achievement and personality.

THE EMINENCE OF FIRST-BORNS

In the past quarter-century, birth-order research has become something of a fad among psychologists. Studies have been published about the links between people's birth order and almost every conceivable psychological characteristic, from pain tolerance (later-borns seem to be able to withstand more pain) to the likelihood of becoming a stripper (first-born women have been found to be more likely to enter this profession) (Skipper and McCaghy, 1970).

Some of the hundreds of birth-order findings are undoubtedly statistical flukes, and each of them should be taken with a grain of salt. But the research as a whole con-

firms that people's position of birth in their families can have an impact both on their childhood experiences and on the sorts of adults they will become.

The clearest and most consistent of these findings is the tendency for first-born children to have greater academic and occupational achievements than later-borns. First-borns have been found to have higher grades in college than later-borns and to be overrepresented in various listings of eminent men and women (Schachter, 1963). Of the first twenty-three American astronauts to travel into space, all but two were first-borns or only children. And in a recent study of twenty-five of the top female business executives in America, *all* twenty-five turned out to be first-borns or onlies (Hennig and Jardim, 1977).

Why is it that first-born children tend to achieve greater eminence than their kid brothers and sisters? Even though they are "number 1," first-borns apparently try harder, especially in the school setting. This academic striving seems to reflect the aspirations and pressures of their parents—after all, their first child is their first entry in the race for success. Indeed, even when babies are as young as 18 months, mothers have been found to demand more mature behavior from first-borns than from later-borns (Snow, 1981).

There is also a well-documented tendency for first-borns to be more intelligent than later-borns. As one goes down the family roster, first-borns have the highest IQs, second-borns the next highest, and so on down the line, with the last-borns tending to get the lowest scores (Belmont and Marolla, 1973). The differences are quite small, and they are not found in all families. But when the scores are averaged over thousands of cases, a clear pattern emerges.

Although the pattern is clear, the causes for it are not. It is possible that some physical factors are involved—for example, that the uterine environment may become less nourishing for later-born children—but there is no evidence for such ideas. Another speculation, put forth by Robert Zajonc (1976) is that the later-born child's intellectual development is held back by the presence of older siblings who are themselves infants or toddlers when the new baby is born. Whereas first-borns are exposed to concentrated intellectual stimulation by their parents in the first two or three years of life, later-borns receive less concentrated stimulation. If the older children are *much* older (five or more years), however, the younger child's intelligence is not expected to suffer.

But being a later-born isn't all bad. The need to get along with older siblings may teach later-born children valuable lessons about dealing with powerful others. Perhaps as a result of such learning, later-borns tend to be a bit more socially skilled and better liked than first-borns (Miller and Maruyama, 1976). In addition, parents, now that they have had some experience, tend to be less anxious with their later-born children than they were with their first-born. And it has been found that, on the average, later-borns grow up to be less anxious adults (Howarth, 1980).

SIBLINGS IN INFANCY AND CHILDHOOD

The ambivalence of sibling relationships begins at the beginning: when a second child is born into a family. The older child, who until this time has had the ex-

The birth of a younger sibling typically arouses mixed feelings in the older child.

clusive attention of the parents, is likely to feel distressed and envious, even as he feels excited and proud.

Two British psychologists, Judy Dunn and Carol Kendrick (1982), conducted an extensive study of sibling relationships in infancy and early childhood. The first-born children in their study were between 1½ and 3 years old when their younger brother or sister was born. Almost all of the first-borns showed signs of distress at the time of the new arrival. They were likely to become more demanding, clinging, and tearful. Many of the first-borns began to act more like newborns themselves at times, babbling like babies or demanding to be carried around.

At the same time, however, most of the first-born children were affec-

tionate toward their new brother or sister and were eager to help their mother care for the baby. "When she cries, he's very concerned," one mother reported. "He gets her pacifier, then comes and tells me." And despite their occasional relapses into babyishness, more than half of the first-borns also showed increased independence upon the birth of their sibling. Most commonly, they showed a new insistence on feeding or dressing themselves and an increase in the length of time they were able to play alone. Several children gave up the bottle in the first two weeks after the baby's birth. Once the baby is born, it seems, the first-born is often motivated to show that he is *not* a baby himself.

As the younger siblings grow up, they are likely to have mixed feelings toward their older siblings as well. Infants may become attached to their older brothers and sisters and, when parents are not available, may be reassured by big brother's or big sister's presence (Stewart, 1983). Younger children look up to their older siblings and frequently imitate their behavior (Abramovitch, Corter, and Lando, 1979). On the other hand, young siblings may also feel victimized and tormented by the older ones—and often with good reason.

It is difficult to determine what leads some pairs of siblings to develop friendly relationships in childhood whereas other pairs always seem to be at each other's throats. But Dunn and Kendrick did find a surprisingly high degree of continuity over time in sibling relationships. For example, those first-born children who had shown the most positive reactions toward the new baby were also the most likely to respond with concern three or four years later when the younger child was hurt or distressed.

The ties between siblings are the longest lived of all human relationships.

SIBLINGS IN ADULTHOOD

Ties between siblings are the longest-lived of human relationships. Even as childhood friends are forgotten, as marriages are made and unmade, and as parents pass away, brothers and sisters remain related for life. Even siblings who no longer keep in close touch with each other are still expected to come to each other's aid in times of economic or emotional need.

And even in adulthood, sibling rivalry is likely to continue. Men seem especially likely to compare their own accomplishments with those of their brothers. When a man hears that one's brother has received an honor, a raise, or a promotion, he is likely to feel both proud ("That's my brother!") and envious ("Is he outdoing me?").

Such rivalry was strong in the case of William James, the pioneering American psychologist, and his younger brother, Henry, the world-renowned novelist. William was highly critical of Henry's writing—so much so that Henry once wrote to him, "I am always sorry when I hear of you reading something of mine, and always hope you won't—you seem to be constitutionally unable to enjoy it" (Edel, 1953–72). And yet, there was also a lifelong relationship of love and admiration between the two brothers.

William Arkin (1981) has pointed out that although brothers may feel great loyalty toward each other, it is often hard for them to maintain intimate relationships. The ideal of brotherly love often seems to come into conflict with an ideal of masculinity that stresses achievement, competition, and keeping one's cool. Because of these unfortunate demands to "be a man," men often want to let their brothers know about their successes but cannot tell them about their problems.

Sisters, too, are likely to have rivalrous feelings, especially as they are growing up. But after they leave home, sisters usually keep in closer contact with each other than brothers do, confide more in each other, and maintain more intimate relationships (Cicirelli, 1982). Sisters commonly decide to live together in their old age, often after they have been widowed; brothers rarely do.

In their traditional role as the "kin keepers" of the family, women usually maintain closer ties with their relatives than men do, whether through letters, phone calls, or visits (Adams, 1968). In families with at least two brothers and one sister, sisters often have the role of channeling news from one brother to another. In times of crisis, men more often prefer to get in touch with their sister than with their brother (Arkin, 1981). In all this, it may be argued, brothers get a better bargain than their sisters do. Victor Cicirelli (1982) has gone so far as to conclude, on the basis of questionnaire results, that "The more sisters an elderly man has, the happier he is." There are no comparable data to suggest that brothers are central to the happiness of elderly women.

THE ONLY CHILD

With all of this talk about the pleasures and pains of having siblings, what of those people who have none? About 5 percent of Americans are only children, and, by at least some accounts, they are a disadvantaged minority. In national surveys, about 80 percent of those polled say they think being an only child is a handicap (Blake, 1974). And, when asked, college students described only children as more self-centered, temperamental, unhappy, and unlikeable than children with siblings (Thompson, 1974). Parents, too, seem to have accepted a negative view of the only child. They often decide to have a second child in order to keep their first child from being lonely.

Is there any reality behind this picture of only children as selfish, lonely, and maladjusted? Psychologist Toni Falbo (see Chapter 1, Box 3) decided to check it out. After reviewing the available studies that compared only children with those who have siblings and after conducting additional studies of her own, Falbo (1979) concluded that there is little basis for the negative stereotype. Only children attending college do say they have fewer friends and belong to fewer clubs and organizations, on the average, than those with siblings. But the only children report just as many *close* friends, and they are likely to be the *leaders* of their organizations. Only children also seem to be especially independent and autonomous, perhaps because they are more likely to have grown up in "adult-centered" families, without a lot of youngsters running about.

In Falbo's opinion, there is nothing wrong with being an only child; in fact, it may be an advantage. She advises parents to stop thinking that they must have a second child "in order to keep the first from being neurotic, selfish, and lonely."

T*here is little basis for the negative stereotype of only children.*

SUMMARY

- *1* Research on birth order has consistently found a tendency for first-born children to achieve greater academic and occupational success than later-born children. This may be because parents put greater pressure on their first-borns to be successful. However, later-borns tend to be more socially skilled and better liked than first-borns.
- *2* Children show a great deal of ambivalence when a new baby arrives. On the one hand, they may show distress and relapse into babyishness; on the other hand, they show concern for the baby's well-being. Such ambivalence toward siblings can continue throughout life.
- *3* In adulthood, sibling rivalry is especially prevalent among brothers. Perhaps because of traditional masculine stereotypes, brothers are more likely to compete than to share intimacies.
- *4* Although sisters may also have rivalries, they tend to keep in closer contact than brothers do and to maintain more intimate relationships with both brothers and sisters well into old age.
- *5* Research has revealed that there is little basis for the stereotype of the only child as being selfish, lonely, and maladjusted.

ADULTHOOD AND AGING

Development continues throughout the years of adulthood.

If you are now in your late teens or early twenties, a vast span of life stretches out before you. In your twenties you may complete your formal education, start your first real job, perhaps get married and start a family. In your thirties, you may be working hard at a career, raising children, reaffirming—or maybe ending—an intimate relationship. In your forties, you may begin to cope with physical changes caused by growing older and with psychological questions about the meaning of your life, now that it is half over. In your fifties you may be a different person in some respects—perhaps more relaxed, more reflective, more mellow than you were earlier in life. In your sixties you may retire, begin to collect Social Security, and establish new relationships with your children and grandchildren. In your seventies and the years beyond, you are likely to experience chronic illnesses, although they may not limit your daily functioning, and you may turn to new interests and endeavors. You are also likely to experience the death of a spouse or other loved ones. Your own death becomes more imminent.

The specific progression of events through the span of life varies greatly from one individual to another. For all of us, though, development continues throughout life. Most research on human development has focused on the years of infancy, childhood, and adolescence, when physical and psychological changes are most rapid and dramatic. In recent years, however, psychologists have paid increasing attention to the development that takes place later in the life span, as people proceed through the years of adulthood.

We will begin this chapter by considering the nature of adult development, including the ways in which it is similar to and different from development earlier in life. We will then examine three broad stages of life: early adulthood (roughly from age 18 to age 40), middle adulthood (40 to 65), and late adulthood (from 65 on). The age boundaries between these stages are fuzzy, and indeed some social scientists would prefer not to discuss adulthood in terms of stages at all. Nevertheless, the intellectual skills, self-perceptions, and social circumstances of a 20-year-old are likely to differ from those of a 45-year-old, and both are likely to differ from those of a 70-year-old. We will consider these differences as we examine the course of adult life.

THE NATURE OF ADULT DEVELOPMENT

Just like development during infancy and childhood, development in adulthood involves an interplay between maturation (changes that are biologically preprogrammed) and learning (changes that are caused by experience). For example, when a woman will go through menopause and whether and when a man will grow bald are changes that are primarily maturational. But development through most of adulthood is influenced to a greater extent by the experiences of life than by maturation.

Paul Baltes (1979) and others have found it useful to distinguish between two sorts of factors that influence adult development: age-graded influences and non-age-graded influences. *Age-graded influences* are experiences and events that commonly occur at a given stage of life. For example, it is common for people to get married and start a family in their

THE AGE-IRRELEVANT SOCIETY

Although an adult's age is likely to be related to her physical and psychological development, it seems to be becoming a poorer predictor of how people live. "It no longer surprises me," notes Bernice Neugarten (1980), "to hear of a 22-year-old mayor or a 29-year-old university president—or a 35-year-old grandmother or a retiree of 50. No one blinks at a 70-year-old college student or at the 55-year-old man who becomes a father for the first time." Neugarten believes that we are on our way to becoming an age-irrelevant society—and she thinks that's the way it ought to be.

twenties and thirties, to ascend the occupational ladder in their forties, and to retire and experience widowhood in their sixties and seventies. *Non-age-graded influences* are experiences and events that are unique to the individual rather than associated with a particular stage of life. For example, a person may have a serious accident at age 25, inherit a sum of money at 35, get divorced at 45, or move to a new job assignment at 55.

Baltes points out that age-graded influences are especially common in infancy and childhood. At that time physical and cognitive growth and specific life events (such as going through the school grades) are highly correlated with age. After adoles-

cence, however, age-graded influences become less central. Thus, there are no clear stages of physical and intellectual development in adulthood, and there is a greater diversity of social paths in adulthood than in childhood. Some adults go to college and some do not; some get married and some remain single; some write poetry and some sell insurance. It is not until the years of late adulthood, when such predictable events as retirement, widowhood, and certain physical declines are common, that age-graded influences once again become relatively strong. Because of the greater importance of non-age-graded influences during adulthood, people seem to be-

Development in adulthood is marked by both stability and change. Billy Martin (top) was playing ball for the New York Yankees in 1952 and was managing the same team 30 years later. John Glenn (bottom) shifted careers from astronaut in 1961 to senator and presidential aspirant in 1984. Even when people's occupations change, however, certain aspects of personality tend to remain relatively stable through the adult years.

come more diverse as they age: two 50-year-olds are likely to be more different from each other in their personalities and values than two 10-year-olds or two 20-year-olds.

Despite the diversity of adult lives certain psychological tasks and challenges do seem to characterize particular stages of life. Erik Erikson (1950) influenced much of the current research on adult development by outlining three major stages of adult development. (These are the last three of Erikson's stages of psychosocial development that were presented in Chapter 8, Box 1.) In early adulthood, Erikson believes, the central psychological challenge is to establish *intimacy*—a close bond with another person, usually a husband or wife. In middle adulthood, the central psychological challenge is *generativity*—having an impact on the next generation, whether through guiding one's own children or through one's contribution to society. And in late adulthood or old age, Erikson emphasizes the theme of *integrity*, the ability to look back at one's life with satisfaction. We will return to each of these themes later in this chapter.

A central issue in the study of adult development is the extent to which it is characterized by *stability* or *change*. For example, will the artistic and literary woman of 23 remain absorbed in cultural matters as she grows older, or will these interests become overshadowed by the demands of career and family when she reaches 33? Will the ambitious, aggressive man of 35 still be so hard-driving when he is 50, or will he become more inward-looking and mild-mannered? The best way to answer these questions about stability and change in development is through *longitudinal* studies, in which the same people are assessed periodically through their adult years.

Although the evidence to date is limited, longitudinal studies have provided evidence for both stability and change. Despite the fact that people often turn to different activities as they age—a middle-aged man may give up basketball and take up golf—a person's overall level of activity seems to be quite stable through the life span, with those who are most

energetic and active in their youth also being the most energetic and active in late adulthood (Haan and Day, 1974). Similarly, studies have found a great deal of stability in certain personality traits, such as sociability, over the adult years (McCrae and Costa, 1984).

At the same time, recent studies have also emphasized the potential for significant changes in skills, values, and self-concept through the course of adulthood. As people deal with the tasks and challenges of adult life, they may also come to view themselves in new ways and in some respects become "different people" (Brim and Kagan, 1980). For example, a quiet and deferential housewife who enters law school at 32, after her children are in school, may emerge several years later as a more forceful, outspoken woman, not only in her professional life as a corporate lawyer but in her family roles as well. Robert Butler (1963) suggests that substantial reorganization of personality may also take place in old age, leading to the wisdom and serenity that are characteristic of many old people.

EARLY ADULTHOOD

When is a person an adult? There is no single criterion. Legal definitions of adulthood rely on chronological age. In most states, for example, one can vote at 18 and drink at 20 or 21. But a person's age is not really a good indicator of her physical and psychological development. One 18-year-old may support herself and feel quite independent, while another may remain her parents' "little girl" until she is well into her twenties. Nevertheless, all of us must at some time, usually in our late teens or early twenties, leave the relatively sheltered world of adolescence and enter the world of adulthood. The period of early adulthood extends from this time until about the age of 40, when people make the transition into the middle years of life.

Physical and cognitive changes take place in early adulthood, just as they do in infancy, childhood, and adolescence. For example, physical

One of the signposts marking one's entry into adulthood is voting for the first time.

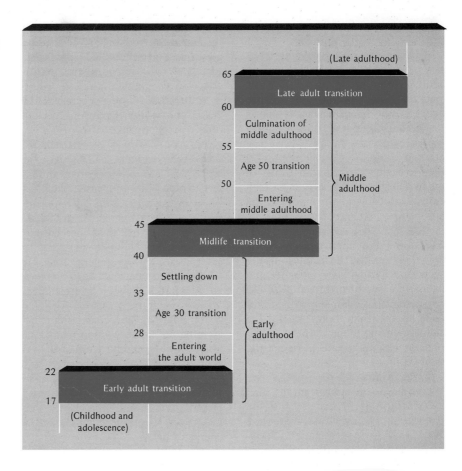

strength is usually greatest and the heart usually functions most efficiently in the mid-twenties, with a gradual decline from then on (Hershey, 1974). Sensory acuity and reaction time also tend to be at their peaks in the twenties and to decline gradually thereafter (Birren, 1964). But the physical and cognitive changes of early adulthood are much less noticeable than the corresponding changes of childhood or of old age, and they play a comparatively minor role in development. Instead, the most significant aspects of early adult development involve the ways in which individuals deal with several central psychological tasks and decisions: separating from the world of childhood and becoming one's own person, choosing an occupation, establishing an intimate relationship, and starting a family.

The stages of early adulthood

On the basis of an intensive study of the lives of forty men, Daniel Levin-

son (1978) has proposed that early adulthood—at least for men—consists of several discrete stages, involving an alternating sequence of relatively stable periods and periods of transition. Through all of the stages, each person engages in a continuing struggle to evolve a *life structure:* the basic pattern or design of one's life at a given time. A life structure includes both external features, such as career, marriage, and family, and one's internal view of oneself, or sense of identity. Many other researchers (for example, Costa and McCrae, 1980) doubt that the stages of men's lives are as clear and unvarying as Levinson suggests. Nevertheless, these proposed stages (depicted in Figure 9.1) provide valuable starting points for further research on the course of adult development.

The early adult transition (ages 17–22). During these years, Levinson notes, the man must start moving out of the preadult world of his childhood and take his first steps into the adult world. College is one setting in which many men (and women) work on their separation from the family and expand their outlook on life.

Entering the adult world (ages 22–28). Now the young man is a "novice adult," with a life of his own. At this stage, he must find the right balance between two opposing tasks. One is to explore the possibilities of adult life, keeping his options open. The other is to create a stable life structure, to begin to "make something" of his life. During this period, most men embark on careers, form intimate relationships, and start families.

The age 30 transition (ages 28–33). As the man approaches 30, he is drawn to examine the initial adult life structure that he has established and in many cases to modify it. Life becomes more serious—now it's "for real." Some men make major life changes during the age 30 transition, such as changing careers or getting married.

Settling down (ages 33–40). Following the age 30 transition, the man invests himself in his "second life structure." He tries to establish a place for himself in society, to solidify his family life, and to make it in the world of work. Toward the end of this stage (during the years between 36 and 40), Levinson speaks of the period of "becoming one's own man," when the man is most concerned with becoming a full-fledged senior member of the adult world.

Settling down and "becoming one's own man" do not conclude the story of adult development, from Levinson's perspective. To the contrary, this stage is typically followed by a new period of self-doubt and questioning, the midlife transition, which we will consider later in this chapter.

A question of great interest is the extent to which Levinson's stages might be applicable to women's development. Levinson himself conjectures that women go through the same basic adult developmental periods as men, but other researchers believe that there are fundamental differences between women's and men's development. As Rosalind Barnett and Grace Baruch (1978) note, Levinson's stages reflect in large measure men's preoccupations with careers. For women, however, careers are less taken for granted. Carol Gilligan (1982) suggests, moreover, that "becoming one's own woman" may be a less central theme for women than it is for men. Whereas men are likely to place great emphasis on gaining independence from others, women may place a greater emphasis on their attachments to others throughout the course of life.

Choosing an occupation

People's initial decisions about an occupation may be made in childhood or adolescence. These early decisions are often quite unrealistic, however. For example, as many as half of all teenagers indicate a preference for professional occupations, whereas only about 14 percent actually be-

Work and career are a central focus of adult life. When people enter the work world, they sometimes discover a gap between their idealized images of the job and their actual experiences.

CHAPTER NINE: ADULTHOOD AND AGING

come professionals (Cosby, 1974). Observing the work roles of one's parents can have a major impact on career decisions. In particular, having a working mother as a model often plays a crucial role in women's decisions to enter professions (Lopate, 1968). It is not until early adulthood, however, that one must crystallize and implement one's career plans, by getting appropriate training and by finding one's first job.

When people actually enter the work world, they may discover that there is a gap between their idealized images of the job and the skills taught in school, on the one hand, and the real rewards and demands of the job, on the other. Even students who major in such "practical" fields as journalism and engineering find themselves unprepared for the actualities of the work world. Such "reality shock" contributes to the high turnover in certain professions, including nursing and teaching (Ritzer, 1977). In most cases, however, the young workers get over their initial shock and strive to advance in their chosen field. The years between the late twenties and about 40 are typically ones in which the worker advances in status and seniority and in which job satisfaction increases.

In the 1980s more and more people are questioning the traditional model of having a single career in their lifetime. Instead, they are feeling freer to explore many occupations, perhaps interspersed with periods away from work (Sarason, 1977). Some people switch between related fields, such as a photographer becoming a photography instructor or a scientist becoming a science writer. Still others switch between radically different fields. Ronald Reagan was a radio announcer and then an actor long before he became a politician.

Establishing an intimate relationship

For Erik Erikson, the central psychological challenge of early adulthood is to establish an intimate relationship. Such intimacy involves a high degree of sharing and communication between two people. With the achievement of intimacy, the person feels enriched and connected to others; without it, he is lonely and isolated.

"In youth," Erikson (1974) writes, "you find what you *care to do* and where you *care to be*. . . . In young adulthood you learn whom you *care to be with*—at work and in private life, not only exchanging intimacies, but sharing intimacy" (page 124). As this implies, Erikson believes that a clear sense of one's own identity—who one is and what one believes in—is a prerequisite for the establishment of intimacy. A truly intimate relationship requires "a fusing of identities" while at the same time retaining

A central challenge of early adulthood is to establish an intimate relationship with another person without losing one's own identity.

a sense of self. A person with a weak identity will be too fearful of losing that fragile sense of self to be able to achieve intimacy. At best, such a person might form unstable or highly dependent relationships.

Recent studies have provided support for Erikson's view. In one study, measures of college students' "identity status" and "intimacy status" were derived from interviews about their life commitments and interpersonal relationships. Men and women who had achieved a clear sense of identity were found to have deeper and more committed relationships than those who had not yet developed a clear identity (Kacerguis and Adams, 1980). The results of this and other correlational studies do not show that identity achievement necessarily precedes intimacy, however. In fact, intimacy has an impact on one's identity, as well. As David Matteson (1975) observes, "In every real sharing experience both persons grow; identities are rediscovered and altered" (page 161). We will return to the themes of intimacy and commitment in Chapter 17 and the Psychological Issue on marriage and divorce that follows it.

Starting a family

Early adulthood is the time when most people not only get married but also have children. A large majority of married couples have at least one child, and almost all of these children are born during the parents' early adult years. Most of the psychological research on parents and children has focused on the parents' impact on the children. In Chapter 8, for instance, we considered the ways in which different approaches to child rearing may affect children's development. It is important to recognize, however, that having and raising children also has a great impact on the *parents'* development. Parents typically report that having children makes them feel "more like an adult" and more responsible. Parents also feel that their children provide them with affection, fun, and a sense of purpose (Hoffman and Manis, 1979). But child rearing has its negative side as well. Once they have children, couples have greater financial difficulties, less time to spend with each other, and greater difficulty balancing work and family demands.

Until relatively recent years, married couples were expected to have children if they were biologically able to do so, and this expectation was one that few couples thought to defy. In the last decade and a half, however, the option of not having children—*voluntary childlessness*—has become more acceptable for young couples. Couples are now considering more carefully the decision of whether to have children, and a significant minority are deciding that the costs would outweigh the rewards.

In addition to deciding whether to have children, couples decide *when* to have them. Whereas in previous generations most couples launched their families when they were in their early twenties, more and more couples today are waiting until their late twenties or early thirties to have their first child.

Pamela Daniels and Kathy Weingarten (1981) interviewed couples in three different generations who had their children "early" (in their early twenties) or "later" (in their late twenties or early thirties). Their interviews emphasized the major impact that family timing has on people's lives. The couples who had their children later generally believed that the postponement helped give them a chance to solidify their marriage, to advance both the husband's and wife's careers, and in general to do more "growing up" before bringing a child into the world. For example, an artist who became a mother at 32 felt that if she had had children when she was younger, her work "never would have formed itself." As she put it, "The twenties were the years I was putting everything together, without even knowing what I was doing, evolving a style, and getting my work going." But many later mothers also found that the arrival of a baby created new conflicts with their rising careers that they had not anticipated. Moreover, some of the early parents stressed the advantage of having their children grow up sooner. One early mother, now a systems analyst, summarized the tradeoff involved:

More and more couples are waiting until their late twenties or thirties to launch a family.

LOOKING YOUR AGE

Because age is often judged on the basis of physical appearance—how old one looks— *it is important to maintain a clear sense of how old one* is. *On Gloria Steinem's fortieth birthday, a friend paid her what she intended to be a compliment: "You don't look 40!" Steinem had a quick and sensible reply: "This is what 40 looks like."*

I like the fact that my children are as old as they are, and that I'm as young as I am and my career is so open ahead of me. I'd hate to be in my career position, wanting to have children and not knowing when to make the break. On the other hand, I missed that early period of freedom, of trying my wings and doing things on my own. (Daniels and Weingarten, 1981)

The issue of family timing serves to illustrate the importance of the links between the different tasks of early adulthood: work, intimacy, and the family. Today people are able to make a wide range of decisions about each of these tasks. But the decisions are not independent of one another. It is the interplay of these decisions, including their timing, that affects the person's development through the course of early adulthood.

MIDDLE ADULTHOOD

The years between 40 and 65 often seem to be a stable, even static period of life. People in middle age have "gotten there." They run our nations and most of our major institutions. They have reached some stability in their struggles to establish a career, a family, and a life-style. But in fact,

middle age is characterized by development and change as well as by stability. It is a time of adaptation to physical changes, of new demands from one's work and family, and of evaluation of one's past and future.

The midlife transition

Some time around the age of 40, people must make the transition from early to middle adulthood. They must come to a new conception of themselves as middle-aged people, with new tasks, limitations, and opportunities. This shift is called the *midlife transition.*

In his study of men's lives, Daniel Levinson (1978) found that the midlife transition begins at about age 40 and lasts about five years. For 80 percent of the men he studied, Levinson reports, the midlife transition involved a painful and disruptive struggle. In such cases, the men were seen as having a *midlife crisis:*
Every aspect of their lives comes into question, and they are horrified by much that is revealed. . . . A profound reappraisal of this kind cannot be a cool, intellectual process. It must involve emotional turmoil, despair, the sense of not knowing where to turn or of being stagnant and unable to move at all. (Levinson, 1978, page 199)

The midlife transition sometimes involves a painful struggle, as people appraise their values and talents and the extent to which they have lived up to them.

For other men, the midlife transition is smoother and less turbulent (see examples in Box 1). Whether the midlife transition is rocky or smooth, however, Levinson believes that it is a normal and necessary developmental stage. As a man reaches the middle of his life, he is drawn to appraise his values and talents and the degree to which he has lived up to them. One man may decide that as a result of his youthful ambition to get to the top he has become an overly aggressive, grasping person. Another man may regret the fact that he gave up his early dream to become a musician and may decide that he must find a way to recapture this side of himself. Through the course of the midlife transition, the man must come to terms with himself and build a new life structure that is better suited for the years of middle adulthood. Through the remaining stages of middle adulthood (see Figure 9.1), the man proceeds to solidify and further modify this new life structure.

As noted previously, the relevance of Levinson's stages to women has been questioned. But there are additional reasons to expect a period of transition in midlife, for women as well as for men. Hormonal changes and the awareness of a physical slowdown may force the middle-aged person to recognize that he or she is not "young" anymore. Midlife may also

bring on a new time orientation (Neugarten, 1958). The person stops counting "time since birth" and begins to view life in terms of "life left to live." Instead of thinking, "I'm only 41," he or she might begin to think, "I have maybe 25 good years left." In some cases the shift in perspective may come rapidly, in other cases as a gradual shift from a "younger" to an "older" self-conception (Vaillant, 1977).

Physical changes in middle adulthood

The physical changes that begin in early adulthood continue through the middle adult years (ages 40 to 65). In middle age, there are changes in physical appearance, health and energy, sensory acuity, and sexual functioning. These changes are usually gradual, continuing the physical declines that begin in the early twenties and extend through the course of life. What is most important in many cases is not the changes themselves but how the middle-aged person reacts to them. Sometimes the changes are hardly noticed, sometimes they are welcomed, and sometimes they lead to worry and concern.

One sort of change that one can hardly avoid noticing, especially in a society that gives inordinate emphasis to a "youthful" physical appear-

THE INCREDIBLE SHRINKING MAN
One of the lesser known aspects of adult development is that as we get older, we get shorter. Our bodies can withstand the force of gravity for only so long. As our muscles weaken, our back slumps. And as the disks between the bones of the spine deteriorate, our bones move closer together. As a result, a man who measures 5'10" at age 30 can expect to be 5'9⅞" at 40, 5'9⅝" at 50, 5'9¼" at 60, and 5'8⅞" at 70 (Tierney, 1982).

BOX 1

PATHS THROUGH THE MIDLIFE TRANSITION

In Daniel Levinson's view, there are many possible paths through the midlife transition, ranging from relatively smooth, uneventful movement from early to middle adulthood to painful, tormented struggles with one's life. The cases of two of the blue-collar workers in Levinson's study provide examples (Levinson, 1978, pages 280–281):

Perhaps the most stable, yet continually evolving life was that of Ralph Ochs. At 45, he is still working in the plumbing department of the factory where, at 18, he started as an apprentice to his father. A man of great integrity and modest aspirations, he enriched his life over the course of early adulthood by his active involvement in organizing and running a union, becoming a shop steward, and, as he passed 40, serving as an informal adviser to younger workers. His major investment is now in his family. He speaks with unusual perceptiveness and caring about his three adolescent children. He would like all three to go to college. His eldest son is graduating from high school and has no interest in college. Ochs recognizes that this is a source of tension between them, and he is trying with considerable tact and insight to be helpful but not overly controlling. He takes considerable delight in the talents and projects of his youngest daughter, the brightest and most successful of the children. He enjoys and works at being an active father.

Contrasting sharply with Ralph Ochs's stable midlife transition was the more stressful passage of another worker:

Larry Strode left a black middle-class home in the South following military service in World War II. At 40, after fifteen years in the same factory, he was a skilled worker, shop steward, and occasional foreman. He was oppressed by the realization that he could advance no further in industry and that his life was of little value. During his midlife transition (age 40 to 45) he started his own barber shop, continued at the factory, completed high school, explored the work world for alternative occupations, and tried desperately to improve his failing mar-

riage. The son of a minister, he had long wanted a career that would more directly benefit human minds and souls. At 45, Strode began to build a new life structure. He left the factory and became a mental health worker at a local hospital while continuing to manage his barber shop. He separated from his wife, and divorced her a few years later. During the late forties he tried to develop a new occupation and family life (including the children of his former marriage, with whom he was strongly involved). At 49, when we last saw him, he was just beginning to succeed in making a life different from that of his early adulthood.

Whether the transition is easy or painful, Levinson believes that it involves important tasks of self-examination and development. In all cases, the individual's life in the late forties will differ in important respects from that in the late thirties.

ance, is changes in one's face and body. The middle-aged person looking in the mirror will find an image quite different from her high-school graduation picture. The eyes are deeper set, the lips are thinner, the facial contours are less pronounced. The skin is becoming wrinkled, and the hair is thinning and may be turning gray. Weight gain, especially in the stomach and hips, is common. Although some changes in appearance are inevitable, the amount of change depends on behavior as well as on biology. "Middle-aged spread," for example, is in part a result of the redistribution of fatty tissues that naturally occurs as we get older, but it also reflects a life-style common to many middle-aged people—eating more, eating richer foods, and getting less exercise.

Changes in health may also be quite important in middle age. Even if one has no immediate health problems, one begins to take seriously the threat of death or disease. The concern is not unfounded. The risk of heart diseases, which are the primary cause of death for men in the United States, increases after age 30, and the highest risk is between the ages of 50 and 60. Similarly, the risk of breast cancer for women is greatest in middle age (Owen, 1978). As with changes in appearance, declining health is not a necessary product of getting older. It is related not only to

biologically "preprogrammed" processes but also to one's habits throughout life. Stress in the job or family, tobacco or alcohol abuse, overeating, and lack of exercise all increase one's susceptibility to disease (see Chapter 12).

Even when he is in the best of health, the middle-aged person may notice some changes in what he can do. Heart and lung capacity continue to decline in middle adulthood, leading to a gradually diminishing capacity for strenuous work (see Figure 9.2). Changes in the brain's capacity to initiate and coordinate sets of movements leads to decreasing speed in the performance of clerical sorts of tasks, such as copying sets of numbers. Changes in sexual functioning may also occur in middle adulthood. For men, decreases in the volume of blood in the penis can cause erection and ejaculation to occur more slowly. For women, drops in hormone levels can cause vaginal walls to thin and vaginal secretions to be reduced (Masters and Johnson, 1966). But in the domains of both physical ability and sexuality, the extent of change is largely determined by individual physical condition, attitudes, and habits. Many people remain active in sports throughout middle adulthood, and exercise programs begun even late in life can yield marked improvements in physical capacity (deVries, 1970). Both men and women with

Some of the physical changes that take place in adulthood can be seen in the face of John F. Kennedy as he aged from 22 (left) to 29 (center) to 46 (right).

CHAPTER NINE: ADULTHOOD AND AGING

FIGURE 9.2

Physical changes with age. As we get older, our physical functioning becomes less efficient, as indexed by decrements in the cardiac index (the heart's output of blood to the body), vital capacity (the volume of air that can be exhaled from the lungs after a deep breath), and maximal breathing capacity (the volume of air that can be breathed in 15 seconds).

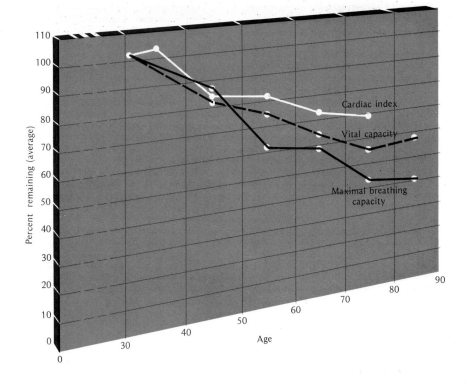

THE EMPTY NEST

When the last child leaves home, do parents sit tearfully over faded baby pictures, or do they break out the champagne? More often than not, it's the champagne. Studies have found that the majority of men and women actually look forward to the "empty nest" (Lowenthal and Chiriboga, 1972). There may be a feeling of regret, to be sure. But after having had children in the home for some 20 or 25 years, parents may find the prospect of a more private life to be a relief. And parents' relationships with their children often improve after the children have left home (Sullivan and Sullivan, 1980).

positive attitudes toward sexuality usually maintain active sex lives throughout middle adulthood. Contrary to some people's assumptions, the woman's menopause, at about age 45 to 55, need not interfere with her sexual functioning (see Box 2).

Personality in middle adulthood

Regardless of the precise timing and nature of the midlife transition, there is no doubt of the importance of the shift from early to middle adulthood in people's lives, from a time when men and women think of themselves as young to a time when they think of themselves as middle-aged. There is evidence that the period of middle adulthood is associated with greater introspection and inward-turning for many people, a process of increasing self-knowledge that often continues into the years of old age (Neugarten, 1968). At the same time, it has also been suggested that middle adulthood in many cultures—including our own—is a time of sex-role reversal when many men become more interpersonally sensitive and nurturant,

while many women become more outgoing and assertive (Gutmann, 1977). To the extent that such changes take place, middle adulthood may be a time during which both men and women recapture "lost" parts of themselves and become more fully human. (In Chapter 16 we will return to the theme of transcending the limitations of one's sex role.)

In Erik Erikson's view, the major psychological challenge in middle adulthood is achieving generativity— to feel that one is making significant contributions to the next generation. Without such generativity, one may feel a sense of worthlessness or stagnation. Middle-aged parents may achieve generativity by guiding their children through the transition from adolescence into early adulthood. Generativity can also be achieved in the world of work, as middle-aged people strive to make contributions that they feel will have some lasting importance. One of the most important career rewards for many middle-aged people is the opportunity to be a mentor—someone who can influence and further the development of young adults, such as students or younger coworkers.

BOX 2

MENOPAUSE

Some time during the years of middle adulthood women experience a developmental change that is not shared by men: *menopause*. Medically, menopause is defined as 12 consecutive months without a menstrual period. Over a span of about two years, usually between ages 45 and 55, a woman's hormonal function is reorganized. By the end of this reorganization period, estrogen levels are quite low and the ovaries no longer release eggs; the woman can no longer bear children. This process is sometimes accompanied by uncomfortable physical symptoms, such as "hot flashes" and headaches.

Many psychologists and physicians have assumed that menopause is a disturbing, even traumatic event in a woman's life. Such an attitude toward menopause is captured in the writing of Helene Deutsch (1944), a prominent psychoanalytic theorist: "Woman has ended her existence as a bearer of a new future, and has reached her natural end—a partial death—as servant of the species. . . . With the lapse of her reproductive service, her beauty vanishes, and usually the warm vital flow of her feminine emotional life as well" (page 477). Such views betray a pervasive sort of sexism: Since women's roles have traditionally been limited to those of wife and mother, it is assumed that the end of the childbearing years must represent a terrible loss for a woman.

In fact, both men and women go through a *climacteric*, a process of physical and sexual slowing down spread out over 15 or 20 years as the adult moves from middle to late adulthood. Menopause is one aspect of the female climacteric. There is no comparable "male menopause" in the sense that fertility ends, but male sex hormone levels do tend to drop throughout the climacteric.

What role does menopause actually play in women's development? Does the loss of reproductive ability really mean the loss of sexuality and attractiveness? Is the nonfertile woman so grief-stricken by her loss that she considers her life over? The evidence suggests not. Far from mourning the loss of their sexuality, many women, now freed from worry over pregnancy, enjoy sex more than ever (Weideger, 1977).

In a recent national survey, menopause was found to be distressing to women when it was "off time"—that is, when it came considerably earlier than the mid-forties or later than the mid-fifties. Menopause that comes either "too soon" or "too late" may be difficult to deal with because it does not fit into one's life in a predictable and "appropriate" way. Early menopause, in particular, may lead women to feel they are aging too quickly. When menopause comes at the expected time, however, it is not generally related to psychological distress (Lennon, 1982).

In reviewing the research on menopause, Malkah Notman (1979) concludes that other events of the middle years, such as release from child-care responsibilities, return to the work force, and changes in marital relationships, are usually much more important to women than menopause itself. The "partial death" that Deutsch described seems to have more reality for the psychologists and psychiatrists who write about it than for the women who are supposed to be experiencing it.

According to Erik Erikson, the challenge of middle age is to achieve generativity—to make a contribution to members of the younger generation either by raising them, teaching them, or serving as an example for them.

FIGURE 9.3

Over the course of the twentieth century, the elderly population of the United States has greatly increased. (Data from U.S. Census Bureau)

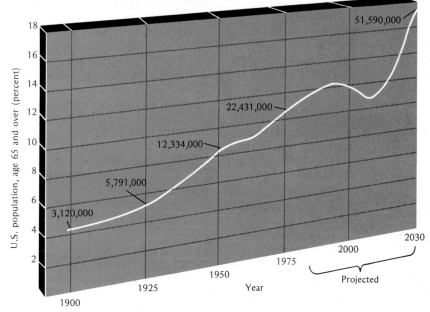

LATE ADULTHOOD

As medical advances extend life expectancies, the elderly are becoming a larger and larger proportion of the U.S. population (see Figure 9.3). A man of 65 can now expect to live to almost age 79, on the average, and a woman to age 83. Many researchers are now addressing the question, "What does it mean to be old?"

We must begin by recognizing that late adulthood may itself encompass several stages of life, from the 70-year-old who continues to lead an active, vigorous life to the 85-year-old whose activities may have greatly slowed down. Because of such differences, Bernice Neugarten (1975) suggests that we distinguish between the "young-old" and the "old-old," rather than talking about old age as a single category. Some of our prevailing cultural attitudes and prejudices about old age are examined in Box 3.

BOX 3

AGEISM

When one group of college students were asked how they felt about old age, their responses included: "Dread, disgust, I will not get old"; "It's frightening. . . . I wish I didn't have to"; "I hope I die before I get there"; "It will never happen to me" (Barrow, 1976). At least for this group of students, old age is clearly not something desirable.

Our society places a high value on the attributes of youth, and we tend to demean old age. The resulting bias against old people is a form of discrimination called *ageism*. Ageism is reflected in our stereotypes of elderly women and men. The stereotypical old person is not someone most of us would care to become: dependent on others, mentally unreliable, uninterested in sex (and unable to perform anyway), cranky, fretful, and rigid. "Old age is seen as pathological," writes Richard Kalish (1979), "a time of sickness and strangeness and falling-apartness. It is also seen as a static period without much chance for change in a positive direction."

Even young children latch onto this negative view of old people. In one study, preschool children were shown photographs of young, middle-aged, and old people and asked to indicate which pictures "went with" each of a list of adjectives. The children linked negative adjectives—such as sad, bad, ugly, poor, and dirty—much more often with photographs of old people than with photographs of the young or middle-aged (Chitwood and Bigner, 1980).

Some aspects of the ageist stereotype may have a grain of truth. Older people are more prone to disease than younger people. The mental processes of the elderly tend to be slower (though not necessarily less powerful) than they were in youth. And there is some evidence that older people tend to be more cautious and less flexible than younger people (Riley, Foner et al., 1968). But most of the research reveals what we should have known in the first place: that the personalities of old people are quite as diverse as the personalities of people at any other

The popularity of cosmetic treatments to make old people "look younger" is one reflection of ageism in our society.

stage of life (Maddox and Douglas, 1974). The stereotype fools us into viewing a 70-year-old or an 80-year-old as an "old person" rather than as a distinctive individual with unique strengths and weaknesses.

Ageism is also reflected in the discomfort that many younger people feel when they are with older adults, perhaps because of the mental link between old age and sickness and death. Even doctors, nurses, and social workers tend to avoid working with the elderly, preferring to work instead with children or younger adults (Palmore, 1977). In hospital emergency rooms, old people typically get a less thorough examination than young people, are less likely to elicit the fullest efforts of the medical staff, and are more often declared "dead on arrival" (Sudnow, 1967).

In addition to the stereotype of old persons, there is another, more subtle form of ageism. Because advanced age is so little valued in our society, there is only one way to age "successfully," and that is not to age at all. As a result, older people are seen as aging "successfully" to the extent that they continue to behave the way they did

when they were younger—that is like middle-aged people. "She looks like a woman twenty years younger" or "He still plays a set of tennis every day" is often taken as the highest compliment one can pay to an older person. As Kalish (1975) points out, this definition of "successful aging" is an example of ageism at its worst, because it presumes that one age group's pattern of behavior is inherently superior to that of another age group.

With the increasing proportion of old people in our society, negative attitudes toward the old may decline. There are already signs of such change: Large numbers of college students now take courses on aging, and increasing numbers of younger adults are becoming interested in careers that involve service to older people. But such change requires us to learn what to respect and admire in the elderly. That means shifting from a youth-biased set of values that emphasize competition, glamour, and power and that underemphasize wisdom, freedom from competitiveness, and self-knowledge.

The biology of aging

Like every other period of life, late adulthood is marked by its own set of changes. Many of the physical changes that were barely noticeable in middle age become marked in the late sixties. Vision and hearing may become noticeably impaired. Changes in the spinal column can produce stooped posture. Muscles and joints may become stiff enough to reduce physical activity. Blood vessels lose their elasticity, which can lead to circulatory problems. Changes in the central nervous system produce a general slowing down of behavior. The body's system of immune responses for fighting disease becomes less efficient.

All these changes relate to aging. Why do they occur? Can aging and ultimate death be slowed or even eliminated? No one knows for sure why we age and die. But there are several biological theories of aging, and each may provide part of the answer. One group of theories focuses on changes in the individual cells that make up our bodies. Some of our cells, such as those of the heart and brain, do not divide; when they die, they can never be replaced. Theorists have suggested that these cells "wear out" over time, as a result of such influences as exposure to radiation and excessive changes in body temperature. In addition, certain chemical reactions within cells produce waste materials that the cells cannot dispose of and that may ultimately lead to the death of the cell (Timiras, 1978). One such substance is *lipofuscin*, the chemical that causes brown "age spots" to appear on the skin of older persons. Even those body cells that do divide eventually stop reproducing themselves, for reasons that are not yet well understood (Hayflick, 1980).

Over the course of time there may also be damage to the genetic information stored in cells. The genetic code used to construct the proteins required by cells for their survival is stored in DNA molecules in each cell's nucleus. The information is copied and carried to other parts of the cell by another complex molecule, RNA. Damage to the DNA itself, or errors in copying the information in it, could lead to cell death. A single copying error would not necessarily kill the cell, but because cells are constantly renewing themselves, the error would repeat and accumulate over time until the cell eventually died (Timiras, 1978).

Although beauty is often associated with youth, the age-weathered faces of the elderly can also be considered beautiful.

Other theories of aging examine larger systems of the body rather than single cells. The immune system normally protects the body from foreign and mutant cells, such as cancer cells. Late in life this system appears to be less efficient in detecting mutant cells and in fighting them off (Makinodan, 1977). This may be one cause of the higher cancer rates in old people. Further, in old age the immune system may become disorganized and start attacking normal cells, producing an *autoimmune reaction* (Walford, 1969).

Still other theories suggest that the endocrine system (see Chapter 2) is primarily responsible for aging. Age-related changes occur in the endocrine glands, leading to lowered or less efficient endocrine function. Just as the brain controls the hormonal activity that directs physical growth and development, it may induce hormonal changes that lead to aging and death, as well. As Paola Timiras (1978) notes, it is as if there is a "biological master plan" to prevent us from living forever.

In some cases, especially in extreme old age, damage to the brain's cells leads to *senile dementia*, or senility, which can include such symptoms as memory loss, disorientation in time and place, impaired attention, and the loss of the ability to acquire new information. Contrary to many people's assumptions, senility is not a "normal" or usual aspect of old age, but rather a disease that afflicts only about 5 percent of old people, usually after age 75. The most common form of senile dementia is *Alzheimer's disease*, a brain disorder believed to be caused by the degeneration of nerve cells that release the neurotransmitter acetylcholine. Alzheimer's disease can strike as early as age 40, but it usually descends on people after the age of 60. In the future it may be possible to treat Alzheimer's disease with drugs (see Chapter 6, Box 3), but at present there is no cure.

Although most forms of senile dementia, including Alzheimer's disease, are incurable, memory loss and mental confusion may also be produced by other medical or psychological conditions that *can* be treated.

Unfortunately, these diseases are sometimes misdiagnosed as senile dementia. One study found a treatable medical or psychological condition in 35 percent of a group of patients who were originally diagnosed as having irreversible senile dementia (Altman, 1980).

Intelligence in late adulthood

Until recently, psychologists believed that people's intellectual capacity leveled off in their twenties and thirties and then started to decline rapidly in middle age and more rapidly in old age. Those people now in their thirties and forties should therefore be gratified to learn of recent research suggesting that in fact intelligence does not generally decline with advancing years. According to these studies, intelligence may actually increase on some measures well into the seventies (Schaie, 1982).

One reason that earlier studies indicated more serious declines in intelligence with greater age is that they compared old people's performances with younger people's at a single point in time. Using this *cross-sectional approach*, the younger people outscored the older ones on intelligence tests. But the younger people were also born in a time of greater educational opportunities, and this situation almost certainly contributed to their higher scores on some measures of intelligence. This sort of difference between two generations as a result of the different times in which they lived is called a *cohort effect. Longitudinal studies*, in which the same people are followed over many years, tend to show less decline, and the declines come later in life.

In studying intellectual changes in late adulthood, researchers have found it useful to consider two different types of intellectual abilities: fluid intelligence and crystallized intelligence (Horn, 1978). *Fluid intelligence* refers to the kind of mental agility, especially nonverbal, that allows people to make sense of unfamiliar stimuli and to see old problems

HOW LONG CAN WE LIVE?

All forms of life have some upper limit on their life span—from 10 to 20 days for the house fly to about 2000 years for some trees. Human beings live longer than any other mammals, and our maximum life span is probably about 110 years (Medvedev, 1975). Claims that eating yogurt or living in high altitudes produces much longer life spans than 110 have not been substantiated. Some scientists have been experimenting with ways to increase the maximum life span, such as "antiaging" diets (Rosenfeld, 1982). A more immediate prospect is progress in controlling diseases of old age so that more and more people will live into their nineties or even past 100.

in new ways. Such skills as finding the pattern in a string of letters, visualizing an object in space, and piecing together a jigsaw puzzle rely on fluid intelligence. *Crystallized intelligence* includes verbal skills, the ability to define words, and other information accumulated through the course of living in society. Most formal education is concerned with crystallized intelligence.

Fluid intelligence is thought to be more sensitive to changes in the central nervous system. Because aging is accompanied by such changes, fluid intelligence might be expected to decline over time. Crystallized intelligence on the other hand, relies more on ongoing experience, so it might be expected to improve with age. In fact, these predictions have been supported by research findings. Fluid intelligence seems to begin a gradual decline in middle age and may drop more sharply for many people in late adulthood (Botwinick, 1978). Crystallized intelligence appears to remain the same or to improve well into the seventies (Nesselroade, Schaie, and Baltes, 1972). These patterns are summarized in Figure 9.4.

Even in the domain of fluid intelligence, age-related declines do not seem to be inevitable. Some of the decline may, indeed, result from age-related changes in the central nervous system, so that certain messages cannot be communicated between neurons as efficiently. But the decline may also reflect older people's decreased interest in certain sorts of intellectual tasks. Doing jigsaw puzzles, for example, simply may not be as involving to older people as to younger people. In some cases, old people may decline intellectually because of a self-fulfilling prophecy: Because people *expect* their abilities to go downhill, they no longer make as much effort to remain intellectually active. As a result, they let some of their intellectual skills fall into disuse. On the other hand, older people whose professional careers require them to keep using certain intellectual skills, such as mathematics and extensive reading, seem to be the least likely to experience declines in fluid intelligence (Schaie and Geiwitz, 1982). And when old people from all walks of life are given practice and coaching sessions on fluid intelligence tasks, their scores increase significantly (Baltes and Willis, 1981). The writer I. F. Stone, who decided in his seventies to take up the study of ancient Greek language and civilization, may have been right when he concluded, "The mind is like a muscle—you must exercise it."

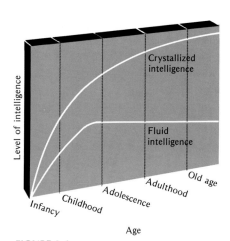

FIGURE 9.4

Changes in two types of intelligence with age. While crystallized intelligence (use of accumulated information and verbal skills) continues to increase through most of the life span, fluid intelligence (mental agility) typically reaches its peak in early adulthood and then gradually declines.

Old people whose careers require them to keep using their intellectual skills seem to be the least likely to show declines in fluid intelligence.

Memory in late adulthood

One area of intellectual functioning that clearly does decline as we get older is memory. Our memories seem to be best in early adulthood and to slowly head downhill from there, with a marked downturn after about age 60 (Schaie, 1980). Short-term memory—the amount of material we can keep in mind for a few seconds (Chapter 6)—does *not* seem to decline with age. But older people commonly find that their long-term memories are not as good as they used to be. It becomes harder for them to remember people's names, where they put things, or things they planned to do. (In Box 4, Malcolm Cowley provides a firsthand account of this and other changes experienced in late adulthood.)

Studies suggest that older people do not organize information for storage into long-term memory as efficiently as younger people do. As a result, they have more trouble retrieving material. Old people do almost as well as young people on tests of *recognition* (for example, deciding whether they have seen a particular word or object before) but not as well on tests of *recall* (which require them to retrieve the word or object on their own) (Erber, 1982).

How can older people best deal with declining memory? It is useful, first of all, to recognize the fact that for most of us memory does decline, from early adulthood on. Even though older people often complain about their failing memories, they also tend to overestimate how good their memories really are. In one study, adults of different ages were asked to predict how well they would do on a word-recall test. The older subjects (in their sixties and seventies) made predictions that were only slightly under the predictions made by the younger subjects (in their late teens and twenties). But when they actually performed the task, the older subjects did considerably less well than the younger ones (Bruce, Coyne, and Botwinick, 1982). Once people recognize that their memory is not as good as it used to be, they may be able to arrange their lives in ways that minimize the problem. When he was 78, psychologist B. F. Skinner (1983) recommended several helpful methods for older people to deal with memory problems. One of his recommendations was to execute as much of a behavior as you can at the moment that it occurs to you. For example, if as you dress to go out you hear a weather report predicting rain, hang the umbrella on the doorknob *right then*, so you won't have to remember it later. Skinner also recommended using a pocket notebook or a tape recorder to help compensate for declining memory.

Social changes in late adulthood

As people move through the years of late adulthood, they inevitably experience changes in the social fabric of their lives—how they spend their time and whom they spend it with. Among the most important social changes of late adulthood are retirement, widowhood, and changing relationships with family and friends. In still later years, a number of old people experience institutionalization.

Retirement. If we have any recognized marker of the onset of late adulthood, it is retirement. Unlike other life-markers, such as college graduation, marriage, or a first child, retirement seems to signal an ending more than a new beginning; it isn't clear what is coming next. The average worker can expect to spend the last fourteen years of life in retirement (Butler, 1977).

As long as individuals maintain their health and have an adequate income, they usually find retirement a satisfying stage of life. Richard Barfield and James Morgan (1978) asked retired men and their wives how they felt about retirement. Some of the most positive responses were: "Enjoy every minute of it! Have the time at last to do just what I want or not do anything if I want that." "I like it! We enjoy life a lot more if we're out of the rat race." The negative responses were usually related to poor health: "Not much to think about—you got the black lung; you just sit and wait." "He feels helpless and lost. It gives him a sad feeling seeing the land lying

OLD IS OLD—OR IS IT?

When is someone "old"? There is not much agreement on the matter. Alfred Zipser (1982), a retired public relations executive, believes that when we call people in their sixties "senior citizens," we are using a silly euphemism. At 63, Zipser writes without embarrassment, "I am old." "One of the tricks of old age," he adds, "is to face it squarely." When Corinna Marsh (1982) read Zipser's comments, she was greatly amused. At 91, she considers people of Zipser's age to be "youngsters." "Old at 63?" she writes in amazement. "Bah, humbug!"

BOX 4

THE VIEW FROM 80

Malcolm Cowley

"To enter the country of age is a new experience," writes the literary historian Malcolm Cowley (1980), "different from what you supposed it to be. Nobody, man or woman, knows the country until he has lived in it and taken out his citizenship papers" (page 3).

At the age of 80, therefore, Cowley decided to provide his own road map of this "country of age." His book, called *The View from 80*, is a witty and insightful account of the experience of old age. Here are some excerpts.

WHEN YOU KNOW YOU ARE OLD
The body and its surroundings have their messages for [the man of 80], or only one message: "You are old." Here are some of the occasions when he receives this message:
- when it becomes an achievement to do thoughtfully, step by step, what he once did instinctively
- when his bones ache
- when there are more and more little boxes in the medicine cabinet, with instructions for taking four times a day
- when he spends more time looking for things misplaced than he spends using them after he (or more often his wife) has found them
- when he forgets names, even of people he saw last month ("Now I'm beginning to forget nouns," the poet Conrad Aiken said at 80)
- when everything takes longer to do— bathing, shaving, getting dressed or undressed—but when time passes quickly, as if he were gathering speed while coasting downhill. The year from 79 to 80 is like a week when he was a boy. (pages 3–4)

GROWING OLD IN OTHERS' EYES
We start by growing old in other people's eyes, then slowly we come to share their judgment. [I remember the first time that] a young woman rose and offered me her seat in a Madison Avenue bus. That message was kind and also devastating. "Can't I even stand up?" I thought as I thanked her and declined the seat. But the same thing happened twice the following year, and the second time I gratefully accepted the offer, though with a

sense of having diminished myself. (pages 5–6)

THOUGHTS OF DEATH
Like many old people—or so it would seem from various reports—I think less about death than might be expected. As death comes nearer, it becomes less frightening, less a disaster, more an everyday fact to be noted and filed away. The question that obsesses me is what to do with those 6.7 years, more or less, that the Census Bureau has grudgingly allowed me. (pages 29–30)

INEQUALITIES AMONG THE AGED
As a group, we compose a disadvantaged minority, but some of us are vastly more fortunate than others. Although we are all in the same boat, with tickets for the same destination, we do not enjoy the same comforts during the voyage. The boat turns out to be an old-fashioned liner with first-, second-, and third-class accommodations, not to mention a crowded steerage. Age has inequalities that are even greater than those of youth. In the matter of income, for example, most of the old are well below the national median, but others are far about it. (pages 38–39)

TURNING INWARD
More and more the older person is driven back into himself; more and more he is occupied with what goes on in his mind. In middle age that absorption in the self had been a weakness to be avoided, a failure to share and participate that ended by diminishing the self. For the very old it becomes a pursuit appropriate to their stage in life. It is still their duty to share affection and contribute to the world as much as possible, but they also have the task of finding and piecing together their personalities. (page 55)

In retirement, older people must develop new ways of spending time and making contributions to society. This man has become active in a foster grandparent program.

vacant and not being able to plant something" (page 20).

It is often hard for people to adjust to their retirement. Our society places its highest value on the work-oriented life, and it takes time to switch to a leisure-oriented life and still feel important. To help make this transition, it is useful for people to plan for their retirement ahead of time and to develop interests outside of work that are most fulfilling to them. To facilitate this process, some companies have introduced phased retirement plans—for example, a plan that allows the employee to gradually increase the number of days taken for volunteer work in the community.

Widowhood. Most married women can expect to outlive their husbands, so there are many more widows than widowers. More than half of married women in the United States are widowed by their early sixties, and 80 percent are widowed by their early seventies. Among people over 65, widows outnumber widowers four to one (Hendricks and Hendricks, 1977).

Widowhood, for both men and women, can shatter a person's social world. Most of our society's social activities are built around couples, and there is no obvious social position for the single adult. This social isolation may be underscored by

physical isolation as well: three-fourths of widowed adults live alone. In at least one study, people who were single throughout their lives felt more satisfied in late adulthood than did widows and widowers of the same age. This may be because the single people had chosen a single life-style for themselves and had become adjusted to it (Gubrium, 1974).

Although widowers tend to be better off financially than widows, they have their own problems. In a study of 403 older men and women, Carol Barrett (1978) found that widowers felt lonelier, had a harder time with routine household tasks, and were generally less happy with their lives than widows. Many men have become highly dependent on their wives for emotional support, as well as for their housekeeping, and they are also less likely than women to have close friendships and family ties to fall back on (Stroebe and Stroebe, 1983).

Family relationships. After their children have established their own independent lives, older people find that the old bases of their parent-child relationship have been removed and new ones must be formed. Although 80 percent of older people in the United States have living children, only 12 percent of them live with a grown child. One reason for living

Relationships between grandparents and grandchildren can play a vital role in the lives of both the old and the young.

apart is a mutual wish for independence and privacy. Neither children nor parents want to be viewed as dependent on the other.

Relationships between elderly parents and their adult children can be stressful. Parents may impose demands for time and assistance that the children have difficulty meeting. Children may make too many demands themselves or may disappoint their parents by seeming aloof. But there are important rewards as well. Grown children can often help their parents with household repairs, care in illness, and finances. Elderly parents can provide their children with similar sorts of help and often assist in child care, too.

Relationships with grandchildren are often particularly rewarding for older people, who now have the opportunity to establish a loving link to a new generation of young people (Kivnick, 1982). Psychiatrist Arthur Kornhaber believes that grandparent-grandchild relationships often play a vital role in the lives of both the old and the young (Kornhaber and Woodward, 1981). It is a myth, Kornhaber (1983) asserts, that "grandparents spoil grandchildren." Instead, grandparents have a valuable chance to rectify the mistakes they made with their own children. In addition, he reports that children with close rela-

tionships to at least one grandparent tend to have a deeper sense of belonging to a family and community and to be less "ageist" (see Box 3) than children without such a close connection to a grandparent.

Institutionalization. Despite the prevalent image of the aged person spending his last days in an old-age home, only 4 to 5 percent of the aged population live in institutions. But for very old adults, institutionalization becomes an increasingly likely possibility. Women face a higher probability of institutionalization than men because they live longer, and people who never married or had children are more likely than others to be institutionalized because of the limited number of people in their lives available to take care of them (Palmore, 1976).

The decision of whether or not an old person should be placed in an institution is often a wrenching one for the person and his family. The decision by middle-aged children to allow an old parent to be institutionalized is sometimes equated with abandonment. In many cases, however, strained relations between old people and their children are improved when an institution assumes primary responsibility for the parent's care. With the reduction of day-to-day demands on the children, they may be

A small proportion of older adults live in institutions for the aged.

able to relate to the parent in more loving and less conflicted ways (Smith and Bengtson, 1979).

While some of the residents of institutions for the aged are truly unable to care for themselves, many have only limited disabilities. They are not helpless—only poor and alone. Some psychologists suspect that institutionalization contributes to a decline in intellectual skills among old people, because the institutional environment does little to encourage people to keep thinking for themselves. Programs that encourage and reward cognitive activity by institutionalized old people may be able to halt or reverse the decline in such skills as short-term memory (Langer et al., 1979). Partly because of the prevalent negative view of old-age facilities, there is a growing movement to provide these persons with the services they need within the community, rather than through an institution. Day centers and retirement communities extend to elderly persons the daily services they need while allowing them to live in their own homes, doing as much for themselves as possible (Kane and Kane, 1980).

Successful aging

Which person does a more "successful" job of growing old—the person who spends most of his time in a rocking chair reflecting on his past life, or the person who continues to work actively as an interior decorator and keeps up an active round of social activities? In fact, there seems to be no single way to age successfully; different types of people will find different ways of adapting to old age and enjoying it (Neugarten, 1972). In general, a person will select a style of aging that is suited to her personality. Thus, the book editor who has always been active in political groups, has kept a large circle of friends, and has enjoyed traveling will probably maintain many of these pursuits after retirement and would be unhappy without them. But the accountant who has spent most of his recreational time working on his vegetable garden and who has always avoided social gatherings will probably spend his later years in quiet withdrawal and be just as satisfied with his life as the retired editor is with hers.

Erik Erikson (1950) believes that the developmental task of the old is to establish *integrity*—the sense that one has lived a whole and fulfilling life. In Erikson's framework, the achievement of integrity represents successful aging. Robert Butler (1963) suggests that much of the reminiscing that is common late in life may be a valuable way of "sorting out" the past and the present. Butler calls this process of reminiscing the *life review*. "My life is in the background of my mind much of the time," one 76-year-old man reported, "it cannot be any

There is no single way to age "successfully." For some people, successful aging involves remaining physically active, for others it involves establishing a more leisurely style of life.

other way" (Butler, 1963, page 68). As Malcolm Cowley writes (see Box 4), old people "have the task of finding and piecing together their personalities."

Some individuals review their lives privately and internally; others share their memories and reflections with those around them. For this lat-

ter group, the life review serves a double purpose: It organizes a final perspective on their lives for themselves, and it leaves a record that will live on with others. One very old woman described her feelings about participating in a "living history" class where elderly people shared their pasts: "The memories came up in me like lava. So I felt I enriched myself. And I am hoping maybe I enriched somebody else. All this, it's not only for us. It's for the generations" (Myerhoff, 1978, page 39).

The last stage of life, of course, is not old age but death. We will discuss the challenge of facing death in the Psychological Issue that follows this chapter. One task of life, and especially of late adulthood, is to prepare for death. And the most important part of this preparation may be the feeling that one has lived a satisfying and meaningful life. "In such final consolidation," Erik Erikson writes, "death loses its sting."

SUMMARY

The nature of adulthood

• **1** Development in adulthood continues to involve an interplay between maturation and learning. *Age-graded influences* are experiences and events that commonly occur at a given stage of life. *Non-age-graded influences* are experiences and events that are unique to the individual. Whereas age-graded influences are central in child development, non-age-graded influences take on greater importance in adult development.

• **2** Longitudinal studies have shown that adult development is characterized by both stability and change over time.

Early adulthood

• **3** According to Levinson, early adulthood consists of several discrete stages: the early adult transition (ages 17–22), entering the adult world (ages 22–28), the age 30 transition (ages 28–33), and settling down (ages 33–40). Throughout all the stages an individual engages in a continuing struggle to evolve a *life structure.*

• **4** One of the tasks of early adulthood is to choose, prepare for, and enter an occupation. Entering the work world can produce "reality shock"—discovery of the gap between idealized images of a job and the actual job itself.

• **5** According to Erikson, the central psychological challenge of early adulthood is to establish an inti-

mate relationship. Most people get married in early adulthood, and a majority have children at this time, although a significant number are choosing *voluntary childlessness.* Many couples are also waiting until their late twenties or early thirties to have children.

Middle adulthood

• **6** Around the age of 40 people make the *midlife transition,* in which they must come to see themselves as "middle-aged," with new tasks, limitations, and opportunities. Some individuals experience a *midlife crisis,* a painful and disruptive struggle in which they reevaluate their lives.

• **7** Middle adulthood (ages 40 to 65) is a time of adaptation to physical changes, including changes in appearance, health and energy, sensory acuity, and sexual functioning. One of the most noticeable changes is the *menopause,* or cessation of menstruation, in women. Rather than being a "partial death," menopause is usually a comparatively minor event in the life of a middle-aged woman.

• **8** Erikson sees the major psychological challenge of middle adulthood as the need to achieve *generativity*—to feel that one is making a significant contribution to the next generation. Generativity can be achieved by guiding children into adulthood, by making lasting contributions in one's work, and by serving as a *mentor* for young adults.

Late adulthood

• **9** Although late adulthood (ages 65 and over) is often discussed as a single period, it might be thought of as encompassing both the "young-old" and the "old-old."

• **10** *Ageism* refers to discrimination against old people. The stereotype of old people as all being alike is far from the truth, because individual differences are as marked in old age as at any other time of life. Ageism is also reflected in our society's praise of those people who don't "show" their age.

• **11** Late adulthood is marked by numerous physical changes. According to one theory of aging, cells wear out over time and die. Another theory suggests that damage to

DNA or RNA over time leads to cell death. In addition, the immune system becomes less efficient. The endocrine system may also undergo changes that eventually lead to aging and death.

• **12** *Senile dementia* (senility) is a disorder that affects a small minority of the elderly. It is characterized by memory loss, disorientation in time and place, impaired attention, and loss of the ability to acquire new information.

• **13** Contrary to popular opinion, intelligence does not generally decline with advancing years. *Fluid intelligence,* or mental agility in solving problems, is likely to decline with age. But *crystallized intelligence,* or acquired knowledge and verbal skills, is likely to remain the same or even improve well into one's seventies.

• **14** One aspect of mental functioning that does decline with age is memory. Older adults have more trouble storing and retrieving material from long-term memory than younger people do.

• **15** Among the most important social changes of late adulthood are retirement, widowhood, and changing relationships with family and friends.

• **16** Only a small percentage of old people are institutionalized, some because of illnesses and handicaps and others simply because they are poor and alone.

• **17** Different types of people will find different ways of adapting to old age. Erikson sees the primary task of old age as the establishment of *integrity*—the sense that one has lived a whole and fulfilling life. Old people engage in a *life review,* a process of sorting out one's previous life. An additional task of old age is preparing to face death.

KEY TERMS

age-graded influences
ageism
Alzheimer's disease
autoimmune reaction
cohort effect
cross-sectional studies
crystallized intelligence
early adulthood
fluid intelligence
generativity
institutionalization
integrity
intimacy
late adulthood
life review
life structure
longitudinal studies
menopause
middle adulthood
midlife crisis
midlife transition
non-age-graded influences
senile dementia

FACING DEATH

Death can occur at any time in the life span. A sudden accident or fatal disease can cut short even the youngest life. But the fact is that most people in today's North America die when they are old. The fact that people are living longer than they used to is reflected in changing causes of death. In 1900, influenza, pneumonia, and tuberculosis were the three leading causes of death in the United States. But once such infectious diseases were conquered with antibiotics and vaccines, they were replaced as the leading causes of death by heart disease, cancer, and strokes. These degenerative diseases are more likely to affect older people; their increased frequency is in large measure the result of people living long enough to develop them. At present, the most common cause of death for people between 25 and 34 is accidents, for people between 35 and 44 it is cancer, and for people 45 and over it is heart disease.

Regardless of when we die and what we die from, there is nothing in life more certain than death. People through the ages have fantasized about immortality, but no one has ever escaped death permanently. Death is a reality that each of us must face. But our society, as we will see, encourages us to avoid the issue.

THE DENIAL OF DEATH

If you are under 40 and in good health, your own death probably has little reality for you. You probably have not considered where you would like to die, how your body should be disposed of, or whether you are willing to have an autopsy performed on your body. These issues don't seem compelling to healthy young people, because they consider death to be something that happens to old people. As Robert Kastenbaum (1979) has written, "One of our society's odd customs is to 'save' death for the elderly." Meanwhile, younger people avoid thoughts of death. Try asking people at a party, "Do you prefer burial or cremation?" The stunned reactions you would receive would probably convince you that death is an improper subject for open discussion—it's "too morbid" or "in bad taste." Instead, people push death out of their minds, engaging in what some social scientists call an "illusion of immortality" (Barrow and Smith, 1979).

Children are curious about death, but adults are generally reluctant to discuss the issue with them. One mother first realized how much she had been influenced by a death-denying society when she read a children's book about death to her 4-year-old son. She had borrowed a book called *The Dead Bird* (Brown and Charlip, 1965) from the library without examining its contents. She felt a sense of panic and a desire to protect her son as she began reading the words:

The bird was dead when the children found it. . . . it was still warm and its eyes were closed . . . but there was no heart beating. That was how they knew it was dead. . . . It began to get cold. . . . The children were very sorry the bird was dead and could never fly again.

The mother had an urge to hide the book and not read the story. But her son treated the material matter-of-factly and learned about both life and death from the book (Barrow and Smith, 1979).

The denial—or avoidance—of death extends even to medical personnel. Although doctors generally agree that patients should be told of terminal conditions, and most patients themselves want to be told,

Our society often tries to "protect" children from death. But it is better for children to learn about death as a fact of life than to be taught that death is a topic to be avoided.

Doctors tend to avoid informing patients that they are dying.

doctors tend to avoid informing patients that they are dying. Doctors may also avoid contact with dying patients. One professional, who leads seminars to help hospital personnel come to grips with their own anxieties about death, noted that physicians and nurses feel an involuntary anger toward the dying patient, whom they associate with their own failure and helplessness: "When you've exhausted everything you can do for a patient medically, it becomes difficult to walk into the room every day and talk to that patient" (Barrow and Smith, 1979).

THE DYING PATIENT

What of people who know they are dying? How do they face impending death? In an influential book called *On Death and Dying* (1969), Elisabeth Kübler-Ross outlined five stages that dying persons pass through. She based her stages on interviews with terminally ill adults, both young and old. Not all people experience all five stages, and individuals can experience more than one stage at a time.

Although this framework does not necessarily apply to all dying patients (Schulz and Aderman, 1974), the stages can still help us understand some of the emotions experienced by those facing death.

In the first stage, *denial,* the individual refuses to believe that she is terminally ill. She might insist that the test results are inaccurate, or may change doctors. She may refuse to discuss her illness with anyone, or may treat it lightly. A few people maintain this attitude right up to death.

The second stage is *anger.* The enraged patient asks, "Why me?" Medical staff and family may be subjected to angry demands and tantrums as the patient works through her resentment of her illness and envy of others' health.

In the third stage, *bargaining,* the person tries to postpone death. He may offer his body to science if the

doctors can extend his life, or he may promise to devote himself to God if his life can last a little longer. A common theme in this stage is that there is one more place to be visited, one final task to be completed, one important wrong that must be righted before the patient can give in to death.

The fourth stage is *depression;* it often accompanies advancing symptoms of disease. The overwhelming sense is one of loss—loss of one's memories, loss of close relationships, and loss of a future.

The final stage is *acceptance.* Acceptance can be achieved with the support and help of surrounding family, friends, and medical personnel. Having worked through anger and grief, the dying patient can come to her end in peace.

DEATH AND THE LIFE SPAN

Attitudes toward death appear to change as we age. Richard Kalish and David Reynolds (1976) questioned 434 Los Angeles residents in three age groups: 20–39, 40–59, and over 60. They probed such issues as where individuals would prefer to die, how often they thought about death, and how frightening death was to them. Kalish and Reynolds found that the oldest group both thought more about death and were less frightened by it than the other two groups. The fact that older people think more about death, as more of their agemates are dying, is not surprising. The lessened fear of death in old age may result from many factors. In old age one's own death may take on an appropriateness it lacked in earlier years. And some of the increased thinking about death, as well as the achievement of a sense of integrity, may help the person to accept death (Kalish, 1976).

But even among old people, attitudes toward death are as individual

as the people who hold them. Robert Kastenbaum and Avery Weisman (1972) describe two very different responses to impending death. Some people are "acceptors"; they view their coming death as timely and appropriate. "One 90-year-old woman was a very alert, independent person. . . . As her health began to decline she initiated arrangements for her funeral. She also expressed a readiness for death in the most straightforward manner. She declared that she had lived her life and was now ready to see it come to an end" (page 215). Other elderly patients are more annoyed than anything else by the prospect of dying. "One 82-year-old woman . . . became quite involved in the social and recreational life of the institution. [Three years later] she faced death as though it were a regrettable interruption of her participation in activities and relationships" (page 215).

HUMANIZING DEATH

Facing death at any age is a complex and painful experience. But there are ways that the terminally ill patient of any age can be helped and supported through the process. Richard Schulz (1978) lists three major needs of dying persons: control of physical pain, maintaining a sense of dignity and self-worth, and receiving love and affection.

The terminally ill patient often faces severe physical pain. Standard medical practice is to treat the pain with heavy doses of narcotics, which can leave the patient fuzzy-headed or unconscious much of the time. Experiments with nonnarcotic substances, including LSD and marijuana, have suggested that patients can be freed from pain while staying alert. Involving the patient himself in determining the dosages and timing of medication can also help

*O*ld people think about death more but fear it less.

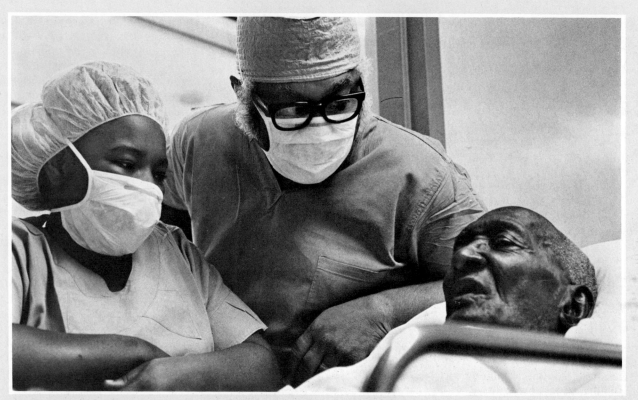

The needs of dying patients are not easily met in hospitals, although medical personnel are becoming more aware of people's need to die with dignity.

to anticipate and prevent pain, rather than simply to reduce it when it occurs.

Like anyone else, a dying person needs to feel effective, competent, and in control of his life; these are basic components of dignity. By participating in his own treatment, a dying patient can maintain a sense of competence and self-worth. The love and recognition of the people around the dying person can relieve the loneliness of his situation and provide reasons for enjoying whatever time is left to him.

These needs are not easily met in the institutions, such as hospitals and nursing homes, where over 60 percent of us die. Such institutions are frequently more concerned with efficient control of patients than with cooperative responses to them. One alternative to such institutions are *hospices*. In the Middle Ages a "hospice" was a traveler's rest station; in the 1800s the name was applied to places where nuns cared for the dying. Modern hospices are

facilities designed for the care of the dying. They are committed to helping the terminally ill die without pain, in peace and dignity, surrounded by their loved ones. Patients' family members are involved in their care and may even move into the hospice for closer contact with the patient. Hospice staff members also provide services to individuals who prefer to live their final weeks at home. One of the major goals of the hospice movement is to break down the isolation that usually surrounds a dying individual (Kastenbaum, 1978).

GLIMPSES OF THE WORLD BEYOND?

Is there a life after death? This is a religious question, not a medical or psychological one. And yet recent medical advances and psychological research have given a new focus to this ultimate mystery.

Until recently, anyone whose heart stopped pumping simply died—

and took his experiences with him. But advanced medical technology has altered this age-old reality. Because it is now possible to maintain basic vital functions mechanically, people can survive accidents or illnesses that temporarily stop the heart.

A few people believe that this technology has produced something entirely new in human history, a group of individuals who have "come back"—people whose hearts had stopped beating as a result of an illness or accident and who were then "restored to life." Such people sometimes report experiences "from the other side," raising the possibility that they had had a glimpse of the afterlife (Moody, 1975).

Most scientists remain skeptical of such an interpretation of the patients' reports. Nevertheless, research has been carried on to investigate the meaning of the "near-death" experience. When psychologist Kenneth Ring (1980) interviewed over 100 hospital patients who had

Hospices are places that help terminally ill people die in peace and dignity, surrounded by their loved ones.

experiences? Most researchers believe that these are not glimpses of the afterlife but rather hallucinations brought on either by the patient's physical condition or by the deep emotion aroused by the crisis of facing death (Siegel, 1980).

While most researchers don't take these reports very seriously, some consider them potentially dangerous. Robert Kastenbaum (1978) believes that the positive picture of death presented in such reports could encourage suicide attempts, particularly among the terminally ill. Kastenbaum is also concerned that a belief in death as an uplifting experience could reduce the quality of care given to terminally ill and elderly patients, in a misguided effort to "release" these people to a "better place."

But then, of course, there is always that lingering—if unlikely—possibility that the reports really reflect a glimpse of the world beyond. As Woody Allen (1971) put it, "I don't believe in an afterlife, although I am bringing along a change of underwear."

SUMMARY

- **1** Our society tends to deny the idea of death and to reserve it for the elderly.
- **2** Kübler-Ross suggested that the dying person goes through five stages in dealing with impending death: denial, anger, bargaining, depression, and acceptance.
- **3** Older people tend to be less fearful of death than younger people, although attitudes toward death vary widely.
- **4** Hospices are facilities that are committed to helping terminally ill people die without pain and in dignity, surrounded by their loved ones.
- **5** People who have had near-death experiences sometimes report having felt a detachment from their bodies and a spiritual encounter of some kind. Such experiences have been interpreted both as glimpses of an "afterlife" and as hallucinations.

come close to death, he found that 48 percent of them had some recollection of the event. Among those reporting such recollections, Ring found that the reported "near-death" experience included five stages that occur in a particular order. People seem to pass from an initial stage of great peace and contentment to a second stage in which they feel detached from their bodies. The third stage involves some experience of darkness that gives way to the fourth stage, in which people see a brilliant light. In the

fifth and final stage people report a variety of spiritual experiences, including reunions with departed relatives. The whole experience is accompanied by feelings of comfort and serenity. The descriptions are not explicitly religious but they share much of the imagery that many religious groups, particularly Christians, associate with death. Ring found, however, that religious persons were no more likely to have such experiences than people who were not religious.

What is the meaning of these

288

FACING LIFE'S CHALLENGES

Life is full of challenges for each of us—goals to be strived for, obstacles to be overcome, disappointments to be coped with. The three chapters in this part all touch on the ways in which people face these challenges.

Chapter 10 deals with Motivation and Emotion. Our motives are the inner needs that direct our behavior and point us toward specific goals. Our emotions not only spur many of our actions, but also provide the greatest highs and lows of our lives. The Psychological Issue on Violence discusses a domain in which people's motives and emotions are turned to destructive ends.

The study of Personality, our topic in Chapter 11, concerns the unique ways in which people adapt to the situations of life. Different personality theories—from Sigmund Freud's psy-choanalytic theory to the humanistic theories of Carl Rogers and Abraham Maslow—provide different perspectives on the ways in which life's challenges are faced. The Psychological Issue that follows discusses what is perhaps people's most elusive challenge—the pursuit of Happiness.

In Chapter 12, we explore some of the many links between Psychology and Health. We will see that the stresses of life can be harmful to our physical health, as well as to our emotional well-being. But people can also learn to cope successfully with stress, by viewing stressful situations as challenges to be overcome. The Psychological Issue on Alcohol Abuse focuses on one of the most tragic ways in which some people deal with life's challenges—by turning to the bottle.

MOTIVATION AND EMOTION

What needs and desires move us to behave in particular ways? Our motives and our emotions turn out to be closely linked.

THE NATURE OF MOTIVATION

The range of motives
Drives, needs, and incentives

Human motivation, from hunger to the need to confirm our competence, depends on both internal needs and external incentives.

MOTIVATIONAL SYSTEMS

Hunger and eating
Sexual motivation
Work and intrinsic motivation
Motives in conflict

We eat, we make love, we work. What motivates our behavior in each of these areas? What happens when motives conflict?

THE NATURE OF EMOTION

The components of emotion
What are the basic emotions?
The physiology of emotion
Are emotions universal and innate?

Each emotion includes subjective feelings, physiological changes, and expressive behaviors. People throughout the world seem to have the same basic set of emotions.

HOW IS EMOTION ACTIVATED?

From physiological arousal to felt
 emotion: The James-Lange theory
Cognitive labeling theory
The facial feedback hypothesis
Imagination and emotion

Different theories propose different mechanisms for how people come to experience emotions.

PSYCHOLOGICAL ISSUE
VIOLENCE

Violence seems to have become an almost expected part of life.

BOXES
1 A hierarchy of human needs
2 Thin eaters and fat eaters
3 The achievement motive
4 The label of love

Freshman David Green stopped to look at the sign announcing the semi-annual Red Cross blood drive at his college. He had never given blood before. But the sign said, "We need blood to help save lives," and David told himself, "I really should go in and give. After all, it's my obligation to do my part to help out." After making the initial decision, David felt a surge of apprehension. "I wonder if it's going to hurt," he thought. As he formed a mental image of a needle entering his vein and blood being drawn out, he felt a mounting fear. Nevertheless, he steadied himself and walked across campus to the Blood-mobile.

A few minutes later, David was leaning back in a big padded chair, watching the technician prepare to draw his blood. Now David could feel his heart race and his pulse quicken. Although he was scared, he tried his best not to let the fear show in his face. After the technician had inserted the needle and began to take the blood, David's fear gradually subsided. When it was over, the volunteers at the Bloodmobile thanked him warmly. And after collecting himself for a moment, David felt a warm glow of pride spread through his body. He found himself smiling, and it was all he could do to keep himself from breaking into exultant laughter. Six months later—the next time the Bloodmobile came to campus—David gave blood again, and afterward he felt the same glow of satisfaction.

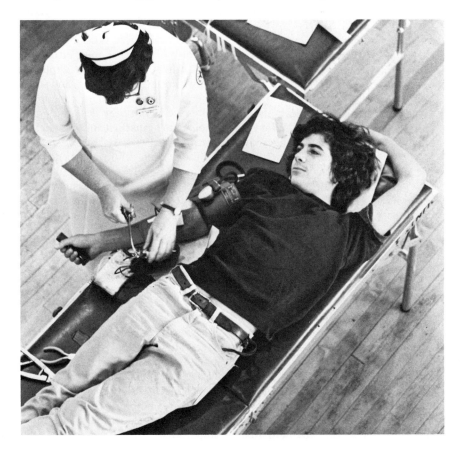

Why is this young man donating his blood? A variety of motives may be involved. And these motives are closely related to emotions, ranging from fear to pride.

Why did David give blood the first time? And why did he give blood again on later occasions? To answer these questions, we must enter the realm of *motivation:* our needs and desires to behave in a particular way, whether to eat a meal, to start a business, or to donate blood. As David's story suggests, our motives to behave in certain ways are closely related to our *emotions,* or feelings. Our emotions, whether terror, rage, or delight, are often primary forces in motivating our behavior. In this chapter we will delve into the origins and workings of human motivation and emotion. First we will survey the range of human motives that psychologists have studied and will consider the basic concepts of *drive, need,* and *incentive.* Then we will look more closely at three particular motivational systems: hunger and eating, sexual motivation, and work and intrinsic motivation. After that we will address some central questions about human emotion, including the question of whether emotions are innate or learned. Finally, we will examine several explanations of the way that our emotions arise in particular situations.

THE NATURE OF MOTIVATION

In trying to solve a murder case, one of the detective's first questions is, "What was the *motive?*" Was the crime committed for revenge, for money, or for the "thrill" of it? The detective is not unique in wanting to know why people do things. In fact, we are always asking questions about the underlying "whys" of human behavior—in other words, about motivation.

The entire study of psychology concerns the underlying causes of human behavior. But motives are certain kinds of causes—the internal needs and desires that energize and direct our actions. Our motives channel our energy to the pursuit of particular goals. When we are hungry, for example, we are likely to devote our energy to finding food. When we are motivated to do well on an exam, we will devote many hours to studying for it. In this section, we will first

explore the wide range of human motives and then look at some of the concepts psychologists have used in describing motives.

The range of motives

At one level, the number of human motives is almost limitless. Jim needs to buy a new pair of shoes, Frank badly wants to learn to play the guitar, and Marie is dying to be elected class president. But beyond these specific needs, desires, and goals, psychologists have long been interested in identifying the general categories of motives that underlie human action. At the turn of the century, many psychologists equated motives with *instincts*—inherited tendencies to seek certain goals. One leading instinct theorist, William McDougall (1908) set forth a list of twelve "basic" instincts, including hunger, sex, curiosity, and self-assertion, and other psychologists put forth even longer lists. One problem with these lists was that it was easy to fall into the trap of thinking that one had explained the forces underlying a particular sort of behavior simply by giving it a name. Thus, if people liked to walk around, there must be a "locomotion" instinct; if they often imitated others, that could be explained by an "imitation" instinct, and so on. One psychologist poked fun at his colleagues' efforts by describing psychologists' "instinct of a belief-in-instincts" (Ayres, 1921).

Today such catalogues of needs or instincts are no longer popular, and there is no single list of basic motives that all psychologists agree on. For our purposes, however, it is useful to consider three broad categories of motives that underlie much of our behavior: basic needs, social motives, and competence motives.

Basic needs, such as hunger, thirst, and avoidance of pain, are needs that must be satisfied if the organism, whether human or animal, is to survive. These basic needs are the motives that are most clearly based on biological functioning. There is reason to believe that if a person's basic needs are not satisfied, the other types of motives will not be of much importance to him (see Box 1).

A MOST STIMULATING EXPERIENCE

James Olds (1958) has provided some leads into the brain mechanisms that may underlie certain of our motives—especially our basic needs. Olds found that rats that normally press a bar 25 times an hour for food will press it more than 100 times a minute to receive electrical stimulation to locations in the lateral hypothalamus in the brain. Rats and even monkeys will forego food, sometimes to the point of starvation, in order to obtain such brain stimulation. More recent studies have shown that areas of the frontal lobe in the cerebral cortex are also involved in the brain's reward system (Routtenberg, 1978). These studies suggest that there are "pleasure centers" in the brain and that rewards in everyday life, such as food, drink, and sex, may affect these brain centers.

Our motives include basic needs *such as hunger and thirst (above), social motives, such as the desire to affiliate with others (top right), and* competence motivation, *or the desire to master the challenges of our environment (bottom right).*

Social motives, such as the desire to affiliate with others or the desire to have an impact on others, are needs related to our involvement with other people (see Chapter 17). Whereas we are born with our basic needs, our social motives are largely learned as we grow up, as a result of our interaction with others.

Competence motivation is perhaps the most distinctively human form of motivation. Robert White (1959) has suggested that the "master reinforcer" that keeps most of us motivated for long periods of time is the need to confirm our personal competence—our ability to master the challenges of our environment. Being able to deal effectively with our environment is rewarding, whether it involves a child's learning to ride a bike, a student's mastering an academic subject, or keeping one's head in times of crisis.

BOX 1

A HIERARCHY OF HUMAN NEEDS

When people are very hungry or very thirsty, they can think of little else but finding something to eat or to drink. At such times, other needs—whether for security, love, or competence—become unimportant. On the other hand, when a person's needs for food and water have been met, such needs become less central and other motives are likely to take on greater importance. These observations provide part of the rationale for an influential view of human motivation that was put forth over 40 years ago by Abraham Maslow (1943).

Maslow proposed that human needs exist at five different levels, ranging from the "lowest" and most basic needs to the "highest" level, represented by people's need to fulfill their own unique potential. This hierarchy is often depicted as a pyramid, with the most basic needs at the base of the pyramid and the higher levels building upon this base. The five categories of needs, starting from the bottom and moving up, are:

1 *Physiological needs*—the basic biological needs for food, water, and pain reduction, and the biological aspects of sexual needs.
2 *Safety needs*—the needs to feel physically and psychologically safe and secure. They include the need for safety from physical danger and the need for economic security.
3 *Love needs*—the need to love others and to be loved by others, and the need to be an accepted member of a community of friends.
4 *Esteem needs*—the needs to achieve, to be competent, and to receive respect and appreciation from others.
5 *Self-actualization needs*—the need to fulfill our own unique potential. "A musician must make music, an artist must paint, a poet must write if he is to be ultimately happy. What a man [or woman] *can* be, he *must* be" (Maslow, 1954, page 46).

In relation to the three main categories of motivation described in the text, Maslow's physiological and safety needs fall for the most part under basic needs, the love needs under social motives, and the esteem needs and perhaps the self-actualization needs under the category of competence motivation.

Maslow believed that a person must first satisfy needs at the lower levels of the pyramid before being able to devote attention to needs at higher levels. A hungry person, for example, will strive for nothing but food. But when food is plentiful and other biological needs are met, the needs for safety become most important. And once these needs are met, the person becomes most concerned, in turn, with the needs for love and esteem. Even if all these needs are satisfied, Maslow suggested, people will often become discontent if they feel they are not fulfilling their unique potential.

Maslow noted that because few people in our society have satisfied all their lower needs, self-actualization remains rare. In his later writing, Maslow (1970) added that self-actualization, unlike the other needs, may take an entire lifetime to unfold, so it is unlikely to occur in young people. We will return to Maslow's view of self-actualization when we discuss his theory of personality in Chapter 11.

Not all of the details of Maslow's hierarchy of needs have been supported by more recent research (Lawler and Suttle, 1972). It *is* well established that people who have not satisfied their basic physiological needs are unlikely to be concerned with much else (Wahba and Bridwell, 1976). But beyond the lowest level of the pyramid there is little evidence that people's needs are necessarily ordered in the way that Maslow proposed. Instead, the relative importance of our needs—for example, for love and for esteem—seems to vary from one person to another. In addition, as Maslow himself acknowledged, several different needs typically motivate our behavior at the same time.

But even while the specifics of Maslow's hierarchy may be questioned, Maslow's theory has done a great deal to establish the central role of motivation in human life. We are, as Maslow writes, "perpetually wanting animals." Our personality and behavior are determined to a large extent by our needs and desires, in a way that is consistent with the uniqueness of each human being.

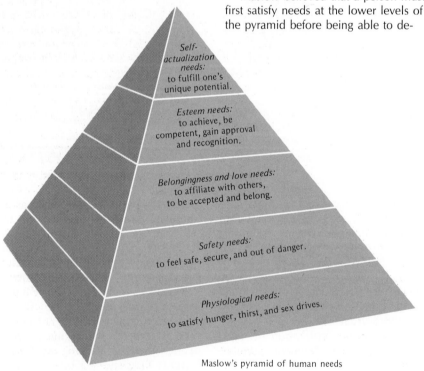

Maslow's pyramid of human needs

CHAPTER TEN: MOTIVATION AND EMOTION

It is not always easy to figure out which specific motive is directing a person's actions. Part of the problem is that in most cases more than one motive is likely to be involved. What motivated David to give blood, for example? Basic needs did not seem to be involved. But social motives, such as the desire to fulfill an obligation to his fellow human beings, may well have played a major role. And competence motivation—the desire to master a difficult situation—may also have had great importance. Thus, our answer to the detective's question "What was the motive?" will often involve several different motives.

An additional difficulty in figuring out what motives underlie particular actions—especially our own actions—is that people are often unaware of their own motives. In Sigmund Freud's terms, motives are often *unconscious,* or outside of awareness. Freud believed that certain of our motives are *repressed,* or banished from consciousness, because they are too anxiety-arousing for us to deal with. But these motives still may have clear effects on our behavior. An accident-prone woman may complain that fate has been unkind to her, while those around her may see that her accidents are unconscious ways of expressing a desire to hurt herself. Or an obese man may claim that he eats because he has "too many fat cells" or has no willpower, when his unconscious motivation for eating may be to use food as a substitute for love.

Freud paid special attention to people's slips of the tongue as one reflection of unconscious motivation. In his honor, these are commonly referred to as *Freudian slips.* For instance, people may express unconscious feelings toward others by "accidentally" mispronouncing their names. What would you conclude, for example, if your professor were to begin her next lecture with "Today we will consider the contributions of the great psychologist Sigmund Fraud"? Such a slip might betray the fact that the professor doesn't really think Freud was that great after all. We will return to the topic of unconscious motives in Chapter 11, when we discuss Freud's theory of personality.

Drives, needs, and incentives

For much of the present century psychologists explained human motivation in terms of *drive reduction theory.* According to this theory, motivation begins with a bodily need, such as the need for food or the need for water. Through various physiological mechanisms (which we will get to later), this need becomes experienced as a psychological *drive.* The drive, such as hunger or thirst, is an internal tension or pressure that becomes increasingly uncomfortable. It leads the organism—whether human or other animal—to act in a certain way, such as to look for food or water. The food or water is the *goal* toward which the drive is directed. When the goal is obtained, the physiological deficit is corrected and the unpleasant drive is reduced.

In recent decades, the drive reduction theory has come to be viewed as an inadequate account of most human motivation. Although drive reduction may help to explain eating behavior, how can it account for our strong motive to explore our surroundings? This desire to explore seems to underlie much of human behavior, from the manipulation of objects by babies to the quest of scientists to understand the workings of the universe. Some psychologists did try to explain such behavior in terms of drive reduction theory, by proposing the existence of a "curiosity drive" that can build up over time and that can be reduced only by exploring our surroundings. But in fact, acquiring knowledge about the environment often motivates us to seek out still more knowledge, not less as the drive reduction theory would suggest. Similarly, Abraham Maslow (1970) noted that the need for self-actualization (see Box 1) is not reduced by initial experiences of self-actualization; rather, it is a motive that continues to grow and expand. Thus, the notion of drive does not seem to be the most useful way of viewing curiosity or other "higher motives."

Instead of considering "drives" and "goals," today's researchers more often speak of "needs" and "incentives." *Needs* are the internal aspect

of motivation: the desires within us for particular objects or experiences. *Incentives* are the external aspect of motivation: the objects or opportunities in our environment that we strive for. To understand most sorts of motivated behavior, we must take both the internal needs and the external incentives into account. Laboratory studies show, for example, that rats will run down an alley toward food in a goal box faster when they have been deprived of food and therefore are hungry (the need) than when they are not. But rats will also run faster to get to a larger piece of food (the incentive) than a small one. Both the need and the incentive are necessary to motivate running. A rat will not run even for a huge chunk of food if it is not hungry, and even a ravenously hungry rat won't bother to run if there is no food at the end of the alley.

A similar kind of analysis is equally relevant to human behavior and to "higher motives." A person may be highly motivated to do well at tennis, for example, perhaps in part as a result of a broader need for achievement. But this need will be activated only when appropriate incentives are present, such as the chance to play against a challenging opponent. If the only available opponent is a pushover, the achievement-oriented person may not be particularly interested in playing. As in the case of the hungry rat, both the need and the incentive are necessary to motivate the person's behavior.

MOTIVATIONAL SYSTEMS

To understand human motivation more fully, we must look closely at particular motivational systems. A motivational system is a set of needs, incentives, and associated behaviors that operate in a particular sphere of life. Among the many motivational systems that might be considered, we will focus on three: hunger and eating, sexual motivation, and work and achievement.

Hunger and eating

Most of us eat at least three meals a day, and some of us eat a lot more than that. Why? The place to begin in examining eating behavior is with the physiology of hunger.

Hunger comes from the body's need for nutrients used in growth, energy, and body repair. One way that we know we are hungry is through *hunger pangs*, which are caused by contraction of the stomach muscles when the stomach is empty. In fact, an early theory of hunger, put forth by

Motivation involves both internal needs and external incentives. People may be motivated to eat or drink, for example, both by their internal state of hunger or thirst (the need) and by the food or drink available in their environment (the incentive).

Why do we eat when we do? Hunger pangs are not the main reason.

Walter Cannon (1911), held that these stomach contractions are primarily responsible for the experience of hunger and for motivating us to eat. But as Cannon himself realized, there are problems with trying to explain hunger and eating solely in terms of stomach activity. For one thing, people in affluent cultures rarely experience hunger pangs. We fill ourselves up too often for such feelings to occur more than once in a while. So hunger pangs themselves can't explain why we eat when we do. In addition, there is evidence that humans whose stomachs have been surgically removed still feel hungry and that rats whose stomachs have been removed still behave like hungry rats.

Although the stomach does play a role in regulating our eating patterns, other physiological mechanisms, involving the hypothalamus in the brain, seem to play a greater role. First, the hypothalamus monitors the level of sugar in the blood. When blood sugar is low, the hypothalamus causes the person to feel hungry and to eat. Conversely, when the blood-sugar level is high, the hypothalamus inhibits eating. Second, the hypothalamus keeps track of the fat content of the body, as indicated by substances in the blood. The hypothalamus increases our desire to eat when the fat content goes below a certain predetermined level, or *set point*, and it de-

creases our desire to eat when the fat content goes above that level. Thus, the hypothalamus acts something like a thermostat for the level of body fat (Bennett and Gurin, 1982).

When the functioning of the hypothalamus is impaired, an animal can no longer monitor blood-sugar levels or fat content, and weight can no longer remain stable. This was demonstrated dramatically in a series of experiments in which researchers destroyed the hypothalamus in laboratory animals (Teitelbaum, 1967). This operation had startling effects: The animals began to eat compulsively over an extended period of time, ultimately assuming monstrous proportions—often two to three times their normal body weight (see Figure 10.1). Such effects have been obtained in rats, dogs, cats, monkeys, and chickens, among others. These animals are called *hyperphagic*, from the Greek words for "overeating."

The regulatory activity of the hypothalamus is one of the main reasons why most people find it so difficult to lose weight. Almost anyone can diet for a few weeks and take off some weight. The hard part is keeping it off. After a person brings his weight below his set point, the receptors in the hypothalamus detect the lower level of fat in the blood, eventually leading to heightened cravings for food. "You're getting too thin," our

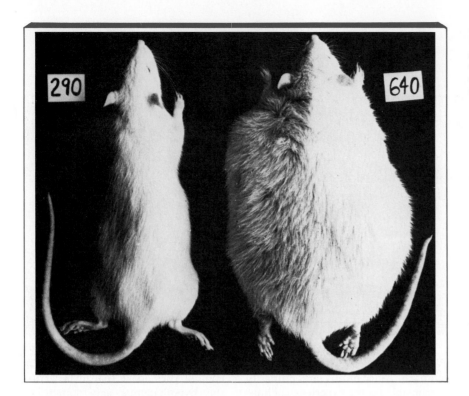

FIGURE 10.1
When portions of the hypothalamus in the brain are destroyed, a rat (such as the one on the right) may become hyperphagic and overeat so much that it grows to two or three times its normal body weight.

body tells us, and the proverbial Jewish or Italian mother in our brain sends us a chemical message, "Eat, eat!" that is hard to defy. This set-point mechanism contributes to a situation in which many people repeatedly lose 5 or 10 pounds only to gain it back a few months later, their weights going up and down like yo-yos.

An individual's set point for body fat is influenced to a large extent by heredity. Nevertheless, it seems possible for people to alter their body's set points. Continuing exposure to the taste and smell of rich food seems to raise the set point, apparently as a way of allowing the body to take advantage of scarce resources. Recent studies also suggest that active physical exercise programs can lower people's set points, making it possible for them to maintain a lower body weight (Bennett and Gurin, 1982). Other research, discussed in Box 2, has focused on differences in the eating habits of overweight and average-weight people.

Sexual motivation

People are sexually active for many reasons—to relieve boredom, to express love, to expand self-esteem, even to attain social status. Although sex seems to be a motive in and of itself, it also encompasses many other motives. We commonly speak of a "sex drive," but sex does not fit the usual conception of drive as a felt need that gets stronger and stronger until it is satisfied. In fact, people do not necessarily become increasingly motivated to have sex the longer they go without it. Indeed, sexual abstinence probably decreases sexual motivation over the long run (Masters and Johnson, 1970). And there is no good evidence that abstinence from sexual activity is detrimental to a person's health (Katchadourian and Lunde, 1975).

To understand sexual motivation, we must consider the role of biological processes. Our sexual and reproductive functioning is regulated by hormones, the products of the endocrine system we discussed in Chapter 2. In both men and women, hormones called *androgens* have an influence on sexual motivation. In men, an androgen called testosterone is produced by the testes. Men whose testes have been removed for medical reasons show a decline in sexual motivation, and injections of testosterone

BOX 2

THIN EATERS AND FAT EATERS

Why are some people fat while others are of average weight or thin? There is no single answer to this question. Genetic factors clearly play a major role. Some people simply have more fat cells than others. Some people, born with high rates of metabolism, burn off their calories quickly and easily, while others burn them off much more slowly. In addition, some people have a higher set point for body fat—or "natural weight"—than others, and overcoming this set point is by no means a simple matter.

Another part of the difference between overweight and average-weight persons involves their eating patterns. Our eating behavior is influenced by two sets of factors: *internal cues* (or needs) signaling how hungry we feel, and *external cues* (or incentives) such as the taste of food, its availability, and its visibility. Sometimes we eat because we really are hungry, but at other times we eat simply because there is good food around.

Psychologist Stanley Schachter has argued that average-weight and overweight people differ in the relative degree to which they are influenced by these two types of cues. Schachter's theory is that average-weight people rely primarily on internal cues—how hungry they feel—to regulate the amount of food they eat, whereas overweight people respond more to external cues, such as the sight, smell, taste, and availability of food.

To explore the importance of internal cues of hunger, Schachter and two colleagues set up a study in which half of their subjects—both average-weight and overweight college students—were deprived of food for a period of time, while the other half were fed roast beef sandwiches until they were full. After that, all the subjects were asked to take part in a cracker-tasting test. The results were what the researchers predicted: Average-weight subjects ate fewer crackers when their stomachs were full of sandwiches than when they were empty, but the eating behavior of the overweight subjects was unrelated to the fullness of their stom-

achs (Schachter, Goldman, and Gordon, 1968).

Although overweight subjects do not seem to be greatly affected by internal cues, Schachter (1971) found that they are highly responsive to external cues. In one study both average-weight and overweight subjects were offered sandwiches. For some of the subjects, the sandwiches were left out on a table, while for the rest the food was left out of sight. Average-weight subjects ate about the same number of sandwiches in both conditions. Overweight subjects, on the other hand, ate many sandwiches if they were in direct view on the table but very few if they were out of sight.

In a more recent study, average-weight and overweight persons were observed as they decided what—if anything—to order for dessert at a good French restaurant in Toronto. In some cases, the waitress, who was part of the research team, happened to be carrying one of the scrumptious-looking desserts at the time that she took the dessert orders. When the waitress was not carrying the dessert, average-weight and overweight diners were equally likely to order dessert. But when she was carrying the dessert—thus making the external cue highly visible—the overweight diners

were three times as likely than the average-weight diners to order it (Herman, Olmsted, and Polivy, 1983).

These studies all seem to indicate that overweight people often eat in response to external cues—the visibility and availability of food—rather than to internal cues of hunger. Schachter's hypothesis remains a controversial one, however. Whereas a number of studies have found the differences that he postulated, many other studies have not (Rodin, 1981). It is clear that many people who are highly responsive to external food cues *don't* get fat, perhaps because of a high metabolism rate or a low set point for body fat. Nevertheless, the Schachter studies do suggest some ideas for overweight persons who suspect that they are overly dependent on external cues for eating. For example: Avoid cooking big meals or eating in cafeterias, because if there is a lot of food around you will probably eat it. Keep your soft drinks in a cabinet and your bread in a breadbox. Above all, never leave jellybeans sitting out in a candy dish. For you, at least as far as food is concerned, out of sight is out of mind.

can help to restore their sexual interest. In women, androgen is produced not by the ovaries but by the adrenal glands. Among women, removal of the ovaries does not decrease sexual desire, but removal of the adrenals does (Rose, 1972).

In most animals, hormones totally control sexual motivation. Female monkeys and apes, for example, are receptive to males only at the midpoint of their menstrual cycle, when estrogen levels peak and when they are also the most fertile. At such times, very specific stimuli, such as the odor of a receptive animal of the opposite sex, will lead to an instinctive sexual response. Humans, in contrast, are not limited to specific mating times, nor are they totally controlled by their hormones. Humans are capable of being sexually aroused at any time and in response to a wide variety of stimuli. Rather than serving as driving forces, human sex hormones sensitize people to erotic stimulation. These hormones make it more likely that a stimulus that a person already finds to be arousing—whether a sight, a sound, a touch, or even a thought—will in fact arouse the person on a particular occasion.

What is considered erotic varies greatly from one culture to another and, within a culture, from one individual to another. Whether one is turned on by brains or brawn, lace or leather seems to be a product both of cultural learning and personal experience. For example, a teenage girl may become sexually aroused by a movie scene in which a long-haired muscular man nibbles on a woman's ear. As learning theorists might suggest, her initial associations may become strengthened if she subsequently fantasizes about the man while masturbating, and she may in the future be highly aroused by long hair, muscles, and ear nibbling. Other boys and girls, with their own sets of learning experiences, may be especially aroused by champagne and candlelight or by strobe lights and dancing to heavy metal music. We will consider the cultural, as well as the biological, aspects of sexual behavior in further detail in Chapter 16.

Work and intrinsic motivation

Most adult Americans spend at least one of every three waking hours working. We are part of a culture that has a deep-rooted belief in achievement through ambition, energy, and perseverance. At the heart of this ideology is the assumption that people can find satisfaction in work.

How does work provide this sense of satisfaction? Many different sets of motives are likely to be involved. To start with, a person who works can purchase adequate food, shelter, and clothing and can contribute to the support of a family. So work helps people to satisfy their basic physical needs. Second, many people gratify social needs through their work, such as the opportunity to influence other people or simply to have pleasant social interaction. Perhaps most important, work is one of the primary ways in which many people develop a feeling of competence—of exercising skills and meeting challenges effectively. These competence motives are similar to the needs for esteem and self-actualization described by Maslow (see Box 1).

One way of looking at the link between work and competence is in terms of the distinction between *intrinsic motivation* and *extrinsic motivation*. When you engage in an activity solely for the pleasure of it, psychologists say you are intrinsically motivated. If you do something for an outside reward, such as to earn money or to avoid criticism, you are extrinsically motivated. People often receive both intrinsic and extrinsic rewards from doing a job: they are paid for it, but they also enjoy the work itself. But it is the intrinsic rewards—the pleasures of mastering the challenges of the job—rather than the financial or social rewards that satisfy the need for competence. Whether it is the baseball player's pleasure at executing a successful bunt or the financier's pleasure at swinging a successful deal, people's work can be rewarding for its own sake. And the more competent a person feels he is at his work, the more highly motivated he probably will be

When we are intrinsically motivated, we engage in an activity for the sheer pleasure of it or the sense of mastery that it gives us. When we are extrinsically motivated, we engage in an activity to gain external rewards, such as a salary. Work usually involves some combination of intrinsic and extrinsic motivation.

to pursue the same activity in the future (Deci and Ryan, 1980).

Paradoxically, the promise of external rewards, such as a high salary or good fringe benefits, can sometimes reduce or undermine a person's intrinsic motivation. Edward Deci (1975) used an involving three-dimensional puzzle called a Soma cube to explore intrinsic and extrinsic motivation. He gave each subject four puzzle problems to solve. Half of the subjects were told they would get a dollar for each correct solution, while the other half were not paid. Once the subjects had completed the puzzles, they were left alone to do whatever they wanted. Deci found that subjects who had not been paid to solve the puzzles spent more time playing with the puzzles when alone than had the subjects who were paid. In other words, intrinsic motivation decreased when subjects had been given an external reward.

Why does external reward decrease intrinsic motivation? One explanation focuses on people's interpretations of their own behavior. Imagine asking one of Deci's subjects why he was working on the puzzle. The subjects who were not being paid would probably say, "Because I like to" or "Because it's an interesting challenge." But, the subjects who *were* being paid might say, "Because I earn money." In the postsession period the nonpaid subjects would continue to play with the puzzle because it is still an interesting challenge that enlists their need for competence. But the rewarded subjects might not continue with the puzzle because they are no longer being rewarded for doing so. For similar reasons, a highly paid professional athlete may be less likely than an amateur to play "just for fun" in the off season.

We have been talking about competence motivation as something that all of us have. There is also reason to believe, however, that some people are more highly motivated than others to exercise competence of certain sorts. As discussed in Box 3, the desire to exercise competence is especially central to people with a strong *achievement motive.*

Motives in conflict

A single motive seldom operates in isolation, and sometimes our motives interfere with one another. Motives can conflict in several ways. The major types of conflict are termed approach-approach, avoidance-avoidance, and approach-avoidance.

In *approach-approach conflict,* two equally attractive goals compete with each other. For example, two of your favorite TV programs may be on at the same time, so you can watch only one. Or you may have trouble deciding what to order in a restaurant because two items on the menu are equally enticing. On a grander scale, people must make choices about how to spend large amounts of money (buy a car or take a trip) or about what to do with their lives at a major choice point (continuing on in college or taking a promising job offer). These conflicts may seem pleasant to an outsider, but they can be agonizing to the person who must make a decision that will inevitably result in the loss of something he or she desires.

In an *avoidance-avoidance conflict,* there are two goals, neither of which is desirable but one of which must be chosen. This was the kind of conflict faced by 1960s war protestors when, for reasons of conscience, they had to choose between the draft and going to prison. Neither choice was attractive, but no other real alternatives were available. Similarly, a man who has been in a serious accident

WORKAHOLICS

Workaholics are people who love their work so much that they are practically addicted to it. They are likely to be intense, energetic, and competitive people who set high standards for themselves and who live life as if it were a race against time. One workaholic liked to get to work hours before anyone else: "By 9 a.m. I had done a day's work—I was already a day ahead of everybody." Workaholics are often scorned by others as single-minded people who are missing out on many of life's pleasures. But Marilyn Machlowitz (1980), who has conducted an extensive study of workaholics, reports that most workaholics are remarkably satisfied with their lives. For a workaholic to be happy, however, she must find—or create—a job that fits her abilities and in which she can feel competent.

CHAPTER TEN: MOTIVATION AND EMOTION

may have to decide between having his leg amputated or risking gangrene. And voters in an election may have to choose between equally undesirable candidates. A decision in such cases is often based on choosing the "lesser of two evils."

In an *approach-avoidance conflict,* there is one goal but two motives. One motive tells us to approach the goal and the other tells us to avoid it. Such conflict is seen in the hungry dieter who wants to eat but who also wants to leave food alone. This conflict may be visible as the person alternately approaches and withdraws from the refrigerator, unable to decide which impulse to follow. This type of conflict can also be seen in the case of David Green: he *wants* to give blood but he is also afraid to. When motives are in conflict in this way, we typically feel mixed emotions.

THE NATURE OF EMOTION

Clearly, David Green's *motivation* to give blood and his *emotions* before, during, and after the donation were closely linked. Before deciding to give blood, David had certain feelings—perhaps of obligation or guilt—that contributed to his initial decision to give. Just before the medical bloodletting, David felt frightened, but he went ahead despite his fright. And afterward he felt strong emotions of pride and happiness. One of the reasons he gave blood again was almost certainly the desire to perpetuate these good feelings.

More generally, many psychologists argue that all of our motivated behavior is influenced to a large extent by our emotions (e.g., Izard, 1979). Some "motives" themselves resemble emotions, such as our feeling of hunger when we need food. In some cases, emotions directly impel our actions, such as the all too common tendency for the emotion of anger to impel people to acts of violence. In other cases, the rewards of motivated behavior are themselves emotions, such as our feeling of heightened interest and enjoyment when we are intrinsically motivated by an activity, or our feeling of pride when we know that we have contributed to other people's welfare.

In this section we will consider some basic issues concerning the nature of emotion. First we will provide a definition of emotion in terms of three components that all emotions have. Then we will try to zero in on the "basic" emotions. After that we will consider the extent to which human emotions are innate and universal and the extent to which they are the product of specific cultures.

The components of emotion

Suppose when human beings finally explore the distant reaches of the universe we stumble onto a planet occupied by beings much like ourselves, with only one major exception: they are incapable of experiencing emo-

BOX 3

THE ACHIEVEMENT MOTIVE

What do you see in this picture?

Your answer to this question may help to reveal whether your *achievement motive* is strong or weak. The achievement motive is the need to maintain or increase one's competence in activities in which a standard of excellence is thought to apply. One can either succeed or fail in such activities. The person who is highly motivated to achieve is one who will keep trying to succeed, by matching or exceeding her existing standard.

David McClelland and his colleagues (1953) devised a way of measuring people's achievement motive by asking them to make up stories about a series of pictures like the one above. Subjects are asked to tell what is happening in the picture, what led up to the situation, what is being thought, and what the outcome will be. The responses are then scored for the number of achievement-related themes. For example, if a subject were to write the following as part of his story about the daydreaming boy, it would be coded as an achievement-related theme: "He is thinking about his ambition to become an astronaut and be the first person to visit Mars." In contrast, if the subject were to write that "He is thinking about how much fun he had when he went to the beach with his family," it would not be coded as achievement-related.

When subjects are asked directly about their desire for achievement, their answers do not usually agree very closely with the themes that emerge in the stories they make up. People may not always be aware of the extent of their own achievement needs—and, if they are, they may not always want to admit them. McClelland believes that people's fantasies about achievement provide a less direct, but more useful way to measure the strength of achievement motives. (This and other methods of assessing personality will be discussed in Chapter 11.)

Childhood training seems to have an impact on the achievement motive. For example, Marian Winterbottom (1953) found that the mothers of 8- to 10-year-old boys who were high in the achievement motive expected their children to have mastered at an early age such independent behaviors as obeying traffic signals, earning their own spending money, and choosing their own clothes. Mothers of boys low in the achievement motive reported that they did not expect this level of independence until a significantly later age. Recent research has suggested that child rearing practices may influence children's level of achievement motivation when they become adults (McClelland and Pilon, 1983).

People with high levels of achievement motivation have been found to be more likely than people with lower levels of the motive to enter a field of work that involves risk and challenge, such as starting a small business, and to do better at such work (McClelland, 1971). Because of this link between achievement motivation and business success, McClelland and David Winter (1969) set up a program to train small businessmen in India to be more achievement oriented. They report that the program succeeded. Those businessmen in one town who were trained to think more about their personal standards of excellence started more new businesses, employed more workers, and increased the standard of living in their town, as compared to businessmen in another town who did not receive training in achievement motivation. Such training has also

The achievement motive spurs us to match our own standards of excellence.

been used to improve small business performance and increase employment among minorities in the United States (McClelland, 1978).

Almost all of the early research on the achievement motive was done with male subjects. After all, men are the ones who have traditionally been taught to get ahead in society, while women have traditionally been taught to emphasize other motives and traits, such as nurturance and sociability. In recent decades, however, these assumptions about the goals and motives of the two sexes have been radically changed. (See the Psychological Issue, "Changing Sex Roles," following Chapter 16.) And in the past decade, considerable research has been conducted on the achievement motivation of women as well as men (Spence, 1983).

tion. Suppose these beings exist without the feelings of triumph or failure, joy or sorrow, pleasure or disgust. To us, it would be like life with all the juices wrung out of it—a colorless, monotonous, one-dimensional existence.

It would be difficult to relate to these beings; to do so would be like making friends with a computer or a television set. They could think, react, and respond, but they would have no feelings. This difference between us and these hypothetical extraterrestrials suggests some of the essential hallmarks of emotion. Emotions invariably seem to contain three components, each of which is lacking among these unfeeling beings from outer space:

1 *Subjective experience.* An emotion includes a subjective experience or "feeling" that involves elements of pleasure or displeasure, of liking or disliking, or of arousal. In the last analysis, people's subjective experiences of this sort are probably the best single way to define emotion. And in studying emotion, psychologists must rely to a large extent on the subjective reports that people provide. "I'm thrilled!" "What a disgusting place!" and "Wow!" are a few of the ways in which people put their subjective experience of emotion into words.

2 *Physiological arousal.* Emotions always seem to involve changes in our bodies. In some cases, the physiological changes are quite dramatic. When we are very angry or afraid, our hearts may accelerate from their normal rate of about 72 beats per minute to as much as 180 beats per minute. Our breathing may become rapid and uneven, and our blood pressure may rise alarmingly. In other cases, the physiological changes may be smaller and more subtle.

3 *Expressive behavior.* Our emotions also involve expressive behaviors, particularly facial expressions—the smiles, the pouts, the frowns, and the many other expressions that typically signal that the person is experiencing a particular emotion. In addition, emotions are often expressed by changes in posture and tone of voice. When we are sad, for example, we tend to slouch our

shoulders and speak in a lower, less variable pitch than when we are angry or afraid (Scherer, 1979).

What are the basic emotions?

People experience an almost limitless variety of emotions. We speak of being ecstatic, depressed, proud, nervous, jealous, guilty, afraid, bored, amused, amazed—not to mention happy, sleepy, grumpy, and sometimes even dopey. What's more, our emotional states often seem to be complex mixtures of more basic emotions. How would you feel, for example, if you were to learn that you received an A in your psychology course but your best friend got a D? Elated, perhaps, and somewhat superior, but also sorry for your friend and quite possibly a bit embarrassed and worried that he will be angry with you.

Given such a broad spectrum of emotions, psychologists have tried to identify a smaller number of "primary" emotions that might serve as the building blocks of more complex emotions. In taking this approach, we look at the range of emotions in a way that is similar to the way we look at the range of colors. Just as all of the hundreds of shades of color can be made through mixtures of a small number of primary colors (such as red, blue, and yellow), it has been suggested that all of the hundreds of shades of emotion can be formed by mixtures of small numbers of primary emotions.

In a well-known scheme of classifying emotions developed by Robert Plutchik (1980), there are eight primary emotions: joy, acceptance, fear, surprise, sadness, disgust, anger, and anticipation. These emotions can be arranged around an "emotion wheel" (see Figure 10.2), similar to the color wheels often used for arranging colors. The closer any two emotions are to each other on the wheel, the more they resemble each other, as assessed by subjects' ratings of these feelings. Thus, the emotions of fear and surprise, which are adjacent to each other on the wheel, are typically experienced as being similar in certain ways—both seem to involve an ele-

FIGURE 10.2

Robert Plutchik's emotion wheel. The closer any two emotions are on the wheel, the more they resemble each other. The emotions labeled outside the wheel (e.g., contempt) are often described as blends of the more basic emotions labeled inside the wheel (e.g., anger and disgust).

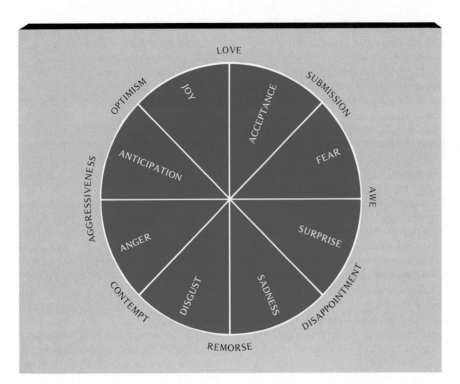

ment of the unknown. Emotions that are opposite each other on the wheel, such as joy and sadness, are typically judged to be opposites. And people commonly agree in their descriptions of particular mixtures of the primary emotions. For example, a blend of joy and acceptance is often described as love, while a mixture of anger and disgust is described as contempt.

Whereas Plutchik derived his model largely from people's subjective reports of what different emotions feel like, other researchers have put forward slightly different typologies that are based on the different facial expressions of emotion. According to this approach, the "primary emotions" are those for which distinctive facial expressions have evolved over the course of human evolution. Those who take this approach, including Carroll Izard (1977), suggest that there are at least six primary emotions: joy, surprise, sadness, anger, disgust, and fear. If you compare this list to Plutchik's, you will see the typologies are quite similar.

The physiology of emotion

All strong emotions are accompanied by the same general pattern of physio-

logical arousal. When we are afraid or angry, for example, our heartbeat speeds up, our pulse races, and our breathing rate tends to increase. Our body's metabolism speeds up and sugar in the bloodstream and fats in the tissues are burned off at a faster rate. In addition, the salivary glands become less active, causing a feeling of dryness in the mouth. Our sweat glands may overreact, producing a dripping forehead, clammy hands, and "cold sweat." Finally, our pupils may enlarge, producing the wide-eyed look that is characteristic of both terror and rage.

The physiological changes that take place when we are afraid or angry are part of our body's preparation to act in a threatening situation, whether by escaping (as in the case of fear) or fighting back (as in the case of anger). Our increased heart rate, breathing, and metabolism provide us with the additional energy we need for quick action. Such bodily reactions can be very helpful in coping with an emergency, whether the situation is perceived as terrifying or as infuriating. If we were to remain angry or fearful for long periods, however, these reactions could take a severe toll. We will discuss such harmful effects of emotional arousal in

CHAPTER TEN: MOTIVATION AND EMOTION

Chapter 12, when we consider the consequences of stress.

Not all emotions have such noticeable physiological components. When we experience emotions that are weaker and more subtle than fear and anger, the physiological changes are less clear. There are also certain differences between the physiological changes associated with different emotions. While both fear and anger tend to increase blood pressure, the increases appear to be greater with anger (Schwartz, Weinberger, and Singer, 1981). On the other hand, there is some evidence that heart rate, respiration, muscle tension, and sweat gland activity increase more with fear (Ax, 1953). Studies with animals also suggest that different emotions may involve the structures of the brain's limbic system in distinctive ways and that they may be associated with changed levels of various neurotransmitters in the brain (Izard and Saxton, in press). But despite the evidence of such differences, it remains clear that the internal changes associated with different strong emotions are quite similar to one another and involve increases in the body's general level of arousal.

Are emotions universal and innate?

In what ways are our basic emotions common to people throughout the world, and in what ways are they specific to a person's culture? Most of the research on this question has focused on facial expressions of emotions. For example, does a smile mean pleasure and a frown mean displeasure in all cultures, or do such expressions depend on the conventions of the particular society? If the same facial expressions are found to be associated with the same feelings for all human beings, then it may be argued that our basic emotions are innate—that they are biologically "wired in" for all people.

The question of the origin of emotional expressions was asked over a century ago by Charles Darwin. Darwin believed that our expressions of emotion are a part of our evolutionary heritage and that they are common to all human beings. In *The Expression of Emotions in Man and Animals*, published in 1872, Darwin suggested that many of our ways of expressing emotion are left over from a time when such expressions were an important part of survival. Before the development of language, emotional expression was our ancestors' primary mode of communication. If people (or their apelike ancestors) were to cooperate with one another, whether in hunting, building homes, or defending against predators, they needed to have ways of understanding each other. Darwin speculated that modes of emotional expression evolved for this reason. For example, the emotion of anger prompted our forebears to scowl and bare their teeth, discouraging their enemies and warning that they were ready to bite. We still make such expressions of anger, even though we rarely bite our enemies nowadays. Similarly, positive emotional expressions, such as smiling, evolved as a means to promote cooperation between individuals. This evolutionary view points up the links between emotion and motivation: Our emotions seem to have evolved because they motivate us to behave in adaptive ways—ways that increased our ancestors' chances of survival.

Recent evidence supports Darwin's contention that particular emotional expressions are inborn characteristics of the human species. When Paul Ekman (1975) showed posed photographs of facial expressions representing six basic emotions— happiness, sadness, anger, fear, surprise, and disgust—to college students in countries around the world, he found that a large majority recognized the emotions accurately. To eliminate the possibility that the subjects responded similarly because all had been exposed to Western culture, Ekman and his associates (1969) traveled to the South East Highlands of New Guinea, in the South Pacific, where they found a group of people called the Fore who were almost totally isolated from Western culture. First the researchers showed Fore adults and children photographs depicting three different emotions as expressed by Caucasians (Figure 10.3). Then they read a story to the subjects,

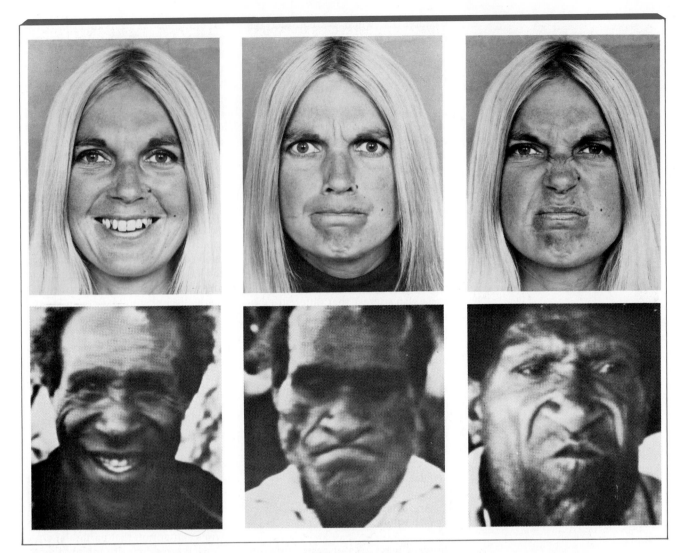

in their native language, and asked them to select the face that fit the story. In the story about fear, for example, the subjects were told, "A wild pig is standing in the door of the house and the woman is looking at the pig and is very afraid of it." Using this technique, the researchers found a high level of agreement among both adults and children; the isolated New Guinea tribespeople made essentially the same links between emotions and facial expressions as Westerners.

Ekman and his team also asked the Fore subjects to demonstrate how *they* would look if they were in the situation described in the stories. They then took photographs of the tribespeople's expressions (see examples in Figure 10.3) back to America and had them rated by college students. The results: The American students understood Fore face lan-

guage almost perfectly, just as the Fore subjects had understood American face language. Ekman's data strongly indicate that there are universal links between basic emotions and the way they are expressed facially. There is increasing evidence that all human beings share the same biological program, which links specific facial muscles with specific emotions (Rinn, 1984).

Ekman's research indicates, then, that the links between basic emotions and facial expressions are innate. They do not have to be learned by observing other people in one's particular culture. Recent studies of infants provide further evidence for the innateness of our basic emotions. These studies suggest that a range of distinctive emotional expressions—happiness, surprise, disgust, distress, and interest—are present at birth

FIGURE 10.3

When Fore tribespeople in New Guinea were shown photographs of emotions as expressed by Caucasians, such as happiness, anger, and disgust (top, left to right), they were able to identify the emotions accurately. Similarly, American subjects were able to identify the same emotions as expressed by Fore people (bottom).

CHAPTER TEN: MOTIVATION AND EMOTION

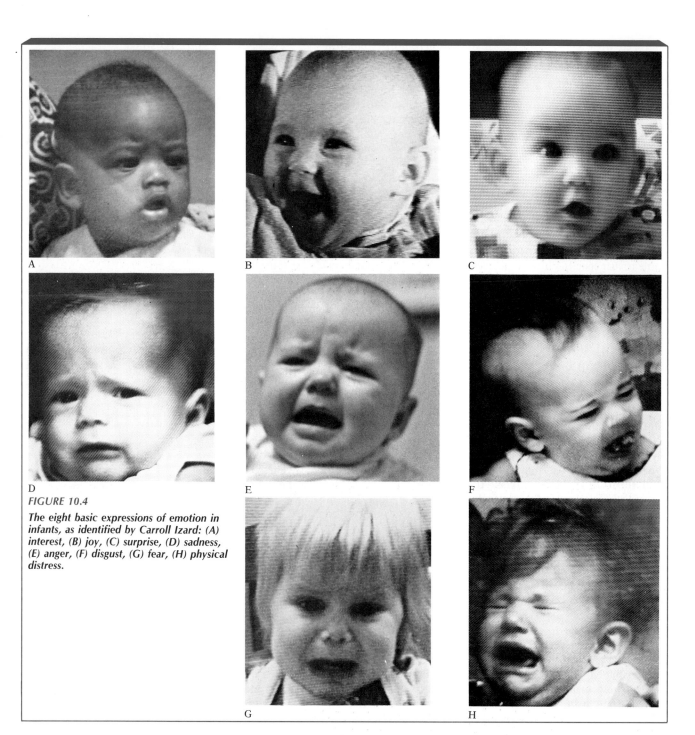

FIGURE 10.4

The eight basic expressions of emotion in infants, as identified by Carroll Izard: (A) interest, (B) joy, (C) surprise, (D) sadness, (E) anger, (F) disgust, (G) fear, (H) physical distress.

(Izard, 1978). By the time infants are 8 or 9 months old, they seem to be capable of displaying—under what seem to be appropriate circumstances—distinctive expressions of happiness, surprise, sadness, anger, disgust, contempt, and fear (see Figure 10.4) (Izard et al., 1980). Expressions of these common emotions occur even in blind infants, who have never seen a laughing or mourning face (Eibl-Eibesfeldt, 1970). Since these infants cannot imitate the expressions on others' faces, their expressions presumably reflect our inborn disposition to express particular emotions in particular ways.

The evidence from different cultures and from studies of infants converges to suggest that certain basic aspects of our emotional patterns are universal and innate. Babies, whether they are born in Boston or Borneo, seem to come into the world equipped with the same basic set of emotions and the same ways of expressing them. It remains, clear, however, that people's experiences in particular cultures and environments also have an influence on their emotions. Whereas our capacity to experience happiness, surprise, or anger—and the facial expressions that go along with these emotions—seems to be innate, the specific things that elate us, surprise us, or enrage us depend to a large extent on what we learn. Thus, for example, although the emotion of fear is innate, people come to fear specific things as a result of their personal experiences, their families, and their cultures. Some children learn to fear animals, others to fear flying, and others to fear academic failure, by observing and adopting the attitudes of people around them. In some societies people come to fear ghosts and demons, in other societies to fear soldiers, and in still others to fear nuclear accidents. A similar analysis can be applied to things that elate, depress, surprise, enrage, and disgust people. While our basic repertoire of emotions seems innate and universal, the objects of these emotions are influenced to a large degree by experience and culture.

HOW IS EMOTION ACTIVATED?

Our emotions are triggered by a wide range of events and thoughts. When David saw the technician prepare to take his blood, he felt a surge of fear. When Sarah learned that she had received a scholarship, she felt a glow of pride and elation. When Peter recalled his grandfather's funeral, he was again filled with sadness. For the past century, psychologists have been trying to understand precisely how these links between events, thoughts, and feelings take place. In particular, they have tried to explain the interplay of the different components of emotion: the physiological arousal, the expressive behaviors, and the subjective feeling. In this section, we will survey several different explanations for the activation of emotion.

From physiological arousal to felt emotion: The James-Lange theory

Common sense suggests that a specific event causes a person to feel a particular emotion (the subjective experience) and this emotion then causes certain physiological changes as well as certain behaviors and expressions (crying, striking back, smiling, and so on). For example, when David was about to have a needle inserted into his vein, he felt scared; as a result, his heart began to pound, his breath quickened, and his muscles tightened up. But William James, the great American psychologist, was not satisfied with this "common-sense" explanation. He proposed that in fact the sequence is quite the reverse: An event or stimulus causes bodily changes (both internal responses, such as increased heart rate, and overt actions, such as crying or running), and these bodily effects in turn produce the experienced emotion. The experience of emotion, according to James, is a direct result of a person's perception of his own bodily changes and behaviors: "We feel sorry because we cry, angry because we strike, afraid because we tremble" (James, 1890).

In developing his theory, James drew on the related ideas of a Danish physiologist named Carl Lange. As a result, the theory that the experience of emotion results from the perceptions of one's bodily changes is known as the *James-Lange theory*. In David's case, this theory suggests, the sight of the needle and the anticipation of the blood being taken led directly to the pounding heart and tightened muscles, and it was David's subsequent perception of these physiological changes that constituted his feeling of fear.

Although the James-Lange theory has been influential, it does not seem to provide a fully adequate account of emotion. The theory presupposes that each emotion has its own distinct pattern of physiological change—that joy, fear, anger, and so on must each lead to its own distinct set of bodily changes. Otherwise, the person would not be able to distinguish between the different emotions. But on

A SMILE TO SHARE

Why do you smile? To express a feeling of happiness, even when you're by yourself, or to communicate friendliness to others? Robert Kraut and Robert Johnston (1979) have found that among bowlers, at least, smiling is a social expression. They observed hundreds of bowlers in Ithaca, New York, and found that they often smiled while looking and talking to others but not necessarily when they scored a strike or a spare. Bowlers were also much more likely to smile when facing their friends than when facing the pins. Human smiling probably developed in the first place as a means of communication, not private expression.

the whole, as noted earlier, similar physiological responses seem to accompany all emotions, varying primarily in intensity. There is no evidence that each of the many shades of emotion we are capable of feeling has its own distinct pattern of internal bodily changes. Thus, the James-Lange theory fails to adequately explain the relationship between the physiological and subjective aspects of emotion.

Cognitive labeling theory

The *cognitive labeling theory* of emotional activation, put forth by Stanley Schachter (1964), is one approach to dealing with the basic problem of the James-Lange theory. In accord with the James-Lange theory, Schachter proposed that bodily changes precede the experience of emotion. But instead of assuming that each emotion has its own characteristic pattern of physiological changes, Schachter made the more plausible assumption that the patterns of physiological change associated with different emotions are quite similar. A person who feels physiologically aroused must, in fact, *decide* which particular emotion she is feeling. The interpretation or labeling of an emotion, Schachter went on to postulate, depends on the situation in which the arousal occurs. If you feel a racing pulse and a shortness of breath at a party, where everyone is making merry, you may interpret the emotion as elation. If you experience the same arousal after someone has insulted you, you may interpret it as anger. The same form of physiological arousal, therefore, may lead to two different emotions, depending on the surrounding circumstances. Figure 10.5 provides a summary of the "common-sense" view of emotional activation, the James-Lange theory, and cognitive labeling theory.

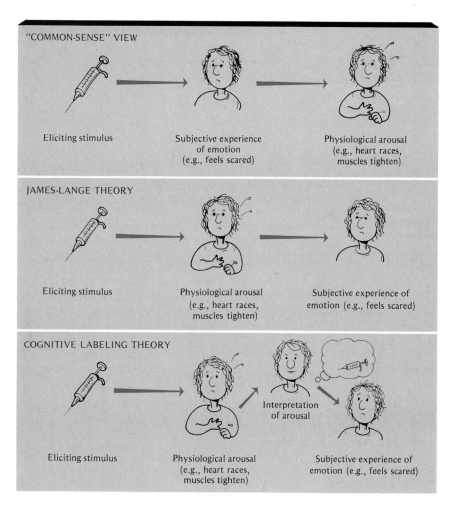

FIGURE 10.5

Three views of the way in which emotion is activated: a "common-sense" view, the James-Lange theory, and Schachter's cognitive labeling theory.

In David's case, the sight of the needle had its most immediate impact on his internal reactions—the racing pulse and tightened muscles. If David were in a different situation— say on a first date with a woman he finds very attractive—he might interpret his own reaction as indicating sexual arousal or even "love" (see Box 4). But given that he was in a Bloodmobile with a needle about to enter his arm, the more appropriate emotional label was clearly "fear."

Schachter's theory has been called the "jukebox theory of emotion" (Mandler, 1962). According to this analogy, the state of physiological arousal is like the state of a jukebox after a coin has been inserted. It is all set to go, ready to play its tune. But just which tune it will play—a love song, a lament, an exultant march— will depend on which button is pushed. And which button is pushed, in Schachter's view, depends on the way in which the individual interprets his environment.

To demonstrate the validity of his theory, Schachter and Jerome E. Singer (1962) had a physician inject subjects with epinephrine. As noted in Chapter 2, epinephrine is a hormone that produces physiological reactions usually associated with strong emotions—pounding heart, rapid breathing, sweating palms. Some subjects were told what the effects of the injection would be (the "epinephrine-informed" group), while other subjects were not told about these effects (the "epinephrine-uninformed" group). Schachter and

FIGURE 10.6

Two subjects in Schachter and Singer's experiment. When subjects were informed about the drug's arousing effects, they tended not to experience strong emotion. But when they were not informed about the drug's effects, they tended to "catch" the emotion displayed by the confederate.

CHAPTER TEN: MOTIVATION AND EMOTION

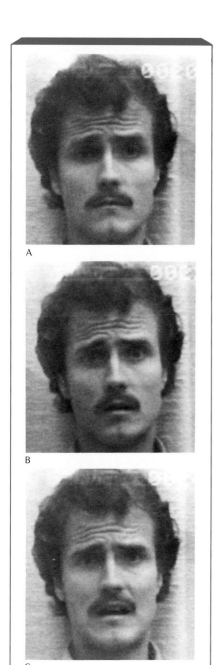

FIGURE 10.7

This subject was asked to move his facial muscles in a particular way: (A) "raise your brows and pull them together," (B) "now raise your upper eyelids," (C) "now also stretch your lips horizontally, back toward your ears." Having assumed such a facial expression of fear, subjects also tended to show the physiological effects of real fear.

Singer predicted that subjects who knew that the drug caused their arousal would not experience any strong emotion—they would say to themselves, in effect, "I'm aroused; I guess it's because of the epinephrine." On the other hand, subjects who were not informed of the effects of the drug should attribute their arousal to an emotion relevant to the situation they were in. To test this prediction, Schachter and Singer created two situations. In the first, the subjects watched another student (actually a confederate of the experimenters) act in a wild and silly way, playing with a hula hoop and shooting wads of paper at a wastebasket. In the second situation, the confederate objected strenuously to a questionnaire that he and the real subject were filling out. He escalated his protest until he finally tore up the questionnaire and left the room. Schachter and Singer expected their epinephrine-uninformed subjects to use the confederate's behavior as a cue in identifying their own emotions. The data suggested that this may indeed have happened. The subjects tended to attribute their physiological arousal to elation or anger, depending on the social context (see Figure 10.6). Once they had interpreted their physiological state as an emotion, they then proceeded to behave in ways appropriate to that particular emotion, acting either giddy or irritated themselves.

It should be noted, however, that Schachter and Singer's results were not really clear-cut, and more recent studies have not obtained similar results (Maslach, 1979; Marshall and Zimbardo, 1979). Consequently, the validity of the cognitive labeling model is currently a topic of debate among psychologists. Nevertheless, the cognitive labeling theory does seem quite applicable to many aspects of our emotional experience—even romantic love, as discussed in Box 4.

The facial feedback hypothesis

You are watching your favorite football team score a winning touchdown in the final minutes of the game, and a broad smile lights up your face. Or you are watching a sad movie in which a boy's pet collie dies, and your face becomes a mask of sorrow. Facial expressions such as these have long been thought to play a central role in emotion. As we have seen, the links between particular facial expressions and particular emotions seem to be very much the same in cultures throughout the world, suggesting that there is an innate, biological basis to these links. Noting that there may be built-in connections between particular facial expressions and particular emotions, some psychologists have proposed that our awareness of our own facial expressions is a primary ingredient in the experience of emotion (Tomkins, 1962; Izard, 1977). This approach is called the *facial feedback hypothesis.*

Several recent studies have provided evidence for the facial feedback hypothesis. In one such study, subjects were first asked to hold their facial muscles in positions that are characteristic of particular emotions, such as joy or fear. For example, a subject might be told, "Raise your brows and pull them together; now raise your upper eyelids; now also stretch your lips horizontally back toward your ears" (Figure 10.7). The subjects were not told which emotion the facial movements were supposed to mimic (in this instance it was fear). As a result of moving the facial muscles in this way, subjects' heart rate went up and skin temperature went down—effects known to accompany real fear (Ekman, Levenson, and Friesen, 1983). It has been suggested that facial expressions are likely to call to mind thoughts or memories that are consistent with the expression. As one subject told researcher James Laird at the end of a session, "When my jaw was clenched and my brow was down, I tried not to be angry, but I found my thoughts wandering to things that made me angry" (Laird, 1974, page 480).

Actually, William James anticipated facial feedback theory when he proposed that emotion is produced by people's perceptions of their own bodily changes, including facial expres-

BOX 4

THE LABEL OF LOVE

Recent studies of falling in love have indicated that love is like a Brooks Brothers suit or a Saks Fifth Avenue dress. For one's feelings toward another to be experienced as "love," they must not only feel good and fit well, they must also have the appropriate label. Sometimes a sexual experience contributes to such labeling. One college student told an interviewer that she was surprised to discover that she enjoyed having sex with her boyfriend, because until that time she had not been sure that she loved him. The pleasant experience helped to convince her that she was actually "in love" (Peplau, Rubin, and Hill, 1977).

Paradoxically, however, people sometimes label as "love" experiences that seem to be negative rather than positive (Berscheid and Walster, 1974). Consider the rather interesting case of fear. Ovid noted in *The Art of Love*, written in first century Rome, that an excellent time for a man to arouse passion in a woman was while watching gladiators disembowel one another

in the arena. Presumably the emotions of fear and revulsion stirred up by the grisly scene would somehow be converted to romantic interest.

Ovid himself did not conduct any controlled experiments to check the validity of the fear-breeds-love principle, but two psychologists at the University of British Columbia have done so (Dutton and Aron, 1974). They conducted their experiment on two footbridges that cross the Capilano River in North Vancouver. One of the bridges is a narrow, rickety structure that sways in the wind 230 feet above the rocky canyon; the other is a solid structure upriver, only 10 feet above a shallow stream. An attractive female experimenter approached men who were crossing one or the other bridge and asked if they would take part in her study on "the effects of exposure to scenic attractions on creative expression." All they had to do was write down their associations to a picture she showed them. The researchers found that the men accosted on the fear-arousing bridge were more sexu-

ally aroused than the men on the solid bridge, as measured by the amount of sexual imagery in the stories they wrote. The men on the high-fear bridge were also more likely to telephone the young woman afterward, ostensibly to get more information about the study.

The best available explanation of these results comes from Schachter's cognitive labeling theory of emotion. Schachter's experiments suggested that the experience of emotion has two necessary elements. The first is physiological arousal—a racing heart, heightened breathing, sweating, and the like. These symptoms tend to be much the same for any intense emotion, whether it be anger, fear, or love. The second necessary element, therefore, is the person's subjective labeling of her arousal. In order to determine which emotion she is experiencing, the person must look around and decide what external stimulus is causing the inner upheaval.

This labeling is a complicated process, and (as Ovid apparently knew some 2000 years ago) mistakes can happen. In the Capilano Canyon study, subjects apparently relabeled their inner stirrings of fear, at least in part, as sexual arousal and romantic attraction. This sort of relabeling is undoubtedly encouraged by the fact that the popular stereotype of falling in love—a pounding heart, shortness of breath, trembling hands—bears an uncanny resemblance to the physical symptoms of fear. With such traumatic expectations of what love should feel like, it is no wonder that it is sometimes confused with other emotions. As the Supremes put it in a song of the 1960s, "Love is like an itching in my heart."

There is, of course, much more to love than cognitive labeling. Indeed, love cannot be regarded as only an emotion. As we will see in Chapter 17, it is also a particular sort of social relationship that takes time to grow and develop.

sions and other overt behaviors. The possibility that our actions—and especially our facial expressions—can produce our emotions has the interesting implication that we may sometimes be able to gain control over our emotions by consciously altering our behavior.

George Miller (1962) noted that James developed his theory at a time when both his parents had just died and when he was wrestling with deep grief. But James had learned to live with his feelings, to rise above grief and depression. And the way to do so, he maintained, was to act *as if* one were not affected. "If we wish to conquer undesirable emotional tendencies in ourselves," James (1884) wrote, "we must assiduously, and in the first instance cold-bloodedly, go through the *outward motions* of those contrary dispositions we prefer to cultivate." If we act cheerful, for example, the emotion of happiness will replace the gloom we want to get rid of. Thus, by consciously altering our behavior, we may be able to alter our feelings.

William James's advice along these lines will not always work. In some cases, suppressing or disguising one's feelings is likely to have harmful effects. A person who behaves perfectly calmly after the death of a close friend may suffer a great deal internally. Nevertheless, there is evidence that such conscious masquerading can sometimes have the desired effect. In one experiment, students received electric shocks and were asked either to conceal or to exaggerate the facial expressions associated with anticipating and receiving the shocks (Lanzetta, Cartwright-Smith, and Kleck, 1976). Thus, some subjects did their best not to show any outward signs of pain, while others made an effort to express their feelings quite fully. As the shocks were presented, the researchers also obtained written self-reports of the subjects' feelings and physiological measures of the extent of their arousal. The researchers found that the subjects who suppressed their fear and pain also reported that they felt less upset, and they showed fewer physiological signs of arousal than did the subjects who expressed their feelings.

Imagination and emotion

When an actor has to portray a particular emotion, he is likely to use the technique of recalling or imagining a situation that would give rise to the emotion. If he wants to portray anger, for example, he may imagine that the person he is speaking to has just ridiculed him. Such exercises of the imagination can lead to vivid experiences of emotion, almost as if the eliciting stimulus were directly present. Thus, when Peter thinks back to his grandfather's funeral, the sad feelings again well up in him. And when Sarah recalls getting the letter that informed her about her scholarship, she again feels elated. Studies have confirmed that such images and memories can elicit both subjective feelings and patterns of facial muscle movement that are similar to those elicited by more immediate stimuli (Schwartz et al., 1976). William James, who was ahead of his time in anticipating advances in our understanding of emotion, also discussed the power of imagery in activating emotion. Because of this power, James believed that a good imagination is a prerequisite for a rich emotional life.

The different approaches to the activation of emotion that we have discussed in this section are not mutally exclusive. Each of the approaches may explain a part of the process by which emotion is activated. For example, it is quite possible that when we are feeling angry or afraid, physiological arousal, our interpretation of the situation, facial expression, and images or memories of other upsetting situations all contribute to the experienced emotion. Recent approaches to emotion have, in fact, attempted to combine all these elements into a more complex and comprehensive model (for example, Izard, 1977).

As we have seen, our motives and emotions are closely linked. In the case of David, giving blood involved considerable fear. Yet by going ahead despite the fear, he experienced the emotions of elation and pride, which heightened his motivation to give blood in the future. Indeed, studies have suggested that certain activities, from skydiving to blood donation, are sometimes especially pleasurable—even addictive—because they involve bouncing back from pain or fear to relief and satisfaction (Piliavin, Callero, and Evans, 1982).

More generally, our emotions play a role in motivating practically all of our behavior, from making money to making love. Our emotions often determine whether we will be motivated to help or hurt other people. When we are feeling happy, we are especially likely to help other people out. In one series of studies, some people were put in a good mood when they unexpectedly found a dime in the coin return of a pay telephone. These happy people were then found to be much more likely than those who had not found a dime to help a passerby pick up a folder full of papers she had dropped (Isen and Levin, 1972) or to mail a lost letter (Levin and Isen, 1975). It seems that when we're feeling good ourselves, we're often motivated to spread the goodwill to others. On the other hand, when we are feeling afraid or angry, we are especially likely to take our bad feelings out on others. This negative side of emotion—the case of violence—is the topic of the Psychological Issue that follows.

SUMMARY

The nature of motivation
- **1** *Motives* are the internal needs and desires that energize and direct our actions. Although there are many ways of cataloging and categorizing human motives, it is useful to think of motives as falling into three broad categories: *basic needs, social motives,* and *competence motives.*
- **2** Maslow proposed a hierarchy of human needs, with physiological needs at the bottom and self-actualization needs at the top. He suggested that the needs at the lower levels must be satisfied before one can begin to satisfy needs at the higher levels.
- **3** According to *drive reduction theory,* motivation begins with a

physiological *need* that is experienced psychologically as a *drive.* The drive leads the individual to satisfy the need; once the need is satisfied, the drive is reduced. Drive reduction theory is inadequate for explaining many aspects of motivation, such as the curiosity motive and the self-actualization motive.
- **4** Understanding most sorts of motivated behavior requires taking into account both the internal needs and the external *incentives* involved.

Motivational systems
- **5** Hunger is a basic physiological motive. Although hunger pangs play some role in regulating eating patterns, the major role is played by the hypothalamus, which monitors both blood-sugar level and body fat content and subsequently stimulates or inhibits eating behavior. The hypothalamus's regulatory activity serves to maintain remarkably constant body weight. Animals in which part of the hypothalamus has been destroyed become compulsive eaters and double or triple in body weight.
- **6** Stanley Schachter has suggested that overweight humans base their eating habits on external cues, such as food taste or availability, rather than on internal cues, such as hunger pangs.
- **7** Whereas hormones totally control sexual motivation in many other animals, in humans a variety of factors—including cultural learning and personal experience—can influence sexual motivation.
- **8** The motivation to work may be *intrinsic* (the activity is rewarding in itself) or it may be *extrinsic* (an outside reward is required). In some cases an extrinsic reward may actually decrease intrinsic motivation.
- **9** People vary in their level of *achievement motivation*—the need to match or exceed one's standard of excellence.
- **10** Motives can conflict with one another in several ways. The major types of conflict have been identified as: *approach-approach* (a choice between two desirable goals), *avoidance-avoidance* (a choice between two undesirable goals), and *ap-*

CHAPTER TEN: MOTIVATION AND EMOTION

proach-avoidance (in which there is one goal with both advantages and disadvantages).

The nature of emotion

• **11** An *emotion* appears to have three aspects: the subjective experience ("feeling"), physiological arousal (the bodily response), and expressive behavior (such as facial expressions, posture, and tones of voice).

• **12** Plutchik has suggested that there are eight primary emotions: joy, acceptance, fear, surprise, sadness, disgust, anger, and anticipation. Similarly, Ekman and Izard have identified six primary emotions, based on distinctive facial expressions: joy, surprise, sadness, anger, disgust, and fear.

• **13** All strong emotions appear to be accompanied by a similar pattern of physiological arousal that includes increased heartbeat and breathing rate, a shutting down of digestive functions, dry mouth because of decreased salivary function, overreaction of sweat glands, and enlargement of pupils. Not all emotions have such noticeable physiological components, and there are a few differences in physiological response patterns for different emotions.

• **14** Modern research has supported Darwin's contention that particular facial expressions of emotion are inborn characteristics of the human species. Ekman's research has shown that even people in remote cultures can recognize the emotions being expressed in American photographs, and Izard's research with infants indicates that all infants come into the world equipped with the same basic set of emotions.

How is emotion activated?

• **15** According to the *James-Lange theory*, an event or stimulus causes bodily changes, which in turn produce the subjective experience of emotion. One problem with this theory is that it assumes that each emotion has its own characteristic pattern of physiological changes.

• **16** Schachter has suggested that the experience of an emotion depends on what label a person puts on his physiological arousal. This label in turn depends on the particular situation in which the arousal occurs. Schachter's approach is called *cognitive labeling theory*. In some situations, the emotion of love, for example, can be explained in terms of cognitive labeling theory.

• **17** According to the *facial feedback hypothesis*, our awareness of our own facial expressions can influence our experience of emotions.

• **18** Subjective feelings and facial expressions that originally accompanied an experience can later be elicited by imagining or remembering that experience.

• **19** The different approaches to the activation of emotion—the James-Lange theory, the cognitive labeling theory, the facial feedback hypothesis, and the role of imagination—are not mutually exclusive. Each may explain a different aspect of how an emotion is activated.

KEY TERMS

achievement motive
approach-approach conflict
approach-avoidance conflict
avoidance-avoidance conflict
basic needs
cognitive labeling theory
competence motivation
drive
drive reduction theory
emotions
extrinsic motivation
facial feedback hypothesis
Freudian slips
hyperphagic
incentives
instincts
intrinsic motivation
James-Lange theory
motivation
motives
needs
set point
social motives

VIOLENCE

YOUTHS ASSAULT GUARD, FLEE
MASS THURSDAY FOR SLAIN OFFICER
Man Gets Prison in Strangling of His Stepfather
10 ARRESTED IN ATTACK ON 5 SAILORS
TV Film to Act Out Big Dan's Gang Rape

These headlines all appeared in the Boston *Globe* during a one-week period in March 1984. The newspaper is a respectable one and the week was not particularly violent or eventful, as weeks go nowadays. The unfortunate fact of the matter is that violence has become an expected part of American life. Violence has always been a part of the American tradition, and in recent years the situation has gotten worse than ever. In 1982, there were 22,000 murders in the United States. Every hour, it is estimated, more than 2 people are murdered, 194 people are assaulted, and 18 women are raped (McGrath, 1983). The homicide rate in the United States is one of the highest in the world—about four times the rate in Canada, eight times the rate in England, and thirteen times the rate in Denmark, Norway, and Greece.

ARE PEOPLE NATURALLY VIOLENT?

Although homicide rates are higher in the United States than almost anywhere else, violence is not an exclusively American commodity. In fact, Konrad Lorenz (1966), the Nobel prize-winning biologist, has argued that violence is an inherent part of human nature. Lorenz and other

Violence has always been a part of the American tradition.

writers claim that through the course of evolution, people—especially men—developed the capacity for violence, because violence was useful for survival. The aggressive man, they assert, controls territory, women, food, and other "resources."

But the "human nature" assumption does not account for the fact that there are some human cultures in which there is very little violence. Although we all share the same "human nature," some of us are more aggressive than others, and some situations are more likely than others to elicit aggressive responses. As a result, we need to go beyond "human nature" to a consideration of when and where aggression is most likely to occur.

FRUSTRATION AND AGGRESSION

Did you ever sit down, intending to watch your favorite TV show, only to have someone else barge in and change the channel? Have you ever searched a crowded city street for a parking space only to have another driver sneak into the last available spot? Did you ever settle down to a good night's sleep only to be blasted out of bed by a neighbor's stereo? If so, then you've experienced what psychologists call *frustration*—the blocking of efforts to attain some desired goal. At times like these, you probably became angry and perhaps even felt a strong urge to punch someone in the nose.

Almost 50 years ago, John Dollard and his associates (1939) at Yale University put forth the *frustration-aggression hypothesis*—the idea that frustration leads to aggression. The aggression may be physical, such as a punch in the nose, or it may be verbal, such as a hostile joke or an insult. It may be directed toward the person who caused the frustration (the person who stole your parking spot), or it may be *displaced* toward an innocent bystander (such as a passenger in your car).

Driving on clogged city streets can be a frustrating experience that leads people to verbal, if not physical, aggression.

Although there is a great deal of evidence for the frustration-aggression hypothesis, it also needs to be carefully qualified. Frustration often leads to aggression, but not always. For example, imagine how various people would respond to the frustrating experience of losing money in a Coke machine. One person might kick the machine and curse at it. Another might jot down the name and address of the company and write a letter demanding his money back. And a third person might become painfully depressed, wondering, "Why does this sort of thing always happen to me?" So, while aggression is one possible response to frustration, it is by no means the only one. And although frustration seems to be one common cause of aggression, it is certainly not the only cause.

GETTING IT OUT OF YOUR SYSTEM: CATHARSIS

The movie *Rollerball* portrayed a future society in which citizens get rid of their violent and rebellious urges by watching a bloody hybrid of football and roller derby. The idea is that when frustrations mount up, we can reduce our aggressive drives by engaging in—or even just watching—violent activity. If this idea were correct, we might be able to make the world a more peaceful place by taking time each day to watch a bloody movie, scream at a wall, or pound a pillow. For centuries, people have been telling each other to "blow off steam" whenever they feel angry or tense. Psychologists refer to this method of releasing emotional tension as *catharsis*.

Unfortunately, aggressive catharsis probably doesn't work the way its proponents say it should. If you are angry at someone, striking out at that person may make you feel better, at least temporarily. But there is no evidence that harming anyone other than the person you're angry at will have a cathartic effect. And the evidence suggests that when people shout and scream at each other, they are more likely to rehearse and reinforce their anger than to get rid of it. Married couples who yell at each other, for example, actually feel even angrier afterward (Tavris, 1983).

Nor is there any evidence that watching someone else behave aggressively, whether in a violent movie or on the football field, will help you get rid of hostile feelings. In fact, as we will see, quite the opposite is more likely.

OBSERVING VIOLENCE

If there is a single principle that accounts for violent behavior, it is that violence begets violence. One reason for this principle is that people—especially children—tend to imitate what they see. When children have many opportunities to observe physical aggression, whether in real life or on television, they become more likely to behave aggressively themselves.

In one well-known experiment, one group of nursery-school children observed an adult model punch and pound an inflated plastic "Bobo doll," while other groups of children observed a nonaggressive adult or no adult at all (Bandura, Ross, and Ross, 1963). Later, each of the children was observed at play in a room containing a Bobo doll. The researchers found that the children who had observed an aggressive model engaged in more aggression themselves than did children who had not observed an aggressive model. Sometimes the children attacked the Bobo doll in just the same way the model had, such as by slamming it with a rubber mallet. This is known as *imitative aggression*. At other times, the children devised their own distinctive ways of attacking the doll, such as kicking it in the head, which is something the model had not done. This is called *nonimitative aggression*, because it does not involve exact imitation of the model's actions.

The children's imitative aggression is not too surprising. We've all seen children imitating adults in all sorts of ways. The adult demonstrates some action that is new to

Observing violence teaches new ways to be violent and makes violence seem acceptable.

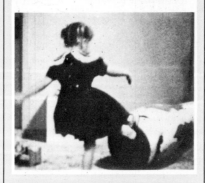

Frames taken from movies of Bandura's studies of the imitation of aggression. Children who saw a model punching and kicking a "Bobo doll" were likely to exhibit similar aggressive behavior themselves.

the child, like reading a newspaper or eating with a fork, and the child wants to try it out. The children's nonimitative aggression suggests that observing violence can have even more far-reaching effects. The aggressive model seems to have made a wide range of aggressive behaviors acceptable to the children. It is a case of social learning (Chapter 5), in which actions speak louder than words. Whereas children are often taught not to hurt others, seeing aggressive models lets them know that these teachings do not always apply. Thus, observing violence can actually produce violence in two ways: It teaches new ways to be violent, and it makes violence seem acceptable.

TELEVISION AND VIOLENCE

Many critics decry the high level of violence on television, especially the shows watched by children. One recent sampling showed that 70 percent of prime time shows contained acts of violence. And fully 92 percent of children's cartoon shows contained violent acts, with an average of four beanings, brainings, beatings, or bashings per hour (Signorelli, Gross, and Morgan, 1982). Although the television networks would like us to think otherwise, a large body of research conducted over the past 15 years leaves little doubt that children's TV watching tends to increase their levels of aggressive behavior.

In some cases, specific acts of violence have been traced to ideas that children got from television. In one case, a child set fire to a house after seeing a similar instance of arson on a TV drama (Schorr, 1981). In other, less dramatic cases, TV shows have provided children with an arsenal of aggressive behaviors to imitate. Just like imitating an adult's act of hitting a Bobo doll with a mallet, a child who sees one cartoon character happily slam another over the head with a frying pan may decide to try it on her little

Watching violence on television may have a long-term effect on children's attitudes and behavior. In one study, children who spent the most time watching TV violence when they were 8 years old were rated as most aggressive ten years later.

GETTING USED TO IT

Continual exposure to violence may have still another undesirable effect: the more we see or read about, the less it seems to bother us. Just as we become habituated to loud noises or other sensory stimuli, so that we no longer notice them, we may also become habituated to violence, so that it no longer seems notable or upsetting.

In one experiment (Drabman and Thomas, 1975) third- and fourth-grade children were taken individually into a game room, where half of them watched a violent eight-minute segment of a western movie and the other half just played without being exposed to violence. Afterward, each child was asked to watch a video monitor in order to keep an eye on two younger children who were playing in another room. Although the younger children's interaction was actually videotaped, the subjects believed it was live. The experimenter left the room while the subjects observed the younger children, but he instructed them to call him right away if anything seemed to go wrong. About a minute into the observed interaction, the children on the videotape started hitting each other fiercely, were soon crying, and even seemed to have smashed the camera.

It turned out, as the researchers had predicted, that the third- and fourth-graders who had watched the violent movie took longer to call for help than the children who hadn't seen the movie. The children who had seen the film had apparently become habituated to violence, so that it took longer for them to consider the children's fight significant. If these results can be extended to adolescents and adults (and it seems likely that they can), the conclusion is clear: the more violence we observe—in movies, on the news, or in the streets—the more we may come to accept it as a natural part of life.

brother. As noted in Chapter 5, social learning theory postulates that we learn by observing others—both their behavior and its consequences. Much of television portrays both inappropriate behavior and unrealistically positive consequences.

Television violence may have a long-term, cumulative input on children's attitudes and behavior. In one extensive longitudinal study, children who spent the most time watching violent television shows when they were 8 were rated as most aggressive by their peers 10 years later, when they were 18 (Eron, 1982). Similarly, a British study found that prolonged exposure to television was correlated

with the degree to which London teenagers engaged in serious acts of violence (Muson, 1978).

More than a decade ago, a commission appointed by the U.S. Surgeon General (1972) concluded that there was a clear link between viewing televised aggression and behaving aggressively. The research done since that time bolsters that conclusion. Nevertheless, the television networks have continued to air violent shows to both children and adults. If anything, the amount of violence has increased, as in the new wave of rock videos. Television producers have apparently, and unfortunately, concluded that violence sells.

LEGITIMIZING VIOLENCE

Television is not the only force that serves to expose people to violence. As noted at the beginning of this Issue, the headlines of our daily papers are full of violence, from muggings around the corner to bloody wars in distant corners of the globe. In at least some cases, such an atmosphere can make violence seem a legitimate and acceptable way to settle disputes.

The ultimate legitimation of violence comes when governments decide to resolve their disputes by going to war. Going to war, in turn, has been found to increase the level of violent crimes at home. During the period of the Vietnam war, for example, the murder rate in the United States increased by 42 percent. During the same period, by contrast, the murder rate in Canada (a country not involved in the war) increased by only 11 percent (Archer and Gartner, 1983).

Dane Archer and Rosemary Gartner (1983) analyzed homicide rates in 110 nations for the decades between 1900 and 1970, during which time different countries were involved in the two world wars and many regional wars. They found that warring nations were considerably more likely to experience increased levels of homicide at home than were nations not involved in war.

As Archer and Gartner note, when your own nation is at war, several ingredients are present that can increase violence at home. Many violent killings take place in the war; these killings are given official approval and, indeed, the most successful killers are given conspicuous praise. "What all wars have in common," write Archer and

Wars can make violence seem a legitimate way to settle disputes. During the period of the Vietnam war, the U.S. murder rate increased by 42 percent.

Gartner, "is the unmistakable moral lesson that homicide is an acceptable, or even praiseworthy, means to the attainment of certain ends." This moral lesson is apparently not lost on at least some of the citizens of nations at war. If violence at war seems legitimate, then people are more likely to resort to violence at home as well.

SUMMARY

- **1** Some theorists have suggested that violence is a part of human nature. However, this explanation falls short of accounting for actual patterns of aggression and violence.
- **2** According to the frustration-aggression hypothesis, aggression often results from a frustrating experience. Nevertheless, there are many acts of aggression that cannot be accounted for by this theory, nor does all frustration lead to aggression.
- **3** According to the catharsis theory, people can reduce aggressive drives by engaging in or simply observing violent behavior. However, there is little evidence that such effects actually occur.
- **4** Most studies have shown that observing violence, including violence on TV, is likely to increase the incidence of violent behavior by the observer.
- **5** Observing violence can also lead to habituation—the more you are exposed to violence, the less it bothers you.
- **6** Violence can sometimes be seen as a legitimate way to settle disputes. When countries are at war, they are also likely to experience increased violence at home.

Going to war has been found to increase the level of violent crimes at home.

PERSONALITY

Each of us has a distinctive personality— our own unique way of approaching the situations of our life.

CHAPTER **11**

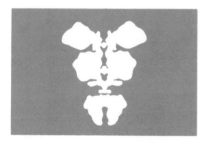

Imagine you are in a restaurant, looking around at some of the people ordering, eating, and drinking. You notice that one woman sits right down, calls the waiter, and places her order without even looking at the menu. When the food arrives, she puts salt and ketchup on it without tasting it first. Then a man comes in. He spends a long time looking around trying to decide where to sit—he almost sits at one table, then tries another, and finally sits (without much assurance) at a third. Before ordering, he seems to consider every item on the menu, and after placing his order he proceeds to call back the waiter and change the order two different times. Some of the other diners exhibit still other patterns of behavior. When the waiter says that one of the items on the menu is not available, one patron gets furious while another smiles understandingly and orders something else. Some of the diners seem to savor every bit of food, letting it slowly roll around in their mouths; others seem to gulp the food down without tasting it. Some are sociable and talkative, others sit by themselves in silence.

In a restaurant, as in many other situations, each of us seems to have a distinctive temperament and style of behaving. We each have our own concerns, priorities, likes and dislikes, and ways of dealing with conflict and frustration. These differences between people are a central focus of the study of personality.

Personality refers to the distinctive patterns of behavior, thoughts, and emotions that characterize the individual's adaptation to the situations of his or her life (Mischel, 1981). In studying personality, we want to know how any given person is unique. But we are also interested in the ways in which people are alike and in understanding how both the differences and the similarities come about.

We will begin this chapter with an examination of the roots of personality: the ways that each person's biological heritage and life experiences interact to produce his or her unique personality. Then we will discuss three influential theories of personality. The first, Sigmund Freud's psychoanalytic theory, emphasizes the role of unconscious forces underlying people's feelings and behavior. The second, social learning theory, draws on the mechanisms of social learning we introduced in Chapter 5 and helps to explain why people often behave very differently in different situations. And finally, the humanistic theories of Carl Rogers and Abraham Maslow focus on people's sense of their own worth and their striving for self-fulfillment. After describing these theories, we will look at the various methods that psychologists use to assess, or measure, people's personalities.

THE ROOTS OF PERSONALITY

Bjorn Borg and John McEnroe are both world-class tennis players. They resemble each other in their tremendous skill and in their dedication to the game. But their personalities —at least in the view of spectators at their matches—are very different. Borg is methodical, steady, and unflappable. He rarely shows emotion, even when he has made an error or a close call goes against him. McEnroe, on the other hand, is flamboyant, hot-tempered, and erratic. When he makes an error, he sometimes throws his racquet to the ground or growls at himself in disgust. When a close call goes against him, he will sometimes lose control of himself and start shouting at the line judge.

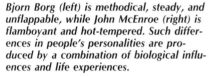

Bjorn Borg (left) is methodical, steady, and unflappable, while John McEnroe (right) is flamboyant and hot-tempered. Such differences in people's personalities are produced by a combination of biological influences and life experiences.

What leads to these sorts of differences in people's personalities—in their tempers and their emotional control under stress, for example? And equally important, what leads to the similarities that we often observe between aspects of different people's personalities? In Chapter 8 we discussed two sets of processes central in psychological development: maturation (the unfolding of biologically preprogrammed patterns) and learning (the effects of experience). Each individual's personality is forged by a unique combination of biological and genetic influences, on the one hand, and life experiences, on the other. In this section we will consider both of these influences on personality.

Biological and genetic influences on personality

There is an old notion that people can be classified into certain personality types, with each type being defined by a single central characteristic. Such personality types were often thought to be determined by physical characteristics. The ancient Greek physician Hippocrates proposed that everyone could be classified as one of four main "temperaments": choleric (irritable), melancholic (depressed), sanguine (optimistic), and phlegmatic (listless). Hippocrates believed that each temperament was related to a predominance of one of the four bodily "humors," or fluids. The choleric type of person, for example, had too much yellow bile, and the sanguine type had too much blood.

More recently, William H. Sheldon (1940, 1954) suggested an association between people's body type—or *somatotype*—and their personality. In Sheldon's system of rating body build, the *ectomorph* is thin, poorly muscled, and delicate; the *mesomorph* is well-muscled and athletic; and the *endomorph* is heavy and fat (see Figure 11.1). According to Sheldon, the delicate ectomorphs are typically sensitive, solitary, and intellectual; the muscular mesomorphs are assertive, daring, and independent; and the heavy endomorphs are relaxed, self-indulgent, and approval seeking.

Although Sheldon's research was influential, studies of the past several decades have not confirmed the existence of close links between body type and personality. Some ectomorphs are indeed intellectual loners, but so are many mesomorphs and endomorphs. Sheldon's type theory may have failed because he tried to explain personality in terms of too simple a set of categories.

Despite the inadequacy of body types as an explanation of personal-

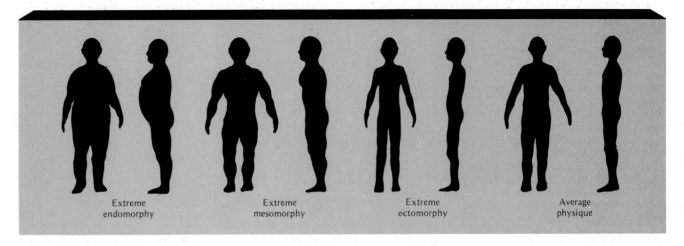

Extreme
endomorphy

Extreme
mesomorphy

Extreme
ectomorphy

Average
physique

ity, the notion that personality has biological roots has become widely accepted. As mentioned in Chapter 2, research in *behavior genetics* has explored genetic effects on personality by examining personality similarities and differences between family members with differing degrees of relatedness. These studies have shown that there is a large genetic component in several personality traits, including people's degree of *sociability* (the extent to which a person seeks out or avoids social contacts), *activity level* (the extent to which a person is always "on the go" or is more placid and passive), *emotionality* (the extent to which a person reacts to events with intense feelings or remains rela-

tively cool and calm), and *impulsivity* (the extent to which a person makes decisions quickly or more slowly and deliberately). About half of the variation among people on these four traits can be attributed to inherited predispositions or tendencies (Buss and Plomin, 1975). Thus, it seems quite likely that a high degree of emotionality runs in John McEnroe's family while a lesser degree runs in Bjorn Borg's. Some especially striking evidence of the genetic component of personality comes from studying pairs of identical twins who were brought up separately, as discussed in Box 1.

How might genes work to influence personality? The precise mecha-

FIGURE 11.1

The human body types (or somatotypes) identified by William Sheldon. He believed that each body type was typically associated with a particular pattern of personality.

Certain traits tend to run in families, at least in part because of genetic influences. Thus, the Jacksons' shared musical talent and performing flair may be attributed in part to inherited predispositions.

BOX 1

IDENTICAL PERSONALITIES?

Jim Lewis and Jim Springer are identical twins who were separated at birth, were raised in different families, and first met each other at the age of 39. When reunited, they found remarkable similarities in their lives. Both were first married to women named Linda and then remarried women named Betty. Both had clerical jobs and both had worked as volunteers for police agencies. Both did woodworking as a hobby, chewed their fingernails, and had suffered migraine headaches since adolescence.

The "Jim twins" were the first subjects in an extensive study of pairs of identical twins who had been reared apart conducted by psychologist Thomas Bouchard and his coworkers (1981) at the University of Minnesota. Financial difficulties or other events sometimes lead parents to place one or both of their twins up for adoption, leading to their separation. Because such twins have the same genes yet have different life experiences, observing them provides researchers with a unique opportunity to sort out the contributions of heredity and environment to different aspects of personality and intellect.

In the first years of his study, Bouchard found twenty-five such sets of twins from all over the world and flew them to Minneapolis, often for their first reunion since their separation in infancy. In the six days they spent at Bouchard's laboratory, the twins took numerous IQ and personality tests and underwent a complete medical examination. The team of researchers also interviewed the twins and members of their families and examined all available school and medical records (Bouchard et al., 1981; Holden, 1980).

The first shock for the researchers, and for the twins themselves, was how much the twins resemble each other in appearance and mannerisms. Not only do they usually have the same body build, but they often have the same tastes in clothing and the same non-verbal gestures. One pair of twins first met on the plane on their way to Min-

Jim Lewis and Jim Springer are identical twins who were separated at birth and raised in different families.

neapolis and each was wearing seven rings and many bracelets. Another pair, dubbed the "giggle sisters," punctuated the proceedings with the same nervous laughter.

The similarities go far beyond appearance, however. Most of the twin pairs obtained highly similar scores on IQ and personality tests. In fact, the researchers note that in most cases the scores were as similar as they would be if one person took the test on two different days. The researchers also found great similarities in the twins' emotional well-being. One set of female twins was claustrophobic and both balked at going into a booth for some medical tests. Another pair both reported having nightmares about smothering to death. The "Jim twins" both had felt increasing anxiety over the last seven years and were both being treated with Valium, an anti-anxiety drug.

Paradoxically, identical twins who are reared apart may tend to be more similar in many respects than identical twins who are reared in the same household (Farber, 1981). When identical twins are brought up together, they often adopt different interests or styles as a way of asserting their individuality. One twin, for example, may come to be viewed as "the athletic one," the other as "the studious one." This sort of typecasting may lead to

enduring differences in personality. When identical twins are brought up apart, however, there is no such motivation to assert individual differences, so their genetically identical predispositions may come through more clearly in their personality and behavior.

To be sure, there are also important differences between the twins. For example, one twin is often more aggressive, outgoing, and confident than the other. In some cases major differences between twins can be traced to major differences in their upbringings. In one instance, one twin was brought up by intellectually oriented parents and was given good educational opportunities, while his identical twin brother was given little intellectual stimulation and never finished high school. The first twin turned out to have an IQ score 20 points higher than his brother's. Further differences are likely to emerge as the extensive data from the study are more fully analyzed.

So far, however, it is the unexpected and overwhelming similarity of the twins that has impressed researchers. And for now, at least, the study's most striking message is that our genetic endowment exerts considerable influence on a wide range of traits and capacities.

nism of such influences is far from clear, but in general genes exert their effects on the development of bodily structures, including the brain and nervous system, and on the body's chemical processes. These, in turn, influence our styles of thinking, feeling, and behaving. One intriguing set of studies examined the physiological basis of a heritable personality characteristic called *sensation seeking*—the degree to which a person is ready to take risks and try new experiences. People who score high on a self-report test of sensation seeking have been found to have relatively low blood levels of monoamine oxidase (MAO), an enzyme that regulates the concentration of certain neurotransmitters in the brain (Zuckerman, 1983).

The evidence suggests, then, that although our personalities cannot be explained by our body types, biological and genetic factors do have an importance influence on our personalities. But we cannot look at these biological influences in isolation. We must go on to examine the ways in which our life experiences contribute to the shaping of personalities.

The role of experience

Many of our experiences add to, detract from, or modify our genetic tendencies to respond to the world in particular ways. Certain experiences —especially during the childhood years—play a central role in the formation of personality. We are all toilet trained, we all learn to eat at a table, we all go to school, and so on. These common experiences, shared by almost everyone in a culture, help to ensure that we will all grow up to be adults who relate to the world with certain common modes of thinking and feeling. But the influence of common experiences on personality does not mean that we all come to be more and more alike. In fact, these common experiences affect each of us in different ways, depending at least in part on our biological predispositions. For example, sitting at a dinner table may be pleasurable and rewarding to a sociable and not-too-active child but sheer torture to a highly active and not-too-sociable child.

In addition to common experiences, each person has his or her own unique experiences that may have a major effect on personality. Bob grew up on a farm, where he had to get up at 5:30 each morning and do chores. Sam grew up in the city, where he lived in an apartment and had a maid who picked up after him. Given these different experiences, it would not be surprising to learn that Bob and Sam have developed rather different views of the world and different ways of dealing with life's daily challenges.

The impact of unique experiences

DESIGNER'S GENES?

Does being a travel agent or a fashion designer run in the blood? When tests of occupational interests were given to adolescents and their parents, fairly high correlations were found between the interests of parents and their biological children but no such correlations were found for parents and their adoptive children (Scarr and Weinberg, 1978). These results suggest that shared genes, rather than shared family experiences, may account in large measure for the similarities. Of course, we are not actually born with genes for being politicians or plumbers. But genes influence broader sorts of temperaments and talents, such as sociability and artistic ability, which in turn may predispose us to certain vocational interests.

The environments in which people grow up—for example, the city (left) and the suburbs (right)—can have a major impact on people's developing personalities.

CHAPTER ELEVEN: PERSONALITY

Some aspects of personality seem to remain quite stable over the course of time. Even though President Ronald Reagan changed his occupation and his political philosophy since his radio broadcasting days, he seems to have retained his genial personal style.

helps to explain why siblings often have very different personalities (Scarr and Grajek, 1982). For example, younger siblings are born to older and wiser parents, who often treat their younger children differently from older ones. In addition, the experience of growing up and dealing with an older brother or sister can be quite different from the experience of dealing with a younger sibling (as described in the Psychological Issue for Chapter 8). And siblings who are even a few years apart are likely to experience the same events in different ways. For example, parental divorce might evoke quite different reactions from a 4-year-old than from a 10-year-old.

In the last analysis, biology and experience interact with each other to shape our personalities. In some cases, a person's biological makeup will influence the experience he will have. For example, a thin delicate boy (whom Sheldon would classify as an ectomorph) may be sheltered from rough activities and therefore never learn to behave aggressively. In other cases, a person's biological makeup may influence the way he responds to particular experiences. Thus, a person who is biologically predisposed to be emotional may be affected rather differently by a family crisis than a person without such a predisposition.

Stability and change in personality

In past years it was widely believed that personality is formed in child-hood and adolescence and that it changes little over the rest of a person's life. "In most of us," wrote William James in 1887, "by the age of 30, the character has set like plaster and will never soften again." Sigmund Freud believed that the plaster of personality was set even earlier than that—in the early years of childhood. Although our bodies may become bent by the years and our opinions changed by the times, it was believed that the central core of personality remains basically unchanged. According to a more recent view, however, personality continues to change throughout life.

In fact, there is evidence for both sides of this argument, because personalities typically show both stability and change. As noted in Chapter 9, longitudinal studies have found that certain personality traits, such as activity level and sociability, remain relatively stable from childhood through early adulthood and even through later adulthood (McCrae and Costa, 1984).

Genetic predispositions may provide part of the explanation for this stability. A person who is biologically predisposed to be sociable, for example, may continue to have this predisposition throughout life. In addition, our environment typically plays a large role in keeping aspects of our personality constant. Most of us live within the same culture, hold the same sorts of jobs, and maintain contact with the same sorts of people for most of our lives. Thus, to some extent, all of us get locked into certain roles and expectations that serve to keep our personalities relatively constant.

Nevertheless, people do change over the course of their lives. Certain specific sorts of personality changes are common: on the average, levels of sensation seeking, activity, hostility, and impulsiveness drop slightly as people get older (Rubin, 1981). Beyond such general changes with age, most people's personalities change in their own distinctive ways, often as a result of new experiences. Some people become more doctrinaire and traditional, while others become more open-minded and flexible.

In sum, both stability and change contribute to successful adjustment to life. On the one hand, having a relatively constant personality seems necessary for us to make good decisions about our future. If we are to make intelligent choices—whether of careers, spouses, or friends—we must know what we are like and what we will continue to be like. On the other hand, the potential for growth and change may well be a central hallmark of humanity. As Orville G. Brim, Jr. and Jerome Kagan (1980) have written, "Each person is, by nature, a purposeful, striving organism with a desire to be more than he or she is now."

The various personality theories that we will examine in the next three sections of this chapter take different perspectives on the issue of personality stability and change. Sigmund Freud's psychoanalytic theory emphasizes the enduring influences of early life experiences on personality. Social learning theory points to the ways in which personality may remain stable *and* change, depending on one's learning experiences. And the humanistic theories of Carl Rogers and Abraham Maslow place their major emphasis on people's capacity for lifelong growth and change.

As you consider these various theories of personality, keep in mind that no single theory is necessarily "right" or "wrong." Rather, each theory provides another lens through which we can view the nature and development of human personality. The richest understanding of personality may be gained by considering for yourself the insights offered by each of these theories.

FREUD'S PSYCHOANALYTIC THEORY

Sigmund Freud devised the best-known and most widely studied of all the personality theories, *psychoanalytic theory*. Freud believed that instinctual biological urges, primarily sexual and aggressive, are the forces that motivate every aspect of a person's behavior. Because these impulses are strongly disapproved of by society, they are *repressed*—banished from conscious awareness. Yet these unconscious forces continue to dominate our personality and behavior.

From Freud's viewpoint, we all begin life as biological organisms but become fully civilized and human by taming our biology. But the need to subdue biological impulses inevitably leads to emotional conflicts. Freud's model of personality depicts people as creatures who are perpetually at war with themselves.

Freud grew up in the sexually repressed Victorian climate of nineteenth-century Austria (see Box 2). Perhaps that's why his initial theories of human psychology emphasized people's sexual urges. Later on, after he had lived through the horrors of World War I, Freud was so struck by the spectacle of millions of young men marching to their deaths that he modified his theory to include aggressive urges as well. In Freud's later work, the "death" instincts (aggression) held a place of prominence equal to that of the "life" instincts (or sexuality).

In addition to his emphasis on unconscious instincts and motives, Freud placed a major emphasis on the shaping of personality in the early years of life. He believed that the personality is almost fully formed by the time a child enters school and that personality development after this time consists of elaborating and refining the basic structure.

Freud's psychoanalytic theory is relevant both to normal personality development and to the development of psychological disorder. Thus, after

Sigmund Freud in 1922.

BOX 2

SIGMUND FREUD

Born in Moravia (now Czechoslovakia) in 1856, Sigmund Freud was the son of middle-class Jewish parents. Freud's family emigrated to Vienna, Austria, when he was three, and he spent most of his life there.

As a young man, Freud received a medical degree and opened a practice as a neurologist. But his interests soon came to center on the psychological rather than the physical aspects of mental disturbance. As a young physician, Freud treated many cases of *hysteria,* an emotional disorder in which patients suffered physical symptoms such as twitches, paralyses, and even blindness without any discernible physical basis. At first Freud treated these patients with the "cathartic" method developed by his friend Josef Breuer. In this method, the patient was asked—usually while under hypnosis—to recall the first time she experienced a symptom. This often led to a report of a highly emotional, anxiety-arousing experience earlier in life that the patient had forgotten. Once the patient could recapture the experience and "relive" the emotion felt at the time, the symptoms were likely to disappear. (Such expression of a bottled-up emotion is called *catharsis.*) Later Freud replaced the use of hypnosis in his treatment with the method of *free association,* in which the patient is encouraged to say whatever comes to mind, without holding anything back.

Freud and his family. The 22-year-old Sigmund is standing behind his mother.

Sigmund Freud and his fiancée.

(Freud's approach to therapy is discussed in further detail in Chapter 14.)

Freud's work with his patients gradually led him to his theory that repressed memories and wishes lie at the base of emotional disorder and that personality involves a perpetual conflict between different mental forces. Between 1895 and 1900 Freud published his ideas about anxiety and the defense mechanisms used to control it. In his book *The Interpretation of Dreams,* published in 1900, he developed these ideas further, making use of patients' dreams to probe their unconscious motives.

Most of Freud's work was ignored by scientists until 1905, when he published an explicit account of his theory of sexuality in infants and children. *Three Essays on the Theory of Sexuality* shocked the intellectuals of nineteenth-century Vienna, and Freud quickly became the most unpopular scientist of his day. At the same time, Freud attracted a band of brilliant disciples, some of whom (such as Carl Jung and Alfred Adler) went on to develop major psychological theories of their own.

Freud continued to expand and modify his theories throughout his life. His model of the three mental functions of id, ego, and superego, representing a significant revision of some of his earlier work, was published in 1923, when he was 67.

Most of Freud's books were denounced by other scientists, primarily because his theories attacked many previously unquestioned beliefs. In his later years, however, Freud began to receive the recognition he deserved for his courageous exploration of the human mind. When the Nazis invaded Austria in 1938, Freud was persuaded to emigrate to England. He died one year later at the age of 83.

Freud is now viewed as one of the great thinkers of modern times. His psychoanalytic theory profoundly influenced psychologists of all theoretical persuasions, has been a dominant force in therapy, and has had a major impact on sociology, anthropology, and history. Many ideas that Freud developed have become part of our everyday vocabulary—repression, superego, Oedipus complex, death wish, and many others. In short, Freud has been one of the few people in history to exert a major impact on the way people think about themselves.

outlining psychoanalytic theory here, we will return to it in Chapter 13, in connection with disorder, and in Chapter 14, where we discuss the psychoanalytic approach to therapy.

The structure of personality

For Freud, each person's personality consists of three functions that he labeled the id, the ego, and the superego—three distinct but interrelated systems of psychological functioning. The *id*, according to Freud, is the reservoir of basic biological urges that motivate the individual. The id is hunger, thirst, sexual impulses, and other needs that assure survival, bring pleasure, or provide relief from pain. The id remains an unchanging, powerful, active force throughout life, but its insistent demands are tempered by the ego. The actions of the id usually remain unconscious and out of our awareness.

The *ego* moderates and restrains the id by requiring it to seek gratification of impulses within realistic and socially acceptable bounds. If the id wants to destroy another human being who is frustrating the id's quest for gratification, the ego decides whether or not this can be done easily and safely. Unlike the id, most of the ego's actions are conscious. The ego thus acts like an executive who sees

to it that the gratification of impulses will not be painful, dangerous, or self-destructive.

The *superego* is that force within the self that acquires the values and ideals of parents and society. The superego is the moral part of the personality—similar to what most people call "conscience." It looks to the ideal rather than the real, to what ought to be rather than what is. Further, the superego limits the sexual and aggressive impulses of the id. It pressures the ego to respond to socially approved goals rather than impulse-gratifying ones.

In this three-part structure, the ego mediates between the impulses of the id and the controls of the superego. The id powers the human vehicle, the ego steers it on a safe course, and the superego insists that it obey the traffic laws. As we will see, the conflict of id, ego, and superego causes anxiety, which, in turn, leads to the creation of defense mechanisms to control the anxiety.

Psychosexual development

To the staid turn-of-the-century Victorians, Freud's theory seemed outrageous, because it emphasized the importance of sexual drives not only in adults but also in infants and children. Freud's concept of the sexual

GUILT

Guilt, in Freud's view, is the way our superego punishes us for violating its standards. We can feel guilty for a wide range of "transgressions," from actually harming another person to just thinking unacceptable thoughts. Some people feel guilty when they act assertive, or if they survive a plane crash in which others perished, or if they fail to realize their potential. Some therapists regard guilt as a destructive force and seem bent on erasing it from their patients' minds. But most psychologists distinguish between the "neurotic guilt" that one would best be rid of and the "normal guilt" that is a valuable part of our personalities because it helps us to enforce our positive values (Adams, 1979).

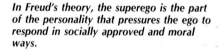

In Freud's theory, the superego is the part of the personality that pressures the ego to respond in socially approved and moral ways.

CHAPTER ELEVEN: PERSONALITY

urge was very broad, however. In fact, his theory deals with not one but three separate pleasure-giving areas of the body. These areas, known as the *erogenous zones,* are the oral zone (mouth, lips, tongue), the anal zone, and the genital zone (penis or vagina). In each case, physical stimulation of the zone can be highly pleasurable, and it is such bodily pleasure that Freud equated with sexuality.

As the child goes through successive stages of development, the different erogenous zones become prominent—first the oral, then the anal, then the genital. And the way in which a child goes through these *psychosexual stages* is a major determinant of personality in later life. For example, if a child receives too much gratification (is overindulged) or too little gratification (is deprived or frustrated) at the earlier stages, he may become *fixated* at that stage—his sexual impulses may stay focused on that stage, and his character structure may reflect the unresolved difficulties of that period. This idea will become clearer as we discuss each of Freud's developmental stages: the oral, anal, phallic, latency, and genital stages.

The oral stage. The *oral stage,* in the first year of life, is the first stage in the child's psychosexual development. According to Freud, during the oral stage the child's sexual energies are focused on the mouth area, in such activities as feeding, sucking, chewing, and biting. Psychologically, the infant has to deal with issues of oral gratification, personal dependency, and trust, because he must depend on and trust adults for his sustenance. Freud believed that an infant who passes successfully through the oral stage will develop into an adult who is able to enjoy oral gratification but is not obsessed with it. Such a person will be basically trusting of other people but not overly dependent on them. But Freud also believed that infants can become fixated in the oral stage if being fed is *too* pleasurable for them or if nursing is painful or frustrating. Overgratification at the sucking stage can lead to an unreasonably self-assured adult, whereas a painful sucking period can produce excessive dependency in the adult. Frustration

during the oral stage might also lead to aggressive oral habits, such as sarcasm or verbal hostility in later life.

The anal stage. During the *anal stage,* in the second and third years of life, the child's sexual energies focus around the anus and the act of defecation. When children are toilet trained, they can decide for themselves whether or not to defecate and, in the process, whether or not to satisfy their parents' desires. The central psychological issues of the anal stage involve giving and holding back, cleanliness and messiness, resistance and compliance. An infant who passes successfully through the anal stage should, according to Freud, develop into an adult who is flexible rather than obstinate or submissive, generous rather than stingy or a spendthrift, and tidy rather than excessively fastidious or messy. If too much anxiety is present at toilet training, the child may grow up to be compulsively clean and orderly and may become intolerant of those who are less so. If the parents lose in the toilet-training contest and the child learns he can always get his way, he may develop a lifelong pattern of messiness, negativism, and attempts to dominate others.

The phallic stage. In the *phallic stage* of development (about ages 3 to 5), the sex organs become the focus of attention. (The term "phallic" comes from *phallus,* the Greek word for penis.) The key event in this stage, Freud believed, is the child's feeling of sexual attraction toward the opposite-sex parent, together with envy of the same-sex parent. Freud labeled this situation, and the psychological conflicts it produces, the *Oedipus complex,* alluding to the Greek myth about Oedipus, who killed his father and married his mother, unaware of their true identity. Of course, killing one's father and sexually possessing one's mother represents an extremely unusual and pathological resolution to the Oedipus conflict. But Freud believed that all children have to resolve such a conflict in one way or another and that the way one goes about doing so has a large impact on subsequent personality development.

According to Freud, the boy at this stage fears that his father will find out

A

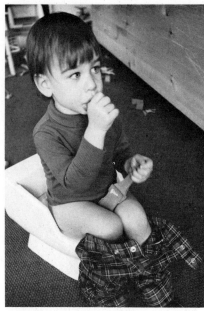

B

In Freud's oral stage of psychosexual development (A), pleasure is focused on the mouth area. In the anal stage (B), the child develops control over a basic bodily function, thereby developing control in other areas of life as well. During the phallic stage (C), the child feels attraction toward the opposite-sex parent, while during the latency period (D), the child's attention is turned away from sexuality and toward such activities as school and play. Sexuality resurfaces in the genital stage (E), when the adolescent becomes interested in heterosexual relationships.

C

E

FREUD AND HIS FATHER

Psychoanalytic theory suggests that unconscious conflicts may influence virtually everything we do, including the way psychologists themselves view personality. As a case in point, it has been observed that Freud himself was unable to develop his theory of the Oedipus complex, which emphasizes a son's resentment and fear of his father, until after his own father had died, when Freud was 40.

D

about the boy's desire to replace him and will punish him by castrating him; this fear is called *castration anxiety.* If the Oedipus conflict is adequately managed, the boy learns to control his envy, fear, and hostility toward his father. He identifies with his father's power and masculinity and converts his hostility into motivation for accomplishment in life. Now the boy wants to be like his father—to be an active, assertive male. This *identification* also leads to the development of the superego—the boy incorporates parental ideals and values into his own personality. Failure to resolve the Oedipus conflict means growing up with an intense fear that a powerful and jealous father might punish the boy for his feelings toward his mother. The boy who fails to resolve the conflict will, Freud be-

lieved, become a man who is timid, passive, and effeminate.

What about girls? Well, to be honest, Freud hardly thought about the problem of female psychosexual development until after he had worked out the Oedipus scenario for boys. As a result, his theory for females (which he named the *Electra complex* after another character in Greek mythology) seems rather strained. According to Freud, girls start, as boys do, loving their mother and resenting their father, because the father is a rival for the mother's attention. During the phallic stage, however, girls realize that they are lacking the more "desirable" sexual organ: the penis. As a result of *penis envy,* the girl becomes attracted to her father as a love object. But eventually the girl must renounce her attraction to her father and, if the Electra conflict is successfully resolved, decide to identify with her mother and find another man to replace her father as a sex object.

Freud's notion of the Oedipus complex and its resolution, even though it may sound a bit far-fetched, provides an interesting explanation for the learning of sex roles (to be discussed in Chapter 16). Adherents of Freud's theory add that the reason that this sequence of early life events seems far-fetched is that, because the conflict is so full of threat and anxiety, we adults have had to banish it from consciousness.

Recent research on the Oedipus complex has led to a mixed verdict on its validity. Studies reviewed by Roger Greenberg and Seymour Fisher (1977) indicate that children generally do have to cope with erotic feelings toward the opposite-sex parent and hostility toward the same-sex parent, as Freud suggested. But there is little proof that this problem becomes especially marked at ages 4 to 5, when Freud thought it did. And boys don't seem to develop a conscience primarily out of fear of castration and punishment, as Freud theorized. Parental nurturance and warmth seem to be more important than fear and punishment in promoting moral development.

The latency period. At the end of the phallic stage (at about age 5), the child enters a period of psychosexual *latency*. During this period, Freud believed, the child's attention is turned away from particular erogenous zones, previous sexual feelings are forgotten, and sexual urges lie dormant.

The genital stage. At puberty, when sexual interest is reawakened, the child enters the *genital stage*. During this stage, sexual energies are again focused on the genital organs—the penis and the vagina. This is the stage of adult heterosexual relationships. Freud didn't have very much to say about the genital stage; he seemed to hold the view that if you passed successfully through the oral, anal, and phallic periods, you would be O.K. Freud's analysis of "adult" problems almost always involved presumed fixations at the earlier oral, anal, and phallic stages.

Anxiety and defense mechanisms

Anxiety is a fear that seems unjustified by any objective threat or danger. It is an exceptionally uncomfortable experience that is hard to cope with because it has no easily identifiable source. Freud believed that anxiety stems from people's unconscious fear that their instincts will cause them to do something they will be punished for. When the pressure of anxiety is excessive and cannot be relieved by practical, problem-solving methods,

the ego must use maneuvers called *defense mechanisms*. Defense mechanisms have two primary characteristics. First, they deny or distort reality. Second, they operate unconsciously, so that the person is not aware of them. Such defensive maneuverings begin in the early years of childhood as we deal with the many threats, conflicts, and frustrations that are a part of growing up. In Freud's view, the methods we develop to handle thousands of little contests with anxiety and frustration are a central part of our personality. Let us look briefly at how some of the defense mechanisms work.

Repression. Repression, the most basic and probably the most widely used defense mechanism, is the exclusion of unacceptable unconscious impulses from consciousness. For instance, you might repress aggressive impulses toward your spouse, or sexual urges toward somebody else's spouse, because of the anxiety such urges would produce if allowed into consciousness.

Projection. Projection is the unconscious attribution of one's own thoughts and feelings to other people. These thoughts, feelings, and impulses are projected onto someone else because they would create anxiety if attributed to oneself. Thus, the censor who thinks modern movies are filthy may be concealing his own strong interest in such sexual activity—an interest that would produce anxiety if allowed into consciousness.

Reaction formation. Reaction formation is the development of behavior patterns that are the opposite of those that might create anxiety. For instance, a person with strong unconscious aggressive urges might become a pacifist. Through reaction formation, the individual is able to avoid the anxiety that would be produced if her unacceptable impulses were actually brought into consciousness.

Displacement. Sometimes the object that will gratify an instinctual urge is not accessible. In such a situation, the urge may be displaced or redirected toward a substitute object. If a young man unconsciously desires to sleep with his mother, he will look for a woman who resembles his mother instead. If an executive is angry at her superior, she may displace her aggressive urge by yelling at her secretary. Substitute objects are rarely as satisfying as the original objects, but they are also less anxiety arousing.

Rationalization. Rationalization is the attempt to substitute "good" reasons for our real reasons. We use rationalization to conceal from ourselves the fact that our real motives conflict with our standards. The man who mistreats his wife may rationalize his behavior by claiming that she needs a strong, dominant male as a mate.

Intellectualization. Through intellectualization, anxiety is kept away by analyzing emotional issues and converting them to theory rather than action. By intellectualizing, problems become detached from the self and removed from unpleasant emotional consequences. Discussions of sexuality in college dorms and coffee shops may sometimes be examples of such intellectualization.

Defense mechanisms are designed to help us escape the pain of anxiety. Most of us would not survive very well without occasionally resorting to such defenses. The trouble is that these defenses may become habitual, characteristic patterns of reacting to conflict; indeed, they may become permanent character traits. As a result, the use of defense mechanisms to deal with anxiety and conflict can sometimes be costly. We will return to the psychic costs of defense mechanisms in Chapter 13, when we discuss anxiety disorders.

Evaluating Freud's theory

When Freud's ideas began to sweep the Western world in the 1930s, there was virtually no proof of their validity. Freud's theory was based on his observations of a limited number of patients and, like all personal observations, they were highly susceptible to bias and distortion. Even today, it is not easy to evaluate psychoanalytic theory scientifically, because it typically does not make specific predictions about personality that can be tested.

Consider, for example, Freud's suggestion that if a nursing baby is afraid her mother will reject or leave her, she will develop a fixation at the oral stage that will lead to an adult with an *oral-dependent* character structure. Such an adult takes a passive, dependent attitude toward the world. She expects to have things given to her when she is good and taken from her when she is bad, instead of learning to satisfy her needs through her own efforts. But does everyone who experiences oral anxiety in infancy develop such a character structure? Well, no. Because dependency of this sort is likely to arouse anxiety, such a person may also develop a character structure that defends *against* dependency. One person may adopt the defense of reaction formation, leading her to resist being dependent on anyone; she can't ask for anything, because that would call forth the anxiety. Another person may use the defense of projection and see *other* people as dependent and feel obligated to help them; such a person may enter a helping profession such as nursing or public service law (Hall, 1954).

Because of the abundance of possibilities, psychoanalytic theory cannot predict the outcome of a particular set of early childhood experiences. Freud himself recognized this limitation: "We never know beforehand which of the determining factors will prove the weaker or the stronger. We only say at the end that those which succeeded must have been the stronger" (1933, page 227). This state of affairs creates a problem for Freud's theory; almost anything can be neatly explained after the fact, while almost nothing can be predicted ahead of time.

Despite the difficulty of testing psychoanalytic theory, there is considerable evidence for the validity of some of Freud's central ideas, including the importance of unconscious motives and conflicts, the impact of early life events on later personality, and the role of defense mechanisms in handling anxiety. Most psychologists now believe, however, that Freud overemphasized sexual and aggressive instincts as the sole source of motivation and that he underestimated the potential for continuing personality development and change

TEDDY BEARS AND SMOKING

A team of British psychologists recently compared the habits of 4-year-old children with certain aspects of their personality and behavior when they were 16. Among their findings: "cuddly" children—those who took stuffed animals to bed with them when they were 4—were less likely than "noncuddly" children to be regular smokers when they were 16. The finding should probably be taken with a grain of salt, but the researchers nevertheless offered an explanation for it. They suggested that having a cuddly object helps make the young child feel secure and, thus, prevents "persistent oral habits," such as smoking (Newson et al., 1982).

after the childhood years. As Greenberg and Fisher (1977) have concluded, "Psychoanalysis is not an entity that must be totally accepted or rejected as a package. It is a complex structure consisting of many parts, some of which should be accepted, others rejected, and the rest at least partially reshaped" (page 28).

Freud's followers

Freud attracted an inner circle of brilliant followers, including the Swiss psychiatrist Carl Jung and the Viennese psychiatrist Alfred Adler. Both Jung and Adler later had differences of opinion with Freud, however, and each broke off to take psychoanalytic theory in his own direction.

For Jung, personality was a product of the balance achieved between conscious and unconscious forces. However, Jung had a different conception of the unconscious than Freud did. Jung distinguished two levels of unconscious: (1) the *personal unconscious*, which encompasses repressed or forgotten material, and (2) the *collective unconscious*, which is common to all humans. According to Jung, the collective unconscious consists of representations of universal human experiences—including mothers, the earth, and even the caves in which our ancestors once lived—which Jung called *archetypes*. Jung believed that these unconscious images are a central part of the healthy personality.

Alfred Adler developed a theory of personality that focused on real or imagined feelings of inferiority. He was the inventor of the term *inferiority complex*. Adler had overcome a series of handicaps early in his own life. Because of rickets, he did not walk until age 4; he then developed pneumonia, which was followed by a series of accidents. These experiences suggested to him that people are strongly motivated to compensate for their felt inferiority. In the Adlerian system of psychology, which has many adherents today, people are seen as overcoming their feelings of inferiority through the attainment of some master goal in life.

Several other psychoanalytic theorists, referred to as *neo-Freudians*,

were strongly influenced by Freud's theory but, like Jung and Adler, gave less priority to the role of instinctual drives and fixed stages of development. Rather than viewing all human motives as derived from the biological urges of the id, they emphasized people's strivings to form satisfying social relationships. The neo-Freudians also gave greater attention than Freud did to the influence of society and culture in shaping human personality. For example, Erich Fromm insisted that ideals like truth, justice, and freedom were genuine human strivings, not just rationalizations of baser motives. Another neo-Freudian, Karen Horney, focused on people's simultaneous needs for acceptance and independence in their social relationships. And Erik Erikson, as noted in Chapter 8, reformulated Freud's theory of psychosexual stages to encompass the entire life span. In addition to the influence of their work in its own right, the neo-Freudians provided an important bridge between Freudian theory and the more recent humanistic theories, to be discussed later in this chapter.

SOCIAL LEARNING THEORY

Whereas psychoanalytic theory emphasizes people's underlying motives and traits, the *social learning theory* of personality focuses directly on people's behavior and is not concerned with underlying motives or traits. The emphasis is on what people *do* rather than on the attributes they *have* (Mischel, 1981).

One of the strongest arguments for such a social learning approach to personality comes from research that calls into question the very existence of "personality traits." This research suggests that, contrary to what you might expect, there is relatively little consistency in people's behavior from one situation to another. Here, we will first consider this issue of behavioral consistency across situations. Then we will look more closely at the mechanisms that social learning theorists propose to help account for people's patterns of behavior in different situations.

Carl Jung

Alfred Adler

Karen Horney

The issue of cross-situational consistency

In the first section of this chapter, we discussed the genetic and environmental roots of personality and we considered ways in which people's personalities remain constant or change over the course of time. In the second section, we examined Freud's theory of personality, including his idea that enduring personality traits are established early in life. Before proceeding further, it is time to take a close look at an important set of findings that may be viewed as challenging the idea that we have "personalities" at all.

In much of our discussion so far we have referred to people's personality traits, such as traits of activity level, sociability, and emotionality. A *trait* is a relatively enduring quality or characteristic of thought, feeling, or behavior that some people have more of than others. We commonly refer to many traits in our daily conversation: "He's such a ruthless person" or "She's the most generous person I know." When we describe people in terms of traits such as ruthlessness or generosity, we usually assume that people will act in accord with these traits in a wide range of situations. From a psychoanalytic perspective, for example, an "oral-dependent" man would be expected to act in his characteristically dependent ways regardless of whether he is with his

wife, his coworkers, or his tennis partner. Similarly, when we describe a person as "conscientious," we are implying that she acts conscientiously in a variety of situations: she always hands in her homework on time, does all the work assigned by her employer, and never fails to send a thank-you note when she receives a present.

But this assumption of *cross-situational consistency*—the notion that people behave in accord with underlying traits in a wide range of situations—has been challenged by a number of studies in which people's behavior has been observed in a variety of situations. After reviewing hundreds of studies of such traits as dependency, masculinity-femininity, and self-control, Walter Mischel (1968) concluded that in fact our behavior is not very consistent across situations. Rather than being determined by underlying traits, our behavior is more often determined by the demands or requirements of the particular situation we happen to be in.

After a little reflection, this inconsistency across situations may not seem surprising. Consider your own behavior. Are you talkative and sociable when out with friends? Well, then maybe you are extraverted. But aren't you sometimes shy and anxious with strangers? Oh, then you must be introverted. You are stubborn at times, right? Yet at other times you are flexi-

People's behavior depends to a large extent on the situations they are in. Thus, Meryl Streep may seem to be a different sort of person when she is shopping for vegetables than when she is accepting an Academy Award.

ble. You are easygoing but sometimes irritable; you are cheerful but occasionally grumpy. In fact, you are all of these things because your behavior depends not only on *you* but also on your situation—whom you are with, where, and when.

One reason for the common tendency to overestimate other people's consistency is that we typically see them in only a small range of situations. Perhaps when you go places with your friend Joe he is almost always jolly and outgoing. But it may well be that Joe is subdued and pensive much of the time when you are not around. When we judge people's consistency with respect to particular traits, we also tend to focus on certain situations and to ignore others. When you say that Joe is "extraverted," for example, what you may really be saying is that Joe is almost always outgoing in a certain set of situations, such as parties. If you stopped to think about Joe's behavior in class, when he rarely says anything at all, you might be led to qualify your statement (Mischel and Peake, 1982).

This is not to say that there is *no* consistency in our behavior across situations. Most of us believe that we are consistent in some respects, and although we may be biased judges, we may also be right. Daryl Bem and Andrea Allen (1974) obtained extensive reports of students' friendliness and conscientiousness in a wide variety of situations. The data came not only from students' self-reports but also from reports by their parents and friends and from observations made by psychologists in several laboratory situations. In general, there was only a small degree of consistency in a person's friendliness or conscientiousness across situations. But there was much greater consistency for those students who themselves stated that they did not vary much from situation to situation on a particular trait. Some students felt that they were consistently conscientious or unconscientious, but not consistently friendly or unfriendly; others felt that they were consistently friendly or unfriendly but not consistently conscientious or unconscientious. In both cases, the students' self-assessments generally seemed to be correct.

We are presumably more consistent in those matters that are central aspects of our personality and that relate to our basic values. In other respects we are more likely to remain flexible and to behave in accordance with the situation.

On the whole, however, Mischel's conclusion that our behavior is not very consistent has been supported by studies in which people are observed in a wide range of situations. Our behavior in specific situations often remains stable over the course of time, but we are not notably consistent from one situation to another (Mischel and Peake, 1982).

Mechanisms of social learning

Psychoanalytic theory and other approaches to personality that emphasize underlying traits and motives have difficulty dealing with evidence suggesting that there is relatively little consistency in people's behavior. In contrast, social learning theory, as developed by such researchers as Albert Bandura (1977) and Walter Mischel (1981), finds such lack of consistency to be quite understandable. The social learning approach tries to explain both consistency and inconsistency by focusing on the mechanisms by which patterns of behavior are learned and on the situations in which the learning takes place.

As already noted, social learning theory focuses directly on people's behavior and is not concerned with underlying motives or traits. In this respect, social learning theory is heavily influenced by B. F. Skinner's behavioristic approach to learning (see Chapter 5). According to this approach, people are most likely to behave in ways that have been reinforced in the past. If Johnny hits his younger brother and thus gets to eat his brother's candy bar—and if he successfully avoids punishment for this behavior—he is likely to do it again. What's more, he may learn from his experience that it is profitable to hit younger children in a variety of circumstances, such as when he wants to ride someone else's bicycle or play with someone else's toys. This learning process, as discussed in

GRANOLA, YOGURT, AND ANTINUKE

We choose to eat particular sorts of foods not only because of their taste or nutritional value but also because the kind of food we eat is a statement—both to others and to ourselves—of the sort of people we are. In one study of college students, it was found that health-food fans, who liked such foods as protein shakes, granola, and yogurt, tended to view themselves as noncompetitive and intellectual, to oppose nuclear power, and to enjoy concerts and plays. Gourmets, who thrived on fresh oysters and lobster Newburg, described themselves as sensual and sophisticated and said they enjoyed sailing and mountain climbing. And fast-food freaks, who subsisted on Big Macs and pizza, tended to describe themselves as logical, conservative, and family-oriented (Sadalla and Burroughs, 1981).

Chapter 5, is called *generalization*. Johnny generalizes the behavior (hitting) to a variety of situations in which it will be rewarding. Similarly, Sally may learn that it is rewarding to cling to her mother's skirt in a variety of situations.

But social learning theory does not predict that Johnny will be aggressive all the time or that Sally will be consistently dependent. If Johnny is encouraged by his success and tries to hit his *older* brother, he may end up with a bloody nose. Or if he tries hitting his younger brother while his parents are around, he may end up sitting in his room without dinner. Because these new behaviors are punished rather than rewarded, he is unlikely to try them again. This learning process, as noted in Chapter 5, is known as *discrimination*—Johnny learns to discriminate between situations in which a particular sort of behavior is likely to be rewarded and situations in which it is not.

From the standpoint of the social learning theorist, these processes of generalization and discrimination explain why there is typically only a small degree of cross-situational consistency in people's behaviors. As Mischel points out, social learning theory suggests that people will behave consistently across situations only to the extent to which similar behavior is expected to have positive consequences. Because most social behaviors (such as aggression) are not reinforced in the same ways in different situations, a high degree of consistency cannot be expected.

Mischel (1981) gives the example of a woman who seems hostile and independent some of the time and passive and dependent at other times. Social learning theory allows for the fact that this woman can have all these characteristics—hostility, independence, passivity, dependence. The qualities that she displays at any particular time depend on where she is, whom she is with, and what she is doing. Rather than considering such a woman to be inconsistent or fickle, social learning theorists would emphasize her adaptability and flexibility. Social learning theory extends Skinner's behavioristic theory of learning by emphasizing the roles of modeling and of other sorts of learning that do not depend on direct rewards and reinforcements. (See the section on cognitive learning in Chapter 5.) According to this viewpoint, behavior is shaped by people's *expectations* of reward or punishment in a particular situation. We form these expectations not only from our own experience but also by watching other people, reading, and listening to other people's explanations. Thus, if Annie saw another girl steal an apple and get

We learn to behave in particular ways not only through direct rewards or punishments, but also through observing the behavior of others.

away with it, Annie might be tempted to try the same thing herself. On the other hand, if Annie saw the other girl get caught and punished, or if she had been convinced by her parents that "crime does not pay," she would not expect this behavior to lead to positive consequences and she would refrain from trying it herself. People may also form more generalized expectations of what will bring rewards, as discussed in Box 3.

In recent years, social learning theory has become an extremely popular and influential approach to the study of personality. Like most popular and influential approaches, however, it also has its critics. Some of these critics contend that by concerning themselves only with people's behavior and not with their underlying attributes, social learning theorists have ended up with a theory of personality that ignores the *person* (Bowers, 1973). In response to such criticisms, Mischel (1981) denies that social learning theorists have lost sight of the person. Instead, he maintains, they have been moving toward an image of the person that stresses the ability to learn from experience and to respond flexibly in a variety of situations.

HUMANISTIC THEORIES

Humanistic theories of personality have been so named because they focus on what their proponents consider to be the unique characteristics of the human species. Humanistic psychologists see people as rational, free to make their own choices about how to live, and motivated to maximize this freedom and to achieve personal growth. Whereas psychoanalytic theory emphasizes some of the baser impulses of the human animal that must be controlled, humanistic theories emphasize the noble strivings of the human being that must be fulfilled.

Humanistic theories also emphasize the way each person views and interprets his or her experience. Most important is each person's image of himself or herself, especially the person's view of his or her own worth, or *self-esteem*. Among the humanistic theorists, Carl Rogers stresses the importance of the self-concept in determining behavior and Abraham Maslow stresses the person's striving to perfect the self.

Carl Rogers

Carl Rogers has practiced psychotherapy since 1927. Like Freud's theory of personality, Rogers's theory evolved from what he saw in his patients; but here the similarity ends. From the beginning, Rogers rejected most of the assumptions of psychoanalysis and focused on each person's unique, conscious, and immediate experiences and his or her need to fulfill the self. "At bottom," Rogers believes, "each person is asking, 'Who am I, *really?* How can I get in touch with this real self, underlying all my surface behavior? How can I become myself?'" (Rogers, 1961, page 108).

According to Rogers, we each try to maintain an organized, consistent image of ourselves, and it is this *self-concept* that directs our behavior and determines how we see reality. The image of the self—as "strong" or "weak," for example—may or may not correspond to the way others see us. Each of us develops our own view of events in the world, so that no one else can precisely understand someone else's unique reality. But we are by no means unconcerned about other people's views of us. To maintain a positive view of ourselves, Rogers believes, we all need *unconditional positive regard*—a general acceptance and appreciation of who we are—from those most important to us.

Almost inevitably, conflicts arise between the values we have incorporated into our self-concept and our actual experiences. For example, Chris may view himself as a "good student" (the self-concept) and yet discover that he does not enjoy his courses (the experience). Or there may be a conflict between the person's *real self* (for example, Mary's view of herself as a gregarious and popular person) and her *ideal self* (she would like to see herself as making a greater contribution to humanity). Such discrepancies—or *incongru-*

Carl Rogers

BOX 3

INTERNAL AND EXTERNAL CONTROL

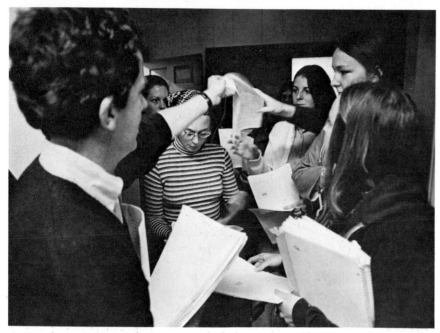

Some students believe that their grades result from their own efforts, while others believe that they have little control over the grades they get.

Would you say that your grades are the result of your own efforts, or do you sometimes feel that you have little to do with the grades you get?

Is making a varsity team usually the result of hard work and persistence, or is it largely a matter of getting the right breaks?

Are you the master of your fate, or is most of what happens to you a matter of chance?

People answer these questions differently. Some think they can easily control their successes in school, in sports, or in life in general. Others feel that their outcomes are controlled by fate, luck, chance, or God's will. These differences are a topic of active current research, showing one application of social learning theory to the study of personality.

Julian Rotter (1966) has argued that people form generalized expectancies about their own behavior. The people who come to believe that they themselves control what happens to them are said to have an *internal locus of control*. The people who come to believe that their outcomes depend on external forces (fate, God, the govern-

ment) are said to have an *external locus of control*. The questions listed at the beginning of this box are adapted from a scale Rotter designed to measure locus of control.

Where does an internal or external locus of control come from? Rotter believes that we generate these expectancies from our everyday experiences. If you repeatedly discover that your efforts are rewarded, you will come to expect to be able to exert control over your outcomes in the future. If you discover that your efforts are of no avail, you will become resigned to lack of control.

Recent studies have shown that experiences that reduce people's opportunities in life are likely to make them more external. For example, women who have children "too soon"—before the age of 19—are likely to face new constraints on their educational and occupational development, and they tend to become more external (McLaughlin and Micklin, 1983).

But other sorts of experiences can give people a greater sense of control over their own destinies—and, as a

result, make them more internal. In one study, unionized workers were found to be more internal than nonunion workers, perhaps because the union workers felt that they had greater control over their wages and work conditions (Seeman, 1966).

How does the behavior of internals differ from that of externals? The most important difference is that people who believe they can control their outcomes will try harder to exert that control. For example, internal people have been found to play a more active role than externals in planning their families. External people are less likely to use effective contraceptives, apparently believing that the decision of whether or not to have children is not really in their own hands (Chilman, 1979).

Similarly, smokers who successfully quit smoking have been found to be more internal than those who were unsuccessful (James, Woodruff, and Werner, 1965). The internal smokers can apparently take themselves in hand and say, "I'm going to kick this habit," whereas externals are more likely to say, "Well, I'm hooked and there's nothing I can do about it." And in a study of executives who faced stressful events, those with an internal locus of control handled their problems more directly and were less likely to suffer from stress-related illness than those with an external locus (Kobasa, 1979). It seems, then, that an internal locus of control can be good for your health.

ences, in Rogers's terms—may propel people to change either their behavior or their self-concept, in the service of personal growth. The person comes to recognize that "it rests within himself to choose; that the only question which matters is, 'Am I living in a way which is deeply satisfying to me, and which truly expresses me?'" (Rogers, 1961, page 119). Rogers's method of therapy, which is intended to help people attain such personal growth and satisfaction, is described in Chapter 14.

Abraham Maslow

Abraham Maslow began his career in 1934 as a behaviorist, persuaded by the view that behavior can be understood in terms of rewards and punishments, without regard to conscious experience. He broke with this tradition, however, following the birth of his first child. Watching a child grow and change, he felt, made behaviorism look "foolish." Maslow spent most of his career, until his death in 1970, developing a new theory of motivation and personality that emphasized positive strivings of human beings.

Maslow accepted the assumption that we have basic biological and social needs that direct our actions, but he felt that these needs were not sufficient to explain all human behavior. As we saw in Chapter 10 (Box 1), he believed each person progresses through a hierarchy of needs. Once the more basic needs (such as for food, safety, and acceptance) are met, the individual pursues the need for *self-actualization,* or the fulfillment of one's total potential. "What a man can be he must be," Maslow wrote in 1954. "He must be true to his own nature. This we may call self-actualization" (page 46).

Maslow felt that too much of psychological theory had been derived from the study of neurotic patients. He sought instead to characterize the healthy, or self-actualized, person. He examined the lives of people who seemed to have lived up to their potential most fully, including Albert Einstein and Eleanor Roosevelt. Maslow found that self-actualized individuals shared certain attributes:

They were accepting of themselves and others, deeply committed to their work, spontaneous in the expression of emotion, and relatively unconcerned about the opinions of others. In addition, these people had a notable lack of guilt, shame, or anxiety.

Maslow's criteria for identifying particular people as "self-actualized" have been criticized as being too subjective and vague. Nevertheless, Maslow made an important contribution by discussing self-actualization as a central human motive. Although few of us can attain this ideal, most of us experience at least a glimpse of self-actualization in moments that Maslow called *peak experiences.* Such experiences of fulfillment may occur in scholarly insight or athletic achievement, in sexual experiences or childbirth, in moments of intense appreciation of music or art, or even in mundane activities when one suddenly feels total appreciation of that moment in time. According to Maslow, such moments play a role in making each of us continue to strive for self-actualization.

Recent research has suggested that people are likely to have peak experiences that are consistent with other aspects of their needs and personalities. People with a strong need for interpersonal intimacy and closeness, for example, are likely to report peak experiences related to intimacy, while people with a strong need to have an impact on others are likely to report peak experiences related to power (McAdams, 1982).

PERSONALITY ASSESSMENT

Much of the research discussed in this chapter relies on the use of various techniques of *personality assessment:* methods of measuring aspects of personality. Personality assessment is a difficult endeavor. Most theories of personality are concerned not only with observable behavior but with traits, dispositions, defense mechanisms, and other such concepts that are presumed to underlie thoughts, feelings and behavior. These constructs are intangible and invisible—no one has ever seen a

Abraham Maslow

"trait" or a "defense mechanism"; instead, they must be inferred from the person's responses or actions. But psychologists have risen to the challenge of assessing personality and have developed several approaches that are currently in use. The particular technique chosen to assess personality is likely to depend on the psychologist's orientation and on the specific purpose of the assessment, whether for research, vocational counseling, or diagnosing psychological problems. In this section we will consider four main approaches to personality assessment: interviews, behavioral observation and rating scales, self-report inventories, and projective techniques.

Each of these methods has its own advantages and liabilities. For one thing, the methods vary in their *reliability*. A method is highly reliable if it can be counted on to lead to the same conclusions about a person's characteristics on successive testings or when administered by different testers. A method is not highly reliable if it is likely to lead to different conclusions from one testing to another or from one tester to another. Just as important as the reliability of a measure is its *validity:* the extent to which the conclusions it leads to about an

individual's personality are accurate. But the validity of any particular personality assessment technique is likely to be debatable; whether someone considers a method valid may depend greatly on that person's underlying conception of personality.

Interviews

The *interview* is a face-to-face session in which a person is asked questions about himself. The interview method is the oldest of the personality assessment techniques. Most of Freud's ideas about personality were derived from his intensive interviews of his own patients, and interviews are still used by researchers and counselors. The specific questions asked depend on the interviewer's purpose. Thus, a vocational counselor may ask an individual questions about the academic subjects that interest her most, whereas a researcher interested in temperament may ask her about the occasions on which she prefers to be alone or with others.

An advantage of interviews is that the questions can be tailored to the individual. Certain areas can be pursued in greater depth where it seems useful, or questions can be rephrased if the person does not fully under-

Interviewers assess people's personalities by asking them questions about themselves. Skilled interviewers pay attention not only to what a person says, but also to how she says it.

stand them. Skilled interviewers not only listen to what the person says but pay attention to how he says it. An interviewer may notice, for example, that the person hesitates in his speech and drums his fingers whenever he speaks of his "wonderful experience" at his last job. These nonverbal signals can sometimes tell the interviewer more than words can.

Despite these advantages, the interview method also has its weaknesses. Because two different interviewers may approach an individual in their own distinctive ways, they may each come away with rather different views of the individual's personality. Indeed, the subject may present himself differently with different interviewers: he may be warm and engaging with one interviewer but cold and aloof with another. As a result, interview results tend to have low reliability: two different interviewers will often disagree in their assessments of the same person. To help overcome this problem, more highly structured interviews are frequently used. The interviewers are trained to ask each person the same questions in the same ways. In some cases, interviewers try to maintain "the best of both worlds" by using interviews that are structured to a large extent but that also allow the interviewer a degree of flexibility in dealing with individual subjects.

Behavioral observations and rating scales

Another approach to personality assessment is to observe people's behavior in various situations. Social learning theorists, with their emphasis on the ways people learn to behave in different situations, are especially likely to employ observational techniques. In one sort of *behavioral observation*, the observer makes precise counts of particular acts that occur during preestablished time periods. For example, an observer may unobtrusively record the number of statements a child makes to his peers and teachers during free-play time at school, as a measure of the child's sociability or extraversion in that situation (Billman and McDevitt, 1980).

Such an observational approach

has the advantage of great reliability and precision. A drawback is that the researcher may be forced to rely on a very small sample of the subject's behaviors in a very small number of situations. This may lead to a rather limited view of the subject's personality. One attempt to remedy this problem is the use of *rating scales*, on which people who know the subject are asked to check off statements that best describe his behavior. Thus, a parent, teacher, friend, or coworker of the subject might be given a series of items such as the following:

_____ shows up for appointments on time.

1	2	3	4	5
Almost never	Rarely	Occasionally	Usually	Almost always

_____ pays careful attention to what he/she wears.

1	2	3	4	5
Almost never	Rarely	Occasionally	Usually	Almost always

_____ keeps his/her work materials carefully organized.

1	2	3	4	5
Almost never	Rarely	Occasionally	Usually	Almost always

Such rating scales can provide valuable information about how the person behaves in a variety of situations, because the information comes from someone who knows the person well. Of course, these raters may also be biased. Parents, for example, may emphasize the positive characteristics of their child and minimize the negative ones. To help overcome this problem, researchers often try to get several different observers to rate the same person and then compare the observers' reports.

Self-report inventories

Other people may know how we behave, but they cannot always know our thoughts and feelings. One way to try to discover these aspects of personality is through *self-report inventories*. The individual is typically presented with a set of statements and asked to rate each of them as true or untrue of her. Or she is asked to choose which of a pair of statements describes her better. Some inventories, such as Rotter's scale of internal versus external locus of control (described in Box 2), measure one specific dimension of personality. Other inventories, such as the *Minnesota Multiphasic Personality Inventory* (MMPI), look at many aspects of personality. Because the MMPI is used extensively in research on personality, we will look at it in greater detail.

The MMPI (Hathaway and McKinley, 1942) was originally designed to diagnose psychological disorders. Its originators gave a large number of statements to psychiatric patients who had already been diagnosed as having specific disorders, as well as to normal individuals. The researchers then made up the final test with only those items that distinguished the patients from normals and that distinguished among the different categories of disorder. The resulting MMPI consists of 550 items that deal with such matters as moods, fears, physical concerns, and preferences for activities. The person rates each item as being "true" of himself, "false," or "cannot say." The items are grouped into ten scales measuring particular personality dimensions. For example, the Social Introversion scale distinguishes people who are socially outgoing and confident from those who are withdrawn and inhibited. It in-

cludes such items as "I enjoy social gatherings, just to be with people." The Depression scale distinguishes pessimistic people from those with more positive outlooks on the basis of such items as "I wish I could be as happy as others seem to be."

In addition to the ten scales, the MMPI includes a Lie scale that tries to check up on how honestly the person is responding. The Lie scale includes such items as "I gossip a little at times" and "Once in a while I laugh at a dirty joke." A person who denies a large number of these statements is presumed to be either a saint or—more likely—answering inaccurately in order to present himself in a favorable light. If a person gets a high score on the Lie scale, the rest of his scores must be interpreted with special caution.

To score the MMPI, psychologists look at the total profile over the scales and compare it to that of others who have taken the test. A sample profile is shown in Figure 11.2. In order to arrive at the best interpretation, computer programs are now widely used to score the tests and to compare each person's profile with that of thousands of others who have taken the test.

FIGURE 11.2

A client's profile of scores on the Minnesota Multiphasic Personality Inventory (MMPI) (left), together with the first page of a computerized interpretation of her profile (right). This client has especially high scores on the "Hypomania" (Ma) and "Psychopathic Deviate" (Pd) scales, suggesting that she is an outgoing, uninhibited person who tends to form superficial and manipulative social relationships.

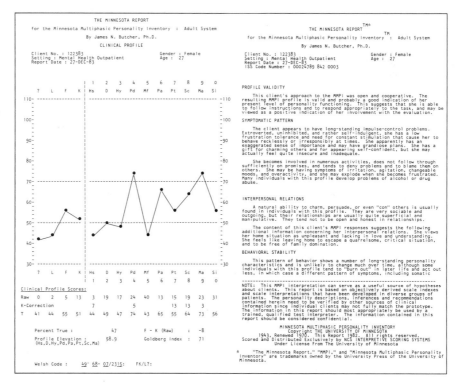

The MMPI was designed to help diagnose psychological disorder and it is often effective in doing so. It has also been widely used as a personality test for normal individuals. We all vary in the extent to which we are trustful of others (Paranoia scale), are concerned about physical health (Hypochondriasis scale), are energetic and impulsive (Hypomania scale), and so on. The MMPI may sometimes be a useful tool for assessing these variations. In one study, for example, scores on the Hypomania scale predicted the speed with which business school students climbed the corporate ladder during the ten years after their graduation (Harrell, 1972). Nevertheless, many psychologists are dubious about the value of using the MMPI for purposes other than the diagnosis of psychological disorder. Other personality inventories, such as the California Psychological Inventory (1957), have been specifically designed to assess personality in normal populations.

Projective techniques

How a person describes herself does not always tell the whole story. Psychoanalytic theorists, in particular, believe that thoughts and feelings that we are not consciously aware of are fundamental to personality. *Projective tests* are methods used to explore these unconscious thoughts and feelings. In a projective test, the individual is given some ambiguous material, such as a picture of a group of people, and is asked what she sees in the picture. Because there are no guidelines or "correct" answers, the person is assumed to "project" her own thoughts and feelings into her response (similar to the way people use the defense mechanism of projection).

One such projective technique is the *Rorschach inkblot test*, named for its developer, the Swiss psychiatrist Hermann Rorschach (1921). This test consists of a series of ten cards on which inkblots are printed. For each card, the subject is asked, "What might this be?" What do *you* see in the inkblot that follows?

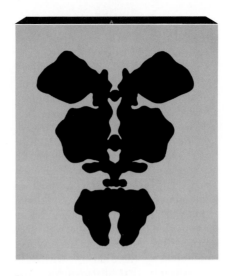

One college student we asked described this blot as having at the bottom "Siamese bears . . . two bears attached at the spine." Another student saw something quite different: "a flower pot . . . that's the pot on the bottom and the flowers on top of it."

Interpretation of inkblot responses requires a great deal of training and experience. In addition to the specific content of the response, Rorschach experts generally focus on how much of the blot the person refers to in his response and which features produce the response. For example, using only a small portion of the blot, as the first student did, is often taken as an indication of a need for precision and attention to details. Giving many responses that seem fairly common and obvious, such as the second student's flower pot, can be taken to indicate that the person is fairly conventional. Such interpretation is difficult and subjective, and even the experts do not always agree on how a response should be interpreted. Thus, there is some doubt about the reliability of the Rorschach technique as a means of assessing personality. Nevertheless, Rorschach inkblots are widely used by therapists—in conjunction with other sorts of evidence, such as intensive interviews—to provide insight into a person's inner needs.

Another commonly used projective technique is the *Thematic Apperception Test* (TAT) devised by Henry Murray in 1938. Murray used a series of drawings such as the one that follows.

THE NAZI PERSONALITY

It is easy to assume that the leaders of Nazi Germany, who were responsible for the annihilation of millions of people, were madmen. Molly Harrower (1976) had the Rorschach responses of leading Nazi officials (obtained when they were awaiting trial at Nuremberg) scored by a panel of 15 experts who didn't know whom they were evaluating. They did not identify the Nazis as being mentally disordered. Nor did they discover any particular commonalities in the personality profiles of the men. Harrower doubts that the Nazi leaders were insane, suggesting instead that they may have been normal people, caught in the grip of strong social forces.

The person being tested is asked to indicate who the people are, what led up to the situation, and what the outcome will be. Before you read further, think about what *you* see happening in this picture. Here is the story that one college student constructed: *The young woman has lived in a small town all her life but has never found happiness there. She has just told her mother she is leaving to go to New York City to see what life is all about. She will not find wealth and happiness there but will return to her hometown, happy that she at least tried, and will take care of her mother in her last years.*

Another college student saw something quite different in this picture: *The women are standing in an elevator. The older woman is a pickpocket and is trying to take the younger woman's wallet. The younger woman is daydreaming and has no idea of what is going on. When she gets home she will curse herself for being so stupid.*

To interpret such responses on the TAT, psychologists note consistent themes running across several stories. If, for example, the first student tells several stories about leaving loved ones and having to meet personal goals, a psychologist might conclude that she has some guilt about seeking independence. Or if the second student tells several stories about being incompetent, it might suggest that she has low self-esteem. Many precise systems for scoring TAT responses have been developed, such as the

scoring for the need for achievement described in Chapter 10 (Box 3). In some of these cases, TAT responses seem to provide valuable information about people's motives and to correlate highly with their observed behavior. As with the Rorschach, however, some psychologists question the reliability of the TAT. You can probably think of several stories to match the adjoining picture, each with a very different theme. Which story will give the appropriate insights into the "real" you?

As we have seen, there are many different approaches to assessing personality, and some of them are surrounded by a good deal of controversy. Perhaps this should not be surprising. After all, the concept of "personality" itself is a complex one, and different theories make different basic assumptions about what personality is and how it develops. Nevertheless, most psychologists believe that it is essential to understand people's distinctive patterns of needs, temperaments, and values. And so efforts continue to find good ways to assess personality and, ultimately, to come to a fuller understanding of the differences and similarities in the ways in which people adapt to the situations of life.

SUMMARY

- **1** *Personality* is the pattern of characteristic behaviors, thoughts, and emotions we use to deal with our environment.

The roots of personality
- **2** Personality has both genetic and environmental roots. There seems to be a large genetic component in several aspects of personality, including such traits as sociability, activity level, emotionality, and impulsivity. However, experiences modify genetic predispositions in a number of ways. Each person not only shares general experiences with others in his or her culture but also has unique experiences that help shape personality.
- **3** Personality is characterized by both stability and change. Although certain aspects of personality re-

main remarkably stable over a lifetime, other aspects change, often as a result of new experiences.

Freud's psychoanalytic theory

• **4** *Psychoanalytic theory*, as formulated by Sigmund Freud, views personality formation in terms of an inner struggle between our basic biological urges and our need to subdue them.

• **5** In Freud's view, personality consists of three parts: the *id*, which seeks to gratify instinctual needs; the *ego*, which controls gratification of the id; and the *superego*, which embodies the standards and ideals of parents and society.

• **6** Freud identified five stages of *psychosexual development*, the first three of which center around a particular *erogenous zone*. Failure to resolve conflicts at any of the earlier stages can result in *fixation* at that stage, as reflected in lifelong personality traits.

• **7** In infancy one goes through the *oral* and *anal* stages. At about age 3 the child enters the *phallic* stage. During this period the boy must resolve the *Oedipus complex* and overcome castration anxiety, while the girl must deal with the corresponding *Electra complex*. The childhood years are called the *latency period*, while puberty brings on the *genital* stage.

• **8** Freud thought that individuals use *defense mechanisms* to unconsciously distort or deny reality so that *anxiety* will be reduced. Common defense mechanisms include repression, projection, reaction formation, displacement, rationalization, and intellectualization.

• **9** Freud's theory is difficult to evaluate scientifically, because his ideas can be used to explain things after the fact but not to predict behavior ahead of time. Nevertheless, some of his central ideas appear to be valid, while others have been called into question.

• **10** Carl Jung postulated that personality is the outcome of the balance between conscious and unconscious forces. In Jung's view, the unconscious consists of two parts: the *personal unconscious* of the individual and the *collective unconscious* that is common to all human beings.

• **11** Alfred Adler believed that personality development is a result of people's need to overcome inferiority by striving to master a major goal in life.

• **12** The *neo-Freudians*, such as Horney, Fromm, and Erikson, accepted many of Freud's basic ideas but emphasized the role of society and culture in influencing personality.

Social learning theory

• **13** Most theories of personality assume the existence of *cross-situational consistency* in personality. However, many studies have found a minimal amount of consistency in people's behavior from situation to situation.

• **14** The *social learning theory* approach to personality focuses on the person's behavior rather than on underlying motives or traits. It was influenced by Skinner's behaviorist approach. People develop ways of behaving on the basis of rewards and punishments, generalization and discrimination. People can also learn from observing models and by developing expectations about what kinds of rewards and punishments will be connected with a particular situation.

• **15** People who learn that their behaviors will in general be rewarded come to expect success, and their perceived *locus of control* is *internal*. People who come to believe that their behaviors have no effect generally may come to expect failure; their locus of control is *external*.

Humanistic theories

• **16** *Humanistic theories* of personality focus on the individual—on how each human being makes choices of how to live and how to maximize his or her potential.

• **17** According to Carl Rogers, one's *self-concept* directs one's behavior and determines how one sees reality. All of us need *unconditional positive regard* from others who are important to us, in order to develop a positive self-view.

• **18** According to Abraham Maslow, individuals who have satisfied their basic needs are then motivated to pursue *self-actualization*. Most people get at least a glimpse of self-actualization through moments called *peak experiences*.

Personality assessment

• **19** Psychologists use a wide variety of techniques to measure personality. The major approaches to personality assessment include interviews, behavioral observations and rating scales, self-report inventories, and projective techniques.

• **20** The *interview* method is the oldest assessment technique. It can be used for a number of different purposes and can be tailored to the individual. However, interview results tend to have low reliability because of variations among interviewers.

• **21** With the *behavioral observation* technique, the researcher observes the subject's behavior and records information. A related technique is to have people who know the subject respond to *rating scales* containing items about the subject's behavior.

• **22** *Self-report inventories* can be used to measure one specific aspect or several aspects of personality. One of the most widely used inventories is the *Minnesota Multiphasic Personality Inventory* (MMPI), which was originally developed to diagnose mental disorders.

• **23** *Projective tests* are designed to gain insight into unconscious thoughts and feelings. These tests include the *Rorschach inkblot test* and the *Thematic Apperception Test* (TAT). Because interpretation of tests results is difficult and subjective, there is some debate about the reliability of projective tests as a means of assessing personality.

KEY TERMS

cross-situational consistency
defense mechanisms
ego
erogenous zones
fixation
humanistic theories
id
identification
interview
locus of control
MMPI
neo-Freudians
Oedipus complex
peak experience
personality
projective tests
psychoanalytic theory
psychosexual development
reliability
Rorschach inkblot test
self-actualization
self-concept
self-report inventories
social learning theory
somatotype
superego
Thematic Apperception Test
trait
unconditional positive regard
validity

HAPPINESS

William James defined it as "the agreement of a person's inner life with his outer experiences." Jean Jacques Rousseau was more concrete: it is "a good bank account, a good cook, and good digestion." Howard Mumford Jones was probably right when he concluded that it "belongs to the category of words, the meaning of which everyone knows but the definition of which no one can give."

Each of these men was referring to the concept of "happiness." People differ in how they define it, how they pursue it, and how completely they attain it. But for all of us happiness is an ultimate goal. We make the major decisions of our lives based not necessarily on what is

practical but on what we think will make us happy. Indeed, Thomas Jefferson wrote into the Declaration of Independence that the pursuit of happiness is a basic right, ranked alongside life and liberty. And now psychologists are trying to determine just what happiness is and how we get it.

WHAT IS HAPPINESS?

In one attempt to pin down this elusive concept, Jonathan Freedman (1979) asked a large number of people for their definitions of happiness. About half of the sample spoke of happiness in terms of fun, excitement, and good times. To them, happiness was a life full of

pleasurable activities. Rousseau's definition, emphasizing plenty of money and good food, probably falls into this category. For the other half of the people, happiness was defined in terms of contentment, satisfaction, and freedom from worries. For them, happiness was a quieter, internal state of being, often described as "peace of mind." But even though some people stress pleasurable activity and others stress quiet contentment, the difference is really a matter of emphasis. Almost everyone recognizes both good times *and* peace of mind as central to happiness. People merely differ in the mixture of these two aspects that they consider to be necessary.

When most people speak of hap-

Both good times and peace of mind are central to happiness.

*F*or all of us happiness is an ultimate goal.

piness, they are referring to a relatively enduring state of mind, which may last for months or years. Such an enduring state can be contrasted to momentary moods or emotions, such as the "happiness" we feel when our team wins a game or the "unhappiness" we feel when dinner is burned. Data from surveys suggest, however, that the momentary moods and more enduring states of happiness are related. For example, Norman Bradburn (1969) asked peo-

ple about the number of good and bad feelings they had experienced in recent weeks—how often they felt pleased, excited, lonely, restless, or upset. He found that the extent to which good feelings outnumbered bad feelings was related to people's ratings of their overall state of happiness. In other words, even burned dinners will not make you miserable as long as there are enough winning games and other good moments to compensate.

WHO IS HAPPY?

Over the past 30 years, the University of Michigan's Institute for Social Research has conducted national surveys, asking Americans to rate their level of happiness as well as asking them about many other aspects of their lives. In a 1978 survey that asked people about the positive and negative emotions they had experienced within the previous few weeks, 87 percent of the respondents reported that they had felt pleased about accomplishing something; 74 percent had felt that things were going their way; and 74 percent had felt particularly excited or interested in some-

Satisfying social relationships are among the most important ingredients of happiness.

Money and prestige are not the keys to happiness.

thing. During the same period, 30 percent had felt depressed or very unhappy; 48 percent had felt restless; and 22 percent had been upset by personal criticism. Thus, although life has its highs and lows, it seems that for most people the good moments are more common than the bad ones. Not surprisingly, then, people report fairly high levels of overall happiness. In the same survey, 30 percent of the respondents rated themselves as "very happy," 55 percent as "pretty happy," and only 10 percent as "not too happy" (Campbell, 1981).

By relating these reports of moods and overall happiness to other information, we can get some notions of what contributes to happiness. As it turns out, few objective characteristics are related to happiness. Younger people, in the so-called "prime of life," are not generally happier than elderly people. People who live in rural areas are no more nor less happy, on the average, then city-dwellers.

Money and prestige do not seem to be the keys to happiness either. While there is a slight tendency for the rich to be happier than the poor, the differences are not as large as one might expect. People living in extreme poverty are unlikely to be very happy, but beyond this extreme, comparing the lowest and highest income groups in the 1978 survey, the percentage rating themselves as "very happy" were 25 percent and 32 percent respectively—really not that different.

If objective characteristics do not predict happiness, what does? The surveys find that social relationships are important. On the average, people who are married are happier than those who are single, divorced, or widowed. Especially among single people, those with close friendships are happier than

those without them. Whether it is provided through marriage, relatives, or friendship, caring about others and feeling cared about in return seems to be an important component of happiness. (As we will see in the next chapter, satisfying social relationships can be good for our health as well.)

Even more important than social relationships are people's feelings about themselves. Those who report that they are satisfied with themselves and feel in control of their lives are happier than those who take less pride in their abilities and who feel like a pawn of external forces.

The overall pattern of findings is quite consistent with Abraham Maslow's hierarchy of needs, presented in Chapter 10 (Box 1). Maslow proposed that human beings first try to satisfy survival needs, such as those for food and safety, and then strive for love and self-esteem. Since most Americans have achieved at least a minimal level of health and wealth (the basic survival needs), it is the higher needs of love and self-esteem that make the most difference in whether or not they are happy.

WHEN GOOD FORTUNE WEARS OFF

Even good fortune—say, winning a million dollars—has relatively little enduring impact on our state of happiness (Brickman et al., 1978). One explanation for this anomaly is that we adapt to whatever conditions we live in (Brickman and Campbell, 1971). As we saw in Chapter 4, our sensory organs quickly adapt to a certain level of stimulation. For example, if someone is used to living near a superhighway, he does not "hear" the noise. In the same way, we get used to a certain standard of living.

Winning a state lottery is a thrilling experience. Over the long run, however, it does not seem to make the winners any happier.

DEFINITIONS OF HAPPINESS
Happiness is wanting what you want, getting what you get, and hoping the two will coincide.

HOWARD MUMFORD JONES

Happiness is when I can do the things I want without having to look for a ride or be home by dinner.

A 9-YEAR-OLD BOY (FREEDMAN, 1979)

What makes me happy? Freedom . . . freedom to be alone or with others. Freedom to move about and choose my professions. Freedom from pressures. Freedom even now, when I am physically handicapped, to use my time as I please.

A 79-YEAR-OLD WOMAN (FREEDMAN, 1979)

If you can't be happy—and who the hell is—you can at least have a good time.

ALEXANDER KORDA

After a while, our current circumstances come to seem "normal"— and not a cause for happiness or sadness. What makes us happy, then, depends on what we are used to.

A study by Philip Brickman and his colleagues (1978) dramatically illustrated this process of adaptation. They interviewed a group of people who had recently won a state lottery and a comparable group of people who had not had the thrill of suddenly coming into a lot of money. The subjects were asked how happy they were now, how happy they had been six months earlier, and how happy they expected to be in another six months. They were also asked to rate how pleasurable they found several routine experiences, such as having breakfast, talking with a friend, getting a compliment, or reading a magazine. Lottery winners were not significantly different from the comparison group in their past, present, or expected level of happiness. And in some respects, they were worse off than the nonwinners. They found less pleasure in the more mundane activities of life. After a major positive change in their lives, the simple pleasures took on less meaning for them.

Our expectations are an important determinant of how we perceive our situation. In the Institute of Social Research surveys, one of the happiest groups of people consisted of those who had little education, and hence low expectations about earnings, but who had managed to earn a great deal; those with similar income but higher education were somewhat less happy, perhaps because they had expected this income all along. By the same token, people who have had an unhappy childhood are not necessarily unhappy as adults (Freedman, 1979). When they compare their current life with their past life, they feel happy to be where they are. If we are to gain the greatest pleasure from our good fortune, we would do well to remember our humble origins.

A TALENT FOR HAPPINESS?

We all know some people who are always making the best of a situation and others who always seem to look at the dark side of things. Is there some talent for happiness that some of us have and others don't? Paul Costa and Robert McCrae (1979) think so. They gave a large number of men a series of personality tests and asked them to rate the number of positive and negative feelings they had recently experienced. They found that high scores on the personality dimension of "extraversion" (being sociable, active, and involved in life) related to the number of positive feelings the men reported.

And high scores on the personality dimension of "neuroticism" (being anxious, impulsive, and hostile) related to the number of negative feelings they reported. This suggests that people high in extraversion and low in neuroticism will find the most satisfaction with life. Indeed, Costa and McCrae found that scores on these personality traits—which seem to be based in part on heredity—predicted the men's ratings of their happiness ten years later.

In all of this, can we find a recipe for happiness? Not with any great degree of certainty. People with certain characteristics—who are married, have an adequate income, and have a positive sense of self—are happier than people without these resources. But there is no one set of factors that absolutely ensures happiness. And even good fortune will have little impact on happiness if it leads us to raise our standards and expectations. It seems that happiness is not a possession that one can acquire and hold on to, but rather a process that we keep working at. Thomas Jefferson chose his words carefully: we cannot possess happiness, but only pursue it.

SUMMARY

- *1* Happiness is a relatively enduring state of mind that has elements of both pleasurable activities and peace of mind. A majority of Americans report high levels of overall happiness.
- *2* Happiness does not seem to be significantly related to objective characteristics such as age and income. Rather, the most important factors in happiness appear to be strong social relationships and high self-esteem.
- *3* Happiness depends to a large extent on the conditions people are adapted to and on their expectations.
- *4* Certain personality traits, such as extraversion and a lack of neuroticism, seem to predispose people toward happiness.

PSYCHOLOGY AND HEALTH

Our physical health is closely related to our states of mind and our behavior. The new field of health psychology is concerned with these links.

CHAPTER 12

STRESS

What is stress?
The biology of stress
Stress and illness
Coping with stress

Stress can take a heavy toll on our emotional and physical health. We need to learn how to cope with stress effectively.

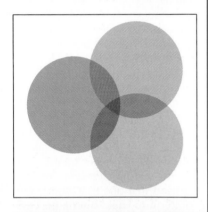

PSYCHOLOGICAL PROCESSES AND ILLNESS

Psychology and heart disease
Psychology and cancer

Our emotions, personality, and behavior are directly linked to the development of many illnesses, including heart disease and cancer.

PSYCHOLOGY AND HEALTH CARE

Behavioral medicine
Doctors and patients
Patients in hospitals

Psychological approaches to health care emphasize the need for people to take responsibility for their own health.

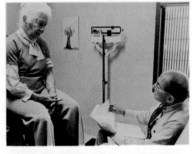

PREVENTING ILLNESS

Smoking
Exercise
Wellness

We can prevent illness before it happens by adopting healthier patterns of behavior.

PSYCHOLOGICAL ISSUE
ALCOHOL ABUSE

BOXES
1 Life Change and Illness
2 The Power of Placebos
3 "Friends Can Be Good Medicine"

Alcohol misuse can do damage to virtually every system of the body.

- Emily Brown has been promoted to the position of division head in her company. She receives a higher salary, but is now under great pressure to improve her division's performance. Every week she must report her division's sales figures to the company president. After a few months in the new job, Janet starts suffering from severe headaches and soon afterward is diagnosed as having ulcers.
- Mary Peters and Arlene Delano both had breast cancer. The disease had been discovered at the same stage of progression in the two women, and both received the same treatment—a mastectomy (breast removal), followed by intensive drug treatment. Mary died within two years. Arlene has lived for five years without a reappearance of cancer and may well live a normal life span. What made the difference?
- Mark Berry has been in the hospital for three weeks, following surgery for a stomach condition. Many doctors and nurses pop in and out of Mark's room, but their relationship with him is detached and impersonal. Although he is given several medicines, he doesn't know why he is taking them. Mark is beginning to feel that he has no role in managing his own health.
- Stanley Warnock has been smoking two packs of cigarettes a day since his late teens. Now in his early forties, he knows that if he keeps smoking he is greatly increasing his risk of heart disease, cancer, and other illnesses. He has quit several times, but each time has gone back to smoking within two months. Stanley's problem is how to stop for good.

These cases give us glimpses of some of the many ways in which psychology relates to people's health.

Since ancient times, people have known that there are links between the state of people's minds and the condition of their bodies. Throughout history, people have thought that faith and belief can modify the course of an illness. In modern times, however, there has been a split between the approaches of medical science and of psychology. Modern medicine has emphasized the physical causes of illness—genetics, microorganisms, injuries—and physical approaches to treating them, such as drugs and surgery. Only in the past 15 years has it become increasingly recognized that people's thoughts, moods, personality, and behavior can have a large impact on the development of illness, its treatment, and its prevention.

As part of this new recognition, the field of *health psychology* has grown rapidly in the past decade (Matarazzo, 1980). Health psychologists study the role of psychological factors in the development of disease, in coping with illness, and in the promotion of health. They frequently work with physicians and other health care professionals in developing and applying behavioral procedures to treat illness and maintain health. Health psychology builds on work in various areas of psychology, including research on learning, motivation, emotion, personality, and social behavior. Health psychology is also concerned with the close links between mental health (to be discussed in Chapters 13 and 14) and physical health.

In this chapter, we will explore some of the major areas of intersection between psychology and health. First we will examine stress—sometimes viewed as the greatest health risk of modern times—and ways in which people can better cope with it. Then we will look at psychological factors in two of the most prevalent and lethal illnesses, heart disease and cancer. Next we will explore psychological aspects of health care, including techniques of behavioral medicine, the nature of doctor-patient communication, and the psychological effects of hospitalization. Finally, we will consider psychological aspects of the prevention of disease and the maintenance of "wellness." A central theme to be emphasized throughout the chapter is that it is valuable for people to become actively involved in managing their own health—both when they are sick and when they are well.

STRESS

Almost everyone knows what it means to experience stress. We perceive some threat or challenge in our environment and we feel uncomfortable and pressured. We may feel tense, anxious, or depressed—sometimes all at the same time. And we may experience unwelcome physical symptoms, such as a tightening of the muscles or a sense of fatigue. Stress is especially acute among poor people,

who must continually worry about scraping together a living, feeding their children, and simply surviving in crumbling and crime-ridden neighborhoods. Even among people who live in relative comfort, however, modern life often seems to be full of stresses, including competition at school or work, worries about financial security, family strains, and even concerns about our very survival in a perilous nuclear age. Stress, especially when it continues over a period of time, can contribute to a wide range of illnesses. Thus, health psychologists are particularly concerned about understanding stress and learning how people can cope with it more effectively.

What is stress?

The term *stress* has been defined in several different ways. Sometimes the term is applied to stimuli or events in our environment that make emotional and physical demands on us, and sometimes it is applied to our emotional and physical reactions to such stimuli. In this discussion, we will refer to the environmental stimuli or events as *stressors* and to the emotional and physical reactions as *stress*.

Stress commonly involves both emotional reactions, such as feelings of anxiety or depression, and psychological symptoms, such as tightened muscles and a sense of fatigue.

Driving in heavy traffic to school or work can take a toll not only on your car, but also on your health. Daniel Stokols and his coworkers (1978) studied 100 commuting workers at two California companies. The commuters' blood pressure was measured as they pulled into the company parking lot each day, and it was checked again periodically on the job. The researchers found that the longer the commute and the worse the traffic, the more the workers' blood pressure increased, and the higher it remained during the workday. Long commutes were also found to be associated with bad moods at work.

Many sorts of events can be stressors, including disasters such as hurricanes or tornadoes, major life events such as divorce or the loss of a job, and daily hassles such as having to wait in line at the supermarket when you need to be somewhere else in ten minutes. What all these events have in common is that they interfere with or threaten our accustomed way of life. When we encounter such stressors, we must pull together our mental and physical resources in order to deal with the challenge. How well we succeed in doing so will determine how serious a toll the stress will take on our mental and physical well-being.

The Canadian physiologist Hans Selye (1976) has been the most influential researcher and writer on stress. Selye has proposed that both humans and other animals react to any stressor in three stages, collectively known as the *general adaptation syndrome*. The first stage, which occurs when the person or animal first becomes aware of the stressor, is the *alarm reaction*. In this stage, the organism becomes highly alert and aroused, energized by a burst of epinephrine. After the alarm reaction comes the stage of *resistance*, as the organism tries to adapt to the stressful stimulus or to escape from it. If these efforts are successful, the state of the organism returns to normal. If the organism cannot adapt to continuing stress, however, it enters a stage of *exhaustion*, or collapse.

Selye developed his model of the general adaptation syndrome as a result of research with rats and other animals. In rats, certain stressors, such as painful tail-pulling, consistently lead to the same sorts of stress reactions. In humans, however, it is harder to predict what will be stressful to a particular person at a particular time. Whether a particular stimulus will be stressful depends on the person's subjective appraisal of that stimulus: How threatening is it? How well have I handled this sort of thing in the past? How well will I be able to handle it this time? For one person, being called upon to give a talk in front of class is a highly stressful stimulus that will immediately produce such elements of an alarm reaction as a pounding heart and a dry mouth. For another person, being called on to give a talk is not threatening at all, but facing a deadline to complete a term paper is extremely stressful. In humans, moreover, the specific stress reaction is likely to vary widely: Some stressful situations give rise predominantly to emotions of fear, some to anger, some to helplessness and depression.

The biology of stress

It is the dawn of human history, and Homo sapiens steps out from his cave to watch the rising sun paint the horizon. Suddenly he hears a rustling in the forest. His muscles tense, his heart pounds, his breath comes rapidly as he locks eyes with a saber-toothed tiger. Should he fight or run for his life? He reaches down, picks up a sharp rock and hurls it . . . .

It is the start of another working day, and Homo sapiens steps out of his apartment building into the roar of rush hour. He picks his way through traffic and arrives at the corner just in time to watch his bus pull away. Late for work, he opens his office door and finds the boss pacing inside. His report was due an hour ago, and the client is furious . . . . The man eyes a paperweight on his desk and longs to throw it at his oppressor. Instead, he sits down, his stomach churning, his back muscles knotting, his blood pressure climbing. He reaches for a Maalox and an aspirin. . . . (Wallis, 1983, page 48)

Our bodies' reactions to stressors originated, in the course of our evolution, to deal with physical threats, such as attacking animals. When faced with stress, the body mobilizes for action, in what is often called the *fight-or-flight reaction* (Cannon, 1932): The heart speeds up, the breath comes quickly, the muscles tense, whether in preparation to throw a rock or to run away. In twentieth-century society, this reaction is usually brought on by circumstances in which neither "fight" nor "flight" is quite appropriate—traffic jams, financial problems, grim news reports, job pressures, and other frustrations of modern life.

The fight-or-flight reaction is similar to the alarm reaction described by Selye. When the organism identifies a threat, activity in the sympathetic nervous system increases and the adrenal medulla (a portion of the adrenal gland) secretes the hormones epinephrine (adrenalin) and norepinephrine into the bloodstream. At the same time, hormones called *corticosteroids*, which release fatty acids for energy, are secreted by the outer shell (or cortex) of the adrenal gland. As a result of this nervous system and hormonal activity, digestion stops, the level of blood sugar rises, and the heart pumps more blood to the muscles. These reactions are quite the same as the physiological aspects of strong emotions, such as fear and anger (see Chapter 10).

Most descriptions of the biology of stress have focused on this initial alarm (or "fight-or-flight") reaction, the first stage of Selye's general adaptation syndrome. But the body continues to react to stressful situations in later stages as well. If the stress persists, the body recovers from the initial alarm reaction and the organism begins coping with the situation. During this stage, the activity of the sympathetic nervous system decreases, epinephrine secretion is reduced, but there is still an above-normal level of corticosteroid secretion. Finally, if the stress continues and the body cannot cope with it, there is likely to be a breakdown of bodily resources. In this exhaustion stage, there may be a reduction of the levels of epinephrine and norepinephrine in the brain, a state associated with depression. All of these reactions, if continued over a long period of time, can be harmful to the body.

Stress and illness

In many stressful situations, the body's responses can improve our performance—we become more energetic, more alert, better able to take effective action. But when stress is encountered continually, the body's reactions are more likely to be harmful than helpful to us. As will be seen later in this chapter, the continual speeding up of bodily reactions and the production of stress-related hormones seems to make people more susceptible to heart disease. And stress reactions can reduce the disease-fighting effectiveness of the body's immune system, thereby increasing susceptibility to illnesses ranging from colds to cancer. Other diseases that can result at least in part from stress include arthritis, asthma, migraine headaches, and ulcers. Workers who experience the greatest degree of job pressures have been found to be especially likely to suffer from a large number of illnesses (House, 1981). Moreover, many studies have shown that people who have experienced major changes in their lives are at unusually high risk for a variety of illnesses, as discussed in Box 1.

As an example of stress-induced illness, take the case of stomach ulcers, small lesions in the stomach wall that afflict one out of twenty people at some point in their lives. Ulcers are a common disorder among people who work in occupations that make heavy psychological demands, from assembly line workers to air traffic controllers. In many of these cases, stress is the culprit. Stress leads to increased secretion of hydrochloric acid in the stomach. Hydrochloric acid normally helps to break down foods during digestion, but in excess amounts it can eat away at the stomach lining, producing ulcers.

Stress may also contribute to disease in less direct ways, by influencing moods and behavior. People under stress may become anxious or depressed and as a result may eat too much or too little, have sleep difficulties, smoke or drink more, or fail to exercise. These behavioral changes may, in turn, be harmful to their health. In addition, people are more likely to pay attention to certain bodily sensations, such as aches and pains, when they are under stress and to decide that they are "sick" (Mechanic, 1968). If the person were not under stress, the same bodily sensations might not be perceived as symptoms and the person might continue to feel "well." Some researchers have suggested that assuming the role of a "sick person" is one way in which certain people try to cope with stress (Cohen, 1979). Instead of dealing with

MEDICAL STUDENT'S DISEASE
Two people may interpret the same set of bodily sensations—say, a tightness in the muscles of the neck—in very different ways. One person may disregard the sensations, while another may consider them to be symptoms of illness (Pennebaker, 1982). People's activities and goals help to determine how much attention they will pay to such sensations. Athletes who are deeply involved in a competitive race or game may well be unaware of such physical discomforts as sprains, muscle pulls, and sometimes even broken bones. Medical students, in contrast, are constantly having their attention directed toward bodily functions. As a result, they often report having a large collection of symptoms—a phenomenon sometimes called "medical student's disease" (Mechanic, 1972).

CHAPTER TWELVE: PSYCHOLOGY AND HEALTH

BOX 1

LIFE CHANGE AND ILLNESS

Soon after Richard Nixon resigned the presidency in 1974, he became seriously ill with phlebitis, and his wife, Pat, suffered a stroke.

After a major earthquake in Athens in 1981, the incidence of fatal heart attacks there rose sharply.

People who lose their jobs are highly prone to illness. One study found that for each 1 percent increase in the national unemployment rate there was a 2 percent increase in deaths due to heart disease and liver cirrhosis (Brenner, 1973).

As these events and findings suggest, the stresses caused by major changes in people's lives are likely to give rise to serious illness.

The impact of life changes on illness was first studied systematically in the 1950s by Thomas Holmes. When Holmes interviewed thousands of tuberculosis patients, he discovered that in a strikingly large number of cases the disease had begun after the occurrence of a major life change, such as a death in the family or a new job. These events clearly did not *cause* the illness—tuberculosis is caused by a bacterium—but the stress seemed to lower people's resistance to the disease.

To establish a scale that might predict the onset of disease, Holmes and Richard Rahe (1967) asked several hundred people to rate the degree of social readjustment required by each of forty-three major life events. The single event rated as the most traumatic in terms of necessary readjustment was the death of a spouse. The other events on the "Top 10" list of crises, in descending order of severity, were divorce, marital separation, a jail term, death of a close family member, personal injury or illness, marriage, loss of a job, marital reconciliation, and retirement. Among the runners-up were pregnancy, gain of a new family member, and career change.

The relation of illness to life crisis was confirmed in a detailed study of 2500 officers and enlisted men aboard three Navy cruisers (Rahe, 1968). Life-change data were gathered for six

Stressful life changes, such as the death of a loved one, can make people more susceptible to illness.

months and then health-change records were obtained after the sailors had spent six months at sea. In the first month of the cruise men in the high-risk group (those who had been exposed to major life changes before embarking) had nearly 90 percent more illnesses, on the average, than the men in the low-risk group. And the high-risk group continued to have more illnesses each month than their lower-risk shipmates.

Note that the life changes on the Holmes and Rahe scale include several events that are generally considered to be positive, such as getting married or having a child. Even a positive event such as marriage may require extensive readjustment of one's life patterns and, as a result, can be stressful. Not surprisingly, however, when two events require the same

amount of readjustment, negative life changes are likely to take a greater physical toll than positive life changes (Johnson and Sarason, 1979).

Although a great deal of research has focused on the effects of major life events, Richard Lazarus and his colleagues have argued that life's daily hassles and frustrations—the petty quarrels, the pile of bills to be paid, the traffic jams—have at least as great an effect on mental and physical health (DeLongis et al., 1982). No single hassle may have much of an impact, but when taken together these annoyances can lead to anxiety, depression, and illness. This focus on daily hassles does not contradict the research on major life changes, how-

The daily hassles of life can also take their toll on people's health.

ever. In fact, one of the reasons that major life changes—the loss of a job, for example—are so devastating is that they have a "ripple effect" on people's daily lives, multiplying the number of minor stresses and strains that must be coped with.

Of course, the same life event will be more stressful for some people than for others, depending on their unique situations and expectations. A job change, for example, may be relatively smooth for a person who has sought out the change and prepared for it but traumatic for someone who is abruptly transferred by his company. Remember that events in themselves are not necessarily "stressful" or "nonstressful"— what makes all the difference is the way that a person deals with them.

the stressful situation directly, these people fall sick. After all, it is often more acceptable in our society to be sick and to seek medical help than it is to admit that one cannot cope with the stresses of life.

Coping with stress

It is Friday evening and two young lawyers, both associates in a large firm, get phone calls at home from the senior partner who is supervising them. The trial date for an important case has been moved up. Each of the lawyers will now have to have her portion of the trial brief completed by Monday morning. It is a threatening situation for both. Each must do extensive research and then complete a cogent document of some forty pages, all in the space of a single weekend. What's more, each knows that her work will be evaluated by the firm's partners, and how well she does may greatly influence her future in the firm. One of the lawyers finds the situation extremely stressful: she feels tremendous anxiety, experiences headaches and stomach upset, and finds it impossible to work effectively. She somehow manages to produce a report, but she is not at all happy with it. The other lawyer, although she too feels the pressure of the situation, sees it not so much as a threat but as a challenge—an opportunity to rise to the occasion. She moves into the firm's offices for the weekend and, sleeping only about three hours a night, completes her portion of the brief with a clear mind and a surge of energy.

As this example helps illustrate, stress is caused not so much by events themselves as by the ways in which people perceive and react to events. As the Greek philosopher Epictetus declared almost 2000 years ago, "We are not disturbed by things, but by our opinions about things." To cope with stress effectively, we often need to redefine the situation from one of threat to one of challenge or opportunity.

An important influence on people's ability to cope with stressful situations is the degree of control they feel they can exercise over the situation. Both animals and humans have been found to cope better with painful or threatening stimuli when they feel that they can exercise some degree of control, rather than being passive and helpless victims (Thompson, 1981). Such a sense of control can help minimize the negative consequences of stress, both psychological and physical. In one well-known experiment, Jay Weiss (1972) administered electric shocks to pairs of rats. In each pair, one of the two animals was given a degree of control over the situation: it could reach through a hole in its cage and press a panel that would turn off the shock both for itself and for its partner. Thus, the two rats received exactly the same number of shocks, but one was passive and helpless while the other was in control. After a continuous 21-hour session, the animals were sacrificed and their stomachs examined for ulcers. Those rats who could exert control had much less ulceration than their helpless partners.

The ability to control painful stimuli often benefits humans too. For example, the loud music coming from your stereo is probably not stressful; in fact, it's quite enjoyable. But the same music coming from the place next door can be terribly irritating and stressful. As noted in the Psychological Issue on noise pollution (Chapter 4), merely knowing that one can control a noise seems to make it less bothersome (Cohen and Weinstein, 1981). That's one reason why your blaring stereo doesn't bother you—you know you can always turn it off.

Even when you can't control them, unpleasant events tend to be less stressful if they are predictable—if you at least know *when* they will occur. This was demonstrated by Weiss (1972) in another study with rats. One group of rats heard a buzzer about ten seconds before they would receive a shock; although the animals could not escape the shock, at least they had a chance to prepare themselves for the expected pain. A second group of rats received no such warnings; the shocks came unpredictably. Weiss found that the rats who were forewarned of the shocks developed fewer ulcers than the rats who were not forewarned. This finding, too, has

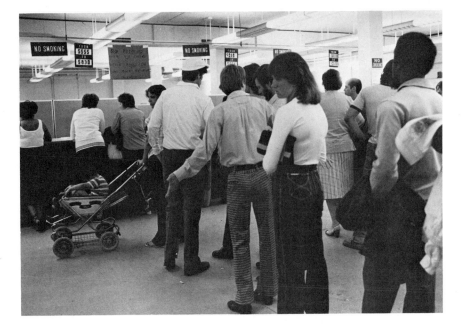

People can cope better with the stress of unemployment if they are prepared for the layoff and if they experience some control over the situation.

WHY PRESIDENTS STAY HEALTHY

Being President of the United States might seem to be a stressful job. Yet the presidency does not seem to have been harmful to the health of its occupants. The first eight Presidents, from George Washington to Martin van Buren, lived an average of 79.4 years. On the average, those Presidents who died natural deaths exceeded the life spans of their Vice-presidents by a good margin. And not a single President is known to have suffered from the common stress-related illness of ulcers. As Martin Tullai (1984) points out, although the President is faced with tough problems, he is also given the means to cope with them. Rather than being a "stressful" job, the presidency seems to be a challenging one, which may actually have a positive effect on health.

parallels in human life. The death of a loved one, for example, is usually less traumatic when it is anticipated than when it is unexpected. On a less tragic level, many students find surprise quizzes to be more upsetting than scheduled quizzes that they can prepare for.

The fact that events tend to be less stressful when we control them—or, at least, when we know that they are coming—has implications for the treatment of patients with various illnesses. As we will see later, patients often feel helpless, without the ability to control their destinies or even to predict the course of their illnesses. If the patient's sense of control can be increased, he is more likely to feel better about himself and even, in some instances, to achieve a better recovery.

Are some people generally better than others at coping with stress? Recent research suggests that the answer is yes—that there is a certain kind of person who has a relatively *stress-resistant personality*. Suzanne Kobasa (1982) has found that people who cope well with stress tend to be committed to what they are doing (rather than alienated), to feel in control (rather than powerless), and to welcome moderate amounts of change and challenge. In studies of men and women in various occupations, Kobasa and her associates

(1982) have used self-report personality tests to measure these interlocking components of commitment, control, and challenge. They have found that among people who are facing stressful life events, those with stress-resistant personalities—that is, those who are high in commitment, control, and challenge—experience fewer physical illnesses than those whose personalities are less hardy.

Until recently, it was generally believed that to maintain good health people should strive to avoid stressors in their lives. Such a strategy can be quite limiting, however. The desire to avoid stress may also lead people to avoid potentially beneficial changes in their lives, such as job changes or promotions. Moreover, the attempt to avoid stress is often unrealistic: How, for example, can a person avoid such shocks as a parent's death? But the finding that some people manage to cope effectively with stress provides a useful counterpoint to the one-sided message, "Avoid stress." Indeed, if people do not confront a certain amount of stress in their lives, they will end up being bored and unstimulated, which can also be physically harmful. In the last analysis, each person needs to come to terms with stress in his or her own way, sometimes trying to avoid it but sometimes accepting it or even seeking it out, as a challenge to be mastered.

PSYCHOLOGICAL PROCESSES AND ILLNESS

Even in ancient times it was believed that people's states of mind—their emotions, their beliefs, their religious faith—could influence their health. As medical knowledge advanced, however, the direct causes of many diseases were traced to such external agents as bacteria and viruses. These discoveries helped extricate medical science from superstition, but they also led to the premature conclusion that mind and body were entirely separate.

It is now clear, however, that psychological factors often interact closely with biological factors in causing illness. As indicated in Figure 12.1, the causes of disease can be divided into three major categories (Borysenko, 1983). Two of these sets of causes are biological: hereditary predispositions and environmental factors. The third cause is psychological. The hereditary predispositions include inherited weaknesses in certain body tissues or organs that increase susceptibility to disease. The environmental factors include microorganisms that cause disease, chemical pollutants in the air or water, and even some natural ingredients of the food we eat, such as saturated fats (which may contribute to heart disease). Psychological factors include stress and other aspects of our emotions, states of mind, and behavioral styles.

Psychological factors are sometimes the primary determinants of disease, as in certain types of headache, certain skin rashes, and stomach ulcers. Such diseases are sometimes called *psychosomatic*—which, needless to say, does not make them any less real. In other cases, perhaps even more prevalent, psychological factors interact with biological factors in producing disease; that is, states of mind can determine whether processes that are initiated by hereditary or environmental factors will in fact cause disease or will be fought off. In the remainder of this section, we will look at the ways in which psychological factors can contribute

to two of the most serious diseases of our times, heart disease and cancer.

Psychology and heart disease

Heart disease is Western society's number one killer. It accounts for one-third of all deaths in America and for well over half the deaths among middle-aged men. Heart disease was relatively rare in America at the turn of the century, but it has risen dramatically since then, with a slight downturn since 1960. Heart disease is often viewed as a disease of modern living, spurred on by the habits and the stresses of industrialized society. Evidence for this idea comes from the fact that non-Western societies have relatively low rates of heart disease. And there is a higher rate of heart disease among immigrants to America, such as Japanese-Americans and Chinese-Americans, than among those who remain in their native country, suggesting that something about the Western environment promotes the development of the disease (Shapiro, 1983).

Heart disease usually involves the formation of a fatty substance called *plaque* in the walls of the coronary arteries that supply blood to the heart. If the arteries become narrowed enough or blocked, the person may suffer a heart attack (death of a region of heart muscle tissue). Among the many factors that have been found to be related to the risk of developing heart disease are high blood pressure (or *hypertension*), a history of heart disease among one's close relatives (indicating a possible genetic predisposition to the disease), cigarette smoking, being greatly overweight, and a high level of a fatty substance called cholesterol in the blood. In addition to all of these well-established risk factors, it is now clear that stress can have a major impact on the development of heart disease. People who continually undergo a great deal of stress—and who lack the ability to control it—are at significantly greater risk for heart disease than people who undergo less stress or who can manage stress successfully. Jobs that impose high psychological demands but that provide the worker with little

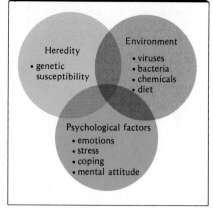

FIGURE 12.1

Hereditary, environmental, and psychological factors can interact with one another in causing disease.

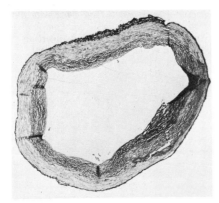
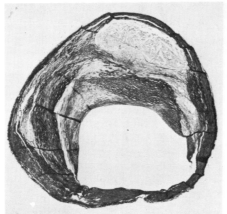
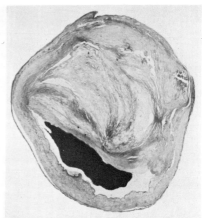

Heart disease involves the blockage of the arteries that supply blood to the heart. Depicted here are a normal artery (left), an artery with fatty deposits (center), and a plugged artery with fatty deposits and a blood clot (right).

control—such as cook, waiter, and hospital orderly—seem to breed heart disease (Karasek, 1981).

Whereas some jobs may make heavier psychological demands than others, certain sorts of people, regardless of their occupation, seem to make heavy psychological demands on themselves—and, as a result, run a greater risk of heart disease. People with a particular personality style, called the *coronary-prone behavior pattern* and commonly labeled *Type A*, have been found to be especially susceptible to heart disease (Friedman and Rosenman, 1974). Type A people

are hard-driving, competitive, and aggressive. They experience great time urgency, always trying to do more and more in less and less time. People who have an opposite, more laid-back sort of personality are termed *Type B*. Others are categorized somewhere in between. The best measure of the Type A behavior pattern is a structured interview, intentionally designed to be stressful, in which people are asked challenging questions about their life-styles. The responses are judged not just in terms of what the people say but in terms of how they say it: Type A people are

Jobs that make heavy demands and provide the worker with little control over his activities, such as the job of a short-order cook, increase the risk of heart disease.

People who display a Type A behavior pattern—hard-driving, tense, and competitive (top)—are more susceptible to heart disease than people with a more relaxed, laid-back Type B pattern (bottom).

likely to speak in a fast, loud, explosive style and to display clenched fists and aggressive facial expressions (Chesney, Eagleston, and Rosenman, 1981).

Many studies have confirmed that Type A people are more susceptible to heart disease than Type B people (Dembroski et al., 1984). One probable reason is that Type A people tend to make greater demands on themselves and to expose themselves to more stressful situations than do Type B people. One study of college football players found, for example, that Type A players were rated by their coaches as playing harder than Type B players when they were injured (Carver, DeGregorio, and Gillis, 1981). Type A people also tend to have an unusually intense physiological reaction to the stress that they encounter. When they are faced with a challenging situation, they tend to manifest higher blood pressure and greater increases in heart rate and in the level of epinephrine in their blood than Type B people. Some researchers believe that this greater physiological reactivity when under stress—sometimes called *hot reactivity*—is the key to the link between the Type

CHAPTER TWELVE: PSYCHOLOGY AND HEALTH

A pattern and heart disease (Dembroski et al., 1984).

The bulk of the research on psychological factors in heart disease has focused on men, rather than women. Even among women who face highly stressful situations, whether at work or at home, the risk for heart disease remains considerably lower than for men. Many biological and psychological factors may contribute to this difference. Among them is the consistent finding that although women tend to express their emotions more openly than men do, their physiological reactions to stress tend to be less intense (Frankenheuser, 1983). In terms of the risk of heart disease, then, it may be better to let one's emotions show outwardly than to bury them inside where they may eventually cause damage to one's body.

Because of the links between the Type A behavior pattern and heart disease, various approaches have been taken to changing this pattern of behavior. For example, Type A people have been taught relaxation exercises and other techniques to manage stress. They have been encouraged to develop nonstressful hobbies, and they have been given therapy sessions to help change their pressured view of the world. Some programs have had a degree of success in altering the behavioral and psychological reactions of Type A individuals (Suinn, 1982). So far, however, the success has been limited. The Type A pattern seems to be learned over the course of many years, and it is supported by the competitive, achievement-oriented aspects of Western society. As such, it is not a simple matter to change this pattern. Indeed, as Joan Borysenko (1984) notes, "One of the most stressful things for a Type A is to be told to relax."

Psychology and cancer

Cancer is the second leading cause of death in America. It remains one of the least understood diseases and, partly for that reason, one of the most feared. In cancer, cells of the body become altered and then multiply rapidly, creating clusters of cells whose growth is uncontrollable. These cell clusters, or malignant *tumors*, can proceed to invade bodily tissue and cause damage to the body's organs. In many cases, the eventual outcome is death.

Medical scientists are just beginning to understand the biological mechanisms of cell behavior that underlie the onset and development of cancer. But even though these mechanisms remain mysterious, it's clear that in several respects cancer can be linked to behavior. The likelihood of cancer can be greatly increased by exposure to certain substances in the environment, including cigarette smoke, asbestos, chemical wastes, and radiation. We cannot always control our own exposure to such *carcinogens* (cancer-causing agents), but in at least some instances we can. Another aspect of behavior that can affect the course of cancer is a person's efforts to help detect cancer at an early stage, when it is more likely to be treated successfully. That is why, for example, women are encouraged to examine their breasts regularly and to seek medical advice if they note any unusual changes.

There is also increasing evidence that people's emotions are involved in the progression of cancer once it has begun. In a study of women who underwent mastectomy for early-stage breast cancer, Steven Greer and his coworkers in England (Greer and Morris, 1981) found that women who reacted to their diagnosis with either a fighting spirit or strong denial were more likely to be free of disease eight years later than were women who reacted with stoic acceptance or with feelings of helplessness. Other recent research suggests that those women who complain the most about their breast cancer—who express their anger outwardly, instead of keeping it inside—have a better chance for recovery (Levy, 1984).

Recent studies have begun to shed light on the biological mechanisms that may account for such links between emotions and cancer. These links involve the functioning of the body's *immune system*, a collection of billions of cells that travel through the bloodstream and defend the body against invasion by foreign agents,

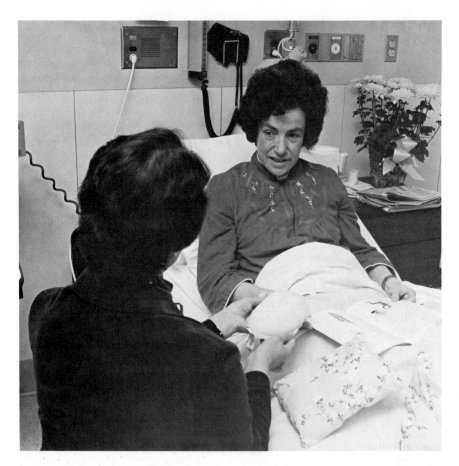

A cancer patient's emotional reactions may affect the course of her illness. Women who react to their diagnosis with a fighting spirit have been found to have a better chance of recovery than women who feel resigned and helpless.

including bacteria and viruses, and against cells that become cancerous. Psychological factors can influence immune functioning, and the expanding field of research on these influences is called *psychoimmunology* (Borysenko, 1983). It is believed that small cancers form frequently in everyone but that our immune systems usually reject them. However, prolonged stress may lead to elevated levels of corticosteroids and to lower levels of the neurotransmitter norepinephrine in the brain. These and other changes apparently make it harder for the immune system to reject cancer cells. When the organism copes with the stress in an active way, these changes in the immune system seem to be minimized; when the organism reacts with helplessness and depression, the changes are maximized.

These links between stress, helplessness, immune function, and cancer have been demonstrated experimentally in studies with animals. In one study, Lawrence Sklar and Hymie Anisman (1979) injected three groups of mice with the same number of cancer cells. One group was then exposed to an electric shock that they could learn to escape by jumping over a barrier to safety. A second group was exposed to the same duration of shock but had no means of actively coping with the stress. The third group was never shocked. The cancers grew fastest and led to earliest death among the animals that had no means of coping with their stress. In contrast, the animals that could mount an effective escape response did not differ in tumor growth from those that had not been shocked at all. Other studies have directly linked such inescapable stress to changes in the animal's immune system—for example, to a suppression of the proliferation of disease-fighting lymphocytes in the bloodstream (Laudenslager et al., 1983).

The link between stress, helplessness, and cancer has been demonstrated in humans as well. In one dramatic study, Richard Shekelle and his coworkers (1981) studied over 2000 men who had taken a psychological

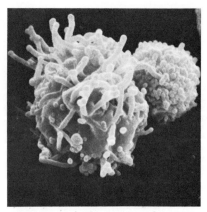

This electron micrograph shows a cancer cell (magnified about 8000 times) in the foreground. The smaller cell in the background is a type of white blood cell called a "natural killer cell." The killer cell produces chemical changes that cause the cancer cell to swell up and burst like a balloon. But when people are under stress, the functioning of their natural killer cells may be impaired.

CHAPTER TWELVE: PSYCHOLOGY AND HEALTH

test that diagnoses depression and other emotional states. Seventeen years later, the researchers found that those men who had been highly depressed at the time of the testing had twice the chance of dying of cancer as men who had not been depressed. Since depressed people might drink more alcohol or smoke more cigarettes, which might in turn increase the risk of cancer, Shekelle took this into account when he analyzed the data: the association between depression and cancer still held, regardless of drinking or smoking rates. In another study, widowed husbands were found to have a decline in the function of their white blood cells—part of the immune system—within two months of their wives' deaths (Schleifer et al., 1980).

Findings on the links between emotional reactions to stress and the progression of cancer have given rise to some recommendations for the treatment of cancer patients. In particular, programs that can help give cancer patients a greater feeling of control over their own destinies and that can help them to adopt a "fighting spirit" might just increase their odds. So far, however, there is no solid evidence that such programs can in fact extend people's lives (Levy, 1984). Developing programs that might have such an impact is an exciting frontier in health psychology.

PSYCHOLOGY AND HEALTH CARE

The traditional medical approach to health care has emphasized the direct biological treatment of illness—in particular, the use of drugs and, when necessary, surgery. In this traditional model, the patient is viewed as a relatively passive participant in the health care process. The "good patient" does little more than follow the doctor's orders and take his medicine when he is supposed to. In the past decade, however, this traditional model has begun to change. Psychologists are joining forces with other health care professionals to develop behavioral treatments for a variety of illnesses, as well as to prevent ill-

nesses from occurring. In these approaches, patients become more active participants in their own treatment. Psychologists have also been seeking ways to improve the relationships between physicians and patients and to humanize the situation of hospitalized patients.

Behavioral medicine

Behavioral medicine refers to the application of a wide variety of behavioral techniques to the treatment and prevention of illness. Most of these techniques represent applications of learning principles, as discussed in Chapter 5 and the Psychological Issue on "Behavior Control." These learning techniques may be applied to both voluntary responses, such as keeping one's medical appointments or taking prescribed medications, and involuntary physiological responses, such as altering one's blood pressure or stomach activity.

So far, the most widely used and successful programs in behavioral medicine have focused on the management of stress and anxiety. One commonly used stress-management technique is *progressive muscle relaxation*, in which people are taught to discriminate tension in various muscle groups and then to relax these muscles. If you were in such a relaxation program, you might first be asked to wrinkle your forehead and notice the feeling of strain in the forehead muscles. After maintaining the tension for about ten seconds, you would be instructed to let the forehead muscles completely relax and to notice the difference in the sensations. You would then move on to other groups of muscles—in your neck, your arms, your legs, and so on. Over a period of time, people who master this technique can learn to be more relaxed in day-to-day situations.

In another approach to managing stress and anxiety, certain techniques of meditation (see Chapter 3, Box 4) have been adapted by behavioral medicine practitioners. Herbert Benson (1975) has found that people can learn to produce a *relaxation response* by following four simple steps for 15 to 20 minutes, once or twice a day: Sit in a comfortable position, close your

Psychologist Arnold Lazarus (right) conducts a relaxation therapy session, teaching people to progressively relax different groups of muscles.

eyes, concentrate on a single word, phrase, or sound, and cast off all other thoughts. When distracting thoughts arise, just let them come in and go out, and then return to your focus. The relaxation response produced by such training is the physiological opposite of the fight-or-flight stress response; for example, the heart rate and breathing rate slow down and blood pressure decreases. By learning to produce this response, people can sometimes relieve such stress-related conditions as high blood pressure and headaches.

Other behavioral treatments make use of *biofeedback* to help people gain control over their physiological responses. In biofeedback, electronic devices are used to monitor various physiological responses so the person can see just what his body is doing. As discussed in Chapter 5 (Box 3), biofeedback has been used with some success to teach people to control their heart rate and blood pressure (Goldstein, 1982). Efforts have also been made to apply biofeedback to a variety of other physiological responses, including muscular tension in people who suffer from certain backaches and headaches, breathing responses in asthma patients, and even brain-wave patterns in epileptic patients (see Chapter 2, Box 2).

Many other techniques of behavioral medicine are being developed and used. For example, hypnosis (discussed in Chapter 3) has been used effectively in the treatment of certain psychosomatic disorders and in the alleviation of pain. As we will see later, behavior modification techniques have been successfully applied to such health-related goals as helping people to stop smoking or to keep exercising. In addition, techniques of cognitive behavior therapy (see Chapter 14), in which people's erroneous beliefs about themselves and their health are altered, have been used to help people cope with serious illnesses. As noted in Box 2, one factor that contributes to the success of various techniques is the patient's expectation that the technique will in fact be effective.

Techniques of behavioral medicine typically give patients a more active role in their own treatment than traditional medical treatments do. The patient herself must be motivated to learn to manage stress, to alter her physiological responses, or to change her health-related habits. These techniques have the added benefit of increasing the patient's sense of control over her own health—and this in itself can be helpful in coping with stress and promoting health.

BOX 2

THE POWER OF PLACEBOS

The history of medicine lists many remedies that seem outlandish in light of modern science. Moss scraped from the skull of a hanged criminal, powdered reindeer horns, and crocodile dung have all had their day as wonder drugs. The real wonder of such treatments is that in some cases they have actually worked.

These and other nostrums, from snake oil to swine's teeth, could not have exerted their effects through any specific biological action. In many instances, however, such "drugs" have had real physical effects, including improvements in skin condition and recovery from fever (Jospe, 1978). In such cases, certain physiological reactions of the patient are apparently put into gear by his faith in the healer or the treatment.

Until recently, medical researchers have not taken seriously the possibility that belief or faith could modify the course of illness. In recent decades, however, researchers have begun to bridge the gap between mental and physical events. We have already seen how people's emotions and states of mind can be involved in the development of such diseases as heart disease and cancer. It now seems clear that if psychological factors can contribute to causing diseases, they can help cure diseases as well. The mind is indeed a two-edged sword that can both wound and heal.

The unorthodox treatments of faith healers can help because of *placebo effects*. A placebo is any treatment that has no specific biological influence on the condition being treated. If you have a bacterial infection and are given a sugar pill, that pill is a placebo because sugar does not affect bacteria. Placebos do not have to be pills, however. They can be any treatment, such as special diets, hot compresses, exercises, or even surgical procedures that do not really have a direct effect on the source of your pain or discomfort. The placebo effect is the effect of your *expectations* on your bodily reactions.

Placebo effects play an important role not only in faith healing, but also in conventional medical practice. Placebos are especially useful in controlling pain. Chronic pain—continuing, often severe pain associated with such maladies as recurring headaches and lower-back problems—is among the greatest of human miseries. The pain is sometimes incapacitating, and physicians are often at a loss in treating it effectively. At the same time, it is clear that such pain is highly influenced by psychological factors. There is not necessarily a direct link between tissue damage and pain, and how much pain a person experiences may depend greatly on his emotional state.

In most studies of the effects of sugar pills and other placebos on pain, about one-third of the patients are helped (Beecher, 1959). When placebo drugs were given in eight different studies to patients with tension headaches, there was an average of 35 percent improvement in their condition (Blanchard and Andrasik, 1982). Part of the effectiveness of other pain treatments, such as hypnosis (discussed in Chapter 3) and acupuncture (discussed in Chapter 4), may also be due to placebo effects. If patients *expect* these treatments to work, they have a better chance of being effective.

Placebos may work to alleviate illness and reduce pain in several different ways. First, the patient's expectation that he will get better may

enhance his motivation to behave in healthy ways. The patient who has "faith" may try harder—he may drink more fluids, eat healthier foods, and exercise more—and these behaviors may help to improve his condition. Second, the patient's positive expectations may influence his interpretation of bodily sensations. While one person may interpret a particular pattern of sensations as "painful," another person—who expects the pain to subside—may reinterpret the same sensations as aches or twinges that are not really painful.

Third, positive states of mind can have direct effects on physiological processes, including the activity of the autonomic nervous system and of hormones, which may in turn influence one's state of health. Indeed, there is evidence that placebos may stimulate the release of endorphins, the brain's "natural pain-killers" (see Chapter 2). In one study, volunteer dental patients were given only placebos to reduce pain following tooth extraction. For some individuals, the placebos worked. But for these people, the administration of naloxone, a chemical that is known to block the effects of the endorphins, worsened the pain. This result clearly suggested that the placebo worked by affecting the patients' brain chemistry (Fields, 1978).

It has been said that wise physicians use new drugs while they still have the power to work. The saying refers to the high expectations that exist for all new treatments—and which sometimes help them to succeed. After a while, as failures become more widely known, the drug becomes less effective. The power of placebos is relevant to medical treatment more generally and, especially, to doctor-patient relationships. The most effective physicians may be those who inspire the confidence of their patients—and, as a result, can help bolster the patient's faith that she will get well.

Doctors and patients

After complaining of chest pain for several weeks, Ralph Bissinger, a 46-year-old truck driver, went to see his family doctor. Following a series of tests, Dr. Kaiser diagnosed Ralph as having angina (a discomfort in the chest caused by a deficiency of blood to the heart muscle) and high blood pressure. If treated, these conditions could be kept under control; if left untreated, they would make Ralph a prime candidate for a heart attack. Dr. Kaiser prescribed methyldopa (a medication for high blood pressure), a diuretic (a medication that increases urine flow and thus helps to remove excess fluid from the body), and a salt-free diet. He also told Ralph to "take it easy" and to lose weight. These recommendations were sound medical advice. However, Ralph stopped taking the methyldopa when he found that it made him feel dizzy. He kept forgetting to take the diuretic. And because he was on the road so often in his job, the salt-free diet was almost impossible for him to follow. He did cut back on desserts and was able to lose a few pounds. But he could not "take it easy" because he was determined to save the money needed to send his three children to college. When Dr. Kaiser saw Ralph on a follow-up visit, he reprimanded his patient for not following medical advice. Dr. Kaiser considered Ralph to be a "noncompliant patient" (adapted from DiMatteo and Friedman, 1982, page 35).

This case illustrates one of the biggest obstacles to effective medical treatment, the problem of *patient compliance* with doctors' recommendations. An estimated one-third to one-half of all patients fail to follow fully the treatments prescribed for them, and this noncompliance often represents a hazard to the patient's health (Stone, 1979).

In recent years social psychologists studying the problem of patient compliance have focused on the nature of the interactions and relationships between doctors and patients. They have found that several factors contribute to the high rate of noncompliance. One contributing factor is that in too many cases patients don't understand what their doctors are telling them (Golden and Johnston, 1970). Some of the miscommunication occurs because doctors often make use of technical medical terms that are simply not in their patients' vocabulary. Such miscommunications as the following would be funny, if the consequences were not likely to be so serious:

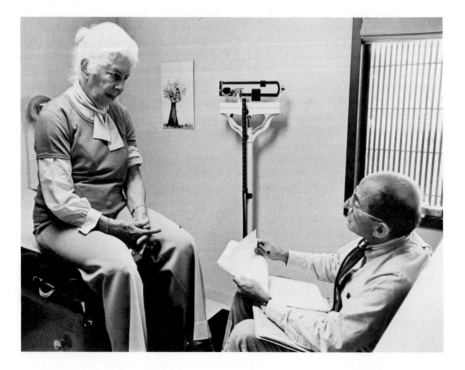

Patients are most likely to follow their doctors' recommendations if there is clear communication and mutual respect.

DOCTOR: *Have you ever had a history of cardiac arrest in your family?*

PATIENT: *No, we never had any trouble with the police.*

(DiMatteo and Friedman, 1982, page 87)

Doctors often use such jargon out of habit, without pausing to consider that the patient's vocabulary and understanding of the body may be rather different from their own. In addition, some observers suggest that doctors sometimes use medical jargon as a way of demonstrating their greater expertise and emphasizing their power over the dependent patient. Patients, for their part, contribute to the problem by failing to ask enough questions and, by their silence, lead the doctor to feel that they understand her completely even when they really don't. The ideal of the "good patient" seems to be someone who listens to the doctor carefully, without taking up the doctor's valuable time with too many questions.

In addition to such miscommunication, doctors frequently fail to be sufficiently sensitive to their patients' individual situations and to the factors that may make it difficult for a particular patient to comply with the doctors' recommendations. If, for example, Dr. Kaiser had learned more about Ralph Bissinger's motives and life-style, he might have been able to work out a treatment plan with Ralph that would have been easier for Ralph to follow. Doctors also need to pay attention to their patients' emotions—for example, the anxiety that people commonly feel when they learn that they are seriously ill—which may interfere with their ability to comprehend and to follow certain recommendations (Stone, 1979).

The problem of patient compliance directs our attention to the nature of the doctor-patient relationship. When doctors simply instruct their patients to follow their orders, speaking as competent but distant "experts," the patients do not always heed the instructions. In contrast, when doctors and patients first establish a relationship of trust and mutual respect, the patients are more likely to be motivated to follow the doctors' recommendations. Under these conditions, a recommendation is more likely to be *internalized*, to be viewed by the patient as something he himself wants to do, rather than as an order imposed upon him by an external agent (Rodin and Janis, 1982). The establishment of personal, respectful relationships between doctors and patients is helpful not only in motivating patients to follow their doctors' recommendations, but, just as important, in motivating them to see the doctor in the first place (DiMatteo and Friedman, 1982).

The training of physicians has typically emphasized the biological aspects of medicine and has given little attention to matters of interpersonal sensitivity and communication. Because of the importance of interpersonal skills in medical practice, however, health psychologists have been joining forces with medical educators in trying to incorporate training in such skills into medical school curricula. In addition, many health psychologists, as well as increasing numbers of physicians, advocate a redefinition of the doctor-patient relationship, from the model of the "expert" physician giving orders to the compliant (or, too often, noncompliant) patient to a model of more equal cooperation between two people—professional and patient—who share the responsibility for maintaining the patient's health (Stone, 1979).

Patients in hospitals

The words *hospital* and *hotel* come from the same Latin root, meaning "host." Before the twentieth century, hospitals were places where travelers, soldiers, and poor wanderers could find rest and nourishment. It is only recently that hospitals have taken their present form as centers of advanced medical care, complete with computerized diagnostic tools, sophisticated physiological monitoring equipment, and gleaming operating rooms. The modern hospital allows physicians and other health care practitioners to provide their services in a convenient and well-equipped envi-

PATIENTS TEACH DOCTORS

In 1984, a teaching hospital in New York made an elderly woman an honorary faculty member, even though she has no medical degree. For years the woman has been teaching medical students—by letting them listen to her unique heart murmur. More generally, using patients as instructors to doctors is an idea whose time has come. Physicians rarely receive any direct feedback on their performance from their patients. But certain patients with chronic illnesses are in an excellent position to evaluate how well a young doctor is doing, both technically and interpersonally. In some training programs, such patients are recruited to instruct medical students, and in this way provide an important new dimension to medical training (DiMatteo and Friedman, 1982).

ronment. In the process of change, however, hospitals have lost much of their traditional "hospitality."

Despite the importance of hospitals in treating sick people, there are aspects of the social patterns of the modern hospital that may actually be harmful to patients' health. As Shelley Taylor (1982) notes, hospitals tend to *depersonalize* their patients, stripping away many elements of their individual identities and instead putting them in the anonymous and usually passive role of "patient." The patient is asked to wear a standard hospital gown, to live in a strange room, to submit to the hospital's rules about when to eat and sleep, and to give up much of her privacy. Much of the time the patient is isolated from family and friends, but dozens of staff persons—including doctors, nurses, technicians, and housekeepers—may continually walk in and out of her room. When medical personnel visit a patient, they sometimes talk about her in medical jargon that she cannot understand, almost as if she were not there. After a while the patient may come to feel that she is nothing more to the staff than "the gallbladder in Room 302." Of course, the hospital staff is not really trying to strip patients of their identity or to make them feel uncomfortable. Nev-

ertheless, the procedures that were instituted in order to run the hospital smoothly and efficiently often lead to such depersonalizing treatment.

In addition to such depersonalization, patients are typically given little involvement in their own care and little control over their own daily lives. They often receive minimal information about their illness or their treatment. Doctors and nurses may fear that telling the patient too much will lead to painful emotional reactions or will cause the patient to ask new questions or make new demands that will disrupt the hospital's routines. Instead, patients are expected to play the role of "good patient," which calls for them to do exactly what they are told and not to rock the boat. In some cases, however, the lack of control leads patients to feel depressed and helpless—states that may diminish their ability to cope with stress and may even increase their susceptibility to further illness. A minority of patients reject the "good patient" role and instead become angry and frustrated about their lack of control, and these reactions, too, can interfere with their recovery.

To help reduce these unhealthy aspects of hospitalization, Taylor and other psychologists advocate procedures that increase patients' sense of

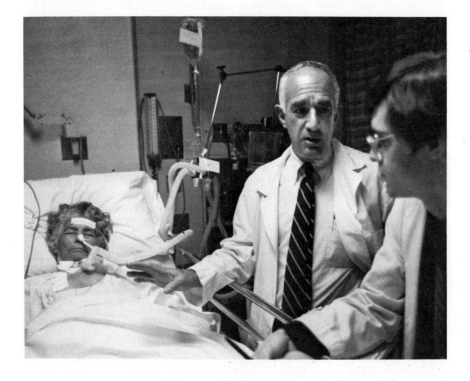

On their hospital rounds, doctors sometimes talk among themselves in medical jargon, almost as if the patient was not there.

CHAPTER TWELVE: PSYCHOLOGY AND HEALTH

control over their outcomes. One recommendation is that patients be given more extensive information about their condition and treatment. Studies have shown, for example, that giving surgical patients extensive advance information about the operation and the discomfort that may follow it can improve their postoperative adjustment (Langer, Janis, and Wolfer, 1975). A second recommendation is to involve patients more actively in their own care. In some facilities for long-term patients, those patients who can get around are encouraged to perform such tasks as making their own beds or helping other patients who are too sick to care for themselves. In other self-help units, some patients administer their own medications, take their own temperatures, and monitor their own condition (Kornfeld, 1972).

Both increased information and increased self-care can have important positive effects. Not only can these innovations make patients feel better about the hospital experience, but they can also contribute to a better medical recovery. In one study, patients who had had heart attacks were found to make the best recoveries when they were given both full information about their disease and an opportunity to participate in their own treatment (Cromwell et al., 1977). The opportunity for participation included access to a switch that the patient could flick to activate his own cardiac monitor to get an electrocardiogram whenever he felt some symptom. In addition, patients in the high-participation condition were taught mild isometric and foot-pedaling exercises that they could undertake on their own initiative.

Many health psychologists would like to see such innovations more widely adopted. Other new ideas are being tried at various hospitals in the hope of combating the depersonalizing effects of the hospital environment. These practices include allowing patients to exchange their hospital gowns for more normal clothing, letting patients or their families do some of their own cooking, establishing support groups of patients who have similar problems, and having a single doctor and nurse (rather than a constantly shifting army) coordinate the care of each patient. Such innovations may improve health care, even as they help the modern hospital to recover some of its traditional values of hospitality.

PREVENTING ILLNESS

Throughout the history of health care, the greatest strides have been made in preventing disease and promoting health rather than in curing disease (McKeown, 1979). It makes more sense, for example, to provide good sanitation, good nutrition, and

Community-based prevention programs can help to head off heart disease. One such program was established in 1980 in Mankato, Minnesota, emphasizing heart-healthy foods, physical fitness, and smoking prevention.

BOX 3

"FRIENDS CAN BE GOOD MEDICINE"

In 1981, the California Department of Mental Health published a valuable booklet entitled *Friends Can Be Good Medicine*. The booklet's basic premise was that friendships and other supportive social relationships are just as important to people's physical well-being as they are to their emotional health.

It has repeatedly been found, for example, that adults who are single, divorced, or widowed have a higher death rate and a higher rate of heart disease than do adults who are married. By one recent estimate, being married rather than single, is associated among white males with a greater life expectancy of about six years (Cohen and Lee, 1982). Although more than one interpretation might be offered for this finding, the most plausible seems to be that marriage can provide the kind of support that helps people to cope with stress and to prevent illness (Lynch, 1977). Other studies have found clear links between the extent of people's networks of friends and their risk of suffering illness (Berkman and Syme, 1979).

Family, friends, and colleagues can help to prevent illness by providing affection and approval, confidence and encouragement, information and advice. Taken together, the benefits that others provide to us in facing the challenges of life are called *social support*. Social support is particularly necessary in times of stress and crisis. For example, a study of men who had lost their jobs found less illness, lower cholesterol levels, and less depression among those men who had supportive marriages and friendships (Gore, 1978).

Social support seems to help people cope with stress and maintain their health in two main ways. First, supportive family members and friends can provide emotional benefits that directly reduce the harmful effects of stress. Our family and friends can help us to understand and interpret potentially stressful situations in ways that are less threatening. They can help us to relax, to maintain a sense of humor, and to feel more optimistic about the

In times of stress and crisis, the support of friends can help people maintain their health.

future. All of these influences can, in turn, have a beneficial effect on our bodies.

Second, supportive others can provide information and encouragement that helps us to behave in healthier ways, such as remembering to take a prescribed drug or staying on a diet. As noted in this chapter, the encouragement of family and friends can help people to stay away from cigarettes after they have quit and to adhere to exercise programs.

When people do suffer serious illnesses, they usually need a great deal of reassurance, comfort, and understanding. In such situations, the support of family and friends can be extremely important. In addition, people with long-term illnesses can often profit from participating in peer support groups consisting of others in the same situation. For example, "Make Today Count" is a national organization that sponsors groups in which cancer patients and their families can share information and feelings about living with cancer.

Despite the benefits of social support, having close family ties and

friendships is not *always* healthy (Suls, 1982). One California sociologist noted that the *Friends Can Be Good Medicine* booklet could be harmful if it led people to think that friendships are a panacea for all of life's ills (Fischer, 1983). We must not forget that marriages and friendships involve obligations as well as benefits, and the need to *provide* support to relatives or friends in times of crisis can itself be highly stressful. Some social scientists point out that women are more often cast in the role of emotional support-givers than men are—and that this, in turn, may add considerable stress to women's lives (Bernard, 1982).

Like all "good medicines," then, social support is not a cure-all. It may sometimes even have harmful side effects. All things considered, however, the love and support of family and friends is one of the best prescriptions for good health that you can get.

CHAPTER TWELVE: PSYCHOLOGY AND HEALTH

an unpolluted environment—and, thus, to prevent disease—than it does to focus exclusively on the treatment of infectious diseases, malnutrition, and poisonings. It is because of prevention, not pills, that you have probably never encountered malaria, polio, or typhoid fever. The same arguments apply to aspects of health that are directly linked to behavior. If we could prevent an adolescent from developing bad eating habits or starting to smoke, he would be much less likely to require treatment for serious illness when he reaches middle age. In fact, the major causes of death in our society are closely tied to behavior. By promoting good eating habits and proper exercise, and by discouraging cigarette smoking, our society could prevent illness in millions of people. As noted in Box 3, the support of family and friends can also play a major role in preventing illness.

Smoking

In 1964, the Surgeon General of the United States issued a famous report concluding that cigarette smoking is a direct cause of lung cancer. And since 1966, every pack of cigarettes sold in the United States has carried a health warning. More recently, the major role of smoking in causing heart disease has been firmly established. Smoking has been conclusively linked to many other diseases as well, including bronchitis, emphysema, larynx cancer, and pancreatic cancer. There is also mounting evidence that simply being exposed to other people's smoke increases the risk of lung disease, especially in children. Despite these deadly effects, however, about 35 percent of adult men and 25 percent of adult women in the United States smoke cigarettes, averaging one and a half packs a day, for a national grand total of some 600 billion packs a year (U.S. Department of Health and Human Services, 1981). Because cigarette smoking is generally viewed as the most important behavioral risk to health, it has become a central concern of health psychologists.

Given the general knowledge of the health risks of smoking, it is no wonder that the majority of smokers

have tried at some time in their lives to quit. But in most cases their attempts have been unsuccessful. People begin smoking, often when they are adolescents, for a variety of reasons, including the example of parents and pressure from peers. If others in one's group of friends are starting to smoke, it can be hard to resist going along with the crowd. (Such conformity to peer pressures is discussed in greater detail in Chapter 15.) Once people start smoking, they are likely to get hooked. The addiction to smoking is partly physiological; smokers become used to the effects of nicotine and can experience painful withdrawal symptoms when they give it up. In addition, people become psychologically dependent on smoking, as a way of reducing anxiety and of coping with particular situations. Because of these physiological and psychological forces, quitting is difficult and the relapse rate is high.

Psychologists have developed a variety of behavior modification techniques to help people stop smoking. In the *rapid smoking* technique, smokers in a clinic or lab are asked to smoke continually, puffing every six to eight seconds, until they can't tolerate it any longer. This technique is an example of a form of classical conditioning called *aversive conditioning*. Making smoking a painful (or aversive) rather than a pleasant experience can create a conditioned aversion in the smoker, motivating her to avoid smoking even when she leaves the clinic. Smoking cessation programs also commonly teach people techniques of *stimulus control*, in which smokers learn first to become aware of the stimuli and situations that commonly lead to smoking, and then to avoid these situations or to develop alternative behaviors. If you find, for example, that you usually smoke while drinking an after-dinner cup of coffee, you might do well to give up the coffee and take an invigorating, smokeless after-dinner walk instead.

Programs that include such techniques often help people stop smoking for a period of weeks or months. The problem is that within six months to a year 80 to 85 percent of the "quitters" return to their smoky

"YOU'VE COME A LONG WAY, BABY"

One of the negative side effects of the move toward equality of the sexes in America has been a dramatic increase in the rate of smoking among women. Because of social taboos, far fewer women than men have traditionally been smokers. But in the 1940s, 1950s, and 1960s more and more women started to smoke, and in the past two decades the percentage of smokers has dropped more slowly among women than among men. By 1979, 37 percent of men and 28 percent of women were smokers—a much smaller gap than in previous decades. And for the first time the proportion of smokers in their twenties was as high among women as among men. (U.S. Department of Health and Human Services, 1980). As the unsettling slogan of Virginia Slims cigarettes puts it, "You've come a long way, baby."

ways (Lichtenstein, 1982). One factor that often seems to help a reformed smoker stay off cigarettes is the encouragement and support of a spouse or of other close family members or friends (Ockene et al., 1982). There is reason to believe that a large proportion of smokers *can* quit for good if they are strongly enough motivated to do so (Schachter, 1982). But the fact remains that so far there is no program that can consistently enable people to stay off the weed.

The difficulty of quitting emphasizes the importance of *preventing* cigarette smoking by young people. Various sorts of smoking prevention programs have been attempted, often in junior high schools. Traditionally, these efforts have focused on explaining the long-term health risks of smoking. But people often have the knack of putting such gloomy long-term warnings out of their minds, and these programs have not been notably effective. More recently, Richard Evans and his coworkers (1981) have emphasized teaching children and adolescents how to resist the social pressures that often lead young people to try smoking. For example, stu-

dents are shown videotapes of a situation in which an adolescent is offered a cigarette by a friend but turns down the offer. The students are then given opportunities to practice, or role play, the behavior of refusing a cigarette. Such training helps prepare the 12- or 13-year-old to deal effectively with similar social influence situations in real life and seems to have been successful in influencing students in the direction of deciding not to smoke.

A total solution to our society's smoking problem will not come, however, until society's expectations change in a major way; that is, until smoking is no longer viewed as a "grown-up" or approved thing to do. Such a change has begun to take place in recent years, and there have been significant reductions in the numbers of smokers in America. More smokers have been quitting and fewer young people have been deciding to take up smoking in the first place.

Exercise

In recent decades, large numbers of Americans have led physically inactive lives. People shuffle out to their

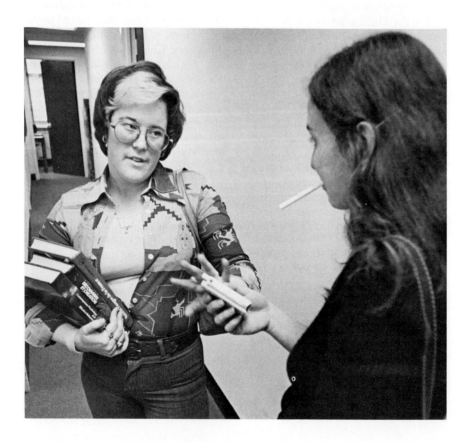

Role-playing exercises have been used to help teach children and adolescents how to resist the social pressures to start smoking.

Jogging is a form of exercise that can reduce the risk of heart disease and other diseases.

cars in the morning, sit or stand in one place most of the day, ride home, and settle into easy chairs to watch other people play baseball or football on television. In the process, people get little vigorous exercise. Today, however, more and more people are jogging, swimming, bicycling, and engaging in other forms of *aerobic exercise*—exercise that requires a constant flow of oxygen (Cooper, 1968). The exercise boom is a good example of how general social values and expectations affect health-related behaviors. There were few joggers 20 years ago, but there are millions today.

The health benefits of aerobic exercise are not as obvious as the health risks of cigarette smoking. Nevertheless, people who lead a sedentary life, without much exercise, have been found to be at greater risk for heart disease and other illnesses. Researchers at Harvard and Stanford recently reported the results of a major study of 17,000 middle-aged and older men who were first studied as college students between 1916 and 1950 and then followed up periodically for many decades (Paffenberger et al., 1984). The researchers found that those men who exercised regularly, even at moderate levels, lived longer than those who did not. Even after correcting for such factors as family history, the death rate due to heart disease of the least active group was

almost twice as high as that for the most active group. Another recent study found that both men and women who kept physically fit were much less likely to develop high blood pressure (a common precursor of heart disease) than those who did not keep fit (Blair et al., 1984).

Exercise may reduce the risk of heart disease and other diseases in several ways. First, there is evidence that regular exercise can favorably alter blood levels of different forms of cholesterol, which in turn may be related to the likelihood of plaque forming in coronary arteries (Wood and Haskell, 1979). Second, exercise can improve the health of overweight people by helping them to lose weight. Third, exercise often has psychological benefits, helping to relieve depression (McCann and Holmes, 1984) and increasing people's general sense of well-being (Folkins and Sime, 1981). These psychological benefits can, in turn, make people better able to cope with stress and to engage in other health-producing behaviors, such as cutting down on smoking and drinking.

Despite the physical fitness boom, a large proportion of Americans still fail to exercise regularly. In particular, people who begin exercise programs because of an identified health risk are as likely as not to drop out within three to six months (Martin and Dubbert, 1982). Thus, psycholo-

People can profitably incorporate exercise into their daily lives. For example, they can be encouraged to take the stairs instead of the escalator.

gists have been trying to develop exercise programs that will keep people exercising. As in the case of smoking cessation programs, the encouragement and support of spouses have been found to play a major role in keeping people from dropping out of exercise programs (Andrew et al., 1981). In addition, people are more likely to continue exercising when they are in group rather than individual programs (Martin and Dubbert, 1982). Finally, people are more likely to adhere to a fitness program if they can incorporate the exercise into their daily lives—for example, by walking instead of driving short distances, or by walking up and down a few flights of stairs instead of taking the elevator. Because no special places, equipment, or times are needed, long-term adherence becomes more likely.

Wellness

As we have seen, the focus of medical care in our society has been shifting from curing disease to preventing disease—especially in terms of changing our many unhealthful behaviors, such as poor eating habits, smoking, and failure to exercise. (In the Psychological Issue that follows, another unhealthful set of behaviors is discussed—drinking too much alcohol.) The line of thought involved in this shift from curing disease to preventing it can be pursued further. Imagine a person who is about the right weight but does not eat very nutritious foods, who feels OK but exercises only occasionally, who goes to work every day but is not an outstanding worker, who drinks a few beers at home most nights but does

CHAPTER TWELVE: PSYCHOLOGY AND HEALTH

not drive while intoxicated, and who has no tumors or chest pains or abnormal blood counts but sleeps a lot and often feels a bit tired. This person is not ill. He may not even be at risk for any particular disease. But we can imagine that this person could be a lot healthier.

The field of medicine has not traditionally distinguished between someone who is merely "not ill" and someone who is in robust health and paying active attention to the special needs of his body. Both types have simply been called "well." In recent years, however, some health practitioners have begun to apply the terms *well* and *wellness* only to those people who are actively striving to maintain and improve their health. People who are well are concerned with nutrition and exercise, and they make a point of monitoring their body's condition—for example, through regular breast self-examinations or blood pressure checkups. Most important, perhaps, people who are well take active responsibility for all matters pertaining to their health. Even people who have a physical disease or handicap may be "well," in this new sense, if they make an active effort to maintain the best possible health they can in the face of their physical limitations. "Wellness" may perhaps best be viewed not as a state that people can achieve but as an ideal that people can strive for.

Unfortunately, as M. Robin DiMatteo and Howard Friedman (1982) note, wellness is sometimes viewed as a crazy new fad or as some sort of mystical road to truth and self-fulfillment. In fact, wellness is a sensible antidote to the narrow view that health involves the "fixing" of a passive, diseased body. People who are well are likely to be better able to resist disease and to fight disease when it strikes. And by focusing attention on healthy ways of living, the concept of wellness can have a beneficial impact on the ways in which people face the challenges of daily life.

SUMMARY

- *1* The relatively new field of *health psychology* is concerned with the role of psychological factors in the development of disease, in coping with illness, and in the promotion of health.

Stress

- *2* *Stressors* are stimuli or events in our environment that make emotional and physical demands on us; *stress* is our emotional and physical reaction to such stimuli. When we encounter stressors, we must pull together our mental and physical resources to deal with the challenge.

- *3* Selye has suggested that animals, including humans, react to stressors in a regular way, termed the *general adaptation syndrome.* This syndrome consists of three stages: the *alarm reaction,* the stage of *resistance,* and the stage of *exhaustion.*

- *4* When faced with stress, the body mobilizes for action in what is called the *fight-or-flight reaction.* Activity in the sympathetic nervous system increases; epinephrine, norepinephrine, and corticosteroids are released; and body systems necessary to "fight" or "flight" speed up while less necessary systems slow down.

- *5* When stress continues over a long period of time, the body becomes more susceptible to many illnesses. Holmes and other researchers have found that, in particular, major life changes can give rise to serious illness.

- *6* Stress is caused not so much by events themselves as by the ways in which people perceive and react to these events. Thus, effectively coping with stress often requires redefining the situation from one of threat to one of challenge or opportunity.

- *7* Both animals and humans can better cope with stress if they feel they have some control over the stressful situation. Even if unpleasant events cannot be controlled, they will tend to be less stressful if they are predictable.

- *8* People who cope well with stress tend to be committed to what they are doing, to feel in control, and to welcome moderate amounts of change and challenge.

Psychological processes and illness

- *9* Psychological factors often interact closely with biological factors in causing illness. Diseases in which the primary determinants are psychological are called *psychosomatic* diseases.

- **10** Stress can have a major impact on the development of heart disease. People in certain types of high-stress jobs that offer little control are particularly prone to heart disease, as are people with a particular personality style, termed the *coronary-prone behavior pattern*, or *Type A*.

- **11** Although cancer is still a poorly understood disease, there is increasing evidence that people's emotions are involved in the progression of cancer once it has begun. It has been suggested that psychological factors can affect functioning of the *immune system*, interfering with its ability to fight cancer cells. In particular, emotional reactions to stress—particularly feelings of helplessness—and depressive states have been implicated in increasing the risk of cancer.

Psychology and health care

- **12** *Behavioral medicine* is the application of a wide variety of behavioral techniques to the treatment and prevention of illness. The most widely used behavioral techniques have focused on the management of stress and anxiety, through such methods as *progressive muscle relaxation*, production of a *relaxation response*, and *biofeedback*.

- **13** One factor that contributes to the success of various medical therapies is the patient's expectation that the treatment will in fact work. This is called the *placebo effect*. Placebo effects account for the success of such unorthodox treatments as faith healing. Placebos have been particularly effective in controlling pain, in part because the patient's expectations may stimulate the release of the body's own natural pain-killers, endorphins.

- **14** One of the biggest obstacles to effective medical treatment is patients' noncompliance with doctors' recommendations. Factors that contribute to noncompliance include miscommunication and failure of the doctor to be sensitive to the patient's individual situation and emotions. It is important for

patients and doctors to establish a relationship of trust and mutual respect.

- **15** Hospitals tend to depersonalize patients and give them little involvement in their own care, allowing them little control over their own lives. Giving patients more information about their condition and treatment and involving them more actively in their own care can have important positive effects.

Preventing illness

- **16** Health psychology is particularly concerned with promoting behaviors that will help prevent illness. In this regard, a number of programs have been developed to try to help smokers quit their habit and to try to encourage people to maintain regular exercise programs.

- **17** The *social support* of family, friends, and colleagues can help prevent illness by providing affection and approval, confidence and encouragement, information and advice.

- **18** Although medicine has traditionally defined healthy people as those who are "not ill," in recent years there has been a movement toward the concept of *wellness*—striving actively to maintain and improve one's health.

KEY TERMS

aerobic exercise
alarm reaction
behavioral medicine
biofeedback
carcinogens
coronary-prone (Type A) behavior pattern
corticosteroids
exhaustion stage
fight-or-flight reaction
general adaptation syndrome
health psychology
hot reactivity
immune system
progressive muscle relaxation
psychoimmunology
psychosomatic
relaxation response
resistance stage
stress
stress-resistant personality
stressors
wellness

ALCOHOL ABUSE

Alcohol is a drug that has been used and abused by human beings for thousands of years. It is used to enhance social gatherings and celebrations, it is a part of religious rituals, and it also brings personal tragedy and social disgrace to those who regularly abuse it. "Alcohol has been appreciated, craved, respected, abhorred, and feared," writes Morris Chafetz (1979), "but it has never been fully understood."

Alcohol misuse has been a factor in more than 10 percent of all deaths in the United States—about 200,000 deaths per year. It has been associated with half of all traffic deaths, many involving teenagers. With prolonged abuse, alcohol can damage virtually every system of the body; it is the primary cause of cirrhosis of the liver, one of the ten leading causes of death.

The damage goes beyond the costs to life and health. The person who abuses alcohol becomes less and less able to work effectively or to fulfill family responsibilities. Emotional problems, such as depression and anxiety, stalk the alcohol abuser.

Despite these well-publicized risks, large numbers of Americans continue to abuse alcohol. An estimated 10 million people over the age of 18 (about 7 percent of all adults) are *problem drinkers*—people who get drunk at least once a month. Perhaps half of these may be categorized as *alcoholics*—people who consistently abuse alcohol in a way that drowns out most of life's interests and activities. About one in three Americans has a person with a drinking problem in the family.

Alcoholics are said to be *physiologically addicted* to alcohol—their bodies crave alcohol in such a way that painful physical withdrawal effects may take place if they can't get a drink. Other problem drinkers may show no signs of physiological addiction but they have become *psychologically dependent* on alcohol—they become anxious without a drink. In increasing numbers of cases, people who abuse alcohol have problems with other drugs, such as barbiturates and cocaine, as well.

To understand these problems, we will first consider the reasons that people drink in the first place, and then turn to problem drinking and alcoholism.

WHY DO PEOPLE DRINK?

It can't be because it tastes good. That might be the reason for drinking a fine French wine at an expensive dinner, but it doesn't explain the cheap wines and beers that many teenagers start out with. Reasons for drinking usually have more to do with a desire to relax, to reduce inhibitions, and to be part of the crowd.

In small amounts, alcohol reduces the inhibitions on one's impulses and for a brief period, may lift one's spirits. Especially at social gatherings, when they want to feel less tense or self-conscious, people may turn to drink. On such occasions, alcohol gives people "permission" to behave in ways that would otherwise be disapproved. The normally strait-laced executive knows that he can relax and tell a few crude jokes at the annual office Christmas party—everyone will attri-

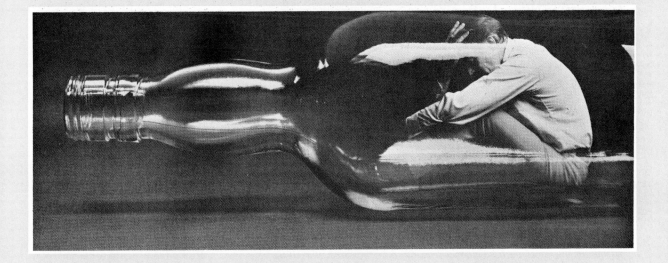

bute any inappropriate behavior to the alcohol, not to *him*.

But whereas alcohol can have these relaxing effects for a short period of time, it is actually a depressant that lessens the efficiency of many bodily systems. It impairs one's motor skills and, after a point, scrambles one's sensations and perceptions. By next morning, the executive who has had "one too many" may wish he had had one less.

Most people take their first drinks when they are teenagers. For many adolescents, drinking is considered a sign of being grown-up (Hawkins, 1982). Teenagers tend to copy the drinking behavior of their peers, in order to be a part of things and to avoid rejection. Unfortunately, the pressures on teenagers to drink have increased in recent years. The large majority of American teenagers drink some alcoholic beverage at least once a month, and an estimated 3.5 million of them have had problems with

*O**nly a tiny proportion of alcoholics fit the skid-row stereotype.*

alcohol. Among college students, both drinking and drinking problems have been increasing steadily over the past half-century (Chafetz, 1979). The increase in teenage problem drinking—and its strong association with traffic fatalities—has led to a move to return the national minimum age for drinking to 21.

WHO BECOMES AN ALCOHOLIC?

When you think of an alcoholic, you are likely to picture the classic derelict wino: the dirty, unshaven, bleary-eyed, uneducated, skid-row bum who staggers through the streets drinking from bottles in paper bags (Regestein and Howe, 1972). Perhaps we maintain the skid-row ster-

eotype because we don't like to think that the fate of alcoholism could befall people like *ourselves*. But in fact, only a tiny proportion of alcoholics fit the skid-row image. The vast majority can be found in all walks of life, including large numbers of alcoholics in business and professional positions.

A lot of people drink, but relatively few are alcoholics. In past years, many psychological and moral speculations about the causes of alcoholism were bandied about. Alcoholism was attributed to fixation at the oral stage of psychosexual development, to an unstable personality, and to a basic lack of self-restraint. More recently, however, it has become clearly established that the tendency to become alcoholic has an important biological component. Certain people are biologically predisposed to become alcoholic, while others are not.

Many family studies of alcoholics have indicated that the predisposition to become alcoholic is genetically transmitted; for example, the children of alcoholic parents have unusually high rates of alcoholism themselves, even if they were adopted and brought up by parents who were not alcoholic. People with a family history of alcoholism have been found to be relatively insensitive to the intoxicating effects of alcohol. Thus, they may drink more without throwing up or passing out, while the alcohol wrecks their bodies (Schuckit, 1983).

Recent research has begun to shed light on the biochemical basis of this predisposition to alcoholism. This research suggests that some people may be predisposed to become alcoholic because they metabolize alcohol by a different chemical route than nonalcoholics (Rutstein et al., 1983). In part because of the

Most people take their first drinks when they are teenagers. Among college students, both drinking and drinking problems have increased steadily over the past half-century.

Alcoholics and problem drinkers can be found in every walk of life. A small proportion of alcoholics fit the skid-row image (top), but many others can be found in more affluent settings (bottom).

major role of such biological factors, some experts consider alcoholism to be a physical disease.

But whereas biology predisposes certain people to become alcoholic, not all of these people actually do become alcoholic. Both personality factors and social influences may also play important roles. In one study, Mary Cover Jones (1968, 1971) was able to classify the drinking patterns of middle-aged men and women who had taken part in a longitudinal study of personality development ever since they were in junior high school. She found that those boys who went on to become problem drinkers were rated during their school years as assertive, rebellious, and hostile. For these boys, turning to alcohol may have been an expression of rebellion against authority. Girls who became problem drinkers were rated as unstable, impulsive, and prone to depression.

Cultural influences also play a role in alcohol abuse. George Vaillant (1982) has found that alcoholism is most prevalent among certain cultural and ethnic groups in which alcohol is officially forbidden, but in which at some level drunkenness is actually admired. In contrast, cultural and ethnic groups that frown on drunkenness but allow moderate drinking with one's family and at meals have low rates of alcoholism.

Social norms and attitudes may also contribute to the fact that men are much more likely than women to become alcoholic. Drinking is often considered to be a "manly vice" and someone who wants to be a "real man" may have to learn how to get loaded. The potential risk for women seems to be greatest when they are changing life-styles: among women, those who are divorced and separated and under the age of 35 have the highest incidence of alcoholism.

There is still considerable controversy about the nature of alcoholism, however. One view that has long been influential is that alcoholism is a disease that makes it impos-

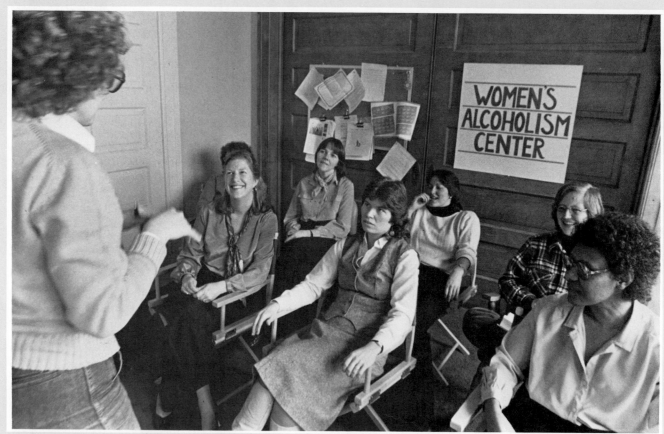

"Society expects a lady to drink, but not to have a drinking problem"—Betty Ford. These women have taken the first step toward solving their alcohol problems, by admitting that they have a problem.

sible for people to exert control over their drinking. Another view, which has been gaining acceptance among psychologists, is that alcohol problems are primarily problems in living—life-style habits that people have acquired as attempts to deal with stress. From this point of view, "Excessive drinking can be redefined as behavior that people *do*, not a symptom of what people *are* (i.e., you *are* an alcoholic)" (Marlatt, 1983, page 1108).

As we will see, these differing conceptions of alcoholism and problem drinking lead to different approaches to treatment. The view of alcoholism as a disease underlies the approach of Alcoholics Anonymous, while the behavioral view of alcohol problems underlies controlled drinking approaches.

TREATING ALCOHOL PROBLEMS

One of the hardest aspects of treating alcohol problems is getting people to admit that they have a problem. Especially among people who are trying to maintain a respectable facade, the problem is often denied for years. The derelict image adds shame to the alcoholic's list of difficulties. This shame makes it difficult for him—or his family—to admit his

condition and seek help. Of course, if an alcohol problem is not acknowledged, it cannot be treated effectively.

Women have found it particularly difficult to admit to having alcohol problems. As Betty Ford, the wife of former President Gerald Ford, put it, "Society expects a lady to drink, but not to have a drinking problem." In 1978, Mrs. Ford herself announced that she was entering a hospital for treatment of her dependency on alcohol and pain-killers. Her example was credited with influencing many other "respectable" people to own up to their alcohol problems and seek treatment.

One of the hardest aspects of treating alcohol problems is getting people to admit that they have a problem.

Role playing is used to teach problem drinkers how to refuse a drink.

Many different approaches have been taken to treating alcohol problems, from psychoanalytic therapy to LSD treatment, with greater or lesser success. Here we will examine two of the best-known approaches, Alcoholics Anonymous and controlled drinking.

Alcoholics Anonymous. The most publicized approach to helping those who can't handle alcohol is Alcoholics Anonymous (AA). The basic principles of AA are that only an alcoholic can help another alcoholic, that alcoholics can manage to lead normal lives through mutual support and self-examination, and that they must seek faith in a higher power to surmount their "obsession" with alcohol. Most important, an alcoholic must never again take even one drink.

Founded in 1935, AA has been the preeminent approach toward treating alcoholism. Since 1968, the membership of AA has more than tripled, from 170,000 to 586,000, and women now make up one-third of its membership. In recent years, AA has also become increasingly involved in other forms of drug abuse, since alcohol problems are frequently linked to the use of other drugs.

AA has maintained that 50 percent of all alcoholics coming into AA get sober and stay that way. Twenty-five percent have one or two slips before they see the light, and the other 25 percent are not sufficiently motivated to stop drinking. Although these statistics are probably overestimates of the success of AA, the fact remains that AA has worked where other approaches have failed.

Controlled drinking. Until recently, the AA creed that an alcoholic must abstain totally from alcohol—that even one drink is an invitation to disaster—went uncon-

tested. But this approach scares some problem drinkers and alcoholics away from seeking help because they regard the goal of total abstinence as unattainable.

In recent years, some psychologists have tried a new tack with alcoholics and problem drinkers—applying techniques of behavior modification to teach them to control their own drinking behavior. According to this *controlled drinking* approach, total abstinence is not necessarily the key to overcoming a drinking problem. Instead, problem drinkers are taught specific skills and techniques that will enable them to drink in moderation.

Controlled drinking skills include methods of monitoring one's own consumption and of setting limits. Behavioral medicine techniques, such as those discussed in Chapter 12, are also utilized to help the person manage stress and adopt a healthier life-style (Marlatt, 1983). Role playing is often used to teach problem drinkers how to refuse a drink when one is offered (Foy et al., 1976).

The effectiveness of controlled drinking has been the subject of great controversy. In a pioneering study a decade ago, Mark and Linda Sobell (1973) published results indicating that a controlled drinking program had been used successfully with a group of male alcoholic patients at a California state hospital. Other researchers subsequently challenged the Sobells' results, and even charged that the study had been fraudulent (Pendery, Maltzman, and West, 1982). The Sobells have since been exonerated of fraud, and many psychologists are convinced of the validity of their conclusions.

Because the idea of controlled drinking directly challenges the established AA credo of total absti-

nence, it continues to arouse strong negative reactions from adherents of AA. Whereas controlled drinking has been gaining recognition as a treatment for problem drinking and alcoholism in Europe, especially Great Britain and Scandinavia, it has not yet been widely accepted in America.

In fact, there seems to be room for both AA and controlled drinking approaches in the arsenal of techniques to combat alcohol abuse. Controlled drinking does not work for everyone. It seems to work best for people under the age of 40 who have been problem drinkers for less than ten years and who tend not to view themselves as alcoholics. If controlled drinking does not prove successful after a carefully observed trial period, the client is usually told to consider abstinence as an alternative goal. For some people, however, controlled drinking may be an effective way to learn to have a drink without letting the drink get the better of them.

SUMMARY

- *1* Despite the physical, economic, and social costs of alcohol abuse, an estimated 10 million American adults are problem drinkers and about half of these are alcoholics—people who are physically addicted to the drug.
- *2* People drink primarily out of the desire to relax, to reduce inhibitions, or to go along with the crowd. Only a small percentage of those who drink actually become alcoholics. Some people have a genetic predisposition toward alcoholism. However, personality factors, social influences, and culture all play a role in determining whether a person will actually become an alcoholic.
- *3* Two major approaches to treatment of alcohol abuse are Alcoholics Anonymous, which emphasizes complete abstinence from drinking, and the controlled drinking approach, based on techniques of behavior modification.

The study of psychological disorders is often known as abnormal psychology. As we will see, however, it is by no means easy to determine which patterns of thought, feeling, and behavior are "normal" and which are "abnormal." Indeed, what is considered "normal" or "healthy" in one culture may be considered "abnormal" or "pathological" in another.

But in spite of such debates about the nature of abnormality, we cannot deny that millions of people suffer painfully from mental and emotional problems. In Chapter 13, on Psychological Disorder, we will examine several of the most prevalent psychological disorders, including anxiety disorders, depression, schizophrenia, and the disorders of childhood. Then, in the Psychological Issue, we will consider one of the most tragic outcomes of psychological disorder, Suicide.

Chapter 14 examines several forms of Therapy currently used in the treatment of psychological problems and disorders. We will find that theory and research in different areas of psychology have given rise to specific approaches to therapy. Thus, Freud's theory of personality (discussed in Chapter 11) has led to psychoanalytic approaches to therapy, research on learning (Chapter 5) to the behavior therapies, and research on brain mechanisms (Chapter 2) to certain forms of drug treatment. The Psychological Issue on The Therapy Marketplace provides a quick tour of some of the many new forms of therapy that have recently arrived on the scene—from est to primal screams—and attempts to provide some perspective on what to make of them.

PSYCHOLOGICAL DISORDER

Psychological disorders range from relatively minor problems to afflictions that make normal living impossible.

DEFINING DISORDER

Psychological adequacy
The medical model
Culture and disorder
Classifying disorder

It is not always easy to determine what is "normal" and "abnormal" in human behavior and experience.

ANXIETY DISORDERS

Panic attacks
Phobias
Obsessive-compulsive disorders

Anxiety can overwhelm people, in the form of panic attacks, or saddle people with irrational fears and compulsions.

DEPRESSION

The range of depression
Cognitive patterns in depression
What causes depression?

Depression has been called the "common cold" of mental illness. Over 25 percent of Americans suffer from it at some time in their lives.

SCHIZOPHRENIA

The nature of schizophrenia
Cognitive disorders in schizophrenia
What causes schizophrenia?

People with schizophrenia live in a mental world that is different from the one the rest of us inhabit.

THE DISORDERS OF CHILDHOOD

Hyperactivity
Autism

Hyperactivity and autism are two of the disorders that strike in infancy or childhood.

PSYCHOLOGICAL ISSUE
SUICIDE

Suicide is the tragic escape route that some people take from a seemingly insoluble problem in living.

BOXES
1 *Abnormality through history*
2 *The insanity defense*
3 *Multiple personality*
4 *The antisocial personality*
5 *A child called Noah*

• Mary T., a wife and mother of five children, has spent almost all of the past three years inside her house. On the two occasions that she went out, she was filled with anxiety and dread. Mary T. is suffering from an *anxiety disorder*.

• John F. has not smiled for months, does his job poorly and with little ambition, feels worthless, and can't seem to enjoy anything any more. John F. is suffering from *depression*.

• Cathy P. rocks on the floor in the corner all day, mumbling to herself, occasionally telling passers-by that she is the president's wife, and screaming answers to voices only she seems to be able to hear. Cathy P. has been diagnosed as having *schizophrenia*.

• Richard S. is 4 years old, has no interest in communicating with people, spends most of his day staring at fans or other spinning objects, and has unpredictable tantrums. Richard S. suffers from a childhood disorder called *autism*.

These cases illustrate some of the many psychological disorders that can affect people. There is a wide range of disorders, from relatively minor problems that barely disrupt people's lives to major disorders that make any semblance of normal living impossible. Some disorders, such as autism, appear in the first year of life; others, such as certain cases of depression, do not make their first appearance until middle age or later. Recent research has indicated that the most serious diseases usually have biological origins, but these disorders are in many cases triggered by stressful life experiences.

Psychological disorder affects a large number of people. Some of the disorders that will be examined in this chapter, such as multiple person-

ality disorder, are very rare; but others, such as anxiety disorders and certain forms of depression, are quite common. A recent national study arrived at the estimate that 29.4 million American adults—almost one person in five—suffer from at least one psychological disorder or have suffered from one within the past 6 months (Schmeck, 1984).

In this chapter we will survey the range of psychological disorders. First, we will consider the difficult issue of defining disorder: How can we distinguish a "psychological disorder" from day-to-day problems that do not reflect disorder? We will base our discussion on the third edition of the American Psychiatric Association's *Diagnostic and Statistical Manual of Mental Disorders*, commonly known as *DSM-III*, which was published in 1980. This manual provides the system currently used by most professionals to diagnose psychological disorders. A summary of the major *DSM-III* categories is shown in Table 13.1. Then we will focus on four of the more common categories of disorder: anxiety disorders, depression, schizophrenia, and childhood disorders. Two other sorts of disorder are discussed in boxes: multiple personality (Box 3) and anti-social personality disorder (Box 4).

The various types of psychological disorders have traditionally been divided into two main groupings, neuroses and psychoses. *Neuroses* are characterized by anxiety and by an inability to cope effectively with life's challenges, but do not involve a loss of contact with reality. (In *DSM-III* the term "neurosis" has generally been abandoned, and many of the neuroses are now called "anxiety disorders.") *Psychoses*, in contrast, are disorders that do involve a loss of contact with reality. People with psychoses may experience delusions

TABLE 13.1

MAJOR CATEGORIES OF PSYCHOLOGICAL DISORDER IN DSM-III

Category	General description	Examples of specific disorders
Anxiety disorders *[handwritten: neurotic in nature / neurosis]*	Disorders in which anxiety is the main symptom, or in which the symptom seems to be an attempt to defend against anxiety.	*Panic attacks *[handwritten: treatment / medication / 1 on 1 Therapy / Freud analysis]* *Phobias *Obsessive-compulsive disorders *[handwritten: anxiety that result from things happen in early life]*
Affective disorders *[handwritten: neurotic]*	Disturbances of mood that color one's entire life.	*Depression *Bipolar disorder (alternating mania and depression)
Schizophrenic disorders *[handwritten: Psychotic in nature]*	Disorders involving serious alterations of thought and behavior that represent a split from reality.	*Disorganized, catatonic, paranoid, and undifferentiated types of schizophrenia
Disorders arising in childhood or adolescence	Disorders that are usually first evident in infancy, childhood, or adolescence.	*Hyperactivity (attention deficit disorder) *Infantile autism *[handwritten: chemically induced substance]* Mental retardation (see Chapter 7) *[handwritten: base on IQ level]*
Dissociative disorders *[handwritten: Psychotic in nature]*	Sudden alteration in the normally integrated functions of consciousness or identity.	Amnesia (when not caused by an organic mental disorder) *Multiple personality (Box 3)
Personality disorders *[handwritten: No what dying but believe they right society wrong]*	Deeply ingrained, inflexible, and maladaptive patterns of thought and behavior.	*Antisocial personality disorder (Box 4)
Organic mental disorders *[handwritten: Psychotic type]*	Psychological or behavioral abnormalities associated with a temporary or permanent dysfunction of the brain.	Senile dementia (see Chapter 9) Korsakoff's syndrome (see Chapter 6)
Substance use disorders *[handwritten: Can exhibit all different behavior / Psychotic type]*	Undesirable behavioral changes associated with drugs that affect the central nervous system.	Alcohol abuse or dependence (see Psychological Issue for Chapter 12) Amphetamine abuse or dependence Cannabis (marijuana) abuse or dependence
Somatoform disorders *[handwritten: sugar tablets / neurotic type]*	Disorders marked by physical symptoms for which no physical causes can be found, and which may be linked to psychological stresses or conflicts.	Conversion disorder (physical symptoms that cannot be explained by known physical causes) Psychogenic pain disorder (severe pain that cannot be explained by known physical causes)
Psychosexual disorders *[handwritten: neurotic]*	Disorders of sexual functioning or sexual identity. *[handwritten: check for physical causes / Tactile stimulation]*	Sexual dysfunctions, e.g., impotence; inhibited orgasm (see Chapter 16) Transsexualism (see Chapter 16, Box 3)
Adjustment disorder	Impairment of functioning due to identifiable life stresses, such as family or economic crises.	Adjustment disorder with depressed mood Adjustment disorder with anxious mood
Factitious disorders	Physical or psychological symptoms that are voluntarily produced by the patient, often involving deliberate deceit.	Factitious disorder with psychological symptoms Factitious disorder with physical symptoms

*Asterisks denote specific disorders that are discussed in this chapter.
Source: Based on the *Diagnostic and Statistical Manual of Mental Disorders* (American Psychiatric Association, 1980).

(false beliefs about themselves or the world), disturbed thought processes, and loss of control over feelings and actions.

DEFINING DISORDER

The study of psychological disorder is often referred to as *abnormal psychology*, reflecting the idea that disorder is characterized by actions, thoughts, or feelings that are not normal. But it is not always easy to determine what is "normal" and what is "abnormal" in human behavior and experience. If we were to take the term "abnormal" literally, any large deviation from what the majority of people do would be considered abnormal—that is, differing from the general norm. But such a definition would hardly do. Some people have very unusual and outstanding talents and we would not want to say that they are "abnormal" or suffering from a psychological disorder. On the other hand, certain disorders, such as depression, are so common that from a purely statistical standpoint they are not "abnormal" at all. Throughout history, as discussed in Box 1, people have frequently changed their ideas about what constitutes abnormality and disorder. In this section we will consider some of the issues involved in defining disorder.

Psychological adequacy

A central aspect of most approaches to disorder is *psychological adequacy*—that is, how well people adjust to and cope with their environment. If a man is willing and able to feed and dress himself, to hold a job, to support himself, and to communicate rationally with others, he would be regarded as functioning more adequately than a man who cannot or will not do these things. Adequacy can also be judged in terms of the amount of distress or discomfort an individual feels in the course of everyday experiences.

Psychological adequacy plays a central role in the "official" definition of mental disorder put forth in *DSM-III:*

[A] mental disorder is conceptualized as a clinically significant behavioral or psychologic syndrome or pattern that occurs in an individual that is typically associated with either a painful symptom or impairment in one or more important areas of functioning.

This definition makes explicit that the "mentally disordered" person must either experience personal distress or be incapable of functioning adequately in an important area. The task force that developed *DSM-III* conceded that the definition is imperfect. It is often difficult to tell how "distressed" a person is, for example, and it is not always clear what constitutes an "impairment in an important area of functioning."

The medical model

The notion that abnormal behavior results from mental illness became popular around the middle of the nineteenth century. Advances in the field of medicine convinced many physicians that some form of physical or organic disorder was responsible not only for physical ailments but for psychological difficulties as well. As a result, doctors came to view psychological disorders as *illnesses*—each with its own distinctive causes, symptoms, and treatment, just like physical illnesses. This *medical model* clearly underlies the approach to psychological disorder put forth in *DSM-III*. The psychiatrist or psychologist makes use of information about a patient's behaviors, thoughts, and feelings to diagnose a psychological disorder, much in the same way that physicians make use of physical symptoms to diagnose pneumonia or influenza.

Can psychological disorders really be viewed as illnesses, as the medical model suggests? This question is the focus of controversy among mental health professionals. Many professionals believe that the medical model provides a useful approach to psychological disorder because it first classifies the problem as belonging to a particular category before a treatment is chosen. Advocates of the medical model also point out that

Psychiatrists tend to be more favorable to the medical model of abnormality than psychologists. In one study, about half of the psychiatrists surveyed agreed with the statement "I believe that mental illness is an illness like any other," while two-thirds of the clinical psychologists surveyed disagreed with this statement (Morrison and Hanson, 1978). This is not surprising, because psychiatrists are themselves M.D.s who view their work as a branch of medicine, whereas psychologists typically view their field as being distinct from medicine. But there is a good deal of disagreement within each profession as well.

BOX 1

ABNORMALITY THROUGH HISTORY

Throughout history people have tried to explain and to deal with abnormal behavior and psychological disturbance. Through the ages, two very different approaches have prevailed. At some times, the dominant view has been religious: abnormality is seen as a punishment from God or the work of the devil. At other times, the scientific or medical view has been prevalent: abnormality is seen as an illness or disease.

In early Greece, mental disorders were attributed to the gods. The "psychiatrists" were priests, and the "mental hospitals" were temples. This approach continued into the Roman era, where the temples dedicated to Saturn were not unlike lavish resorts for the mentally disturbed, where the guests walked in the gardens, attended concerts, and were treated to other entertainment.

But ancient Greece was also the birthplace of a more scientific approach to mental disorder. The great physician Hippocrates (460–377 B.C.) believed that mental disorders had physical origins, linked to disorders of the brain. His treatment for psychological disturbances included dietary changes, exercise, and abstinence from alcohol.

Because of Hippocrates' influential belief in the physical causes of mental disorder, treatment passed out of the hands of priests and into the hands of physicians for the first—but by no

A trepanning operation used in the Middle Ages to rid a person of evil spirits.

means the last—time in history. But after the fall of Rome, it was not until the nineteenth century that physicians regained the influence in treating disorder that we so naturally accord to them today.

In the Middle Ages, madness was thought to be the will of God, and its cure was religious ritual. By the end of this period, deviant behavior had come to be viewed as witchcraft, in the service of the devil. Treatment of

"witches" consisted of exorcism—a ritual designed to cast the evil spirits from the body. This process involved incantation and prayer, as well as such severe measures as flogging and starvation.

This medieval view of abnormality prevailed well into the seventeenth century, and even today mentally disturbed persons are sometimes referred to as "madmen" and are regarded with a mixture of fear and revulsion.

Hippocrates believed that mental disorders had physical origins.

An insane asylum in the United States in the late nineteenth century.

The establishment of special institutions for the mentally disturbed began in the sixteenth century. Unlike the idyllic temples of ancient Rome, these institutions were very unpleasant. Patients were chained and kept in dungeonlike cells. In London, visitors would come to observe patients as if they were animals in a zoo.

In the late eighteenth century, shortly before the French Revolution, a young doctor, Philippe Pinel, arrived in Paris and revolutionized mental health care by freeing his patients from their chains and instituting humane methods of treatment. The influence of the Enlightenment made it possible once more to view mental disorders as the result of natural causes.

In the first half of the nineteenth century, a number of small and relatively humane mental hospitals were established in both England and America. The hospital superintendent knew all the patients by name and took his meals with them. But these hospitals could not accommodate all the people who needed treatment. By the end of the nineteenth century, therefore, the large mental asylum had become a familiar landmark in the United States.

Unfortunately, such institutions did not work as well as had been hoped: Psychotic patients, criminals, and mentally retarded people were often confined together in a hopeless jumble, without the opportunity for adequate treatment. A subsequent storm over conditions in mental hospitals launched the *mental hygiene* movement in the early 1900s, which endeavored to educate people about mental illness.

Today, scientific advances have stimulated new progress in the diagnosis and treatment of mental disorders. The present era is one of optimism— hope that scientific methods will finally solve one of humanity's most tragic and burdensome problems. And, most significantly, we are finally beginning to admit the difficulty of defining the whole idea of "abnormality."

biological causes for many psychological disturbances are now being discovered. Finally, proponents of the medical model believe that it is more appropriate for a disturbed person to be regarded as suffering from an illness than to be stigmatized for having some basic moral defect (Blaney, 1975).

But critics of the medical model argue that most people who are having psychological problems are not suffering from a "disease" as the word is usually defined. Such people do not necessarily show any signs of physical damage or dysfunction in their brain or nervous system. Psychiatrist Thomas Szasz (1970) has gone so far as to claim that the idea of mental illness is a myth. He argues that the "mentally ill" individual is not really sick; rather, she or he is having difficulty coping with the stresses of everyday life. By attributing the problems to an "illness" rather than to the individual's own inappropriate behaviors, Szasz believes, mental health professionals may encourage the individual to disclaim any responsibility for his or her actions. Indeed, in criminal cases a person judged to be mentally ill is frequently relieved of responsibility for having committed a criminal act (see Box 2).

Culture and disorder

An additional objection to the medical model stems from the fact that what constitutes psychological dis-

order often depends on the norms of a particular culture. Whereas people in all societies would agree that a broken arm is a medical problem, they might differ about whether fits of crying, for instance, is a psychological problem.

If most people in a particular culture have a common type of dance, manner of speech, or mode of dress, these behaviors are declared normal. If you behave in a way that does not follow the norms of your society, your actions will be labeled abnormal. Because abnormality is culturally defined, abnormal behavior in one society may be normal behavior in another. For example, women in one tribe of Melanesian islanders never leave their cooking pots unguarded because they are afraid of being poisoned—a behavior that in our culture would be considered paranoid (Arieti and Meth, 1959). Furthermore, when a society's norms change, what was once considered to be abnormal behavior may come to be considered normal.

The example of homosexuality shows how the dividing line between normal and abnormal is continually shifting. Until recently, homosexuality was considered abnormal in American society, and for 23 years it was listed as a mental disorder in the American Psychiatric Association's diagnostic manual. More recently, however, homosexuality has become more acceptable in our society (see Chapter 16), and in 1974 the American Psychiatric Association removed

BOX 2

THE INSANITY DEFENSE

President Ronald Reagan had just finished giving a speech at the Washington Hilton Hotel. As the President left the hotel, a young man waiting outside pulled out a pistol, crouched down, and fired repeatedly at the President. The man, John W. Hinckley, Jr., wounded the President and three other men. One of them, the President's press secretary, was left with permanent brain damage.

No one disputed that Hinckley had fired the shots on that day in March 1981. Yet he was not convicted of any crime. Instead, a jury found him "not guilty by reason of insanity." Rather than being sent to prison for many years, he was sent to a mental institution, from which he may be released as soon as he is declared to be "sane."

The insanity defense has long been an accepted aspect of our criminal justice system. It rests on the idea that a civilized society should not punish a person who is mentally unable to regulate his own conduct. Yet John Hinckley's acquittal was viewed with indignation by a large majority of the American public, who saw this as a case of a would-be assassin getting off on a legal loophole (Hans and Slater, 1983). The Hinckley verdict has intensified efforts to abolish the insanity defense.

Insanity is a legal term, not a psychological one. And legal definitions of insanity have long been debated. In 1843, Daniel M'Naghten fatally shot the secretary of Britain's prime minister. He said that he had intended to kill the prime minister, on instructions from the "voice of God." The judges decided he was innocent by reason of insanity. Afterward, the British parliament issued the M'Naghten rule, which states that a defendant is legally insane if he does not know what he is doing at the time of the crime or cannot distinguish right from wrong. This rule provided the basic definition of insanity in United States law for over a century.

In 1954, legal insanity received a new definition in the United States.

After his attempt to assassinate President Reagan, John Hinckley was found "not guilty by reason of insanity."

The Durham decision, handed down in a federal appeals court, stated that a person is not criminally responsible for any act that was "the product of either a mental disease or a mental defect." Thus, the court endorsed an explicit medical view of insanity, in contrast to the moral ("knowing right from wrong") view of the M'Naghten rule.

In practice, the Durham rule has led to great uncertainty about who is insane and who is not. Getting two experts to agree on a psychiatric diagnosis has always been difficult.

At John Hinckley's trial, for example, defense psychiatrists and psychologists argued that Hinckley was suffering from a psychosis that left him unable to control his inner drives or to distinguish between reality and fantasy. In contrast, prosecution psychiatrists depicted him as a self-centered young man who decided to try assassination as a way of "becoming famous without working." The jurors were required to evaluate these conflicting opinions and then to decide for themselves whether Hinckley was "sane" or "insane."

An additional problem in determining insanity is that the law asks only whether the accused person was insane *at the time of the crime.* This

means that the experts—and juries—must make judgments about a person's state of mind as it was at some point in the past. This is by no means an easy judgment to make.

Critics of the insanity defense also note that, even in the case of violent crimes, offenders judged to be not guilty by reason of insanity may be back on the streets before long—as soon as they are pronounced "sane." In some cases, newly declared "sane" people have been released from mental institutions only to commit another violent crime soon afterward.

In light of these problems, many people would like to do away with the insanity defense. One new approach, already taken in some states, is to abandon the verdict "not guilty by reason of insanity" and replace it with a verdict of "guilty but mentally ill." "Guilt," in this view, is determined by the person's commission of a crime and not by his mental state. The person judged "guilty but mentally ill" would receive treatment in a mental institution and would be sent to prison, if ever, only after such treatment.

Most mental health professionals oppose this change, however. They contend that, in practice, the "guilty but mentally ill" verdict deprives offenders suffering from mental disorders from needed treatment: many persons judged "guilty but mentally ill" do not in fact receive any treatment before serving their prison sentences.

Most psychiatrists and psychologists favor a tightening of the insanity defense, limiting its use to people with the most serious disorders. At the same time, however, they believe that abandoning the insanity defense would amount to a retreat from justice: that the truly psychotic person who cannot control his behavior or understand its consequences should not be held legally responsible for what he does. A humane system of justice simply must make such distinctions, difficult as they may be.

What is considered normal in one context may be considered abnormal in another.

LOCAL DISORDERS

Certain cultures have psychological disorders that are not found anywhere else. For example, windigo *is a psychosis among Algonquin Indians in which a starved man believes he is being controlled by some supernatural being that has an insatiable craving for human flesh.* Ufufunyane *is an affliction among some South African tribes involving attacks of shouting, loss of vision, and loss of consciousness. And in* Amok *(Malaysia), people suddenly go berserk and assault or kill anyone in their path—hence the expression "to run amok."*

homosexuality from its list of disorders.

The impact of culture on definitions of disorder is emphasized by the fact that the very same behaviors may be viewed as either normal or abnormal, depending on the situation in which they are performed. Thus, it is considered quite "normal" to cry at weddings or funerals but "abnormal" to do so in a laundromat or a grocery store. Experiencing extreme anxiety may be "normal" if it occurs immediately prior to undergoing major surgery, but "abnormal" if it occurs immediately prior to brushing one's teeth (Mahoney, 1980).

But not all is relative in the diagnosis of psychological disorder. Certain sorts of experiences and behav-

ior, such as hearing voices or talking to people who do not exist, are regarded as abnormal in all of the world's cultures. Jane Murphy (1976) found that people living in various non-Western cultures had invented their own terms to classify "crazy" people and that those terms were defined in much the same way as schizophrenia is defined in the Western world. It may be that many individuals who have relatively minor adjustment problems would be classified as normal in one culture and as abnormal in another. But when someone is seriously disturbed, he is not merely marching to the beat of "a different drummer"; he is suffering from a psychological disorder that needs to be treated.

Classifying disorder

To be able to discuss psychological disorders meaningfully and to make progress in treating them effectively, it is important to be able to classify them into various categories—anxiety disorders, depression, schizophrenia, and so on. The diagnostic system employed by mental health professionals, as set forth in *DSM-III*, provides a guide to such categorization.

Before *DSM-III* was introduced in 1980, psychiatric diagnoses were notoriously low in *reliability*. That is, experts were likely to disagree about which category particular people should be placed in. A major reason for the lack of reliability was the fact that the old system of diagnosis lacked criteria that were sufficiently clear and specific. *DSM-III* has helped to remedy this problem by providing more precise criteria. In order to be diagnosed as having depression, for example, a patient must have at least four symptoms from a list that includes poor appetite, sleep difficulties, loss of ability to feel pleasure or enjoy sex, loss of ability to think or concentrate, fatigue, excessive guilt, and suicidal thoughts. The clearer criteria of *DSM-III* have led to much higher levels of reliability (Spitzer, Forman, and Nee, 1979), although the reliability of psychiatric diagnoses is still far from perfect.

The fact that a group of professionals can agree about whether a patient suffers from disorder X or disorder Y does not necessarily mean that they have an accurate understanding of the causes of the disorder or that they can predict its future course. In other words, even if a diagnosis is reliable, such reliability does not guarantee *validity*—the extent to which the diagnosis is in fact correct. Some psychologists and psychiatrists have raised questions about the validity of the distinctions made by *DSM-III*, arguing that its criteria are too rigid to be applicable to all patients (Finn, 1982). It remains clear, however, that without agreement about what constitutes a particular disorder, little progress can be made in understanding the disorder's causes or predicting

its course. In other words, without reliability, there cannot be much validity.

Related to these problems of classification is the fact that a diagnosis becomes a label that can in itself have major effects on the way the patient is viewed. Even if the diagnosis is incorrect, it can come to take on a reality of its own (Scheff, 1975). As we will discuss in Chapter 17, people's reputations can affect the way they are viewed by others. Once people are labeled "mentally ill," it may be difficult for them to get "well" again, because others continue to view them as sick and to treat them that way. In one dramatic and controversial study, psychologist David Rosenhan (1973) and seven other normal people faked symptoms of psychological disorder, in order to get a firsthand view of the life of mental patients. After they were admitted to mental institutions, these pseudopatients took extensive notes about their experiences. At first they worried that the hospital personnel who saw them taking notes would catch on that they were really observers and not patients. But because the personnel had already categorized the pseudopatients as mentally ill, they typically viewed the patients' odd "writing behavior" as another aspect of the patients' illnesses.

ANXIETY DISORDERS

Anxiety is that vague, unpleasant feeling that suggests something bad is about to happen. It is so closely related to fear that there is no sharp dividing line between the two. Physiologically, anxiety and fear are quite similar; they include the same physical symptoms, such as sweating, difficulty in sleeping, and increased heart rate (see Chapter 10). We all feel anxious in certain situations, such as when we are taking an important test or are interviewing for a job. But in *anxiety disorders*, the anxiety is far out of proportion to the situation. Anxiety disorders are the most prevalent psychological disorders, affecting about 8 percent of American adults.

Panic attacks

Anxiety sometimes expresses itself in sudden overwhelming episodes called *panic attacks*. One person described such an attack as "a knot in my stomach, a feeling of hot flashes and warmth through my entire body, tightening of the muscles, a lump in my throat, and a constant feeling that I am going to throw up." Another person said, "I noticed that my hands began to sweat, my legs crumpled under me, I saw white spots floating before my eyes. I felt like getting up and running" (Sarnoff, 1957).

Richard Lazarus (1974) describes the case of a college student who suffered periodic panic attacks. The student complained that he was extremely jittery and uneasy, that he couldn't sleep, that he couldn't concentrate on his studies, and that his stomach hurt. The campus psychologist noted that these panic attacks occurred just before a long holiday when the student would have to return home to his family. According to the student, he looked forward to these visits home. Yet when the end of the semester approached, and with it the prospect of another trip home, the student once again experienced waves of anxiety. It finally came out in sessions with the psychologist that the student's home environment was filled with conflict—a fact the student was able to deny as long as he was away at school. Because the student was unable to acknowledge to himself his repressed negative feelings toward his parents, he tried to hide them. But whenever the prospect of experiencing the reality of his family situation came close, anxiety over those buried feelings gave him away.

Whereas in panic attacks the person experiences anxiety directly, psychoanalytic theorists view other anxiety disorders as resulting from the defense mechanisms that people use to avoid experiencing anxiety. As noted in Chapter 11, all of us occasionally make use of defenses to deal with anxiety and conflict, and this can be perfectly healthy. But defense mechanisms can have their psychic costs, as well, producing (according to the psychoanalytic view) the phobias and obsessive-compulsive disorders to be discussed in the following sections.

Phobias

Phobias are intense fears of particular objects or activities that seem out of proportion to the real dangers involved. Some fears are quite normal—everyone is frightened by what he only partly comprehends. For example, a school-age child may express a dislike for dogs and be uneasy around them. But if the child becomes preoccupied with the possibility of encountering a dog and lives in a constant state of anticipatory anxiety, his feeling goes beyond a normal fear and becomes a phobia.

Phobias are relatively common in childhood. As children grow up they tend to leave these irrational fears behind. Nevertheless, many adults suffer from phobias. Among the most common adult phobias are *agoraphobia* (fear of open places), *claustrophobia* (fear of closed, cramped places), and *acrophobia* (fear of heights). Such phobias can be quite debilitating—a person with agoraphobia, for example, might refuse to go out of the house. It is easy to see how each of these phobias might lead to additional problems. Since people with such phobias cannot feel comfortable in many places, they are likely to feel inadequate and tense and to have problems with interpersonal rela-

Anxiety is a vague feeling that something bad is about to happen. It is closely related to fear, and it upsets us both physically and psychologically.

BOX 3

MULTIPLE PERSONALITY

- Sue is a part-time secretary and a hard-working, conscientious mother of two boys. She accepts what life dishes out but occasionally suffers bouts of depression because of her many responsibilities.
- Ellen is a fun-loving and sexually promiscuous young woman, quick to express her emotions. She has difficulty accepting any responsibility. She has attempted suicide on several occasions.
- Sue-Sue is 6 years old. She is a timid and fearful child who withdraws from contact with others. She prefers to be left alone to play with her dolls.

Each of these people seems to need help, but their problems are more complex than they appear. Sue, Ellen, and Sue-Sue are three personalities in the body of one woman (Spitzer et al., 1983).

Multiple personality is classified as a *dissociative disorder*—a disorder in which the individual dissociates, or loses access to, part of her consciousness. It is one of the rarest psychological disorders, but several cases of multiple personality have achieved wide attention. The popular book *Sybil* (Schreiber, 1975), for example, recounted the struggle of a young woman and her psychiatrist to integrate sixteen different personalities into one. In recent years, researchers have begun to conduct systematic studies on larger numbers of patients with multiple personalities. About 85 percent of these patients are women.

Are the different "faces" of people with this disorder really separate "personalities"? Or is the disorder, as some clinicians have suspected, merely a matter of very convincing role playing? To determine just how distinct the personalities really are, Frank Putnam (1982) gave a series of tests to each of the personalities of ten people diagnosed as having a multiple personality. He found that there were remarkable differences in the memories, mannerisms, and abilities of each personality.

For example, one "person" may recall a happy childhood, while the others within the same body remember only bad experiences; one personality may speak with a severe stutter, while another may be exceptionally articulate. The most striking finding was that the separate personalities showed clear differences in their brain-wave patterns—as large as the differences normally found between two different people. Such differences seem almost impossible to "fake."

Putnam and other researchers have found certain common features in cases of multiple personality. Each personality seems to be a "specialist," taking on a particular role or emotional experience for the others. In the case of Sue/Ellen/Sue-Sue, for example, one personality was practical and diligent, one was outgoing and assertive, and one was passive and dependent. Each personality emerged in response to particular situations. One or two of the personalities may be in control of the body most of the time. In times of crisis, however, there may be a rapid alternation of personalities, known to clinicians as the "revolving door syndrome."

The dominant personalities are typically unaware of the activities of the others. As a result, "losing time" is a common experience in cases of multiple personality. One young woman reported that she had gotten used to the experience of waking up in bed with a strange man and not knowing how she got there. Another woman complained of waking up with headaches every morning; only when she entered therapy and became aware of another self, who drank to excess, did she realize the headaches were hangovers (Bliss, 1980).

It is also common for one personal-

ity to behave violently toward another. In one case, the dominant personality woke up with the pain of her own slashed wrists. She did not understand how or why this occurred until she discovered a note written from one personality to another, threatening her life (Hale, 1983).

What is the cause of multiple personality? The most important common factor, occurring in some 90 percent of the reported cases, is a history of physical or sexual abuse in childhood. When faced with stresses that cannot be explained or coped with, some children apparently learn to escape emotionally by devising separate personalities to deal with the torment. For example, there may be the "bad one" who deserves the punishment, the "good one" who is loved and never hurt, the "sexual one" who permits the fondling, and the "angry one" who wants to strike back. Each emotional experience is sequestered and forgotten, as if it happened to someone else. As multiple personalities get older and escape the abuse, the different personalities still serve as a device for coping with difficulties.

The treatment of multiple personality is a long and difficult process. In the case of Sybil, it took 11 years to integrate her sixteen personalities into one. Some therapists have suggested that the integration may not always be necessary. In at least some cases, people with multiple personality seem to function reasonably well and they may fear that "integration" would lead to the loss of valuable and productive parts of themselves (Hale, 1983). But most therapists do try to help the person integrate the multiple parts of the personality.

Hypnosis is one valuable tool in this process. Hypnosis often succeeds in helping patients recognize the "others." After acknowledging the others' existence, the person—or the dominant personality—can begin to understand how her emotions and skills have been delegated. She can then begin to recapture some of those feelings and abilities, accepting some and rejecting others, as part of a single personality.

People with an extreme fear of heights (acrophobia) may not even want to look at the adjacent photograph.

PHOBIAS FOR ALL OCCASIONS

It is possible, at least in theory, to develop an extreme fear or phobia of practically anything. And when you do, rest assured the psychological wordsmiths already have a word for it. Here are some of the more esoteric phobias (Wallechinsky and Wallace, 1975):

anthophobia: fear of flowers
cyberphobia: fear of computers
decidophobia: fear of making decisions
ergophobia: fear of work
gephydrophobia: fear of crossing bridges
iatrophobia: fear of doctors
ombrophobia: fear of rain
taphophobia: fear of being buried alive
trichophobia: fear of hair

tions. Nevertheless, people with specific phobias—for example, a fear of flying—can often function perfectly well in other areas of their lives.

According to the psychoanalytic view, phobias are symptoms of the repression of unacceptable basic urges. When repression is effective, phobic symptoms need not exist. But when repression fails, the anxiety may become attached to some other object, person, or situation. That is, instead of fearing one's unacceptable impulses, one fears a symbolic substitute for these impulses and thereby avoids having to deal with them. As a result, harmless objects such as snakes or heights or open spaces come to produce enormous fear and are anxiously avoided. In this way the phobia protects the individual from recognizing the true nature of the emotional problem.

The classic example of phobia was the case of "Little Hans," a 5-year-old

boy who lived in terror of horses. Hans's phobia, according to Freud, was not so much fear of horses as fear of his own frightening impulses. First, Hans repressed his wish to attack his father. Then, fearing the father might somehow learn of this wish and punish him horribly, Hans "solved" the problem by fearing horses instead of his father. Now Hans could hate horses while loving his father.

In contrast to psychoanalytic theory, the behavioral view contends that phobias are learned—the person learns to connect intense fear responses with otherwise neutral objects or situations. Wolpe and Rachman (1960) note, for example, that Little Hans experienced a series of traumatic exposures to horses during the time his phobia developed and suggest that these experiences provide a more reasonable explanation of Hans's phobia than the explanation provided by Freud.

The behaviorist's version of Little Hans is John Watson and Rosalie Rayner's (1920) "Little Albert." As noted in Chapter 5, the 11-month-old Albert acquired a phobia as a result of classical conditioning. The experimenters struck a steel bar near Albert's head, producing a terrifying noise, whenever the baby reached to touch a rat. As a result, Albert came to fear the rat and, through a process of stimulus generalization, to fear other furry objects as well. In addition to firsthand learning experiences, such as those of Little Albert, people may become phobic about particular objects or situations by observing others or as a result of verbal descriptions. If, for example, a child's parents are afraid of flying and are always making comments about the dangers of airplanes, the child may develop an unrealistic fear of flying himself.

Why do particular experiences lead some people, but not others, to develop phobias? At least part of the answer may be biological and genetic. There is evidence that certain people are more likely to develop phobias than others. These are the "jumpy" people whose autonomic nervous systems are easily aroused by a wide range of stimuli; such an arousable pattern is to some extent heritable. If such people are placed into a frightening situation, they are more likely to develop a phobia about such situations.

Obsessive-compulsive disorders

Obsessive-compulsive disorders involve two sets of related patterns. First, the person keeps thinking certain thoughts over and over and is unable to put those thoughts out of her head (the obsession). Second, seemingly against her will, the individual engages in ritualistic acts, such as stepping over cracks, knocking on wood, or repeatedly washing her hands (the compulsion). One relatively common form of this disorder is compulsive neatness, in which people attempt to ward off anxiety by keeping their possessions, homes, or workplaces in extremely neat order; any deviation from the prescribed order—a pencil out of place or a rec-

ord out of its jacket—may give rise to anxiety.

Gerald Davison and John Neale (1982) report the extreme case of a woman who compulsively washed her hands over 500 times a day in spite of the painful sores that resulted. She reported that she had a strong fear of being contaminated by germs and that she could temporarily alleviate this concern only by washing her hands. Psychoanalytic theorists speculate that this sort of repetitious handwashing represents an unconscious attempt to make penance for one's forbidden thoughts or impulses. Behaviorists, for their part, believe that compulsive behaviors persist because they have been repeatedly reinforced by their consequences (Meyer and Chesser, 1970). That is, each time the woman washed her hands, she was rewarded by a reduction in anxiety, produced by the knowledge that her hands were now temporarily clean (Hodgson and Rachman, 1972).

In a famous scene in Shakespeare's play Macbeth, *Lady Macbeth washes her hands repeatedly and compulsively, as a result of the guilt she feels for participating in a murder.*

DEPRESSION

Almost all of us feel depressed at one time or another: times when we are discouraged or dejected, when nothing seems to go right, when we feel there is little chance that things will turn out for the better. At such times, thoughts like "I'm a hopeless case" and "I'll never amount to anything" may go through our minds. Such feelings are especially likely to come after a loss or disappointment, whether in love, school, or work. Through such experiences, most of us have some idea of what the psychological disorder called *depression* is like.

However, even though we say we are "depressed," we are usually not suffering from a psychological disorder, or clinical depression. Clinical depression is classified as an *affective disorder,* which means that it is a disturbance of mood or emotion. The difference between clinical depression (depression that would be diagnosed as a psychological disorder) and our normal depression is largely a matter of degree. Clinical depression

Almost all of us feel "depressed" at one time or another. But some people suffer from deep and long-lasting depressions that interfere with their ability to function in their daily lives.

includes such symptoms as a predominantly sad mood, difficulty in sleeping (or, in some cases, difficulty in getting out of bed), loss of appetite, loss of energy, feelings of worthlessness and guilt, and thoughts of suicide. If a person has several of these symptoms for some period of time, he would be diagnosed as depressed.

Even without counting the normal times when people feel down, depression is a very common psychological disorder. It has been estimated that over 25 percent of Americans suffer from serious depression at some time in their lives (Weissman and Myers, 1978). Because it is so widespread, depression has been called "the common cold of mental illness." But whereas colds never kill anyone, depression often does. As many as half of the suicides in the United States are committed by persons suffering from depression (see the Psychological Issue that follows this chapter). Far too many serious cases of depression go unrecognized and untreated. This is especially unfortunate because, of all psychological disorders, depression is probably the most responsive to effective treatment, whether through psychotherapy or drug treatment.

The range of depression

A middle-aged woman presented herself to me for psychotherapy. Every day, she says, is a struggle just to keep going. On her bad days she cannot bring herself to get out of bed, and her husband comes home at night to find her still in her pajamas. . . . She cries a great deal; even her lighter moods are continually interrupted with thoughts of failure and worthlessness. Small chores such as shopping or dressing seem very difficult, and every minor obstacle seems like an impassable barrier. (Seligman, 1975, page 1)

Depression takes many forms, some of which are more severe than others. Some people experience symptoms of depression, including feelings of sadness and despair, to a moderate degree but are still able to continue their day-to-day functioning. In more se-

vere cases, people suffering from depression may remain motionless and mute for hours on end, their faces frozen in expressions of grief. The case described above is somewhere near the middle of this range of depression.

Many depressions can be traced at least in part to difficult life events. The depression of the middle-aged woman described above may have been triggered by specific incidents in her life: her twin sons went away to college and her husband was promoted to a job that frequently took him away from home. In other cases, however, depressions do not have any apparent external causes. These cases are sometimes chronic conditions that can last an entire lifetime.

In some people, episodes of depression alternate with episodes of *mania*, an opposite state of extreme elation or agitation. The alternation between mania and depression is known as *bipolar disorder*. One lawyer spent most of his life alternating between the highs and lows of bipolar disorder. "I literally enjoyed the manic phases," he reported. "I was a big shot, on top of the world. I spent not only my own money, but everybody else's I could get my hands on— I bought six suits at a time, a lot of stupid unnecessary things." Some people in manic states also become loud and aggressive and show little concern about what other people will think of them. After being in such a phase for a while, however, the manic individual comes crashing down into the low phase. In this phase, the lawyer reported, "I feared getting out of bed, and was anxious to get into bed at night because I could block out the horror of my daily life" (*Newsweek*, 1973). It is now clear that bipolar disorders are caused at least in part by biochemical imbalances in the brain.

Cognitive patterns in depression

Although depression is primarily an affective (or emotional) disorder, one important approach to depression suggests that underlying the disturbed moods and feelings is a *cognitive* disorder—a particular style of thinking about the world and oneself. Aaron Beck (1967) suggests that depressed people tend to perceive whatever happens to them in unrealistically negative ways. Thus, a nondepressed person might perceive a flat tire on his car as irritating and inconvenient; a depressed person might perceive it as yet another example of his own failings and the utter hopelessness of life.

Recent experiments have documented the sort of cognitive style that may underlie depression. In one study, subjects peered for a fraction of a second into a box with two eyepieces and were asked to describe what they had seen (Gilson, 1983). In fact, two different pictures—such as a happy face and a sad face—were shown to the subjects simultaneously, one to each eye. Subjects who were relatively depressed, as measured by a mood questionnaire, were more likely to see the sad face, while nondepressed subjects were more likely to see the happy face. People seem to filter their perceptions of the world in their own ways, and these biased perceptions may in turn determine their moods. Another cognitive pattern in depression is the tendency to overgeneralize from negative experiences. Thus, depressed students are likely to agree with such statements as "When even one thing goes wrong, I begin to feel bad and wonder if I can do anything at all" (Carver and Ganellen, 1983).

Where do such cognitive patterns come from? Researchers do not yet have a full answer to this question. But it seems that some combination of biochemical factors and past experiences cause certain people to think in distorted ways that predispose them to depression. There is also evidence that when people stop feeling depressed, their cognitive distortions subside as well (Hamilton and Abramson, 1983).

What causes depression?

Almost all of us experience losses or disappointments at certain points in our lives, yet only some people become seriously depressed. What accounts for this difference? It is now clear that certain types of depression can be traced to the chemistry of the brain. One likely possibility is that

depression involves a depletion of norepinephrine and serotonin, two of the neurotransmitters that convey impulses from one neuron to another in the brain and nervous system (see Chapter 2). As we will see in Chapter 14, drugs that have been effective in treating depression have, as one of their effects, the ability to increase the levels of norepinephrine and serotonin in parts of the nervous system.

The role of brain chemistry is especially clear in cases of bipolar disorder, in which the depressive phase appears to be associated with low levels of the neurotransmitter dopamine (as well as of norepinephrine and serotonin) in certain areas of the brain. The manic phase of bipolar disorder is associated with excessively high levels of some of these chemicals. The biochemical imbalances that lead to bipolar disorder are highly heritable. It is estimated that a child with one parent who suffers from bipolar disorder has a 25 percent chance of being affected by the disorder, and if both parents are affected, the child has a 50 to 75 percent chance of having the disorder (Alper, 1983).

Although certain kinds of depression clearly have a biological basis, in many cases stressful life experiences are necessary to bring the disorder to the fore. On the average, depressed persons have experienced more stress, including physical illnesses, family problems, and work problems, than nondepressed persons (Billings, Cronkite, and Moos, 1983). People who already have a biological predisposition to depression seem to find it particularly difficult to cope with such stresses. In many cases, then, the onset of depression can be attributed to a combination of biochemical factors and stressful experiences.

Early life experience may also contribute to people's susceptibility to depression. Sigmund Freud (1917) suggested that some people become excessively dependent on others for the maintenance of their self-esteem, as a result of either too much or too little gratification of their needs during the oral stage of psychosexual development (see Chapter 11). When these people experience a loss during adulthood, such as the death of a loved one or a rejection, they feel un-

WHEN TASKS BECOME ORDEALS

Although depressed patients often do poorly on various tasks, they tend to believe that they are even worse than they really are—that their actions don't have any chance of succeeding. For example, Martin Seligman (1975) was giving patients a graded-task assignment as therapy for depression. He brought one of the patients, a middle-aged woman, into the testing room, chatted with her, and then said, "I have some tasks here I should like you to perform." When he said the word "tasks," the woman burst into tears and could not continue. As Seligman put it, "A mere task is seen by a depressive as a labor of Hercules" (page 85).

CHAPTER THIRTEEN: PSYCHOLOGICAL DISORDER

People sometimes feel helpless in the face of difficulties. Repeated experiences of helplessness may lead people to believe that they cannot affect their own outcomes. Such people may become passive and depressed.

conscious anger toward this person for leaving them. This anger, however, is not directly expressed but is instead turned inward against the self, leading to the self-blame and self-hatred that are characteristic of depression. Although many psychologists and psychiatrists agree with aspects of Freud's theory of depression, there is little firm evidence for it.

Learning theorists have also proposed that the predisposition to become seriously depressed may have roots in childhood experience. Rather than talking about oral deprivation, however, they focus on the person's history of reinforcement. Martin Seligman (1975) has suggested that depression may be the result of *learned helplessness*—that is, of experiences in which the person learns that her efforts have little to do with the outcome of the situation. People with such experiences may learn that when faced with difficulties, it is useless to try to surmount them. Instead, they become helpless, passive, and depressed. Some researchers believe that the phenomenon of learned helplessness may help to explain why women have been found to be twice as susceptible to depression as men. Women have traditionally been trained to act and feel helpless, and society often keeps them that way. If women learn to be overly dependent on others—parents, boyfriends, husbands, bosses—for their reinforcements, they may ultimately come to feel ineffective and, as a result, prone to depression.

SCHIZOPHRENIA

We had half an hour or so of pleasant chatter about old friends . . . Then he came out with the remark: "I saw you in Cleveland last week, you know." That rocked me a bit as I had not been in Cleveland. And then it all came out. My guest believed that his entire circle of high school friends—who had, in fact, gone their separate ways for years—had had him under surveillance since high school. (Roger Brown, in Brown and Herrnstein, 1975, page 631)

Although most of us can understand pretty well what it is like to be depressed, schizophrenia remains a strange, unfathomable disorder to most people. But it is a condition that afflicts approximately 1 percent of the American population and accounts for half the patients confined to mental institutions. Other schizophrenic people live outside the hospital, in many cases returning periodically for treatment. Regardless of where they may live physically, these people inhabit a mental world that is different from the one the rest of us experience.

The nature of schizophrenia

The term *schizophrenia* was coined by a Swiss psychiatrist, Eugen Bleuler, in 1911. The word literally means

People with schizophrenia may engage in a variety of behaviors that seem inappropriate or bizarre to others. Carrying on a conversation with a statue is one example.

"split mind." But schizophrenia should not be confused with the rare cases of multiple personality that were described in Box 3. The "splitting" that Bleuler was referring to was the patient's departure from social reality. The hallmarks of schizophrenia are serious alterations of perception, activity, emotion, and thought. Sometimes people with schizophrenia are extremely withdrawn and unresponsive and seem oblivious to things going on around them. They may display extremely unusual motor behavior, ranging from frenzied excitement to complete immobility. They sometimes react with emotions that seem totally inappropriate, and they may entertain thoughts about themselves and others that are far out of touch with reality. But schizophrenic patients may sometimes appear at first glance to be perfectly normal. Roger Brown observes that hospital volunteers who converse informally with patients usually find it difficult to tell some of the patients from some of the doctors (Brown and Herrnstein, 1975).

People with schizophrenia sometimes experience *hallucinations*, in which they hear, see, or smell things

that are not really there. And sometimes they entertain *delusions:* thoughts about themselves, others, or the world that seem to be totally divorced from reality. For example, they may have *delusions of grandeur*, believing themselves to be saviors or famous people (such as Napoleon or Jesus Christ), or they may have *delusions of persecution*, believing that others are conspiring against them.

Not all schizophrenic people have all these symptoms, and, depending on which symptoms are most prevalent, a schizophrenic person may be diagnosed as belonging to one of four subtypes. The person with the *disorganized* type of schizophrenia exhibits bizarre behavior, including strange facial expressions and speech and inappropriate or silly emotional reactions. *Catatonic* schizophrenic patients display severe motor disturbances; such persons may show either extreme immobility or agitation. *Paranoid* schizophrenic patients sometimes seem fairly normal; their thinking often seems clear and logical in its own terms, but they are plagued by unrealistic fears, suspicions, and sometimes delusions of persecution. The man described at the beginning

DELUSION OR REALITY?

It's not always easy to decide what is delusion and what is reality. One woman appeared at a local mental hospital at 2 A.M., complaining of disturbances of perception and mood that were triggered, she said, by her discovery that the Mafia had a contract out on her because she was testifying against them in a big government case. "Sure," said the psychiatrist on duty, and admitted the obviously deluded woman. The next day the FBI showed up at the hospital and asked to put a guard on the patient's room. They needed her testimony in a big organized-crime case and had found out that there was a contract out on her.

BOX 4

THE ANTISOCIAL PERSONALITY

It has been some 15 years since Charles Manson was sentenced to jail, but many people still actively fear his release. Manson, along with a group of young people who followed him as their leader and called themselves his "family," was convicted of murdering three men and two women, including actress Sharon Tate, in 1969. The mass murder took place in an expensive home in Hollywood. The killers left the word *pig* scrawled in blood on the front door.

Charles Manson would probably be diagnosed as having an antisocial personality disorder.

Almost as alarming as the mass murder itself was the reaction of the murderer. "I have no guilt," Manson stated at his trial. Throughout his past, he had delighted in escaping from reformatories, getting away with criminal acts, and emerging from prisons totally unrepentant, having learned only to be more careful and more determined in the future. He had always

been described as charming, charismatic, and captivating, able to adapt himself easily to different roles in accordance with the needs and expectations of those around him. He would become "what each person wanted him to be—without ever really being what anyone thought he was" (Nathan and Harris, 1980, page 358). He seemed to be a man without any real emotion.

It is difficult and a bit dangerous to diagnose people on the basis of newspaper stories about them. Yet it seems very likely, as Peter Nathan and Sandra Harris (1980) suggest, that Charles Manson would be diagnosed as having an *antisocial personality disorder*. (More familiar terms for the antisocial personality are *psychopath and sociopath*.) The antisocial personality is one of a larger category of *personality disorders*. A person with a personality disorder has a rigid and narrow range of responses that significantly restrict his way of relating to the environment. Because the disorder is so deeply ingrained a part of personality, the person is typically not made anxious or troubled by his behaviors, even though they disturb other people.

The antisocial personality is characterized by superficial charm and intelligence, insincerity, lack of remorse or guilt, failure to learn from experience, self-centeredness, inability to love, and failure to follow any life plan. An individual with this disorder cannot tolerate frustration. If he wants something *now*, he will do anything to get it, unconcerned about the harm he may do to others along the way.

There is some evidence that the antisocial personality disorder has a biological basis. People with this disorder do not show the same physiological responses that other people do when they are put into a stressful situation—for example, when they are told they are about to receive a strong electric shock (Hare, 1978). As a result, these people may have trouble learning behaviors that most people learn out of fear, and they may not become anxious about the outcome of

their behaviors. The many jail sentences that Charles Manson served never taught him to avoid those actions that put him in jail.

In addition to any biological predisposition that may exist to develop an antisocial personality disorder, such people are quite likely to come from broken homes or from homes with sociopathic or alcoholic fathers (Robins, 1966), and they are also likely to have lost a parent at an early age (Greer, 1964). These findings suggest that antisocial personality disorder may be caused in part by inadequate love and discipline in childhood, especially on the part of one's father. Charles Manson never knew his real father and spent his childhood being shunted between an alcoholic mother, other relatives, boarding schools, and juvenile institutions.

Most research on the antisocial personality disorder has been confined to males. It may be that our society does not breed this type of personality as readily in women as it does in men. With changing sex roles, this situation, too, may change. In fact, recent cases of repeating crimes by female criminals have been linked to diagnoses of antisocial personality disorder (Martin, Cloninger, and Guze, 1978).

SCHIZOPHRENIA 407

of this section would be diagnosed as having paranoid schizophrenia. Finally, many schizophrenics are diagnosed as having *undifferentiated* schizophrenia, which means that they have so many overlapping symptoms that they can't be classified in any of the four subtypes.

Schizophrenia sometimes develops slowly and gradually, with the individual plagued by adjustment difficulties beginning in childhood; this is called *process* schizophrenia. In other cases, schizophrenia strikes more suddenly, sometimes in reaction to a stressful event; this is called *reactive* schizophrenia.

Cognitive disorders in schizophrenia

Whether or not they have delusions or hallucinations, most schizophrenic persons have *thought disorders* of one sort or another. Sometimes these disorders are revealed in incoherent, rambling conversations, such as the following:

DOCTOR: *What would you like, Mr. Kelley?*
PATIENT: *The power of the ancients. The Asunder. I want the Asunder.*
DOCTOR: *Did you ever have the power before? Was it something you lost?*
PATIENT: *Holy, Holy, Holy, Adonai Echod. Te Deum Laudamus. Ex Post Christo, Ex Post Facto, Ex Rel Post Office. There you have it. (Viscott, 1972, page 224)*

In addition, some schizophrenic patients make up new words to use in their conversations, as in the following excerpt:

PATIENT: *I was sent by the government to the United States to Washington to some star, and they had a pretty nice country there. Now you have a body like a young man who says he is of the prestigitis.*
DOCTOR: *Who was this prestigitis?*
PATIENT: *Why, you are yourself. You can be prestigitis. They make you say bad things; they can read you; they bring back Negroes from the dead. (White, 1932, page 228)*

Such manufactured words, meaningful only to the speaker and no one else, are called *neologisms*.

Schizophrenic thought is also likely to be characterized by *loose associations*. The person may be talking about one thing and then drift off on a train of thought that listeners find hard to follow. Schizophrenics may also make *clang associations*, in which the words seem to follow because they rhyme or sound similar rather than because they make sense. For example, "I'll swamp you for a got you and a fair-haired far for a bar and jar for tar" (Rodgers, 1982, page 86).

At the heart of schizophrenic thought disorders seems to be a basic *cognitive deficit*, or abnormal style of processing information. In laboratory studies, people with schizophrenia have been found to be unusually distractable and to have poor recall. Instead of keeping their attention on the task at hand, they are easily diverted by irrelevant stimuli in their environment or by their own thoughts (Oltmanns, O'Hayon, and Neale, 1978). As a result of such distractability, their train of thought and speech becomes disorganized. "My thoughts get all jumbled up," one schizophrenic patient reported. "I start thinking or talking about something but I never get there" (McGhie and Chapman, 1961, page 108).

Another related cognitive deficit found in schizophrenic patients has been termed a *perceptual organization deficit*. Schizophrenic patients sometimes have trouble organizing the features of an object so that they can see the object as a single unit. They seem to deal with stimuli as parts, not as wholes. Raymond Knight (1984) suggests that because schizophrenic persons must process pieces of information individually instead of organizing the information more efficiently, they do not have enough attention left to devote to other aspects of information processing. They may lack the cognitive capability to sift out irrelevant information (so they are more distractable) and to rehearse information (so their recall suffers). Such deficits in basic cognition may lead these people to think, talk, and act abnormally, even to see and hear things that we do not, until they live in worlds that others cannot understand.

Not all schizophrenic patients

These four pictures of cats were painted by an English painter who suffered from schizophrenia. The pictures are arranged in the order in which he painted them (reading from left to right, first top, then bottom), as his disease worsened. The paintings seem to reflect the gradual movement of the painter into his own private and bizarre mental world.

show such cognitive deficits, however. Those that do are most likely to be chronic, or long-term, patients (Knight, 1984). Antipsychotic drugs (see Chapter 14) have been useful in reducing these cognitive deficits, as well as the thought disorders that they produce.

What causes schizophrenia?

Many different explanations for schizophrenia have been proposed. Schizophrenia usually strikes between the ages of 16 and 25, but the seeds for it are sown much earlier. Freud proposed that in schizophrenic breakdowns people regress to the oral stage of development (see Chapter 11), in part because their egos are not strong enough to handle intense sexual urges. Other theorists have focused on family patterns in childhood that they believe give rise to schizophrenia. But there is little hard evidence to support these psychoanalytic or family-pattern approaches. Instead, the breakthroughs in recent research have involved genetic and biochemical factors that seem central to schizophrenia.

Schizophrenia is highly heritable. People with close relatives who are schizophrenic are much more likely to develop schizophrenia themselves than people who do not have schizophrenic relatives. If one identical twin has the disorder, there is about a 50 percent chance that the other twin will have it as well. In the case of fraternal twins, on the other hand, there is only a 10 percent chance that one will have schizophrenia if the other does (Kety, 1983). Some of the cognitive deficits found in schizophrenic patients have also been found in their close relatives, even when the relatives themselves are not schizophrenic (DeAmicus, Huntzinger, and Cromwell, 1981). All of these data converge to indicate that schizophrenia has a large genetic component.

There is almost certainly a biochemical factor predisposing people to schizophrenia that is passed on through the genes. Researchers are hard at work trying to pin down this biochemical factor. Some of the latest evidence suggests that schizophrenia is associated with an increased level of the neurotransmitter dopamine or an overresponsiveness to dopamine in certain brain regions (Nicol and Gottesman, 1983). As noted in Chapter 2, dopamine transmits messages to portions of the limbic system that regulate emotional responses. An excess of dopamine in these areas may give rise to the hallucinations and other disruptions of thought and emotion that characterize schizophrenia. The most direct support for this hypothesis comes from recent studies that have found high levels of dopamine in the brains—especially in the limbic system—of deceased schizophrenic persons (Mackay et al., 1982).

Although genetic factors clearly play a central role in schizophrenia, they cannot explain it entirely. Only about half of the identical twins of schizophrenic patients have schizophrenia themselves, even though they share the same genes and therefore the same biochemical makeup (Nicol and Gottesman, 1983). The fact that one twin develops schizophrenia and the other doesn't reinforces the view that events in the lives of people with a predisposition to schizophrenia often determine whether they will actually develop the disorder. It seems clear, moreover, that stressful events such as failure or rejection in love or work, can sometimes trigger a schizophrenic episode. Just how such events may interact with a person's biological predisposition to cause schizophrenia remains to be understood.

A final complication in discovering the causes of schizophrenia is that researchers are becoming convinced that schizophrenia is not a single disease but rather a family of diseases that may result from a variety of underlying problems. Some of these diseases may be linked to specific inherited biochemical abnormalities; others may even be linked to a virus that strikes prenatally (Torrey, 1980). As researchers learn to distinguish more clearly between the different subtypes and forms of schizophrenia, they hope to move closer to ways of effectively treating it.

THE DISORDERS OF CHILDHOOD

Like the disorders of adulthood, the psychological disorders of childhood span a wide range. For example, *conduct disorders* are marked by repeated violations of social rules to a degree far beyond childish mischief. The most common forms of conduct disorder involve aggression and occur among boys. *Childhood anxiety disorders* are marked by excessive anxiety, fears, or worrying. Two childhood disorders that have particularly puzzled psychologists and have had serious consequences on the families involved are hyperactivity and infantile autism.

Hyperactivity

Hyperactivity, now officially listed under the heading of *attention deficit disorder*, is characterized by short attention span, poor concentration, and excessive motor activity. The case of Larry is illustrative. As a toddler, Larry frequently got up early in the morning and messed up his room before anyone else was awake. In nursery school, at age 4, he was far more active than the other children and could not get along with his peers. By first grade, he had great difficulty in sticking to academic tasks. His handwriting was very sloppy and his notebooks were illegible. He shouted out

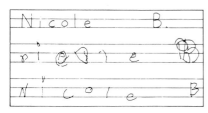

FIGURE 13.1

These handwriting samples show the effects of drug treatment on a hyperactive child. The teacher printed a model on the top line and the child tried to copy it on the second. After taking a stimulant drug, the child tried again on the bottom line. The drug clearly seemed to improve the child's concentration.

in class and could not wait his turn in games. At home Larry was constantly knocking things off tables. By the time he was 8, he had destroyed three television sets. By the age of 10 he was on the verge of being thrown out of school because of his destructiveness and short attention span (Spitzer et al., 1983).

Hyperactive children are impulsive and distractable, find it difficult to focus in school, and may not be able to sit still to eat dinner. Between 3 and 5 percent of all children are affected by hyperactivity, with hyperactive boys outnumbering hyperactive girls by about ten to one.

Signs of hyperactivity are often noticeable shortly after birth. A normal 1-month-old baby will stop moving when he sees someone's face or is given a toy, but a hyperactive baby squirms about constantly. Hyperactive behavior becomes more obvious when the child starts school. The teacher is often unable to manage such a child in the classroom, and his behavior may disrupt other students. The hyperactive child often cannot succeed with schoolwork because of his problem in paying attention. As he grows older, he may continue to be impulsive, inattentive, and unable to make friends.

The exact cause of hyperactivity is unknown, but many researchers assume that it involves an underlying brain abnormality. Treatment for hyperactivity ranges from restricted diets to behavior modification procedures to medication. None of these treatments is foolproof, but since the 1930s stimulant drugs such as Ritalin have been widely used as a means of treatment. Even though these drugs are stimulants they have the paradoxical effect of reducing the child's restlessness and improving his concentration (Solanto, 1984) (see Figure 13.1). Such medications seemed to be effective in Larry's case: Although his schoolwork remained poor, he was no longer a behavior problem and was able to complete assignments. Many parents and professionals object to the use of Ritalin, however, claiming that its benefits may not be worth the possible side effects, such as interference with the child's sleep and appe-

tite or dulling of his senses in the long run (Axelrod and Bailey, 1979).

Autism

Infantile autism is a rare disorder, affecting fewer than 1 out of every 10,000 children born. Autistic children usually are male and frequently are first-borns.

The predominant signs of autism are self-imposed isolation, insistence on sameness in the environment, and major language difficulties. The autistic child often spends hours alone, staring into space, motionless, and his attention cannot be distracted even by loud calling of his name. He may display violent temper tantrums if a single piece of furniture has been moved. And he may have peculiar speech patterns or even fail to speak at all. The autistic child typically shows no interest in people and an excessive interest in mechanical objects. In addition to all these difficulties, the child usually performs at a low level intellectually. But autistic children may also perform well in certain isolated areas, such as rote memorization, calculation, mechanics, and music (see Chapter 7, Box 4).

As an infant, the autistic child may be described as a "good baby who never fusses," probably because he demands little human stimulation. However, he may terrify his mother or father when he shows no interest in being held and begins prolonged head banging, both in his parents' arms and while alone. As he grows older, such self-injurious behavior, as well as intense tantrums, feeding problems, and toilet-training difficulties, all make the autistic child difficult to live with (see Box 5).

It was once thought that autism was produced by cold and unloving parents (Bettelheim, 1967), but the past decade of research has shed considerable doubt on this explanation. Recent biochemical and neurological studies have strongly supported the view that autism is a biological disorder. Autism has been found to be associated with abnormalities in the brain's left hemisphere, which, as discussed in Chapter 2, is largely responsible for linguistic abilities, while the

BOX 5

A CHILD CALLED NOAH

Noah Greenfeld (right) with his older brother, Karl.

Childhood disorders affect the families of disturbed children, as well as the children themselves. A severely disturbed child may require so much care that his needs become the center of attention and thus disrupt normal family life. The daily burden of these needs may evoke devotion and love, but they may also give rise to frustration and resentment. Josh Greenfeld has published two books (1972, 1978) describing the experiences he, his wife, Foumi, and his older son, Karl, have faced in dealing with his severely disturbed son, Noah, who would probably be diagnosed as autistic. The following journal entries from those books give some insight into the family's reactions to Noah, who was born in July, 1966.

4–16–67
We've decided to stop worrying about Noah. He isn't retarded, he's just pushing the clock hands at his own slow speed. Yet . . .

3–11–68
Noah kept us up half the night, giggling to himself and bouncing in his

crib. *I became annoyed with him and finally slapped him. He laughed back at me.*

7–1–68
Noah is two. He still doesn't talk, but I do think he is trying to teach himself how to stand up. We're still concerned. And I guess we'll remain concerned until he stands up and walks like a boy.

6–6–69
Our fears about Noah continue to undergo dramatic ups and downs. Because . . . he doesn't respond when we call his name and fails to relate completely to his immediate environment—a pattern of retardation or autism—we took him to a nearby hospital. . . . I guess we both fear that what we dread is so, that Noah is not a normal child, that he is a freak, and his condition is getting worse.

8–1–69
Last night, as I tried to fall asleep I heard Foumi crying. Why? She was crying for Karl, for the difficulties he would have with other children because he had an abnormal brother. I tried to comfort her, but I know she's right.

9–13–69
I'm a lousy father. I anger too easily. I get hot with Karl and take on a four-year-old kid. I shout at Noah and further upset an already disturbed one. Pehaps I am responsible for Noah's problems.

2–19–70
Foumi keeps complaining about how it's impossible to keep Noah from being destructive about the house. Anything on a table, in a cabinet, on a floor is fodder for him to break. Poor Foumi, she can't afford to take her eyes off him for a second. Poor Noah.

Five years later, when Noah is 8, the family's struggles continue.

9–24–74
Noah refused to eat last night, was up again at an ungodly hour this morning. I've lost my patience with him; I'm beginning to hate him. He ruins my weekends, spoils my days, ravages my sleep, consumes my freedom.

11–30–74
I have to drive him to school in the morning, I have to return from work early because of him. I have to walk him, I have to bathe him, I have to wipe his ass, I have to attend to so many ridiculous chores because of him. And yet . . . I do not look forward to the day when he leaves our lives.

11–17–76
I asked Karl: "What does it feel like being in a family with a brain-damaged brother?"

Karl shrugged. "I don't know what it feels like being in a family without a brain-damaged brother."

1–16–77
I bemoan the kids, especially Noah, but I cannot visualize a life without him. . . . No matter what I say, no matter what I do, I love Noah more than I can do or say. I want him in my house. I want him in my home. That is his place.

An autistic child often spends hours alone, motionless and staring into space. His attention cannot be distracted, even by loud calling of his name.

right-hemisphere abilities (such as musical and spatial abilities) remain essentially intact. But there remains considerable controversy among researchers about the specific biological causes of autism (Fein et al., 1984).

Treatment of autistic children centers on behavior modification procedures (Lovaas and Newsom, 1976). For example, a child who engages in self-injurious behavior might be punished every time she hurts herself and rewarded every time she refrains from hurting herself and attempts some desirable activity. Although these procedures often help to eliminate some of the autistic child's disturbing behaviors and to teach her certain tasks, they do not return the child to normalcy. The long-term outlook for the autistic child is most closely linked with intelligence and speaking ability. Those children who are verbal have the best chance of reaching relatively normal adjustment in adult life. Most autistic children have poor outcomes, however. Only 2 percent of

autistic children recover to be fully normal adults, while 60 percent are classed as making poor adjustments as adults (DeMyer et al., 1973.).

We have sampled only a relatively small number of the psychological disorders that afflict adults and children. It is evident that psychological disorders can, quite as much as physical diseases, cause great suffering in people's lives. Psychological disorders can even take people's lives, as we will see in the Psychological Issue that follows. Then, in Chapter 14, we will move to a more hopeful topic—the ways in which such disorders can be treated.

SUMMARY

Defining disorder

• *1* Throughout history people have had different ideas about what constitutes and causes abnormality. Over the years the religious view of disordered persons as being "possessed" has given way to a more humane medical approach.

• **2** Disorder is often defined in terms of *psychological adequacy*—the person's ability to adjust to and cope with his or her environment.

• **3** According to the *medical model*, mental disorders should be seen as illnesses, with diagnoses, symptoms, and treatments. Szasz and other critics of the medical model say that it absolves the disturbed person from responsibility for his or her condition. An additional objection to the medical model is that it does not take cultural norms into account.

• **4** Cases such as John Hinckley, Jr.'s illustrate the current controversy over the insanity plea in court cases. Critics of the insanity plea see it as a legal loophole to absolve wrongdoers for their crimes, while advocates believe that it is humane and serves justice.

• **5** The diagnostic categories that are used to classify psychological disorders provide a means for mental health professionals to communicate about abnormal behavior. Such categories tended to be unreliable until the introduction of *DSM-III*. However, *reliable* diagnoses (that experts agree on) are not necessarily *valid* (or correct).

• **6** The labels given to patients—such as "mentally ill"—can affect the way they view themselves and are viewed by others.

Anxiety disorders

• **7** *Anxiety* is a vague, unpleasant feeling that something bad is about to happen. In *anxiety disorders*, the anxiety is far out of proportion to the situation. Anxiety is sometimes expressed in the form of *panic attacks*.

• **8** A *phobia* is an intense fear of something that is out of proportion to the real danger involved. According to psychoanalytic theory, phobias displace fears from one's unacceptable impulses onto harmless objects. According to the behavioral view, phobias are learned responses.

• **9** In *obsessive-compulsive disorders*, the person, seemingly against his will, keeps thinking certain thoughts (obsession) and engaging in repetitive acts (compulsion).

Depression

• **10** The most common psychological problem is *depression*. Depression ranges widely in severity. It is characterized by feelings of worthlessness, hopelessness, and lethargy. Depressions may be triggered by external events or may appear as the result of forces within the individual. In *bipolar disorder*, the individual alternates between states of deep depression and extreme elation *(mania)*.

• **11** Depression seems to involve a cognitive disorder—a tendency to filter one's perceptions of the world in negative ways or to overgeneralize from negative experiences.

• **12** What causes depression? Depression may have a biochemical basis, involving the depletion of the neurotransmitters norepinephrine and serotonin. Freud believed that depressed persons turn inward their anger toward a person who has rejected or abandoned them, leading to self-hatred. Seligman has suggested that depression is the result of *learned helplessness*—the person has found that her actions have little effect on the world.

• **13** *Multiple personality* is a rare dissociative disorder in which two or more distinct personalities have developed in the same individual.

Schizophrenia

• **14** The primary characteristics of *schizophrenia* include serious alterations of perception, activity, emotion, and thought. Schizophrenic persons may experience *delusions of persecution* and believe that other people are conspiring against them. They may also have *delusions of grandeur*, believing themselves to be famous persons or religious figures.

• **15** The person with *disorganized* schizophrenia exhibits bizarre behavior. *Catatonic* schizophrenics may show either extreme immobility or agitation. *Paranoid* schizophrenics are plagued by delusional fears and suspicions. And *undifferentiated* schizophrenics have overlapping symptoms of the other types.

• *16* Schizophrenia may strike suddenly (*reactive* schizophrenia) or it may develop slowly and gradually (*process* schizophrenia).

• *17* Schizophrenia is also characterized by thought disorders, and schizophrenic patients' conversations are often incoherent and rambling. They sometimes invent words—*neologisms*—and make *loose associations* or *clang associations* in building sentences. At the heart of these thought disorders is some kind of *cognitive deficit*.

• *18* Schizophrenia is highly heritable, suggesting that there is a predisposing biochemical factor for this disorder. However, environmental factors are involved as well.

• *19* *Antisocial personality disorder* is characterized by superficial charm and intelligence, insincerity, lack of remorse or guilt, inability to learn from experience, self-centeredness, and a lack of concern for other people.

Disorders of childhood

• *20* Psychological disorders of childhood include *conduct disorders, childhood anxiety disorders,* hyperactivity, and infantile autism.

• *21* *Hyperactivity* (classified as *attention deficit disorder*) is characterized by short attention span, poor concentration, and excessive motor activity. Treatment for hyperactivity ranges from behavior modification to stimulant drugs such as Ritalin.

• *22* *Infantile autism* is characterized by self-imposed isolation, in-sistence on sameness in the environment, and major language difficulties. This disorder may be related to abnormalities in the brain's left hemisphere. Treatment usually involves behavior modification procedures, but few autistic children reach normal adjustment.

KEY TERMS

abnormal psychology
antisocial personality disorder
anxiety
anxiety disorders
bipolar disorder
cognitive deficit
delusions
depression
DSM-III
hallucinations
hyperactivity
infantile autism
insanity
learned helplessness
medical model
multiple personality
neuroses
obsessive-compulsive disorders
panic attacks
perceptual organization deficit
personality disorder
phobias
psychological adequacy
psychoses
reliability
schizophrenia
thought disorders
validity

SUICIDE

In ancient times suicide was considered a heroic way of dealing with an impossible life situation. The Japanese hero confronted with an intolerable "loss of face" committed hara-kiri, just as the Greek or Roman warrior fell on his own sword to save his honor. Today suicide is rarely seen as heroic, and it is frowned upon by virtually all religions. Yet suicide remains a major cause of death in America today.

THE MEASURE OF SUICIDE

According to official figures, someone in the United States commits suicide about every 20 minutes—a total of almost 30,000 a year. And these "official" suicides are actually a vast underestimate of the number of people who take their own lives.

Who commits suicide? It is sometimes difficult to know for sure. Many suicides are never reported as such because of the shame attached to the act by family members. Furthermore what looks like an accident may actually be a deliberate suicide. About 50,000 people die each year in automobile accidents, but no one knows how many of these drivers consciously or unconsciously set up the conditions for a fatal crash.

Even if we confine ourselves to the officially recorded suicides, we find that suicide is a personal and social tragedy of tremendous magnitude. Suicide has ranked tenth among causes of death for adults and it is the third leading cause of death for teenagers, after accidents and homicides (Holinger, 1979). And until recently suicide rates have been on the increase.

Suicides are three times as common among men as among women

(Steffensmeier, 1984). However, women are three times as likely as men to attempt suicide unsuccessfully. Some think that most of these unsuccessful attempts are pleas for help rather than real attempts to take one's life. Men are most likely to use guns to commit suicide, while women tend to use pills.

The older a man is, the more likely he is to commit suicide—the rate for men 65 and over is almost twice as great as that for men between 15 and 24. Among women, the rate increases until middle age and declines after that. But suicides among young people have shown the most striking increases in recent years.

THE MOTIVES FOR SUICIDE

Why do people take their lives? Many possible reasons have been suggested. They include: turning aggression inward, retaliating against others by making them feel guilty, trying to make amends for perceived past wrongs, trying to rid oneself of unacceptable feelings, desiring to rejoin a dead loved one, and escaping from pain, stress, or emotional problems (Mintz, 1968).

Gerald Davison and John Neale (1982) suggest that at a fundamental level a person chooses suicide as the best means available for withdrawing from a seemingly unsolvable problem in living. But they are quick to point out that this explanation does not account for the fact that not all people faced with the same sorts of problems commit suicide.

Suicide is related to psychological disorder, especially depression. One study found that four out of five people hospitalized after attempting suicide were suffering from depression. And autopsies have suggested that there are abnormally low levels of the neurotransmitter serotonin in the brains of suicide victims. Low levels of serotonin have been linked to depression, and some investigators see this biochemical deficiency as play-

Dear Folks:

I know this won't seem the right thing to do but from where I stand, it seems like the best solution, considering what is inevitably in store for the future.

You know I am in debt. Probably not deeply compared to a lot of people but at least they have certain abilities, a skill or trade, or talents with which to make financial recovery. Yes, I am still working but only "by the grace of the gods." You know how I feel about working where there are a lot of girls. I never could stand their cattiness and I couldn't hope to be lucky enough again to find work where I had my own office and still have someone to rely on like Betty. . . .

One reason for doing this now is that Bill will be back and may want his .22. But the primary reason is one I think you already know—Mike. I love him more than anyone knows and it may sound silly to you but I can't go on without him. What is there that's worth living for without him?

Partial contents of a suicide note left by a 23-year-old woman who shot herself to death.

ing a critical role in the decision to commit suicide (Greenberg, 1982).

Not everyone who attempts or commits suicide is depressed, however. Some suffer from other disorders that involve feelings of agitation, aggression, or impulsivity. It has been found that seriously depressed people are especially vulnerable to suicide just at the time that their spirits begin to rise. When these people are most severely depressed, they may not have enough energy to do anything, let alone commit suicide. When they first start to feel better, they may still be quite depressed but now have the energy to take their own lives.

Among people who are already depressed or suffering from other disorders, personal crises may trigger the act of suicide. Such crises may include failures at work or desertion by a lover. However, most suicides are planned, rather than sudden, impulsive acts.

The suicide rate among married persons is lower than the rate among persons who are single, widowed, or divorced, suggesting that marriage may provide some degree of protection against the stresses that lead people to take their lives.

TEENAGE SUICIDE

On a December evening in 1973, while her parents were at a neighborhood party and her sister was upstairs playing the piano, Vivienne Loomis, an attractive ninth-grader who was a remarkably gifted writer, hanged herself in the basement of her home. She was 14 years old.

In Plano, Texas in 1983, after one teenaged boy was killed in an accident, his best friend turned on a car engine in a closed garage and poisoned himself with carbon monoxide. In the next few months, two more Plano teenagers committed suicide, and sixteen made unsuccessful attempts.

Over the past three decades, the suicide rate among teenagers (and even children) has reached epidemic proportions. Each year some 5,000 teenagers kill themselves, and half a million make unsuccessful attempts. The suicide rate for this age group has more than tripled since the 1950s, although it has apparently remained level since 1978.

Why do so many young people try to kill themselves, and why has the rate of teenage suicide increased so dramatically? Some observers point to today's relaxed morality, which may give teenagers too many decisions to make too soon. Others point to the rootlessness that many young people feel. Suicidal adolescents have described feeling "a void in their lives—the lack of anything to stand for."

Vivienne Loomis left behind a diary and poems that offer us a glimpse of the pain that she, and perhaps other teenagers, experienced (Mack and Hickler, 1981). Over and over, she described herself as worthless and unattractive. "I am of no use to anyone, and no one is of any use to me" (page 63). She described the intense loneliness and emptiness that she felt: "I need people and there aren't any who care" (page 63). And she expressed her frequent feelings of hopelessness, as in this poem written a year before her death (page 53):

And then
There are times
When I have nothing
To look forward to
In life
At all.
Like now.

THE OTHER VICTIMS

Suicide is not only the ultimate act of self-destruction but also the ultimate act of abandonment. It affects the lives of all those connected with the victim. In the past decade, more attention and research has been focused on the special problems of the survivors that suicides leave behind.

Particularly devastating are cases of parents whose child commits suicide. The tremendous grief that is felt no matter how a child dies is compounded by feelings of ultimate failure and guilt. The parents blame themselves for not preventing the tragedy or for raising a child to be so unhappy that he would choose to die. Vivienne Loomis's father said he knew what it was like to feel "just utterly damned." Her mother still wonders whether she burdened Vivienne with too many of her own concerns.

When a parent commits suicide, especially when the child is young, the child may decide that she was somehow to blame. "Twenty-five years ago my mother committed suicide," a young woman writes. "I was seven. No one told me how she died or why. I thought perhaps I had driven her away" (Bergson, 1982). Added to this is a feeling of anger at the parent who decided to leave the child instead of raising her.

The child must now live with a legacy of suicide in the family. Children become fearful that they are destined to follow the parent's example—and in fact children of parents who committed suicide are at an increased risk for suicide themselves. This association may be due in part to a genetic predisposition to depression or other psychological disorders. But some psychotherapists describe "an identification in the children of suicides, setting up a sense of doom that is eventually acted on" (Bergson, 1982, page 104).

Across the country, organizations and support groups have formed to help suicide survivors learn to cope with their tragedies. No one ever gets over a suicide, but psychotherapists believe that talking through experiences and feelings can help. The tragedy is even worse for survivors when the topic is hushed, as it traditionally had been, leaving the survivors feeling overwhelmed, isolated, and ashamed.

PREVENTING SUICIDE

How can we prevent the tragedy of suicide? One approach is through community suicide prevention centers, which offer 24-hour services to people who are feeling suicidal. When people call the center, the staff members try to determine how serious their threats are and to establish personal contact. Workers on such suicide "hotlines" have specific goals in talking to callers. These goals include communicating empathy to the caller, conveying understanding of the problem, providing information on where to go for professional help, convincing the caller to agree to measures that will take her a step away from the suicide, and providing hope that the caller's crisis will end (Speer, 1972).

Another approach to preventing suicide is to make it harder to do. For example, a fence was put around the observation platform of the Empire State Building to eliminate one "popular" method of suicide. Physicians limit the number of sedative and antidepressant tablets prescribed at one time so that the means to commit suicide will be less readily available (Hudgens, 1983). And because firearms, especially handguns, are used in the majority of successful suicides, it has been suggested that the rise in the suicide rate might be controlled by enforcing stricter handgun laws (Boyd, 1983).

Finally, therapists urge people to notice warning signals—the signs suicidal individuals often put out. Among these signals are indirect comments about how they might as well be dead, giving away treasured possessions, and marked personality changes. If you notice these signals in a friend or family member, confront him and ask him what is going on. If you suspect that he is feeling suicidal, do your utmost to see that he gets professional help (Langone, 1981).

Why are we so concerned about preventing suicide? Why not let individuals decide for themselves when they have had enough of liv-

Suicide affects the lives of all those connected with the victim.

At suicide prevention hotlines, workers try to communicate empathy to callers. They try to convince callers to take measures that will take them a step away from suicide, and they encourage callers to get further professional help.

ing? One reason for our concern is that people who attempt suicide often go on to lead happy, productive lives. Most people who attempt suicide don't want to die and would not try to kill themselves if they could find any other solution to life's problems.

As Martin Seligman (1975) points out, moreover, depression, which is often central in suicide, usually dissipates with time. The depressed person has a bleak view of his future and feels hopeless. But in a few weeks or months this attitude is likely to change, and when the depression goes, so will the compulsion to commit suicide.

One woman who had attempted suicide several times supported this point when she wrote, "By the way: to all the doctors, nurses, and psy-chiatrists who forced me to live when I didn't want to—thank you for keeping breath in my lungs and my heart beating and encouraging hope in me when I didn't have any hope. I'm glad I'm alive to say that" (Scheinin, 1983).

SUMMARY

- **1** Suicide is a major cause of death in America. Men are more likely to commit suicide than women, although women are more likely to make unsuccessful suicide attempts.
- **2** There are many possible reasons for suicide, but the fundamental reason is the inability to cope with a seemingly unresolvable problem. The majority of those who attempt or commit suicide are suffering from depression or other psychological disorders.
- **3** The most dramatic increases in suicide rates have been among teenagers. It has been suggested that this increase in young suicides is related to today's relaxed morality and to the rootlessness that many young people feel.
- **4** Suicide affects not only the victim but the lives of all those connected with the victim. The victim's loved ones have special problems that often require outside help, either from support groups or therapists.
- **5** Suicide prevention centers and hotlines are designed to help potential suicides change their minds and seek professional help for their problems.

CHAPTER 14

INSIGHT THERAPIES

Psychoanalytic therapy
Client-centered therapy

Insight therapies emphasize talking out problems and getting feelings out in the open.

BEHAVIOR THERAPIES

Desensitization
Operant therapy
Modeling and role playing

Behavior therapies use principles of learning to help people change their patterns of behavior.

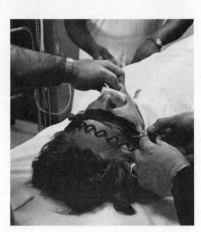

SOMATIC THERAPIES

Psychopharmacology
Electroconvulsive therapy
Psychosurgery

Somatic therapies include the use of drugs and the application of electric shocks to treat psychological disorders.

EVALUATING THERAPY

Does therapy work?
Therapy and responsibility

How effective is therapy? And what are the special responsibilities of the therapist?

PSYCHOLOGICAL ISSUE
THE THERAPY MARKETPLACE

A wide variety of alternative therapies, from "rebirthing" to est, are now being offered. The consumer must be discriminating.

BOXES
1 **Gestalt therapy**
2 **Rational-emotive therapy**
3 **The right to refuse treatment**
4 **In and out of the mental hospital**
5 **Community mental health**

We have seen that psychological disorders take many forms and can cause individuals and their families considerable distress. What can psychology and psychiatry do to help people who suffer from these disorders? This question brings us to the domain of *therapy*, the professional application of techniques intended to treat psychological disorders and reduce distress. It is estimated that some 6 million Americans receive therapy each year—1.5 million in therapists' offices, 2.4 million in outpatient psychiatric clinics, 1.5 million in community mental health centers, and several hundred thousand in mental hospitals (Gross, 1978).

The field of therapy is so diverse that it might be more appropriate to speak of *therapies*. There are more than 250 different schools of therapy, from the well-established and traditional approaches (such as psychoanalysis) to the avant-garde and way-out approaches, some of which will be discussed in the Psychological Issue that follows this chapter. New therapies are continually being developed, almost always with high claims and expectations. As Morris Parloff (1976) notes, "No school has ever been withdrawn for failure to live up to its claims, and as a consequence all continue to coexist" (page 14).

Therapy may be conducted individually or in groups, in settings that range from hospital rooms to private offices to auditoriums. It may be administered by psychiatrists, clinical psychologists, social workers, psychiatric nurses, and sometimes by members of other professions, such as the clergy. It may take years of several sessions per week to be considered successful, or it may consist of a single session. The techniques for therapy range from listening quietly as the client talks to administering powerful drugs.

Therapy addresses itself to a wide spectrum of problems, from serious disorders such as major depression and schizophrenia to mild problems of adjustment that are not really "psychological disorders" at all. Particularly because of these latter kinds of problems, it is often difficult to distinguish between therapy and counseling. For the most part, however, *counseling* focuses on specific decisions or adjustments that a person needs to make (such as decisions about schoolwork, occupation, or marriage), whereas therapy is concerned with more generalized or deeper-rooted psychological problems.

Despite the wide variations in therapies, all approaches attempt to give the patient or client some relief from anxiety, depression, and other symptoms. They try to give clients a better understanding of their own feelings, motives, and social relationships. They attempt to help clients develop a sense of adequacy and self-esteem. And they try to help clients adjust to their culture and society. Different therapies may emphasize some of these goals more than others, however, and they may differ in what they consider to be "adequacy" or "adjustment."

In this chapter, we will focus on three major categories of therapies. First, we will examine the major "insight therapies," which emphasize talking through one's problems. Second, we will discuss the behavior therapies, which are based on principles of experimental psychology, especially principles of learning. Third, we will consider the somatic therapies, which involve direct physiological intervention, including the use of drugs. After our tour of this variety of therapies, we will consider some general issues regarding their effectiveness and ethics.

INSIGHT THERAPIES

The basic idea of the "insight therapies" is that open discussion of a problem can bring insights into its causes and suggest possible solutions. Insight therapies emphasize getting one's feelings out into the open—bringing out the concealed thoughts and emotions that are often the cause of psychological problems.

Two major varieties of insight therapy are psychoanalysis and client-centered therapy. Although both types emphasize expression of inner feelings by the client, they differ greatly in their theoretical basis and in their approach to the client-therapist relationship. Another variety of insight therapy, Gestalt therapy, is discussed in Box 1 (page 425).

Psychoanalytic therapy

Psychoanalysis is the system of therapy developed by Sigmund Freud, and it is part and parcel of his general theory of personality (see Chapter 11). Psychoanalysis was born with the case of "Anna O." In the early 1880s a physician named Josef Breuer told Freud of a patient he was treating, a woman whom he called "Anna O.," who was suffering from hysteria—the presence of physiological symptoms with no organic basis. At various times, Anna had a severe cough, paralysis of parts of her body, and speech disturbances, none of which had any apparent physical cause. Breuer found that when he hypnotized Anna she could remember long-buried, painful events from her past that were associated with the first appearance of specific symptoms. During hypnosis Breuer helped his patient to reexperience the painful events and to express the feelings that accompanied them. Upon being awakened, Anna expressed a great relief—both physical and emotional. For example, Anna traced the origin of her nervous cough to an occasion when she was at her dying father's bedside. She heard dance music coming from a neighbor's house and felt a wish to be there, coupled with intense guilt for having such a feeling. Anna covered up her feelings at the time with a cough, and from then on

coughed uncontrollably whenever she heard dance music. After Anna had recalled this repressed episode, the symptom disappeared (Breuer and Freud, 1895).

The case of Anna O. illustrates the basic tenet of the theory Freud subsequently developed: that painful thoughts and emotions are often hidden in the unconscious mind. The goal of psychoanalysis is to open the doors to the unconscious to discover the underlying causes of patients' problems and to help the patient achieve *catharsis*—the release of pent-up emotions—as Breuer did with Anna. Freud discovered that hypnosis was unnecessary to achieve these goals. Instead, he developed the techniques of *free association*, in which patients are asked to let their thoughts flow freely and to say whatever comes to mind. Freud would say to his patients:

*You will notice that as you relate things various thoughts will occur to you which you would like to put aside on the ground of certain criticisms and objections. You will be tempted to say to yourself that this or that is irrelevant here, or is quite unimportant, or nonsensical, so that there is no need to say it. You must never give in to these criticisms, but must say it precisely be-*cause *you feel an aversion to doing so. (Freud, 1913, page 135)*

Freud believed that even the most "irrelevant" thoughts can have meaning and that pauses or breaks in a train of thought indicate the patient's *resistance* to touch on sensitive topics. The psychoanalyst is trained to notice points of resistance and to try to help the patient overcome them. In the process of *interpretation*, the analyst points out resistances and offers some reasons for them. Freud also asked his patients to recount their dreams, and he made use of this material as a gateway to the patients' unconscious minds.

Some patients find themselves at times becoming furious at their psychotherapists or at other times forming strong attachments to them. Freud believed that these emotions had less to do with the patients' actual relationship with the therapists than with residues from the patients'

REFRESHER COURSES FOR PSYCHOANALYSTS

Freud believed that psychoanalysts, like their patients, were likely to react emotionally to their patients as figures from their own past. Such feelings are called countertransference. *Partly to help them handle such countertransferences, psychoanalysts must undergo psychoanalysis themselves before beginning to practice. Freud also recommended refresher courses for analysts: "Every analyst should periodically—at intervals of five years or so—submit himself to analysis once more without feeling ashamed of taking this step" (1964, page 249).*

relationships to people in the past, usually their parents, which are then shifted to the therapists. Freud called this process of shifting emotions *transference,* and he believed it to be a central ingredient of successful psychoanalysis. By permitting patients to reexperience and express conflicts from their earlier life, the transference relationship helps them to gain awareness of the unconscious forces underlying their behavior.

The process of transference can be seen in the following excerpt from a psychoanalytic session:

PATIENT (a 50-year-old male business executive): *I really don't feel like talking today.*

ANALYST (remains silent for several minutes, then): *Perhaps you'd like to talk about why you don't feel like talking.*

PATIENT: *There you go again, making demands on me, insisting I do what I just don't feel up to doing.* (Pause) *Do I always have to talk here, when I don't feel like it?* (Voice becomes angry and petulant) *Can't you just get off my back? You don't really give a damn how I feel, do you?*

ANALYST: *I wonder why you feel I don't care.*

PATIENT: *Because you're always pressuring me to do what I feel I can't do.*

(Davison and Neale, 1982, page 564)

The patient in this excerpt had been in therapy for about a year. In previous sessions the analyst had learned enough about the patient to suspect that, although he was a successful businessman, he had feelings of weakness and incompetence that seemed to stem from childhood experiences with his father. The father had been highly critical and never seemed satisfied with his son's efforts. The analyst interpreted the above comments by the patient as an expression of resentment against the father, not against the analyst. "The patient's tone of voice (petulant), as well as his overreaction to the analyst's suggestion that he talk about his feelings of not wanting to talk, indicated that the patient was angry not at his analyst but at his father" (Davison and Neale, 1982, page 564). The therapist used this transference as the basis for subsequent sessions.

Freud believed that therapists should remain somewhat aloof and provide a neutral screen on which patients can project whatever image (such as father, mother, or spouse) they require for working out basic conflicts. In Freud's words, the therapist should be "impenetrable to the patient, and, like a mirror, reflect nothing but what is shown him" (1956, page 331). This is one of the reasons why the patient traditionally lies on a couch, while the psychoana-

In the traditional psychoanalytic session, the patient lies on a couch, while the analyst sits behind the patient where she cannot be seen.

lyst sits behind the patient where she cannot be seen.

From the psychoanalytic viewpoint, the patient's need to discover and reexperience deeply buried psychological forces is a time-consuming process. Traditional psychoanalysis involves hour-long sessions three to five times a week, often extending over several years. In recent years, however, traditional psychoanalysis has become less prevalent, at least in part because of the high costs involved. At $75 to $100 an hour, four days a week, it can cost well over $15,000 a year. Now psychoanalytic therapy is more likely to be conducted in once- or twice-weekly sessions. There is also a trend toward limiting the length of such therapy, often to 20 or 30 sessions. The therapist and patient typically sit facing each other, and the therapist plays a more active role than in traditional psychoanalysis, providing guidance in exploring current, as well as past, problems. Contemporary psychoanalytic therapists also tend to be eclectic, borrowing techniques from other schools when appropriate rather than relying solely on free association, transference, and other Freudian techniques. Nevertheless, the emphasis remains on the individual gaining insight into the unconscious forces governing her behavior.

How effective is psychoanalytic therapy? As with all of the therapies we will consider, this is a matter of considerable dispute, especially in the absence of many well-controlled studies. It is known that psychoanalytic therapy, as Freud himself acknowledged, is not effective with schizophrenic or other psychotic patients. Rather, it is best directed at patients with anxiety disorders or relatively mild depression—what Freud called neuroses. Psychoanalytic therapy seems to work best with highly educated and verbal people who already have some skill in exploring their own emotions. Certainly many people feel better over the course of this type of extended therapy. We will return to the question of the effectiveness of various forms of therapy later in this chapter.

Client-centered therapy

According to Carl Rogers, the humanistic psychologist who developed *client-centered therapy*, the aim of therapy is to help clients become their true selves by allowing them to test out the feelings that they have previously refused to admit are part of their life. As discussed in Chapter 11, Rogers believes that maladjustment is a result of denying those feelings and behaviors that do not conform to one's image of oneself, even when that image is false. Rather than correcting that self-image, the individual keeps evading the contradictory experiences. When these attempts fail, the inconsistency brings intense anxiety.

Client-centered therapists help individuals express and experience their true feelings by providing *unconditional positive regard.* That is, the therapist continues to respect the client no matter what he says or does. With such unconditional positive regard, the client worries less about how he will be evaluated by others and instead concentrates on the primary goals of evaluating his behavior for himself and considering how it will contribute to his personal growth.

Unlike the psychoanalyst, the client-centered therapist does not probe or make interpretations of the client's hidden thoughts and feelings. Instead, the therapist's main task is to create conditions that will help the client to change *by herself.* These conditions include acceptance, unconditional positive regard, and clarification of feelings, in the context of a warm relationship.

During the therapy session, the therapist will often rephrase clients' statements in such a way as to highlight the things the client seems to be suggesting but will not admit to in so many words. The following example from a client-centered therapy session shows how this technique is used:

CLIENT: (an 18-year-old female college student): *My parents really bug me. First it was Arthur they didn't like, now it's Peter. I'm just fed up with all their meddling.*

THE BEST SHRINKS IN LIFE ARE FREE
Freud (1913/1958) believed that the patient's payment of a fee contributed to the success of psychotherapy. More recently, psychologists have argued that fee-paying patients will try harder to improve, in order to justify their financial commitment. To investigate these notions, Carol Yoken and Jeffrey Berman (1984) randomly divided college students into two groups: half who paid for a therapy session and half who did not. Following the session, the students who had not paid reported lower levels of distress, suggesting that the therapy had been more effective for them. In at least some cases, people who receive free therapy may perceive their therapist as warmer and more caring—and, as a result, are more likely to improve. So far, however, the study has not led any of my therapist friends to lower their fees.

BOX 1

GESTALT THERAPY

While Freud sought to cure patients' problems by helping them to understand their complicated pasts, Fritz Perls (1894–1970) emphasized becoming whole through awareness and appreciation of the here and now. His approach to achieving such wholeness is called *Gestalt therapy,* from the German "gestalt," meaning "configuration" or "arrangement of parts in a whole."

According to Perls (1969), people tend to block out awareness of aspects of themselves and their experience and look at only a part of who they are or what they are doing. The therapist's job is to make such individuals "whole" again by helping them recognize all facets of their personalities and experiences.

Fritz Perls, founder of Gestalt therapy.

Gestalt therapy stresses feeling rather than thinking. "Intellect is the whore of intelligence," Perls (1969) wrote. "It's a drag on your life." Perls frowned on asking the question "why?" and said that the question to be asked is "how?" "Why" implies a search for intellectual understanding of what went wrong in the past; "how" implies a search for an understanding of what *is*. What *is* needs to be accepted, not criticized.

Gestalt therapy makes use of *psychodrama,* in which one acts out scenes in order to bring out their emotional significance. In this technique, the person might "talk to his father," trying to picture his father on the empty chair across from him. The client might then switch chairs and be his father, replying to him. Gestalt therapy is typically done in groups, although the focus remains on the distinctive experiences of individual group members.

Gestalt therapy takes the view that people are responsible for their own lives and can make their own choices. Perls made this philosophy explicit in a memorable credo:
I do my thing and you do your thing. I am not in this world to live up to your expectations. And you are not in this world to live up to mine. You are you and I am I. And if by chance we find each other, it's beautiful. If not, then not. (Perls, 1969)

Gestalt therapy has been criticized by some for being anti-intellectual and unscientific. Like other "growth-oriented" therapies, its lack of clear criteria for measuring personal growth makes it difficult to evaluate. But Gestalt therapy's emphasis on emotional experience has had a major impact on the human potential movement of recent decades, and some of its specific techniques have been adopted by therapists from a wide variety of theoretical persuasions.

THERAPIST: *You really are angry at your folks.*

CLIENT: *Well, how do you expect me to feel? Here I am with a 3.5 GPA, and providing all sorts of other goodies, and they claim the right to pass on how appropriate my boyfriend is.* (Begins to sob)

THERAPIST: *It strikes me that you're not just angry with them.* (Pause) *Maybe you're worried about disappointing them.*

CLIENT: (Crying even more): *I've tried all my life to please them. Sure their approval is important to me. They're really pleased when I get the A's, but why do they have to pass judgment on my social life as well?* (Davison and Neale, 1982, page 575)

In this example, the therapist had learned from previous sessions that the client's efforts to do well academically were motivated by a need to please her parents and avoid their criticism. Even though at first the client is expressing anger at her parents,

the therapist is helping her to realize that she really is afraid of their disapproval.

According to Rogers, warmth and empathy from the therapist are the most important factors in the success of therapy. Rather than emphasizing specific techniques, he stresses the personal qualities and emotional style of the therapist (Rogers, 1951). Studies of the effectiveness of various therapies seem to bear this idea out. They suggest that therapists who are genuine, warm, and empathic (having an accurate understanding of the client) obtain the best outcomes (Truax and Mitchell, 1971). These qualities are likely to be helpful to therapists of any orientation, not just client-centered therapists. As one client of a warm, helpful therapist put it, "Right from the start, I felt she really cared about me. She seemed to be upset by my problems and to be happy when I made progress. I felt so relaxed with her that it was easy to talk about very personal things" (Derlega and Chaikin, 1975, page 104).

TELEPHONE THERAPY

The value of the telephone in treating psychological disorder has only recently been recognized. Psychiatrist Gerald Grumet (1979) suggests that the phone may be the ideal form of communication for certain clients who are too anxious to tolerate face-to-face therapy sessions. Grummet describes one woman who was prone to extreme anxiety and occasional fits of rage during treatment sessions. After several crisis-type phone calls, the therapist realized that the client communicated better on the telephone. The client herself eventually eliminated visits, but therapy proceeded in nightly phone calls for ten years.

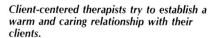

Client-centered therapists try to establish a warm and caring relationship with their clients.

CHAPTER FOURTEEN: THERAPY

BEHAVIOR THERAPIES

The *behavior therapies* are based on the principles of experimental psychology, especially of learning theory (see Chapter 5). Behavior therapists do not typically focus on deep underlying causes for psychological problems, nor do they see therapy as a process of drawing out buried emotions or hidden thoughts. Rather, they concentrate on the factors that are currently maintaining the person's inappropriate or self-defeating behaviors. The tasks of behavior therapy are to help the client learn to replace inappropriate or unsatisfying behaviors with more appropriate or satisfying ones, and to help the client acquire skills needed to cope effectively with life's challenges.

Behavior therapists use a variety of techniques, either alone or in combination, depending on the client's problem. The techniques to be examined here are desensitization, operant conditioning, and modeling and role playing.

Desensitization

As noted in Chapter 5, fears can be acquired through a process of classical conditioning. Recall, for example, the case of Little Albert, who was conditioned to fear rats by having a loud noise sounded near his head whenever he reached toward a rat. The fear response was generalized from the initial object of fear (the noise) to the objects that were associated with it. *Desensitization therapy* is an attempt to reverse this process by linking feared objects or situations with new responses that replace the fear. The feared object or situation becomes linked to something pleasant, and the client is "desensitized" to the object or situation.

What later came to be called desensitization therapy was first introduced by Mary Cover Jones (1925), a colleague of John Watson, the psychologist who had conditioned Little Albert. She was able to eliminate a fear of rabbits in a 3-year-old named Peter by giving him candy and other foods he liked while he was in the presence of a rabbit. At first the animal was kept at the far end of the room, then it was brought closer and closer on successive occasions. Jones proceeded to study seventy other children using variations of this strategy. The underlying idea of this approach is *counterconditioning:* the fearful stimulus (in Peter's case, the rabbit) is repeatedly paired with an object that produces positive, non-fearful responses (candy and food). This new conditioned association crowds out the previous association between the object and fear (see Figure 14.1).

Several decades after Jones's pioneering work, Joseph Wolpe (1958), a psychiatrist from South Africa, developed the technique of *systematic desensitization* to treat a wide range of fears and anxieties. Because most of the fears that therapists are called upon to treat are not as concrete as the fear of rabbits, Wolpe had subjects *imagine* the anxiety-evoking event or situation, whether it was fear of taking tests, of asserting oneself, or of speaking in public. And instead of giving patients candy, he taught subjects techniques of deep muscle relaxation. In systematic desensitization, the client is asked to arrange scenes in an *anxiety hierarchy,* from the least arousing to the most arousing. The patient then relaxes while imagining the least fearful scene and progressively moves on to more and more anxiety-arousing scenes, analogous to the way Jones brought the rabbit closer and closer to Peter. The ability to imagine more and more fearful scenes while relaxing has been found to reduce anxiety in the real-life situations, as well. The client learns to associate relaxation, not fear, with these situations.

In one experimental study of systematic desensitization, researchers were concerned with reducing test anxiety, a common problem among students (Freeling and Shemberg, 1970). A group of students rated high in test anxiety met once a week for six weeks. At the first meeting they were asked to develop an anxiety hierarchy of fifteen items, ranging from "You are sitting in a classroom of 100 students listening to a lecture" to "The test papers are being passed out

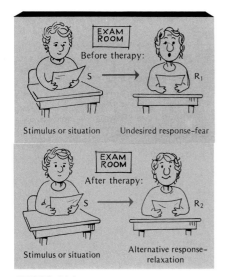

FIGURE 14.1

In desensitization therapy, a stimulus or situation (S) that elicits an undesirable response (R₁), such as fear or anxiety, is now associated with relaxation (R₂). Because the new response of relaxation is incompatible with the old response of fear, the old response disappears.

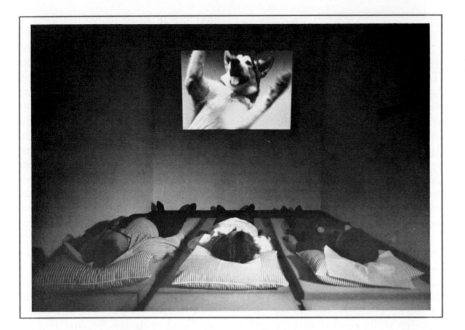

In one type of desensitization, the client learns to relax while viewing films of the feared object (in this case, dogs). The next step is to learn to relax while being within sight of a live dog, and progressively work toward being close to a dog without feeling fearful.

and you are sitting in your seat waiting to receive your paper." The students were then taught techniques for deep muscle relaxation and were told to practice them at home every day. At the subsequent sessions the group first relaxed. Then the experimenter presented items from the anxiety hierarchy, starting with the least anxiety-arousing scene. The students were asked to imagine the scene, and when they could do so without feeling anxious, the next higher item was presented. No more than four items were introduced at each meeting. In between items, the subjects were repeatedly told to relax, to feel calm and heavy. The whole process went slowly, step by step, until the entire hierarchy was covered. At the end of the six weeks, the students were less anxious, as measured both by anxiety questionnaires and performance in an actual test situation. Similar desensitization techniques have been used to help treat a variety of problems, including claustrophobia, fear of heights, and sexual impotence.

Operant therapy

Whereas desensitization was suggested by the principles of classical conditioning, *operant therapy* relies heavily on the operant conditioning procedures developed by B. F. Skinner and his followers, also discussed in

Chapter 5. Positive reinforcement is the main tool in operant therapy. By rewarding desired behaviors—for example, dressing oneself by a retarded person or homework completion by a child in school—one can add these behaviors to the person's repertoire or increase their frequency. To be successful, the reward administered must be something geared to motivate the specific client, it must be given only after performance of the desired behavior, and there must be a method for gradually molding existing behavior into more complex behaviors not yet in the person's repertoire (Bandura, 1967).

We have already discussed some examples of operant therapy in the Psychological Issue for Chapter 5, where we considered such behavior modification techniques as the token economy, in which residents of institutions (such as mental hospitals and juvenile detention homes) receive tokens for desired behaviors. The tokens can in turn be exchanged for rewards. Operant therapy techniques are used widely—and often successfully—with children (Ross, 1981). Behavior therapists teach parents or teachers how to administer rewards more effectively at home and in school. For example, teachers at one nursery school were concerned about the socially withdrawn behavior of one little boy who spent about 80 per-

THERAPY IS GOING TO THE DOGS

Psychologists have adapted certain psychotherapeutic techniques for use with household pets. One team of psychologists (Tuber, Hothersall, and Voith, 1974) reported success in using desensitization to cure Higgins (an Old English sheep dog) of his intense fear of thunderstorms. They began by playing a recording of a thunderstorm very softly. If Higgins remained calm, he was rewarded with chocolate bars. As long as Higgins remained calm, the intensity of the artificial thunderstorm was gradually increased. When a real thunderstorm came along, Higgins was able to keep his anxiety under control.

cent of his time playing alone (Harris, Wolf, and Baer; cited by Bandura, 1967). Because the teacher's attention seemed to serve as a reward for this behavior, the procedure was for the teacher to ignore the boy's solitary activities but to give her full attention whenever the boy played with other children. Before long he was spending 60 percent of his time with others. Eventually the enjoyment of playing in the group came to be a reward in itself and the teacher was able to reduce her role in providing reinforcement.

A major goal of operant therapy is to insure that the behavior change will persist even after the therapist, teacher, or parent stops providing the reinforcement. After all, we don't want to teach people to behave in new and better ways only when other people keep patting them on the back. One approach to this challenge is to move from total reinforcement to a partial reinforcement schedule, in which the desired behavior is rewarded only some of the time. As discussed in Chapter 5, behavior rewarded on such a partial

reinforcement schedule is likely to become more resistant to extinction. In addition, behavior therapists often attempt to teach clients to evaluate their own behavior and then to reward themselves when appropriate, rather than relying on reinforcement from external sources. Finally, as in the case of the little boy who was rewarded for playing with others, once a desired behavior is established, it is often rewarded by the natural environment of the person so that special efforts to reward the behavior are no longer necessary.

Modeling and role playing

One of the best ways to acquire a new response or skill is to watch another person demonstrate it. For example, we can sometimes reduce our fears of certain situations—say, flying in airplanes—by observing other people take the situation in stride. Behavior therapists have put the potential of such *modeling* to good use. One experiment demonstrated, for example, that people could reduce their fear of

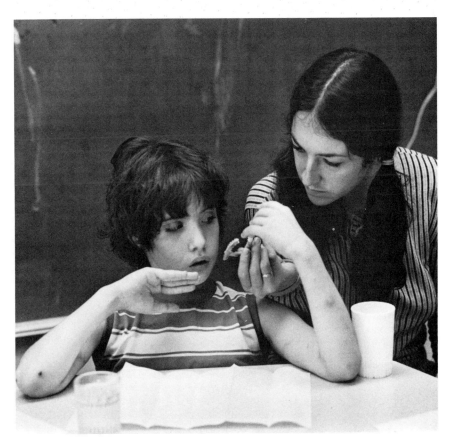

Behavior therapy has been used successfully with many autistic children. Here an autistic child is receiving a pretzel from a therapist as reinforcement for desired behavior.

snakes by watching other people, both in person and on videotape, move gradually closer to snakes without any dire consequences (Bandura, Blanchard, and Ritter, 1969). Other studies have used modeling to help children overcome their fear of dogs (Hill, Liebert, and Mott, 1968), and even of dentists (Adelson et al., 1972).

Another use of modeling is to show people how to handle social situations more effectively. Thus, the therapist may demonstrate how to join others in conversation or—as noted in the Psychological Issue for Chapter 12—may show problem drinkers how to refuse a drink gracefully. Videotaped models are also commonly used in such social skills instruction.

Modeling is often augmented by *role playing,* in which the client practices the desired behavior and gets feedback on his performance. By practicing in a protective setting, such as a therapy session, clients need not become anxious about the initial mistakes they make. It is something like practicing a new dance step at home before trying it out in public. In one application of role playing, college men and women volunteered for a program to improve their dating skills (Christensen and Arkowitz, 1974). Each participant went on a series of "practice dates" with participants of

the opposite sex. After each date the students exchanged feedback forms on which they had listed four positive things about the other person as well as one behavior that they felt the other should change. At the end of the program the participants reported that they felt more confident and skillful in dating situations and they began to have more interaction with people of the opposite sex. Both modeling and role playing are often used as part of programs of *assertiveness training,* which are designed to help previously timid people stand up for themselves.

Modeling and role playing are techniques that reflect the current emphasis on integrating cognitive learning (as discussed in Chapter 5) into behavior therapy. The prevailing view is that people's understandings and expectations of themselves are central determinants of their behavior. Following this line of reasoning, some approaches to behavior therapy stress *cognitive restructuring,* or modification of the client's thoughts. For example, Aaron Beck (1976) has developed a *cognitive therapy* that is often highly effective in treating people with depression. In keeping with Beck's cognitive theory of depression, discussed in Chapter 13, the therapist tries to persuade the depressed person to change his erroneous negative

Assertiveness training makes use of role playing in helping people to be less timid and to stand up for themselves.

BOX 2

RATIONAL-EMOTIVE THERAPY

Rational-emotive therapy (RET) is a form of cognitive behavior therapy that assumes that emotional difficulties are caused by irrational thinking. Albert Ellis (1962), the founder of rational-emotive therapy, believes that events themselves do not cause emotional reactions. Rather, it is a person's belief system that leads her to interpret events in particular ways, which in turn causes her emotional reactions. A person's belief system is like a set of internal sentences that the person continually repeats to herself. A disturbed patient's belief system may include unrealistic expectations, such as "It is necessary for me to succeed in everything I do," or illogical reasoning, such as "If he doesn't love me, then I am a worthless person." Thus, when the patient inevitably confronts situations in which she is unsuccessful or feels unloved, she comes to the distorted—and crushing—conclusion: "I am a failure."

Albert Ellis.

According to Ellis, the bases of psychoanalytic therapy and most of the humanistic therapies are "just nonsense" (Gross, 1978). What Ellis criticizes most in these therapies is their focus on emotion. He particularly scorns Gestalt therapy (see Box 1) for its tendency to overemphasize feelings at the expense of rational thinking and to encourage all feelings, regardless of whether or not they are appropriate.

Ellis argues that letting out one's emotions rarely cures anyone. Like Aaron Beck (see text), Ellis advocates cognitive restructuring—getting the patient to substitute more rational beliefs for irrational ones. The patient is made to recognize the faulty reasoning on which his distorted conclusions are based. Thus, for example, he is made to see that it is unrealistic to expect to succeed in everything and is led from his distorted "I am a failure" to the rational "I have failed in this situation."

The rational-emotive therapist attempts to change the patient's thinking through logic, persuasion, occasional lecturing, and even prescribing specific activities. Whereas psychoanalytic and client-centered therapists are relatively nondirective, with the emphasis on helping the patient find his own way, the rational-emotive therapist is highly directive—she *tells* the patient what to think and do if he wants to get better.

A common complaint is that rational-emotive therapists do not try to build a warm, caring relationship with their patients. This complaint is based on the assumption that it is important to build such a relationship before moving on to the patient's specific problems. But rational-emotive therapists have a different view of the matter. "If you give clients a lot of warmth, support, attention, and caring," they contend, "you may be reinforcing their dire needs for love, which frequently and even usually are the central core of their disturbances. You also run the risk of making the client dependent on you and therapy instead of helping him or her cope with life's difficulties directly" (Saltzberg and Elkins, 1980, page 326).

Like the founders of many other therapeutic schools, Albert Ellis believes that his approach is the single right way. Although most therapists would not go so far as Ellis in his belief in RET to the exclusion of all other approaches, RET has influenced many of them to give more emphasis to their patients' belief systems.

opinions of events and of himself. For example, when a client says that he is worthless because "Every time I try to do something I botch it up," the therapist offers concrete examples that are contrary to the client's overgeneralization. Cognitive behavior therapists also try to teach their clients to talk to themselves in new ways—for example, to tell themselves to "slow down" or to "remember the way you did it last time." Studies have shown that such "self-talk" can help people to perform more effectively in many situations (Dush, Hirt, and Schroeder, 1983). One cognitive behavioral approach that has gained great popularity is Albert Ellis's *rational-emotive therapy,* described in Box 2.

Although we have described several behavior therapy techniques, in practice the behavior therapist rarely uses a single technique in isolation. Rather, the typical procedure is to use several techniques, either simultaneously or in succession, to provide the most effective program for changing the client's behavior in desired ways. The behavior therapist often takes a stance of experimentation, trying out different approaches to see which work best for the problems of a particular client.

SOMATIC THERAPIES

Somatic therapies make use of direct physiological interventions—drugs, electric shocks, or brain surgery—to treat the symptoms of a psychological disorder (the term *somatic* comes from the Greek *soma,* or "body"). Somatic methods can be used only by medical doctors. These methods are often used in conjunction with other therapies, such as those already described in this chapter.

Psychopharmacology

Sigmund Freud himself predicted that drugs would ultimately be used in the treatment of psychological disorder. "The future may teach us how to exercise a direct influence by particular chemical substances," he wrote. The future that Freud foresaw is now. Perhaps the most promising frontier in the treatment of psychological disorder is *psychopharmacology,* the use of drugs that affect the patient's mood and behaviors. Drugs have been used to treat mental illness since ancient times. But only in the past third of a century have several classes of drugs been developed that seem truly effective in relieving the symptoms of certain disorders, even if they can't actually cure them. And recent advances in our understanding of brain chemistry (see Chapter 2) have begun to explain how these drugs work and have offered a promise that even more effective drugs will be developed in the near future.

Three major classes of drugs are now in widespread use in the treatment of psychological disorders: antianxiety drugs, antidepressants, and antipsychotics.

The *antianxiety drugs* (also known as "minor tranquilizers") are prescribed to millions of Americans to take the edge off their anxiety and tension and to help them function more effectively. Before the 1950s the most widely used antianxiety drugs were barbiturates—strong sedatives that cause drowsiness and sometimes depression and that have the potential for addiction and lethal overdose. The antianxiety drugs that are most widely prescribed today belong to a chemical family called the *benzodiazepines,* including diazepam (better known by the trade name Valium) and chlordiazepoxide (Librium). These drugs have the valuable ability of relieving anxiety without having a sedative effect, and they are less susceptible than barbiturates to abuse (Rickels et al., 1983). As a result, they are now among the most widely used prescription drugs in America. The antianxiety drugs work by influencing the sensitivity of specific receptors in the brain to neurotransmitters that regulate moods. Although antianxiety drugs have been a great boon to many people, they can also be habit-forming, and health authorities have recently voiced great concern about the possibility that they are being overprescribed and used too freely.

Drugs are often used in the treatment of psychological disorders. Antianxiety drugs, such as Valium and Librium, are among the most widely used of all prescription drugs.

The *antidepressant drugs* are able to lift the spirits of many depressed patients. The most widely used group of antidepressants, first used for this purpose in the 1950s, are the *tricyclics*, which include imipramine (Tofranil) and amitriptyline (Elavil). As noted in Chapter 13, one likely cause of depression is a deficiency of the neurotransmitters norepinephrine and serotonin in certain areas of the brain. The antidepressant drugs seem to work by increasing the available levels of these neurotransmitters. Antidepressants are not effective with all depressed patients, but they are effective in a large number of cases. In many cases of depression, the most effective treatment has been a combination of antidepressant drugs and psychotherapy, often of the insight-oriented variety (Weissman et al., 1981).

In addition to the tricyclics, another drug, *lithium carbonate*, has been used in recent years for the treatment of bipolar disorder—the disorder that involves extreme mood swings between agitated highs (mania) and depressed lows. Although researchers are not yet certain about how it works, lithium is often extremely successful in bringing people down from their highs and in preventing them from plunging to the depths of their lows. In many cases, these patients will continue to take lithium for many years, perhaps the rest of their lives.

The most controversial of the psychopharmacological agents are the *antipsychotic drugs* (once called "major tranquilizers"). Among the several chemical families of antipsychotic drugs, the most widely used are the *phenothiazines*, including chlorpromazine (or Thorazine) and trifluoperazine (Stelazine), and the *butyrophenones*, such as haloperidol (Haldol). These drugs act to relieve the agitation, delusions, and thought disorders of schizophrenia. Although the drugs do not cure the underlying disorder, they relieve its symptoms to a point that allows a majority of patients taking them to live outside the hospital, in the general community. For example, one New York man who had spent a dozen years in mental hospitals was able to live at home after he was put on a regimen of one drug to overcome his lethargy and tendency to withdraw, another drug to prevent his becoming overly agitated, and a third to control paranoid delusions. Because of his schizophrenia he is unable to live a totally "normal" life but, as his mother put it, at

BOX 3

THE RIGHT TO REFUSE TREATMENT

As a mental patient at Boston State Hospital, Rubie Rogers was forced to take the antipsychotic drug Haldol. After more than three years, Ms. Rogers was so distraught over the drug's painful muscle-tightening side effects that she set herself on fire, in order to provoke a transfer to another hospital where she would not be forced to take such drugs.

In 1975, patients' rights lawyers filed a suit on behalf of Rogers and six other patients to stop hospitals from forcing patients to take drugs. Now a landmark case, *Mills v. Rogers* (Mills was the Massachusetts Commissioner of Mental Health), established for the first time the right of a patient to refuse antipsychotic drug treatment. In 1979 a federal court ruled that except in emergency situations, those mental patients who are "legally competent" have the right to refuse such treatment (Appelbaum, 1983).

The issue of a patient's right to refuse antipsychotic medication is a difficult one. Psychiatrists have argued that if the patient does not accept medication, he causes tremendous expense and inconvenience. This is especially true of patients confined to mental hospitals because they are dangerous to themselves or to others. Without medication, the patient may have to be watched more carefully, physically restrained more often, or hospitalized longer. The antipsychotic drugs are very effective in reducing the symptoms of schizophrenic and other psychotic patients and in making their behavior more acceptable.

From the patient's point of view, however, the drugs have side effects that can range from the slightly uncomfortable to the severely painful. Especially in cases in which the patient may act strangely but is not dangerous, what right does the doctor have to forcibly medicate him? In addition, patients have sometimes been overmedicated, in order to make them easier to manage. Without the right to refuse treatment, patients have no protection against such medical abuses. In recent years, patients' rights groups have forcefully advocated these concerns, and increasing numbers of psychologists and psychiatrists have come to agree with them.

The court's decision in the case of *Mills v. Rogers* has not ended the controversy. A central issue, still being debated in the courts, is how the patient's "legal competence" to decide whether to accept medication is to be determined. It remains clear that in many cases the patient will benefit from taking antipsychotic drugs—whether or not the patient himself realizes it.

Although the controversy continues, with the case of *Mills v. Rogers* we have come a long way from the situation where medical personnel could indiscriminately force patients to take drugs that would "calm them down." It has now been established that mental patients, like all other adults, have certain rights regarding their own treatment that must be respected.

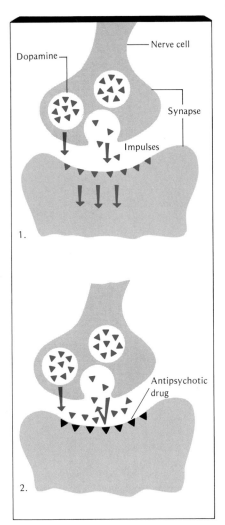

FIGURE 14.2

How antipsychotic drugs are thought to work. Dopamine, a transmitter substance that affects movement, thought, and mood, crosses the synapse and activates other neurons. It is suspected that in schizophrenia, dopamine levels are excessively high. The antipsychotic drugs block the receptor sites on neurons, preventing them from accepting the dopamine at the synapse.

In electroconvulsive therapy, brief electrical currents are applied to the brain, producing convulsions. This treatment is often successful in relieving the symptoms of severe depression.

least "he has an identity, a feeling of being useful" (Clark, 1979, page 99).

Researchers' best guess about the primary cause of schizophrenia is an excess of the neurotransmitter dopamine in certain brain areas, in both the limbic system and the cerebral cortex. The antipsychotic drugs seem to work by attaching themselves to dopamine receptors in the brain, thereby preventing dopamine from reaching them (Iversen, 1979) (see Figure 14.2).

The widespread use of the antipsychotic drugs is a hotly debated issue. Proponents of these drugs argue that they not only help schizophrenic patients return to socially acceptable behavior but also make it easier for them to be treated with other therapies. But critics contend that the drugs are no more than chemical constraints, used to keep patients under control. Many professionals feel that the drugs have been used too often to replace talking to people and making them feel cared about (Sobel, 1980). The antipsychotic drugs also have unpleasant side effects, including tremors of the fingers, muscular rigid-ity, and a twisted posture—reasons why patients are not always eager to take them. Prolonged use can bring on *tardive dyskinesia*, a neurological condition that involves uncontrollable facial twitches and grimaces. These side effects can be reduced to some extent by other drugs.

Most psychiatrists and psychologists who work with schizophrenic patients are convinced of the value of antipsychotic drugs for their patients. But there is currently a heightened awareness of their possible overuse and of the rights of patients themselves to decide whether or not to accept such medication (see Box 3).

Electroconvulsive therapy

Electroconvulsive therapy (or ECT) is the application of brief electrical currents to the brain, producing a seizure. It is often referred to as "shock treatment." First an anesthetic is given to the patient to put him to sleep; then a muscle relaxant is injected into the patient so there will be

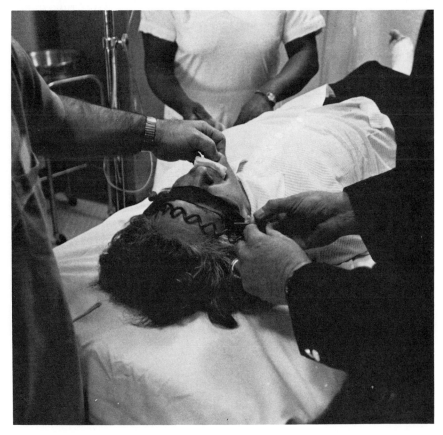

no bodily convulsion. Electrodes are then placed at one or both sides of the head, and from 70 to 130 volts are applied for less than a second. The patient experiences a brain convulsion, lasting about a minute, that is identical to an epileptic seizure. Treatment usually consists of about six sessions, spaced over a period of several weeks.

"Perhaps more than any other form of medical treatment," observes Maggie Scarf (1978), ECT "arouses fantasies and fears of the Frankenstein-style physician who is tinkering with matters that ought to be beyond human intervention." But ECT, first introduced in 1938, continues to be widely used because of its success in alleviating the symptoms of severe depression, often within one or two weeks. As many as 100,000 Americans a year receive ECT treatment. Nobody knows just how ECT works, but the seizure apparently restores balance to the imbalanced brain chemistry that underlies many severe depressions. Especially for severely depressed patients who do not respond well to antidepressant drugs and for the patients who are suicidal,

ECT appears to be the best available treatment (Scovern and Kilmann, 1980).

It is clear that ECT has been overused. In the 1940s and 1950s it was used for a large variety of hospitalized patients, and there are reports—the best known, perhaps, in Ken Kesey's 1962 novel *One Flew Over the Cuckoo's Nest*—that it was used to punish or sedate troublemakers. ECT has such side effects as headaches, nausea, and—perhaps most troublesome—memory loss that can last for days, months, or even longer. Current research with new forms of electroshock—using less powerful currents, using shorter intervals of administration, and applying currents to only one brain hemisphere—give promise of reducing the side effects.

Because of the rather violent aspects of ECT, its side effects, and the possibility for its abuse, some psychologists and psychiatrists oppose its use (for example, Breggin, 1979). In 1982 the voters of Berkeley, California went so far as to ban the use of ECT in that city. The referendum was subsequently overturned in court, however, on the ground that it de-

Some people consider electroconvulsive therapy to be a cruel and dangerous form of treatment. In 1982 the voters of Berkeley, California passed a referendum that banned the use of electroconvulsive therapy in that city.

prived severely depressed patients of their right to treatment. Despite the heightened awareness of the potential for abusing ECT, it is generally regarded as a useful form of treatment in a restricted set of cases, in which the benefits of the treatment outweigh its liabilities (American Psychiatric Association, 1978).

Psychosurgery

Psychosurgery refers to the surgical destruction or disconnection of portions of the brain in an attempt to regulate disordered behavior. It was introduced in the 1930s by Antonio de Egas Moniz, a Portuguese neurologist, who surgically severed the frontal lobes from the rest of the brain in some agitated patients. Thousands of such operations, called *prefrontal lobotomies*, were performed in the United States in the 1940s and 1950s. But the overall results of the operations were not encouraging. The surgery calmed down some agitated patients, but it also made vegetables of others—they walked, they talked, they looked like human beings, but they were without ambition, imagination, or self-awareness (Greenblatt, 1967). With the introduction of the antipsychotic drugs in the mid-1950s, the number of lobotomies decreased dramatically.

Several hundred psychosurgical operations are still performed in the United States each year. Surgical procedures have been greatly improved, so that it is possible to separate the frontal cortex from lower brain areas that regulate emotional response, with minimal destruction of brain tissue (Shevitz, 1976). And there is evidence that such operations do help a small minority of patients who are totally incapacitated by obsessions or depression and for whom no other techniques are helpful (Goodwin, 1980). For the most part, however, the current view of psychosurgery is one of extreme caution.

The use of somatic therapies—especially the use of antipsychotic drugs—has had a large impact on mental hospitals. Some of the controversial issues involved are discussed in Box 4.

EVALUATING THERAPY

Now that we have reviewed a wide range of approaches to therapy, let us consider some of the larger issues raised by the enterprise of therapy. How well does therapy really work, and what are the special responsibilities of therapists and clients?

Does therapy work?

There has been a great deal of debate over whether psychotherapy—especially the nonsomatic therapies, which do not involve direct physiological manipulation of the brain—works at all. In 1952 Hans Eysenck created a storm when he reviewed the existing studies of therapy (mainly psychoanalytic) and concluded that it had no favorable effect at all. He claimed that as many patients "improved" as would have improved anyway with the passage of time. Others disputed Eysenck's interpretation, and by now, with many more studies having been conducted, it is fair to conclude that although therapy does not help everybody (and in some cases it may even be harmful), on the whole it has modest positive effects (Smith, Glass, and Miller, 1980).

In one representative study (Sloane et al., 1975), ninety outpatients at the Temple University outpatient clinic were randomly assigned to one of three groups: one that received behavior therapy, one that received short-term psychoanalytic therapy, and a "waiting list" group that was given only minimal treatment. The clients were generally anxious, depressed, or otherwise troubled—not severely disturbed or psychotic. The therapists were experienced. After four months of treatment (or waiting), the clients were assessed by an independent rater who did not know to which groups the clients were assigned. On the average, clients in all three groups improved, even those on the waiting list, which shows that time itself can sometimes heal psychic wounds. But clients in the two treatment groups improved more than the waiting-list clients. Neither

BOX 4

IN AND OUT OF THE MENTAL HOSPITAL

At any one time, several hundred thousand Americans are patients in mental hospitals. Some of these patients need short-term hospitalization for acute (brief and intense) psychological disorders or episodes. But the majority of hospitalized mental patients suffer from long-term disorders, such as chronic schizophrenia, and are likely to require special care for the rest of their lives. We are now learning, however, that this special care need not necessarily be provided in mental hospitals.

Until the 1950s, many of the patients admitted to mental hospitals could expect to remain there for years—often for life. In the last few decades, however, there has been a movement to allow chronically disturbed people who are not dangerous to themselves or others to return to community life—a process referred to as *deinstitutionalization*. Between 1955 and 1975, the patient population of mental hospitals decreased by 65 percent, and the average number of days spent in the hospital decreased by more than two-thirds (Bassuk and Garson, 1978).

The movement toward deinstitutionalization was made possible by the introduction of antipsychotic drugs, which could reduce severe symptoms, and by the community mental health movement (see Box 5), which included plans for rehabilitating chronic mental patients within the community. The idea was initially welcomed because it would reduce the drain on taxpayer dollars spent on state mental hospitals and would, at least in the ideal case, allow patients to lead more normal lives.

These goals sound good in theory, but many mental health professionals have serious questions about the way deinstitutionalization has been implemented in practice. Even though chronic mental patients leave the hospital with their most troubling symptoms relieved, they are by no means "cured." They often require supervised living units, such as halfway houses, as well as job training and continued outpatient treatment programs. Unfortunately, many of these services have

Formerly hospitalized mental patients, with staff members, at a halfway house.

not been run very well. Too many ex-patients live in poorly supervised and rundown housing, and thousands live on their own with no money and no work. They wander the streets, and their sometimes bizarre appearance and behavior often frightens neighborhood residents, who then may actively protest the deinstitutionalization process.

Another challenge to deinstitutionalization is the fact that, although the number of patients in state hospitals at any one time has dropped sharply, the number of admissions has increased—about half of the discharged patients are readmitted within a year of leaving. What exists, in many cases, is a revolving door policy, with patients shuttling in and out of the hospital.

While some consider deinstitutionalization a failure, others believe that well-run programs can eliminate many of the problems. In San Jose, California, for example, an organization run by the state university provided a large corps of volunteers to work with the former mental patients housed in the nearby community (Williams, 1977). According to a survey of the ex-patients, 75 percent felt they had benefited from community living and only

5 percent wanted to return to the hospital. More generally, it is estimated that if the necessary community facilities existed, more than half of the revolving door readmissions could be avoided.

Some psychologists, such as Charles Kiesler (1982), believe that we must go beyond deinstitutionalization to a policy of *noninstitutionalization*, in which initial admissions to mental hospitals are kept to a minimum. Kiesler maintains that people who have never been institutionalized are less likely to fall into a pattern of dependency that may be perpetuated throughout their lives. As a result, they usually fare better than those who are hospitalized for the same conditions.

Kiesler and others argue persuasively that with the proper alternative facilities and care, many patients could be treated more effectively—and less expensively—outside than inside the mental hospital. Such facilities and care could give mentally disturbed individuals, who in prior years would have spent their lives in the impersonal environments of state hospitals, their best chance of leading relatively normal lives.

CHAPTER FOURTEEN: THERAPY

The personal characteristics of therapists may often be more important than the techniques they use. In one study, students seeking therapy who were treated by understanding college professors improved just as much, on the average, as students who were treated by professional therapists.

GREAT EXPECTATIONS

Will therapy be more effective if the therapist expects the client to improve? Jeffrey Berman and Richard Wenzlaff (1983) devised an experiment to find out. Therapists at the University of Texas counseling center were told that one of their new clients had scored extremely high on a scale that predicted rapid improvement in therapy. They received no such information about a second new client. The information was actually fabricated; the client "expected" to improve was chosen randomly. Nevertheless, when the therapists' expectations were raised in this way, both therapists and clients reported greater improvement over the course of six sessions. When a therapist expects a client to improve, he or she seems to be more likely to take an approach that will actually produce improvement—a clear case of a self-fulfilling prophecy.

psychoanalytic therapy nor behavior therapy was superior overall.

As this study illustrates, one method of therapy is not necessarily better than another. This is the general consensus of recent research (Smith, Glass, and Miller, 1980). There is reason to believe, moreover, that the personal characteristics of therapists, such as their supportiveness and empathy, are often more important than the specific techniques they use. In one study, male students seeking therapy were treated either by highly experienced psychotherapists (both psychiatrists and psychologists) or by college professors chosen for their ability to form understanding relationships; they included professors of English, history, mathematics, and philosophy. The patients treated by the professors were found to show just as much improvement, on the average, as the patients treated by the professional therapists (Strupp and Hadley, 1979).

The effectiveness of therapy will depend, of course, on the nature and severity of the patient's disorder. In addition, particular techniques may be more effective for particular sorts of patients or problems. As noted earlier, psychoanalytic therapy seems to work best with people who already

have some skill in exploring their own emotions. Specific behavioral techniques, such as systematic desensitization, seem especially useful in treating certain phobias and anxieties. But the superiority of one therapy over another, even for specific problems, is not yet well established.

One of the difficulties in evaluating the relative effectiveness of different forms of therapy is that different schools of therapy have their own criteria for what constitutes "improvement." There is a great need for further research to specify which sorts of therapy are most effective in producing specific types of change (Garfield, 1983). Meanwhile, more and more therapists have become "eclectic," drawing on psychoanalytic, client-centered, behavioral, or other techniques as they seem appropriate, rather than maintaining an unyielding allegiance to a single approach (Smith, 1983).

In addition to their attempts to make therapy more effective, psychologists and other mental health professionals are increasingly concerned with ways of *preventing* the emergence of psychological disorder. This is the primary focus of the community mental health movement, described in Box 5.

BOX 5

COMMUNITY MENTAL HEALTH

- A recently widowed father feels lonely and goes to a single-parents group to meet and talk with other parents who are alone.
- A single mother on welfare frequently feels depressed and goes to a local mental health center for weekly therapy.
- A high-school student worries about his growing dependence on drugs and calls a hotline when he feels tempted to get high.

The *community mental health* movement was founded on the idea of preventing psychological disorder by helping people deal with their problems in their own community, rather than waiting until their problems are serious enough to land them in a mental hospital.

Perhaps the best known community mental health programs in the United States are the some 650 federally funded Community Mental Health Centers. Through legislation passed in 1963, funds were made available to establish centers and staffs in local communities. Staff members get to know the people and their needs, give educational presentations to community groups (on problems of child rearing, for example), and work closely with schools and health clinics, in order to help detect problems early enough to prevent them from becoming more serious.

Community mental health centers also offer treatment for existing problems to people for whom services have not been available in the past. People can obtain help without making an appointment or paying a high fee. Mental health centers are most likely to offer brief or short-term therapy, rather than the unhurried, detailed exploration of the person provided in expensive traditional therapies. In these centers, only a specific problem is typically addressed, and therapy usually lasts four to six weeks.

In cases of *crisis intervention,* both prevention and treatment are emphasized. Help provided following a particularly stressful event in a person's life, such as rape or the death of a

A community mental health center in New York City.

family member, can often ward off more serious difficulties later. A mental health center might offer one session and a follow-up call to help the person restore equilibrium and make necessary decisions.

Community mental health programs often rely on the use of *paraprofessionals*—community residents who are trained by professionals to provide therapy or support. In some cases *peer counseling*—for example, mothers on welfare working with other mothers on welfare—helps to bridge gaps and bring services to those who may not have access to professionals. In other cases, parents or teachers are trained to work with troubled children, or volunteers are trained to work with a particular group in need of help. For example, adult community residents in

Hawaii were trained by psychologists to act as "buddies" for 11- to 17-year-old youths referred by the family court for behavior and academic problems. (Fo and O'Donnell, 1974).

Community mental health has its critics. They say that community centers still reach only a small proportion of community members who need help and that nonprofessional groups or individuals often do not deliver adequate therapy. But despite such criticisms, community mental health efforts have made support and guidance available to many people who badly needed it. As a result, such efforts have furthered the vital goal of preventing psychological disorder.

CHAPTER FOURTEEN: THERAPY

Therapy and responsibility

The enterprise of therapy places important responsibilities on the therapist—and on the client, as well. By virtue of his role as an "expert" to whom one turns in times of personal trouble, the therapist is likely to have great impact on her clients: Many schools of therapy emphasize the therapist's neutrality—she is there to help the client achieve the goals that the client himself wants, not to impose her own. But, as Seymour Halleck (1971) argues, the notion of a "neutral" therapist may to a large extent be a myth: "In the very process of defining his needs in the presence of a figure who is viewed as authoritarian, the patient is profoundly influenced. He ends up wanting some of the things the [therapist] thinks he should want." Clients often adopt not only the ideals but even the mannerisms of the therapist. Having this sort of impact is a responsibility that the therapist must come to terms with. She must always keep aware of the primary need to work in the client's best interests, even if that means the client will live a life very different from what the therapist would choose for herself.

Particular techniques of therapy are sometimes singled out as ethically questionable, such as the physical assaults of electroconvulsive therapy and psychosurgery and the occasional use of physical punishment in certain forms of behavior therapy. Any instance in which physical damage or pain is inflicted in the process of therapy must, of course, be examined carefully. As Gerald Davison and John Neale (1982) point out, however, pain can be psychological, as well as physical: "Shall we permit a Gestalt therapist to make a patient cry by confronting him with feelings he has turned away from for years? Shall we forbid a psychoanalyst from guiding a patient to an insight that will likely cause great anguish, all the more so for the conflict's having been repressed for years?" (page 709). What Davison and Neale are implying, quite appropriately, is that in *all* forms of therapy the therapist must consider whether the pain being in-

flicted is justified by the expected gains.

In the 1980s, therapy is more popular than ever. "In prior times, people would take care of ordinary life crises by themselves, or with the help of their families," one psychologist notes. "Now they all want psychotherapy" (quoted by Gross, 1978, page 7). But the very popularity of therapy itself brings up ethical questions about its impact on mental health. As Jerome Frank (1973) has observed, the more treatment facilities are available and the more widely they are known, the more people will seek their services. As result, mental health professionals, by focusing attention on people's disappointments and dissatisfactions, may at times stimulate personal insecurity. Frank puts the proposition most boldly: "Psychotherapy is the only form of treatment which, at least to some extent, appears to create the illness it treats" (page 8). In the case of long-term treatment, moreover, psychotherapy may create a dependency on the part of the client that runs counter to the goal of increasing the client's autonomy. These possibilities add to the ethical dilemma of the therapist, who is dedicated to the reduction of distress, not its creation.

At the same time, the client, or prospective client, must share the responsibility for therapy. It is up to her to decide what sort of help she needs, to choose a therapist or treatment facility, to participate actively in her own treatment, and to discontinue the therapy if she feels it is not helping. There are, of course, some patients, such as children or people with serious disorders, who cannot exercise this responsibility fully; in such cases therapists, family members, and the legal system have to take on added responsibility for the patient's welfare. In most cases, however, people must assume major responsibility for their own treatment.

The choice of a therapist is a particularly important one. Even within any single school of therapy, treatment is by no means standardized; each therapist has his own distinctive style. When in the market for therapy, don't be afraid to ask a prospective therapist specific questions about his orientation and approach. Important criteria include not only the therapist's competence and commitment but also the "fit" between the therapist and the client. "You have to get along," one psychologist emphasizes. "It could be Sigmund Freud himself, but if he rubs you the wrong way, you should get another therapist" (quoted by Sobel, 1980). Such careful shopping becomes especially important with the wide range of new therapies and quasi-therapies on the market, as we will see in the Psychological Issue that follows.

SUMMARY

- **1** *Therapy* is the professional application of techniques intended to treat psychological disorders and reduce distress. There are many kinds of therapy, and they differ in setting, time frame, professionals involved, and techniques used. All types share similar goals, however, such as relieving symptoms and increasing feelings of adequacy.

Insight therapies

- **2** *Insight therapies*, such as psychoanalysis and client-centered therapy, emphasize expression of inner feelings by the patient or client.

- **3** Freud's system of *psychoanalysis* is based on the idea that psychological distress is caused by painful thoughts and emotions buried in the unconscious mind. Freud developed the techniques of *free association* and *interpretation* to help the patient release buried emotions. Freud also believed that the therapist should remain neutral so that the process of *transference* could occur.

- **4** Modern-day psychoanalytic therapy uses many of Freud's techniques but is usually less time consuming. The therapist generally faces the patient and plays a more active role than in classical psychoanalysis.

- **5** In Carl Rogers's *client-centered therapy*, the therapist provides *unconditional positive regard*, encouraging the client to express his true feelings and desires. The warmth and acceptance of the therapist are emphasized in this approach.

- **6** The aim of *Gestalt therapy*, developed by Fritz Perls, is to put individuals in touch with all facets of their personalities and experiences.

Behavior therapies

- **7** *Behavior therapies* see the client as someone who has learned inappropriate ways of behaving rather than having deep underlying psychological problems. Behavior therapists use such techniques as desensitization, operant conditioning, modeling, and role playing to eliminate the inappropriate behavior and create a desired behavior.

- **8** In *desensitization therapy*, the client learns to substitute a new response (such as relaxation) for an old response (fear or anxiety) associated with a particular stimulus. *Systematic desensitization* involves arranging fear-causing stimuli in an *anxiety hierarchy* and learning to relax in the presence of the least anxiety-arousing items first.

- **9** In *operant therapy*, the client is rewarded for performing a desired behavior or for refraining from performing an undesired behavior.

- **10** In *modeling*, the client observes someone else perform the desired behavior before trying it herself. In *role playing* the client tries out the desired behavior in an unthreatening setting.

- **11** The idea that irrational thinking is the basis of emotional problems forms the foundation for Albert Ellis's *rational-emotive therapy*. In RET, the therapist attempts to convince the patient to change his belief system.

Somatic therapies

- **12** *Somatic therapies* make use of physiological techniques—drugs, electric shocks, or brain surgery—to treat the symptoms of psychological disorder.

- **13** *Psychopharmacology* is the use of drugs to affect a patient's mood or behavior. The most widely used drugs for this purpose are the *antianxiety drugs* (minor tranquilizers), *antidepressants*, and *antipsychotic drugs* (major tranquilizers).

- **14** The last few decades have

seen a movement toward *deinstitutionalization*—returning mental patients to the community. This movement has been the focus of a great deal of controversy.

• **15** *Electroconvulsive therapy* is the application of brief electrical currents to the brain, producing convulsions. This treatment is used with severely depressed patients.

• **16** *Psychosurgery* is the surgical destruction or disconnection of portions of the brain in an attempt to regulate disordered behavior. Such procedures are rarely used today.

Evaluating therapy

• **17** Although psychotherapy does not help everyone, on the whole it seems to have a positive effect. No one type of therapy seems to be superior, and many people improve without professional help. Among the most important factors in the success of therapy are the therapist's personal characteristics.

• **18** In an effort to help people with their problems in their own communities, community mental health centers have been established throughout America. Among services available are counseling, educational programs, crisis intervention, and hotlines.

• **19** The enterprise of therapy places important responsibilities on the therapist, including not imposing his own values on the client,

and assessing the potential pain inflicted by certain therapeutic techniques. It is also important that the client share the responsibility for therapy.

KEY TERMS

antianxiety drugs
antidepressant drugs
antipsychotic drugs
anxiety hierarchy
behavior therapies
client-centered therapy
cognitive restructuring
community mental health
counseling
crisis intervention
deinstitutionalization
desensitization therapy
electroconvulsive therapy
free association
Gestalt therapy
modeling
operant therapy
psychoanalysis
psychopharmacology
psychosurgery
rational-emotive therapy
role playing
somatic therapies
systematic desensitization
therapy
transference
unconditional positive regard

THE THERAPY MARKETPLACE

In the past 20 years many new forms of psychological assistance have been offered to the public— forms that go far beyond the relatively traditional types of psychotherapy we have discussed thus far. In the 1980s, no one is limited to therapists' offices or counseling centers in their search for ways to ease emotional distress. Help for the depressed, the anxious, and the desperate is offered in urban basements, hotel ballrooms, bathtubs, over the radio, on television, and in the great outdoors. Help is even offered to those who don't really feel distressed at all but would still like to move toward greater self-fulfillment. Nor are clients limited to talking their way to inner peace. They can scream, chant mantras, float in warm water, or subject themselves to verbal abuse from strangers. Various therapy programs use such props as snorkels and nose clips, hot tubs, baby bottles, mattresses, and punching bags.

There are now at least 250 different forms of therapy available to the troubled person, including the traditional forms already described. Primal therapy, est, co-counseling, rebirthing, Arica, transcendental meditation, biofeedback, psychosynthesis, bioenergetics, and past-lives therapy are just a few of the offerings in the therapy marketplace. There is even soap opera therapy, in which clients approach their own problems through television sagas.

Some people doubt whether many of these "therapies" are really therapies at all, suggesting that they are fads, crazes, or social movements. Furthermore, some of these approaches state clearly to their clients that they are not "cures" for anything. But they all share the stated goals of their founders to

reduce psychological problems and to increase individual happiness and self-fulfillment. The therapy marketplace also includes hundreds of psychological self-help books that profess to contain the answers to your problems within their covers.

With so many forms of therapy— or therapylike programs—available, it is important to be a discriminating consumer in the therapy marketplace. Although each of the therapies may have something to offer some people, many of them are commercially packaged operations that offer overly "easy" solutions for problems and in some cases may even be dangerous.

A THERAPY SAMPLER

The following is just a small sampling of some of the new therapies on the market.

Primal therapy. Primal therapy was introduced in the late 1960s by Arthur Janov, a psychologist who established the Primal Institute in Los Angeles. Janov's approach centers on the idea of pain. Each time a child is not held when he cries, not fed when hungry, or ignored when he needs attention, it contributes to a "primal pool of pain," which, when deep enough, can produce neurosis as a way of life. The goal of primal therapy is to achieve the

A primal therapy session.

primal state, an emotional return to infancy in which the client screams, weeps, thrashes, writhes, and (for extra psychological credit) babbles baby talk. This state is achieved by talking to a therapist trained at Janov's Institute, by acting out scenes of childhood, or by introspection. It may take several months of primalling to expel all the pain, but Janov claims the effort is worth it. "Primal man," he writes, "is indeed a new kind of human being with a different kind of brain functioning and a new physiology" (Janov, 1973). Brushing aside Freud and Jung, from whom primal therapy derives, Janov states, "this renders all other psychological theories obsolete and invalid" (Gross, 1978, page 278). Although Janov doesn't say so, we can assume that "primal man" is also free of excessive modesty.

Scream therapy. Scream therapy sounds a lot like primal therapy, but its originator, Daniel Casriel, contends that it is different. He created scream therapy after observing encounter groups at Synanon, the drug addiction halfway house. Scream therapy is practiced in groups, where individuals one by one share their problems with the others. Then all hold hands and are instructed to scream. Individuals are encouraged to scream whenever they feel especially overwhelmed, which, what with one thing or another, is pretty often. Casriel disdains primal therapy, claiming that its therapy is oversimplified and that most of Janov's clients fake their primals. But, like Janov, Casriel believes he has wrought a psychological revolution: "I believe I've found what professionals are looking for, a quick way to get to feelings, the science of emotions" (Gross, 1978, page 284).

Rebirthing. The opportunity to reexperience one's own birth is offered by Theta, an organization developed by Leonard Orr. Rebirthing is designed to eliminate The Big Feeling—the panic we all experienced at birth when the umbilical

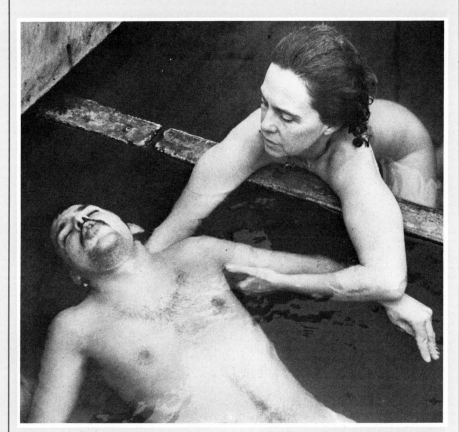

Rebirthing.

The goal is to get rid of "the creeping crud."

cord was cut and we had to breathe by ourselves. Orr claims that The Big Feeling has blighted all our lives and is most clearly evidenced in improper breathing habits. His therapy involves learning new breathing patterns and reexperiencing the trauma of birth in order to exorcise the pain. After a few dry runs, the client strips, dons a snorkel and nose clips, and enters a tub of warm water. Nude assistants suspend the client in water and murmur reassuring words. The client eventually experiences a kind of primitive panic, which Orr calls "the creeping crud." The client is then removed from the tub, towelled off, and congratulated on being reborn. It often takes several dunks to become completely free of "the creeping crud."

Encounter groups. One of the longest established routes to "consciousness raising" is the encounter group. The aim of encounter groups is to bring people together to increase trust, openness, and sensitivity. Encounter groups have been around since the 1940s but were developed into therapeutic tools in the 1950s by such prominent psychologists as Abraham Maslow and Carl Rogers. Most contemporary encounter groups stress emotional experience and include a great deal of kissing, weeping, hugging, yelling, and professions of love. Many people report that encounter groups have helped them greatly in experiencing and expressing their feelings.

Some critics of encounter groups say that the "instant emotion" de-

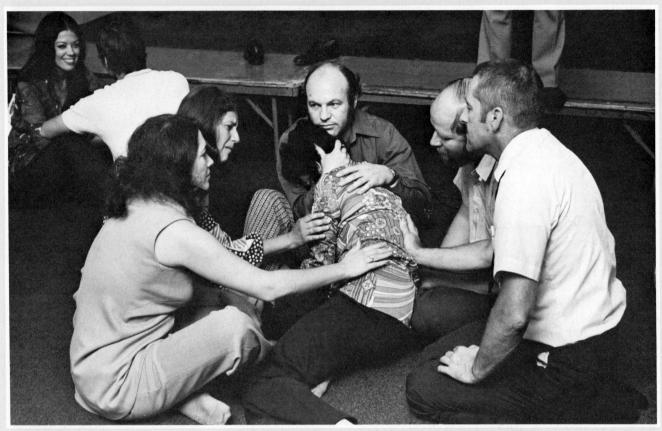

An encounter group session.

manded of participants actually undercuts real intimacy. One veteran of these groups says, "Going around hugging people in the encounter groups I went to didn't make me feel any less lonely. I suppose there are some people who can't hug anyone and it's good for them to go around getting practice hugging people, but that isn't my problem. I can hug people, but I like to hug selectively. In encounter groups, I've been told, you're supposed to enjoy hugging anyone, people for whom you have no feeling. It's just unselective hugging, and it doesn't make me feel very good" (Gordon, 1976, page 277).

Fifteen years ago Carl Rogers (1970) expressed his own doubts about the turns some encounter groups seemed to be taking: "The faddists, the cultists, the nudists, the manipulators, those whose needs are for power or recognition,

may come to dominate the encounter group horizon. In this case, I feel it is headed for disaster."

est. Erhard Seminars Training (est) was established in 1971 by Werner Erhard. The est organization claims that over 375,000 people in 103 countries, ranging in age from 6 to 96, have completed the training, which consists of seminars held in hotels or other public facilities for a 60-hour period stretching over two weekends. The program uses a variety of techniques, from aggressive confrontation of participants to relaxation and "trust" exercises borrowed from Gestalt therapy and renamed "processes." Here is how one participant described a process: "We were asked to lie down on the floor and imagine that we were afraid of the people next to us. Then . . . people began to moan and cry. . . . I'm not the kind of person to be afraid of other people.

But as the process went on and on I began to be afraid of people in the room—they were people who were so incredibly suggestible they had become a mob" (Gordon, 1976, page 296).

est offers no specific changes. Basically, it tries to persuade people to accept themselves. Once participants have done so, they have, in the parlance of est, "gotten It." *It* remains undefined. A participant described the conclusion of an est seminar as follows: "At the end of the training the trainer asks if people 'got it.'" One group of people say they got it; they are applauded. Then another group says they weren't sure they got it; the trainer talks to them and they all say they got it. One group says they definitely didn't get it. He talks to all but one, and finally this last person says he didn't get it, and the trainer says, 'Well, you got it, 'cause there's

CHAPTER FOURTEEN: THERAPY

A "self-actualization" training session, similar to those offered by est.

nothing to get' and they turn the whole thing into a joke" (Gordon, 1976, pages 298–299). Getting It and not getting It are considered equally successful and cost the same—about $450.

Transpersonal therapies. In 1968 Abraham Maslow termed humanistic psychology, which focuses on people's inner potential for growth, the "Third Force" in psychology, following psychoanalytic theory and behaviorism. He predicted that the Third Force would give way to a "still higher Fourth Psychology which would be transpersonal, transhuman, centered on the cosmos, rather than human needs and interest" (Maslow, 1968). Transpersonal

psychology appears to have arrived, as more and more organizations concern themselves not with psychological problems but with the individual's state of consciousness and relationship with the universe.

One such approach to enlightened consciousness is Arica, developed by Oscar Ichazo. Arica includes selected elements of a variety of mystic disciplines such as yoga, Zen, Sufism (the mystical branch of Islam), and the Oriental martial arts. The Arica Institute has plush headquarters in New York City and branches across the United States and in Europe. Its followers are trained in dietary rules, certain forms of meditation, breathing pat-

terns, sensory awareness, and "energy generation." The results of Arica training are said to be primarily mystical alterations in consciousness, but presumably these alterations have some positive effects on day-to-day living, as well.

EVALUATING ALTERNATIVE THERAPIES

Most of the creators of alternative therapies claim high rates of success for their programs, but little research has been done to substantiate their claims. One of the problems with investigating such claims is that it is difficult to define "success."

"**G**oing around hugging people in encounter groups didn't make me any less lonely."

In a major study of encounter groups conducted at Stanford University, more than 200 students were randomly assigned to seventeen groups representing ten major styles of encounter. Control subjects did not participate in any group. Participants were assessed six months and one year after taking part in the study. In general, the results were not encouraging: about one-third of the students showed positive effects, about one-third showed negative effects (including some who experienced psychological damage), and the remaining third showed no effects. Generally, the encounter subjects showed no more change for better or worse than the control subjects (Lieberman, Yalom, and Miles, 1973).

For a few individuals, some of these alternative therapies may actually be dangerous. The confrontation aspects of est, for example, may be more than some people can handle. There have been several reports of psychotic breakdowns in persons without previous psychiatric histories after completing est training (Glass, Kirsch, and Parris, 1977). One 39-year-old man developed a sudden increase in self-esteem and energy after the second day of training. His feelings rapidly expanded until he felt he had godlike powers. At home he jumped into the swimming pool and tried to breathe under water. After two days of manic activity, he was finally hospitalized. He was released six days later, and after four months of treatment he returned to his pre-est level of functioning. This and other such episodes cannot be attributed exclusively to the impact of est; nevertheless, est may be threatening to people with certain types of personalities. Unfortunately, few alternative therapies screen their applicants carefully, to warn off those who might be adversely affected.

Some social commentators have decried the explosion of alternative therapies, saying that they are merely exploitations of our society's increasing narcissism. Martin Gross

The line between traditional therapies and the new "pop" therapies is not always clear.

(1978) describes "the apparently rotating clientele that has been analyzed by Freudians, screamed for Casriel . . . and confronted one another in Encounter" (page 311). Many psychologists see a dangerous anti-intellectualism in the alternative therapies, in that most of the organizations condemn the "thinking" person in favor of the "feeling" person.

On the other hand, it should be recognized that the line between the more traditional therapies and the new "pop" therapies is not always a clear one (Appelbaum, 1982). Gestalt therapy (Chapter 14, Box 1) was initially viewed as a "way out" approach, but its methods gradually came to exert an important influence on more traditional therapists. Similarly, despite Werner Erhard's lack of the "appropriate" credentials, est has recently been gaining a surprising degree of acceptance in traditional circles.

A BETTER YOU THROUGH READING

For those unwilling or unable to undertake a course in primal therapy, est, or any of the other alternative therapies, there are other opportunities for psychological self-improvement. These other approaches are outlined in self-help books, which tell you how to get along with other people, how to assert yourself, how to improve your sex life, how to overcome depression, how to like yourself more or worry less, how to take risks, and how to start or end a marriage. It is hard to come up with a human problem that isn't addressed in a self-help book.

Even a small paperback bookstore is likely to have at least a hundred psychological how-to books in stock. And they move fast. Wayne

Dyer's *Your Erroneous Zones* (1976) sold 150,000 hardbound copies in its first six months of publication and millions of copies in paperback. Other best-selling psychological how-to books in recent years have had such titles as *How to Be Your Own Best Friend, How to Take Charge of Your Life, How to Live with Another Person, How to Survive the Loss of a Love, How to Break Your Addiction to a Person, Learning to Love Yourself,* and even *The Do-It-Yourself Psychotherapy Book.* Best-seller lists almost always contain a few self-help books.

Like the leaders of the new therapies, some of the authors of these books are well-trained psychologists and psychiatrists, while other authors have no professional credentials. Many mental health professionals are skeptical of the value of self-help books. They charge that many of the books mislead potential buyers with excessive claims. Who could resist a book that claims to "give you ways to create a new life for yourself, whoever you are, whatever you are now"? Another book claims to be "an admission ticket to a happier life," and still another describes itself as "the proven new method for coping successfully with other people every day of your life."

Raphael Bevcar (1978) adds that self-help books may give rise to new problems. The routine stresses of everyday life can produce perfectly normal anxiety, depression, and anger. By suggesting that negative emotions are neurotic or unnecessary, self-help books may create "pseudoproblems" for people who are actually coping quite well. On the other hand, seriously troubled people may delay or avoid seeing a professional therapist, confident that these books can solve their problems.

***I**t is hard to come up with a human problem that is not addressed in a self-help book.*

Personal Growth

The "personal growth" section of a bookstore. Best-seller lists almost always contain a few self-help books.

While acknowledging the need for caution, other professionals believe that the self-help literature can be valuable. Josiah Dilley (1978) suggests that particularly in the areas of reducing tension, increasing self-esteem, and improving personal relationships, self-help books can provide useful insights. "There is a gold mine of exciting possibilities in the self-help literature," Dilley advises fellow professionals, "techniques, suggestions, ideas and success stories not to be found elsewhere. Don't knock it 'til you try it" (page 295).

There is no doubt that some self-help books have helped their readers sort out particularly trying problems. But there are also drawbacks to relying on them as psychological counselors. In the final analysis, we shouldn't rule out self-help books or the new therapies in the marketplace, but we should caution the buyer to beware.

SUMMARY

- *1* In recent years there has been a proliferation of "alternative" therapies that are often oriented toward personal growth rather than toward solving specific psychological problems.
- *2* Among the alternative therapies in the marketplace are primal therapy, scream therapy, rebirthing, various types of encounter groups, est, and transpersonal therapies such as Arica.
- *3* Alternative therapies have been criticized as anti-intellectual fads that are possibly dangerous to some people.
- *4* Hundreds of self-help books offer solutions to psychological problems and insights into personal growth. Some books may be helpful to readers with specific problems, but they may also be misleading.

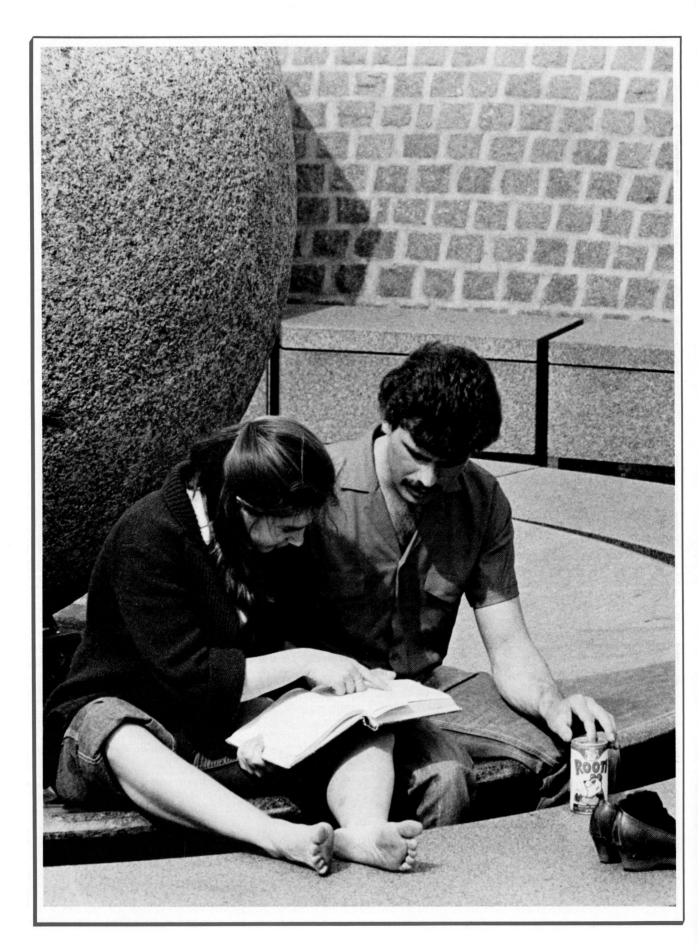

RELATING TO ONE ANOTHER

Psychology cannot confine itself to studying individuals as if they were isolated organisms, each in his own private world. A fundamental aspect of being human is the way in which we affect— and, in turn, are affected by— our fellow human beings. In this part we will focus on the ways in which people relate to one another, drawing from the field of social psychology.

Chapter 15 is concerned with the interrelated topics of Attitudes and Influence. We will discover that people's attitudes, whether they concern political candidates, consumer goods, or social values, are all formed in large measure through interactions with other people. We will also examine some of the techniques people use to influence the views and actions of others. The Psychological Issue concerns Prejudice and Racism, dangerous sets of attitudes that directly influence our behavior toward entire groups of people.

Chapter 16, entitled Male and Female, deals with relations between the two sexes. It focuses on the differences and similarities between men and women, and examines the ways in which
people come to assume patterns of behavior that are considered appropriate to their sex. This chapter also explores the interactions between women and men in the domain of sexuality. The Psychological Issue discusses the controversial topic of Changing Sex Roles *and the possibility of moving toward a society in which people's traits and opportunities are not affected by their sex.*

Chapter 17 explores some of the central themes that run through our Social Relationships—needing others, perceiving others, liking others, loving others, and leaving others. Several of these themes relate closely to psychological processes that we discussed in previous chapters—"needing others" to social aspects of motivation, "perceiving others" to social aspects of perception, and "loving others" to social aspects of emotion. The Psychological Issue discusses some of the challenges and problems of social relationships in a sphere of tremendous importance both to individuals and to society as a whole, that of Marriage and Divorce.

ATTITUDES AND INFLUENCE

The ways in which our attitudes are formed and changed are central to our lives and to the workings of society.

CHAPTER 15

THE NATURE OF ATTITUDES

Measuring attitudes
Attitudes and behavior

Our attitudes toward people, groups, and issues serve as guides to our actions.

THE FOUNDATIONS OF ATTITUDES

Emotional foundations of attitudes
Cognitive foundations of attitudes
Behavioral foundations of attitudes
Social foundations of attitudes

Our attitudes are built on a foundation of emotions, beliefs, behaviors, and social relationships.

PERSUASION

The communicator
The message
The medium
The audience

The persuasiveness of a message depends on who delivers it, what he says, what medium he uses, and whom he is addressing.

OBEDIENCE TO AUTHORITY

Milgram's experiment
Legitimate authority
Reducing obedience

We are prone to obey the dictates of authorities, sometimes in a blind and unquestioning way.

PSYCHOLOGICAL ISSUE
PREJUDICE AND RACISM

Although racial prejudice seems to have been reduced in recent years, it has by no means been erased.

BOXES
1 Conformity
2 Brainwashing
3 Resisting persuasion
4 Deception in research

• How good a job do you think the President is doing?

• Do you approve or disapprove of sexual intercourse between unmarried people?

• Are you in favor of capital punishment for certain crimes?

• All in all, what is your opinion of the college you attend?

• How do you feel about your psychology professor?

• What brand of mouthwash, if any, do you prefer?

These questions all ask about your attitudes—the ways in which you evaluate people, objects, and issues. Attitudes are people's likes and dislikes, and as such they play a major role in determining social behavior, from trivial choices to crucial life decisions. Your attitudes are likely to play a major role in determining whom you vote for, what groups you join, what courses you take, and what products you buy.

No wonder, then, that attitudes have been a central focus of theory and research in social psychology— the branch of psychology that deals with social interactions and relationships. In fact, "attitude" is probably the single most widely used term in all the social sciences (Berkowitz, 1972). Attitudes have also been a central concern of people with an interest in shaping and changing other people's opinions and behavior, including pollsters and politicians, manufacturers and merchandisers, and advocates of every cause from lower taxes to cleaner air. Changing people's attitudes is central to most instances of social influence. More generally, *social influence* refers to the ways in which people's attitudes or behavior are changed—whether intentionally or unintentionally—by other people or groups. In this chapter, we will focus on how attitudes are formed

and how they can be changed. In the last section of the chapter, we will turn from attitude change to another sort of social influence—obedience to authority.

THE NATURE OF ATTITUDES

Attitudes are people's relatively enduring sets of thoughts (or beliefs) and feelings about particular people, objects, or issues. Thoughts are generally referred to as the *cognitive* component of an attitude, and feelings as the *affective* component. For example, the cognitive component of Carl's attitude toward capital punishment might include the beliefs that capital punishment is immoral and that it does not effectively deter crime anyway. The affective component of this attitude might include the feeling of sadness and revulsion that Carl experiences whenever he hears about an execution.

In general, we expect the cognitive and affective aspects of an attitude to be consistent with each other. If, for example, you favor the positions of a particular candidate, you are also likely to feel good when that candidate gets elected. Or, if you have negative beliefs about a particular group of people, you may well feel uneasy when you come into contact with a member of that group.

Measuring attitudes

Psychologists and other social scientists have devoted a great deal of attention to the problem of measuring attitudes. Many different measurement techniques have been developed, but most of them involve asking people direct questions about

Market researchers are interested in measuring people's attitudes about various products.

their views. One technique is to ask *open-ended questions*, which allow the respondents (the people being questioned) to make any response they wish. For example, a political pollster might ask, "When you think of Jesse Jackson, what are the first things that come to your mind?" Or a marketing researcher might ask a parent, "Now that you've had a chance to use our disposable diapers for a month, could you tell me how you feel about them?"

Answers to such open-ended ques-

tions can provide rich information about people's attitudes, but they may also be difficult to analyze quantitatively. Thus, most attitude measurement devices make use of *fixed-response questions*, in which the respondents are asked to select one of a given set of answers to a question. One common approach is to present people with a series of statements about some object or issue and to ask them to indicate how much they agree or disagree with each statement. For example, Table 15.1 repre-

TABLE 15.1

SAMPLE ITEMS TO ASSESS PEOPLE'S ATTITUDES TOWARD CAPITAL PUNISHMENT

For each statement circle the number that expresses how much you agree or disagree.

1. Executing murderers is an effective way to deter other people from committing murder.

−3	−2	−1	+1	+2	+3
Strongly Disagree	Moderately Disagree	Slightly Disagree	Slightly Agree	Moderately Agree	Strongly Agree

2. Although capital punishment may have been appropriate in other times, today it can only be regarded as a "cruel and inhuman punishment."

−3	−2	−1	+1	+2	+3
Strongly Disagree	Moderately Disagree	Slightly Disagree	Slightly Agree	Moderately Agree	Strongly Agree

3. Capital punishment only serves to perpetuate violence in our society.

−3	−2	−1	+1	+2	+3
Strongly Disagree	Moderately Disagree	Slightly Disagree	Slightly Agree	Moderately Agree	Strongly Agree

4. There are times when a person has committed a crime so hideous that the only appropriate punishment is death.

−3	−2	−1	+1	+2	+3
Strongly Disagree	Moderately Disagree	Slightly Disagree	Slightly Agree	Moderately Agree	Strongly Agree

DO YOUR EYES REVEAL YOUR ATTITUDES?

Twenty years ago, Eckhard Hess (1965) reported that people's positive and negative attitudes toward other people or objects are reflected in the widening or narrowing of the pupils of their eyes. In one study, Hess found that men's pupils widened most when they were shown female pinups, and women's pupils widened most when they were shown male pinups and pictures of babies. On the other hand, both men's and women's pupils tended to get smaller when they viewed photographs of cross-eyed and crippled children. But most subsequent studies failed to confirm Hess's results (Woodmansee, 1970). The current verdict of experts is that physiological measures, including pupil size and skin conductance, may be useful indices of emotional arousal, but they are not reliable measures of attitudes.

sents a series of questions that might be used to assess people's attitudes toward capital punishment. The respondent's overall attitude score is determined by summing her answers on each of the individual questions. The more strongly a person agrees with items 1 and 4 and the more strongly she disagrees with items 2 and 3, the more favorable the person's attitude toward capital punishment would be said to be. In this case, as in many others, researchers are likely to assume that the attitude they are interested in is too complex to be adequately measured with a single question; therefore, they make use of a combination of questions, each of which gets at a slightly different aspect of the underlying attitude.

Attitude measures are not infallible. They will produce accurate results only to the extent that the respondent in fact *has* an attitude about the object in question and is motivated to respond honestly. Because attitude questionnaires and public opinion polls often ask questions about matters that the respondent has never thought about before, they may sometimes *create* attitudes rather

than simply measure them. Furthermore, people's expressed attitudes can sometimes be influenced by the specific situation in which the interview or questionnaire is administered. For example, Robert Shomer and Richard Centers (1970) had three groups of male students fill out a questionnaire measuring attitudes about men's and women's roles. Those men who completed the questionnaire in a classroom with other men proved to have the most "male chauvinist" attitudes; those who filled out the questionnaire in a room containing half men and half women expressed in-between attitudes; and those who answered it in a room containing eighteen men and only one woman had the the least male-chauvinist attitudes. The testing situation, ranging from the all-male "locker room atmosphere" to the perhaps consciousness-raising atmosphere of a lone woman in a group of men, apparently had an effect on the attitudes that the men chose to express. In spite of problems such as this, however, researchers are usually able to assess people's attitudes with a reasonable degree of accuracy.

THE NATURE OF ATTITUDES   455

Attitudes and behavior

People's attitudes toward particular objects are usually closely related to their behavior toward those objects. If you approve of a political candidate, you will probably act on your attitude by voting for her. If you disapprove of premarital sex, you will probably act on your attitude by refraining from such activity. Thus, our attitudes are not only reflections of our views of the world but they also serve as guidelines for our actions. As a result, we can often do a good job of predicting people's behavior if we know their attitudes.

In practice, people don't act on every occasion in ways that seem consistent with their attitudes. For example, people's reported attitudes toward the nation's energy problems have not been found to be good predictors of their own energy-conserving practices (Olson, 1981). Similarly, people's expressed attitudes toward their churches are not very good predictors of whether they will in fact attend church on any given Sunday (Wicker, 1969). On reflection, this lack of perfect consistency between attitudes and actions may not be too surprising. After all, attitudes are not the *only* influences on our behavior. Our behavior is also influenced by rewards, punishments, laws, regulations, and the subtler "rules" pro-

duced by the expectations of other people. Thus, even a person who believes that energy conservation is important may still turn up the thermostat on a cold day. And even a person with a positive attitude toward his church may decide to join friends for a picnic on a Sunday morning.

An additional problem in predicting behavior on the basis of attitudes is the fact that we have many attitudes and they are sometimes in conflict with one another. You may have a strong positive attitude toward Robert Redford and a strong negative attitude toward war movies. What do you do if a new war film comes out starring Redford? Which of your attitudes will prevail? "A few people will go to the stake for a single value," writes Howard Schuman (1972), "but history and common sense tell us that most people work out compromises."

Despite these problems of prediction, on the whole our attitudes do play a powerful role in guiding our behavior. In many domains, from consumers' decisions about products to voters' decisions about candidates, knowing a person's attitudes provides the best possible prediction of his future actions. Attitudes are especially good predictors of general patterns of behavior, as opposed to isolated actions. Although a person's religious attitudes may not be a good predictor of church attendance on a given Sun-

Some of these people have a strongly positive attitude toward church-going. Others may have a less positive attitude, but are in church this Sunday for other reasons. Attitudes influence our behaviors, but they are not the only influences.

FIGURE 15.1

Our attitudes are founded in our emotions, our beliefs (or cognitions), our behaviors, and our social relationships.

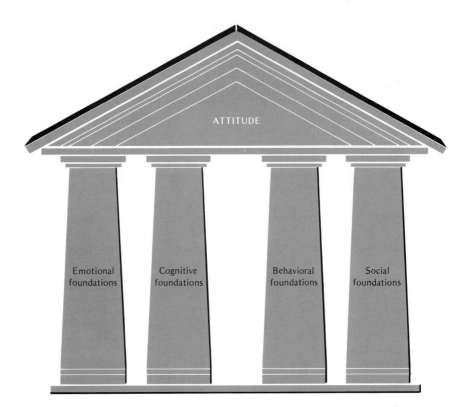

ATTITUDE

Emotional
foundations

Cognitive
foundations

Behavioral
foundations

Social
foundations

MUSICAL CONDITIONING

Can background music really affect our attitudes toward products? Apparently it can. In one marketing study, students heard either pleasant or unpleasant background music while they were shown a slide of either a light blue or a beige pen. Later the subjects were allowed to choose either a blue or a beige pen as a gift. Seventy-nine percent of the subjects who had heard the pleasant music chose the pen of the color that they had seen, while 70 percent of those who heard the unpleasant music chose the pen of the color that they had not seen. The subjects were apparently unaware of the strong effects of the music. When asked what had influenced their choice, only 5 of the 195 subjects mentioned the music (Gorn, 1982).

day, for example, they can predict his church-going frequency rather well when averaged over a period of time (Kahle and Berman, 1979).

THE FOUNDATIONS OF ATTITUDES

We are not born with attitudes—they are learned, through our experience in the world and our interactions with other people. In this section we will examine four important ways in which our attitudes are acquired and sustained. These four foundations of attitudes can be categorized, following the terminology of Daryl Bem (1970), as the *emotional*, the *cognitive*, the *behavioral*, and the *social* (see Figure 15.1).

Emotional foundations of attitudes

Remember the last time you had a Coke? It probably seemed like a simple, uncomplicated event—you were thirsty and you got something to drink. Right? Wrong, according to the advertisers who spend millions shaping your attitudes toward their prod-

ucts. You not only had something to drink, you had "a Coke and a smile." According to its advertisers, Coca-Cola "makes you feel good" because it "adds life." They not only sold you a Coke but a sense of well-being and vigor. Even cigarette manufacturers, who are hawking a distinctly unwholesome product, try to link their product with positive emotions. Take a recent magazine advertisement showing a young man and woman playing in a tree—he is hanging upside down, she is rightside up—clearly having a wonderful, carefree time. They are Newport smokers, "Alive with Pleasure!"

Commercial appeals like these are often remarkably successful, and they illustrate ways in which attitudes can be formed by linking particular objects to positive emotions. The basic technique was described in Chapter 5. Based on the principles of classical conditioning, a product is repeatedly paired with images and ideals we are likely to feel good about. The goal is for us to associate the good feelings with the product.

Many of our most strongly held attitudes are also likely to have emotional foundations, often dating back to childhood. Imagine, for example, that a child's parents display an aversion to homosexuals, referring to gay people in disparaging terms and showing disdain whenever they see a gay couple. Such a child may well come to associate homosexuality with negative emotions himself, thus acquiring an attitude of homophobia (see Chapter 16, Box 4). Our positive attitude of pride in our country is also likely to have a strong emotional foundation, derived from the pairing of references to and symbols of our country (such as the national flag and anthem) with uplifting experiences and sentiments. Have you ever had tears come to your eyes or a lump in your throat when "The Star Spangled Banner" or "O Canada" was played? If so, classical conditioning is likely to have been involved.

Cognitive foundations of attitudes

Most of our attitudes fit into a larger structure of beliefs and attitudes that we have. This larger structure serves as the *cognitive* foundation of the attitude. For example, if you were to ask a person why she favors the legalization of marijuana, she might give you an answer something like the following: "Well, there's no good evidence that marijuana is harmful, laws against marijuana limit people's freedom, and people are going to use it anyway." Each element in this answer can be converted into a chain of reasoning, or *syllogism*. The implied syllogisms in this particular person's cognitive structure are depicted in Figure 15.2. As the figure shows, each syllogism begins with two premises. One of these premises is a belief that corresponds to the person's stated reason for favoring the legalization of marijuana (for example, "There's no good evidence that marijuana is harmful"). The second premise is a belief or attitude that the person has not stated but that is implied in her reasoning (for example, "Nonharmful substances should be legal"). When these two beliefs or attitudes are put together, they point logically to the conclusion ("Marijuana should be legalized"). Needless to say, other people will begin with different premises and will therefore come to different conclusions. Typically, the more arguments we have for a particular attitude, the more resistant that attitude is to change.

Many of our attitudes have cognitive foundations of this sort. For example, Donald Granberg (1982) assessed the beliefs of the members of two groups with diametrically opposing views on abortion—the Abortion

Our attitude of pride in our country is strongly linked to emotions that were instilled in childhood. We have learned to pair symbols of our country, such as the flag, with uplifting sentiments.

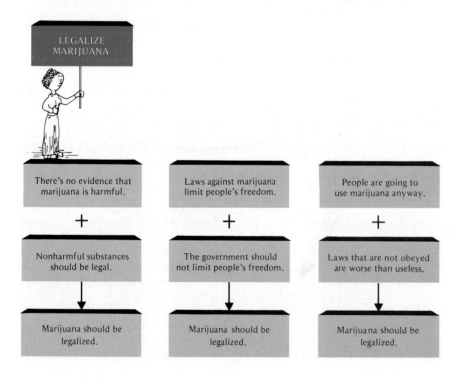

LEGALIZE MARIJUANA

There's no evidence that marijuana is harmful.	Laws against marijuana limit people's freedom.	People are going to use marijuana anyway.
+	+	+
Nonharmful substances should be legal.	The government should not limit people's freedom.	Laws that are not obeyed are worse than useless.
↓	↓	↓
Marijuana should be legalized.	Marijuana should be legalized.	Marijuana should be legalized.

FIGURE 15.2

The cognitive structure of one hypothetical person's attitudes about legalizing marijuana. Other people will begin with different premises and, as a result, will come to different conclusions.

Rights Alliance of Missouri (a group advocating each woman's right to choose abortion) and the Missouri Citizens for Life (an antiabortion group). Granberg found that members of the two groups had sharply divergent beliefs about a variety of related issues as well as abortion. Members of the Missouri Citizens for Life were much more likely to believe that a person's life begins at conception, that the fetus is a person, and that the heart of the fetus is formed and beating by the fourth week of pregnancy. Members of the Abortion Rights Alliance were much more likely to believe that abortion has become safer

in recent years, that the United States has a serious population problem, and that if abortions were illegal the number of teenage mothers would increase. It is not hard to see how these differing beliefs of the two groups helped to prop up their respective attitudes toward abortion.

Our attitudes are not always consistent and logical, however. We have already seen that people's attitudes often have emotional bases that do not seem logical at all. And as we will see in the next section, people often achieve "consistency" among their attitudes by means of cognitive contortions that are far from logical.

People who have strong attitudes either in favor of a woman's right to choose abortion or against abortion are likely to have an extended structure of beliefs that is consistent with this attitude.

Behavioral foundations of attitudes

As noted earlier, people's attitudes play a major role in guiding their behavior toward the object of their attitudes. If I like modern art I will go to museums to see it, and if I disdain panhandlers I will do whatever I can to avoid them. It is important to note, however, that the links between attitudes and behaviors go in both directions. Not only do our attitudes influence our actions, but our actions also serve to shape our attitudes. Thus, once a person has been induced to act in a particular way, his attitudes are likely to follow. Many studies have shown, for example, that favorable attitudes toward racial integration typically follow, rather than precede, actual desegregation (see the Psychological Issue at the end of this chapter).

Along similar lines, if a person makes a statement (the behavior) that does not initially agree with her real views, that person's views are likely to change to come into greater conformity with the statement she has made. Suppose, for example, that you were somewhat in favor of the registration of young men for the draft but were nevertheless induced by a friend to sign a petition opposing registration. It is quite likely that after signing the petition you would become less favorable to draft registration than you had been previously. Such an attitude shift can be explained in terms of Leon Festinger's (1957) theory of *cognitive dissonance*. According to Festinger's theory, it is psychologically uncomfortable to entertain two clashing thoughts or cognitions—in this case, the cognitions that (a) I am in favor of registration and (b) I've just signed a petition opposing registration. Therefore, you will be motivated to reduce the dissonance; and the best way to do so may be to focus on the negative aspects of registration and decide that they may in fact outweigh the positive aspects.

The theory of cognitive dissonance also maintains that attitude change is most likely if you were not forced or bribed to sign the petition, but agreed to do so of your own free will. If you signed the petition only because someone "made you an offer you couldn't refuse" (like $20, or a threat to blackball you in a fraternity election), then your signing of the petition was not really inconsistent or "dissonant"—you did it for reasons that you were well aware of. And in such an event, there is no need to reduce dissonance by changing your attitudes. But if you signed the petition in the absence of such pressures, the dissonance is greater, and, hence, there is a stronger motive to change your attitude in such a way as to restore consistency. This line of reasoning was supported in a famous study by Festinger and J. Merrill Carlsmith (1959). In this study, students who had taken part in a boring experiment were offered either a token reward of $1 or a large bribe of $20 for telling other students that they really enjoyed the experiment. Later, Festinger and Carlsmith asked the subjects what they really thought about the experiment. The researchers found that subjects who had told the $1 lie now believed the experiment had been more fun than did subjects who had told the $20 lie (see Figure 15.3). After all, Festinger and Carlsmith pointed out, it's not really "dissonant" or inconsistent to tell a white lie if you're being paid a lot of money to do so. But to tell a lie for only one lousy dollar does arouse dissonance—and that's why the subjects were motivated to decide that they really believed what they had said.

Another way of explaining the tendency for people's behavior to affect their attitudes is Daryl Bem's (1972) *self-perception theory*. Whereas dissonance theory postulates an inner motive or drive to reduce inconsistency, self-perception theory does not assume that we have any such motive. Instead, it focuses on inferences we make from observing our own behavior. According to Bem, just as we often infer other people's attitudes by observing their actions, we may also determine our *own* attitudes by observing our own actions. Bem (1970) writes:
Most people agree that the question, "Why do you eat brown bread?" can properly be answered with "Because I like it." I should like to convince you, however, that

DISSONANCE AFTER THE FLOOD

People who rebuild their homes in a previously flooded valley often seem unrealistically confident that they will not be washed out again. Some of the flood-plain dwellers interviewed by Robert Kates (1962) even believed that they were protected by dams that were actually downstream. The theory of cognitive dissonance may help to explain this sort of irrational thinking. It is, after all, highly dissonant to believe that (a) this area is dangerous and (b) I've decided to live here anyway. To reduce the dissonance, people are prone to seize upon whatever evidence they can find that is consistent with their behavior—even evidence that might seem awfully flimsy to a more objective observer.

FIGURE 15.3

In Festinger and Carlsmith's study, subjects who were paid only $1 to tell a lie seemed to experience cognitive dissonance. But subjects who were paid $20 to tell the same lie did not seem to experience dissonance.

After signing a petition, a person may reflect on his behavior and conclude that he really agrees with the position that he has endorsed.

the question, "Why do you like brown bread?" frequently ought to be answered with "Because I eat it." (Page 54)

According to Bem's analysis, a person may say to himself, "Well, I've just signed a petition opposing draft registration—and I wasn't even forced to do it. I guess I must be opposed to registration after all." Of course, there are limits to the applicability of Bem's theory. Sometimes we know full well what our attitudes about an issue are, and we don't need to spend time figuring them out. In many other cases, however, Bem's approach makes sense. Our attitudes about many issues *are* initially vague and confused, and they may finally take shape only after we have had a chance to reflect upon our own behavior. For myself, I recently figured out that I am in favor of banning handguns (by noting that I had just contributed to the National Coalition to Ban Handguns) and that I like rippled potato chips (by acknowledging that I keep sneaking into the kitchen to find some).

Social foundations of attitudes

In addition to having emotional, cognitive, and behavioral foundations, attitudes are social products, the result of our interactions with other people. For example, children often use their parents as models for the attitudes they should hold. It is no accident that the large majority of Americans adhere to their parents' choice of political party (Stone, 1974) or that children are more likely to smoke if their parents do (Wohlford, 1970). As children reach adolescence, the influence of parents must often compete with the influence of peers.

In the 1930s, Theodore Newcomb conducted a classic study of the way in which parents and peers shaped people's attitudes at Bennington College, an elite women's school in Ver-

mont (Newcomb, 1943). Almost all the young women attending Bennington came from affluent, upper-crust families—they *had* to be affluent to send their daughters to an expensive college during the years of the Depression. As was generally characteristic of people of their social and economic background, the parents of Bennington students were socially and economically conservative. In the 1936 presidential election, for example, two-thirds of the parents preferred the conservative Republican candidate, Alfred Landon, to the liberal Democratic incumbent, Franklin D. Roosevelt. In sharp contrast to the conservative family backgrounds of its students, Bennington had an extremely liberal or, by some people's reckoning, even radical atmosphere.

This liberal atmosphere quickly enveloped incoming students. A majority of the students abandoned the conservative attitudes of their parents and adopted the liberal views of the campus community. As Table 15.2 shows, a majority of the freshmen women entering Bennington in 1936 shared their parents' preference for

One of Theodore Newcomb's psychology classes at Bennington College in the 1930s. Newcomb is at the far right.

TABLE 15.2

BENNINGTON COLLEGE STUDENTS' PREFERENCES IN THE 1936 PRESIDENTIAL ELECTION

Candidate favored	Freshmen	Juniors and seniors
Alfred M. Landon (Republican)	62 percent	15 percent
Franklin D. Roosevelt (Democrat)	29 percent	54 percent
Socialist or Communist	9 percent	30 percent

Source: Adapted from Newcomb (1943).

CHAPTER FIFTEEN: ATTITUDES AND INFLUENCE

Landon, but five out of six juniors and seniors, who had had a few years to soak up the prevailing political atmosphere, preferred either Roosevelt or, to their parents' undoubted chagrin, one of the more radical candidates. In addition, the juniors and seniors had more liberal views than the freshmen on the political and economic issues of the day, such as unemployment, public relief, and the rights of organized labor—issues that had been made prominent by President Roosevelt's New Deal.

These dramatic shifts in attitudes attest to the power of a social group to shape people's views. In Newcomb's terms, the college community became a *reference group* for many of the Bennington women—a group with which they identified and from which they derived many of their opinions. One of the reasons that people are likely to adopt group opinions is that having "popular" opinions often helps gain acceptance and prestige. Newcomb found, for example, that the Bennington women who were best liked and most respected among their classmates tended to be among those with the most liberal views. Some of the women whom Newcomb interviewed during their senior year admitted that they changed their opinions at least in part in order to gain acceptance and popularity. Other examples of conformity to the attitudes or actions of a group are discussed in Box 1. Identifying with the more liberal attitudes of the college community was also a way for many women to assert their independence from their parents.

The fact that many of the students adopted new attitudes in order to gain acceptance and assert their indepen-

People often adopt a particular attitude or behavior in order to identify with a group.

CONFORMITY

To most of us, *conformity* is a dirty word suggesting robotlike acceptance of the attitudes and actions of others. Buckling under to group pressure suggests that we are too weak to think for ourselves. Our heroes are likely to be the nonconformists of the world who march to the sound of a different drummer.

At the same time, however, we recognize that conformity to the norms of our groups and culture is the price of living in social groups without anarchy and chaos. We conform to common standards of expression and behavior because they make our day-to-day interaction smoother and more predictable. And we conform to certain beliefs—from the notion that the earth is round to the tenet that all people should have equal rights—because they provide a common basis for life in society. The issue, then, is not *whether* to conform or to remain independent, but *when* to conform and when to hold out for an unpopular position.

Solomon Asch (1951) conducted an experiment that dramatically illustrated the dilemma of conformity to group pressures. Asch assembled groups of eight subjects to participate in a study of visual judgment. The subjects sat around a table and judged the length of various lines. But only one member of each group was a genuine subject. All the others were Asch's confederates, and on prearranged trials they reported ridiculously incorrect judgments. In a case such as that in the figure below, the confederates each reported confidently that Line 1 was

In Asch's experiment, several subjects were asked by the experimenter (right) *to compare the length of lines (as in the figure at the bottom of the page). Six of the subjects have been instructed ahead of time to give unanimously wrong answers. The seventh (sixth from the left) has merely been told that it is an experiment in perception.*

most similar in length to the comparison line on the left.

These events put the real subject, who was one of the last to call out his decision, in a difficult situation. Should he report his real judgment, even though it would make him look silly in the eyes of other group members, or should he go along with the crowd? The situation was extremely uncomfortable for many of Asch's subjects, and different subjects resolved the dilemma in different ways: some of the subjects never conformed, while others conformed almost all of the time. Overall, subjects conformed to the false group consensus on 32 percent of the trials.

In some cases, subjects' confidence was genuinely shaken by the reports of the unanimous majority. One subject who went along with the group on almost every trial explained afterward, "If they had been doubtful I probably would have changed, but they answered with such confidence." Most of the subjects who went along with the majority admitted later that they really didn't believe that the majority was correct, but they were afraid of seeming foolish in the eyes of their fellow students.

Similar effects can take place outside the laboratory. In jury deliberations, for example, a juror who finds herself to be a lone dissenter on the

initial ballot will find it extremely difficult to hold out for her point of view (Hastie, Penrod, and Pennington, 1983). On the other hand, if there is at least one additional dissenter to provide support for one's minority opinion, conformity is greatly reduced. Asch found that when just one of the confederates in his groups was instructed to give the right answers instead of going along with the majority, the amount of conformity declined sharply from 32 percent to 5 percent.

Social psychologist Irving Janis (1982) has identified a particularly dangerous form of conformity that he calls *groupthink*. Groupthink refers to the tendency for members of policy-making groups to suppress all individual doubts and dissent, creating an illusion of unanimity. Both in President Kennedy's inner circle of advisers who gave the go-ahead to the ill-fated Bay of Pigs invasion of Cuba and in the council who advised President Johnson to escalate the Vietnam war, critical judgment seems to have been suspended in favor of shared illusions. Janis has also suggested that groupthink may have contributed to the decision by President Carter and his advisers to attempt a poorly conceived rescue mission of U.S. hostages in Iran.

Especially in a group that has high morale, no individual wants to be the

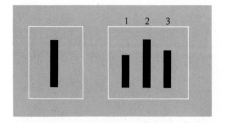

Example of stimulus used in Asch's experiment. Which of the three lines matches the line on the left?

one to burst the balloon by raising doubts or reservations. And the group as a whole acts to suppress such expression of doubts. Having suppressed all dissent, the group feels invulnerable, that nothing can go wrong—and, as a result, it is likely to make dangerous, ill-considered decisions.

Despite the strong pressures to conform, people with minority viewpoints within a group are not powerless. Many studies have demonstrated that minorities of as few as two people within a larger group can sometimes manage to convert the group to their position. For such *minority influence* to be effective, the people in the minority must be consistent and confident—to convince the larger group that their view is a plausible one that deserves to be considered seriously (Maass and Clark, 1984). Even if the group does not ultimately adopt the minority viewpoint, the minority—by sticking to its guns—can play a constructive role in the decision-making process. They can help to insure that the group considers critically a range of alternatives rather than reaching a quick decision simply because "we all seem to agree."

dence from their families does not mean that their attitude change was superficial or cosmetic. "I became a liberal at first because of its prestige value," one woman acknowledged, "[but] I remain so because the problems around which my liberalism centers are important" (Newcomb, 1965, page 222). Once people have adopted a new set of attitudes, for whatever reasons, these new attitudes can become a central part of their self-definition. And when new issues arise, people tend to view them from the perspective of these attitudes.

In addition to providing us with new attitudes, our social groups and relationships also support and reinforce the attitudes we already have. If you know that your friends share your opinions about politics, religion, or drugs, you are likely to hold these opinions more securely and confidently than if you feel you are alone in your view. People who hold a particular attitude or engage in a particular behavior have also been found to overestimate the number of people who share their views. This phenomenon has been called the *false consensus effect*. For example, when adolescents were asked what percentage of all students in their school smoked, those who were themselves smokers gave higher estimates than did nonsmokers (Sherman et al., 1983). The false consensus effect may be another way in which people can find "social support" for their attitudes—by assuming that their views or behaviors are endorsed by others.

The emotional, cognitive, behavioral, and social foundations of attitudes are not independent of one another. For example, social groups may make use of emotional techniques to instill attitudes in us. Thus, liberal attitudes may have taken on positive emotional connotations for many Bennington students because these attitudes were associated with people whom they liked and admired. These attitudes were also embedded in interconnected cognitive structures, and they were fortified by behaviors— political activities and discussions that students engaged in. In general, the emotional, cognitive, behavioral, and social factors work together to produce our attitudes.

PERSUASION

Although people's attitudes tend to be relatively enduring, they sometimes change. People often reflect on their attitudes or have experiences that lead them to change their minds about important issues. One way in which attitudes may be changed is through *persuasion*—messages from other people that are designed to change the views of the people who receive them.

Persuasion takes place every day, in forms ranging from a Washington lobbyist's success in convincing a representative to change his vote to a doctor's success in convincing a patient to start an exercise program. (A less common form of persuasion— brainwashing—is discussed in Box 2.) Social psychologists have made extensive attempts to discover just what sorts of persuasive appeals are most likely to work. Every attempt at persuasion can be seen as having four components: a *communicator* delivers a *message* through a particular *medium* to an *audience* (see Figure 15.4). Researchers have tried to determine what characteristics of the communicator, of the message she delivers, of the medium used, and of the particular audience addressed are most likely to result in attitude change.

The communicator

Who would be more successful in convincing you that you need only five or six hours of sleep at night—a Nobel Prize-winning physiologist or an unknown YMCA director? Which article about the effectiveness of antihistamine drugs would you be more likely to believe—one that appears in a prestigious medical journal or one that appears in a mass-circulation pictorial magazine? If you are like most of the subjects in experiments that used these materials, the messages of the famous physiologist (Bochner and Insko, 1966) and of the medical journal (Hovland and Weiss, 1953) would have a better chance of success. Within each of these experiments, subjects in different conditions were presented with precisely

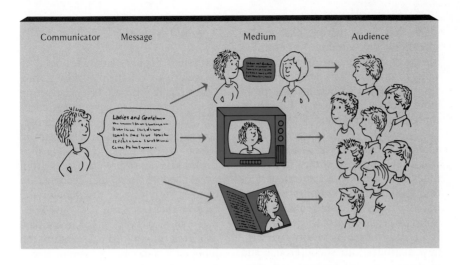

Communicator   Message   Medium   Audience

Ladies and Gentlemen

FIGURE 15.4

The components of a persuasive communication are the communicator, the message, the medium through which the message is communicated, and the audience to whom the message is addressed.

the same message, but the message was attributed to one or the other source. Not surprisingly, the same message was more effective when subjects thought it had been delivered by the more expert communicator.

The *credibility*, or believability, of a communicator is a factor that television advertisers are highly concerned with. The more expert a source seems to be, the more credible he will be. That is why aspirin commercials are often delivered by a dignified man in a white coat and why orange juice commercials feature biology teachers and nutritionists. From the standpoint of credibility, Robert Young—remembered by many TV viewers as Marcus Welby, M.D.— was an inspired choice as the spokesman for Sanka decaffeinated coffee. After all, who should know more about the effects of caffeine than a "doctor"?

Besides expertise, a second important factor in a communicator's credibility is sincerity. We sometimes suspect communicators of trying to convince us of something for their own ulterior motives. But a sincere communicator makes clear that she really believes what she is saying. For this reason, we are likely to be more convinced by a message if we overhear it than if it is directly addressed to us (Walster and Festinger, 1962). When we overhear a communication, we are less likely to reason that "he's just trying to persuade me." Consequently, we are less likely to discount the validity of the message. That is

why advertisers sometimes present "candid" commercials in which we "overhear" housewives praising particular detergents in the privacy of their own homes.

The message

Many studies of persuasion have focused on the content of the message itself. For example, is it more effective for a communicator to present only one point of view, or is it better to deal with opposing arguments, as well? Let's say you're trying to convince your classmates that capital punishment should be abolished. Should you stick to describing what you believe to be the failings of capital punishment, or should you also mention other people's views that capital punishment can deter crime and then try to refute these views? Research suggests that the best strategy would depend on the characteristics of your audience. If your classmates are predisposed to agree with you anyway (Hovland, Lumsdaine, and Sheffield, 1949), and if they don't know there is an opposing view (Jones and Brehm, 1970), the one-sided message is likely to be more effective. After all, why muddy the water with negative arguments that would never otherwise occur to your audience? But if your classmates have a somewhat positive view of capital punishment and if they already know there are arguments for it, you will be better off acknowledging these arguments and trying to deal with them.

BOX 2

BRAINWASHING

Brainwashing is a loaded term, with different meanings for different people. For some, it has come to mean almost any case of a person's being persuaded to do or think something that he later regrets having done or thought. For example, consumers complain that they are brainwashed into buying products they don't really want. For others, "brainwashing" has a sinister ring to it, with connotations of torture and mind-altering drugs. Most accurately, however, brainwashing refers to a set of techniques that is used in an attempt to change a captured person's basic attitudes and values. These techniques do not depend on physical torture, drugs, or gadgets. Rather, they are based on a recognition of the social foundations of attitudes; they work (when they are successful) by tearing down the existing social foundations of a person's attitudes and erecting new ones in their place.

The word *brainwash* comes from the Chinese expression *hsi nao*, which literally means "wash brain." The Chinese Communists developed brainwashing techniques as part of the program of thought reform that followed their takeover of mainland China in 1949. These techniques were used to convert Chinese young people and intellectuals, and similar techniques were also applied to Westerners in China and to American prisoners captured by the Chinese during the Korean War.

Brainwashing has two major phases. The first is to destroy the person's existing group ties and, in so doing, to break down his sense of identity. This may be done by isolating prisoners from other people, by restricting communication to them, and by making them feel guilty for their actions. For example, the Chinese would deliver American prisoners their mail only if it contained bad news. And they told the prisoners that their failure to receive mail proved that their loved ones at home had abandoned them (Schein, 1957).

The second phase of brainwashing is to give the prisoner a new set of relationships, tied to the new ideals that the brainwashers want the prisoners to adopt. Edgar Schein (1957) reports that Chinese "instructors" sometimes lived with American prisoners for long periods of time in order to establish close relationships with them. They offered the prisoners special privileges if they would make public confessions or engage in other propaganda activities. By inducing the prisoners to engage in public behaviors that betrayed their old group and ideas, the brainwashers hoped that their private attitudes would change, as well.

Was Patricia Hearst a victim of brainwashing?

Brainwashing was back in the news in 1976 when Patricia Hearst was placed on trial for taking part in a bank robbery while she was a captive of the militant radical group called the Symbionese Liberation Army (SLA). One of the experts testifying in Patty's defense claimed that the SLA employed many brainwashing techniques that came right out of the Communist Chinese book. They toppled Patty's sense of self by locking her in a closet for weeks, and they created feelings of guilt and self-blame by branding her as "the daughter of a ruling class family,

the Hearsts." When Patty emerged from the closet, they induced her to take steps to renounce her old identity, such as making a tape on which she publicly called her parents "the pig Hearsts." And the bank robbery itself—which, the defense claimed, Patty was forced to take part in—further cut off her links to the past. Instead, Patty took on a new name ("Tania") and a new identity, as a member of the group that had captured her.

It is extremely difficult to brainwash someone successfully. Schein found that although the Chinese were successful in obtaining behavioral compliance and collaboration from many of their American prisoners, they produced very few ideological conversions. People's attitudes and ideals are rooted in decades of training in their original groups, and breaking down these strongly held attitudes is no easy matter.

Nevertheless, there is no doubt that by systematically destroying and replacing people's group supports and self-images, lasting changes in beliefs and attitudes can in some cases be produced.

The advantages of presenting both sides of an argument can also extend to marketing. Advertisers usually accentuate the positive aspects of their products and ignore the negative. But mentioning the weak points of a product, along with its stronger points, can sometimes make an ad more credible—and, as a result, may increase its effectiveness (Swinyard, 1981). For example, an effective mouthwash commercial might say, "Our mouthwash doesn't taste very good and it costs a little more, but it fights bad breath all day long."

Researchers have also examined the effectiveness of attempts to scare us into changing our attitudes. Scare tactics, or *fear appeals*, are often used

for laudable reasons, such as to induce people to stop smoking or to drive more carefully. In general, the more frightening the message, the more persuasive it is likely to be. For example, frightening films showing diseased lungs and gory cancer operations tend to produce greater shifts in smokers' attitudes toward their habit than do less scary films of statistical charts and graphs demonstrating the dangers of smoking (Leventhal, 1970). But simply scaring people out of their wits will not persuade them of anything. If it is to work, the frightening message must be accompanied by a reassuring one. The audience must be convinced that the recommendations offered by the communicator—such

PEANUTS, MUSIC, AND THOUGHTS OF YOU

Different techniques can be used to make an audience feel good about a product or message. In one study, subjects who were given a snack of peanuts and Pepsi-Cola while they read were more persuaded by a written message than were subjects who went snackless (Janis, Kaye, and Kirschner, 1965). In another study, subjects were more influenced by messages that were accompanied by folk music than by those that were unaccompanied (Galizio and Hendrick, 1972). And journalist Joe McGinnis (1969) reported that the people in charge of "selling" Richard Nixon in 1968 made a point of including pleasant background music in all of his spot commercials.

Mark Waters was a chain smoker. Wonder who'll get his office?

Too bad about Mark. Kept hearing the same thing everyone does about lung cancer. But, like so many people, he kept right on smoking cigarettes. Must have thought, "been smoking all my life... what good'll it do to stop now?" Fact is, once you've stopped smoking, no matter how long you've smoked, the body begins to reverse the damage done by cigarettes, provided cancer or emphysema have not developed. Next time you reach for a cigarette, think of Mark. Then think of your office—and your home.

American Cancer Society

Fear appeals can be effective in changing people's attitudes.

as to stop smoking or to wear seat belts—will in fact serve to reduce or avert the danger (Mewborn and Rogers, 1979). If a frightening message is presented without such reassurance, it may backfire: people will be so scared that they will defend themselves by dismissing the message completely.

The medium

Will a persuasive message be more effective when delivered face-to-face, on television, over the radio, or in a newspaper? Research makes clear that different media are likely to be more effective for different sorts of messages. Written messages, especially if they are complex, are usually easier to understand than spoken or televised messages (Wilson, 1974). The reader can go along at his own speed and is likely to think about the message more carefully (Wright, 1974). On the other hand, a face-to-face or television message is likely to have more immediate emotional impact. Following from these considerations, Shelly Chaiken and Alice Eagly (1976) found that when subjects were given a message that was easy to understand, it was more effective when presented by a communicator on videotape. But when the message was more complicated, it was best understood and most readily accepted

when presented in print. Political candidates often make practical use of this principle. They present simple, sometimes emotional appeals in their televised speeches and relegate their more complicated arguments to written position papers.

Some media, such as face-to-face or television presentations, make the personal qualities of the communicator highly noticeable. We see the person who is trying to persuade us, we monitor his facial expressions, and listen to his tone of voice. As a result, our feelings about the communicator are especially likely to influence our evaluation of his message. In written material, the characteristics of the communicator are less prominent, and the message is more likely to be evaluated in its own right. These differences between media have important practical implications: if a communicator is especially likable, she is likely to be more persuasive in face-to-face or video presentations; if she is not likable, she is better off using a written message (Chaiken and Eagly, 1983).

The audience

An effective communicator must tailor his message to the characteristics of the particular group he is trying to persuade. Some people may be generally easier to persuade than oth-

Many of our attitudes are shaped by the multimedia society in which we live.

ers. Perhaps you know such people, who are likely to be convinced by practically anything they hear or read. Sometimes we call such people "open-minded." Sometimes we call them "gullible." Studies have shown that in many instances people who have low self-esteem—that is, who do not think highly of themselves—are more easily influenced than people with high self-esteem (Eagly, 1980). People with low self-esteem lack confidence in their own judgment and hence are more quickly swayed by the judgments of others. It should be noted, however, that a person's overall level of self-esteem is less strongly related to her persuasibility than is her feeling of competence with regard to the specific issue at hand. The more a person feels she knows about a particular subject, the harder it typically will be to change her mind. Thus, for example, it will usually be harder to change a physician's mind than a musician's about the merits of a new drug, and harder to change a musician's mind than a physician's about the merits of a new symphony.

Regardless of the personal characteristics of the people you are trying to convince, a generally good rule is that the more actively you can involve them in the attempt to persuade them, the more likely they are

to be persuaded. Communicators can sometimes get the audience involved by asking rhetorical questions that the listeners must answer for themselves. Thus, the political challenger may find it more effective to ask, "Are you better off now than you were four years ago?" than simply to assert, "The value of your paycheck has declined over the past four years." By inducing the listeners to answer the question themselves, the candidate gets them to assist her in making her case (Petty et al., 1981). Television advertisers frequently try to involve the audience in their commercials. "Fill it to the rim," the man says to the woman, pausing dramatically so that we, who have already seen the commercial 247 times, can fill in the answer for ourselves ("with Brim") before she does. This technique of audience involvement is part of Brim's answer to Sanka's use of the supercredible Robert Young, in the never-ending battle of television persuaders.

Even though we are often influenced by persuasive messages, most of us would also like to feel that we are considering the choices for ourselves, rather than being coerced by the persuader. If we feel that a communicator is trying to take away our freedom of choice, we may feel motivated to reassert this freedom—a

BOOING THE TEAM TO VICTORY

It's well known that home teams have an advantage over visiting teams in athletic contests. Among the explanations for this home advantage is the influence of a home-team crowd that boos the visitors. In a careful study of college basketball games, Donald Greer (1983) found that immediately after periods of crowd booing, the home team's performance improved slightly and the visiting team's performance declined significantly. It's also possible that booing crowds exert an influence on the judgment of referees. Booing may not be sportsmanlike, but it does seem to help.

CHAPTER FIFTEEN: ATTITUDES AND INFLUENCE

BOX 3

RESISTING PERSUASION

To resist unwarranted persuasion, listen to messages critically, considering objections that might be raised.

Whether in politics, marketing, or other areas, the free commerce of ideas—with people attempting to persuade others of their positions—is the hallmark of a free society. Persuasion becomes dangerous, however, when it is accomplished with manipulative techniques that obscure the ideas being presented. To avoid being taken in by others, it is important for us to know how to resist persuasion.

When we are addressed by "experts," for example, we are sometimes lulled into instant acquiescence. After all, we think, the expert knows more about the subject than we do. In some cases, however, such "experts" lead people to surrender their own better judgment. Susan Andersen and Philip Zimbardo (1980) estimate, for example, that two million Americans a year undergo surgical operations that they don't need, at a cost of over $4 billion—a testimony to the power of the "experts."

To be able to resist being persuaded when we don't want to be, several techniques are recommended:

1 Become sensitive to the techniques that are used in persuasion attempts, such as the ways in which an aura of expertise or credibility may be established. Ask yourself whether Robert Young really knows more than you do about decaffeinated coffee, just because he once played a TV doctor. Ask yourself whether an insurance agent's well-practiced "sincerity" has any relevance to the merits of his argument. Ask yourself *why* the communicator is presenting his message: What's in it for him? Remember that "experts" can generally be found on both sides of every controversial issue. In the last analysis, when it comes to what you should think, *you're* the best expert.

2 When someone is presenting arguments to you, don't be afraid to argue back. In a face-to-face setting, you may be able to argue back publicly: to ask questions, raise objections, and point out holes in the argument. If you are listening to a speech or reading an article, then argue back privately. Instead of passively absorbing the message, consider the various objections that might be raised. When you are tired or distracted, you may not be able to counterargue effectively. This is one reason why persuasive messages are sometimes more effective when the audience is distracted by other matters. When the listeners are unable to generate their own counterarguments, they may accept the message uncritically (Petty, Wells, and Brock, 1976). If the conditions do not permit you to be an active listener, it may be better not to listen at all.

3 When you are evaluating a persuasive message, discuss it with other people, such as your friends or family. Other people can help you to raise new questions, consider the evidence more carefully, and arrive at a more considered conclusion. As suggested in Box 1 (on conformity) and Box 2 (on brainwashing), when people are isolated from others, they are most likely to accept persuasive messages uncritically.

In general, one should try to build up resistance to uncritical persuasion without becoming closed to valid messages. The best way to do this is to become an active, involved, and questioning listener.

motive that is called *psychological reactance* (Brehm and Brehm, 1981). Because of this motive, persuasive methods that seem too controlling are likely to backfire. If, for example, the communicator concludes, "You have no choice but to adopt my point of view," people are likely to react by rejecting the message (Worchel and Brehm, 1970). The communicator is better advised to make his arguments as compelling as possible and then to let the audience members feel that they are free to draw their own conclusions. For the audience members' part, they are well advised to listen to persuasive messages carefully and to evaluate them critically (see Box 3).

OBEDIENCE TO AUTHORITY

The most direct and time-honored form of social influence is *obedience*—doing something because an authority tells you to. Obedience is usually regarded as a positive quality—and, indeed, society would not be able to survive if people did not regularly follow the orders of their superiors. When obedience becomes blind and unquestioning, however, it may conflict with other important values, such as the value of the life and worth

of our fellow human beings. It was obedience to orders that allowed so many Germans to participate in the massive human exterminations that took place during the Nazi era: "Gas chambers were built, death camps were guarded, daily quotas of corpses were produced with the same efficiency as the manufacture of appliances. These inhuman policies may have originated in the mind of a single person, but they could only be carried out on a massive scale if a very large number of people followed orders" (Milgram, 1963, page 373).

Milgram's experiment

Stanley Milgram (1963; 1974) conceived of an experimental situation to investigate the conditions that lead people to obey an authority, even when it requires them to betray their own values and to harm innocent victims. Milgram's experiment, one of the classic studies of social psychology, began with an impressive-looking prop, a "shock generator" that had an instrument panel with thirty switches set in a horizontal line. Each switch had voltage designations ranging from 15 to 450 volts, with accompanying verbal labels ranging from "Slight Shock" to "Danger: Severe Shock." The last two switches were simply—and ominously—labeled

Milgram's experiment. (A) The "shock generator" that subjects used, with designations ranging from "Slight Shock" to "Danger: Severe Shock." (B) The experimenter (right) asks the subject (left) to help affix the shock electrodes to the "learner" (seated). (C) The experimenter instructs the subject in the use of the shock generator. (D) A subject defies the experimenter and refuses to administer shocks.

"XXX." The machine was so carefully custom-built that no subject suspected that it was fake. (The deceptions employed in many experiments, including Milgram's, raise serious ethical questions, which are discussed in Box 4).

The subjects in Milgram's experiment were adults between 20 and 50 years of age from a wide variety of educational backgrounds and occupations. They were recruited by mail and through newspaper advertisements to take part in a study of the effects of punishment on learning. When a pair of subjects arrived at Milgram's laboratory at Yale University, one of them was assigned to the role of "teacher" and the other to the role of "learner." As the teacher looked on, the experimenter escorted the learner to an adjacent room, strapped him down to an "electric chair" apparatus, and attached an electrode to each wrist. The teacher was then seated in front of the shock generator in a different room from the learner. The teacher was to read a list of word pairs to the learner over an intercom; then he was to read the first word of each pair along with four possible responses. The learner was to indicate the correct response by pressing one of four switches in front of him, which lit up the corresponding number in a box at the top of the shock generator. Each time the learner got the answer wrong, the teacher was to administer a shock as "punishment." And after each error, the teacher was to increase the voltage by one level on the shock generator.

The learner was in fact a confederate of Milgram's, a mild-mannered 47-year-old accountant. He never actually received any shocks, although the teachers (who were the only real subjects) were thoroughly convinced that he did. To aid in the illusion, the teachers themselves were given a sample shock of 45 volts before the experiment began—and this shock was quite real. As the learning task progressed, the learner made frequent errors, according to a preprogrammed sequence. In one condition of the experiment—one of many that Milgram ran—no protests were heard from the learner until the 300-volt level was reached. At that point, the learner pounded loudly on the wall of the room where he sat strapped to the shock apparatus. After 315 volts, the learner pounded again, and his answers no longer appeared on the panel.

What was the subject to do now? When the pounding began, subjects usually turned to the experimenter for guidance. The experimenter instructed them to treat the absence of an answer as a wrong answer and to continue to shock the learner as previously instructed. If at this point or thereafter subjects exhibited any reluctance to continue, the experimenter ordered them to continue, using one of a set of standard prods, such as "Please continue," "The experiment requires that you continue," and "You have no other choice; you must go on." If the subjects expressed concern that the learner might suffer serious injury, the experimenter politely, but firmly, replied, "Although the shocks may be painful, there is no permanent tissue damage, so please go on."

What would you have done in this situation? The vast majority of people who are asked this question confidently answer that once the learner stopped answering they would refuse to continue shocking him. But this is not what actually happened. Milgram's subjects found themselves in an extremely tense and uncomfortable situation. They were observed to sweat, tremble, bite their lips, and dig their fingernails into their flesh. Many of them repeatedly expressed concern about the learner's well-being. But in the face of the experimenter's stern orders, fully 65 percent of the subjects were obedient to the end, continuing to shock the learner until they reached the maximum level on the generator. In another condition of the experiment, the learner screamed, shouted, and begged to be released (the voice was actually a tape recording, but a very convincing one), but more than 60 percent of the subjects continued to shock him in spite of his protests.

When I tell students in my classes about these results, their first response is usually to focus on the personal characteristics of Milgram's

BOX 4

DECEPTION IN RESEARCH

Many psychological studies of attitude change and social influence share a troubling feature: they involve misinforming the research subjects—usually college students—about the nature of the research.

In Solomon Asch's experiments on conformity, described in Box 1, the subjects were told that they were participating in a study of perception (involving the ways in which people judge the length of lines), rather than a study of social influence. They were led to believe that the other group members were fellow subjects, whereas they were really confederates of the experimenter who were following a carefully programmed script.

In Stanley Milgram's experiments on obedience, deception played an equally central role. The subjects were made to believe that they were participating in a study of learning and that they were inflicting painful shocks on the "learner." In fact, the learner was an employee of the experimenter, the shocks were not real, and the purpose of the study was not to study learning but to see how far the subjects would go in following the dictates of an authority.

Many of the studies of persuasion described earlier in this chapter also involved deception. In all of these cases, the researchers argue that if we are to learn more about processes of social influence—and about how people can better resist such influence—deceptive studies are necessary. After all, if subjects were told in advance that the researcher was studying persuasion, conformity, or obedience, the situation would be stripped of its reality and subjects' behavior would tell us little about social influence in real life.

The researchers also emphasize that the deceptions that they employ are short-lived. After the study is over, the researchers carefully explain to the subject what the study was really about and conscientiously deal with the subject's questions or concerns.

But the use of deception in research raises serious ethical questions. For one thing, deceptive research deprives potential subjects of the right to decide for themselves in an informed way whether to take part in a particular study. If the subject is misinformed about what the study involves, his consent to participate is really being obtained under false pretenses.

Deceptive research also contributes to an atmosphere of suspicion and mistrust between researchers and research participants. Some psychologists feel that deceptive studies poison the whole atmosphere for psychological research. The large majority of psychological studies do not involve deception. But even honest experiments are sometimes contaminated by the fact that subjects are trying to figure out what the researcher "is really up to" rather than addressing themselves to the experimental task at hand.

More generally, deceptive research can be seen as contributing to a general trend of viewing human beings as objects to be manipulated at will (Kelman, 1967). One may also wonder about what the effect of conducting deceptive research may be on the *researchers*. "When we learn to stage events and manage impressions," asks Thomas Murray (1980), "are we led to do the same with our other relationships? Do we come to see people as so easily duped outside the laboratory as inside it?"

The ethics of deception have been debated extensively by psychologists (for example, American Psychological Association, 1981; Milgram, 1977; Murray, 1980). Researchers who wish to conduct deceptive (or, for that matter, nondeceptive) studies must first have their procedures approved by human subjects review boards at their college or university. But there is no consensus about when deception is or is not justified.

My own view is that some studies employing deception, such as those conducted by Asch and by Milgram, have been of truly great importance. Indeed, the large majority of Milgram's subjects, when later questioned about the study, said they were glad they had taken part; many of them felt they had learned something important about themselves from their experience. In the case of such studies, the ethical costs may be outweighed by the gain to knowledge. But most deceptive studies, for my money, are not ethically justified (Rubin, 1970; 1983). They make the arrogant presumption that psychologists have the right to lie in the name of "research," and they perpetrate an atmosphere of mistrust between researchers and subjects. I believe that deceptive research should be kept to an absolute minimum. Perhaps most important, it should never be taken for granted as a "normal" way of conducting research.

sample of subjects. These men must have been sadists, some students suggest. Or if they were not sadists, they must have been weak-willed, or uneducated, or politically reactionary, or too stupid to know any better. What the students really seem to be saying is, "Perhaps *they* acted in this way, but *I* never would." If this is your own feeling, the likelihood is that you are wrong. In fact, when Milgram conducted a similar experiment using students at Yale University as subjects, he obtained quite similar results. In another condition, he employed women as subjects and again found almost the identical pattern. If you had asked Milgram's subjects themselves how they thought they would behave in this situation, very few would have predicted that they would continue to shock the learner. But asking a hypothetical question about how you *would* behave is one thing, and actually placing you in a situation of this sort is quite another. The situation in which Milgram's subjects found themselves has a force that is much greater than most people realize.

Legitimate authority

Just what was it about Milgram's experimental situation that compelled his subjects to keep following orders, even when they thought they might be seriously injuring another human being? There were no physical constraints in the situation. If they had wanted to, subjects could have simply gotten up and left the laboratory—and, indeed, a few subjects did. Moreover, the experimenter was not a physically imposing man, and he spoke in a soft and calm voice. But he was wearing a gray technician's coat, was doing "scientific research," and was obviously in full charge of his elegant laboratory. As a result, he was

At his trial in Jerusalem, Nazi official Adolf Eichmann testified that his war crimes were not his responsibility—he was merely "following orders."

perceived by the subjects as being a *legitimate authority*—someone who had the right to dictate their behavior within the laboratory setting.

Obedience to legitimate authorities is deeply ingrained in all of us. If a person were to come up to you on the street and politely ask you to take your clothes off, you would regard that person as a weirdo and would certainly not comply. But if a doctor were to ask you the same question in her office, you would obey immediately. Similarly, if a young man were to approach you in the school cafeteria and ask you to clear the dishes off your table and take them to the kitchen, you would look at him unbelievingly. But if you were in the Army and the young man wore an officer's uniform, you would probably obey without even thinking about it. Milgram's results indicate that it is extremely difficult to defy such a legitimate authority, even when the authority's orders require one to injure an innocent human being.

When you stop to think about it, perhaps Milgram's results should not be so surprising after all. There have been several well-publicized events in our recent history in which apparently moral, well-meaning people followed the immoral orders of people perceived as legitimate authorities. The massacre of innocent civilians at My Lai, during the Vietnam war, was one of the most notable of these incidents. Defendants in the My Lai case tried to absolve themselves of guilt by pleading: "I was just following orders." The killings at My Lai bring to our attention the dilemma of obedience to authority versus personal responsibility. At what point must obedience give way to individual conscience? Milgram's experiment dramatizes this dilemma by showing how powerful the forces eliciting obedience can be. As Milgram wrote, "If in this study an anonymous experimenter could successfully command adults to subdue a 50-year-old man and force on him painful electric shocks against his protests, one can only wonder what government, with its vastly greater authority and prestige, can command of its subjects" (1965a, page 262).

Reducing obedience

As most elementary-school teachers know, a disobedient child can set a bad example. Once one child begins to defy the teacher's authority, the other children may follow suit. In a variation of his experiment, Milgram found that a disobedient person can also set a *good* example. In this experimental condition, Milgram (1965b) assigned three-man teams of subjects to share the role of teacher. Once the learner began to protest, however, two members of the team (Milgram's confederates) announced that they would not continue to take part in the experiment, and they took seats on the sidelines. The experimenter continued to order the real subject, the only teacher left, to administer shocks. In this condition, however, the subjects were much more likely to defy the experimenter's orders: Only 10 percent of the subjects went up to the highest shock level. The other team members' acts of defiance undermined the experimenter's authority and provided a concrete model of resistance for the subject. We need such principled models outside the laboratory as well, if we are to resist the dangers of blind obedience.

Although most of this chapter has focused on people's attitudes, Milgram's experiments demonstrate that people's actions are sometimes influenced more strongly by the pressures of specific situations than by their enduring attitudes. If you were to ask Milgram's subjects how they *felt* about shocking the learner, almost all of them would have told you that they were strongly against it. But in the face of the pressures of the situation they were in, this attitude fell by the wayside. Social psychologists have come increasingly to recognize that studying people's attitudes is not enough, just as personality psychologists have come to rely less on studying people's underlying traits (see Chapter 11). We must also pay close attention to situational forces and how they work, for, as Milgram suggests, it is often not so much the kind of person one is as it is the kind of situation in which one is placed that determines one's actions.

WHAT WOULD YOU HAVE DONE AT MY LAI?

Many Americans were outraged by the trial of Lieutenant William Calley for his participation in killing civilians at My Lai during the Vietnam war. These Americans believed he was simply carrying out the policy set forth by his superiors. In a national sample, 51 percent said that if they had been soldiers in Vietnam and were ordered to kill innocent civilians, they would have done so. Given their view that one must obey orders, these people viewed the Army's case against Calley as a betrayal. For these people, "It is as if a subject in the Milgram experiment were brought to trial for administering shocks to another subject, and the chief of the laboratory came to testify against him" (Kelman and Lawrence, 1972, page 209). But other people in the sample took a different view, holding that we must each accept ultimate responsibility for our own actions.

SUMMARY

The nature of attitudes

● *1 Attitudes* are the ways in which we evaluate people, objects, and issues. Attitudes have both a *cognitive* component (thoughts) and an *affective* component (feelings).

● *2* Among the devices used for measuring attitudes are *open-ended questions* and *fixed-response questions.* Sometimes the questions themselves or the testing situation can influence an individual's responses.

● *3* Although attitudes serve as guidelines for actions, they are not always good predictors of how people will behave in particular situations.

The foundations of attitudes

● *4* Attitudes are acquired through emotional, cognitive, behavioral, and social means. Emotionally, attitudes can be established by using classical conditioning to link positive emotions to a product or idea.

● *5* Cognitively, attitudes can be acquired through a reasoning process that links the particular object or idea to one's already existing structure of beliefs and attitudes. Not all of one's attitudes are logical or consistent, however.

● *6* The link between attitudes and behaviors goes both ways. If one is somehow induced to behave as if he holds a particular attitude, that person's attitudes tend to change in alignment with this behavior. This phenomenon can be accounted for by Festinger's theory of *cognitive dissonance* or by Bem's *self-perception theory.*

● *7* The social acquisition of attitudes, as seen in the example of Bennington College students, involves identification with a *reference group* and adopting the attitudes of that group.

● *8* Group pressure can give rise to *conformity,* even when the conforming individuals know that the group is wrong. Asch found that people may distort their judgments and statements in order to avoid being a lone dissenter. When a group comes to a decision that members are afraid to challenge (for the sake of keeping group solidarity), they are victims of *groupthink.*

● *9 Brainwashing* refers to a set of techniques used to change a captured person's basic attitudes and values. Brainwashing has two major phases: breaking down the person's existing group ties and sense of identity, and providing a new set of relationships tied to new ideals.

Persuasion

● *10* Changing people's attitudes through *persuasion* involves four components: a *communicator,* a *message,* a *medium,* and an *audience.*

● *11* The *credibility* or believability of a communicator will influence that person's ability to change our attitudes. A communicator has credibility to the extent that he is regarded as an expert and as being sincere.

● *12* Whether or not a communicator should include opposing arguments in her message depends on the characteristics of the audience— a one-sided approach is better if the audience is already predisposed to agree and is unaware of opposing viewpoints. Otherwise, it is better to take opposing arguments into account.

● *13* Scare tactics, or *fear appeals,* are sometimes highly effective. But a fear appeal will succeed only if specific information is supplied for dealing with the fear-arousing situation.

● *14* Different media are likely to be more effective for different types of messages. Complex messages are better transmitted through written media, whereas simple emotional appeals typically work best when delivered face-to-face or over television.

● *15* The more actively audience members can be involved in the attempt to persuade them, the more likely they are to be persuaded. Techniques include asking rhetorical questions that the listeners must answer for themselves. However, persuasive methods that seem too controlling can create *psychological reactance* in the audience.

• **16** You can resist being persuaded by becoming sensitive to persuasion techniques, by arguing back, and by discussing the message with others.

Obedience to authority

• **17** Milgram's experiment showed that under certain conditions people will obey an authority even if it means betraying their values or harming another human being. Obedience is most likely to occur in the presence of a *legitimate authority* and in the absence of dissenters. It seems, then, that the pressures of a specific situation can sometimes influence actions more strongly than do enduring attitudes.

• **18** Studies that involve deceiving subjects about the nature of the research raise serious ethical questions.

attitudes
audience
brainwashing
cognitive dissonance
communicator
conformity
credibility
false consensus effect
fear appeals
fixed-response questions
groupthink
legitimate authority
medium
message
minority influence
obedience
open-ended questions
persuasion
psychological reactance
reference group
self-perception theory
social influence
syllogism

PREJUDICE AND RACISM

Racism runs deep in American culture. Thomas Jefferson believed in the innate inferiority of black people. Although he personally opposed slavery, he agreed to compromise with Southern slavery interests and to delete an antislavery statement from the Declaration of Independence. Abraham Lincoln was also convinced that black people were inferior to whites and felt that equality was not attainable as long as blacks and whites lived in the same society. And these are two of the Presidents who were *most* sympathetic to the plight of black people in America (Jones, 1972). Although overt racism has declined in recent decades, more subtle forms of racism, as we will see, remain strong in America.

This Psychological Issue will focus on *racism*, differential attitudes and behavior toward individuals on the basis of their racial group membership, grounded in a belief (whether conscious or nonconscious) that one race is inherently superior to another. But the discussion will illustrate the more general process of *prejudice*, the prejudgment of people in negative ways on the basis of their group membership. Whether it is the prejudice of whites against blacks, Anglos against Chicanos, young people against old people, or men against women, it is an attitude that we need to understand as well as we can if we are ever to succeed in eliminating it.

Racism encompasses discrimination as well as prejudice. Whereas

prejudice refers to unfairly negative *attitudes* toward members of a particular group, *discrimination* refers to unfairly negative *actions* toward such groups. As we have seen in Chapter 15, attitudes and actions are usually closely intertwined, and so are prejudice and discrimination.

RACIAL ATTITUDES IN AMERICA

Ever since 1942, researchers at the National Opinion Research Center have been asking questions about racial attitudes to representative national samples of white Americans. Through the years, whites have been asked such questions as, "Do you think white students and black students should go to the same schools or to separate schools?" and whether they agree or disagree that "White people have a right to keep blacks out of their neighborhoods if they want to." These surveys have indicated that racial attitudes have steadily become more positive and tolerant (Taylor, Sheatsley, and Greeley, 1978; National Opinion Research Center, 1980).

In at least some respects, then, racial prejudice in America seems to be on the wane. But when it comes to many important spheres of behavior, racism remains strong. In the early 1980s as many as 93 percent of white Americans agreed that "Blacks have a right to live wherever they can afford to, just like whites" (ABC News poll, 1981). At the same time, however, most white Americans are reluctant to live in neighborhoods that have more than a handful of black families (Farley et al., 1978).

In addition, recent studies of whites' behavior toward blacks, including many studies using college students as subjects, have shown that antiblack sentiments remain much stronger than the survey data might lead one to expect (Crosby, Bromley, and Saxe, 1980).

These studies have involved the measurement of prejudice through people's actual behavior. In one study, a completed application to graduate school was "planted" in an airport telephone booth. Half of the time the applicant (shown in a photograph) was white, and the other half he or she was black. In all cases, a stamped, addressed envelope and a note asking "Dad" to mail the form were attached. The context made it clear that "Dad" had lost the letter in the airport. The researchers found that more of the white subjects who found the application bothered to mail it when the applicant was white than when the applicant was black (Benson, Karabenick, and Lerner, 1976).

It seems, then, that among white Americans there has been a shift from blatant forms of discrimination to more subtle forms. Whereas many whites will deny that they are prejudiced against blacks if you ask them directly—indeed, they may truly believe they are unprejudiced—their prejudice may reveal itself in their actions.

What perpetuates such prejudice and discrimination? There are many factors to be considered, each of which may provide one piece of the answer. Here we will consider three such factors: the workings of stereotypes, personality predispositions, and the impact of social norms.

STEREOTYPES

The literal meaning of *prejudice* is "prejudgment." We prejudge members of other groups when we view them in terms of *stereotypes* that are applied to entire groups of people (the idea of stereotypes was introduced in Chapter 7). If we were capable of responding to every person as an individual—if we didn't categorize people at all—we would be free of

prejudices about blacks, gay people, or old people. But freeing ourselves of such categorizations completely is an unattainable ideal. We depend on categories in order to handle the tremendous amount of information that constantly confronts us.

However, most of the racial and national stereotypes that we hold—aggressive blacks, shrewd Jews, inscrutable Orientals—have little if any basis in reality. And by relying on such stereotypes, we are blinded to the immense diversity among individuals. We expect people to behave like our stereotypes of those who happen to have the same skin color, speak with the same accent, or have the same background, rather than to behave like themselves.

If our stereotypes have little basis in reality, why do they persist as strongly as they do? A large part of the answer lies in the phenomenon of *selective perception*, discussed in Chapter 4. We tend to focus on information that is consistent with our stereotypes and to screen out or reinterpret information that is inconsistent with these preconceived notions (Hamilton, 1979). For instance, once you have reached the conclusion that all Cubans are "lazy," you will be more likely to notice examples of lazy Cubans. If you see a lazy Anglo, you will pay little attention or else you will interpret his behavior quite differently— "He must be resting after doing some hard work."

An experiment by Birt Duncan (1976) illustrates such selective perception. White college students viewed a videotaped interaction between two other students who were supposedly taking part in a discussion. After some initial conversation, the students got into an

argument that became more and more heated until finally Student B shoved Student A. The subjects were later asked for their impressions of the two students. When the shover was black and the person he shoved was white, 70 percent of the subjects classified the shove as an instance of "violent behavior." But when the shover was white and the person he shoved was black, only 17 percent of the subjects considered this "violent behavior," while 42 percent described it as either "playing around" or "dramatizing." Blacks are often viewed by whites as being prone to violence. As Duncan's study demonstrates, selective perception can serve to maintain this stereotype.

Without being fully aware of it, we all become skilled at perceiving only those events that are consistent with our prejudices. After a while, we amass a pile of evidence that assures us that our prejudices are justified. In addition, movies and television often portray members of various groups in ways that conform to popular stereotypes and, as a result, help to perpetuate them.

THE PREJUDICED PERSONALITY

There is evidence that some people tend to be generally prejudiced—not just toward blacks or toward Mexican-Americans or toward Jews, but toward practically *all* "outgroups." Eugene Hartley (1946) helped to make this point when he obtained measures of people's attitudes toward various minority groups, including three minorities that Hartley made up: Walonians, Pirenians, and Danerieans. People who were prejudiced toward blacks and other out-

We all become skilled at perceiving only those events that are consistent with our prejudices.

groups expressed prejudice toward the made-up groups as well. "I don't know anything about them," one prejudiced respondent replied. "Therefore, I would exclude them from my country."

In the 1940s a group of psychologists at the University of California at Berkeley, influenced by Freud's psychoanalytic theory of personality (see Chapter 11), looked intensively into the origins of a prejudiced personality. The researchers (Adorno et al., 1950) concluded that highly prejudiced people are likely to have *authoritarian personalities*. These people tend to see the world as divided sharply into two categories—the weak and the strong. They tend to be power oriented in their personal relationships. They are most comfortable when they are either taking orders from a superior or dishing it out to a subordinate. The Berkeley researchers believed that these were the sorts of people who would have been likely to be drawn to the fascist ideology of Nazi Germany.

As the centerpiece of their research, the Berkeley researchers developed a personality scale, known as the *F* scale (the *F* stands for fascism), to measure the extent to which a person has an authoritarian personality. "High *F*s," or authoritarians, tend to agree with such statements as "Obedience and respect for authority are the most important virtues children should learn" and "No weakness or difficulty can hold us back if we have enough will power."

The researchers found that authoritarian people tend to come from families that stress harsh discipline and obedience and in which there is anxiety about family status. People from such backgrounds may often find it difficult to accept personal weakness or to acknowledge their own sexual or aggressive motives. Instead, they make use of the Freudian defense mechanism of *projection*, seeing themselves and their own groups as being without weakness and, instead, seeing the unde-

sirable traits that they are afraid of in members of outgroups. In this way the authoritarian personality arrives at his racial and religious prejudice.

SOCIAL NORMS AND DISCRIMINATION

Although research on the authoritarian personality has been valuable, individual bigotry can explain only a small pro-

portion of the racial discrimination that is found in America. For example, even though overt discrimination against blacks has traditionally been greater in the South than in the North, white Southerners have not scored higher than white Northerners on measures of authoritarianism. Rather, the discrimination patterns against blacks in the South have been mainly a result of conformity to *social norms* that developed through the course of history.

When whites and blacks work together on the job, they may be friendly. However, the same people may be unlikely to visit each other's homes because of social norms that permit interracial interaction in some contexts but not in others.

For integrated classrooms to be successful in reducing prejudice, they must foster cooperation and equal-status contact among the children.

The fact that social norms bear much of the responsibility for prejudice and discrimination helps to explain certain apparent inconsistencies in interracial behavior. R. D. Minard (1952) reported, for example, that black and white coal miners in West Virginia followed a pattern of almost complete integration below the ground and almost complete segregation above the ground. This pattern makes sense only when viewed in terms of people's conformity to changing norms of acceptable and unacceptable conduct (Pettigrew, 1971). We must recognize that prejudice, like our other attitudes, has a strong social foundation. We learn to be prejudiced not as a general way of life, but in the form of specific attitudes and behaviors illustrated to us by our parents, our peers, and the mass media.

To reduce prejudice, therefore, massive psychotherapy is not the answer. Instead, we need to develop ways of changing the social norms that perpetuate discriminatory behavior.

REDUCING PREJUDICE

The best way to reduce prejudice is to take seriously the principle (discussed in Chapter 15) that attitudes often follow behavior. Rather than preaching lofty ideals of equality, we need to *create* greater equality, by law or by individual action.

Each of the long series of moves toward greater racial integration and equality in America has been met by resistance. Whites, and sometimes blacks as well, have argued that by integrating the buses, or the lunch counters, or the schools, we will

only cause tension and discomfort, and as a result we will only make matters worse.

Of course, these critics have been right about the tension and discomfort. It is impossible to change long-standing and deeply ingrained behavior patterns without generating a great deal of tension. Nevertheless, the general experience has been that once such changes are instituted, people gradually come to accept them. Surveys reveal, for example, that attitudes toward integration on the part of both black and white Americans are most favorable among those who have experienced it and least favorable among those who have had no interracial contacts (Pettigrew, 1971).

MAKING DESEGREGATION WORK

Despite people's general tendency to accept moves toward integration, it would be a mistake to conclude that integration is a cure-all for problems of prejudice and racism. The desegregation of American schools—beginning with the famous U.S. Supreme Court decision in 1954 that separate schools for blacks and whites were inherently unequal—is a case in point. It had been hoped that desegregation would lead to decreasing prejudice and discrimination. Many studies have found, however, that when black children enter desegregated schools, the prejudice of white schoolchildren toward blacks increases at least as often as it decreases (Stephan, 1978).

Simply increasing the amount of contact between members of different racial groups will not necessarily make them like each other. In fact, such contact may simply fortify negative stereotypes. An intensive study of a newly integrated middle school (sixth and seventh graders) in the Northeast conducted by Janet Ward Schofield (1982) illustrates some of the difficulties in making desegregation work. The "Wexler School" seemed to have a lot going for it. It had open enrollment rather than

To break down prejudices, members of the two groups must meet on an equal plane.

forced assignment of children to the school, and the school administrators were both blacks and whites with a strong commitment to effective desegregation. Nevertheless, Schofield found that very few of the children's friendships crossed racial lines, and these friendships almost never extended beyond the school setting.

Schofield found that the white children tended to place a greater emphasis on academic achievement than the black children did, while the black children tended to be "tougher" and more aggressive. These differences may well have had more to do with the children's social-class backgrounds than with their race: the whites came from more affluent homes than the blacks did. Not surprisingly, however, the children associated these attributes with race.

White children typically regarded themselves as intellectually superior to the blacks, and the black children were quite aware of this white attitude of superiority. And because the whites viewed the blacks as aggressive, even playful behaviors by blacks toward whites were interpreted as threatening. "Even innocuous acts, like a black girl lightly touching a white girl's hair, can result in tears and a situation that ends in the vice-principal's office" (Schofield, 1981, page 82). Thus, the upshot of the interracial contact at the "Wexler School" was not so much to shatter negative stereotypes as to reinforce them.

The situation is not hopeless, however. For desegregation to succeed in breaking down prejudices, it seems that it must be instituted in a way that places members of the two groups on an equal plane and that encourages a cooperative classroom atmosphere. Educators are now more aware of these needs

than they used to be, and various programs to foster cooperative and equal-status interaction in the classroom show promise of success (Cook, 1979).

One such program, developed by Elliot Aronson and his coworkers (1978) is called the *jigsaw technique* because it works much like a jigsaw puzzle, whose pieces must be fitted together. In this technique, children are assigned to small interracial learning groups. Each child in the group gets material that represents one piece of the lesson to be learned. For example, in a lesson for fifth graders on the life of the publisher Joseph Pulitzer, one child received a paragraph about Pulitzer's ancestors, another on his childhood, another on his early adulthood, and so on. Each child had to learn her part and then communicate it to the others in the group. At the end of the period, the entire group was to be tested on the lesson.

With this technique, the majority and minority children are forced—sometimes for the first time—to pay attention to each other, to teach and learn from each other, and to respect each other's contributions. Aronson and his coworkers have found that children in jigsaw classrooms grow to like each other better, and the minority children come to achieve more academically and to develop higher self-esteem. Aronson adds that the technique works best with young children, before prejudicial attitudes have a chance to become deeply ingrained.

The jigsaw technique and other methods of fostering cooperative interdependence in the classroom are not, to be sure, cure-alls for prejudice and racism. Prejudice must be battled on many fronts, including more equitable exposure of minorities in the mass media and

greater educational and job opportunities for minorities. As long as there are large economic and social inequalities between racial groups in the society at large, it will be very difficult to defeat prejudice and racism in the classroom.

Although racism is far from dead in America, efforts are being made to combat it on all these fronts. These efforts must continue if the United States is to become a truly just and tolerant society.

SUMMARY

- **1** *Prejudice* is prejudgment of people on the basis of their membership in a particular group. *Discrimination* is acting differentially toward people on the basis of their membership in a particular group. *Racism* is holding negative attitudes toward and discriminating against people on the basis of a belief that one race is inherently superior to another.
- **2** Although racial attitudes of whites about blacks seem to have become less prejudiced in recent years, whites still show subtle behavioral discrimination toward blacks.
- **3** Although racial *stereotypes* have little basis in reality, they tend to be perpetuated by *selective perception*, in which people notice only those aspects of others that coincide with their stereotypes.
- **4** People who appear prejudiced toward all outgroups are likely to have *authoritarian personalities*.
- **5** Prejudice and discrimination in America are perpetuated by *social norms* that dictate appropriate and inappropriate conduct.
- **6** Studies have shown that it takes contact with the outgroup people for ingroup people to break down their prejudices. However, this contact must be on an equal-status basis and should be of the sort that encourages cooperation if it is to produce the desired effect.

MALE AND FEMALE

People's identity as male or female is a major influence on their lives.

PSYCHOLOGICAL DIFFERENCES BETWEEN MEN AND WOMEN

Stereotypes about sex differences
Facts about sex differences
Evaluating sex differences

There are psychological differences between men and women, but on the whole the two sexes are more similar than they are different.

EXPLAINING THE DIFFERENCES: BIOLOGY AND CULTURE

Biological influences
Cultural influences
Learning gender roles in childhood
Playing gender roles in adulthood

Although biology may play a role, social learning is central in shaping the differences between the sexes.

HUMAN SEXUALITY

Human sexual response
Gender roles and sexual attitudes
The impact of the sexual revolution

The two sexes have similar capacities for sexual response. But society's "double standard" imposes different sexual expectations on men and women.

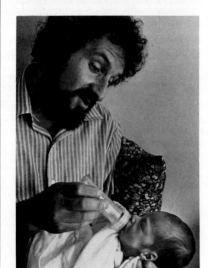

PSYCHOLOGICAL ISSUE
CHANGING SEX ROLES

BOXES
1 Face-ism
2 Psychology's sex bias
3 Transsexuals
4 Homosexuality and homophobia

The roles of men and women are undergoing important changes, both at work and in the family. The changes are not easy.

There are many things about you that are central to your identity as a distinctive human being—your talents, your habits, your appearance, your occupational aspirations, your political views, your ideals. Yet of all the elements of individual identity, the one that is quite regularly singled out for special attention is your sex. When we hear someone described, it is often in a sentence like "He's the guy who . . ." or "She's the woman who . . ." Even before we hear the end of the sentence, we already know the person's sex. And for each of us, our gender becomes one of the most central elements of our self-definition. Ask a child as young as 3 or 4 the question, "Who are you?" The chances are that the child will not give such answers as "I'm a child" or "I'm a Canadian," even though these answers would be perfectly logical. Instead, the child is most likely to answer, "I'm a boy" or "I'm a girl."

Not only do people identify themselves in terms of their gender, but this identification serves to influence many of their choices and behaviors. For example, schoolchildren often make a point of associating only with those of their own gender. "The chairs in Mr. Socker's [seventh grade] room are arranged in the shape of a wide shallow U," an observer reported. "As the first few kids come into the room, Harry says to John, who is starting to sit down in an empty section of the room along one side of the U, 'Don't sit there, that's where all the girls sit.' Harry and John sit elsewhere" (Schofield, 1981, page 62).

Adults, too, typically regard their identity as female or male, or their *gender identity*, as one of the most important facts about themselves. The importance of one's sex is reflected in the fact that men and women often behave differently from each other. Are there, in fact, basic psychological differences between women and men? If so, how important are they? These are the questions we will address at the beginning of this chapter. We will discover that there are some real sex differences in personality and behavior, although these differences are smaller than many people believe them to be. Then we will consider some explanations for the differences that do exist, including the possibility of biological predispositions and the force of cultural dictates about how males and females *should* behave. Next, we will turn to one of the central aspects of the interactions between men and women, sexual behavior, and discuss some of the important changes in sexual attitudes and behavior that have occurred in the past two decades. Finally, in the Psychological Issue for this chapter, we will focus on the ways that sex roles have been changing in our society, as well as on the continuing obstacles to such change.

A note on terminology: The words "sex" and "gender" will be used more or less interchangeably in this chapter. However, there is a subtle distinction between the two that some psychologists find useful. The term *sex* is more often used to refer to biological differences between male and female, while the term *gender* is more often used in connection with the social roles and expectations that go along with being male or female.

PSYCHOLOGICAL DIFFERENCES BETWEEN MEN AND WOMEN

Some of the differences between men and women are obvious: the two sexes differ in genital organs, internal reproductive systems, and secondary sex characteristics, such as breasts and facial hair. There are other physical differences, as well. Although there is considerable overlap between the two sexes, on the average men are taller, heavier, and more muscular than women. Men are also more likely to be bald, to be color-blind, and to live shorter lives. In and of themselves, however, these physical differences do not have much to do with men's and women's personalities or with their social and occupational roles. Only a few occupations, such as playing professional basketball, place much emphasis on a person's height. Physical strength was once important in human affairs, but in today's push-button age it is no longer a crucial quality.

In this section, we will consider psychological rather than physical differences between men and women—differences in social behavior, personality traits, and cognitive skills. First we will consider stereotypes about sex differences—the assumptions that people frequently make about what members of the groups "men" and "women" are like. As we will see, these stereotypes can lead people to make inaccurate and unfair evaluations of individual men and women. Then we will turn to what recent research has shown about the actual differences—and similarities—between men and women.

Stereotypes about sex differences

When Shakespeare wrote, "Men have marble, women waxen, minds" he was expressing one sort of belief about sex differences. He was suggesting that men are decisive and independent, whereas women are uncertain and compliant. As noted in Chapter 7, such beliefs are called *stereotypes*—concepts about entire groups of people. "Blacks are musical," "Italians are emotional," and "football players are dumb" are other examples of stereotypes. Such concepts about the categories of males and females are called *gender stereotypes*.

What are the gender stereotypes held in America today? In a study done by Inge Broverman and her colleagues (1972), subjects were given a list of over a hundred traits and were asked to rate "an adult male" or "an adult female" according to these characteristics. The researchers found that men were consistently described as being more aggressive, independent, dominant, active, competitive, and self-confident than women. Women were consistently described as being more tactful, gentle, sensitive, emotional, expressive, neat, and quiet than men. Such stereotypes can be dangerous. Even if we assume that, *on the average*, men and women differ in some of these ways, the stereotypes are misleading, because they encourage us to overgeneralize—to assume that the stereotype accurately describes *all* (or, at least, the large majority of) members of the group. In reality, stereotypes are never accurate in this blanket sense, as evidenced by the existence of large numbers of tone-deaf blacks, calm Italians, and intellectual football players, not to mention submissive men and insensitive women.

Yet we are all likely to make errors of overgeneralization in which we react to individuals as if they had all the stereotypical characteristics of their group (Wallston and O'Leary, 1981). I once showed my wife, Carol, the work of two different editors who had worked on material for a book. I had told Carol that one of the editors was a man and the other was a woman. In discussing the material, Carol began referring to one of the editors as "he" and the other as "she." It turned out that she had assumed that the editor whose work was tighter and more compact was a man and that the one whose work was more expansive and expressive was a woman. Needless to say, her assumptions were wrong; in fact, "he" was a she, and "she" was a he.

As this example suggests, gender stereotypes can lead to bias in the way we evaluate people's work. This point was demonstrated in an experiment conducted by Kay Deaux and Tim Emswiler (1974). Students were told that either a man or a woman had done very well on a task involving

IT FEELS LIKE A BOY

Michael Lewis (1972) found in his research on fetal behavior in the last three months of pregnancy that mothers seemed to respond to the activity of their unborn child in a sex-differentiated manner. Mothers who had an active fetus that kicked and moved a great deal assumed that their child was probably a male. Many people also seem to believe in the old wives' tale that relates a child's prenatal position to its sex—boys supposedly are carried high and girls are carried low.

The two sexes are commonly viewed in terms of stereotypes—for example, males are expected to be aggressive and competitive, females to be tender and nurturant.

identification of mechanical objects. When the person was identified as a man, the subjects indicated that they thought he was quite skillful. When the person who turned in an identical performance was a woman, the subjects gave her lower skill ratings and instead gave her high ratings on "luck." The stereotype that men are more mechanical than women apparently led the subjects to assume that the man's performance reflected greater ability than the woman's identical performance. Another reflection of gender stereotypes—the tendency to depict men and women in different ways—is discussed in Box 1.

Facts about sex differences

Some aspects of prevailing gender stereotypes seem to have little basis in reality. I know of no evidence that

BOX 1

FACE-ISM

It is no surprise to learn that men and women are depicted differently in our popular culture, from children's books to magazine ads, in ways that correspond to common stereotypes about the sexes. Thus, men are more likely to be portrayed in active, work-oriented, powerful roles, while women are more likely to be portrayed as passive and dependent (Weitzman et al., 1972; Goffman, 1976).

Now a team of researchers led by Dane Archer (1983) has uncovered a more surprising and subtle difference in the portrayals of men and women in the media. By carefully measuring thousands of photographs of men and women in newspapers and magazines, they discovered that photos of men in both news stories and advertisements tend to emphasize their faces, while photos of women give greater emphasis to their bodies. Almost two-thirds of the average male photo was devoted to the face, compared to less than half of the average female photo. Always ready to turn a phrase, Archer dubbed this phenomenon of greater male facial prominence *face-ism*.

Face-ism seems to be a universal phenomenon. When Archer and his coworkers examined over 5000 photos in magazines from twelve different countries, from Kenya to Hong Kong, they found the same tendency in every magazine. It was also found in paintings and drawings from the seventeenth, eighteenth, and nineteenth centuries, as well as in the twentieth.

Does the tendency toward face-ism extend beyond the mass media to people's everyday images of men and women? The answer seems to be yes. Archer and his colleagues asked college students to draw a picture of either a woman or a man. Their only instruction was "try to capture the character of a real person in your drawing." When the subjects (both male and female) drew men, the faces were much more prominent than in the drawings of women. In addition, the subjects tended to provide more detail in the facial features of men.

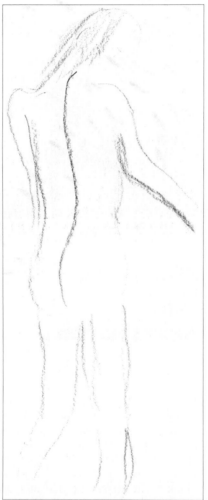

When people draw pictures of men, they tend to make the faces more prominent; when they draw pictures of women, they tend to make the bodies more prominent.

The adjoining pictures, drawn by subjects in Archer's study, are examples.

How can we explain this pervasive tendency to emphasize men's faces—or, to put it another way, to emphasize women's bodies? Archer suggests that it may be related to the common view of men as more intellectual (the head) and of women both as more emotional and as sexual objects (the body). Indeed, the researchers found the same people were rated as more intelligent when they were seen in close-up photos emphasizing the face than when they were seen in photos of the entire body. If this is the case, then face-ism may be one more way in which stereotypes of men and women are perpetuated. You might want to check for yourself whether the photographs of men and women in this textbook reflect face-ism.

supports the notion, for example, that men are generally more active than women or that women are generally neater than men. Recent research suggests that other aspects of the prevailing gender stereotypes may have a grain of truth to them, in the sense that there are small but real differences between the "average" man and the "average" woman. But stereotypes to the contrary, the two sexes are hardly "opposite." In almost every respect, men and women are far more similar to each other than they are different. And in almost every respect, the range of variation *within* each sex is much greater than the average difference *between* the sexes. When asked whether man or woman was more intelligent, the famous English writer Samuel Johnson gave an appropriate reply: "Which man? Which woman?"

Nevertheless, researchers have found men and women do differ—at least on the average—with respect to a number of psychological attributes:

• Males have been found to be more aggressive than females, on the average, in both childhood and adulthood. Boys tend to fight more than girls, to taunt and insult others

Women's closest same-sex friendships tend to be more intimate than those of men. Women are more likely to disclose personal feelings to their friends, while men are more likely to base their friendships on joint activities.

more, and to fantasize more about aggressive themes (Maccoby and Jacklin, 1974; Eron, 1980). Among adults, men commit many more violent crimes than women. And opinion polls show that men tend to have more favorable attitudes toward violence than women do in a wide range of spheres: men are more likely to endorse military intervention in international disputes, to favor capital punishment, and to oppose gun control (Smith, 1984).

• On the average, females are more attuned to other people's feelings than males are. Girls and women have consistently been found to be more accurate than boys and men at "reading" other people's nonverbal expressions (Hall, 1978). Females also tend to be more empathic than males—that is, they seem more predisposed to put themselves in another's place and to feel that person's joy or pain (Hoffman, 1977). Perhaps related to their concern about other people's feelings, females also tend to have more intimate same-sex friendships than males do, both in childhood (Rubin, 1980) and in adulthood (Caldwell and Peplau, 1982). Although her argument remains speculative, Carol Gilligan (1982) suggests that women place greater value on close social relationships than men do. She sees women as defining themselves in terms of their attachments to others, while men are more concerned with forming their own separate identities.

• For centuries, male philosophers and scientists have assumed—and loudly declared—that men are more intelligent than women. In fact, there is no evidence that either sex is more intelligent than the other. But there are differences in particular cognitive domains. Girls tend to acquire language more quickly than boys, and there is some indication that females' verbal skills exceed those of males (Hyde, 1981). It is clear, on the other hand, that on the average males' spatial abilities (for example, the ability to mentally rotate geometric figures) and mathematical skills exceed those of females (Benbow and Stanley, 1980; Hyde, 1981).

Evaluating sex differences

The study of sex differences in personality traits, cognitive skills, and social behaviors has become a political minefield, loaded with dissent and controversy. Although the sex differences summarized above are reasonably well-established, some psychologists believe that the differences are too small to be of any practical importance. Only a small fraction of the variation in people's scores on measures of personality traits or cognitive skills—usually not more than 5 percent—can be predicted simply by knowing people's sex (Deaux, 1985).

Critics also warn of the dangers of paying attention to psychological sex differences. For one thing, some people may equate these differences with deficiencies and assume that one sex is better than the other. In fact, such assumptions have often been made over the years by predominantly male psychologists, as discussed in Box 2. For another thing, when a difference between the sexes is noted and publicized, it can become a self-fulfilling prophecy. For example, Jacquelynne Eccles and her coworkers (1982) interviewed parents of 10- to 12-year-old boys and girls about their children's mathematical skills. When boys did well at math in school, the parents were likely to think that their sons had naturally high mathematical ability. When girls did equally well, the parents tended to downplay their ability and to feel that their daughters had to work very hard to get their good grades. Such assumptions may well lead parents to discourage their daughters from pursuing training in math and science. Such a course of action would, of course, serve to widen the relatively small existing difference between the sexes.

My own view is that although the differences between the sexes are relatively small, they are still worthy of serious attention. At the extremes of certain dimensions, the sex differences may be rather dramatic. For example, extremely violent criminals are much more likely to be male than female. So are people with prodigious mathematical skills: Among a select group of seventh-grade "math ge-

BOX 2

PSYCHOLOGY'S SEX BIAS

Psychology is supposed to be the science of human behavior. But is it really? In fact, a great deal of psychological research makes use of subjects of only one sex, and that sex is usually male. According to one count of studies in personality and social psychology, males were used as subjects twice as often as females (Holmes and Jorgensen, 1971).

What lies behind this preference for male subjects? One possible explanation is that psychological researchers, who have been predominantly male, feel they can understand men better than women. In addition, psychologists may share society's implicit assumption that the male sex is somehow more important than the female sex and therefore more worthy of study.

But even though psychologists often focus their research on men, they still tend to discuss the results as if they pertain to everyone. As a result, researchers run the risk of enshrining men's typical patterns of behavior as the "normal" patterns for all people. "We have a psychology of men," writes Joanna Bunker Rohrbaugh (1979), "but it is called simply 'psychology.'"

The equation of "normal human development" with *male* development is found in the work of many of psychology's most influential theorists. Sigmund Freud, for one, declared that women cannot develop as strong a superego (or conscience) as men because they do not have a clear and easily resolved Oedipus complex (see Chapter 11). As a result, Freud concluded, women "show less sense of justice than men . . . [and] are more influenced in their judgments by feelings of affection or hostility" (1925, pages 257–258).

Similarly, the great developmental psychologist Jean Piaget (see Chapter 8) focused on boys' childhood games and concluded that an appreciation of laws and rules "is far less developed in girls than in boys" (1932, page 77). Following in this tradition, boys have been found to score at higher levels

than girls on Lawrence Kohlberg's widely used scale of moral development (also discussed in Chapter 8)—itself based on research conducted with boys.

In the past decade, however, the tide has begun to turn, as psychologists have begun to investigate women's development in its own terms. One of those who has led the movement to remove male blinders from psychological theory and research is developmental psychologist Carol Gilligan. Her influential book *In a Different Voice* (1982) has helped to awaken psychologists to the dual recognition that there *are* important differences between men and women and that the patterns of one sex cannot be taken as the standard for the other.

Carol Gilligan

Are men really more "moral" than women, as Freud, Piaget, and Kohlberg would all suggest? No, Gilligan replies. Instead, she believes, we need to redefine our views of morality to encompass interpersonal caring (which tends to be more characteristic of females) as well as impersonal standards of justice (which tend to be more characteristic of males).

Gilligan also takes issue with the male-oriented account of psychosocial development offered by Erik Erikson (see Chapter 8, Box 1) and with the account of adult development put forth by Daniel Levinson, based on his re-

search with men in middle adulthood (see Chapter 9). Levinson speculated that women go through the same basic adult developmental periods as men do, but Gilligan has found that "becoming one's own person"—a major theme in Levinson's discussion of men's midlife development—is typically less central for women than for men. Whereas men are likely to place great emphasis on gaining independence from others, women typically place greater emphasis on their attachment to others through the course of life.

Along with a growing number of other psychologists, Gilligan believes that a closer examination of women's development is needed to broaden the perspective of a psychology that has been dominated by male conceptions of "humanity." "The disparity between women's experience and the representation of human development . . . has generally been seen to signify a problem in women's development," Gilligan (1982) writes. "Instead, the failure of women to fit models of human growth may point to a problem in the representation, a limitation in the conception of human condition, an omission of certain truths about life" (pages 1–2).

niuses" who scored over 700 on the College Board Scholastic Aptitude Test in math, there were thirteen times as many boys as girls (Benbow and Stanley, 1982). (No, this doesn't imply that violent criminals are gifted at math.) We must bear in mind, as Carol Gilligan (1982) forcefully argues, that differences do *not* imply deficiencies. In fact, each sex seems to have unique strengths—and each can learn from the other. Moreover, the recognition that there are average differences between the sexes does not imply that individuals' traits and skills are immutable. Both men and women can *learn* to be less aggressive, to be more socially concerned, or to develop their verbal or mathematical skills.

Finally, it is essential to note that recognizing differences between men and women is not the same as *explaining* these differences. Do they result from biological predispositions, from cultural conditioning, or from some combination of biology and culture? In the next section, we turn to this central question of explaining the differences.

EXPLAINING THE DIFFERENCES: BIOLOGY AND CULTURE

Do any of the psychological differences between men and women have a biological basis? Or are they entirely the product of social and cultural conditioning, reflecting the fact that men and women tend to become the sort of people they are expected to be? We will consider this issue with respect to one of the psychological sex differences that has been consistently found—the tendency for males to be more aggressive than females. As we will see, it does not turn out to be a simple question of biology *or* culture. In fact, both biology *and* culture are involved in determining a person's level of aggressive behavior, and both forces interact to produce the sex differences that have been observed.

Biological influences

Many scientists believe that sex differences in aggression emerged as part of the biological evolution of the human species (see Chapter 2). During the period in which our species evolved, it is argued, there was a strict division of labor between men and women, with men taking the role of fighters and hunters and women remaining close to home to care for their children. In order to be successful hunters, men may have evolved not only physically (for example, larger muscles for hurling spears) but also psychologically (for example, a greater readiness to be aggressive). This particular account of the evolution of sex differences in aggression remains speculative, and it seems

Men tend to have larger muscles than women, a difference that is part of our biological heritage. But people's physical strength may also be shaped by the activities they choose, such as body-building.

Yes, there are sex differences in the brain—and there is a lot of controversy about their importance. Studies of animals such as rats and songbirds have shown that certain clusters of brain cells, including areas involved in sexual behavior, are larger in males than in females. In humans, brain-wave studies suggest that men have a greater degree of hemispheric specialization than women. When performing spatial tasks, men tend to activate their right hemispheres, while women are more likely to activate both hemispheres, suggesting that a larger portion of the female brain is involved in spatial ability (McGlone, 1980). Some observers are convinced that such differences contribute importantly to sex differences in skills and behavior. Others are just as convinced that they don't.

impossible to test directly. Nevertheless, there is a great deal of evidence suggesting that the sex differences in aggression are, at least in part, biologically based.

If sex differences in aggression were based in part on biology, we would expect to see the same sex differences in societies throughout the world. After all, even though cultures may differ, the basic biological nature of all people is the same. In fact, the male's greater aggressiveness is not peculiar to American society. Men are the hunters, the warriors, and the aggressors in virtually every society that has been studied (D'Andrade, 1966). Boys roughhouse more and exchange insults more than girls do in societies throughout the world (Whiting and Edwards, 1973).

A second sort of evidence that points to the role of biological predisposition comes from observations of our animal relatives. Because culture, as we know it, does not play a large role in shaping the behavior of other animals, any consistent sex differences in other animals must almost certainly have a biological basis. And, in fact, males are more aggressive than females in almost all species of monkeys and apes, our closest relatives in the animal kingdom, as well as in most other mammals.

Neither the cross-cultural generalities nor the biological sex differences in other animals proves beyond doubt

that sex differences in humans have a biological basis. Nevertheless, both sorts of evidence are consistent with the idea that a predisposition toward greater male aggressiveness is part of our evolutionary heritage.

If there is a biological predisposition for males to be more aggressive than females, how is it brought about? In other animals—and quite possibly in humans, as well—the predisposition toward greater male aggressiveness seems to result from the action of the male hormones on the brain and, through the brain, on behavior. At the time of conception and shortly thereafter, "male" and "female" embryos are essentially identical. The only difference is that the female has two X chromosomes while the male has an X and a Y. Sexual differentiation begins when the XY chromosomes send a biochemical signal that leads to the production of the male hormone testosterone. The hormone causes certain embryonic tissues to develop into male sex organs. If no male hormone is produced, these tissues develop instead into female organs. Were it not for this hormonal influence, all of us would develop as females (Money and Ehrhardt, 1972).

In addition to its effects on the genitals and reproductive system, the male hormone causes certain changes in brain pathways, which in turn has an impact on the individual's temperament and behavior. In one study,

A young female rhesus monkey who had been exposed prenatally to male hormones engages in characteristically male rough-and-tumble play with a young male monkey.

testosterone was administered to pregnant monkeys (Young, Goy, and Phoenix, 1964). The female offspring of these monkeys were born with masculinized genitals, with an enlarged clitoris that resembles a penis, attesting to the physical effect of the hormone. What's more, these female monkeys showed elevated levels of rough-and-tumble play, behaving in this respect more like male than female monkeys. The prenatal hormones had affected not only anatomy but also behavior.

The link between prenatal hormones and aggressiveness is not as clear in humans as it is in other primates (Jacklin, Maccoby, and Doering, 1983), but there is at least some evidence for such a link. In certain rare cases, a female infant becomes exposed to an excess of male hormone before birth, as a result of a glandular defect or the use of certain drugs. Such an infant may have masculinized genitals, but this condition can be corrected surgically; with proper medical treatment, the infant can grow into a normal woman. Anke Ehrhardt and Susan Baker (1973) studied seventeen girls who had received an excess of male hormone prenatally and compared them with their normal sisters. Even though the masculinized girls did not look any different from normal girls, they did tend to act in more "tomboyish" ways. Compared to their sisters, they liked outdoor sports more, liked dolls less, and were somewhat more likely to start fights. Although these data are not conclusive—it is certainly possible that these girls were also treated somewhat differently by their parents—they suggest that the male hormones may have predisposed them to behave more aggressively. These cases also provide indirect support for the hypothesis that the average difference in aggressiveness between normal males and normal females may be due in part to the effects of male hormones.

Needless to say, most instances of girls who like sports, climb trees, or start fights have absolutely nothing to do with an excess of male hormones. Such behavior is perfectly normal for girls as well as for boys and in the overwhelming majority of cases has no link to unusual hormone levels.

Cultural influences

Having said all this about biological influences on aggressive behavior, it is now time to look at the other side of the coin. I have been using the word *predisposition* quite regularly in this chapter. A *predisposition* is a readiness to behave or to develop in a particular way. On the average, men apparently have more of a readiness to be aggressive than women, for reasons that seem to be partly biological. But human behavior rarely, if ever, reflects such predispositions in a simple or direct way. As noted in the Psychological Issue on violence following Chapter 10, whether or not someone will in fact behave aggressively in a particular situation depends to a large extent on what the person has learned about the appropriate situations in which to express aggression. In our culture men are permitted or encouraged to be aggressive to a much greater degree than women are. Boys are given toy guns and toy soldiers to play with and are expected to make loud noises with them, while girls are given dolls and tea sets and are expected to play more quietly. On television children are more likely to see aggressive men, whether they are cowboys, cops, or robbers, than aggressive women. This sort of cultural shaping probably has considerably more impact on patterns of aggressive behavior than does biological predisposition.

One example of the role of culture in shaping aggressive behavior comes from a study done among the Luo people of Kenya (Ember, 1973). Among the Luo, boys and girls are typically assigned to different sorts of household tasks, such as heavy work for boys and child care for girls. When there is no older girl in the family to take care of the "female" tasks, however, a boy will be assigned to do this work. It was found that boys who were assigned to do female work tended to be less aggressive, less dominant, and more dependent than other boys; in these respects their behavior was more like that of girls. These boys were of course no different from other boys biologically. Rather, the fact that they were placed in a traditionally female role had a direct effect on their temperament and behavior.

Television portrayals of men and women may both reflect and shape sex differences in personality. In All in the Family, *Archie Bunker played a tough, dominant role, while his wife Edith was more timid and submissive.*

Further evidence for the cultural shaping of sex differences in aggression comes from studies showing that under some conditions women are *not* less aggressive than men. These include situations in which there is a clear justification for the aggression, such as when the subjects were first provoked by another person and were then given the opportunity to retaliate. Under such conditions, women have sometimes been found to be just as aggressive as men are (Frodi, Macaulay, and Thome, 1977).

In the last analysis, my own conclusion—and that of most psychologists—is that differences in the aggressive behavior of men and women are shaped to a much larger extent by culture than by biology. A similar argument can be made about a number of other sex differences, such as men's greater mathematical skill. Biology does set certain of the boundaries of male and female behavior. Moreover, very small differences that are biologically based are likely to be magnified as a result of social influences. If, for example, boys are biologically predisposed to be more aggressive than girls, and if boys also tend to play with other boys, and girls tend to play with other girls, the sex differences in aggression are likely to widen. But the biological boundaries are extremely broad. The actual de-

velopment of traits, skills, and aspirations depends in large measure on society's values about what men and women can and should do with their lives. In the next two sections, we will look more closely at how these values help to shape the characteristics of men and women.

Learning gender roles in childhood

Our expectations about what men and women should do and what they should be like are called *gender roles* (or sex roles). Whereas stereotypes are widely held assumptions of what men and women *are like*, gender roles are widely held notions about the way men and women *ought to be.* Each of us learns about these expectations as we grow up, and the expectations can have a major impact on our personalities and behavior.

Even before a child is born, the parents-to-be have notions of what they would like their sons and daughters to be like, and they proceed to communicate these expectations to their children, beginning in infancy. Boys are taught to "get ahead" and "stay cool" (Pleck and Sawyer, 1974). They are encouraged to be ambitious and assertive and are discouraged from expressing their weaknesses or their

Children are taught early in life about the qualities they need to be a "woman" or a "man." As part of the process of learning gender roles, children model themselves after parents or other adults of the same sex.

tender feelings. Girls, on the other hand, learn to play a more submissive and dependent role. They are taught to be well-behaved and cooperative and to act as if they have no aggressive impulses at all. Girls are also expected to be tender and nurturant, whether with their dolls or with baby sisters and brothers.

Children learn gender roles not only at home but in their interactions with friends, neighbors, teachers, and other adults. Through their experience with doctors and nurses, plumbers and nursery-school teachers, even kindergarten children come to learn the "proper" occupations for men and women. Indeed, experience with occupational models outside of the home can overshadow learning within the home, as in the case of the child of the woman physician who says that women can't be doctors (Turkington, 1984).

A great deal of gender-role learning takes place through the mass media, especially television. Even though there have been some changes recently, men are still portrayed as strong, competent, resourceful people who occupy such exalted roles as physician, lawyer, or police detective. These male role models are some-

times permitted to show warmth and sensitivity, but only when coupled with great achievement and self-reliance. Women, on the other hand, are depicted as gentler, more sensitive beings who frequently reveal their weaknesses and their emotions. Even when women have achieved high-status occupations (police officer, news reporter, lawyer), they typically remain subordinate to their bosses and dependent on their husbands and boyfriends. These gender-role stereotypes can also be seen in Saturday morning children's shows. One study found that male characters on these shows are portrayed as being more active, independent, and capable of solving problems than female characters (McArthur and Eisen, 1976). Such television images are likely to have an influence on children's own aspirations and styles of behavior.

The process of gender-role learning is not a passive one on the part of the child. To the contrary, as Lawrence Kohlberg (1966) has emphasized, once the child learns his or her sex—which virtually all children do by age 3—the child invariably wants to demonstrate that he or she can behave like a member in good standing of that sex. This reflects every child's motivation

WE FROWN ON GIRLS WHO PLAY ROUGH

The two preschool children were roughhousing in the snow, their sexes disguised by their snowsuits (Condry and Ross, 1985). When the children, shown on a videotape, were described to college students as girls, their behavior was rated as more aggressive than when the same two children were described as boys. Since boys are generally expected to act rougher than girls, the "boys'" behavior was apparently more likely than the "girls'" to be passed off as normal roughhousing. The study illustrates one way in which our expectations of boys and girls may lead us to stifle the assertive side of young females. "Roughhousing" can be tolerated, but "aggression" is dangerous—and, therefore, must be discouraged.

BOX 3

TRANSSEXUALS

In 1974, Dr. Richard Raskind was a successful physician with a large practice. He also played amateur tennis and ranked thirteenth nationally in the men's division for players 35 and over. In 1977, Dr. Renée Richards had discontinued her active medical practice in order to concentrate on professional tennis. She ranked tenth among women players in America, an unprecedented accomplishment for a 42-year-old who had never before played professionally. Richard Raskind had undergone sex-change surgery to become Renée Richards after years of feeling that he was a woman locked inside a man's body.

Similarly, James Morris, a noted British journalist, withdrew from circulation for a brief period and emerged as Jan Morris. She went on to write *Conundrum* (1974), a moving account of her life as a *transsexual*—a person who felt that her anatomy conflicted with her true sexual identity—and of her decision to have this "mistake of nature" corrected surgically.

Between 10,000 and 20,000 men and women in the United States, by one rough estimate, are transsexuals (Restak, 1979). These people share the feeling that they are trapped in a body of the wrong sex. About four out of five transsexuals seen by doctors have been males, although the number of females has recently been increasing.

The transsexual's feeling that his body is "the wrong sex" usually begins early in life. Transsexuals commonly report that as children they preferred activities characteristic of the opposite sex and that they enjoyed cross-dressing (wearing clothes made for members of the opposite sex). They also report that they were upset by the development of their bodies at puberty, since these changes heightened the conflict between their sexual anatomy and their personal sense of sexual identity.

No one knows what causes transsexualism. Transsexuals show no abnormalities in their sex organs or hormone levels, and no biological explanation for their desire to change their sex has been found. Psychologi-

James Morris (top) was a foreign correspondent and father of four children before he had a sex-change operation and became Jan Morris (bottom).

cal theories, such as an unusually intense identification with the opposite-sex parent, have been put forth. But so far, there is no conclusive evidence in support of any such theories.

Regardless of what its underlying causes might be, transsexualism is a condition that places a person in a state of extreme conflict—between the state of his body, on the one hand, and the state of his mind, on the other.

Attempts to change transsexuals' gender identities through psychotherapy have generally been unsuccessful. But if psychotherapists could not change transsexuals' minds to match their bodies, some surgeons decided that they could change transsexuals' bodies to match their minds. The sex-change operation was first performed in the United States at the Johns Hop-

kins Hospital in 1966 and later was performed at other hospitals as well.

Sexual reassignment through surgery is no simple procedure. In the male-to-female operation the patient's testicles are cut away and his penis is cored out, leaving the skin, which is used to line an artificially formed vagina. In the female-to-male operation, the breasts, uterus, and ovaries are removed, the vagina is sealed, and an artificial penis is created. All patients are treated with opposite-sex hormones prior to the surgery, and many obtain additional cosmetic surgery to make their facial features, hair growth, and skin texture seem more appropriate to the sex they want to be. After the operation, transsexuals are incapable of reproduction, but they can experience some degree of sexual stimulation.

The sex-change operation was initially greeted with great enthusiasm. Where psychiatrists and psychologists had failed, surgeons had succeeded. In recent years, however, professionals' views about sexual reassignment have become much more guarded. Although some transsexuals, such as Renée Richards and Jan Morris, apparently made good adjustments after the operation, many others still had serious psychological problems. Some became seriously depressed, suicidal, or psychotic after the surgery, and their family lives were often ruined. (Lothstein, 1982).

By 1979, in the wake of such negative outcomes, Johns Hopkins, the hospital that had pioneered the surgery in this country, refused to continue to perform it. Other hospitals, however, continue to carry out sex-change surgery, making use of extensive psychological screening of applicants that is believed to increase the chances of the operation's success. But sex-change surgery is now viewed only as a last resort for a highly select group of patients (Lothstein, 1982). Meanwhile, there are many transsexuals who continue—with greater or lesser degrees of distress—to inhabit the bodies of the "wrong sex."

EXPLAINING THE DIFFERENCES: BIOLOGY AND CULTURE   497

to be a competent and consistent human being. As a result, the child actively seeks clues as to how a "boy" or a "girl" should behave by observing their same-sex parent and other same-sex models. This desire to behave "consistently" with one's sex helps to explain why gender roles often seem so difficult to change. Even in nonsexist nursery schools that make every effort to treat boys and girls alike, one is still likely to see boys and girls playing separately at different sorts of activities—often more boisterous and aggressive in the case of boys, quieter and more sedate in the case of girls (Rubin, 1980). In the process, the children confirm their own identity as "boy" or "girl." (In Box 3, we consider a fascinating exception to the normal tendency of children and adults to identify themselves with their biological sex—the case of *transsexuals.*)

With all these opportunities to learn gender roles—in the family, in school, on television—coupled with the child's own desire to behave consistently with his or her sex, it is no wonder that by the time they finish elementary school boys and girls typically behave in quite different ways.

Playing gender roles in adulthood

The process of shaping "male" and "female" behavior does not end in childhood. In fact, most men and women have the potential to behave in a broad range of ways—more or less assertively, more or less sensitively, and so on. How they actually behave depends to a large extent on the life choices that they make and the expectations that others have for them. Even as adults, we continue to play gender roles—much like the roles of a play—in ways that are influenced by the parts into which we are cast and by the performances of other actors.

Roles are the positions that people occupy in life, together with the sets of behaviors that are expected of people in those positions. They include family roles, such as "father" and "mother," and work roles, such as "division manager" and "assistant bookkeeper." The family and work roles that are chosen by men and women—or that are chosen for them—are clearly central in patterning their behavior. Although there have been striking changes in the past two

When men and women who occupy the same occupational roles are compared, relatively few psychological differences are found between them.

CHAPTER SIXTEEN: MALE AND FEMALE

Men's dominance over women has now been found on a higher plane. Not long ago, a team of researchers observed over 800 men and women on airline flights and found that when a man and a woman were sitting next to each other, the man was using the armrest between them five times as often as the woman. Even when the woman was at least as big as the man, the man still had possession of the armrest three times as often as the woman. In subsequent interviews, many men admitted that they got very annoyed when "their" armrest was usurped—especially if the usurper was a woman (Hai et al., 1982).

decades (see the Psychological Issue that follows this chapter), men are still much more likely than women to be the primary breadwinners for their families, and women still devote much more time and effort than men to homemaking and child care. In addition, men and women tend to be employed in different sorts of jobs— for example, mechanical jobs for men and secretarial jobs for women. In business organizations *he* is much more likely to be *her* boss than the other way around (Nieva and Gutek, 1981). All of these differences are likely to shape the ways in which men and women think about themselves, as well as the ways in which they behave.

It is interesting to note that when men and women who occupy the *same* occupational roles are compared, few psychological differences between the two are found. In a study of blue-collar workers in the steel industry, for example, Kay Deaux and Joseph Ullman (1983) found almost no evidence of sex differences: Men and women were alike in their self-evaluations, aspirations, and likes and dislikes about their work. Similarly, comparisons of male and female leaders show little difference between them (Hollander, in press). It may be that similar sorts of people, regardless of their sex, tend to choose particular occupational roles. It is also likely, however, that the role has a major impact on the characteristics of the person playing it.

Our roles come to shape our behavior through specific sequences of social interaction. We often make assumptions about what is expected of us by the people we associate with, and we then try to conform to their expectations. This is not usually a matter of consciously manipulating our identities. It reflects, rather, the deeply ingrained and typically automatic human tendency to interact with others in predictable and "appropriate" ways. In one study that illustrates this process, college women took part in a simulated job interview with a male interviewer (von Baeyer, Sherk, and Zanna, 1981). Before the interview, half of the women were led to think that the interviewer was a typical male chauvinist—that he be-

lieved working women should be unassertive, gentle, and demure. The other half of the women were led to believe that the interviewer had more egalitarian views of working women—that he believed they should be independent and assertive. These expectations affected the women's behavior in subtle but revealing ways. The women who expected to meet the chauvinist interviewer presented themselves in a more traditionally feminine way—they wore more makeup and accessories and were judged to be more attractive. In addition, as compared to the women who expected to meet the egalitarian interviewer, these women talked less during the interview and were less likely to look directly at the interviewer while they were talking. Their behavior, in other words, reflected precisely the sort of feminine demeanor that they believed the interviewer expected.

It is not only the behavior of women or of subordinates that is affected by such social expectations. The behavior of men and of leaders is influenced, too, by what they perceive to be the expectations of others. In these ways, the social interactions of men and women can exert a major influence on their behavior and even on their modes of thought. To the extent that men and women are expected to think, feel, and act differently, the psychological differences between the two sexes will be widened.

HUMAN SEXUALITY

Our maleness and femaleness are most obviously reflected in the area of sexuality—our sexual responses, experiences, and relationships. We have already discussed human sexual motivation in Chapter 10, focusing on the influence of both biological and cultural factors on people's sexual behavior. There have long been basic differences between men and women in the experience and expression of sexuality. Although some of these differences may have a basis in biology, recent research has shown that the physiology of sex in men and women is much more similar than had previously been suspected. But cultural attitudes have perpetuated differences between men's and women's orientations toward sexuality.

Human sexual response

Much of what we know about our body's sexual responses comes from the research of William Masters and Virginia Johnson (1966). These investigators were the first to scientifically examine physical responses to sexual stimulation in the laboratory.

One of Masters and Johnson's most important findings was that patterns of sexual response are very similar in women and men. For both sexes there are four stages of sexual arousal (see Figure 16.1). The first stage, the *excitement phase,* can be initiated by physical factors (such as genital stimulation), or by psychological factors (such as fantasy). In this phase, heart rate and respiration increase and blood flows into the genitals, making the penis erect and causing the clitoris to swell. Moisture forms on the vaginal walls. Both women's and men's nipples may become erect. In the second, or *plateau phase,* the genitals reach their maximum engorgement. The clitoris retracts into the clitoral hood and the uterus raises slightly, expanding the vagina. The glans of the penis enlarges and darkens in color, while the testes swell, pulling up into the scrotum. At the end of the plateau phase both sexes

may have a sense that orgasm is inevitable. In the *orgasmic phase,* muscular contractions push the blood in the genitals back into the bloodstream. The vaginal walls move in and out and the uterus pulsates. Muscles in and around the penis pulse to cause ejaculation, the discharge of semen. Some people experience muscular contractions in other parts of the body, such as in the face, arms, or legs. In the *resolution phase* the body returns to its preexcitement state.

Although men and women share these basic stages of sexual response, there are a few differences in their physiological reactions. Women do not ejaculate—although women's orgasms may in some cases be accompanied by release of fluid from the urethra (Belzer, 1981). And Masters and Johnson's findings indicate that men undergo a *refractory period* in the resolution stage, during which further excitement to orgasm is impossible. Women, however, may skip the refractory period and can be stimulated to orgasm again. This is a finding that contradicts prevalent social attitudes. Rather than being less sensual than men, it appears that women have a greater sexual capacity than men do. There is more recent evidence, however, that at least some men, too, can have a series of orgasms in a short period of time (Robbins and Jensen, 1978).

Masters and Johnson also found that the same kinds of orgasms can be achieved through masturbation, in-

FIGURE 16.1

Typical sexual response patterns in the human male and female (after Masters and Johnson, 1966). In both sexes, sexual excitement increases until it reaches a plateau. The orgasm is a sudden surge of arousal beyond this plateau. After orgasm, men have a refractory period during which further excitement to orgasm is impossible. For women, several different patterns are typical. The woman may remain at the plateau stage without proceeding to orgasm (line B); she may have an orgasm followed by resolution (return to the preexcitement stage) (line C); or she may have two or more orgasms in succession before resolution (line A).

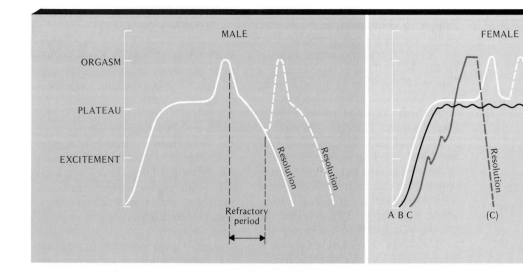

For human beings, sex is as much psychological as it is genital.

tercourse, or in some cases even fantasy for both men and women. The fact that mere fantasy can prompt the same sexual response as actual intercourse points up a fundamental fact about human sexuality: for humans, sex is as much psychological as it is genital.

The importance of cognitive activity in sexual arousal is apparent in the ease with which humans become aroused—an erotic novel or picture can be as effective as direct genital stimulation. It has traditionally been believed that men are more easily aroused by explicit pornographic materials than women, while women have been thought to be more responsive to romantic or sentimental stimuli. But recent studies of men's and women's reactions to erotic material suggest otherwise (Fisher, 1983). Julia Heiman (1975) studied male and female college students' sexual responses to a variety of tape-recorded stories. Some subjects heard erotic or explicit sexual material, some heard romantic but nonsexual material, and some heard combined erotic-romantic material. Sexual arousal was measured by devices placed on the penis (to record the size of erections) or in the vagina (to record increased blood flow during arousal). Heiman found that both men and women who listened to the romantic tapes showed low levels of sexual arousal, while men and women who listened to the erotic or erotic-romantic tapes

showed high levels of arousal. Furthermore, women who listened to the erotic material were as aroused as men, while the romantic tapes had no more effect on women than on men. These findings indicate that sexual response occurs as a result of *mental* stimulation and in the presence of the same stimuli for men and women.

The psychological aspect of sexuality becomes particularly apparent in cases of *sexual dysfunction.* Sexual dysfunction takes a number of forms, including problems with performing intercourse, enjoying sex, or reaching orgasm. All of these problems are very common. Couples who are distressed by such problems can now seek *sex therapy*, which utilizes techniques pioneered by Masters and Johnson (1970). As it turns out, very few sexual dysfunctions are caused by physical problems (Kaplan, 1974). A major contributor to sexual dysfunction is worrying: worry about becoming pregnant, worry about having orgasms, worry about how one's body looks and smells, worry about rejection. Sex therapists try to combat these worries by encouraging people with sexual problems to focus on sensual pleasure rather than on sexual expertise (Heiman, 1979).

Gender roles and sexual attitudes

If you had grown up on the Polynesian island of Mangaia, you would

Sex therapists encourage people to focus on sensual pleasure, rather than on sexual expertise.

probably be having sexual intercourse every night, with two or three orgasms each time. You would have been taught the value of mutual pleasure in sex. Sex is of such importance in Mangaia that the people have many different words for intercourse, just as the Eskimos have many different words for snow in all its various forms (Marshall, 1971). On the other hand, if you had grown up on the Irish island of Inis Beag, you would find sex to be a rushed, secretive matter, with no knowledge or expectation of female orgasm. The main thing you would have learned about sex is that it depletes your energy and should be kept to a minimum (Messenger, 1971). The natives of Mangaia and of Inis Beag are not different from each other biologically, but their culture shapes their sexuality in profoundly different ways.

Our own sexual attitudes and values are just as much affected by the time and place we live in as the attitudes and values of the people of these two contrasting cultures. Our most recent and influential cultural legacy concerning sexuality stems from the Victorian era, which spanned approximately the last two-thirds of the nineteenth century, when Queen Victoria ruled England. For the Victorians, sex was considered a necessary evil for men and as something basically foreign to the nature of women. A "good" husband would impose sex on his wife as sel-

dom as possible, and a "good" wife would tolerate sex as one of her marital duties. The idea that a woman could derive pleasure from sex was regarded as an insult. According to an old English joke, when a Victorian girl asked her mother what to do on her wedding night, the mother advised, "Lie still and close your eyes, dear, and think of England" (Tavris and Offir, 1977, page 61). It is doubtful that all Victorian men and women lived up to these cultural standards. Yet the era unmistakably created a legacy of sexual restraint and repression in both Europe and America that has been difficult to shake. A central part of this legacy is the *sexual double standard*, which mandates very different patterns of sexual behavior for men and women.

During the first half of the twentieth century, significant changes in sexual attitudes and behavior took place. In his widely influential theory of personality (see Chapter 11), Sigmund Freud viewed sex as a central motivational force and thus helped establish the normality of sexual desire for both sexes. But Freud believed that women's sexual motivation derived mainly from the wish to have children, while men experienced sexual desire as an end in itself. In Freud's view, it was "normal" for men to play the active role in sex and for women to play a passive role. Thus, although Freud's influence led people to be more open and accepting

IS MASTURBATION DANGEROUS?

In the Victorian era, masturbation was considered evil and disgusting. Victorian physicians warned that stimulating yourself sexually could lead to acne, blindness, impotence, warts, coughing spells, and even insanity. To protect little girls from themselves, some doctors went so far as to apply a hot iron to the clitoris or to sew the vaginal lips together. In the 1940s and 1950s Kinsey stunned the American public when he announced that 92 percent of the men in his sample and (even more shocking) 62 percent of the women had masturbated. More recent surveys have shown that women are beginning to masturbate earlier and with greater frequency than in previous decades (Hunt, 1974). In fact, masturbation does not seem to cause acne, blindness, impotence, warts, coughing spells, or even insanity.

about sex, it left the sexual double standard as strong as ever.

In recent decades, sexual attitudes and behaviors in America have undergone massive change—so much so that many people refer to the changes since 1960 as a "sexual revolution." Compared to previous periods in history, many more people now view sex as a normal and natural source of pleasure, rather than as something to be engaged in with guilt or anxiety. But the "sexual revolution" notwithstanding, the sexual double standard lives on.

In the 1950s an estimated 25 percent of unmarried college women and 55 percent of unmarried college men had had sexual intercourse (Hopkins, 1977). By 1983, the estimated figures were 60 percent of women and 75 percent of men (Gallup Organization, 1983). But more important than the discrepancy in the numbers of sexually active men and women are other fundamental differences between the orientations of the two sexes toward sexual behavior. Men are still expected to be the initiators of sexual activity, while women are still expected to play more passive roles and to be the ones to set the limits on sexual activity.

In a study of college dating couples in the Boston area, Letitia Anne Peplau, Zick Rubin, and Charles Hill (1977) found that among couples who were having sex, it was much more common for the boyfriend than for the girlfriend to be more interested in sex. And among couples who were not having sex, the woman's background and attitudes were usually the major restraining force. Other recent studies echo the conclusion that men are expected to push for sex and women are expected to make sure that it doesn't happen too soon (McCormick and Jesser, 1983). These continuing expectations can put strong pressures on both men and women. Women may fear that if they are sexually active and assertive they will seem to be "bad girls" or scare men off. And men may feel they are inadequate if they don't play a sexually active and assertive role.

The sexual double standard is buttressed by stereotypes about the sex drives of men and women. Even in the 1980s, a century after the Victorian era, 56 percent of a national sample of college students, both men and women, said they believed that men have a stronger sex drive than women do. About 7 percent believed that women have a stronger sex drive, and 37 percent thought there was no dif-

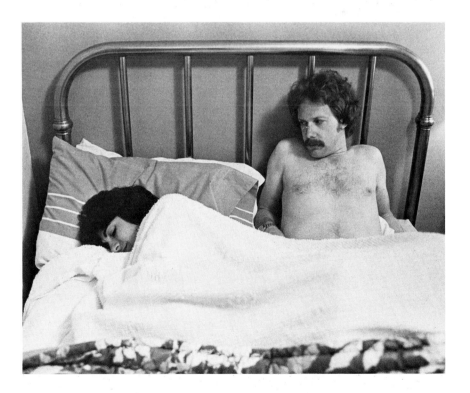

According to traditional gender roles, men are more eager to have sex than women. This difference is one aspect of the sexual double standard.

ference (Gallup Organization, 1983). Although this belief seems to have no basis in the biology of the two sexes, it reflects the continuing influence of different sets of expectations for the sexual behavior of men and women.

Some observers see value in the persistence of the sexual double standard. At the least, these observers note, the double standard helps to avoid ambiguity and confusion in heterosexual behavior, as the man plays his socially assigned role of sexual initiator and the woman plays her socially assigned role of sexual limit-setter. For the most part, however, the double standard seems to have had harmful rather than beneficial effects on interaction between the sexes, turning relationships into power struggles that do not foster real intimacy.

There is reason to believe that the sexual double standard is finally beginning to fade. Women are freer now than they were in the past to make the first move in a flirtation, and men may be freer than in the past to forgo making sexual advances (McCormick and Jesser, 1983). Such a shift—albeit a slow and uneasy one—toward a single sexual standard may be applauded for its potential to provide both men and women with greater flexibility and more rewarding relationships.

The impact of the sexual revolution

Masters and Johnson's research was one of the influences that led to a further move away from the sexual repression of the Victorian era toward a new emphasis on sexual enjoyment and openness in the 1970s and 1980s. The values of humanistic psychology (see Chapter 11) also contributed to this shift, by stressing that people can move toward self-actualization by doing the things they personally find enjoyable and fulfilling.

As a result of these new attitudes, sex became more pleasurable for many people during the 1970s than it had been in previous decades. Not only was there more premarital sex than there used to be, but there was more enjoyment of sex in marriage. According to one national survey, the average duration of sexual intercourse

for married couples increased from two minutes to ten minutes, as couples began to think of sex less as an obligation and more as a pleasurable experience (Hunt, 1974). People also reported using more variations in sexual foreplay, engaging in oral sex more often, and experimenting more with different positions for intercourse. Homosexuality, though not necessarily on the increase, clearly came out of the closet (see Box 4).

Many aspects of the sexual revolution have been seen as welcome changes, but the revolution has created new problems, as well. Although people's values about premarital sex range widely, one clearly negative aspect of the increase in premarital sex has been an increase in unwanted adolescent pregnancies. More than half of the 21 million 15- to 19-year-olds in the United States have sexual intercourse at least on occasion (Zelnik and Kantner, 1977) and no more than 20 percent use contraceptives regularly. The result is almost 700,000 unwanted teenage pregnancies a year. Of these, about 300,000 are ended by abortion and 100,000 by miscarriages, while 200,000 lead to out-of-wedlock births and 100,000 end in quick and often short-lived marriages (Byrne, 1977). One in six of the sexually active college women surveyed by Katz and Cronin (1980) reported having undergone an abortion at some time.

The sexual revolution also created a need in many people to keep up with what they perceived as the new sexual standards. Many people began to feel that they were missing out on something sexually, even when they were really not. Sex therapists reported that couples were beginning to come to them even though they didn't have any sexual problems; they just wanted their sex lives to be "better." Thus, a couple might be dissatisfied because the woman was having "only" one orgasm during intercourse or because the man wanted to have sex "only" three times a week (Tavris and Offir, 1977).

In the years since 1980 there has been an increasing recognition of these dangers of the sexual revolution. There have been downturns in the amount of sexual activity re-

SEXUAL ATTITUDES AND BIRTH CONTROL

Despite the widespread availability of contraceptives, many adolescents and young adults—including many college students— fail to use them. In one survey, fewer than a third of sexually active undergraduate women said they always used contraceptives, and more than a third said they never did. The failure to use contraceptives regularly may reflect negative or ambivalent feelings about sex. After all, using a contraceptive means admitting to yourself that you may have sex, and it involves dealing with doctors or druggists, discussing birth control plans with your partner, and actually taking a pill every day or using a device. Donn Byrne and William Fisher (1983) find that people who are anxious about sex tend to avoid these sexually oriented behaviors and, as a result, run the greatest risk of unwanted pregnancy.

CHAPTER SIXTEEN: MALE AND FEMALE

BOX 4

HOMOSEXUALITY AND HOMOPHOBIA

A recent issue of my college alumni magazine included an advertisement announcing the formation of a new organization, the Yale Gay and Lesbian Association. In 1984, with the increasing readiness of homosexual men and women to acknowledge their sexual orientation openly, the announcement did not seem particularly unusual.

To many Yale alumni, however, the advertisement was both embarrassing and infuriating. "I have always been proud to be a Yale man until I received the February 1984 issue . . . ," one chagrined member of the class of 1959 wrote to the editor. "I hid the magazine so that none of the members of my family or friends would see it." "Why in God's name," a member of the class of 1934 demanded, "do we tolerate the use of Yale's name for an organization composed of perverts and deviates . . . ? Their life-style may not be illegal but it is immoral, unnatural, and against the principles of Christianity."

As these responses suggest, the prevalent attitude toward homosexuality in America has been strongly negative. As recently as 1982, over two-thirds of Americans polled in nationwide surveys said that homosexual relations are "always wrong" (Schneider and Lewis, 1984). Many people believe that homosexuality is a sickness, and many others believe that it is immoral or perverse.

In fact, research suggests that homosexuals are no "sicker" than heterosexuals and that gay people are not a dangerous or corrupting influence on society (Bell and Weinberg, 1978). Gay people are as diverse as straight people, and they differ from heterosexuals only in their preference for sexual partners of the same sex rather than of the opposite sex. But the strongly negative attitudes toward homosexuals persist. These attitudes can best be explained as a reflection of *homophobia,* an irrational fear or intolerance of homosexuals (Morin and Garfinkle, 1978).

Homophobia can be demonstrated

In recent years, increasing numbers of homosexual people, such as this couple who live together, have begun to acknowledge their sexual orientation openly.

in laboratory situations. In one study, college students were interviewed by a male or female experimenter about their attitudes toward homosexuality and other issues (Morin, Taylor, and Kielman, 1975). In one experimental condition, the experimenter wore a "Gay and Proud" button and was introduced as working for the Association of Gay Psychologists. In a second condition, the experimenter wore no button and was simply introduced as a graduate student. It was found that subjects placed their chairs significantly further away from the experimenter identified as a homosexual than from the experimenter who was not so identified.

Heterosexual men tend to be even more threatened by homosexuality than heterosexual women are. In the experiment just described, for example, male subjects showed much more aversion to a "homosexual" man than female students showed to a "homosexual" woman. Stephen Morin and Ellen Garfinkle (1978) suggest that heterosexual men fear homosexual men because of their own need to preserve traditional sex roles. Heterosexual men often view gay men as being effeminate—as more delicate, passive, small, and yielding than heterosexual men (Karr, 1975). Men who are strongly

homophobic also tend to suspect any man who exhibits "feminine" characteristics of being homosexual (Dunbar, Brown, and Amoroso, 1973). Even among boys on the playground, terms like "fag," "queer," and "fairy" are commonly hurled at anyone who shows any lack of "male" toughness and bravado. The heterosexual man's aversion to homosexuals—and his fear of being labeled homosexual himself—serves as a powerful force for him to remain in a traditionally masculine role—unemotional, tough, and assertive.

In the past fifteen years gay men and lesbians (homosexual women) have been more likely to come "out of the closet" and acknowledge their sexual orientation openly, and gay people have banded together to fight for their civil rights. As a result of these efforts, many states and cities have passed laws that forbid discrimination against homosexuals in jobs and housing, and many large corporations have announced nondiscrimination policies. In addition, both the American Psychological Association and the American Psychiatric Association have explicitly declared that homosexuality is not a sickness.

The increasing number of gay people who have "come out" has made it easier for other gay men and lesbians to acknowledge their sexual orientation to themselves and others, without shame or guilt. In addition, we can expect the greater openness and self-acceptance of a vanguard of gay people to increase the overall level of tolerance in society. Recent surveys have shown that those Americans who personally know someone who is openly gay are much more likely to have tolerant attitudes toward homosexuals.

As more and more gay people come out, such personal contacts will become more common, whether on college campuses, in workplaces, or in neighborhoods. Such person-to-person contact between gay and straight people may be the best way to combat the oppressive effects of homophobia.

One negative consequence of the "sexual revolution" has been the increase in unwanted pregnancies among adolescents.

ported by students at many colleges, and more young people are saying that sex without love is unenjoyable or unacceptable (Rubenstein, 1983). People seem freer than they used to be to make the decision *not* to have sex as well as the decision to have it. Indeed, a cover story in *Time* magazine in April 1984 went so far as to declare that the "revolution is over." In the wake of the revolution, there seems to be a swing back from the emphasis on sexual experience toward a greater emphasis on love and commitment. "Veterans of the revolution," the *Time* article observed, "are reinventing courtship and romance and discovering, often with astonishment, that they need not sleep together on the first or second date. Many individuals are even rediscovering the traditional values of fi-

delity, obligation, and marriage" (Leo, 1984, page 74).

The sexual revolution may have succeeded, at least to some degree, in freeing people to make their own decisions about sexuality. As we have seen, however, the freedom is hardly complete. The sexual double standard persists, and with it come severe limitations in the approach that individual men and women can take toward sexuality. Thus, in the domain of sexuality, as in so many other spheres of life, differences between the roles of the two sexes persist. Over the past two decades, concerted efforts have been made to change these sex roles in order to achieve greater equality between women and men. These attempts to change sex roles are the focus of the Psychological Issue that follows this chapter.

CHAPTER SIXTEEN: MALE AND FEMALE

SUMMARY

Psychological differences between men and women

• **1** *Gender stereotypes* characterize men as basically more aggressive, independent, dominant, active, competitive, and self-confident and women as more tactful, gentle, sensitive, emotional, neat, and quiet. These stereotypes can lead to differential treatment and perception of males and females.

• **2** Men and women are far more similar to each other than they are different. But the sexes do differ, on the average, in the areas of aggressiveness, empathy, and certain cognitive skills.

• **3** Psychological research tends to be biased toward men: male subjects are used more often than female subjects, and "normal" human development has often been equated with male development.

Explaining the differences: biology and culture

• **4** Sex differences in aggression seem to reflect a biological *predisposition* for males to behave more aggressively. This predisposition apparently results from the action of male hormones on the brain. Most psychologists agree, however, that culture plays a greater role than biological predispositions in shaping psychological differences between men and women.

• **5** Our expectations about what men and women should do and what they should be like are called *gender roles.* Gender-role learning occurs through parental teaching and expectations and the child's motivation to be a member in good standing of his or her sex. Gender-role learning also occurs in schools and through the mass media, especially television.

• **6** *Transsexuals* are people who believe that they are trapped in a body of the wrong sex. Although sex-change surgery for transsexuals was initially greeted enthusiastically, it is now regarded with greater caution.

• **7** Adults continue to play gender roles, especially in their family and at work. These family and work roles in turn shape behavior through specific sequences of social interaction.

Human sexuality

• **8** The patterns of sexual response in men and women are remarkably similar. Masters and Johnson identified four stages of sexual response: the *excitement phase*, the *plateau phase*, the *orgasmic phase*, and the *resolution phase.*

• **9** Human sexual response depends greatly on psychological factors. This is apparent from the fact that fantasy can produce sexual arousal in both men and women and that few sexual dysfunctions can be traced to physical disorders.

• **10** In recent times sexual attitudes and behaviors have undergone massive changes. Nevertheless, there continues to be a double standard in sexuality, with men expected to be the initiators of sexual activity and women expected to play a more passive role.

• **11** Although the "sexual revolution" has brought benefits to many people, it has also brought an increase in teenage pregnancies and new kinds of anxieties about sexual performance.

• **12** The prevalent attitude of heterosexuals toward homosexuals has been strongly negative, reflecting an attitude of *homophobia.* During the past decade, however, social attitudes toward homosexuals have begun to become more tolerant, as more gay people themselves have openly acknowledged and accepted their sexual orientation.

KEY TERMS

excitement phase
face-ism
gender identity
gender roles
gender stereotypes
homophobia
orgasmic phase
plateau phase
predisposition
refractory period
resolution phase
roles
sexual double standard
sexual dysfunction
stereotypes
transsexual

CHANGING SEX ROLES

In the past two decades, there has been a growing feeling in America that our traditional sex roles (or gender roles) are in need of change. No longer, it is often declared, should men rule our governments and our corporations. No longer, it is frequently maintained, should women be solely responsible for the upkeep of our homes and the care of our children. And no longer, it is increasingly argued, should a major portion of the scripts for people's lives be written for them in childhood, simply on the basis of their gender. These ideas about sex roles have been accompanied by a good deal of actual change, especially in women's increased entry into the workforce and into formerly "male" occupations. Nevertheless, as we will see, the changes have not been easy.

THE LEGACY OF SEXISM

The attempt to change sex roles flies in the face of a long history of *sexism*, in which the sexes have been viewed not only as different but also as inherently unequal. Male supremacy has been a dominant theme of societies throughout the world. Men have had a virtual monopoly on power and prestige, holding most positions of political and religious leadership and enjoying the respect that goes with these positions. Within the family, the father is usually considered the "boss," despite the fact that the mother takes care of the house and children.

The notion that men are superior to women is part of the ideology of the world's major religions. Consider the following passage, for example, from the New Testament: *Let your women keep silence in the churches; for it is not permitted unto them to speak, but they are commanded to be under obedience . . . And if they will learn anything, let them ask their husband at home. (1 Cor. 11:14)*

And the idea that women are men's intellectual inferiors has persisted through the generations. "Direct thought is not an attribute of femininity," wrote the inventor Thomas Edison, in one of his less illuminating moments. A survey of the jokes in *Reader's Digest* in the 1940s, 1950s, and 1960s found six times as many antifemale jokes as antimale ones (Zimbardo and Meadow, 1976). Most typically, women were depicted as stupid or foolish. For example: "Sweet young thing to husband: 'Of course I know what's going on in the world. I just don't understand any of it, that's all.'"

The legacy of sexism continues in our political institutions today. Even at the start of the 1980s, the official code of Georgia stated, "The husband is the head of the family, and the wife is subject to him." In 1984 the Oklahoma state legislature— itself, needless to say, dominated by men—passed a law providing that the man is the head of the family.

So when we think about changing sex roles—even in the supposedly enlightened 1980s—we should realize that we are up against a long and deeply rooted tradition of sexism. The primary force in fighting this tradition in the past 20 years has been the women's movement.

THE WOMEN'S MOVEMENT

The women's movement surfaced in the 1960s as a resurgence of earlier feminist movements in America. An important event in the birth of the move-

Although the Equal Rights Amendment to the U.S. Constitution has not been ratified, the women's movement remains a strong force in America.

ment was the publication in 1963 of Betty Friedan's *The Feminine Mystique*. Friedan argued against the pervasive belief that a woman's place is in the home. Although many American women were well-housed and well-fed, they were bored and discontent, in need of challenges that extended beyond giving children baths and doing laundry.

As women began to question the mold into which they had been cast, they began to try to broaden their opportunities. Since the 1960s the goals of the women's movement have included equal pay for equal work, an end to job discrimination by sex, adequate child-care programs, an equal sharing of family responsibilities, an end to all forms of sexual exploitation, and most fundamentally, a restructuring of women's roles to achieve equality in all spheres of life.

Much of the social and legal history of the 1970s is a history of gains of the women's movement. For example (from a chronology assembled by Sweet, 1979):

1971: The University of Michigan becomes the first university to incorporate an affirmative action plan for the hiring and promotion of women.

1973: The Supreme Court outlaws sex-segregated classified advertisements for employment.

1974: The national Little League agrees to admit girls to teams.

1977: AT&T agrees to allow dual listings of married couples (both the husband's and wife's names) in phone directories.

1978: More women than men enter college for the first time in U.S. history.

The gains have continued into the 1980s. In 1981, for example, Sandra Day O'Connor became the first female justice of the U.S. Supreme Court. In 1983, Sally Ride became the first American woman to soar into space. In 1984, Geraldine Ferraro became the first woman nominated by one of the major parties to run for vice-president of the United States.

The women's movement has also had an impact on the mass media and on education. School textbooks have been scrutinized for their presentation of sex-role stereotypes and have been revised to reduce their sexist bias. In the first edition of this text, published in 1974, the major sections had such titles as "Of Mind and Man," "Thinking Man," and "Relating Man." It is now recognized, however, that it is misleading to use the word "man" to refer to all human beings. This usage makes it seem as though males are really psychology's central concern. In the subsequent editions, therefore, I switched to nonsexist titles and I began using the pronoun "she" as well as the pronoun "he" to refer to people in general.

But despite all these changes, women's march toward equality has been slow and uneasy. Women are forging new paths, but not without difficulties—both in achieving their career goals and in managing the competing demands of work and family. Almost 20 years after her first book encouraged women to leave the home, Betty Friedan wrote *The Second Stage* (1981), in which

she cautioned that as women strive for careers they should beware of sacrificing their equally important needs for home and family life. Women have won a few battles, she argues, but the real war involves much more fundamental changes in women's *and* men's roles, both in the workplace and in the home.

MEN, WOMEN, AND WORK

Women are entering the workforce in increasing numbers. In 1950 only 34 percent of American women worked outside the home, including only 12 percent of women with children under age 6. By 1981, 52 percent of American women—including half of those with children under 6—were in the workforce (Spain and Bianchi, 1983). In many cases, women have had to work in order to support their families. But in one recent survey, three out of four young working women stated that they would keep working even if they could maintain their current standard of living without doing so (La Farge, 1983). Jobs provide many women with a sense of mastery and a chance to exercise talents that

It is misleading to use the word "man" to refer to all human beings.

Sandra Day O'Connor (left) was the first female justice of the U.S. Supreme Court; Sally Ride (center) was the first American woman in space; and Geraldine Ferraro (right) was the first woman to run for vice-president on a major party ticket.

In recent years, many women have entered previously "male" occupations.

housework and motherhood alone do not provide. And even housewives now report a new sense of freedom because staying at home has now become a choice, rather than a mandatory life sentence.

Not only are more women working, but they are entering new fields. In 1970 only 5 percent of all law degrees and 10 percent of all medical degrees went to women, but by 1980 women earned 20 percent of the degrees in each of these fields (Spain and Bianchi, 1983). Between 1971 and 1981, the number of women receiving doctorates in sciences and engineering doubled. In the field of psychology, the percentage of women among the recipients of new doctorates increased from 25 percent in 1971 to 44 percent in 1981 (National Science Foundation, 1982).

But many obstacles to equality of the sexes in the workplace remain. Although women are entering new fields, they are not always accepted in these roles. In one recent national survey, fully half of the *women* polled said they preferred a male doctor to a female doctor (Dowd, 1983). And as women trailblazers enter totally new fields—as surgeons, movie directors, and corporate executives—they are often regarded more as curiosities than as full-fledged members of their profession. When Sally Ride became the first woman in space, a great deal of media attention was given to such issues as how she would handle her hairdo and personal hygiene in space (Goodman, 1983).

Perhaps the most serious inequity is that women workers earn far less than men. On the average, a female worker earns about 60 cents for every dollar a male earns. In part, this is because women workers, on the average, have less education and work experience than men do. But even when women are in jobs requiring the same amount of education and experience as men, they are typically paid considerably less. In one survey in the Washington, D.C. area, nurses were found to make less than house painters, and teachers less than liquor-store clerks or truck drivers (Tolley, 1983). And even though women are beginning to enter "men's" fields, very few men are entering "women's" fields. As long as large numbers of women remain the sole occupants of undervalued and underpaid jobs, there will not be full sexual equality in the workplace.

MEN, WOMEN, AND THE FAMILY

If changing sex roles at work is a difficult undertaking, changing sex roles in the family is even more difficult. Even as most men and women have come to accept in the abstract the principle that the two sexes should be treated equally in the work world, many men have found it difficult to accept the idea of their own wives working. In fact, there is evidence that men whose wives work outside the home tend to have lower self-esteem than men whose wives are homemakers (Kessler and McRae, 1982). Especially in working-class families, in which the wife works out of economic necessity, the husband may take the wife's employment as a sign of his own failure as a provider—and, by extension, as a man (Rubin, 1983).

Even in two-earner families, women continue to do the lion's share of homemaking and child rearing. No country in the world has ever been fully successful in getting men and women to share domestic work equally (Tavris and Offir, 1977). Taking care of young children and, more generally, being tender and nurturant, have not traditionally been regarded as manly activities.

Within the past decade, however, more and more men have decided that they themselves want to change their roles—not primarily in order to give more power to women, but because they believe that the male role has been as limiting and stifling, in its own way, as the female role has been. As part of their dominant role, men have learned to place tremendous emphasis on achievement and competition. Men are taught to put women in weak, dependent roles, while remaining tough and independent themselves. Men are taught that a "real man" never shows weakness, never cries, never lets his emotions show. One group of "men's liberationists," the Berkeley Men's Group, has expressed their goals as follows: *We, as men, want to take back our full humanity. We no longer want to strain and compete to live up to an impossible oppressive masculine image—strong, silent, cool, handsome, unemotional, successful, master of women, leader of men, wealthy, brilliant, athletic, and "heavy." . . . We want to love, nurture, and support ourselves and* other men, as well as women. (Berkeley Men's Center, 1974)

One area in which men have been making progress in reshaping their roles, albeit slowly and uncertainly, is the domain of fatherhood. An increasing number of men, especially those now in their twenties and thirties, have been taking an active role in the care of their children. Men whose own fathers played traditional family roles as breadwinners and somewhat distant patriarchs are now spending larger amounts of time with their own small children—making dinners, giving baths, providing emotional comfort. These changes have often involved considerable ambivalence. As one man admits, "There are moments when I really resent having to do more than my own father did and more than I thought I was going to do when I was growing up" (Bell, 1982).

At the same time, however, many men are discovering that increased involvement with their children brings rich rewards—including an ability to get back in touch with

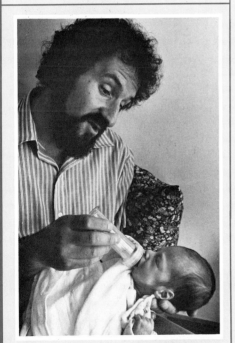

An increasing number of fathers have been taking an active role in the care of their babies and young children.

nurturant parts of themselves that were suppressed by the expectations of the male role. Some employers are facilitating these changes by making it possible for men to alter their work schedules in order to be able to play a greater role in child rearing (Klinman et al., 1984).

TOWARD ANDROGYNY

Some people believe that the best way to change sex roles is to change the basic personality makeup of men and women. Indeed, studies have found that the healthiest people are not those who are highly "masculine" males or highly "feminine" females but rather individuals who incorporate some of the traits traditionally associated with the other sex—that is, men who can be warm and expressive and women who can be strong and assertive. Sandra Bem (1972, 1975) has called the ability to combine masculine and feminine traits *psychological androgyny*. (The word *androgyny* is derived by combining the Greek words for "man" and "woman.") Bem measured androgyny by asking students how often various adjectives were descriptive of themselves. Subjects were categorized as androgynous if they indicated that they had both masculine and feminine traits.

Bem found some evidence that androgynous students of both sexes behaved more effectively in a variety of laboratory situations than students who were highly feminine or highly masculine. Highly masculine men were independent and assertive but they lacked the ability to express warmth and playfulness. Highly feminine women showed concern for others, but they were not independent or assertive. "In contrast," Bem writes, "the androgynous men and women . . . could be independent and assertive when they needed to be, and warm and responsive in appropriate situations" (1975, page 62). Instead of having to defend against behavior

that might seem inappropriate or inconsistent for their sex, they were able to behave in a more flexible and fully human manner.

Is androgyny the wave of the future? There is evidence that American parents are treating their sons and daughters more alike in certain respects than they used to; for example, they are encouraging girls to participate in competitive sports and are having boys do more domestic tasks (Klemesrud, 1980). Should we encourage our children to develop both masculine and feminine traits and interests and look forward to a time when we transcend sex roles and "masculine" and "feminine" become outmoded notions? Some people believe that this is the way to go. Others are not so sure. If we do away with all the traditional differences between men and women, might we lose something in the process? These are questions that all of us are now being called upon to answer.

SUMMARY

- **1** The idea of male supremacy has been a dominant theme of societies throughout the world, and there are still many signs of this sexist belief in our culture.
- **2** The women's movement has met with many successes in restructuring women's roles in the past two decades, especially in the sphere of employment.
- **3** Inequities still exist between men and women in the workforce, particularly in the area of pay, and at home, where women continue to bear the lion's share of homemaking and child-care responsibilities. However, some men are trying to break out of the traditional male role and devote more time to fathering.
- **4** There is some evidence that androgynous people (those who have a combination of both masculine and feminine characteristics) behave more flexibly and effectively in a variety of situations.

Social relationships provide many of the greatest satisfactions, as well as many of the greatest challenges, of being human.

CHAPTER 17

NEEDING OTHERS

Seeking company
What relationships provide
Being lonely

People need both emotional attachments and a network of friends. Without them, they may feel painfully lonely.

PERCEIVING OTHERS

Physical appearance
Reputations
Attribution processes

We are continually forming impressions of what other people are like, often on the basis of limited information.

LIKING OTHERS

The nearness of you
Birds of a feather

Our friends tend to be people who are similar to us and who are close at hand.

LOVING OTHERS

Measuring love
Love and sex
Love and commitment

Love includes components of attachment, caring, and intimacy, but it does not necessarily involve long-term commitment.

LEAVING OTHERS

Responses to dissatisfaction
Breaking up

Relationships end for many reasons. Breakups can be painful, but they also teach us valuable lessons.

PSYCHOLOGICAL ISSUE
MARRIAGE AND DIVORCE

BOXES
1 Is beauty best?
2 Reading nonverbal clues
3 Should we study love?
4 Three couples

Nearly half of all marriages may end in divorce, yet people keep coming back for more.

Unless you've made a firm decision to spend the rest of your days sitting on top of a flagpole, your relationships with other people will undoubtedly remain among the most important aspects of your life. From your earliest attachments to your parents to your later relationships with playmates, work associates, friends, and lovers, social relationships provide many of the greatest satisfactions, as well as many of the greatest challenges, of being human.

The term *social relationship* refers to the pattern of interactions between two people that extends over a period of time, as well as to the thoughts and feelings that the two people have about each other. Relationships can vary greatly in their degree of intimacy, from the casual relationship between a bus driver and an occasional passenger to the lifelong relationship between siblings or the highly involved relationship between spouses. In this chapter, we will place much of our emphasis on close relationships—those that have the greatest impact on our lives.

We will discuss, in turn, phenomena that relate to *needing* others, *perceiving* others, *liking* others, *loving* others, and *leaving* others. "Needing others" refers to our human needs to seek the company of others and to form social relationships. In the section on "perceiving others," we refer to the processes by which we form impressions of other people. In the section "liking others," we discuss some of the factors that lead particular people to become friends. In the section on "loving others," we will consider the qualities of that special attitude called "love," including its links to sex and commitment. Finally, we will consider "leaving others"—how and why relationships end.

NEEDING OTHERS

All of us have a need for other people—sometimes simply for the company of another human being, and sometimes to form relationships with particular people. Our needs for others are *social motives;* they are a part of the more general family of human motives that were discussed in Chapter 10.

Seeking company

Suppose you've just heard on the news that the Martians have landed. At such a time, would you take a walk by yourself to contemplate the meaning of the news? Or would you feel a strong desire to seek the company of other humans? One of the major reasons we seek out other people is the need for *social comparison*—to be able to compare our own emotions and attitudes with those of other people. Especially in fearful and uncertain situations—the landing of the Martians would certainly qualify—people often don't know quite how they should think or feel. To help find out, they are motivated to affiliate with others in the same situation.

This tendency to seek the company of others when we are afraid or uncertain was demonstrated by Stanley Schachter (1959) in an experiment with college women. Half of the subjects (the high-fear group) were told that as part of an important scientific study they would receive a series of extremely painful electric shocks. The other half of the subjects (the low-fear group) were told that they would experience mere "tingles" and that they would enjoy the experiment. Then the experimenter told the subjects that while he was setting up the equipment, they could choose to

wait either in a room by themselves or in a room together with other subjects. Fully two-thirds of the high-fear subjects chose to wait with others, compared to only one-third of the low-fear subjects. Thus, the fearful subjects tended to seek company, just as people are likely to huddle together during power failures or, presumably, Martian landings. In a follow-up study, Schachter demonstrated that fearful subjects did not want to wait with just anybody, but only with other subjects who were in the same situation they were in. "Misery doesn't love just any kind of company," Schachter observed, "only miserable company." And the reasons subjects gave for this preference reflected the need for social comparison. In fact, the subjects were probably not sure just how they should react and behave in this strange set of circumstances. Should they feel fear for their safety? Anger at the diabolical experimenter? Gratitude for being allowed to suffer for the sake of science? Should they submit bravely to their fate or mount a protest? The subjects wanted to affiliate with others in the same situation in order to find out how they should feel and behave.

In addition to the impact of fear and uncertainty on our desire for company, some of us are by nature more sociable than others. Whereas a highly sociable person may enjoy having dinner with friends almost every evening, a less sociable person may prefer to dine alone much of the time. As noted in Chapter 11, there is evidence that the personality trait of *sociability* is to at least some degree inherited. A lack of sociability should not be confused with *shyness*—the tendency to feel anxious and uncomfortable in the presence of others. It is quite possible to be both sociable and shy—that is, to desire the company of others even though one is often uncomfortable and inhibited in social situations. It is also quite possible to be unsociable without being shy. Self-report measures of these two traits have been found to be only slightly correlated with each other (Cheek and Buss, 1981).

What relationships provide

We are motivated not only to seek the company of others in general but to form close and enduring relationships with specific other people. Robert Weiss (1974) believes that each of us needs to form two different kinds of social relationships: *emotional attachments* to one other person (usu-

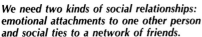
We need two kinds of social relationships: emotional attachments to one other person and social ties to a network of friends.

THE BENEFITS OF PETS

Our relationships with other people can provide us with companionship, affection, and the opportunity to care for someone. Pets can apparently provide some of the same benefits. Over the course of the 1970s, as the divorce rate increased and the size of families became smaller, the number of dogs and cats in American households increased by about 50 percent. There are now about 49 million dogs and 42 million cats living as pets in America; together they far exceed the number of children under 18. The pet boom seems to reflect, among other things, people's continuing needs for the provisions of social relationships (Robey, 1983).

ally a lover or a spouse) and *social ties* to a network of friends. Each type of relationship provides its own special set of provisions. Emotional attachments make available a sense of comfort and security, and social ties provide a sense of group identity and integration. The adult's need for an emotional attachment seems to develop from the infant's attachment to its parents. The infant feels secure and comfortable only when in the parent's presence and terrified when the parent leaves (see Chapter 8). As adults, we no longer require the constant physical presence of an attachment figure, but we still retain a strong need for an emotional attachment in order to feel secure. Social ties, usually to a group of friends of one's own age, become important in childhood and even more so in adolescence. Adolescents achieve a sense of belonging and of identity by affiliating with and comparing themselves to other members of their peer group. And this need for a network of friends with whom we can share activities and concerns persists into adulthood.

In addition to emotional attachments and ties to friends, there are other sorts of social relationships that supply us with important provisions. Many people have significant relationships with relatives (such as par-

ents and siblings), with teachers and employers, and with counselors or therapists. For many parents, relationships with children play a central role in life. Each of these relationships may fill a distinctive need. Weiss suggests that a fundamental challenge for each person is to establish and maintain a set of relationships that satisfactorily fulfill his or her set of social needs.

But relationships are not simply a matter of having one's needs fulfilled by others. For relationships to succeed, they must be reciprocal, with each person fulfilling certain needs of the other. In the view of Harold Kelley and his associates (1983), the hallmark of close social relationships is *interdependence*—the way in which each person has an impact on the other's thoughts, feelings, and behavior. In these researchers' view, the closeness of a relationship can be measured in terms of the degree of this mutual impact. In "close" relationships the two people have a frequent and intense impact on each other over a period of time; in less close relationships, the impact is less frequent and less enduring. Close relationships are not necessarily pleasant or satisfying. Two business partners may feel great mutual hostility, for example, but still have a strong impact on each other, and thus have a "close" relationship.

Being lonely

When people lack either an emotional attachment or a social network, the outcome is likely to be the condition called *loneliness*—an experience of longing and of emptiness that one noted psychiatrist, Harry Stack Sullivan, has described as "so terrible that it practically baffles clear recall" (Sullivan, 1953, page 261). One does not have to be physically isolated in order to be lonely. Indeed, it's quite possible to feel lonely in the midst of a crowd. Rather, loneliness stems from the lack of social relationships and of their provisions.

Robert Weiss (1973) has identified two kinds of loneliness, each linked to the absence of one of the basic provisions of social relationships. The loneliness of *emotional isolation* results from the loss or absence of an emotional attachment, and the loneliness of *social isolation* results from the loss or absence of social ties. Each

of these conditions is likely to be extremely painful, including symptoms of restlessness and depression. Weiss has found, moreover, that one sort of relationship cannot readily substitute for another in alleviating loneliness. Thus, a person suffering from the loss of a love relationship is likely to feel painfully lonely, even though she may have children at home or friends to spend time with. One divorced mother described her experience in the following terms:

Your house is so noisy all day long, phones, people, kids, all kinds of action going on and come eight o'clock everybody's in bed, and there's this dead silence. Like the whole world has just come to an end. All of a sudden you get this feeling that you're completely alone, that there is no one else in the world. You look out the window, you walk back and forth from room to room, you watch television, and you're dead. (Weiss, 1973, page 136)

And people who have close emotional attachments may still feel

Loneliness results from the lack of an emotional attachment or a network of friends.

Old people are more likely than young people to be alone. But the popular conception that old people, as a group, are especially prone to loneliness is apparently a myth. In fact, people in their sixties, seventies, and eighties report that they are less lonely than younger adults (Peplau et al., 1982). In particular, older widows and widowers seem to be better protected from loneliness than younger ones, perhaps because the loss of a spouse is a more expected occurrence in late adulthood than in earlier years.

great loneliness if they lack a network of friends. Many college students feel painfully lonely because of this lack. Students often leave behind the familiar worlds of high school, hometown, and family and must struggle to establish a new social network. "After being voted in junior high and senior high 'Best Personality' and 'Most Popular,'" one college freshman reported, "I had to start over. Walking a long distance, seeing nothing but strangers was rather difficult . . ." (Cutrona, 1982). Although entering the world of college can lead to loneliness in almost anyone, loneliness is especially prevalent among students who are shy or who are relatively unskilled in interacting with others (Jones, 1982). One approach to curing loneliness, therefore, is to help people develop the social skills, such as the ability to be a good listener, that can help them to make friends (Rook and Peplau, 1982).

As noted earlier, being lonely is not the same thing as being alone. Although it is painful to be lonely, most people value periods of solitude. Especially in big cities, people are often overloaded with stimuli—including other people—to a point that can be physically and emotionally stressful. "No one would deny that loneliness can hurt," writes Peter Suedfeld (1982), "but it is equally certain that aloneness can heal" (page 65). Unfortunately, Suedfeld points out, we have been conditioned to dread solitude. If we want to be alone, people may think there is something wrong with us. Such negative views of being alone can have the effect of poisoning the experience of solitude. That is, if we expect aloneness to be painful, it probably will be. But in fact, surveys suggest that people who live alone by choice are no more likely to be lonely than people who live with others (Rubenstein and Shaver, 1982). To prevent loneliness it seems less important to be in the physical presence of a spouse, sweetheart, or friend than to know that he will be there when needed.

Loneliness is especially prevalent among unmarried, widowed, and divorced people (Weiss, 1973), but none of us is entirely immune to it. In one recent survey of Americans, two out

of ten people interviewed said they were lonely during their spare time (United Media Enterprises, 1982). Far from being a sign of weakness, loneliness is a manifestation of the basic need for social relationships—a need we all share. Although various activities can help us to cope with our loneliness, the only real cure seems to be the establishment of relationships that will provide the resources that we so badly need.

PERCEIVING OTHERS

You arrive in biology class on the first day of the term, and a bearded man wearing a rumpled suit stands up in front of the class and begins telling jokes about the sex life of planaria. On the cafeteria line at lunchtime you find yourself standing behind a petite woman with long dark hair who keeps looking around the room furtively as if she were a foreign spy. In the afternoon you go to the library and see someone whom you recognize from the newspaper as the star tackle on the football team and are surprised to discover that he is immersed in a book of Emily Dickinson's poetry. In each of these cases, you inevitably begin to ask yourself questions: What sort of a person is this? Why is this person behaving in these particular ways? Is this the sort of person I would like to get to know better? We are continually forming impressions of other people, both out of sheer curiosity and because such impressions have a large impact on the way we relate to others. This process of forming inferences about other people on the basis of what we observe about them is analogous to the way we come to perceive the qualities of the physical environment on the basis of the input to our sense organs; therefore, this process is called *person perception*.

Physical appearance

Even though we are warned not to judge a book by its cover, we can hardly avoid forming impressions of people on the basis of their physical appearance. A person's size, shape, color, and manner of dress often have a powerful impact on the inferences we make about the person's personality. We usually notice a person's physical characteristics before we have any other information about him or her. By the time we come to notice that a woman is "soft-spoken," for example, we may have already identified her as "obese" (McArthur, 1982). These initial impressions are especially important because they establish the context in which any other information about the person will be interpreted.

The impressions that we form on the basis of a person's physical characteristics often reflect the operation of stereotypes, similar to the gender stereotypes discussed in Chapter 16 and the racial stereotypes discussed in the Psychological Issue following Chapter 15. We mentally place a person in the category of those who have a particular physical characteristic, and we then infer that the person resembles other members of that category in other respects as well (McArthur, 1982). Redheads may be assumed to be hot-tempered, people who wear glasses to be studious, fat people to be jolly. Diane Berry and Leslie McArthur (1985) recently studied the stereotype attached to having a "baby face," with such features as large, round eyes and a small chin. Because these characteristics are associated with babies, they give rise to a set of impressions that are unconsciously applied when judging adults as well: men with baby faces were rated as being unusually warm, kind, and naive. We also have preconceived notions about what physically attractive and unattractive people are apt to be like (see Box 1). Whether or not these stereotypes have any basis in reality, they often serve to organize our initial impressions of people.

Reputations

We sometimes begin to form impressions of people even before we meet them. This is because people are likely to be preceded by their reputations. Students learn what to expect from their professor by talking to students who took the same course the previous year. And before going out on a blind date, we are usually given a good deal of information about what our date will be like. In each case, the person's reputation is likely to have an impact on the way she is later perceived.

In a famous experiment, Harold

We often make inferences about people's personalities from their appearance. For example, people who wear glasses may be assumed to be studious or intellectual.

BOX 1

IS BEAUTY BEST?

We are all taught that "beauty is skin deep," that a person's character and behavior are what really count. It remains clear, however, that people's physical attractiveness greatly influences the way they are perceived by others. For example, Karen Dion, Ellen Berscheid, and Elaine Hatfield (1972) asked subjects to provide their impressions of male and female students on the basis of photographs. The researchers found that the better-looking students were rated as more sensitive, kind, interesting, poised, and sociable than the less attractive students. The subjects also believed that the better-looking people had a greater chance of achieving success in their careers, becoming good husbands or wives, and finding happiness in their lives.

Dion and her colleagues concluded that there is a stereotype of beautiful people that extends to characteristics that lie beneath the surface. This stereotype can even affect our judgments of children. Margaret Clifford and Elaine Hatfield (1973) found that fifth-grade teachers expected attractive children to be more intelligent than unattractive children, and they predicted that the attractive children would achieve a higher level of education.

Beautiful people are favored in other ways, as well. Physically attractive people are likely to be given an edge over less attractive people in many domains in which beauty is supposed to be irrelevant, such as getting jobs (Dipboye, Fromkin, and Wiback, 1975), getting lighter sentences in criminal trials (Efran, 1974), and winning national elections (Efran and Patterson, 1974). In all of these respects, good looks seem to be just as much an advantage for men as they are for women. Perhaps because of the advantages they receive, physically attractive people have also been found to be more self-confident, to speak more fluently, and to be more persuasive, on the average, than less attractive people (Chaiken, 1979). And perhaps because of the harsh treatment they receive from others, unattractive people seem to be at greater risk of

When one of Robert Redford's movies is praised, he may wonder whether it's because of his acting or his looks. Woody Allen doesn't have this problem.

developing mental illness (O'Grady, 1982).

Beauty isn't always an advantage, however. Strikingly beautiful people may be seen as vain and egotistical (Dermer and Thiel, 1975), and they are sometimes more likely to be rejected—perhaps because of jealousy—

by peers of their own sex (Krebs and Adinolfi, 1975).

Another problem with being strikingly attractive is that it sometimes makes it harder for a person to know whether she is getting favored treatment because of her accomplishments or because of her looks. One study found that highly attractive men and women were less likely than unattractive people to accept at face value the praise they received for an essay they had written (Major et al., 1984).

For all of the advantages that beauty may bring, it should be borne in mind that once people become known by others, they are judged by a much larger set of characteristics than their appearance. In addition, beauty remains to a large extent "in the eye of the beholder," with different people varying in their physical preferences. We often perceive people whom we love as being beautiful, regardless of what anyone else may think.

Kelley (1950) demonstrated how a person's reputation can affect the way he is perceived. Kelley's students were told that their class would be taken over by a new instructor, whom they would be asked to evaluate at the end of the period. Before the instructor arrived, the students were given a brief description of him to read. Half of the students were told that the instructor was a 26-year-old graduate student who was considered "a rather warm person, industrious, critical, practical, and determined." The other half of the students received precisely the same information, except that the adjective "warm" was replaced with "cold." This difference of a single word proved to have a large impact on the students' reactions to the instructor. After the instructor had led the class in a 20-minute discussion, the students who had been told that he was "warm" rated him as more consider-ate, sociable, good-natured, and hu-morous than did the students who had been told that he was "cold." The instructor's reputation also affected students' willingness to interact with him: 56 percent of the "warm" sub-jects took part in the class discussion, compared to only 32 percent of the "cold" subjects.

It seems that people's reputations, just like stereotypes based on physi-cal appearance or group membership, provide a context within which we interpret their behavior. For example, if a woman is told in advance that her blind date is extremely witty, she will be primed to categorize his remarks as witty ones. Such expectations also influence the other person to behave in a way that actually lives up to the expectation. When others treat us as if they expect us to be witty or charm-ing or hostile, we are more likely to behave in just the way that they ex-pect (Darley and Fazio, 1980).

"HI, I'M HOWARD—OR MAKE THAT HOWIE"

James E. Carter, Jr., the thirty-ninth Presi-dent of the United States, insisted on being referred to as Jimmy. On the other hand, Major Charles Emerson Winchester, III, on the TV series M*A*S*H, made it clear that he was never to be called anything so common as "Charlie." The first names that we choose to go by can influence the im-pressions that others form of us. In one study, students read descriptions of other people who went either by their formal first names (such as "Lawrence" or "Patri-cia") or by more familiar first names (such as "Larry" or "Patty"). When they went by their formal names, the same people were rated as more cultured, more conscien-tious, and less outgoing than when they went by familiar names (Leirer, Hamilton, and Carpenter, 1982).

People who listen to a celebrated come-dian like Richard Pryor will often burst out laughing at just about anything he says. The comedian's reputation for being up-roariously funny affects the way he is per-ceived.

Attribution processes

In forming impressions of people, a primary goal is to make inferences about a person's underlying traits or dispositions on the basis of his observable actions. Such inferences are important because they allow us to predict how the person is likely to behave in the future. This inference process is not always an easy one, however. Suppose that you observe a person donating blood as part of the annual Red Cross drive. Do you infer that she is an unusually altruistic person who decided to give blood because of her commitment to helping others? And, as a result, can you expect her to behave altruistically in the future? Perhaps. But what if you also knew that intense pressure had been put on all of the residents of her dormitory to give blood, and that the names of all those who refused to do so were to be posted publicly? In that case, it would be more difficult to infer anything about the woman's altruism from her behavior. Instead, her behavior might simply reflect conformity to group pressure. We are constantly confronted with dilemmas of this sort as we form impressions of people. In particular, we must try to determine whether a person's behavior reflects an underlying disposition

of that person—something about her enduring personality—or whether it is primarily a consequence of the situation in which the person was placed. The ways in which we try to sort out the causes of people's behavior are called *attribution processes*.

In recent years, attribution processes have been the topic of a large outpouring of research (Harvey and Weary, 1984). One of the central conclusions of this research is that people have a tendency to focus on the dispositional causes rather than on the situational causes of other people's behavior (Watson, 1982). For example, when students see a film of one of the subjects in Milgram's obedience experiment (Chapter 15) repeatedly administering shocks to the "learner," they often assume that the subject is an unusually sadistic person. In attributing this person's behavior to his distinctive personality trait (his "sadism"), the students underestimate the pressures that cause *most* people in this situation to behave in quite the same way. Even when we *know* that there are strong situational pressures affecting a person's behavior, we are still likely to emphasize the role of personal dispositions. In one study (Jones and Harris, 1967), students read statements that they were told had been written

Why is this woman giving blood? Is she an unusually altruistic person, or is she conforming to social pressure? The ways in which we try to sort out the causes of people's behavior are called attribution processes.

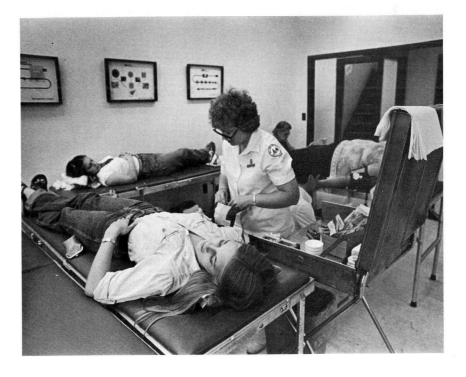

by a college debater who had to argue in favor of an assigned position. Even though the students knew that the debater had no choice in deciding which position to argue, they still tended to conclude that he privately supported the position that he was arguing for.

One of the reasons for this tendency to overestimate the role of personal dispositions is that the behaviors themselves, such as the debater's speech, tend to grab more of our attention than do the contexts of the behaviors, such as the fact that the debater was assigned his position. As a result, the impact of the context is slighted in our attributions. In addition, we typically observe people's behavior in only a limited range of situations. We may observe an army sergeant barking at his men and conclude that he is an unusually nasty person. If we had the chance to observe the sergeant at home, playing gently with his children, we would be more likely to appreciate the impact of situational constraints on his behavior.

In forming impressions of people, finally, we rely not only on their overt actions and statements but also on subtler nonverbal clues, as discussed in Box 2.

LIKING OTHERS

Liking, perhaps even more than love, is what makes the world go round. Our patterns of liking and disliking determine in large measure which people we will spend time with and which people we will avoid. Psychologists have explored many factors that lead us to like and become friends with certain other people. In this section we will explore two such factors: proximity and similarity. In both cases, liking can be explained by a basic economic principle: We like people who can provide us with the greatest possible rewards at the least possible cost. Of course, these rewards and costs are not usually financial ones. Rather, they are the social rewards that we gain from interacting with particular others and the social costs of interactions that are difficult or unpleasant.

The nearness of you

If you live in San Diego and I live in Boston, it is not very likely that we will become fast friends or even get to meet each other. But even at much closer range, the physical *proximity* of any two people has a direct impact

The closer people live to each other, the more likely they are to be friends.

CHAPTER SEVENTEEN: SOCIAL RELATIONSHIPS

BOX 2

READING NONVERBAL CLUES

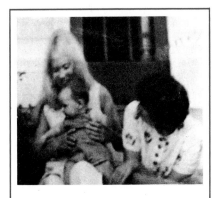

SCENE 1
Which one of these two women is the mother of the baby?
a. The woman on the left.
b. The woman on the right.
c. Neither woman.

SCENE 2
Are these two people:
a. Friends who have known each other for at least six months?
b. Acquaintances who have had several conversations?

In forming impressions of people—what they are like, what they are feeling, and what their behavior really means—we must take into account not only their overt actions and statements but also subtler nonverbal messages.

Take the case of sarcasm. If someone says to us, "That's wonderful!" how do we decide whether the remark is sincere or sarcastic? As Dane Archer (1979) points out, there is a specific nonverbal "script" for sarcasm, just as there is a script for other messages. When North Americans perform the sarcasm script, they usually employ one or more nonverbal devices, such as raising both eyebrows in an exaggerated way, saying the sentence very slowly, or changing the tone of voice and placing unusual emphasis on the word "wonderful."

All of us learn to read nonverbal messages such as these. But some people seem to be better readers of nonverbal clues than others. To assess people's ability in this domain, Archer and Robin Akert (1977) developed a measure called the Social Interpretation Task (SIT), in which subjects are presented with videotaped scenes of people interacting and then asked to make certain inferences about the actors. Two examples of these situations are presented on the left.

What were your answers? Although the still photos provide much less information than the 30-second videotaped scenes that Archer and Akert used, they still provide an opportunity to exercise our nonverbal reading abilities. Interested in the correct answers? In Scene 1, the woman on the right is the mother of the baby. In Scene 2, the two people are strangers. After watching the entire videotape, 64 percent of the subjects Archer and Akert studied got the right answer for Scene 1, and 62 percent were correct for Scene 2.

In many cases the videotape provides types of information that words could not. In Scene 1, for example, one videotape viewer explained that the woman on the left was holding the baby gingerly, "as if he were made of porcelain." The viewer correctly interpreted this as indicating unfamiliarity with the baby. Another viewer correctly concluded that the people in Scene 2 were strangers because "there was no eye contact on the part of the woman, while the man has an appraising gaze, watching her and the impression he's making." These clues suggested that while the two people were trying to hold a relaxed conversation, they were not succeeding.

Researchers have found that on the whole, women are better at reading nonverbal clues than men are (Hall, 1978). In addition, parents of small children have been found to be better readers of nonverbal clues than people without small children, perhaps because of the practice they get in reading the unspoken messages of their prelinguistic children (Rosenthal et al., 1979). Archer (1980) also believes that we can all train ourselves to be better readers of nonverbal clues by recognizing their importance and consciously paying greater attention to them.

on their likelihood of becoming friends. College students assigned to be roommates become friends far more often than one would expect simply on the basis of their other characteristics (Newcomb, 1961). And one study in a college dormitory found a striking tendency for students to like the person next door more than the person two doors away, to like that person more than the person three doors away, and so on (Priest and Sawyer, 1967).

To be sure, physical proximity doesn't *always* foster liking. Close and frequent contact can also breed hostility. It is common enough for people who are assigned to be roommates to end the year, if they stick it out for that long, as mortal enemies. Nevertheless, researchers have found that frequent contact more often leads to liking than to disliking. Interaction with all sorts of people is likely to bring us certain social rewards, such as the opportunity to engage in joint activities or to compare our reactions and experiences. But with a roommate or someone else who lives close by, we can obtain these rewards without having to go far out of our way. Thus, physical proximity is

likely to bring us rewards at low cost. And this interpersonal "profit" is translated into liking. It may sound crass, but that is the way liking often works—we like those who can bring us the biggest profit on the "interpersonal marketplace" (Rubin, 1973).

The same principle of proximity also applies to love and marriage. Studies by sociologists have documented that the closer a man and a woman live within a city, the more likely they are to marry one another (Katz and Hill, 1958). The tendency to be attracted to people who are close at hand makes perfect sense in terms of the profit motive of the interpersonal marketplace. If a suitable mate lives next door, there is no need for a man in search of a partner to scour the entire block. If she lives in the neighborhood, there is no need for him to spend time and money on the crosstown bus.

Birds of a feather

Once we have had an opportunity to meet another person, the single factor that plays the largest role in determining whether we will like each other is how *similar* we are. The prin-

Similarity in age, background, and interests are important foundations of friendship.

ciple that "Birds of a feather flock together" is not a new discovery of social psychologists. They were beaten to the punch by Aristotle many centuries ago:

And they are friends who have come to regard the same things as good and the same things as evil, they who are friends of the same people, and they who are enemies of the same people. . . . We like those who resemble us, and who are engaged in the same pursuits.

As Aristotle's statement suggests, we tend to choose friends who are similar to us in many different respects, including age, occupational status, educational level, and political preferences (Fischer, 1982). Similarities are important in our choice of husbands and wives, as well. Hundreds of statistical studies have found husbands and wives to be much more similar to each other than one would expect by chance, on characteristics ranging from height to intelligence (Rubin, 1973).

The most critical similarities, however, are similarities of people's beliefs and attitudes. We already had a glimpse of the link between attitude similarity and liking in Chapter 15, when we discussed the social foundations of attitudes. In his study at Bennington College, Theodore Newcomb found that many students adopted a liberal set of attitudes in order to gain the liking and acceptance of their classmates. In a later study, Newcomb provided a more direct demonstration of the influence of attitude similarity on liking. Newcomb (1961) rented a boarding house at the University of Michigan and provided one term's free room and board to students transferring to the university in exchange for their participation in his study of friendship formation. As the term progressed, Newcomb discovered that friendship patterns among the students were determined primarily by similarities of attitudes and values. For example, one group of friends consisted of five men who were all enrolled in the liberal arts college and who had liberal political views and strong intellectual and artistic interests. Another clique consisted of three veterans, all in the college of engineering, politically conservative, and with interests that were more "practical" than "theoretical."

Why does similarity of attitudes have such a large impact on our likes and dislikes? Psychologists have suggested that it is rewarding to be agreed with for several reasons (Rubin, 1973):

• Agreement may provide a basis for engaging in joint activities, whether it be attending a prayer meeting or a rock concert.

• A person who agrees with you helps increase your confidence in your own opinion—and this, in turn, will bolster your self-esteem.

• Most people are vain enough to believe that anyone who shares their views must be a sensible and praiseworthy individual, while anyone who does not must have his head on backward.

• People who agree about things that matter to them generally find it easier to communicate with each other.

• We often assume that people whose attitudes are similar to ours will like *us*—and, therefore, we tend to like them in turn.

Yes, there are exceptions to the "birds of a feather" principle. We are sometimes attracted to people who are quite different from ourselves, especially if those people provide a fresh perspective that we would like to learn more about. Robert White provides an example of such a "friendship of opposites" between two teenage boys:

Ben, whose school experience had been so unstimulating that he never read a book beyond those assigned, discovered in Jamie a lively spirit of intellectual inquiry and an exciting knowledge of politics and history. Here was a whole world to which his friend opened the door and provided guidance. Jamie discovered in Ben a world previously closed to him, that of confident interaction with other people. Each admired the other, each copied the other, each used the other for practice. (White, 1976, page 337)

Ben and Jamie became friends not because they were merely different from each other but because they

WHAT IS A "FRIEND"?

Friendship is portrayed in song and story as a relationship of great intimacy and loyalty. But in fact the term "friend" seems to be applied rather loosely in America. In a survey of 1050 adults in Northern California, the respondents applied the term "friend" to fully five-sixths of the people they associated with who were not relatives. Many more people were called "friends" than were described as "close" (Fischer, 1982). Rather than denoting any special closeness, "friend" often seems to be a catchall category for a wide range of people whom we come in contact with. "People brush up against one another, on the job or at leisure," notes Harry Stein (1980), "and bang! they identify one another as friends."

were in certain respects *complementary*—each could supply certain qualities that the other was lacking. The close working partnership and intimate friendship between two comic actors, Dan Aykroyd and the late John Belushi, was also a complementary one. Belushi was a hard-to-control, undisciplined person whom Aykroyd idolized, while Aykroyd provided a steadiness and protectiveness that Belushi needed. "Aykroyd was 'nice,' mild, and internal; Belushi was 'mean,' wild, and external," writes David Michaelis (1983). "Aykroyd softened Belushi's hardness and Belushi brought a polish to Aykroyd's rough edges."

Even in such cases of complementarity, however, there are almost always central similarities between close friends. Belushi and Aykroyd, for example, were bonded by their shared passion for a certain outrageous brand of comedy and adventurous style of life. Diversity is valuable and enriching, and under certain conditions people actively seek it. But we also need to recognize that people with fundamentally different approaches to life are unlikely to become fast friends.

LOVING OTHERS

"Love is really ambiguous," mused one student. "I have a feeling for her; I don't know what to call it. It's a warm feeling—an appreciation of her, an understanding of her . . . If you want to call it love, sure."

Many of us, like this student, are uncertain about just how to define "love." The phenomena of love are not easy to pin down scientifically. Indeed, as noted in Box 3, some people doubt that love is a proper topic for scientific research. In the past 15 years, however, psychologists—myself included—have been making concerted efforts to study love. In Chapter 10 (Box 4), we discussed one approach to love, in the context of Stanley Schachter's labeling theory of emotion. From this perspective, love can be viewed as a label that people learn to place on their own physiological arousal. Most of the time, however, love does not involve intense physical reactions. Instead, love can be viewed as a particular sort of attitude that one person has toward another person.

Dan Aykroyd and John Belushi, shown here in the movie "The Blues Brothers," had a close personal friendship. Their friendship was cemented both by their shared passion for an outrageous brand of comedy and by their complementary personalities. Belushi had a wild streak that Aykroyd admired, and Aykroyd provided a steadiness that Belushi needed.

CHAPTER SEVENTEEN: SOCIAL RELATIONSHIPS

BOX 3

SHOULD WE STUDY LOVE?

As psychologists began to investigate love, shouts of criticism were being voiced by those who believed that love is not a proper object of study. Perhaps the most vocal of these critics has been United States Senator William Proxmire of Wisconsin. In his role as chairman of the Senate committee that oversees appropriations to the National Science Foundation, Proxmire has habitually kept a sharp eye out for federally funded projects that seem impractical or frivolous. When he discovered in 1975 that the National Science Foundation had awarded a grant to a social psychologist to study aspects of romantic love, Proxmire was enraged. He fired off a press release in which he called the project "the biggest waste of the taxpayer's money for the month of March." He went on to say that "I believe that 200 million Americans want to leave some things in life a mystery, and right at the top of the things we don't want to know about is why a man falls in love with a woman and vice versa."

Soon afterward Proxmire expanded

Senator William Proxmire believes that love should be left a mystery.

his attack to include other programs of research on social relationships. "I think it is time the National Science Foundation put a stop to the Federal version of 'The Love Machine,'" he declared, "and rearrange its research priorities to address our scientific, not our erotic curiosity."

Many other people agree wholeheartedly with Senator Proxmire's indictment of research on love. One psychologist went so far as to declare that "The scientist in even attempting to interject love into a laboratory situation is by the very nature of the proposition dehumanizing the state we call love" (Karmel, 1970). Many newspaper columnists and editorialists jumped on Proxmire's bandwagon, echoing his conclusion that trying to understand love is a ridiculous and money-wasting enterprise.

But many others strongly disagree with Proxmire's point of view. I am among them. Social relationships are extremely complicated phenomena, and psychologists have no illusions that they will ever unlock all of love's mysteries. But social relationships are also the source of great confusion and distress for many people. For example, divorce rates in America have been skyrocketing, leaving a tremendous amount of human suffering in their wake. If research of the sort that is reported in this chapter can make even a small contribution to people's understanding of their relationships with others, then the relatively small amount of money expended for such research will be more than justified.

You will have to draw your own conclusion about this controversy. But I personally liked a response to Senator Proxmire that was offered by *New York Times* columnist James Reston (1975): "If the sociologists and psychologists can get even a suggestion of the answer to our patterns of romantic love, marriage, disillusion, divorce—and the children left behind—it could be the best investment of Federal money since Mr. Jefferson made the Louisiana Purchase."

Measuring love

Through the course of history love has been defined in countless ways, as everything from "a spirit all compact of fire" (by Shakespeare) to "a state of perceptual anesthesia" (by H. L. Mencken) to "not ever having to say you're sorry" (by Erich Segal). Not wishing to be outdone by these people of letters, I made an initial attempt to define and measure this attitude (Rubin, 1970; 1973). On the basis of a questionnaire administered to several hundred dating couples at the University of Michigan, I developed an attitude measure that I called a love scale. On this scale, respondents are asked to indicate how much they agree or disagree with a series of statements about their feelings toward another person, usually their boyfriend or girlfriend (see Table 17.1). As defined by my scale, love consists of three components: *attachment*, *caring*, and *intimacy*.

• *Attachment* refers to a person's need for the physical presence and emotional support of the other person. It corresponds to the emotional attachment discussed by Robert Weiss, described earlier in this chapter.

• *Caring* refers to a person's feelings of concern and responsibility for another person. Caring corre-sponds to Erich Fromm's (1956) definition of love as "the active concern for the life and growth of that which we love."

• *Intimacy* refers to a person's desire for close and confidential communication with another person. When we love someone, we want to share certain of our thoughts and feelings with that person more fully than with anyone else.

I came to view love as an attitude held by one person toward another that includes all three of these components. Skeptics may point out that a paper-and-pencil love scale does not really measure how much people love each other but simply how much they *say* they love each other. But I also obtained behavioral evidence for the love scale's validity. Consider the well-known folk wisdom that lovers spend a great deal of time staring into each other's eyes. After all, eye contact frequently seems central to intimate communication; one psychiatrist calls it "the core of interpersonal relatedness" (Grumet, 1983). In my study (Rubin, 1970) couples were observed through a one-way mirror in the psychological laboratory while they were waiting for an experiment to begin. These surreptitious observations confirmed that "strong lovers" (couples whose members received above-average scores on the love

---

TABLE 17.1

Sample Items From Rubin's Love Scale

[ATTACHMENT]

If I could never be with _____, I would feel miserable.

1	2	3	4	5	6	7	8	9
Not at all true; Disagree completely								Definitely true; Agree completely

[CARING]

One of my primary concerns is _____'s welfare.

1	2	3	4	5	6	7	8	9
Not at all true; Disagree completely								Definitely true; Agree completely

[INTIMACY]

I feel that I can confide in _____ about practically everything.

1	2	3	4	5	6	7	8	9
Not at all true; Disagree completely								Definitely true; Agree completely

According to the well-known folk wisdom, lovers spend a great deal of time gazing into each other's eyes.

scale) made significantly more eye contact than "weak lovers" (couples whose scores on the love scale were below average). Or, as the popular song has it, "I only have eyes for you."

At the same time that I developed a love scale, I developed a parallel liking scale, to help pinpoint the distinctions between these two sentiments. The items on the liking scale do not refer to attachment, caring, or intimacy but rather to having a favorable evaluation of the other person (for example, "Most people would react favorably to _____ after a brief acquaintance") and respect for her (for example, "I have great confidence in _____'s good judgment"). As one might expect, students' love scores were highly correlated with their estimates of the likelihood that they and their partner would get married. The correlation between liking scores and marriage estimates were much lower. This pattern of correlations is perhaps not too surprising. After all, the link between love and marriage in our society is taken almost as a matter of faith, while the link between liking and marriage is too often a well-kept secret.

The love scale can be applied to friendships, as well as to romantic or sexual relationships. I found that when students filled out the love scale in terms of their feelings toward their closest same-sex friends, women reported that they loved their friends more than men did. There were no such differences in liking scores. This result makes sense in terms of what we know about differences between the two sexes. As noted in Chapter 16, women's friendships tend to be more intimate than men's, involving more spontaneous joint activities and more exchanging of confidences (Caldwell and Peplau, 1982). Men may often channel their love into a single romantic or sexual relationship, while women may be more able to experience attachment, caring, and intimacy in other relationships, as well.

Love and sex

Within opposite-sex, romantic relationships, what are the links between love and sex? One view, suggested by Sigmund Freud (1905), is that sex can diminish love. Love, for Freud, was "aim-inhibited sex"—that is, a channeling of sexual impulses into the less overt form of tender and affectionate feelings. As a result, when lovers express their sexual needs directly, their love for each other is likely to become less intense. Most other observers would take exception to this idea, however, maintaining that sexual communication between two people can heighten their love for each other.

Sexual attraction and emotional intimacy sometimes go hand in hand.

In one experiment, Marshall Dermer and Thomas Pyszczynski (1978) found that sexual arousal tended to increase male college students' love for their girlfriends. These men were aroused sexually by reading an explicit account of the sexual behaviors and fantasies of a college woman. Afterward, the men were asked to complete my love and liking scales in terms of their feelings toward their own girlfriends. The love scores—but not the liking scores—of these men increased. Although the love scale itself does not include items referring to sexual attraction, it seems that sexual feelings can lead to increases in the feelings of attachment, caring, and intimacy that are measured by the love scale.

In practice, the link between love and sex is likely to depend in large measure on the sexual values of the people involved. Whereas many men and women in dating couples believe that their sexual relationship helps to strengthen their love and commitment, many others believe that their love will remain just as strong or stronger without sex (see Box 4). In a study of college student dating couples, Anne Peplau, Charles Hill, and I (1977) found that whether or not a couple had sexual intercourse was not related to the future of their relationship. Couples who had had intercourse were no more nor less likely to stay together over a two-year period than couples who had not had intercourse.

Love and commitment

In 1979 the singer Michelle Triola sued actor Lee Marvin for a share of the financial assets he had acquired during the six years they had been living together—a relationship he had broken off. During this highly publicized "palimony" court trial, Marvin was asked whether he had ever loved Triola "even a little bit." He hedged in his reply, noting that there are different kinds of love and that the love he once had for Triola was not the sort that involved long-term loyalty. Indeed, the real issue in this case was not one of love at all, but one of *commitment* (Rubin, 1979). And loving

someone is not the same thing as a commitment to remain in a relationship with that person.

Commitment is a pledging of oneself to continue a course of action over a period of time. If one is committed to the goal of halting the nuclear arms race, for example, one will steadfastly continue to work toward that goal. If one is committed to the continuation of a relationship, one will stick with that relationship, even in the face of obstacles. Commitment operates on both a public and a private level. On a public level, we often make commitments through public statements, actions, or rituals. Participating in a wedding ceremony is the prime example of a commitment to continue a couple's relationship. On a private level, we make commitments by coming to define ourselves in terms of particular lines of action. Thus, a person who is committed to halting the nuclear arms race will come to regard that cause as a central part of her identity. And a person who is committed to a relationship with another person will come to regard his participation in that relationship as an integral part of who he is.

Love and commitment do not quite go together like a horse and carriage. Whereas love refers to one's present feelings toward one's partner, commitment refers to a decision to continue the relationship into the future. A person may love a partner a great deal without having a major stake in the long-term survival of the relationship. Conversely, someone may remain loyal to a partner even after most of the love and affection have faded (Kelley, 1983).

In practice, however, love and commitment commonly coexist. The factors that attract people to each other are also the factors that are likely to keep them together. Because of this overlap, it is easy for people to confuse love and commitment. Thus, as Harold Kelley (1983) notes, Lee Marvin may once have loved Michelle Triola without feeling or making any commitment to her. But this distinction may not have been accurately communicated to Triola, who may have honestly believed that he was both in love with her and committed to her.

BOX 4

THREE COUPLES

Couples on today's college campuses show a wide range of orientations toward love and sex. In our study of 231 student dating couples, Anne Peplau, Charles Hill, and I (1977) identified three types of couples. For *sexually traditional couples,* love alone is not a sufficient justification for sexual intercourse—the more permanent commitment of marriage is a necessary prerequisite. For *sexually moderate couples,* sex is considered permissible if a man and woman love each other; in this view, sex is an expression of love and caring. For *sexually liberal couples,* sex is acceptable even without love; sex is considered an enjoyable activity to be valued for its own sake.

The following are examples of each of the three types of couples:

A SEXUALLY TRADITIONAL COUPLE:
PAUL AND PEGGY
Peggy believes that intercourse before marriage is wrong. She explained that "even if I were engaged, I wouldn't feel right about having sex." Many of Peggy's girlfriends are having sexual affairs, which Peggy accepts "for them." It's not right for Peggy, however, and she believes that Paul respects her views. For his part, Paul indicated that he would like to have intercourse with Peggy, but he added that intercourse "just isn't all that important for me." (Page 97)

A SEXUALLY MODERATE COUPLE:
TOM AND SANDY
Three weeks after their first date, Tom told Sandy that he loved her. She was in love, too, and their relationship grew quickly. In a few months they were spending weekends together at one of their dorms. They slept in the same bed but did not have intercourse. Although Tom was very attracted to Sandy, he was slow to initiate intercourse. "I didn't want to push it on her," he said. "I felt that we shouldn't have sex until our relationship reached a certain point. [Sex] is something I just can't imagine on a first date." Tom and Sandy first had intercourse with each other just before becoming engaged. For Tom, "Sex added another dimension to our relationship; it's a landmark of sorts." (Page 98)

A SEXUALLY LIBERAL COUPLE:
DIANE AND ALAN
About two weeks after they started dating, Alan asked if Diane would like to make love. She declined, saying she wasn't ready yet, but implying that she would be soon. Since they were alone in Alan's apartment, she jokingly suggested that he go "exhibit himself" across the room so she could get used to his body. They spent the weekend together, and by Sunday Diane felt ready for intercourse. Diane told us that she and Alan were not in love when they first had intercourse. Nonetheless, she enjoyed the sex and felt it was "part of our getting to know each other. It led to an obvious closeness." (Pages 98–99)

The central distinction between these three orientations concerns the links between sexual intimacy and emotional intimacy. For traditionalists, emotional intimacy develops in the context of limited sexual activity; sexual intercourse is tied not only to love but to a permanent commitment, as well. For moderates, emotional intimacy sets the pace for sexual intimacy. As feelings of closeness and love increase, greater sexual exploration is possible. For liberals, sexual intimacy and emotional intimacy need not be related. Sex can be enjoyed in its own right, or sexual intimacy can be a route to developing emotional intimacy.

As you may have noticed, in all three of the couples the man was the one who took the lead in increasing sexual intimacy, while the woman played a more passive or limit-setting role. In all types of couples—traditional, moderate, and liberal—aspects of the sexual double standard that we described in Chapter 16 live on.

LEAVING OTHERS

Love does not necessarily last forever. Although love often leads to long-term relationships or to marriage, in many other cases true love runs its course and dies. Friendships, too, sometimes last a lifetime, but other times fade away. In this section we will discuss some aspects of the ending of close relationships.

Responses to dissatisfaction

People may become dissatisfied with their close relationships for many reasons, ranging from simple boredom to major disagreements about life-styles. And people may respond to such dissatisfaction in many different ways. Caryl Rusbult and Isabella Zembrodt (1983) have identified four major categories of responses to dissatisfaction in couples' relationships, which they call *exit, voice, loyalty,* and *neglect:*

• *Exit.* Ending the relationship—for example, formally separating, moving out, or deciding to be "just friends."

• *Voice.* Actively trying to improve the situation—for example, discussing the problems openly or seeking the help of a counselor or therapist.

• *Loyalty.* Staying in the relationship, waiting and hoping that things will improve.

• *Neglect.* Passively allowing the relationship to deteriorate—for example, ignoring the problems or treating the partner badly.

Rusbult and her coworkers (1982) have found that the more satisfying a relationship has been in the past, the more likely the partners are to respond to dissatisfaction with "voice" or "loyalty," as opposed to "exit" or "neglect." Of course, the partners' initial responses to dissatisfaction are not necessarily their final responses. "Neglect," for example, seems likely to lead sooner or later to an "exit" of one or both partners. "Voice" and "loyalty" responses may sometimes succeed in maintaining the relationship but in other cases may give way to "neglect" or "exit."

Breaking up

In our study of student dating couples, my coworkers and I investigated some of the factors that lead people to take the "exit" route (Hill, Rubin, and Peplau, 1976). Over a two-year period, about half of the couples in our sample stayed together and the other half broke up. We found that the people who stayed together tended to be more similar to each other in age, intelligence, career plans, and physical attractiveness than the people who broke up. In addition, when people who had broken up were asked to explain why the relationship had ended, they frequently mentioned differences in interests, backgrounds, sexual attitudes, and ideas about marriage. It seems that similarities between people not only lead to attraction in the first place but also encourage the continuation of relationships. Partners who have serious differences or disagreements are likely to end up going their separate ways.

Our study also found that relationships were most likely to end if one of the partners was considerably more involved in the relationship than the other. Of the couples in which both members initially reported that they were equally involved in the relationship, only 23 percent broke up during the subsequent two-year period. But among those couples in which one partner was more involved than the other, 54 percent broke up. There seems to be an inherent lack of stability in relationships in which one partner is more invested than the other. In such a relationship, the more involved partner may feel overly dependent and exploited, while the less involved partner may feel restless and guilty. "Commitments must stay abreast for a love relationship to develop into a lasting mutual attachment," writes sociologist Peter Blau (1964). "Only when two lovers' affection for and commitment to one another expand at roughly the same pace do they tend mutually to support their love" (page 84).

The ending of a close relationship often leads to feelings of pain and distress, similar to the symptoms of loneliness discussed earlier. These feelings are likely to be most acute for the partner who was broken up with (assuming that the ending was not completely mutual), but they affect the partner who wanted to break up as well. There is also evidence that the more satisfying the relationship had been in the past, the longer it takes for the couple to break up and the more acute the partners' distress over the breakup (Lee, 1984).

But in spite of the pain involved, the ending of close relationships can teach us valuable lessons. By experiencing firsthand the difficulties of close relationships, we are likely to learn more about our own interpersonal needs, preferences, strengths, and weaknesses. These lessons can be of value to us as we enter new relationships. After the ending of her relationship with David, for example, Ruth told an interviewer, "I don't regret having the experience at all. But after being in the supportive role, *I* want a little support now. That's the main thing I look for" (Hill, Rubin, and Peplau, 1976, page 156). And after his breakup with Kathy, Joe indicated that he would exercise greater caution in future relationships. "If I fall in love again," he said, "it might be with the reservation that I'm going to keep awake this time" (page 155). Breakups are most valuable if they take place before marriage. For, as we will see in the Psychological Issue that follows, marital breakups are likely to be considerably more painful and stressful than breakups that take place before marriage. As an anonymous wise person once said, "The best divorce is the one you get before you get married."

SUMMARY

Needing others

• **1** People often seek the company of others because of the need for *social comparison*—the need to compare one's experiences and reactions with those of other people. This is especially true when people are afraid or uncertain.

• **2** According to Weiss, people have a need for two kinds of social relationships: *emotional attach-*ments to one other person, and *social ties* to a network of friends. When people lack either type of relationship they are likely to experience *loneliness*. Lack of emotional attachment brings the loneliness of *emotional isolation*, while lack of social ties produces the loneliness of *social isolation.*

Perceiving others

• **3** The way we form impressions of people is called *person perception.* Our perceptions of others are highly influenced by their physical appearance and by their reputations.

• **4** Studies have shown that physical attractiveness has a major impact on how we view people. Attractive people tend to be rated as more interesting, poised, and sociable, and to be given favored treatment by others.

• **5** A person's actions often lead us to form ideas about her underlying traits. The ways in which we try to infer the causes of people's behavior are called *attribution processes.* There is a pervasive tendency to overestimate the role of personal dispositions and to underestimate the role of situational constraints affecting people's behavior.

• **6** In forming impressions of people, we also try to interpret their nonverbal messages, such as facial expressions and tones of voice. On measures such as the Social Interpretation Task, women have been found to be better at reading nonverbal clues than men.

Liking others

• **7** The physical *proximity* of any two people has a direct impact on their likelihood of becoming friends. For example, studies have shown that people who live next door to each other are more likely to become friends than people who live two doors away.

• **8** A major factor in whether two people will become friends is their *similarity* to each other. Friends and married couples tend to be similar in age, occupational status, and educational level. However, the most important area of similarity is beliefs and attitudes—people who agree with us provide us with many kinds of rewards. In addition to being similar, close friends may be *complementary* in certain respects.

Loving others

• **9** How does one measure love? Zick Rubin's love scale defines love in terms of three components: *attachment*, *caring*, and *intimacy*. Some people believe, however, that love is not a proper object of scientific study.

• **10** The link between love and sex is likely to depend on the sexual values of the people involved. Some people believe that sexual intercourse is acceptable without love, some believe that love should precede sex, and some believe that the permanent commitment of marriage is a necessary prerequisite for sex.

• **11** Loving someone is not the same thing as a *commitment* to remain in a relationship with that person. However, love and commitment commonly occur together.

Leaving others

• **12** Love does not necessarily last forever. People may respond to dissatisfaction in a relationship in four main ways: exit, voice, loyalty, and neglect. Many factors can contribute to the ending of a relationship, in-cluding differences in interests, background, sexual attitudes, and ideas about marriage. Also, relationships are more likely to end if one partner is considerably more involved in the relationship than the other.

KEY TERMS

attachment
attribution processes
caring
commitment
complementary
emotional attachments
emotional isolation
interdependence
intimacy
loneliness
person perception
proximity
shyness
similarity
sociability
social comparison
social isolation
social relationship
social ties

MARRIAGE AND DIVORCE

My wife and I are survivors. We recently celebrated our fifteenth anniversary with a four-day vacation in Bermuda, where we were surrounded by honeymooners—most of them in their twenties—enjoying their blissful first days of marriage. If current projections hold true, about half of these marriages will eventually end in divorce—usually within 10 years (Glick, 1984).

Over the past 20 years, the divorce rate in America has more than doubled, with over a million divorces now taking place each year. Although there are signs that the divorce rate may finally have leveled off in the 1980s, it remains at a level that is among the highest in the world.

These statistics might lead us to believe that Americans are becoming disillusioned about marriage—that they are deciding that the burdens of married life outweigh the benefits it might bring. But the news that about five in ten marriages are destined to fail hasn't dissuaded young people from trying marriage out for themselves. Over 90 percent of Americans marry at least once, and this pattern is expected to continue into the 1990s (Masnick and Bane, 1980). What's more, about three-fourths of the women and five-sixths of the men who divorce eventually remarry. Even though these people decided that their first marriages were not very satisfactory, they still insist on coming back for more.

Indeed, we are in the midst of a marriage boom in America. The number of marriages has been increasing year after year, topping the 2.5 million mark in 1982. And 45 percent of these weddings involve at least one partner who has been married before.

The number of marriages in the United States has been increasing year after year, topping the 2.5 million mark in 1982.

What can account for these contradictions? Even though the usual sequence is marriage before divorce, let's look at these two phenomena in reverse order. Perhaps we can gain some insights into both the causes of the divorce boom and the undiminished popularity of marriage.

DIVORCE IN AMERICA

Why are so many American couples deciding to get divorced? Many different culprits have been identified, from the fading of traditional religious values to the failure of couples to give adequate consideration to their decision to marry. But of all the possible factors, two seem to have had the greatest impact.

First, there has been a gradual shift from the notion that marriage is forever, "for better or worse," to the notion that personal happiness and self-fulfillment are the most important goals for individuals. Second, the shift in values has been accompanied by changes in laws that make it much easier than it used to be to end a marriage. Since 1970, forty-nine of the fifty states have instituted "no-fault" divorce laws that declare that if a husband and wife agree to divorce it is essentially their own business.

Taken together, these ideological and legal changes have drastically changed the balance of forces acting on a couple with a troubled relationship. In the past, many couples would stay together even when their relationship was no longer satisfying. In some cases, these couples' marital bonds seemed more like the walls of a prison, but staying together was still the respectable thing to do. There are still many such unsatisfactory marriages in America. But it is no longer as clear as it used to be that remaining in such a marriage is the "right" thing. Today the "success" of a marriage is less likely to be judged by how long it lasts and more likely to be judged by the extent to which it brings happiness and personal fulfillment (Levinger, 1979).

Still another factor contributing to the increase in divorce is the

"No-fault" divorce laws make the legal aspect of ending a marriage much easier than it used to be.

entry of more women into the workforce (see the Psychological Issue following Chapter 16). When wives, as well as husbands, are employed, the wife is less dependent on the marriage for her economic survival, and divorce becomes more likely (Levinger, 1979). Indeed, the most highly educated women—those with graduate and professional degrees—have been especially likely to divorce (Houseknecht, Vaughan, and Macke, 1984). In the future, however, this state of affairs may well change. Among couples married in the 1960s, a woman's decision to enter a professional career may have introduced unexpected new strains on the marriage. In the 1980s, on the other hand, such career decisions are more likely to be made before marriage and couples may have clearer expectations ahead of time.

UNTYING THE MARITAL KNOT

The divorce boom and the rising ethic of self-realization might suggest that ending a marriage is an easy matter. It might even suggest to some young people that there's no reason not to marry someone you're drawn to at the moment; after all, if it doesn't work, you can always get a divorce. This is an interesting theory, but nothing could be further from the truth. No matter how good or bad a marriage has been, ending it is almost always an extremely painful, wrenching experience.

Robert Weiss (1975) has conducted an extensive study of people in the process of separation or divorce. He concludes, "Most separations . . . come about only after a long and anguished process of mutual alienation from which both partners emerge bruised, their morale depleted, their self-esteem low, their ability to function damaged by the varied assaults of the failing marriage" (page 28).

Once a man and woman have divorced, their problems are by no means over. Instead, the experience of being on one's own after being married is often a terrifying one. One woman reported, "When the idea occurred to me that I could live without Dave and be happier, my immediate next feeling was just gut fear. It's really hard to explain. It was just terror" (Weiss, 1979, page 203).

Many divorcing couples are surprised to discover that even though they found life with their partner to be intolerable, after the separation they remain strongly attached to the partner:

Here I was, three days with someone of the opposite sex, trying to start rebuilding, and I just got overwhelmed with panic and being three thousand miles from Laura. And these waves built up until I was just white. It is an unbearable feeling. (Weiss, 1979, page 203)

Moreover, divorce is near the

Ending a marriage is almost always a painful experience.

"Most divorces come about only after a long and anguished process of mutual alienation."

top of the list of events that can cause stress in people's lives (see Chapter 12). Reflecting the impact of such stress, many studies have suggested that divorce increases people's susceptibility to both psychological and physical disorders (Bloom, White, and Asher, 1978). And as we saw in Chapter 8, Box 3, the divorce of one's parents is invariably a highly stressful event for children.

Janet Kohen and her coworkers at the Women's Research Center of Boston (1979) believe that in some cases divorce can be the chance for a new and better life for women. "Despite the drawbacks," they write, "their experiences of heading a family [without a husband] are often better for these women than were their marriages" (page 234).

Nevertheless, the problems should not be underestimated. Even though divorce may sometimes be liberating for women—and for men as well—there are few divorces that are not filled with tremendous pain and distress.

COMING BACK FOR MORE

There are some people who have tried marriage, decided that they didn't like it, and resolved to remain single in the future. This was true of most of the sample of thirty divorced women interviewed by Kohen and her co-workers (1979). But these women are in the minority. As noted earlier, the large majority of the women and men who divorce eventually remarry. These people are not disillusioned with marriage as an institution. Their feeling seems to be that marriage itself is a good thing, even though their own first marriage was unsuccessful.

Robert Weiss (1975) stresses that the process of getting back into circulation and forming new attachments is a difficult one. He finds that it usually takes a divorced person between two and four years to recover fully from the distress produced by the breakup. During this period, the divorced person may need to rely heavily on networks of friends, organizations like Parents Without Partners, or professional counselors for support and advice. But eventually most divorced people find satisfactory new attachments. Human beings learn from experience, and we are not doomed to make the same mistakes twice.

One divorced woman whom Weiss interviewed summed it up as follows:

I have a friendship with this guy that has gone on for a long period of time. Every once in a while we will have a conversation and I will

expect certain responses, because that is what I am conditioned to. And his reactions are entirely different from my husband's. He's a different person, that's all. So with one partner you can do everything and say everything wrong, but with another partner it's fine. So you shouldn't give up hope because you batted out once. (Page 308)

WHY MARRY?

The desire of most divorced people to try marriage again brings us back to one of the questions we started with: Why do such a large majority of people choose to marry at all? Part of the answer is that society has always put strong pressures on women and men to marry, as the only "appropriate" or "normal" thing to do. In colonial America, older single women were ridiculed as "old maids" and treated as failures in life. Bachelors were placed in practically the same category as criminals; in some colonies bachelors were assigned to live with "licensed" families and had to pay special taxes. This treatment of unmarried individuals provided an inducement for them to marry (Scanzoni and Scanzoni, 1976).

Such negative attitudes, albeit in somewhat more subtle form, have persisted until the present day. Boys and girls learn from their parents and from the mass media that they are expected to marry and to "live happily ever after." Even if many marriages don't achieve the latter goal, the injunction to marry still comes through loud and clear.

The notion that marriage is the ideal life-style for everyone has recently begun to be questioned. The women's movement has supported the idea that staying single can be more fulfilling than marriage for many women. As Letha and John Scanzoni (1976) note, there are enough examples of successful single women in business, education, government, the professions, and the arts to invalidate old notions about a woman's being a failure if

Forty-five percent of the marriages in America today involve at least one partner who has been married before.

she doesn't marry. In fact, there is evidence that single women tend to have higher levels of intelligence, education, and occupational status than married women (Spreitzer and Riley, 1974). It is no longer a stigma to be over 30 and unmarried in America.

In recent years, moreover, there has been a clear trend toward getting married at a later age. In 1960, for example, 28 percent of women between 20 and 24 were still single; by 1983 the proportion had increased to 56 percent, and it is still on the rise (Norton, 1983). Going along with this trend toward later marriage is the sharply increasing number of unmarried couples who are living together, in many cases as part of the process of deciding whether or not to marry.

But the greater tolerance for remaining single has not diminished most Americans' desire to marry. In a recent national survey of women (Virginia Slims Poll, 1980), 94 percent said they favored marriage as a way of life, and recent surveys have shown similar high rates of endorsement by men.

Many reasons can be suggested for the continuing appeal of mar-

riage—love, the desire for security, the desire for sex on a regular basis, the desire to have children, the desire to "make it legal," pressure from parents, and the force of tradition. One student in the study of dating couples conducted by my coworkers and me listed three reasons for deciding to get married:

- *1* I loved her and wanted to spend the rest of my life with her.
- *2* I felt lonesome when not seeing her for long periods.
- *3* I wanted to take her out of circulation.

Another student explained her decision in the following terms:
Our parents never knew we were living together. One reason for marrying was to make a public statement that we were committed to each other. It would make things such as bank account, insurance and renting an apartment easier. We already felt married so there didn't seem to be any reason not to. Being married was a state I had always unquestionably known I would enter.

Perhaps most important, by committing men and women to one another, marriage serves to keep people together even in the face of

temporary fluctuations in their feelings of attraction for one another. Marriage makes it more likely that a relationship will withstand the ups and downs that are an inevitable part of any close relationship. As such, marriage can play a valuable stabilizing role in satisfying people's needs for close interpersonal relationships (Levinger, 1979).

In addition, the fact that marriage has existed in every human society and in every era suggests that the institution of marriage is useful for society as a whole. As sociologist John Finley Scott (1966) writes, marriage "combines the functions of reproduction, child care, sexual gratification, and economic cooperation with an overall efficiency that no alternate arrangement has been able to match."

And so we can expect Americans to keep getting married, even though they may be in somewhat less of a rush to do so than in previous generations. And if at first they don't succeed, they'll try, try again.

SUMMARY

- *1* The American divorce rate is at an all-time high and 50 percent of current marriages appear destined to end in divorce. However, about 80 percent of people who divorce eventually remarry, and the popularity of marriage itself does not seem to have diminished.
- *2* The current high rate of divorce is the result of many factors, including a major change in attitudes toward marriage and in divorce laws making it easier to dissolve marriages.
- *3* Despite the "ease" of divorce today, it is still a highly traumatic experience.
- *4* Even though staying single has become an increasingly legitimate life-style, the large majority of men and women *do* want to marry. Apparently marriage fulfills both strong emotional needs and the needs of society.

PSYCHOLOGY AND NUMBERS

A basic understanding of statistics is essential to being a well-informed member of society.

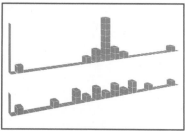

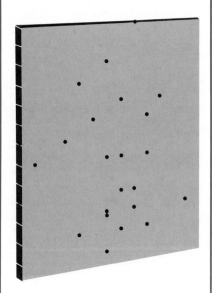

DESCRIPTIVE STATISTICS

Descriptive statistics are numbers used to describe sets of observations or scores.

SAMPLING AND STATISTICAL SIGNIFICANCE

Tests of statistical significance help us to determine whether observed differences between groups are simply a matter of chance.

CORRELATION COEFFICIENTS

Correlation coefficients describe the degree to which two sets of scores are related to one another.

You need to know something about statistics if you want to become a sophisticated consumer of the products of psychological research. Indeed, a basic understanding of statistics has become increasingly essential to being a well-informed member of modern society. Your daily newspaper is filled with statistics about food prices, crime rates, income distributions, marriage and divorce rates, and other matters that directly relate to your personal well-being. Every time you turn on the television you are bombarded by statistical claims about calories, miles per gallon, or pain relief, attesting to the superiority of one product over another. In this day and age, there is no escape from numbers.

Statistics are simply numbers that are used to describe and interpret facts or observations. Social scientists often use such numbers to communicate, because words can be too imprecise. Imagine doing research in which you had to report your findings using only such terms as "quite a lot," "not nearly as much," or "a whole bunch." It's hard to know whether "fast, fast, fast relief" is faster or slower than "immediate relief" or whether a "huge" crowd is bigger or smaller than a "tremendous" one. Such terms have no precise meaning.

Even though statistics are necessary tools for psychologists and other scientists, they have their pitfalls as well. Numbers can be used in confusing and misleading ways, especially by people who are trying to sell you something—whether a product, an idea, or a point of view. An advertiser's "Four out of five dentists recommend sugarless gum for their patients who chew gum" needs to be examined very carefully. It may also be the case that nine out of ten dentists would advise their patients not to chew gum at all. Similarly, a psychol-

ogist's statement that "There is a significant relationship between training in psychology and interpersonal sensitivity" (to use an example we introduced in Chapter 1) also needs to be closely scrutinized: What does it really mean for a relationship to be "significant"? How were each of the two variables measured? What group of subjects was used in computing this relationship? The importance of the psychologist's findings for you depends on the answer to questions like these.

In the next few pages we will take a brief tour of some of the statistical tools that are used by psychologists and other scientists to help describe and interpret their observations. First, we will discuss the basic statistics used to describe a single set of observations or scores. Then we will discuss the use of samples and the concept of statistical significance. Finally, we will discuss the use of correlation coefficients to describe the relationship between two sets of observations.

DESCRIPTIVE STATISTICS

Both scientists and nonscientists are often confronted with sets of numbers that represent a set of observations or scores. For example, we may have a set of numbers representing the IQ scores of each student in a school, or the annual incomes of each of the employees of a company, or the number of pounds lifted by each of fifty weight lifters. In order to make sense out of such sets of numbers, we must first be able to describe these *raw data* clearly and efficiently. For purposes of illustration, we can make up some numbers to use as our raw data. To make sure that our numbers represent something close to your heart and important to your survival, let's take examination scores.

Suppose your class is given a multiple-choice examination consisting of 25 questions, with 1 point for every correct answer and 0 points for each one you miss. The range of possible scores is 0 to 25. In practice, of course, it's quite likely that no one will get a score as low as 0 or as high as 25. Let's suppose that there are 23 students in the class, and the test-score data look like those in Table 1.

In summarizing such a set of scores, the first thing that an instructor is likely to do is to make a *frequency distribution* indicating how many students obtained each score, as in Table 2. Because no one in this class received a score of less than 13, the possible scores from 0 to 12 are lumped into a single category.

The information in this frequency distribution can also be displayed pictorially, by drawing a *histogram* (see Figure 1). In the histogram, each little box represents one test score. By showing how many boxes are piled on top of each other for each obtained score, the overall pattern of test results becomes easier to visualize.

Both the frequency distribution and the histogram provide a good overall description of the test scores in this class. In presenting results, however, it is often inefficient to provide the entire frequency distribution. Instead, we often make use of statistics that *summarize* the overall distribution. There are two important types of summary statistics: measures of the *central tendency* of a distribution, to indicate the "average" or "typical" score, and measures of the *variability* of a distribution, to indicate how spread out the scores are.

The most frequently used measure of central tendency is the *mean*. The mean is another term for what we often call the *average* score. To compute the mean of a set of scores, first add up the individual scores (13, 15, 16, 16, 17, and so on) and then divide the sum by the number of cases (in this instance 23). In our illustration, the mean score turns out to be 433/23 = 18.8. This number provides an index of how well the class as a whole did on the exam.

The *median* is a slightly different sort of measure of central tendency. The median is simply the middle-most score in any set of scores. In our set of 23 scores for example, the median would be the twelfth highest (or twelfth lowest) score—that is, the score that falls right in the middle of the overall distribution. In our example, the median score turns out to be 19. Although the mean is the measure of central tendency that is most commonly used by psychologists, the median may sometimes provide a more useful summary of a distribution of scores than the mean. Let's say that we wanted to provide an indication of the "average" age of a group of five people, aged 18, 19, 20, 21 and 70. The mean age of these five people is 29.6. But the median age (20) would be more representative of the ages of most members of the group. Similarly, distributions of people's income are often summarized in terms of their median, rather than their mean, to avoid giving too much weight to the small number of people with extremely high incomes.

The final measure of central tendency, the *mode* of a distribution, is simply the score that is more common than any other score. In our illustration, the mode is 18, since more students obtained that score than any

TABLE 1

CLASS MEMBERS' SCORES ON EXAMINATION

Student	Examination score
Leonard Ahern	20
Catherine Baskin	16
Patricia Breen	18
Michael Cavanaugh	18
Harold Costopoulos	19
Arlene DiNapoli	20
Noam Feinberg	22
Julia Hernandez	20
Mary Jameson	19
Joel King	13
Robert Liu	19
Fred Luna	18
Frances Mazurek	18
Denise Moeller	17
Elihu Noyes	21
William Piper	15
Louise Randolph	18
Kenneth Roderick	21
Delores Santos	24
Janet Slovin	21
Harmon Stewart	19
John Thibodeau	16
Helen Welsh	21

TABLE 2

FREQUENCY DISTRIBUTION OF EXAMINATION SCORES IN TABLE 1

Examination score	Number of students receiving that score
0–12	0
13	1
14	0
15	1
16	2
17	1
18	5
19	4
20	3
21	4
22	1
23	0
24	1
25	0

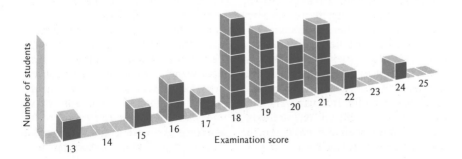

FIGURE 1

A histogram representing pictorially the distribution of examination scores given in Table 2. Each box represents one student's score on the exam.

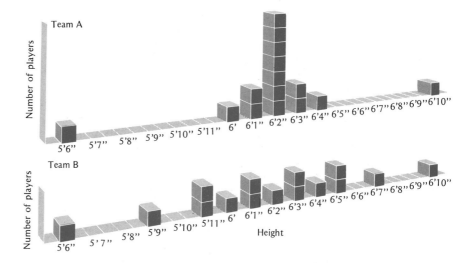

other single score. Modes are most useful when we want to indicate which one of a small number of categories is most prevalent or "popular."

In addition to describing the central tendency of a set of scores, it is also useful to describe the variability of a set of scores—that is, how widely the scores are dispersed. The simplest way to summarize the variability of a distribution is to specify its *range*—that is, to indicate the lowest and highest scores actually obtained. In our illustration, the range of scores was from 13 to 24. In another class the range might have been narrower—say, from 17 to 21. The range is not a perfect summary of variability, however, because it can be radically changed as a result of one or two "oddball" scores. A fuller description of the variability of a set of scores is provided by its *standard deviation*. The standard deviation is computed by means of a formula that takes into account how far each individual score is from the mean of the distribution. The more closely packed the scores are around the mean, the lower the standard deviation of that distribution. The more widely dispersed the scores are, the higher the standard deviation.

Consider, for example, the heights of two fifteen-member basketball teams, presented in the form of two histograms in Figure 2. Although both teams include the same range of heights (from 5'6" to 6'10") and both teams have the same mean height (6'2"), on the whole there is more va-

riety in the heights of members of Team A than of Team B. And, as a result, we would find that the standard deviation of the heights of Team A is greater than the standard deviation of the heights of Team B.

SAMPLING AND STATISTICAL SIGNIFICANCE

Let's say that you wanted to know which sex spends more time studying at your school—women or men. (This example is adapted from Wing, 1969.) One way to find out would be to do a complete survey of the students at your school; ask each person how many hours per day he or she spends studying, and then compare the mean scores of the men and of the women. But such a complete survey would be difficult, if not impossible, to do. Instead, it may be possible to answer your question more conveniently by interviewing a *random sample* of female and male students. A random sample is one in which each member of the overall population being studied has an equal chance of ending up in the sample. If you stood in front of the gymnasium or in front of the library, you would be unlikely to obtain a random sample of students, because students are not equally likely to be found at these locations. A better sampling technique would be to begin with a complete list of students, and then choose every tenth or every fiftieth name for your sample.

Let's say you obtained a random sample of twenty men and twenty women at your school, interviewed these students, and found out how much time each spends studying—or, at least, how much time each student claims to spend studying. You find that women spend an average (mean) of 3.7 hours a day and the men spend an average (mean) of 3.3 hours a day. A remaining question is whether this difference between the two samples reflects a real difference between the two populations to which you want to generalize. Is it really true that women at your school study more than men, or is the difference that you found simply a matter of chance? Maybe an unusually large number of studious women or nonstudious men just happened, by the luck of the draw, to turn up in your sample. To evaluate this possibility, tests of *statistical significance* are employed.

There are three elements of any comparison between samples that are important in deciding whether the observed differences reflect real population differences. First, the greater the difference between the means of the two samples, the more likely it is that there will be a corresponding difference in the total population. Second, the larger the number of subjects in the samples, the more likely it is that the sample accurately reflects population data. And third, the smaller the variation of scores (or the standard deviation) within each sample, the more likely it is that the difference between samples reflects a real population difference. All of these factors are taken into account in tests that assess the statistical significance of differences between groups.

The significance level of any obtained difference between groups is the probability that the difference was simply due to chance, rather than reflecting a true population difference. Thus, a significance level of .25 would indicate that there was a 25 percent (or 1 in 4) chance that the difference in mean scores that we obtained was due to chance. A significance level of .05 indicates that there is only a 5 percent chance that the

total populations are not really different. In general, psychologists accept a significance level of .05 as sufficiently small to make it reasonable to consider the difference to be a real one. The significance level of any difference is also called a *p* value, with *p* standing for "probability." Psychologists often compute *p* values when they conduct experiments, in order to determine whether any obtained differences in behavior between subjects in different experimental conditions are worth taking seriously.

CORRELATION COEFFICIENTS

The *correlation coefficient* is a statistic that describes the degree to which one set of scores is related to a second set of scores. For example, we can make use of correlations to tell us what the relationship is between how much students study and those students' grades, or to indicate the size of the relationship between people's scores on two different personality measures.

The best way to view the correlation coefficient is as a measure of the extent to which knowing one set of scores helps us to predict a second set of scores. Let's say that a class is given two examinations, one early in the term and one later in the term. We can represent the two sets of scores graphically by means of *scatterplots*, as in Figure 3. Each point on the scatterplot represents an individual student's score on both of the two tests. In Figure 3A, there is a good deal of consistency between students' scores on the two tests. As a result, it is possible to make a reasonably good prediction of how well the student will do on the second test on the basis of his performance on the first test. In Figure 3B, on the other hand, there is little consistency between scores on the two tests. In this case, knowing how well a student did on the first test is of little or no help in predicting her score on the second test. Although it is unlikely to be the case in this example, we may sometimes find *inverse* relationships between two sets of scores, so that a higher score

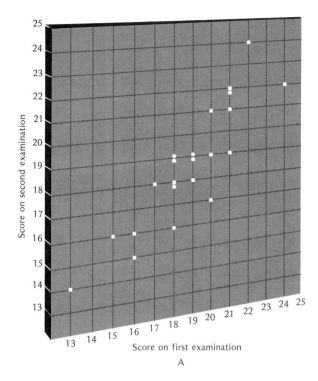

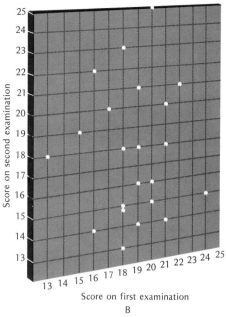

FIGURE 3

Each of these scatterplots shows the relationship between students' scores on two examinations. In A, there is a high positive correlation between scores on the two exams. In B, the correlation is near zero.

Score on second examination

on one measure is associated with a lower score on a second measure.

When such relationships between two sets of scores are converted into the form of a number, the obtained correlations can range from +1.00 (a perfect positive correlation) through .00 (no correlation at all) to −1.00 (perfect inverse correlation). In practice, it is unusual to find "perfect" correlations of +1.00 or −1.00. Virtually all of the correlations that psychologists encounter take the form of numbers between −1.00 and +1.00, such as +.43 or −.37. The larger this number, whether in a positive or a negative direction, the stronger is the relationship between the two sets of scores. In Figure 3A, the correlation between the two sets of test scores is quite high—approximately +.80. In Figure 3B, the correlation is close to .00.

Table 3 presents a set of correlation coefficients obtained in a study of 231 dating couples that I conducted with Charles Hill and Anne Peplau (1976). (Some of the findings of this study were discussed in Chapter 17.) Each of the correlations in the table represents the relationship between boyfriends' and girlfriends' scores on a particular measure. Thus, boyfriends' and girlfriends' scores on a

measure of sex-role attitudes were rather highly related (with a correlation of +.47). In other words, men with traditional sex-role attitudes tended to be paired with women with traditional attitudes; men with egalitarian sex-role attitudes tended to be paired with women with egalitarian attitudes. There was also a relationship between the physical attractiveness of the two partners, as rated from individual photographs—people tended to be dating others at their own level of attractiveness—but this relationship was not as strong (correlation of only +.24).

The correlation between two sets of scores provides an index of the extent to which two measures or events vary together. As we noted in Chapter 1, however, the fact that two measures are highly correlated with one another does not indicate that one event *caused* the other. If we found, for example, that there was a high positive correlation between students' hours of studying and their grades, it would not necessarily mean that studying led to higher grades. It is possible, for example, that the causal link actually went in the other direction, so that getting high grades encouraged students to study more. Similarly, the high correlation be-

TABLE 3

CORRELATION BETWEEN BOYFRIENDS' AND GIRLFRIENDS' SCORES ON VARIOUS CHARACTERISTICS

Characteristic	Correlation
Sex-role traditionalism (10-item scale)	.47
Number of children wanted	.51
Self-report of how religious one is	.37
Score on Scholastic Aptitude Test (verbal)	.24
Physical attractiveness (rated from photos)	.24
Height	.21

From Hill, Rubin, and Peplau (1976)

tween boyfriends' and girlfriends' sex-role attitudes does not indicate that one person's attitudes influenced the other's. It seems more likely, in this case, that men and women selected each other in the first place in part as a result of their similar attitudes. A significant correlation—that is, one that is unlikely to come about by chance—indicates only that a relationship is present. We must supplement our correlational analysis with other methods, such as experiments, if we want to *explain* that relationship.

GLOSSARY

The number of the page on which each term was introduced is given in parentheses.

abnormality See *medical model; psychological adequacy.*

abnormal psychology The study of psychological disorder. *(393)*

achievement motive The striving to maintain or increase one's competence in activities in which a standard of excellence is thought to apply. *(304)*

activation-synthesis model The idea that dreams begin with the firing of giant cells in the brain stem, leading to activation of certain areas of the brain. The dreams then synthesized depend on which areas of the brain are stimulated. *(76)*

acupuncture A medical practice, developed by the Chinese, in which the insertion of needles into various sites on the body surface relieves pain in either the surrounding area or distant body parts. *(110)*

adaptation See *perceptual adaptation; sensory adaptation.*

addiction See *physiological addiction.*

aerobic exercise Exercise that requires a constant flow of oxygen. *(379)*

affective disorder A disturbance of mood or emotion, such as depression and mania. *(402)*

afferent neurons The neurons that collect messages from inside and outside the body and transmit them to the central nervous system; sensory neurons. *(39)* See also *efferent neurons.*

affiliation motive The need of human beings to associate with one another.

afterimages The sensory impressions that persist after the removal of a stimulus. *(101)*

age-graded influences Experiences and events that commonly occur at a given stage of life. *(258)* See also *non-age-graded influences.*

ageism The high value placed on youth in our society, resulting in a negative view of old people and discrimination against them. *(272)*

alarm reaction According to Selye, the first stage in an animal's response to stress; it involves general physiological arousal. *(359)* See also *exhaustion stage; resistance stage.*

alcoholism A physiological addiction to alcohol, often viewed as a physical disease. *(383)*

all-or-none principle The idea that a stimulus must be of a minimum strength to stimulate an axon to fire and that once this threshold is reached the axon will fire completely. *(43)*

alpha wave A rhythmic electrical impulse of the brain, occurring during wakefulness and relaxation. *(47)*

Alzheimer's disease A brain disorder believed to be caused by degeneration of certain nerve cells; it usually occurs after age 60. *(274)*

amnesia A loss of memory. *(175)* See *childhood amnesia, retrograde amnesia, transient global amnesia.*

amniocentesis Extracting and analyzing cells from a pregnant woman's uterus to determine the genetic and health status of the fetus. *(62)*

amphetamine psychosis A psychosislike state produced by long-term or excessive use of amphetamines. It is characterized by paranoid delusions, compulsions, and stereotyped behaviors. *(82)*

amphetamines A group of drugs that act to stimulate the central nervous system. *(81)*

amygdala A structure in the limbic system that appears to be involved in rage and violent behavior. *(48)*

anal stage According to Freud, the second stage of psychosexual development (ages 2 to 3), during which bowel control is achieved and gratification centers on the anal area. *(333)*

androgyny See *psychological androgyny.*

antianxiety drugs The minor tranquilizers, such as Valium and Librium, which are commonly prescribed to relieve tension and anxiety. *(432)*

antidepressant drugs Drugs prescribed to lift the spirits of depressed patients. *(433)*

antipsychotic drugs The major tranquilizers, used primarily to treat the symptoms of schizophrenia. *(433)*

antisocial personality A type of personality disorder characterized by superficial charm, insincerity, lack of remorse or guilt, failure to learn from experience, and inability to tolerate frustration. *(407)*

anxiety A vague, unpleasant feeling that something bad is about to happen. *(398)*

anxiety disorders Mental disorders characterized by excessive anxiety, such as phobias and obsessive-compulsive disorder. *(398)*

anxiety hierarchy In systematic desensitization, arranging a series of related scenes in an order from least anxiety-arousing to most anxiety-arousing. *(427)*

aphasia Loss of language ability because of brain damage. *(51)*

applied research Research designed to help solve a practical problem. *(23)*

approach-approach conflict Having to choose between two equally attractive goals. *(302)*

approach-avoidance conflict Having to choose between temptation and denial. *(302)*

archetypes Mental representations of universal human experiences that, according to Carl Jung, are part of the collective unconscious. *(338)*

assertiveness training A program designed to help timid people stand up for themselves. *(430)*

association neurons Neurons found primarily in the central nervous system that make the connection between incoming and outgoing messages. *(39)*

attachment An infant's bond or affectional tie to her parent or a parent figure *(236)*; the need for the physical presence and emotional support of a loved one. *(528)*

attention The process of selectively responding to certain stimuli while ignoring others. *(117)*

attitudes People's relatively enduring sets of thoughts and feelings about particular people, objects, or issues. *(453)*

attribution processes People's methods of trying to infer the underlying causes of other people's behavior. *(521)*

audience In persuasion, the persons at whom a message is directed. *(465)*

auditory nerve The nerve that carries messages from the ear to the hearing portion of the brain. *(106)*

authoritarian child rearing A child-rearing style in which the parent attempts to shape and control the behavior of the child according to specific standards of conduct. *(243)* See also *permissive child rearing.*

authoritarian personality A personality type characterized by admiration of strength, hatred of weakness, and a strong belief in obedience to authority. *(481)*

authority See *legitimate authority.*

autism See *infantile autism.*

autoimmune reaction A situation in which the immune system begins to attack the body's own cells. *(274)*

autonomic nervous system The part of the peripheral nervous system that controls glands and involuntary movements. *(40)* See also *somatic nervous system.*

aversive conditioning A form of classical conditioning in which an undesired behavior is repeatedly paired with an unpleasant experience, in order to eliminate the behavior. *(377)*

avoidance-avoidance conflict Having to choose between two undesirable goals. *(302)*

axon A long fiber extending from a neuron and transmitting messages to other neurons, to muscles, or to glands. *(42)*

axonal transmission The movement of electrical impulses along the surface of a neuron. *(43)*

basic needs Needs (such as hunger and thirst) that must be satisfied if an organism is to survive. *(292)*

basic research Research conducted to advance knowledge, without any immediate concern for the practical uses of that knowledge. *(23)*

behavior control See *behavior modification.*

behavior genetics The study of the hereditary factors that affect personality and behavior. *(30)*

behavior modification Alteration or control of behavior through systematic application of principles of learning. *(139)*

behavior shaping Producing a desired behavior by rewarding responses that come closer and closer to the desired response. *(139)*

behavior therapy Applications of the principles of experimental psychology, especially principles of learning, to treat psychological problems. *(427)* See also *desensitization; operant therapy; role playing; token economy.*

behavioral medicine The application of behavioral techniques to the treatment and prevention of illness. *(369)*

behavioral observation See *observation.*

behaviorism A school of psychology that emphasizes observable behavior as opposed to unobservable conscious processes. *(6)*

benzodiazepines Tranquilizers such as Valium and Librium that relieve anxiety without having a sedative effect. *(432)*

binocular vision The cooperation of the two eyes in giving solidity and distance to viewed objects. *(104)*

biofeedback A technique for monitoring bodily processes (such as brain waves and blood pressure) so that a person can identify fluctuations in these processes and try to control them. *(47)*

biological rhythms Daily, monthly, annual, and other rhythms or cycles that characterize behavior and experience. *(90)* See also *circadian rhythm, infradian rhythm, ultradian rhythm.*

biorhythms The idea, now discredited, that people are influenced by three biological rhythms initiated at the time of birth: a 23-day physical rhythm, a 28-day emotional rhythm, and a 33-day intellectual rhythm. *(30)*

bipolar disorder A psychological disorder characterized by alteration between states of deep depression and extreme elation. *(403)*

birth order People's order of birth in their families (first-born, second-born, and so on). *(253)*

blind spot The area of the retina where the optic nerve leaves the eye. *(100)*

blood flow measurement Monitoring of the amount of blood flowing to different parts of the brain to determine what parts of the brain are involved in various activities. *(46)*

brain stem The central core of the brain; its functions are connected to the fundamental processes of survival and the emotions. *(48)*

brain-tissue transplant The procedure of grafting neurons from another organism or another part of the body into a damaged portion of the brain. *(63)*

brain waves Rhythmic electrical impulses given off by the neurons in the cerebral cortex. *(45)*

brainwashing A set of techniques used to destroy a person's existing group ties and sense of identity in order to provide a new set of relationships tied to new ideals. *(467)*

brightness constancy The tendency for objects to appear to be the same brightness no matter what the lighting conditions. *(122)*

Broca's area An area of the left frontal lobe of the brain that is involved with language. *(51)*

butyrophenones A group of antipsychotic drugs used in the treatment of schizophrenia. *(433)*

carcinogens Cancer-causing agents. *(367)*

caring Feelings of concern and responsibility for another person, viewed as a component of love. *(528)*

case study Research based on long-term examination of an individual subject. *(17)*

castration anxiety According to Freud, a boy's fear that his father will discover the boy's attraction to his mother and will punish him by castration. *(335)*

catatonic schizophrenia A type of schizophrenia characterized by alternation between long periods of extreme immobility and bursts of aggressive or violent behavior. *(406)*

catharsis The release of emotional tension thought to occur when a person engages in or observes violent activity *(319)*; in psychoanalysis, the release of pent-up emotions as the result of bringing buried thoughts to the surface of consciousness. *(422)*

central nervous system The brain and spinal cord. *(39)*

cerebellum A structure at the back of the brain concerned primarily with the control of body position and movement. *(48)*

cerebral cortex The largest area of the human brain, covering the rest of the brain parts; it is responsible for sensory and perceptual processes and is the site of thought, consciousness, and memory. *(49)*

cerebral hemispheres The two halves of the cerebral cortex; each controls one side of the body and is somewhat specialized in its functions. *(51)*

childhood amnesia The tendency to forget the events and emotions of the first few years of life. *(173)*

circadian rhythm A biological rhythm that occurs about every 24 hours, such as the sleep-waking cycle. *(90)*

clairvoyance The ability to know about an object or event without employing the usual senses; a form of extrasensory perception. *(115)*

clang associations In schizophrenics, creation of sentences by associating words with similar sounds. *(408)*

classical conditioning A type of learning in which a neutral stimulus, as the result of being paired with an unconditioned stimulus, comes to elicit a response originally elicited by the unconditioned stimulus. *(132)*

client-centered therapy A humanistic approach to therapy, developed by Rogers, in which the client is encouraged to express her true feelings and become her true self. *(424)*

clinical psychology The subfield of psychology that focuses on diagnosing psychological problems and providing psychotherapy. *(25)*

clinical retardation Moderate to profound mental retardation, usually diagnosed at birth. It usually has a specific neurological, metabolic, or genetic cause that can be determined. *(212)* See also *sociocultural retardation.*

closure The tendency to perceptually fill in the gaps in an incomplete figure. *(116)*

cocaine A stimulant drug extracted from the leaves of the coca plant. *(82)*

cochlea The spiral-shaped part of the inner ear that contains the receptor cells for hearing. *(106)*

cognitive deficit An abnormal style of processing information, found in schizophrenic patients. *(408)*

cognitive development The changes in modes of thought that take place through the course of infancy, childhood, and adolescence. *(234)*

cognitive dissonance An internal state of unease produced when one perceives inconsistencies between one's attitudes or between one's attitudes and one's actions. *(460)*

cognitive labeling theory Schachter's idea that an emotion is the result of mental appraisal of physiological sensations that arise in a particular context. *(311)*

cognitive learning The acquisition of information and ways of dealing with information. *(148)*

cognitive map A mental representation of the relationships between locations. *(151)*

cognitive psychology The modern study of thought processes. *(7)*

cognitive restructuring In behavior therapy, the modification of a client's thoughts about events and herself. *(430)*

cognitive skills Approaches or procedures that are useful in solving a particular set of problems. *(153)*

cognitive therapy Beck's method of treating depressed people, in which the therapist tries to persuade the person to change his erroneous negative opinions of events and of himself. *(430)*

cohort effects Differences between people who grow up during different historical periods. *(274)*

collective unconscious According to Jung, a part of the human mind that is filled with archetypes of universal human experience and that is shared by all human beings. *(338)* See also *personal unconscious.*

color blindness See *dichromatic color blindness; monochromatic color blindness.*

color constancy The tendency for objects to appear to be the same color despite changes in lighting conditions or proximity to other colors. *(122)*

commitment A pledging of oneself to continue a course of action over a period of time. *(531)*

communicator In persuasion, the one who conveys the message. *(465)*

community mental health Approach toward preventing psychological disorder by helping people deal with their problems in their own community. *(440)*

community psychology The subfield of psychology that focuses on preventing and treating psychological problems at a community level. *(26)*

comparative psychology The subfield of psychology concerned with comparing the behavior patterns of different animal species. *(25)*

competence motivation The need to confirm one's ability to interact effectively with one's environment. *(292)*

complementary In friendships, the ability of each person to supply certain qualities the other is lacking. *(526)*

compulsion An irrational desire to engage in ritualistic acts. *(402)*

computer-aided instruction (CAI) The use of computers to provide individualized educational instruction. *(142)*

computer simulations Programming computers to simulate human thought processes. *(202)*

concept A word or idea that represents a category of things with related characteristics. *(195)*

concrete operational stage According to Piaget, the third stage of cognitive development (ages 7 to 12), during which the child learns to mentally manipulate objects and to understand concepts such as conservation. *(235)*

condensation According to Freud, the fact that symbols in a dream can have multiple meanings. *(74)*

conditioned response A response that has come to be elicited by a stimulus that does not naturally elicit that response. *(133)*

conditioned stimulus A previously neutral stimulus that, through repeated pairing with an unconditioned stimulus, comes to elicit a response. *(133)*

cones Light-sensitive cells in the retina

that are responsible for color vision. *(98)*

conformity Acceptance of the norms of a group or society. *(464)*

consciousness A level of thought that integrates and regulates experience; it is sometimes necessary for normal activities but often is not. *(66)*

conservation The fact that a substance's weight, mass, or volume remains the same even when the substance changes shape. *(240)*

consolidation phase The time it takes for chemical changes of memory to have a permanent impact on the brain. *(174)*

constancy See *perceptual constancy.*

consumer psychology The subfield of psychology that is concerned with the application of psychological principles to the purchase and consumption of goods and services. *(27)*

contact comfort The infant's innate tendency to derive pleasure from contact with another body, especially that of his mother. *(237)*

continuous reinforcement Reinforcement of a response every time it is emitted. *(143)*

control group In an experiment, a group of subjects against which the experimental group is compared. *(22)*

controlled drinking The use of behavior modification techniques to teach problem drinkers to control their own drinking behavior. *(387)*

cornea The transparent protective coating on the front part of the eye. *(97)*

coronary-prone behavior pattern See *Type A behavior.*

corpus callosum A mass of nerve fibers connecting the two hemispheres of the cerebral cortex. *(52)*

correlation The degree to which two sets of measures are associated with each other. *(20)*

correlational studies Research in which psychologists try to discover a relationship between two factors by measuring each separately and then comparing results. *(20)*

correlation coefficient A statistic that describes the degree to which one set of scores is related to a second set of scores. *(544)*

corticosteroids Hormones released by the adrenal cortex that release fatty acids for energy. *(360)*

counseling psychology The subfield of psychology that focuses on helping people with such issues as career decisions, marital problems, and readjustment to life after an illness or injury. *(26)*

countertransference In psychoanalysis, the phenomenon that occurs when a patient begins to react to the therapist on the basis of the therapist's problems and not her own. *(422)*

creationism The idea that the biblical account of creation is a valid explanation of the origins of the human species. *(35)*

creativity The ability to produce a novel and appropriate solution to a problem. *(203)*

credibility The believability of a communicator. *(466)*

crisis intervention Providing help following a particularly stressful event in a person's life, such as rape or death of a family member. *(440)*

critical period A point early in an animal's life during which a relatively small amount of learning can produce a major and lasting effect; if the behavior is not learned at this time, it may never be learned at all. *(227)*

cross-sectional study A research study based on subjects of different ages all measured at a single point in time. *(274)* See also *longitudinal study.*

cross-situational consistency The assumption that people have the same personality at all times and in all situations. *(339)*

crystallized intelligence The kind of mental ability that includes verbal skills, the ability to define words, and accumulated knowledge. *(275)* See also *fluid intelligence.*

cumulative deficit The finding that as disadvantaged children grow older their IQ scores tend to fall farther behind the scores of more advantaged children. *(211)*

cystic fibrosis A serious genetic disease, affecting the respiratory and digestive systems. *(39)*

decibel Unit for measuring the loudness of a sound. *(126)*

defense mechanism A method used by the ego to deny, change, or channel unacceptable impulses or ideas so that they need not be dealt with consciously. *(336)*

deinstitutionalization The process of returning chronically disturbed mental patients to community life. *(438)*

delayed reinforcement Reward administered long after the response was emitted. *(141)*

delta sleep The stage of sleep in which the sleeper is hardest to waken; deep sleep. *(72)*

delusion A false belief about oneself or one's environment. *(406)*

delusion of grandeur The irrational belief that one is a famous person or religious figure. *(406)*

delusion of persecution The irrational belief that other people are conspiring against one. *(406)*

dendrites Short fibers projecting from a neuron that receive messages from other neurons. *(42)*

dependent variable In an experiment, the behavior that is being measured—which may be affected by changes in the independent variable. *(21)*

depressants Drugs that depress the activity of the central nervous system and decrease its ability to respond to stimuli. *(78)*

depression A psychological disorder marked by feelings of worthlessness, hopelessness, lethargy, and helplessness. *(402)*

depth perception The ability to perceive

that objects are three-dimensional and at a certain distance just by looking at them. *(104)*

descriptive studies Research in which the scientist is primarily concerned with setting forth a clear account of the subject's behavior or self-reports. *(20)*

desensitization therapy A method of behavior therapy in which the client is taught to relax in anxiety-producing situations. *(427)*

development The relatively enduring changes in people's capacities and behavior that occur as they grow older. *(225)*

developmental psychology The subfield of psychology concerned with human development through the life cycle. *(25)*

dichromatic color blindness The inability to distinguish between red and green or between yellow and blue. *(103)*

discrimination In learning, the ability to distinguish between stimuli; responding to one stimulus while not responding to a similar stimulus *(136)*. In social psychology, behaving differently toward members of a specific group on the basis of prejudice toward that group. *(479)*

discriminative stimulus A stimulus that becomes associated with the delivery of reinforcement because reinforcement occurs in its presence. *(140)*

disorganized schizophrenia Schizophrenia characterized by bizarre behavior, including strange facial expressions, speech, and emotional reactions. *(406)*

displacement Redirecting unconscious urges toward a more accessible or more socially acceptable object. *(336)*

dissociated consciousness A separation between different aspects of consciousness. *(87)*

dissociative disorder A psychological disorder in which the individual unconsciously dissociates or loses access to some part of consciousness. *(400)*

dominant gene A gene whose instructions always prevail. *(36)* See also *recessive gene.*

dopamine A neurotransmitter in the brain. *(55)*

Down's syndrome A disorder caused by incorrect distribution of genetic material in the zygote; it is characterized by mental retardation and various physical abnormalities. *(212)*

drive The psychological experiencing of a biological need. *(295)*

drive reduction theory The idea that motivation involves a basic physiological need that is experienced as a psychological drive; this drive is reduced when the physiological need is satisfied. *(295)*

DSM-III *The Diagnostic and Statistical Manual of Mental Disorders*, 3rd. ed., of the American Psychiatric Association. It provides the system currently used to diagnose psychological disorders. *(391)*

dual coding Storing information in memory on the basis of both verbal and visual coding. *(179)*

ectomorph The slender physical type of person, with long bones, poor muscula-

ture, and delicate constitution. *(325)* See also *endomorph; mesomorph.*

educational psychology The subfield of psychology involved with the design of educational settings and teaching techniques and with the training of teachers. *(26)*

EEG See *electroencephalograph.*

efferent neurons Neurons that carry messages from the central nervous system to the muscles and glands; motor neurons. *(39)* See also *afferent neurons.*

ego According to Freud, the part of the personality that directs and controls basic biological urges by seeking to gratify them within socially acceptable bounds. *(332)*

egocentrism The inability to see things from perspectives other than one's own. *(240)*

electrical stimulation of the brain (ESB) The application of an electrical current to specific areas of the brain in order to discover the functions of the areas and to alter behavior. *(45)*

electroencephalograph (EEG) A machine used to record brain waves. The printed-out record of the brain waves is called an electroencephalogram. *(45)*

electroconvulsive therapy Application of electrical current to the brain in order to relieve symptoms of depression. *(435)*

Electra complex According to Freud, a young girl's attraction to her father and envy of her mother that occurs during the phallic stage of psychosexual development. *(335)*

embryo In humans, the prenatal organism from the fourth day after conception through the eighth week. *(230)*

emotion The physiological changes, subjective experience, and expression of reactions involved in such phenomena as joy, fear, grief, and anger. *(303)*

emotional attachment A close social relationship to one other person, usually a lover or spouse. *(514)*

emotional isolation See *loneliness.*

encoding Linking information to concepts and categories that one has already learned in order to store it in long-term memory. *(164)*

encounter groups Therapy groups in which people can meet for the purpose of increasing their openness and sensitivity to one another. *(445)*

endocrine glands A group of glands that secrete chemicals directly into the bloodstream. *(41)*

endomorph The heavy, fat physical type of person. *(325)* See also *ectomorph; mesomorph.*

endorphins Morphinelike chemicals in the brain that seem to be involved in mood and pain control. *(58)*

engineering psychology The subfield of psychology that focuses on appropriate design of equipment to be used by human beings. *(26)*

enkaphalins Morphinelike chemicals in the brain that seem to be involved in mood and pain control. *(58)*

epilepsy A convulsive brain disorder

characterized by mental blackouts and sometimes seizures. *(54)*

epinephrine A hormone secreted by the adrenal glands that is involved in physiological arousal. *(56)*

equilibrium The sense of balance. *(111)*

erogenous zones Pleasure-giving areas of the body. *(333)*

ESB See *electrical stimulation of the brain.*

ESP See *extrasensory perception.*

est A seminar program in which participants go through a series of exercises designed to help them accept themselves. *(446)*

estrogen A female sex hormone. *(56)*

evoked potential A computer-derived average of the brain waves produced in response to a particular stimulus. *(46)*

excitatory message A neurotransmitter message that increases the likelihood that a neuron will fire *(43)*

excitement phase In human sexual response, the first stage or arousal period. *(500)*

exhaustion stage According to Selye, the final stage in an animal's physiological response to long-term stress. *(359)* See also *alarm reaction; resistance stage.*

experiment A study in which the researcher places subjects in different conditions and compares the effects. *(21)*

experimental group In an experiment, the group of subjects being studied. See also *control group. (21)*

experimental psychology The subfield of psychology that focuses on research on such fundamental psychological processes as perception, learning, memory, motivation, and emotion. *(24)*

experimenter expectancy effects Cases in which the results of research are unintentionally affected by what the researcher expects to find. *(22)*

extinction The weakening of a learned response. In classical conditioning, it results from repeated presentation of the conditioned stimulus without the unconditioned stimulus; in operant conditioning, it results from withdrawal of reinforcement. *(135)*

extrasensory perception (ESP) Perception of objects, events, or thoughts by other than normal sensory means. *(115)*

extrinsic motivation Doing something for an external reward. *(300)* See also *intrinsic motivation.*

face-ism The fact that photos of men in newspapers and magazines tend to emphasize their faces, whereas photos of women give greater emphasis to their bodies. *(488)*

facial feedback hypothesis The idea that awareness of one's facial expressions is a primary ingredient in one's experiencing of emotions. *(312)*

false consensus effect People's tendency to overestimate the number of others who share their views. *(465)*

farsightedness Poor visual acuity for close objects, caused by the image falling behind the retina. (100) See also *near-sightedness*.

fear appeals Using scare tactics in an attempt to change people's attitudes. (468)

fetus In humans, the prenatal organism from the ninth week following conception until birth. (230)

fight-or-flight reaction Mobilization of the body for action in response to stressful situations. (359)

figure-ground perception The tendency to differentiate between an object and the background against which the object stands. (116)

fissures Two grooves that divide the cerebral cortex into lobes. (49)

fixation According to Freud, a focusing of sexual energy at an early stage of psychosexual development because of unresolved conflicts at that stage. (333)

fixed-interval schedule Administering reinforcement after a set period of time. (143) See also *variable-interval schedule*.

fixed-ratio schedule Administering reinforcement after a fixed number of responses. (143) See also *variable ratio schedule*.

fixed-response questions In opinion polling, measuring devices in which respondents are asked to select one answer from a given set of answers to a questions. (454) See also *open-ended questions*.

flashbulb memories Sharp, vivid memories of the setting and manner in which one heard of a major event that has had an impact on one's life. (10)

fluid intelligence The kind of mental ability, especially nonverbal, that allows people to see old problems in new ways and to solve puzzles and visual problems. (274) See also *crystallized intelligence*.

forgetting curve The fact that the greatest memory loss occurs immediately after learning and that the rate of loss declines as time passes. (168)

formal operational stage According to Piaget, the adolescent stage of cognitive development, during which the individual learns to deal with complex concepts and with abstract notions. (235)

fovea Depressed spot on the retina directly behind the lens, with a high concentration of cones but no rods. (99)

fraternal twins Individuals conceived at the same time but developed from separate eggs fertilized by separate sperm. (37) See also *identical twins*.

free association A method used in psychoanalysis in which the client is asked to say whatever comes to mind. (422)

frequency distribution A summary of the number of subjects who receive each score. (542)

Freudian slip Slips of the tongue that reflect unconscious motives. (295)

frontal lobe The section of the cerebral cortex believed to be the site of personality and to be concerned with some aspects of speech. (49)

frustration The blocking of one's efforts to achieve a desired goal. (319)

frustration-aggression hypothesis The idea that most aggressive behavior results from frustration. (319)

F scale A personality scale used to measure the extent to which a person has an authoritarian personality. (481)

functional fixedness The inability to see a new use for a familiar object. (201)

functionalism An early school of psychology that emphasized practical applications of the study of conscious processes. (6)

g According to Spearman, a single general-intelligence factor on which individuals can vary. (208)

gate control theory of pain The idea that the transmission of pain signals in the body depends on "gates" in the central nervous system that allow or prevent passage of pain signals. (110) See also *specificity theory*.

gender identity One's perception of oneself as male or female. (485)

gender roles Social expectations about what men and women should do and be like. (495)

gender stereotypes The widely held assumptions that men are aggressive, independent, dominant, active, competitive, and self-confident whereas women are tactful, gentle, sensitive, emotional, expressive, neat, and nurturant. (486)

gene The unit of heredity. (36)

general adaptation syndrome Selye's term for the sequence of physical responses that compose the body's reaction to stress. (359) See also *alarm reaction*; *exhaustion stage*; *resistance stage*.

generalization Making the same response to separate but similar stimuli. (136)

generativity According to Erikson, having an impact on the next generation. (260)

genetic counseling Examining a couple's genetic background and advising them on the risks of producing a defective child. (62)

genetics The study of heredity. (36)

genital stage According to Freud, the final period of psychosexual development. Beginning with puberty, sexual energies are again focused on the genitals, and the individual seeks adult heterosexual relationships. (336)

genotype The fundamental hereditary constitution of an organism. (36) See also *phenotype*.

Gestalt psychology A school of psychology that identified the basic principles of perceptual organization. (116)

gestalt therapy A humanistic approach to therapy in which the client attempts to pull together all aspects of her personality into a unified whole. (425)

glia Cells in the brain that surround, cushion, and nourish nerve cells. (43)

graphology Handwriting analysis. (30)

groupthink The tendency for members of a policy-making group to suppress all individual doubts and dissent, creating the illusion of unanimity. (464)

hair cells The receptor cells for hearing, located inside the cochlea. (106)

hallucination Seeing or hearing things that aren't there. (406)

health psychology Study of the role of psychological factors in the development of disease, in coping with illness, and in the promotion of health. (357)

heritability An estimate of how much of the variation between individuals on a particular trait is due to genetic factors. (210)

"hidden observer" A part of the hypnotized person's mind that watches and remembers everything that is going on. (87)

hippocampus A structure in the brain's limbic system that appears to play a role in short-term memory. (49)

homophobia An irrational fear or intolerance of homosexuals. (505)

hormones Chemicals secreted by glands of the endocrine system. (55)

hospices Facilities designed for terminally ill people to die in peace and dignity. (286)

hot reactivity A greater physiological reactivity when under stress found in Type A persons. (366)

humanistic theories A set of approaches to personality that emphasizes the uniqueness, self-esteem, and dignity of the individual. (342)

hyperactivity A childhood psychological disorder characterized by short attention span, poor concentration, and excessive motor activity. (410)

hyperphagic Pertaining to animals whose hypothalamus has been lesioned, resulting in compulsive overeating and excessive weight gain. (297)

hypnosis A state of increased suggestibility, or willingness to comply with another person's directions, that is brought about through use of relaxation-producing techniques. (84)

hypothalamus A structure in the brain stem that monitors body activities such as eating and sleeping and that plays a major role in controlling emotional behavior. (48)

hypothesis An educated guess as to why something occurs as it does. (11)

id According to Freud, the reservoir of basic biological urges that motivate the individual. (332)

identical twins Two individuals developed from the same fertilized egg. (37) See also *fraternal twins*.

identification The child's desire to be like another person, usually the same-sex parent. (335)

identity formation The development of a clearly defined sense of self, seen as a central task of the adolescent years. (247)

imitative aggression Aggressive acts that duplicate those observed in another person. (320) See also *nonimitative aggression*.

immune system A collection of billions of cells that travel through the body, protecting it from invasion by foreign agents and against cells that become cancerous. *(367)*

imprinting A form of learning in which certain stimuli very early in life produce behavior patterns that are not generally reversible. *(227)*

in vitro fertilization Fertilizing an egg outside a woman's body, and then replacing it in her uterus. *(61)*

incentives The external aspect of motivation: the objects or opportunities that one strives for. *(296)*

incongruence According to Rogers, a discrepancy between a person's self-concept and his experience, or between his real self and ideal self. *(342)*

incubation The process of moving toward the solution to a problem while consciously thinking about something else. *(202)*

incus One of the three small bones of the middle ear. *(106)*

independent variable In an experiment, a factor manipulated by the experimenter in order to see what effect it has on the dependent variable. *(21)*

infantile autism A rare childhood disorder characterized by self-imposed isolation, insistence on sameness in the environment, and major language difficulties. *(411)*

inferiority complex According to Adler, the real or imagined feelings of inferiority that motivate people to achieve goals. *(338)*

information-processing approach Analyzing human thought processes and developing computer simulations of those processes to produce a general problem-solving strategy. *(202)*

infradian rhythm A biological cycle that occurs over a period longer than a day, such as the menstrual cycle. *(91)*

inhibitory message A neurotransmitter message that decreases the likelihood that a neuron will fire. *(43)*

insanity A legal concept, relieving a person of full responsibility for a crime on the grounds that he was suffering from psychological disorder. *(396)*

insight A sudden understanding of a problem—seeing it in a new light, thereby finding a solution. *(200)*

insomnia Difficulty in falling or staying asleep. *(73)*

instincts Inborn, unlearned, biologically purposeful responses. *(131)*

institutionalization Placing a person in an institution for the aged *(279)*; or in a mental hospital. *(438)*

integrity According to Erikson, the ability to look back at one's life with satisfaction. *(260)*

intellectualization Reducing anxiety by analyzing threatening issues intellectually, thereby detaching them from the self. *(337)*

intellectually gifted Those with IQs higher than 135. *(214)*

intelligence The capacity to acquire and apply knowledge. *(205)*

intelligence quotient (IQ) A measure of mental ability obtained by dividing a child's mental age by his chronological age and multiplying by 100. In adults, IQ is determined by comparing test scores to those of a standardized sample. *(205)*

intelligence tests Tests of people's intellectual capacity, yielding IQ scores. *(205)*

interdependence In a social relationship, the way in which each person has an impact on the other's thoughts, feelings, and behavior. *(515)*

interference See *proactive interference; retroactive interference.*

interpretation In psychoanalysis, pointing out aspects of the patient's narrative that are important and explaining their significance. *(422)*

interval schedule See *fixed-interval schedule; variable-interval schedule.*

interview A research method in which subjects are verbally questioned by a researcher. *(20, 345)*

intimacy A close bond with another person. *(260, 528)*

intrinsic motivation Doing something for the pleasure of the activity itself. *(300)* See also *extrinsic motivation.*

introspection The careful examination of one's own conscious experience. *(67)*

IQ See *intelligence quotient.*

iris The colored portion of the eye that contains muscles that control the widening and narrowing of the pupil *(98)*

James-Lange theory The idea that an event or stimulus causes bodily changes, which then produce the subjectively experienced emotion. *(310)*

jigsaw technique A teaching method designed to foster cooperative interdependence among learners. *(483)*

key word method A method of learning a foreign language vocabulary that involves linking a foreign word to an English key word on the basis of similar sound and a related mental image. *(180)*

kinesthesis The sensation of the body's position, movement, and tension. *(110)*

Korsakoff's syndrome A memory disorder in which the patient is permanently unable to place new information in long-term storage in the brain. *(175)*

language A rule-governed system of symbols used for communicating information, thoughts, or feelings. *(188)*

latency period According to Freud, the period of psychosexual development (about ages 6 to 12) during which sexual urges are dormant. *(336)*

latent dream content According to Freud, the hidden meaning of a dream. *(76)*

latent learning Learning that occurs without any direct reinforcement or intent to learn. *(149)*

learned helplessness The discovery that one's actions are ineffective, leading to passivity and depression. *(405)*

learning A relatively permanent change in behavior as the result of experience or practice. *(131)*

learning by observation See *modeling.*

legitimate authority Someone who appears to have the right to dictate one's behavior in a particular setting. *(476)*

lens The portion of the eye that captures light and focuses it on the retina. *(98)*

levels of generality A concept's grouping of objects in broader or narrower categories (for example a "fruit" vs. an "apple"). *(196)*

life review A self-examination that many old people undergo when they realize they are approaching death. *(280)*

life structure The basic pattern or design of one's life at a given time. *(261)*

limbic system A set of structures attached to the bottom of the cerebral cortex that appear to be involved in emotional expression. *(48)*

lipofuscin The chemical that causes brown "age spots" to appear on the skin of older persons. *(273)*

lithium carbonate An antidepressant drug used to treat bipolar disorders. *(433)*

locus of control The perceived set of factors that influence what happens to a person. Persons with an *internal* locus of control believe their own behaviors generally determine their outcomes, whereas those with an *external* locus of control believe that external forces control their lives. *(343)*

loneliness A feeling of longing and emptiness caused by a lack of emotional attachments (*emotional isolation*) or of social ties (*social isolation*). *(516)*

longitudinal study A research study in which subjects are followed over a long period of time. *(274)* See also *cross-sectional study.*

long-term memory Mental storage of information for an indefinite period of time. *(164)*

long-term potentiation Elevated neural response following high-frequency stimulation, proposed as a physiological basis for long-term memory. *(174)*

loudness Variation in sound perception in relation to changes in the amplitude of the sound wave. *(106)*

LSD (lysergic acid diethylamide) A drug chemically derived from ergotic alkaloids that is capable of producing vivid imagery, hallucinations, and mental disorganization. *(80)*

mainstreaming Allowing retarded students to attend regular school classes for at least part of the school day. *(214)*

malleus One of the three small bones of the middle ear. *(106)*

mania A state of intense excitement that may be so extreme that the individual becomes disoriented, incoherent, unresponsive to others, and potentially violent. *(403)*

manic-depressive disorder See *bipolar disorder.*

manifest dream content According to

Freud, the surface meaning of a dream, hiding its latent content. *(76)*

marijuana A psychoactive drug made from the hemp plant, *Cannabis sativa.* *(80)*

maturation The unfolding of inherited biological patterns that are preprogrammed into each individual. *(225)*

mean A measure of central tendency that is determined by adding individual scores and dividing by the total number of scores in order to arrive at an average. *(542)* See also *median; mode.*

means-end analysis A problem-solving strategy in which the person goes back and forth between goals to be achieved (ends) and methods (or means) to achieve these goals. *(204)*

median A measure of central tendency represented by the score that falls in the exact middle of the distribution; half the scores fall above this number and half fall below. *(542)* See also *mean; mode.*

medical model Defining normality in terms of health and disease and treating mental illness as a disease to be cured. *(393)*

meditation A state of consciousness achieved by relaxing the body and focusing the mind on one thought or object. *(86)*

medium In persuasion, the means by which a message is conveyed— face-to-face, by radio, in newsprint, and so on. *(465)*

medulla A structure in the brain stem that controls such basic rhythms as heartbeat and breathing and that contains reflex centers for vomiting, sneezing, coughing, and swallowing. *(48)*

menarche The first menstrual period. *(246)*

menopause The cessation of menstruation. *(270)*

menstrual syndrome The physical and emotional experiences many women are thought to undergo each month at the time of menstruation. *(57)*

mental age A measure of intellectual ability obtained from tests that have been standardized using average scores of children at each age level. *(205)*

mental retardation Intellectual deficits marked by IQ scores lower than 70. Retardation ranges from mild (IQ of 55–69) to profound (IQ lower than 25). *(212)* See also *clinical retardation; sociocultural retardation.*

mesomorph The muscular or athletic physical type. *(325)* See also *ectomorph; endomorph.*

message In persuasion, the content of the argument being conveyed. *(465)*

method of loci A memory system in which items to be learned are mentally placed in a set of familiar locations that follow some logical order. *(179)*

midlife crisis The sudden recognition, at around age 40, that one's life is half over, accompanied by a questioning of the meaning of one's life and a reassessment of one's goals. *(265)*

midlife transition The shift, at around age 40, from early to middle adulthood, involving changes in tasks, limitations, and opportunities. *(265)*

Minnesota Multiphasic Personality Inventory (MMPI) A personality test, consisting of 550 items, originally designed to assess psychological disorders. *(347)*

minority influences The ability of minorities within a larger group to convert the group to their position. *(465)*

mode The score that occurs most often in a frequency distribution—the most "popular" score. *(542)* See also *mean; median.*

modeling Observing the behavior of others and emulating their behavior. *(151)*

monochromatic color blindness The inability to perceive color caused by a lack of cone cells. *(103)*

monocular depth cues Clues to an object's distance that can be perceived with only one eye. *(104)*

moral development Changes in a child's views of right and wrong that occur with changes in cognitive abilities. *(242)*

moral independence According to Piaget, the ability to devise and modify rules to fit particular situations. *(242)*

moral realism According to Piaget, morality based on acceptance of rules given by an authority. *(242)*

motion parallax The fact that images of objects close to the eye move across the retina faster than images of objects farther away. *(104)*

motivated forgetting Forgetting things because remembering them would be embarrassing or painful. *(172)*

motivation A tendency to act to achieve a particular goal or state. *(292)*

motives The internal factors that arouse and direct behavior. *(292)*

motor neurons See *efferent neurons.*

motor skills The ability to control the movement of body parts. *(234)*

Müller-Lyer illusion An optical illusion demonstrating that lines of equal length will appear unequal if arrow shapes pointing inward are placed on one line and arrow shapes pointing outward are placed on the other. *(122)*

multiple personality A dissociative disorder characterized by the existence of two or more distinct personalities in the body. *(400)*

myelin sheath A white, fatty substance encasing certain nerve fibers. *(42)*

narcolepsy A disorder characterized by brief attacks of deep sleep. *(74)*

natural childbirth Childbirth without medication or instruments, usually involving relaxation training by the mother to reduce the pain of delivery. *(230)*

natural selection Darwin's principle that those organisms best able to adapt to their environment are the ones that will survive to produce offspring. *(34)*

nearsightedness Poor visual acuity for distant objects, caused by the image falling in front of the retina. *(100)* See also *farsightedness.*

Necker cube An ambiguous graphic presentation of a cube. *(123)*

need A biological condition of deprivation that stimulates activity toward correcting the condition. *(295)*

need to achieve See *achievement motive.*

negative reinforcement The strengthening of a response by removing an unpleasant stimulus. *(141)*

neo-Freudians Psychoanalytic theorists who were strongly influenced by Freud's theory but gave less priority to the role of instinctual drives and fixed stages of development. *(338)*

neologisms Invented words that have meaning only to the inventor. *(408)*

nervous system See *central nervous system; peripheral nervous system.*

neural transmission The process by which neurons communicate with one another. *(42)*

neurons The basic cells of the nervous system. *(42)*

neuropeptides A recently discovered family of chemicals in the brain that has major effects on experience and behavior. *(58)*

neuroscience The modern interdisciplinary study of the neurological bases of behavior and mental processes. *(7)*

neuroses Relatively mild psychological disorders characterized by anxiety, inability to cope effectively with challenges, and difficulty in interpersonal relationships. *(391)*

neutral stimulus A stimulus that does not produce a specific unconditioned response. *(133)*

neurotransmitters A group of chemicals in the nervous system that carries messages across synapses. *(55)*

non-age-graded influences Experiences and events that are unique to the individual rather than associated with a particular stage of life. *(259)* See also *age-graded influences.*

nonimitative aggression Aggressive acts engaged in by children who have observed an aggressive model but whose aggression does not duplicate that of the model. *(320)* See also *imitative aggression.*

non-REM sleep That period of sleep during which the person passes through four sleep stages, each characterized by specific EEG patterns, but does not dream. *(73)* See also *REM sleep.*

norepinephrine A hormone secreted by the adrenal glands that is involved in physiological arousal; also, a neurotransmitter in the brain. *(55)*

normal distribution Distribution of scores on a test in which the majority of the test-takers achieve scores in the middle range, while increasingly fewer achieve scores toward the higher and lower ends of the range. *(206)*

norms See *social norms.*

obedience Doing something because an authority tells one to. *(472)*

object permanence The recognition that a physical object continues to exist even when it is out of sight or out of reach. *(236)*

observation A method of research in which the researcher observes behavior as it occurs in a particular situation. *(20, 346)*

obsession A persistent unwanted thought. *(402)*

obsessive-compulsive disorder An anxiety disorder characterized by persistent unwanted thoughts and repeated, ritualistic behavior. *(402)*

occipital lobe The section of the cerebral cortex primarily involved in seeing and perhaps in memory. *(49)*

Oedipus complex According to Freud, the young boy's feeling of sexual attraction toward his mother and hostility toward his father. *(333)*

olfaction The sense of smell. *(112)*

olfactory neurons Sensory receptors for smell. *(112)*

open-ended questions In opinion polling, measuring devices that allow respondents to give any answer they wish. *(454)* See also *fixed-response questions.*

operant conditioning A type of learning in which behaviors increase or decrease in frequency as the result of application or withdrawal of rewards. *(136)*

operant therapy A method of behavior therapy in which rewards are used to motivate a client to perform a desired behavior or to refrain from performing an undesired behavior. *(428)*

operations The ability to mentally manipulate objects or ideas. *(240)*

opponent cells Cells in the retina responsible for coding color information passed on from the cones. *(100)*

optic nerve The nerve tract that carries messages from the eye to the visual portion of the brain. *(99)*

oral stage According to Freud, the first stage in psychosexual development (from birth to age 2), during which the mouth is the primary focus of pleasure. *(333)*

organizational psychology The subfield of psychology that focuses on devising methods for businesses and other organizations to function more effectively. *(26)*

orgasmic phase In human sexual responses, the phase in which sexual tension is released in the form of orgasm. *(500)*

overregularization In language learning, a child's tendency to apply a grammatical rule in all instances—even when it is incorrect. *(194)*

panic attacks Overwhelming attacks of dread, uneasiness, and apprehension, accompanied by various physical symptoms. *(399)*

paranoid schizophrenia A type of psychosis characterized by intense delusions and hallucinations. *(406)*

parascience Ways of looking at the world that do not employ the traditional methods of science. *(29)*

parasympathetic nervous system A subdivision of the autonomic nervous system; it acts to slow down bodily functions, especially after a stress reaction. *(40)* See also *sympathetic nervous system.*

parietal lobe The section of the cerebral cortex concerned with the skin senses and the sense of bodily position. *(49)*

partial reinforcement Rewarding a particular response some but not all of the time. *(143)*

peak experience According to Maslow, a feeling of total appreciation of a moment in time or of intense fulfillment. *(344)*

peer counseling An approach to therapy in which people with problems and backgrounds similar to those of clients are used as counselors. *(440)*

penis envy In psychoanalytic theory, the young girl's wish to possess the more "desirable" sexual organ—the penis. *(335)*

perception The processes by which people come to experience the stimuli in their environment. *(97)*

perceptual adaptation The tendency to adjust our perceptions and judgments on the basis of comparisons to previous experiences. *(121)*

perceptual constancy The tendency to perceive objects as unchanging, despite changes in lighting or distance. *(120)*

perceptual illusions Instances in which perception and reality do not agree. *(120)*

perceptual organization The way individual sensations are organized into meaningful perceptions of reality. *(116)*

perceptual organization deficit A type of cognitive deficit in which schizophrenic patients have trouble organizing the features of an object so that they can see the object as a single unit. *(408)*

peripheral nervous system Nerve fibers and tissues lying outside the brain and spinal cord. *(39)*

permissive child rearing A child-rearing style in which the parent avoids attempts to actively control the child's behavior. *(245)* See also *authoritarian child rearing.*

personal unconscious According to Jung, repressed or forgotten material. *(338)* See also *collective unconscious.*

personality The distinctive patterns of behavior, thought, and emotions that characterize an individual's adaptation to the situations of his or her life. *(324)*

personality disorder A psychological disorder characterized by a rigid and narrow range of responses that significantly restrict the person's way of relating to his or her environment. *(407)*

personnel psychology The subfield of psychology concerned with selecting workers for particular jobs and with issues of morale and job satisfaction. *(26)*

person perception Forming inferences about other people on the basis of their physical appearance, reputation, or observable behavior. *(517)*

perspective The apparent convergence of parallel lines as they extend into the dis-

tance, thus providing a cue to help perceive depth. *(104)*

persuasion Messages designed to change the views of people who receive them. *(463)*

peyote The Mexican name for the mescale cactus, from which mescaline is derived. Used as a drug, peyote produces intense sensory experiences and hallucinations. *(80)*

phallic stage According to Freud, the stage of psychosexual development (ages 4 to 5) during which the sex organs become the focus of pleasure and the Oedipal and Electra conflicts must be resolved. *(333)*

phenothiazines A group of antipsychotic drugs used in the treatment of schizophrenia. *(433)*

phenotype The outward expression of an organism's genetic makeup—its observable characteristics. *(36)* See also *genotype.*

phenylketonuria (PKU) A genetic disease caused by impaired protein metabolism; if left untreated, it is characterized by mental retardation, hyperactivity, and seizures. *(39)*

phobia An intense irrational fear of a particular object or activity. *(399)*

phonemes The recognizable sound units of a language. *(193)*

phrenology A discredited approach to the study of personality based on the idea that the bumps and hollows of the skull represent specific personality traits. *(29)*

physiological addiction The body's physical dependence on a drug such that its removal produces a withdrawal syndrome. *(80)*

physiological psychology The subfield of psychology concerned with the biological foundations of behavior and mental processes. *(25)*

pitch The high or low quality of a sound. *(106)*

PKU See *phenylketonuria.*

placebo effect The power of expectations that a treatment will work to alleviate the condition. *(371)*

placenta A network of blood vessels and membranes connecting the fetus's umbilical cord to the uterus and serving as a passageway for nutrients and waste products. *(230)*

plateau phase In human sexual response, the phase between arousal and orgasm. *(500)*

Ponzo illusion An optical illusion in which equal horizontal lines placed over converging vertical lines appear to be unequal in length. *(123)*

positive reinforcement Rewarding a behavior in order to increase its frequency. *(141)*

positive transfer Applying past experience in solving problems to new situations. *(201)*

positron-emission tomography (PET) A technique for studying the brain that monitors the concentration of glucose in different parts of the functioning brain. *(46)*

posthypnotic amnesia Forgetting that is induced by hypnotic suggestion. *(85)*

posthypnotic suggestion An instruction given during hypnosis to perform some behavior once the trance is over. *(84)*

PQ4R method A studying technique comprising six stages: preview, question, read, reflect, recite, and review. *(179)*

predisposition A readiness to behave or develop in a particular way. *(494)*

prefrontal lobotomy An operation in which the frontal lobes are separated from the rest of the brain. *(437)*

prejudice An unfavorable attitude held about a particular group of people. *(479)*

prenatal development Development in the uterus from conception to birth. *(228)*

preoperational stage According to Piaget, the second stage of cognitive development (ages 2 through 7), during which the child has not yet mastered such basic mental operations as conservation. *(235)*

primal therapy Arthur Janov's method of therapy, in which the client is encouraged to reexperience childhood pain and to release emotions built up over a lifetime. *(444)*

primary reinforcers Stimuli that naturally increase a response, such as food, water, and affection. *(140)* See also *secondary reinforcers.*

proactive interference Interference with a learning task that is caused by previously learned material. *(170)* See also *retroactive interference.*

problem A mental task that involves figuring out how to achieve a goal. *(197)*

process schizophrenia Schizophrenia that develops gradually and slowly; it is more resistant to treatment than reactive schizophrenia. *(408)*

projection The unconscious attribution of one's own unacceptable thoughts and feelings to other people. *(336)*

progressive muscle relaxation A stress-management technique in which people are taught to discriminate tension in various muscle groups and then to relax those muscles. *(369)*

projective tests Personality tests in which the individual is asked to provide her own interpretation of materials such as pictures or inkblots. *(348)*

prosopagnosia An inability to identify people from their faces. *(51)*

protocol analysis The research method of obtaining and analyzing subjects' streams of thoughts while solving problems. *(202)*

prototypical concepts Instances of a concept that are most representative of that concept. *(195)*

proximity In social psychology, the physical distance between people. *(522)* In perception, the tendency to link objects that are close to one another. *(116)*

psilocybin A psychedelic drug derived from mushrooms. *(80)*

psychedelic drugs Drugs that cause extreme alterations in perception and thought processes, often producing delu-sions, hallucinations, and intensified sensory awareness. *(78)*

psychiatrist A medical doctor who specializes in the diagnosis and treatment of mental disorders. *(25)*

psychoactive drugs Drugs that have a noticeable impact on consciousness and behavior. *(78)*

psychoanalysis The method of psychotherapy based on Freud's psychoanalytic theory of personality; its basic premise is that the unconscious mind contains buried impulses and desires that must be brought to the surface if anxiety is to disappear. *(422)*

psychoanalytic theory Freud's theory that all human behavior is dominated by instinctual biological urges that must be controlled; it is the conflict between the urges and the efforts to control them that leads to emotional problems. *(330)*

psychodrama A method of therapy in which one acts out scenes in order to bring out their emotional significance. *(425)*

psychoimmunology Study of the psychological factors that can influence immune system functioning. *(368)*

psychological adequacy How well people adjust to and cope with their environment. *(393)*

psychological androgyny The ability to integrate both "masculine" and "feminine" traits into one's personality. *(511)*

psychological dependence A strong psychological need to continue taking a drug at practically any cost. *(80)*

psychological reactance The motive to restore or reassert a threatened freedom, sometimes by doing the opposite of whatever we feel others are trying to make us do. *(472)*

psychology The science of behavior and mental processes. *(5)*

psychopharmacology The use of drugs to affect patients' moods and behaviors. *(432)*

psychoses Major psychological disorders characterized by loss of contact with reality, loss of control over feelings and actions, and such symptoms as delusions and hallucinations. *(391)*

psychosexual stages According to Freud, stages that children go through in which their sexual energy is focused on different areas of the body. *(333)* See also *anal stage; genital stage; latency period; oral stage; phallic stage.*

psychosocial stages Eight stages of personality development through the life cycle, as proposed by Erikson. At each stage the individual must resolve a different crisis. *(229)*

psychosomatic disease Physical disorder caused at least in part by stress or other psychological factors. *(364)*

psychosurgery Brain surgery designed to relieve psychological symptoms. *(437)*

punishment An unpleasant event or outcome following a response. *(145)*

pupil The opening in the eye that allows light rays to enter. *(98)*

racism The differential attitudes toward and treatment of individuals on the basis of their racial group membership, grounded in a belief (whether conscious or unconscious) that one race is inherently superior to another. *(479)*

random sample In statistics, a sample in which each member of the population being studied has an equal chance of being chosen. *(543)*

range The variability of a set of scores as indicated by the lowest and highest scores in the distribution. *(543)*

rating scales A method of personality assessment in which people who know the subject are asked to rate descriptions of him. *(346)*

ratio schedule See *fixed-ratio schedule; variable-ratio schedule.*

rational-emotive therapy Albert Ellis's approach to therapy, which assumes that emotional difficulties are caused by irrational thinking. *(431)*

rationalization Justifying one's actions by substituting an acceptable explanation for the real, unacceptable reason. *(337)*

reaction formation Developing behavior patterns the opposite of those that would create anxiety. *(336)*

reactive schizophrenia Schizophrenia that strikes suddenly, in reaction to a stressful life event. *(408)* See also *process schizophrenia.*

rebirthing A therapy designed to help the individual reexperience the trauma of birth in order to exorcise the pain. *(445)*

recall A measure of retention in which the individual must recount or reproduce something previously learned. *(169)*

receptor cells Sensitive cells in sense organs. *(97)*

recessive gene A gene that is expressed only when a dominant gene for that trait is not present. *(36)*

recognition A measure of retention in which the individual must identify something previously encountered. *(169)*

reconstructive memory The idea that our wider knowledge of the world affects the way we remember a specific event. *(166)*

reference group A group with which one identifies and from which one derives many of one's attitudes. *(463)*

reflex An automatic action involving sensory nerves, motor nerves, and the spinal cord, with no intervention from higher brain centers. *(39)*

refractory period In men, a period following orgasm during which further excitation is impossible. *(500)*

rehearsal Repeating of information to oneself in order to store it in long-term memory. *(164)*

reinforcement Any event following a response that strengthens that response or that increases the probability of the response occurring again. *(140)* See also *delayed reinforcement; negative reinforcement; partial reinforcement; positive reinforcement; schedules of reinforcement.*

relaxation response A reduction in heart rate, breathing rate, blood pressure, and similar physiological responses through meditation and other relaxation techniques. *(369)*

relearning A measure of retention in which an individual is asked to relearn material previously learned; the speed with which relearning takes place is an indication of how much information has been retained. Also called the *savings method*. *(169)*

reliability In personality testing, the extent to which a method can be counted on to lead to the same conclusions about a person's characteristics on successive testings or when administered by different testers. *(345)* In abnormal psychology, the extent to which experts agree on the particular diagnostic category to place a patient in. *(398)* See also *validity*.

REM sleep A period of sleep during which rapid eye movements and a specific EEG pattern occur and the individual appears to be dreaming. *(73)* See also *non-REM sleep*.

repression The exclusion of unpleasant or painful memories or impulses from conscious awareness. *(172, 336)*

research See *applied research; basic research*.

resistance In psychoanalysis, the reluctance to bring important ideas into consciousness. *(422)*

resistance stage According to Selye, the second stage in an animal's physiological response to stress; it involves mobilizing the body to deal with the stressful situation. *(359)* See also *alarm reaction; exhaustion stage*.

resolution phase In human sexual response, the phase following orgasm in which the body gradually returns to its preexcitement state. *(500)*

reticular formation Nerve tissue in the brain stem that serves to screen incoming messages and alert higher brain centers to important information. *(54)*

retina An inner lining at the back of the eye that contains the light-sensitive rods and cones. *(98)*

retrieval The ability to locate information in long-term memory. *(166)*

retrieval failure Forgetting that is due to the inability to locate material in long-term memory. *(171)*

retroactive interference Inability to recall previously learned material caused by interference of more recently learned material. *(170)* See also *proactive interference*.

retrograde amnesia Loss of memory for events immediately preceding an accident or electroshock therapy. *(174)*

reversibility Understanding that manipulations of a substance's weight, mass, or volume can be reversed. *(240)*

rhodopsin (visual purple) A chemical in the rods of the retina that changes when exposed to light. *(98)*

rods Light-sensitive cells in the retina that are insensitive to color. *(98)*

role playing In behavior therapy, practicing a set of desired behaviors in a protective setting in which clients need not worry about the consequences of their behavior. *(430)*

roles The positions that people occupy in life, together with the sets of behaviors that are expected of people in those positions. *(497)*

Rorschach inkblot test A personality test in which individuals are asked to respond to a series of ambiguous inkblots. *(348)*

sample A group of subjects representing a larger population. *(15, 543)*

savings See *relearning*.

schedules of reinforcement Administration of reinforcement according to a fixed or varying number of responses or time interval. *(143)*

schizophrenia A type of psychosis characterized by serious alterations of perception, activity, emotion, thought, and personality. *(405)* See also *catatonia; disorganized schizophrenia; paranoid schizophrenia; process schizophrenia; undifferentiated schizophrenia*.

secondary reinforcers Stimuli that become reinforcers as a result of association with primary reinforcers. *(140)*

selective perception The tendency to perceive what one expects to. *(119)*

self-actualization According to Maslow, full realization of one's potential as a human being. *(294)*

self-concept An organized, consistent image of oneself. *(342)*

self-esteem One's positive regard for oneself. *(342)*

self-perception theory Bem's idea that people arrive at attitudes after they behave in certain ways and reflect on that behavior. *(460)*

self-report inventories Personality assessment instruments, such as the MMPI, that ask people to rate statements about themselves. *(346)*

self-reports People's own assessments of their thoughts and feelings, as reported to researchers. *(18)*

semicircular canals The sense organs for equilibrium located in the inner ear. *(111)*

senile dementia A disease caused by damage to brain cells in old age, producing such symptoms as memory loss, disorientation in time and place, and impaired attention. *(274)*

sensation seeking The degree to which a person is ready to take risks and try new experiences. *(328)*

senses The organs and neural pathways through which information about the environment is received, including vision, hearing, the skin senses, smell, and taste. *(97)*

sensorimotor stage According to Piaget, the first stage of cognitive development (from birth to age 2), during which the child learns to coordinate sensory information and motor (muscle) activities. *(235)*

sensory adaptation The tendency of sense organs to adjust themselves to a particular level of stimulation. *(121)*

sensory deprivation Placing a person in a specially designed environment devoid of sensory stimulation, producing alterations in perception and consciousness. *(108)*

sensory neurons See *afferent neurons*.

sensory storage The momentary retention of sensory information after it has been received. *(163)*

sensory threshold The smallest amount of stimulation that can be detected by a particular sense organ. *(99)*

serotonin A transmitter substance in the brain that apparently plays a role in temperature regulation and sensory perception. *(55)*

set point A certain predetermined level of fat content in the body at which the desire to eat is in equilibrium. *(297)*

sexism The idea that one sex is inherently superior to the other. *(508)*

sex therapy Various techniques used to treat sexual dysfunction. *(501)*

sexual double standard The idea that the rules governing male sexual behavior are different from the rules governing female sexual behavior. *(502)*

sexual dysfunction Problems with performing intercourse, enjoying sex, or reaching orgasm. *(501)*

short-term memory Information that has just been learned and that may be retained for up to 20 seconds before being forgotten or transferred to long-term memory. *(163)*

shyness The tendency to feel anxious and uncomfortable in the presence of others. *(514)*

sickle-cell anemia A serious genetic disorder among blacks, in which abnormally shaped blood cells cut off oxygen supplies to vital tissues. *(39)*

similarity In perception, the tendency to perceive as a unit elements that are similar to one another. *(117)* In social psychology, the tendency to choose friends with similar backgrounds and beliefs. *(522)*

size constancy The process by which we take into account changing distances and other cues in order to perceive objects as remaining the same size. *(120)*

skin senses The receptors in the skin for pressure, temperature, and pain. *(109)*

Skinner box An apparatus, developed by B. F. Skinner, used for studying operant conditioning of animals. *(136)*

sociability The disposition to spend time with and socialize with others. *(514)*

social comparison The idea that people have a need to compare themselves with others in a similar situation in order to clarify their own feelings and experiences. *(513)*

social influence The ways in which people's attitudes or behavior are changed by other people or groups. *(453)*

social isolation See *loneliness*.

social learning theory An approach to personality that focuses on the role of imitation and social rewards in the learning of patterns of behavior. *(338)*

social motives Motives that involve our orientation toward other people, such as the need to affiliate. *(292)*

social norms Rules that dictate appropriate and inappropriate behavior in a society. *(481)*

social psychology The subfield of psychology that focuses on the ways in which people's behavior is affected by other people and by the social environment. *(25)*

social relationship The pattern of interactions between two people that extends over a period of time, plus the thoughts and feelings these two people have about each other. *(513)*

social support The benefits that others provide in helping us face the challenges of life. *(376)*

social ties Social relationships with a network of friends. *(515)*

sociocultural retardation Mild mental retardation that is not usually diagnosed until a child enters school and that has multiple causes related to economic and social disadvantages. *(212)* See also *clinical retardation.*

somatic nervous system The part of the peripheral nervous system that controls voluntary muscles and hence most body movements. *(40)* See also *autonomic nervous system.*

somatic therapy The use of drugs, electroshock, or psychosurgery to treat the symptoms of psychological disorder. *(432)*

somatotypes The three basic body types identified by Sheldon. *(325)* See also *ectomorph; endomorph; mesomorph.*

specificity theory of pain The idea that there are specific pain receptors throughout the body that relay signals of pain directly to the brain. *(110)* See also *gate control theory.*

spinal cord A cylindrical structure of nerve tissue stretching from the base of the spine down through the center of the backbone; it provides basic connections between motor and sensory neurons and serves as a pathway for messages traveling to and from the brain. *(39)*

split-brain surgery Severing of the corpus callosum, thereby greatly reducing communication between the two cerebral hemispheres. *(54)*

spontaneous recovery The later reappearance of an extinguished response. *(135)*

stage A description of the way children's thought or behavior is organized during a particular period of time. *(228)*

standard deviation A statistic that indicates the amount of variability in a set of scores. It is computed on the basis of the distance of each score from the mean. *(543)*

standardization Administration of a test to a large sampling of subjects to determine the usual distribution of scores on the test. *(206)*

Stanford-Binet An intelligence test emphasizing verbal and mathematical skills. *(206)*

stapes One of the three small bones of the middle ear. *(106)*

state-dependent memory The tendency for people's memories to be best when they recall material in the same locale or same physical or mental state as when they first learned it. *(171)*

statistical significance The extent to which an observed difference between samples reflects real differences and not chance. *(544)*

statistics Numbers used to describe and interpret data and observations. *(541)*

stereotypes Notions of what entire groups of people are like based on their race, sex, occupation, or other group membership. *(197)*

stimulants Drugs that stimulate the activity of the central nervous system and thus may intensify perceptions and produce heightened activity and restlessness. *(178)*

stimulus control A situation in which a response occurs only in the presence of a specific discriminative stimulus. *(140)*

stranger anxiety The tendency of an infant to protest or withdraw when approached by an unfamiliar person. *(236)*

stress The emotional and physical reactions to stressful stimuli or events in the environment. *(358)*

stressor Pressure from the environment that makes physical and emotional demands on a person. *(358)*

stress-resistant personality Traits found in people who cope well with stress: a commitment to what they are doing, a feeling of being in control, and welcoming of moderate changes and challenges. *(363)*

structuralism An early school of psychology that emphasized the structure of conscious processes. *(6)*

subjects Persons or animals who take part in an experimental study. *(9)*

superego According to Freud, the part of the personality that acquires the values and ideals of the parents and society and imposes constraints on the id and ego; the conscience. *(332)*

surrogate mother An artificial or substitute mother, such as those used by Harlow in his experiments with infant monkeys. *(237)*

survey A study in which hundreds or even thousands of subjects are questioned. *(17)*

syllogism A logical statement comprising a major premise, a minor premise, and a conclusion. *(458)*

symbolism In Freud's view, the translation of unacceptable ideas into more acceptable or symbolic forms. *(74)*

sympathetic nervous system A subdivision of the autonomic nervous system; it acts to accelerate certain bodily processes in response to stress. *(40)* See also *parasympathetic nervous system.*

synapse The microscopic gap that separates the end of each axon from the dendrite or cell body of another neuron and across which transmitter substances travel. *(43)*

synaptic transmission The movement of nerve impulses across a synapse from one neuron to another. *(43)*

synesthesia The blending of senses, such as hearing color or seeing tastes. *(106)*

systematic desensitization A behavioral approach to treating fears and anxieties; it involves arranging fearful scenes in an anxiety hierarchy and then learning to relax while imagining each scene, in the order from least fearful to most fearful. *(427)*

tardive dyskinesia A neurological condition caused by prolonged use of antipsychotic drugs. *(435)*

taste buds Receptor cells for the sense of taste. *(113)*

TAT See *Thematic Apperception Test.*

Tay-Sachs disease A fatal genetic disease striking infants descended from Eastern European Jews. *(39)*

telepathy The awareness of another person's thoughts without benefit of normal sensory channels; a form of extrasensory perception. *(115)*

temperament A consistent style of responding to the world. *(239)*

temporal lobe The section of the cerebral cortex that contains centers for hearing and speech and possibly sites for memory and learning. *(49)*

testosterone The male sex hormone. *(56)*

texture gradient An apparent change in the surface of an object as it extends away in space; texture gradients provide cues for depth perception. *(104)*

Thematic Apperception Test (TAT) A personality test in which the person is asked to react to a series of drawings. *(348)*

theory A set of ideas and principles that fits together to provide a perspective on some aspect of the world. *(15)*

therapy The professional application of techniques intended to treat psychological problems and reduce stress. *(421)*

thought The mental manipulation of ideas and concepts. *(188)*

thought disorders Abnormal patterns of language, logic, and information processing that are characteristic of schizophrenia. *(408)*

thyroid gland An endocrine gland that helps control the body's metabolism. *(55)*

thyroxin A hormone, released by the thyroid gland, that regulates aspects of metabolism. *(55)*

timbre The richness or quality of a sound that comes from a particular sound source. *(106)*

tip-of-the-tongue (TOT) phenomenon The feeling of almost, but not quite, being able to recall a word or name. *(167)*

token economy A form of behavior therapy in which the individual is given a token for each task accomplished; the tokens can later be traded for items that are rewarding to the individual. *(157)*

trait A relatively enduring quality or characteristic of thought, feeling, or behavior that some people have more than others. *(339)*

transcendental meditation (TM) A system of meditation developed by Maharishi Mahesh Yogi. *(86)*

transference In psychoanalysis, the patient's tendency to treat the analyst in the same way he would treat an important authority figure in his life. *(423)*

transformational grammar A set of rules about how words are usually joined in a sentence and how sentences can be transformed, or changed around, without changing their meaning. *(190)*

transient global amnesia A disorder in which brain damage causes the patient to suffer attacks in which he is unable to hold onto information for more than a few seconds before forgetting it. *(175)*

transsexual A person who believes that he or she is trapped in a body of the wrong sex. *(498)*

trial and error Trying many solutions to a problem, one after another, in hopes that one will finally work. *(200)*

tricyclics Widely used antidepressant drugs. *(433)*

twins See *fraternal twins; identical twins.*

tympanic membrane The eardrum. *(106)*

Type A behavior pattern A hard-driving, competitive, aggressive personality style that has been linked to increased risk of heart attack. *(365)*

ultradian rhythm A biological rhythm or cycle that occurs more often than once a day, such as the heartbeat. *(91)*

unconditional positive regard In client-centered therapy, the idea that the therapist should accept and respect the client and whatever she has to say. *(424)*

unconditioned response A response that naturally occurs for a given stimulus, before any conditioning takes place. *(133)*

unconditioned stimulus A stimulus that produces an unconditioned response. *(133)*

unconscious Ideas or impulses that a person has but is not aware of. *(67)* See also *collective unconscious; personal unconscious.*

undifferentiated schizophrenia Schizophrenia characterized by a wide variety of symptoms. *(408)*

validity In personality testing, the extent to which the conclusions of a test about an individual's personality are accurate. *(345)* In abnormal psychology, the extent to which a diagnostic category provides an accurate understanding of the causes and future course of the disorder. *(398)* See also *reliability.*

variable See *dependent variable; independent variable.*

variable-interval schedule Administering reinforcement after a time period has passed, with the interval varying around some average. *(144)* See also *fixed-interval schedule.*

variable-ratio schedule Administering reinforcement after a number of responses, with the number varying around some average. *(143)* See also *fixed-ratio schedule.*

verbal learning Retention in memory of words, letters, or other verbal material. *(169)*

visual acuity The ability to discriminate details in the field of vision. *(100)*

visual cliff An experimental apparatus designed to test depth perception in infants. *(105)*

visual purple See *rhodopsin.*

visual threshold The smallest amount of stimulation the rods and cones will respond to. *(99)*

Wechsler Adult Intelligence Scale (WAIS) A test of adult mental ability assessing both verbal abilities and performance skills. *(206)*

wellness Actively striving to maintain and improve one's health. *(380)*

Wernicke's area An area of the left temporal lobe of the brain that is involved in language. *(51)*

withdrawal syndrome A painful illness that occurs when an addicted person stops taking a drug. *(80)*

zygote The fertilized egg. *(230)*

BIBLIOGRAPHY

Aarons, L. Sleep-assisted instruction. *Psychological Bulletin*, 1976, *83*, 1–40.

ABC News/Washington Post Survey. February 26–March 6, 1981. Reported in *Public Opinion*, April–May, 1981.

Abell, G. O. The Mars effect. *Psychology Today*, July 1982.

Abramovitch, R.; Corter, C.; and Lando, B. Sibling interaction in the home. *Child Development*, 1979, *50*, 997–1003.

Adams, B. N. *Kinship in an urban setting.* Chicago: Markham, 1968.

Adams, B., and Cromwell, R. Morning and night people in the family: A preliminary statement. *Family Coordinator*, 1978, *27*, 5–13.

Adams, V. Behavioral scientists argue guilt's role. *New York Times*, July 24, 1979.

Adelson, R., et al. A modeling film to reduce children's fear of dental treatment. *International Association of Dental Research Abstracts*, March 1972.

Adler, A. The significance of early recollections. *International Journal of Individual Psychology*, 1937, *3*, 283–287.

Adorno, T. W., et al. *The authoritarian personality.* New York: Harper & Row, 1950.

Ainsworth, M. *Patterns of attachment.* Hillside, N.J.: Lawrence Erlbaum, 1978.

Allport, G. W. *The nature of prejudice.* Reading, Mass.: Addison-Wesley, 1954.

Alper, J. Biology and mental illness. *Atlantic Monthly*, December 1983.

Altman, L. K. Perceptions hinder treatment of senility. *New York Times*, June 24, 1980.

Amabile, T. M. Motivation and creativity: Effects of motivational orientation on creative writers. *Journal of Personality and Social Psychology*, 1985 (in press).

Amabile, T. M. *The social psychology of creativity.* New York: Springer-Verlag, 1983.

American Psychiatric Association, *Electroconvulsive therapy: Task force report 14.* Washington, D.C.: APA, 1978.

American Psychiatric Association. *Diagnostic and statistical manual of mental disorders.* (3rd ed.) Washington, D.C.: APA, 1980.

American Psychological Association. Ethical principles of psychologists. *American Psychologist*, 1981, *36*, 633–638.

Andersen, K. Crashing on cocaine. *Time*, April 13, 1983.

Andersen, S. M., and Zimbardo, P. G. Resisting mind control. *USA Today*, November 1980.

Anderson, J. R. *Cognitive psychology and its implications.* San Francisco: W. H. Freeman, 1980.

Andrew, S. M., et al. Reasons for dropout from exercise programs in postcoronary patients. *Medicine and Science in Sports and Exercise*, 1981, *13*, 164–168.

Anthony, D. S. Is graphology valid? *Psychology Today*, August 1967.

Appelbaum, P. S. Can mental patients say no to drugs? *New York Times Magazine*, March 21, 1982.

Appelbaum, S. Challenge to traditional psychotherapy from the "new therapies." *American Psychologist*, 1982, *37*, 1002–1008.

Appleyard, D., and Lintell, M. The environmental quality of city streets: The residents' viewpoint. *Journal of the American Institute of Planners*, 1972, *38*, 84–101.

Archer, D. Reading nonverbal clues. In Z. Rubin and E. B. McNeil, *The psychology of being human.* (Brief update ed.) New York: Harper & Row, 1979.

Archer, D. *How to expand your S.I.Q. (Social Intelligence Quotient).* New York: M. Evans, 1980.

Archer, D., and Akert, R. Words and everything else: Verbal and nonverbal cues in social interpretation. *Journal of Personality and Social Psychology*, 1977, *35*, 443–449.

Archer, D., and Gartner, R. War and violent crime. In S. H. Kadish (Ed.), *The encyclopedia of crime and justice*, New York: Free Press, 1983.

Archer, D.; Iritani, B.; Kimes, D. D.; and Barrios, M. Face-ism: Five studies of sex differences in facial prominence. *Journal of Personality and Social Psychology*, 1983, *45*, 725–735.

Arehart-Treichel, J. The great pain plan. *Science News*, October 14, 1978.

Arend, R.; Gove, F.; and Sroufe, L. A. Continuity of individual adaptation from infancy to kindergarten: A predictive study of ego-resiliency and curiosity in preschoolers. *Child Development*, 1979, *50*, 950–959.

Arieti, S., and Meth, J. M. Rare, unclassifiable, collective, and exotic psychotic syndromes. In S. Arieti (Ed.), *American handbook of psychiatry*, vol. 1. New York: Basic Books, 1959.

Arkin, W. Prolegomenon to the study of "brother" as a male family role. *Family Coordinator*, 1981, *28*, 630–637.

Aronson, E., et al. *The jigsaw classroom.* Beverly Hills, Calif.: Sage Publications, 1978.

Asch, S. E. Effects of group pressure upon the modification and distortion of judgments. In H. Guetzkow (Ed.), *Groups, leadership, and men.* Pittsburgh: Carnegie Press, 1951.

Atkinson, R. C. Teaching children to read using a computer. *American Psychologist*, 1974, *29*, 169–178.

Atkinson, R. C. Mnemotechnics in second-language learning. *American Psychologist*, 1975, *30*, 821–828.

Atkinson, R. C., and Shiffrin, R. M. Human memory: A proposed system and its controlled processes. In K. W. Spence and J. T. Spence (Eds.), *The psychology of learning and motivation*, vol. 2. New York: Academic Press, 1968.

Attarian, P. J. Early recollections: Predictors of vocational choice. *Journal of Individual Psychology*, 1978, *34*, 56–62.

Ax, A. F. The physiological differentiation of emotional states. *Psychosomatic Medicine*, 1953, *15*, 433–442.

Axelrod, S., and Bailey, S. L. Drug treatment for hyperactivity: Controversies, alternatives, and guidelines. *Exceptional Children*, 1979, *45*, 544–550.

Ayllon, T., and Azrin, N. *The token economy: A motivational system for therapy and rehabilitation.* New York: Appleton-Century-Crofts, 1968.

Ayres, C. E. Instinct and capacity: I. The instinct of belief-in-instincts. *Journal of Philosophy*, 1921, *18*, 561–566.

Bahrick, H. P.; Bahrick, P. O.; and Wittlinger, R. P. Fifty years of memory for names and faces: A cross-sectional approach. *Journal of Experimental Psychology: General*, 1975, *104*, 54–75.

Bainbridge, W. S., and Stark, R. Superstitions: Old and new. *Skeptical Inquirer*, 1980, *4*, 18–32.

Baltes, P. B. Life-span developmental psychology: Some converging observations on history and theory. In P. B. Baltes and O. G. Brim (Eds.), *Life-span development and behavior*, vol. 2. New York: Academic Press, 1979.

Baltes, P. B., and Willis, S. L. Enhancement (plasticity) of intellectual functioning in old age: Penn State's Adult Development and Enrichment Project (ADEPT). In F. I. M. Craik and S. E. Trehub (Eds.), *Aging and cognitive processes.* New York: Plenum, 1981.

Bandura, A. Behavioral psychotherapy. *Scientific American,* March 1967.

Bandura, A. *Aggression: A social learning analysis.* Englewood Cliffs, N.J.: Prentice-Hall, 1973.

Bandura, A. Behavior theory and the models of man. *American Psychologist,* 1974, *12,* 859–869.

Bandura, A. *Social learning theory.* Englewood Cliffs, N.J.: Prentice-Hall, 1977.

Bandura, A.; Blanchard, E. B.; and Ritter, B. Relative efficacy of desensitization and modeling approaches for inducing behavioral, affective, and attitudinal changes. *Journal of Personality and Social Psychology,* 1969, *13,* 173–199.

Bandura, A.; Ross, D.; and Ross, S. Imitation of film-mediated aggressive models. *Journal of Abnormal and Social Psychology,* 1963, *67,* 601–607.

Bank, S. P., and Kahn, M. D. *The sibling bond.* New York: Basic Books, 1982.

Bardwick, J. *The psychology of women.* New York: Harper & Row, 1971.

Barfield, R. E., and Morgan, J. N. Trends in satisfaction with retirement. *The Gerontologist,* 1978, *18,* 19–23.

Barnett, R. C., and Baruch, G. K. Women in the middle years: A critique of research and theory. *Psychology of Women Quarterly,* 1978, *3,* 187–197.

Baron, R. A., and Byrne, D. *Social psychology.* (2nd ed.) Boston: Allyn and Bacon, 1977.

Barrett, C. J. Effectiveness of widows' groups in facilitating change. *Journal of Consulting and Clinical Psychology,* 1978, *46,* 20–31.

Barrett, D. The first memory as a predictor of personality traits. *Journal of Individual Psychology,* 1980, *36,* 136–149.

Barrow, G. Personal reactions to growing old. Unpublished study, Santa Rosa Junior College, 1976.

Barrow, G. M., and Smith, P. A. *Aging, ageism, and society.* St. Paul, Minn.: West, 1979.

Bartlett, F. C. *Remembering.* Cambridge, England: Cambridge University Press, 1932.

Bassuk, E. L., and Gerson, S. Deinstitutionalization and mental health services. *Scientific American,* February 1978.

Batson, C. D. Latent aspects of "From Jerusalem to Jericho . . ." In M. P. Golden (Ed.), *The Research Experience.* Itasca, Ill.: F. E. Peacock, 1976.

Baum, D. R., and Jonides, J. Cognitive maps: Analysis of comparative judgments of distance. *Memory and Cognition,* 1979, *7,* 462–468.

Baumrind, D. Current patterns of parental authority. *Developmental Monographs,* 1971, *4,* 1–103.

Beck, A. T. *Depression: Clinical, experimental and theoretical aspects.* New York: Harper & Row, 1967.

Beecher, H. K. *Measurement of subjective responses: Quantitative effects of drugs.* New York: Oxford University Press, 1959.

Begley, S. How the brain works. *Newsweek,* February 7, 1983.

Bell, A. P., and Weinberg, M. *Homosexualities: A study of human diversity.* New York: Simon & Schuster, 1978.

Bell, D. *Being a man.* Lexington, Mass.: Lewis Publishing Company, 1982.

Belmont, L., and Marolla, F. A. Birth order, family size, and intelligence. *Science,* 1973, *182,* 1096–1101.

Belsky, J., and Steinberg, L. D. The effects of day care: A critical review. *Child Development,* 1978, *49,* 929–949.

Belzer, E. G. Orgasmic expulsions of women: A review and heuristic inquiry. *Journal of Sex Research,* 1981, *17,* 1–12.

Bem, D. J. *Beliefs, attitudes, and human affairs.* Belmont, Calif.: Brooks/Cole, 1970.

Bem, D. J. Self-perception theory. In L. Berkowitz (Ed.), *Advances in experimental social psychology,* vol. 6. New York: Academic Press, 1972.

Bem, D. J., and Allen, A. On predicting some of the people some of the time: The search for cross-situational consistencies in behavior. *Psychological Review,* 1974, *81,* 506–520.

Bem, S. L. Psychology looks at sex roles: Where have all the androgynous people gone? Paper presented at UCLA Symposium on Women, May, 1972.

Bem, S. L. Androgyny vs. the tight little lives of fluffy women and chesty men. *Psychology Today,* September 1975.

Bem, S. L., and Bem, D. J. Does sex-biased job advertising "aid and abet" sex discrimination? *Journal of Applied Social Psychology,* 1973, *3,* 6–18.

Benbow, C. P., and Stanley, J. C. Sex differences in mathematical ability: Fact or artifact? *Science,* 1980, *210,* 1262–1264.

Benbow, C. P., and Stanley, J. C. Sex differences in mathematical reasoning: More facts. *Science,* 1983, *222,* 1029–1031.

Bennett, W., and Gurin, J. Do diets really work? *Science 82,* March 1982.

Benson, H. *The relaxation response.* New York: William Morrow, 1975.

Benson, P. L.; Karabenick, S. A.; and Lerner, R. M. Pretty pleases: The effects of physical attractiveness, race, and sex on receiving help. *Journal of Experimental Social Psychology,* 1976, *12,* 409–415.

Bergson, L. Suicide's other victims. *New York Times Magazine,* November 14, 1982.

Berkeley Men's Center Manifesto. In J. H. Pleck and J. Sawyer (Eds.), *Men and masculinity.* Englewood Cliffs, N.J.: Prentice-Hall, 1974.

Berkman, L. F., and Syme, S. L. Social networks, host resistance, and mortality: A nine-year follow-up study of Alameda County residents. *American Journal of Epidemiology,* 1979, *109,* 186–224.

Berkowitz, L. *Social psychology.* Glenview, Ill.: Scott, Foresman, 1972.

Berlyne, D. E. Attention as a problem in behavior theory. In D. I. Mostofsky (Ed.), *Attention: Contemporary theory and analysis.* New York: Appleton-Century-Crofts, 1970.

Berman, J. S., and Wenzlaff, R. M. The impact of therapist expectations on the outcome of psychotherapy. Paper presented at the meeting of the American Psychological Association, Anaheim, 1983.

Bernard, J. *The future of marriage,* second edition. New Haven: Yale University Press, 1982.

Berndt, T. J. The features and effects of friendship in early adolescence. *Child Development,* 1982, *53,* 1447–1460.

Bernstein, A. C. *The flight of the stork.* New York: Delacorte, 1978.

Bernstein, I. L. Learned taste aversions in children receiving chemotherapy. *Science,* 1978, *200,* 1302–1303.

Berry, D. S., and McArthur, L. Z. Some components and consequences of a baby face. *Journal of Personality and Social Psychology,* 1985 (in press).

Berscheid, E., and Walster, E. Physical attractiveness. In L. Berkowitz (Ed.), *Advances in experimental social psychology,* vol. 7. New York: Academic Press, 1974.

Bersoff, D. N. Testing and the law. *American Psychologist,* 1981, *36,* 1042–1056.

Bettelheim, B. *The empty fortress.* New York: Free Press, 1967.

Bevcar, R. J. Self-help books: Some ethical questions. *Personnel and Guidance Journal,* 1978, *56,* 160–162.

Bever, T. G., and Chiarello, R. J. Cerebral dominance in musicians and nonmusicians. *Science,* 1974, *185,* 137–139.

Billings, A. G.; Cronkite, R. C.; and Moos, R. H. Social-environmental factors in unipolar depression: Comparisons of depressed patients and nondepressed controls. *Journal of Abnormal Psychology,* 1983, *92,* 119–133.

Billman, J., and McDevitt, S. C. Convergence of peer and observer ratings of temperament with observations of peer interaction in nursery school. *Child Development,* 1980, *51,* 395–400.

Birren, J. E. *The psychology of aging.* Englewood Cliffs, N.J.: Prentice-Hall, 1964.

Bixler, E. O., et al. Prevalence of sleep disorders in the Los Angeles metropolitan area. *American Journal of Psychiatry,* 1979, *136,* 1257–1262.

Blair, S. N.; Goodyear, N. N.; Gibbons, L. W.; and Cooper, K. H. Physical fitness and incidence of hypertension in healthy normotensive men and women. *Journal of the American Medical Association,* 1984, *252,* 487–490.

Blake, J. Can we believe recent data on birth expectations in the United States? *Demography,* 1974, *11,* 25–44.

Blaney, P. H. Implications of the medical model and its alternatives. *American Journal of Psychiatry,* 1975, *132,* 911–914.

Blau, P. M. *Exchange and power in social life.* New York: Wiley, 1964.

Bliss, E. L. Multiple personalities: A report of 14 cases with implications for schizophrenia and hysteria. *Archives of General Psychiatry,* 1980, *37,* 1388–1397.

Block, J. H. Generational continuity and discontinuity in the understanding of societal rejection. *Journal of Personality and Social Psychology,* 1972, *22,* 333–345.

Bloom, B. L.; White, S. W.; and Asher, S. J. Marital disruption as a stressful life event. *Psychological Bulletin,* 1978, *85,* 867–894.

Bochner, S., and Insko, C. A. Communicator discrepancy, source credibility, and opinion change. *Journal of Personality and Social Psychology,* 1966, *4,* 614–621.

Bolles, R. Species specific defense reactions in avoidance learning. *Psychological Review,* 1970, *71,* 32–48.

Borysenko, J. Psychoimmunology: Mind, body, and health. In Z. Rubin, and E. B. McNeil, *The psychology of being human,* Brief/Update 3rd ed. New York: Harper & Row, 1983.

Borysenko, J. Ways to control stress and make it work for you (interview). *U.S. News & World Report,* March 12, 1984.

Botwinick, J. *Aging and behavior.* (2nd ed.) New York: Springer, 1978.

Bouchard, T. J., Jr.; Heston, L.; Eckert, E.; Keyes, M.; and Resnick, S. The Minnesota study of twins reared apart: Project description and sample results in the developmental domain. In *Twin research 3: Intelligence, personality, and development.* New York: Alan R. Liss, 1981.

Bower, G. H. Stimulus sampling theory of encoding variability. In A. W. Melton and E. Martin (Eds.), *Coding processes in human memory.* Washington, D.C.: Winston, 1972.

Bower, G. H. Memorizing with imaginary maps. In G. Lindzey, C. Hall, and R. F. Thompson, *Psychology.* New York: Worth, 1975.

Bower, G. H. Mood and memory. *American Psychologist,* 1981, *36,* 129–148.

Bower, G. H., and Clark, M. C. Narrative stories as mediators for serial learning. *Psychonomic Science,* 1969, *14,* 181–182.

Bowers, K. Situationism in psychology: An analysis and a critique. *Psychological Review,* 1973, *80,* 307–336.

Bowlby, J. *Attachment and loss.* New York: Basic Books, 1969.

Boyd, J. H. The increasing rate of suicide by firearms. *New England Journal of Medicine,* 1983, *308,* 872–874.

Brackbill, Y. Obstetrical medication and infant behavior. In J. D. Osofsky (Ed.), *Handbook of infant development.* New York: Wiley-Interscience, 1978.

Bradburn, N. M. *The structure of psychological well-being.* Chicago: Aldine, 1969.

Brainerd, C. J. Cognitive development and concept learning: An interpretive review. *Psychological Bulletin,* 1977, *84,* 919–939.

Breggin, P. *Electroshock: Its brain disabling effects.* New York: Springer, 1979.

Brehm, S., and Brehm, J. W. *Psychological reactance: A theory of freedom and control.* New York: Academic Press, 1981.

Brennan, T. Loneliness at adolescence. In L. A. Peplau and D. Perlman (Eds.), *Loneliness: A sourcebook of current theory, research and therapy.* New York: Wiley-Interscience, 1982.

Brenner, M. H. *Mental illness and the economy.* Cambridge, Mass.: Harvard University Press, 1973.

Breuer, J., and Freud, S. *Studies on hysteria* (1895). New York: Basic Books, 1957.

Brickman, P., and Campbell, D. T. Hedonic relativism and planning the good society. In M. H. Appley (Ed.), *Adaptation-level theory: A symposium.* New York: Academic Press, 1971.

Brickman, P.; Coates, D.; and Janoff-Bulman, R. Lottery winners and accident victims: Is happiness relative? *Journal of Personality and Social Psychology,* 1978, *36,* 917–927.

Brigham, J. C. The accuracy of eyewitness evidence: How do attorneys see it? *The Florida Bar Journal,* 1981, *55* (10).

Brim, O. G., Jr., and Kagan, J. Constancy and change: A view of the issues. In O. G. Brim, Jr., and J. Kagan (Eds.), *Constancy and change in human development.* Cambridge, Mass.: Harvard University Press, 1980.

Broad, W. J. Pentagon is said to focus on ESP for wartime use. *The New York Times,* January 10, 1984.

Broadbent, D. E. *Perception and communication.* London: Pergamon Press, 1958.

Brody, J. D. Noise poses a growing threat, affecting hearing and behavior. *The New York Times,* November 16, 1982.

Broverman, I. K., et al. Sex-role stereotypes: A current appraisal. *Journal of Social Issues,* 1972, *28* (2), 59–78.

Browman, C. P.; Sampson, M. G.; Gujavarty, K. S.; and Mitler, M. M. The drowsy crowd. *Psychology Today,* August 1982.

Brown, B. B. Recognition of aspects of consciousness through association with EEG alpha activity represented by a light signal. *Psychophysiology,* 1970, *6,* 442–452.

Brown, M. W., and Charlip, R. *The dead bird.* Reading, Mass.: Addison-Wesley, 1965.

Brown, R. *Words and things.* New York: Free Press, 1958.

Brown, R. *Social psychology.* New York: Free Press, 1965.

Brown, R. *A first language: The early stages.* Cambridge, Mass.: Harvard University Press, 1973.

Brown, R., and Herrnstein, R. J. *Psychology.* Boston: Little, Brown, 1975.

Brown, R., and Kulik, J. Flashbulb memories. *Cognition,* 1977, *5,* 73–99.

Brown, R. W., and McNeill, D. The "tip of the tongue" phenomenon. *Journal of Verbal Learning and Verbal Behavior,* 1966, *5,* 325–327.

Bruce, P. R.; Coyne, A. C.; and Botwinick, J. Adult age differences in metamemory. *Journal of Gerontology,* 1982, *3,* 354–357.

Bruner, J. S. On perceptual readiness. *Psychological Review,* 1957, *64,* 123–152.

Bruner, J. S., and Goodman, C. C. Value and need as organizing factors in perception. *Journal of Abnormal and Social Psychology,* 1947, *42,* 33–44.

Bryant, J.; Comisky, P.; and Zillmann, D. Teachers' humor in the college classroom. *Communication Education,* 1979, *28,* 110–118.

Buckhout, R., et al. Memory, hypnosis, and evidence: Research on eyewitnesses. *Social Action and the Law,* 1982, *7,* 67–72.

Buckhout, R.; Figueroa, D.; and Hoff, E. Psychology and eyewitness identification. Center for Responsive Psychology, Report No. CR-1, November 1972.

Bullough, V. L. Age at menarche: A misunderstanding. *Science,* 1981, *213,* 365–366.

Burnam, M. A.; Pennebaker, J. W.; and Glass, D. C. Time consciousness, achievement striving, and the Type A coronary-prone behavior pattern. *Journal of Abnormal Psychology,* 1975, *84,* 76–89.

Busch, F., et al. Primary transitional objects. *Journal of the American Academy of Child Psychiatry,* 1973, *12,* 193–214.

Buss, A. H., and Plomin, R. *A temperament theory of personality development.* New York: Wiley, 1975.

Bustillo, M.; Buster, J. E., et al. Delivery of a healthy infant following nonsurgical ovum transfer. *Journal of the American Medical Association,* 1984, *251,* 889.

Butler, R. N. The life review: An interpretation of reminiscence in the aged. *Psychiatry,* 1963, *26,* 65–76.

Butler, R. N. Alternatives to retirement. Testimony before the Subcommittee on Retirement Income and Employment, House Subcommittee on Aging. Department of Health, Education, and Welfare No. (NIH) 78-243. Washington, D.C.: U.S. Government Printing Office, 1977.

Butterfield, E. C., and Siperstein, G. N. Influence of contingent auditory stimulation upon non-nutritional suckle. In *Proceedings of the third symposium on oral sensation and perception: The mouth of the infant.* Springfield, Ill.: Charles C Thomas, 1974.

Byck, R., and Ritchie, J. M. Nine-tetrahydrocannabinol: Effects on mammalian nonmyelinated nerve fibers. *Science,* 1973, *180,* 84–85.

Byrne, D. A pregnant pause in the sexual revolution. *Psychology Today,* July 1977.

Byrne, D., and Fisher, W. A. (Eds.). *Adolescents, sex, and contraception.* New York: Academic Press, 1983.

Cain, W. S. Educating your nose. *Psychology Today*, July 1981.

Cain, W. S. To know with the nose: Keys to odor identification. *Science*, 1979, *203*, 467–470.

Caldwell, M., and Peplau, L. A. Sex differences in same-sex friendship, *Sex Roles*, 1982, *8*, 721–732.

California Department of Mental Health. *Friends can be good medicine*. Sacramento, Calif., 1981.

Camer, R. I like me. *Psychology Today*, December 1983.

Campbell, A. *The sense of well-being in America: Recent patterns and trends.* New York: McGraw-Hill, 1981.

Campbell, D., and Beets, J. Lunacy and the moon. *Psychological Bulletin*, 1978, *85*, 1123–1129.

Cannon, W. B. *The mechanical factors of digestion.* London: Arnold, 1911.

Cannon, W. B. *The wisdom of the body.* New York: W. W. Norton, 1932.

Caputo, D. V.; Goldstein, K. M.; and Taub, H. Neonatal compromise and later psychological development: A 10-year longitudinal study. In S. L. Freedman and M. Sigman (Eds.), *Preterm birth and psychological development.* New York: Academic Press, 1981.

Carey, J. The mind of the machine. *Newsweek*, February 7, 1983.

Cartwright, R. D. Happy endings for our dreams. *Psychology Today*, December 1978.

Carver, C. S.; DeGregorio, E.; and Gillis, R. Challenge and Type A behavior among intercollegiate football players. *Journal of Sport Psychology*, 1981, *3*, 140–148.

Carver, C. S., and Ganellen, R. J. Depression and components of self-punitiveness: High standards, self-criticism, and overgeneralization. *Journal of Abnormal Psychology*, 1983, *92*, 330–337.

Cederlöf, R., et al. Studier över ljudnivaer och hygieniska olägenheter au trafikbuller samt förslag till atgärder. *Nordisk Hygienisk Tidskrift*, 1961, *42*, 101–192.

Chafetz, M. E. Alcohol and alcoholism. *American Scientist*, May–June 1979.

Chaiken, S. Communicator physical attractiveness and persuasion. *Journal of Personality and Social Psychology*, 1979, *37*, 1387–1397.

Chaiken, S., and Eagly, A. H. Communication modality as a determinant of message persuasiveness and message comprehensibility. *Journal of Personality and Social Psychology*, 1976, *34*, 605–614.

Chaiken, S., and Eagly, A. H. Communication modality as a determinant of persuasion: The role of communicator salience. *Journal of Personality and Social Psychology*, 1983, *45*, 241–256.

Chase, M. Every 90 minutes a brainstorm. *Psychology Today*, November 1979.

Cheek, J. M., and Buss, A. H. Shyness and sociability. *Journal of Personality*

and Social Psychology, 1981, *41*, 330–339.

Chesney, M. A.; Eagleston, J. R.; and Rosenman, R. H. Type A behavior: Assessment and intervention. In C. K. Prokop and L. A. Bradley (Eds.), *Medical psychology*. New York: Academic Press, 1981.

Child, I. L. Parapsychology and psychology. In *Research in parapsychology 1981*. Metuchen, N.J.: Scarecrow Press, 1982.

Chilman, C. S. *Adolescent sexuality in a changing American society: Social and psychological perspectives.* Washington, D.C.: U.S. Government Printing Office, 1979.

Chitwood, D. G., and Bigner, J. J. Young children's perceptions of old people. *Home Economics Research Journal*, 1980, *8*, 369–374.

Chomsky, N. *Language and mind*, rev. ed. New York: Harcourt Brace Jovanovich, 1972.

Chomsky, N. Language and the mind. *Psychology Today*, February 1968.

Christensen, A., and Arkowitz, H. Preliminary report on practice dating and feedback as treatment for college dating problems. *Journal of Counseling Psychology*, 1974, *21*, 92–95.

Chukovsky, K. *From two to five*, tr. and ed. M. Morton. Berkeley: University of California Press, 1963.

Cicirelli, V. G. Sibling influence throughout the lifespan. In M. E. Lamb and B. Sutton-Smith (Eds.), *Sibling relationships: Their nature and significance across the lifespan.* Hillsdale, N.J.: Lawrence Erlbaum, 1982.

Clark, M. Drugs and psychiatry: A new era. *Newsweek*, November 12, 1979.

Clark, M. The new gene doctors. *Newsweek*, May 18, 1981.

Clarke, A., and Ruble, D. Young adolescents' belief concerning menstruation. *Child Development*, 1978, *49*, 321–324.

Clifford, M. M., and Walster, E. The effect of physical attractiveness on teacher expectation. *Sociology of Education*, 1973, *46*, 248–258.

Clingempeel, W. G., and Reppucci, N. D. Joint custody after divorce: Major issues and goals for research. *Psychological Bulletin*, 1982, *91*, 102–127.

Cohen, B. L., and Lee, F. *Health Physics*, 1982, *36*, (6).

Cohen, F. Personality, stress, and the development of physical illness. In G. C. Stone, F. Cohen, and N. E. Adler (Eds.), *Health psychology.* San Francisco: Jossey-Bass, 1979.

Cohen, N. J., and Squire, L. R. Perceived learning and retention of pattern-analyzing skill in amnesia: Dissociation of knowing how and knowing that. *Science*, 1980, *210*, 207–210.

Cohen, S. Marijuana as medicine. *Psychology Today*, April 1978.

Cohen, S.; Glass, D. C.; and Singer, J. E. Apartment noise, auditory discrimination, and reading ability in children. *Journal of Experimental Social Psychology*, 1973, *9*, 407–422.

Cohen, S., and Weinstein, N. Nonauditory effects of noise on behavior and health. *Journal of Social Issues*, 1981, *37* (1), 36–70.

Cohen, S., et al. Physiological, motivational, and cognitive effects of aircraft noise on children: Moving from the laboratory to the field. *American Psychologist*, 1980, *35*, 231–243.

Colegrove, F. W. Individual memories. *American Journal of Psychology*, 1899, *10*, 228–255.

Coleman, J., et al. *Equality of educational opportunity.* Washington, D.C.: U.S. Government Printing Office, 1966.

Colletta, N. D. Stressful lives: The situation of divorced mothers and their children. *Journal of Divorce*, 1983, *6* (3), 19–31.

Collins, G. U. S. social tolerance of drugs found on rise. *The New York Times*, March 21, 1983.

Condon, W. S., and Sander, L. W. Neonate movement is synchronized with adult speech: Interactional participation and language acquisition. *Science*, 1974, *183*, 99–101.

Condry, J. C. and Ross, D. F. Sex and aggression: The influence of gender label on the perception of aggression in children. *Child Development*, 1985 (in press).

Consumer Reports, Is breast feeding best for babies? March 1977.

Cook, S. W. Social science and school desegregation: Did we mislead the Supreme Court? *Personality and Social Psychology Bulletin*, 1979, *5*, 420–437.

Cooper, K. H. *Aerobics.* New York: Bantam, 1968.

Coopersmith, S. *Antecedents of self-esteem.* San Francisco: W. H. Freeman, 1967.

Cornelius, R. R., and Averill, J. R. Sex differences in fear of spiders. *Journal of Personality and Social Psychology*, 1983, *45*, 377–383.

Cory, C. T. When verse is worse. *Psychology Today*, May 1982.

Cosby, A. Occupational expectations and the hypothesis of increasing realism of choice. *Journal of Vocational Behavior*, 1974, *5*, 53–65.

Costa, P. T., Jr., and McCrae, R. R. Still stable after all these years: Personality as a key to some issues in aging. In P. B. Baltes and O. G. Brim (Eds.), *Life-span development and behavior*, vol. 3. New York: Academic Press, 1980.

Côté, L. Basal ganglia, the extra pyramidal motor system, and diseases of transmitter metabolism. In E. R. Kandel and J. H. Schwartz (Eds.), *Principles of neural science.* New York: Elsevier North-Holland, 1981.

Cowart, B. J. Development of taste perception in humans: Sensitivity and preference throughout the life span. *Psychological Bulletin*, 1981, *90*, 43–73.

Cowley, M. *The view from 80.* New York: Viking Press, 1980.

Cox, C. M. *The early mental traits of three hundred geniuses.* (Vol. 2 of *Ge-*

netic studies of genius.) Stanford, Calif.: Stanford University Press, 1926.

Coyle, J. T.; Price, D. L.; and DeLong, M. R. Alzheimer's disease: A disorder of cortical cholinergic innervation. *Science,* 1983, *219,* 1184–1190.

Craik, F. I., and Lockhart, R. S. Levels of processing: A framework for memory research. *Journal of Verbal Learning and Verbal Behavior,* 1972, *11,* 671–684.

Craik, F. I., and Tulving, E. Depth of processing and the retention of words in episodic memory. *Journal of Experimental Psychology: General,* 1975, *104,* 268–294.

Crawford, J. W. Mother-infant interaction in premature and full-term infants. *Child Development,* 1982, *53,* 957–962.

Crick, F. H. C. Thinking about the brain. *Scientific American,* September 1979.

Crick, F., and Mitchison, G. The function of dream sleep. *Nature,* July 14, 1983.

Cromwell, R. L.; Butterfield, E. C.; Brayfield, F. M.; and Curry, J. J. *Acute myocardial infarction: Reaction and recovery.* St. Louis: C. V. Mosby, 1977.

Crosby, F.; Bromley, S.; and Saxe, L. Recent unobtrusive studies of black and white discrimination and prejudice: A literature review. *Psychological Bulletin,* 1980, *87,* 546–563.

Csikszentmihalyi, M.; Larsen, R.; and Prescott, S. The ecology of adolescent activity and experience. *Journal of Youth and Adolescence,* 1977, *6,* 281–294.

Cunningham, M. R. Weather, mood, and helping behavior: Quasi-experiments with the sunshine Samaritan. *Journal of Personality and Social Psychology,* 1979, *37,* 1947–1956.

Curtis, H. *Biology.* (2nd ed.) New York: Worth, 1975.

Cutrona, C. E. Transition to college: Loneliness and the process of social adjustment. In L. A. Peplau and D. Perlman (Eds.) *Loneliness: A sourcebook of current theory, research, and therapy.* New York: Wiley-Interscience, 1982.

Damon, W., and Killen, M. Peer interaction and the process of change in children's moral reasoning. *Merrill-Palmer Quarterly,* 1982, *28,* 347–367.

D'Andrade, R. G. Sex differences and cultural institutions. In E. E. Maccoby (Ed.), *The development of sex differences.* Stanford, Calif.: Stanford University Press, 1966.

Daniels, P., and Weingarten, K. *Sooner or later: The timing of parenthood in adult lives.* New York: W. W. Norton, 1981.

Darley, J. M., and Batson, C. D. From Jerusalem to Jericho: A study of situational and dispositional variables in helping behavior. *Journal of Personality and Social Psychology,* 1973, *27,* 100–108.

Darley, J. M., and Cooper, J. The "clean for Gene" phenomenon: The effects of

students' appearance on political campaigning. *Journal of Applied Social Psychology,* 1972, *2,* 24–33.

Darley, J. M., and Fazio, R. H. Expectancy confirmation sequences arising in the social interaction sequences. *American Psychologist,* 1980, *35,* 867–881.

Darwin, C. R. *The expression of emotions in man and animals.* London: John Murray, 1872.

Davison, G. C., and Neale, J. M. *Abnormal psychology.* (3rd ed.) New York: Wiley, 1982.

De Amicus, L. A.; Huntzinger, R. S.; and Cromwell, R. L. Magnitude of reaction time crossover in process schizophrenia patients in relation to their first-degree relatives. *Journal of Nervous and Mental Disease,* 1981, *169,* 64–65.

Deaux, K. From individual differences to social categories: Analysis of a decade's research on gender. *American Psychologist,* 1984, *39,* 105–116.

Deaux, K. Sex and gender. *Annual review of psychology,* vol. 36. Palo Alto, Calif.: Annual Reviews, Inc., 1985.

Deaux, K., and Emswiler, T. Explanation of successful performance on sex-linked tasks: What is skill for the male is luck for the female. *Journal of Personality and Social Psychology,* 1974, *29,* 80–85.

Deaux, K., and Ullman, J. C. *Women of steel.* New York: Praeger, 1983.

Deci, E. *Intrinsic motivation.* New York: Plenum, 1975.

Deci, E. L., and Ryan, R. M. The empirical exploration of intrinsic motivational processes. In L. Berkowitz (Ed.), *Advances in experimental social psychology,* vol. 13. New York: Academic Press, 1980.

De Longis, A.; Coyne, J.; Dakof, G.; Folkman, S.; and Lazarus, R. S. Relationship of daily hassles, uplifts, and major life events to health status. *Health Psychology,* 1982, *1,* 119–136.

Dembroski, T. M.; MacDougall, J. M.; Eliot, R. S.; and Buell, J. C. Moving beyond Type A. *Advances,* 1984, *1,* 16–25.

Dement, W. C. The effect of dream deprivation. *Science,* 1960, *131,* 1705–1707.

Dement, W. *Some must watch while some must sleep.* San Francisco: W. H. Freeman, 1972.

Dempsey, D. Noise. *New York Times Magazine,* November 23, 1975.

DeMyer, M. K., et al. Prognosis in autism: A follow-up study. *Journal of Autism and Childhood Schizophrenia,* 1973, *3,* 199–246.

Derlega, V. J., and Chaikin, A. L. *Sharing intimacy: What we reveal to others and why.* Englewood Cliffs, N.J.: Prentice-Hall, 1975.

Dermer, M., and Pyszczynski, T. A. Effects of erotica upon men's loving and liking responses for women they love. *Journal of Personality and Social Psychology,* 1978, *36,* 1302–1309.

Dermer, M., and Thiel, D. L. When beauty may fail. *Journal of Personality and Social Psychology,* 1975, *31,* 1168–1176.

Deutsch, H. *The psychology of women,* vol. 2. New York: Grune & Stratton, 1944.

deVilliers, P. A., and deVilliers, J. G. *Early language.* Cambridge, Mass.: Harvard University Press, 1979.

deVries, H. A. Physiological effects of an exercise training regimen upon men aged 52 to 88. *Journal of Gerontology,* 1970, *25,* 325–336.

Dewhirst, J. R. Biological rhythms and behavior. In Z. Rubin and E. B. McNeil, *The psychology of being human.* (Brief update ed.) New York: Harper & Row, 1979.

Dienstbier, R. A. Aerobic exercise, catecholamines, and temperament. *SASP Newsletter,* 1982, *8* (6), 29–30.

Dilley, J. Self-help literature: Don't knock it till you try it. *Personnel and Guidance Journal,* 1978, *57,* 293–295.

DiMatteo, M. R., and Friedman, H. S. *Social psychology and medicine.* Cambridge, Mass.: Oelgeschlager, Gunn, & Hain, 1982.

Dion, K. K.; Berscheid, E.; and Walster, E. What is beautiful is good. *Journal of Personality and Social Psychology,* 1972, *24,* 285–290.

Dipboye, R. L.; Fromkin, H. L.; and Wiback, H. Relative importance of applicant sex, attractiveness, and scholastic standing in evaluation of job applicant resumés. *Journal of Applied Psychology,* 1975, *60,* 39–43.

Doering, C., et al. A cycle of plasma testosterone in the human male. *Journal of Clinical Endocrinology and Metabolism,* 1975, *40,* 492–500.

Dollard, J., et al. *Frustration and aggression.* New Haven, Conn.: Yale University Press, 1939.

Douvan, E., and Adelson, J. *The adolescent experience.* New York: Wiley, 1966.

Dowd, M. Many women in poll value jobs as much as family life. *The New York Times,* December 4, 1983.

Doyle, A. C. A study in scarlet. In *The complete Sherlock Holmes.* Garden City, N.Y.: Doubleday, 1927.

Drabman, R. S., and Thomas, M. H. Does TV violence breed indifference? *Journal of Communication,* Autumn 1975.

Dullea, G. Is joint custody good for children? *New York Times Magazine,* February 3, 1980.

Dunbar, J.; Brown, M.; and Amoroso, D. Some correlates of attitudes toward homosexuality. *Journal of Social Psychology,* 1973, *89,* 271–279.

Duncan, B. L. Differential social perception and attribution of intergroup violence: Testing the lower limits of stereotyping of blacks. *Journal of Personality and Social Psychology,* 1976, *34,* 590–598.

Duncker, K. On problem solving. *Psychological Monographs,* 1945, *58,* No. 270.

Dunn, J., and Kendrick, C. *Siblings.* Cambridge, Mass.: Harvard University Press, 1982.

Dush, D. M.; Hirt, M. L.; and Schroeder, H. Self-statement modification with adults: A meta-analysis. *Psychological Bulletin*, 1983, *94*, 408–422.

Dutton, D. G., and Aron, A. P. Some evidence for heightened sexual attraction under conditions of high anxiety. *Journal of Personality and Social Psychology*, 1974, *30*, 510–517.

Dywan, J., and Bowers, K. The use of hypnosis to enhance recall. *Science*, 1983, *22*, 184–185.

Dyer, W. W. *Your erroneous zones.* New York: Thomas Y. Crowell, 1976.

Eagly, A. H. Recipient characteristics as determinants of responses to persuasion. In R. E. Petty, T. M. Ostrom, and T. C. Brock (Eds.) *Cognitive responses to persuasion.* Hillsdale, N.J.: Erlbaum, 1980.

Ebbinghaus, H. M. *Memory: A contribution to experimental psychology.* (1885). H. A. Ruger and C. E. Bussenius (Trs.). New York: Teachers College, Columbia University, 1913.

Eccles, J.; Adler, T. F.; and Kaczala, C. M. Socialization of achievement attitudes and beliefs: Parental influences. *Child Development*, 1982, *53*, 310–321.

Edel, L. *Henry James* (5 vols.) Philadelphia: Lippincott, 1953–1972.

Edgerton, R. B. *Mental retardation.* Cambridge, Mass.: Harvard University Press, 1979.

Edmiston, S. Out from under! A major report on women today. *Redbook*, May 1975.

Efran, M. G. The effect of physical appearance on the judgment of guilt, interpersonal attraction, and severity of recommended punishment in a simulated jury task. *Journal of Research on Personality*, 1974, *8*, 45–54.

Efran, M. G., and Patterson, E. W. J. Voters vote beautiful: The effect of physical appearance on a national election. *Canadian Journal of Behavioral Science*, 1974, *6*, 352–356.

Ehret, C. F., and Scanlon, L. W. *Overcoming jet lag.* New York: Berkley Publishing, 1983.

Ehrhardt, A. A., and Baker, S. W. Fetal androgens, human central nervous system differentiation, and behavior sex differences. In R. C. Friedman, R. M. Richart, and R. L. Vande Wiele (Eds.), *Sex differences in behavior.* New York: Wiley, 1973.

Eibl-Eibesfeldt, I. *Ethology: The biology of behavior.* New York: Holt, Rinehart and Winston, 1970.

Einstein, A. Autobiography. In P. Schilpp, *Albert Einstein: Philosopher-scientist.* Evanston, Ill.: Library of Living Philosophers, 1949.

Ekman, P. The universal smile: Face muscles talk every language. *Psychology Today*, September 1975.

Ekman, P.; Levenson, R. W.; and Friesen, W. V. Autonomic nervous system activity distinguishes among emotions. *Science*, 1983, *221*, 1208–1210.

Ekman, P.; Sorenson, E. R.; and Friesen, W. V. Pan-cultural elements in facial displays of emotion. *Science*, 1969, *164*, 86–88.

Ellis, A. *Reason and emotion in psychotherapy.* Secaucus, N.J.: Lyle Stuart, 1962.

Ember, C. R. Feminine task assignment and the social behavior of boys. *Ethos*, 1973, *1*, 424–439.

Emery, R. E. Interparental conflict and the children of discord and divorce. *Psychological Bulletin*, 1982, *92*, 310–330.

Engen, T. *The perception of odors.* New York: Academic Press, 1982.

Erber, J. T. Memory and age. In T. Field, et al. (Eds.), *Review of human development.* New York: Wiley, 1982.

Erikson, E. *Childhood and society.* New York: Norton, 1950.

Erikson, E. H. *A healthy personality for every child. A fact finding report: A digest.* (Mid-century White House Conference on Children and Youth.) Raleigh, N.C.: Health Publications Institute, 1951.

Erikson, E. H. *Dimensions of a new identity.* New York: Norton, 1974.

Erlich, J. W. *The lost art of cross-examination.* Cited in *Social Action and the Law Newsletter*, February 1974.

Eron, L. D. Parent-child interaction, television violence, and aggression of children. *American Psychologist*, 1982, *37*, 197–211.

Eron, L. D. Prescription for reduction of aggression. *American Psychologist*, 1980, *35*, 244–252.

Evans, R. I., et al. Social modeling films to deter smoking in adolescents: Result of a three-year field investigation. *Journal of Applied Psychology*, 1981, *66*, 399–414.

Everett, P. B.; Hayward, S. C.; and Meyers, A. W. The effects of a token reinforcement procedure on bus ridership. *Journal of Applied Behavior Analysis*, 1974, *7*, 1–9.

Eysenck, H. J. The effects of psychotherapy: An evaluation. *Journal of Consulting Psychology*, 1952, *16*, 319–324.

Falbo, T. Does the only child grow up miserable? *Psychology Today*, May 1976.

Falbo, T. Only children, stereotypes, and research. In M. Lewis and L. A. Rosenblum (Eds.), *The child and its family.* New York: Plenum, 1979.

Farber, S. L. *Identical twins reared apart: A reanalysis.* New York: Basic Books, 1981.

Farley, R.; Schuman, H.; Bianchi, S.; Colasanto, D.; and Hatchett, S. Chocolate city, vanilla suburbs: Will the trend toward racially separate communities continue? *Social Science Research*, 1978, *7*, 319–344.

Fein, D.; Humes, M.; Kaplan, E.; Lucci, D.; and Waterhouse, L. The question of left hemisphere dysfunction in infantile autism. *Psychological Bulletin*, 1984, *95*, 258–281.

Ferrell, T. A pioneering cognitive psychologist has everyone's mind on his. *The New York Times*, October 12, 1982.

Festinger, L. *A theory of cognitive dissonance.* Stanford, Calif.: Stanford University Press, 1957.

Festinger, L., and Carlsmith, J. M. Cognitive consequences of forced compliance. *Journal of Abnormal and Social Psychology*, 1959, *58*, 203–210.

Field, D. Can preschool children really learn to conserve? *Child Development*, 1981, *52*, 326–334.

Finn, S. E. Base rates, utilities, and DSM-III: Shortcomings of fixed-rule systems of psychodiagnosis. *Journal of Abnormal Psychology*, 1982, *9*, 294–302.

Fischer, C. S. *To dwell among friends.* Chicago: University of Chicago Press, 1982.

Fischer, C. S. The friendship cure-all. *Psychology Today*, January 1983.

Fischer, C. S. What do we mean by "friend"? An inductive study. *Social Network*, 1982, *3*, 287–306.

Fisher, W. A. Gender, gender-role identification, and response to erotica. In E. R. Allgeier and N. B. McCormick (Eds.), *Changing boundaries.* Palo Alto, Calif.: Mayfield, 1983.

Fitzgerald, H., and Bundy, R. S. *Rhythm, time, and human behavior.* Homewood, Ill.: Learning Systems Company, 1975.

Flavell, J. H. *Cognitive development.* Englewood Cliffs, N.J.: Prentice-Hall, 1977.

Flavell, J. H. On cognitive development. *Child Development*, 1982, *53*, 1–10.

Floody, D. R. Further systematic research with biorhythms. *Journal of Applied Psychology*, 1981, *66*, 520–521.

Fo, W. S. O., and O'Donnell, C. R. The buddy system: Relationship and contingency conditions in a community intervention program for youth with nonprofessionals as behavior change agents. *Journal of Consulting and Clinical Psychology*, 1974, *42*, 163–169.

Folkins, C. H., and Sime, W. E. Physical fitness training and mental health. *American Psychologist*, 1981, *36*, 373–389.

Foltz, D. Psychologists in the media. *APA Monitor*, May 1980.

Foy, D. W., et al. Social-skills training to teach alcoholics to refuse drinks effectively. *Journal of Studies on Alcohol*, 1976, *37*, 1340–1345.

Francke, L. B., et al. The children of divorce. *Newsweek*, February 11, 1980.

Frank, J. D. *Persuasion and healing: A comparative study of psychotherapy.* (2nd ed.) Baltimore: Johns Hopkins University Press, 1973.

Frankenheuser, M. Psychoneuroendocrine approaches to the study of emotion as related to stress and coping. In R. A. Dienstbier (Ed.), *1978 Nebraska Symposium on Motivation.* Lincoln: University of Nebraska Press, 1979.

Frankenheuser, M. The sympathetic-adrenal and pituitary-adrenal response to challenge: Comparison between the sexes. In T. M. Dembraski, G. Schmidt, and G. Blumchen (Eds.), *Behavioral bases of coronary heart disease.* New York: Karger, 1983.

Freed, W. J.; Cannon-Spoor, H. E.; Krauthamer, E.; Hoffer, B. J.; and Wyatt, R. J. Catecholaminergic brain grafts: A behavioral, histochemical, and biochemical comparison of substantia nigra and adrenal medulla grafts. *Psychopharmacology Bulletin,* 1983, *19,* 305–307.

Freedman, J. L. *Happy people: What happiness is, who has it and why.* New York: Harcourt Brace Jovanovich, 1979.

Freeling, N. R., and Shemberg, K. M. The alleviation of test anxiety by systematic desensitization. *Behavior Research and Therapy,* 1970, *8,* 293–299.

Freud, S. *Group psychology and the analysis of the ego.* London: Hogarth Press, 1922.

Freud, S. The interpretation of dreams (1900). In J. Strachey (Ed. and tr.), *The standard edition of the complete psychological works of Sigmund Freud,* vols. 4 and 5. London: Hogarth Press, 1953.

Freud, S. Mourning and melancholia (1917). In *Collected papers,* vol. 4. London: Hogarth Press, 1950.

Freud, S. The psychogenesis of a case of homosexuality in a woman. In *Collected papers,* vol. 2. London: Hogarth Press, 1933.

Freud, S. Some psychical consequences of the anatomical distinction between the sexes (1925). In J. Strachey (Ed. and tr.), *The standard edition of the complete psychological works of Sigmund Freud,* vol. 19. London: Hogarth Press, 1961.

Freud, S. Three essays on sexuality (1905). In J. Strachey (Ed. and tr.), *The standard edition of the complete psychological works of Sigmund Freud,* vol. 7. London: Hogarth Press, 1954.

Freud, S. Recommendations for physicians on the psychoanalytic method. In *Collected papers,* vol. 2. London: Hogarth Press, 1956.

Freud, S. Further recommendations on the technique of psychoanalysis. I: On beginning the treatment (1913). In J. Strachey (Ed. and tr.), *The standard edition of the complete psychological works of Sigmund Freud,* vol. 12. London: Hogarth Press, 1958.

Freud, S. Analysis terminable and interminable. In J. Strachey (Ed. and tr.), *The standard edition of the complete psychological works of Sigmund Freud,* vol. 23. London: Hogarth Press, 1964.

Friedan, B. *The feminine mystique.* New York: Norton, 1963.

Friedan, B. *The second stage.* New York: Summit Books, 1981.

Friedman, M., and Rosenman, R. H. *Type A behavior and your heart.* New York: Knopf, 1974.

Frodi, A.; Macaulay, J.; and Thome, P. R. Are women always less aggressive than men? A review of the experimental literature. *Psychological Bulletin,* 1977, *84,* 634–660.

Fromm, E. *The art of loving.* New York: Harper & Row, 1956.

Galanter, E. Contemporary psychophysics. In R. Brown et al., *New directions in psychology,* vol. 1. New York: Holt, Rinehart and Winston, 1962.

Galizio, M., and Hendrick, C. Effect of musical accompaniment on attitude: The guitar as a prop for persuasion. *Journal of Applied Social Psychology,* 1972, *2,* 350–359.

Gallup Organization. Newsweek on Campus poll, September 1983. Reported in *Newsweek on Campus,* April 1984.

Garcia, J. The logic and limits of mental aptitude testing. *American Psychologist,* 1981, *36,* 1172–1180.

Garcia, J., and Koelling, R. A. Relation of cue to consequence in avoidance learning. *Psychonomic Science,* 1966, *4,* 123–124.

Gardner, H. *Artful scribbles.* New York: Basic Books, 1980.

Gardner, H. *Frames of mind: The theory of multiple intelligences.* New York: Basic Books, 1983.

Gardner, H. *The shattered mind.* New York: Knopf, 1975.

Gardner, R. A., and Gardner, B. T. Teaching sign language to a chimpanzee. *Science,* 1969, *165,* 664–672.

Garfield, S. L. Effectiveness of psychotherapy: The perennial controversy. *Professional Psychology: Research and Practice,* 1983, *14,* 35–43.

Gastorf, J. W. Time urgency of Type A behavior pattern. *Journal of Consulting and Clinical Psychology,* 1980, *48,* 299.

Gazzaniga, M. S. The split brain in man. *Scientific American,* August 1967.

Geller, E. S.; Paterson, L.; and Talbott, E. A behavioral analysis of incentive prompts for motivating seat belt use. *Journal of Applied Behavior Analysis,* 1982, *15,* 403–413.

Geschwind, N. Specializations of the human brain. *Scientific American,* September 1979.

Gibson, E. J., and Levin, H. *The psychology of reading.* Cambridge, Mass.: MIT Press, 1975.

Gibson, E. J., and Walk, R. D. The visual cliff. *Scientific American,* April 1960.

Gilligan, C. *In a different voice.* Cambridge, Mass.: Harvard University Press, 1982.

Gilson, M. Depression as measured by perceptual bias in binocular rivalry. Doctoral dissertation, Georgia State University, 1983.

Glass, D. C., and Singer, J. E. Experimental studies of uncontrollable and unpredictable noise. *Representative Research in Social Psychology,* 1973, *4,* 165–183.

Glass, L. L.; Kirsch, M. A.; and Parris, J. N. Psychiatric disturbances associated with Erhard Seminars Training: I. Report of cases. *American Journal of Psychiatry,* 1977, *134,* 245–247.

Gleick, J. Exploring the labyrinth of the mind. *New York Times Magazine,* August 21, 1983.

Gleitman, H. Place-learning. *Scientific American,* October 1963.

Glick, P. C. Children of divorced parents in demographic perspective. *Journal of Social Issues,* 1979, *35* (4), 170–182.

Glick, P. C. Marriage, divorce, and living arrangements: Prospective changes. *Journal of Family Issues,* 1984, *5,* 7–26.

Gmelch, G. Baseball magic. *Transaction,* June 1971.

Godden, D. R., and Baddeley, A. D. Context-dependent memory in two natural environments: On land and underwater. *British Journal of Psychology,* 1975, *66,* 325–331.

Goffman, E. *Gender advertisements.* New York: Harper & Row, 1976.

Goldberg, S. Prematurity: Effects on parent-infant interaction. *Journal of Pediatric Psychology,* 1978, *3,* 137–144.

Goldberg, V. What can we do about jet lag? *Psychology Today,* August 1977.

Golden, J. S., and Johnston, G. D. Problems of distortion in doctor-patient communications. *Psychiatry in Medicine,* 1970, *1,* 127–149.

Goldfarb, W. Variations in adolescent adjustment of institutionally reared children. *American Journal of Orthopsychiatry,* 1947, *17,* 449–457.

Goldfoot, D. A., et al. Behavioral and physiological evidence of sexual climax in the female stump-tailed macaque (*Macaca arctoides*). *Science,* 1980, *208,* 1477–1479.

Goldsmith, H. H. Genetic influences on personality from infancy to adulthood. *Child Development,* 1983, *54,* 331–335.

Goldstein, I. B. Biofeedback in the treatment of hypertension. In L. White and P. Tursky (Eds.), *Clinical biofeedback: Efficacy and mechanisms.* New York: Guilford Press, 1982.

Goldstein, M. J.; Baker, B. L.; and Jamison, K. R. *Abnormal psychology.* Boston: Little, Brown, 1980.

Goleman, D. Braintapping on Madison Ave. *Psychology Today,* April 1979.

Goleman, D. 1,528 little geniuses and how they grew. *Psychology Today,* February 1980.

Goodman, E. Tribulations of a first woman. *Boston Globe,* June 28, 1983.

Goodwin, D. W. Biological psychiatry. In A. W. Kazdin, A. S. Bellack, and M. Hersen (Eds.), *New perspectives in abnormal psychology.* New York: Oxford University Press, 1980.

Gordon, S. *Lonely in America.* New York: Simon & Schuster, 1976.

Gore, S. The effect of social support in moderating the health consequences of unemployment. *Journal of Health and Social Behavior,* 1978, *19,* 157–165.

Gorn, G. The effects of music in advertising on choice behavior: A classical conditioning approach. *Journal of Marketing,* 1982, *46,* 94–101.

Granberg, D. Comparison of pro-choice and pro-life activists: Their values, attitudes, and beliefs. *Population and Envi-*

ronment: *Behavioral and Social Issues*, 1982, 5, 75–94.

Gray, R.; Graubard, P. S.; and Rosenberg, H. Little brother is changing you. *Psychology Today*, March 1974.

Greenberg, J. Shaping behavior contest for minds. *Miami Herald*, October 3, 1976.

Greenberg, J. Suicide linked to brain chemical deficit. *Science News*, 1982, 121, 355.

Greenberg, R. P., and Fisher, S. *The scientific credibility of Freud's theories and therapy.* New York: Basic Books, 1977.

Greenblatt, M. Psychosurgery. In A. M. Freedman and H. I. Kaplan (Eds.), *Psychiatry.* Baltimore: Williams & Wilkins, 1967.

Greenfeld, J. *A child called Noah.* New York: Holt, Rinehart and Winston, 1972.

Greenfeld, J. *A place for Noah.* New York: Holt, Rinehart and Winston, 1978.

Greer, D. L. Spectator booing and the home advantage: A study of social influence in the basketball arena. *Social Psychology Quarterly*, 1983, 46, 252–261.

Greer, S. Study of parental loss in neurotics and sociopaths. *Archives of General Psychiatry*, 1964, 11, 177–180.

Greer, S., and Morris, T. Psychological response in breast cancer and survival: Eight-year followup. Paper presented at the American Psychological Association convention, Los Angeles, 1981.

Gregory, R. L. Visual illusions. *Scientific American*, May 1968.

Grinspoon, L., and Bakalar, J. Cocaine: A social history. *Psychology Today*, March 1977.

Groninger, L. D. Mnemonic imagery and forgetting. *Psychonomic Science*, 1971, 23, 161–163.

Gross, C. G. Inferotemporal cortex and vision. In E. Stellar and J. M. Sprague (Eds.), *Advances in physiological psychology.* New York: Academic Press, 1973.

Gross, M. L. *The psychological society.* New York: Random House, 1978.

Grumet, G. W. Eye contact: The core of interpersonal relatedness. *Psychiatry*, 1983, 46, 172–180.

Grumet, G. W. Telephone therapy: A review and case report. *American Journal of Orthopsychiatry*, 1979, 49, 574–584.

Gubrium, J. F. Marital desolation and the evaluation of everyday life in old age. *Journal of Marriage and the Family*, 1974, 36, 107–113.

Gutmann, D. The cross-cultural perspective: Notes toward a comparative psychology of aging. In J. E. Birren and K. W. Schaie (Eds.), *Handbook of the psychology of aging.* New York: Van Nostrand-Reinhold, 1977.

Haan, N., and Day, D. A longitudinal study of change and sameness in personality development: Adolescence to later adulthood. *International Journal of Aging and Human Development*, 1974, 5, 11–39.

Haan, N.; Smith, M. B.; and Block, J. Moral reasoning of young adults: Political-social behavior, family background, and personality correlates. *Journal of Personality and Social Psychology*, 1968, 10, 183–201.

Hai, D. M.; Khairullah, Z. Y.; and Coulmas, N. Sex and the single armrest: Use of personal space during air travel. *Psychological Reports*, 1982, 51, 743–749.

Haith, M. M. *Rules that babies look by: The organization of newborn visual activity.* Hillsdale, N.J.: Lawrence Erlbaum, 1980.

Halcomb, R. Winning the war against birth defects. *Parents' Magazine.* May 1977.

Hale, E. Inside the divided mind. *New York Times Magazine*, April 17, 1983.

Hall, C. S. *A primer of Freudian psychology.* New York: World, 1954.

Hall, C. S. A ubiquitous sex difference in dreams revisited. *Journal of Personality and Social Psychology*, 1984, 46, 1109–1117.

Hall, C. S. *The meaning of dreams.* New York: McGraw-Hill, 1966.

Hall, J. A. Gender effects in decoding nonverbal cues. *Psychological Bulletin*, 1978, 85, 845–857.

Halleck, S. L. *The politics of therapy.* New York: Science House, 1971.

Hamilton, D. L. A cognitive-attributional analysis of stereotyping. In L. Berkowitz (Ed.), *Advances in experimental social psychology*, vol. 12. New York: Academic Press, 1979.

Hamilton, E. W., and Abramson, L. Y. Cognitive patterns and major depressive disorder: A longitudinal study in a hospital setting. *Journal of Abnormal Psychology*, 1983, 92, 173–184.

Haney, W. Validity, vaudeville, and values: A short history of social concerns over standardized testing. *American Psychologist*, 1981, 36, 1021–1034.

Hans, V. P., and Slater, D. John Hinckley, Jr. and the insanity defense: The public's verdict. *Public Opinion Quarterly*, 1983, 47, 202–212.

Hare, R. D. Psychophysiological studies of psychopathy. In D. C. Forles (Ed.), *Clinical applications of psychophysiology.* New York: Columbia University Press, 1978.

Harlow, H. F. Love in infant monkeys. *Scientific American*, March 1959.

Harrell, T. W. High earning MBAs. *Personnel Psychology*, 1972, 25, 523–550.

Harris, B. Whatever happened to Little Albert? *American Psychologist*, 1979, 34, 151–160.

Harrower, M. Were Hitler's henchmen mad? *Psychology Today*, July 1976.

Hartley, E. L. *Problems in prejudice.* New York: Kings Crown, 1946.

Hartmann, E. L. *The functions of sleep.* New Haven, Conn.: Yale University Press, 1973.

Harvey, J. H., and Weary, G. Current issues in attribution theory and research. In *Annual Review of Psychology*, vol. 35. Palo Alto, Calif.: Annual Reviews, 1984.

Hastie, R.; Penrod, S. D.; and Pennington, N. *Inside the jury.* Cambridge, Mass.: Harvard University Press, 1983.

Hathaway, S. R., and McKinley, J. C. *The Minnesota multiphasic personality inventory.* Minneapolis: University of Minnesota Press, 1942.

Hauserman, N.; Waylen, S. R.; and Behling, M. Reinforced racial integration in the first grade: A study in generalization. *Journal of Applied Behavior Analysis*, 1973, 6, 193–200.

Hawkins, R. O., Jr. Adolescent alcohol abuse: A review. *Developmental and Behavioral Pediatrics*, 1982, 3, 83–87.

Hayes, D. S.; Chemelski, B. E.; and Palmer, M. Nursery rhymes and prose passages: Preschoolers' liking and short-term retention of story events. *Developmental Psychology*, 1982, 18, 49–56.

Hayes, J. R. *The complete problem solver.* Philadelphia: The Franklin Institute Press, 1981.

Hayflick, L. The cell biology of human aging. *Scientific American*, January 1980.

Heiman, J. R. A psychophysiological exploration of sexual arousal patterns in females and males. *Psychophysiology*, 1977, 14, 266–274.

Heiman, J. R. Continuing revolutions in sex research. In Z. Rubin and E. B. McNeil, *The psychology of being human.* (Brief update ed.) New York: Harper & Row, 1979.

Helson, H. *Adaptation-level theory.* New York: Harper & Row, 1964.

Hendricks, J. H., and Hendricks, C. D. *Aging in mass society: Myths and realities.* Cambridge, Mass.: Winthrop, 1977.

Hennig, M., and Jardim, A. *The managerial woman.* Garden City, N.Y.: Anchor Press/ Doubleday, 1977.

Herink, R. (Ed.) *The psychotherapy handbook.* New York: New American Library, 1980.

Herman, C. P.; Olmsted, M. P.; and Polivy, J. Obesity, externality, and susceptibility to social influence: An integrated analysis. *Journal of Personality and Social Psychology*, 1983, 45, 926–934.

Heron, W. The pathology of boredom. *Scientific American*, January 1957.

Herridge, C. F., and Chir, B. Aircraft noise and mental hospital admissions. *Sound*, 1972, 6, 32–36.

Hershey, D. *Life span and factors affecting it.* Springfield, Ill.: Charles C Thomas, 1974.

Hess, E. H. Attitude and pupil size. *Scientific American*, February 1965.

Hetherington, E. M.; Cox, M.; and Cox, R. The aftermath of divorce. In J.H. Stevens Jr. and M. Mathews (Eds.), *Mother/child father/child relationships.* Washington, D.C.: National Association for the Education of Young Children, 1978.

Hetherington, E. M.; Cox, M.; and Cox, R. Play and social interaction in children following divorce. *Journal of Social Issues*, 1979, 35 (4), 26–46.

Hiatt, J., and Kripke, D. Ultradian rhythms in waking gastric activity. *Psy-*

chosomatic Medicine, 1975, 37, 320–355.

Hicks, R. F., and Kinsbourne, M. Human handedness: A partial cross-fostering study. *Science,* 1976, *192,* 908–910.

Hilgard, E. R. *Hypnotic susceptibility.* New York: Harcourt, Brace and World, 1965.

Hilgard, E. R. *Divided consciousness: Multiple controls in human thought and action.* New York: Wiley-Interscience, 1977.

Hilgard, E. R., and Hilgard, J. R. *Hypnosis in the relief of pain.* Los Altos, Calif.: William Kaufmann, 1975.

Hilgard, J. R. *Personality and hypnosis,* (2nd ed.) Chicago: University of Chicago Press, 1979.

Hill, A. L. An investigation of calendar calculating by an idiot savant. *American Journal of Psychiatry,* 1975, *132,* 557–560.

Hill, C. T.; Rubin, Z.; and Peplau, L. A. Breakups before marriage: The end of 103 affairs. *Journal of Social Issues,* 1976, *32* (1), 147–168.

Hill, J. H.; Liebert, R. M.; and Mott, D. E. W. Vicarious extinction of avoidance behavior through films: An initial test. *Psychological Reports,* 1968, *12,* 192.

Hilts, P. J. Mind machines. *Omni,* October 1982.

Hobson, J. A. and McCarley, R. W. The brain as a dream state generator: An activation-synthesis hypothesis of the dream process. *American Journal of Psychiatry,* 1977, *134,* 1335–1348.

Hochberg, J. E. *Perception.* (2nd ed.) Englewood Cliffs, N.J.: Prentice-Hall, 1978.

Hodgson, R. J., and Rachman, S. J. The effects of contamination and washing on obsessional patients. *Behaviour Research and Therapy,* 1972, *10,* 111–117.

Hoff-Ginsburg, E., and Shatz, M. Linguistic input and the child's acquisition of language. *Psychological Bulletin,* 1982, *92,* 3–26.

Hoffman, L. W., and Manis, J. D. The value of children in the United States: A new approach to the study of fertility. *Journal of Marriage and the Family,* 1979, *41,* 583–596.

Hoffman, M. L. Sex differences in empathy. *Psychological Bulletin,* 1977, *84,* 712–722.

Holden, C. Identical twins reared apart. *Science,* 1980, *207,* 1323–1327.

Holinger, P. C. Violent deaths among the young: Recent trends in suicide, homicide, and accidents. *American Journal of Psychiatry,* 1979, *136,* 1144–1147.

Hollander, E. P. Leadership and power. In G. Lindzey and E. Aronson (Eds.), *Handbook of social psychology* (3rd ed.) Reading, Mass.: Addison-Wesley, (in press).

Holmes, D. S. Meditation and somatic arousal reduction: A review of the experimental evidence. *American Psychologist,* 1984, *39,* 1–10.

Holmes, D. S., and Jorgensen, B. W. Do personality and social psychologists study men more than women? *Representative Research in Social Psychology,* 1971, *2,* 71–76.

Holmes, D. S., et al. Biorhythms: Their utility for predicting postoperative recuperative time, death, and athletic performance. *Journal of Applied Psychology,* 1980, *65,* 233–236.

Holmes, T. H., and Rahe, R. H. The social readjustment rating scale. *Journal of Psychosomatic Research,* 1967, *11,* 213–218.

Homa, D. An assessment of two extraordinary speed-readers. *Bulletin of the Psychonomic Society,* 1983, *21,* 123–126.

Hopkins, J. R. Sexual behavior in adolescence, *Journal of Social Issues,* 1977, *33* (2), 67–85.

Horn, J. L. Human ability systems. In P. B. Baltes (Ed.), *Life-span developmental psychology,* vol. 1. New York: Academic Press, 1978.

House, J. S. *Work, stress, and social support.* Reading, Mass.: Addison-Wesley, 1981.

Houseknecht, S. K.; Vaughan, S.; and Macke, A. S. Marital disruption among professional women: The timing of career and family events. *Social Problems,* 1984, *31,* 273–284.

Hovland, C. I.; Lumsdaine, A. A.; and Sheffield, F. D. *Experiments on mass communication.* Princeton, N.J.: Princeton University Press, 1949.

Hovland, C. I., and Weiss, W. The influence of source credibility on communication effectiveness. *Public Opinion Quarterly,* 1951, *15,* 635–650.

Howard, J. W., and Dawes, R. M. Linear prediction of marital happiness. *Personality and Social Psychology Bulletin,* 1976, *2,* 478–480.

Howarth, E. Birth order, family structure, and personality variables. *Journal of Personality Assessment,* 1980, *44,* 299–301.

Hubel, D. H. The brain. *Scientific American,* September 1979.

Hubel, D. H., and Wiesel, T. N. Brain mechanisms of vision. *Scientific American,* September 1979.

Hudgens, R. W. Preventing suicide. *New England Journal of Medicine,* 1983, *308,* 897–898.

Hunt, J. V., and Rhodes, L. Mental development of preterm infants during the first year. *Child Development,* 1977, *48,* 204–210.

Hunt, M. *Sexual behavior in the 1970s.* Chicago: Playboy Press, 1974.

Hunt, M. *The universe within.* New York: Simon and Schuster, 1982.

Hurvich, L. M., and Jameson, D. An opponent process theory of color vision. *Psychological Review,* 1957, *64,* 384–404.

Huyghe, P. Of two minds. *Psychology Today,* December 1983.

Hyde, J. S. How large are cognitive gender differences? A meta-analysis using ω^2 and *d. American Psychologist,* 1981, *36,* 892–901.

Hyman, A. The influence of color on the taste perception of carbonated water preparations. *Bulletin of the Psychonomic Society,* 1983, *21,* 145–148.

Inhelder, B., and Piaget, J. *The growth of logical thinking from childhood to adolescence.* New York: Basic Books, 1958.

Isen, A. M., and Levin, P. F. The effect of feeling good on helping: Cookies and kindness. *Journal of Personality and Social Psychology,* 1972, *21,* 384–388.

Israel, R. J. Bee hives and blisters. *Moment,* October 1982.

Iversen, L. I. The chemistry of the brain. *Scientific American,* September 1979.

Izard, C. E. Emotions as motivations: An evolutionary-developmental perspective. In R. A. Dientbier (Ed.), *Nebraska symposium on motivation 1978.* Lincoln: University of Nebraska Press, 1979.

Izard, C. E. *Human emotions.* New York: Plenum, 1977.

Izard, C. E. On the development of emotions and emotion-cognition relationships in infancy. In M. Lewis and L. Rosenblum (Eds.), *The development of affect.* New York: Plenum, 1978.

Izard, C. E., et al. The young infant's ability to produce discreet emotion expressions. *Developmental Psychology,* 1980, *16,* 132–140.

Izard, C. E., and Saxton, P. M. Emotions. In R. C. Atkinson, R. J. Herrnstein, G. Lindzey, and D. Luce (Eds.), *Handbook of experimental psychology.* New York: Wiley-Interscience (in press).

Jacklin, C. N.; Maccoby, E. E.; and Doering, C. H. Neonatal sex-steroid hormones and timidity in 6–18 month old boys and girls. *Developmental Psychology,* 1983, *16,* 163–168.

James, W. What is an emotion? *Mind,* 1884, *9.*

James, W. *The principles of psychology.* New York: Holt, 1890.

James, W. H.; Woodruff, A. B.; and Werner, W. Effects of internal and external control upon changes in smoking behavior. *Journal of Consulting Psychology,* 1965, *29,* 184–186.

Janis, I. L. *Groupthink* (2nd ed.) Boston: Houghton Mifflin, 1982.

Janis, I. L. In rescue planning, how did Carter handle stress? *The New York Times,* May 18, 1980.

Janis, I. L.; Kaye, D.; and Kirschner, P. Facilitating effects of "eating-while-reading" on responsiveness to persuasive communications. *Journal of Personality and Social Psychology,* 1965, *1,* 181–186.

Janov, A. (Ed.) *The Journal of Primal Therapy,* 1973, *1.*

Jason, L. A. Preventive community interventions: Reducing school children's smoking and decreasing smoke exposure. *Professional Psychology,* 1979, *10,* 744–752.

Jensen, A. R. Cumulative deficit in IQ of blacks in the rural South. *Developmental Psychology,* 1977, *13,* 184–191.

Jensen, A. R. Reaction time and psychometric g. In H. J. Eysenck (Ed.), *A model for intelligence.* Heidelberg: Springer-Verlag, 1982.

Johnson, J. H., and Sarason, I. G. Recent developments in research on life stress. In V. Hamilton and D. M. Warburton (Eds.), *Human stress and cognition*. Chichester, England: Wiley, 1979.

Johnson, M. P., and Leslie, L. Couple involvement and network structure. A test of the dyadic withdrawal hypothesis. *Social Psychology Quarterly*, 1982, 4, 34–43.

Jones, E. E., and Harris, V. A. The attribution of attitudes. *Journal of Experimental Social Psychology*, 1967, 3, 1–24.

Jones, J. M. *Prejudice and racism*. Reading, Mass.: Addison-Wesley, 1972.

Jones, M. C. A laboratory study of fear: The case of Peter. *Pedagogical Seminary*, 1925, 31, 308–315.

Jones, M. C. The later careers of boys who were early or late maturing. *Child Development*, 1957, 28, 113–128.

Jones, M. C. Personality correlates and antecedents of drinking patterns in adult males. *Journal of Consulting and Clinical Psychology*, 1968, 32, 2–12.

Jones, M. C. Personality antecedents and correlates of drinking patterns in women. *Journal of Consulting and Clinical Psychology*, 1971, 36, 61–69.

Jones, R. A., and Brehm, J. W. Persuasiveness of one- and two-sided communications as a function of awareness that there are two sides. *Journal of Experimental Social Psychology*, 1970, 6, 47–56.

Jones, W. H. Loneliness and social behavior. In L. A. Peplau and D. Perlman (Eds.), *Loneliness: A sourcebook of current theory, research, and therapy*. New York: Wiley-Interscience, 1982.

Jospe, M. *The placebo effect*. Lexington, Mass.: Lexington Books, 1978.

Jung, C. *Man and his symbols*. Garden City, N.Y.: Doubleday, 1964.

Kacerguis, M. A., and Adams, G. R. Erikson stage and resolution: The relationship between identity and intimacy. *Journal of Youth and Adolescence*, 1980, 9, 117–126.

Kagan, J.; Kearsley, R. B.; and Zelazo, P. R. *Infancy: Its place in human development*. Cambridge, Mass.: Harvard University Press, 1978.

Kagan, J., and Moss, H. *From birth to maturity: A study in psychological development*. New York: Wiley, 1962.

Kahle, L. R., and Berman, J. Attitudes cause behaviors: A cross-lagged panel analysis. *Journal of Personality and Social Psychology*, 1979, 37, 315–321.

Kahn, M.; Baker, B. L.; and Weiss, J. M. Treatment of insomnia by relaxation training. *Journal of Abnormal Psychology*, 1968, 73, 556–558.

Kahneman, D. *Attention and effort*. Englewood Cliffs, N.J.: Prentice-Hall, 1973.

Kahneman, D., and Tversky, A. Choices, values, and frames. *American Psychologist*, 1984, 39, 341–350.

Kalish, R. A. *Late adulthood: Perspectives on human development*. Monterey, Calif.: Brooks/Cole, 1975.

Kalish, R. A. Death and dying in a social context. In R. H. Binstock and E. Shanas (Eds.), *Handbook of aging and the social sciences*. New York: Van Nostrand Reinhold, 1976.

Kalish, R. A. The new ageism and the failure models: A polemic. *The Gerontologist*, 1979, 19, 398–402.

Kalish, R. A., and Reynolds, D. K. *Death and ethnicity: A psycho-cultural study*. Los Angeles: University of Southern California Press, 1976.

Kane, R. L., and Kane, R. A. Alternatives to institutional care: Beyond the dichotomy. *The Gerontologist*, 1980, 20, 249–259.

Kaplan, H. S. *The new sex therapy*. New York: Brunner/Mazel, 1974.

Kaplan, M. A woman's view of *DSM-III*. *American Psychologist*, 1983, 38, 786–792.

Karasek, R.; Baker, D.; Marxer, F.; Ahlbom, A.; and Theorell, T. Job decision latitude, job demands, and cardiovascular disease: A prospective study of Swedish men. *American Journal of Public Health*, 1981, 71, 694–705.

Karmel, L. The case for love. Paper presented at meeting of the American Psychological Association, Miami Beach, 1970.

Karr, R. *Homosexual labeling: An experimental analysis*. Doctoral dissertation, University of Washington, 1975.

Kassarjian, H. H. Voting intentions and political perception. *Journal of Psychology*, 1963, 56, 85–88.

Kastenbaum, R. Death, dying, and bereavement in old age. *Aged Care and Services Review*, May–June, 1978.

Kastenbaum, R. *Humans developing: A lifespan perspective*. Boston: Allyn & Bacon, 1979.

Kastenbaum, R., and Weisman, A. D. The psychological autopsy as a research procedure in gerontology. In D. P. Kent, R. Kastenbaum, and S. Sherwood (Eds.), *Research planning and action for the elderly*. New York: Behavorial Publications, 1972.

Katchadourian, H. A., and Lunde, D. T. *Fundamentals of human sexuality*. (2nd ed.) New York: Holt, Rinehart and Winston, 1975.

Kates, R. *Hazards and choice perception in flood plain management*. Chicago: University of Chicago Press, 1962.

Katkin, E. S.; Fitzgerald, C. R.; and Shapiro, D. Clinical applications of biofeedback: Current status and future prospects. In H. L. Pick et al. (Eds.), *Psychology: From research to practice*. New York: Plenum, 1978.

Katz, A. M., and Hill, R. Residential propinquity and marital selection: A review of theory, method, and fact. *Marriage and Family Living*, 1958, 20, 27–34.

Katz, J., and Cronin, D. M. Sexuality and college life. *Change*, February–March, 1980.

Kazdin, A. E. *Behavior modification*. Homewood, Ill.: Learning Systems Company, 1975.

Kazdin, A. E. The token economy: A decade later. *Journal of Applied Behavior Analysis*, 1982, 15, 431–445.

Keating, D. P. Thinking processes in adolescence. In J. Adelson (Ed.), *Handbook of adolescent psychology*. New York: Wiley-Interscience, 1980.

Kelley, H. H. Love and commitment. In H. H. Kelley et al., *Close relationships*. San Francisco: W. H. Freeman, 1983.

Kelley, H. H. The warm-cold variable in first impressions of persons. *Journal of Personality*, 1950, 18, 431–439.

Kelley, H. H., et al. *Close relationships*. San Francisco: W. H. Freeman, 1983.

Kelman, H. C. Human use of human subjects: The problem of deception in social psychological experiments. *Psychological Bulletin*, 1967, 67, 1–11.

Kelman, H. C., and Lawrence, L. H. Assignment of responsibility in the case of Lt. Calley: Preliminary report on a national survey. *Journal of Social Issues*, 1972, 28, 177–212.

Kenrick, D. T., and Gutierres, S. E. Contrast effects and judgments of physical attractiveness: When beauty becomes a social problem. *Journal of Personality and Social Psychology*, 1980, 38, 131–140.

Kesey, K. *One flew over the cuckoo's nest*. New York: Viking, 1962.

Kessler, R. C., and McRae, J. A., Jr. The effect of wives' employment on the mental health of married men and women. *American Journal of Sociology*, 1982, 47, 216–226.

Kety, S. S. Mental illness in the biological and adoptive relatives of schizophrenic adoptees: Findings relevant to genetic and environmental factors in etiology. *American Journal of Psychiatry*, 1983, 140, 720–727.

Kevan, S. M. Season of life—season of death. *Social Science and Medicine*, 1979, 12 (D), 227–232.

Kiesler, C. A. Mental hospitals and alternative care: Noninstitutionalization as potential public policy for mental patients. *American Psychologist*, 1982, 37, 349–360.

Kihlstrom, J. F., and Harackiewicz, J. M. The earliest recollection: A new survey. *Journal of Personality*, 1982, 50, 134–148.

Kivnick, H. Q. Grandparenthood: An overview of meaning and mental health. *The Gerontologist*, 1982, 22, 59–66.

Klein, M., and Stern, L. Low birth weight and the battered child syndrome. *American Journal of Diseases of Childhood*, 1971, 122, 15–18.

Kleitman, N. The basic rest-activity cycle. In N. Wuhlfson and A. Sances (Eds.), *The nervous system and electric currents*. New York: Plenum, 1970.

Klemesrud, J. Survey finds major shifts in attitudes of women. *The New York Times*, March 13, 1980.

Klima, E. S., and Bellugi, U. *The signs of language*. Cambridge, Mass.: Harvard University Press, 1979.

Klinman, D.; Kohl, R.; and the Fatherhood Project. *Fatherhood USA.* New York: Garland, 1984.

Klos, D. S., and Paddock, J. R. Relationship status: Scales for assessing the vitality of late adolescents' relationships with their parents. *Journal of Youth and Adolescence,* 1978, 7, 353–369.

Knight, R. A. Converging models of cognitive deficit in schizophrenia. In W. D. Spaulding and J. K. Cole (Eds.), *Nebraska symposium on motivation, 1983: Theories of schizophrenia and psychosis.* Lincoln: University of Nebraska Press, 1984.

Knox, R. A. Brain tissue implants: Opening a new door. *Boston Globe,* June 13, 1983.

Kobasa, S. C. The hardy personality: Toward a social psychology of stress and health. In G. S. Sanders and J. Suls (Eds.), *Social psychology of health and illness.* Hillsdale, N.J.: Lawrence Erlbaum, 1982.

Kobasa, S. C. Stressful life events, personality, and health: An inquiry into hardiness. *Journal of Personality and Social Psychology,* 1979, 37, 1–11.

Kobasa, S. C.; Maddi, S. R.; and Kahn, S. Hardiness and health: A prospective study. *Journal of Personality and Social Psychology,* 1982, 42, 168–177.

Kohen, J. A.; Brown, C. A.; and Feldberg, R. Divorced mothers: The costs and benefits of female family control. In G. Levinger and O. C. Moles (Eds.), *Divorce and separation.* New York: Basic Books, 1979.

Kohlberg, L. A. Cognitive-developmental analysis of children's sex-role concepts and attitudes. In E. E. Maccoby (Ed.), *The development of sex differences.* Stanford, Calif.: Stanford University Press, 1966.

Kohlberg, L. The cognitive-developmental approach to socialization. In D. A. Goslin (Ed.), *Handbook of socialization theory and research.* Chicago: Rand McNally, 1969.

Köhler, W. *The mentality of apes.* New York: Harcourt, Brace, 1925.

Kojima, S., and Goldman-Rakic, P. S. Functional analysis of spatially discriminative neurons in prefrontal cortex of rhesus monkey. *Brain Research,* 1984, 291, 229–240.

Komarovsky, M. *Dilemmas of masculinity: A study of college youth.* New York: Norton, 1976.

Kornfeld, D. S. The hospital environment: Its impact on the patient. *Advances in Psychosomatic Medicine,* 1972, 8, 252–270.

Kornhaber, A. The vital connection— 1983. *Children Today,* July-August 1983.

Kornhaber, A., and Woodward, K. L. *Grandparents/grandchildren: The vital connection.* New York: Doubleday, 1981.

Kosslyn, S. M. Mental images. In Z. Rubin and E. B. McNeil, *The psychology of being human* (3rd ed.) Brief/Update. New York: Harper & Row, 1983.

Kraut, R. E., and Johnston, R. E. Social and emotional messages of smiling: An

ethological approach. *Journal of Personality and Social Psychology,* 1979, 37, 1539–1553.

Krebs, D., and Adinolfi, A. A. Physical attractiveness, social relations, and personality style. *Journal of Personality and Social Psychology,* 1975, 31, 245–253.

Kripke, D., and Sonneschein, D. A 90 minute daydream cycle. *Proceedings of the Association for the Psychophysiological Study of Sleep,* 1973, 2, 177.

Krosnick, J. A., and Judd, C. M. Transitions in social influence at adolescence: Who induces cigarette smoking? *Developmental Psychology,* 1982, 3, 359–368.

Krueger, A. P., and Reed, E. J. Biological impact of small air ions. *Science,* 1976, 193, 1209–1213.

Kübler-Ross, E. *On death and dying.* New York: Macmillan, 1969.

Kulik, J. A.; Bangert, R. L.; and Williams, G. W. Effects of computer-based teaching on secondary school students. *Journal of Educational Psychology,* 1983, 75, 19–26.

Kulka, R. A., and Weingarten, H. The long-term effects of parental divorce in childhood on adult adjustment. *Journal of Social Issues,* 1979, 35 (4), 50–76.

Lackner, J. R., and Graybiel, A. Perceived orientation in free-fall depends on visual, postural, architectural factors. *Aviation Space and Environmental Medicine,* 1983, 54, 47–51.

La Farge, P. The new woman. *Parents,* October 1983.

Laird, J. D.; Wagener, J. J.; Halal, M.; and Szegda, M. Remembering what you feel: Effects of emotion on memory. *Journal of Personality and Social Psychology,* 1982, 42, 646–657.

Lamb, M. E. *The role of the father in child development.* New York: Wiley, 1981.

Langer, E.; Janis, I. L.; and Wolfer, J. A. Reduction of psychological stress in surgical patients. *Journal of Experimental Social Psychology,* 1975, 11, 155–165.

Langer, E. J., et al. Environmental determinants of memory improvement in late adulthood. *Journal of Personality and Social Psychology,* 1979, 37, 2003–2013.

Langone, J. Too weary to go on. *Discover,* November 1981.

Langway, L. Bringing up superbaby. *Newsweek,* March 28, 1983.

Lanzetta, J. T.; Cartwright-Smith, J.; and Kleck, R. E. Effects of nonverbal dissimulation on emotional experience and autonomic arousal. *Journal of Personality and Social Psychology,* 1976, 33, 354–370.

Larkin, J. Cognition of learning physics. *American Journal of Physics,* 1981, 49, 534–541.

Lashley, K. S. In search of the engram. In *Symposium of the Society for Experimental Biology,* vol. 4. New York: Cambridge University Press, 1950.

Lassen, N. A.; Ingvar, D. H.; and Skinhøj, E. Brain function and blood flow. *Scientific American,* October 1978.

Laudenslager, M. L.; Ryan, S. M.; Drugan, R. C.; Hyson, R. L.; and Maier, S. F. Coping and immunosuppression: Inescapable but not escapable shock suppresses lymphocyte proliferation. *Science,* 1983, 221, 568–570.

Lawler, E. E., and Suttle, J. L. A causal correlational test of the need hierarchy concept. *Organizational Behavior and Human Performance,* 1972, 7, 265–287.

Lazar, I., and Darlington, R. S. *Lasting effects after preschool.* Washington, D.C.: Department of Health, Education, and Welfare, 1979.

Lazarus, R. S. *The riddle of man.* Englewood Cliffs, N.J.: Prentice-Hall, 1974.

Lee, L. Sequences in separation: A framework for investigating endings of the personal (romantic) relationships. *Journal of Social and Personal Relationships,* 1984, 1, 49–73.

Leeper, R. The role of motivation in learning: A study of the phenomenon of differential motivation control on the utilization of habits. *Journal of Genetic Psychology,* 1935, 46, 3–40.

Leirer, V. O.; Hamilton, D. L.; and Carpenter, S. Common first names as cues for inferences about personality. *Personality and Social Psychology Bulletin,* 1982, 8, 712–718.

Lenneberg, E. *The biological foundations of language.* New York: Wiley, 1967.

Lennon, M. C. The psychological consequences of menopause: The importance of timing a life stage event. *Journal of Health and Social Behavior,* 1982, 23, 353–366.

Leo, J. Take me out of the ball game. *Time,* August 15, 1983.

Leo, J. The revolution is over. *Time,* April 9, 1984.

Lerner, R. M., and Knapp, J. R. Actual and perceived intrafamilial attitudes of late adolescents and their parents. *Journal of Youth and Adolescence,* 1975, 4, 17–36.

Lerner, R. M., and Spanier, G. B. *Adolescent development: A life-span perspective.* New York: McGraw-Hill, 1980.

Leventhal, H. Findings and theory in the study of fear communications. In L. Berkowitz (Ed.), *Advances in experimental social psychology,* vol. 5. New York: Academic Press, 1970.

Levin, P. F., and Isen, A. M. Further studies on the effect of feeling good on helping. *Sociometry,* 1975, 38, 141–147.

Levinger, G. A social psychological perspective on marital dissolution. In G. Levinger and O. C. Moles (Eds.), *Divorce and separation.* New York: Basic Books, 1979.

Levinson, D. J., et al. *The seasons of a man's life.* New York: Knopf, 1978.

Levinthal, C. F. *Introduction to physiological psychology.* Englewood Cliffs, N.J.: Prentice-Hall, 1983.

Levy, S. M. Emotions and the progression of cancer: A review. *Advances,* 1984, 1, 10–15.

Lewis, J. L. Semantic processing of unattended messages using dichotic listening.

Journal of Experimental Psychology. 1970, *85*, 225–228.

Lewis, M. Culture and gender roles: There's no unisex in the nursery. *Psychology Today,* May 1972.

Lichtenstein, E. The smoking problem: A behavioral perspective. *Journal of Consulting and Clinical Psychology,* 1982, *50*, 804–819.

Lieber, A., and Sherin, C. Homicides and the lunar cycle: Toward a theory of lunar influence on human emotional disturbance. *American Journal of Psychiatry,* 1972, *129*, 69–74.

Lieberman, M. A.; Yalom, I. D.; and Miles, M. *Encounter groups: First facts.* New York: Basic Books, 1973.

Lipscomb, D. M. Killing your ears with the sound of music. *Science year.* Chicago: World Book, 1982.

Loehlin, J. C.; Lindzey, G.; and Spuhler, J. N. *Race differences in intelligence.* San Francisco: W. H. Freeman, 1975.

Loftus, E. F. Eyewitness testimony: Does the malleable human memory interfere with legal justice? *Social Action and the Law Newsletter,* April 1975.

Loftus, E. F. *Eyewitness testimony.* Cambridge, Mass.: Harvard University Press, 1979.

Loken, B. Heavy smokers', light smokers', and nonsmokers' beliefs about cigarette smoking. *Journal of Applied Psychology,* 1982, *67*, 616–622.

Lopate, C. *Women in medicine.* Baltimore: Johns Hopkins University Press, 1968.

Lorayne, H. and Lucas, J. *The memory book.* New York: Ballatine, 1974.

Lorenz, K. The companion in the bird's world. *Auk,* 1937, *54*, 245–273.

Lorenz, K. *On aggression.* New York: Harcourt, Brace, and World, 1966.

Lothstein, L. M. Sex reassignment surgery: Historical, bioethical, and theoretical issues. *American Journal of Psychiatry,* 1982, *139*, 417–426.

Louis, A. M. Should you buy biorhythms? *Psychology Today,* April 1978.

Lovaas, O. I., and Newsom, C. D. Behavior modification with psychotic children. In H. Leitenberg (Ed.), *Handbook of behavior modification and behavior therapy.* New York: Appleton-Century-Crofts, 1976.

Lowenthal, M. F., and Chiriboga, D. Transition to the empty nest. *Archives of General Psychiatry,* 1972, *26*, 8–14.

Luce, G. G. *Body time.* New York: Pantheon, 1971.

Lynch, G., and Baudry, M. The biochemistry of memory: A new and specific hypothesis. *Science,* 1984, *224*, 1057–1063.

Lynch, J. J. The broken heart: The medical consequences of loneliness. New York: Basic Books, 1977.

Maass, A., and Clark, R. D., III. Hidden impact of minorities: Fifteen years of minority influence research. *Psychological Bulletin,* 1984, *95*, 428–450.

Maccoby, E. E., and Jacklin, C. N. *The psychology of sex differences.* Stanford, Calif.: Stanford University Press, 1974.

Macfarlane, A. *The psychology of childbirth.* Cambridge, Mass.: Harvard University Press, 1977.

Machlowitz, M. *Workaholics.* Reading, Mass.: Addison-Wesley, 1980.

Mack, J. E., and Hickler, H. *Vivienne: The life and suicide of an adolescent girl.* Boston: Little, Brown, 1981.

Mackay, A. V. P., et al. Increased brain dopamine and dopamine receptors in schizophrenia. *Archives of General Psychiatry,* 1982, *39*, 991–997.

Maddox, G., and Douglas, E. Aging and individual differences. *Journal of Gerontology,* 1974, *29*, 555–563.

Mahoney, M. J. *Abnormal psychology.* San Francisco: Harper & Row, 1980.

Main, M., and Weston, D. R. The quality of the toddler's relationship to mother and to father: Related to conflict behavior and the readiness to establish new relationships. *Child Development,* 1981, *52*, 932–940.

Major, B.; Carrington, P. I.; and Carnevale, P. J. D. Physical attractiveness and self-esteem: Attribution for praise from an other-sex evaluator. *Personality and Social Psychology Bulletin,* 1984, *10*, 43–50.

Makinodan, T. Immunity and aging. In C. B. Finch and L. Hayflick (Eds.), *Handbook of the biology of aging.* New York: Van Nostrand Reinhold, 1977.

Mandler, G. Emotion. In R. Brown et al., *New directions in psychology,* vol. 1. New York: Holt, Rinehart and Winston, 1962.

Marek, G. R. *Toscanini.* London: Vision Press, 1975.

Mark, V. H., and Ervin, F. R. *Violence and the brain.* New York: Harper & Row, 1970.

Marks, L. E. Synesthesia: The lucky people with mixed-up senses. *Psychology Today,* June 1975.

Marlatt, G. A. The controlled-drinking controversy: A commentary. *American Psychologist,* 1983, *38*, 1097–1010.

Marsh, C. Age has nothing to do with being old. (Letter) *The New York Times,* December 25, 1982.

Marshall, D. S. Too much in Mangaia. *Psychology Today,* February 1971.

Marshall, G. D., and Zimbardo, P. G. Affective consequences of inadequately explained physiological arousal. *Journal of Personality and Social Psychology,* 1979, *37*, 970–988.

Marshall, J. The evidence: Do we see and hear what is? Or do our senses lie? *Psychology Today,* February 1969.

Martin, J. E., and Dubbert, P. M. Exercise applications and promotion in behavioral medicine: Current status and future directions. *Journal of Consulting and Clinical Psychology,* 1982, *50*, 1004–1017.

Martin, R. L.; Cloninger, C. R.; and Guze, S. B. Female criminality and the prediction of recidivism. *Archives of General Psychiatry,* 1978, *35*, 207–214.

Maslach, C. Negative emotional biasing of unexplained arousal. *Journal of Personality and Social Psychology,* 1979, *37*, 953–969.

Maslow, A. H. A theory of human motivation. *Psychological Review,* 1943, *50*, 370–396.

Maslow, A. H. *Motivation and personality.* New York: Harper & Row, 1954.

Maslow, A. H. *Toward a psychology of being.* New York: Van Nostrand Reinhold, 1962.

Maslow, A. *Motivation and personality.* (2nd ed.) New York: Harper & Row, 1970.

Masnick, G., and Bane, M. J. *The nation's families, 1960–1990.* Cambridge, Mass.: Joint Center for Urban Studies of MIT and Harvard University, 1980.

Mastellone, M. Aversion therapy: Another use for the old rubber band. *Journal of Behavior Therapy and Experimental Psychiatry,* 1974, *5*, 311.

Masters, W. H., and Johnson, V. E. *Human sexual inadequacy.* Boston: Little, Brown, 1970.

Masters, W. H., and Johnson, V. E. *Human sexual response.* Boston: Little, Brown, 1966.

Matarazzo, J. D. Behavioral health and behavioral medicine: Frontiers for a new health psychology. *American Psychologist,* 1980, *35*, 807–817.

Matas, L.; Arend, R.; and Sroufe, L. A. Continuity and adaptation in the second year of life: The relationship between quality of attachment and later competence. *Child Development,* 1978, *49*, 547–556.

Mathews, K. E., Jr., and Canon, L. K. Environmental noise level as a determinant of helping behavior. *Journal of Personality and Social Psychology,* 1975, *32*, 571–577.

Matteson, D. R. *Adolescence today: Sex roles and the search for identity.* Homewood, Ill.: Dorsey, 1975.

Maugh, T. H. Marijuana: Does it damage the brain? *Science,* August 30, 1974.

McAdams, D. P. Experiences of intimacy and power: Relationships between social motives and autobiographical memory. *Journal of Personality and Social Psychology,* 1982, *42*, 292–302.

McArthur, L. Z. Judging a book by its cover: A cognitive analysis of the relationship between physical appearance and stereotyping. In A. H. Hastorf and A. M. Isen (Eds.), *Cognitive social psychology.* New York: Elsevier-North Holland, 1982.

McArthur, L. Z., and Eisen, S. V. Television and sex-role stereotyping. *Journal of Applied Social Psychology,* 1976, *6*, 329–351.

McCall, R. B. Environmental effects on intelligence: The forgotten realm of discontinuous nonshared within-family factors. *Child Development,* 1983, *54*, 253–259.

McCall, R. B. *Intelligence and heredity.* Homewood, Ill.: Learning Systems Company, 1975.

McCann, I. L., and Holmes, D. S. Influence of aerobic exercise on depression. *Journal of Personality and Social Psychology*, 1984, *46*, 1142–1147.

McCartney, K. The effect of quality of daycare environment upon children's language development. *Developmental Psychology*, 1984, *20*, 244–260.

McCaul, K. D., et al. Predicting adolescent smoking. *Journal of School Health*, 1982, *52*, 342–346.

McClelland, D. C. *Motivational trends in society.* New York: General Learning Press, 1971.

McClelland, D. C. Testing for competence rather than for "intelligence." *American Psychologist*, 1973, *28*, 1–14.

McClelland, D. C. Managing motivation to expand human freedom. *American Psychologist*, 1978, *33*, 201–210.

McClelland, D. C., and Pilon, D. A. Sources of adult motives in patterns of parent behavior in early childhood. *Journal of Personality and Social Psychology*, 1983, *44*, 564–574.

McClelland, D. C., and Winter, D. G. *Motivating economic achievement.* New York: Free Press, 1969.

McClelland, D. C., et al. *The achievement motive.* New York: Appleton-Century-Crofts, 1953.

McConnell, J. V. Memory transfer through cannibalism in planarians. *Journal of Neuropsychiatry*, 1962, *3*, 542–548.

McCormick, N. B., and Jesser, C. J. The courtship game: Power in the sexual encounter. In E. R. Allgeier and N. B. McCormick (Eds.), *Changing boundaries.* Palo Alto, Calif.: Mayfield, 1983.

McCrae, R. R., and Costa, P. T., Jr. *Emerging lives, enduring dispositions.* Boston: Little, Brown, 1984.

McDougall, W. *Social psychology.* New York: G. P. Putnam's Sons, 1908.

McGaugh, J. L. Preserving the presence of the past: Hormonal influences on memory storage. *American Psychologist*, 1983, *38*, 161–174.

McGaugh, J. L. Time-dependent processes in memory storage. *Science*, 1966, *153*, 1351–1358.

McGhie, A., and Chapman, J. S. Disorders of attention and perception in early schizophrenia. *British Journal of Medical Psychiatry*, 1961, *34*, 103–116.

McGinniss, J. *The selling of the president, 1968.* New York: Simon & Schuster, 1969.

McGlone, J. Sex differences in human brain asymmetry: A critical survey. *Behavioral and Brain Sciences*, 1980, *3*, 215–264.

McGrath, R. J. Newsletter to constituents. June 5, 1983.

McHale, S. M. Social interactions of autistic and nonhandicapped children during free play. *American Journal of Orthopsychiatry*, 1983, *53*, 81–91.

McKean, K., and Brownlee, S. Facing up to man's past. *Discover*, July 1983.

McKeown, T. *The role of medicine.* Princeton, N.J.: Princeton University Press, 1979.

McKernon, P. E. The development of first songs in young children. In H. Gardner and D. Wolf (Eds.), *Early symbolization.* San Francisco: Jossey-Bass, 1979.

McLaughlin, S. D., and Micklin, M. The timing of the first birth and changes in personal efficacy. *Journal of Marriage and the Family*, 1983, *46*, 47–56.

McNeil, B. J.; Pauker, S. G.; Sox, H. C., Jr.; and Tversky, A. On the elicitation of preferences for alternative therapies. *New England Journal of Medicine*, 1982, *306*, 1259–1262.

Mechanic, D. *Medical sociology.* New York: Free Press, 1968.

Medrich, E. A.; Roizen, J. A.; Rubin, V.; and Buckley, S. *The serious business of growing up.* Berkeley: University of California Press, 1982.

Medvedev, Z. A. Aging and longevity: New approaches and new perspectives. *The Gerontologist*, 1975, *15*, 196–201.

Melzack, R. *The puzzle of pain.* New York: Basic Books, 1973.

Messenger, J. C. The lack of the Irish. *Psychology Today*, February 1971.

Mewborn, C. R., and Rogers, R. W. Effects of threatening and reassuring components of fear appeals on physiological and verbal measures of emotion and attitudes. *Journal of Experimental Social Psychology*, 1979, *15*, 242–253.

Meyer, V., and Chesser, E. S. *Behavior therapy in clinical psychiatry.* Baltimore: Penguin, 1970.

Michaelis, D. *The best of friends.* New York: William Morrow, 1983.

Milgram, S. Behavioral study of obedience. *Journal of Abnormal and Social Psychology*, 1963, *67*, 371–378.

Milgram, S. Some conditions of obedience and disobedience to authority. *Human Relations*, 1965, *18*, 57–75. (a)

Milgram, S. Liberating effects of group pressure. *Journal of Personality and Social Psychology*, 1965, *1*, 127–134. (b)

Milgram, S. *Obedience to authority: An experimental view.* New York: Harper & Row, 1974.

Milgram, S. Subject reaction: The neglected factor in the ethics of experimentation. *Hastings Center Report*, October 1977.

Miller, G. A. The magical number seven, plus or minus two: Some limits on our capacity for processing information. *Psychological Review*, 1956, *63*, 81–97.

Miller, G. A. *Psychology: The science of mental life.* New York: Harper & Row, 1962.

Miller, J. D. Effects of noise on people. *Journal of the Acoustical Society of America*, 1974, *56*, 729–764.

Miller, N., and Maruyama, G. Ordinal position and peer popularity. *Journal of Personality and Social Psychology*, 1976, *33*, 123–131.

Miller, N., et al. Speed of speech and persuasion. *Journal of Personality and Social Psychology*, 1976, *34*, 615–624.

Miller, N. E. Behavioral medicine: Symbiosis between laboratory and clinic. In *Annual Review of Psychology, 34.* Palo Alto, Calif.: Annual Reviews, Inc., 1983.

Miller, R. A.; Pople, H. E., Jr.; and Myers, J. D. INTERNIST-1, an experimental computer-based diagnostic consultant for general internal medicine. *New England Journal of Medicine*, 1982, *307*, 468–476.

Miller, R. R., and Marlin, N. A. Amnesia following electroconvulsive shock. In J. F. Kihlstrom and F. J. Evans (Eds.), *Functional disorders of memory.* Hillsdale, N.J.: Lawrence Erlbaum, 1979.

Milner, B. Amnesia following operation on the temporal lobes. In C. W. M. Whitty and O. L. Zangwill (Eds.), *Amnesia.* London: Butterworth, 1966.

Minard, R. D. Race relations in the Pocahontas coal field. *Journal of Social Issues*, 1952, *8* (1), 29–44.

Mindess, H.; Turek, J.; Miller, C.; Bender, A.; and Corbin, S. Development of the Antioch sense of humor inventory. Unpublished report, Antioch University, 1983.

Mintz, R. S. Psychotherapy of the suicidal patient. In H. L. P. Resnik (Ed.), *Suicidal behaviors.* Boston: Little, Brown, 1968.

Mischel, W. *Introduction to personality* (3rd ed.) New York: Holt, Rinehart, and Winston, 1981.

Mischel, W. *Personality and assessment.* New York: Holt, Rinehart and Winston, 1968.

Mischel, W., and Peake, P. K. Beyond déjà vu in the search for cross-situational consistency. *Psychological Review*, 1982, *89*, 730–755.

Money, J., and Ehrhardt, A. A. *Man & woman, boy & girl.* Baltimore: Johns Hopkins University Press, 1972.

Moody, R. A. *Life after life.* Atlanta: Mockingbird Books, 1975.

Moore-Ede, M. C. What hath night to do with sleep? *Natural History*, September 1982.

Morin, S. F., and Garfinkle, E. M. Male homophobia. *Journal of Social Issues*, 1978, *34* (1), 29–47.

Morin, S. F.; Taylor, K.; and Kielman, S. Gay is beautiful at a distance. Paper presented at meeting of the American Psychological Association, Chicago, August 1975.

Morris, D. *The naked ape.* New York: McGraw-Hill, 1967.

Morris, S., and Charney, N. Nipping nail-biting. *Psychology Today*, February 1983.

Morrison, J. K., and Hanson, G. D. Clinical psychologists in the vanguard: Current attitudes toward mental illness. *Professional Psychology*, 1978, *9*, 240–248.

Morse, W., and Skinner, B. F. A second type of "superstition" in the pigeon. *American Journal of Psychology*, 1957, *70*, 308–311.

Moskowitz, H. R., et al. Cross-cultural differences in simple taste preferences. *Science*, 1975, *190*, 1217–1218.

Muir, K. A., and Milan, M. A. Parent

reinforcement for child achievement: The use of a lottery to maximize parent training effects. *Journal of Applied Behavior Analysis,* 1982, *15,* 455–460.

Murphy, J. M. Psychiatric labeling in cross-cultural perspective. *Science,* 1976, *191,* 1019–1028.

Murray, H. A. *Explorations in personality.* New York: Oxford University Press, 1938.

Murray, J. B. What is meditation? Does it help? *Genetic Psychology Monographs,* 1982, *106,* 85–115.

Murray, T. H. Learning to deceive. *Hastings Center Report,* April 1980.

Muson, H. Teenage violence and the telly. *Psychology Today,* March 1978.

Mussen, P. H., and Jones, M. C. Self-conceptions, motivations, and interpersonal attitudes of late and early maturing boys. *Child Development,* 1957, *28,* 243–256.

Myerhoff, B. *Number our days.* New York: Simon & Schuster, 1978.

Nabokov, P. The peyote road. *New York Times Magazine,* March 9, 1969.

Nathan, P. E., and Harris, S. L. *Psychopathology and society.* (2nd ed.) New York: McGraw-Hill, 1980.

National Academy of Sciences. *Marijuana and health.* Washington, D.C.; National Academy Press, 1982.

National Institute of Drug Abuse. *National Survey on Drug Abuse,* 1982.

National Opinion Research Center. *General social surveys, 1972–1980: Cumulative codebook.* Storrs, Conn.: Roper Opinion Research Center, University of Connecticut, 1980.

National Science Foundation. Women's S/E doctorates double between 1971 and 1981. *NSF Mosaic,* 1982.

Nesselroade, J. R.; Schaie, K. W.; and Baltes, P. B. Autogenic and generational components of structural and quantitative change in adult behavior. *Journal of Gerontology,* 1972, *27,* 222–228.

Neugarten, B. L. Adult personality: Toward a psychology of the life cycle. In B. L. Neugarten (Ed.), *Middle age and aging.* Chicago: University of Chicago Press, 1968.

Neugarten, B. L. Personality and the aging process. *The Gerontologist,* 1972, *12,* 9–15.

Neugarten, B. L. The future and the young-old. *The Gerontologist,* 1975, *15,* no. 1, part 2, 4–9.

Neugarten, B. L., interviewed by E. Hall. Acting one's age: New rules for old. *Psychology Today,* April 1980.

Newcomb, M. D.; Huba, J. G.; and Bentler, P. M. Mothers' influence on the drug use of their children: Confirmatory tests of direct modeling and mediation theories. *Developmental Psychology,* 1983, *19,* 714–726.

Newcomb, T. M. *Personality and social change.* New York: Dryden Press, 1943.

Newcomb, T. M. *The acquaintance process.* New York: Holt, Rinehart and Winston, 1961.

Newcomb, T. M. Attitude development as a function of reference groups: The Bennington study. In H. Proshansky and B. Seidenberg (Eds.), *Basic studies in social psychology.* New York: Holt, Rinehart and Winston, 1965.

Newell, A., and Simon, H. A. *Human problem solving.* Englewood Cliffs, N.J.: Prentice-Hall, 1972.

Newport, E. L., and Ashbrook, E. F. The emergence of semantic relations in American Sign Language. *Papers and Reports in Child Language Development,* 13, 1977.

Newson, J., et al. Persistant infant comfort habits and their sequelae at 11 and 16 years. *Journal of Child Psychology and Psychiatry,* 1982, *23,* 421–436.

Newsweek. Coping with depression. January 8, 1973.

Nicol, S. E., and Gottesman, I. J. Clues to the genetics and neurobiology of schizophrenia. *American Scientist,* 1983, *71,* 398–404.

Nieva, V. F., and Gutek, B. A. *Women and work: A psychological perspective.* New York: Praeger, 1981.

Nisbet, B. C. An ostensible case of auditory ESP. *Journal of the Society for Psychical Research,* 1977, *49,* 440–445.

Nisbett, R. E., and Ross, L. *Human inference.* Englewood Cliffs, N.J.: Prentice-Hall, 1980.

Norman, D. A., and Bobrow, D. G. On data-limited and resource-limited processes. *Cognitive Psychology,* 1975, *7,* 44–64.

Norton, A. J. Keeping up with households. *American Demographics,* May 1983.

Notman, M. Midlife concerns of women: Implications of the menopause. *American Journal of Psychiatry,* 1979, *136,* 1270–1274.

Ockene, J. K.; Benfari, R. C.; Nuttall, R. L.; Hurwitz, I.; and Ockene, I. S. Relationship of psychosocial factors to smoking behavior change in an intervention program. *Preventive Medicine,* 1982, *11,* 13–28.

Offer, D., and Offer, J. B. *From teenage to young manhood.* New York: Basic Books, 1975.

O'Grady, K. E. Sex, physical attractiveness, and risk for mental illness. *Journal of Personality and Social Psychology,* 1982, *43,* 1064–1071.

Ojemann, G. A. Prospects for further brain-stimulation studies during neurosurgical operations under local anesthesia. In M. Studdert-Kennedy (Ed.), *Psychobiology of Language.* Cambridge, Mass.: MIT, Press, 1983.

Olds, J. Self-stimulation of the brain. *Science,* 1958, *127,* 315–324.

Olmedo, E. L. Testing linguistic minorities. *American Psychologist,* 1981, *36,* 1078–1085.

Olson, M. E. Consumers' attitudes toward energy conservation. *Journal of Social Issues,* 1981, *37* (2), 108–131.

Oltmanns, T. F.; O'Hayon, J.; and Neale, J. M. The effects of antipsychotic medication and diagnostic criteria on distractibility in schizophrenia. *Journal of Psychiatric Research,* 1978, *14,* 81–92.

Orlansky, H. Infant care and personality. *Psychological Bulletin,* 1949, *46,* 1–48.

Orne, M. T. The use and misuse of hypnosis in court. *International Journal of Clinical and Experimental Hypnosis,* 1979, *27,* 311–341.

Orne, M. T., and Wilson, S. K. On the nature of alpha feedback training. In G. E. Schwartz and D. Shapiro (Eds.), *Consciousness and self-regulation: Advances in research.* New York: Plenum, 1978.

Ornstein, R. E. *The psychology of consciousness.* San Francisco: W. H. Freeman, 1972.

Orwell, G. *1984.* New York: Harcourt, Brace, 1949.

Paffenberger, R. S., Jr.; Hyde, R. T.; Wing, A. L.; and Steinmetz, C. H. A natural history of athleticism and cardiovascular health. *Journal of the American Medical Association,* 1984, *252,* 491–495.

Paige, K. Women learn to sing the menstrual blues. *Psychology Today,* September 1973.

Paivio, A. *Imagery and verbal processes.* New York: Holt, Rinehart and Winston, 1971.

Palmore, E. Total change of institutionalization among the aged. *The Gerontologist,* 1976, *16,* 504–507.

Palmore, E. Facts on aging. *The Gerontologist,* 1977, *17,* 315–320.

Parlee, M. The rhythms in men's lives. *Psychology Today,* April 1978.

Parloff, M. B. Shopping for the right therapy. *Saturday Review,* February 21, 1976.

Pendery, M. L.; Maltzman, I. M.; and West, L. J. Controlled drinking by alcoholics? New findings and a reevaluation of a major affirmative study. *Science,* 1982, *217,* 169–174.

Penfield, W. The interpretive cortex. *Science,* 1959, *129,* 1719–1725.

Pennebaker, J. D. *The psychology of physical symptoms.* New York: Springer-Verlag, 1982.

Peplau, L. A.; Bikson, T. K.; Rook, K. S.; and Goodchilds, J. D. Being old and living alone. In L. A. Peplau and D. Perlman (Eds.), *Loneliness: A sourcebook of current theory, research, and therapy.* New York: Wiley-Interscience, 1982.

Peplau, L. A.; Rubin, Z.; and Hill, C. T. Sexual intimacy in dating relationships. *Journal of Social Issues,* 1977, *33* (2), 86–109.

Perls, F. S. *Gestalt therapy verbatim.* Moab, Utah: Real People Press, 1969.

Peterson, L. R., and Peterson, M. J. Short-term retention of individual verbal items. *Journal of Experimental Psychology,* 1959, *58,* 193–198.

Pettigrew, T. F. Regional differences in anti-Negro prejudice. *Journal of Abnor-*

mal and Social Psychology, 1959, 59, 28–36.

Pettigrew, T. F. Racially separate or together? New York: McGraw-Hill, 1971.

Petty, R. E.; Cacioppo, J. T.; and Heesacker, M. Effects of rhetorical questions on persuasion: A cognitive response analysis. Journal of Personality and Social Psychology, 1981, 40, 432–440.

Petty, R.; Wells, G.; and Brock, T. Distraction can enhance or reduce yielding to propaganda: Thought disruption versus effort justification. Journal of Personality and Social Psychology, 1976, 34, 874–884.

Piaget, J. The moral judgment of the child (1932). Glencoe, Ill.: Free Press, 1948.

Piaget, J. The origins of intelligence in children. New York: International Universities Press, 1952.

Piaget, J., and Inhelder, B. The growth of logical thinking from childhood to adolescence. New York: Basic Books, 1958.

Pierrel, R., and Sherman, J. G. Train your pet the Barnabus way. Brown Alumni Monthly, February 1963.

Piliavin, J. A.; Callero, P. L.; and Evans, D. E. Addiction to altrusim? Opponent-process theory and habitual blood donation. Journal of Personality and Social Psychology, 1982, 43, 1200–1213.

Pillemer, D. B. Flashbulb memories of the assassination attempt on President Reagan. Cognition, 1984, 16, 63–80.

Pleck, J. H., and Sawyer, J. (Eds.). Men and masculinity. Englewood Cliffs, N.J.: Prentice-Hall, 1974.

Plutchik, R. Emotion: A psychoevolutionary synthesis. New York: Harper & Row, 1980.

Pope, H., and Mueller, C. W. The intergenerational transmission of marital instability: Comparison by race and sex. In G. Levinger and O. C. Moles (Eds.), Divorce and separation: Context, causes, and consequences. New York: Basic Books, 1979.

Porter, R. H., and Moore, J. D. Human kin recognition by olfactory cues. Physiology and Behavior, 1981, 27, 493–495.

Powledge, T. M. Windows on the womb. Psychology Today, May 1983.

Priest, R. F., and Sawyer, J. Proximity and peership: Bases of balance in interpersonal attraction. American Journal of Sociology, 1967, 72, 633–649.

Proust, M. Swann's way. Translated by C. K. S. Moncrieff. New York: Modern Library, 1928.

Putnam, F. Traces of Eve's faces. Psychology Today, October 1982.

Rahe, R. H. Life change measurement as a predictor of illness. Proceedings of the Royal Society of Medicine, 1968, 61, 1124.

Raloff, J. Occupational noise—the subtle pollutant. Science News, May 22, 1982, 121, 347–350.

Ramsey, R., and Toye, K. The goodbye book. New York: Van Nostrand Reinhold, 1979.

Raskin, M.; Bali, L. R.; and Peeke, H. U. Muscle biofeedback and transcendental meditation: A controlled evaluation of efficacy in the treatment of chronic anxiety. Archives of General Psychiatry, 1980, 37, 93–97.

Raudsepp, E. More creative gamesmanship. Psychology Today, July 1980.

Rechtschaffen, A.; Gilliland, M. A.; Bergmann, B. M.; and Winter, J. B. Physiological correlates of prolonged sleep duration in rats. Science, 1983, 21, 182–184.

Regestein, Q. R., and Howe, L. P. A psychotherapy group for skid-row alcoholics. Massachusetts Journal of Mental Health, 1972, 2, 4–24.

Reiss, M. L., and Bailey, J. S. Visiting the dentist: A behavioral community analysis of participation in a dental health screening and referral program. Journal of Applied Behavior Analysis, 1982, 15, 353–362.

Restak, R. Genetic counseling for defective parents—the danger of knowing too much. Psychology Today, September 1975.

Restak, R. The brain: The last frontier. New York: Doubleday, 1979.

Restak, R. Islands of genius. Science 82, May 1982.

Reston, J. Proxmire on love. The New York Times, March 14, 1975.

Rheingold, H. Our machine Friday. Psychology Today, December 1983.

Rhine, J. B. Extra-sensory perception. Boston: Boston Society for Psychic Research, 1934.

Rice, B. Going for the gifted gold. Psychology Today, February 1980.

Rickels, K.; Case, W. G.; Downing, R. W.; and Winokur, A. Long-term diazepam therapy and clinical outcome. Journal of the American Medical Association, 1983, 250, 767–771.

Riley, M. W.; Foner, A.; and Associates. Aging and society, vol. 1: An inventory of research findings. New York: Russell Sage Foundation, 1968.

Ring, K. Life at death: A scientific investigation of the near death experience. New York: Coward, McCann, & Geoghegan, 1980.

Rinn, W. E. The neuropsychology of facial expression: A review of the neurological and psychological mechanisms for producing facial expressions. Psychological Bulletin, 1984, 95, 52–77.

Ritzer, G. Working: Conflict and change. (2nd ed.) Englewood Cliffs, N.J.: Prentice-Hall, 1977.

Robbins, M. B., and Jensen, G. D. Multiple orgasm in males. Journal of Sex Research, 1978, 14, 21–26.

Robey, B. The two-cat family. American Demographics, May 1983.

Robins, L. N. Deviant children grow up. Baltimore: Williams & Wilkins, 1966.

Rock, I., and Kaufman, L. The moon illusion, Science, 1962, 136, 1023–1031.

Rodgers, J. E. Roots of madness. Science 82, July-August 1982.

Rodin, J. Current status of the internal-external hypothesis for obesity: What went wrong? American Psychologist, 1981, 36, 361–372.

Rodin, J., and Janis, I. L. The social power of health-care practitioners as agents of change. In H. S. Friedman and M. R. DiMatteo (Eds.), Interpersonal issues in health care. New York: Academic Press, 1982.

Rogers, C. R. Client-centered therapy. Boston: Houghton Mifflin, 1951.

Rogers, C. On becoming a person. Boston: Houghton Mifflin, 1961.

Rogers, C. On encounter groups. New York: Harper & Row, 1970.

Rohrbaugh, J. B. Women: Psychology's puzzle. New York: Basic Books, 1979.

Rook, K. S., and Peplau, L. A. Perspectives on helping the lonely. In L. A. Peplau and D. Perlman (Eds.), Loneliness: A sourcebook of current theory, research, and therapy. New York: Wiley-Interscience, 1982.

Rorschach, H. Psychodiagnostik. Bern: Bircher, 1921. English translation: Psychodiagnostics. New York: Grune & Stratton, 1942.

Rosch, E. H. On the internal structure of perceptual and semantic categories. In T. E. Moore (Ed.), Cognitive development and the acquisition of language. New York: Academic Press, 1973.

Rosch, E. H.; Simpson, C.; and Miller, R. S. Structural bases of typicality effects. Journal of Experimental Psychology: Human Perception and Performance, 1976, 2, 491–502.

Rose, R. J., and Ditto, W. B. A developmental genetic analysis of common fears from early adolescence to early adulthood. Child Development, 1983, 54, 361–368.

Rose, R. M. The psychological effects of androgens and estrogens—a review. In R. I. Shader (Ed.), Psychiatric complications of medical drugs. New York: Raven Press, 1972.

Rosenblatt, P. Communication in the practice of love magic. Social Forces, 1971, 49, 482–487.

Rosenfeld, A. In search of youth. GEO, June 1982.

Rosenhan, D. L. On being sane in insane places. Science, 1973, 179, 250–258.

Rosenthal, A. M. Thirty-eight witnesses. New York: McGraw-Hill, 1964.

Rosenthal, M. K., Vocal dialogues in the neonatal period. Developmental Psychology, 1982, 18, 17–21.

Rosenthal, R. Experimenter effects in behavioral research. (Enlarged edition) New York: Irvington, 1976.

Rosenthal, R., et al. Sensitivity to nonverbal communication: The PONS test. Baltimore: Johns Hopkins University Press, 1979.

Ross, A. O. Psychological disorders of childhood: A behavioral approach to theory, research, and practice. (2nd ed.) New York: McGraw-Hill, 1981.

Rotter, J. B. Generalized expectancies for internal and external control of reinforcements. Psychological Monographs, 1966, vol. 80, no. 1, whole no. 609.

Routtenberg, A. The reward system of the brain. *Scientific American*, November 1978.

Rowe, I., and Marcia, J. E. Ego identity status, formal operations, and moral development. *Journal of Youth and Adolescence*, 1980, 9, 87–99.

Rubenstein, C. Psychology's fruit flies. *Psychology Today*, July 1982.

Rubenstein, C. The modern art of courtly love. *Psychology Today*, July 1983.

Rubenstein, C. M., and Shaver, P. The experience of loneliness. In L. A. Peplau and D. Perlman (Eds.), *Loneliness: A sourcebook of current theory, research, and therapy*. New York: Wiley-Interscience, 1982.

Rubin, Z. Are working wives hazardous to their husbands' mental health? *Psychology Today*, May 1983.

Rubin, Z. Does personality really change after 20? *Psychology Today*, May 1981.

Rubin, Z. Jokers wild in the lab. *Psychology Today*, December 1970.

Rubin, Z. Los Angeles says it with love on a scale. Op-Ed page, *Los Angeles Times*, February 14, 1979.

Rubin, Z. Measurement of romantic love. *Journal of Personality and Social Psychology*, 1970, 16, 265–273.

Rubin, Z. *Liking and loving: An invitation to social psychology.* New York: Holt, Rinehart and Winston, 1973.

Rubin, Z. Seasonal rhythms in behavior. *Psychology Today*, December 1979.

Rubin, Z. Taking deception for granted. *Psychology Today*, March 1983.

Rubin, Z. *Children's friendships.* Cambridge, Mass.: Harvard University Press, 1980.

Rusbult, C. E., and Zembrodt, I. M. Responses to dissatisfaction in romantic involvements: A multidimensional scaling analysis. *Journal of Experimental Social Psychology*, 1983, 19, 274–293.

Rusbult, C. E., Zembrodt, I. M., and Gunn, L. K. Exit, voice, loyalty, and neglect: Responses to dissatisfaction in romantic involvements. *Journal of Personality and Social Psychology*, 1982, 43, 1230–1242.

Rutstein, D. D., et al. 2,3-butanediol: An unusual metabolite in the serum of severely alcoholic men during acute intoxication. *Lancet*, 1983, 534–537.

Rutter, M. Maternal deprivation, 1972–1978: New findings, new concepts, new approaches. *Child Development*, 1979, 50, 283–305.

Sachs, J.; Bard, B.; and Johnson, M. L. Language learning with restricted input: Case study of two hearing children of deaf parents. *Applied Psycholinguistics*, 1981, 2, 33–54.

Sachs, M. L. The runner's high. In M. L. Sachs and G. W. Buffone (Eds.), *Running as therapy: An integrated approach.* Lincoln: University of Nebraska Press, 1984.

Sackeim, H. A., et al. Hemispheric asymmetry in the expression of positive and negative emotions: Neurologic evidence. *Archives of Neurology*, 1982, 39, 210–218.

Sadalla, E., and Burroughs, J. Profiles in eating: Sexy vegetarians and other diet-based social stereotypes. *Psychology Today*, October 1981.

Salaman, E. *A collection of moments: A study of involuntary memories.* London: Longman, 1970.

Saltzberg, L., and Elkins, G. R. An examination of common concerns about rational-emotive therapy. *Professional Psychology*, 1980, 11, 324–330.

Sarason, S. B. *Work, aging, and social change.* New York: Free Press, 1977.

Sarnoff, C. A. *Medical aspects of flying motivation.* Randolph Air Force Base, Texas: Air University School of Aviation Motivation, 1957.

Scanzoni, L., and Scanzoni, J. *Men, women, and change: A sociology of marriage and the family.* New York: McGraw-Hill, 1976.

Scarf, M. Shocking the depressed back to life. *New York Times Magazine*, June 17, 1979.

Scarr, S., and Grajek, S. Similarities and differences among siblings. In M. E. Lamb and B. Sutton-Smith (Eds.), *Sibling relationships through the lifespan.* Hillsdale, N.J.: Lawrence Erlbaum, 1982.

Scarr, S., and Weinberg, R. A. IQ test performance of black children adopted by white families. *American Psychologist*, 1976, 31, 726–739.

Scarr, S., and Weinberg, R. A. Attitudes, interests, and IQ. *Human Nature*, April 1978.

Schachter, S. *The psychology of affiliation.* Stanford, Calif.: Stanford University Press, 1959.

Schachter, S. Birth order, eminence, and higher education. *American Sociological Review*, 1963, 28, 757–767.

Schachter, S. The interaction of cognitive and physiological determinants of emotional state. In L. Berkowitz (Ed.), *Advances in experimental social psychology*, vol. 1. New York: Academic Press, 1964.

Schachter, S. Some extraordinary facts about obese humans and rats. *American Psychologist*, 1971, 26, 129–144.

Schachter, S. Recidivism and self-cure of smoking and obesity. *American Psychologist*, 1982, 37, 436–444.

Schachter, S.; Goldman, R; and Gordon, A. Effects of fear, food deprivation, and obesity on eating. *Journal of Personality and Social Psychology*, 1968, 10, 91–97.

Schachter, S., and Singer, J. E. Cognitive, social, and physiological determinants of emotional state. *Psychological Review*, 1962, 69, 379–399.

Schaeffer, J.; Andrysiak, T.; and Ungerleider, J. T. Cognition and long-term use of ganja (cannabis). *Science*, 1981, 213, 465–466.

Schaie, K. W. Cognitive development in aging. In L. K. Obler and M. Alpert (Eds.), *Language and communication in the elderly.* Lexington, Mass.: D. C. Heath, 1980.

Schaie, K. W. The Seattle longitudinal study: A twenty-one-year exploration of psychometric intelligence in adulthood. In K. W. Schaie (Ed.), *Longitudinal studies of adult psychological development.* New York: Guilford Press, 1982.

Schaie, K. W., and Geiwitz, J. *Adult development and aging.* Boston: Little, Brown, 1982.

Scheff, T. J. (Ed.) *Labeling madness.* Englewood Cliffs, N.J.: Prentice-Hall, 1975.

Schein, E. H. Reaction patterns to severe chronic stress in American army prisoners of war of the Chinese. *Journal of Social Issues*, 1957, 13, 21–30.

Scheinin, A. The burden of suicide. *Newsweek*, February 7, 1983.

Scherer, K. R. Non-linguistic vocal indicators of emotion and psychopathology. In C. E. Izard (Ed.), *Emotions in personality and psychopathology.* New York: Plenum, 1979.

Schleidt, M. Personal odor and nonverbal communication. *Ethology and Sociobiology*, 1980, 1, 225–231.

Schleifer, S. J.; Keller, S. E.; McKegney, F. P.; and Stein, M. Bereavement and lymphocyte function. Paper presented at the annual meeting of the American Psychiatric Association, San Francisco, 1980.

Schmeck, H. M., Jr. Almost one in five may have mental disorder. *The New York Times*, September 1984.

Schmeck, H. M., Jr. Research on marijuana finds many risks, some benefits. *The New York Times*, October 9, 1979.

Schmidt, W. E. Gifted retardates: The search for clues to mysterious talent. *The New York Times*, July 12, 1983.

Schneider, W., and Lewis, I. A. The straight story on homosexuality and gay rights. *Public Opinion*, February/March 1984.

Schofield, J. W. Complementary and conflicting identities: Images and interaction in an interracial school. In S. R. Asher and J. M. Gottman (Eds.), *The development of children's friendships.* Cambridge, Mass.: Cambridge University Press, 1981.

Schofield, J. W. *Black and white in school: Trust, tension, or tolerance?* New York: Praeger, 1982.

Schorr, D. Go get some milk and cookies and watch the murders on television. *The Washingtonian*, October 1981.

Schreiber, F. R. *Sybil.* Chicago: Henry Regnery, 1973.

Schukit, M. A. The genetics of alcoholism. In B. Tabakoff, P. B. Sutker, and C. L. Randall (Eds.), *Medical and social aspects of alcohol abuse.* New York: Plenum, 1983.

Schulz, R. *The psychology of death, dying and bereavement.* Reading, Mass.: Addison-Wesley, 1978.

Schulz, R., and Aderman, D. Clinical research and the stages of dying. *Omega*, 1974, 5, 137–143.

Schuman, H. Attitudes vs. actions versus attitudes vs. attitudes. *Public Opinion Quarterly*, 1972, *36*, 347–354.

Schwartz, G. E.; Fair, P. L.; Salt, P.; Mandel, M. R.; and Klerman, G. L. Facial muscle patterning to affective imagery in depressed and non-depressed subjects. *Science*, 1976, *192*, 489–491.

Schwartz, G. E.; Weinberger, D. A.; and Singer, J. A. Cardiovascular differentiation of happiness, sadness, anger, and fear following imagery and exercise. *Psychosomatic Medicine*, 1981, *43*, 343–364.

Scott, J. F. Marriage is not a personal matter. *New York Times Magazine*, October 30, 1966.

Scovern, A. W., and Kilmann, P. R. Status of electroconvulsive therapy: Review of the outcome literature. *Psychological Bulletin*, 1980, *87*, 260–303.

Seeman, M. Alienation, membership and political knowledge: A comparative study. *Public Opinion Quarterly*, 1966, *30*, 359–367.

Segal, J., and Segal, Z. Video-tripping. *Health*, June 1983.

Segal, M. W. Alphabet and attraction: An unobtrusive measure of the effect of propinquity in a field setting. *Journal of personality and Social Psychology*, 1974, *30*, 654–657.

Seligman, C., and Darley, J. M. Feedback as a means of decreasing residential energy consumption. *Journal of Applied Psychology*, 1977, *62*, 363–368.

Seligman, M. E. P. *Helplessness: On depression, development, and death.* San Francisco: W. H. Freeman, 1975.

Seligman, M. E. P. Phobias and preparedness. In M. E. P. Seligman and J. L. Hager (Eds.), *Biological boundaries of learning.* New York: Appleton-Century-Crofts, 1972.

Selman, R. L. *The growth of interpersonal understanding: Developmental and clinical analyses.* New York: Academic Press, 1980.

Selye, H. *The stress of life.* (2nd ed.) New York: McGraw-Hill, 1976.

Serbin, L. A.; Tonick, I. J.; and Sternglanz, S. H. Shaping cooperative cross-sex play. *Child Development*, 1977, *48*, 924–929.

Shapiro, S. Epidemiology of ischemic heart disease and cancer. In D. Mechanic (Ed.), *Handbook of health, health care, and the health professions.* New York: Free Press, 1983.

Sheils, D. A cross-cultural study of beliefs in out-of-the-body experiences, waking and sleeping. *Journal of the Society for Psychical Research*, 1978, *49*, 697–741.

Shekelle, R. B., et al. Psychological depression and 17-year risk of death from cancer. *Psychosomatic medicine.* 1981, *43*, 117–125.

Sheldon, W. H. *Varieties of human physique.* New York: Harper & Row, 1940.

Sheldon, W. H. *Atlas of man: A guide for somatotyping the adult male of all ages.* New York: Harper & Row, 1954.

Shepard, R. W., and Metzler, J. Mental rotation of three-dimensional objects. *Science*, 1971, *171*, 701–703.

Sherman, S. J.; Presson, C. C.; Chassin, L.; Corty, E.; and Olshavsky, R. The false consensus effect in estimates of smoking prevalence: Underlying mechanisms. *Personality and Social Psychology Bulletin*, 1983, *9*, 192–207.

Shevitz, S. A. Psychosurgery: Some current observations. *American Journal of Psychiatry*, 1976, *133*, 266–270.

Shomer, R. W., and Centers, R. Differences in attitudinal responses under conditions of implicitly manipulated group salience. *Journal of Personality and Social Psychology*, 1970, *15*, 125–132.

Shulman, L. S. Educational psychology returns to school. In A. G. Kraut (Ed.), *The G. Stanley Hall lecture series*, vol. 2. Washington, D.C.: American Psychological Association, 1982.

Shuttleworth, E. C.; Syring, V.; and Allen, N. Further observations on the nature of prosopagnosia. *Brain and Cognition*, 1982, *1*, 302–332.

Siegel, A. W.; Kirasic, K. C.; and Kail, R. W. Stalking the elusive cognitive map. In I. Altman and J. F. Wohlwill (Eds.), *Children and the environment.* New York: Plenum, 1978.

Siegel, R. K. The psychology of life after death. *American Psychologist*, 1980, *35*, 911–931.

Siegel, R. K., and Jarvik, M. E. Drug-induced hallucinations in animals and man. In R. K. Siegel and L. J. West (Eds.), *Hallucinations: Behavior, experience, and theory.* New York: Wiley, 1975.

Sigman, M., and Parmelee, A. H. Longitudinal evaluation of the high risk infant. In T. Field, et al. (Eds.), *Infants born at risk.* Holliswood, N.Y.: Spectrum, 1979.

Signorelli, N.; Gross, L.; and Morgan, M. *Violence in television programs: Ten years of scientific progress and implications for the 80's.* Washington, D.C.: U.S. Government Printing Office, 1982.

Siipola, E. M. A study of some effects of preparatory set. *Psychological Monographs*, 1935, *46*, 210.

Silveira, J. Incubation: The effect of interruption, timing, and length on problem solution and quality of problem processing. Doctoral dissertation, University of Oregon, 1971.

Simmons, J. E.; Ottinger, D.; and Haugh, E. Maternal variables and neonate behavior. *Journal of the American Academy of Child Psychiatry*, 1967, *6*, 174–182.

Simmons, R. G., et al. Entry into early adolescence: The impact of school structure, puberty, and early dating on self-esteem. *American Sociological Review*, 1979, *44*, 948–967.

Simon, H. A. Studying human intelligence by creating artificial intelligence. *American Scientist*, 1981, *69*, 300–309.

Singer, B., and Benassi, V. A. Occult beliefs. *American Scientist*, 1981, *69*, 49–55.

Singer, D. G., and Singer, J. L. Is human imagination going down the tube? *Chronicle of Higher Education*, April 23, 1979.

Singer, I. B. Contribution to "Psychology tomorrow: The Nobel view." *Psychology Today*, December 1982.

Singer, J. L. Navigating the stream of consciousness: Research in daydreaming and related inner experience. *American Psychologist*, 1975, *30*, 727–738.

Singer, J. L. Fantasy: The foundation of serenity. *Psychology Today*, July 1976.

Singer, J. L., and Antrobus, J. Eye movements during fantasies. *A.M.A. Archives of General Psychiatry*, 1965, *12*, 71–76.

Skinner, B. F. *Walden two.* New York: Macmillan, 1948.

Skinner, B. F. "Superstition" in the pigeon. *Journal of Experimental Psychology*, 1953, *38*, 168–172.

Skinner, B. F. *Verbal behavior.* New York: Appleton-Century-Crofts, 1957.

Skinner, B. F. Teaching machines. *Science*, 1958, *128*, 969–977.

Skinner, B. F. *Beyond freedom and dignity.* New York: Knopf, 1971.

Skipper, J. K., Jr., and McCaghy, C. H. Strip-teasers: The anatomy and career contingencies of a deviant occupation. *Social Problems*, 1970, *17*, 391–405.

Sklar, L. S., and Anisman, H. Stress and coping factors influence tumor growth. *Science*, 1979, *205*, 513–515.

Sloane, R. B., et al. *Psychotherapy versus behavior therapy.* Cambridge, Mass.: Harvard University Press, 1975.

Slobin, D. I. Cognitive prerequisites for the development of grammer. In C. Ferguson and D. I. Slobin (Eds.), *Studies of child language development.* New York: Holt, Rinehart and Winston, 1973.

Smith, D. Trends in counseling and psychotherapy. *American Psychologist*, 1982, *37*, 802–809.

Smith, K. F., and Bengtson, V. L. Positive consequences of institutionalization: Solidarity between elderly parents and their middle-aged children. *The Gerontologist*, 1979, *19*, 438–447.

Smith, M. C. Hypnotic memory enhancement of witnesses: Does it work? *Psychological Bulletin*, 1983, *94*, 387–407.

Smith, M. L.; Glass, G. V.; and Miller, T. I. *The benefits of psychotherapy.* Baltimore: Johns Hopkins University Press, 1980.

Smith, T. W. Happiness: Time trends, seasonal variations, inter-survey differences, and other mysteries. *Social Psychology Quarterly*, 1979, *47*, 18–30.

Smith, T. W. (Ed.) The polls: Gender and attitudes toward violence. *Public Opinion Quarterly*, 1984, *48*, 384–396.

Snow, C. E. Mothers' speech to children learning language. *Child Development*, 1972, *43*, 549–564.

Snow, M. E. Birth order differences in young children's interactions with mother, father, and peer. Paper presented to the Society for Research on Child Development, Boston, 1981.

Snyder, S. H. The true speed trip: Schizophrenia. *Psychology Today*, January 1972.

Snyder, S. H. (Interviewed by D. Goleman.) Mind over matter: The big issues raised by newly discovered brain chemicals. *Psychology Today*, June 1980.

Sobel, D. For stage fright, a remedy proposed. *The New York Times*, November 20, 1979.

Sobel, D. Psychiatric drugs widely misused, critics charge. *The New York Times*, June 3, 1980.

Sobell, M. B., and Sobell, L. C. Alcoholics treated by individualized behavior therapy: One year treatment outcome. *Behavior Research and Therapy*, 1973, *11*, 599–618.

Solanto, M. V. Neuropharmacological basis of stimulant drug action in attention deficit disorder with hyperactivity: A review and synthesis. *Psychological Bulletin*, 1984, *95*, 387–409.

Sorenson, S. On the possibilities of changing the annoyance reaction to noise by changing the attitude to the source of annoyance. *Nordisk Hygienisk Tidskrift*, Supplementum 1, 1970, 1–76.

Spain, D., and Bianchi, S. M. How women have changed. *American Demographics*, May 1983.

Spanos, N. P., and Barber, T. X. Toward a convergence in hypnosis research. *American Psychologist*, 1974, *29*, 500–511.

Spearman, C. "General intelligence," objectively determined and measured. *American Journal of Psychology*, 1904, *15*, 201–293.

Speer, D. C. An evaluation of a telephone crisis service. Paper presented at meeting of the Midwestern Psychological Association, Cleveland, 1972.

Spelke, E.; Hirst, W.; and Neisser, U. Skills of divided attention. *Cognition*, 1976, *4*, 215–230.

Spence, J. T. (Ed.) *Achievement and achievement motives: Psychological and sociological approaches.* San Francisco: W. H. Freeman, 1983.

Sperling, H. The information available in brief visual presentations. *Psychological Monographs*, 1960, vol. *74*, whole no. 498.

Spitzer, R. L.; Forman, J. B. W.; and Nee, J. *DSM-III* field trials; I. Initial interrater diagnostic reliability. *American Journal of Psychiatry*, 1979, *136*, 815–817.

Spitzer, R. L.; Skodol, A. E.; Gibbon, M.; and Williams, J. B. W. *Psychopathology: A Case book.* New York: McGraw-Hill, 1983.

Spreitzer, E., and Riley, L. Factors associated with singlehood. *Journal of Marriage and the Family*, 1974, *36*, 533–542.

Sprott, R. L., and Statts, J. Behavioral studies using genetically defined mice: A bibliography. *Behavior Genetics*, 1975, *5*, 27–82.

Sroufe, L. A. Wariness of strangers and the study of infant development. *Child Development*, 1977, *48*, 731–746.

Stapp, J., and Fulcher, R. The employment of APA members: 1982. *American Psychologist*, 1983, *38*, 1298–1320.

Starker, S. Daydreaming styles and nocturnal dreaming. *Journal of Abnormal Psychology*, 1974, *83*, 52–55.

Steffensmeier, R. H. Suicide and the contemporary woman: Are male and female suicide rates converging? *Sex Roles*, 1984, *10*, 613–631.

Stein, H. Just good friends. *Esquire*, August 1980.

Stephan, W. G. School desegregation: An evaluation of predictions made in *Brown v. Board of Education. Psychological Bulletin*, 1978, *85*, 217–238.

Stepney, R. Why do people smoke? *New Society*, July 28, 1983.

Sterman, M. B. Biofeedback and epilepsy. *Human Nature*, May 1978.

Stern, J. A.; Brown, M.; Vlett, G. A.; and Sletten, I. A comparison of hypnosis, acupuncture, morphine, valium, aspirin, and placebo in the management of experimentally induced pain. In W. E. Edmonston, Jr. (Ed.), *Conceptual and investigative approaches to hypnosis and hypnotic phenomena. Annals of the New York Academy of Sciences*, 1977, *296*, 175–193.

Sternberg, R. J. The nature of mental abilities. *American Psychologist*, 1979, *34*, 214–230.

Sternberg, R. J. Toward a triarchic theory of human intelligence. *Behavioral and Brain Sciences*, 1984, *7*, 269–287.

Stevens, C. F. The neuron. *Scientific American*, September 1979.

Stewart, R. B. Sibling attachment relationships: Child-infant interactions in the strange situation. *Developmental Psychology*, 1983, *19*, 192–199.

Stockton, W. Creating computers that think. *New York Times Magazine*, December 7 and 14, 1980.

Stokols, D.; Novaco, R. W.; Stokols, J.; and Campbell, J. Traffic congestion, Type A behavior, and stress. *Journal of Applied Psychology*, 1978, *63*, 467–480.

Stone, G. C. Patient compliance and the role of the expert. *Journal of Social Issues*, 1979, *35* (1), 34–59.

Stone, W. F. *The psychology of politics.* New York: Free Press, 1974.

Stroebe, M. S.; and Stroebe, W. Who suffers more? Sex differences in health risks of the widowed. *Psychological Bulletin*, 1983, *93*, 279–301.

Strupp, H. H., and Hadley, S. W. Specific vs. nonspecific factors in psychotherapy: A controlled study of outcome. *Archives of General Psychiatry*, 1979, *36*, 1125–1136.

Sudnow, D. Dead on arrival. *Transaction*, November 1967.

Suedfeld, P. The benefits of boredom: Sensory deprivation reconsidered. *American Scientist*, January–February 1975.

Suedfeld, P. Aloneness as a healing experience. In L. A. Peplau and D. Perlman (Eds.), *Loneliness: A sourcebook of current theory, research, and therapy.* New York: Wiley-Interscience, 1982.

Suinn, R. M. Intervention with Type A behaviors. *Journal of Consulting and Clinical Psychology*, 1982, *50*, 933–949.

Sulin, R. A., and Dooling, D. J. Intrusion of a thematic idea in retention of prose. *Journal of Experimental Psychology*, 1974, *103*, 255–262.

Sullivan, H. S. *The interpersonal theory of psychiatry.* New York: Norton, 1953.

Sullivan, K., and Sullivan, A. Adolescent-parent separation. *Developmental Psychology*, 1980, *16*, 93–99.

Suls, J. Social support, interpersonal relations, and health: Benefits and liabilities. In G. S. Sanders and J. Suls (Eds.), *Social psychology of health and illness.* Hillsdale, N. J.: Lawrence Erlbaum, 1982.

Swanson, J. M., and Kinsbourne, M. State-dependent learning and retrieval: Methodological cautions and theoretical considerations. In J. F. Kihlstrom and F. J. Evans (Eds.), *Functional disorders of memory.* Hillsdale, N.J.: Lawrence Erlbaum, 1979.

Sweet, E. A. '70s chronology. *Ms.*, December 1979.

Swinyard, W. R. The interaction between comparative advertising and copy claim variation. *Journal of Marketing Research*, 1981, *18*, 175–186.

Szasz, T. S. *Ideology and insanity.* Garden City, N.Y.: Anchor, 1970.

Tanner, J. M. Sequence, tempo, and individual variation in growth and development of boys and girls aged twelve to sixteen. In J. Kagan and R. Coles (Eds.), *Twelve to sixteen: Early adolescence.* New York: Norton, 1972.

Tavris, C. *Anger: The misunderstood emotion.* New York: Simon & Schuster, 1983.

Tavris, C., and Offir, C. *The longest war: Sex differences in perspective.* New York: Harcourt Brace Jovanovich, 1977.

Taylor, D. G.; Sheatsley, P. B.; and Greeley, A. M. Attitudes toward racial integration. *Scientific American*, June 1978.

Taylor, S. E. Hospital patient behavior: Resistance, helplessness, or control? In H. S. Friedman and M. R. DiMatteo (Eds.), *Interpersonal issues in health care.* New York: Academic Press, 1982.

Teitelbaum, P. Motivation and control of food intake. In C. F. Code (Ed.), *Handbook of physiology: Alimentary canal*, vol. 1. Washington, D.C.: American Physiological Society, 1967.

Television and growing up: The impact of televised violence. (Report of the Surgeon General's Scientific Advisory Committee on Television and Social Behavior.) Washington, D.C.: U.S. Government Printing Office, 1972.

Terman, L. M. The discovery and encouragment of exceptional talent. *American Psychologist*, 1954, *9*, 221–230.

Terman, L. M., and Merrill, M. A. *Measuring intelligence: A guide to the administration of the new revised Stanford-Binet tests for intelligence.* Boston: Houghton Mifflin, 1937.

Terrace, H. *Nim.* New York: Knopf, 1979.

Thomas, A., and Chess, J. *Temperament and development.* New York: Bruner/Mazel, 1977.

Thomas, E. L., and Robinson, H. A. *Improving memory in every class: A sourcebook for teachers.* Boston: Allyn and Bacon, 1972.

Thompson, J. C. Will it hurt less if I can control it? A complex answer to a simple question. *Psychological Bulletin,* 1981, *90,* 89–101.

Thompson, R. A., and Lamb, M. E. Security of attachment and stranger sociability in infancy. *Developmental Psychology,* 1983, *19,* 184–191.

Thompson, V. D. Family size: Implicit policies and assumed psychological outcomes. *Journal of Social Issues,* 1974, *30* (4), 93–124.

Thorndyke, P. W., and Hayes-Roth, B. Differences in spatial knowledge acquired from maps and navigation. *Cognitive Psychology,* 1982, *14,* 560–569.

Thurstone, L. L. Primary mental abilities. *Psychometric Monographs,* no. 1, Chicago: University of Chicago Press, 1938.

Tierney, J. The aging body. *Esquire,* May 1982.

Timiras, P. Biological perspectives on aging. *American Scientist,* September–October 1978.

Timson, J. Is coffee safe to drink? *Human Nature,* December 1978.

Tobin-Richards, M.; Boxer, A.; and Petersen, A. C. The psychological impact of pubertal change: Sex differences in perceptions of self during early adolescence. In J. Brooks-Gunn and A. C. Petersen (Eds.), *Girls at puberty: Biological and psychosocial perspectives.* New York: Plenum, 1983.

Tolley, H. B., Jr. Challenging discriminatory wages for women's work. *USA Today,* May 1983.

Tolman, E. C. Determiners of behavior at a choice point. *Psychological Review,* 1938, *45,* 1–41.

Tolman, E. C.; Ritchie, B. F.; and Kalish, D. Studies in spatial learning. Part II: Place learning versus response learning. *Journal of Experimental Psychology,* 1946, *36,* 221–229.

Tomkins, S. S. *Affect, imagery, consciousness, vol. 1.: The positive affects.* New York: Springer, 1962.

Torrey, E. F. *Schizophrenia and civilization.* New York: Jason Aronson, 1980.

Trefil, J. S. A consumer's guide to pseudoscience. *Saturday Review,* April 29, 1978.

Trickett, P. K.; Apfel, N. H.; Rosenbaum, L. K.; and Zigler, E. F. A five year follow-up of participants in the Yale Child Welfare Research Program. In E. F. Zigler and E. W Gordon (Eds.), *Day care: Scientific and social policy issues.* Boston: Auburn House Publishing, 1983.

Truax, C. B., and Mitchell, K. M. Research on certain therapist interpersonal skills in relation to process and outcome. In A. E. Bergin and S. L. Garfield (Eds.), *Handbook of psychotherapy and behavior change.* New York: Wiley, 1971.

Tuber, D. S.; Hothersall, D.; and Voith, V. L. Animal clinical psychology: A modest proposal. *American Psychologist,* 1974, *29,* 762–766.

Tulving, E. Cue-dependent forgetting. *American Scientist,* January–February 1974.

Turkington, C. Parents found to ignore sex stereotypes. *APA Monitor,* April 1984.

Turnbull, C. M. Some observations regarding the experiences and behavior of the Ba Mbuti pygmies. *American Journal of Psychology,* 1961, *74,* 304–308.

Underwood, B. J. Interference and forgetting. *Psychological Review,* 1957, *64,* 49–60.

United Media Enterprises. Leisure time survey. Reported in *Time,* December 27, 1982.

U.S. Department of Health and Human Services. *The health consequences of smoking for women. A report of the Surgeon General.* Washington, D.C.: Public Health Service, 1980.

U.S. Department of Health and Human Services. *The health consequences of smoking: The changing cigarette.* Washington, D.C.: Public Health Service, 1981.

U.S. Surgeon General's Report. *Healthy people.* Washington, D.C.: Department of Health, Education, and Welfare, 1979.

Vaillant, G. *Adaptation to life.* Boston: Little, Brown, 1977.

Vaillant, G. E. *The natural history of alcoholism.* Cambridge, Mass.: Harvard University Press, 1982.

Valenstein, E. *Brain control.* New York: Wiley, 1973.

Valins, S. Cognitive effects of false heart-rate feedback. *Journal of Personality and Social Psychology,* 1966, *4,* 400–408.

Veroff, J.; Douvan, E.; and Kulka, R. *The inner American: A self-portrait from 1957 to 1976.* New York: Basic Books, 1981.

Virginia Slims American Women's Poll, 1980. As reported by J. Klemesrud, *The New York Times,* March 13, 1980.

Viscott, D. S. *The making of a psychiatrist.* New York: Arbor House, 1972.

Von Baeyer, C. L.; Sherk, D. L.; and Zanna, M. P. Impression management in the job interview: When the female applicant meets the male (chauvinist) interviewer. *Personality and Social Psychology Bulletin,* 1981, *7,* 45–52.

Wachs, T. D. Proximal experience and early cognitive-intellectual development: The physical environment. *Merrill-Palmer Quarterly of Behavior and Development,* 1979, *25,* 3–41.

Wahba, N. A., and Brickwell, L. G. Maslow reconsidered: A review of research on the need hierarchy theory. *Organizational Behavior and Human Performance,* 1976, *15,* 212–240.

Wald, G. The receptors of human color vision. *Science,* 1964, *145,* 1007–1017.

Walford, R. L. *The immunologic theory of aging.* Copenhagen: Munksgard, 1969.

Walker, L. J. The sequentiality of Kohlberg's stages of moral development. *Child Development,* 1982, *53,* 1330–1336.

Wallace, R. K., and Benson, H. The physiology of meditation. *Scientific American,* 1972, *226,* 84–90.

Wallechinsky, D., and Wallace, I. *The people's almanac.* Garden City, N.Y.: Doubleday, 1975.

Wallerstein, J. S., and Kelly, J. B. *Surviving the break-up: How children and parents cope with divorce.* New York: Basic Books, 1980.

Wallis, C. Stress: Can we cope? *Time,* June 6, 1983.

Wallston, B. S., and O'Leary, V. E. Sex and gender make a difference: The differential perceptions of men and women. *Review of Personality and Social Psychology,* 1981, *2,* 9–41.

Walster, E., and Festinger, L. The effectiveness of "overheard" persuasive communications. *Journal of Abnormal and Social Psychology,* 1962, *65,* 395–402.

Waterman, A. S. Identity development from adolescence to adulthood: An extension of theory and a review of research. *Developmental Psychology,* 1982, *18,* 341–358.

Watson, D. The actor and the observer: How are their perceptions of causality divergent? *Psychological Bulletin,* 1982, *92,* 682–700.

Watson, J. B. Psychology as the behaviorist views it. *Psychological Review,* 1913, *20,* 158–177.

Watson, J. B., and Rayner, R. Conditioned emotional reactions. *Journal of Experimental Psychology,* 1920, *3,* 1–14.

Watts, B. L. Individual differences in circadian activity and their effects on roommate relationships. *Journal of Personality,* 1982, *50,* 374–384.

Webb, E. J., et al. *Unobtrusive measures: Nonreactive research in the social sciences.* Chicago: Rand McNally, 1966.

Webb, W. B. *Sleep: The gentle tyrant.* Englewood Cliffs, N.J.: Prentice-Hall, 1975.

Webb, W. B., and Bonnet, M. H. Sleep and dreams. In M. E. Meyer (Ed.), *Foundations of contemporary psychology.* New York: Oxford University Press, 1979.

Webb, W. B., and Campbell, S. S. Relationships in sleep characteristics of identical and fraternal twins. *Archives of General Psychiatry,* 1983, *40,* 1093–1095.

Weideger, P. *Menstruation and menopause.* (Revised and Expanded Ed.) New York: Delta Books, 1977.

Weingartner, H.; Rudorfer, M. W.; Buchsbaum, M. S.; and Linnoila, M. Effects of serotonin on memory impairments produced by ethanol. *Science*, 1983, *221*, 472–474.

Weingartner, H., et al. Effects of vasopressin on human memory functions. *Science*, 1981, *211*, 601–603.

Weiss, J. M. Psychological factors in stress and disease. *Scientific American*, June 1972.

Weiss, R. S. *Loneliness: The experience of emotional and social isolation.* Cambridge, Mass.: M.I.T. Press, 1973.

Weiss, R. S. The provisions of social relationships. In Z. Rubin (Ed.), *Doing unto others; Joining, molding, conforming, helping, loving.* Englewood Cliffs, N.J.: Prentice-Hall, 1974.

Weiss, R. S. *Marital separation.* New York: Basic Books, 1975.

Weiss, R. S. The emotional impact of marital separation. In G. Levinger and O. C. Moles (Eds.), *Divorce and separation.* New York: Basic Books, 1979.

Weiss, R. S. Growing up a little faster: The experience of growing up in a single-parent household. *Journal of Social Issues*, 35 (4), 97–111.

Weissman, M. M.; Klerman, G. L.; Prusoff, B. A.; Sholomskas, D.; and Padian, N. Depressed outpatients: Results one year after treatment with drugs and/or interpersonal psychotherapy. *Archives of General Psychiatry*, 1981, *38*, 51–56.

Weissman, M. M., and Myers, J. K. Affective disorders in a U.S. urban community. *Archives of General Psychiatry*, 1978, *35*, 1304–1310.

Weitzman, L. J., et al. Sex role socialization in picture books for preschool children. *American Journal of Sociology*, 1972, *77*, 1125–1150.

Welles, C. Teaching the brain new tricks. *Esquire*, March 1983.

Wessells, M. G. *Cognitive psychology.* New York: Harper & Row, 1982.

White, B. L. An experimental approach to the effects of environment on early human behavior. In J. P. Hill (Ed.), *Minnesota symposium on child psychology*, vol. I. Minneapolis: University of Minnesota Press, 1967.

White, B. L. *The first three years of life.* Englewood Cliffs, N.J.: Prentice-Hall, 1975.

White, R. M. Sleep length and variability: Measurement and relationships. Doctoral dissertation, University of Florida, 1975.

White, R. W. Motivation reconsidered: The concept of competence. *Psychological Review*, 1959, *66*, 297–333.

White, R. W. *The enterprise of living: A view of personal growth.* (2nd ed.) New York: Holt, Rinehart and Winston, 1976.

White, S. H., and Pillemer, D. B. Child-hood amnesia and the development of a socially accessible memory system. In J. F. Kihlstrom and P. J. Evans (Eds.), *Functional disorders of memory.* Hillsdale, N.J.: Lawrence Erlbaum, 1979.

White, W. A. *Outlines of psychiatry.* (13th ed.) New York: Nervous and Mental Disease Publishing Company, 1932.

Whiting, B., and Edwards, C. P. A cross-cultural analysis of sex differences in the behavior of children aged three through 11. *Journal of Social Psychology*, 1973, *91*, 171–188.

Whorf, B. L. *Language, thought, and reality.* New York: MIT Press-Wiley, 1956.

Whybrow, P. C. Where there's mud, there's momentum. *Yankee Magazine*, April 1979.

Wicker, A. W. Attitudes versus actions: The relationship of verbal and overt behavioral responses to attitude objects. *Journal of Social Issues*, 1969, *25* (4), 41–78.

Wickler, W. *The sexual code.* Garden City, N.Y.: Anchor, 1973.

Wilson, C. E. The effect of medium on loss of information. *Journalism Quarterly*, 1974, *51*, 111–115.

Wing, R. An introduction to statistics. Mimeographed handout, Department of Social Relations, Harvard University, 1969.

Wingfield, A. *Human learning and memory: An introduction.* New York: Harper & Row, 1979.

Winterbottom, M. R. The relation of childhood training in independence to achievement motivation. Doctoral dissertation. University of Michigan, 1953.

Wohlford, P. Initiation of cigarette smoking: Is it related to parental smoking behavior? *Journal of Consulting and Clinical Psychology*, 1970, *34*, 148–151.

Wolcott, J. H., et al. Correlation of general aviation accidents with the biorhythm theory. *Human Factors*, 1977, *19*, 283–293.

Wolfe, J. B. Effectiveness of token rewards for chimpanzees. *Comparative Psychological Monographs*, 1936, *12*, 50.

Wolpe, J. *Psychotherapy by reciprocal inhibition.* Stanford, Calif.: Stanford University Press, 1958.

Wolpe, J., and Rachman, S. Psychoanalytic "evidence": A critique based on Freud's case of Little Hans. *Journal of Nervous and Mental Disease*, 1960, *131*, 135–147.

Wood, P. D., and Haskell, W. L. The effect of exercise on high density lipoproteins. *Lipids*, 1979, *14*, 417–427.

Woodmansee, J. J. The pupil response as a measure of social attitudes. In G. F. Summers (Ed.), *Attitude measurement*, Chicago: Rand McNally, 1970.

Worchel, S., and Brehm, J. W. Effects of threats to attitudinal freedom as a function of agreement with the communicator. *Journal of Personality and Social Psychology*, 1970, *14*, 18–22.

Wright, P. L. Analyzing media effects on advertising responses. *Public Opinion Quarterly*, 1974, *38*, 192–205.

Wurtman, R. Brain muffins. *Psychology Today*, October 1978.

Yoken, C., and Berman, J. S. Does paying a fee for psychotherapy alter the effectiveness of treatment? *Journal of Consulting and Clinical Psychology*, 1984, *52*, 254–260.

Young, W. C.; Goy, R. W.; and Phoenix, C. H. Hormones and sexual behavior. *Science*, 1964, *143*, 212–218.

Zajonc, R. B. *Animal social behavior.* Morristown, N.J.: General Learning Press, 1972.

Zajonc, R. B. Family configurations and intelligence. *Science*, 1976, *192*, 227–236.

Zeigarnik, B. Uber das Behalten von erlededigten und unerledigten Handlungen. *Psychologische Forschung*, 1927, *9*, 1–85.

Zelnik, M., and Kantner, J. F. Sexual and contraceptive experience of young unmarried women in the United States, 1976 and 1971. *Family Planning Perspectives*, 1977, *9*, 55–71.

Zillmann, D.; Williams, B. R.; Bryant, J.; Boynton, K. R.; and Wolf, M. A. Acquisition of information from educational television programs as a function of differently paced humorous inserts. *Journal of Educational Psychology*, 1980, *72*, 170–180.

Zimbardo, P. G., and Meadow, W. Sexism springs eternal—in the *Reader's Digest. Women's Studies Abstracts*, 1976, *5*, 61.

Zinberg, N. The war over marijuana. *Psychology Today*, December 1976.

Zipser, A. R. Old is old is old. Face it squarely. Avoid delusions. *The New York Times*, December 18, 1982.

Zuckerman, M. A biological theory of sensation seeking. In M. Zuckerman (Ed.), *Biological bases of sensation seeking, impulsivity, and anxiety.* Hillsdale, N.J.: Lawrence Erlbaum, 1983.

Zung, W. W., and Wilson, W. P. Time estimation during sleep. *Biological Psychiatry*, 1971, *3*, 159–164.

Zurif, E. B. Language mechanisms: A neuropsychological perspective. *American Scientist*, 1980, *68*, 305–306.

Zweigenhaft, R. L. The empirical study of signature size. *Social Behavior and Personality*, 1977, *5*, 177–185.

Jones, M.C., 247, 385, 427
Jones, R.A., 466
Jones, W.H., 517
Jonides, J., 151
Jorgensen, B.W., 491
Jospe, M., 371
Judd, C.M., 249
Jung, C., 70, 77, 331, 338

Kacerguis, M.A., 264
Kagan, J., 227, 239, 260, 330
Kahle, L.R., 457
Kahn, M.D., 253
Kahneman, D., 148, 198
Kail, R.W., 151
Kalish, R., 272, 285
Kane, R.A., 280
Kane, R.L., 280
Kantner, J.F., 504
Kaplan, H.S., 501
Kaplan, M., 398
Karabenick, S.A., 480
Karasek, R., 365
Karmel, L., 527
Karr, R., 505
Kass, L., 63
Kassarjian, H.H., 119
Kastenbaum, R., 284, 285, 286, 287
Katchadourian, H.A., 298
Kates, R., 460
Katkin, E.S., 146
Katz, A.M., 524
Katz, J., 504
Kaufman, L., 122
Kaye, D., 468
Kazdin, A.E., 158, 160
Kearsley, R.B., 227
Keating, D.P., 247
Kelley, H., 515, 520, 531
Kelly, J., 244
Kelman, H.C., 474, 476
Kendrick, C., 254
Kenrick, D.T., 121
Kesey, K., 436
Kessler, R.C., 510
Kety, S.S., 410
Kevan, S.M., 92
Kielman, S., 505
Kiesler, C., 438
Kihlstrom, J., 173
Killen, M., 243
Kilman, P.R., 436
Kinsbourne, M., 38, 172
Kinsey, A.C., 502
Kirasic, K.C., 151
Kirsch, M.A., 448
Kirschner, P., 468
Kivnick, H.Q., 279
Kleck, R.E., 315
Klein, M., 233
Kleitman, N., 91
Klemesrud, J., 511
Klima, E.S., 192
Klinman, D., 511
Klos, D.S., 251
Knapp, J.R., 249
Knight, R., 408, 409
Knox, R.A., 64
Kobasa, S.C., 343, 363
Koelling, R.A., 132
Kohen, J., 538
Kohlberg, L., 228, 242–243, 491, 496
Köhler, W., 200

Kojima, S., 46
Korda, A., 355
Kornfeld, O.S., 375
Kornhaber, A., 279
Korsakoff, S.S., 175
Kosslyn, S.M., 151
Kraut, R., 310
Krebs, D., 519
Kripke, D., 68, 91
Krosnick, J.A., 249
Krueger, A.P., 92
Kübler-Ross, E., 285
Kulik, J.A., 10–13, 142
Kulka, R.A., 25, 244

Lackner, J.R., 111
LaFarge, P., 509
Laird, J., 313
Lamb, M.E., 238
Lando, B., 254
Lange, C., 310
Langer, E.J., 280, 375
Langone, J., 418
Langway, L., 227, 228
Lanzetta, J.T., 315
Larkin, J., 199
Lashley, K., 172, 174
Lassen, N.A., 46, 54
Laudenslager, M.L., 368
Lawler, E.E., 294
Lawrence, L.H., 476
Lazar, I., 228
Lazarus, R., 361, 399
Lee, 376
Lee, L., 534
Leeper, R., 119
Leirer, V.O., 520
Lenneberg, E.H., 190
Lennon, M.C., 270
Leo, J., 84, 506
Lerner, R.M., 180, 249, 250
Leslie, L., 531
Levenson, R.W., 313
Leventhal, H., 468
Levin, H., 100
Levin, P.F., 316
Levinger, G., 537, 539
Levinson, D., 14, 261–262, 265, 267, 491
Levinthal, C.F., 58
Levy, S.M., 367, 369
Lewis, I.A., 505
Lewis, J.L., 118
Lewis, M., 486
Lichtenstein, E., 378
Lieber, A., 92
Lieberman, M.A., 448
Liebert, R.M., 430
Lindzey, G., 210
Linnaeus, C., 112
Lintell, M., 129
Lipscomb, D.M., 127
Locke, J., 6, 226
Lockhart, R.S., 166
Loehlin, J., 210
Loftus, E., 184, 185
Loken, B., 459
Lopate, C., 263
Lorayne, H., 179
Lorenz, K., 227, 318
Lothstein, L.M., 497
Louis, A.M., 31
Lovaas, O.I., 413
Lowenthal, M.F., 269

Lucas, J., 179
Luce, G.G., 90
Lumsdaine, A.A., 466
Lunde, D.T., 298
Luria, A.R., 106, 175
Lynch, G., 174
Lynch, J.J., 376

Maass, A., 465
McAdams, D.P., 344
McArthur, L., 496, 518
McCaghy, C.H., 253
McCall, R.B., 207, 208, 210
McCann, I.L., 379
McCarley, R., 76, 77
McCartney, K., 195
McCaul, K.D., 153
Macaulay, J., 495
McClelland, D.C., 208, 304
Maccoby, E.E., 490, 494
McConnell, J., 174
McCormick, N.B., 503, 504
McCrae, R.R., 260, 261, 329, 355
McDevitt, S.C., 346
McDougall, W., 292
Macfarlane, A., 233, 234
McGaugh, J., 174, 175
McGhie, A., 408
McGinnis, J., 468
McGlone, J., 493
McGrath, R.J., 318
McHale, S.M., 411
Machlowitz, M., 302
Mack, J.E., 418
Mackay, A.V.P., 410
Macke, A.S., 537
McKean, K., 35
McKeown, T., 375
McKernon, P.E., 228
McKinley, J.C., 347
McLaughlin, S.D., 343
McNeil, B.J., 198
McNeil, E., 27
McNeill, D., 167
McRae, J.A., 510
Maddox, G., 272
Mahoney, M.J., 397
Main, M., 238
Major, B., 519
Makinodan, T., 274
Maltzman, I.M., 387
Mandler, G., 312
Manis, J.D., 264
Marcia, J.E., 248
Marek, G.R., 172
Mark, V.H., 49
Marks, L.E., 106
Marlatt, G.A., 386, 387
Marlin, N.A., 174
Marolla, F.A., 253
Marsh, C., 276
Marshall, D.S., 502
Marshall, G.D., 313
Marshall, J., 183
Martin, J.E., 379, 380
Martin, R.L., 407
Maruyama, G., 254
Maslach, C., 313
Maslow, A., 294, 295, 330, 344, 354, 445, 447
Masnick, G., 536
Mastellone, M., 429

AUTHOR INDEX

Masters, W.H., 268, 298, 500, 501, 504
Matarazzo, J.D., 357
Matas, L., 238
Mathews, K., 129
Matteson, D., 264
Maugh, T.H., 81
Maury, A., 76
Meadow, W., 508
Mechanic, D., 360
Medrich, E.A., 243
Medvedev, Z., 274
Melanchton, P., 5
Melzack, R., 109, 110
Mencken, H.L., 528
Merrill, M.A., 206, 207
Mesmer, A., 84
Messenger, J.C., 502
Meth, J.M., 395
Metzler, J., 151
Mewborn, C.R., 469
Meyer, V., 402
Meyers, A.W., 158
Michaelis, D., 526
Micklin, M., 343
Milan, M.A., 158
Miles, M., 448
Milgram, S., 13, 472–473, 474, 475, 476, 521
Miller, G., 163, 220, 315
Miller, J.D., 128
Miller, N., 254, 466
Miller, N.E., 146
Miller, R.A., 219
Miller, R.R., 174
Miller, R.S., 196
Miller, T.I., 437, 439
Milner, B., 175
Minard, R.D., 482
Mindess, H., 347
Minsky, M., 221
Mintz, R.S., 417
Mischel, W., 324, 338, 339, 340, 341, 342
Mitchell, K.M., 426
Mitchison, G., 70
Money, J., 493
Moniz, A. de Egas, 437
Moody, R.A., 286
Moore, J.S., 113
Moore-Ede, M.C., 91
Moss, R.H., 404
Morgan, J., 276
Morgan, M., 320
Morin, S., 505
Morris, D., 34
Morris, J., 497
Morris, S., 160
Morris, T., 367
Morrison, J.K., 393
Morse, W., 138
Moskowitz, H.R., 114
Moss, H., 239
Mott, D.E.W., 430
Mueller, C.W., 244
Muir, K.A., 158
Murphy, J., 397
Murray, H., 348–349
Murray, J.B., 86
Murray, T.H., 474
Muson, H., 321
Mussen, P.H., 247
Myerhoff, B., 282
Myers, J.D., 219
Myers, J.K., 403

Nabokov, P., 80
Nathan, P., 407
Neale, J., 402, 408, 417, 423, 424, 426, 441
Necker, L.S., 123
Nee, J., 398
Neisser, U., 154
Nesselroade, J.R., 275
Neugarten, B., 259, 266, 269, 271, 280
Newcomb, M.D., 153
Newcomb, T.M., 462–463, 465, 524
Newell, A., 197, 202, 204
Newport, E.L., 192
Newsom, C.D., 413
Newson, J., 337
Nicol, S.E., 410
Nieva, V.F., 499
Nisbet, B.C., 115
Nisbett, R., 32
Norman, D.A., 117
Norton, A.J., 539
Notman, M., 270

Ockene, J.K., 378
O'Donnell, C.R., 440
Offer, D., 249
Offer, J.B., 249
Offir, C., 502, 504, 510
O'Grady, K.E., 519
O'Hayon, J., 408
Ojemann, G., 45
Olds, J., 292
O'Leary, V.E., 486
Olmedo, E.L., 208
Olmsted, M.P., 299
Olson, M.E., 456
Oltmanns, T.F., 408
Orlansky, H., 226
Orne, M.T., 47, 186
Ornstein, R.E., 52
Ottinger, D., 230
Owen, B.D., 268

Paddock, J.R., 251
Paffenberger, R.S., Jr., 379
Paige, K., 57
Paivio, A., 179
Palmore, E., 272, 279
Papert, S., 221
Parlee, M.B., 92
Parloff, M., 421
Parmelee, A.H., 232
Parris, J.N., 448
Paterson, L., 158
Patterson, E.W.J., 519
Pavlov, I., 13, 132–134, 135
Peake, P.K., 340
Peeke, H.J., 86
Pendery, M.L., 387
Penfield, W., 45
Pennebaker, J.D., 360, 366
Pennington, N., 464
Penrod, S.D., 464
Peplau, L.A., 314, 490, 503, 517, 530, 531, 532, 533, 534, 545
Perls, F., 425
Petersen, A.C., 247
Peterson, L.R., 164
Peterson, M.J., 164
Pettigrew, T.F., 482
Petty, R.E., 470, 471

Phoenix, C.H., 494
Piaget, J., 228, 234, 239–240, 241, 242, 247, 491
Piliavin, J.A., 316
Pillemer, D.B., 13, 173
Pilon, D.A., 304
Pinel, P., 395
Pleck, J.H., 495
Plomin, R., 326
Plutchik, R., 305, 306
Polivy, J., 299
Pope, H., 244
Pople, H.E., Jr., 219
Porter, R.H., 113
Powledge, T.M., 231
Priest, R.F., 524
Proxmire, W., 527
Putnam, F., 400
Pyszczynski, T., 531

Rachman, S.J., 401, 402
Rahe, R., 361
Raloff, J., 127
Ramsey, R., 280
Raskin, M., 86
Raudsepp, E., 200–201
Rayner, R., 134, 402
Rechtschaffen, A., 69
Reed, E.J., 92
Regestein, Q.R., 384
Reiss, M.L., 158
Reppucci, N.D., 245
Restak, R., 63, 74, 213, 497
Reston, J., 527
Reynolds, D., 285
Rheingold, H., 219
Rhine, J.B., 115
Rhodes, L., 232
Rice, B., 215
Rickels, K., 432
Riley, L., 539
Riley, M.W., 272
Ring, K., 287
Rinn, W.E., 308
Ritchie, J.M., 81
Ritter, B., 430
Ritzer, G., 263
Robbins, M.B., 590
Robey, B., 515
Robins, L.N., 407
Robinson, H.A., 179
Rock, I., 122
Rodgers, J.E., 408
Rodin, J., 299, 373
Rogers, C., 160, 330, 342, 344, 424, 426, 445
Rogers, R.W., 469
Rohrbaugh, J.B., 491
Rook, K.S., 517
Rorschach, H., 348
Rosch, E., 195, 196
Rose, R.J., 37
Rose, R.M., 300
Rosenberg, H., 159
Rosenblatt, P., 528
Rosenfeld, A., 274
Rosenhan, D., 398
Rosenman, R.H., 365, 366
Rosenthal, A.M., 8
Rosenthal, M.K., 233
Rosenthal, R., 22, 523
Ross, A.O., 428

Ross, D., 320
Ross, D.F., 496
Ross, L., 32
Ross, S., 320
Rotter, J., 343
Rousseau, J.J., 226, 352
Routtenberg, A., 292
Rowe, I., 248
Rubenstein, C.M., 16, 506, 517
Rubin, Z., 19, 248, 314, 330, 474, 490,
    498, 503, 510, 524, 525, 528, 531, 532,
    533, 534
Ruble, D., 57
Rusbult, C., 533
Rutstein, D.D., 384
Rutter, M., 228
Ryan, R.M., 301–302

Sachs, J., 189
Sachs, M.L., 83
Sadalla, E., 340
Salaman, E., 173
Saltzberg, L., 431
Sander, L.W., 233
Sarason, I.G., 361
Sarason, S.B., 208, 263
Sarnoff, C.A., 399
Saxe, L., 480
Saxton, P.M., 307
Sawyer, J., 495, 524
Scanlon, L.W., 91
Scanzoni, J., 538
Scanzoni, L., 538
Scarf, M., 369, 436
Scarr, S., 211, 328, 329
Schachter, S., 253, 299, 311, 314, 378,
    513–514
Schaeffer, J., 81
Schaie, K.W., 274, 275, 276
Scheff, T.J., 398
Schein, E., 467
Scheinin, A., 419
Scherer, K.R., 305
Schleidt, M., 113
Schleifer, S.J., 369
Schmeck, H.M., Jr., 81, 391
Schmidt, W.E., 213
Schneider, W., 505
Schofield, J.W., 482–483, 485
Schorr, D., 320
Schreiber, F.R., 400
Schroeder, H., 432
Schuckit, M.A., 384
Schulz, R., 285
Schuman, H., 456
Schwartz, G.E., 307, 315
Scovern, A.W., 436
Sears, P., 215
Sears, R., 215
Seeman, M., 343
Segal, E., 528
Segal, J., 142
Segal, M., 524
Segal, Z., 142
Seligman, C., 158
Seligman, M., 403, 404, 405, 419
Selman, R.L., 241
Selye, H., 359
Serbin, L.A., 139
Shapiro, D., 146
Shapiro, S., 364
Shatz, M., 195

Shaver, P., 517
Sheatsley, P.B., 479
Sheffield, F.D., 466
Sheils, D.A., 115
Shekelle, R., 368–369
Sheldon, W.H., 325
Shemberg, K.M., 427
Shepard, R.W., 151
Sherin, C., 92
Sherk, D.L., 499
Sherman, S.J., 465
Shevitz, S.A., 437
Shiffrin, R., 162
Shomer, R., 455
Shulman, L., 153
Shuttleworth, E.C., 51
Siegel, A.W., 151
Siegel, R.K., 80, 287
Sigman, M., 232
Signorelli, N., 320
Siipola, E.M., 119
Silveira, J., 202
Sime, W.E., 379
Simmons, J.E., 230
Simmons, R.G., 247
Simon, H.A., 197, 202, 204, 218
Simon, T., 205
Simonton, O.C., 369
Simpson, C., 196
Singer, B., 32
Singer, D.G., 243
Singer, J.A., 307
Singer, J.E., 128, 312–313
Singer, J.L., 68, 243
Siperstein, G.N., 193
Skinhøj, E., 46, 54
Skinner, B.F., 7, 136, 138, 142, 144, 148,
    157, 159, 189, 276, 340, 428
Skipper, J.K., Jr., 253
Sklar, L., 368
Slater, D., 396
Sloane, R.B., 437
Slobin, D.I., 192
Smith, D., 439
Smith, K.F., 280
Smith, M.B., 250
Smith, M.C., 186
Smith, M.L., 437, 439
Smith, P.A., 284, 285
Smith, T.W., 92, 490
Snow, C.E., 192
Snow, M.E., 253
Snyder, S.H., 55, 82
Sobel, D., 307, 435, 442
Sobell, L., 387
Sobell, M., 387
Solanto, M.V., 411
Sonneschein, D.A., 68, 91
Sorenson, S., 127
Spain, D., 510
Spanier, G., 249, 250
Spanos, N.P., 87
Spearman, C., 208
Speer, D.C., 418
Spelke, E., 154
Spence, J.T., 304
Sperling, H., 163
Sperry, R., 54
Spitzer, R.L., 398, 400, 411
Spreitzer, E., 539
Sprott, R.L., 37
Spuhler, J.N., 210
Squire, L.R., 177

Sroufe, L.A., 236, 238
Stanley, J.C., 490, 492
Stapp, J., 27
Stark, R., 32
Starker, S., 68
Statts, J., 37
Steffensmeier, R.H., 417
Stein, H., 525
Steinberg, L.D., 239
Steinem, G., 265
Stephan, W.G., 482
Stepney, R., 79
Sterman, M.B., 47
Stern, J.A., 85
Stern, L., 233
Sternberg, R., 208, 209, 210
Sternglanz, S.H., 139
Stevens, C.F., 43
Stewart, R.B., 254
Stockton, W., 221
Stokols, D., 359
Stone, G.C., 372, 373
Stone, W.F., 462
Stroebe, M.S., 278
Stroebe, W., 278
Strupp, H.H., 439
Sudnow, D., 272
Suedfeld, P., 108, 517
Suinn, R.M., 367
Sulin, R.A., 168
Sullivan, A., 269
Sullivan, K., 269
Sullivan, H.S., 516
Suls, J., 376
Suttle, J.L., 294
Swanson, J.M., 172
Sweet, E.A., 509
Swinyard, W.R., 468
Szasz, T., 395
Syme, S.L., 376

Talbott, E., 158
Tanner, J.M., 247
Taub, H., 232
Tavris, C., 320, 502, 504, 510
Taylor, D.G., 479
Taylor, K., 505
Taylor, S., 374
Teitelbaum, P., 297
Terman, L.M., 207, 214
Terrace, H., 191
Thiel, D.L., 519
Thomas, A., 239
Thomas, E.L., 179
Thomas, M.H., 321
Thome, P.R., 495
Thompson, J.C., 362
Thompson, R.A., 238
Thompson, V.D., 255
Thorndyke, P.W., 151
Thurstone, L.L., 208
Tierney, J., 266
Timiras, P., 273, 274
Timson, J., 79
Titchener, E.B., 67
Tobin-Richards, M., 247
Tolley, H.B., 510
Tolman, E.C., 149, 151
Tomkins, S.S., 313
Tonick, I.J., 139
Torrey, E.F., 410
Toye, K., 280
Trefil, J., 29, 32

SUBJECT INDEX

Berkeley Men's Group, 510–511
Beyond Freedom and Dignity (Skinner), 159
Big Feeling, 445
Binocular vision, 104–105
Biofeedback techniques, 23, 47, 370
  blood pressure and, 146
  heart rate and, 146
Biological clock, 92
Biological engineering, 58, 61–64
Biological rhythms, 30, 90–93
Biology
  of aging, 273
  alcoholism and, 384–385
  genetics and, 36–39
  intelligence and, 210
  language acquisition and, 190–192, 195
  learning and, 132
  personality and, 325–328, 329, 407
  schizophrenia and, 409–410
  sex differences and, 492–494
  stress and, 359–360
Biorhythms, 29, 30–31
Bipolar disorder, 392, 403, 404, 433
Birth control, 504
Birth defects, genetic counseling and, 62–63
Birth order, personality and, 253
Blacks, prejudice and, 479–483
Blind spot, of the retina, 100, 101
Blood flow measurement, of the brain, 46
Blood pressure, operant conditioning and, 146
Body type, personality and, 325–326
Bottle feeding, 234
Brain, 39, 43–54
  chemicals and, 55
  diet and, 55
  hemispheres, 52, 54, 190, 213
  language and, 190
  memory and the, 172, 174–177
  psychosurgery and, 437
  sex differences in, 493
Brain damage, 45, 52–53
Brain stem, 48
Brain surgery, 45
Brain transplants, 63–64
Brainwashing, 467, 471
Brain waves, 45–46, 47, 71
Brave New World (Huxley), 62
Breaking up, of a relationship, 533–534
Breast feeding, 234
Brightness constancy, 122
Broca's area, 51, 54, 190
Brothers. *See* Sibling relationships
Butyrophenones, 433

Caffeine, 78, 79
California Psychological Inventory, 348
Cancer, 284
  in middle age, 268
  psychology and, 367–369
  stress and, 360
Cannabis sativa, 80
Carcinogens, 367
Career. *See* Occupation
Caring, in love, 528
Case studies, 17
Castration anxiety, 335
Catatonic schizophrenia, 406

Categories. *See* Concepts
Catharsis, 319–320, 422
  for aggression, 331
  in psychoanalytic theory, 331
CAT scans, 53
Cause and effect, in infancy, 235–236
Cause-and-effect hypotheses, 21–22
Cell body, of neuron, 42
Central nervous system, 39. *See also* Brain; Spinal cord
  in late adulthood, 273
Central tendency, measures of, 542–543
Cerebellum, 48
Cerebral cortex, 49–51, 52, 54, 190
Cerebral hemispheres, 51
Child abuse, premature infants and, 233
Childhood
  child rearing methods, 243–246, 264
  cognitive development in, 234–236, 239–241
  competence in, 243
  gender roles in, 239, 495–498
  language development in, 188–195, 226, 239
  moral development in, 242–243
  personality development in, 14, 239
  psychological disorders of, 410
  sibling relationships in, 254
Childhood amnesia, 173
Childhood and Society (Erikson), 229
Childhood anxiety disorders, 410
Childhood memories, 173
Child rearing methods, 243–244, 264
Children
  decision to have, 264–265
  divorce of parents and, 538
Chimpanzees. *See* Apes
Chlordiazepoxide, 432
Chlorpromazine, 433
Chronic schizophrenia, 438
Cigarette smoking, 79, 343, 377–378, 459
Circadian rhythms, 90–91
Clairvoyance, 115
Clang associations, 408
Classical conditioning, 13, 132–136, 148, 377. *See also* Desensitization
  attitudes and, 135, 457–458
Classifications. *See* Concepts
Claustrophobia, 399
Client-centered therapy, 424, 426
Climacteric, 270
Clinical depression, 402–403
Clinical psychology, 17, 25–26, 27
Clinical retardation, 212, 214
Closure, perceptual organization and, 116
Cocaine, 78, 82–84
Cochlea, 106
Codeine, 79
Cognitive activity, in sexual arousal, 501
Cognitive behavior therapy, 370
Cognitive development, 228, 234–235. *See also* Intelligence
  in adolescence, 247–248
  in childhood, 239–241
  concrete operations and, 235, 240, 247
  in early adulthood, 260, 261
  formal operations and, 235, 247–248
  in infancy, 234–236
  language and, 194
Cognitive disorders, 403, 404

in schizophrenia, 408, 409, 410
Cognitive dissonance, 460
Cognitive labeling theory of emotion, 311–313, 314
Cognitive learning, 132, 148–154, 430, 432
Cognitive maps, learning and, 149, 151
Cognitive psychology, 7
Cognitive restructuring, 430
Cognitive stage, of cognitive skill learning, 153
Cognitive therapy, 430, 432
Cohort effect, 274
Cold, sensation of, 109
Cold-pressor response, 85
Colds, stress and, 360
Collective unconscious, 338
Color blindness, 103
Color constancy, 122
Color vision, 100–103
Commitment, love and, 531
Communicator, in persuasion, 465–466
Community Mental Health Centers, 440
Community mental health movement, 438, 439, 440
Community psychologist, 26
Community suicide prevention centers, 418
Company, need for, 513–517
Comparative psychologist, 25
Competence
  in childhood, 243
  dreams and, 77
Competence motivation, 293, 295, 300, 302
Complementarity, in friendship, 526
Components, in solving a problem, 209
Computer-aided instruction (CAI), 142
Computers
  artificial intelligence and, 204, 218–221
  brain versus, 44
  operant conditioning and, 142
Computer simulation, human thought processes and, 202, 204
Concentrative meditation, 85
Concepts, 195–197, 198
Concrete-operational stage, 235, 240, 247
Condensation, in dreams, 75
Conditioned response, 133, 135–136
Conditioned stimulus, 133, 135
Conditioning. *See also* Classical conditioning; Desensitization therapy
  aversive, 377
  operant, 136–148, 157
Conduct disorders, 410
Cones, of eye, 98–99, 100
Conformity, 464–465, 471, 474
Consciousness, 66–87
Conservation, Piaget on, 240
Consolidation phase, memory and, 174
Consumer psychologist, 27
Contact comfort, 237
Continuous reinforcement, 143
Contraceptives. *See* Birth control
Contrast, attention and, 117
Control group, 22
Controlled drinking, 387
Conundrum (Morris), 497
Conventional level, of moral reasoning, 242, 243

Conversion disorder, 392
Coping, stress and, 362–363
Cornea, 97, 98
Coronary-prone behavior pattern, 365–367
Corpus callosum, 52
Correlational study, 12, 20–21
Correlation coefficient, 544–546
Corticosteroids, 360
Counseling, 421. *See also* Therapy
Counseling psychologist, 26
Counterconditioning, 427
Creationism, 35
Creativity, 14, 203
Credibility, of a communicator, 466
Crisis intervention, 440
Critical period
    in development, 227
    for language learning, 190
Cross-dressing, 497
Cross-sectional approach, 274
Cross-situational consistency, 339–340, 341
Crystallized intelligence, 275
Cues, for retrieval, 166
Culture
    alcoholism and, 385
    concepts and, 197
    psychological disorders and, 395, 397
    sex differences and, 494–499
Cumulative
    development as, 226
    psychology as, 13, 15
Cumulative deficit, in intelligence, 211
Cystic fibrosis, 39

Day-care programs, 239
Day centers, for elderly, 280
Daydreaming, 67–68
DDAVP, 176
Dead Bird, The (Brown and Charlip), 284
Deaf children, sign language and, 190, 192
Death and dying, 284–287
Deception, in research, 474
Decisions, mental accounts for, 198
Defense mechanisms, 336–337
Deinstitutionalization, 438
Delayed reinforcement, 141
Delta sleep, 72
Delta waves, 72
Delusions, 406
Dendrites, of neuron, 42
Denial, as stage of dying, 285
Deoxyribonucleic acid (DNA), 36, 273
Dependent variable, 21
Depressants, 78, 80
Depression, 391, 392, 398, 402–405, 419
    antidepressant drugs for, 433
    cognitive therapy for, 430, 432
    electroconvulsive therapy for, 436
    insomnia and, 73
    psychoanalysis for, 424
    as stage of dying, 285
    suicide and, 417
Depth perception, 104–106
Description, in psychological research, 20
Descriptive statistics, 541–543
Desegregation, 460, 482–483
Desensitization therapy, 135, 427–428

Determinism, behaviorists and, 159–160
Development. *See also* Childhood; Cognitive development
    adolescence, 246–251
    adulthood, 229, 258–282
    infancy, 227, 233–239
    nature of, 225–228
    newborn, 226, 230–233
    prenatal, 228, 230
Developmental psychologists, 25
Diagnostic and Statistical Manual of Mental Disorders (DSM-III), 391, 392, 393, 398
Diazepam, 432
Dichromatic color blindness, 103
Discrimination
    classical conditioning and, 136
    as learning process, 341
    operant conditioning and, 139
    racism and, 479–483
Discriminative stimulus, 140
Disease. *See* Health; Illness
Disorganized schizophrenia, 406
Displacement, 336–337
    in dreams, 75–76
Dissociated, consciousness as, 87
Dissociative disorders, 392, 400
Divorce, 244–245, 516, 536–539
Doctor-patient relationship, 372–373
Dominant gene, 36
Dopamine, 55
    depression and, 404
    schizophrenia and, 410, 435
Double standard, sexual, 502–506, 532
Down's syndrome, 212
Dreaming, 68, 69, 70, 71, 73, 74–77, 239
    daydreaming, 67–68
Drive reduction theory, 295
Drives, 295
Drugs
    consciousness and, 77–84
    for memory, 176
    prenatal development and, 230
    psychopharmacology, 432–433, 435
    for terminally ill patient, 285–286
Dual coding, as memory system, 179
Durham decision, 396

Ear, 106–107. *See also* Hearing
    equilibrium and, 111
Eardrum, 106, 107
Early adulthood, 260–268
Early adult transition, in early adulthood, 261–262
Early experience, development and, 226–228
Eating behavior, 296–298, 299, 340
Ectomorph, 325, 326
Educational psychology, 26, 27
    cognitive learning and, 148–149, 150
Efferent neurons, 39
Ego, 331, 332
Egocentric, children as, 240–241
Elavil, 433
Elderly. *See* Late adulthood
Electra complex, 335
Electrical stimulation, of brain, 45
Electroconvulsive therapy (ECT), 174, 435–437, 441
Electroencephalograms (EEGs), 45–46
Embryo, 230

Emotional attachment, 514–515, 516–517
Emotional isolation, 516
Emotionality, 326
Emotional wheel, 305–306
Emotions. *See also* Stress
    attitudes and, 452, 457–458
    brain and, 53
    cancer and, 367–369
    classical conditioning and, 134–135
    disorders relating to, 392, 402
    prenatal development and maternal, 230
    sex differences in, 490
Empty nest, 269
Encoding
    long-term memory and, 164–165
    in solving a problem, 209
Encounter groups, 445–446
Endocrine system, 41, 274. *See also* Hormones
Endomorph, 325, 326
Endorphins, 58, 80, 371
Engineering psychologist, 26–27
Engrams, 172, 174
Enkephalins, 58
Entering the adult world, in early adulthood, 262
Environment, 7, 329
    heredity and, 38
    intelligence and, 210
Epilepsy, 47
Epinephrine, 13, 56, 312–313
    fight-or-flight reaction and, 360
    memory and, 174–175
Equilibrium, 111
Erogenous zones, 333
ESP, 29, 115
est (Erhard Seminars Training), 446–447, 448
Estrogen, 56, 57
Ethics
    in research, 474
    in therapy, 441
Evoked potential, 45
Evolution, 34–36, 307
Excitatory message, 43
Excitement phase, 500
Exercise, 378–380
Exhaustion, in general adaptation syndrome, 359
Exit, in ending relationships, 533
Expectations
    behavior and, 341–342, 343
    happiness and, 355
    of researcher, 22–23
Experience. *See also* Early experience
    intelligence and, 210
    personalities and, 328–329
Experiment, 12
Experimental group, 21–22
Experimental psychology, 24–25, 427. *See also* Behavior therapies
Experimentation, 21–22
Experimenter expectancy effects, 22–23
Expertise, of a communicator, 466
Expert systems, in artificial intelligence, 219
Expression of Emotions in Man and Animals, The (Darwin), 307
Expressive behavior, 305
Extension, of words, 193

External cues, 299
External locus of control, 343
Extinction, of a learned response, 135, 141, 143
Extrasensory perception (ESP), 29, 115
Extraversion, 355
Extrinsic motivation, 203, 300, 302
Eye, 97–100. See also Vision
Eye contact, love and, 528–529
Eyewitness testimony, unreliability of, 183–186

Face-ism, 488
Facial expressions, emotions and, 313, 315
Facial feedback hypothesis, 313, 315
Factitious disorder, 392
False consensus effect, 465
Fame, depression and, 403
Family. See also Parents
    gender roles in, 510–511
    illness prevention and, 376
    in late adulthood, 278
    starting a, 264
Farsightedness, 100
Fatherhood, 511
    infant/father relationship and, 238
Fear, 307, 310, 313
    classical conditioning and, 134–135
    love and, 314
Fear appeals, in persuasion, 468
Feedback
    in behavior modification, 158
    in cognitive-skills learning, 154
    computers learning from, 221
Feelings. See Emotions
Feminine Mystique, The (Friedan), 508
Fetus, 230
Fight-or-flight reaction, 359–360
Figure, perception of, 116
Fired, in axonal transmission, 43
First-born, personality and, 253
Fissures, of cerebral cortex, 49–50
Fixation, 333
Fixed-interval schedules of reinforcement, 143, 144
Fixed-ratio schedules of reinforcement, 143, 144
Fixed response questions, for attitude measurement, 454–455
Flashbulb memory, 10–13, 22, 23, 174
Flashcards, 227
Fluid intelligence, 274–275
Food and Drug Administration, 82
Foreign language, learning of, 180
Forgetting, 166, 171–172
Forgetting curve, 168
Formal-operational stage, 235, 247–248
Fourth psychology, 447
Fovea, 99
Free association, 422
Free recall test, 169
Free will, humanists and, 159–160
Frequency distribution, 542
Freudian slips, 295
Friends Can Be Good Medicine (California Department of Health), 376
Friendships, 522, 524–526. See also Peers; Social relationships
    in adolescence, 248

illness prevention and, 376
    in late adulthood, 278
    love scale for, 528–530
    proximity and, 522, 524
    sex differences in, 530
Frontal lobes, 49–50
FRUMP, 221
Frustration, 319
Frustration-aggression hypothesis, 319
F scale, 481
Functional fixedness, 201
Functionalism, 6

g, as factor in intelligence, 208, 209
Gate-control mechanisms, 110
Gender identity, 485
Gender roles, 495–499, 508–511
    reversal in middle adulthood, 269
    sexual attitudes and, 501–504
Gender stereotypes, 486–491
Gene, 36–37
Gene pair, 37
General adaptation syndrome, 359
Generality, concepts and, 196–197
Generalizations, 341
    classical conditioning and, 136
    operant conditioning and, 139
General Problem Solver (GPS), 202, 204, 218
Generativity, 260
    in middle adulthood, 269
Generativity versus self-absorption, 229
Genetic counseling, 62–63
Genetic counselors, 62–63
Genetic disorders, 39
Genetics, 36–39. See also Biology
Genital stage, 336
Genotype, 36
Gestalt psychologists, perception and, 116–117
Gestalt therapy, 425, 431, 448
Giant cells, 76
Gifted individuals, 214–215
Givens, of problems, 197
Glaucoma, 81
Glia cells, 43
Goal
    of a drive, 295
    of problems, 197
Gonads, 56–57
Good Samaritan study, 8–10, 14, 22, 23
Grandparent/grandchildren relationship, 279
Graphology, 29, 30
Ground, perception of, 116
Groupthink, 465
Growth hormone, 55
Guilt, 332

Hair cells, of cochlea, 106
Haldol, 433
Hallucinations, 406
Hallucinogens, 78
Haloperidol, 433
Handedness, heredity and, 38
Handwriting analysis, 30
Happiness, 352–355
Health, psychology and, 356–381. See also Illness
Health psychology, 357, 358, 373

Hearing, 106–107
    in late adulthood, 273
    in newborns, 231
    pollution and, 126–127
    threshold of, 99
Heart disease, 284
    exercise and, 379
    in middle age, 268
    psychology and, 364–367
    smoking and, 377
Heart rate, operant conditioning and, 145, 146
Heat, sensation of, 109
Helping behavior, 8–10, 14, 22, 23, 129
Hemispheres of brain, 52, 54, 190, 213
Heredity. See Biology
Heritability, of a trait, 210–211
Heroin, 78
Hidden observer, 87
Hierarchy of needs, 344, 354
Higher mental processes, 188. See also Intelligence; Language; Thought
Hippocampus, 49
Histogram, 542
Homophobia, 458, 505
Homo sapiens, 34, 35
Homosexuality, 395, 397, 458, 504, 505
Hormones, 41, 55–57, 274, 298
    aggression and, 492–494
    cycles in, 91–92
    memory and, 174–175
    sexual motivation and, 300
Horoscopes, 31–32
Hospice, 286
Hospitals, patients in, 373–375
Hot reactivity, 366
Humanistic psychology, 447, 504
    behavior modification and, 159
Humanistic theories, 330, 342, 344
Human sexuality. See Sexuality
Human sexual response, 500–501
Humor, learning process and, 150
Humors, theory of, 92
Hunger, 296–297, 299
Hunger pangs, 296–297
Huntington's chorea, 64
Hydrocephalus, 61, 63
Hyperactivity, 392, 410–411
Hyperphagic animals, 297
Hypertension, 364
Hypnosis, 84–87
    eyewitnesses and, 186
    for multiple personality, 400
    for pain, 370, 371
    in psychoanalytic theory, 331, 422
    stress dealt with by, 370
Hypothalamus, 48, 57, 297
Hypotheses, 11, 13
Hysteria, 331

Id, 331, 332
Ideal self, 342
Ideas, for research, 13–15
Identification, 15
Identity
    in adolescence, 247–248
    in early adulthood, 264
    gender, 485
Identity versus role confusion, 229
Idiot savants, 213
Ill-defined, problem as, 199

Illness. *See also* Health
  friends and prevention of, 376
  in late adulthood, 273
  mental. *See* Psychological disorders;
    Therapy
  in middle age, 268
  patients, 372–375
  psychological processes and, 364–369
  stress and, 360–362
Illusions, perceptual, 121–123
Imagination, emotion and, 315–316
Imaginative reconstruction, 183–184
Imipramine, 433
Imitative aggression, 320
Immune system
  cancer and, 367–368
  in late adulthood, 274
Imprinting, 227
Impulsivity, 326
In a Different Voice (Gilligan), 491
Incentives, 296–297
Incongruence, 342
Incubation, for problem solving, 202
Incus, 106, 107
Independent variable, 21
Individual differences, in infancy, 239.
    See also Sex differences
Individualized instruction, computer for,
  142
Industry versus inferiority, 229, 243
Infancy, 227, 233–239
  emotions in, 309
  oral stage and, 333
  siblings in, 254
Infantile autism, 411
Inferiority complex, 338
Inferring, in solving a problem, 209
Information-processing approach
  to intelligence, 209
  problem solving and, 202, 204
Infradian rhythms, 91–92
Inhibitory message, 43
Initiative versus guilt, 229, 243
Inner ear, 106, 111
Input, 44
Insanity defense, 396
Insight, 200–202
Insight therapies, 421, 422–426
Insomnia, 73
Instincts, 292, 330
Institutionalization, in late adulthood,
  279–280
Integration, prejudice and racism and,
  482–483
Integrity, 260
  in late adulthood, 280
Integrity versus despair, 229
Intellectualization, 337
Intellectually gifted, 214–215
Intelligence, 188, 205–215. *See also*
    Cognitive development; Learning;
    Memory; Thought
  artificial, 204, 218–221
  crystallized, 275
  early experience and, 227–228
  first born and, 253–254
  fluid, 274–275
  in late adulthood, 274
  noise and, 128–129
  prematurity and, 232
  sex differences in, 490
Intelligence quotient (IQ), 205
Intelligence tests, 205–208

Interdependence, in social relationships,
  515–516
Interference, memory and, 170
Internal clocks, 92
Internal cues, 299
Internal locus of control, 343
INTERNIST-1, 219
Interpretation, in psychoanalysis, 422
Interpretation of Dreams, The (Freud),
  75, 351
Interval schedule of reinforcement,
  143–144
Interviews
  personality assessed with, 345–346
  in psychological research, 20
Intimacy, 260
  in early adulthood, 263–264
  in love, 528
Intimacy versus isolation, 229
Intrinsic motivation, 203, 300
Introspection, 67
Inverse relationships, 544–545
In vitro fertilization, 61
IQ tests, 205–208
Iris, 98

James-Lange theory, 310–311
Jet lag, 91
Jigsaw technique, 483
Joint custody, 244–245
Jukebox theory, of emotion, 312

Key word method, for foreign language
  learning, 180
Kinesthesis, 110–111
Korsakoff's syndrome, 175, 392

Labeling, love and, 314
Laboratory, for psychological research,
  19–20
Language, 188–195, 226, 239
  brain and, 51
  computers understanding, 221
  concepts and, 195–197
  private use of, 195. *See also* Thoughts
Late adulthood, 271–282. *See also* Death
    and dying
  loneliness and, 517
Latency period, 336
Latent content, in dreams, 76
Latent learning, 149
Lateralization, 190
Law
  insanity defense in, 396
  memory and the, 183–186
Learned helplessness, 405
Learning, 130–154. *See also* Memory
  concepts, 195–196
  development and, 225–226
  language learning and, 189–190
  in newborn, 233
  observational. *See* Modeling
  rote, 168, 178
  social learning theory and, 338–342,
    343
Learning theorists, depression and, 405.
    See also Behavior therapies
Leaving others, 533–534
Left hemisphere, of brain, 52, 53, 54
Legitimate authority, 475–476
Lens, 98

Lesbians, 505. *See also* Homosexuality
Levels of generality, concepts and,
  196–197
Librium, 432
Life events
  depression and, 403, 404–405
  illness and, 361
Life review, in late adulthood, 280–282
Life span, 274
Life structure, 261
Liking others, 522, 524–526, 529–530
Liking scale, 529–530
Limbic system, 48–49
Lipofuscin, 273
Lithium carbonate, 433
Lobes, of cerebral cortex, 49–50
Lobotomies, 437, 441
Loci, method of, 179–180
Loneliness, 516–517
Longitudinal studies, 260, 274, 329
Long-term memory, 162–163, 164–166,
  167, 171, 174, 175, 276
Long-term potentiation, 174
Loose associations, 408
Loudness, of sound waves, 106
Love, 314, 354, 524, 526–533
Love magic, 528
Love scale, 19, 528–530, 531
Loyalty, in ending relationships, 533
LSD-25 (lysergic acid diethylamide), 55,
  78, 80

Mainstreaming, 214
Major tranquilizers. *See* Antipsychotic
  drugs
Make Today Count, 376
Male hormone, aggression and, 492–494
Malleability, of memory, 185–186
Malleus, 106, 107
Mania, 403, 404, 433
Manifest content, in dreams, 76
Marijuana, 78, 80–81, 392, 458
Marriage
  divorce and, 244–245, 516, 536–539
  proximity and, 524
  similarities of mates in, 525
Marriage counseling, 26
Masturbation, 500–501, 502
Maturation
  in adolescence, 246–247
  development and, 225–226
Mean, 542
Meaning
  long-term memory and, 166
  for studying, 178–179
Means-end analysis, as problem-solving
  method, 204
Measures of central tendency, 542–543
Median, 542
Medical model, of abnormality, 393, 395
Medical student's disease, 360
Meditation, 86
  stress and anxiety relieved by,
  369–370
Medium, in persuasion, 469
Medulla, 48
Memory, 109, 162–181. *See also*
    Learning
  brain structure and, 49
  flashbulb, 10–13, 174
  hypnosis and, 84–85
  in late adulthood, 276
  law and, 183–186

Memory (Continued)
  long-term, 162–163, 164–166, 167,
    171, 174, 175, 276
  senile dementia and, 274
  short-term, 162–164, 175, 276
Memory disorders, 175, 177
Memory research, 175, 176
Memory systems, 179–180
Menarche, 57, 246
Menopause, 57, 269, 270
Menstrual syndrome, 57
Menstruation, 56–57, 91–92, 246
Mental accounts, 198
Mental age, 205
Mental health. See also Psychological
    disorders; Therapy
Mental hospitals, 438
Mental hygiene movement, 395
Mental images, cognitive maps as, 151
Mental representation
  insight and, 200–201
  of the problem, 199
Mental retardation, 39, 212–214, 392
Mentor, 269
Mescaline, 78
Mesomorph, 325, 326
Message, in persuasion, 466, 468–469
Metabolism, 55
Method of loci, as memory system,
    179–180
Microelectrodes, brain waves studied
    with, 46
Middle adulthood, 14, 265–269
Middle ear, 106, 107
Midlife transition, 265–266, 267
Migraine headaches, 360
Mild retardation, 212, 214
Mills v. Rogers, 434
Minnesota Multiphasic Personality
    Inventory (MMPI), 347–348
Minority groups, prejudice towards,
    479–483
Minority influence, 465
Minor tranquilizers. See Antianxiety
    drugs
Mixed schedules of reinforcement, 144
Mnemonics, for improving memory, 180
Mode, 542–543
Modeling, 15, 151–153, 429–430
  aggressive behavior and, 153, 320
  personality shaping and, 153, 338–342,
    343
  sex-role development and, 153,
    495–496, 498
Moderate retardation, 212
Mongolism. See Down's syndrome
Monoamine oxidase (MAO), 328
Monochromatic color blindness, 103
Monocular cues, 104
Moon, behavior and, 92
Moon illusion, 123
Moral development, 228, 242–243, 491
Moral dilemmas, 242–243
Moral independence, 242
Moral realism, 242
Morning people, 90–91
Morphine, 78
Mother-infant relationship, 236–239
Motion parallax, 104
Motivated forgetting, 172
Motivation, 203, 292–303, 304, 344. See
    also Emotions
Motivational systems, 296–303

Motives, 292–293, 295, 302–303, 304,
    330
Motor memory, 177
Motor neurons, 39
Motor skills, in infancy, 234
Motor strip, 50–51
Müller-Lyer illusion, 122–123
Multiple personality, 392, 400
Music
  attitudes and, 457
  language of, 190
  in persuasion, 468
MYCIN, 219

Name recognition test, 169
Narcolepsy, 74
Narcotics, 78, 79
Natural childbirth, 230
Natural selection, 34–35, 36
Nazi personality, 348
Nearsightedness, 100
Necker cube, 123
Needing others, 513–517
Needs, 292, 294, 295–296, 344, 354
Negative instances, 195
Negative reinforcement, 141, 145
Neglect, in ending relationships, 533
Neo-Freudians, 338
Neologisms, 408
Nervous system, 34, 39–54
Neural transmission, 42–43
Neurons, 39, 42–43, 55
Neuropeptides, 58
Neuroscience, 7, 13, 63
Neuroses, 381, 424
Neurotic guilt, 332
Neuroticism, 355
Neurotransmitters, 43, 55
  depression and, 404
  memory and, 174
Neutral stimulus, 133
Newborn, 226, 230–233
Nicotine, 79
Night-before syndrome, 176
Night dreaming, 68, 69, 70, 71, 73
Night people, 90–91
Night terrors, 74
Noise, 106, 127–129
Noise pollution, 126–129
Non-age-graded influences, 259–260
Nonimitative aggression, 320
Noninstitutionalization, 438
Non-REM (NREM) sleep, 73, 77
Nonverbal clues, in attribution process,
    523
Noradrenalin. See Norepinephrine
Norepinephrine, 13, 55, 56, 83
  depression and, 404
  fight-or-flight reaction and, 360
  memory and, 174–175
  sleep and, 70
Normal distribution, of scores, 206, 207
Normal guilt, 332
Normalization, for mentally retarded,
    214
Norms. See Social norms
Nostrums, 371
Note taking, for studying, 178–179
Novelty, attention and, 117

Obedience, to authority, 472–476
Objective method, of research, 15
Object permanence, 236

Observation
  behavioral, 346
  by psychologists, 18–20
Observational learning. See Modeling
Observational study, 20
Obsessive-compulsive disorder, 392, 402
Occipital lobes, 49, 52
Occupation. See also Work
  choosing, 262–263
  vocational counseling, 26
Oedipus complex, 333, 335, 336, 491
Old age. See Late adulthood
Olfaction. See Smell
Olfactory bulbs, 112
Olfactory neurons, 112
On Death and Dying (Kübler-Ross), 285
One Flew Over the Cuckoo's Nest
    (Kesey), 436
Only children, 255–256
  personalities of, 14
On the Origin of Species By Means of
    Natural Selection (Darwin), 34
Open-ended questions, for attitude
    measurement, 454
Opening-up meditation, 86
Operant conditioning, 136–148, 157. See
    also Operant therapy
Operant therapy, 428–429
Operations, 240
  concrete, 235, 240, 247
  formal, 235, 247–248
Opponent cells, 100
Optic nerve, 99
Oral stage, 333
Organic mental disorders, 392
Organizational psychology, 26, 27
Orgasmic phase, 500
Orgasms, 500
Outer ear, 106, 107
Output, 44
Ovaries, 56
Overregularizing, as rule of language, 194
Overweight, 299
Ovum transfer, 62

Pain
  placebos for, 371
  primal therapy and, 444–445
  psychogenic, 392
  sensation of, 109–110
Pain memory, 109
Panic attacks, 392, 399
Paranoid schizophrenia, 82, 406, 408
Paraprofessionals, 440
Parasciences, 29–32
Parasympathetic nervous system, 40–41
Parents. See also Family
  adolescence and, 248–251
  child rearing by, 264
  infant relationship with, 236–239
  styles of, 243, 245–246
Parents Without Partners, 538
Parietal lobes, 49
Parkinson's disease, 55, 61, 63–64
Partial reinforcement schedule, 143, 429
Patient compliance, 372–373
Patients. See also Health; Illness
  doctors and, 372–373
  hospitals and, 373–375
Peak experiences, 344
Peers. See also Friendships
  in adolescence, 248–251
  counseling by, 440

Penis envy, 335
Pep pills. *See* Amphetamines
Perception, 97–124
Perceptual adaptation, 121
Perceptual constancy, 120–121
Perceptual illusions, 122–124
Perceptual organization, 116–117
  schizophrenia and, 408
Performance, learning and, 151–152
Peripheral nervous system, 39–40
Permissive parents, 245
Personality, 37, 239, 294, 324–355, 407
  alcoholism and, 385
  assessment of, 304, 344–349
  authoritarian, 481
  coronary-prone behavior pattern,
    365–367
  early memories and, 173
  in middle adulthood, 269
  multiple, 392, 400
  of only children, 14
  prejudiced, 480–481
  shyness, 514
  sociability and, 514
Personality disorders, 392, 407
Personality psychologist, 25, 26
Personal unconscious, 338
Person perception, 517–522
Persuasion, 465–470
Pets, social relationship provided by, 515
Phallic stage, 333, 335
Phenothiazine, 433
Phenotype, 36
Phenylketonuria (PKU), 39
Phobias, 135, 392, 399, 401–402
Phonemes, 193
Phrenology, 29–30
Physical appearance, 517–518, 519
Physical change and development
  in adolescence, 246–247
  in early adulthood, 260–261
  in late adulthood, 273
  in middle adulthood, 266, 268–269
Physiological addiction, 383
  drugs and, 80
Physiological arousal, 305
Physiological psychologists, 25
Physostigmine, 176
Pitch, 106
Pituitary gland, 55, 57
Placebo, 371
Placebo effects, 371
Placenta, 230
Plaque, heart disease and, 364
Plateau phase, 500
Ponzo illusion, 122, 123
Porteus Maze Test, 208
Positive instances, 195
Positive reinforcement, 141, 428
Positive transfer, 201
Positron-emission tomography (PET), 46
Postconventional level, of moral
  reasoning, 242, 243
Posthypnotic amnesia, 85
Posthypnotic suggestion, 84
PQ4R method, 179
Practice of psychology, 23
Preconventional level, of moral
  reasoning, 242–243
Predisposition, 494
Prefrontal lobotomies, 437
Pregnancy, 228, 230, 231
Prejudice, 479–483

Prejudiced personality, 480–481
Premarital sexual activity, 503, 504
Prematurity, 230, 232–233
Prenatal development, 228, 230
Preoperational period, 235, 239–240
Pressure, sensation of, 109
Primal therapy, 444–445
Primary emotions, 305, 306
Primary reinforcers, 140
Proactive interference, 170
Probability, 544
Problem, definition of, 197, 199. *See also*
  Problem solving
Problem drinkers. *See* Alcohol abuse
Problem solving, 197, 199–204, 209. *See*
  also Intelligence
  by computers, 204, 218–221
  infancy and, 238
Process schizophrenia, 408
Profound retardation, 212
Progesterone, 56, 57
Progressive muscle relaxation, 369
Projection, 336
Prosopagnosia, 51–52
PROSPECTOR, 219
Protective techniques, 348–349
Protocol analysis, 202
Prototypes, concepts and, 195–196
Proximity
  friendship and, 522, 524
  perceptual organization and, 116
Psilocybin, 78, 80
Psychedelic drugs, 78, 80
Psychiatrist, 25–26
Psychoactive drugs, 77–84
Psychoanalytic theory, 7, 15, 330–338,
  422–424
  obsessive-compulsive disorders and,
    402
  phobias and, 401
Psychoanalytic therapy, 437, 439
Psychodrama, 425
Psychogenic pain disorder, 392
Psychoimmunology, 368
Psychological adequacy, 393
Psychological androgyny, 511
Psychological dependence, 383
  on drugs, 80
Psychological development. *See*
  Development
Psychological disorders, 390–419. *See*
  also Psychopharmacology
Psychological laboratories, 19–20
Psychological reactance, 472
Psychological research, 7–27
  ethics and, 474
  sex bias in, 491
  statistics for, 540–546
Psychology, 5, 7, 29
  roots of, 6–7
  subfields of, 24–27
Psychopath, 407
Psychopharmacology, 432–433, 435
Psychoses, 391, 393
  antipsychotic drugs for, 433–435
Psychosexual development, 332–336
Psychosexual disorders, 392
Psychosexual stages, 333
Psychosocial development, 229, 260
Psychosomatic disorders, 364, 370
Psychosurgery, 437, 441
Psychotherapy, 157, 441. *See also*
  Therapies

Puberty, 247. *See also* Adolescence
Public opinion polls, as attitude
  measure, 455
PUFF, 219
Punishment, 145, 147–148
  behavior modification and, 139
  operant conditioning and, 136
Pupil, of eye, 97–98
p value, 544

Questionnaires, as attitude measure, 455

Racial differences, in intelligence, 210,
  211
Racism, 479–483
Random sample, 543–544
Range, 543
Rapid smoking technique, 377
Rating scales, for personality assessment,
  346
Rational-emotive therapy (RET), 431
Rationalization, 337
Ratio schedule of reinforcement, 143,
  144
Raw data, 541–542
Reaction formation, 336
Reactive schizophrenia, 408
Readiness, for language learning, 226
Reading rate, 105
Real self, 342
Rebirthing, 445
Recall, 169
  tests of, 276
Receptor cells, 97, 98
Recognition, 169
  tests of, 276
Reconstructive memory, 166, 168
Red-green color blindness, 103
Reference group, 463
Reflex action, 39–40
Refractory period, 500
Rehearsal, long-term memory and,
  164–165
Reinforcement, 15
  operant conditioning and, 136, 138,
    140–145
  operant therapy and, 428–429
  positive, 428
  self, 160
Relationships. *See* Social relationships
Relaxation response, 86, 369–370
Relaxation training, 146
Relearning, 169
Reliability
  of assessment measures, 345
  of psychiatric diagnoses, 398
Remarriage, 538
REM (rapid eye movement) sleep, 70, 73,
  74, 76, 77
Repression, 172, 173, 330, 336
  of motives, 295
Reproduction, child's view of, 241
Reputations, 518, 520
Research. *See* Psychological research
Resistance
  in general adaptation syndrome, 359
  in psychoanalysis, 422
Resolution phase, 500
Resource room, 214
Responses, 132
  conditioning and, 132, 133, 135–136
Reticular formation, 54
Retina, 98

Retirement, 276–278
Retirement communities, 280
Retrieval, long-term memory and, 166, 167
Retrieval failure, 171
Retroactive interference, 170
Retrograde amnesia, 174, 175
Reversibility, Piaget on, 240
Reviewing, for studying, 178
Rewards. *See also* Reinforcement
    behavior and, 341–342, 343
    behavior modification and, 139
Rhodopsin, 98
Right hemisphere, of brain, 52, 53, 213
Right to refuse treatment, 434
Ritalin, 411
RNA, 273
Rods, of eye, 98–99
Role confusion, 248
Role playing, 430, 432
    for problem drinkers, 387
Roles, 498. *See also* Gender roles
Rorschach inkblot test, 348
Rote learning, 168, 178
Rotter's scale, 343, 346
Route maps, cognitive maps as, 151
Rules of language, 194
Runner's high, 80

Sample, 15–17
Sampling, 543–544
Savants, 213
Savings method, relearning as, 169
Scare tactics, in persuasion, 468
Scatterplots, 544
Schedules of reinforcement, 141, 143–144
Schizophrenia, 55, 82, 391, 392, 398, 405–406, 408–410, 433, 434, 435
School psychologist, 26
Scientific psychology, 6
Scores, correlation between, 544–546
Scream therapy, 445
Seasonal rhythms, 92–93
Secondary reinforcers, 140–141
Secondary sex characteristics, 56
Second Stage, The (Friedan), 509
Securely attached, infants as, 238
Sedatives, 78, 79
Selective perception, 119–120, 480
Self-actualization, 295, 344, 504
Self-concept, 342, 344
Self-esteem, 342, 354
    dreams and, 77
Self-fulfilling prophecy, in therapy, 439
Self-modification, of behavior, 160
Self-perception theory, 461–463
Self-reinforcement, 160
Self-report inventories, 18, 346–348
Semicircular canals, equilibrium and, 111
Senile dementia, 274, 392
Sensation seeking, 328
Sense of Humor Inventory, 347
Senses, 97–124
    in newborns, 231
Sensorimotor stage, 235
Sensory adaptation, 121
Sensory deprivation, 108
Sensory neurons, 39
Sensory storage, 163
Sensory strip, 50–51
Sensory threshold, 99

Sentences, early formation of, 194
Sequences, of development, 228
Serendipity, 13
Serotonin, 55, 80
    depression and, 404
    suicide and, 417
Sesame Street, 150
Set point, 298
Settling down, in early adulthood, 262
Severe retardation, 212
Sex-change operation, 497
Sex differences, 485–499
    in dreams, 77
    in friendships, 530
    in psychological disorders, 398
Sex glands. *See* Gonads
Sexism, 508
Sex roles. *See* Gender roles
Sex therapy, 501
Sexual double standard, 502–506, 532
Sexual dysfunction, 392, 501
Sexuality, 499–506
    dreams and, 75–76
    homosexuality, 395, 397, 458, 504, 505
    love and, 314, 530–531, 532
    in middle adulthood, 268–269, 270
    psychoanalytic theory and, 331, 332–336
    transsexuals, 497
Sexually liberal couples, 532
Sexually moderate couples, 532
Sexually traditional couples, 532
Sexual motivation, 298, 300
Sexual response, 500–501
Sexual revolution, 502–506
Shaping behavior, 139–140
Shock treatment. *See* Electroconvulsive therapy
Short-term memory, 162–164, 175, 276
Shyness, 514
Sibling relationships, 253–256
Sickle-cell anemia, 39, 63
Sick person, role of, 360, 362
Significance level, 544
Sign language, 190, 191, 192
Similarity, perceptual organization and, 117
Sincerity, of a communicator, 466
Singlehood, 538–539
Sisters. *See* Sibling relationships
Size constancy, 120, 122
Skinner box, 136, 139, 140, 141, 144
Skin senses, 109–110
Sleep, 69–74
    learning in, 152
    prolonged sleep deprivation, 77
    retroactive interference and, 170
Sleep disorders, 73–74
Sleeping pills, 73, 78, 79
Sleeplessness. *See* Insomnia
Sleepwalking, 74
Smell, 112–113
    taste and, 114
    threshold of, 99
Smile, 310
Smoking, 79, 343, 377–378, 459
Sociability, 326, 514
Social change and development
    in infancy, 236–239
    in late adulthood, 276–280
Social-class differences, in intelligence, 210, 211
Social comparison, 513

Social foundations, of attitudes, 462–465
Social influences, 453. *See also* Attitudes
Social Interpretation Task (SIT), 523
Social isolation, 516
Social learning theory, 15, 330, 338–342, 343, 346
    aggressive behavior and, 320, 321
Social motives, 293. *See also* Needing others
Social norms
    alcoholism and, 385
    discrimination and, 481–482
Social psychology, 25, 27
Social relationships, 513–534. *See also* Friendships; Marriage; Peers
    moral development and, 243
Social support, illness prevention and, 376
Social ties, 515
Sociocultural retardation, 214
Sociopath, 407
Somatic nervous system, 40
Somatic therapies, 421, 432–437, 438
Somatoform disorders, 392
Somatotype, 325
Sound waves, 106
Specialization, of brain functions, 52–54
Specificity of pain, 110
Speed freaks, 82
Spinal cord, 39
Spindles, brain waves and, 72
Spontaneous recovery, 135, 136
Stability, in adult development, 260
Stage fright, 307
Stages, of development, 228, 229
Standard deviation, 543, 544
Standardized tests, 206
Standard perfect vision, 100
Stanford-Binet test, 206
Stanford Hypnotic Susceptibility Scale, 85
Stapes, 106, 107
State-dependent memory, 171–172
Statistical significance, 21, 543–544
Statistics, 540–546
Stelazine, 433
Stereotypes, 197
    ageism and, 272
    physical characteristics and, 518, 519
    prejudice and, 480
    sex differences and, 486–491
    sex drives and, 503–504
Stimulants, 78, 79, 81–84, 411
Stimulus, 132
    classical conditioning and, 135–136
    conditioning and, 132, 133
    discriminative, 140
Stimulus control, 140
    behavior modification and, 160
    smoking cessation and, 377
Stimulus-response learning, 148. *See also* Conditioning
Stranger anxiety, 236
Stress, 56, 358–363
    depression and, 404–405
    memory and, 174–175
    prenatal development and, 230
Stressors, 358–359, 363
Stress-resistant personality, 363
Structuralism, 6, 67
Studying, strategies for, 177–179
Subgoal, in problem solving, 204
Subjective experience, 305